CENSUS OF INDIA 1921

CENSUS OF INDIA, 1921

BOOK - 19: VOLUME - X

BURMA

PART II - TABLES

PART III - ADMINISTRATIVE VOLUME

S. G. GRANTHAM

GYAN

Published by

Gyan Publishing House
5, Ansari Road
Daryaganj, New Delhi-110002
Phone: 011-47034999, 9811692060
E-mail: books@gyanbooks.com

Distribution Network
gyanbooks.com
India, USA, Canada, UK, Australia

ISBN: 978-81-212-7125-7 (Set) 25 Vols. In 44 Bindings

ISBN: 978-81-212-7679-5 (PB) Vol. X, Pt. II, III

First Published, 1923

2nd Impression 2024

Printed at: Gyan Press, Delhi.

CENSUS OF INDIA 1921

CENSUS OF INDIA, 1921

Volume X

BURMA

PART II.—TABLES

BY

S. G. GRANTHAM, I.C.S.

SUPERINTENDENT OF CENSUS OPERATIONS, BURMA

RANGOON

OFFICE OF THE SUPERINTENDENT, GOVERNMENT PRINTING, BURMA

1923

LIST OF AGENTS FOR THE SALE OF GOVERNMENT PUBLICATIONS.

IN INDIA.

AMERICAN BAPTIST MISSION PRESS, Rangoon.
INTERNATIONAL BUDDHIST BOOK DEPÔT, Post Box No. 971, Rangoon.
MODERN PUBLISHING HOUSE, Ltd., Rangoon.
RANGOON TIMES PRESS, Rangoon.
MAUNG LU GALE, Law Book Depôt, 42, Ayo-o-gale, Mandalay.
BUTTERWORTH & Co. (India). Ltd., Calcutta.
W. NEWMAN & Co., Calcutta.
THACKER, SPINK & Co., Calcutta and Simla.
D. B. TARAPOREVALA, SONS & Co., Bombay.*
THACKER & Co., Ltd., Bombay.
HIGGINBOTHAM & Co, Madras.
MANAGER, THE "HITAVADA," Nagpur.

IN EUROPE.

A. CONSTABLE & Co., 10, Orange Street, Leicester Square, W.C.
BERNARD QUARITCH, 11, Grafton Street, New Bond Street, W.
EAST & WEST, LTD., 3, Victoria Street, S.W. 1.
GRINDLAY & Co., 54, Parliament Street, S.W.
HENRY S. KING & Co., 65, Cornhill, E.C.
KEGAN PAUL, TRENCH, TRUBNER & Co., Ltd., 68–74, Carter Lane, E.C., and 39, New Oxford Street, W.C.
LUZAC & Co., 46, Great Russell Street, W.C.
P. S. KING & SON, 2 and 4, Great Smith Street, Westminster, S.W.
T. FISHER UNWIN, Ltd., 1, Adelphi Terrace, W.C.
WHELDON & WESLEY, Ltd., 2, 3 and 4, Arthur Street, New Oxford Street, London, W.C. 2.
W. THACKER & Co., 2, Creed Lane, Ludgate Hill, E.C.
B. H. BLACKWELL, 50 and 51, Broad Street, Oxford.
DEIGHTON BELL & Co., Ltd., Trinity Street, Cambridge.
OLIVER & BOYD, Tweeddale Court, Edinburgh, Scotland.
E. PONSONBY, Ltd., 116, Grafton Street, Dublin, Ireland.
ERNEST LEROUX, 28, Rue Bonaparte, Paris, France.
MARTINUS NIJHOFF, The Hague, Holland.
OTTO HARRASSOWITZ, Leipzig, Germany.
R. FRIEDLANDER & SOHN, 11, Carlstrasse, Berlin, Germany.

* For the sale of official publications excluding those of the Legislative Department.

NOTES ON THE IMPERIAL TABLES.

1. All the Imperial Tables except Nos. I and II cover the whole population of 13,169,099 persons enumerated in the synchronous and non-synchronous areas, and exclude all estimated population-figures. Imperial Tables I and II include also 43,093 persons estimated as mentioned in Note 2 of Imperial Table I and so relate to 13,212,192 persons.

2. In all tables in which statistics are given by districts the province has been divided into two parts named Divisional Burma and the Eastern States. The latter includes the Federated Shan States and the Karenni States, while the former includes all the rest of the province. The administrative divisions in which the districts have been grouped in the tables are those which existed on the date of the synchronous census, namely, the 18th March 1921.

3. For the purposes of all the Imperial Tables the statistics given for the Rangoon Town District represent Rangoon Town itself, including the municipality, the cantonments and the port. The statistics given for Mandalay District always cover Mandalay City as well as the rest of the district; but generally separate figures for the city are also given.

4. All ages are stated in the tables in terms of fully completed years, and every age-group includes all who have reached its lower but have not yet reached its higher limit, *e.g.*, age-group 20–40 means all from age 20 to just not 40, and includes all who have completed 20 years but have not completed 40 years.

TABLE OF CONTENTS

IMPERIAL TABLES.

PROVINCIAL TABLES.

NOTE.—Provincial Tables III to VIII inclusive are omitted from copies of this volume supplied to Government Officers in Burma who do not require those tables and from most copies supplied free to recipients outside Burma. They are included in all copies kept in the Government Book Depôt for sale.

CORRIGENDA.

Page 1. NOTE 3.—For ***Thangdut*** read ***Thaungdut.***

13. NOTE 7.—At the end of the second paragraph correct 56,179 to 56,079.

17. NOTE 1.—In line 2, for ***Note*** 3 read *Note* 1.

18. Column 3; in heading; for ***preceding page*** substitute *page* 13.

Irrawaddy Division, Ma-ubin town; column 13 is indistinct in some copies; read 1159.

20. Serial No. 7, Thôngwa; column 7 is indistinct in some copies; read 3269.

Serial No. 37, Shwegyin; column 4 is indistinct in some copies; read 2874.

Above Serial No. 72 for Eastern States; in column 8 correct 2005 to 1605.

21. Serial No. 4, Rangoon; in column 15 for 237 read 273.

28. In the heading above columns 2 and 3 for ***Race-group*** read ***Race-groups*** (plural) and delete S at the beginning of the second line.

In the footnote delete the words: ***and*** 1 ***female Buddhist Thinchi.***

30. In column 32 transpose 6 Chinese Mahomedan males from Hanthawaddy district (line 7) to Insein district (line 6). For Hanthawaddy read ***nil.***

34. Mahomedans born outside Burma, age 0–5; in some copies column 2 is indistinct; read 2022.

38. Animists, age 15–20; in some copies column 10 is indistinct; read 5422.

51. Rangoon Town, ***Others,*** age 40–50; in column 2 for 898 read 1,898.

63. Pyapôn district, Buddhists, total for all ages; read 254,072.

83. Sagaing district, Mahomedans, total for all ages; in the last column for 314 read 134.

84. Upper Chindwin district, Buddhists, age 15–20; in column 6 for 7,144 read 7,444.

102. Delete the words ***City of Rangoon*** in the left-hand portion of column 1.

IMPERIAL TABLE I.

Area, Houses and Population.

NOTE 1.—The figures contained in this table represent the whole of the administered portion of Burma except that part of the Putao District which is not included in the eight Hkāmti Lông Shan States or Fort Hertz; they include also the "unadministered" portion of the Pakôkku Hill Tracts. The areas omitted from the census and excluded from this table are—

(1) All Putao District except the eight Hkāmti Lông Shan States and Fort Hertz.

(2) Unadministered territory associated with the Upper Chindwin District.

(3) Unadministered territory associated with the Hill District of Arakan, but not yet assigned to any administrative division; bounded on the east by the Haka Subdivision of the Chin Hills District, on the North and West by the Lushai Hills and on the South by the Hill District of Arakan.

(4) The uncontrolled portion of the Wa States.

NOTE 2.—All the figures in the table have been obtained by actual enumeration except in the areas shown in the following statement. In these an estimate was made by local officers on the basis of the number of houses and other available information.

	District, etc.	Portion.	Estimate.			
			Number of houses.	Persons.	Males.	Females.
26	Pakôkku Hill Tracts	Unadministered territory.	1,802	8,756	4,207	4,549
35	Upper Chindwin ...	Somra Tract ...	1,834	7,636	3,719	3,917
41	Northern Shan States.	East Manglün ...	4,855	26,701	13,527	13,174
	Total Estimated Area ...		8,491	43,093	21,453	21,640

NOTE 3.—The figures given for the Upper Chindwin District include Kanti (or Singkaling Hkāmti) and Thangdut (or Hsawnghsup), which are two small Shan states situated in that district and administered by hereditary chiefs under the supervision of the Deputy Commissioner. Their total populations are 2,287 and 7,043 respectively.

NOTE 4.—The figures for each hill-tract are included in those for the district or state with which it is associated for administrative purposes.

NOTE 5.—Some of the entries for area given in column 2 of the table include estimates or approximations reached by rough surveys, and in some such cases revised figures have been adopted since the census of 1911. In some other cases area figures, although based on complete survey, have been changed by a revision of the survey or as a consequence of erosion or accretion by rivers. Some district boundaries and areas have been changed since 1911 by the transfer of land which in some cases had no population in 1911. If therefore a comparison with Table I of 1911 is made, Table II below should also be consulted.

NOTE 6.—In the Hill District of Arakan, the Chin Hills District, the Eastern States and all hill-tracts included in other districts, the figures in column 4 represent villages. In practically all the remainder of Burma they represent administrative units called village-tracts. (See Note 8 below.) The figures in column 4 for the Upper Chindwin District and the Northern Shan States do not include any figures for the estimated areas mentioned in Note 2 above although the other columns do cover these areas.

[See page 4.

Serial No.	District or State.	Area in square miles.	Census Towns. (See Note 7.)	Villages or Village-tracts outside Census Towns. (See Note 6.)	Occupied Houses. Total.	Occupied Houses. In Census Towns.	Occupied Houses. In other places.
	1	2	3	4	5	6	7
	Provincial Total	233,707	79	† 35,048	2,727,451	256,977	2,470,474
	Divisional Burma	173,114	71	† 16,334	2,427,151	249,249	2,177,902
	Arakan Division	*14,807*	*3*	*1,442*	*189,892*	*8,886*	*181,507*
1	Akyab	5,136	1	870	117,396	6,716	110,680
2	Hill District of Arakan ...	1,500	...	41	5,303	...	5,303
3	Kyaukpyu	4,387	1	354	44,659	902	43,757
4	Sandoway	3,784	1	177	22,534	767	21,767
	Pegu Division	*13,707*	*16*	*2,273*	*462,141*	*89,901*	*372,240*
5	Rangoon Town	76	1	...	58,047	58,047	...
6	Insein	1,904	1	375	60,110	2,759	57,351
7	Hanthawaddy	1,866	2	468	70,571	4,802	65,769
8	Tharrawaddy	2,863	7	549	101,359	8,531	92,828
9	Pegu	4,083	2	438	88,699	5,569	83,130
10	Prome	2,915	3	443	83,355	10,193	73,162
	Irrawaddy Division	*13,437*	*16*	*2,580*	*395,938*	*30,827*	*365,111*
11	Bassein	4,127	3	688	95,041	10,142	84,899
12	Henzada	2,872	3	621	114,800	7,968	106,832
13	Myaungmya	2,650	3	588	71,604	3,830	67,774
14	Ma-ubin	1,640	3	311	62,692	4,122	58,570
15	Pyapôn	2,148	4	372	51,801	4,765	47,036
	Tenasserim Division	*35,788*	*9*	*1,708*	*311,372*	*31,318*	*280,054*
16	Toungoo	6,135	3	560	85,827	6,901	78,926
17	Salween	2,666	...	89	11,256	...	11,256
18	Thatôn	4,831	2	385	87,569	4,181	83,388
19	Amherst	7,059	2	348	71,480	11,870	59,610
20	Tavoy	5,308	1	179	29,949	5,205	24,744
21	Mergui	9,789	1	147	25,291	3,161	22,130
	Magwe Division	*21,040*	*8*	*2,532*	*306,218*	*16,421*	*289,797*
22	Thayetmyo	4,750	2	641	57,172	4,230	52,942
23	Pakôkku	6,210	1	742	98,422	4,188	94,234
24	Minbu	3,293	2	339	60,888	2,806	58,082
25	Magwe	3,687	3	465	83,424	5,197	78,227
26	Pakôkku Hill Tracts ...	3,100	...	345	6,312	...	6,312
	Mandalay Division	*28,788*	*7*	*2,852*	*184,882*	*47,551*	*136,881*
27	Mandalay	2,117	4	332	83,630	42,331	41,299
28	Bhamo	6,903	1	555	24,532	1,838	22,694
29	Myitkyina	10,651	1	771	24,954	1,266	23,688
30	Katha	8,917	1	685	49,762	2,116	47,646
31	Putao	200	...	* 9	1,504	...	1,504
	Sagaing Division	*35,056*	*5*	*2,219*	*317,058*	*9,111*	*307,942*
32	Shwebo	5,714	2	632	90,799	3,209	87,590
33	Sagaing	1,825	1	282	72,488	2,789	69,699
34	Lower Chindwin	3,480	1	361	92,176	2,586	89,590
35	Upper Chindwin	16,037	1	† 465	38,107	527	37,580
36	Chin Hills	8,000	...	479	23,483	...	23,483
	Meiktila Division	*10,491*	*7*	*1,228*	*260,155*	*15,735*	*244,420*
37	Kyauksè	1,282	1	277	36,509	1,589	34,920
38	Meiktila	2,287	1	400	62,335	2,131	60,204
39	Yamèthin	4,176	3	356	69,654	6,337	63,317
40	Myingyan	2,746	2	195	91,657	5,678	85,979
	Eastern States	60,593	8	† 18,714	300,300	7,728	292,572
41	Northern Shan States ...	20,156	3	† 6,610	113,979	3,896	110,083
42	Southern Shan States ...	36,157	5	11,412	170,494	3,832	166,662
43	Karenni	4,280	...	692	15,827	...	15,827

* Really one Civil Station and eight Shan States. † *See* Note 6.

POPULATION.									
Persons.			Males.			Females.			Serial No. of Dist. or State (col. 1).
Total.	In Census Towns.	In other places.	Total.	In Census Towns.	In other places.	Total.	In Census Towns.	In other places.	
8	9	10	11	12	13	14	15	16	
13,212,192	1,291,527	11,920,665	6,756,969	777,114	5,979,855	6,455,223	514,413	5,940,810	
11,714,800	1,256,529	10,458,271	5,999,549	756,024	5,243,525	5,715,251	500,505	5,214,746	
909,246	*44,216*	*865,031*	*472,227*	*31,966*	*440,261*	*437,019*	*12.249*	*424,770*	
576,430	36,569	539,861	309,564	27,693	281,871	266,866	8,876	257,990	1
20,914	...	20,914	10,790	...	10,790	10,124	...	10,124	2
199,873	3,884	195,989	96,569	2,226	94,343	103,304	1,658	101,646	3
112,029	3,762	108,267	55,304	2,047	53,257	56,725	1,715	55,010	4
2,309,293	*498,639*	*1,810,654*	*1,258,914*	*327,039*	*931,875*	*1,050,379*	*171,600*	*878,779*	
341,962	341,962	...	236,689	236,689	...	105,273	105,273	...	5
293,083	14,308	278,775	156,794	9,520	147,274	136,289	4,788	131,501	6
364,624	23,346	341,278	201,043	16,253	184,790	163,581	7,093	156,488	7
492,429	43,429	449,000	246,261	23,501	222,760	246,168	19,928	226,240	8
445,620	26,265	419,355	235,324	15,073	220,251	210,296	11,192	199,104	9
371,575	49,329	322,246	182,803	26,003	156,800	188,772	23,326	165,446	10
2,030,044	*164,501*	*1,865,543*	*1,048,377*	*97,232*	*951,145*	*981,667*	*67,269*	*914,398*	
489,473	56,224	433,249	252,947	35,478	217,469	236,526	20,746	215,780	11
550,920	38,508	512,412	273,439	20,485	252,954	277,481	18,023	259,458	12
370,551	20,842	349,709	196,757	12,287	184,470	173,794	8,555	165,239	13
330,106	21,016	309,090	168,513	11,936	156,577	161,593	9,080	152,513	14
288,994	27,911	261,083	156,721	17,046	139,675	132,273	10,865	121,408	15
1,613,523	*166,465*	*1,447,058*	*847,445*	*94,716*	*752,729*	*766,078*	*71,749*	*694,329*	
381,883	31,541	350,342	197,505	17,752	179,753	184,378	13,789	170,589	16
50,379	...	50,379	26,811	...	26,811	23,568	...	23,568	17
471,100	22,259	448,841	245,909	11,972	233,937	225,191	10,287	214,904	18
417,910	67,888	350,022	223,348	41,634	181,714	194,562	26,254	168,308	19
156,786	27,480	129,306	80,994	13,818	67,176	75,792	13,662	62,130	20
135,465	17,297	118,168	72,878	9,540	63,338	62,587	7,757	54,830	21
1,447,530	*77,884*	*1,369,646*	*709,454*	*40,285*	*669,169*	*738,076*	*37,599*	*700,477*	
255,406	21,987	233,419	125,283	11,382	113,901	130,123	10,605	119,518	22
465,771	19,507	446,264	223,943	9,665	214,278	241,828	9,842	231,986	23
274,302	12,237	262,065	134,495	6,225	128,270	139,807	6,012	133,795	24
423,252	24,153	399,099	211,686	13,013	198,673	211,566	11,140	200,426	25
28,799	...	28,799	14,047	...	14,047	14,752	...	14,752	26
849,361	*198,521*	*650,840*	*435,894*	*107,674*	*328,220*	*413,467*	*90,847*	*322,620*	
356,621	177,411	179,210	182,999	94,831	88,168	173,622	82,580	91,042	27
112,960	7,741	105,219	56,888	4,933	51,955	56,072	2,808	53,264	28
118,382	4,956	113,426	63,419	3,107	60,312	54,963	1,849	53,114	29
253,725	8,413	245,312	128,444	4,803	123,641	125,281	3,610	121,671	30
7,673	...	7,673	4,144	...	4,144	3,529	...	3,529	31
1,358,032	*36,845*	*1,321,187*	*645,009*	*19,696*	*625,313*	*713,023*	*17,149*	*695,874*	
391,284	13,347	377,937	184,708	7,131	177,577	206,576	6,216	200,360	32
326,908	11,858	315,050	155,054	5,784	149,270	171,854	6,074	165,780	33
342,880	9,225	333,655	156,693	5,109	151,584	186,187	4,116	182,071	34
186,881	2,415	184,466	94,432	1,672	92,760	92,449	743	91,706	35
110,079	...	110,079	54,122	...	54,122	55,957	...	55,957	36
1,197,771	*69,459*	*1,128,312*	*582,229*	*37,416*	*544,813*	*615,542*	*32,043*	*583,499*	
142,677	6,107	136,570	70,449	3,037	67,412	72,228	3,070	69,158	37
289,897	8,868	281,029	137,573	5,240	132,333	152,324	3,628	148,696	38
323,189	28,459	294,730	160,913	15,134	145,779	162,276	13,325	148,951	39
442,008	26,025	415,983	213,294	14,005	199,289	228,714	12,020	216,694	40
1,497,392	34,998	1,462,394	757,420	21,090	736,330	739,972	13,908	726,064	
585,924	15,096	570,828	299,227	10,338	288,889	286,697	4,758	281,939	41
847,618	19,902	827,716	427,064	10,752	416,312	420,554	9,150	411,404	42
63,850	...	63,850	31,129	...	31,129	32,721	...	32,721	43

NOTE 7.—The figures in columns 3, 6, 9, 12 and 15 of the statement relate to a number of areas of an urban character arbitrarily selected and described as Census Towns for the purposes of Imperial Tables IV and V below. The selection includes all towns to which the Burma Towns Act applies and also all municipalities and notified areas and all cantonments, and some other areas in addition. Areas of an urban character which are not included are either smaller or less important than included areas or lack defined boundaries and administrative unity.

NOTE 8.—A village-tract is defined by law as the local area under the jurisdiction of a headman, including a village or group of villages and adjacent lands. In practice it may include no true village at all but only a number of small clusters of houses scattered through a comparatively extensive area. On the other hand a village may be shared by two or more village-tracts some of which may include parts or wholes of other villages. Some Census Towns include more than one village-tract or include parts of one or more village-tracts. In every such case, if the same area is not to be counted twice, the number of village-tracts shown in this table must differ from the correct number of statutory village-tracts which is shown in Provincial Table I. Imperial Table III agrees with the present table.

NOTE 9.—The definition of a house on which the numbers in columns 5 to 7 depend was ordinarily as follows :—

A *House* means the separate residence of a family. A residence is considered to be separate when it has a separate entrance from a common way.

If one building is jointly occupied by two or more families it should be treated as one house if the families share meals, but as two or more if they cook and eat separately.

Monasteries, Zayats, Schools, Godowns and Field Huts and all other buildings are to be included in the term *House* if used as dwelling-places, whether used at night or not. They must always be included if a watchman or durwan lives there.

In Rangoon Town and occasionally in other towns *house* was taken to mean a tenement ; and this definition was generally substituted for the ordinary one for lodging-houses and coolie-lines and similar cases. Amongst some tribes in which there is a custom of building extensions of a house for all descendants of the original house-holder the term house was generally taken to mean the residence of the whole group of relations ; this variation from the normal definition would only affect the figures in a few remote areas.

IMPERIAL TABLE II.

Variation in Population since 1872.

NOTE 1.—No census was taken in Upper Burma prior to 1891, nor in the Eastern States or the Pakôkku Hill Tracts or the Chin Hills District prior to 1901.

NOTE 2.—In columns 9 and 10 the figures for Total Variation in some lines of totals or sub-totals are not the sum of the figures given for the component parts of the corresponding area. This is due to the inclusion of the figures for the Chin Hills for the first time in 1901 and of the other districts of Upper Burma in 1891.

NOTE 3.—Two new districts have been created since the census of 1911. The Insein District has been formed of parts of the Hanthawaddy and Pegu Districts, and the Putao District has been established in hitherto unadministered territory north of the Myitkyina District.

NOTE 4.—Separate figures for Karenni are given here for the first time. In previous censuses they were included in those of the Southern Shan States.

NOTE 5.—In 1920 the Ruby Mines District was divided into two parts; the Möngmit State, including the Kodaung and Ngadaung Hill Tracts, was transferred to the Northern Shan States and the remainder was added to the Katha District.

NOTE 6.—Except in the cases mentioned in Notes 7 and 13, the populations shown in the table for 1911 and previous years have been adjusted to correspond to districts as constituted on the 18th March 1921. The districts for which the figures now given differ from those given in the corresponding table of 1911 are shown below; there have been changes in the boundaries of other districts besides these, but the areas transferred were reserved forests or wild tracts without population :

7. Hanthawaddy.
9. Pegu.
18. Thatôn.
23. Pakôkku.
24. Minbu.
25. Magwe.
30. Katha.
37. Kyauksè.
38. Meiktila.
39. Yamèthin.
40. Myingyan.
41. Northern Shan States.

In all cases, however, the figures given for a district in any year exclude all areas omitted from the census of that year. Notes 7 and 8 below give some particulars of such cases; for further information earlier census reports should be consulted.

NOTE 7.—The large increases shown in columns 11 and 13 for the whole province and for Thayetmyo District are due to the inclusion for 1891 of certain areas which were omitted from previous enumerations because they were outside British Burma. Similarly in column 10 for Bhamo and Katha Districts owing to the omission of certain areas from the census of 1891.

NOTE 8.—Columns 2, 8, 13, 14 and 20 of the table include increases to the extent shown below on account of extension of the area of enumeration in 1921 to include areas which were omitted from the enumeration of 1911:

District.		Area omitted in 1911.				
			Census of 1921.			
Serial No.	Name.	Description.	Kind of Enumeration.	Persons.	Males.	Females.
7	Hanthawaddy ...	Coco Islands ...	Synchronous ...	46	40	6
29	Myitkyina ...	Htawgaw Kachin Hill Tracts.	Non-synchronous.	17,305	8,745	8,560
		Sana Kachin Hill Tracts.	Do. (a)	979	484	495
			(b)	2,773	1,331	1,442
31	Putao ...	Hkamti Lông Shan States and Fort Hertz.	Do.	7,673	4,144	3,529
35	Upper Chindwin ...	Somra Tract ...	Estimate ...	7,636	3,719	3,917
41	Northern Shan States	East Manglün ...	Do. ...	26,701	13,507	13,174
Notes (a) Portion in Myitkyina Hill Tracts. (b) Portion in Mogaung Hill Tracts.			Total ...	63,113	31,990	31,123

NOTE 9.—Further notes relating to this table will be found on page 8.

Serial No.	District or State.	Persons. 1921.	1911.	1901.	1891.	1881.	1872.	Variation. Increase (+), Decrease (−). 1911—1921	1901—1911	1891—1901	1881—1891	1872—1881
	1	2	3	4	5	6	7	8	9	10	11	12
	Provincial Total	**13,212,192**	**12,115,217**	**10,490,624**	**7,722,053**	**3,736,771**	**2,747,148**	**+1,096,975**	**+1,624,593**	**+2,768,571**	**+3,985,282**	**+ 989,623**
	Divisional Burma	**11,714,800**	**10,702,849**	**9,308,472**	**7,704,675**	**3,736,771**	**2,747,148**	**+1,011,951**	**+1,394,377**	**+1,590,681**	**+3,967,904**	**+ 989,623**
	Arakan Diun.	*909,246*	*839,896*	*762,102*	*673,274*	*588,690*	*484,963*	*+ 69,350*	*+ 77,794*	*+ 88,828*	*+ 84,584*	*+ 103,727*
1	Akyab ...	576,430	529,943	481,666	416,305	359,706	276,671	+ 46,187	+ 48,277	+ 65,361	+ 56,599	+ 83,035
2	Hill District of Arakan.	20,914	22,234	20,682	14,628	14,499	8,790	− 1,320	+ 1,552	+ 6,054	+ 129	+ 5,709
3	Kyaukpyu ...	199,873	184,916	168,827	163,832	149,303	144,177	+ 14,957	+ 16,089	+ 4,995	+ 14,529	+ 5,126
4	Sandoway ...	112,029	102,803	90,927	78,509	65,182	55,325	+ 9,226	+ 11,876	+ 12,418	+ 13,327	+ 9,857
	Pegu Division	*2,309,293*	*2,085,487*	*1,830,710*	*1,580,584*	*1222,555*	*852,725*	*+ 223,806*	*+ 254,777*	*+ 300,176*	*+ 307,979*	*+ 369,830*
5	Rangoon Town	341,962	293,316	245,430	182,080	134,176	98,745	+ 48,646	+ 47,886	+ 63,350	+ 47,904	+ 35,431
6	Insein ...	293,083	265,245	227,300	184,064	138,746	86,831	+ 27,838	+ 37,945	+ 43,236	+ 45,318	+ 51,915
7	Hanthawaddy	304,624	332,569	297,015	244,057	182,607	115,321	+ 32,055	+ 35,554	+ 52,958	+ 61,450	+ 67,286
8	Tharrawaddy	492,429	433,320	395,570	339,240	272,001	171,202	+ 59,109	+ 37,750	+ 56,330	+ 67,239	+ 100,799
9	Pegu ...	445,620	382,166	299,591	212,116	166,120	100,338	+ 63,454	+ 82,575	+ 87,475	+ 45,996	+ 65,782
10	Prome ...	371,575	378,871	365,804	368,977	328,905	280,288	− 7,296	+ 13,067	− 3,173	+ 40,072	+ 48,617
	Irrawaddy Dun.	*2,030,044*	*1,869,485*	*1,663,669*	*1,300,119*	*989,978*	*680,315*	*+ 160,559*	*+ 205,816*	*+ 363,550*	*+ 310,141*	*+ 309,663*
11	Bassein ...	489,473	440,988	391,427	320,973	268,169	202,428	+ 48,485	+ 49,561	+ 70,454	+ 52,804	+ 65,741
12	Henzada ...	550,920	532,357	484,558	437,620	363,899	256,753	+ 18,563	+ 47,799	+ 46,938	+ 73,721	+ 107,146
13	Myaungmya	370,551	334,852	282,932	181,792	105,369	56,845	+ 35,699	+ 51,920	+ 101,140	+ 76,423	+ 48,524
14	Ma-ubin ...	330,106	305,073	278,309	213,738	173,315	124,442	+ 25,033	+ 26,764	+ 64,571	+ 40,423	+ 48,873
15	Pyapôn ...	288,994	256,215	226,443	145,996	79,226	39,847	+ 32,779	+ 29,772	+ 80,447	+ 66,770	+ 39,379
	Tenasserim Dun.	*1,618,523*	*1,417,544*	*1,149,486*	*904,539*	*765,988*	*572,329*	*+ 195,979*	*+ 268,058*	*+ 244,947*	*+ 138,551*	*+ 193,659*
16	Toungoo ...	381,883	351,076	279,315	211,784	190,385	136,816	+ 30,807	+ 71,761	+ 67,531	+ 21,399	+ 53,569
17	Salween ...	50,379	46,608	37,837	31,439	30,009	26,117	+ 3,771	+ 8,771	+ 6,398	+ 1,430	+ 3,892
18	Thatôn ...	471,100	405,225	333,438	259,108	223,309	160,429	+ 65,875	+ 71,787	+ 74,330	+ 35,799	+ 62,880
19	Amherst ...	417,910	367,918	300,173	233,539	180,738	129,948	+ 49,992	+ 67,745	+ 66,634	+ 52,801	+ 50,790
20	Tavoy ...	156,786	135,293	109,979	94,921	84,988	71,827	+ 21,493	+ 25,314	+ 15,058	+ 9,933	+ 13,161
21	Mergui ...	135,465	111,424	88,744	73,748	56,559	47,192	+ 24,041	+ 22,680	+ 14,996	+ 17,189	+ 9,367
	Magwe Diun.	*1,447,580*	*1,308,267*	*1,124,353*	*1,033,523*	...	...	*+ 139,263*	*+ 183,914*	*+ 77,714*	...	...
22	Thayetmyo	255,406	248,275	239,706	250,161	169,560	156,816	+ 7,131	+ 8,569	− 10,455	+ 80,601	+ 12,744
23	Pakôkku ...	465,771	409,823	357,557	312,877	...	...	+ 55,948	+ 52,266	+ 44,680	...	...
24	Minbu ...	274,302	262,380	232,902	215,485	...	...	+ 11,922	+ 29,478	+ 17,117	...	...
25	Magwe ...	423,252	361,538	281,972	255,000	...	...	+ 61,714	+ 80,466	+ 26,072	...	...
26	Pakôkku Hill Tracts.	28,799	26,251	13,116	...	...	...	+ 2,548	+ 13,135	...	...	...
	Mandalay Diun.	*849,361*	*779,755*	*733,758*	*576,057*	...	...	*+ 69,606*	*+ 45,997*	*+ 157,701*	...	...
27	Mandalay ...	356,621	340,770	366,507	375,055	...	...	+ 15,851	− 25,737	− 8,548	...	...
28	Bhamo ...	112,960	107,811	79,515	41,939	...	...	+ 5,149	+ 28,296	+ 37,576	...	...
29	Myitkyina ...	118,382	85,577	68,527	51,831	...	...	+ 32,805	+ 17,050	+ 16,696	...	...
30	Katha ...	253,725	245,597	219,209	107,232	...	...	+ 8,128	+ 26,388	+ 111,977	...	...
31	Putao ...	7,673	...	...	...	...	...	...	...	...	...	...
	Sagaing Diun.	*1,358,032*	*1,274,827*	*1,081,655*	*816,463*	...	...	*+ 83,205*	*+ 193,172*	*+ 265,192*	...	...
32	Shwebo ...	391,284	356,363	286,891	230,779	...	...	+ 34,921	+ 69,472	+ 56,112	...	...
33	Sagaing ...	326,908	312,111	277,769	241,645	...	...	+ 14,797	+ 34,342	+ 36,124	...	...
34	Lower Chindwin.	342,880	316,175	276,383	233,316	...	...	+ 26,705	+ 39,792	+ 43,067	...	...
35	Upper Chindwin.	186,881	170,622	153,423	110,723	...	...	+ 16,259	+ 17,199	+ 42,700	...	...
36	Chin Hills ...	110,079	119,556	87,189	...	...	...	− 9,477	+ 32,367	...	...	...
	Meiktila Diun.	*1,197,771*	*1,127,588*	*962,739*	*870,166*	...	...	*+ 70,183*	*+ 164,849*	*+ 92,573*	...	...
37	Kyauksè ...	142,677	141,598	141,398	126,756	...	...	+ 1,079	+ 200	+ 14,642	...	...
38	Meiktila ...	289,897	280,690	253,066	217,845	...	...	+ 9,207	+ 27,624	+ 35,221	...	...
39	Yamèthin ...	323,189	306,379	242,291	205,858	...	...	+ 16,810	+ 64,088	+ 36,433	...	...
40	Myingyan ...	442,008	398,921	325,984	319,707	...	...	+ 43,087	+ 72,937	+ 6,277	...	...
	Eastern States	**1,497,392**	**1,412,368**	**1,182,152**	...	...	...	**+ 85,024**	**+ 230,216**	...	...	...
41	Northern Shan States.	585,924	512,166	365,798	17,378*	...	...	+ 73,758	+ 146,368	+ 348,420*	...	...
42	Southern Shan States.	847,618	836,574	770,561	...	...	...	+ 11,044	+ 66,013	...	...	...
43	Karenni ...	63,850	63,628	45,793	...	...	...	+ 222	+ 17,835	...	...	...

* Figures for Northern Shan States

: *Population since* 1872.

Net Variation in period 1872—1921. Increase (+) Decrease (—)	Males.						Females.						Serial No. of District or State (col. 1).
	1921.	1911.	1901.	1891.	1881.	1872.	1921.	1911.	1901.	1891.	1881.	1872.	
13	14	15	16	17	18	19	20	21	22	23	24	25	
+10,465,044	6,756,969	6,183,494	5,342,033	3,937,936	1,991,005	1,435,518	6,455,223	5,931,723	5,148,591	3,784,117	1,745,766	1,311,630	
+8,938,853	5,999,549	5,477,004	4,753,815	3,927,103	1,991,005	1,435,518	5,715,251	5,225,845	4,554,657	3,777,572	1,745,766	1,311,630	
+ 424,283	472,227	441,925	405,587	357,640	318,417	254,363	437,019	397,971	356,515	315,634	270,273	230,600	
+ 299,759	309,564	289,474	267,980	230,414	203,124	148,180	266,866	240,469	213,686	185,891	156,582	128,491	1
+ 12,124	10,790	11,405	10,557	7,600	7,467	4,784	10,124	10,829	10,125	7,028	7,032	4,006	2
+ 55,696	96,569	89,571	81,075	79,943	74,476	73,056	103,304	95,345	87,752	83,889	74,827	71,121	3
+ 56,704	55,304	51,475	45,975	39,683	33,350	28,343	56,725	51,328	44,952	38,826	31,832	26,982	4
+1,456,568	1,258,914	1,142,331	1,000,468	828,932	672,148	456,038	1,050,379	943,156	830,242	701,602	550,407	396,687	
+ 243,217	236,689	208,111	174,587	126,001	91,504	62,374	105,273	85,205	70,843	56,079	42,672	36,371	5
+ 206,252	156,794	141,346	121,297	98,251	74,020	46,307	136,289	123,899	106,003	85,813	64,726	40,524	6
+ 249,303	201,043	185,331	162,941	136,910	109,065	66,195	163,581	147,238	134,074	107,147	73,542	49,126	7
+ 321,227	246,261	216,442	201,033	171,295	140,295	85,714	246,168	216,878	194,537	167,945	131,706	85,488	8
+ 345,282	235,324	204,888	162,148	114,862	92,500	54,136	210,296	177,278	137,443	97,254	73,620	46,202	9
+ 91,287	182,803	186,213	178,462	181,613	164,764	141,312	188,772	192,658	187,342	187,364	164,141	138,976	10
+1,349,729	1,048,377	962,913	865,917	674,086	511,799	342,459	981,667	906,572	797,762	626,033	478,179	337,856	
+ 287,045	252,947	226,773	203,977	166,122	140,174	104,701	236,526	214,215	187,450	154,851	127,995	97,727	11
+ 294,167	273,439	264,319	241,557	219,729	182,732	124,774	277,481	268,038	243,001	217,891	181,167	131,979	12
+ 313,706	196,757	176,165	149,141	94,581	60,152	28,214	173,794	158,387	133,791	87,271	45,217	28,631	13
+ 205,664	168,513	155,715	145,122	112,956	83,440	65,318	161,593	149,358	133,187	100,782	89,875	59,124	14
+ 249,147	156,721	139,641	126,120	80,758	45,301	19,452	132,273	116,574	100,323	65,238	33,925	20,395	15
+1,041,194	847,445	744,487	602,888	475,949	401,333	301,336	766,078	673,057	546,598	428,590	364,655	270,993	
+ 245,067	197,505	181,488	143,685	109,684	103,775	75,075	184,378	169,588	135,630	102,100	86,610	61,741	16
+ 24,262	26,811	24,741	19,464	16,521	15,509	13,509	23,568	21,867	18,373	14,918	14,500	12,608	17
+ 310,671	245,909	211,631	174,955	136,202	106,286	77,022	225,191	193,594	158,483	122,906	117,023	83,407	18
+ 287,962	223,348	198,130	163,930	128,211	104,659	75,714	194,562	169,488	136,243	105,328	76,079	54,234	19
+ 84,959	80,994	68,667	54,574	46,542	41,785	35,616	75,792	66,626	55,405	48,379	43,203	36,211	20
+ 88,273	72,878	59,530	46,280	38,789	29,319	24,400	62,587	51,894	42,464	34,959	27,240	22,792	21
...	709,454	636,929	540,787	499,776	...	...	738,076	671,888	583,616	533,747	...	...	
+ 98,590	125,283	122,231	118,948	125,474	87,308	81,322	130,123	126,044	120,758	124,687	82,252	75,494	22
...	223,943	196,118	168,308	147,362	...	...	241,828	213,705	189,249	165,515	...	...	23
...	134,495	128,096	111,520	102,660	...	...	139,807	134,284	121,382	112,825	...	...	24
...	211,686	177,517	135,412	124,280	...	...	211,566	184,021	145,660	130,720	...	...	25
...	14,047	12,967	6,549	...	...	...	14,752	13,284	6,567	...	...	...	26
...	435,894	399,536	371,978	294,314	...	...	418,467	380,219	361,780	281,748	...	...	
...	182,999	170,750	183,374	184,392	...	...	173,622	170,020	183,133	190,663	...	...	27
...	56,888	55,528	41,530	23,346	...	...	56,072	52,283	37,985	18,593	...	...	28
...	63,419	47,863	36,956	29,569	...	...	54,963	37,714	31,571	22,262	...	...	29
...	128,444	125,395	110,118	57,007	...	...	125,281	120,202	109,091	50,225	...	...	30
...	4,144	...	...	...	...	...	3,529	...	...	...	...	...	31
...	645,009	601,851	505,519	378,584	...	...	713,028	672,976	576,136	437,879	...	...	
...	184,708	168,070	134,045	108,773	...	...	206,576	188,293	152,846	122,006	...	...	32
...	155,054	147,816	129,808	112,277	...	...	171,854	164,295	147,961	129,368	...	...	33
...	156,693	141,262	121,967	101,791	...	...	186,187	174,913	154,416	131,525	...	..	34
...	94,432	86,141	76,532	55,743	...	...	92,449	84,481	76,891	54,980	...	...	35
...	54,122	58,562	43,167	...	...	...	55,957	60,994	44,022	...	...	...	36
...	582,229	547,032	460,721	417,822	...	...	615,542	580,556	502,018	452,844	...	...	
...	70,449	68,950	69,399	62,828	...	...	72,228	72,648	71,999	63,928	...	...	37
...	137,573	134,807	119,608	102,419	...	...	152,324	145,883	133,458	115,426	...	...	38
...	160,913	152,504	119,753	102,980	...	...	162,276	153,875	122,538	102,878	..	...	39
...	213,294	190,771	151,961	149,595	...	...	228,714	208,150	174,023	170,112	...	...	40
...	757,420	706,490	588,218	...	...	...	739,972	705,878	593,934	...	...	...	
...	299,227	257,785	184,635	10,833*	...	...	286,697	254,381	181,163	6,545*	...	...	41
...	427,064	417,237	380,916	...	...	...	420,554	419,337	389,645	...	...	...	42
...	31,129	31,468	22,667	...	...	...	32,721	32,160	23,126	...	...	...	43

in 1891 relate only to Möng Mit State; all other States omitted.

NOTE 10.—No areas enumerated in 1911 were omitted in 1921.

NOTE 11.—The areas omitted from the enumeration of 1921 were as follows:—

(1) All Putao District except the eight Hkamti Lông Shan States and Fort Hertz.

(2) Unadministered territory associated with the Upper Chindwin District.

(3) Unadministered territory associated with the Hill District of Arakan, but not yet assigned to any administrative division; bounded on the east by the Haka subdivision of the Chin Hills District, on the north and west by the Lushai Hills and on the south by the Hill District of Arakan.

(4) The uncontrolled portion of the Wa States.

NOTE 12.—The areas for which figures were obtained by estimation in 1911 or 1921 and the districts in which the corresponding figures are included in the table are shown in the following statement:—

District.		Description of Area.	1921.				1911.			
Serial No.	Name.		Kind of Enumeration	Persons.	Males.	Females.	Kind of Enumeration.	Persons.	Males.	Females.
34	Upper Chindwin	Somra Tract ...	Estimated	7,636	3,719	3,917	Omitted	...	...	...
40	Northern Shan States.	East Manglün	Do.	26,701	13,527	13,174	Do.	...	...	...
		West Manglün	Non-synchronous.	20,597	10,436	10,161	Estimated	18,562	9,061	9,501
		Kokang ...	Do.	31,820	16,461	15,359	Do.	25,604	13,389	12,215
42	Karenni * ...	Brè Circle ...	Do.	3,365	1,566	1,799	Do.	5,717	2,606	3,111
		Wiwa Circle ...	Do.	3,144	1,501	1,643				
43	Pakôkku Hill Tracts.	Unadministered territory.	Estimated	8,756	4,207	4,549	Do.	9,123	4,478	4,645

* Karenni was included in the Southern Shan States in the Census Tables of 1911. The Brè Circle was known in 1911 as the Tuchaung East Circle, while the Wiwa Circle of 1921 includes both the Wiwa and the Tuchaung West Circles of 1911. The Brè and the Wiwa Circles of 1921 together constitute the area described for the census of 1911 as the Brè Tract.

NOTE 13.—In the case of Rangoon Town there is some doubt about the adjustment required for the years 1872 and 1881. The present Rangoon Town District consists of Rangoon Town and the Rangoon River down to its mouth, and the population recorded for it consists of persons in Rangoon Town and persons enumerated on ships which were in the river on the night of the census or arrived in Rangoon within 15 days of that date without having been enumerated at any other Indian port. The Rangoon Town of 1891 differed from this by excluding a land area which had in that year a population of 1,756. The same area (and perhaps other areas) was excluded in 1872 and 1881, but it is not possible to discover the corresponding excluded population in those years for which therefore the population shown in the table for the Rangoon Town District is really that of Rangoon Town as it was constituted in those years. Any population which may have been in 1872 or 1881 on the area subsequently taken into Rangoon Town has thus been included in the figures of those years for the Insein and Hanthawaddy Districts.

IMPERIAL TABLE III.

Village-tracts and Census Towns Classified by Population.

NOTE 1.—Except as indicated in Note 2 below this table deals with village-tracts and not with villages. A village-tract is defined by law as the local area under the jurisdiction of a headman, including a village or group of villages and adjacent lands. In practice it may include no true village at all but only a number of small clusters of houses scattered through a comparatively extensive area. On the other hand a village may be shared by two or more village-tracts some of which may include parts or wholes of other villages. Some Census Towns (*see* Note 3 below) include more than one village-tract or include parts of one or more village-tracts. In every such case, if the same area is not to be counted twice, the number of village-tracts shown in this table must differ from the correct number of statutory village-tracts which is shown in Provincial Table I. Imperial Table I agrees with the present table.

NOTE 2.—For the Hill District of Arakan, the Chin Hills District, the Pakôkku Hill Tracts, the Eastern States and in all hill-tracts included in other districts, the figures given in columns 2, 4, 6, etc., represent villages. For other areas there is no record of the number of villages available ; but the numbers of villages which have more than 40 or more than 100 houses are shown in Provincial Table I of this volume.

NOTE 3.—The *Census Towns* are a number of areas of an urban character arbitrarily selected and described as Census Towns for the purposes of Imperial Tables IV and V below. The selection includes all towns to which the Burma Towns Act applies and also all municipalities and notified areas and all cantonments, and some other areas in addition. Areas of an urban character which are not included are either smaller or less important than included areas or lack defined boundaries and administrative unity.

NOTE 4.—The description *Adventitious Population* in the last column of the table includes all persons who were not enumerated as residents of a village-tract or town. The term thus includes—

(1) the inmates (not the staff) of jails, reformatories, hospitals, lunatic or leper asylums,

(2) the inhabitants of military areas or of military police lines,

(3) travellers enumerated in boats or trains or at railway stations or in camps or travelling on roads on which travellers were comparatively numerous, and all persons on boats and ships in ports who were not local shore residents,

(4) persons (not local residents) assembled at a pagoda festival,

(5) residents in such forest reserves (or other areas) as are not included in the ordinary village-tract administrative system nor in recognised forest villages,

(6) railway construction camps,

(7) other classes of persons enumerated away from home either in groups simultaneously assembled or at points where the number of such persons appearing successively justified the appointment of a special enumerator.

Visitors staying in hotels, etc., or with friends in private houses were treated as residents, as also were occasional travellers at places at which the appointment of special enumerators as described in item (7) above was not required.

NOTE 5.—The adventitious population shown in the last column of the table is excluded from the figures in columns 5 to 21. All Census Towns are thus classified according to their Normal Civil Population as shown in Part II of Imperial Table V.

NOTE 6.—The table covers the whole area of actual enumeration but does not take any account of the areas described in Notes 1 and 2 of Imperial Table I in which either an estimate was made without actual enumeration or no census was taken at all. For this reason the figures in column 2 for the Pakôkku Hill Tracts (and for all areas including these) differ from the corresponding figure of Imperial Table I.

TABLE III.—*Village-Tracts and Census*

Serial No.	District or State.	Total number of Census Towns and Village-Tracts outside Census Towns. (See Notes 1 and 2.)	Population.	Village-Tracts: Under 500. Number.	Under 500. Population.	500 to 1,000. Number.	500 to 1,000. Population.	1,000 to 2,000. Number.	1,000 to 2,000. Population.
	1	2	3	4	5	6	7	8	9
	Provincial Total ...	85,084	13,169,099	27,131	3,482,951	4,913	3,492,354	2,398	3,209,686
	Divisional Burma ...	16,362	11,698,403	8,522	2,136,540	4,823	3,433,985	2,385	3,191,261
	Arakan Division ...	*1,445*	*909,246*	*735*	*217,278*	*495*	*349,059*	*194*	*252,117*
1	Akyab	871	576,430	424	122,634	304	212,988	125	160,507
2	Hill District of Arakan ...	41	20,914	23	7,354	16	11,364	2	2,136
3	Kyaukpyu	355	199,873	198	57,601	115	82,331	41	55,666
4	Sandoway	178	112,029	90	29,689	60	42,376	26	33,808
	Pegu Division ...	*2,289*	*2,309,293*	*797*	*256,391*	*912*	*661,173*	*482*	*637,785*
5	Rangoon Town ...	1	341,962	...	...	...	...	...	...
6	Insein	376	293,083	146	47,151	146	104,326	71	94,781
7	Hanthawaddy ...	470	364,624	185	61,648	195	138,683	79	103,592
8	Tharrawaddy ...	556	492,429	161	51,092	233	170,359	140	181,923
9	Pegu	440	445,620	117	36,348	169	125,931	117	157,387
10	Prome	446	371,575	188	60,152	169	121,874	75	100,102
	Irrawaddy Division ...	*2,598*	*2,030,044*	*941*	*321,090*	*1,139*	*805,739*	*455*	*591,286*
11	Bassein	691	489,473	276	91,346	324	227,244	86	107,894
12	Henzada	624	550,920	162	58,501	311	223,650	139	185,372
13	Myaungmya	591	370,551	299	101,059	223	155,299	61	76,060
14	Ma-ubin	314	330,106	67	22,768	112	81,549	110	147,303
15	Pyapôn ...	376	288,994	137	47,416	169	117,997	59	74,657
	Tenasserim Division ...	*1,717*	*1,618,523*	*602*	*162,051*	*586*	*432,847*	*416*	*566,148*
16	Toungoo	563	381,883	296	68,697	152	110,025	95	125,401
17	Salween	89	50,379	44	13,541	37	25,794	8	11,044
18	Thatôn	387	471,100	62	20,358	140	108,890	143	199,750
19	Amherst	350	417,910	85	27,106	129	95,142	96	130,319
20	Tavoy	180	156,786	67	17,464	68	48,073	38	49,721
21	Mergui	148	135,465	48	14,885	60	44,414	36	48,913
	Magwe Division ...	*2,497*	*1,438,774*	*1,603*	*371,935*	*545*	*384,803*	*263*	*359,625*
22	Thayetmyo	643	255,406	515	136,534	110	71,333	13	15,287
23	Pakôkku	743	465,771	426	113,438	198	139,321	98	136,059
24	Minbu	341	274,302	166	44,414	90	66,523	63	85,361
25	Magwe	468	423,252	194	57,728	147	107,626	89	122,918
26	Pakôkku Hill Tracts ...	302	20,043	302	19,821	...	...	...	...
	Mandalay Division ...	*2,359*	*849,361*	*2,013*	*340,224*	*253*	*170,349*	*72*	*94,407*
27	Mandalay	336	356,621	192	49,607	96	65,885	39	50,810
28	Bhamo	556	112,960	531	85,791	21	14,105	3	3,680
29	Myitkyina	772	118,382	727	73,100	34	23,356	9	11,950
30	Katha	686	253,725	558	130,502	100	65,791	20	26,761
31	Putao	9	7,673	5	1,224	2	1,212	1	1,206
	Sagaing Division ...	*2,224*	*1,350,396*	*1,349*	*325,751*	*524*	*370,388*	*274*	*362,611*
32	Shwebo	634	391,284	351	95,826	186	131,127	77	103,350
33	Sagaing	283	326,908	70	24,707	106	78,770	82	107,933
34	Lower Chindwin ...	362	342,880	136	44,659	109	78,869	88	116,863
35	Upper Chindwin ...	466	179,245	357	83,674	85	57,038	21	27,538
36	Chin Hills	479	110,079	435	76,885	38	24,584	6	6,927
	Meiktila Division ...	*1,285*	*1,197,771*	*482*	*141,820*	*369*	*260,127*	*229*	*328,282*
37	Kyauksè	278	142,677	172	45,693	83	56,990	19	24,287
38	Meiktila	401	289,897	182	56,690	138	95,379	67	93,380
39	Yamèthin	359	323,189	124	38,156	139	100,772	77	104,237
40	Myingyan	197	442,008	4	1,281	9	6,986	66	106,448
	Eastern States ...	18,722	1,470,691	18,609	1,346,411	90	58,369	13	18,425
41	Northern Shan States ...	6,613	559,223	6,569	506,209	35	22,739	5	6,833
42	Southern Shan States ...	11,417	847,618	11,358	785,825	47	30,268	7	10,038
43	Karenni	692	63,850	682	54,377	8	5,362	1	1,554

Towns Classified by Population.

and Census Towns with a Population of :—

2,000 to 5,000.		5,000 to 10,000.		10,000 to 20,000		20,000 to 50,000.		50,000 to 100,000.		Over 100,000.		Adventitious Population.	
Number.	Population.	Number.	Population.	Number.	Population.	Number.	Population.	Number.	Population.	Number.	Population.		Serial No.
10	11	12	13	14	15	16	17	18	19	20	21	22	
567	1,530,936	54	374,188	13	194,510	5	134,095	1	56,029	2	460,329	234,021	
560	1,509,731	51	355,561	13	194,510	5	134,095	1	56,029	2	460,329	226,367	
20	*52,305*	...	...	...	...	*1*	*23,437*	...	...	...	...	*15,050*	
17	42,959	...	...	...	...	1	23,437	...	...	...	...	13,905	1
...	...	...	...	...	...	...	...	...	...	...	...	60	2
1	3,518	...	...	...	...	...	...	...	...	...	...	757	3
2	5,828	...	...	...	...	...	...	...	...	...	...	328	4
81	*222,346*	*11*	*77,188*	*4*	*58,765*	*1*	*23,951*	...	...	*1*	*317,687*	*54,007*	
...	...	...	...	...	...	...	...	...	...	1	317,687	24,275	5
12	32,100	...	...	1	11,774	...	...	...	...	...	...	2,951	6
7	19,024	3	19,227	1	15,072	...	...	...	...	...	...	7,378	7
18	54,748	4	30,616	...	...	...	...	...	...	...	...	3,691	8
33	87,573	3	18,277	1	17,985	...	...	...	...	...	...	2,119	9
11	28,901	1	9,068	1	13,934	1	23,951	...	...	...	...	13,593	10
49	*133,062*	*10*	*72,113*	...	...	*2*	*59,725*	...	...	...	...	*47,029*	
2	5,623	2	13,261	...	...	1	37,199	...	...	...	...	6,906	11
9	21,787	2	14,536	...	...	1	22,526	...	...	...	...	24,548	12
6	19,798	2	13,528	...	...	...	...	...	...	...	...	4,807	13
23	58,483	2	14,957	...	...	...	...	...	...	...	...	5,036	14
9	27,371	2	15,821	...	...	...	...	...	...	...	...	5,732	15
104	*280,939*	*4*	*25,518*	*3*	*49,230*	*1*	*26,982*	*1*	*56,029*	...	...	*15,279*	
17	46,003	2	11,903	1	18,034	...	...	...	...	...	...	1,820	16
...	...	...	...	...	...	...	...	...	...	...	...	...	17
40	117,924	1	7,062	1	14,090	...	...	...	...	...	...	3,017	18
38	96,085	1	6,553	...	...	...	...	1	56,029	...	...	6,676	19
6	14,048	...	...	...	...	1	26,982	...	...	...	...	498	20
3	6,879	...	...	1	17,106	...	...	...	...	...	...	3,268	21
75	*202,241*	*9*	*70,455*	*2*	*30,306*	...	...	...	...	...	...	*19,409*	
3	9,093	1	9,561	1	11,109	...	...	...	...	...	...	2,489	22
20	55,166	...	...	1	19,197	...	...	...	...	...	...	2,590	23
20	56,792	2	11,867	...	...	...	...	...	...	...	...	9,345	24
32	81,190	6	49,027	...	...	...	...	...	...	...	...	4,763	25
...	...	...	...	...	...	...	...	...	...	...	...	222	26
16	*42,078*	*3*	*22,509*	*1*	*12,515*	...	...	...	...	*1*	*142,642*	*24,638*	
6	16,299	1	8,497	1	12,515	...	...	...	...	1	142,642	10,366	27
...	...	1	5,940	...	...	...	...	...	...	...	...	3,444	28
2	5,484	...	...	...	...	...	...	...	...	...	...	4,492	29
7	17,417	1	8,072	...	...	...	...	...	...	...	...	5,182	30
1	2,878	...	...	...	...	...	...	...	...	...	...	1,153	31
70	*202,473*	*6*	*43,306*	*1*	*11,737*	...	...	...	...	...	...	*34,130*	
19	49,046	1	9,384	...	...	...	...	...	...	...	...	2,551	32
22	65,415	2	14,090	1	11,737	...	...	...	...	...	...	24,856	33
26	80,983	3	19,832	...	...	...	...	...	...	...	...	1,074	34
3	7,029	...	...	...	...	...	...	...	...	...	...	3,966	35
...	...	...	...	...	...	...	...	...	...	...	...	1,683	36
145	*374,287*	*8*	*44,472*	*2*	*31,957*	...	...	...	...	...	...	*16,826*	
1	2,554	3	11,643	...	...	...	...	...	...	...	...	1,510	37
13	34,376	1	6,943	...	...	...	...	...	...	...	...	3,159	38
17	47,718	1	7,404	1	14,527	...	...	...	...	...	...	10,375	39
114	289,639	3	18,482	1	17,430	...	...	...	...	...	...	1,742	40
7	21,205	3	18,627	...	...	...	...	...	...	...	...	7,654	
3	9,249	1	7,699	...	...	...	...	...	...	...	...	6,494	41
3	9,399	2	10,928	...	...	...	...	...	...	...	...	1,100	42
1	2,557	...	...	...	...	...	...	...	...	...	...	...	43

IMPERIAL TABLE IV.

Variation since 1872 of the Population of Census Towns.

NOTE 1.—The *Census Towns* are a number of areas of an urban character arbitrarily selected and described as Census Towns for the purposes of Imperial Tables IV and V. The selection includes all* towns to which the Burma Towns Act applies, and also all municipalities and notified areas and all cantonments, and some other areas in addition. Areas of an urban character which are not included are either smaller or less important than included areas or lack defined boundaries and administrative unity. In the present table the Census Towns are arranged in descending order of magnitude according to population.

NOTE 2.—The name of No. 21 is shown as Allanmyo, that being the name generally used by the Local Government; the municipal committee however uses the name Allanmyo-Ywataung for the same area.

NOTE 3.—In column 3, M is shown against towns which are Municipalities and N against those which are Notified Areas: T is shown against those which are administrative towns under the Burma Towns Act; C is shown against those which have a cantonment associated with them.

NOTE 4.—Zalun, Lemyethna, Sinbyugyun and Kindat, which were included in Table IV of 1911, have been excluded from the table.

NOTE 5.—The following towns have now been included in the table for the first time:—

35. Thôngwa.
40. Namtu-Panghai.
42. Nyaunglebin.
46. Zigôn.
53. Pyu.
56. Mawlamyainggyun.
58. Taunggyi.
60. Këngtüng.
65. Nattalin.
68. Yawnghwe.
70. Hsipaw.
71. Minhla.
73. Tharrawaddy.
74. Lashio.
75. Myitngè.
76. Kalaw.
77. Ye-u.
78. Mawlaik.
79. Loilem.

No. 52, Kawkareik, which was omitted from the table of 1911, has also been included again.

NOTE 6.—The figures given for each town in this table include both the Normal Civil Population and the Adventitious Population as defined in Note 1 of Imperial Table V. The portion belonging to each of these classes in 1921 is shown by Parts II and III of that table.

NOTE 7.—The figures given for each town at each successive Census represent the population of the area recognized as the town at the census dates.

In this respect the figures for Rangoon Town for 1901 and 1891, but not earlier years, differ from the corresponding figures shown in Table IV of the census of 1911, which had been adjusted to correspond to the area occupied by the Town in 1911, which was the same as that occupied by it in 1921; the population of that area in 1901 was 174,587 males and 70,843 females; in 1891 it was 126,001 males and 56,179 females.

The boundaries of Mandalay City have not been changed since 1891 except in 1917 when an area was added which in 1921 included 141 males and 83 females.

NOTE 8.—Figures for the population of Cantonments and Ports are included in those given in this table for the respective towns with which they are associated, but are shown separately in Note 16 on page 16. The names of such towns are marked with an asterisk in column 1.

NOTE 9.—The towns are grouped in classes according to their magnitude in 1921. Except for 1921 the totals given for each class in the various columns do not correspond to the specific towns which belonged to that class in 1921 but represent the total population enumerated at each census in towns of that magnitude. The same applies to the second line of the table.

NOTE 10.—As in the table of 1911 the figures given for No. 36 Pyapôn include the population of the Municipality and also that of the Civil Station which is outside although adjacent to the municipality and is also not subject to the Burma Towns Act although the municipality is. Figures for the civil station are given in the table of Note 16 on page 16.

NOTE 11.—The separate populations of Namtu and Panghai (see No. 40), which, though they form at present separate administrative units in different Shan states, make up a single block of residences, are also given in Note 16 on page 16.

NOTE 12.—At the census of 1901 the populations of railway premises were omitted in compiling the figures for the following towns. In the present table corrections have been made for this, and accordingly the figures shown in it for these towns for 1901 differ from those shown for the same year in the census tables of 1901 and 1911:—

10. Toungoo.
11. Myingyan.
20. Sagaing.
23. Shwebo.
25. Letpadan.
32. Amarapura.
41. Gyobingauk.
51. Thônzè.
73. Tharrawaddy.

NOTE 13.—Similarly a correction has been made for the population in 1911 of No. 55 Myaungmya by excluding the population of the jail which is outside the town.

NOTE 14.—See also Notes 15 and 16 on page 16.

---

* It is not certain whether the Act applies to Zalun, which has been omitted (*see* Note 4).

Serial No.	Town.	District or State.	Municipality, Cantonment, etc. (*See* Note 3 on preceding page.)				Population.					
							1921.	1911.	1901.	1891.	1881.	1872.
	1	2	3				4	5	6	7	8	9
	Total for all towns tabulated for 1921 ...		...	...	...	...	**1,281,527**	...	...	...	...	...
	Total enumerated in towns above 10,000 ...		...	...	...	...	**947,014**	**875,175**	**818,184**	**732,088**	...	...
	Class I, 100,000 and over	......	...	...	...	...	490,879	431,615	418,697	369,139	...	...
1	Rangoon *	Rangoon ...	M	...	T	C	341,962	293,316	234,881	180,324	134,176	98,745
2	Mandalay *	Mandalay ..	M	...	T	C	148,917	138,299	183,816	188,815	...	...
	Class II, 50,000—100,000	......	...	...	...	...	61,301	57,582	58,446	55,785	53,107	[illegible]
3	Moulmein *	Amherst ...	M	...	T	...	61,301	57,582	58,446	55,785	53,107	46,472
	Class III, 20,000—50,000	......	...	...	...	...	156,330	172,082	142,046	128,370	90,949	81,845
4	Bassein *	Bassein ...	M	...	T	...	42,563	37,081	31,564	30,177	28,147	20,968
5	Akyab *	Akyab ...	M	...	T	...	36,569	37,893	35,680	37,938	33,989	19,230
6	Tavoy ...	Tavoy ...	M	...	T	...	27,480	25,074	22,371	15,099	13,372	14,469
7	Prome	Prome ...	M	...	T	...	26,057	26,911	27,375	30,022	28,813	31,157
8	Henzada	Henzada ...	M	...	T	...	23,651	25,052	24,756	19,762	16,724	15,307
	Class IV, 10,000—20,000	......	...	...	...	...	238,504	223,957	198,995	188,787	...	...
9	Pakôkku	Pakôkku ...	M	...	T	...	19,507	20,010	19,456	19,972	...	...
10	Toungoo	Toungoo ..	M	...	T	...	19,332	18,546	16,146	19,232	17,199	10,752
11	Myingyan	Myingyan ...	M	...	T	...	18,931	16,379	16,205	19,790	...	...
12	Pegu	Pegu	M	...	T	...	18,769	17,104	14,132	10,762	5,891	4,416
13	Mergui	Mergui ...	M	..	T	...	17,297	14,889	11,987	10,137	8,633	9,737
14	Maymyo *	Mandalay ...	...	N	T	C	16,558	11,974	1,259	228	...	...
15	Syriam	Hanthawaddy ...	M	...	T	...	15,193	10,807	...	...	...	...
16	Thatôn	Thatôn ...	M	...	T	...	15,091	14,392	14,342	9,683	6,338	...
17	Pyinmana	Yamèthin ...	M	...	T	...	14,886	14,074	14,388	12,926	..	...
18	Insein	Insein ...	M	...	T	...	14,203	13,992	...	...	...	...
19	Paungdè	Prome ...	M	...	T	...	14,154	12,104	11,105	10,233	6,787	8,630
20	Sagaing	Sagaing ...	M	...	T	...	11,853	10,937	10,039	9,924	...	...
21	Allanmyo	Thayetmyo ...	M	...	T	...	11,2[illegible]9	12,894	10,207	9,012	8,825	9,697
22	Thayetmyo * ...	Thayetmyo ...	M	...	T	C	10,[illegible]68	11,577	15,824	17,101	16,097	15,142
23	Shwebo *	Shwebo ...	M	...	T	C	10,605	10,629	9,792	9,368	...	...
24	Yenangyaung ...	Magwe ...	...	N	...	...	10,028	8,896	3,245	4,258	...	...
	Class V, 5,000—10,000	......	...	...	...	...	285,834	...	...	...	...	...
25	Letpadan	Tharrawaddy ...	M	...	T	...	9,901	9,247	9,107	2,151	775	...
26	Yandoon	Ma-ubin ...	M	...	T	...	9,344	12,570	12,779	20,235	12,673	9,680
27	Mônywa	Lower Chindwin	M	...	T	...	9,225	8,628	7,869	6,316	...	...
28	Kyaiklat	Pyapôn ...	M	...	T	...	9,224	8,438	...	...	...	...
29	Shwedaung	Prome ..	...	N	...	...	9,108	9,021	10,787	12,424	12,373	12,684
30	Yamèthin	Yamèthin ...	M	...	T	...	8,869	8,083	8,680	6,534	...	...
31	Meiktila *	Meiktila ...	...	N	...	C	8,863	7,076	7,203	4,155	...	...
32	Amarapura	Mandalay ...	...	...	T	...	8,497	7,565	9,151	11,004	...	...
33	Wakèma	Myaungmya ...	M	...	T	...	8,447	7,031	...	...	...	...
34	Mogôk ¶	Katha ...	...	...	...	...	8,413	11,[illegible]69	10,864	...	...	...
35	Thôngwa	Hanthawaddy ...	M	...	T	...	8,153	..	...	...	...	...
36	Pyapôn †	Pyapôn ...	M	...	T	...	8,107	7,066	..	...	...	...
37	Magwe	Magwe ...	...	N	T	...	7,819	4,967	6,232	6,673	...	...
38	Myanaung	Henzada ...	M	...	T	...	7,793	8,331	6,351	5,489	5,416	5,696
39	Bhamo *	Bhamo ...	M	...	T	C	7,741	9,762	10,734	8,048	...	...
40	Namtu-Panghai § ...	North Shan States	...	...	...	...	7,699	449	...	...	...	...
41	Gyobingauk ...	Tharrawaddy ...	M	...	T	...	7,665	7,410	6,083	3,008	837	...
42	Nyaunglebin ...	Pegu	M	...	...	...	7,495	6,642	...	...	...	...
43	Kyaikto	Thatôn ...	M	...	T	...	7,168	6,127	6,637	5,164	3,859	...
44	Nyaung-u	Myingyan ...	...	N	...	...	7,094	5,726	...	...	...	...
45	Kyangin	Henzada ...	M	...	T	...	7,064	8,386	7,183	8,116	7,965	8,477
46	Zigôn	Tharrawaddy ...	M	...	...	...	6,916	5,218	...	...	...	...
47	Kyônpyaw	Bassein ...	...	N	...	...	6,910	5,429	...	...	...	...
48	Salin	Minbu ...	M	...	T	...	6,834	7,547	7,957	10,345	...	...
49	Ma-ubin	Ma-ubin ...	M	...	T	...	6,812	7,022	6,623	5,327	1,567	...
50	Ngathainggyaung-Daunggyi	Bassein ...	M	...	T	...	6,751	7,182	7,182	5,608	..	...
51	Thônzè ‡ ..	Tharrawaddy ...	M	...	T	...	6,574	6,929	6,648	2,257	1,505	...
52	Kawkareik	Amherst ...	...	N	...	...	6,587	5,559	3,919	3,097	...	...
53	Pyu	Toungoo ...	...	N	T	...	6,451	...	...	...	...	...
54	Taungdwingyi ...	Magwe ...	M	...	T	...	6,306	6,402	5,941	5,687	...	...
55	Myaungmya ...	Myaungmya ...	M	..	T	...	6,280	5,461	4,711	2,929	...	...
56	Mawlamyainggyun ...	Myaungmya ...	...	N	...	...	6,215	...	...	...	...	...
57	Kyauksè	Kyauksè ...	M	...	T	...	6,107	5,877	5,430	7,201	...	...
58	Taunggyi	South Shan States	...	N	...	...	6,016	5,180	...	...	...	...
59	Shwegyin	Toungoo ...	M	...	T	...	5,758	8,037	7,616	8,754	7,519	7,872
60	Kengtung	South Shan States	...	...	...	...	5,718	5,742	...	...	...	...
61	Dedayè	Pyapôn ...	...	...	...	...	5,563	6,189	...	...	...	...
62	Minbu	Minbu ...	M	...	T	...	5,403	5,501	5,780	7,270	...	...
63	Bogale	Pyapôn ...	...	...	...	...	5,012	3,279	...	...	...	...
	Class VI, under 5,000	......	...	...	...	...	58,679	...	...	...	...	...
64	Myitkyina	Myitkyina ...	...	...	...	...	4,956	5,663	...	...	...	...
65	Nattalin	Tharrawaddy ...	...	N	...	...	4,898	4,165	...	...	...	...
66	Danubyu	Ma-ubin ...	...	N	T	...	4,863	7,695	...	...	...	...
67	Pyawbwè	Yamèthin ...	...	N	...	...	4,704	4,571	...	...	...	...
68	Yawnghwe	South Shan States	...	...	...	...	4,173	...	...	...	...	...
69	Kyaukpyu	Kyaukpyu ...	M	...	T	...	3,884	3,323	3,145	3,548	3,235	...
70	Hsipaw	North Shan States	...	...	...	...	3,949	5,455	...	...	...	...
71	Minhla	Tharrawaddy ...	...	N	...	...	3,819	...	...	...	...	...
72	Sandoway	Sandoway ...	M	...	T	...	3,762	3,360	2,845	2,531	1,617	...
73	Tharrawaddy ‡ ...	Tharrawaddy ...	...	N	T	...	3,625	3,246	2,666	...	...	...
74	Lashio	North Shan States	...	N	...	...	3,448	4,055	...	...	...	...
75	Myitngè	Mandalay ...	...	N	...	...	3,439	...	...	...	...	...
76	Kalaw	South Shan States	...	N	...	...	2,937	-	...	...	...	...
77	Ye-u .. .	Shwebo ...	...	N	...	...	2,744	...	...	...	...	...
78	Mawlaik	Upper Chindwin	...	N	...	...	2,415	...	...	...	...	...
79	Loilem	North Shan States	...	N	...	...	998	...	...	...	...	...

* *See* Notes 8 and 16. † *See* Notes 10 and 16. ‡ *See* Note 6. § *See* Notes 12 and 16. ¶ The figures given for Mogôk in 1921 are possibly deficient.

of the Population of Census Towns.

Variation: Increase (+), Decrease (−). 1911—1921.	1901—1911.	1891—1901.	1881—1891.	1872—1881.	Variation in period 1872—1921. Increase (+). Decrease (−).	Males. 1921.	Males. 1911.	Males. 1901.	Females. 1921.	Females. 1911.	Females. 1901.	Serial No. of Town.
10	11	12	13	14	15	16	17	18	19	20	21	
...	...	...	...	...	...	777,114	...	...	514,413	...	...	
+ 71,839	+ 58,901	+ 88,101	...	...	...	585,853	541,853	489,309	381,961	333,322	328,875	
+ 59,264	+ 12,918	+ 49,558	...	...	...	314,452	277,829	259,128	176,427	153,786	159,569	
+ 48,646	+ 58,435	+ 54,557	+ 46,148	+ 35,431	+ 243,217	236,689	203,111	165,545	105,273	85,205	69,336	1
+ 10,618	− 45,517	− 4,999	...	...	...	77,763	69,718	93,583	71,154	68,581	90,233	2
+ 5,719	− 864	+ 2,661	+ 2,678	− 92,110	− 83,926	38,076	35,130	46,650	23,225	22,452	21,756	
+ 3,719	− 864	+ 2,661	+ 2,678	+ 6,635	+ 14,829	38,076	35,130	36,690	23,225	22,452	21,756	3
− 15,691	+ 29,975	+ 23,674	+ 27,423	+ 39,104	+ 104,485	97,231	104,380	86,201	59,099	67,641	58,845	
+ 5,482	+ 5,217	+ 1,687	+ 2,030	+ 7,459	+ 21,875	28,406	24,246	20,122	14,157	12,835	11,442	4
− 1,324	+ 2,213	− 2,258	+ 3,949	+ 14,759	+ 17,339	27,693	29,509	27,581	8,876	8,384	8,099	5
+ 2,406	+ 2,703	+ 7,278	+ 1,727	− 1,097	+ 13,011	13,818	12,573	10,904	13,662	12,501	11,467	6
− 844	− 464	− 2,647	+ 1,209	− 2,344	− 5,090	14,340	14,385	14,037	11,727	12,526	13,338	7
− 1,401	+ 296	+ 4,994	+ 3,038	+ 1,117	+ 8,344	12,974	14,009	13,237	10,677	11,043	11,499	8
+ 24,567	+ 14,962	+ 10,208	...	...	...	135,294	124,524	107,290	103,220	89,443	91,708	
− 508	+ 554	− 516	...	...	...	9,665	9,638	9,123	9,842	10,352	10,333	9
+ 786	+ 2,400	− 3,086	+ 2,033	+ 6,467	+ 8,600	11,150	11,106	8,892	8,182	7,440	7,254	10
+ 2,552	+ 174	− 3,585	...	...	...	10,374	8,765	8,322	8,557	7,614	7,883	11
+ 1,665	+ 2,972	+ 3,370	+ 4,871	+ 1,475	+ 14,353	10,728	10,232	8,375	8,041	6,872	5,757	12
+ 2,408	+ 2,902	+ 1,850	+ 1,504	− 1,104	+ 7,560	9,540	8,100	6,169	7,757	6,789	5,818	13
+ 4,584	+ 10,715	+ 1,031	...	...	...	10,749	8,003	1,037	5,809	3,966	323	14
+ 4,296	...	...	...	...	...	11,741	8,434	...	3,452	2,463	...	15
+ 699	+ 50	+ 4,659	+ 3,295	...	...	8,076	7,932	8,315	7,015	6,410	6,027	16
+ 818	− 314	+ 1,462	...	...	...	7,938	7,475	7,169	6,898	6,590	7,219	17
+ 316	...	...	...	...	...	9,520	10,046	...	4,788	3,946	...	18
+ 2,050	+ 999	+ 872	+ 3,506	+ 1,097	+ 8,524	7,289	6,328	5,683	6,865	5,782	5,482	19
+ 928	+ 898	+ 105	...	...	...	5,784	5,427	4,931	6,074	5,310	5,108	20
− 1,675	+ 2,687	+ 1,295	+ 5,187	− 3,872	+ 1,532	5,480	6,384	4,816	5,739	6,510	5,391	21
− 809	− 4,247	− 1,277	+ 1,004	+ 935	− 4,374	5,902	6,374	9,101	4,865	5,303	6,783	22
− 24	+ 837	+ 424	...	...	...	5,635	6,059	5,510	4,920	4,570	4,282	23
+ 1,138	+ 5,650	− 1,018	...	...	...	5,623	5,085	1,736	4,405	3,811	1,510	24
...	...	...	...	...	...	138,656	...	...	127,278	...	...	
+ 654	+ 140	+ 6,956	+ 1,376	...	...	5,411	5,099	4,933	4,490	4,148	4,169	25
− 3,156	− 279	− 7,456	+ 7,562	+ 2,993	− 336	5,134	6,793	7,028	4,210	5,707	5,751	26
+ 597	+ 759	+ 1,553	...	...	...	5,103	4,614	4,382	4,116	4,014	3,487	27
+ 786	...	...	...	...	...	5,600	5,042	...	3,624	3,396	...	28
+ 87	− 1,766	− 1,637	+ 51	− 281	− 3,546	4,374	4,187	4,892	4,734	4,834	2,895	29
+ 786	− 587	+ 2,096	...	...	...	4,830	4,289	4,522	4,039	3,794	4,158	30
+ 1,792	− 127	+ 3,048	...	...	...	5,140	3,085	4,287	3,628	3,091	2,916	31
+ 631	− 1,285	− 1,853	...	...	...	3,918	3,619	4,166	4,579	4,217	4,985	32
+ 1,416	...	...	...	...	...	4,161	4,125	...	3,556	2,905	...	33
− 2,656	+ 285	...	...	...	...	4,803	7,007	7,405	3,610	4,062	2,459	34
...	...	...	...	...	...	4,518	...	...	2,641	...	...	35
+ 1,042	...	...	...	...	...	4,877	4,393	...	3,230	2,668	...	36
+ 2,852	− 1,265	− 441	...	...	...	4,258	2,834	3,305	3,561	2,133	2,422	37
− 538	+ 2,980	+ 861	+ 73	− 220	+ 2,157	3,907	4,262	3,118	3,886	4,069	3,233	38
− 2,081	− 972	+ 2,636	...	...	...	4,933	6,703	7,129	2,808	5,059	3,605	39
+ 7,259	...	...	...	...	...	6,031	212	...	1,663	208	...	40
+ 856	+ 1,327	+ 5,075	+ 2,171	...	...	4,169	4,067	3,252	3,497	3,343	2,831	41
+ 854	...	...	...	...	...	4,345	3,772	...	3,151	2,870	...	42
+ 1,041	− 510	+ 1,473	+ 1,305	...	...	3,896	3,280	3,734	3,272	2,847	2,903	43
+ 1,368	...	...	...	...	...	3,631	2,852	...	3,463	2,874	...	44
− 1,322	+ 1,203	− 933	+ 551	− 912	− 1,413	3,604	4,220	3,379	3,160	4,186	3,804	45
...	...	...	...	...	...	3,805	2,755	...	3,111	2,463	...	46
+ 1,481	...	...	...	...	...	3,617	2,889	...	3,293	2,540	...	47
− 713	− 410	− 2,388	...	...	...	3,278	3,161	5,641	3,556	3,936	4,316	48
− 218	+ 999	+ 1,295	+ 3,760	...	...	4,090	4,377	4,301	2,722	2,645	2,319	49
− 431	Nil	+ 1,574	...	...	...	3,455	3,677	3,963	3,295	3,505	2,214	50
− 238	+ 288	+ 4,384	+ 752	...	...	3,343	3,586	3,455	3,246	3,343	3,183	51
+ 1,028	+ 1,640	+ 822	...	...	...	3,558	2,955	2,134	3,009	2,604	1,788	52
...	...	...	...	...	...	3,504	...	...	2,947	...	...	53
− 96	+ 461	+ 254	...	...	...	3,132	3,179	2,883	3,174	3,223	3,058	54
+ 829	+ 790	+ 1,782	...	...	...	3,755	3,551	2,922	2,525	2,100	1,789	55
...	...	...	...	...	...	3,671	...	...	2,444	...	...	56
+ 230	+ 457	− 1,781	...	...	...	3,037	2,900	2,712	3,070	2,977	2,708	57
...	...	...	...	...	...	3,311	2,856	...	2,705	2,324	...	58
− 2,379	+ 421	− 1,138	+ 1,235	− 352	− 2,113	3,093	4,355	4,029	2,660	3,682	3,287	59
− 34	...	...	...	...	...	3,033	2,945	...	2,680	2,790	...	60
− 622	...	...	...	...	...	3,403	3,656	...	2,160	2,533	...	61
− 98	− 279	− 1,490	...	...	...	2,947	2,967	2,977	2,456	2,534	2,803	62
+ 1,733	...	...	...	...	...	3,161	1,970	...	1,851	1,309	...	63
...	...	...	...	...	...	33,405	...	...	25,274	...	...	
− 707	...	...	...	...	...	3,107	3,794	...	1,849	1,869	...	64
+ 733	...	...	...	...	...	2,584	2,159	...	2,314	2,006	...	65
− 2,835	...	...	...	...	...	2,712	4,426	...	2,148	3,269	...	66
+ 133	...	...	...	...	...	2,316	2,395	...	2,388	2,176	...	67
...	...	...	...	...	...	2,029	...	...	2,141	...	...	68
+ 561	+ 178	− 403	+ 383	...	...	2,226	1,896	1,770	1,658	1,457	1,375	69
− 1,586	...	...	...	...	...	2,161	2,891	...	1,638	2,564	...	70
...	...	...	...	...	...	2,105	...	...	1,724	...	...	71
+ 402	+ 515	+ 514	+ 514	...	...	2,047	1,816	1,462	1,715	1,544	1,383	72
+ 379	+ 580	...	...	...	...	2,079	2,895	1,600	1,546	1,358	1,066	73
− 687	...	...	...	...	...	2,046	2,691	...	1,409	1,364	...	74
...	...	...	...	...	...	2,401	...	...	1,038	...	...	75
...	...	...	...	...	...	1,822	...	...	1,175	...	...	76
...	...	...	...	...	...	1,446	...	...	1,296	...	...	77
...	...	...	...	...	...	1,672	...	...	742	...	...	78
...	...	...	...	...	...	552	...	...	446	...	...	79

NOTE 15.—The figures given for No. 39 Bhamo in 1921 exclude passengers on steamboats which reached the town the morning after the census; this was probably but not certainly the case also in 1911. Similarly the figures given for No. 67 Pyawbwè in 1921 exclude 532 males and 220 females in the military police lines, for which the corresponding figures were probably but not certainly included in 1911; these lines are outside the town.

NOTE 16.—The following table gives details for the cantonments and ports associated with certain towns and for divisions of Pyapôn and of Namtu-Panghai. (See Notes 8, 10 and 11 above.) For 1921, the description *Port* corresponds throughout to persons enumerated in vessels within the limits of the port (which may extend beyond the limits of the town) and excludes all enumerated on shore; it is believed the same holds good for earlier years. The division of the Rangoon Cantonment is into civil and military areas, not civil and military population; and all compounds of military quarters are included in the military area. In the case of Mandalay the whole of the Fort, including the jail and other areas not associated with military purposes, is regarded as a military area. Maymyo and Meiktila Cantonments include only purely military areas. In the case of Thayetmyo the figures given for the Sudder Bazaar include all the Cantonment except the military lines; in 1921 there was no longer any garrison. At Shwebo also there was no longer any garrison in 1921. Bhamo Cantonment in 1921 included a civil area which had a population of 258 persons, of whom 154 were males and 104 females.

Town.		Division of Town.	Persons.				Males.				Females.			
No.	Name.		1921.	1911.	1901.	1891.	1921.	1911.	1901.	1891.	1921.	1911.	1901.	1891.
1	2	3	4	5	6	7	8	9	10	11	12	13	14	15
1	Rangoon*	Cantonment—												
		Civil	3,897	} 8,381	13,721	14,556	2,870	} 6,292	9,095	10,852	1,027	} 2,089	4,626	3,704
		Military	2,574				1,670				904			
		Port	13,801	9,968	10,641	7,747	13,400	9,681	10,393	7,574	401	287	248	173
		Remainder	321,690	274,967	210,519	158,021	218,749	192,138	146,057	106,341	102,941	82,829	64,462	51,680
2	Mandalay	Cantonment—												
		Civil Area	9,513	10,405	} 16,095	18,744	4,903	5,540	} 9,922	11,921	4,610	4,865	} 6,173	6,823
		Military Lines and Fort.	4,565	2,980			3,758	2,362			807	618		
		Remainder	134,839	124,914	167,721	170,071	69,102	61,816	83,661	81,582	65,737	63,098	84,060	88,489
3	Moulmein	Port	3,646	} 37,582	2,252	3,135	3,586	} 35,130	2,248	3,069	60	} 22,452	4	66
		Remainder	57,655		56,194	52,650	34,490		34,442	31,183	23,165		21,752	21,467
4	Bassein	Port	3,521	} 37,081	492	399	3,276	} 24,246	476	398	245	} 12,835	16	1
		Remainder	39,042		31,372	29,778	25,130		19,946	18,615	13,912		11,426	11,163
5	Akyab	Port	7,246	} 37,893	3,993	5,979	7,185	} 29,509	3,988	5,945	61	} 8,384	5	34
		Remainder	29,323†		31,687	31,959	20,508		23,593	23,263	8,815		8,094	8,696
14	Maymyo	Cantonment	3,719	} 11,974	1,259	228	2,903	} 8,008	1,037	226	816	} 3,966	222	2
		Remainder	12,839				7,846				4,993			
22	Thayetmyo	Sudder Bazaar	690	} 11,577	1,081	} 4,218	319	} 6,374	533	} 3,363	371	} 5,203	548	} 855
		Military Lines	—		1,528		—		1,387		—		141	
		Remainder	10,078		13,215	12,883	5,583		7,181	6,491	4,495		6,034	6,392
23	Shwebo	Cantonment	894	} 10,629	1,751	} 9,368	442	} 6,059	1,397	} 5,558	452	} 4,570	354	} 3,810
		Remainder	9,711		8,041		5,243		4,113		4,468		3,928	
31	Meiktila	Cantonment	1,637	} 7,076	1,011	686	1,316	} 3,985	834	597	321	} 3,091	177	89
		Remainder	7,231		6,192	3,469	3,924		3,453	1,840	3,307		2,739	1,609
36	Pyapon	Municipality	7,659	} 7,066	—	—	4,536	} 4,126	—	—	3,123	} 2,905	—	—
		Civil Station	448				341				107			
39	Bhamo	Cantonment	1,213	} 9,762	1,600	1,184	1,009	} 6,703	1,476	1,155	104	} 3,059	124	29
		Remainder	6,528		9,134	6,864	3,924		5,653	4,392	2,604		3,481	2,472
40	Namtu-Panghai	Total	7,699	449	Uncertain.	No Census.	6,031	241	Uncertain.	No Census.	1,668	208	Uncertain.	No Census.
		Namtu	5,463	265			4,524	160			939	105		
		Panghai	2,236	84			1,507	81			729	103		

* The corresponding figures for Rangoon in 1881 were :—

	Persons.	Males.	Females.
Cantonment	9,652	6,975	2,677
Port	9,388	8,855	533
Remainder	115,136	75,674	39,462

It should be noted that some lands were transferred between the Cantonment and Municipality in 1887, 1901, 1903, 1905, 1907, 1908 and 1910.

† These figures for the *Remainder* of Akyab Town include 5,207 males chiefly employed in rice mills who were only present temporarily and proposed to leave the town shortly after the Census.

IMPERIAL TABLE V.

Population of Census Towns classified by Religion.

NOTE 1.—In all the three parts in which this table has been constructed the census towns tabulated in Imperial Table IV (and defined in Note 3 of that table) have been arranged according to the division and district in which they are situated. In Part I the population shown for each town in 1921 in Imperial Table IV is classified by religion. These numbers include not only persons actually present in the town on the night of the census but also some persons who although they did not reach the town at any time that night were enumerated in some special circumstances, *e.g.*, as travellers in boats or trains, which resulted in the record of the enumeration being collected, according to the usual custom, with those of the town. In Parts II and III the numbers tabulated in Part I are tabulated again after division into two parts described as the *Normal Civil Population* and *Adventitious Population* respectively. The latter term includes all population of the classes described in Note 4 of Imperial Table III, of which the following are the most important in census towns—

(1) the inmates (not the staff) of jails, reformatories, hospitals, lunatic or leper asylums,
(2) the inhabitants of Military Areas or of Military Police Lines,
(3) travellers enumerated in boats or trains or at railway stations or in camps or travelling on roads on which travellers were comparatively numerous, and all persons on boats or ships in ports who were not local shore-residents,
(4) persons (not local residents) assembled at a pagoda festival,
(5) In the case of Akyab town the male temporary immigrants present in the town on the date of the census, numbering 2,483 Hindus and 2,724 Mahomedans.

Visitors staying in hotels, etc., or with friends in private houses have been included in the Normal Civil Population.

NOTE 2.—In Part I of the table the classification is strictly by religion; but in Parts II and III all persons of Christian races have been tabulated as Christians whether they profess the Christian religion or not. The numbers of such persons are as follows :—

Totals by Religion.					Details by Towns.					
Area.	Religion, etc.	Persons.	Males.	Females.		Town.	Religion, etc.	Persons.	Males.	Females.
The whole Province.	Agnostic ...	17	15	2	1	Rangoon	Agnostic ...	10	10	...
	Atheist ...	1	1	...			Buddhist ...	21	11	10
	Buddhist ...	30	14	16			Freethinker ...	9	7	2
	Freethinker ...	9	7	2	15	Syriam	Atheist ...	1	1	...
	Theosophist ...	1	1	...			Buddhist ...	9	3	6
					7	Prome	Agnostic ...	6	4	2
							Theosophist ...	1	1	...
	Total ...	58	38	20	64	Myitkyina	Agnostic ...	1	1	...

NOTE 3.—In Part I separate figures are given for every religion; a few religions have been grouped under the heading *Other Religions* in columns 40, 41 and 42, but details of these are given on page 22. In Parts II and III all the religions of comparatively few adherents are grouped together under the description *Others*.

NOTE 4.—The serial numbers in column 2 (*a*) of Part I are taken from column 2 of Imperial Table IV and therefore indicate the position of each town in the descending order of magnitude. In the last column of the same table are given the serial numbers of Parts II and III.

NOTE 5.—Notes 1 to 9 inclusive and Note 15 prefixed to Imperial Table IV apply to this table, except as regards the order in which the towns are shown.

NOTE 6.—The populations of Cantonments are included in those of the town with which they are associated but are separately tabulated on page 22. The towns concerned are indicated by C in column 3. In this connection Note 16 of Imperial Table IV should be consulted.

District and Division.	TOWN. Serial No. in Table IV.	TOWN. Name.	Municipality, Cantonment, etc. (See Note 1 on the preceding page.)				TOTAL POPULATION. Persons.	Males.	Females.	BUDDHISTS. Persons.	Males.	Females.	ANIMISTS. Persons.	Males.	Females.	HINDUS. Persons.	Males.	Females.
1	2a	2b	3				4	5	6	7	8	9	10	11	12	13	14	15
Provincial Total	...	All tabulated Towns.	...	...	...	.	1,291,527	777,114	514,413	769,198	386,984	382,214	25,180	19,593	5,587	253,497	203,972	49,525
Divisional Burma	...		...	...	..	..	1,256,529	756,024	500,505	746,792	375,640	371,152	23,226	17,883	5,343	246,949	198,705	48,244
Arakan Division	...	...	..	...	...	..	44,215	31,966	12,249	17,731	9,157	8,574	514	386	128	8,757	8,276	481
Akyab ...	5	Akyab ...	M		T	...	36,569	27,693	8,876	12,979	6,645	6,291	446	328	118	8,277	7,852	425
Kyaukpyu ..	69	Kyaukpyu ...	M	...	T	...	3,884	2,230	1,653	2,780	1,458	1,322	46	38	8	263	242	21
Sandoway ...	72	Sandoway ...	M	...	T	...	3,762	2,047	[illegible]	2,012	1,053	959	22	20	2	217	182	35
Pegu Division ...	...	...	...	...	...	...	498,629	327,039	171,630	219,603	112,211	107,392	6,973	5,204	1,769	151,228	123,376	27,852
Rangoon ..	1	Rangoon ...	M	...	T	C	241,962	136,689	105,273	111,771	58,033	53,453	2,883	2,136	747	125,003	102,313	22,689
Insein ...	18	Insein ...	M	...	T	.	14,303	9,520	4,788	6,779	4,546	2,233	130	114	16	4,349	3,032	1,317
Hanthawaddy	15	Syriam ...	..	...	T	...	15,193	11,741	3,452	4,051	1,991	2,067	138	105	33	7,098	6,644	454
Do. ...	35	Thônzwa ...	M	...	T	.	8,153	4,512	3,641	6,620	3,345	3,275	193	151	42	839	688	151
Tharrawaddy ...	51	Thônzè ...	M		T	..	6,594	3,348	3,246	5,353	2,538	2,815	105	79	27	508	385	123
Do ...	73	Tharrawaddy ..	.	N	T	..	3,623	2,079	1,546	1,832	918	914	46	38	8	838	607	231
Do. ...	25	Letpadan ...	M	..	T	..	9,901	5,411	4,490	7,617	3,746	3,871	263	203	54	1,105	841	264
Do. ...	41	Gyobingauk ..	M		T	.	7,669	4,169	3,497	5,832	2,796	3,036	298	233	75	858	695	163
Do. ...	46	Zigon ...	M		...		6,915	3,803	3,112	5,381	2,590	2,791	151	121	30	853	724	129
Do. ...	65	Nattalin ...	.	N	...	...	4,898	2,584	2,314	4,031	1,913	2,118	89	63	21	398	337	61
Do. ...	71	Minhla ...	.	N	.	..	3,829	2,105	1,724	3,020	1,470	1,550	121	87	34	433	352	81
Pegu ...	12	Pegu ...	M	...	T	..	18,759	10,728	8,031	12,601	6,352	6,249	443	344	99	3,778	2,786	992
Do. ...	42	Nyaunglebin ...	M	..	...	...	7,491	4,345	3,146	5,014	2,563	2,451	281	237	84	1,284	980	304
Prome ...	7	Prome ...	M	...	T		25,057	13,340	11,717	19,401	9,741	9,660	1,398	977	421	2,634	1,963	663
Do. ...	19	Paungdè ...	M		T	...	13,454	7,289	6,165	12,072	5,652	6,420	316	261	55	1,064	881	183
Do. ...	29	Shwedaung ...	.	N	...	.	9,108	4,374	4,734	8,418	3,929	4,489	87	64	23	187	146	41
Irrawaddy Divn.	...	...	.	..	...	..	164,501	97,232	67,269	116,858	59,923	56,935	4,222	3,445	777	22,925	19,521	3,404
Bassein ...	4	Bassein .	M	..	T	...	42,563	28,406	14,157	23,164	12,957	10,207	1,141	933	208	10,770	9,465	1,305
Do. ...	50	Ngathainggyaung-Daungyi.	M	..	T		6,751	3,455	3,296	5,855	2,801	3,054	88	65	23	304	259	45
Do. ...	47	Kyônpyaw ...	...	N	.	...	6,910	3,617	3,293	6,032	2,955	3,077	39	39	..	356	299	57
Henzada ...	8	Henzada ...	M		T	.	23,651	12,974	10,677	18,478	9,281	9,197	580	478	102	2,347	1,800	547
Do. ...	38	Myanaung ...	M	..	T	.	7,793	3,907	3,886	6,502	3,030	3,472	91	72	19	333	262	76
Do. ...	45	Kyangin ...	M	.	T	..	7,034	3,604	3,430	6,370	3,099	3,271	51	42	9	324	289	35
Myaungmya ...	55	Myaungmya ..	M	...	T		6,280	3,755	2,525	4,017	2,000	2,017	439	349	90	742	654	88
Do. ...	33	Wakèma ...	M	.	T	...	8,447	4,861	3,586	6,523	3,262	3,261	386	341	45	593	542	51
Do. ...	86	Mawlamyainggyun	...	N	..	...	6,115	3,671	2,444	4,656	2,440	2,210	198	163	35	669	608	61
Ma-ubin ..	49	Ma-ubin ...	M	...	T	...	6,812	4,090	2,722	4,493	2,355	2,138	...	...	..	1,119	[illegible]	214
Do. ...	26	Yandoon ...	M	...	T	...	9,944	5,834	4,110	7,377	3,701	3,676	87	67	20	1,021	810	211
Do. ...	66	Danubyu ...		N	T	..	4,860	2,712	2,148	2,942	1,896	1,046	36	28	8	467	403	64
Pyapôn ...	36	Pyapôn ...	M	...	T	...	8,107	4,877	3,230	5,229	2,657	2,572	346	261	85	1,655	1,314	341
Do. ...	28	Kyaiklat ...	M	...	T	..	9,224	5,600	3,624	6,809	3,566	3,243	236	201	35	916	778	138
Do. ...	63	Bogale ..	..	..	...	.	5,012	3,161	1,851	3,617	1,960	1,657	266	228	38	600	506	94
Do. ...	61	Dedayè ...	...	.	...	...	5,561	3,403	2,150	3,891	1,937	1,957	238	178	60	664	587	77
Tenasserim Divn.	...	...	...	...	...	..	165,465	94,716	70,749	103,499	51,013	52,486	4,975	3,625	1,350	28,691	22,401	6,290
Toungoo ...	10	Toungoo ...	M	...	T	...	19,333	11,150	8,183	10,739	5,460	5,279	584	411	173	3,481	2,617	864
Do. ...	89	Shwegyin ...	M	...	T	...	5,758	3,098	2,660	4,107	2,010	2,097	174	155	19	442	355	87
Do. ...	53	Pyu ...	..	N	T	.	6,451	3,504	2,947	4,600	2,251	2,349	303	218	85	820	617	203
Thatôn ...	16	Thatôn ..	M	..	T	...	15,091	8,076	7,015	11,314	5,533	5,781	258	195	63	1,607	1,201	406
Do. ...	43	Kyaikto ...	M	...	T	...	7,163	3,895	3,272	4,998	2,419	2,579	195	134	61	1,190	837	353
Amherst ...	3	Moulmein ...	M		T	...	61,301	38,076	23,225	28,259	14,503	13,756	1,484	1,071	413	17,566	13,804	3,762
Do. ...	52	Kawkareik ...	..	N	...	..	6,587	3,558	3,029	4,647	2,395	2,252	183	129	54	475	334	141
Tavoy ...	6	Tavoy ...	M	...	T	..	27,480	15,818	11,662	23,469	11,019	12,450	557	417	140	1,299	1,094	205
Mergui ...	13	Mergui ...	M	...	T	..	17,297	9,540	7,757	11,367	5,394	5,973	1,137	895	242	1,811	1,542	269
Magwe Division	...	...		...	...	..	77,884	40,285	37,599	68,261	33,820	34,441	996	742	254	3,598	2,693	905
Thayetmyo ..	22	Thayetmyo ..	M	..	T	C	10,768	5,903	4,865	8,435	4,525	3,910	224	136	88	969	657	312
Do. ...	21	Allanmyo ...	M	...	T	..	11,219	5,480	5,739	10,092	4,739	5,353	94	69	25	408	300	108
Pakôkku ...	9	Pakôkku ...	M	..	T	.	19,507	9,665	9,842	18,211	8,784	9,427	143	115	28	366	285	81
Minbu ...	62	Minbu ...	M	...	T	...	5,403	2,947	2,455	4,279	2,177	2,102	151	109	42	438	337	101
Do. ...	48	Salin ...	M	.	T	...	6,834	3,278	3,556	6,508	3,040	3,468	42	33	9	104	88	16
Magwe ...	37	Magwe ...	..	N	T	...	7,819	4,258	3,561	6,561	3,370	3,191	162	127	35	526	399	127
Do. ...	24	Yenangyaung ...	...	N	.	...	10,018	5,613	4,405	8,361	4,368	3,993	144	123	21	610	498	112
Do. ...	84	Taungdwingyi ...	M	...	T	...	6,306	3,132	3,174	5,814	2,817	2,997	35	30	6	177	129	48
Mandalay Divn.	...	...	...	...	...	...	198,521	107,674	90,847	138,271	68,195	70,076	4,276	3,453	823	22,841	15,892	6,949
Mandalay ...	8	Mandalay City ..	M	...	T	C	148,917	77,763	71,154	115,154	56,811	58,343	1,612	1,320	292	10,995	7,434	3,561
Do. ...	32	Amarapura ...	...	...	T	...	8,497	3,918	4,579	8,009	3,663	4,346	28	19	9	138	85	53
Do. ...	14	Maymyo ...	...	N	T	C	16,558	10,749	5,809	3,977	2,038	1,939	948	877	71	5,305	3,887	1,419
Do. ...	75	Myitngè ...	...	N	...	...	2,439	2,401	1,038	486	295	191	...	...	...	2,308	1,688	620
Bhamo ...	39	Bhamo ...	M	...	T	C	7,741	4,933	2,808	3,325	1,505	1,820	642	480	162	799	598	201
Myitkyina ...	64	Myitkyina ..	..	...	...	...	4,956	3,107	1,849	1,109	571	538	358	281	77	2,394	1,528	866
Katha ...	34	Mogôk ...	...	...	...	...	8,413	4,803	3,610	6,211	3,312	2,899	688	476	212	901	672	229
Sagaing Division	...	...	...	...	...	..	36,845	19,696	17,149	28,836	14,133	14,703	364	314	50	3,360	2,496	864
Shwebo ...	23	Shwebo ...	M	...	T	C	10,605	5,685	4,920	8,004	3,912	4,092	131	101	30	970	722	248
Do. ...	77	Ye-u ...	...	N	..	...	2,742	1,446	1,296	2,314	1,162	1,152	42	35	7	185	139	46
Sagaing ...	20	Sagaing ...	M	...	T	...	11,858	5,784	6,074	9,879	4,599	5,280	25	19	6	775	515	260
Lower Chindwin	27	Mônywa ...	M	..	T	...	9,225	5,109	4,116	7,221	3,636	3,585	87	87	...	979	645	334
Upper Chindwin	78	Mawlaik ...	...	N	...	...	2,415	1,672	743	1,418	824	594	79	72	7	551	475	76
Meiktila Division	..	...	...	...	...	...	69,459	37,416	32,043	53,733	27,188	26,545	906	714	192	5,549	4,050	1,499
Kyaukse ...	57	Kyaukse ...	M	...	T	...	6,107	3,037	3,070	5,207	2,453	2,754	27	22	5	348	261	87
Meiktila ..	31	Meiktila ...	..	N	...	C	8,868	5,240	3,628	5,789	3,243	2,546	65	49	16	1,036	732	304
Yamèthin ...	30	Yamèthin ...	M	...	T	.	8,869	4,830	4,039	5,373	2,769	2,604	70	62	8	822	579	243
Do. ...	17	Pyinmana ...	M	..	T	..	14,836	7,938	6,898	10,215	4,990	5,225	294	225	69	1,810	1,281	529
Do. ...	67	Pyawbwè ...	.	N	...	..	4,704	2,316	2,388	3,850	1,756	2,094	125	98	27	315	200	115
Myingyan ...	11	Myingyan ...	M	...	T	...	18,931	10,374	8,557	16,534	8,595	7,939	282	218	64	1,097	892	205
Do. ...	44	Nyaung-u ...	...	N	...	...	7,094	3,631	3,463	6,765	3,382	3,383	43	40	3	121	105	16
Eastern States	...	...	...	..	...	...	24,998	11,090	13,908	22,406	11,344	11,062	1,954	1,710	244	6,548	5,267	1,281
N. Shan States	74	Lashio ...	...	N	...	...	3,448	2,045	1,402	1,881	978	903	199	139	60	1,178	818	360
Do.	70	Hsipaw ..	...	...	...	...	3,949	2,261	1,688	3,049	1,535	1,514	228	195	33	275	240	35
Do.	40	Namtu-Panghai*	...	...	...	...	7,699	6,031	1,668	2,488	1,429	1,059	1,134	1,052	82	2,536	2,328	208
S. Shan States	58	Taunggyi ...	...	N	...	...	6,016	3,311	2,705	3,439	1,670	1,769	137	109	28	1,447	987	460
Do.	76	Kalaw ...	..	N	...	...	2,997	1,822	1,175	1,735	848	887	123	103	20	751	644	107
Do.	79	Loilem ...	...	N	..	..	998	552	446	681	329	352	14	12	2	239	173	66
Do.	60	Kengtung ...	...	...	...	...	5,718	3,038	2,680	5,162	2,655	2,507	92	81	11	36	19	17
Do.	68	Yawnghwe ...	...	...	...	...	4,173	2,029	2,144	3,971	1,900	2,071	27	19	8	86	58	28

* See the note at the foot of page 22.

territorially with Total Population by Religion.

MAHOMEDANS.			CHRISTIANS.			ARYAS.			BRAHMOS.			CONFUCIANS.			JAINS.			JEWS.			SIKHS.			OTHER RELIGIONS.			Serial No. in Parts II and III.
Persons.	Males.	Females.	Persons.	Males.	Females.	Persons.	Males.	Females.	Persons.	Males.	Females.	Persons.	Males.	Females.	Persons.	Males.	Females.	Persons.	Males.	Females.	Persons.	Males.	Females.	Persons.	Males.	Females.	
16	17	18	19	20	21	22	23	24	25	26	27	28	29	30	31	32	33	34	35	36	37	38	39	40	41	42	
169,192	122,409	46,783	54,656	30,216	24,450	233	168	65	410	325	85	13,243	9,286	3,957	690	487	203	1,106	567	539	3,682	2,837	845	430	270	160	
166,753	120,659	46,094	53,205	29,347	23,853	233	163	65	410	325	85	13,243	9,286	3,957	690	487	203	1,106	567	539	3,492	2,687	805	430	270	160	
16,387	13,598	2,789	721	465	255	10	6	4	...	...	...	11	10	1	35	33	2	10	4	6	21	16	5	18	14	4	
14,250	12,393	1,857	552	391	161	10	6	4	...	...	...	11	10	1	35	33	2	10	4	6	21	16	5	18	14	4	1
771	478	293	21	10	14	...	...	...	...	...	...	...	...	...	...	...	...	...	...	...	...	...	...	...	...	...	2
1,366	727	639	145	65	80	...	...	...	...	...	...	...	...	...	...	...	...	...	...	...	...	...	...	...	...	...	3
75,059	58,791	16,268	29,916	16,597	13,319	190	142	43	345	289	57	12,465	8,610	3,855	494	326	168	986	505	481	1,033	770	263	346	218	128	
61,954	49,520	12,431	25,275	14,208	11,057	191	142	48	329	272	57	12,361	8,505	3,855	472	310	162	966	493	473	630	493	137	329	203	121	4
1,338	954	384	1,656	835	821	...	...	...	...	...	...	...	...	...	...	...	...	...	...	...	92	67	25	4	2	2	5
2,921	2,362	559	629	391	255	...	...	...	...	...	...	104	104	...	1	1	...	9	4	5	196	130	66	5	2	3	6
459	312	147	42	16	23	...	...	...	...	...	...	...	...	...	...	...	...	...	...	...	...	...	...	...	...	...	7
352	223	129	272	120	153	...	...	...	...	...	...	...	...	...	2	2	...	...	...	...	1	1	...	...	...	...	8
491	308	183	408	200	208	...	...	...	...	...	...	...	...	...	2	2	...	2	2	...	6	4	2	...	...	...	9
738	521	217	173	90	83	...	...	...	...	...	...	...	...	...	...	...	...	...	...	...	6	4	2	1	1	...	10
490	343	147	169	93	76	...	...	...	15	16	...	...	...	...	...	...	...	...	...	...	3	3	...	...	...	...	11
458	333	125	72	35	36	...	...	...	...	...	...	...	...	...	...	...	...	1	1	...	...	...	...	...	...	...	12
293	203	97	31	14	17	...	...	...	...	...	...	...	...	...	...	...	...	...	...	...	...	...	...	...	...	...	13
237	183	54	8	3	5	...	...	...	...	...	...	...	...	...	...	...	...	...	...	...	...	...	...	...	...	...	14
1,491	997	494	398	205	193	...	...	...	...	...	...	...	...	...	...	...	...	8	5	3	49	38	11	...	...	...	15
607	437	170	275	135	140	...	...	...	...	...	...	...	...	...	...	...	...	...	...	...	5	3	2	...	...	...	16
2,154	1,420	734	424	219	205	...	...	...	...	...	...	...	...	...	11	8	3	...	...	...	8	5	3	7	5	2	17
665	448	217	44	22	22	...	...	...	...	...	...	...	...	...	6	3	3	...	...	...	37	22	15	...	...	...	18
395	228	167	20	6	14	...	...	...	1	1	...	...	...	...	...	...	...	...	...	...	...	...	...	...	...	...	19
15,837	11,699	4,138	4,303	2,356	1,947	...	...	...	...	...	...	293	254	39	13	10	3	6	2	4	44	22	22	...	...	...	
5,757	4,116	1,641	1,731	935	795	...	...	...	...	...	...	...	...	...	...	...	...	...	...	...	...	...	...	...	...	...	20
483	318	165	21	12	9	...	...	...	...	...	...	...	...	...	...	...	...	...	...	...	...	...	...	...	...	...	21
434	290	144	59	24	35	...	...	...	...	...	...	...	...	...	...	...	...	...	...	...	...	...	...	...	...	...	22
1,336	919	417	872	479	393	...	...	...	...	...	...	...	...	...	6	3	3	...	...	...	32	14	18	...	...	...	23
795	497	298	61	43	18	...	...	...	...	...	...	...	...	...	...	...	...	...	...	...	6	3	3	...	...	...	24
270	147	123	46	24	22	...	...	...	...	...	...	...	...	...	...	...	...	...	...	...	3	3	...	...	...	...	25
766	588	178	316	154	152	...	...	...	...	...	...	...	...	...	...	...	...	...	...	...	...	...	...	...	...	...	26
869	673	196	70	37	33	...	...	...	...	...	...	6	6	...	...	...	...	...	...	...	...	...	...	...	...	...	27
554	433	121	38	21	17	...	...	...	...	...	...	...	...	...	...	...	...	...	...	...	...	...	...	...	...	...	28
697	529	168	355	173	182	...	...	...	...	...	...	101	85	15	...	...	...	6	2	4	1	1	...	...	...	...	29
762	506	255	71	43	28	...	...	...	...	...	...	123	105	18	1	1	...	...	...	...	2	1	1	...	...	...	30
376	292	84	74	33	41	...	...	...	...	...	...	63	58	5	2	2	...	...	...	...	...	...	...	...	...	...	31
567	474	93	310	171	139	...	...	...	...	...	...	...	...	...	...	...	...	...	...	...	...	...	...	...	...	...	32
1,024	888	136	175	103	72	...	...	...	...	...	...	...	...	...	4	4	...	...	...	...	...	...	...	...	...	...	33
465	416	49	34	21	13	...	...	...	...	...	...	...	...	...	...	...	...	...	...	...	...	...	...	...	...	...	34
682	613	69	90	73	17	...	...	...	...	...	...	...	...	...	...	...	...	...	...	...	...	...	...	...	...	...	35
22,964	14,334	8,630	6,180	3,234	2,946	...	...	...	12	7	5	10	10	...	42	30	12	23	10	13	61	47	14	8	5	2	
2,792	1,766	1,026	1,713	841	872	...	...	...	12	7	5	...	...	...	...	...	...	4	4	...	3	2	1	5	3	2	36
857	471	386	178	107	71	...	...	...	...	...	...	...	...	...	...	...	...	...	...	...	...	...	...	...	...	...	37
698	401	297	30	17	13	...	...	...	...	...	...	...	...	...	...	...	...	...	...	...	...	...	...	...	...	...	38
1,615	987	628	297	160	137	...	...	...	...	...	...	...	...	...	...	...	...	...	...	...	...	...	...	...	...	...	39
749	496	253	36	20	16	...	...	...	...	...	...	...	...	...	...	...	...	...	...	...	...	...	...	...	...	...	40
10,856	7,096	3,760	3,026	1,525	1,501	...	...	...	...	...	...	10	10	...	42	30	12	14	4	10	44	33	11	...	...	...	41
1,251	681	570	31	19	12	...	...	...	...	...	...	...	...	...	...	...	...	...	...	...	...	...	...	...	...	...	42
1,699	1,036	663	441	243	198	...	...	...	...	...	...	...	...	...	...	...	...	5	2	3	7	5	2	3	2	1	43
2,447	1,400	1,047	428	302	126	...	...	...	...	...	...	...	...	...	...	...	...	...	...	...	7	7	...	...	...	...	44
4,064	2,451	1,613	741	409	332	...	...	...	20	12	8	...	...	...	52	48	4	4	1	3	147	108	39	1	1	...	
955	496	459	169	85	84	...	...	...	...	...	...	...	...	...	...	...	...	...	...	...	5	2	3	1	1	...	45
601	358	243	24	14	10	...	...	...	...	...	...	...	...	...	...	...	...	...	...	...	...	...	...	...	...	...	46
620	380	240	135	78	53	...	...	...	15	7	8	...	...	...	...	...	...	...	...	...	16	16	...	...	...	...	47
425	261	165	74	41	33	...	...	...	...	...	...	...	...	...	...	...	...	...	...	...	35	22	13	...	...	...	48
149	95	54	15	10	5	...	...	...	...	...	...	...	...	...	...	...	...	...	...	...	16	12	4	...	...	...	49
431	291	140	122	61	61	...	...	...	...	...	...	...	...	...	4	2	2	4	1	3	9	7	2	...	...	...	50
684	460	224	142	94	48	...	...	...	5	5	...	...	...	...	48	46	2	...	...	...	34	29	5	...	...	...	51
188	110	78	59	26	33	...	...	...	...	...	...	...	...	...	...	...	...	...	...	...	32	20	12	...	...	...	52
22,012	13,491	8,521	8,837	4,825	4,012	5	5	...	28	13	15	451	392	59	36	28	8	72	40	32	1,636	1,309	327	56	31	25	
16,373	9,638	6,735	4,160	2,083	2,077	3	3	...	28	13	15	5	5	...	8	7	1	20	9	11	520	415	105	39	25	14	53
300	139	161	18	9	9	...	...	...	...	...	...	2	2	...	...	...	...	...	...	...	1	1	...	1	...	1	54
2,389	1,654	735	3,837	2,211	1,500	2	2	...	...	...	...	10	10	...	6	6	...	31	14	17	48	36	12	14	4	10	55
500	200	100	163	89	74	...	...	...	...	...	...	...	...	...	...	...	...	...	...	...	182	129	53	...	...	...	56
1,470	1,127	343	302	197	105	...	...	...	...	...	...	433	371	57	22	15	7	21	17	4	731	622	109	1	1	...	57
695	457	238	240	160	80	...	...	...	...	...	...	5	3	2	...	...	...	...	...	...	154	106	48	1	1	...	58
485	276	209	127	66	61	...	...	...	...	...	...	1	1	...	...	...	...	...	...	...	...	...	...	...	...	...	59
2,946	1,954	992	1,066	603	463	28	15	13	3	3	...	13	10	3	8	4	4	...	...	...	221	164	57	...	...	...	
877	560	317	448	271	177	25	12	13	3	2	...	1	1	...	8	4	4	...	...	...	139	100	39	...	...	...	60
70	45	24	131	64	67	...	...	...	...	...	...	...	...	...	...	...	...	...	...	...	...	...	...	...	...	...	61
968	546	422	170	78	92	...	...	...	...	...	...	13	9	3	...	...	...	...	...	...	29	18	11	...	...	...	62
757	570	187	265	155	110	...	...	...	...	...	...	...	...	...	...	...	...	...	...	...	16	16	...	...	...	...	63
274	232	42	52	35	17	3	3	...	1	1	...	...	...	...	...	...	...	...	...	...	37	30	7	...	...	...	64
7,484	4,341	3,143	1,441	857	584	...	...	...	1	1	...	...	...	...	10	8	2	5	5	...	329	251	78	1	1	...	
350	216	134	122	50	72	...	...	...	...	...	...	...	...	...	...	...	...	...	...	...	53	35	18	...	...	...	65
1,324	733	591	465	339	126	...	...	...	1	1	...	...	...	...	3	3	...	5	5	...	180	135	45	...	...	...	66
2,245	1,212	1,033	289	145	144	...	...	...	...	...	...	...	...	...	...	...	...	...	...	...	69	62	7	1	1	...	67
2,306	1,335	970	243	141	102	...	...	...	...	...	...	...	...	...	...	...	...	...	...	...	18	15	3	...	...	...	68
382	246	136	29	15	14	...	...	...	...	...	...	...	...	...	...	...	...	...	...	...	3	1	2	...	...	...	69
717	497	220	288	164	124	...	...	...	...	...	...	...	...	...	7	5	2	...	...	...	6	3	3	...	...	...	70
160	101	59	5	3	2	...	...	...	...	...	...	...	...	...	...	...	...	...	...	...	...	...	...	...	...	...	71
2,439	1,750	689	1,451	869	592	...	...	...	...	...	...	...	...	...	...	...	...	...	...	...	190	150	40	...	...	...	
94	49	45	80	49	31	...	...	...	...	...	...	...	...	...	...	...	...	...	...	...	16	13	3	...	...	...	72
339	260	79	58	31	27	...	...	...	...	...	...	...	...	...	...	...	...	...	...	...	...	...	...	...	...	...	73
899	785	114	468	300	168	...	...	...	...	...	...	...	...	...	...	...	...	...	...	...	174	137	37	...	...	...	74
679	374	305	314	171	143	...	...	...	...	...	...	...	...	...	...	...	...	...	...	...	...	...	...	...	...	...	75
201	134	67	187	93	94	...	...	...	...	...	...	...	...	...	...	...	...	...	...	...	...	...	...	...	...	...	76
41	25	16	23	13	10	...	...	...	...	...	...	...	...	...	...	...	...	...	...	...	...	...	...	...	...	...	77
106	76	30	322	207	115	...	...	...	...	...	...	...	...	...	...	...	...	...	...	...	...	...	...	...	...	...	78
80	47	33	9	5	4	...	...	...	...	...	...	...	...	...	...	...	...	...	...	...	...	...	...	...	...	...	79

IMPERIAL TABLE V, PART II.—*Normal Civil Population of Census Towns.*

Serial No.	District and Division.	Town.	TOTAL.			BUDDHISTS.		ANIMISTS.		HINDUS.		MAHOMEDANS.		CHRISTIANS.		OTHERS.	
			Persons.	Males.	Females.	Males.	Females.	Males.	Females.	Males.	Females.	Males.	Females.	Males.	Females.	Males.	Females.
	1	2	3	4	5	6	7	8	9	10	11	12	13	14	15	16	17
	Provincial Total	...	1,197,197	693,902	503,295	357,655	375,853	17,723	5,409	179,151	46,950	100,399	45,899	26,371	23,546	10,603	5,638
	Arakan Division	...	30,389	18,285	12,104	7,976	8,495	331	126	4,672	434	4,985	2,775	270	252	51	22
1	Akyab ...	Akyab ...	23,437	14,631	8,806	5,891	6,258	280	117	4,353	402	3,860	1,849	196	158	51	22
2	Kyaukpyu ...	Kyaukpyu ...	3,518	1,903	1,615	1,263	1,293	34	7	177	14	419	287	10	14	...	...
3	Sandoway ...	Sandoway ..	3,434	1,751	1,683	822	944	17	2	142	18	706	639	64	80	...	...
	Pegu Division ...	...	467,501	299,457	168,044	102,319	104,832	4,893	1,731	113,129	27,344	53,220	16,125	15,287	13,042	10,609	4,960
4	Rangoon ...	Rangoon ...	317,687	215,053	102,634	52,540	51,729	1,896	717	93,051	22,234	44,406	11,327	12,943	10,806	10,207	4,822
5	Insein ...	Insein ...	11,774	7,007	4,767	2,357	2,210	70	16	2,835	1,309	853	384	827	821	65	27
6	Hanthawaddy	Syriam ...	15,072	11,634	3,438	1,961	2,054	106	33	6,592	451	2,339	566	396	260	240	74
7	Do.	Thôngwa ...	8,046	4,413	3,633	3,313	3,269	150	42	635	149	301	147	14	26	...	...
8	Tharrawaddy ...	Thônzè ...	6,556	3,314	3,242	2,514	2,811	79	27	379	123	219	129	120	152	3	...
9	Do. ...	Tharrawaddy ...	3,398	1,913	1,485	858	87	37	8	520	222	296	183	194	197	8	2
10	Do. ...	Letpadan ...	9,674	5,243	4,431	3,649	3,816	205	54	800	262	497	215	87	82	5	5
11	Do. ...	Gyobingauk ...	7,603	4,125	3,478	3,769	3,018	220	75	694	163	333	146	93	76	17	...
12	Do. ...	Zigôn ...	6,783	3,700	3,083	2,550	2,772	115	97	676	128	322	120	38	36	1	...
13	Do. ...	Nattalin ...	4,898	2,584	2,314	1,963	2,118	68	21	337	61	202	97	14	17	...	...
14	Do. ...	Minhla ...	3,829	2,105	1,724	1,480	1,550	87	34	352	81	185	54	3	5	...	...
15	Pegu ...	Pegu ...	17,985	10,133	7,852	6,044	6,086	337	94	2,594	984	936	489	200	191	22	8
16	Do. ...	Nyaunglebin ...	7,243	4,130	3,113	2,453	2,425	225	84	905	299	414	163	130	135	3	2
17	Prome ...	Prome ...	23,951	12,653	11,298	8,423	9,285	973	421	1,771	656	1,270	728	203	202	13	6
18	Do. ...	Paungdè ...	13,934	7,114	6,820	5,520	6,327	261	55	843	181	443	217	22	22	25	18
19	Do. ...	Shwedaung ...	9,068	4,336	4,732	3,925	4,489	64	23	135	41	206	165	6	14	...	...
	Irrawaddy Divn.	...	151,384	85,637	65,747	53,461	55,534	3,262	775	17,245	3,373	9,200	4,098	2,091	1,899	278	68
20	Bassein ...	Bassein ...	37,199	23,464	13,735	9,955	9,820	900	208	8,313	1,296	3,464	1,625	831	786	...	...
21	Do. ...	Ngathainggyaung-Daunggyi.	6,515	3,257	3,258	2,665	3,022	65	23	254	45	278	159	11	9	...	...
22	Do ...	Kyônpyaw ...	6,746	3,500	3,246	2,870	3,030	39	...	294	57	273	144	24	15	..	...
23	Henzada ...	Henzada ...	22,526	11,909	10,617	8,583	9,146	467	100	1,701	547	693	416	454	387	11	21
24	Do. ...	Myanaung ...	7,538	3,690	3,848	2,915	3,434	72	19	234	76	428	298	40	18	1	3
25	Do. ...	Kyangin ...	6,998	3,543	3,455	[illegible]	3,266	38	9	248	35	139	123	24	22	3	...
26	Myaungmya ...	Myaungmya ...	5,925	3,469	2,456	1,880	1,954	347	90	570	84	510	176	162	152	...	...
27	Do. ...	Wakèma ...	7,839	4,412	3,427	2,987	3,106	328	45	500	49	558	196	33	38	6	...
28	Do. ...	Mawlamyainggyun	5,689	3,297	2,392	2,223	2,162	162	35	553	61	340	117	19	17	...	...
29	Ma-ubin ...	Ma-ubin ...	6,125	3,501	2,624	2,027	2,054	...	..	808	203	414	166	165	181	87	20
30	Do. ...	Yandoon ...	8,842	4,709	4,133	3,304	3,602	60	20	765	208	432	256	42	28	106	19
31	Do. ...	Danubyu ...	4,629	2,539	2,090	1,777	1,894	28	8	376	64	265	78	33	41	60	5
32	Pyapôn ...	Pyapôn ...	7,489	4,364	3,125	2,435	2,477	259	85	1,134	339	386	93	150	131	...	...
33	Do. ...	Kyaiklat ...	8,332	4,786	3,546	3,287	3,173	197	35	637	138	573	135	88	65	4	...
34	Do. ...	Bogale ...	4,309	2,576	1,733	1,720	1,542	214	38	424	94	198	49	10	10	...	...
35	Do. ...	Dedayè ...	4,083	2,621	2,062	1,737	1,851	176	60	454	77	249	67	5	6	...	...
	Tenasserim Divn.	...	157,759	86,749	71,010	47,773	52,026	3,543	1,349	19,704	6,172	12,603	8,527	3,023	2,901	103	45
36	Toungoo ...	Toungoo ...	18,034	9,984	8,050	4,721	5,188	405	173	2,404	835	1,664	991	774	855	16	8
37	Do. ...	Shwegyin ...	5,509	2,874	2,635	1,872	2,085	145	19	296	81	457	381	104	69	...	...
38	Do. ...	Pyu ...	6,394	3,451	2,943	2,231	2,345	217	85	[illegible]	203	392	297	17	13	...	...
39	Thatôn ...	Thatôn ...	14,090	7,348	6,742	5,103	5,562	182	63	1,080	391	835	597	148	129	...	...
40	Do. ...	Kyaikto ...	7,062	3,833	3,229	2,378	2,550	134	61	812	351	489	251	20	16	...	...
41	Amherst ...	Moulmein ...	56,029	33,010	23,019	12,970	13,644	1,057	412	11,728	3,715	5,761	3,729	2,432	2,488	72	[illegible]
42	Do. ...	Kawkareik ...	6,553	3,530	3,023	2,394	2,252	129	54	318	139	675	568	14	10	..	...
43	Tavoy ...	Tavoy ...	26,982	13,356	13,626	10,844	12,433	394	140	946	895	937	1,056	227	196	8	6
44	Mergui ...	Mergui ...	17,106	9,363	7,743	5,260	5,967	880	342	1,526	262	1,393	1,047	297	125	7	...
	Magwe Division	...	75,081	37,837	37,244	32,073	34,257	722	254	2,380	843	2,117	1,513	286	282	159	54
45	Thayetmyo ...	Thayetmyo ...	9,561	4,751	4,807	3,498	3,878	128	88	569	295	473	464	81	81	5	3
46	Do. ...	Allanmyo ...	11,109	5,404	5,705	4,699	5,325	69	25	300	103	322	237	14	10	...	...
47	Pakôkku ...	Pakôkku ...	19,197	9,410	9,787	8,682	9,403	114	23	245	73	292	218	61	57	26	8
48	Minbu ...	Minbu ...	5,111	2,698	2,413	2,034	2,091	98	42	313	95	190	242	41	30	22	13
49	Do. ...	Salin ...	6,756	3,209	3,547	3,020	3,465	33	9	52	11	85	53	10	5	9	4
50	Magwe ...	Magwe ...	7,308	3,827	3,481	3,107	3,166	127	35	320	109	201	103	61	61	9	7
51	Do. ...	Yenangyaung ...	9,941	5,557	4,384	4,339	3,978	123	21	476	112	445	218	54	48	80	7
52	Do. ...	Taungdwingyi ...	6,098	2,980	3,118	2,692	2,951	30	6	105	40	109	78	24	31	20	12
	Mandalay Divn.	...	184,497	96,374	88,123	65,771	69,485	2,289	711	12,662	5,779	11,148	8,203	3,419	3,579	1,085	366
53	Mandalay ...	Mandalay City ...	142,642	72,435	70,207	54,767	57,938	1,210	288	6,432	3,407	8,104	6,568	1,620	1,879	302	127
54	Do. ...	Amarapura ...	8,497	3,918	4,579	3,663	4,346	19	9	85	53	139	161	9	9	3	1
55	Do. ...	Maymyo ...	12,515	7,586	4,929	1,828	1,793	85	25	2,878	1,008	1,429	681	1,314	1,384	62	38
56	Do. ...	Myitngè ...	3,439	2,401	1,038	293	191	...	...	1,688	620	200	100	89	74	129	53
57	Bhamo ...	Bhamo ...	5,940	3,426	2,514	1,457	1,795	326	123	337	117	590	265	167	95	549	119
58	Myitkyina ...	Myitkyina ...	3,392	2,096	1,296	550	528	232	67	694	376	425	219	156	78	39	28
59	Katha ...	Mogôk ...	8,072	4,512	3,560	3,211	2,894	417	193	548	193	271	209	64	60	1	...
	Sagaing Division	...	33,735	17,197	16,538	13,032	14,347	288	50	1,916	765	1,418	918	435	426	108	42
60	Shwebo ...	Shwebo ...	9,384	4,723	4,661	3,469	3,948	78	30	517	229	442	289	180	144	37	21
61	Do. ...	Ye-u ...	2,742	1,446	1,296	1,162	1,152	35	7	139	46	46	24	64	67	...	...
62	Sagaing ...	Sagaing ...	11,737	5,681	6,056	4,503	5,262	19	6	511	260	543	422	77	92	27	21
63	Lower Chindwin	Mônywa ...	8,121	4,181	3,940	3,314	3,532	87	...	393	171	280	141	91	96	16	...
64	Upper Chindwin	Mawlaik ...	1,751	1,166	585	584	453	69	7	355	59	107	42	23	17	28	7
	Meiktila Division	...	63,922	32,847	31,075	24,016	25,849	690	192	3,476	1,391	3,997	3,057	596	540	72	44
65	Kyauksè ...	Kyauksè ...	5,865	2,879	2,986	2,366	2,685	22	5	220	83	209	131	50	72	12	10
66	Meiktila ...	Meiktila ..	6,943	3,656	3,287	2,326	2,370	48	16	497	234	651	556	107	90	26	21
67	Yamèthin ...	Yamèthin ...	7,404	3,737	3,667	1,996	2,274	51	8	481	235	1,068	1,006	124	141	17	3
68	Do. ...	Pyinmana ...	14,527	7,703	6,824	4,845	5,181	221	69	1,197	512	1,294	959	137	100	9	3
69	Do. ...	Pyawbwè ...	4,659	2,288	2,371	1,782	2,077	98	27	199	115	243	136	35	14	1	2
70	Myingyan ...	Myingyan ...	17,430	8,953	8,477	7,369	7,879	210	64	777	196	430	220	160	123	7	5
71	Do. ...	Nyaung-u ...	7,094	3,631	3,463	3,382	3,383	40	3	105	16	101	59	3	2	...	...
	Eastern States	...	32,929	19,519	13,410	11,234	11,088	2,005	221	3,967	849	1,781	683	864	590	138	37
72	N. Shan States	Lashio ...	2,612	1,431	1,181	937	891	72	38	331	176	42	45	48	31	1	...
73	Do.	Hsipaw ...	3,750	2,079	1,671	1,470	1,501	157	32	190	32	235	79	27	27	...	...
74	Do.	Namtu-Panghai *	7,699	6,031	1,668	1,429	1,059	1,052	82	2,328	208	785	114	300	108	137	37
75	S. Shan States	Taunggyi ...	5,210	2,734	2,476	1,666	1,760	103	28	420	246	368	299	171	148	...	...
76	Do.	Kalaw ...	[illegible]	1,737	1,164	848	887	103	20	549	96	134	67	93	94	...	...
77	Do.	Loilem ...	876	450	426	329	352	12	2	72	46	24	26	13	10	...	...
78	Do.	Kengtung ...	5,718	3,038	2,680	2,655	2,507	81	11	19	17	76	30	207	115	...	...
79	Do.	Yawnghwe ...	4,173	2,029	2,144	1,900	2,071	19	8	58	28	47	33	5	4	...	...

* See the note at the foot of page 22; there is no adventitious population.

IMPERIAL TABLE V, PART III.—*Adventitious Population of Census Towns.*

Serial No.	District and Division.	Town.	TOTAL. Persons.	TOTAL. Males.	TOTAL. Females.	BUDDHISTS. Males.	BUDDHISTS. Females.	ANIMISTS. Males.	ANIMISTS. Females.	HINDUS. Males.	HINDUS. Females.	MAHOMEDANS. Males.	MAHOMEDANS. Females.	CHRISTIANS. Males.	CHRISTIANS. Females.	OTHERS. Males.	OTHERS. Females.
	1	2	3	4	5	6	7	8	9	10	11	12	13	14	15	16	17
	Provincial Total	...	94,330	83,212	11,118	29,315	6,345	1,870	178	24,821	2,575	22,020	884	3,883	924	1,313	212
	Arakan Division	...	13,826	13,681	145	1,181	79	55	2	3,604	47	8,613	14	196	3	32	...
1	Akyab ...	Akyab ...	13,132	13,062	70	755	35	48	1	3,499	23	8,533	8	195	3	32	...
2	Kyaukpyu ...	Kyaukpyu ...	366	323	43	195	29	4	1	65	7	59	6	...	...	...	...
3	Sandoway ...	Sandoway ...	328	296	32	231	15	3	...	40	17	21	...	1	...	...	...
	Pegu Division	...	31,138	27,582	3,556	9,878	2,544	311	38	10,247	508	5,571	133	1,347	297	228	36
4	Rangoon ...	Rangoon ...	24,275	21,636	2,639	5,537	1,744	240	30	9,252	455	5,114	107	1,293	237	200	30
5	Insein ...	Insein ...	2,534	2,513	21	2,159	13	44	...	197	8	101	...	8	..	4	..
6	Hanthawaddy	Syriam ...	121	107	14	30	7	...	...	52	3	23	3	2	1	...	...
7	Do. ...	Thôngwa ...	107	99	8	32	6	1	...	53	2	11	...	2	...	...	...
8	Tharrawaddy ...	Thônzè ...	38	34	4	24	4	...	...	6	...	4	...	...	...	...	...
9	Do. ...	Tharrawaddy ...	227	166	61	60	41	1	...	87	9	12	...	6	11	...	...
10	Do. ...	Letpadan ...	227	168	59	97	55	3	...	41	2	24	2	3	...	...	...
11	Do. ...	Gyobingauk ...	63	44	19	27	18	3	...	1	...	10	1	1	...	2	...
12	Do. ...	Zigôn ...	133	105	28	40	19	6	3	48	1	11	5	...	...	...	...
13	Do. ...	Nattalin ...	...	...	...	...	...	...	...	...	...	...	...	...	...	...	...
14	Do. ...	Minhla ...	...	...	...	...	...	...	...	...	...	...	...	...	...	...	...
15	Pegu ...	Pegu ...	784	595	189	308	163	7	5	191	8	61	5	6	2	21	6
16	Do. ...	Nyaunglebin ...	253	215	38	110	26	2	...	75	5	23	2	5	5	...	...
17	Prome ...	Prome ...	2,116	1,687	429	1,318	405	4	...	194	13	150	6	21	5	...	...
18	Do. ...	Paungdè ...	220	175	45	132	43	...	...	38	2	5	...	...	...	...	...
19	Do. ...	Shwedaung ...	40	38	2	4	...	...	...	11	...	22	2	...	...	1	...
	Irrawaddy Divn.	...	13,117	11,595	1,522	6,462	1,401	83	2	2,276	31	2,499	40	265	48	10	...
20	Bassein ...	Bassein ...	5,364	4,942	422	3,001	387	35	...	1,152	9	652	16	104	10	...	...
21	Do. ...	Ngathainggyaung-Daunggyi.	236	198	38	132	32	...	...	25	...	40	6	1	...	...	...
22	Do. ...	Kyônpyaw ...	164	117	47	95	47	...	..	5	...	17	...	...	...	...	...
23	Henzada ...	Henzada ...	1,125	1,065	60	698	51	11	2	99	...	226	1	25	6	6	...
24	Do. ...	Myanaung ...	255	217	38	115	38	...	...	28	...	69	...	3	...	2	...
25	Do. ...	Kyangin ...	66	61	5	8	5	4	...	41	...	8	...	...	...	...	...
26	Myaungmya ...	Myaungmya ...	355	286	67	120	63	2	...	84	4	78	2	2	...	...	...
27	Do. ...	Wakèma ...	608	449	157	275	155	13	...	42	2	115	...	4	2	...	...
28	Do. ...	Mawlamyainggyun	426	374	52	223	48	1	..	55	...	93	4	2	...	...	...
29	Ma-ubin ...	Ma-ubin ...	687	589	98	328	84	...	...	137	11	115	2	8	1	1	...
30	Do. ...	Yandoon ...	502	425	77	297	74	7	...	45	3	74	...	1	...	1	...
31	Do. ...	Danubyu ...	231	173	58	119	52	...	...	27	...	27	6	...	...	...	...
32	Pyapôn ...	Pyapôn ...	618	513	105	222	95	2	...	180	2	88	...	21	8	...	...
33	Do. ...	Kyaiklat ...	892	814	78	339	70	4	...	241	...	315	1	15	7	...	...
34	Do. ...	Bogale ...	703	585	118	270	115	4	...	82	...	218	...	11	3	...	...
35	Do. ...	Dedayè ...	885	787	98	220	85	2	...	133	...	364	2	68	11	...	...
	Tenasserim Divn.	...	8,706	7,967	739	3,240	460	82	1	2,697	128	1,731	113	211	45	6	2
36	Toungoo ...	Toungoo ...	1,298	1,166	132	778	51	6	...	213	29	102	35	67	17	...	...
37	Do. ...	Shwegyin ...	249	224	25	138	12	10	...	59	6	14	5	3	2	...	...
38	Do. ...	Pyu ...	57	53	4	20	4	1	...	23	...	9	...	—	—	...	..
39	Thatôn ...	Thaton ...	1,001	728	273	430	219	13	...	121	15	152	31	12	8	...	...
40	Do. ...	Kyaikto ...	106	63	43	31	39	...	...	25	2	7	2	...	...	...	...
41	Amherst ...	Moulmein ...	5,272	5,066	206	1,533	112	14	1	2,076	47	1,335	31	103	13	8	2
42	Do. ...	Kawkareik ...	34	28	6	1	...	...	...	16	2	6	2	5	2	...	...
43	Tavoy ...	Tavoy ...	498	462	36	275	17	23	...	148	10	99	7	16	2	1	...
44	Mergui ...	Mergui ...	191	177	14	134	6	15	...	16	7	7	...	5	1	...	...
	Magwe Division	...	2,803	2,448	355	1,747	184	20	...	313	62	334	100	43	9	11	...
45	Thayetmyo ...	Thayetmyo ...	1,207	1,150	57	1,037	32	8	...	88	17	23	5	4	3	...	...
46	Do. ...	Allanmyo ...	110	76	34	40	28	...	...	...	...	36	6	...	...	...	...
47	Pakôkku ...	Pakôkku ...	310	255	55	102	24	1	...	40	8	88	22	17	1	7	...
48	Minbu ...	Minbu ...	292	249	43	143	11	11	...	24	6	71	23	...	3	...	...
49	Do. ...	Salin ...	78	69	9	20	3	...	...	36	8	10	1	...	...	3	...
50	Magwe ...	Magwe ...	511	431	80	261	25	...	...	79	18	90	37	...	...	1	...
51	Do. ...	Yenangyaung ...	87	66	21	29	15	...	...	22	...	15	6	...	...	...	...
52	Do. ...	Taungdwingyi ...	208	152	56	125	46	...	...	24	8	1	...	2	2	...	...
	Mandalay Divn.	...	14,024	11,300	2,724	2,424	591	1,264	112	3,230	1,170	2,343	318	2,407	433	730	100
53	Mandalay ...	Mandalay City ...	6,275	5,328	947	2,044	405	110	4	1,002	154	1,534	167	463	198	175	19
54	Do. ...	Amarapura ...	...	...	...	...	...	...	...	...	...	...	...	...	...	..	...
55	Do. ...	Maymyo ...	4,043	3,163	880	210	146	792	46	1,009	411	235	54	907	222	10	1
56	Do. ...	Myitngè ...	...	...	...	...	...	...	...	...	...	...	..	...	...	...	...
57	Bhamo ...	Bhamo ...	1,801	1,507	294	48	25	154	39	261	84	537	78	30	10	477	58
58	Myitkyina ...	Myitkyina ...	1,564	1,011	553	21	10	49	10	834	490	32	19	5	3	70	22
59	Katha ...	Mogôk ...	341	291	50	101	5	59	13	124	31	5	...	2	1	...	...
	Sagaing Divn. ...	...	3,110	2,499	611	1,201	356	26	...	580	99	536	74	168	47	88	35
60	Shwebo ...	Shwebo ...	1,221	962	259	443	144	23	...	205	19	118	28	91	33	82	35
61	Do. ...	Ye-u ...	...	...	...	...	...	...	...	...	...	...	...	...	...	...	...
62	Sagaing ...	Sagaing ...	121	103	18	96	18	...	..	3	...	3	...	1	...	...	...
63	Lower Chindwin	Mônywa ...	1,104	928	176	322	53	...	...	252	63	290	46	64	14	...	...
64	Upper Chindwin	Mawlaik ...	664	506	158	240	141	3	...	120	17	125	...	12	..	6	...
	Meiktila Divn.	...	5,537	4,569	968	3,172	696	24	...	574	108	344	86	261	40	194	36
65	Kyauksè ...	Kyauksè ...	242	158	84	87	62	...	...	41	4	7	3	...	...	23	8
66	Meiktila ...	Meiktila ...	1,925	1,584	341	917	176	8	...	235	70	81	35	232	36	118	24
67	Yamèthin ...	Yamèthin ...	1,465	1,093	372	773	330	11	...	98	8	144	27	21	3	46	4
68	Do. ...	Pyinmana ...	359	285	74	245	44	4	...	84	17	42	11	4	2	6	...
69	Do. ...	Pyawbwè ...	45	28	17	24	17	...	...	1	..	3	...	...	...	...	...
70	Myingyan ...	Myingyan ...	1,501	1,421	80	1,226	60	8	...	125	9	67	20	4	1	1	...
71	Do. ...	Nyaung-u ...	...	...	...	...	...	...	...	...	...	...	...	...	...	...	...
	Eastern States	...	2,069	1,571	498	110	34	105	23	1,300	432	39	6	5	...	12	3
72	N. Shan States	Lashio ...	836	615	221	41	12	67	22	487	184	7	...	1	...	12	3
73	Do.	Hsipaw ...	199	182	17	65	13	38	1	50	3	25	...	4	...	...	...
74	Do.	Namtu-Panghai	...	...	...	...	...	...	...	...	...	...	...	..	...	...	..
75	S. Shan States	Taunggyi ...	806	577	229	4	9	...	...	567	214	6	6	...	...	...	...
76	Do.	Kalaw ...	106	95	11	...	...	...	...	95	11	...	...	...	...	...	...
77	Do.	Loilem ...	123	102	20	...	...	...	...	101	20	1	...	...	...	...	...
78	Do.	Kengtung ...	...	...	...	...	...	...	...	...	...	...	...	...	...	...	...
79	Do.	Yawnghwe ...	...	...	...	...	...	...	...	...	...	...	...	...	...	...	...

Details for Other Religions in Census Towns in Imperial Table V, Part I (*see Note 3 on page 17*).

Town. Serial No.	Town. Name.	Persons.	Males.	Females.	Town. Serial No.	Town. Name.	Persons.	Males.	Females.
	Zoroastrians.					**Agnostics.**			
	Total ...	*341*	*204*	*137*		*Total* ...	*19*	*17*	*2*
5	Akyab ...	18	14	4	1	Rangoon Town ...	10	10	...
1	Rangoon Town ...	263	152	111	7	Prome ..	6	4	2
15	Syriam ...	4	1	3	22	Thayetmyo ...	1	1	...
18	Insein ...	4	2	2	64	Myitkyina ...	1	1	...
25	Letpadan .	1	1	...	30	Yamèthin ...	1	1	...
10	Toungoo ..	5	3	2					
6	Tavoy ...	3	2	1		**Atheists.**			
2	Mandalay City ..	34	24	10		*Total* ...	*5*	*5*	...
32	Amarapura ...	1	...	1	1	Rangoon Town ...	4	4	...
14	Maymyo ...	7	4	3	15	Syriam ...	1	1	...
39	Bhamo ..	1	1	...					
						Freethinkers.			
	Shintoists.				1	Rangoon Town ...	19	11	8
	Total ...	*44*	*31*	*13*		**Theosophists.**			
1	Rangoon Town ..	32	30	2		*Total* ...	*2*	*2*	...
2	Mandalay City ..	5	1	4	1	Rangoon Town ...	1	1	...
14	Maymyo ...	7	..	7	7	Prome ..	1	1	...

Population of Cantonments Classified by Religion (*see Note 6 on page 17*).

Cantonment.	Total Population.			Buddhists.		Animists.		Hindus.		Mahomedans.		Christians.		Others.	
	All.	Males.	Females.	Males.	Females.	Males.	Females.	Males.	Females.	Males.	Females.	Males.	Females.	Males.	Females.
1	2	3	4	5	6	7	8	9	10	11	12	13	14	15	16
Rangoon ..	6,471	4,540	1,931	575	509	34	12	1,980	779	530	118	1,393	508	28	5
Civil Area ...	*3,897*	*2,870*	*1,027*	*81*	*57*	...	..	*1,345*	*559*	*325*	*65*	*1,118*	*345*	*1*	*1*
Military Area ...	*2,574*	*1,670*	*904*	*494*	*452*	*34*	*12*	*635*	*220*	*205*	*53*	*275*	*163*	*27*	*4*
Thayetmyo ...	690	319	371	122	180	2	10	131	129	27	21	37	31	...	...
Mandalay ...	14,078	8,661	5,417	5,580	4,443	73	7	1,246	396	1,153	339	420	184	189	48
Civil Areas outside Fort	*9,513*	*4,903*	*4,610*	*4,014*	*4,092*	*10*	*4*	*464*	*223*	*282*	*205*	*54*	*56*	*79*	*30*
Civil Areas within Fort	*778*	*510*	*268*	*146*	*113*	*8*	*1*	*182*	*76*	*87*	*34*	*66*	*40*	*21*	*4*
Jail Staff .	*114*	*85*	*29*	*18*	*16*	...	...	*57*	*5*	*7*	*5*	*3*	*3*	...	...
Jail Prisoners ...	*1,228*	*1,214*	*14*	*1,063*	*12*	*55*	*2*	*30*	...	*50*		*12*	...	*4*	...
Military Areas ...	*2,445*	*1,949*	*496*	*339*	*210*	...	...	*513*	*92*	*727*	*95*	*285*	*85*	*85*	*14*
Maymyo ...	3,719	2,903	816	158	128	788	45	882	394	181	45	890	204	4	...
Shwebo ...	894	442	452	217	294	4	3	101	48	111	102	8	5	1	...
Meiktila ...	1,637	1,316	321	750	164	1	...	161	65	57	33	232	36	115	23
Bhamo ...	1,213	1,009	204	96	100	36	...	100	32	403	39	14	2	360	31
Civil Area ...	*258*	*154*	*104*	*80*	*89*	*25*	...	*36*	*11*	...	..	...	...	*13*	*4*
Military Area ...	*955*	*855*	*100*	*16*	*11*	*11*	...	*64*	*21*	*403*	*39*	*14*	*2*	*347*	*27*

Details for Namtu-Panghai.

(*Column-headings as in Cantonment Statement above.*)

1	2	3	4	5	6	7	8	9	10	11	12	13	14	15	16
Total ...	7,699	6,031	1,668	1,429	1,059	1,052	82	2,328	208	785	114	300	168	137	37
Namtu ...	*5,463*	*4,524*	*939*	*693*	*440*	*550*	*29*	*2,222*	*172*	*649*	*98*	*293*	*168*	*117*	*32*
Panghai ...	*2,236*	*1,507*	*729*	*736*	*619*	*502*	*53*	*106*	*36*	*136*	*16*	*7*	...	*20*	*5*

IMPERIAL TABLE VI-A.

Religion.

NOTE 1.—Table VI-A classifies by religion the population actually enumerated throughout the province, and omits, besides the population of the areas shown in Note 11 of Table II as entirely omitted from the Census, the population of the following areas in which no complete enumeration was made but only an estimate :—

	Administration.	Description of Area.	Persons.	Males.	Females.
26	Pakôkku Hill Tracts	Unadministered Territory.	8,756	4,207	4,549
35	Upper Chindwin District.	Somra Tract .	7,636	3,719	3,917
41	Northern Shan States	East Manglün ...	26,701	13,527	13,174

The succeeding table, numbered VI-B, classifies according to race the adherents shown in the present table for each of the principal religions, and for some races distinguishes those born in Burma from those born elsewhere. A later table, XIII, classifies by religion the population of each race.

NOTE 2.—Details for the various religions represented by columns 38, 39 and 40 of this table under the heading *Remainder* are given in a subsidiary table on page 26.

NOTE 3.—In this table the classification is strictly by religion, in which respect it differs from the corresponding table of the census of 1911, in which the figures given for Christians included, besides all Christians, all non-Christian members of Christian races; but, with the aid of Note 2 prefixed to the table of 1911, comparison with the present table can easily be made. (Allowance should be made however for ten European Buddhist males tabulated in Table VI of 1911 as Buddhists but omitted from Note 2 of that table.) Non-Christian members of Christian races included in the figures for each religion in the present table are as shown in the sub-table below. Of these 2 male Agnostics and 9 male Buddhists in Rangoon, 1 male Freethinker and 2 male Buddhists in Hanthawaddy, and all the female Buddhists described themselves as Anglo-Indian by race; while all the others returned a European or allied race (as defined in Note 1 of Imperial Table XVI).

Totals by Religion.

Area.	Religion.	Persons.	Males.	Females.
The whole Province.	Agnostic	20	18	2
	Atheist	1	1	0
	Buddhist	31	15	16
	Freethinker	11	9	2
	Theosophist	1	1	0
	Unitarian	1	1	0
	Total ...	65	45	20

Details by Districts.

District.	Religion	Persons.	Males.	Females.
5 Rangoon Town.	Agnostic	10	10	0
	Buddhist	21	11	10
	Freethinker	9	7	2
7 Hanthawaddy	Atheist	1	1	0
	Buddhist	9	3	6
	Freethinker	2	2	0
9 Pegu ...	Buddhist	1	1	0
10 Prome ...	Agnostic	7	5	2
	Theosophist	1	1	0
23 Pakôkku ...	Agnostic	1	1	0
29 Myitkyina	Agnostic	1	1	0
32 Shwebo ...	Unitarian	1	1	0
36 Chin Hills	Agnostic	1	1	0

NOTE 4.—The classification by religion of the population of the town of Mandalay is given in Imperial Table V with further details by race in Tables VI-A and XIII. Rangoon Town constitutes the Rangoon Town District for which statistics are given in this table as for other districts.

Serial No.	DISTRICT OR STATE.	TOTAL POPULATION. Persons.	Males.	Females.	BUDDHIST. Persons.	Males.	Females.	ANIMIST. Persons.	Males.	Females.	HINDU. Persons.	Males.	Females.	MAHOMEDAN. Persons.	Males.	Females.
	1	2	3	4	5	6	7	8	9	10	11	12	13	14	15	16
	Provincial Total ...	**13,169,099**	**6,735,516**	**6,433,583**	**11,201,943**	**5,525,159**	**5,676,784**	**702,587**	**369,188**	**333,399**	**484,432**	**378,177**	**106,255**	**500,592**	**314,527**	**186,065**
	Divisional Burma	**11,692,408**	**5,991,623**	**5,700,785**	**10,018,497**	**4,932,849**	**5,085,648**	**456,104**	**243,426**	**212,678**	**471,427**	**367,516**	**103,911**	**495,758**	**311,098**	**184,660**
	Arakan Division ...	**909,246**	**472,217**	**437,029**	**596,694**	**295,258**	**301,436**	**75,601**	**38,968**	**36,633**	**16,304**	**14,748**	**1,556**	**218,737**	**122,108**	**96,629**
1	Akyab ...	576,430	309,564	266,866	315,140	159,722	155,418	36,806	19,124	17,682	14,719	13,401	1,318	208,961	116,736	92,225
2	Hill District of Arakan.	20,914	10,790	10,124	2,225	1,220	1,005	18,051	9,109	8,945	575	407	168	46	43	3
3	Kyaukpyu ...	199,873	96,569	103,304	178,451	84,901	93,550	16,173	8,414	7,759	634	609	25	4,479	2,580	1,899
4	Sandoway ...	112,029	55,304	56,725	100,878	49,415	51,463	4,668	2,321	2,247	376	331	45	5,251	2,749	2,502
	Pegu Division ...	**2,309,293**	**1,258,914**	**1,050,379**	**1,848,999**	**922,203**	**926,796**	**24,406**	**17,273**	**7,133**	**252,530**	**195,953**	**56,577**	**102,095**	**77,881**	**24,214**
5	Rangoon Town ...	341,962	236,689	105,273	111,571	58,088	53,483	2,883	2,136	747	125,002	102,313	22,689	61,954	49,520	12,434
6	Insein ...	293,083	156,794	136,289	241,481	122,368	119,113	3,211	2,358	853	24,658	18,872	5,786	7,990	5,391	2,599
7	Hanthawaddy ...	364,624	201,043	163,581	293,768	148,757	145,011	5,202	3,997	1,205	47,326	35,365	11,961	12,811	9,551	3,260
8	Tharrawaddy ...	492,429	246,261	246,168	467,558	229,477	238,081	2,129	1,600	529	9,179	7,422	1,757	5,421	3,736	1,685
9	Pegu ...	445,620	235,324	210,296	378,338	191,186	187,152	6,707	4,533	2,174	40,856	27,554	13,302	9,745	6,996	2,749
10	Prome ...	371,575	182,803	188,772	356,283	172,327	183,956	4,274	2,649	1,625	5,509	4,427	1,082	4,174	2,687	1,487
	Irrawaddy Division	**2,030,044**	**1,048,377**	**981,667**	**1,835,026**	**917,736**	**917,290**	**14,860**	**11,762**	**3,098**	**54,447**	**46,165**	**8,282**	**38,297**	**28,588**	**9,709**
11	Bassein ...	489,473	252,947	236,526	428,546	213,811	214,735	3,356	2,696	660	14,947	13,151	1,796	9,994	7,082	2,912
12	Henzada ...	550,920	273,439	277,481	525,231	257,027	268,204	1,970	1,632	338	6,703	5,712	991	5,211	3,323	1,888
13	Myaungmya ...	370,551	196,757	173,794	324,315	165,260	159,055	4,027	3,292	735	9,533	8,544	989	11,451	8,990	2,461
14	Maubin ...	330,106	168,513	161,593	302,862	150,413	152,449	1,736	1,244	492	6,833	5,954	879	6,001	4,350	1,651
15	Pyapôn ...	288,994	156,721	132,273	254,072	131,225	122,847	3,771	2,898	873	16,431	12,804	3,627	5,640	4,843	797
	Tenasserim Division	**1,613,523**	**847,445**	**766,078**	**1,359,574**	**690,077**	**669,497**	**58,050**	**32,981**	**25,069**	**76,389**	**56,680**	**19,709**	**63,296**	**39,234**	**24,062**
16	Toungoo ...	381,883	197,505	184,378	297,980	149,783	148,197	20,699	11,268	9,431	19,575	13,316	6,259	8,163	5,498	2,665
17	Salween ...	50,379	26,811	23,568	26,327	14,413	11,914	22,407	11,200	11,207	355	307	48	532	449	83
18	Thatôn ...	471,100	245,909	225,191	430,329	218,580	211,749	2,303	1,615	688	21,112	14,794	6,318	13,405	8,912	4,493
19	Amherst ...	417,910	223,348	194,562	355,175	181,489	173,686	3,442	2,446	996	25,415	19,468	5,947	26,678	16,261	10,417
20	Tavoy ...	156,786	80,994	75,792	145,146	72,612	72,534	2,773	2,194	579	3,319	2,953	366	2,873	1,844	1,029
21	Mergui ...	135,465	72,878	62,587	104,617	53,200	51,417	6,426	4,258	2,168	6,613	5,842	771	11,645	6,270	5,375
	Magwe Division ...	**1,438,774**	**705,247**	**733,527**	**1,376,446**	**667,197**	**709,249**	**29,815**	**10,233**	**19,582**	**12,209**	**10,671**	**1,538**	**7,768**	**5,472**	**2,296**
22	Thayetmyo ...	255,406	125,283	130,123	239,726	116,712	123,014	11,269	5,725	5,544	1,946	1,405	541	1,994	1,177	817
23	Pakôkku ...	465,771	223,943	241,828	460,158	220,495	239,663	3,345	1,756	1,589	842	702	140	1,022	701	321
24	Minbu ...	274,302	134,495	139,807	265,885	129,039	136,846	4,860	2,620	2,240	1,995	1,752	243	1,223	842	381
25	Magwe ...	423,252	211,686	211,566	410,548	200,865	209,683	629	533	96	7,243	6,669	574	3,521	2,748	773
26	Pakôkku Hill Tracts	20,043	9,840	10,203	129	86	43	19,712	9,599	10,113	183	143	40	8	5	3
	Mandalay Division	**849,361**	**435,894**	**413,467**	**638,118**	**316,860**	**321,258**	**128,067**	**65,049**	**63,018**	**37,274**	**26,382**	**10,892**	**28,961**	**17,752**	**11,209**
27	Mandalay ...	356,621	182,999	173,622	299,327	146,205	153,122	2,698	2,301	397	22,061	15,591	6,470	23,209	13,665	9,544
28	Bhamo ...	112,960	56,888	56,072	55,822	28,193	27,629	48,359	22,850	25,509	1,397	1,097	300	1,960	1,541	419
29	Myitkyina ...	118,382	63,419	54,963	39,960	21,587	18,373	66,927	34,135	32,792	8,829	5,980	2,849	1,283	899	384
30	Katha ...	253,725	128,444	125,281	236,886	117,983	118,903	9,620	5,362	4,258	3,990	2,935	1,055	2,478	1,620	858
31	Putao ...	7,673	4,144	3,529	6,123	2,892	3,231	463	401	62	997	779	218	31	27	4
	Sagaing Division	**1,350,396**	**641,290**	**709,106**	**1,210,001**	**568,431**	**641,570**	**111,698**	**54,873**	**56,825**	**10,658**	**7,895**	**2,763**	**12,517**	**7,068**	**5,449**
32	Shwebo ...	391,284	184,708	206,576	378,464	177,347	201,117	388	305	83	2,538	1,925	613	7,610	3,922	3,688
33	Sagaing ...	326,908	155,054	171,854	321,016	151,524	169,492	97	84	13	1,956	1,382	574	2,811	1,563	1,248
34	Lower Chindwin ...	342,880	156,693	186,187	340,065	154,557	185,508	141	126	15	1,299	1,006	293	1,025	794	231
35	Upper Chindwin ...	179,245	90,713	88,532	170,322	84,914	85,408	3,665	1,932	1,733	3,223	2,472	751	1,023	758	265
36	Chin Hills ...	110,079	54,122	55,957	134	89	45	107,407	52,426	54,981	1,642	1,110	532	48	31	17
	Meiktila Division	**1,197,771**	**582,229**	**615,542**	**1,153,639**	**555,087**	**598,552**	**3,607**	**2,287**	**1,320**	**11,626**	**9,032**	**2,594**	**24,087**	**12,994**	**11,093**
37	Kyaukse ...	142,677	70,449	72,228	135,082	66,277	68,805	157	110	47	1,028	821	207	5,740	2,896	2,844
38	Meiktila ...	289,897	137,573	152,324	281,618	132,184	149,434	349	305	44	2,644	2,005	639	4,283	2,369	1,914
39	Yamethin ...	323,189	160,913	162,276	298,565	146,086	152,479	2,719	1,577	1,142	6,220	4,797	1,423	12,908	6,896	6,012
40	Myingyan ...	442,008	213,294	228,714	438,374	210,540	227,834	382	295	87	1,724	1,399	325	1,156	833	323
	Eastern States ...	**1,470,691**	**743,893**	**726,798**	**1,183,448**	**592,310**	**591,138**	**246,433**	**125,762**	**120,721**	**13,005**	**10,661**	**2,344**	**4,834**	**3,429**	**1,405**
41	Northern Shan States	559,223	285,700	273,523	415,893	208,446	207,447	131,057	67,495	63,562	7,804	6,686	1,118	2,286	1,815	471
42	Southern Shan States	847,618	427,064	420,554	748,051	373,450	374,601	81,211	42,672	38,539	4,908	3,721	1,187	2,310	1,467	843
43	Karenni ...	63,850	31,129	32,721	19,502	10,414	9,088	34,215	15,595	18,620	293	254	39	238	147	91

VIA.—*Religion.*

CHRISTIAN.			ARYA.			BRAHMO.			CONFUCIAN.			JAIN.			JEW.			SIKH.			REMAINDER (Details on page 26).			Serial No. of District or State (Column 1).
Persons.	Males.	Females.	Persons.	Males.	Females.	Persons.	Males.	Females.	Persons.	Males.	Females.	Persons.	Males.	Females.	Persons.	Males.	Females.	Persons.	Males.	Females.	Persons.	Males.	Females.	
17	18	19	20	21	22	2	24	25	26	27	28	29	30	31	32	33	34	35	36	37	38	39	40	
257,186	**132,498**	**124,688**	**270**	**190**	**80**	**448**	**355**	**93**	**14,131**	**9,964**	**4,167**	**1,135**	**866**	**269**	**1,135**	**587**	**548**	**4,843**	**3,704**	**1,139**	**477**	**301**	**176**	
234,438	**120,975**	**113,463**	**270**	**190**	**80**	**448**	**355**	**93**	**14,127**	**9,962**	**4,165**	**1,135**	**866**	**269**	**1,135**	**587**	**548**	**4,594**	**3,499**	**1,095**	**475**	**300**	**175**	
1,724	992	732	10	6	4	...	...	...	21	20	1	78	72	6	10	4	6	44	32	12	23	19	4	
618	428	190	10	6	4	...	...	...	21	20	1	78	72	6	10	4	6	44	32	12	23	19	4	1
14	11	3	...	...	...	...	...	...	...	...	...	...	...	...	...	...	...	...	...	...	...	...	...	2
136	65	71	...	...	...	..	..	...	...	...	..	..	...	...	...	...	...	...	...	...	...	...	...	3
956	488	468	...	...	...	...	...	...	...	...	...	..	...	...	...	...	...	...	...	...	...	...	...	4
65,030	34,457	30,573	197	145	52	347	290	57	12,512	8,649	3,863	627	449	178	987	506	481	1,195	875	320	368	233	135	
25,275	14,208	11,067	190	142	48	329	272	57	12,361	8,505	3,855	472	310	162	966	493	473	630	493	137	329	208	121	5
15,579	7,688	7,891	7	3	4	...	..	...	...	..	...	26	23	3	...	...	...	124	87	37	7	4	3	6
5,074	3,022	2,052	...	...	...	...	..	...	106	106	..	79	74	5	9	4	5	227	154	73	22	13	9	7
8,074	3,970	4,104	..	...	...	16	16	...	10	10	...	6	6	...	4	4	...	30	18	12	2	2	...	8
9,790	4,918	4,872	...	...	...	...	...	...	35	27	8	27	25	2	8	5	3	114	80	34	...	...	...	9
1,238	651	587	...	..	.	2	2	...	...	...	..	17	11	6	..	...	...	70	43	27	8	6	2	10
86,608	43,464	43,144	...	...	...	...	...	...	661	554	107	68	60	8	14	10	4	59	34	25	4	4	...	
32,630	16,207	16,423	..	...	...	...	...	...	...	...	...	...	...	...	...	...	...	...	...	..	...	...	...	11
11,742	5,711	6,031	...	...	...	...	...	...	...	...	...	9	5	4	3	...	3	51	29	22	...	...	...	12
21,198	10,645	10,553	...	...	...	...	..	...	9	9	...	16	16	...	2	1	1	...	...	...	...	...	...	13
11,984	5,976	6,008	...	...	...	...	..	...	652	545	107	31	27	4	...	...	...	7	4	3	...	...	...	14
9,054	4,925	4,129	..	...	..	...	..	...	...	...	...	12	12	.	9	9	...	1	1	..	4	4	...	15
55,883	28,250	27,633	2	2	...	12	7	5	143	94	49	49	37	12	38	19	19	78	59	19	10	6	4	
35,442	17,624	17,818	...	...	...	12	7	5	..	...	...	...	...	...	4	4	...	3	2	1	5	3	2	16
758	442	316	...	...	..	...	...	...	...	...	..	...	...	...	...	...	...	...	...	...	...	...	...	17
3,811	1,920	1,891	...	...	...	...	...	...	133	84	49	...	...	...	...	...	...	5	3	2	2	1	1	18
7,074	3,596	3,478	...	...	...	...	...	...	10	10	..	49	37	12	21	7	14	46	34	12	...	...	...	19
2,645	1,371	1,274	1	1	...	...	...	...	...	...	...	...	...	...	10	5	5	16	12	4	3	2	1	20
6,153	3,297	2,856	..	...	...	...	...	...	...	...	...	...	...	...	3	3	...	8	8	...	...	...	...	21
2,210	1,242	768	...	...	...	47	35	12	...	...	...	93	87	6	4	1	3	278	205	73	4	3	1	
465	261	204	...	...	...	...	...	...	...	...	...	...	...	...	..	...	...	5	2	3	1	1	...	22
307	210	97	...	...	...	38	30	8	..	...	...	11	9	2	...	...	...	47	39	8	1	1	...	23
174	118	56	...	...	...	...	...	...	...	...	...	19	19	...	...	...	...	145	104	41	1	1	...	24
1,153	746	407	...	...	...	9	5	4	...	...	...	63	59	4	4	1	3	81	60	21	1	...	1	25
11	7	4	...	...	...	...	...	...	...	...	...	...	...	..	...	...	...	..	...	...	...	...	...	26
14,132	7,638	6,492	21	15	6	28	13	15	743	605	138	37	29	8	73	40	33	1,826	1,460	366	62	31	31	
8,389	4,506	3,833	9	6	3	28	13	15	19	19	...	14	13	1	52	23	29	815	628	187	60	29	31	27
4,058	2,056	1,996	...	...	...	...	..	...	595	496	99	22	15	7	21	17	4	731	622	109	1	1	...	28
994	535	459	...	..	...	...	...	...	124	85	39	1	1	...	...	...	...	263	196	67	1	1	...	29
744	537	207	...	...	...	...	..	...	5	5	..	...	...	...	...	...	...	2	2	...	...	...	...	30
32	24	8	12	9	3	...	...	...	...	...	...	...	...	...	...	...	...	15	12	3	...	...	...	31
4,810	2,501	2,309	41	23	18	12	8	4	45	38	7	71	49	22	4	2	2	536	399	137	3	3	...	
2,008	1,015	993	33	17	16	2	2	...	27	24	3	8	4	4	4	2	2	201	144	57	1	1	...	32
948	446	502	..	...	...	...	..	...	12	9	3	2	1	1	...	...	...	65	44	21	1	1	...	33
334	194	140	...	...	...	...	...	...	...	...	...	...	...	...	...	...	...	16	16	...	...	...	...	34
695	397	298	8	6	2	10	6	4	6	5	1	61	44	17	...	...	...	232	179	53	...	...	...	35
825	449	376	...	...	...	...	...	...	...	...	...	...	...	...	...	...	...	22	16	6	1	1	...	36
4,122	2,311	1,811	...	...	...	2	2	...	2	2	...	112	83	29	5	5	...	578	435	143	1	1	...	
592	292	300	...	...	...	...	...	...	...	...	...	...	...	...	...	...	...	78	53	25	...	...	...	37
772	532	240	...	...	...	2	2	...	...	...	...	4	4	...	5	5	...	220	167	53	...	...	...	38
2,416	1,285	1,131	...	...	...	...	...	...	2	2	...	84	57	27	...	...	...	274	212	62	1	1	...	39
348	202	140	...	...	...	...	...	...	...	...	...	24	22	2	...	...	...	6	3	3	...	...	...	40
22,668	11,523	11,145	...	...	...	...	...	...	4	2	2	...	...	...	...	...	...	249	205	44	2	1	1	
1,929	1,050	879	...	...	...	...	...	...	4	2	2	...	...	...	..	...	...	249	205	44	1	1	...	41
11,137	5,754	5,383	...	...	...	...	...	...	...	...	...	...	...	...	..	...	...	...	...	...	1	...	1	42
9,602	4,719	4,883	..	...	...	...	...	...	...	...	...	...	...	...	...	...	...	...	...	...	...	...	...	43

Details for Religions included in columns 38, 39 and 40 of the Table.

I.—*Totals for the Province.*

Religion.		Persons.	Males.	Females.
Zorastrians	...	380	229	151
Shintoists	...	45	31	14
Unitarians	...	1	1	0
Agnostics	...	22	20	2
Atheists	...	6	5	1
Freethinkers	...	21	13	8
Theosophists	...	2	2	0
Total	...	477	301	176

II.—*Details for each Religion.*

District. Serial No.	District. Name.	Persons.	Males.	Females.
	Zoroastrians.			
	Total ...	380	229	151
1	Akyab ...	23	19	4
5	Rangoon Town ...	263	152	111
6	Insein ..	7	4	3
7	Hanthawaddy ...	19	10	9
8	Tharrawaddy ..	2	2	0
15	Pyapôn ...	4	4	0
16	Toungoo ...	5	3	2
18	Thatôn ...	2	1	1
20	Tavoy ...	3	2	1
24	Minbu ...	1	1	0
27	Mandalay ...	48	28	20
28	Bhamo ...	1	1	0
33	Sagaing ...	1	1	0
41	Northern Shan States	1	1	0
	Shintoists.			
	Total ...	45	31	14
5	Rangoon Town ...	32	30	2
25	Magwe ...	1	0	1
27	Mandalay ...	12	1	11
	Unitarians.			
	Total ...	1	1	0
32	Shwebo ...	1	1	0
	Agnostics.			
	Total ...	22	20	2
5	Rangoon Town ..	10	10	0
10	Prome ...	7	5	2
22	Thayetmyo ...	1	1	0
23	Pakôkku ...	1	1	0
29	Myitkyina ..	1	1	0
36	Chin Hills ...	1	1	0
39	Yamèthin ..	1	1	0
	Atheists.			
	Total ...	6	5	1
5	Rangoon Town ...	4	4	0
7	Hanthawaddy ...	1	1	0
42	Southern Shan States	1	0	1
	Freethinkers.			
	Total ...	21	13	8
5	Rangoon Town ...	19	11	8
7	Hanthawaddy ...	2	2	0
	Theosophists.			
	Total ...	2	2	0
5	Rangoon Town ...	1	1	0
10	Prome ...	1	1	0

IMPERIAL TABLE VI-B.

Religion with further Classification by Race and Birthplace.

NOTE 1.—This table divides according to broad racial classes the figures of Imperial Table VIA for the Buddhist, Animist, Hindu, Sikh, Arya, Brahmo and Mahomedan religions and further classifies the persons of some of these classes according as they were born in Burma or elsewhere. Regarding other religions Note 2 below should be consulted.

NOTE 2.—The Confucians tabulated in Imperial Table VIA were all Chinese. For Christians a racial classification is given by Imperial Tables XV and XVI, further details for some races being given in Imperial Table XIII. The others omitted from the table are the Jains, Jews, Shintoists, Zoroastrians, Unitarians, Agnostics, Atheists, Freethinkers and Theosophists, amounting in all to 1,754 males and 993 females.

NOTE 3.—For details regarding the separate races included in the headings of the several columns of this table reference should be made to Imperial Table XIII.

NOTE 4.—Part V of Imperial Table XIII exhibits in another way the relation between religion and race for the province as a whole.

NOTE 5.—The non-Christian Europeans and Anglo-Indians who are the subject of Note 3 of Imperial Table VIA are classified in this table, as in that, according to their personal religion.

NOTE 6.—The census town of Rangoon is the same as Rangoon Town District.

NOTE 7.—The figures given in this table for Mandalay District include the corresponding figures for Mandalay City which are given immediately below them and are related in the manner described in Note 1 above to the figures for Mandalay City in Imperial Table V.

Serial No.	District or State.	BUDDHISTS. Burma and Mon Race Group S and Buddhist Zerbadis.* Males.	Females.	Karens. Males.	Females.	Other Indigenous Races. Males.	Females.	Chinese. Males.	Females.	Others. Males.	Females.
	1	2	3	4	5	6	7	8	9	10	11
	Provincial Total ...	4,382,832	4,555,629	475,514	468,364	641,393	641,531	19,282	9,677	6,138	1,583
	Divisional Burma ...	4,293,455	4,469,248	397,057	388,985	217,905	216,332	18,474	9,540	5,958	1,543
	Arakan Division ...	288,345	296,081	20	2	5,105	4,791	108	19	1,680	548
1	Akyab	154,387	151,387	...	...	3,771	3,495	75	13	1,489	523
2	Hill District of Arakan	1,076	985	...	...	9	3	...	...	135	17
3	Kyaukpyu	84,822	93,517	...	...	39	29	7	1	33	3
4	Sandoway	48,060	50,192	20	2	1,286	1,264	26	5	23	...
	Pegu Division ...	845,601	855,297	49,537	50,491	17,357	16,354	8,050	4,221	1,658	433
5	Rangoon Town ..	51,980	49,624	165	144	222	255	4,975	3,185	746	275
6	Insein ...	107,110	103,922	11,692	12,225	2,849	2,811	495	131	222	24
7	Hanthawaddy ...	131,926	128,442	13,098	13,296	3,021	3,072	440	138	272	63
8	Tharrawaddy ...	216,504	225,552	10,135	10,233	2,314	2,132	494	159	30	5
9	Pegu	172,534	170,302	12,734	12,748	4,043	3,448	1,533	591	342	63
10	Prome	165,547	177,455	1,713	1,845	4,908	4,636	113	17	46	3
	Irrawaddy Division ...	763,256	767,444	147,831	146,659	2,694	2,257	2,797	762	1,158	168
11	Bassein	173,100	173,084	39,210	40,968	560	427	641	213	300	43
12	Henzada	235,829	247,138	18,899	19,423	1,739	1,503	428	129	132	11
13	Myaungmya ...	122,274	116,729	42,075	42,068	101	99	589	122	221	37
14	Ma-ubin	109,586	115,771	40,091	36,545	39	48	478	46	219	39
15	Pyapôn	122,467	114,722	7,556	7,655	255	180	661	252	286	38
	Tenasserim Division ...	457,651	450,874	198,644	191,253	26,926	23,099	6,055	3,992	801	279
16	Toungoo	124,928	126,181	16,028	14,710	8,179	7,107	358	134	290	65
17	Salween	1,116	799	10,722	9,510	2,495	1,581	42	...	38	24
18	Thatôn	91,160	89,026	121,781	118,445	4,106	3,431	1,438	811	95	36
19	Amherst	130,928	125,778	40.818	39,156	6,853	6,192	2,681	2,438	209	122
20	Tavoy	68,144	68,689	3,727	3,655	50	20	625	154	66	16
21	Mergui	41,375	40,401	5,568	5,777	5,243	4,768	911	455	103	16
	Magwe Division ...	645,311	686,237	58	23	21,509	22,949	161	22	158	18
22	Thayetmyo ...	111,725	118,044	20	11	4,879	4,946	33	2	55	11
23	Pakôkku	212,661	231,463	10	...	7,747	8,198	35	1	42	1
24	Minbu	120,853	128,036	16	12	8,129	8,791	26	7	15	...
25	Magwe	199,986	208,651	12	...	754	1,014	67	12	46	6
26	Pakôkku Hill Tracts ...	86	43	...	...	...	...	...	...	...	...
	Mandalay Division ...	213,728	218,296	134	23	101,712	102,525	920	355	366	59
27	Mandalay ...	142,720	151,210	7	11	3,000	1,823	309	66	169	12
	Mandalay City ...	*56,451*	*58,217*	*6*	*11*	*182*	*86*	*120*	*26*	*52*	*8*
28	Bhamo	11,302	10,612	11	...	16,804	16,882	54	107	22	28
29	Myitkyina	4,745	2,890	20	2	16,676	15,462	92	7	54	12
30	Katha	54,917	53,566	96	10	62,406	65,151	451	171	113	5
31	Putao	44	18	...	...	2,826	3,207	14	4	8	2
	Sagaing Division ...	526,883	597,868	60	19	41,760	43,609	175	70	58	4
32	Shwebo	177,230	201,085	29	16	20	14	52	2	16	...
33	Sagaing	151,105	169,115	27	...	353	373	16	3	23	1
34	Lower Chindwin ...	154,462	185,450	...	2	19	9	68	46	8	1
35	Upper Chindwin ...	43,531	42,192	4	1	41,368	43,213	5	...	6	2
36	Chin Hills	55	26	...	...	...	...	34	19	...	...
	Meiktila Division ...	553,180	497,151	773	515	842	748	208	99	84	39
37	Kyauksè	66,124	68,723	1	...	75	58	57	19	20	5
38	Meiktila	131,984	149,206	61	191	64	22	40	2	35	13
39	Yamèthin	144,540	151,413	711	322	700	665	107	63	28	16
40	Myingyan	210,532	227,809	...	2	3	3	4	15	1	5
	Eastern States ...	89,377	86,381	78,457	79,379	428,488	425,199	808	187	180	40
41	Northern Shan States	17,442	14,975	685	380	189,979	191,972	289	110	51	10
42	Southern Shan States	70,609	70,358	75,865	77,259	225,374	226,929	476	25	126	30
43	Karenni	1,326	1,048	1,907	1,740	7,135	6,298	43	2	3	...

* Also includes 10 male and 7 female Buddhist Kamans and 1 female Buddhist Thinchi.

further classification by Race and Birthplace.

ANIMISTS.								HINDUS.				SIKHS, ARYAS AND BRAHMOS				Serial No. of District, etc. (Column 1).
Indigenous Races.		Chinese.		Indian Races.				Born in Burma.		Born outside Burma.		Born in Burma.		Born outside Burma.		
				Born in Burma.		Born outside Bur.										
Males.	Females.	Males.	Females.	Males.	F'mls.	Males.	F'mls.	Males.	Females.	Males.	Females.	Males.	Females.	Males.	Females.	
12	13	14	15	16	17	18	19	20	21	22	23	24	25	26	27	
293,467	299,355	70,716	32,624	751	546	4,254	874	52,635	44,870	325,542	61,385	506	455	3,748	857	
197,589	200,498	40,877	10,778	744	546	4,216	861	51,559	43,883	315,957	60,028	497	445	3,547	823	
38,134	36,442	504	156	45	32	285	3	985	843	13,763	713	14	12	24	4	
18,456	17,514	384	136	40	30	244	2	834	725	12,567	593	14	12	24	4	1
9,102	8,942	...	...	5	2	2	1	116	98	291	70	...	...	...	...	2
8,317	7,743	81	16	...	...	16	...	25	3	584	22	...	...	...	...	3
2,259	2,243	39	4	...	...	23	...	10	17	321	28	...	...	...	...	4
2,656	2,602	12,067	3,624	424	295	2,126	612	24,911	20,865	171,042	35,712	134	109	1,176	320	
6	9	2,110	725	6	9	14	4	6,721	5,909	95,592	16,780	78	59	829	183	5
217	273	2,099	577	8	2	34	1	3,016	2,367	15,856	3,419	19	12	71	29	6
55	55	2,720	803	217	114	1,005	233	6,498	5,531	28,867	6,430	12	13	142	60	7
162	137	1,351	348	17	16	70	28	805	672	6,617	1,085	...	5	34	7	8
1,184	1,102	2,795	869	112	96	442	107	7,442	6,041	20,112	7,261	17	14	63	20	9
1,032	1,026	992	302	64	58	561	239	429	315	3,998	737	8	6	37	21	10
309	381	10,206	2,546	90	56	1,157	115	4,334	3,035	41,831	5,247	6	11	28	14	
54	60	2,422	583	2	...	218	17	805	589	12,346	1,207	...	...	...	...	11
21	33	1,138	278	8	8	464	19	622	401	5,090	590	6	10	25	12	12
22	15	2,950	687	19	7	301	26	484	379	8,060	610	...	...	...	...	13
210	257	932	208	30	7	72	20	457	353	5,497	526	...	1	4	2	14
1	16	2,764	790	31	34	102	33	1,966	1,313	10,838	2,314	...	...	1	...	15
22,710	22,481	9,741	2,394	112	116	418	78	12,110	10,520	44,570	9,189	7	2	60	22	
9,364	8,855	1,665	482	21	42	218	52	3,088	2,907	10,218	3,352	1	...	8	6	16
11,170	11,206	30	1	...	...	...	...	30	21	277	27	...	...	...	...	17
30	48	1,434	557	68	63	83	20	4,196	3,725	10,598	2,593	...	...	3	2	18
78	135	2,304	848	19	11	45	2	4,466	3,617	15,002	2,330	3	1	31	11	19
352	516	1,841	63	...	...	1	...	164	120	2,789	246	3	1	10	3	20
1,716	1,721	2,467	443	4	...	71	4	166	130	5,676	641	...	...	8	...	21
18,826	19,254	1,256	280	43	84	108	14	1,009	724	9,662	814	37	27	208	58	
5,435	5,427	243	76	37	33	10	8	365	302	1,040	239	...	...	2	3	22
1,561	1,554	191	35	...	...	4	...	97	46	605	94	4	6	65	10	23
2,229	2,158	391	82	...	...	...	...	161	109	1,591	134	28	13	76	28	24
2	2	431	87	6	1	94	6	362	245	6,307	329	5	8	60	17	25
9,599	10,113	...	...	...	...	...	...	24	22	119	18	...	...	...	...	26
59,646	61,611	5,279	1,361	27	9	97	37	5,588	5,673	20,794	5,219	146	158	1,342	229	
886	80	1,379	299	5	2	31	16	3,499	3,762	12,092	2,708	100	96	547	109	27
84	*16*	*1,220*	*262*	*4*	2	*12*	*12*	*2,112*	*2,470*	*5,322*	*1,091*	*50*	42	*379*	*64*	
21,198	25,110	654	399	4	...	...	...	183	132	914	168	42	37	580	72	28
32,306	32,545	1,816	247	1	...	12	...	1,330	1,276	4,650	1,573	1	24	195	43	29
4,019	3,822	1,272	408	17	7	54	21	480	390	2,455	665	...	...	2	...	30
243	54	158	8	...	...	...	...	96	113	683	105	3	1	18	5	31
54,309	56,704	561	120	2	1	1	...	1,555	1,284	6,340	1,529	84	67	346	92	
42	5	261	77	2	1	...	...	331	272	1,594	341	30	26	133	47	32
...	...	83	13	...	...	1	...	355	319	1,027	255	8	14	36	7	33
6	...	120	15	...	...	...	...	131	109	875	184	1	...	15	...	34
1,835	1,718	97	15	...	...	...	...	414	199	2,058	552	42	24	149	35	35
52,426	54,981	...	...	...	...	...	...	384	335	786	197	3	3	13	3	36
999	1,018	1,263	297	1	3	24	2	1,067	989	7,955	1,605	69	59	368	84	
1	2	109	45	...	...	...	...	127	110	694	97	13	16	40	9	37
...	5	299	39	...	...	6	...	258	278	1,747	361	12	22	157	31	38
988	1,011	573	131	1	...	15	...	470	471	4,327	952	41	21	171	41	39
10	...	282	82	...	3	3	2	212	130	1,187	195	3	...	...	3	40
95,878	98,862	29,839	21,846	7	...	38	13	1,076	987	9,585	1,857	9	10	196	34	
38,896	41,954	28,589	21,608	...	...	10	...	402	399	6,284	719	9	10	196	34	41
41,543	38,304	1,094	222	7	...	28	13	662	573	3,059	614	...	...	...	...	42
15,439	18,604	156	16	...	...	...	...	12	15	242	24	...	...	...	...	43

IMPERIAL TABLE VIB.—*Religion with further classification by Race and Birthplace.*

	District or State.	MAHOMEDANS.											
		Zerbadis and Arakan Mahomedans.		Burmans and Kamans.*		Chinese.		Indian Races.				Others (chiefly Malays).†	
								Born in Burma.		Born outside Burma.			
		Males.	Females.	Males.	Females.	Males.	Females.	Males.	F'male.	Males.	F'male.	Males.	Females.
	1	28	29	30	31	32	33	34	35	36	37	38	39
	Provincial Total ...	57,869	59,388	3,727	7,032	1.076	441	103.461	99,429	146,139	17,242	2,255	2,588
	Divisional Burma ...	57,339	59.006	3,712	6,936	860	296	103,069	98,888	143,865	17,002	2,253	2,582
	Arakan Division ...	14,966	13,491	1,139	1,278	...	...	78,109	76,150	27,894	5,710	...	...
1	Akyab	12,721	11,035	557	546	...	...	77,216	75,202	26,242	5,442	...	...
2	Hill District of Arakan	...	...	...	...	...	...	6	2	37	1	...	...
3	Kyaukpyu	243	193	484	579	...	...	758	893	1,095	234	...	...
4	Sandoway	2,002	2,263	98	153	...	...	129	53	520	33	...	...
	Pegu Division ...	8,246	8,509	655	1,341	224	46	8,157	7,634	60,564	6,674	35	10
5	Rangoon Town ...	4,220	4,338	65	345	135	28	3,963	3,493	41,109	4,223	28	7
6	Insein	524	510	440	176	...	...	984	1,270	3,433	640	4	3
7	Hanthawaddy ...	1,558	1,248	...	321	6	...	980	1,074	7,010	617	3	...
8	Tharrawaddy ...	786	737	..	153	13	...	433	480	2,504	315	...	...
9	Pegu	600	623	150	346	56	12	1,199	1,068	4,991	700	...	...
10	Prome	558	1,053	...	...	14	6	598	249	1,517	179	..	...
	Irrawaddy Division ...	3,504	3,561	1,048	1,514	77	11	3,523	3,411	20,434	1,207	2	5
11	Bassein	2,008	2,016	...	...	34	10	685	669	4,355	217	...	...
12	Henzada	388	446	403	356	10	...	645	811	1,875	274	2	1
13	Myaungmya ...	640	585	352	740	16	...	871	829	7,111	303	...	4
14	Ma-ubin	386	391	56	217	13	1	888	835	3,007	207	...	...
15	Pyapôn	82	123	237	201	4	...	434	267	4,086	206	...	...
	Tenasserim Division ...	12,373	13,659	294	574	194	49	7,249	6,097	16,936	1,201	2,188	2,482
16	Toungoo	882	1,406	222	327	65	29	1,019	571	3,310	331	..	1
17	Salween	20	25	...	4	40	4	31	37	358	13	...	...
18	Thatôn	2,114	2,697	...	...	41	5	1,874	1,460	4,880	287	3	44
19	Amherst	5,818	5,803	54	224	25	8	4,102	3,871	6,242	497	20	14
20	Tavoy	727	873	5	2	9	...	153	115	945	39	5	...
21	Mergui	2,812	2,855	13	17	14	3	70	43	1,201	34	2,160	2,423
	Magwe Division ...	1,183	1,262	101	333	26	1	668	385	3,494	314	1	...
22	Thayetmyo ...	437	551	52	89	3	...	190	142	495	35	...	...
23	Pakôkku	123	133	37	60	3	...	81	84	456	44	1	...
24	Minbu	250	230	12	68	...	1	83	40	497	42	...	...
25	Magwe	373	348	...	116	20	...	314	117	2,041	192	...	...
26	Pakôkku Hill Tracts ...	...	...	...	...	...	...	...	2	5	1	..	...
	Mandalay Division ..	7,027	7,908	219	812	272	188	1,661	1,235	8,572	1,059	1	7
27	Mandalay	6,436	7,297	139	588	48	30	1,213	846	5,828	779	1	4
	Mandalay City ...	*4,626*	*5,363*	*66*	*498*	*39*	*24*	*620*	*331*	*4,286*	*516*	*1*	*2*
28	Bhamo	175	145	41	68	...	17	76	66	1,249	120	...	3
29	Myitkyina	149	186	...	7	4	1	112	93	634	97	...	...
30	Katha	266	280	39	149	220	140	259	229	836	60	...	...
31	Putao	1	...	...	...	...	..	1	1	25	3	...	...
	Sagaing Division ...	1,846	2,098	50	60	29	...	2,569	3,008	2,549	268	25	15
32	Shwebo	681	742	...	...	19	...	2,337	2,827	885	119	...	...
33	Sagaing	1,006	1,136	...	...	10	...	72	57	475	55	...	...
34	Lower Chindwin ...	61	91	41	42	...	...	100	46	592	48	...	4
35	Upper Chindwin ...	96	129	9	18	...	...	49	64	579	43	25	11
36	Chin Hills	2	...	...	...	...	...	11	14	18	3	...	...
	Meiktila Division ...	8,194	8,518	206	1,024	38	1	1,133	968	3,422	569	1	13
37	Kyaukse	2,600	2,759	12	...	6	...	102	38	176	47	...	...
38	Meiktila	856	1,046	110	267	6	...	506	434	891	154	1	13
39	Yamethin	4,583	4,464	84	757	13	1	429	482	1,786	308	...	...
40	Myingyan	155	249	...	...	13	...	96	14	569	60	...	...
	Eastern States ...	536	382	15	96	216	145	392	541	2,274	240	2	1
41	Northern Shan States...	191	149	11	24	42	34	172	123	1,397	140	2	1
42	Southern Shan States ...	318	205	...	66	174	111	197	370	778	91	...	...
43	Karenni	21	28	4	6	...	...	23	48	99	9	...	...

* Mahomedan Kamans in Akyab District number 556 M. and 541 F.; in Kyaukpyu District 484 M. and 578 F.; in Sandoway District 4 M. only; in other districts *nil*.

† The total figures for Mahomedan Malays are 2,202 M. and 2,484 F.; these were chiefly found in Mergui District where all the persons shown in columns 38 and 39 belong to this class.

IMPERIAL TABLE VII-A.

Age, Sex, and Civil Condition by Religion.

NOTE 1.—This table is in three parts. Part I gives (subject to Note 4 below) the distribution by age and civil condition of the totals of each religion tabulated in Table VI-A. Parts II and III give similar statistics for Divisional Burma and for the Eastern States respectively, the religions with few adherents being collected in these parts under the description *Others*. The *Eastern States* include the Northern and Southern Shan States and Karenni; *Divisional Burma* includes all the remainder of the province.

NOTE 2.—For all three parts of the table the areas and populations excluded are those excluded from Table VIA, namely those in which the census was by estimate only.

NOTE 3.—The age recorded was the number of completed years. The age-group represented by 5—10 in the table includes all who had completed five but had not yet completed ten years of age; and the other age-groups have a parallel interpretation.

NOTE 4.—Amongst the adherents of some religions were found a few persons for whom the age was not clearly specified. By the records relating to marriage, literacy and occupation most of these could be assigned to classes in which the range of age was limited in one direction or the other. Each class was then distributed amongst the age-groups for whom the age had been specified. In every case the numbers distributed were too small to have any significant effect upon the table.

NOTE 5.—The figures given in columns 11, 12 and 13 of the table under the heading *Widowed* include persons described as divorced and not re-married as well as those described as widowed.

NOTE 6.—In this table all persons belonging to Christian races as well as all professing the Christian religion are included under the description *Christian*. (*See* Note 3 of Table VIA.)

NOTE 7.—Separate figures are given for Hindus born in Burma and for Hindus born outside Burma; both of these are included in the figures given for Total Hindus. Similarly for Mahomedans.

NOTE 8.—Imperial Table XIV gives similar statistics by races instead of by religions. Table VIIB which follows this table immediately gives for each district and for the three parts of the Eastern States statistics similar to those of Parts II and III of this table. Similar statistics for the larger towns are given in Provincial Table V; for Buddhists alone similar statistics for the separate townships into which each district is divided are given in Provincial Table III; and similar statistics for selected races are given for some townships or districts in Provincial Table IV. For Europeans, Anglo-Indians and Armenians statistics for sex and age are given in Imperial Table XVI. Imperial Tables VIB and XIII show relationships between religion and race.

IMPERIAL TABLE VIIA.—*Age, Sex, and Civil Condition by Religion.*

PART I.—THE WHOLE PROVINCE.

RELIGION, AND AGE.	POPULATION. Persons.	POPULATION. Males.	POPULATION. Females.	UNMARRIED. Persons.	UNMARRIED. Males.	UNMARRIED. Females.	MARRIED. Persons.	MARRIED. Males.	MARRIED. Females.	WIDOWED. Persons.	WIDOWED. Males.	WIDOWED. Females.
1	2	3	4	5	6	7	8	9	10	11	12	13
ALL RELIGIONS.	13,169,099	6,735,516	6,433,583	7,042,784	3,764,306	3,278,478	5,045,062	2,621,696	2,423,366	1,081,258	349,514	731,739
0— 1	322,258	157,803	164,455	322,258	157,803	164,455	...	...	...	...	...	...
1— 2	287,785	141,317	146,468	287,785	141,317	146,468	...	...	...	...	...	...
2— 3	321,130	156,256	164,874	321,128	156,254	164,874	2	2	...	...	...	...
3— 4	367,482	181,665	185,817	367,476	181,661	185,815	6	4	2	...	...	...
4— 5	340,342	167,049	173,293	340,337	167,046	173,291	5	3	2	...	...	...
0— 5	1,638,997	804,090	834,907	1,638,984	804,081	834,903	13	9	4	..	...	...
5—10	1,630,390	811,509	818,881	1,630,300	811,490	818,810	53	19	34	37	...	37
10—15	1,504,298	776,040	728,258	1,500,373	775,323	725,050	3,788	705	3,083	137	12	125
15—20	1,347,245	658,235	689,010	1,115,738	610,514	505,224	215,801	45,106	170,695	15,706	2,615	13,091
20—25	1,222,593	612,582	610,011	527,166	344,830	182,336	645,264	251,929	393,335	50,163	15,823	34,340
25—30	1,110,321	583,459	526,862	249,315	173,460	75,855	796,573	384,947	411,626	64,433	25,052	39,381
30—35	1,004,716	547,871	456,845	130,611	90,301	40,310	794,955	425,772	369,183	79,150	31,798	47,352
35—40	776,524	430,426	346,098	70,323	48,090	22,233	633,059	352,856	280,203	73,142	29,480	43,662
40—45	766,725	406,025	360,700	55,436	35,177	20,259	603,766	333,657	270,109	107,523	37,191	70,332
45—50	545,994	293,010	252,984	32,629	19,544	13,085	419,878	242,248	177,630	93,487	31,218	62,269
50—55	542,387	276,397	265,990	30,608	17,717	12,891	372,787	219,284	153,503	138,992	39,396	99,596
55—60	311,194	157,296	153,898	16,892	9,742	7,150	203,425	121,015	82,410	90,877	26,539	64,338
60—65	343,447	176,718	166,729	17,949	10,014	7,935	188,088	126,522	61,566	137,410	40,182	97,228
65—70	158,202	81,901	76,301	9,205	5,285	3,920	79,049	53,732	25,317	69,948	22,884	47,064
70 and over	266,066	119,957	146,109	17,255	8,738	8,517	88,563	63,895	24,668	160,248	47,324	112,924
BUDDHISTS.	11,201,912	5,525,144	5,676,768	6,042,409	3,138,293	2,903,116	4,215,335	2,096,547	2,118,788	944,168	292,304	651,864
0— 1	287,806	140,618	147,188	287,806	140,618	147,188	...	...	...	...	...	...
1— 2	252,562	123,789	128,773	252,562	123,789	128,773	...	...	...	...	...	...
2— 3	276,816	134,103	142,713	276,816	134,103	142,713	...	...	...	...	...	...
3— 4	317,269	156,369	160,900	317,269	156,369	160,900	...	...	...	...	...	...
4— 5	294,342	143,921	150,421	294,342	143,921	150,421	...	...	...	...	...	...
0— 5	1,428,795	698,800	729,995	1,428,795	698,800	729,995	...	...	...	...	...	...
5—10	1,418,341	702,682	715,659	1,418,326	702,677	715,649	15	5	10	...	...	...
10—15	1,326,097	675,679	650,418	1,324,189	675,419	648,770	1,828	257	1,571	80	3	77
15—20	1,167,644	553,361	614,283	977,456	517,993	459,463	176,146	33,304	142,842	14,042	2,064	11,978
20—25	1,009,993	475,994	533,999	423,693	260,822	162,871	541,861	202,056	339,805	44,439	13,116	31,323
25—30	883,878	429,375	454,503	182,028	115,076	66,952	646,868	294,589	352,279	54,982	19,710	35,272
30—35	788,916	398,755	390,161	89,488	54,453	35,035	634,855	320,381	314,474	64,573	23,921	40,652
35—40	637,438	331,329	306,109	50,667	30,602	20,065	525,251	277,472	247,779	61,520	23,255	38,265
40—45	632,340	315,598	316,742	41,253	23,199	18,054	502,037	263,112	238,925	89,050	29,287	59,763
45—50	477,178	246,673	230,505	26,954	14,835	12,119	368,117	205,477	162,640	82,107	26,361	55,746
50—55	463,876	226,628	237,248	24,908	13,289	11,619	319,633	180,780	138,853	119,335	32,559	86,776
55—60	281,527	139,222	142,305	14,946	8,355	6,591	184,156	107,259	76,897	82,425	23,608	58,817
60—65	301,536	151,380	150,156	15,518	8,279	7,239	164,626	108,269	56,357	121,392	34,832	86,560
65—70	145,009	73,684	71,325	8,396	4,697	3,699	72,053	48,165	23,888	64,560	20,822	43,738
70 and over	239,344	105,984	133,360	15,792	7,797	7,995	77,889	55,421	22,468	145,663	42,766	102,897
ANIMISTS.	702,587	369,188	333,399	368,372	208,419	159,953	279,118	147,170	131,948	60,097	18,599	41,498
0— 1	12,098	5,935	6,163	12,098	5,935	6,163	...	...	...	...	...	...
1— 2	13,496	6,641	6,855	13,496	6,641	6,855	...	...	...	...	...	...
2— 3	17,476	8,576	8,900	17,476	8,576	8,900	...	...	...	...	...	...
3— 4	21,158	10,740	10,418	21,158	10,740	10,418	...	...	...	...	...	..
4— 5	17,897	8,915	8,982	17,897	8,915	8,982	...	...	...	...	...	...
0— 5	82,125	40,807	41,318	82,125	40,807	41,318	...	...	...	...	...	...
5—10	86,304	44,511	41,793	86,304	44,511	41,793	...	...	...	...	...	...
10—15	68,927	36,723	32,204	68,708	36,689	32,019	217	32	185	2	2	...
15—20	66,084	33,752	32,332	54,013	30,803	23,210	11,579	2,750	8,829	492	199	293
20—25	66,324	33,479	32,845	31,734	21,144	10,590	32,581	11,523	21,058	2,009	812	1,197
25—30	64,076	33,455	30,621	16,853	12,571	4,282	44,161	19,528	24,633	3,062	1,356	1,706
30—35	71,309	39,178	32,131	11,246	8,451	2,795	53,986	28,328	25,658	6,077	2,399	3,678
35—40	42,922	24,714	18,208	4,192	3,293	899	34,342	19,678	14,664	4,388	1,743	2,645
40—45	50,410	27,512	22,898	3,525	2,405	1,120	38,362	22,522	15,840	8,523	2,585	5,938
45—50	24,528	13,887	10,641	1,321	939	382	18,453	11,381	7,072	4,754	1,567	3,187
50—55	32,703	18,023	14,680	1,507	884	623	21,556	14,584	6,972	9,640	2,555	7,085
55—60	10,827	5,667	5,160	468	274	194	6,841	4,449	2,392	3,518	944	2,574
60—65	17,782	9,085	8,637	685	334	351	9,438	6,789	2,649	7,599	1,962	5,637
65—70	4,926	2,538	2,388	171	102	69	2,500	1,790	710	2,255	646	1,609
70 and over	13,400	5,857	7,543	520	212	308	5,102	3,816	1,286	7,778	1,829	5,949

IMPERIAL TABLE VIIA.—*Age, Sex, and Civil Condition by Religion.*

PART I.—THE WHOLE PROVINCE.

RELIGION AND AGE.	POPULATION.			UNMARRIED.			MARRIED.			WIDOWED.		
	Persons.	Males.	Females.	Persons.	Males.	Females.	Persons.	Males.	Females.	Persons.	Males.	Females.
1	2	3	4	5	6	7	8	9	10	11	12	13
TOTAL HINDUS.	484,482	378,177	106,255	216,488	171,290	45,198	240,621	188,192	52,429	27,323	18,695	8,628
0— 1	5,729	2,827	2,902	5,729	2,827	2,902	...	...	...	...	...	...
1— 2	5,116	2,577	2,539	5,116	2,577	2,539	...	...	...	...	...	...
2— 3	6,889	3,410	3,479	6,888	3,409	3,479	1	1	...	...	...	...
3— 4	7,992	4,082	3,910	7,986	4,078	3,908	6	4	2	...	...	...
4— 5	6,659	3,482	3,177	6,655	3,480	3,175	4	2	2	...	...	...
0— 5	32,385	16,378	16,007	32,374	16,371	16,003	11	7	4	...	...	...
5—10	31,136	16,611	14,525	31,068	16,597	14,471	32	14	18	36	...	36
10—15	27,575	18,601	8,974	26,898	18,336	8,562	653	261	392	24	4	20
15—20	37,782	29,160	8,622	26,213	23,495	2,718	11,212	5,479	5,733	357	186	171
20—25	64,695	52,886	11,809	32,052	30,907	1,145	31,324	21,046	10,278	1,319	933	386
25—30	77,934	65,126	12,808	26,515	25,698	817	48,853	37,389	11,464	2,566	2,039	527
30—35	71,832	60,806	11,026	18,152	17,641	511	50,086	40,301	9,785	3,594	2,864	730
35—40	45,574	39,319	6,255	9,277	9,000	277	33,337	28,017	5,320	2,960	2,302	658
40—45	40,215	34,366	5,849	6,802	6,546	256	29,236	24,894	4,342	4,177	2,926	1,251
45—50	17,210	14,541	2,669	2,408	2,300	108	12,389	10,639	1,750	2,413	1,602	811
50—55	18,117	14,942	3,175	2,400	2,278	122	12,210	10,488	1,722	3,507	2,176	1,331
55—60	5,784	4,595	1,189	686	626	60	3,655	3,089	566	1,443	880	563
60—65	7,896	6,217	1,679	946	862	84	4,562	3,944	618	2,388	1,411	977
65—70	2,425	1,902	523	271	248	23	1,334	1,175	159	820	479	341
70 and over	3,872	2,727	1,145	426	385	41	1,727	1,449	278	1,719	893	826
HINDUS BORN IN BURMA.	97,505	52,635	44,870	74,697	42,028	32,674	19,618	9,287	10,326	3,195	1,325	1,870
0— 1	4,923	2,409	2,514	4,923	2,409	2,514	...	...	...	...	...	...
1— 2	4,338	2,169	2,169	4,338	2,169	2,169	...	...	...	...	...	...
2— 3	5,556	2,723	2,833	5,556	2,723	2,833	...	...	...	...	...	...
3— 4	6,265	3,137	3,128	6,263	3,136	3,127	2	1	1	...	...	...
4— 5	5,196	2,656	2,540	5,194	2,656	2,538	2	...	2	...	...	...
0— 5	26,278	13,094	13,184	26,274	13,093	13,181	4	1	3	...	...	...
5—10	22,251	11,287	10,964	22,231	11,281	10,950	20	6	14	...	...	...
10—15	13,502	7,506	5,996	13,313	7,462	5,851	185	44	141	4	..	4
15—20	8,552	4,711	3,841	5,695	4,015	1,680	2,749	679	2,070	108	17	91
20—25	6,928	3,785	3,143	2,887	2,435	452	3,820	1,286	2,534	221	64	157
25—30	5,999	3,465	2,534	1,871	1,621	250	3,802	1,694	2,108	326	150	176
30—35	4,617	2,852	1,765	1,056	947	109	3,181	1,724	1,457	380	181	199
35—40	2,878	1,907	971	492	428	64	2,052	1,316	736	334	163	171
40—45	2,397	1,530	867	369	326	43	1,614	1,030	584	414	174	240
45—50	1,141	706	435	150	126	24	715	466	249	276	114	162
50—55	1,158	716	442	139	123	16	655	432	223	364	161	203
55—60	532	316	216	67	50	17	269	199	70	196	67	129
60—65	612	387	225	66	47	19	307	232	75	239	108	131
65—70	263	169	94	38	29	9	114	95	19	111	45	66
70 and over	397	204	193	49	40	9	126	83	43	222	81	141
HINDUS BORN OUTSIDE BURMA.	386,927	325,542	61,385	141,791	129,267	12,524	221,008	178,905	42,103	24,128	17,370	6,758
0— 1	806	418	388	806	418	388	...	...	...	...	...	...
1— 2	778	408	370	778	408	370	...	...	...	...	...	...
2— 3	1,333	687	646	1,332	686	646	1	1	...	...	...	...
3— 4	1,727	945	782	1,723	942	781	4	3	1	...	...	...
4— 5	1,463	826	637	1,461	824	637	2	2	...	...	...	...
0— 5	6,107	3,284	2,823	6,100	3,278	2,822	7	6	1	...	...	...
5—10	8,885	5,324	3,561	8,837	5,316	3,521	12	8	4	36	...	36
10—15	14,073	11,095	2,978	13,585	10,874	2,711	468	217	251	20	4	16
15—20	29,230	24,449	4,781	20,518	19,480	1,038	8,463	4,800	3,663	249	169	80
20—25	57,767	49,101	8,666	29,163	28,472	693	27,504	19,760	7,744	1,098	869	229
25—30	71,935	61,661	10,274	24,644	24,077	567	45,051	35,695	9,356	2,240	1,889	351
30—35	67,215	57,954	9,261	17,096	16,694	402	46,905	38,577	8,328	3,214	2,683	531
35—40	42,696	37,412	5,284	8,785	8,572	213	31,285	26,701	4,584	2,626	2,139	487
40—45	37,818	32,836	4,982	6,433	6,220	213	27,622	23,864	3,758	3,763	2,752	1,011
45—50	16,069	13,835	2,234	2,258	2,174	84	11,674	10,173	1,501	2,137	1,488	649
50—55	16,959	14,226	2,733	2,261	2,155	106	11,555	10,056	1,499	3,143	2,015	1,128
55—60	5,252	4,279	973	619	576	43	3,386	2,890	496	1,247	813	434
60—65	7,284	5,830	1,454	880	815	65	4,255	3,712	543	2,149	1,303	846
65—70	2,162	1,733	429	233	219	14	1,220	1,080	140	709	434	275
70 and over	3,475	2,523	952	377	345	32	1,601	1,366	235	1,497	812	685

Imperial Table VIIA.—*Age, Sex, and Civil Condition by Religion.*

PART I.—THE WHOLE PROVINCE.

Religion and Age.	Population. Persons.	Population. Males.	Population. Females.	Unmarried. Persons.	Unmarried. Males.	Unmarried. Females.	Married. Persons.	Married. Males.	Married. Females.	Widowed. Persons.	Widowed. Males.	Widowed. Females.
1	2	3	4	5	6	7	8	9	10	11	12	13
TOTAL MAHOMEDANS.	500,592	314,527	186,065	261,380	166,272	95,108	206,858	134,391	72,467	32,354	13,864	18,490
0—1	10,343	5,280	5,063	10,343	5,280	5,063	...	...	...	...	...	...
1—2	10,843	5,473	5,370	10,843	5,473	5,370	...	...	...	...	...	...
2—3	12,780	6,620	6,160	12,779	6,619	6,160	1	1	...	...	...	...
3—4	13,615	6,791	6,824	13,615	6,791	6,824	...	...	...	...	...	...
4—5	14,177	7,083	7,094	14,176	7,082	7,094	1	1	...	...	...	...
0—5	61,758	31,247	30,511	61,756	31,245	30,511	2	2	...	...	...	...
5—10	60,758	30,775	29,983	60,752	30,775	29,977	5	...	5	1	...	1
10—15	49,914	28,528	21,386	48,960	28,395	20,565	923	130	793	31	3	28
15—20	47,349	28,033	19,316	33,081	24,980	8,101	13,568	2,907	10,661	700	146	554
20—25	54,589	36,083	18,506	24,242	21,745	2,497	28,426	13,512	14,914	1,921	826	1,095
25—30	57,377	40,976	16,401	14,998	13,702	1,296	39,571	25,708	13,863	2,808	1,566	1,242
30—35	49,363	36,029	13,334	7,560	6,811	749	38,365	27,218	11,147	3,438	2,000	1,438
35—40	31,547	23,692	7,855	3,932	3,556	376	24,826	18,576	6,250	2,789	1,560	1,229
40—45	27,601	19,270	8,331	2,376	2,060	316	21,484	15,513	5,971	3,741	1,697	2,044
45—50	15,977	11,487	4,490	1,187	991	196	12,298	9,421	2,877	2,492	1,075	1,417
50—55	17,162	11,060	6,102	1,078	892	186	12,012	8,822	3,190	4,072	1,346	2,726
55—60	7,386	4,670	2,716	408	312	96	4,946	3,705	1,241	2,032	653	1,379
60—65	10,204	6,546	3,658	528	405	123	5,858	4,888	970	3,818	1,253	2,565
65—70	3,683	2,567	1,116	203	165	38	2,089	1,812	277	1,391	590	801
70 and over	5,924	3,564	2,360	319	238	81	2,485	2,177	308	3,120	1,149	1,971
MAHOMEDANS BORN IN BURMA.	335,860	167,529	168,331	199,299	108,279	91,020	114,698	53,202	61,496	21,863	6,048	15,815
0—1	10,093	5,134	4,959	10,093	5,134	4,959	...	...	...	...	...	...
1—2	10,529	5,305	5,224	10,529	5,305	5,224	...	...	...	...	...	...
2—3	12,350	6,359	5,991	12,349	6,358	5,991	1	1	...	...	...	...
3—4	13,135	6,516	6,619	13,135	6,516	6,619	...	...	...	...	...	...
4—5	13,629	6,773	6,856	13,629	6,773	6,856	...	...	...	...	...	...
0—5	59,736	30,087	29,649	59,735	30,086	29,649	1	1	...	...	...	...
5—10	57,650	28,945	28,705	57,647	28,945	28,702	2	...	2	1	...	1
10—15	43,913	23,616	20,297	43,151	23,563	19,588	737	53	684	25	...	25
15—20	33,076	15,227	17,849	21,543	13,843	7,700	10,932	1,303	9,629	601	81	520
20—25	28,385	12,069	16,316	8,636	6,319	2,317	18,365	5,395	12,970	1,384	355	1,029
25—30	27,001	12,990	14,011	3,769	2,605	1,164	21,405	9,708	11,697	1,827	677	1,150
30—35	23,443	12,397	11,046	1,853	1,212	641	19,550	10,406	9,144	2,040	779	1,261
35—40	14,583	7,996	6,587	992	663	329	11,935	6,750	5,185	1,656	583	1,073
40—45	13,528	6,668	6,860	622	345	277	10,544	5,683	4,861	2,362	640	1,722
45—50	8,374	4,539	3,835	374	199	175	6,289	3,863	2,426	1,711	477	1,234
50—55	9,432	4,472	4,960	350	179	171	6,262	3,684	2,578	2,820	609	2,211
55—60	4,640	2,266	2,374	168	76	92	2,949	1,865	1,084	1,523	325	1,198
60—65	6,106	3,138	2,968	203	95	108	3,213	2,456	757	2,690	587	2,103
65—70	2,351	1,396	955	107	73	34	1,234	1,000	234	1,010	323	687
70 and over	3,642	1,723	1,919	149	76	73	1,280	1,035	245	2,213	612	1,601
MAHOMEDANS BORN OUTSIDE BURMA.	164,732	146,998	17,734	62,081	57,993	4,088	92,160	81,189	10,971	10,491	7,816	2,675
0—1	250	146	104	250	146	104	...	...	...	...	...	...
1—2	314	168	146	314	168	146	...	...	...	...	...	...
2—3	430	261	169	430	261	169	...	...	...	...	...	...
3—4	480	275	205	480	275	205	...	...	...	...	...	...
4—5	548	310	238	547	309	238	1	1	...	...	...	...
0—5	2,022	1,160	862	2,021	1,159	862	1	1	...	...	...	...
5—10	3,108	1,830	1,278	3,105	1,830	1,275	3	...	3	...	...	...
10—15	6,001	4,912	1,089	5,809	4,832	977	186	77	109	6	3	3
15—20	14,273	12,806	1,467	11,538	11,137	401	2,636	1,604	1,032	99	65	34
20—25	26,204	24,014	2,190	15,606	15,426	180	10,061	8,117	1,944	537	471	66
25—30	30,376	27,986	2,390	11,229	11,097	132	18,166	16,000	2,166	981	889	92
30—35	25,920	23,632	2,288	5,707	5,599	108	18,815	16,812	2,003	1,398	1,221	177
35—40	16,964	15,696	1,268	2,940	2,893	47	12,891	11,826	1,065	1,133	977	156
40—45	14,073	12,602	1,471	1,754	1,715	39	10,940	9,830	1,110	1,379	1,057	322
45—50	7,603	6,948	655	813	792	21	6,009	5,558	451	781	598	183
50—55	7,730	6,588	1,142	728	713	15	5,750	5,138	612	1,252	737	515
55—60	2,746	2,404	342	240	236	4	1,997	1,840	157	509	328	181
60—65	4,098	3,408	690	325	310	15	2,645	2,432	213	1,128	666	462
65—70	1,332	1,171	161	96	92	4	855	812	43	381	267	114
70 and over	2,282	1,841	441	170	169	8	1,205	1,142	63	907	537	370

IMPERIAL TABLE VIIA.—*Age, Sex, and Civil Condition by Religion.*

PART I.—THE WHOLE PROVINCE.

RELIGION AND AGE.	POPULATION.			UNMARRIED.			MARRIED.			WIDOWED.		
	Persons.	Males.	Females.	Persons.	Males.	Females.	Persons.	Males.	Females.	Persons.	Males.	Females.
1	2	3	4	5	6	7	8	9	10	11	12	13
CHRISTIANS.	257,171	132,543	124,628	148,057	79,028	69,029	92,770	48,008	44,762	16,344	5,507	10,837
0—1	*5,920*	*2,949*	*2,971*	*5,920*	*2,949*	*2,971*	...	...	...	...	...	...
1—2	*5,591*	*2,740*	*2,851*	*5,591*	*2,740*	*2,851*	...	...	...	...	...	...
2—3	*6,779*	*3,347*	*3,432*	*6,779*	*3,347*	*3,432*	...	...	...	...	...	...
3—4	*7,018*	*3,471*	*3,547*	*7,018*	*3,471*	*3,547*	...	...	...	...	...	...
4—5	*6,850*	*3,407*	*3,443*	*6,850*	*3,407*	*3,443*	...	...	...	...	...	...
0—5	32,158	15,914	16,244	32,158	15,914	16,244	...	...	...	...	...	...
5—10	31,873	15,803	16,070	31,873	15,803	16,070	...	...	...	...	...	...
10—15	30,115	15,556	14,559	29,970	15,537	14,433	145	19	126	...	...	...
15—20	26,540	12,672	13,868	23,467	12,115	11,352	2,960	538	2,422	113	19	94
20—25	24,584	12,370	12,214	14,070	8,991	5,079	10,056	3,252	6,804	458	127	331
25—30	24,193	12,357	11,836	7,891	5,449	2,442	15,338	6,558	8,780	964	350	614
30—35	20,373	10,861	9,512	3,400	2,215	1,185	15,614	8,104	7,510	1,359	542	817
35—40	16,777	9,570	7,207	1,813	1,217	596	13,574	7,790	5,784	1,390	563	827
40—45	14,351	7,818	6,533	1,198	698	500	11,263	6,505	4,758	1,890	615	1,275
45—50	10,093	5,607	4,486	648	377	271	7,831	4,685	3,146	1,614	545	1,069
50—55	9,644	5,072	4,572	621	289	332	6,731	4,095	2,636	2,292	688	1,604
55—60	5,318	2,866	2,452	358	150	208	3,576	2,301	1,275	1,384	415	969
60—65	5,753	3,247	2,506	248	114	134	3,396	2,464	932	2,109	669	1,440
65—70	2,029	1,120	909	156	65	91	1,006	732	274	867	323	544
70 and over	3,370	1,710	1,660	186	94	92	1,280	965	315	1,904	651	1,253
ARYAS.	270	190	80	106	65	41	151	116	35	13	9	4
0—1	*8*	*4*	*4*	*8*	*4*	*4*	...	...	...	...	...	...
1—2	*3*	*2*	*1*	*3*	*2*	*1*	...	...	...	...	...	...
2—3	*5*	*4*	*1*	*5*	*4*	*1*	...	...	...	...	...	...
3—4	*10*	*3*	*7*	*10*	*3*	*7*	...	...	...	...	...	...
4—5	*3*	*1*	*2*	*3*	*1*	*2*	...	...	...	...	...	...
0—5	29	14	15	29	14	15	...	...	...	...	...	...
5—10	24	8	16	24	8	16	...	...	...	...	...	...
10—15	15	8	7	15	8	7	...	...	...	...	...	...
15—20	19	15	4	12	12	...	7	3	4	...	...	...
20—25	37	28	9	15	12	3	22	16	6	...	...	...
25—30	38	29	9	7	7	...	29	20	9	2	2	...
30—35	37	30	7	1	1	...	33	26	7	3	3	...
35—40	31	27	4	1	1	...	28	26	2	2	...	2
40—45	15	12	3	1	1	...	13	11	2	1	...	1
45—50	14	9	5	...	...	...	14	9	5	...	...	...
50—55	5	5	...	1	1	...	3	3	...	1	1	...
55—60	1	1	...	...	...	...	...	...	...	1	1	...
60—65	4	3	1	...	...	...	1	1	...	3	2	1
65—70	1	1	...	...	...	...	1	1	...	...	...	...
70 and over	...	...	...	...	...	...	...	...	...	...	...	...
BRAHMOS.	448	355	93	177	138	39	248	200	48	23	17	6
0—1	*5*	*3*	*2*	*5*	*3*	*2*	...	...	...	...	...	...
1—2	*2*	...	*2*	*2*	...	*2*	...	...	...	...	...	...
2—3	*5*	*2*	*3*	*5*	*2*	*3*	...	...	...	...	...	...
3—4	*5*	*1*	*4*	*5*	*1*	*4*	...	...	...	...	...	...
4—5	*6*	*6*	...	*6*	*6*	...	...	...	...	...	...	...
0—5	23	12	11	23	12	11	...	...	...	...	...	...
5—10	18	7	11	18	7	11	...	...	...	...	...	...
10—15	23	7	16	20	6	14	3	1	2	...	...	...
15—20	36	28	8	18	16	2	18	12	6	...	...	...
20—25	84	70	14	38	37	1	46	33	13	...	...	...
25—30	62	54	8	21	21	...	38	31	7	3	2	1
30—35	78	69	9	20	20	...	55	46	9	3	3	...
35—40	42	38	4	8	8	...	33	29	4	1	1	...
40—45	30	26	4	7	7	...	20	17	3	3	2	1
45—50	23	21	2	2	2	...	17	15	2	4	4	...
50—55	18	15	3	...	...	...	13	11	2	5	4	1
55—60	4	4	...	2	2	...	1	1	...	1	1	...
60—65	4	2	2	...	...	...	2	2	...	2	...	2
65—70	...	...	...	...	...	...	...	...	...	...	...	...
70 and over	3	2	1	...	...	...	2	2	...	1	...	1

Imperial Table VIIa.—*Age, Sex, and Civil Condition by Religion.*

PART I.—THE WHOLE PROVINCE.

Religion and Age.	Population. Persons.	Population. Males.	Population. Females.	Unmarried. Persons.	Unmarried. Males.	Unmarried. Females.	Married. Persons.	Married. Males.	Married. Females.	Widowed. Persons.	Widowed. Males.	Widowed. Females.
1	2	3	4	5	6.	7	8	9	10	11	12	13
CONFUCIANS.	14,131	9,964	4,167	7,062	5,041	2,021	6,515	4,684	1,831	554	239	315
0—1	168	91	77	168	91	77	...	...	...	...	...	...
1—2	70	38	32	70	38	32	...	...	...	...	...	...
2—3	239	126	113	239	126	113	...	...	...	...	...	...
3—4	264	133	131	264	133	131	...	...	..	...	...	...
4—5	272	158	114	272	158	114	...	...	...	...	...	...
0—5	1,013	546	467	1,013	546	467	...	...	...	...	...	...
5—10	1,270	734	536	1,270	734	536	...	...	...	...	...	...
10—15	1,156	663	493	1,152	663	489	4	...	4	...	...	...
15—20	1,215	822	393	1,079	779	300	135	43	92	1	...	1
20—25	1,403	1,035	368	884	761	123	512	272	240	7	2	5
25—30	1,679	1,294	385	615	572	43	1,042	715	327	22	7	15
30—35	1,786	1,349	437	431	412	19	1,304	915	389	51	22	29
35—40	1,443	1,106	337	262	245	17	1,138	845	293	43	16	27
40—45	1,196	936	260	172	160	12	951	749	202	73	27	46
45—50	657	521	136	60	56	4	543	441	102	54	24	30
50—55	611	448	163	76	69	7	446	346	100	89	33	56
55—60	240	182	58	15	14	1	180	147	33	45	21	24
60—65	258	181	77	18	15	3	155	121	34	85	45	40
65—70	95	65	30	5	5	...	50	43	7	40	17	23
70 and over	109	82	27	10	10	...	55	47	8	44	25	19
JAINS.	1,135	866	269	493	399	94	588	431	157	54	36	18
0—1	17	13	4	17	13	4	...	...	...	...	...	...
1—2	9	5	4	9	5	4	...	...	...	...	...	...
2—3	24	12	12	24	12	12	...	...	...	...	...	...
3—4	25	13	12	25	13	12	...	...	...	...	...	...
4—5	22	13	9	22	13	9	...	...	...	...	...	...
0—5	97	56	41	97	56	41	...	...	...	...	...	...
5—10	84	56	28	84	56	28	...	...	...	...	...	...
10—15	62	42	20	58	39	19	4	3	1	...	...	...
15—20	107	76	31	58	55	3	49	21	28	...	...	...
20—25	164	130	34	62	62	...	100	67	33	2	1	1
25—30	164	123	41	37	36	1	126	86	40	1	1	...
30—35	184	149	35	44	43	1	130	99	31	10	7	3
35—40	111	100	11	34	34	...	72	62	10	5	4	1
40—45	83	71	12	14	14	...	59	50	9	10	7	3
45—50	30	24	6	4	3	1	21	18	3	5	3	2
50—55	26	23	3	1	1	...	19	19	...	6	3	3
55—60	12	9	3	...	...	..	5	4	1	7	5	2
60—65	5	3	2	...	...	...	3	2	1	2	1	1
65—70	3	1	2	...	...	...	...	...	...	3	1	2
70 and over	3	3	...	...	...	...	...	...	...	3	3	...
JEWS.	1,135	587	548	656	359	297	421	214	207	58	14	44
0—1	27	12	15	27	12	15	...	...	...	..	...	...
1—2	10	7	3	10	7	3	...	...	...	...	...	...
2—3	37	12	25	37	12	25	...	...	...	...	...	...
3—4	35	17	18	35	17	18	...	...	...	...	...	...
4—5	27	11	16	27	11	16	...	...	...	...	...	...
0—5	136	59	77	136	59	77	...	...	...	...	...	...
5—10	158	89	69	158	89	69	...	...	...	...	...	...
10—15	141	65	76	141	65	76	...	...	...	...	...	...
15—20	121	61	60	102	58	44	19	3	16	...	...	...
20—25	105	51	54	60	42	18	44	9	35	1	...	1
25—30	105	51	54	28	21	7	74	29	45	3	1	2
30—35	92	48	44	15	13	2	73	34	39	4	1	3
35—40	77	49	28	3	3	...	65	42	23	9	4	5
40—45	55	37	18	6	5	1	46	32	14	3	...	3
45—50	44	26	18	3	2	1	34	21	13	7	3	4
50—55	38	15	23	1	...	1	30	14	16	7	1	6
55—60	20	12	8	...	...	...	12	10	2	8	2	6
60—65	21	14	7	2	1	1	14	13	1	5	...	5
65—70	9	4	5	1	1	...	3	3	...	5	...	5
70 and over	13	6	7	...	...	...	7	4	3	6	2	4

IMPERIAL TABLE VIIA.—*Age, Sex, and Civil Condition by Religion.*

PART I.—THE WHOLE PROVINCE.

RELIGION AND AGE.	POPULATION.			UNMARRIED			MARRIED.			WIDOWED.		
	Persons.	Males.	Females.	Persons.	Males.	Females.	Persons.	Males.	Females.	Persons.	Males.	Females.
1	2	3	4	5	6	7	8	9	10	11	12	13
SHINTOISTS.	45	31	14	34	25	9	11	6	5	...	...	...
0—5	...	...	...	...	...	...	...	...	...	...	...	...
5—10	2	2	...	2	2	...	...	...	...	...	...	...
10—15	...	...	...	...	...	...	...	...	...	...	...	...
15—20	6	4	2	5	5	2	1	1	...	...	...	...
20—25	11	7	4	10	3	4	1	1	...	...	...	...
25—30	10	7	3	6	6	1	4	2	2	...	...	...
30—35	7	4	3	5	3	2	2	1	1	...	...	...
35—40	4	2	2	2	2	...	2	...	2	...	...	...
40—45	4	4	...	4	4	...	...	...	...	...	...	...
45—50	...	...	...	...	...	...	...	...	...	...	...	...
50—55	1	1	...	...	...	...	1	1	...	...	...	...
55 and over	...	...	...	...	...	...	...	...	...	...	...	...
SIKHS.	4,843	3,704	1,139	2,340	1,848	492	2,249	1,630	619	254	226	28
0—1	*129*	*66*	*63*	*129*	*66*	*63*	...	...	...	...	...	...
1—2	*81*	*45*	*36*	*81*	*45*	*36*	...	...	...	...	...	...
2—3	*74*	*41*	*33*	*74*	*41*	*33*	...	...	...	...	...	...
3—4	*84*	*43*	*41*	*84*	*43*	*41*	...	...	...	...	...	...
4—5	*76*	*47*	*29*	*76*	*47*	*29*	...	...	...	...	...	...
0—5	444	242	202	444	242	202	...	...	...	...	...	...
5—10	373	207	166	372	207	165	1	...	1	...	...	...
10—15	240	149	91	230	147	83	10	2	8	...	...	...
15—20	318	239	79	211	194	17	106	44	62	1	1	...
20—25	577	434	143	290	289	1	280	139	141	7	6	1
25—30	764	581	183	296	284	12	448	279	169	20	18	2
30—35	685	557	128	227	220	7	420	301	119	38	36	2
35—40	522	458	64	128	125	3	361	302	59	33	31	2
40—45	389	353	36	73	73	...	266	236	30	50	44	6
45—50	220	201	19	39	37	2	145	130	15	36	34	2
50—55	166	152	14	14	14	...	117	109	8	35	29	6
55—60	63	60	3	9	9	...	42	42	...	12	9	3
60—65	41	37	4	3	3	...	31	27	4	7	7	...
65—70	17	14	3	2	2	...	9	7	2	6	5	1
70 and over	24	20	4	2	2	...	13	12	1	9	6	3
ZOROASTRIANS.	380	229	151	202	125	77	167	100	67	11	4	7
0—1	*8*	*5*	*3*	*8*	*5*	*3*	...	...	...	...	...	...
1—2	*2*	...	*2*	*2*	...	*2*	...	...	...	...	...	...
2—3	*6*	*3*	*3*	*6*	*3*	*3*	...	...	...	...	...	...
3—4	*7*	*2*	*5*	*7*	*2*	*5*	...	...	...	...	...	...
4—5	*11*	*5*	*6*	*11*	*5*	*6*	...	...	...	...	...	...
0—5	34	15	19	34	15	19	...	...	...	...	...	...
5—10	46	24	22	46	24	22	...	...	...	...	...	...
10—15	33	19	14	32	19	13	1	...	1	...	...	...
15—20	23	11	12	22	10	12	1	1	...	...	...	...
20—25	24	13	11	14	11	3	10	2	8	...	...	...
25—30	37	28	9	18	16	2	19	12	7	...	...	...
30—35	53	35	18	22	18	4	31	17	14	...	...	...
35—40	35	21	14	4	4	...	29	16	13	2	1	1
40—45	34	21	13	5	5	...	27	15	12	2	1	1
45—50	20	13	7	3	2	1	16	11	5	1	...	1
50—55	19	12	7	1	...	1	15	11	4	3	1	2
55—60	12	8	4	...	...	...	11	8	3	1	...	1
60—65	3	3	...	1	1	...	2	2	...	...	...	...
65—70	4	4	...	...	...	...	3	3	...	1	1	...
70 and over	3	2	1	...	...	...	2	2	...	1	...	1
AGNOSTICS, ATHEISTS, FREETHINKERS AND THEOSOPHISTS.	18	11	7	8	4	4	10	7	3	...	...	...
0—5	...	...	...	...	...	...	...	...	...	...	...	...
5—10	3	...	3	3	...	3	...	...	...	...	...	...
10—15	...	...	...	...	...	...	...	...	...	...	...	...
15—20	1	1	...	1	1	...	...	...	...	...	...	...
20—25	3	2	1	2	1	1	1	1	...	...	...	...
25—30	4	3	1	2	2	...	2	1	1	...	...	...
30—35	1	1	...	...	...	...	1	1	...	...	...	...
35—40	1	1	...	...	...	...	1	1	...	...	...	...
40—45	2	1	1	...	...	...	2	1	1	...	...	...
45—50	...	...	...	...	...	...	...	...	...	...	...	...
50—55	1	1	...	...	...	...	1	1	...	...	...	...
55—60	...	...	...	...	...	...	...	...	...	...	...	...
60—65	...	...	...	...	...	...	...	...	...	...	...	...
65—70	1	1	...	...	...	...	1	1	...	...	...	...
70 and over	1	...	1	...	...	...	1	...	1	...	...	...

IMPERIAL TABLE VIIA.—*Age, Sex, and Civil Condition by Religion.*

PART II.—DIVISIONAL BURMA.

RELIGION AND AGE.	POPULATION.			UNMARRIED			MARRIED.			WIDOWED.		
	Persons.	Males.	Females.	Persons.	Males.	Females.	Persons.	Males.	Females.	Persons.	Males.	Females.
1	2	3	4	5	6	7	8	9	10	11	12	13
ALL RELIGIONS.	11,698,408	5,991,623	5,706,785	6,296,904	3,358,733	2,938,171	4,478,435	2,334,655	2,143,780	923,069	298,235	624,834
0—1	288,521	141,374	147,147	288,521	141,374	147,147	...	...	...	...	...	...
1—2	258,685	126,976	131,709	258,685	126,976	131,709	...	...	...	..	...	...
2—3	285,092	138,832	146,260	285,090	138,830	146,260	2	2	...	...	...	...
3—4	326,265	160,908	165,357	326,259	160,904	165,355	6	4	2	...	...	...
4—5	303,405	148,965	154,440	303,400	148,962	154,438	5	3	2	...	...	...
0—5	1,461,968	717,055	744,913	1,461,955	717,046	744,909	13	9	4	...	...	...
5—10	1,446,434	719,047	727,387	1,446,344	719,028	727,316	53	19	34	37	...	37
10—15	1,352,915	696,696	656,219	1,349,380	696,026	653,354	3,405	658	2,747	130	12	118
15—20	1,197,283	585,764	611,519	996,216	543,145	453,071	188,838	40,567	148,271	12,229	2,052	10,177
20—25	1,082,710	544,782	537,928	468,221	304,526	163,695	573,992	227,887	346,105	40,497	12,369	28,128
25—30	988,459	522,472	465,987	224,915	155,360	69,555	709,588	346,649	362,939	53,956	20,463	33,493
30—35	882,347	482,777	399,570	117,359	80,747	36,612	700,097	376,414	323,683	64,891	25,616	39,275
35—40	702,198	390,263	311,935	65,591	44,555	21,036	572,495	320,267	252,228	64,112	25,441	38,671
40—45	668,335	354,611	313,724	51,093	32,346	18,747	527,416	291,211	236,205	89,826	31,054	58,772
45—50	493,663	264,608	229,055	30,802	18,270	12,532	379,535	218,763	160,772	83,326	27,575	55,751
50—55	468,599	237,537	231,062	28,076	16,200	11,876	323,414	188,123	135,291	117,109	33,214	83,895
55—60	281,800	141,073	140,727	15,821	9,054	6,767	184,383	108,673	75,710	81,596	23,346	58,250
60—65	298,430	155,201	143,229	16,503	9,286	7,217	165,860	110,893	54,967	116,067	35,022	81,045
65—70	143,998	74,644	69,354	8,745	5,017	3,728	72,306	48,954	23,352	62,947	20,673	42,274
70 and over	229,269	105,093	124,176	15,883	8,127	7,756	77,040	55,568	21,472	136,346	41,398	94,948
BUDDHISTS.	10,018,466	4,932,834	5,085,632	5,437,724	2,809,761	2,627,963	3,769,831	1,874,288	1,895,543	810,911	248,785	562,126
0—1	259,171	126,700	132,471	259,171	126,700	132,471	...	...	...	...	...	...
1—2	229,643	112,421	117,222	229,643	112,421	117,222	...	...	...	...	...	...
2—3	248,676	120,557	128,119	248,676	120,557	128,119	...	...	...	...	...	...
3—4	284,971	140,161	144,810	284,971	140,161	144,810	...	...	...	...	...	...
4—5	265,034	129,568	135,466	265,034	129,568	135,466	...	...	...	...	...	...
0—5	1,287,495	629,407	658,088	1,287,495	629,407	658,088	...	...	...	...	...	...
5—10	1,270,084	628,896	641,188	1,270,069	628,891	641,178	15	5	10	...	...	...
10—15	1,200,560	610,221	590,339	1,198,926	609,990	588,936	1,561	228	1,333	73	3	70
15—20	1,044,287	494,674	549,613	878,608	462,753	415,855	154,890	30,320	124,570	10,789	1,601	9,188
20—25	899,380	423,585	475,795	376,983	228,971	147,922	486,791	184,574	302,217	35,696	10,040	25,656
25—30	789,128	382,968	406,160	162,717	100,907	61,810	580,464	266,234	314,230	45,947	15,827	30,120
30—35	696,238	350,540	345,698	79,342	47,232	32,110	563,983	284,417	279,566	52,913	18,891	34,022
35—40	579,725	300,686	279,039	46,914	27,835	19,079	478,580	252,872	225,708	44,231	19,979	34,252
40—45	554,239	275,179	279,060	37,770	20,949	16,821	441,679	230,022	211,657	74,790	24,208	50,582
45—50	433,816	223,239	210,577	25,400	13,759	11,641	334,758	186,210	148,548	73,658	23,270	50,388
50—55	402,834	194,775	208,059	22,774	11,986	10,788	278,919	155,424	123,495	101,141	27,365	73,776
55—60	255,955	124,856	131,099	14,007	7,743	6,264	167,503	96,335	71,168	74,445	20,778	53,667
60—65	263,356	133,089	130,267	14,246	7,637	6,609	145,916	95,028	50,888	103,194	30,424	72,770
65—70	132,717	67,261	65,456	7,977	4,451	3,526	66,237	43,984	22,253	58,503	18,826	39,677
70 and over	208,652	93,458	115,194	14,586	7,250	7,336	68,535	48,635	19,900	125,531	37,573	87,958
ANIMISTS.	456,104	243,426	212,678	241,543	136,400	105,143	176,824	94,850	81,974	37,737	12,176	25,561
0—1	8,014	3,930	4,084	8,014	3,930	4,084	...	...	...	...	...	...
1—2	8,213	4,107	4,106	8,213	4,107	4,106	...	...	...	...	...	...
2—3	10,566	5,207	5,359	10,566	5,207	5,359	...	...	...	...	...	...
3—4	13,357	6,782	6,575	13,357	6,782	6,575	...	...	...	...	...	...
4—5	11,267	5,666	5,601	11,267	5,666	5,601	...	...	...	...	...	...
0—5	51,417	25,692	25,725	51,417	25,692	25,725	...	...	...	...	...	...
5—10	54,707	27,977	26,730	54,707	27,977	26,730	...	...	...	...	...	...
10—15	46,456	24,703	21,753	46,334	24,681	21,653	120	20	100	2	2	...
15—20	42,949	21,861	21,088	35,715	20,234	15,481	6,936	1,514	5,422	298	113	185
20—25	41,883	21,345	20,538	21,514	14,349	7,165	19,162	6,491	12,671	1,207	505	702
25—30	42,136	22,592	19,544	12,900	9,662	3,238	27,384	12,121	15,263	1,852	809	1,043
30—35	46,113	25,614	20,499	8,809	6,711	2,098	33,499	17,441	16,058	3,805	1,462	2,343
35—40	29,311	17,398	11,913	5,312	2,790	722	22,883	13,456	9,427	2,916	1,152	1,764
40—45	32,797	18,409	14,388	2,883	2,020	863	24,481	14,681	9,800	5,433	1,708	3,725
45—50	16,922	9,867	7,055	1,133	812	321	12,552	7,944	4,608	3,237	1,111	2,126
50—55	21,384	11,949	9,435	1,190	729	461	13,891	9,499	4,392	6,303	1,721	4,582
55—60	7,528	4,160	3,368	368	226	142	4,802	3,288	1,514	2,358	646	1,712
60—65	11,616	6,316	5,300	541	269	272	6,358	4,735	1,623	4,717	1,312	3,405
65—70	3,183	1,807	1,376	144	88	56	1,653	1,253	400	1,386	466	920
70 and over	7,702	3,736	3,966	376	160	216	3,103	2,407	696	4,223	1,169	3,054

IMPERIAL TABLE VIIA.—*Age, Sex, and Civil Condition by Religion.*

PART II.—DIVISIONAL BURMA.

RELIGION AND AGE.	POPULATION.			UNMARRIED.			MARRIED.			WIDOWED.		
	Persons.	Males.	Females.	Persons.	Males.	Females.	Persons.	Males.	Females.	Persons.	Males.	Females.
1	2	3	4	5	6	7	8	9	10	11	12	13
TOTAL HINDUS.	471,427	367,516	103,911	211,446	167,262	44,184	233,398	182,192	51,206	26,583	18,062	8,521
0—1	5,531	2,725	2,806	5,531	2,725	2,806	...	...	...	...	...	...
1—2	4,931	2,490	2,441	4,931	2,490	2,441	...	..	...	...	...	...
2—3	6,688	3,310	3,378	6,687	3,309	3,378	1	1	...	...	...	...
3—4	7,790	3,981	3,809	7,784	3,977	3,807	6	4	2	...	..	...
4—5	6,497	3,398	3,099	6,493	3,396	3,097	4	2	2	...	...	...
0—5	31,437	15,904	15,533	31,426	15,897	15,529	11	7	4	...	...	...
5—10	30,466	16,231	14,235	30,398	16,217	14,181	32	14	18	36	...	36
10—15	27,088	18,298	8,790	26,428	18,039	8,389	636	255	381	24	4	20
15—20	36,902	28,547	8,355	25,703	23,035	2,668	10,848	5,329	5,519	351	183	168
20—25	62,527	51,020	11,507	31,071	29,934	1,137	30,174	20,185	9,989	1,282	901	381
25—30	75,501	62,944	12,557	25,854	25,044	810	47,177	35,952	11,225	2,470	1,948	522
30—35	69,783	58,973	10,810	17,753	17,246	507	48,566	38,988	9,578	3,464	2,739	725
35—40	44,342	38,208	6,134	9,106	8,834	272	32,364	27,150	5,214	2,872	2,224	648
40—45	39,188	33,456	5,732	6,666	6,413	253	28,459	24,212	4,247	4,063	2,831	1,232
45—50	16,774	14,147	2,627	2,371	2,263	108	12,051	10,333	1,718	2,352	1,551	801
50—55	17,735	14,593	3,142	2,368	2,246	122	11,943	10,245	1,698	3,424	2,102	1,322
55—60	5,683	4,504	1,179	676	616	60	3,598	3,034	564	1,409	854	555
60—65	7,748	6,092	1,656	935	851	84	4,485	3,871	614	2,328	1,370	958
65—70	2,409	1,891	518	270	247	23	1,329	1,170	159	810	474	336
70 and over	3,844	2,708	1,136	421	380	41	1,725	1,447	278	1,698	881	817
HINDUS BORN IN BURMA.	95,442	51,559	43,883	72,900	41,030	31,870	19,364	9,211	10,153	3,178	1,318	1,860
0—1	4,737	2,316	2,421	4,737	2,316	2,421	...	...	...	...	...	...
1—2	4,177	2,095	2,082	4,177	2,095	2,082	...	...	...	...	...	...
2—3	5,376	2,634	2,742	5,376	2,634	2,742	...	...	...	...	...	...
3—4	6,091	3,049	3,042	6,089	3,048	3,041	2	1	1	...	...	...
4—5	5,064	2,586	2,478	5,062	2,586	2,476	2	...	2	...	...	...
0—5	25,445	12,680	12,765	25,441	12,679	12,762	4	1	3	...	...	...
5—10	21,731	10,999	10,732	21,711	10,993	10,718	20	6	14	...	...	...
10—15	13,215	7,342	5,873	13,039	7,301	5,738	172	41	131	4	...	4
15—20	8,374	4,629	3,745	5,592	3,943	1,649	2,675	669	2,006	107	17	90
20—25	6,843	3,748	3,095	2,856	2,409	447	3,767	1,275	2,492	220	64	156
25—30	5,941	3,432	2,509	1,855	1,606	249	3,762	1,678	2,084	324	148	176
30—35	4,579	2,833	1,746	1,049	942	107	3,152	1,710	1,442	378	181	197
35—40	2,868	1,902	966	489	426	63	2,045	1,313	732	334	163	171
40—45	2,373	1,514	859	361	318	43	1,600	1,023	577	412	173	239
45—50	1,130	699	431	150	126	24	708	462	246	272	111	161
50—55	1,149	711	438	139	123	16	647	428	219	363	160	203
55—60	530	316	214	67	50	17	269	199	70	194	67	127
60—65	606	382	224	65	46	19	303	228	75	238	108	130
65—70	263	169	94	38	29	9	114	95	19	111	45	66
70 and over	395	203	192	48	39	9	126	83	43	221	81	140
HINDUS BORN OUT OF BURMA.	375,985	315,957	60,028	138,546	126,232	12,314	214,034	172,981	41,053	23,405	16,744	6,661
0—1	794	409	385	794	409	385	...	...	...	...	...	...
1—2	754	395	359	754	395	359	...	...	...	...	...	...
2—3	1,312	676	636	1,311	675	636	1	1	...	...	...	...
3—4	1,699	932	767	1,695	929	766	4	3	1	...	...	...
4—5	1,433	812	621	1,431	810	621	2	2	...	...	..	...
0—5	5,992	3,224	2,768	5,985	3,218	2,767	7	6	1	...	...	...
5—10	8,735	5,232	3,503	8,687	5,224	3,463	12	8	4	36	...	36
10—15	13,873	10,956	2,917	13,389	10,738	2,651	464	214	250	20	4	16
15—20	28,528	23,918	4,610	20,111	19,092	1,019	8,173	4,660	3,513	244	166	78
20—25	55,684	47,272	8,412	28,215	27,525	690	26,407	18,910	7,497	1,062	837	225
25—30	69,560	59,512	10,048	23,999	23,438	561	43,415	34,274	9,141	2,146	1,800	346
30—35	65,204	56,140	9,064	16,704	16,304	400	45,414	37,278	8,136	3,086	2,558	528
35—40	41,474	36,306	5,168	8,617	8,408	209	30,319	25,837	4,482	2,538	2,061	477
40—45	36,815	31,942	4,873	6,305	6,095	210	26,859	23,189	3,670	3,651	2,658	993
45—50	15,644	13,448	2,196	2,221	2,137	84	11,343	9,871	1,472	2,080	1,440	640
50—55	16,586	13,882	2,704	2,229	2,123	106	11,296	9,817	1,479	3,061	1,940	1,119
55—60	5,153	4,188	965	609	566	43	3,329	2,835	494	1,215	787	428
60—65	7,142	5,710	1,432	870	805	65	4,182	3,643	539	2,090	1,262	828
65—70	2,146	1,722	424	232	218	14	1,215	1,075	140	699	429	270
70 and over	3,449	2,505	944	373	341	32	1,599	1,364	235	1,477	800	677

IMPERIAL TABLE VIIA.—*Age, Sex, and Civil Condition by Religion.*

PART II.—DIVISIONAL BURMA.

RELIGION AND AGE.	POPULATION. Persons.	POPULATION. Males.	POPULATION. Females.	UNMARRIED. Persons.	UNMARRIED. Males.	UNMARRIED. Females.	MARRIED. Persons.	MARRIED. Males.	MARRIED. Females.	WIDOWED. Persons.	WIDOWED. Males.	WIDOWED. Females.
1	2	3	4	5	6	7	8	9	10	11	12	13
TOTAL MAHOMEDANS.	495,758	311,098	184,660	259,247	164,789	94,458	204,489	132,697	71,792	32,022	13,612	18,410
0— 1	*10,238*	*5,220*	*5,018*	*10,238*	*5,220*	*5,018*	...	...	...	...	...	...
1— 2	*10,752*	*5,425*	*5,327*	*10,752*	*5,425*	*5,327*	...	...	...	...	...	...
2— 3	*12,704*	*6,576*	*6,128*	*12,703*	*6,575*	*6,128*	*1*	*1*	...	...	...	...
3— 4	*13,512*	*6,733*	*6,779*	*13,512*	*6,733*	*6,779*	...	...	..	...	...	...
4— 5	*14,077*	*7,032*	*7,045*	*14,076*	*7,031*	*7,045*	*1*	*1*	...	...	...	...
0— 5	61,283	30,986	30,297	61,281	30,984	30,297	2	2	...	...	...	...
5—10	60,312	30,536	29,776	60,306	30,536	29,770	5	...	5	1	...	1
10—15	49,579	28,339	21,240	48,627	28,206	20,421	921	130	791	31	3	28
15—20	46,996	27,815	19,181	32,840	24,789	8,051	13,462	2,884	10,578	694	142	552
20—25	54,020	35,693	18,327	24,006	21,519	2,487	28,113	13,366	14,747	1,901	808	1,093
25—30	56,706	40,463	16,243	14,833	13,547	1,286	39,096	25,381	13,715	2,777	1,535	1,242
30—35	48,753	35,528	13,225	7,462	6,722	740	37,901	26,850	11,051	3,390	1,956	1,434
35—40	31,097	23,318	7,779	3,879	3,503	376	24,477	18,296	6,181	2,741	1,519	1,222
40—45	27,236	18,973	8,263	2,338	2,026	312	21,207	15,287	5,920	3,691	1,660	2,031
45—50	15,781	11,326	4,455	1,164	968	196	12,150	9,296	2,854	2,467	1,062	1,405
50—55	16,982	10,922	6,060	1,062	878	184	11,891	8,724	3,167	4,029	1,320	2,709
55—60	7,329	4,622	2,707	403	307	96	4,907	3,670	1,237	2,019	645	1,374
60—65	10,127	6,486	3,641	525	402	123	5,810	4,847	963	3,792	1,237	2,555
65—70	3,665	2,552	1,113	202	164	38	2,079	1,803	276	1,384	585	799
70 and over	5,892	3,539	2,353	319	238	81	2,468	2,161	307	3,105	1,140	1,965
MAHOMEDANS BORN IN BURMA.	333,761	166,529	167,232	197,928	107,484	90,444	114,058	53,025	61,028	21,780	6,020	15,760
0— 1	*9,989*	*5,075*	*4,914*	*9,989*	*5,075*	*4,914*	...	...	...	...	...	...
1— 2	*10,442*	*5,259*	*5,183*	*10,442*	*5,259*	*5,183*	...	...	...	...	...	...
2— 3	*12,276*	*6,316*	*5,960*	*12,275*	*6,315*	*5,960*	*1*	*1*	...	...	...	...
3— 4	*13,033*	*6,459*	*6,574*	*13,033*	*6,459*	*6,574*	...	...	...	...	...	...
4— 5	*13,542*	*6,727*	*6,815*	*13,542*	*6,727*	*6,815*	...	...	...	...	...	...
0— 5	59,282	29,836	29,446	59,281	29,835	29,446	1	1	...	...	...	...
5—10	57,250	28,729	28,521	57,247	28,729	28,518	2	...	2	1	...	1
10—15	43,639	23,470	20,169	42,879	23,417	19,462	735	53	682	25	...	25
15—20	32,878	15,134	17,744	21,421	13,757	7,664	10,859	1,297	9,562	598	80	518
20—25	28,177	11,992	16,185	8,576	6,269	2,307	18,224	5,373	12,851	1,377	350	1,027
25—30	26,826	12,929	13,897	3,744	2,585	1,159	21,256	9,668	11,588	1,826	676	1,150
30—35	23,320	12,346	10,974	1,831	1,199	632	19,456	10,371	9,085	2,033	776	1,257
35—40	14,494	7,958	6,536	990	661	329	11,859	6,720	5,139	1,645	577	1,068
40—45	13,462	6,642	6,818	620	344	276	10,494	5,662	4,832	2,348	638	1,710
45—50	8,333	4,521	3,812	368	193	175	6,263	3,852	2,411	1,702	476	1,226
50—55	9,392	4,459	4,933	346	177	169	6,242	3,678	2,564	2,804	604	2,200
55—60	4,631	2,262	2,369	167	75	92	2,944	1,864	1,080	1,520	323	1,197
60—65	6,093	3,134	2,959	203	95	108	3,208	2,454	754	2,682	585	2,097
65—70	2,348	1,394	954	106	72	34	1,233	999	234	1,009	323	686
70 and over	3,636	1,721	1,915	149	76	73	1,277	1,033	244	2,210	612	1,598
MAHOMEDAN BORN OUT OF BURMA.	161,997	144,569	17,428	61,319	57,305	4,014	90,436	79,672	10,764	10,242	7,592	2,650
0	*249*	*145*	*104*	*249*	*145*	*104*	...	...	...	...	...	...
1	*310*	*166*	*144*	*310*	*166*	*144*	...	...	...	...	...	...
2	*428*	*260*	*168*	*428*	*260*	*168*	...	...	...	...	...	...
3	*479*	*274*	*205*	*479*	*274*	*205*	...	...	...	...	...	...
4	*535*	*305*	*230*	*534*	*304*	*230*	*1*	*1*	...	...	...	...
0— 5	2,001	1,150	851	2,000	1,149	851	1	1	...	...	...	..
5—10	3,062	1,807	1,255	3,059	1,807	1,252	3	...	3	...	...	...
10—15	5,940	4,869	1,071	5,748	4,789	959	186	77	109	6	3	3
15—20	14,118	12,681	1,437	11,419	11,032	387	2,603	1,587	1,016	96	62	34
20—25	25,843	23,701	2,142	15,430	15,250	180	9,889	7,993	1,896	524	458	66
25—30	29,880	27,534	2,346	11,089	10,962	127	17,840	15,713	2,127	951	859	92
30—35	25,433	23,182	2,251	5,631	5,523	108	18,445	16,479	1,966	1,357	1,180	177
35—40	16,603	15,360	1,243	2,889	2,842	47	12,618	11,576	1,042	1,096	942	154
40—45	13,774	12,329	1,445	1,718	1,682	36	10,713	9,625	1,088	1,343	1,022	321
45—50	7,448	6,805	643	796	775	21	5,887	5,444	443	765	586	179
50—55	7,590	6,463	1,127	716	701	15	5,649	5,046	603	1,225	716	509
55—60	2,698	2,360	338	236	232	4	1,963	1,806	157	499	322	177
60—65	4,034	3,352	682	322	307	15	2,602	2,393	209	1,110	652	458
65—70	1,317	1,158	159	96	92	4	846	804	42	375	262	113
70 and over	2,256	1,818	438	170	162	8	1,191	1,128	63	895	528	367

IMPERIAL TABLE VIIA.—*Age, Sex, and Civil Condition by Religion.*

PART II.—DIVISIONAL BURMA.

RELIGION AND AGE		POPULATION.			UNMARRIED.			MARRIED.			WIDOWED.		
		Persons.	Males.	Females.	Persons.	Males.	Females.	Persons.	Males.	Females.	Persons.	Males.	Females.
1		2	3	4	5	6	7	8	9	10	11	12	13
CHRISTIANS.		234,503	121,020	113,483	135,933	72,565	63,368	83,708	43,387	40,321	14,862	5,068	9,794
	0—1	*5,207*	*2,605*	*2,602*	*5,207*	*2,605*	*2,602*	...	...	...	...	...	...
	1—2	*4,976*	*2,440*	*2,536*	*4,976*	*2,440*	*2,536*	...	...	...	...	...	...
	2—3	*6,072*	*2,986*	*3,086*	*6,072*	*2,986*	*3,086*	...	...	...	...	...	...
	3—4	*6,207*	*3,040*	*3,167*	*6,207*	*3,040*	*3,167*	...	...	...	...	...	...
	4—5	*6,115*	*3,062*	*3,053*	*6,115*	*3,062*	*3,053*	...	...	...	...	...	...
	0—5	28,577	14,133	14,444	28,577	14,133	14,444	...	...	...	...	...	...
	5—10	28,902	14,288	14,614	28,902	14,288	14,614	...	...	...	...	...	...
	10—15	27,573	14,187	13,386	27,428	14,168	13,260	145	19	126	...	...	...
	15—20	24,311	11,613	12,698	21,845	11,209	10,636	2,371	392	1,979	95	12	83
	20—25	22,507	11,380	11,127	13,367	8,537	4,830	8,746	2,737	6,009	394	106	288
	25—30	22,172	11,376	10,796	7,588	5,243	2,345	13,725	5,820	7,905	859	313	546
	30—35	18,595	9,931	8,664	3,235	2,113	1,122	14,146	7,318	6,828	1,214	500	714
	35—40	15,493	8,885	6,608	1,740	1,173	567	12,491	7,197	5,294	1,262	515	747
	40—45	13,087	7,153	5,934	1,154	669	485	10,126	5,918	4,308	1,707	566	1,141
	45—50	9,375	5,224	4,151	623	366	257	7,244	4,342	2,902	1,508	516	992
	50—55	8,784	4,631	4,153	588	276	312	6,129	3,720	2,409	2,067	635	1,432
	55—60	4,956	2,658	2,298	341	137	204	3,325	2,137	1,188	1,290	384	906
	60—65	5,252	2,980	2,272	232	107	125	3,088	2,249	839	1,932	624	1,308
	65—70	1,894	1,043	851	144	59	85	941	686	255	809	298	511
	70 and over	3,025	1,538	1,487	169	87	82	1,131	852	279	1,705	599	1,126
OTHERS.		22,150	15,729	6,421	11,011	7,956	3,055	10,185	7,241	2,944	954	532	422
	0	*360*	*194*	*166*	*360*	*194*	*166*	...	...	...	...	...	...
	1	*170*	*93*	*77*	*170*	*93*	*77*	...	...	...	...	...	...
	2	*386*	*196*	*190*	*386*	*196*	*190*	...	...	...	...	...	...
	3	*428*	*211*	*217*	*428*	*211*	*217*	...	...	...	...	...	...
	4	*415*	*239*	*176*	*415*	*239*	*176*	...	...	...	...	...	...
	0—5	1,759	933	826	1,759	933	826	...	...	...	...	...	...
	5—10	1,963	1,119	844	1,962	1,119	843	1	...	1	...	...	...
	10—15	1,659	948	711	1,637	942	695	22	6	16	...	...	...
	15—20	1,838	1,254	584	1,505	1,125	380	331	128	203	2	1	1
	20—25	2,393	1,759	634	1,370	1,216	154	1,006	534	472	17	9	8
	25—30	2,816	2,129	687	1,023	957	66	1,742	1,141	601	51	31	20
	30—35	2,865	2,191	674	758	723	35	2,002	1,400	602	105	68	37
	35—40	2,230	1,768	462	440	420	20	1,700	1,296	404	90	52	38
	40—45	1,788	1,441	347	282	269	13	1,364	1,091	273	142	81	61
	45—50	995	805	190	111	102	9	780	638	142	104	65	39
	50—55	880	667	213	94	85	9	641	511	130	145	71	74
	55—60	349	273	76	26	25	1	248	209	39	75	39	36
	60—65	331	238	93	24	20	4	203	163	40	104	55	49
	65—70	130	90	40	8	8	...	67	58	9	55	24	31
	70 and over	154	114	40	12	12	...	78	66	12	64	36	28

IMPERIAL TABLE VIIA.—*Age, Sex, and Civil Condition by Religion.*

PART III.—THE EASTERN STATES.

RELIGION AND AGE.	POPULATION.			UNMARRIED.			MARRIED.			WIDOWED.		
	Persons.	Males.	Females.	Persons.	Males.	Females.	Persons.	Males.	Females.	Persons.	Males.	Females.
1	2	3	4	5	6	7	8	9	10	11	12	13
ALL RELIGIONS.	**1,470,691**	**743,893**	**726,798**	**745,880**	**405,573**	**340,307**	**566,627**	**287,041**	**279,586**	**158,184**	**51,279**	**106,905**
0—1	*33,737*	*16,429*	*17,308*	*33,737*	*16,429*	*17,308*	...	...	...	...	...	...
1—2	*29,100*	*14,341*	*14,759*	*29,100*	*14,341*	*14,759*	...	...	...	...	...	...
2—3	*36,038*	*17,424*	*18,614*	*36,038*	*17,424*	*18,614*	...	...	...	...	...	...
3—4	*41,217*	*20,757*	*20,460*	*41,217*	*20,757*	*20,460*	...	...	...	...	...	...
4—5	*36,937*	*18,084*	*18,853*	*36,937*	*18,084*	*18,853*	...	...	...	...	...	...
0—5	177,029	87,035	89,994	177,029	87,035	89,994	...	...	...	...	...	...
5—10	183,956	92,462	91,494	183,956	92,462	91,494	...	...	...	...	...	...
10—15	151,383	79,344	72,039	150,993	79,297	71,696	383	47	336	7	...	7
15—20	149,962	72,471	77,491	119,522	67,369	52,153	26,963	4,539	22,424	3,477	563	2,914
20—25	139,883	67,800	72,083	58,945	40,304	18,641	71,272	24,042	47,230	9,666	3,454	6,212
25—30	121,862	60,987	60,875	24,400	18,100	6,300	86,985	38,298	48,687	10,477	4,589	5,888
30—35	122,369	65,094	57,275	13,252	9,554	3,698	94,858	49,358	45,500	14,259	6,182	8,077
35—40	74,326	40,163	34,163	4,732	3,535	1,197	60,564	32,589	27,975	9,030	4,039	4,991
40—45	98,390	51,414	46,976	4,343	2,831	1,512	76,350	42,446	33,904	17,697	6,137	11,560
45—50	52,331	28,402	23,929	1,827	1,274	553	40,343	23,485	16,858	10,161	3,643	6,518
50—55	73,788	38,860	34,928	2,532	1,517	1,015	49,373	31,161	18,212	21,883	6,182	15,701
55—60	29,394	16,223	13,171	1,071	688	383	19,042	12,342	6,700	9,281	3,193	6,088
60—65	45,017	21,517	23,500	1,446	728	718	22,228	15,629	6,599	21,343	5,160	16,183
65—70	14,204	7,257	6,947	460	258	192	6,743	4,778	1,965	7,001	2,211	4,790
70 and over	36,797	14,864	21,933	1,372	611	761	11,523	8,327	3,196	23,902	5,626	17,976
BUDDHISTS.	**1,183,446**	**592,310**	**591,136**	**604,685**	**326,532**	**278,153**	**445,504**	**222,259**	**223,245**	**133,257**	**43,519**	**89,738**
0—1	*28,635*	*13,918*	*14,717*	*28,635*	*13,918*	*14,717*	...	...	...	...	...	...
1—2	*22,919*	*11,368*	*11,551*	*22,919*	*11,368*	*11,551*	...	...	...	...	...	...
2—3	*28,140*	*13,546*	*14,594*	*28,140*	*13,546*	*14,594*	...	...	...	...	...	...
3—4	*32,298*	*16,208*	*16,090*	*32,298*	*16,208*	*16,090*	...	...	...	...	...	...
4—5	*29,308*	*14,353*	*14,955*	*29,308*	*14,353*	*14,955*	...	...	...	...	...	...
0—5	141,300	69,393	71,907	141,300	69,393	71,907	...	...	...	...	...	...
5—10	148,257	73,786	74,471	148,257	73,786	74,471	...	...	...	...	...	...
10—15	125,537	65,458	60,079	125,263	65,429	59,834	267	29	238	7	...	7
15—20	123,357	58,687	64,670	98,848	55,240	43,608	21,256	2,984	18,272	3,253	463	2,790
20—25	110,613	52,409	58,204	46,800	31,851	14,949	55,070	17,482	37,588	8,743	3,076	5,667
25—30	94,750	46,407	48,343	19,311	14,169	5,142	66,404	28,355	38,049	9,035	3,883	5,152
30—35	92,678	48,215	44,463	10,146	7,221	2,925	70,872	35,964	34,908	11,660	5,030	6,630
35—40	57,713	30,643	27,070	3,753	2,767	986	46,671	24,600	22,071	7,289	3,276	4,013
40—45	78,101	40,419	37,682	3,483	2,250	1,233	60,358	33,090	27,268	14,260	5,079	9,181
45—50	43,362	23,434	19,928	1,554	1,076	478	33,359	19,267	14,092	8,449	3,091	5,358
50—55	61,042	31,853	29,189	2,134	1,303	831	40,714	25,356	15,358	18,194	5,194	13,000
55—60	25,572	14,366	11,206	939	612	327	16,653	10,924	5,729	7,980	2,830	5,150
60—65	38,180	18,291	19,889	1,272	642	630	18,710	13,241	5,469	18,198	4,408	13,790
65—70	12,292	6,423	5,869	419	246	173	5,816	4,181	1,635	6,057	1,996	4,061
70 and over	30,692	12,526	18,166	1,206	547	659	9,354	6,786	2,568	20,132	5,193	14,939
ANIMISTS.	**246,483**	**125,762**	**120,721**	**121,829**	**67,019**	**54,810**	**102,294**	**52,320**	**49,974**	**22,360**	**6,423**	**15,937**
0—1	*4,084*	*2,005*	*2,079*	*4,084*	*2,005*	*2,079*	...	...	...	...	...	...
1—2	*5,283*	*2,534*	*2,749*	*5,283*	*2,534*	*2,749*	...	...	...	...	...	...
2—3	*6,910*	*3,369*	*3,541*	*6,910*	*3,369*	*3,541*	...	...	...	...	...	...
3—4	*7,801*	*3,958*	*3,843*	*7,801*	*3,958*	*3,843*	...	...	...	...	...	...
4—5	*6,630*	*3,249*	*3,381*	*6,630*	*3,249*	*3,381*	...	...	...	...	...	...
0—5	30,708	15,115	15,593	30,708	15,115	15,593	...	...	...	...	...	...
5—10	31,597	16,534	15,063	31,597	16,534	15,063	...	...	...	...	...	...
10—15	22,471	12,020	10,451	22,374	12,008	10,366	97	12	85	...	...	...
15—20	23,135	11,891	11,244	18,298	10,569	7,729	4,643	1,235	3,407	194	86	108
20—25	24,441	12,134	12,307	10,220	6,795	3,425	13,419	5,032	8,387	802	307	495
25—30	21,940	10,863	11,077	3,953	2,909	1,044	16,777	7,407	9,370	1,210	547	663
30—35	25,196	13,564	11,632	2,437	1,740	697	20,487	10,887	9,600	2,272	937	1,335
35—40	13,611	7,316	6,295	680	503	177	11,459	6,222	5,237	1,472	591	881
40—45	17,613	9,103	8,510	642	385	257	13,881	7,841	6,040	3,090	877	2,213
45—50	7,606	4,020	3,586	188	127	61	5,901	3,437	2,464	1,517	456	1,061
50—55	11,319	6,074	5,245	317	155	162	7,665	5,085	2,580	3,337	834	2,503
55—60	3,299	1,507	1,792	100	48	52	2,039	1,161	878	1,160	298	862
60—65	6,106	2,769	3,337	144	65	79	3,080	2,054	1,026	2,882	650	2,232
65—70	1,743	731	1,012	27	14	13	847	537	310	869	180	689
70 and over	5,698	2,121	3,577	144	52	92	1,999	1,409	590	3,555	660	2,895

IMPERIAL TABLE VIIA.—*Age, Sex, and Civil Condition by Religion.*

PART III.—THE EASTERN STATES.

RELIGION AND AGE.	POPULATION.			UNMARRIED.			MARRIED.			WIDOWED.		
	Persons.	Males.	Females.	Persons.	Males.	Females.	Persons.	Males.	Females.	Persons.	Males.	Females.
1	2	3	4	5	6	7	8	9	10	11	12	13
TOTAL HINDUS.	13,005	10,661	2,344	5,042	4,028	1,014	7,228	6,000	1,228	740	633	107
0—1	*198*	*102*	*96*	*198*	*102*	*96*	...	...	...	...	...	...
1—2	*185*	*87*	*98*	*185*	*87*	*98*	...	...	...	...	...	...
2—3	*201*	*100*	*101*	*201*	*100*	*101*	...	...	...	...	...	...
3—4	*202*	*101*	*101*	*202*	*101*	*101*	...	...	...	...	...	...
4—5	*162*	*84*	*78*	*162*	*84*	*78*	...	...	...	...	...	...
0—5	948	474	474	948	474	474	...	...	...	...	...	...
5—10	670	380	290	670	380	290	...	...	...	...	...	...
10—15	487	303	184	470	297	173	17	6	11	...	...	...
15—20	880	613	267	510	460	50	364	150	214	6	3	3
20—25	2,168	1,866	302	981	973	8	1,150	861	289	37	32	5
25—30	2,433	2,182	251	661	654	7	1,676	1,437	239	96	91	5
30—35	2,049	1,833	216	399	395	4	1,520	1,313	207	130	125	5
35—40	1,239	1,111	128	171	166	5	973	867	106	88	78	10
40—45	1,027	910	117	136	133	3	777	682	95	114	95	19
45—50	436	394	42	37	37	...	338	306	32	61	51	10
50—55	382	349	33	32	32	...	267	243	24	83	74	9
55—60	101	91	10	10	10	...	57	55	2	34	26	8
60—65	148	125	23	11	11	...	77	73	4	60	41	19
65—70	16	11	5	1	1	...	5	5	...	10	5	5
70 and over	28	19	9	5	5	...	2	2	...	21	12	9
HINDUS BORN IN BURMA.	2,063	1,076	987	1,797	993	804	249	76	173	17	7	10
0—1	*186*	*93*	*93*	*186*	*93*	*93*	...	...	...	...	...	...
1—2	*161*	*74*	*87*	*161*	*74*	*87*	...	...	...	...	...	...
2—3	*180*	*89*	*91*	*180*	*89*	*91*	...	...	...	...	...	...
3—4	*174*	*88*	*86*	*174*	*88*	*86*	...	...	...	...	...	...
4—5	*132*	*70*	*62*	*132*	*70*	*62*	...	...	...	...	...	...
0—5	833	414	419	833	414	419	...	...	...	...	...	...
5—10	520	288	232	520	288	232	...	...	...	...	...	...
10—15	287	164	123	274	161	113	13	3	10	...	...	...
15—20	178	82	96	103	72	31	74	10	64	1	...	1
20—25	85	37	48	31	26	5	53	11	42	1	...	1
25—30	58	33	25	16	15	1	40	16	24	2	2	...
30—35	38	19	19	7	5	2	29	14	15	2	...	2
35—40	10	5	5	3	2	1	7	3	4	...	...	...
40—45	24	16	8	8	8	...	14	7	7	2	1	1
45—50	11	7	4	...	...	...	7	4	3	4	3	1
50—55	9	5	4	...	...	...	8	4	4	1	1	...
55—60	2	...	2	...	...	...	...	...	...	2	...	2
60—65	6	5	1	1	1	...	4	4	...	1	...	1
65—70	...	...	...	...	...	...	...	...	...	...	...	...
70 and over	2	1	1	1	1	...	...	...	...	1	...	1
TOTAL MAHOMEDANS.	4,834	3,429	1,405	2,138	1,488	650	2,369	1,694	675	332	252	80
0—1	*105*	*60*	*45*	*105*	*60*	*45*	...	...	...	...	...	...
1—2	*91*	*48*	*43*	*91*	*48*	*43*	...	...	...	...	...	...
2—3	*76*	*44*	*32*	*76*	*44*	*32*	...	...	...	...	...	...
3—4	*103*	*58*	*45*	*103*	*58*	*45*	...	...	...	...	...	...
4—5	*100*	*51*	*49*	*100*	*51*	*49*	...	...	...	...	...	...
0—5	475	261	214	475	261	214	...	...	...	...	...	...
5—10	446	239	207	446	239	207	...	...	...	...	...	...
10—15	335	189	146	333	189	144	2	...	2	...	...	...
15—20	353	218	135	241	191	50	106	23	83	6	4	2
20—25	569	390	179	236	226	10	313	146	167	20	18	2
25—30	671	513	158	165	155	10	475	327	148	31	31	...
30—35	610	501	109	98	89	9	464	368	96	48	44	4
35—40	450	374	76	53	53	...	349	280	69	48	41	7
40—45	365	297	68	38	34	4	277	226	51	50	37	13
45—50	196	161	35	23	23	...	148	125	23	25	13	12
50—55	180	138	42	16	14	2	121	98	23	43	26	17
55—60	57	48	9	5	5	...	39	35	4	13	8	5
60—65	77	60	17	3	3	...	48	41	7	26	16	10
65—70	18	15	3	1	1	...	10	9	1	7	5	2
70 and over	32	25	7	...	...	...	17	16	1	15	9	6

Imperial Table VIIa.—*Age, Sex, and Civil Condition by Religion.*

PART III.—THE EASTERN STATES.

Religion and Age.		Population.			Unmarried.			Married.			Widowed.		
		Persons.	Males.	Females.	Persons.	Males.	Females.	Persons.	Males.	Females.	Persons.	Males.	Females.
1		2	3	4	5	6	7	8	9	10	11	12	13
MAHOMEDANS BORN IN BURMA.		2,099	1,000	1,099	1,371	795	576	645	177	468	83	28	55
	0— 1	*104*	*59*	*45*	*104*	*59*	*45*	..	...	...	...	...	...
	1— 2	*87*	*46*	*41*	*87*	*46*	*41*	...	...	...	..	...	...
	2— 3	*74*	*43*	*31*	*74*	*43*	*31*	...	...	...	...	...	...
	3— 4	*102*	*57*	*45*	*102*	*57*	*45*	...	...	...	...	...	...
	4— 5	*87*	*46*	*41*	*87*	*46*	*41*	...	...	...	...	...	...
	0— 5	454	251	203	454	251	203	..	...	...	...	...	...
	5—10	400	216	184	400	216	184	...	...	...	...	...	...
	10—15	274	146	128	272	146	126	2	...	2	...	...	...
	15—20	198	93	105	122	86	36	73	6	67	3	1	2
	20—25	208	77	131	60	50	10	141	22	119	7	5	2
	25—30	175	61	114	25	20	5	149	40	109	1	1	...
	30—35	123	51	72	22	13	9	94	35	59	7	3	4
	35—40	89	38	51	2	2	...	76	30	46	11	6	5
	40—45	66	24	42	2	1	1	50	21	29	14	2	12
	45—50	41	18	23	6	6	...	26	11	15	9	1	8
	50—55	40	13	27	4	2	2	20	6	14	16	5	11
	55—60	9	4	5	1	1	...	5	1	4	3	2	1
	60—65	13	4	9	...	...	...	5	2	3	8	2	6
	65—70	3	2	1	1	1	...	1	1	...	1	...	1
	70 and over	6	2	4	..	...	...	3	2	1	3	...	3
CHRISTIANS.		22,668	11,523	11,145	12,124	6,463	5,661	9,062	4,621	4,441	1,482	439	1,043
	0— 1	*713*	*344*	*369*	*713*	*344*	*369*	...	...	...	...	...	...
	1— 2	*615*	*300*	*315*	*615*	*300*	*315*	...	...	...	...	...	...
	2— 3	*707*	*361*	*346*	*707*	*361*	*346*	...	...	...	...	...	...
	3— 4	*811*	*431*	*380*	*811*	*431*	*380*	...	...	...	...	...	...
	4— 5	*735*	*345*	*390*	*735*	*345*	*390*	...	...	...	...	...	...
	0— 5	3,581	1,781	1,800	3,581	1,781	1,800	...	...	...	...	...	...
	5—10	2,971	1,515	1,456	2,971	1,515	1,456	...	...	...	...	...	...
	10—15	2,542	1,369	1,173	2,542	1,369	1,173	...	...	...	...	...	...
	15—20	2,229	1,059	1,170	1,622	906	716	589	146	443	18	7	11
	20—25	2,077	990	1,087	703	454	249	1,310	515	795	64	21	43
	25—30	2,021	981	1,040	303	206	97	1,613	738	875	105	37	68
	30—35	1,778	930	848	165	102	63	1,468	786	682	145	42	103
	35—40	1,284	685	599	73	44	29	1,083	593	490	128	48	80
	40—45	1,264	665	599	44	29	15	1,037	587	450	183	49	134
	45—50	718	383	335	25	11	14	587	343	244	106	29	77
	50—55	860	441	419	33	13	20	602	375	227	225	53	172
	55—60	362	208	154	17	13	4	251	164	87	94	31	63
	60—65	501	267	234	16	7	9	308	215	93	177	45	132
	65—70	135	77	58	12	6	6	65	46	19	58	25	33
	70 and over	345	172	173	17	7	10	149	113	36	179	52	127
OTHERS.		255	208	47	67	48	19	176	147	28	13	13	...
	0— 1	*2*	...	*2*	*2*	...	*2*	...	...	...	...	..	...
	1— 2	*7*	*4*	*3*	*7*	*4*	*3*	...	...	...	...	...	...
	2— 3	*4*	*4*	...	*4*	*4*	...	...	...	...	...	...	...
	3— 4	*2*	*1*	*1*	*2*	*1*	*1*	...	...	...	...	...	...
	4— 5	*2*	*2*	...	*2*	*2*	...	...	...	...	...	...	...
	0— 5	17	11	6	17	11	6	...	...	...	...	..	...
	5—10	15	8	7	15	8	7	...	...	...	...	...	...
	10—15	11	5	6	11	5	6	...	...	...	...	...	...
	15—20	8	3	5	3	3	...	5	...	5	...	...	...
	20—25	15	11	4	5	5	...	10	6	4	...	...	...
	25—30	47	41	6	7	7	...	40	34	6	...	...	...
	30—35	58	51	7	7	7	...	47	40	7	4	4	...
	35—40	36	34	2	2	2	...	29	27	2	5	5	...
	40—45	20	20	..	...	...	...	20	20	...	...	...	...
	45—50	13	10	3	...	...	...	10	7	3	3	3	..
	50—55	5	5	...	...	...	...	4	4	...	1	1	...
	55—60	3	3	...	...	...	...	3	3	...	...	...	...
	60—65	5	5	...	...	...	...	5	5	...	...	...	...
	65—70	...	...	...	...	...	...	...	...	...	...	...	...
	70 and over	2	1	1	...	...	...	2	1	1	...	...	...

IMPERIAL TABLE VII-B.

Age, Sex and Civil Condition in each District, etc., by Religion.

NOTE 1.—This table gives for each district and for the three parts of the Eastern States statistics similar to those of Parts II and III of Imperial Table VIIA. In every district it relates to the same area and population as that table, thus excluding all areas in which the census was by estimate only, but no others.

NOTE 2.—Rangoon Town constitutes a district and statistics are given for it accordingly as for other districts.

NOTE 3.—The figures given for Mandalay district include those of Mandalay City which are given separately immediately below them.

NOTE 4.—The age recorded was the number of completed years. The age-group represented by 5—10 in the table includes all who had completed five but had not yet completed ten years of age; and the other age-groups have a parallel interpretation.

NOTE 5.—Amongst the adherents of some religions were found a few persons for whom the age was not clearly specified. By the records relating to marriage, literacy and occupation most of these could be assigned to classes in which the range of age was limited in one direction or the other. Each class was then distributed amongst the age-groups in its range in proportion to the numbers in those groups for whom the age had been specified. In every case the numbers distributed were too small to have any significant effect upon the table.

NOTE 6.—The figures given in columns 11, 12 and 13 of the table under the heading *Widowed* include persons described as divorced and not re-married as well as those described as widowed.

NOTE 7.—In this table all persons belonging to Christian races as well as all professing the Christian religion are included under the description *Christian*. (See Note 3 of Table VIA.)

NOTE 8.—The figures given in each district for Hindus or Mahomedans born in Burma are included in those given for Total Hindus or Total Mahomedans. Separate figures are not given as a rule for Hindus or Mahomedans born outside Burma.

NOTE 9.—In some cases in which only few persons are concerned the length of the table has been reduced by omitting the details for separate age-groups of a religion and showing only the totals for all ages of each sex and civil condition.

NOTE 10.—Similar statistics for the larger towns are given in Provincial Table V; for Buddhists alone similar statistics for the separate townships into which each district is divided are given in Provincial Table III; and similar statistics for selected races are given for some townships or districts in Provincial Table IV. For Europeans, Anglo-Indians and Armenians statistics for sex and age are given in Imperial Table XVI. Imperial Tables VIB and XIII show relationships between religion and race.

IMPERIAL TABLE VIIB.—*Age, Sex, and Civil Condition by Religion.*

District, Religion and Age.	Population. Persons.	Population. Males.	Population. Females.	Unmarried. Persons.	Unmarried. Males.	Unmarried. Females.	Married. Persons.	Married. Males.	Married. Females.	Widowed. Persons.	Widowed. Males.	Widowed. Females.
1	2	3	4	5	6	7	8	9	10	11	12	13
AKYAB.												
All Religions ..	*576,430*	*309,564*	*266,866*	*285,238*	*161,244*	*123,994*	*233,512*	*127,537*	*105,975*	*57,680*	*20,783*	*36,897*
0	13,019	6,502	6,517	13,019	6,502	6,517	...	...	...	...	...	...
1—5	62,616	31,391	31,225	62,616	31,391	31,225	...	...	...	...	...	...
5—10	79,574	40,058	39,516	79,574	40,058	39,516	...	...	...	...	...	...
10—15	66,335	35,700	30,635	65,139	35,633	29,506	1,132	64	1,068	64	3	61
15—20	55,982	28,723	27,259	37,364	25,876	11,488	16,628	2,567	14,061	1,990	280	1,710
20—30	102,536	55,503	47,033	20,541	17,372	3,169	72,373	33,923	38,450	9,622	4,208	5,414
30—40	79,991	47,545	32,146	4,170	2,552	1,618	65,773	40,117	25,656	10,048	4,876	5,172
40—50	53,306	30,869	22,437	1,309	931	378	41,578	25,884	15,694	10,419	4,054	6,365
50—60	34,246	18,095	16,151	735	485	250	22,380	14,377	8,003	11,131	3,233	7,898
60 and over	28,825	15,178	13,647	771	444	327	13,648	10,605	3,043	14,406	4,129	10,277
Buddhist ..	*315,140*	*159,722*	*155,418*	*149,870*	*81,821*	*68,049*	*126,349*	*64,182*	*62,167*	*38,921*	*13,719*	*25,202*
0	7,258	3,510	3,748	7,258	3,510	3,748	...	...	...	...	...	...
1—5	29,407	14,620	14,787	29,407	14,620	14,787	..	...	...	...	...	...
5—10	40,271	20,367	19,904	40,271	20,367	19,904	...	...	...	...	...	...
10—15	36,927	19,122	17,805	36,552	19,115	17,437	339	7	332	36	...	36
15—20	31,515	15,551	15,964	22,407	14,315	8,092	7,685	1,081	6,604	1,423	155	1,268
20—30	54,077	26,627	27,450	9,688	7,619	2,069	37,676	16,178	21,498	6,713	2,830	3,883
30—40	43,935	23,259	20,676	2,464	1,097	1,367	34,949	19,133	15,816	6,522	3,029	3,493
40—50	32,851	17,685	15,166	819	576	243	24,929	14,355	10,574	7,103	2,754	4,349
50—60	20,828	10,267	10,561	464	303	161	12,917	7,749	5,168	7,447	2,215	5,232
60 and over	18,071	8,714	9,357	540	299	241	7,854	5,679	2,175	9,677	2,736	6,941
Animist ..	*36,806*	*19,124*	*17,682*	*17,680*	*9,646*	*8,034*	*16,412*	*8,370*	*8,042*	*2,714*	*1,108*	*1,606*
0	731	369	362	731	369	362	...	...	..	...	...	...
1—5	3,873	2,036	1,837	3,873	2,036	1,837	...	...	...	...	...	...
5—10	4,931	2,408	2,523	4,931	2,408	2,523	...	...	...	...	...	...
10—15	4,037	2,197	1,840	4,010	2,197	1,813	27	...	27	...	...	...
15—20	3,364	1,609	1,755	2,474	1,398	1,076	838	189	649	52	22	30
20—30	6,408	3,152	3,256	1,277	967	310	4,801	1,998	2,803	330	187	143
30—40	5,462	2,991	2,471	214	161	53	4,813	2,589	2,224	435	241	194
40—50	3,658	2,004	1,654	69	45	24	3,116	1,755	1,361	473	204	269
50—60	2,342	1,269	1,073	58	36	22	1,749	1,063	686	535	170	365
60 and over	2,000	1,089	911	43	29	14	1,068	776	292	889	284	605
Hindu ..	*14,719*	*13,401*	*1,318*	*5,292*	*4,723*	*569*	*8,345*	*7,779*	*566*	*1,082*	*899*	*183*
0	70	40	30	70	40	30	...	...	...	...	...	...
1—5	340	162	178	340	162	178	...	...	...	...	...	...
5—10	442	237	205	442	237	205	...	..	...	...	...	...
10—15	603	493	110	578	485	93	25	8	17	...	...	...
15—20	1,394	1,265	129	1,121	1,101	20	247	145	102	26	19	7
20—30	4,751	4,458	293	2,127	2,100	27	2,408	2,175	233	216	183	33
30—40	3,740	3,559	181	451	444	7	2,991	2,850	141	298	265	33
40—50	2,041	1,944	97	115	107	8	1,683	1,632	51	243	205	38
50—60	898	844	54	34	34	...	695	676	19	169	134	35
60 and over	440	399	41	14	13	1	296	293	3	130	93	37
Hindus born in Burma.	*1,559*	*834*	*725*	*918*	*510*	*408*	*504*	*267*	*287*	*142*	*57*	*85*
0	53	30	23	53	30	23	...	...	...	...	...	...
1—5	252	117	135	252	117	135	..	...	..	...	...	...
5—10	284	134	150	284	134	150	...	...	...	...	...	...
10—15	165	96	69	154	96	58	11	...	11	...	...	...
15—20	143	64	79	75	61	14	64	3	61	4	...	4
20—30	238	124	114	68	53	15	154	65	89	16	6	10
30—40	198	133	65	15	13	2	149	104	45	34	16	18
40—50	104	57	47	7	2	5	64	40	24	33	15	18
50—60	66	46	20	3	3	...	39	33	6	24	10	14
60 and over	56	33	23	2	1	1	23	22	1	31	10	21
Mahomedan ..	*208,961*	*116,736*	*92,225*	*111,961*	*64,759*	*47,202*	*82,065*	*46,942*	*35,123*	*14,935*	*5,035*	*9,900*
0	4,951	2,576	2,375	4,951	2,576	2,375	...	...	...	...	...	...
1—5	28,954	14,555	14,399	28,954	14,555	14,399	...	...	...	...	...	...
5—10	33,855	17,011	16,844	33,855	17,011	16,844	...	...	...	...	...	...
10—15	24,706	13,857	10,849	23,939	13,807	10,132	739	47	692	28	3	25
15—20	19,641	10,250	9,391	11,304	9,022	2,282	7,848	1,144	6,704	489	84	405
20—30	37,091	21,100	15,991	7,328	6,579	749	27,404	13,516	13,888	2,359	1,005	1,354
30—40	26,664	17,582	9,082	986	800	186	22,892	15,448	7,444	2,786	1,334	1,452
40—50	14,663	9,163	5,500	296	198	98	11,769	8,076	3,693	2,598	889	1,709
50—60	10,139	5,680	4,459	175	109	66	6,990	4,861	2,129	2,974	710	2,264
60 and over	8,297	4,962	3,335	173	102	71	4,423	3,850	573	3,701	1,010	2,691

Imperial Table VIIb.—*Age, Sex, and Civil Condition by Religion.*

District	Religion and Age	Population: Persons	Population: Males	Population: Females	Unmarried: Persons	Unmarried: Males	Unmarried: Females	Married: Persons	Married: Males	Married: Females	Widowed: Persons	Widowed: Males	Widowed: Females
1		2	3	4	5	6	7	8	9	10	11	12	13
AKYAB—*concluded.*	***Mahomedans born in Burma***	*177,277*	*90,494*	*86,783*	*103,155*	*57,103*	*46,052*	*62,344*	*30,170*	*32,174*	*11,778*	*8,221*	*8,557*
	0	4,896	2,542	2,354	4,896	2,542	2,354	...	...	...	...	...	...
	1—5	28,453	14,267	14,186	28,453	14,267	14,186	...	...	...	...	...	...
	5—10	33,010	16,560	16,450	33,010	16,560	16,450	...	...	...	...	...	...
	10—15	23,334	12,889	10,445	22,632	12,855	9,777	679	34	645	23	...	23
	15—20	16,630	7,662	8,968	9,033	6,827	2,206	7,159	776	6,383	438	59	379
	20—30	27,637	12,640	14,997	4,112	3,408	704	21,646	8,627	13,019	1,879	605	1,274
	30—40	19,255	11,096	8,159	554	388	166	16,590	9,901	6,689	2,111	807	1,304
	40—50	10,381	5,671	4,710	188	108	80	8,155	5,010	3,145	2,038	553	1,485
	50—60	7,443	3,660	3,783	130	69	61	4,947	3,117	1,830	2,366	474	1,892
	60 and over	6,238	3,507	2,731	147	79	68	3,163	2,705	463	2,923	723	2,200
	Christian (all ages)	*618*	*428*	*190*	*357*	*232*	*125*	*241*	*181*	*60*	*20*	*15*	*5*
	Others (all ages) ..	*186*	*158*	*33*	*78*	*63*	*15*	*100*	*83*	*17*	*8*	*7*	*1*
HILL DISTRICT OF ARAKAN.	***All Religions*** ..	*20,914*	*10,790*	*10,124*	*9,024*	*5,066*	*3,958*	*10,182*	*5,124*	*5,058*	*1,708*	*600*	*1,108*
	0	338	174	164	338	174	164	...	...	...	...	...	...
	1—5	1,755	895	860	1,755	895	860	...	...	...	...	...	...
	5—10	2,446	1,238	1,208	2,446	1,238	1,208	...	...	...	...	...	...
	10—15	2,291	1,218	1,073	2,291	1,218	1,073	...	...	...	...	...	...
	15—20	2,083	984	1,099	1,305	819	486	723	146	577	55	19	36
	20—30	3,797	1,924	1,873	721	586	135	2,862	1,209	1,653	214	129	85
	30—40	3,277	1,771	1,506	114	99	15	2,922	1,551	1,371	241	121	120
	40—50	2,247	1,169	1,078	31	19	12	1,913	1,042	871	303	108	195
	50—60	1,480	775	705	11	9	2	1,112	687	425	357	79	278
	60 and over	1,200	642	558	12	9	3	650	489	161	538	144	394
	Buddhist ..	*2,225*	*1,220*	*1,005*	*1,105*	*639*	*466*	*918*	*501*	*417*	*202*	*80*	*122*
	0	61	33	28	61	33	28	...	...	...	...	...	...
	1—5	206	99	107	206	99	107	...	...	...	...	...	...
	5—10	272	143	129	272	143	129	...	...	...	...	...	...
	10—15	225	112	113	225	112	113	...	...	...	...	...	...
	15—20	243	130	113	192	124	68	43	4	39	8	2	6
	20—30	400	239	161	122	106	16	249	113	136	29	20	9
	30—40	324	191	133	15	12	3	277	162	115	32	17	15
	40—50	228	126	102	6	4	2	186	105	81	36	17	19
	50—60	165	93	72	2	2	...	120	80	40	43	11	32
	60 and over	101	54	47	4	4	...	43	37	6	54	13	41
	Animist ..	*18,054*	*9,109*	*8,945*	*7,596*	*4,179*	*3,417*	*8,975*	*4,427*	*4,548*	*1,488*	*508*	*980*
	0	262	134	128	262	134	128	...	...	...	...	...	...
	1—5	1,496	767	729	1,496	767	729	...	...	...	...	...	...
	5—10	2,121	1,061	1,060	2,121	1,061	1,060	...	...	...	...	...	...
	10—15	2,020	1,081	939	2,020	1,081	939	...	...	...	...	...	...
	15—20	1,791	824	967	1,086	670	416	658	137	521	47	17	30
	20—30	3,219	1,544	1,675	513	394	119	2,523	1,043	1,480	183	107	76
	30—40	2,826	1,477	1,349	65	53	12	2,562	1,328	1,234	199	96	103
	40—50	1,959	999	960	20	10	10	1,675	900	775	264	89	175
	50—60	1,272	643	629	7	5	2	957	574	383	308	64	244
	60 and over	1,088	579	509	6	4	2	600	445	155	482	130	352
	Hindu (all ages)	*575*	*407*	*168*	*291*	*217*	*74*	*261*	*178*	*83*	*23*	*17*	*6*
	Mahomedan (all ages).	*46*	*43*	*3*	*24*	*24*	...	*22*	*19*	*3*	...	...	...
	Christian (all ages)	*14*	*11*	*3*	*8*	*7*	*1*	*6*	*4*	*2*	...	...	...
KYAUKPYU.	***All Religions*** ..	*199,873*	*96,569*	*103,304*	*94,795*	*49,877*	*44,918*	*84,514*	*41,371*	*43,143*	*20,564*	*5,321*	*15,243*
	0	4,383	2,121	2,262	4,383	2,121	2,262	...	...	...	...	...	...
	1—5	19,933	9,838	10,095	19,933	9,838	10,095	...	...	...	...	...	...
	5—10	26,293	13,194	13,099	26,293	13,194	13,099	...	...	...	...	...	...
	10—15	22,689	11,763	10,926	22,620	11,735	10,885	62	28	34	7	...	7
	15—20	19,961	9,405	10,556	14,523	8,357	6,166	4,809	944	3,865	629	104	525
	20—30	30,281	13,569	16,712	4,455	2,865	1,590	22,882	9,653	13,229	2,944	1,051	1,893
	30—40	28,095	14,113	13,982	1,564	1,194	370	23,607	11,936	11,671	2,924	983	1,941
	40—50	20,444	9,933	10,511	459	254	205	16,705	8,848	7,857	3,280	831	2,449
	50—60	14,516	6,746	7,770	283	167	116	10,164	5,689	4,475	4,069	890	3,179
	60 and over	13,278	5,887	7,391	282	152	130	6,285	4,273	2,012	6,711	1,462	5,249

IMPERIAL TABLE VII.—*Age, Sex, and Civil Condition by Religion.*

DISTRICT, RELIGION, AND AGE.	POPULATION.			UNMARRIED.			MARRIED.			WIDOWED.		
	Persons.	Males.	Females.	Persons.	Males.	Females.	Persons.	Males.	Females.	Persons.	Males.	Females.
1	2	3	4	5	6	7	8	9	10	11	12	13
KYAUKPYU—*concluded.*												
Buddhist ..	*178,451*	*84,901*	*93,550*	*83,984*	*43,592*	*40,392*	*75,523*	*36,706*	*38,817*	*18,944*	*4,603*	*14,341*
0	4,003	1,927	2,076	4,003	1,927	2,076	...	...	...	...	...	...
1—5	17,679	8,715	8,964	17,679	8,715	8,964	...	...	...	...	...	...
5—10	23,408	11,764	11,644	23,408	11,764	11,644	...	...	...	...	...	...
10—15	20,266	10,471	9,795	20,217	10,455	9,762	42	16	26	7	...	7
15—20	17,986	8,415	9,571	13,234	7,530	5,704	4,160	793	3,367	592	92	500
20—30	26,406	11,471	14,935	3,686	2,214	1,472	20,014	8,336	11,678	2,706	921	1,785
30—40	24,769	12,104	12,665	818	472	346	21,322	10,840	10,482	2,629	792	1,837
40—50	18,344	8,680	9,664	409	225	184	14,930	7,753	7,177	3,005	702	2,303
50—60	13,246	6,001	7,245	263	148	115	9,257	5,084	4,173	3,726	769	2,957
60 and over	12,344	5,353	6,991	267	142	125	5,798	3,884	1,914	6,279	1,327	4,952
Animist ...	*16,178*	*8,414*	*7,759*	*8,569*	*4,939*	*3,630*	*6,532*	*2,968*	*3,564*	*1,072*	*507*	*565*
0	304	150	154	304	150	154	...	...	...	...	...	...
1—5	1,901	950	951	1,901	950	951	...	...	...	...	...	...
5—10	2,356	1,184	1,172	2,356	1,184	1,172	...	...	...	...	...	...
10—15	1,890	997	893	1,890	997	893	...	...	...	...	...	...
15—20	1,453	689	764	920	584	336	513	98	415	20	7	13
20—30	2,715	1,301	1,414	449	365	84	2,131	845	1,286	135	91	44
30—40	2,372	1,325	1,047	692	676	16	1,493	519	974	187	130	57
40—50	1,542	877	665	33	15	18	1,335	776	559	174	86	88
50—60	955	550	405	14	13	1	694	448	246	247	89	158
60 and over	685	391	294	10	5	5	366	282	84	309	104	205
Hindu ..	*634*	*609*	*25*	*217*	*213*	*4*	*331*	*361*	*20*	*86*	*85*	*1*
0	...	...	...	...	...	...	...	...	...	...	...	...
1—5	2	2	...	2	2	...	...	...	...	...	...	...
5—10	6	5	1	6	5	1	...	...	...	...	...	...
10—15	21	20	1	20	19	1	1	1	...	...	...	...
15—20	53	49	4	42	40	2	11	9	2	...	...	...
20—30	229	218	11	111	111	...	113	102	11	5	5	...
30—40	170	164	6	21	21	...	140	134	6	9	9	...
40—50	93	92	1	8	8	...	74	73	1	11	11	...
50—60	36	36	...	3	3	...	29	29	...	4	4	...
60 and over	24	23	1	4	4	...	13	13	...	7	6	1
Hindus born in Burma	*28*	*25*	*3*	*11*	*10*	*1*	*16*	*14*	*2*	*1*	*1*	...
0	...	...	...	...	...	...	...	...	...	...	...	...
1—5	1	1	...	1	1	...	...	...	...	...	...	...
5—10	4	3	1	4	3	1	...	...	...	...	...	...
10—15	...	...	...	...	...	...	...	...	...	...	...	...
15—20	3	3	...	2	2	...	1	1	...	...	...	...
20—30	9	7	2	4	4	...	5	3	2	...	...	...
30—40	5	5	...	...	...	...	5	5	...	...	...	...
40—50	4	4	...	...	...	...	3	3	...	1	1	...
50—60	2	2	...	...	...	...	2	2	...	...	...	...
60 and over	...	...	...	...	...	...	...	...	...	...	...	...
Mahomedan ..	*4,479*	*2,580*	*1,899*	*1,955*	*1,105*	*850*	*2,021*	*1,304*	*717*	*503*	*171*	*332*
0	72	43	29	72	43	29	...	...	...	...	...	...
1—5	338	166	172	338	166	172	...	...	...	...	...	...
5—10	509	236	273	509	236	273	...	...	...	...	...	...
10—15	497	269	228	478	258	220	19	11	8	...	...	...
15—20	454	246	208	314	197	117	123	44	79	17	5	12
20—30	900	566	334	201	172	29	605	363	242	94	31	63
30—40	767	509	258	30	23	7	639	435	204	98	51	47
40—50	456	279	177	9	6	3	358	242	116	89	31	58
50—60	272	155	117	3	3	...	178	124	54	91	28	63
60 and over	214	111	103	1	1	...	99	85	14	114	25	89
Mahomedans born in Burma.	*3,150*	*1,485*	*1,665*	*1,522*	*793*	*729*	*1,206*	*578*	*628*	*422*	*114*	*308*
0	65	37	28	65	37	28	...	...	...	...	...	...
1—5	284	145	139	284	145	139	...	...	...	...	...	...
5—10	422	197	225	422	197	225	...	...	...	...	...	...
10—15	394	204	190	394	204	190	...	...	...	...	...	...
15—20	336	149	187	245	135	110	75	9	66	16	5	11
20—30	513	217	296	94	66	28	340	128	212	79	23	56
30—40	465	227	238	12	6	6	383	194	189	70	27	43
40—50	324	161	163	5	2	3	240	136	104	79	23	56
50—60	182	81	101	1	1	...	107	63	44	74	17	57
60 and over	165	67	98	...	...	...	61	48	13	104	19	85
Christian (all ages)	*136*	*65*	*71*	*70*	*8*	*42*	*57*	*32*	*25*	*9*	*5*	*4*

IMPERIAL TABLE VIIB.—*Age, Sex, and Civil Condition by Religion.*

DISTRICT, RELIGION, AND AGE.	POPULATION.			UNMARRIED.			MARRIED.			WIDOWED.		
	Persons.	Males.	Females.	Persons.	Males.	Females.	Persons.	Males.	Females.	Persons.	Males.	Females.
1	2	3	4	5	6	7	8	9	10	11	12	13
SANDOWAY.												
All Religions ...	***112,029***	***55,304***	***56,725***	***57,049***	***29,787***	***27,262***	***46,358***	***23,033***	***23,325***	***8,622***	***2,484***	***6,138***
0	3,073	1,489	1,584	3,073	1,489	1,584	...	...	...	...	...	...
1—5	11,573	5,807	5,766	11,573	5,807	5,766	...	...	...	...	...	...
5—10	14,999	7,539	7,460	14,999	7,539	7,460	...	...	...	...	...	...
10—15	14,098	7,267	6,831	14,098	7,267	6,831	...	...	...	...	...	...
15—20	11,629	5,644	5,985	9,178	5,106	4,072	2,340	517	1,823	111	21	90
20—30	17,723	8,303	9,420	2,939	1,926	1,013	13,613	6,023	7,590	1,171	354	817
30—40	14,819	7,418	7,401	627	322	305	12,992	6,654	6,338	1,200	442	758
40—50	10,858	5,464	5,394	276	169	107	9,111	4,853	4,258	1,471	442	1,029
50—60	7,178	3,365	3,813	154	94	60	5,293	2,861	2,432	1,731	410	1,321
60 and over	6,079	3,008	3,071	132	68	64	3,009	2,125	884	2,938	815	2,123
Buddhist ...	***100,878***	***49,415***	***51,463***	***51,381***	***26,695***	***24,686***	***41,709***	***20,535***	***21,174***	***7,788***	***2,185***	***5,603***
0	2,787	1,354	1,433	2,787	1,354	1,433	...	...	...	...	...	...
1—5	10,507	5,239	5,268	10,507	5,239	5,268	...	...	...	...	...	...
5—10	13,658	6,868	6,790	13,658	6,868	6,790	...	...	...	...	...	...
10—15	12,778	6,581	6,197	12,778	6,581	6,197	...	...	...	...	...	...
15—20	10,431	5,064	5,367	8,216	4,581	3,635	2,120	467	1,653	95	16	79
20—30	15,758	7,229	8,529	2,430	1,547	883	12,253	5,368	6,885	1,075	314	761
30—40	13,263	6,553	6,710	527	247	280	11,655	5,920	5,735	1,081	386	695
40—50	9,650	4,784	4,866	231	138	93	8,112	4,274	3,838	1,307	372	935
50—60	6,517	3,028	3,489	132	79	53	4,815	2,578	2,237	1,570	371	1,199
60 and over	5,529	2,715	2,814	115	61	54	2,754	1,928	826	2,660	726	1,934
Animist ...	***4,568***	***2,321***	***2,247***	***2,194***	***1,169***	***1,025***	***2,017***	***1,027***	***990***	***357***	***125***	***232***
0	130	61	69	130	61	69	...	...	...	...	...	...
1—5	439	218	221	439	218	221	...	...	...	...	...	...
5—10	568	286	282	568	286	282	...	...	...	...	...	...
10—15	537	296	241	537	296	241	...	...	...	...	...	...
15—20	450	209	241	351	186	165	95	21	74	4	2	2
20—30	722	338	384	122	87	35	555	232	323	45	19	26
30—40	667	352	315	18	13	5	600	318	282	49	21	28
40—50	530	283	247	15	13	2	440	241	199	75	29	46
50—60	303	155	148	8	6	2	226	131	95	69	18	51
60 and over	222	123	99	6	3	3	101	84	17	115	36	79
Hindu (all ages) ...	***376***	***331***	***45***	***165***	***146***	***19***	***183***	***159***	***24***	***28***	***26***	***2***
Mahomedan ...	***5,251***	***2,749***	***2,502***	***2,797***	***1,508***	***1,289***	***2,065***	***1,116***	***949***	***389***	***125***	***264***
0	110	55	55	110	55	55	...	...	...	...	...	...
1—5	531	289	242	531	289	242	...	...	...	...	...	...
5—10	664	338	326	664	338	326	...	...	...	...	...	...
10—15	642	328	314	642	328	314	...	...	...	...	...	...
15—20	603	297	306	497	271	226	96	24	72	10	2	8
20—30	922	502	420	257	171	86	628	316	312	37	15	22
30—40	684	364	320	54	37	17	574	305	269	56	22	34
40—50	514	286	228	21	10	11	422	248	174	71	28	43
50—60	300	146	154	10	5	5	215	127	88	75	14	61
60 and over	281	144	137	11	4	7	130	96	34	140	44	96
Mahomedans born in Burma.	***4,698***	***2,229***	***2,469***	***2,588***	***1,309***	***1,279***	***1,759***	***827***	***932***	***351***	***93***	***258***
0	110	55	55	110	55	55	...	...	...	...	...	...
1—5	522	285	237	522	285	237	...	...	...	...	...	...
5—10	658	335	323	658	335	323	...	...	...	...	...	...
10—15	621	308	313	621	308	313	...	...	...	...	...	...
15—20	527	223	304	433	207	226	85	15	70	9	1	8
20—30	748	334	414	173	88	85	542	235	307	33	11	22
30—40	553	240	313	35	18	17	471	209	262	47	13	34
40—50	437	212	225	18	7	11	360	187	173	59	18	41
50—60	272	122	150	8	3	5	192	106	86	72	13	59
60 and over	250	115	135	10	3	7	109	75	34	131	37	94
Christian (all ages)	***956***	***488***	***468***	***512***	***269***	***243***	***384***	***196***	***188***	***60***	***23***	***37***

IMPERIAL TABLE VIIB.—*Age, Sex, and Civil Condition by Religion.*

District, Religion, and Age.	Population.			Unmarried.			Married.			Widowed.		
	Persons.	Males.	Females.	Persons.	Males.	Females.	Persons.	Males.	Females.	Persons.	Males.	Females.
1	2	3	4	5	6	7	8	9	10	11	12	13
RANGOON TOWN.												
All Religions ...	*841,962*	*286,689*	*105,278*	*149,781*	*100,881*	*48,900*	*174,867*	*129,502*	*45,865*	*17,864*	*6,856*	*11,008*
0	5,260	2,664	2,596	5,260	2,664	2,596	..	...	...	...	...	...
1—5	17,492	8,761	8,731	17,481	8,752	8,729	11	9	2	...	...	...
5—10	23,280	12,112	11,168	23,216	12,100	11,116	27	12	15	37	...	37
10—15	25,390	14,913	10,477	24,852	14,696	10,156	512	217	295	26	..	26
15—20	32,480	21,377	11,103	25,606	18,442	7,164	6,704	2,905	3,799	170	30	140
20—30	95,831	72,107	23,724	36,964	31,523	5,441	57,341	39,858	17,483	1,526	726	800
30—40	74,068	57,238	16,830	10,590	8,662	1,928	60,508	47,121	13,387	2,970	1,455	1,515
40—50	39,205	29,173	10,032	3,558	2,596	962	31,723	25,140	6,583	3,924	1,437	2,487
50—60	17,944	11,982	5,962	1,370	853	517	12,552	9,883	2,669	4,022	1,246	2,776
60 and over	11,012	6,362	4,650	834	543	291	5,489	4,357	1,132	4,689	1,462	3,227
Buddhist ...	*111,550*	*58,077*	*58,478*	*61,005*	*88,848*	*27,162*	*42,047*	*21,940*	*20,107*	*8,498*	*2,294*	*6,204*
0	2,565	1,273	1,292	2,565	1,273	1,292	...	...	...	...	...	...
1—5	7,842	3,963	3,879	7,842	3,963	3,879	...	...	...	...	...	...
5—10	10,173	5,036	5,137	10,173	5,036	5,137	...	...	...	...	...	...
10—15	11,598	5,877	5,721	11,565	5,872	5,693	27	5	22	6	...	6
15—20	12,354	6,154	6,200	10,674	5,908	4,766	1,572	238	1,334	108	8	100
20—30	24,242	13,405	10,837	11,590	7,964	3,626	12,119	5,311	6,808	533	130	403
30—40	18,063	9,978	8,085	3,690	2,294	1,396	13,265	7,323	5,942	1,108	361	747
40—50	11,960	6,372	5,588	1,609	873	736	8,600	5,002	3,598	1,751	497	1,254
50—60	7,099	3,419	3,680	752	347	405	4,217	2,560	1,657	2,130	512	1,618
60 and over	5,654	2,600	3,054	545	313	232	2,247	1,501	746	2,862	786	2,076
Animist ...	*2,888*	*2,136*	*747*	*1,568*	*1,218*	*845*	*1,218*	*878*	*845*	*102*	*46*	*57*
0	43	22	21	43	22	21	...	...	...	...	...	...
1—5	159	86	73	159	86	73	...	...	...	...	...	...
5—10	239	140	99	239	140	99	...	...	...	...	...	...
10—15	222	131	91	219	130	89	3	1	2	...	...	...
15—20	244	190	54	233	188	45	10	2	8	1	...	1
20—30	687	549	138	380	367	13	305	182	123	2	...	2
30—40	636	510	126	195	193	2	428	311	117	13	6	7
40—50	404	317	87	76	75	1	299	230	69	29	12	17
50—60	173	136	37	16	14	2	131	111	20	26	11	15
60 and over	76	55	21	3	3	...	42	36	6	31	16	15
Hindu ...	*125,002*	*102,818*	*22,689*	*89,712*	*82,221*	*7,491*	*80,851*	*67,790*	*18,061*	*4,489*	*2,802*	*2,187*
0	1,169	586	583	1,169	586	583	...	...	...	...	...	...
1—5	4,065	2,015	2,050	4,056	2,008	2,048	9	7	2	...	...	...
5—10	5,582	3,039	2,543	5,522	3,027	2,495	24	12	12	36	...	36
10—15	5,801	4,168	1,633	5,429	4,012	1,417	354	156	198	18	...	18
15—20	9,824	7,966	1,858	6,468	6,041	427	3,321	1,910	1,411	35	15	20
20—30	41,454	35,109	6,345	12,139	11,810	329	28,745	22,924	5,821	570	375	195
30—40	33,614	29,393	4,221	3,605	3,486	119	29,049	25,272	3,777	960	635	325
40—50	15,449	13,517	1,932	918	879	39	13,388	12,083	1,305	1,143	555	588
50—60	5,561	4,644	917	286	263	23	4,352	3,970	382	923	411	512
60 and over	2,483	1,876	607	120	109	11	1,609	1,456	153	754	311	443
Hindus born in Burma	*12,680*	*6,721*	*5,909*	*9,893*	*5,488*	*4,410*	*2,478*	*1,159*	*1,319*	*259*	*79*	*180*
0	981	496	485	981	496	485	...	...	.	...	...	...
1—5	2,748	1,343	1,405	2,746	1,342	1,404	2	1	1	...	...	...
5—10	3,040	1,543	1,497	3,028	1,539	1,489	12	4	8	...	...	...
10—15	1,774	970	804	1,707	961	746	65	9	56	2	...	2
15—20	1,034	560	474	693	508	185	335	51	284	6	1	5
20—30	1,781	1,011	770	605	528	77	1,121	464	657	55	19	36
30—40	801	510	291	100	84	16	633	399	234	68	27	41
40—50	313	192	121	21	17	4	227	162	65	65	13	52
50—60	94	60	34	6	4	2	54	47	7	34	9	25
60 and over	64	36	28	6	4	2	29	22	7	29	10	19
Hindus born outside Burma.	*112,872*	*95,592*	*16,780*	*29,819*	*26,738*	*8,081*	*78,873*	*66,631*	*11,742*	*4,180*	*2,228*	*1,957*
0	188	90	98	188	90	98	...	...	...	...	...	...
1—5	1,317	672	645	1,310	666	644	7	6	1	...	...	...
5—10	2,542	1,496	1,046	2,494	1,488	1,006	12	8	4	36	...	36
10—15	4,027	3,198	829	3,722	3,051	671	289	147	142	16	...	16
15—20	8,790	7,406	1,384	5,775	5,533	242	2,986	1,859	1,127	29	14	15
20—30	39,673	34,098	5,575	11,534	11,282	252	27,624	22,460	5,164	515	356	159
30—40	32,813	28,883	3,930	3,505	3,402	103	28,416	24,873	3,543	892	608	284
40—50	15,136	13,325	1,811	897	862	35	13,161	11,981	1,240	1,078	542	536
50—60	5,467	4,584	883	280	259	21	4,298	3,923	375	889	402	487
60 and over	2,419	1,840	579	114	105	9	1,580	1,434	146	725	301	424

IMPERIAL TABLE VIIB.—*Age, Sex, and Civil Condition by Religion.*

District, Religion, and Age.	Population.			Unmarried.			Married.			Widowed.		
	Persons.	Males.	Females.	Persons.	Males.	Females.	Persons.	Males.	Females.	Persons.	Males.	Females.
1	2	3	4	5	6	7	8	9	10	11	12	13
RANGOON TOWN—*concluded.*												
Mahomedan ...	*61,954*	*49,520*	*12,434*	*25,219*	*19,678*	*5,541*	*34,452*	*28,726*	*5,726*	*2,283*	*1,116*	*1,167*
0	685	365	320	685	365	320	..	...	...	...	...	...
1—5	2,539	1,291	1,248	2,537	1,289	1,248	2	2	...	...	...	...
5—10	3,352	1,798	1,554	3,348	1,798	1,550	3	...	3	1	...	1
10—15	4,083	2,821	1,262	3,971	2,770	1,201	110	51	59	2	...	2
15—20	6,166	4,865	1,301	4,795	4,186	609	1,357	672	685	14	7	7
20—30	19,764	16,867	2,897	7,840	7,462	378	11,634	9,216	2,418	290	189	101
30—40	13,912	12,054	1,858	1,474	1,330	144	11,922	10,385	1,537	516	339	177
40—50	6,918	5,906	1,012	380	323	57	6,017	5,341	676	521	242	279
50—60	2,934	2,399	535	122	99	23	2,379	2,140	239	433	160	273
60 and over	1,601	1,154	447	67	56	11	1,028	919	109	506	179	327
Mahomedans born in Burma.	*16,468*	*8,270*	*8,198*	*10,136*	*5,569*	*4,567*	*5,529*	*2,527*	*3,002*	*803*	*174*	*629*
0	646	344	302	646	344	302	...	...	...	...	...	...
1—5	2,161	1,087	1,074	2,160	1,086	1,074	1	1	...	...	...	...
5—10	2,517	1,281	1,236	2,515	1,281	1,234	1	...	1	1	...	1
10—15	2,206	1,202	1,004	2,172	1,195	977	32	7	25	2	...	2
15—20	1,749	805	944	1,254	748	506	488	57	431	7	...	7
20—30	3,138	1,507	1,631	1,008	715	293	2,017	756	1,261	113	36	77
30—40	2,070	1,104	966	252	148	104	1,684	920	764	134	36	98
40—50	1,068	515	553	86	39	47	792	441	351	190	35	155
50—60	527	265	262	29	6	23	345	228	117	153	31	122
60 and over	386	160	226	14	7	7	169	117	52	203	36	167
Mahomedans born outside Burma.	*45,486*	*41,250*	*4,236*	*15,083*	*14,109*	*974*	*28,923*	*26,199*	*2,724*	*1,480*	*942*	*538*
0	39	21	18	39	21	18	...	...	...	...	...	...
1—5	378	204	174	377	203	174	1	1	...	...	...	...
5—10	835	517	318	833	517	316	2	...	2	...	...	...
10—15	1,877	1,619	258	1,799	1,575	224	78	44	34	...	...	...
15—20	4,417	4,060	357	3,541	3,438	103	869	615	254	7	7	...
20—30	16,626	15,360	1,266	6,832	6,747	85	9,617	8,460	1,157	177	153	24
30—40	11,842	10,950	892	1,222	1,182	40	10,238	9,465	773	382	303	79
40—50	5,850	5,391	459	294	284	10	5,225	4,900	325	331	207	124
50—60	2,407	2,134	273	93	93	...	2,034	1,912	122	280	129	151
60 and over	1,215	994	221	53	49	4	859	802	57	303	143	160
Christian ...	*25,816*	*14,286*	*11,079*	*14,562*	*8,545*	*6,017*	*9,271*	*5,298*	*3,973*	*1,482*	*393*	*1,089*
0	608	316	292	608	316	292	...	...	...	...	...	...
1—5	1,940	921	1,019	1,940	921	1,019	...	...	...	...	...	...
5—10	2,481	1,269	1,212	2,481	1,269	1,212	...	...	..	...	...	...
10—15	2,357	1,171	1,186	2,347	1,168	1,179	10	3	7	...	...	...
15—20	2,553	1,325	1,228	2,289	1,303	986	253	22	231	11	...	11
20—30	6,277	3,688	2,589	3,438	2,533	905	2,742	1,134	1,608	97	21	76
30—40	4,476	2,812	1,664	937	710	227	3,264	2,018	1,246	275	84	191
40—50	2,576	1,612	964	342	232	110	1,879	1,289	590	355	91	264
50—60	1,295	752	543	111	57	54	819	598	221	365	97	268
60 and over	752	370	382	69	36	33	304	234	70	379	100	279
Others (all ages) ...	*15,258*	*10,407*	*4,851*	*7,670*	*5,826*	*2,844*	*7,028*	*4,875*	*2,153*	*560*	*206*	*354*
0	190	102	88	190	102	88	...	...	...	...	...	...
1—5	947	485	462	947	485	462	...	...	...	...	...	...
5—10	1,453	830	623	1,453	830	623	...	...	...	...	...	...
10—15	1,329	745	584	1,321	744	577	8	1	7	...	...	...
15—20	1,339	877	462	1,147	816	331	191	61	130	1	...	1
20—30	3,407	2,489	918	1,577	1,387	190	1,796	1,091	705	34	11	23
30—40	3,367	2,491	876	689	649	40	2,580	1,812	768	98	30	68
40—50	898	1,449	449	233	214	19	1,540	1,195	345	125	40	85
50—60	882	632	250	83	73	10	654	504	150	145	55	90
60 and over	446	307	139	30	26	4	259	211	48	157	70	87
INSEIN.												
All Religions ...	*293,083*	*156,794*	*136,289*	*164,446*	*90,739*	*73,707*	*107,754*	*57,787*	*49,967*	*20,883*	*8,268*	*12,615*
0	6,086	3,010	3,076	6,086	3,010	3,076	...	...	...	...	...	...
1—5	30,942	15,422	15,520	30,942	15,422	15,520	...	...	...	...	...	...
5—10	35,963	18,086	17,877	35,962	18,086	17,876	1	...	1	...	...	...
10—15	33,587	17,671	15,916	33,515	17,651	15,864	72	20	52	...	...	...
15—20	29,135	14,619	14,516	24,763	13,554	11,209	4,118	1,032	3,086	254	33	221
20—30	52,894	28,458	24,436	20,808	14,064	6,744	30,169	13,638	16,531	1,917	756	1,161
30—40	42,247	24,651	17,596	7,081	5,231	1,850	31,974	17,908	14,066	3,192	1,512	1,680
40—50	29,457	16,733	12,724	2,863	2,084	779	22,273	12,877	9,396	4,321	1,772	2,549
50—60	17,770	9,489	8,281	1,328	917	411	11,873	7,005	4,868	4,569	1,567	3,002
60 and over	15,002	8,655	6,347	1,098	720	378	7,274	5,307	1,967	6,630	2,628	4,002

Imperial Table VIIb.—*Age, Sex, and Civil Condition by Religion.*

INSEIN—*continued.*

District, Religion, and Age.	Population. Persons.	Population. Males.	Population. Females.	Unmarried. Persons.	Unmarried. Males.	Unmarried. Females.	Married. Persons.	Married. Males.	Married. Females.	Widowed. Persons.	Widowed. Males.	Widowed. Females.
1	2	3	4	5	6	7	8	9	10	11	12	13
Buddhist ...	*241,481*	*122,363*	*119,118*	*136,892*	*72,109*	*64,783*	*86,936*	*43,948*	*42,988*	*17,653*	*5,811*	*11,842*
0	5,213	2,593	2,620	5,213	2,593	2,620	...	...	...	...	...	...
1—5	26,859	13,375	13,484	26,859	13,375	13,484	...	...	...	...	...	...
5—10	31,123	15,537	15,586	31,123	15,537	15,586	...	...	...	...	...	...
10—15	29,427	15,270	14,157	29,384	15,270	14,114	43	...	43	...	...	...
15—20	24,861	11,984	12,877	21,327	11,239	10,088	3,314	725	2,589	220	20	200
20—30	41,262	20,220	21,042	15,377	9,475	5,902	24,287	10,198	14,089	1,598	547	1,051
30—40	31,921	16,811	15,110	4,118	2,503	1,615	25,247	13,242	12,005	2,556	1,066	1,490
40—50	23,402	12,146	11,256	1,740	1,065	675	18,124	9,816	8,308	3,538	1,265	2,273
50—60	14,795	7,454	7,341	920	552	368	9,898	5,671	4,227	3,977	1,231	2,746
60 and over	12,618	6978	5,640	831	500	331	6,023	4,896	1,727	5,764	2,182	3,582
Animist ...	*3,211*	*2,353*	*858*	*1,690*	*1,260*	*430*	*1,338*	*981*	*357*	*183*	*117*	*66*
0	51	29	22	51	29	22	...	...	...	...	...	...
1—5	261	150	111	261	150	111	...	...	...	...	...	...
5—10	295	163	132	295	163	132	...	...	...	...	...	...
10—15	248	169	79	248	169	79	...	...	...	...	...	...
15—20	208	143	65	190	140	50	18	3	15	...	...	...
20—30	575	425	150	310	287	23	249	132	117	16	6	10
30—40	676	550	126	188	182	6	444	331	113	44	37	7
40—50	500	404	96	93	90	3	360	283	77	47	31	16
50—60	242	200	42	33	32	1	179	155	24	30	13	17
60 and over	155	125	30	21	18	3	88	77	11	46	30	16
Hindu ...	*24,658*	*18,872*	*5,786*	*12,434*	*9,798*	*2,636*	*10,686*	*7,962*	*2,724*	*1,538*	*1,112*	*426*
0	315	148	167	315	148	167	...	...	...	...	...	...
1—5	1,487	724	763	1,487	724	763	...	...	...	...	...	...
5—10	1,836	1,048	788	1,836	1,048	788	...	...	...	...	...	...
10—15	1,443	949	494	1,426	932	494	17	17	...	...	...	...
15—20	1,789	1,318	471	1,239	1,069	170	526	240	286	24	9	15
20—30	6,356	5,136	1,220	2,940	2,792	148	3,231	2,197	1,034	185	147	38
30—40	5,969	5,025	944	2,008	1,952	56	3,627	2,817	810	334	256	78
40—50	3,220	2,729	491	771	742	29	2,036	1,670	366	413	317	96
50—60	1,322	1,052	270	263	253	10	772	609	163	287	190	97
60 and over	921	743	178	149	138	11	477	412	65	295	193	102
Hindus born in Burma	*5,383*	*3,016*	*2,367*	*4,297*	*2,517*	*1,780*	*945*	*430*	*515*	*141*	*69*	*72*
0	255	119	136	255	119	136	...	...	...	...	...	...
1—5	1,155	550	605	1,155	550	605	...	...	...	...	...	...
5—10	1,259	691	568	1,259	691	568	...	...	...	...	...	...
10—15	750	441	309	750	441	309	...	...	...	...	...	...
15—20	458	281	177	342	258	84	112	23	89	4	...	4
20—30	717	411	306	322	263	59	372	137	235	23	11	12
30—40	423	291	132	118	107	11	264	158	106	41	26	15
40—50	212	135	77	63	59	4	121	62	59	28	14	14
50—60	89	52	37	17	16	1	48	28	20	24	8	16
60 and over	65	45	20	16	13	3	28	22	6	21	10	11
Mahomedan ...	*7,990*	*5,391*	*2,599*	*4,871*	*2,993*	*1,878*	*3,151*	*2,081*	*1,070*	*468*	*312*	*156*
0	155	66	89	155	66	89	...	...	...	...	...	...
1—5	728	357	371	728	357	371	...	...	...	...	...	...
5—10	823	438	385	822	438	384	1	...	1	...	...	...
10—15	717	426	291	705	423	282	12	3	9	...	...	...
15—20	663	434	229	519	392	127	140	38	102	4	4	...
20—30	1,832	1,341	491	806	731	75	987	580	407	39	30	9
30—40	1,488	1,115	373	403	378	25	978	659	319	107	78	29
40—50	786	630	156	147	137	10	544	425	119	95	68	27
50—60	384	266	118	47	41	6	247	172	75	90	53	37
60 and over	414	318	96	39	35	4	242	204	38	133	79	54
Mahomedans born in Burma.	*3,806*	*1,850*	*1,956*	*2,594*	*1,377*	*1,217*	*1,154*	*514*	*640*	*158*	*59*	*99*
0	153	65	88	153	65	88	...	...	...	...	...	...
1—5	659	318	341	659	318	341	...	...	...	...	...	...
5—10	705	358	347	705	358	347	...	...	...	...	...	...
10—15	514	267	247	511	267	244	3	...	3	...	...	...
15—20	355	173	182	274	160	114	81	13	68	...	...	...
20—30	622	293	329	190	132	58	416	152	264	16	9	7
30—40	439	233	206	59	44	15	345	174	171	35	15	20
40—50	205	104	101	28	21	7	156	79	77	21	4	17
50—60	122	63	59	8	7	1	79	45	34	35	11	24
60 and over	132	76	56	7	5	2	74	51	23	51	20	31

IMPERIAL TABLE VIIB.—*Age, Sex, and Civil Condition by Religion.*

District	Religion and Age	Population: Persons	Population: Males	Population: Females	Unmarried: Persons	Unmarried: Males	Unmarried: Females	Married: Persons	Married: Males	Married: Females	Widowed: Persons	Widowed: Males	Widowed: Females
1		2	3	4	5	6	7	8	9	10	11	12	13
INSEIN—*concluded.*	***Christian*** ...	*15,579*	*7,688*	*7,891*	*8,980*	*4,513*	*4,467*	*5,571*	*2,769*	*2,802*	*1,028*	*406*	*622*
	0	346	169	177	346	169	177	...	...	...	...	...	...
	1—5	1,590	804	786	1,590	804	786	...	...	...	...	...	...
	5—10	1,868	893	975	1,868	893	975	...	...	...	...	...	...
	10—15	1,749	855	894	1,749	855	894	...	...	...	...	...	...
	15—20	1,608	735	873	1,483	709	774	119	26	93	6	...	6
	20—30	2,830	1,311	1,519	1,359	763	596	1,392	522	870	79	26	53
	30—40	2,151	1,117	1,034	353	205	148	1,651	841	810	147	71	76
	40—50	1,529	807	722	111	49	62	1,196	671	525	222	87	135
	50—60	1,016	508	508	64	38	26	770	392	378	182	78	104
	60 and over	892	489	403	57	28	29	443	317	126	392	144	248
	Others (all ages) ...	*164*	*117*	*47*	*79*	*61*	*18*	*72*	*46*	*26*	*13*	*10*	*3*
HANTHAWADDY.	***All Religions*** ...	*364,624*	*201,043*	*163,581*	*206,345*	*117,511*	*88,834*	*134,066*	*73,167*	*60,899*	*29,223*	*10,375*	*18,848*
	0	8,251	4,144	4,107	8,251	4,144	4,107	...	...	...	...	...	...
	1—5	36,983	18,336	18,647	36,983	18,336	18,647	...	...	...	...	...	...
	5—10	44,930	22,398	22,532	44,930	22,398	22,532	...	...	...	...	...	...
	10—15	41,472	22,048	19,424	41,410	22,037	19,373	59	9	50	3	2	1
	15—20	36,040	18,737	17,303	30,583	17,533	13,050	5,184	1,166	4018	273	38	235
	20—30	67,766	38,724	29,042	27,367	20,030	7,337	38,032	17,760	20,272	2,367	934	1,433
	30—40	52,505	31,888	20,617	9,447	7,441	2,006	39,649	22,786	16,863	3,409	1,661	1,748
	40—50	36,653	21,612	15,041	4,164	3,219	945	27,610	16,198	11,412	4,879	2,195	2,684
	50—60	21,188	11,851	9,337	1,770	1,303	467	14,275	8,462	5,813	5,143	2,086	3,057
	60 and over	18,836	11,305	7,531	1,440	1,070	370	9,247	6,776	2,471	8,149	3,459	4,690
	Buddhist ...	*298,769*	*148,764*	*146,005*	*168,554*	*88,746*	*79,808*	*104,476*	*51,865*	*52,611*	*20,729*	*8,148*	*12,586*
	0	7,294	3,685	3,609	7,294	3,685	3,609	...	...	...	...	...	...
	1—5	31,847	15,665	16,182	31,847	15,665	16,182	...	...	...	...	...	...
	5—10	38,823	19,132	19,691	38,823	19,132	19,691	...	...	...	...	...	...
	10—15	36,285	18,661	17,624	36,259	18,661	17,598	25	...	25	1	...	1
	15—20	30,099	14,283	15,816	25,919	13,613	12,306	3,947	642	3,305	233	28	205
	20—30	49,371	24,096	25,275	18,628	11,673	6,955	28,776	11,742	17,034	1,967	681	1,286
	30—40	37,339	19,587	17,752	5,104	3,244	1,860	29,528	15,212	14,316	2,707	1,131	1,576
	40—50	28,580	15,001	13,579	2,415	1,557	858	22,120	11,803	10,317	4,045	1,641	2,404
	50—60	17,626	9,111	8,515	1,179	763	416	12,091	6,765	5,326	4,356	1,583	2,773
	60 and over	16,495	9,533	6,962	1,086	753	333	7,989	5,701	2,288	7,420	3,079	4,341
	Animist ...	*6,202*	*4,997*	*1,205*	*2,742*	*2,158*	*584*	*2,164*	*1,615*	*549*	*806*	*724*	*82*
	0	87	50	37	87	50	37	...	...	...	...	...	...
	1—5	411	238	173	411	238	173	...	...	...	...	...	...
	5—10	433	257	176	433	257	176	...	...	...	...	...	...
	10—15	332	224	108	322	217	105	8	5	3	2	2	...
	15—20	311	246	65	280	236	44	29	10	19	2	...	2
	20—30	1,119	885	234	575	551	24	522	320	202	22	14	8
	30—40	1,247	1,025	222	392	384	8	788	592	196	67	49	18
	40—50	714	605	109	154	144	10	501	415	86	59	46	13
	50—60	315	274	41	54	52	2	193	171	22	68	51	17
	60 and over	233	193	40	34	29	5	113	102	11	86	62	24
	Hindu ...	*47,826*	*35,865*	*11,961*	*24,826*	*19,218*	*5,608*	*20,211*	*14,643*	*5,568*	*2,289*	*1,504*	*785*
	0	548	247	301	548	247	301	...	...	...	...	...	...
	1—5	3,341	1,733	1,608	3,341	1,733	1,608	...	...	...	...	...	...
	5—10	3,923	2,093	1,830	3,923	2,093	1,830	...	...	...	...	...	...
	10—15	3,361	2,245	1,116	3,344	2,245	1,099	17	...	17	...	...	...
	15—20	3,859	2,965	894	2,900	2,522	378	935	437	498	24	6	18
	20—30	12,461	9,949	2,512	5,631	5,445	186	6,572	4,332	2,240	258	172	86
	30—40	10,486	8,548	1,938	3,142	3,045	97	6,891	5,152	1,739	453	351	102
	40—50	5,534	4,623	911	1,310	1,260	50	3,639	2,963	676	585	400	185
	50—60	2,398	1,885	513	434	398	36	1,411	1,123	288	553	364	189
	60 and over	1,415	1,077	338	253	230	23	746	636	110	416	211	205
	Hindus born in Burma	*12,029*	*6,498*	*5,531*	*9,954*	*5,682*	*4,272*	*1,908*	*721*	*1,187*	*217*	*95*	*122*
	0	477	216	261	477	216	261	...	...	...	...	...	...
	1—5	2,781	1,415	1,366	2,781	1,415	1,366	...	...	...	...	...	...
	5—10	3,043	1,567	1,476	3,043	1,567	1,476	...	...	...	...	...	...
	10—15	1,924	1,102	822	1,924	1,102	822	...	...	...	...	...	...
	15—20	1,073	598	475	804	562	242	257	33	224	12	3	9
	20—30	1,546	848	698	651	584	67	849	254	595	46	10	36
	30—40	754	478	276	186	164	22	526	290	236	42	24	18
	40—50	270	175	95	52	43	9	167	108	59	51	24	27
	50—60	99	59	40	17	15	2	49	30	19	33	14	19
	60 and over	62	40	22	19	14	5	10	6	4	33	20	13

IMPERIAL TABLE VIIB.—*Age, Sex, and Civil Condition by Religion.*

DISTRICT, RELIGION, AND AGE.	POPULATION.			UNMARRIED.			MARRIED.			WIDOWED.		
	Persons.	Males.	Females.	Persons.	Males.	Females.	Persons.	Males.	Females.	Persons.	Males.	Females.
1	2	3	4	5	6	7	8	9	10	11	12	13
HANTHAWADDY—concluded.												
Mahomedan ...	*12,811*	*9,551*	*3,260*	*7,120*	*5,412*	*1,708*	*5,083*	*3,799*	*1,284*	*608*	*340*	*268*
0	213	98	115	213	98	115	...	...	...	...	...	...
1—5	801	393	408	801	393	408	...	...	...	...	...	...
5—10	1,042	551	491	1,042	551	491	...	...	...	...	...	...
10—15	977	598	379	972	598	374	5	...	5	...	...	...
15—20	1,306	965	341	1,101	907	194	200	57	143	5	1	4
20—30	3,744	3,134	610	2,031	1,949	82	1,617	1,134	483	96	51	45
30—40	2,454	2,066	388	633	611	22	1,695	1,365	330	126	90	36
40—50	1,240	998	242	200	189	11	911	734	177	129	75	54
50—60	551	390	161	76	68	8	369	263	106	106	59	47
60 and over	483	358	125	51	48	3	286	246	40	146	64	82
Mahomedans born in Burma.	*5,184*	*2,541*	*2,643*	*3,414*	*1,833*	*1,581*	*1,501*	*623*	*878*	*269*	*85*	*184*
0	205	92	113	205	92	113	...	...	...	...	...	...
1—5	748	369	379	748	369	379	...	...	...	...	...	...
5—10	928	477	451	928	477	451	...	...	...	...	...	...
10—15	759	406	353	754	406	348	5	...	5	...	...	...
15—20	550	260	290	419	240	179	126	19	107	5	1	4
20—30	834	384	450	253	182	71	528	189	339	53	13	40
30—40	506	240	266	58	37	21	405	187	218	43	16	27
40—50	315	153	162	31	21	10	228	114	114	56	18	38
50—60	190	78	112	12	5	7	131	57	74	47	16	31
60 and over	149	82	67	6	4	2	78	57	21	65	21	44
Christian ...	*5,086*	*3,028*	*2,058*	*2,948*	*1,860*	*1,088*	*1,860*	*1,016*	*844*	*278*	*152*	*126*
0	105	63	42	105	63	42	...	...	...	...	...	...
1—5	564	298	266	564	298	266	...	...	...	...	...	...
5—10	681	349	332	681	349	332	...	...	...	...	...	...
10—15	495	307	188	494	306	188	1	1	...	...	...	...
15—20	442	265	177	372	248	124	61	14	47	9	3	6
20—30	954	561	393	462	372	90	470	174	296	22	15	7
30—40	853	554	299	157	138	19	642	378	264	54	38	16
40—50	522	330	192	71	55	16	393	245	148	58	30	28
50—60	268	165	103	26	21	5	185	118	67	57	26	31
60 and over	202	136	66	16	10	6	108	86	22	78	40	38
Others (all ages) ...	*440*	*348*	*92*	*155*	*117*	*38*	*272*	*219*	*53*	*13*	*12*	*1*
THARRAWADDY.												
All Religions ...	*492,429*	*246,261*	*246,168*	*264,039*	*137,476*	*126,563*	*191,451*	*97,269*	*94,182*	*36,939*	*11,516*	*25,423*
0	13,883	6,936	6,947	13,883	6,936	6,947	...	...	...	...	...	...
1—5	51,928	25,495	26,433	51,928	25,495	26,433	...	...	...	...	...	...
5—10	62,705	30,899	31,806	62,705	30,899	31,806	...	...	...	...	...	...
10—15	59,647	30,402	29,245	59,631	30,402	29,229	16	...	16	...	...	...
15—20	52,371	25,139	27,232	44,124	23,583	20,541	7,826	1,488	6,338	421	68	353
20—30	83,866	41,476	42,390	22,888	14,767	8,121	57,120	25,432	31,688	3,858	1,277	2,581
30—40	65,847	34,399	31,448	4,861	3,074	1,787	55,564	29,365	26,199	5,422	1,960	3,462
40—50	49,092	24,874	24,218	2,112	1,215	897	39,426	21,364	18,062	7,554	2,295	5,259
50—60	29,577	14,169	15,408	1,028	577	451	19,932	11,395	8,537	8,617	2,197	6,420
60 and over	23,513	12,472	11,041	879	528	351	11,567	8,225	3,342	11,067	3,719	7,348
Buddhist ...	*457,558*	*229,477*	*228,081*	*251,744*	*129,226*	*122,518*	*180,643*	*89,855*	*90,788*	*35,171*	*10,396*	*24,775*
0	13,330	6,657	6,673	13,330	6,657	6,673	...	...	...	...	...	...
1—5	50,151	24,572	25,579	50,151	24,572	25,579	...	...	...	...	...	...
5—10	60,568	29,789	30,779	60,568	29,789	30,779	...	...	...	...	...	...
10—15	57,673	29,249	28,424	57,660	29,249	28,411	13	...	13	...	...	...
15—20	50,170	23,748	26,422	42,365	22,371	19,994	7,399	1,317	6,082	406	60	346
20—30	78,100	37,329	40,771	20,375	12,630	7,745	54,081	23,571	30,510	3,644	1,128	2,516
30—40	60,883	30,589	30,294	3,825	2,104	1,721	52,004	26,811	25,193	5,054	1,674	3,380
40—50	46,208	22,714	23,494	1,770	908	862	37,258	19,766	17,492	7,180	2,040	5,140
50—60	28,094	13,146	14,948	903	476	427	18,956	10,665	8,291	8,235	2,005	6,230
60 and over	22,381	11,684	10,697	797	470	327	10,932	7,725	3,207	10,652	3,489	7,163

IMPERIAL TABLE VIIB.—*Age, Sex, and Civil Condition by Religion.*

DISTRICT, RELIGION, AND AGE.	POPULATION.			UNMARRIED.			MARRIED.			WIDOWED.		
	Persons.	Males.	Females.	Persons.	Males.	Females.	Persons.	Males.	Females.	Persons.	Males.	Females.
1	2	3	4	5	6	7	8	9	10	11	12	13
THARRAWADDY—*concluded.*												
Animist (all ages) ..	*2,129*	*1,600*	*529*	*971*	*729*	*242*	*1,032*	*783*	*249*	*126*	*88*	*38*
Hindu ...	*9,179*	*7,422*	*1,757*	*4,113*	*3,361*	*752*	*4,293*	*3,435*	*858*	*778*	*626*	*1*
0	143	73	70	143	73	70	...	...	...	...	...	...
1—5	418	209	209	418	209	209	...	...	...	...	...	...
5—10	512	267	245	512	267	245	...	...	...	...	...	...
10—15	474	323	151	474	323	151	...	...	...	...	...	...
15—20	675	557	118	480	446	34	187	104	83	8	7	1
20—30	2,606	2,231	375	1,171	1,145	26	1,314	978	336	121	108	13
30—40	2,352	2,039	313	609	603	6	1,532	1,249	283	211	187	24
40—50	1,173	1,043	130	201	196	5	789	692	97	183	155	28
50—60	477	391	86	63	61	2	282	243	39	[illegible]	87	45
60 and over	349	289	60	42	38	4	189	169	20	118	82	36
Hindus born in Burma	*1,477*	*805*	*672*	*1,189*	*653*	*536*	*251*	*131*	*120*	*37*	*21*	*16*
0	125	62	63	125	62	63	...	...	...	...	...	...
1—5	330	161	169	330	161	169	...	...	...	...	...	...
5—10	365	186	179	365	186	179	...	...	...	...	...	...
10—15	216	119	97	216	119	97	...	...	...	...	...	...
15—20	106	64	42	72	54	18	32	8	24	2	2	...
20—30	177	102	75	51	43	8	120	53	67	6	6	...
30—40	99	69	30	23	21	2	67	42	25	9	6	3
40—50	31	24	7	2	2	...	21	17	4	8	5	3
50—60	22	15	7	4	4	...	9	9	...	9	2	7
60 and over	6	3	3	1	1	...	2	2	...	3	...	3
Mahomedan ...	*5,421*	*3,736*	*1,685*	*2,765*	*1,935*	*830*	*2,349*	*1,588*	*761*	*307*	*213*	*94*
0	155	73	82	155	73	82	...	...	...	...	...	...
1—5	418	228	190	418	228	190	...	...	...	...	...	...
5—10	520	270	250	520	270	250	...	...	...	...	...	...
10—15	428	253	175	425	253	172	3	...	3	...	...	...
15—20	546	356	190	396	311	85	145	44	101	5	1	4
20—30	1,327	971	356	546	510	36	743	437	306	38	24	14
30—40	1,012	795	217	222	210	12	721	532	189	69	53	16
40—50	523	414	109	58	55	3	410	316	94	55	43	12
50—60	268	199	69	20	20	...	186	145	41	62	34	28
60 and over	224	177	47	5	5	...	141	114	27	78	58	20
Mahomedans born in Burma.	*2,594*	*1,224*	*1,370*	*1,632*	*857*	*775*	*862*	*338*	*524*	*100*	*29*	*71*
0	150	73	77	150	73	77	...	...	...	...	...	...
1—5	391	212	179	391	212	179	...	...	...	...	...	...
5—10	473	244	229	473	244	229	...	...	...	...	...	...
10—15	324	166	158	324	166	158	...	...	...	...	...	...
15—20	278	108	170	177	93	84	97	14	83	4	1	3
20—30	429	170	259	88	54	34	322	120	212	19	6	13
30—40	274	123	151	24	13	11	232	106	126	18	4	14
40—50	136	64	72	4	1	3	117	57	60	15	6	9
50—60	81	32	49	1	1	...	54	26	28	26	5	21
60 and over	58	32	26	...	...	...	40	25	15	18	7	11
Christian ...	*8,074*	*3,970*	*4,104*	*4,426*	*2,208*	*2,218*	*3,091*	*1,573*	*1,518*	*557*	*189*	*368*
0	205	113	92	205	113	92	...	...	...	...	...	...
1—5	772	378	394	772	378	394	...	...	...	...	...	...
5—10	921	455	466	921	455	466	...	...	...	...	...	...
10—15	897	461	436	897	461	436	...	...	...	...	...	...
15—20	854	387	467	781	370	411	72	17	55	1	...	1
20—30	1,440	657	783	642	334	308	750	310	440	48	13	35
30—40	1,116	578	538	107	64	43	950	489	461	59	25	34
40—50	840	413	427	43	16	27	689	362	328	108	36	72
50—60	580	299	281	27	6	21	398	245	153	155	48	107
60 and over	449	229	220	31	11	20	232	151	81	186	67	119
Others (all ages) ...	*68*	*56*	*12*	*20*	*17*	*3*	*43*	*35*	*8*	*5*	*4*	*1*

IMPERIAL TABLE VIIB.—*Age, Sex, and Civil Condition by Religion.*

District, Religion, and Age.	Population. Persons.	Population. Males.	Population. Females.	Unmarried. Persons.	Unmarried. Males.	Unmarried. Females.	Married. Persons.	Married. Males.	Married. Females.	Widowed. Persons.	Widowed. Males.	Widowed. Females.
1	2	3	4	5	6	7	8	9	10	11	12	13
PEGU.												
All Religions ...	*445,620*	*235,324*	*210,296*	*251,311*	*139,067*	*112,244*	*164,242*	*84,502*	*79,740*	*30,067*	*11,755*	*18,312*
0	9,882	4,928	4,954	9,882	4,928	4,954	...	...	...	...	...	...
1—5	47,837	23,513	24,324	47,837	23,513	24,324	...	...	...	...	...	..
5—10	56,326	27,901	28,425	56,326	27,901	28,425	...	...	...	...	...	...
10—15	52,611	27,679	24,932	52,565	27,665	24,900	45	14	31	1	...	1
15—20	44,237	21,768	22,469	37,017	20,432	16,585	6,821	1,246	5,575	399	90	309
20—30	80,274	42,116	38,158	30,645	21,696	8,949	46,534	19,201	27,333	3,095	1,219	1,876
30—40	64,402	37,167	27,235	10,019	7,807	2,212	49,623	27,043	23,580	4,760	2,317	2,443
40—50	43,224	24,422	18,802	3,819	2,893	926	33,249	19,038	14,211	6,156	2,491	3,665
50—60	25,587	13,763	11,824	1,830	1,302	528	17,156	10,236	6,920	6,601	2,225	4,376
60 and over	21,240	12,067	9,173	1,371	930	441	10,814	7,724	3,090	9,055	3,413	5,642
Buddhist ...	*378,337*	*191,185*	*187,152*	*213,409*	*112,687*	*100,722*	*139,644*	*69,716*	*69,928*	*25,284*	*8,782*	*16,502*
0	8,839	4,413	4,426	8,839	4,413	4,426	...	...	...	...	...	...
1—5	41,557	20,365	21,192	41,557	20,365	21,192	...	...	...	...	...	...
5—10	49,400	24,304	25,096	49,400	24,304	25,096	...	...	...	...	...	...
10—15	47,023	24,293	22,730	47,001	24,291	22,710	21	2	19	1	...	1
15—20	39,006	18,445	20,561	33,030	17,547	15,483	5,649	853	4,796	327	45	282
20—30	65,379	31,875	33,504	23,317	15,117	8,200	39,538	15,967	23,571	2,524	791	1,733
30—40	50,731	27,053	23,678	5,730	3,786	1,944	41,362	21,777	19,585	3,639	1,490	2,149
40—50	36,117	19,164	16 953	2,256	1,453	803	28,740	15,873	12,867	5,121	1,838	3,283
50—60	21,921	11,160	10,761	1,230	760	470	14,933	8,644	6,289	5,758	1,756	4,002
60 and over	18,364	10,113	8,251	1,049	651	398	9,401	6,600	2,801	7,914	2,862	5,052
Animist ...	*6,707*	*4,533*	*2,174*	*3,639*	*2,529*	*1,110*	*2,604*	*1,706*	*898*	*464*	*298*	*166*
0	125	69	56	125	69	56	...	...	...	...	...	...
1—5	606	322	284	606	322	284	...	...	...	...	...	...
5—10	684	372	312	684	372	312	...	...	...	...	...	...
10—15	590	348	242	589	347	242	1	1	...	...	...	...
15—20	501	320	181	426	306	120	74	13	61	1	1	...
20—30	1,245	851	394	602	544	58	594	271	323	49	36	13
30—40	1,396	1,061	335	376	359	17	918	628	290	102	74	28
40—50	839	656	183	139	129	10	582	446	136	118	81	37
50—60	437	322	115	60	57	3	277	207	70	100	58	42
60 and over	284	212	72	32	24	8	158	140	18	94	48	46
Hindu ...	*40,856*	*27,554*	*13,302*	*22,888*	*16,581*	*6,307*	*14,922*	*8,924*	*5,998*	*3,046*	*2,049*	*997*
0	528	256	272	528	256	272	...	...	...	.	...	...
1—5	3,881	1,973	1,908	3,881	1,973	1,908	...	...	...	...	.	...
5—10	4,212	2,219	1,993	4,212	2,219	1,993	...	...	...	...	...	...
10—15	3,037	1,913	1,124	3,020	1,903	1,117	17	10	7	...	...	...
15—20	2,801	1,903	898	1,944	1,559	385	789	300	489	68	44	24
20—30	9,218	6,452	2,766	4,474	4,130	344	4,352	2,005	2,347	392	317	75
30—40	8,814	6,655	2,159	3,055	2,893	162	4,998	3,168	1,830	761	594	167
40—50	4,426	3,348	1,078	1,139	1,067	72	2,626	1,835	791	661	446	215
50—60	2,186	1,627	559	418	384	34	1,280	943	337	488	300	188
60 and over	1,753	1,208	545	217	197	20	860	663	197	676	348	328
Hindus born in Burma	*13,483*	*7,442*	*6,041*	*11,116*	*6,301*	*4,815*	*2,115*	*1,015*	*1,100*	*252*	*126*	*126*
0	476	227	249	476	227	249	...	...	...	...	...	...
1—5	3,381	1,698	1,683	3,381	1,698	1,683	...	...	...	...	...	...
5—10	3,392	1,752	1,640	3,392	1,752	1,640	...	...	...	...	...	...
10—15	1,962	1,124	838	1,962	1,124	838	...	...	...	...	...	...
15—20	1,085	628	457	803	552	251	276	76	200	6	...	6
20—30	1,553	917	636	696	579	117	804	311	493	53	27	26
30—40	1,020	666	354	274	246	28	662	374	288	84	46	38
40—50	333	240	93	84	78	6	213	141	72	36	21	15
50—60	164	114	50	32	29	3	97	65	32	35	20	15
60 and over	117	76	41	16	16	...	63	48	15	38	12	26
Mahomedan ...	*9,745*	*6,996*	*2,749*	*5,804*	*4,355*	*1,449*	*3,435*	*2,285*	*1,150*	*506*	*356*	*150*
0	143	68	75	143	68	75	...	...	...	...	...	...
1—5	772	356	416	772	356	416	...	...	...	...	...	...
5—10	864	447	417	864	447	417	...	...	...	...	...	...
10—15	821	520	301	821	520	301	...	...	...	...	...	...
15—20	894	618	276	686	557	129	208	61	147	...	...	...
20—30	2,621	2,057	564	1,500	1,430	70	1,052	580	472	69	47	22
30—40	1,952	1,577	375	663	640	23	1,168	843	325	121	94	27
40—50	897	728	169	203	195	8	582	450	132	112	83	29
50—60	430	340	90	95	89	6	254	199	55	81	52	29
60 and over	351	285	66	57	53	4	171	152	19	123	80	43

Imperial Table VIIb.—*Age, Sex, and Civil Condition by Religion.*

District, Religion, and Age.	Population. Persons.	Population. Males.	Population. Females.	Unmarried. Persons.	Unmarried. Males.	Unmarried. Females.	Married. Persons.	Married. Males.	Married. Females.	Widowed. Persons.	Widowed. Males.	Widowed. Females.
1	2	3	4	5	6	7	8	9	10	11	12	13
PEGU—concluded.												
Mahomedans born in Burma.	***4,002***	***1,959***	***2,043***	***2,722***	***1,471***	***1,251***	***1,163***	***452***	***711***	***117***	***36***	***81***
0	140	66	74	140	66	74	...	...	...	...	...	...
1—5	689	310	379	689	310	379	...	...	...	...	...	...
5—10	737	377	360	737	377	360	...	...	...	...	...	...
10—15	558	298	260	558	298	260	...	...	...	...	...	...
15—20	418	198	220	285	181	104	133	17	116	...	...	...
20—30	647	279	368	203	150	53	424	123	301	20	6	14
30—40	435	219	216	71	57	14	343	156	187	21	6	15
40—50	213	112	101	21	17	4	166	89	77	26	6	20
50—60	102	63	39	12	9	3	68	47	21	22	7	15
60 and over	63	37	26	6	6	...	29	20	9	28	11	17
Christian ...	***9,791***	***4,919***	***4,872***	***5,467***	***2,834***	***2,633***	***3,566***	***1,822***	***1,744***	***758***	***263***	***495***
0	240	117	123	240	117	123	...	...	...	...	...	...
1—5	1,005	489	516	1,005	489	516	...	...	...	...	...	...
5—10	1,153	549	604	1,153	549	604	...	...	...	...	...	...
10—15	1,129	599	530	1,123	598	525	6	1	5	...	...	...
15—20	1,020	475	545	922	458	464	95	17	78	3	...	3
20—30	1,776	856	920	732	456	276	983	372	611	61	28	33
30—40	1,463	780	683	178	112	66	1,148	603	545	137	65	72
40—50	910	504	416	73	40	33	707	424	283	140	40	100
50—60	605	307	298	26	11	15	408	239	169	171	57	114
60 and over	480	243	237	15	4	11	219	166	53	246	73	173
Others (all ages) ...	***184***	***137***	***47***	***104***	***81***	***23***	***71***	***49***	***22***	***9***	***7***	***2***
PROME.												
All Religions ...	***371,575***	***182,803***	***188,772***	***195,216***	***99,584***	***95,632***	***141,396***	***72,242***	***69,154***	***34,963***	***10,977***	***23,986***
0	9,634	4,776	4,858	9,634	4,776	4,858	...	...	...	...	...	...
1—5	35,282	17,097	18,185	35,282	17,097	18,185	...	...	...	...	...	...
5—10	44,462	22,155	22,307	44,462	22,155	22,307	...	...	...	...	...	...
10—15	43,350	21,902	21,448	43,339	21,902	21,437	10	...	10	1	...	1
15—20	40,587	19,403	21,184	34,124	18,142	15,982	6,122	1,189	4,933	341	72	269
20—30	66,116	32,095	34,021	19,612	10,909	8,703	42,726	19,931	22,795	3,778	1,255	2,523
30—40	51,622	25,971	25,651	4,505	2,475	2,030	41,725	21,702	20,023	5,392	1,794	3,598
40—50	37,350	18,578	18,772	2,213	1,017	1,196	27,835	15,386	12,449	7,302	2,175	5,127
50—60	24,696	11,418	13,278	1,177	620	557	15,207	8,655	6,552	8,312	2,143	6,169
60 and over	18,476	9,408	9,068	868	491	377	7,771	5,379	2,392	9,837	3,538	6,299
Buddhist ...	***356,283***	***172,327***	***183,956***	***187,927***	***94,590***	***93,337***	***134,505***	***67,419***	***67,086***	***33,851***	***10,318***	***23,533***
0	9,388	4,663	4,725	9,388	4,663	4,725	...	...	...	...	...	...
1—5	34,230	16,586	17,644	34,230	16,586	17,644	...	...	...	...	...	...
5—10	43,153	21,460	21,693	43,153	21,460	21,693	...	...	...	...	...	...
10—15	42,301	21,252	21,049	42,296	21,252	21,044	4	...	4	1	...	1
15—20	39,346	18,640	20,706	33,164	17,482	15,682	5,850	1,091	4,759	332	67	265
20—30	62,149	29,177	32,972	17,994	9,487	8,507	40,544	18,550	21,994	3,611	1,140	2,471
30—40	48,403	23,473	24,930	3,799	1,829	1,970	39,454	20,025	19,429	5,150	1,619	3,531
40—50	35,594	17,272	18,322	1,997	833	1,164	26,560	14,415	12,145	7,037	2,024	5,013
50—60	23,824	10,800	13,024	1,084	542	542	14,612	8,202	6,410	8,128	2,056	6,072
60 and over	17,895	9,004	8,891	822	456	366	7,481	5,136	2,345	9,592	3,412	6,180
Animist ...	***4,274***	***2,649***	***1,625***	***2,012***	***1,266***	***746***	***1,938***	***1,216***	***722***	***324***	***167***	***157***
0	60	24	36	60	24	36	...	...	...	...	...	...
1—5	345	160	185	345	160	185	...	...	...	...	...	...
5—10	431	243	188	431	243	188	...	...	...	...	...	...
10—15	319	180	139	316	180	136	3	...	3	...	...	...
15—20	321	176	145	253	153	100	65	23	42	3	...	3
20—30	918	583	335	354	290	64	532	277	255	32	16	16
30—40	849	609	240	160	141	19	633	430	203	56	38	18
40—50	549	371	178	58	47	11	410	279	131	81	45	36
50—60	278	172	106	24	21	3	184	120	64	70	31	39
60 and over	204	131	73	11	7	4	111	87	24	82	37	45
Hindu ...	***5,509***	***4,427***	***1,082***	***2,397***	***1,976***	***421***	***2,740***	***2,155***	***585***	***372***	***296***	***76***
0	79	28	51	79	28	51	...	...	...	...	...	...
1—5	237	114	123	237	114	123	...	...	...	...	...	...
5—10	302	171	131	302	171	131	...	...	...	...	...	...
10—15	239	180	59	236	180	56	3	...	3	...	...	...
15—20	393	315	78	288	266	22	101	45	56	4	4	...
20—30	1,751	1,471	280	747	721	26	939	693	246	65	57	8
30—40	1,439	1,230	209	351	348	3	976	791	185	112	91	21
40—50	646	557	89	99	94	5	459	397	62	88	66	22
50—60	295	246	49	39	36	3	201	174	27	55	36	19
60 and over	128	115	13	19	18	1	61	55	6	48	42	6

Imperial Table VIIb.—*Age, Sex, and Civil Condition by Religion.*

District	Religion, and Age	Population: Persons	Population: Males	Population: Females	Unmarried: Persons	Unmarried: Males	Unmarried: Females	Married: Persons	Married: Males	Married: Females	Widowed: Persons	Widowed: Males	Widowed: Females
	1	2	3	4	5	6	7	8	9	10	11	12	13
PROME—*concluded*.	***Hindus born in Burma***	*774*	*429*	*345*	*576*	*314*	*261*	*171*	*98*	*73*	*28*	*17*	*11*
	0	59	20	39	59	20	39	...	...	...	...	...	...
	1—5	165	74	91	165	74	91	...	...	...	...	...	...
	5—10	155	77	78	155	77	78	...	...	...	...	...	...
	10—15	87	53	34	87	53	34	...	...	...	...	...	...
	15—20	62	39	23	49	36	13	12	2	10	1	1	...
	20—30	102	65	37	39	35	4	61	28	33	2	2	...
	30—40	71	51	20	13	13	...	51	36	15	7	2	5
	40—50	38	27	11	4	3	1	27	19	8	7	5	2
	50—60	22	13	9	1	1	...	13	8	5	8	4	4
	60 and over	13	10	3	3	2	1	7	5	2	3	3	...
	Mahomedan ...	*4,174*	*2,687*	*1,487*	*2,191*	*1,392*	*799*	*1,663*	*1,137*	*526*	*320*	*158*	*162*
	0	91	52	39	91	52	39	...	...	...	...	...	...
	1—5	349	184	165	349	184	165	...	...	...	...	...	...
	5—10	432	211	221	432	211	221	...	...	...	...	...	...
	10—15	360	222	138	360	222	138	...	...	...	...	...	...
	15—20	393	208	185	301	182	119	90	25	65	2	1	1
	20—30	1,025	728	297	411	342	69	556	347	209	58	39	19
	30—40	719	531	188	159	135	24	496	357	139	64	39	25
	40—50	405	277	128	49	37	12	282	209	73	74	31	43
	50—60	213	149	64	23	17	6	146	118	28	44	14	30
	60 and over	187	125	62	16	10	6	93	81	12	78	34	44
	Mahomedans born in Burma.	*2,464*	*1,158*	*1,306*	*1,538*	*786*	*752*	*741*	*325*	*416*	*185*	*47*	*138*
	0	87	48	39	87	48	39	...	...	...	...	...	...
	1—5	333	172	161	333	172	161	...	...	...	...	...	...
	5—10	398	189	209	398	189	209	...	...	...	...	...	...
	10—15	297	172	125	297	172	125	...	...	...	...	...	...
	15—20	290	122	168	225	111	114	65	11	54	...	...	...
	20—30	410	172	238	123	63	60	260	101	159	27	8	19
	30—40	275	124	151	36	16	20	205	95	110	34	13	21
	40—50	185	75	110	19	7	12	118	58	60	48	10	38
	50—60	102	46	56	12	6	6	61	38	23	29	2	27
	60 and over	87	38	49	8	2	6	32	22	10	47	14	33
	Christian *(all ages)*	*1,246*	*657*	*589*	*652*	*336*	*316*	*502*	*287*	*215*	*92*	*34*	*58*
	Others *(all ages)*	*89*	*56*	*33*	*37*	*24*	*13*	*48*	*28*	*20*	*4*	*4*	..
BASSEIN.	***All Religions*** ...	*489,473*	*252,947*	*236,526*	*268,353*	*142,832*	*125,521*	*187,277*	*97,563*	*89,714*	*33,843*	*12,552*	*21,291*
	0	9,752	4,813	4,939	9,752	4,813	4,939	...	...	...	...	...	...
	1—5	50,338	24,579	25,759	50,338	24,579	25,759	...	...	...	...	...	...
	5—10	60,947	30,210	30,737	60,947	30,210	30,737	...	...	...	...	...	...
	10—15	59,333	30,787	28,546	59,277	30,777	28,500	56	10	46	...	...	...
	15—20	51,067	24,837	26,230	44,042	23,399	20,643	6,602	1,367	5,235	423	71	352
	20—30	89,989	46,312	43,677	30,960	20,426	10,534	55,176	24,288	30,888	3,853	1,598	2,255
	30—40	68,720	38,399	30,321	7,565	5,213	2,352	55,787	30,743	25,044	5,368	2,443	2,925
	40—50	47,843	26,095	21,748	2,912	1,935	977	38,178	21,577	16,601	6,753	2,583	4,170
	50—60	29,264	14,889	14,375	1,522	845	677	20,104	11,699	8,495	7,548	2,345	5,203
	60 and over	22,220	12,026	10,194	1,038	635	403	11,284	7,879	3,405	9,898	3,512	6,386
	Buddhist ...	*428,546*	*213,811*	*214,735*	*235,153*	*121,435*	*113,718*	*163,576*	*82,130*	*81,446*	*29,817*	*10,246*	*19,571*
	0	8,740	4,274	4,466	8,740	4,274	4,466	...	...	...	...	...	...
	1—5	45,568	22,174	23,394	45,568	22,174	23,394	...	...	...	...	...	...
	5—10	55,422	27,420	28,002	55,422	27,420	28,002	...	...	...	...	...	...
	10—15	53,626	27,633	25,993	53,580	27,633	25,947	46	...	46	...	...	...
	15—20	45,464	21,640	23,824	39,147	20,432	18,715	5,937	1,156	4,781	380	52	328
	20—30	75,596	36,181	39,415	23,680	14,288	9,392	48,578	20,663	27,915	3,338	1,230	2,108
	30—40	57,121	29,792	27,329	4,989	2,940	2,049	47,680	25,071	22,609	4,452	1,781	2,671
	40—50	41,316	21,537	19,779	2,037	1,194	843	33,411	18,257	15,154	5,868	2,086	3,782
	50—60	25,802	12,644	13,158	1,161	595	566	17,847	10,052	7,795	6,794	1,997	4,797
	60 and over	19,891	10,516	9,375	829	485	344	10,077	6,931	3,146	8,985	3,100	5,885

IMPERIAL TABLE VIIB.—*Age, Sex, and Civil Condition by Religion.*

District	Religion, and Age.	Population. Persons.	Population. Males.	Population. Females.	Unmarried. Persons.	Unmarried. Males.	Unmarried. Females.	Married. Persons.	Married. Males.	Married. Females.	Widowed. Persons.	Widowed. Males.	Widowed. Females.
	1	2	3	4	5	6	7	8	9	10	11	12	13
BASSEIN—concluded.	***Animist (all ages)***	*8,356*	*2,696*	*660*	*1,625*	*1,251*	*274*	*1,630*	*1,301*	*329*	*201*	*144*	*57*
	Hindu ...	*14,947*	*18,151*	*1,796*	*7,017*	*6,322*	*695*	*6,811*	*5,812*	*999*	*1,119*	*1,017*	*102*
	0	94	51	43	94	51	43	...	...	...	...	...	...
	1—5	397	232	165	397	232	165	...	...	...	...	...	...
	5—10	450	250	200	450	250	200	...	...	...	...	...	...
	10—15	620	501	119	620	501	119	...	...	...	...	...	...
	15—20	1,078	934	144	855	800	55	208	121	87	15	13	2
	20—30	5,071	4,553	518	2,608	2,542	66	2,235	1,797	438	228	214	14
	30—40	4,201	3,858	343	1,341	1,319	22	2,482	2,181	301	378	358	20
	40—50	1,935	1,767	168	450	435	15	1,228	1,099	129	257	233	21
	50—60	963	700	63	135	126	9	485	455	30	143	119	24
	60 and over	338	305	33	67	66	1	173	159	14	98	80	18
	Hindus born in Burma.	*1,894*	*805*	*589*	*1,072*	*632*	*440*	*291*	*166*	*136*	*81*	*18*	*18*
	0	78	45	33	78	45	33	...	...	...	...	...	...
	1—5	297	164	133	297	164	133	...	...	...	...	...	...
	5—10	308	161	147	308	161	147	...	...	...	...	...	...
	10—15	163	98	65	163	98	65	...	...	...	...	...	...
	15—20	114	55	59	78	48	30	34	7	27	2	...	2
	20—30	242	151	91	113	83	30	126	65	61	3	3	...
	30—40	104	72	32	22	22	...	73	44	29	9	6	3
	40—50	52	35	17	7	6	1	38	25	13	7	4	3
	50—60	20	14	6	2	1	1	15	12	3	3	1	2
	60 and over	16	10	6	4	4	...	5	2	3	7	4	3
	Mahomedan ...	*9,994*	*7,082*	*2,912*	*5,335*	*8,821*	*1,514*	*8,999*	*2,885*	*1,164*	*660*	*426*	*284*
	0	159	94	65	159	94	65	...	...	...	...	...	...
	1—5	705	356	349	705	356	349	...	...	...	...	...	...
	5—10	679	374	305	679	374	305	...	...	...	...	...	...
	10—15	832	427	405	822	417	405	10	10	...	...	...	...
	15—20	864	544	320	675	500	175	172	40	132	17	4	13
	20—30	2,894	2,242	652	1,446	1,324	122	1,339	836	503	109	82	27
	30—40	2,101	1,686	415	524	475	49	1,413	1,087	326	164	124	40
	40—50	920	733	187	179	162	17	621	498	123	120	73	47
	50—60	457	343	114	64	56	8	276	220	56	117	67	50
	60 and over	383	283	100	82	63	19	168	144	24	133	76	57
	Mahomedans born in Burma.	*5,898*	*2,701*	*2,692*	*8,282*	*1,775*	*1,457*	*1,886*	*808*	*1,028*	*825*	*118*	*207*
	0	154	91	63	154	91	63	...	...	...	...	...	...
	1—5	687	346	341	687	346	341	...	...	...	...	...	...
	5—10	643	349	294	643	349	294	...	...	...	...	...	...
	10—15	725	333	392	721	329	392	4	4	...	...	...	...
	15—20	522	225	297	383	215	168	128	10	118	11	...	11
	20—30	1,070	488	582	362	251	111	663	217	446	45	20	25
	30—40	798	428	370	149	103	46	585	298	287	64	27	37
	40—50	380	219	161	57	42	15	261	155	106	62	22	40
	50—60	223	116	107	26	18	8	126	74	52	71	24	47
	60 and over	191	106	85	50	31	19	69	50	19	72	25	47
	Christians	*82,680*	*16,207*	*16,423*	*19,828*	*10,003*	*9,820*	*11,261*	*5,485*	*5,776*	*2,046*	*719*	*1,827*
	0	713	361	352	713	361	352	...	...	...	...	...	...
	1—5	3,474	1,693	1,781	3,474	1,693	1,781	...	...	...	...	...	...
	5—10	4,170	2,017	2,153	4,170	2,017	2,153	...	...	...	...	...	...
	10—15	4,057	2,087	1,970	4,057	2,087	1,970	...	...	...	...	...	...
	15—20	3,465	1,574	1,891	3,200	1,528	1,672	255	44	211	10	2	8
	20—30	5,754	2,808	2,946	2,894	1,958	936	2,694	786	1,908	166	64	102
	30—40	4,324	2,231	2,093	461	237	224	3,535	1,850	1,685	328	144	184
	40—50	3,143	1,584	1,559	172	72	100	2,521	1,363	1,158	450	149	301
	50—60	2,040	1,026	1,014	128	35	93	1,455	857	598	457	134	323
	60 and over	1,490	826	664	54	15	39	801	585	216	635	226	409
HENZADA.	***All Religions*** ...	*560,920*	*278,439*	*277,481*	*813,277*	*161,259*	*152,018*	*199,276*	*99,427*	*99,848*	*88,868*	*12,758*	*25,615*
	0	11,010	5,380	5,630	11,010	5,380	5,630	...	...	...	...	...	...
	1—5	58,344	28,534	29,810	58,344	28,534	29,810	...	...	...	...	...	...
	5—10	70,472	34,750	35,722	70,471	34,750	35,721	1	...	1	...	...	...
	10—15	67,375	34,822	32,553	67,238	34,817	32,421	135	5	130	2	...	2
	15—20	58,362	27,758	30,604	51,542	26,301	25,241	6,400	1,341	5 059	420	116	304
	20—30	95,621	45,279	50,342	36,300	20,822	15,478	55,721	23,304	32,417	3,600	1,153	2,447
	30—40	73,238	37,932	35,306	9,037	5,285	3,752	58,799	30,658	28,141	5,402	1,989	3,413
	40—50	54,365	27,632	26,733	4,473	2,665	1,808	42,187	22,390	19,797	7,705	2,577	5,128
	50—60	34,899	17,065	17,834	2,778	1,491	1,287	23,153	12,954	10,199	8,968	2,620	6,348
	60 and over	27,234	14,287	12,947	2,084	1,214	870	12,879	8,775	4,104	12,271	4,298	7,973

Imperial Table VIIb.—*Age, Sex, and Civil Condition by Religion.*

HENZADA—*continued.*

District, Religion, and Age.	Population. Persons.	Population. Males.	Population. Females.	Unmarried. Persons.	Unmarried. Males.	Unmarried. Females.	Married. Persons.	Married. Males.	Married. Females.	Widowed. Persons.	Widowed. Males.	Widowed. Females.
1	2	3	4	5	6	7	8	9	10	11	12	13
Buddhist ...	***525,231***	***257,027***	***268,204***	***299,188***	***152,454***	***146,734***	***189,063***	***92,501***	***96,562***	***36,980***	***12,072***	***24,908***
0	10,509	5,119	5,390	10,509	5,119	5,390	...	...	...	...	...	...
1—5	56,222	27,435	28,787	56,222	27,435	28,787	...	...	...	...	...	...
5—10	67,952	33,421	34,531	67,952	33,421	34,531	...	...	...	...	...	...
10—15	64,998	33,486	31,512	64,865	33,484	31,381	131	2	129	2	...	2
15—20	55,995	26,381	29,614	49,500	25,039	24,461	6,082	1,226	4,856	413	116	297
20—30	89,965	41,376	48,589	33,436	18,617	14,819	53,071	21,682	31,389	3,458	1,077	2,381
30—40	68,520	34,491	34,029	8,028	4,456	3,572	55,338	28,209	27,129	5,154	1,826	3,328
40—50	51,549	25,625	25,924	4,088	2,355	1,733	40,067	20,851	19,216	7,394	2,419	4,975
50—60	33,377	16,085	17,292	2,623	1,391	1,232	22,069	12,192	9,877	8,685	2,502	6,183
60 and over	26,144	13,608	12,536	1,965	1,137	828	12,305	8,339	3,966	11,874	4,132	7,742
Animist (all ages)	***1,970***	***1,632***	***338***	***825***	***638***	***187***	***1,053***	***883***	***170***	***92***	***61***	***31***
Hindu ...	***6,703***	***5,712***	***991***	***3,268***	***2,826***	***442***	***3,114***	***2,649***	***465***	***321***	***237***	***84***
0	80	44	36	80	44	36	...	...	...	...	...	...
1—5	275	165	110	275	165	110	...	...	...	...	...	...
5—10	315	182	133	315	182	133	...	...	...	...	...	...
10—15	368	289	79	368	289	79	...	...	...	...	...	...
15—20	540	458	82	437	401	36	103	57	46	...	...	...
20—30	2,105	1,862	243	1,091	1,069	22	966	756	210	48	37	11
30—40	1,641	1,484	157	445	434	11	1,118	986	132	78	64	14
40—50	863	776	87	178	170	8	594	543	51	91	63	28
50—60	336	296	40	50	46	4	234	216	18	52	34	18
60 and over	180	156	24	29	26	3	99	91	8	52	39	13
Hindus born in Burma	***1,023***	***622***	***401***	***727***	***446***	***281***	***253***	***158***	***95***	***43***	***18***	***25***
0	58	30	28	58	30	28	...	...	...	...	...	...
1—5	203	120	83	203	120	83	...	...	...	...	...	...
5—10	176	94	82	176	94	82	...	...	...	...	...	...
10—15	104	61	43	104	61	43	...	...	...	...	...	...
15—20	81	44	37	65	40	25	16	4	12	...	...	...
20—30	147	88	59	58	48	10	85	39	46	4	1	3
30—40	128	100	28	38	35	3	82	58	24	8	7	1
40—50	70	47	23	15	10	5	40	31	9	15	6	9
50—60	31	20	11	5	3	2	18	15	3	8	2	6
60 and over	25	18	7	5	5	...	12	11	1	8	2	6
Mahomedan ...	***5,211***	***3,323***	***1,888***	***2,819***	***1,796***	***1,023***	***2,097***	***1,373***	***724***	***295***	***154***	***141***
0	105	55	50	105	55	50	...	...	...	...	...	...
1—5	521	276	245	521	276	245	...	...	...	...	...	...
5—10	594	304	290	594	304	290	...	...	...	...	...	...
10—15	498	263	235	498	263	235	...	...	...	...	...	...
15—20	451	264	187	346	237	109	101	27	74	4	...	4
20—30	1,167	791	376	449	405	44	676	366	310	42	20	22
30—40	909	681	228	185	163	22	669	478	191	55	40	15
40—50	493	358	135	58	51	7	364	272	92	71	35	36
50—60	226	159	67	29	22	7	154	118	36	43	19	24
60 and over	247	172	75	34	20	14	133	112	21	80	40	40
Mahomedans born in Burma.	***3,055***	***1,441***	***1,614***	***1,971***	***1,019***	***952***	***919***	***377***	***542***	***165***	***45***	***120***
0	102	54	48	102	54	48	...	...	...	...	...	...
1—5	486	254	232	486	254	232	...	...	...	...	...	...
5—10	539	265	274	539	265	274	...	...	...	...	...	...
10—15	416	199	217	416	199	217	...	...	...	...	...	...
15—20	295	132	163	223	122	101	68	10	58	4	...	4
20—30	502	204	298	124	80	44	348	116	232	30	8	22
30—40	333	167	166	45	27	18	266	129	137	22	11	11
40—50	191	80	111	12	9	3	135	60	75	44	11	33
50—60	92	43	49	7	2	5	57	34	23	28	7	21
60 and over	99	43	56	17	7	10	45	28	17	37	8	29

IMPERIAL TABLE VIIB.—*Age, Sex, and Civil Condition by Religion.*

District	Religion, and Age.	Population. Persons.	Population. Males.	Population. Females.	Unmarried. Persons.	Unmarried. Males.	Unmarried. Females.	Married. Persons.	Married. Males.	Married. Females.	Widowed. Persons.	Widowed. Males.	Widowed. Females.
	1	2	3	4	5	6	7	8	9	10	11	12	13
HENZADA—*concluded.*	***Christian*** ...	***11,742***	***5,711***	***6,031***	***7,147***	***3,480***	***3,667***	***3,917***	***2,003***	***1,914***	***678***	***228***	***450***
	0	285	145	140	285	145	140	...	...	...	...	...	...
	1—5	1,216	587	629	1,216	587	629	...	...	...	...	...	...
	5—10	1,482	760	722	1,482	760	722	...	...	...	...	...	...
	10—15	1,408	708	700	1,405	705	700	3	3	...	...	...	...
	15—20	1,246	552	694	1,159	535	624	84	17	67	3	...	3
	20—30	1,969	896	1,073	1,150	562	588	776	322	454	43	12	31
	30—40	1,633	825	808	259	117	142	1,282	662	620	92	46	46
	40—50	1,111	565	546	99	41	58	882	478	404	130	46	84
	50—60	821	398	423	57	15	42	596	332	264	168	51	117
	60 and over	571	275	296	35	13	22	294	189	105	242	73	169
	Others (all ages) ...	***63***	***34***	***29***	***30***	***15***	***15***	***31***	***18***	***13***	***2***	***1***	***1***
MYAUNGMYA.	***All Religions*** ...	***370,551***	***196,757***	***173,794***	***208,430***	***114,946***	***93,584***	***139,773***	***72,894***	***66,879***	***22,298***	***3,917***	***18,881***
	0	7,263	3,563	3,700	7,263	3,563	3700	...	...	...	...	...	...
	1—5	40,159	19,687	20,472	40,159	19,687	20,472	...	...	...	...	...	...
	5—10	47,067	23,479	23,588	47,067	23,479	23,588	...	...	...	...	...	...
	10—15	44,387	23,390	20,997	44,346	23,376	20,970	34	9	25	7	5	2
	15—20	39,021	19,499	19,542	32,400	18,152	14,248	6,335	1,250	5,085	286	77	209
	20—30	67,373	36,165	31,208	24,735	17,569	7,166	40,486	17,717	22,769	2,152	879	1,273
	30—40	51,442	29,949	21,493	7,083	5,529	1,554	40,951	22,760	18,191	3,408	1,660	1,748
	40—50	35,771	19,991	15,780	3,071	2,025	1,046	28,193	16,026	12,167	4,507	1,940	2,567
	50—60	21,266	11,422	9,844	1,351	920	431	14,942	8,836	6,106	4,973	1,666	3,307
	60 and over	16,802	9,632	7,170	1,005	646	359	8,832	6,296	2,536	6,965	2,690	4,275
	Buddhist ...	***324,315***	***165,260***	***159,055***	***181,659***	***96,175***	***85,484***	***122,743***	***61,586***	***61,157***	***19,913***	***7,499***	***12,414***
	0	6,614	3,256	3,358	6,614	3,256	3,358	...	...	...	...	...	...
	1—5	36,473	17,886	18,587	36,473	17,886	18,587	...	...	...	...	...	...
	5—10	42,922	21,353	21,569	42,922	21,353	21,569	...	...	...	...	...	...
	10—15	40,132	20,916	19,216	40,104	20,910	19,194	25	4	21	3	2	1
	15—20	34,515	16,490	18,025	28,526	15,389	13,137	5,743	1,046	4,697	246	55	191
	20—30	55,665	27,335	28,330	18,436	11,923	6,513	35,377	14,739	20,638	1,852	673	1,179
	30—40	42,578	22,992	19,586	4,480	3,065	1,415	35,212	18,658	16,554	2,886	1,269	1,617
	40—50	31,227	16,615	14,612	2,218	1,234	984	25,005	13,762	11,243	4,004	1,619	2,385
	50—60	19,029	9,903	9,126	1,036	647	389	13,430	7,782	5 648	4,563	1,474	3,089
	60 and over	15,160	8,514	6,646	850	512	338	7,951	5,595	2,356	6,359	2,407	3,952
	Animist ...	***4,027***	***3,292***	***735***	***1,934***	***1,568***	***366***	***1,830***	***1,502***	***328***	***263***	***222***	***4***
	0	41	18	23	41	18	23	...	...	...	...	...	...
	1—5	243	144	99	243	144	99	...	...	...	...	...	...
	5—10	282	165	117	282	165	117	...	...	...	...	...	...
	10—15	216	144	72	216	144	72	...	...	...	...	...	...
	15—20	224	183	41	182	162	20	38	17	21	4	4	...
	20—30	883	732	151	454	438	16	392	262	130	37	32	5
	30—40	1,106	991	115	339	332	7	704	600	104	63	59	4
	40—50	618	560	58	117	112	5	437	390	47	64	58	6
	50—60	268	232	36	44	38	6	172	152	20	52	42	10
	60 and over	146	123	23	16	15	1	87	81	6	43	27	16
	Hindu ...	***9,633***	***8,644***	***989***	***5,616***	***5,171***	***445***	***3,471***	***2,970***	***501***	***446***	***403***	***43***
	0	35	12	23	35	12	23	...	...	...	...	...	...
	1—5	281	144	137	281	144	137	...	...	...	...	...	...
	5—10	225	123	102	225	123	102	...	...	...	...	...	...
	10—15	569	483	86	560	475	85	6	5	1	3	3	...
	15—20	942	830	112	774	734	40	152	81	71	16	15	1
	20—30	3,440	3,205	235	2,227	2,191	36	1,120	928	192	93	86	7
	30—40	2,509	2,332	177	1,034	1,019	15	1,330	1,177	153	145	136	9
	40—50	988	924	64	338	335	3	554	503	51	96	86	10
	50—60	349	309	40	102	98	4	203	177	26	44	34	10
	60 and over	195	182	13	40	40	...	106	99	7	49	43	6
	Hindus born in Burma	***363***	***484***	***379***	***664***	***401***	***263***	***179***	***72***	***107***	***20***	***11***	***9***
	0	22	...	22	22	...	22	...	...	...	...	...	...
	1—5	194	93	101	194	93	101	...	...	...	...	...	...
	5—10	96	25	71	96	25	71	...	...	...	...	...	...
	10—15	185	134	51	184	134	50	1	...	1	...	...	...
	15—20	66	33	33	39	30	9	26	3	23	1	...	1
	20—30	144	99	45	79	73	6	62	25	37	3	1	2
	30—40	85	53	32	27	25	2	52	25	27	6	3	3
	40—50	43	27	16	15	14	1	22	9	13	6	4	2
	50—60	17	10	7	6	5	1	10	4	6	1	1	...
	60 and over	11	10	1	2	2	...	6	6	.	3	2	1

IMPERIAL TABLE VIIB.—*Age, Sex, and Civil Condition by Religion.*

DISTRICT, RELIGION, AND AGE.	POPULATION. Persons.	POPULATION. Males.	POPULATION. Females.	UNMARRIED. Persons.	UNMARRIED. Males.	UNMARRIED. Females.	MARRIED. Persons.	MARRIED. Males.	MARRIED. Females.	WIDOWED. Persons.	WIDOWED. Males.	WIDOWED. Females.
1	2	3	4	5	6	7	8	9	10	11	12	13
MYAUNGMYA—*concluded.*												
Mahomedan ...	*11,451*	*8,990*	*2,461*	*7,021*	*5,714*	*1,307*	*3,984*	*2,953*	*1,031*	*446*	*323*	*123*
0	117	57	60	117	57	60	...	...	...	...	...	...
1—5	729	367	362	729	367	362	...	...	...	...	...	...
5—10	798	436	362	798	436	362	...	...	...	...	...	...
10—15	808	507	301	804	507	297	3	...	3	1	...	1
15—20	1,202	924	278	994	858	136	199	63	136	9	3	6
20—30	3,635	3,123	512	2,226	2,174	52	1,330	894	436	79	55	24
30—40	2,447	2,120	327	926	903	23	1,391	1,108	283	130	109	21
40—50	1005	858	147	267	262	5	641	524	117	97	72	25
50—60	431	360	71	111	105	6	267	221	46	53	34	19
60 and over	279	238	41	49	45	4	153	143	10	77	50	27
Mahomedans born in Burma.	*4,021*	*1,863*	*2,158*	*2,669*	*1,460*	*1,219*	*1,210*	*874*	*836*	*142*	*89*	*103*
0	102	51	51	102	51	51	...	...	...	...	...	...
1—5	677	327	350	677	327	350	...	...	...	...	...	...
5—10	726	384	342	726	384	342	...	...	...	...	...	...
10—15	565	280	285	565	280	285	...	...	...	...	...	...
15—20	437	187	250	302	176	126	130	11	119	5	...	5
20—30	690	285	405	197	158	39	467	121	346	26	6	20
30—40	456	195	261	64	50	14	362	133	229	30	12	18
40—50	207	86	121	18	14	4	161	64	97	28	8	20
50—60	104	45	59	12	7	5	70	32	38	22	6	16
60 and over	57	23	34	6	3	3	20	13	7	31	7	24
Christian ..	*21,198*	*10,645*	*10,553*	*12,240*	*6,308*	*5,932*	*7,732*	*3,871*	*3,861*	*1,226*	*466*	*760*
0	456	220	236	456	220	236	...	...	..	...	...	...
1—5	2,431	1,144	1,287	2,431	1,144	1,287	...	...	...	...	...	...
5—10	2,840	1,402	1,438	2,840	1,402	1,438	...	...	...	...	...	...
10—15	2,662	1,340	1,322	2,662	1,340	1,322	...	...	...	...	...	...
15—20	2,136	1,050	1,086	1,922	1,007	915	203	43	160	11	...	11
20—30	3,743	1,763	1,980	1,390	841	549	2,262	889	1,373	91	33	58
30—40	2,793	1,506	1,287	300	206	94	2,310	1,214	1,096	183	86	97
40—50	1,929	1,030	899	131	82	49	1,554	845	709	244	103	141
50—60	1,186	615	571	58	32	26	868	502	366	260	81	179
60 and over	1,022	575	447	50	34	16	535	378	157	437	163	274
Others (all ages) ...	*27*	*26*	*1*	*10*	*10*	...	*13*	*12*	*1*	*4*	*4*	...
MA-UBIN.												
All Religions ...	*330,106*	*168,513*	*161,593*	*191,541*	*100,286*	*91,255*	*116,211*	*60,084*	*56,127*	*22,354*	*8,143*	*14,211*
0	7,854	3,814	4,040	7,854	3,814	4,040	...	...	...	...	...	...
1—5	35,473	17,504	17,969	35,473	17,504	17,969	...	...	...	...	...	...
5—10	42,384	21,315	21,069	42,384	21,315	21,069	...	...	...	...	...	..
10—15	39,946	20,550	19,396	39,898	20,544	19,354	47	6	41	1	...	1
15—20	34,026	16,306	17,720	29,728	15,438	14,290	4,008	819	3,189	290	49	241
20—30	57,169	28,337	28,832	23,182	14,095	9,087	31,765	13,511	18,254	2,222	731	1,491
30—40	43,618	23,495	20,123	6,470	4,161	2,309	33,991	18,050	15,941	3,157	1,284	1,873
40—50	31,803	17,172	14,631	3,808	1,773	2,035	23,720	13,715	10,005	4,275	1,684	2,591
50—60	19,455	9,806	9,649	1,504	921	583	13,222	7,383	5,839	4,729	1,502	3,227
60 and over	18,378	10,214	8,164	1,240	721	519	9,458	6,000	2,858	7,680	2,893	4,787
Buddhist ...	*302,862*	*150,413*	*152,449*	*176,080*	*89,905*	*86,175*	*106,034*	*53,275*	*52,759*	*20,748*	*7,233*	*13,515*
0	7,395	3,564	3,831	7,395	3,564	3,831	...	...	...	...	...	...
1—5	33,278	16,391	16,887	33,278	16,391	16,887	...	...	...	...	..	...
5—10	39,896	20,033	19,863	39,896	20,033	19,863	...	...	...	...	...	...
10—15	37,454	19,083	18,371	37,408	19,077	18,331	45	6	39	1	...	1
15—20	31,396	14,670	16,726	27,450	13,916	13,534	3,675	707	2,968	271	47	224
20—30	50,860	23,736	27,124	19,878	11,355	8,523	28,975	11,794	17,181	2,007	587	1,420
30—40	38,687	19,792	18,895	5,084	2,918	2,166	30,779	15,815	14,964	2,824	1,059	1,765
40—50	28,902	15,053	13,849	3,283	1,294	1,989	21,659	12,273	9,386	3,960	1,486	2,474
50—60	17,932	8,773	9,159	1,306	754	552	12,169	6,649	5,520	4,457	1,370	3,087
60 and over	17,062	9,318	7,744	1,102	603	499	8,732	6,031	2,701	7,228	2,684	4,544
Animist ..	*1,736*	*1,244*	*492*	*921*	*657*	*264*	*723*	*528*	*195*	*92*	*59*	*33*
Hindu ...	*6,833*	*5,954*	*879*	*3,832*	*3,425*	*407*	*2,589*	*2,177*	*412*	*412*	*352*	*60*
0	62	30	32	62	30	32	...	...	...	...	...	...
1—5	210	98	112	210	98	112	...	...	...	...	...	...
5—10	281	166	115	281	166	115	...	...	...	...	...	...
10—15	383	306	77	382	306	76	1	...	1	...	...	...
15—20	640	577	63	534	508	26	101	69	32	5	...	5
20—30	2,130	1,928	202	1,258	1,235	23	781	611	170	91	82	9
30—40	1,703	1,564	139	689	678	11	907	787	120	107	99	8
40—50	847	768	79	267	260	7	493	436	57	87	72	15
50—60	340	306	34	87	86	1	197	174	23	56	46	10
60 and over	237	211	26	62	58	4	109	100	9	66	53	13

Imperial Table VIIb.—*Age, Sex, and Civil Condition by Religion.*

District, Religion, and Age	Population. Persons	Population. Males	Population. Females	Unmarried. Persons	Unmarried. Males	Unmarried. Females	Married. Persons	Married. Males	Married. Females	Widowed. Persons	Widowed. Males	Widowed. Females
1	2	3	4	5	6	7	8	9	10	11	12	13
MA-UBIN—*concluded.*												
Hindus born in Burma	*810*	*457*	*858*	*636*	*868*	*278*	*154*	*87*	*67*	*20*	*7*	*13*
0	53	24	29	53	24	29	...	...	...	...	...	...
1—5	162	70	92	162	70	92	...	...	...	...	...	...
5—10	182	103	79	182	103	79	...	...	...	...	...	...
10—15	102	50	52	101	50	51	1	...	1	...	...	...
15—20	67	37	30	45	32	13	18	5	13	4	...	4
20—30	96	61	35	50	44	6	42	15	27	4	2	2
30—40	92	70	22	30	28	2	58	39	19	4	3	1
40—50	30	22	8	4	4	...	23	17	6	3	1	2
50—60	17	13	4	7	6	1	7	6	1	3	1	2
60 and over	9	7	2	2	2	...	5	5	...	2	...	2
Mahomedan ...	*6,001*	*4,850*	*1,651*	*8,369*	*2,477*	*892*	*2,811*	*1,667*	*644*	*821*	*206*	*115*
0	94	58	36	94	58	36	...	...	...	...	...	...
1—5	491	242	249	491	242	249	...	...	...	...	...	...
5—10	524	258	266	524	258	266	...	...	...	...	...	...
10—15	505	313	192	505	313	192	...	...	...	...	...	...
15—20	546	378	168	420	340	80	120	36	84	6	2	4
20—30	1,605	1,296	309	817	770	47	741	492	249	47	34	13
30—40	1,175	956	219	327	316	11	766	575	191	82	65	17
40—50	567	470	97	120	116	4	376	303	73	71	51	20
50—60	273	207	66	42	37	5	183	148	35	48	22	26
60 and over	221	172	49	29	27	2	125	113	12	67	32	35
Mahomedans born in Burma.	*2,775*	*1,831*	*1,444*	*1,816*	*985*	*881*	*824*	*306*	*518*	*135*	*40*	*95*
0	86	52	34	86	52	34	...	...	...	...	...	...
1—5	456	215	241	456	215	241	...	...	...	...	...	...
5—10	482	239	243	482	239	243	...	...	...	...	...	...
10—15	391	212	179	391	212	179	...	...	...	...	...	...
15—20	292	140	152	195	125	70	91	13	78	6	2	4
20—30	449	191	258	137	93	44	291	88	203	21	10	11
30—40	321	149	172	45	36	9	250	102	148	26	11	15
40—50	145	71	74	13	9	4	111	56	55	21	6	15
50—60	83	30	53	6	1	5	50	24	26	27	5	22
60 and over	70	32	38	5	3	2	31	23	8	34	6	28
Christian ...	*11,984*	*5,976*	*6,008*	*7,010*	*8,551*	*8,459*	*4,225*	*2,157*	*2,068*	*749*	*268*	*481*
0	258	136	122	258	136	122	...	...	...	...	...	...
1—5	1,300	665	635	1,300	665	635	...	...	...	...	...	...
5—10	1,475	729	746	1,475	729	746	...	...	...	...	...	...
10—15	1,425	737	688	1,425	737	688	...	...	...	...	...	...
15—20	1,264	554	710	1,160	552	608	97	2	95	7	...	7
20—30	2,108	1,022	1,086	988	514	474	1,048	484	564	72	24	48
30—40	1,534	760	774	251	136	115	1,167	583	584	116	41	75
40—50	1,135	576	559	78	45	33	933	481	452	124	50	74
50—60	750	384	366	45	20	25	563	318	245	142	46	96
60 and over	735	413	322	30	17	13	417	289	128	288	107	181
Others (all ages) ...	*690*	*576*	*114*	*329*	*271*	*58*	*329*	*280*	*49*	*32*	*25*	*7*
PYAPÔN.												
All Religions ...	*288,994*	*156,721*	*132,273*	*163,438*	*92,187*	*71,246*	*107,587*	*56,934*	*50,653*	*17,974*	*7,600*	*10,874*
0	5,757	2,905	2,852	5,757	2,905	2,852	...	...	...	...	...	...
1—5	31,699	15,780	15,919	31,697	15,780	15,917	2	...	2	...	...	...
5—10	36,624	18,153	18,471	36,617	18,153	18,464	7	...	7	...	...	...
10—15	32,468	17,030	15,438	32,393	16,990	15,403	75	40	35	...	...	...
15—20	29,347	14,950	14,397	24,038	14,049	9,989	5,122	880	4,242	187	21	166
20—30	54,071	30,073	23,998	20,312	15,322	4,990	32,016	14,081	17,935	1,743	670	1,073
30—40	40,575	24,037	16,538	6,443	5,268	1,175	31,473	17,534	13,939	2,659	1,235	1,424
40—50	28,486	16,859	11,627	3,438	2,064	1,374	21,177	12,989	8,188	3,871	1,806	2,065
50—60	15,901	8,922	6,979	1,300	937	363	10,938	6,517	4,421	3,663	1,468	2,195
60 and over	14,066	8,012	6,054	1,438	719	719	6,777	4,893	1,884	5,851	2,400	3,451
Buddhist ...	*254,7 2*	*131,225*	*122,847*	*143,049*	*76,579*	*66,470*	*94,556*	*48,013*	*46,543*	*16,467*	*6,683*	*9,884*
0	5,268	2,657	2,611	5,268	2,657	2,611	...	...	...	...	...	...
1—5	29,029	14,358	14,671	29,029	14,358	14,671	...	...	...	...	...	...
5—10	33,659	16,534	17,125	33,659	16,534	17,125	...	...	...	...	...	...
10—15	29,793	15,322	14,471	29,763	15,309	14,454	30	13	17	...	...	...
15—20	26,280	12,739	13,541	21,483	12,006	9,477	4,619	718	3,901	178	15	163
20—30	44,601	22,617	21,984	15,132	10,429	4,703	27,883	11,625	16,258	1,586	563	1,023
30—40	33,264	18,145	15,119	3,921	2,855	1,066	27,025	14,303	12,722	2,318	987	1,331
40—50	24,900	13,980	10,920	2,548	1,234	1,314	18,861	11,195	7,666	3,491	1,551	1,940
50—60	14,287	7,674	6,613	894	653	341	9,929	5,736	4,193	3,364	1,285	2,079
60 and over	12,991	7,199	5,792	1,252	544	708	6,209	4,483	1,786	5,530	2,032	3,298

IMPERIAL TABLE VIIB.—*Age, Sex, and Civil Condition by Religion.*

PYAPÔN—*concluded.*

DISTRICT, RELIGION, AND AGE.	POPULATION.			UNMARRIED.			MARRIED.			WIDOWED.		
	Persons.	Males.	Females.	Persons.	Males.	Females.	Persons.	Males.	Females.	Persons.	Males.	Females.
1	2	3	4	5	6	7	8	9	10	11	12	13
Animist ...	***3,771***	***2,898***	***873***	***2,023***	***1,608***	***415***	***1,551***	***1,162***	***389***	***197***	***128***	***69***
0	19	...	19	19	...	19	...	...	...	...	...	...
1—5	270	171	99	270	171	99	...	...	...	...	...	...
5—10	338	207	131	338	207	131	...	...	...	...	...	...
10—15	252	163	89	248	159	89	4	4	...	...	...	...
15—20	226	158	68	188	150	38	38	8	30	...	...	...
20—30	872	717	155	509	488	21	354	225	129	9	4	5
30—40	921	758	163	277	270	7	587	443	144	57	45	12
40—50	552	456	96	126	118	8	370	303	67	56	35	21
50—60	198	166	32	24	23	1	139	124	15	35	19	16
60 and over	123	102	21	24	22	2	59	55	4	40	25	15
Hindu ...	***16,431***	***12,804***	***3,627***	***9,762***	***8,082***	***1,680***	***5,998***	***4,216***	***1,782***	***671***	***506***	***165***
0	196	114	82	196	114	82	...	...	...	...	...	...
1—5	1,091	585	506	1,089	585	504	2	...	2	...	...	...
5—10	1,196	676	520	1,190	676	514	6	...	6	...	...	...
10—15	1,132	806	326	1,108	788	320	24	18	6	...	...	...
15—20	1,451	1,169	282	1,182	1,072	110	263	94	169	6	3	3
20—30	4,820	3,940	880	2,761	2,688	73	1,976	1,190	786	83	62	21
30—40	3,785	3,192	593	1,506	1,463	43	2,106	1,587	519	173	142	31
40—50	1,647	1,403	244	486	461	25	994	813	181	167	129	38
50—60	713	583	130	159	152	7	415	338	77	139	93	46
60 and over	400	336	64	85	83	2	212	176	36	103	77	26
Hindus born in Burma	***3,279***	***1,966***	***1,313***	***2,722***	***1,658***	***1,064***	***483***	***253***	***230***	***74***	***55***	***19***
0	166	101	65	166	101	65	...	...	...	...	...	...
1—5	812	431	381	810	431	379	2	...	2	...	...	...
5—10	799	440	359	793	440	353	6	...	6	...	...	...
10—15	464	267	197	458	267	191	6	...	6	...	...	...
15—20	261	163	98	203	155	48	55	7	48	3	1	2
20—30	384	258	126	184	167	17	190	85	105	10	6	4
30—40	224	168	56	67	60	7	136	94	42	21	14	7
40—50	104	84	20	25	21	4	61	47	14	18	16	2
50—60	37	32	5	9	9	...	16	12	4	12	11	1
60 and over	28	22	6	7	7	...	11	8	3	10	7	3
Mahomedan ...	***5,640***	***4,843***	***797***	***3,268***	***2,877***	***391***	***2,166***	***1,812***	***354***	***206***	***154***	***52***
0	61	36	25	61	36	25	...	...	...	...	...	...
1—5	240	132	108	240	132	108	...	...	...	...	...	...
5—10	245	129	116	244	129	115	1	...	1	...	...	...
10—15	258	186	72	257	186	71	1	...	1	...	...	...
15—20	518	431	87	422	387	35	95	43	52	1	1	...
20—30	2,054	1,861	193	1,204	1,180	24	815	654	161	35	27	8
30—40	1,281	1,170	111	520	512	8	716	625	91	45	33	12
40—50	545	510	35	195	191	4	298	276	22	52	43	9
50—60	274	249	25	84	83	1	156	137	19	34	29	5
60 and over	164	139	25	41	41	...	84	77	7	39	21	18
Mahomedans born in Burma.	***1,348***	***757***	***591***	***881***	***538***	***343***	***411***	***199***	***212***	***56***	***20***	***36***
0	48	27	21	48	27	21	...	...	...	...	...	...
1—5	205	101	104	205	101	104	...	...	...	...	...	...
5—10	198	102	96	197	102	95	1	...	1	...	...	...
10—15	141	74	67	140	74	66	1	...	1	...	...	...
15—20	149	85	64	109	79	30	40	6	34	...	...	...
20—30	282	163	119	111	92	19	160	66	94	11	5	6
30—40	180	112	68	45	41	4	120	67	53	15	4	11
40—50	72	52	20	16	13	3	45	34	11	11	5	6
50—60	43	25	18	7	6	1	31	16	15	5	3	2
60 and over	30	16	14	3	3	...	13	10	3	14	3	11
Christian ...	***9,054***	***4,925***	***4,129***	***5,320***	***3,030***	***2,290***	***3,302***	***1,717***	***1,585***	***432***	***178***	***254***
0	213	98	115	213	98	115	...	...	...	...	...	...
1—5	1,069	534	535	1,069	534	535	...	...	...	...	...	...
5—10	1,186	607	579	1,186	607	579	...	...	...	...	...	...
10—15	1,033	553	480	1,017	548	469	16	5	11	...	...	...
15—20	869	450	419	762	433	329	105	15	90	2	2	...
20—30	1,707	921	786	696	527	169	981	380	601	30	14	16
30—40	1,322	770	552	219	168	51	1,037	574	463	66	28	38
40—50	838	506	332	83	60	23	651	399	252	104	47	57
50—60	429	250	179	39	26	13	299	182	117	91	42	49
60 and over	388	236	152	36	29	7	213	162	51	139	45	94
Others (all ages) ...	***26***	***26***	...	***11***	***11***	...	***14***	***14***	...	***1***	***1***	...

IMPERIAL TABLE VIIB.—*Age, Sex, and Civil Condition by Religion.*

DISTRICT, RELIGION, AND AGE.	POPULATION. Persons.	POPULATION. Males.	POPULATION. Females.	UNMARRIED. Persons.	UNMARRIED. Males.	UNMARRIED. Females.	MARRIED. Persons.	MARRIED. Males.	MARRIED. Females.	WIDOWED. Persons.	WIDOWED. Males.	WIDOWED. Females.
1	2	3	4	5	6	7	8	9	10	11	12	13
TOUNGOO.												
All Religion ...	*381,883*	*197,505*	*184,378*	*205,254*	*110,985*	*94,269*	*146,218*	*75,691*	*70,527*	*30,411*	*10,829*	*19,582*
0	7,916	3,787	4,129	7,916	3,787	4,129	...	...	...	...	...	...
1—5	37,481	18,568	18,913	37,481	18,568	18,913	...	...	...	...	...	...
5—10	48,294	23,741	24,553	48,294	23,741	24,553	...	...	...	...	...	...
10—15	46,258	24,253	22,005	46,105	24,252	21,853	151	1	150	2	...	2
15—20	38,736	18,403	20,333	31,611	16,934	14,677	6,742	1,420	5,322	383	49	334
20—30	67,763	34,316	33,447	23,161	16,023	7,138	41,394	17,099	24,295	3,218	1,194	2,024
30—40	53,112	29,795	23,317	6,158	4,615	1,543	42,183	23,042	19,141	4,761	2,138	2,623
40—50	38,670	21,199	17,471	2,393	1,727	666	29,908	17,079	12,829	6,369	2,393	3,976
50—60	23,253	12,280	10,973	1,193	757	436	15,559	9,544	6,015	6,501	1,979	4,522
60 and over	20,400	11,163	9,237	942	581	361	10,281	7,506	2,775	9,177	3,076	6,101
Buddhist ...	*297,980*	*149,783*	*148,197*	*158,717*	*83,811*	*74,906*	*115,425*	*58,075*	*57,350*	*23,838*	*7,897*	*15,941*
0	6,459	3,090	3,369	6,459	3,090	3,369	...	...	...	...	...	...
1—5	29,484	14,548	14,936	29,484	14,548	14,936	...	...	...	...	...	...
5—10	38,317	18,808	19,509	38,317	18,808	19,509	...	...	...	...	...	...
10—15	37,376	19,602	17,774	37,327	19,601	17,726	47	1	46	2	...	2
15—20	30,577	14,074	16,503	25,178	13,263	11,915	5,065	774	4,291	334	37	297
20—30	50,750	24,337	26,413	15,428	10,204	5,224	32,834	13,333	19,501	2,488	800	1,688
30—40	39,364	20,961	18,403	3,482	2,352	1,130	32,474	17,186	15,288	3,408	1,423	1,985
40—50	30,199	15,895	14,304	1,538	1,029	509	23,803	13,116	10,687	4,858	1,750	3,108
50—60	18,623	9,444	9,179	778	480	298	12,702	7,505	5,197	5,143	1,459	3,684
60 and over	16,831	9,024	7,807	726	436	290	8,500	6,160	2,340	7,605	2,428	5,177
Animist ...	*20,699*	*11,268*	*9,431*	*12,083*	*6,739*	*5,344*	*6,741*	*3,716*	*3,025*	*1,875*	*813*	*1,062*
0	394	194	200	394	194	200	...	...	...	...	...	...
1—5	2,006	1,008	998	2,006	1,008	998	...	...	...	...	...	...
5—10	2,481	1,300	1,181	2,481	1,300	1,181	...	...	...	...	...	...
10—15	2,289	1,224	1,065	2,289	1,224	1,065	...	...	...	...	...	...
15—20	2,025	972	1,053	1,802	944	858	214	28	186	9	...	9
20—30	3,936	2,072	1,864	2,143	1,392	751	1,654	616	1,038	139	64	75
30—40	3,235	1,955	1,280	609	451	158	2,242	1,320	922	384	184	200
40—50	2,204	1,303	901	209	134	75	1,526	965	561	469	204	265
50—60	1,062	668	394	93	59	34	581	452	129	388	157	231
60 and over	1,067	572	495	57	33	24	524	335	189	486	204	282
Hindu ...	*19,575*	*13,316*	*6,259*	*9,551*	*6,551*	*3,000*	*8,753*	*5,960*	*2,793*	*1,271*	*805*	*466*
0	162	57	105	162	57	105	...	...	...	...	...	...
1—5	1,854	926	928	1,854	926	928	...	...	...	...	...	...
5—10	2,062	953	1,109	2,062	953	1,109	...	...	...	...	...	...
10—15	1,348	658	690	1,345	658	687	3	...	3	...	...	...
15—20	1,604	1,183	421	709	642	67	876	531	345	19	10	9
20—30	4,630	3,543	1,087	1,891	1,820	71	2,556	1,586	970	183	137	46
30—40	3,856	2,977	879	999	975	24	2,586	1,799	787	271	203	68
40—50	2,195	1,691	504	362	357	5	1,564	1,163	401	269	171	98
50—60	1,009	775	234	115	113	2	703	536	167	191	126	65
60 and over	855	553	302	52	50	2	465	345	120	338	158	180
Hindus born in Burma	*5,995*	*3,088*	*2,907*	*4,690*	*2,227*	*2,463*	*1,193*	*802*	*391*	*112*	*59*	*53*
0	138	44	94	138	44	94	...	...	...	...	...	...
1—5	1,621	791	830	1,621	791	830	...	...	...	...	..	...
5—10	1,695	742	953	1,695	742	953	...	...	...	...	...	...
10—15	785	285	500	785	285	500	...	...	...	...	...	...
15—20	555	371	184	145	103	42	404	268	136	6	...	6
20—30	568	368	200	177	143	34	368	212	156	23	13	10
30—40	276	198	78	82	76	6	167	104	63	27	18	9
40—50	217	175	42	22	21	1	174	147	27	21	7	14
50—60	67	55	12	17	16	1	40	33	7	10	6	4
60 and over	73	59	14	8	6	2	40	38	2	25	15	10
Mahomedan ...	*8,163*	*5,498*	*2,665*	*4,731*	*3,363*	*1,368*	*2,708*	*1,677*	*1,031*	*724*	*458*	*266*
0	134	66	68	134	66	68	...	...	...	...	...	...
1—5	628	318	310	628	318	310	...	...	...	...	...	...
5—10	713	340	373	713	340	373	...	...	...	...	...	...
10—15	726	421	305	725	421	304	1	...	1	...	...	...
15—20	816	537	279	674	505	169	134	30	104	8	2	6
20—30	2,137	1,596	541	1,126	1,037	89	844	425	419	167	134	33
30—40	1,552	1,194	358	497	464	33	887	612	275	168	118	50
40—50	752	537	215	136	123	13	481	330	151	135	84	51
50—60	411	290	121	57	50	7	254	184	70	100	56	44
60 and over	294	199	95	41	39	2	107	96	11	146	64	82

IMPERIAL TABLE VIIB.—*Age, Sex, and Civil Condition by Religion.*

District, Religion, and Age.	Population. Persons.	Population. Males.	Population. Females.	Unmarried. Persons.	Unmarried. Males.	Unmarried. Females.	Married. Persons.	Married. Males.	Married. Females.	Widowed. Persons.	Widowed. Males.	Widowed. Females.
1	2	3	4	5	6	7	8	9	10	11	12	13
TOUNGOO—*concluded.*												
Mahomedans born in Burma.	*4,476*	*2,152*	*2,324*	*2,779*	*1,505*	*1,274*	*1,362*	*549*	*813*	*335*	*98*	*237*
0	129	66	63	129	66	63	...	...	...	...	...	...
1—5	601	316	285	601	316	285	...	...	...	...	...	...
5—10	687	337	350	687	337	350	...	...	...	...	...	...
10—15	602	316	286	602	316	286	...	...	...	...	...	...
15—20	451	209	242	349	189	160	94	18	76	8	2	6
20—30	811	369	442	292	205	87	470	148	322	49	16	33
30—40	547	253	294	77	53	24	403	180	223	67	20	47
40—50	330	145	185	23	12	11	233	103	130	74	30	44
50—60	192	95	97	16	9	7	126	73	53	50	13	37
60 and over	126	46	80	3	2	1	36	27	9	87	17	70
Christian ...	*35,442*	*17,624*	*17,818*	*20,161*	*10,513*	*9,648*	*12,579*	*6,256*	*6,323*	*2,702*	*855*	*1,847*
0	767	380	387	767	380	387	...	...	...	...	...	...
1—5	3,506	1,765	1,741	3,506	1,765	1,741	...	...	...	...	...	...
5—10	4,720	2,339	2,381	4,720	2,339	2,381	...	...	...	...	...	...
10—15	4,516	2,347	2,169	4,416	2,347	2,069	100	...	100	...	...	...
15—20	3,712	1,636	2,076	3,246	1,579	1,667	453	57	396	13	...	13
20—30	6,306	2,766	3,540	2,562	1,569	993	3,503	1,138	2,365	241	59	182
30—40	5,099	2,705	2,394	580	372	208	3,990	2,124	1,866	529	209	320
40—50	3,316	1,769	1,547	148	84	64	2,530	1,501	1,029	638	184	454
50—60	2,147	1,102	1,045	150	55	95	1,318	866	452	679	181	498
60 and over	1,353	815	538	66	23	43	685	570	115	602	222	380
Others (all ages) ...	*24*	*16*	*8*	*11*	*8*	*3*	*12*	*7*	*5*	*1*	*1*	...
SALWEEN.												
All Religions ...	*50,379*	*26,811*	*23,568*	*29,383*	*16,479*	*12,904*	*16,028*	*8,244*	*7,784*	*4,968*	*2,088*	*2,880*
0	1,425	746	679	1,425	746	679	...	...	...	...	...	...
1—5	5,688	2,845	2,843	5,688	2,845	2,843	...	...	...	...	...	...
5—10	6,513	3,515	2,998	6,513	3,515	2,998	...	...	...	...	...	...
10—15	5,149	2,797	2,352	5,128	2,797	2,331	21	...	21	...	...	...
15—20	5,106	2,497	2,609	4,373	2,417	1,956	693	76	617	40	4	36
20—30	9,529	4,652	4,877	4,352	2,873	1,479	4,758	1,624	3,134	419	155	264
30—40	7,428	4,379	3,049	1,172	876	296	5,197	2,959	2,238	1,059	544	515
40—50	4,865	2,790	2,075	396	237	159	3,113	1,972	1,141	1,356	581	775
50—60	2,810	1,519	1,291	191	99	92	1,526	1,054	472	1,093	366	727
60 and over	1,866	1,071	795	145	74	71	720	559	161	1,001	438	563
Buddhist ...	*26,327*	*14,413*	*11,914*	*14,640*	*8,542*	*6,098*	*9,044*	*4,596*	*4,448*	*2,643*	*1,275*	*1,368*
0	880	465	415	880	465	415	...	...	...	...	...	...
1—5	2,962	1,485	1,477	2,962	1,485	1,477	...	...	...	...	...	...
5—10	3,413	1,819	1,594	3,413	1,819	1,594	...	...	...	...	...	...
10—15	2,770	1,536	1,234	2,754	1,536	1,218	16	...	16	...	...	...
15—20	2,723	1,355	1,368	2,201	1,291	910	488	60	428	34	4	30
20—30	4,800	2,412	2,388	1,729	1,345	384	2,800	954	1,846	271	113	158
30—40	3,847	2,362	1,485	428	379	49	2,808	1,603	1,205	611	380	231
40—50	2,567	1,577	990	157	132	25	1,696	1,093	603	714	352	362
50—60	1,407	819	588	64	50	14	833	569	264	510	200	310
60 and over	958	583	375	52	40	12	403	317	86	503	226	277
Animist ...	*22,407*	*11,200*	*11,207*	*13,851*	*7,273*	*6,578*	*6,340*	*3,180*	*3,160*	*2,216*	*742*	*1,474*
0	516	265	251	516	265	251	...	...	...	...	...	...
1—5	2,596	1,301	1,295	2,596	1,301	1,295	...	...	...	...	...	...
5—10	2,967	1,615	1,352	2,967	1,615	1,352	...	...	...	...	...	...
10—15	2,264	1,198	1,066	2,259	1,198	1,061	5	...	5	...	...	...
15—20	2,256	1,068	1,188	2,075	1,057	1,018	175	11	164	6	...	6
20—30	4,271	1,886	2,385	2,375	1,295	1,080	1,760	554	1,206	136	37	99
30—40	3,226	1,718	1,508	646	400	246	2,160	1,171	989	420	147	273
40—50	2,129	1,067	1,062	213	79	134	1,301	779	522	615	209	406
50—60	1,324	635	689	118	40	78	642	440	202	564	155	409
60 and over	858	447	411	86	28	58	297	225	72	475	194	281
Hindu (all ages) ...	*355*	*307*	*48*	*197*	*181*	*16*	*142*	*112*	*30*	*16*	*14*	*2*
Mahomedan (all ages)	*532*	*449*	*83*	*225*	*191*	*34*	*266*	*224*	*42*	*41*	*34*	*7*
Christian (all ages)	*758*	*442*	*316*	*470*	*287*	*183*	*236*	*132*	*104*	*52*	*23*	*29*

IMPERIAL TABLE VIIB.—*Age, Sex, and Civil Condition by Religion.*

DISTRICT, RELIGION, AND AGE.	POPULATION.			UNMARRIED.			MARRIED.			WIDOWED.		
	Persons.	Males.	Females.	Persons.	Males.	Females.	Persons.	Males.	Females.	Persons.	Males.	Females.
1	2	3	4	5	6	7	8	9	10	11	12	13
THATÔN.												
All Religions ...	*471,100*	*245,909*	*225,191*	*278,888*	*150,727*	*127,656*	*161,240*	*82,275*	*78,965*	*31,477*	*12,907*	*18,570*
0	13,218	6,450	6,768	13,218	6,450	6,768	...	...	...	...	...	...
1—5	55,928	27,759	28,169	55,928	27,759	28,169	...	...	...	...	...	...
5—10	61,354	31,643	29,711	61,354	31,643	29,711	...	...	...	...	...	...
10—15	56,243	29,386	26,857	56,193	29,382	26,811	50	4	46	...	...	...
15—20	48,789	23,801	24,988	43,378	22,967	20,411	5,105	773	4,332	306	61	245
20—30	80,568	40,006	40,562	32,672	21,339	11,333	44,756	17,527	27,229	3,140	1,140	2,000
30—40	64,023	35,907	28,116	8,985	6,580	2,405	50,089	27,054	23,035	4,949	2,273	2,676
40—50	42,171	23,628	18,543	3,533	2,511	1,022	32,305	18,408	13,897	6,333	2,709	3,624
50—60	25,507	13,536	11,971	1,657	1,129	528	17,227	10,002	7,225	6,623	2,405	4,218
60 and over	23,299	13,793	9,506	1,465	967	498	11,708	8,507	3,201	10,126	4,319	5,807
Buddhist ...	*430,829*	*218,580*	*211,749*	*255,658*	*134,919*	*120,739*	*146,171*	*72,752*	*73,419*	*28,500*	*10,909*	*17,591*
0	12,321	6,020	6,301	12,321	6,020	6,301	...	...	...	...	...	...
1—5	52,401	25,938	26,463	52,401	25,938	26,463	...	...	...	...	...	...
5—10	57,182	29,509	27,673	57,182	29,509	27,673	...	...	...	...	...	...
10—15	52,722	27,297	25,425	52,711	27,297	25,414	11	...	11	...	...	...
15—20	45,569	21,788	23,781	40,816	21,097	19,719	4,486	639	3,847	267	52	215
20—30	71,673	33,878	37,795	28,451	17,521	10,930	40,419	15,426	24,993	2,803	931	1,872
30—40	56,042	29,766	26,276	6,565	4,269	2,296	45,120	23,670	21,450	4,357	1,827	2,530
40—50	37,831	20,250	17,581	2,700	1,718	982	29,493	16,321	13,172	5,638	2,211	3,427
50—60	23,236	11,879	11,357	1,292	801	491	15,878	8,997	6,881	6,066	2,081	3,985
60 and over	21,352	12,255	9,097	1,219	749	470	10,764	7,699	3,065	9,369	3,807	5,562
Animist (all ages) ...	*2,308*	*1,616*	*688*	*1,183*	*817*	*366*	*936*	*680*	*256*	*184*	*118*	*66*
Hindu ...	*21,112*	*14,794*	*6,318*	*11,386*	*8,471*	*2,915*	*7,989*	*5,116*	*2,873*	*1,787*	*1,207*	*580*
0	401	194	207	401	194	207	...	...	...	...	...	...
1—5	1,622	852	770	1,622	852	770	...	...	...	...	...	...
5—10	1,985	1,016	969	1,985	1,016	969	...	...	...	...	...	...
10—15	1,606	1,007	599	1,571	1,007	564	35	...	35	...	...	...
15—20	1,571	1,102	469	1,189	999	190	362	98	264	20	5	15
20—30	4,776	3,435	1,341	2,315	2,197	118	2,260	1,114	1,146	201	124	77
30—40	4,500	3,529	971	1,413	1,372	41	2,732	1,888	844	355	269	86
40—50	2,453	1,966	487	515	497	18	1,519	1,155	364	419	314	105
50—60	1,208	903	305	225	208	17	640	480	160	343	215	128
60 and over	990	790	200	150	129	21	441	381	60	399	280	119
Hindus born in Burma	*7,921*	*4,196*	*3,725*	*5,728*	*3,296*	*2,432*	*1,895*	*755*	*1,140*	*298*	*145*	*153*
0	361	171	190	361	171	190	...	...	...	...	...	...
1—5	1,415	734	681	1,415	734	681	...	...	...	...	...	...
5—10	1,658	799	859	1,658	799	859	...	...	...	...	...	...
10—15	1,068	597	471	1,068	597	471	...	...	...	...	...	...
15—20	783	423	360	538	392	146	228	29	199	17	2	15
20—30	1,265	640	625	427	370	57	769	241	528	69	29	40
30—40	772	456	316	156	139	17	553	286	267	63	31	32
40—50	326	201	125	57	53	4	207	113	94	62	35	27
50—60	154	95	59	24	21	3	85	52	33	45	22	23
60 and over	119	80	39	24	20	4	53	34	19	42	26	16
Mahomedan ...	*13,405*	*8,912*	*4,493*	*7,804*	*5,321*	*2,483*	*4,745*	*3,008*	*1,737*	*856*	*583*	*273*
0	320	155	165	320	155	165	...	...	...	...	...	...
1—5	1,270	651	619	1,270	651	619	...	...	...	...	...	...
5—10	1,468	751	717	1,468	751	717	...	...	...	...	...	...
10—15	1,193	687	506	1,189	683	506	4	4	...	...	...	...
15—20	1,128	672	456	902	640	262	211	28	183	15	4	11
20—30	3,117	2,151	966	1,434	1,285	149	1,571	792	779	112	74	38
30—40	2,465	1,930	535	801	762	39	1,487	1,024	463	177	144	33
40—50	1,176	929	247	239	225	14	751	572	179	186	132	54
50—60	638	470	168	110	100	10	392	297	95	136	73	63
60 and over	630	516	114	71	69	2	329	291	38	230	156	74
Mahomedans born in Burma.	*8,201*	*3,997*	*4,204*	*5,393*	*2,995*	*2,408*	*2,447*	*882*	*1,565*	*356*	*120*	*236*
0	315	151	164	315	151	164	...	...	...	...	...	...
1—5	1,235	631	604	1,235	631	604	...	...	...	...	...	...
5—10	1,413	712	701	1,413	712	701	...	...	...	...	...	...
10—15	1,044	559	485	1,040	555	485	4	4	...	...	...	...
15—20	797	370	427	616	364	252	171	6	165	10	...	10
20—30	1,495	612	883	472	331	141	972	267	705	51	14	37
30—40	978	507	471	228	195	33	693	284	409	57	28	29
40—50	463	233	230	47	34	13	336	167	169	80	32	48
50—60	257	110	147	21	13	8	166	81	85	70	16	54
60 and over	204	112	92	11	9	2	105	73	32	88	30	58

IMPERIAL TABLE VIIB.—*Age, Sex, and Civil Condition by Religion.*

District, Religion, and Age.	Population. Persons.	Population. Males.	Population. Females.	Unmarried. Persons.	Unmarried. Males.	Unmarried. Females.	Married. Persons.	Married. Males.	Married. Females.	Widowed. Persons.	Widowed. Males.	Widowed. Females.
1	2	3	4	5	6	7	8	9	10	11	12	13
THATÔN—*concluded.*												
Christian ...	***3,811***	***1,920***	***1,891***	***2,284***	***1,152***	***1,132***	***1,338***	***687***	***651***	***189***	***81***	***108***
0	120	52	68	120	52	68	...	...	...	...	...	...
1—5	426	204	222	426	204	222	...	...	...	...	...	...
5—10	503	243	260	503	243	260	...	...	...	...	...	...
10—15	503	268	235	503	268	235	...	...	...	...	...	...
15—20	360	139	221	331	135	196	26	4	22	3	...	3
20—30	613	268	345	291	178	113	314	89	225	8	1	7
30—40	541	312	229	81	55	26	431	245	186	29	12	17
40—50	353	211	142	15	13	2	293	172	121	45	26	19
50—60	226	120	106	8	2	6	174	105	69	44	13	31
60 and over	166	103	63	6	2	4	100	72	28	60	29	31
Others (all ages) ...	***140***	***88***	***52***	***68***	***47***	***21***	***61***	***32***	***29***	***11***	***9***	***2***
AMHERST.												
All Religions ...	***417,910***	***223,348***	***194,562***	***242,592***	***132,692***	***109,900***	***149,800***	***80,262***	***69,538***	***25,518***	***10,394***	***15,124***
0	11,356	5,667	5,689	11,356	5,667	5,689	...	...	...	...	...	...
1—5	48,130	24,311	23,819	48,130	24,311	23,819	...	...	...	...	...	...
5—10	56,970	28,827	28,143	56,970	28,827	28,143	...	...	...	...	...	...
10—15	49,213	25,614	23,599	49,186	25,609	23,577	26	4	22	1	1	...
15—20	43,481	21,901	21,580	37,764	20,688	17,076	5,399	1,161	4,238	318	52	266
20—30	72,821	38,447	34,374	26,409	18,265	8,144	43,654	19,204	24,450	2,758	978	1,780
30—40	55,615	32,694	22,921	7,317	5,614	1,703	44,347	25,201	19,146	3,951	1,879	2,072
40—50	37,236	21,502	15,734	2,769	1,950	819	29,781	17,467	12,314	4,686	2,085	2,601
50—60	21,701	11,887	9,814	1,320	880	440	15,472	9,228	6,244	4,909	1,779	3,130
60 and over	21,387	12,498	8,889	1,371	881	490	11,121	7,997	3,124	8,895	3,620	5,275
Buddhist ...	***355,175***	***181,489***	***173,686***	***210,652***	***111,674***	***98,978***	***123,088***	***61,648***	***61,440***	***21,435***	***8,167***	***13,268***
0	10,185	5,048	5,137	10,185	5,048	5,137	...	...	...	...	...	...
1—5	42,975	21,537	21,438	42,975	21,537	21,438	...	...	...	...	...	...
5—10	50,484	25,537	24,947	50,484	25,537	24,947	...	...	...	...	...	...
10—15	43,442	22,214	21,228	43,432	22,209	21,223	9	4	5	1	1	...
15—20	37,957	18,498	19,459	33,427	17,644	15,783	4,250	811	3,439	280	43	237
20—30	58,953	28,714	30,239	20,926	13,482	7,444	35,706	14,469	21,237	2,321	763	1,558
30—40	43,655	23,526	20,129	5,119	3,627	1,492	35,391	18,519	16,872	3,145	1,380	1,765
40—50	30,790	16,607	14,183	1,966	1,269	697	24,961	13,716	11,245	3,863	1,622	2,241
50—60	18,440	9,501	8,939	1,017	629	388	13,276	7,480	5,796	4,147	1,392	2,755
60 and over	18,294	10,307	7,987	1,121	692	429	9,495	6,649	2,846	7,678	2,966	4,712
Animist ...	***3,442***	***2,446***	***996***	***1,836***	***1,279***	***557***	***1,371***	***1,004***	***367***	***235***	***163***	***72***
0	78	43	35	78	43	35	...	...	...	...	...	...
1—5	309	183	126	309	183	126	...	.	...	...	...	...
5—10	386	229	157	386	229	157	...	...	...	...	...	...
10—15	305	194	111	305	194	111	...	...	...	...	...	...
15—20	258	146	112	229	141	88	27	5	22	2	...	2
20—30	519	374	145	248	220	28	257	144	113	14	10	4
30—40	622	485	137	151	147	4	436	313	123	35	25	10
40—50	476	383	93	80	74	6	352	283	69	44	26	18
50—60	267	214	53	29	27	2	174	142	32	64	45	19
60 and over	222	195	27	21	21	...	125	117	8	76	57	19
Hindu ...	***25,415***	***19,468***	***5,947***	***10,760***	***8,333***	***2,427***	***12,838***	***9,960***	***2,878***	***1,822***	***1,175***	***647***
0	296	160	136	296	160	136	...	...	...	...	...	...
1—5	1,287	683	604	1,287	683	604	...	...	...	...	...	...
5—10	1,713	904	809	1,713	904	809	...	...	...	...	...	...
10—15	1,489	1,029	460	1,476	1,029	447	13	...	13	...	...	...
15—20	1,976	1,464	512	1,464	1,244	220	501	217	284	11	3	8
20—30	6,647	5,285	1,362	2,596	2,480	116	3,859	2,688	1,171	192	117	75
30—40	6,188	5,238	950	1,230	1,191	39	4,565	3,758	807	393	289	104
40—50	3,050	2,551	499	431	410	21	2,212	1,887	325	407	254	153
50—60	1,507	1,230	277	155	144	11	1,000	859	141	352	227	125
60 and over	1,262	924	338	112	88	24	683	551	132	467	285	182

IMPERIAL TABLE VIIB.—*Age, Sex, and Civil Condition by Religion.*

DISTRICT, RELIGION, AND AGE.		POPULATION.			UNMARRIED.			MARRIED.			WIDOWED.		
		Persons.	Males.	Females.	Persons.	Males.	Females.	Persons.	Males.	Females.	Persons.	Males.	Females.
1		2	3	4	5	6	7	8	9	10	11	12	13
AMHERST—*concluded.*	***Hindus born in Burma***	*8,083*	*4,466*	*3,617*	*5,042*	*3,033*	*2,009*	*2,567*	*1,222*	*1,345*	*474*	*211*	*263*
	0	266	146	120	266	146	120	...	...	...	...	...	...
	1—5	1,136	600	536	1,136	600	536	...	...	...	...	...	...
	5—10	1,397	706	691	1,397	706	691	...	...	...	...	...	...
	10—15	970	582	388	959	582	377	11	...	11	...	...	...
	15—20	820	448	372	602	407	195	210	40	170	8	1	7
	20—30	1,462	764	698	452	396	56	938	344	594	72	24	48
	30—40	1,046	609	437	138	123	15	802	439	363	106	47	59
	40—50	509	325	184	50	44	6	348	232	116	111	49	62
	50—60	261	167	94	26	21	5	144	99	45	91	47	44
	60 and over	216	119	97	16	8	8	114	68	46	86	43	43
	Mahomedan ...	*26,678*	*16,261*	*10,417*	*14,842*	*9,077*	*5,765*	*10,232*	*6,423*	*3,809*	*1,604*	*761*	*843*
	0	671	345	326	671	345	326	...	...	...	...	...	...
	1—5	2,864	1,559	1,305	2,864	1,559	1,305	...	...	...	...	...	...
	5—10	3,384	1,647	1,737	3,384	1,647	1,737	...	...	...	...	...	...
	10—15	2,929	1,648	1,281	2,925	1,648	1,277	4	...	4	...	...	...
	15—20	2,496	1,397	1,099	1,921	1,280	641	550	111	439	25	6	19
	20—30	5,479	3,465	2,014	2,036	1,738	298	3,246	1,650	1,596	197	77	120
	30—40	4,181	2,934	1,247	648	553	95	3,226	2,218	1,008	307	163	144
	40—50	2,318	1,642	676	214	170	44	1,797	1,310	487	307	162	145
	50—60	1,103	730	373	86	65	21	769	576	193	248	89	159
	60 and over	1,253	894	359	93	72	21	640	558	82	520	264	256
	Mahomedans born in Burma.	*19,915*	*9,995*	*9,920*	*12,477*	*6,819*	*5,658*	*6,317*	*2,826*	*3,491*	*1,121*	*350*	*771*
	0	665	341	324	665	341	324	...	...	...	...	...	...
	1—5	2,822	1,527	1,295	2,822	1,527	1,295	...	...	...	...	...	...
	5—10	3,308	1,608	1,700	3,308	1,608	1,700	...	...	...	...	...	...
	10—15	2,751	1,492	1,259	2,751	1,492	1,259	...	...	...	...	...	...
	15—20	2,024	952	1,072	1,519	888	631	482	60	422	23	4	19
	20—30	3,359	1,464	1,895	958	676	282	2,234	740	1,494	167	48	119
	30—40	2,317	1,188	1,129	270	186	84	1,827	917	910	220	85	135
	40—50	1,367	742	625	92	48	44	1,065	620	445	210	74	136
	50—60	635	308	327	45	24	21	405	245	160	185	39	146
	60 and over	667	373	294	47	29	18	304	244	60	316	100	216
	Christian ...	*7,074*	*3,596*	*3,478*	*4,444*	*2,289*	*2,155*	*2,212*	*1,131*	*1,081*	*418*	*126*	*292*
	0	123	69	54	123	69	54	...	...	...	...	...	...
	1—5	682	340	342	682	340	342	...	...	...	...	...	...
	5—10	988	501	487	988	501	487	...	...	...	...	...	...
	10—15	1,043	528	515	1,043	528	515	...	...	...	...	...	...
	15—20	783	390	393	714	373	341	69	17	52	...	...	...
	20—30	1,192	588	604	599	341	258	559	236	323	34	11	23
	30—40	942	489	453	164	91	73	707	376	331	71	22	49
	40—50	590	308	282	76	25	51	450	263	187	64	20	44
	50—60	378	206	172	31	13	18	249	167	82	98	26	72
	60 and over	353	177	176	24	8	16	178	122	56	151	47	104
	Others (all ages) ...	*126*	*88*	*38*	*58*	*40*	*18*	*64*	*46*	*18*	*4*	*2*	*2*
TAVOY.	***All Religions*** ...	*156,786*	*80,994*	*75,792*	*90,990*	*49,385*	*41,605*	*55,168*	*27,940*	*27,228*	*10,628*	*3,669*	*6,959*
	0	3,842	1,898	1,944	3,842	1,898	1,944	...	...	...	...	...	...
	1—5	16,312	8,093	8,219	16,312	8,093	8,219	...	...	...	...	...	...
	5—10	21,466	10,839	10,627	21,466	10,839	10,627	...	...	...	...	...	...
	10—15	19,773	10,347	9,426	19,768	10,345	9,423	5	2	3	...	...	...
	15—20	15,511	7,733	7,778	14,022	7,554	6,468	1,393	174	1,219	96	5	91
	20—30	26,412	13,388	13,024	10,817	7,309	3,508	14,583	5,805	8,778	1,012	274	738
	30—40	21,063	11,787	9,276	2,872	2,113	759	16,728	9,038	7,690	1,463	636	827
	40—50	14,290	7,688	6,602	1,008	692	316	11,431	6,330	5,101	1,851	666	1,185
	50—60	9,026	4,413	4,613	460	288	172	6,297	3,435	2,862	2,269	690	1,579
	60 and over	9,091	4,808	4,283	423	254	169	4,731	3,156	1,575	3,937	1,398	2,539
	Buddhist ...	*145,146*	*72,612*	*72,534*	*84,524*	*44,624*	*39,900*	*50,591*	*24,675*	*25,916*	*10,031*	*3,313*	*6,718*
	0	3,637	1,790	1,847	3,637	1,790	1,847	...	...	...	...	...	...
	1—5	15,610	7,733	7,877	15,610	7,733	7,877	...	...	...	...	...	...
	5—10	20,585	10,411	10,174	20,585	10,411	10,174	...	...	...	...	...	...
	10—15	18,972	9,929	9,043	18,968	9,928	9,040	4	1	3	...	...	...
	15—20	14,679	7,229	7,450	13,337	7,099	6,238	1,247	125	1,122	95	5	90
	20—30	23,311	10,980	12,331	9,119	5,756	3,363	13,250	4,991	8,259	942	233	709
	30—40	18,198	9,379	8,819	1,794	1,072	722	15,077	7,776	7,301	1,327	531	796
	40—50	12,964	6,610	6,354	712	407	305	10,535	5,631	4,904	1,717	572	1,145
	50—60	8,493	4,018	4,475	370	202	168	5,953	3,170	2,783	2,170	646	1,524
	60 and over	8,697	4,533	4,164	392	226	166	4,525	2,981	1,544	3,780	1,326	2,454

IMPERIAL TABLE VIIB.—*Age, Sex, and Civil Condition by Religion.*

DISTRICT, RELIGION, AND AGE.	POPULATION.			UNMARRIED.			MARRIED.			WIDOWED.		
	Persons.	Males.	Females.	Persons.	Males.	Females.	Persons.	Males.	Females.	Persons.	Males.	Females.
1	2	3	4	5	6	7	8	9	10	11	12	13
TAVOY—concluded.												
Animist ...	*2,778*	*2,194*	*579*	*1,671*	*1,375*	*296*	*945*	*712*	*233*	*157*	*107*	*50*
0	41	22	19	41	22	19	...	...	...	...	...	...
1—5	144	80	64	144	80	64	...	...	...	...	...	...
5—10	157	78	79	157	78	79	...	...	...	...	...	...
10—15	133	58	75	133	58	75	...	...	...	...	...	...
15—20	114	58	56	95	51	44	18	7	11	1	...	1
20—30	607	522	85	404	393	11	192	123	69	11	6	5
30—40	911	818	93	501	498	3	371	286	85	39	34	5
40—50	419	363	56	145	144	1	239	190	49	35	29	6
50—60	148	121	27	37	37	...	78	64	14	33	20	13
60 and over	99	74	25	14	14	...	47	42	5	38	18	20
Hindu ...	*3,319*	*2,953*	*866*	*1,741*	*1,585*	*156*	*1,455*	*1,259*	*196*	*123*	*109*	*14*
0	33	18	15	33	18	15	...	...	...	...	...	...
1—5	87	45	42	87	45	42	...	...	...	...	...	...
5—10	86	34	52	86	34	52	...	...	...	...	...	...
10—15	104	84	20	104	84	20	...	...	...	...	...	...
15—20	217	185	32	172	163	9	45	22	23	...	...	...
20—30	1,272	1,156	116	758	748	10	496	391	105	18	17	1
30—40	960	913	47	374	367	7	544	504	40	42	42	...
40—50	356	332	24	89	88	1	238	217	21	29	27	2
50—60	124	114	10	30	30	...	83	79	4	11	5	6
60 and over	80	72	8	8	8	...	49	46	3	23	18	5
Hindus born in Burma	*284*	*164*	*120*	*203*	*116*	*87*	*75*	*44*	*31*	*6*	*4*	*2*
0	27	13	14	27	13	14	...	...	...	...	...	...
1—5	59	35	24	59	35	24	...	...	...	...	...	...
5—10	48	21	27	48	21	27	...	...	...	...	...	...
10—15	38	24	14	38	24	14	...	...	...	...	...	...
15—20	11	6	5	9	6	3	2	...	2	...	...	...
20—30	45	22	23	16	13	3	27	8	19	2	1	1
30—40	33	26	7	6	4	2	26	21	5	1	1	...
40—50	13	9	4	...	...	...	12	8	4	1	1	...
50—60	7	6	1	...	...	...	7	6	1	...	...	...
60 and over	3	2	1	...	...	...	1	1	...	2	1	1
Mahomedan ...	*2,878*	*1,844*	*1,029*	*1,581*	*1,000*	*581*	*1,171*	*754*	*417*	*171*	*90*	*81*
0	61	36	25	61	36	25	...	...	...	...	...	...
1—5	238	123	115	238	123	115	...	...	...	...	...	...
5—10	310	155	155	310	155	155	...	...	...	...	...	...
10—15	211	105	106	211	105	106	...	...	...	...	...	...
15—20	234	139	95	181	124	57	53	15	38	...	...	...
20—30	725	478	247	316	264	52	386	200	186	23	14	9
30—40	561	431	130	149	135	14	381	275	106	31	21	10
40—50	278	207	71	44	39	5	197	145	52	37	23	14
50—60	125	82	43	13	13	...	84	58	26	28	11	17
60 and over	130	88	42	8	6	2	70	61	9	52	21	31
Mahomedans born in Burma.	*1,878*	*888*	*990*	*1,092*	*572*	*520*	*667*	*278*	*389*	*119*	*38*	*81*
0	61	36	25	61	36	25	...	...	...	...	...	...
1—5	230	117	113	230	117	113	...	...	...	...	...	...
5—10	300	149	151	300	149	151	...	...	...	...	...	...
10—15	197	94	103	197	94	103	...	...	...	...	...	...
15—20	176	81	95	135	78	57	41	3	38	...	...	...
20—30	371	141	230	124	72	52	234	65	169	13	4	9
30—40	249	130	119	34	22	12	196	99	97	19	9	10
40—50	134	64	70	6	1	5	105	54	51	23	9	14
50—60	76	34	42	1	1	...	52	27	25	23	6	17
60 and over	84	42	42	4	2	2	39	30	9	41	10	31
Christian ...	*2,645*	*1,371*	*1,274*	*1,508*	*791*	*717*	*993*	*532*	*461*	*144*	*48*	*96*
0	70	32	38	70	32	38	...	...	...	...	...	...
1—5	228	108	120	228	108	120	...	...	...	...	...	...
5—10	325	160	165	325	160	165	...	...	...	...	...	...
10—15	351	170	181	350	169	181	1	1	...	...	...	...
15—20	266	121	145	236	116	120	30	5	25	...	...	...
20—30	491	249	242	218	146	72	256	100	156	17	3	14
30—40	427	241	186	53	41	12	351	193	158	23	7	16
40—50	268	172	96	17	13	4	218	144	74	33	15	18
50—60	135	78	57	10	6	4	98	64	34	27	8	19
60 and over	84	40	44	1	...	1	39	25	14	44	15	29
Others (all ages) ...	*30*	*20*	*10*	*15*	*10*	*5*	*13*	*8*	*5*	*2*	*2*	...

Imperial Table VIIb.—*Age, Sex, and Civil Condition by Religion.*

District, Religion, and Age.	Population. Persons.	Population. Males.	Population. Females.	Unmarried. Persons.	Unmarried. Males.	Unmarried. Females.	Married. Persons.	Married. Males.	Married. Females.	Widowed. Persons.	Widowed. Males.	Widowed. Females.
1	2	3	4	5	6	7	8	9	10	11	12	13
MERGUI												
All Religions ...	*185,465*	*72,878*	*62,687*	*77,619*	*43,182*	*84,437*	*60,838*	*26,919*	*23,414*	*7,518*	*2,777*	*4,786*
0	2,669	1,320	1,349	2,669	1,320	1,349	...	...	...	...	...	...
1—5	13,846	6,880	6,966	13,846	6,880	6,966	...	...	...	...	...	...
5—10	18,973	9,448	9,525	18,968	9,443	9,525	5	5		...	...	...
10—15	16,049	8,464	7,585	16,014	8,455	7,559	34	9	25	1	...	1
15—20	13,471	6,985	6,486	11,761	6,589	5,172	1,633	388	1,245	77	8	69
20—30	25,694	13,826	11,868	10,067	7,222	2,845	14,857	6,328	8,529	770	276	494
30—40	18,841	11,352	7,489	2,597	2,122	475	15,100	8,721	6,379	1,144	509	635
40—50	11,865	7,115	4,750	899	679	220	9,539	5,884	3,655	1,427	552	875
50—60	7,719	3,945	3,774	379	247	132	5,758	3,190	2,568	1,582	508	1,074
60 and over	6,338	3,543	2,795	419	225	194	3,407	2,394	1,013	2,512	924	1,588
Buddhist ...	*104,617*	*53,200*	*51,417*	*60,836*	*32,833*	*28,508*	*87,908*	*18,821*	*19,087*	*5,878*	*2,046*	*3,827*
0	2,179	1,077	1,102	2,179	1,077	1,102	...	...	...	...	...	...
1—5	11,206	5,566	5,640	11,206	5,566	5,640	...	...	...	...	...	...
5—10	15,687	7,693	7,994	15,682	7,688	7,994	5	5	...	...	...	...
10—15	12,982	6,659	6,323	12,951	6,650	6,301	30	9	21	1	...	1
15—20	10,506	5,190	5,316	9,293	4,977	4,316	1,148	209	939	65	4	61
20—30	18,681	9,159	9,522	7,147	4,839	2,308	10,934	4,133	6,801	600	187	413
30—40	13,312	7,205	6,107	1,316	929	387	11,137	5,913	5,224	859	363	496
40—50	8,851	5,016	3,835	485	309	176	7,290	4,315	2,975	1,076	392	684
50—60	6,118	2,911	3,207	246	136	110	4,632	2,389	2,243	1,240	386	854
60 and over	5,095	2,724	2,371	331	162	169	2,732	1,848	884	2,032	714	1,318
Animist ...	*6,426*	*4,258*	*2,168*	*3,415*	*2,331*	*1,084*	*2,615*	*1,695*	*920*	*896*	*282*	*164*
0	125	58	67	125	58	67	...	...	...	...	...	...
1—5	553	268	285	553	268	285	...	...	..	...	...	...
5—10	644	323	321	644	323	321	...	...	...	...	...	...
10—15	507	290	217	505	290	215	2	...	2	...	...	...
15—20	411	215	196	318	195	123	93	20	73	...	..	...
20—30	1,147	693	454	483	425	58	649	260	389	15	8	7
30—40	1,450	1,159	291	489	480	9	888	640	248	73	39	34
40—50	853	664	189	199	196	3	561	413	148	93	55	38
50—60	423	332	91	63	62	1	266	219	47	94	51	43
60 and over	513	256	57	36	34	2	156	143	13	121	79	42
Hindu ...	*6,618*	*5,842*	*771*	*8,209*	*2,937*	*272*	*8,213*	*2,770*	*443*	*191*	*135*	*56*
0	57	32	25	57	32	25	...	...	...	...	...	...
1—5	178	86	92	178	86	92	...	...	...	...	...	...
5—10	219	159	60	219	159	60	...	...	..	...	...	...
10—15	431	386	45	429	386	43	2	...	2	...	...	...
15—20	773	703	70	595	576	19	175	124	51	3	3	...
20—30	2,416	2,160	256	1,031	1,014	17	1,342	1,108	234	43	38	5
30—40	1,680	1,548	132	530	521	9	1,095	984	111	55	43	12
40—50	575	522	53	120	116	4	411	378	33	44	28	16
50—60	203	179	24	33	32	1	145	133	12	25	14	11
60 and over	81	67	14	17	15	2	43	43	...	21	9	12
Hindus born in Burma	*296*	*166*	*180*	*248*	*127*	*116*	*49*	*86*	*13*	*4*	*8*	*1*
0	40	18	22	40	18	22	...	...	...	...	...	...
1—5	85	29	56	85	29	56	...	...	...	...	...	...
5—10	43	23	20	43	23	20	...	...	...	...	...	...
10—15	27	15	12	27	15	12	...	...	...	...	...	...
15—20	10	4	6	8	4	4	2	...	2	...	...	...
20—30	51	39	12	24	22	2	26	17	9	1	...	1
30—40	28	26	2	13	13	...	14	12	2	1	1	...
40—50	8	8	...	2	2	...	5	5	...	1	1	...
50—60	2	2	...	...	...	...	1	1	...	1	1	...
60 and over	2	2	...	1	1	...	1	1	...	...	...	...
Mahomedan ...	*11,645*	*6,270*	*5,875*	*6,589*	*8,600*	*2,989*	*4,897*	*2,429*	*1,968*	*709*	*241*	*468*
0	172	93	79	172	93	79	...	...	...	...	...	...
1—5	1,233	628	605	1,233	628	605	...	...	...	...	...	...
5—10	1,518	794	724	1,518	794	724	...	...	...	...	...	...
10—15	1,330	689	641	1,330	689	641	...	...	...	...	..	...
15—20	1,215	593	622	1,057	570	487	151	22	129	7	1	6
20—30	2,252	1,208	1,044	933	643	290	1,247	539	708	72	26	46
30—40	1,585	956	629	184	126	58	1,303	787	516	98	43	55
40—50	1,060	604	456	60	33	27	865	523	342	135	48	87
50—60	662	351	311	26	13	13	488	301	187	148	37	111
60 and over	618	354	264	26	11	15	343	257	86	249	86	163

Imperial Table VIIB.—*Age, Sex, and Civil Condition by Religion.*

District, Religion, and Age.	Population. Persons.	Population. Males.	Population. Females.	Unmarried. Persons.	Unmarried. Males.	Unmarried. Females.	Married. Persons.	Married. Males.	Married. Females.	Widowed. Persons.	Widowed. Males.	Widowed. Females.
1	2	3	4	5	6	7	8	9	10	11	12	13
MERGUI—concluded.												
Mahomedans born in Burma.	***10,086***	***5,057***	***5,029***	***6,082***	***3,208***	***2,874***	***3,424***	***1,679***	***1,745***	***580***	***170***	***410***
0	170	93	77	170	93	77	...	...	...	...	...	...
1—5	1,228	626	602	1,228	626	602	...	...	...	...	...	...
5—10	1,489	778	711	1,489	778	711	...	...	...	...	...	...
10—15	1,277	649	628	1,277	649	628	...	...	...	...	...	...
15—20	1,111	524	587	965	505	460	140	19	121	6	...	6
20—30	1,792	831	961	737	454	283	1,003	365	638	52	12	40
30—40	1,206	624	582	130	72	58	994	520	474	82	32	50
40—50	789	407	382	40	13	27	643	362	281	106	32	74
50—60	533	262	271	20	7	13	391	229	162	122	26	96
60 and over	491	263	228	26	11	15	253	184	69	212	68	144
Christian ...	***6,153***	***3,297***	***2,856***	***3,612***	***1,973***	***1,639***	***2,197***	***1,201***	***996***	***344***	***123***	***221***
0	136	60	76	136	60	76	...	...	...	...	...	...
1—5	676	332	344	676	332	344	...	...	...	...	...	...
5—10	905	479	426	905	479	426	...	...	...	...	...	...
10—15	799	440	359	799	440	359	...	...	...	...	...	...
15—20	564	282	282	496	269	227	66	13	53	2	...	2
20—30	1,195	603	592	470	298	172	685	288	397	40	17	23
30—40	811	481	330	75	63	12	677	397	280	59	21	38
40—50	523	306	217	35	25	10	409	252	157	79	29	50
50—60	313	172	141	11	4	7	227	148	79	75	20	55
60 and over	231	142	89	9	3	6	133	103	30	89	36	53
Others (all ages) ...	***11***	***11***	...	***8***	***8***	...	***3***	***3***	...	...	...	...
THAYETMYO.												
All Religions ...	***255,406***	***125,283***	***130,123***	***133,252***	***68,380***	***64,872***	***99,282***	***49,824***	***49,458***	***22,872***	***7,079***	***15,793***
0	7,159	3,589	3,570	7,159	3,589	3,570	...	...	...	...	...	...
1—5	25,314	12,247	13,067	25,314	12,247	13,067	...	...	...	...	...	...
5—10	31,101	15,305	15,796	31,101	15,305	15,796	...	...	...	...	...	...
10—15	30,801	15,446	15,355	30,745	15,446	15,299	56	...	56	...	...	...
15—20	26,798	12,766	14,032	22,339	11,861	10,478	4,184	862	3,322	275	43	232
20—30	41,612	19,841	21,771	11,112	6,832	4,280	28,134	12,237	15,897	2,366	772	1,594
30—40	33,387	16,881	16,506	2,603	1,475	1,128	27,695	14,296	13,399	3,089	1,110	1,979
40—50	26,927	13,459	13,468	1,404	770	634	21,151	11,307	9,844	4,372	1,382	2,990
50—60	17,860	8,664	9,196	805	455	350	11,952	6,914	5,038	5,103	1,295	3,808
60 and over	14,447	7,085	7,362	670	400	270	6,110	4,208	1,902	7,667	2,477	5,190
Buddhist ...	***239,726***	***116,712***	***123,014***	***125,579***	***64,062***	***61,517***	***92,686***	***46,155***	***46,531***	***21,461***	***6,495***	***14,966***
0	6,821	3,408	3,413	6,821	3,408	3,413	...	...	...	...	...	...
1—5	23,864	11,562	12,302	23,864	11,562	12,302	...	...	...	...	...	...
5—10	29,358	14,425	14,933	29,358	14,425	14,933	...	...	...	...	...	...
10—15	29,153	14,577	14,576	29,102	14,577	14,525	51	...	51	...	...	...
15—20	25,299	12,005	13,294	21,144	11,170	9,974	3,901	797	3,104	254	38	216
20—30	38,702	18,208	20,494	10,270	6,180	4,090	26,231	11,338	14,893	2,201	690	1,511
30—40	30,923	15,371	15,552	2,305	1,227	1,078	25,747	13,157	12,590	2,871	987	1,884
40—50	25,203	12,455	12,748	1,312	703	609	19,778	10,482	9,296	4,113	1,270	2,843
50—60	16,788	8,088	8,700	760	427	333	11,250	6,463	4,787	4,778	1,198	3,580
60 and over	13,615	6,613	7,002	643	383	260	5,728	3,918	1,810	7,244	2,312	4,932
Animist ...	***11,269***	***5,725***	***5,544***	***5,485***	***2,907***	***2,578***	***4,764***	***2,441***	***2,323***	***1,020***	***377***	***643***
0	235	123	112	235	123	112	...	...	...	...	...	...
1—5	1,106	540	566	1,106	540	566	...	...	...	...	...	...
5—10	1,312	654	658	1,312	654	658	...	...	...	...	...	...
10—15	1,292	657	635	1,287	657	630	5	...	5	...	...	...
15—20	1,145	553	592	929	511	418	199	38	161	17	4	13
20—30	1,882	922	960	431	302	129	1,337	566	771	114	54	60
30—40	1,642	889	753	113	83	30	1,393	745	648	136	61	75
40—50	1,223	646	577	38	19	19	1,003	552	451	182	75	107
50—60	820	416	404	25	16	9	541	329	212	254	71	183
60 and over	612	325	287	9	2	7	286	211	75	317	112	205
Hindu (all ages) ...	***1,946***	***1,405***	***541***	***918***	***669***	***249***	***858***	***623***	***235***	***170***	***113***	***57***
Hindus born in Burma (all ages).	***667***	***365***	***302***	***471***	***261***	***210***	***162***	***91***	***71***	***34***	***13***	***21***
Mahomedan (all ages)	***1,994***	***1,177***	***817***	***1,004***	***595***	***409***	***807***	***506***	***301***	***183***	***76***	***107***
Mahomedans born in Burma (all ages).	***1,461***	***679***	***782***	***889***	***486***	***403***	***496***	***216***	***280***	***126***	***27***	***99***
Christian (all ages)	***465***	***261***	***204***	***263***	***146***	***117***	***164***	***97***	***67***	***38***	***18***	***20***
Others (all ages) ...	***6***	***3***	***3***	***3***	***1***	***2***	***3***	***2***	***1***	...	...	...

IMPERIAL TABLE VIIB.—*Age, Sex, and Civil Condition by Religion.*

District, Religion, and Age.	Population. Persons.	Population. Males.	Population. Females.	Unmarried. Persons.	Unmarried. Males.	Unmarried. Females.	Married. Persons.	Married. Males.	Married. Females.	Widowed. Persons.	Widowed. Males.	Widowed. Females.
1	2	3	4	5	6	7	8	9	10	11	12	13
PAKÔKKU.												
All Religions ...	*465,771*	*223,948*	*241,828*	*248,090*	*126,014*	*122,076*	*178,858*	*88,148*	*90,210*	*39,828*	*9,781*	*29,542*
0	16,030	7,786	8,244	16,030	7,786	8,244	...	...	...	...	...	...
1—5	48,769	23,705	25,064	48,769	23,705	25,064	...	...	...	...	...	...
5—10	59,838	29,967	29,871	59,828	29,967	29,861	10	...	10	...	...	...
10—15	52,744	26,854	25,890	52,685	26,853	25,832	54	1	53	5	...	5
15—20	46,986	21,592	25,394	38,680	19,834	18,846	7,739	1,695	6,044	567	63	504
20—30	74,650	35,238	39,412	20,488	12,095	8,393	50,567	22,156	28,411	3,595	987	2,608
30—40	57,106	28,182	28,924	4,882	2,636	2,246	47,525	24,193	23,332	4,699	1,353	3,346
40—50	45,270	21,617	23,653	2,659	1,311	1,348	36,234	18,810	17,424	6,377	1,496	4,881
50—60	31,993	15,111	16,882	1,824	891	933	22,092	12,402	9,690	8,077	1,818	6,259
60 and over	32,385	13,891	18,494	2,245	936	1,309	14,137	8,891	5,246	16,003	4,064	11,939
Buddhist ..	*460,158*	*220,495*	*239,663*	*245,448*	*124,825*	*121,128*	*175,863*	*86,566*	*89,297*	*38,847*	*9,604*	*29,248*
0	15,922	7,732	8,190	15,922	7,732	8,190	...	...	...	...	...	...
1—5	48,302	23,458	24,844	48,302	23,458	24,844	...	...	...	...	...	...
5—10	59,294	29,688	29,606	59,284	29,688	29,596	10	...	10	...	...	...
10—15	52,250	26,577	25,673	52,194	26,577	25,617	51	...	51	5	...	5
15—20	46,557	21,356	25,201	38,339	19,615	18,724	7,660	1,680	5,980	558	61	497
20—30	73,502	34,491	39,011	20,038	11,708	8,330	49,922	21,822	28,100	3,542	961	2,581
30—40	56,017	27,446	28,571	4,722	2,485	2,237	46,682	23,649	23,033	4,613	1,312	3,301
40—50	44,580	21,128	23,452	2,610	1,264	1,346	35,691	18,410	17,281	6,279	1,454	4,825
50—60	31,595	14,864	16,731	1,802	872	930	21,834	12,206	9,628	7,959	1,786	6,173
60 and over	32,139	13,755	18,384	2,235	926	1,309	14,013	8,799	5,214	15,891	4,030	11,861
Animist ..	*8,845*	*1,756*	*1,589*	*1,558*	*876*	*682*	*1,447*	*792*	*655*	*840*	*88*	*252*
Hindu (all ages) ...	*842*	*702*	*140*	*408*	*356*	*52*	*385*	*306*	*79*	*49*	*40*	*9*
Mahomedan (all ages)	*1,022*	*701*	*321*	*491*	*331*	*160*	*463*	*335*	*128*	*63*	*35*	*28*
Christian (all ages)	*308*	*211*	*97*	*147*	*96*	*51*	*142*	*105*	*37*	*19*	*10*	*9*
Others (all ages) ..	*96*	*78*	*18*	*88*	*80*	*8*	*53*	*44*	*9*	*5*	*4*	*1*
MINBU.												
All Religions ...	*274,802*	*134,495*	*139,807*	*141,266*	*73,066*	*68,200*	*107,085*	*53,778*	*53,307*	*25,951*	*7,651*	*18,300*
0	8,354	4,113	4,241	8,354	4,113	4,241	...	...	...	...	...	...
1—5	26,149	12,895	13,254	26,149	12,895	13,254	...	...	...	...	...	...
5—10	30,553	14,879	15,674	30,553	14,879	15,674	...	...	...	...	...	...
10—15	31,851	15,971	15,880	31,833	15,964	15,869	18	7	11	...	...	...
15—20	29,233	14,101	15,132	23,890	12,959	10,931	4,981	1,078	3,903	362	64	298
20—30	46,713	22,809	23,904	13,217	8,284	4,933	31,098	13,691	17,407	2,398	834	1,564
30—40	35,285	17,976	17,309	3,335	1,978	1,357	28,756	14,849	13,907	3,194	1,149	2,045
40—50	27,475	13,718	13,757	1,634	795	839	21,548	11,750	9,798	4,293	1,173	3,120
50—60	20,157	9,825	10,332	1,141	608	533	13,163	7,548	5,615	5,853	1,669	4,184
60 and over	18,532	8,208	10,324	1,160	591	569	7,521	4,855	2,666	9,851	2,762	7,089
Buddhist ...	*265,885*	*129,039*	*136,846*	*136,982*	*70,262*	*66,720*	*103,514*	*51,424*	*52,090*	*25,389*	*7,358*	*18,036*
0	8,143	3,999	4,144	8,143	3,999	4,144	...	...	...	...	...	...
1—5	25,379	12,483	12,896	25,379	12,483	12,896	...	...	...	...	...	...
5—10	29,731	14,468	15,263	29,731	14,468	15,263	...	...	...	...	...	...
10—15	31,086	15,543	15,543	31,070	15,536	15,534	16	7	9	...	...	...
15—20	28,489	13,671	14,818	23,313	12,575	10,738	4,821	1,033	3,788	355	63	292
20—30	44,881	21,488	23,393	12,525	7,647	4,878	30,013	13,049	16,964	2,343	792	1,551
30—40	33,735	16,822	16,913	3,031	1,691	1,340	27,617	14,057	13,560	3,087	1,074	2,013
40—50	26,521	13,045	13,476	1,535	705	830	20,812	11,221	9,591	4,174	1,119	3,055
50—60	19,710	9,519	10,191	1,109	578	531	12,861	7,321	5,540	5,740	1,620	4,120
60 and over	18,210	8,001	10,209	1,146	580	566	7,374	4,736	2,638	9,690	2,685	7,005
Animist ..	*4,860*	*2,620*	*2,240*	*2,552*	*1,440*	*1,112*	*1,981*	*1,072*	*909*	*827*	*108*	*219*
0	145	77	68	145	77	68	...	...	...	...	...	...
1—5	566	302	264	566	302	264	...	...	...	...	...	...
5—10	594	306	288	594	306	288	...	...	...	...	...	...
10—15	553	281	272	553	281	272	...	...	...	...	...	...
15—20	488	248	240	381	226	155	102	21	81	5	1	4
20—30	828	468	360	227	185	42	585	276	309	16	7	9
30—40	652	358	294	47	37	10	571	307	264	34	14	20
40—50	528	299	229	22	14	8	433	263	170	73	22	51
50—60	286	169	117	7	5	2	193	133	60	86	31	55
60 and over	220	112	108	10	7	3	97	72	25	113	33	80
Hindu (all ages) ..	*1,995*	*1,752*	*243*	*933*	*821*	*112*	*919*	*801*	*118*	*143*	*130*	*13*
Hindus born in Burma (all ages).	*270*	*161*	*109*	*213*	*129*	*84*	*51*	*23*	*28*	*6*	*4*	*2*
Mahomedan (all ages)	*1,223*	*842*	*381*	*629*	*417*	*212*	*523*	*382*	*141*	*71*	*48*	*23*
Mahomedans born in Burma (all ages)	*684*	*345*	*339*	*484*	*281*	*203*	*215*	*103*	*112*	*35*	*11*	*24*
Christian (all ages)	*174*	*118*	*56*	*91*	*64*	*27*	*70*	*45*	*25*	*13*	*9*	*4*
Others (all ages)	*165*	*124*	*41*	*79*	*62*	*17*	*78*	*54*	*24*	*8*	*8*	...

IMPERIAL TABLE VIIB.—*Age, Sex, and Civil Condition by Religion.*

District	Religion, and Age.	Population: Persons.	Population: Males.	Population: Females.	Unmarried: Persons.	Unmarried: Males.	Unmarried: Females.	Married: Persons.	Married: Males.	Married: Females.	Widowed: Persons.	Widowed: Males.	Widowed: Females.
1	1	2	3	4	5	6	7	8	9	10	11	12	13
MAGWE.	***All Religions*** ..	*428,252*	*211.686*	*211,566*	*238,617*	*122,747*	*110.870*	*159,874*	*80,889*	*79.486*	*29,761*	*8,550*	*21,211*
	0	12,219	6,118	6,101	12,219	6,118	6,101	...	...	...	...	...	...
	1—5	39,970	19,696	20,274	39,970	19,696	20,274	...	...	...	...	...	...
	5—10	52,492	26,496	25,996	52,492	26,496	25,996	...	...	...	...	...	...
	10—15	49,449	24,961	24,488	49,428	24,960	24,468	21	1	20	...	...	...
	15—20	44,850	21,355	23,495	37,976	20,166	17,810	6,500	1,156	5,344	374	33	341
	20—30	73,533	37,286	36,247	28,484	17,725	10,759	42,690	18,824	23,866	2,359	737	1,622
	30—40	52,103	27,629	24,474	6,201	4,146	2,055	42,504	22,188	20,316	3,398	1,295	2,103
	40—50	42,098	21,425	20,673	3,059	1,677	1,382	33,822	18,111	15,711	5,217	1,637	3,580
	50—60	28,745	14,015	14,730	1,881	911	970	20,556	11,400	9,156	6,308	1,704	4,604
	60 and over	27,793	12,705	15,088	1,907	852	1,055	13,781	8,709	5,072	12,105	3,144	8,961
	Buddhist ...	*410,548*	*200,865*	*209,683*	*227,241*	*117,249*	*109,992*	*154,024*	*75,454*	*78,570*	*29,283*	*8,162*	*21,121*
	0	12,105	6,059	6,046	12,105	6,059	6,046	...	...	...	...	...	...
	1—5	39,444	19,417	20,027	39,444	19,417	20,027	...	...	...	...	...	...
	5—10	51,939	26,190	25,749	51,939	26,190	25,749	...	...	...	...	...	...
	10—15	48,984	24,650	24,334	48,966	24,650	24 316	18	...	18	...	...	...
	15—20	43,806	20,504	23,302	37,159	19,440	17,719	6,275	1,031	5,244	372	33	339
	20—30	69,217	33,453	35,764	26,235	15,527	10,708	40,690	17,243	23,447	2,292	683	1,609
	30—40	48,551	24,385	24,166	5,004	2,974	2,036	40,287	20,242	20,045	3,260	1,169	2,091
	40—50	40,651	20,095	20,556	2,733	1,357	1,376	32,835	17,211	15,624	5,083	1,527	3,556
	50—60	28,256	13,576	14,680	1,773	805	968	20,255	11,123	9,132	6,228	1,648	4,580
	60 and over	27,595	12,536	15,059	1,883	830	1,053	13,664	8,604	5,060	12,048	3,102	8,946
	Animist (all ages) ...	*629*	*588*	*96*	*888*	*278*	*60*	*268*	*285*	*28*	*28*	*20*	*8*
	Hindu ..	*7,248*	*6,669*	*674*	*8,621*	*8,878*	*248*	*8,868*	*8,062*	*801*	*259*	*284*	*25*
	0	36	14	22	36	14	22	...	...	...	...	...	...
	1—5	183	113	70	183	113	70	...	...	...	...	...	...
	5—10	191	115	76	191	115	76	..	...	...	...	...	..
	10—15	206	163	43	204	163	41	2	...	2	...	...	...
	15—20	647	585	62	500	484	16	146	101	45	1	...	1
	20—30	2,634	2,476	158	1,403	1,392	11	1,192	1,051	141	39	33	6
	30—40	2,148	2,045	103	786	776	10	1,286	1,197	89	76	72	4
	40—50	837	818	19	223	221	2	534	519	15	80	78	2
	50—60	264	252	12	79	79	...	152	146	6	53	27	6
	60 and over	97	88	9	16	16	...	51	48	3	30	24	6
	Hindus born in Burma	*607*	*862*	*245*	*450*	*279*	*171*	*139*	*76*	*63*	*18*	*7*	*11*
	0	34	14	20	34	14	20	...	...	...	...	...	...
	1—5	127	75	52	127	75	52	...	...	...	...	...	...
	5—10	108	58	50	108	58	50	...	...	...	...	...	...
	10—15	61	34	27	61	34	27	...	...	...	...	...	...
	15—20	53	24	29	33	20	13	20	4	16	...	...	...
	20—30	114	72	42	38	35	3	72	36	36	4	1	3
	30—40	69	54	15	40	34	6	26	20	6	3	...	3
	40—50	17	15	2	5	5	...	11	9	2	1	1	...
	50—60	14	11	3	4	4	...	7	5	2	3	2	1
	60 and over	10	5	5	...	...	...	3	2	1	7	3	4
	Mahomedan (all ages)	*8,521*	*2,748*	*778*	*1,759*	*1,887*	*872*	*1,624*	*1,260*	*864*	*188*	*101*	*87*
	Christian (all ages)	*1,158*	*746*	*407*	*576*	*391*	*185*	*588*	*329*	*204*	*44*	*26*	*18*
	Others (all ages) ..	*158*	*125*	*88*	*82*	*69*	*18*	*67*	*49*	*18*	*9*	*7*	*2*
PAKÔKKU HILL TRACTS.	***All Religions*** ..	*20,048*	*9,840*	*10,208*	*10,729*	*5,806*	*4,928*	*7,652*	*8,595*	*4,057*	*1,662*	*439*	*1,228*
	0	546	264	282	546	264	282	...	...	...	...	...	...
	1—5	2,986	1,471	1,515	2,986	1,471	1,515	...	...	...	...	...	...
	5—10	2,677	1,379	1,298	2,677	1,379	1,298	...	...	...	...	...	...
	10—15	1,920	1,060	860	1,920	1,060	860	...	...	...	...	...	...
	15—20	1,705	889	816	1,445	845	600	255	44	211	5	...	5
	20—30	3,765	1,659	2,106	976	663	313	2,645	953	1,692	144	43	101
	30—40	3,055	1,444	1,611	128	94	34	2,552	1,253	1,299	375	97	278
	40—50	1,678	832	846	30	17	13	1,255	731	524	393	84	309
	50—60	960	456	504	16	10	6	593	359	234	351	87	264
	60 and over	751	386	365	5	3	2	352	255	97	394	128	266
	Buddhist (all ages)	*129*	*86*	*48*	*68*	*52*	*16*	*54*	*30*	*24*	*7*	*4*	*3*

Imperial Table VIIb.—*Age, Sex, and Civil Condition by Religion.*

District, Religion, and Age.	Population.			Unmarried.			Married.			Widowed.		
	Persons.	Males.	Females.	Persons.	Males.	Females.	Persons.	Males.	Females.	Persons.	Males.	Females.
1	2	3	4	5	6	7	8	9	10	11	12	13
Pakôkku Hill Tracts—*concluded.*												
Animist ..	***19,712***	***9,599***	***10,113***	***10,578***	***5,698***	***4,880***	***7,481***	***3,467***	***4,014***	***1,653***	***434***	***1,219***
0	538	259	279	538	259	279	...	...	...	...	...	...
1—5	2,952	1,456	1,496	2,952	1,456	1,496	...	...	...	...	...	...
5—10	2,653	1,368	1,285	2,653	1,368	1,285	...	...	...	...	...	...
10—15	1,907	1,052	855	1,907	1,052	855	...	...	...	...	...	...
15—20	1,681	872	809	1,426	829	597	251	43	208	4	...	4
20—30	3,641	1,557	2,084	931	618	313	2,570	899	1,671	140	40	100
30—40	2,990	1,391	1,599	121	87	34	2,495	1,208	1,287	374	96	278
40—50	1,652	812	840	29	16	13	1,231	713	518	392	83	309
50—60	949	447	502	16	10	6	583	350	233	350	87	263
60 and over	749	385	364	5	3	2	351	254	97	393	128	265
Hindu (all ages) ..	***188***	***148***	***40***	***75***	***52***	***23***	***106***	***90***	***16***	***2***	***1***	***1***
Mahomedan (all ages)	***8***	***5***	***3***	***3***	***1***	***2***	***5***	***4***	***1***	..	...	...
Christian (all ages)	***11***	***7***	***4***	***5***	***3***	***2***	***6***	***4***	***2***	..	...	...
Mandalay District (including City).												
All Religions ..	***356,621***	***182,999***	***173,622***	***180,593***	***98,181***	***82,412***	***137,856***	***72,795***	***65,061***	***38,172***	***12,023***	***26,149***
0	7,450	3,655	3,795	7,450	3,655	3,795	...	...	...	...	...	...
1—5	29,885	14,516	15,369	29,885	14,516	15,369	...	...	...	...	...	...
5—10	35,485	17,215	18,270	35,485	17,215	18,270	...	...	...	...	...	...
10—15	37,161	18,491	18,670	37,074	18,483	18,591	86	7	79	1	1	...
15—20	36,792	18,580	18,212	30,853	16,998	13,855	5,442	1,419	4,023	497	163	334
20—30	70,976	38,863	32,113	25,550	17,964	7,586	41,726	19,571	22,155	3,700	1,328	2,372
30—40	50,608	27,877	22,731	7,656	5,380	2,276	37,792	20,481	17,311	5,160	2,016	3,144
40—50	39,654	20,790	18,864	3,161	1,988	1,173	28,859	16,213	12,646	7,634	2,589	5,045
50—60	26,413	13,123	13,290	1,751	1,017	734	15,894	9,627	6,267	8,768	2,479	6,289
60 and over	22,197	9,889	12,308	1,728	965	763	8,057	5,477	2,580	12,412	3,447	8,965
Buddhist ..	***299,327***	***146,205***	***153,122***	***151,492***	***79,149***	***72,343***	***114,577***	***57,418***	***57,159***	***33,258***	***9,638***	***23,620***
0	6,423	3,136	3,287	6,423	3,136	3,287	...	...	...	...	...	...
1—5	25,705	12,406	13,299	25,705	12,406	13,299	...	...	...	...	...	...
5—10	30,334	14,628	15,706	30,334	14,628	15,706	...	...	...	...	...	...
10—15	32,628	16,058	16,570	32,574	16,052	16,522	54	6	48	...	...	...
15—20	31,605	15,469	16,136	26,856	14,287	12,569	4,300	1,040	3,260	449	142	307
20—30	55,832	27,943	27,889	18,852	12,192	6,660	33,924	14,822	19,102	3,056	929	2,127
30—40	39,961	20,250	19,711	5,269	3,345	1,924	30,457	15,400	15,057	4,235	1,505	2,730
40—50	33,483	16,543	16,940	2,403	1,388	1,015	24,612	13,161	11,451	6,468	1,994	4,474
50—60	23,197	11,024	12,173	1,479	830	649	13,980	8,162	5,818	7,738	2,032	5,706
60 and over	20,159	8,748	11,411	1,597	885	712	7,250	4,827	2,423	11,312	3,036	8,276
Animist ..	***2,698***	***2,301***	***397***	***1,569***	***1,386***	***183***	***1,023***	***839***	***184***	***106***	***76***	***30***
0	32	18	14	32	18	14	...	...	...	...	...	...
1—5	120	63	57	120	63	57	...	...	...	...	...	...
5—10	99	46	53	99	46	53	...	...	...	...	...	...
10—15	79	58	21	79	58	21	...	...	...	...	...	...
15—20	277	240	37	230	212	18	47	28	19	...	...	...
20—30	1,074	984	90	721	711	10	342	265	77	11	8	3
30—40	565	497	68	193	187	6	352	301	51	20	9	11
40—50	278	243	35	69	66	3	180	156	24	29	21	8
50—60	110	99	11	18	17	1	72	64	8	20	18	2
60 and over	64	53	11	8	8	...	30	25	5	26	20	6
Hindu ..	***22,061***	***15,591***	***6,470***	***9,881***	***7,166***	***2,715***	***10,101***	***7,232***	***2,869***	***2,079***	***1,193***	***886***
0	353	173	180	353	173	180	...	...	...	...	...	...
1—5	1,504	742	762	1,504	742	762	...	...	...	...	...	...
5—10	1,619	830	789	1,619	830	789	...	...	...	...	...	...
10—15	1,310	751	559	1,277	749	528	32	1	31	1	1	...
15—20	1,752	1,147	605	1,114	910	204	610	224	386	28	13	15
20—30	6,479	5,031	1,448	2,510	2,355	155	3,629	2,438	1,191	340	238	102
30—40	4,605	3,659	946	1,038	987	51	3,118	2,382	736	449	290	159
40—50	2,559	1,972	587	305	282	23	1,741	1,389	352	513	301	212
50—60	1,248	894	354	105	94	11	728	588	140	415	212	203
60 and over	632	392	240	56	44	12	243	210	33	333	138	195
Hindus born in Burma	***7,261***	***3,499***	***3,762***	***4,538***	***2,424***	***2,114***	***1,934***	***864***	***1,070***	***789***	***211***	***578***
0	314	155	159	314	155	159	..	...	...	...	...	...
1—5	1,234	591	643	1,234	591	643	...	...	...	...	...	...
5—10	1,263	629	634	1,263	629	634	...	...	...	...	...	...
10—15	868	458	410	858	458	400	10	...	10	...	...	...
15—20	670	314	356	419	269	150	232	41	191	19	4	15
20—30	1,102	543	559	316	235	81	675	271	404	111	37	74
30—40	670	329	341	77	59	18	454	233	221	139	37	102
40—50	515	221	294	32	20	12	321	165	156	162	36	126
50—60	361	149	212	11	3	8	164	94	70	186	52	134
60 and over	264	110	154	14	5	9	78	60	18	179	45	127

Imperial Table VIIb.—*Age, Sex, and Civil Condition by Religion.*

District, Religion, and Age.	Population.			Unmarried.			Married.			Widowed.		
	Persons.	Males.	Females.	Persons.	Males.	Females.	Persons.	Males.	Females.	Persons.	Males.	Females.
1	2	3	4	5	6	7	8	9	10	11	12	13
MANDALAY DISTRICT (including City)—*concluded.*												
Mahomedan ..	*23,209*	*13,666*	*9,544*	*11,851*	*7,106*	*4,745*	*9,189*	*5,662*	*3,527*	*2,169*	*897*	*1,272*
0	470	241	229	470	241	229	...	...	...	...	...	...
1—5	1,831	915	916	1,831	915	916	...	...	...	...	...	...
5—10	2,362	1,200	1,162	2,362	1,200	1,162	...	...	...	...	...	...
10—15	2,131	1,145	986	2,131	1,145	986	...	...	...	...	...	...
15—20	2,104	1,162	942	1,706	1,054	652	380	101	279	18	7	11
20—30	5,415	3,509	1,906	2,180	1,693	487	2,990	1,685	1,305	245	131	114
30—40	3,963	2,601	1,362	791	618	173	2,833	1,817	1,016	339	166	173
40—50	2,463	1,514	949	246	166	80	1,737	1,136	601	480	212	268
50—60	1,405	825	580	88	52	36	843	601	242	474	172	302
60 and over	1,065	553	512	46	22	24	406	322	84	613	209	404
Mahomedans born in Burma.	*16,571*	*7,815*	*8,756*	*9,848*	*4,794*	*4,554*	*5,556*	*2,553*	*3,003*	*1,667*	*468*	*1,199*
0	456	233	223	456	233	223	...	...	...	...	...	...
1—5	1,749	868	881	1,749	868	881	...	...	...	...	...	...
5—10	2,222	1,117	1,105	2,222	1,117	1,105	...	...	...	...	...	...
10—15	1,965	1,010	955	1,965	1,010	955	...	...	...	...	...	...
15—20	1,645	776	869	1,358	726	632	276	50	226	11	...	11
20—30	3,047	1,379	1,668	1,080	618	462	1,804	704	1,100	163	57	106
30—40	2,191	1,009	1,182	311	148	163	1,645	792	853	235	69	166
40—50	1,530	676	854	122	48	74	1,060	528	532	348	100	248
50—60	958	420	538	55	19	36	522	306	216	381	95	286
60 and over	808	327	481	30	7	23	249	173	76	529	147	382
Christian ..	*8,329*	*4,506*	*3,823*	*5,298*	*3,007*	*2,291*	*2,549*	*1,343*	*1,206*	*482*	*156*	*326*
0	145	76	69	145	76	69	...	...	...	...	...	...
1—5	652	354	298	652	354	298	...	...	...	...	...	...
5—10	972	452	520	972	452	520	...	...	...	...	...	...
10—15	962	444	518	962	444	518	...	...	...	...	...	...
15—20	992	515	477	902	497	405	88	17	71	2	1	1
20—30	1,948	1,231	717	1,186	922	264	723	294	429	39	15	24
30—40	1,263	675	588	288	173	115	874	469	405	101	33	68
40—50	736	398	338	113	63	50	508	299	209	115	36	79
50—60	410	242	168	59	22	37	243	186	57	108	34	74
60 and over	249	119	130	19	4	15	113	78	35	117	37	80
Others ..	*997*	*731*	*266*	*502*	*367*	*135*	*417*	*301*	*116*	*78*	*63*	*15*
0	27	11	16	27	11	16	...	...	...	...	...	...
1—5	73	36	37	73	36	37	...	...	...	...	...	...
5—10	99	59	40	99	59	40	...	...	...	...	...	...
10—15	51	35	16	51	35	16	...	...	...	...	...	...
15—20	62	47	15	45	38	7	17	9	8	...	...	...
20—30	228	165	63	101	91	10	118	67	51	9	7	2
30—40	251	195	56	77	70	7	158	112	46	16	13	3
40—50	135	120	15	25	23	2	81	72	9	29	25	4
50—60	43	39	4	2	2	...	28	26	2	13	11	2
60 and over	28	24	4	2	2	...	15	15	...	11	7	4
MANDALAY CITY.												
All Religions ..	*148,917*	*77,763*	*71,154*	*73,464*	*40,817*	*32,647*	*58,649*	*31,808*	*26,841*	*16,804*	*5,138*	*11,666*
0	3,140	1,534	1,606	3,140	1,534	1,606	...	...	...	...	...	...
1—5	10,771	5,160	5,611	10,771	5,160	5,611	...	...	...	...	...	...
5—10	12,843	6,049	6,794	12,843	6,049	6,794	...	...	...	...	...	...
10—15	14,081	6,818	7,263	14,075	6,816	7,259	5	1	4	1	1	...
15—20	15,019	7,944	7,075	12,424	7,117	5,307	2,347	709	1,638	248	118	130
20—30	32,098	18,471	13,627	12,648	9,240	3,408	17,970	8,709	9,261	1,480	522	958
30—40	23,496	13,266	10,230	4,224	2,890	1,334	16,986	9,528	7,458	2,286	848	1,438
40—50	16,825	8,848	7,977	1,740	1,107	633	11,696	6,679	5,017	3,389	1,062	2,327
50—60	11,406	5,679	5,727	880	508	372	6,586	4,063	2,523	3,940	1,108	2,832
60 and over	9,238	3,994	5,244	719	396	323	3,059	2,119	940	5,460	1,479	3,981
Buddhist ..	*115,154*	*56,811*	*58,343*	*56,445*	*30,097*	*26,348*	*45,052*	*22,964*	*22,088*	*13,657*	*3,750*	*9,907*
0	2,563	1,247	1,316	2,563	1,247	1,316	...	...	...	...	...	...
1—5	8,446	3,983	4,463	8,446	3,983	4,463	...	...	...	...	...	...
5—10	9,898	4,589	5,309	9,898	4,589	5,309	...	...	...	...	...	...
10—15	11,272	5,377	5,895	11,270	5,377	5,893	2	...	2	...	...	...
15—20	11,913	6,266	5,647	10,014	5,645	4,369	1,684	512	1,172	215	109	106
20—30	23,555	12,464	11,091	8,904	6,095	2,809	13,541	6,060	7,481	1,110	309	801
30—40	17,174	8,828	8,346	2,770	1,700	1,070	12,639	6,538	6,101	1,765	590	1,175
40—50	13,123	6,414	6,709	1,252	733	519	9,224	4,958	4,266	2,647	723	1,924
50—60	9,349	4,403	4,946	700	387	313	5,411	3,189	2,222	3,238	827	2,411
60 and over	7,861	3,240	4,621	628	341	287	2,551	1,707	844	4,682	1,192	3,490

Imperial Table VIIb.—*Age, Sex, and Civil Condition by Religion.*

MANDALAY CITY—*continued.*

District, Religion, and Age.	Population. Persons.	Males.	Females.	Unmarried. Persons.	Males.	Females.	Married. Persons.	Males.	Females.	Widowed. Persons.	Males.	Females.
1	2	3	4	5	6	7	8	9	10	11	12	13
Animist ...	*1,612*	*1,320*	*292*	*795*	*657*	*138*	*731*	*597*	*134*	*86*	*66*	*20*
0	26	15	11	26	15	11	...	...	...	...	...	...
1—5	82	43	39	82	43	39	...	...	...	...	...	...
5—10	84	40	44	84	40	44	...	...	...	...	...	...
10—15	62	47	15	62	47	15	...	...	...	...	...	...
15—20	129	100	29	99	85	14	30	15	15	...	...	...
20—30	411	359	52	223	216	7	179	137	42	9	6	3
30—40	416	362	54	135	131	4	268	224	44	13	7	6
40—50	243	214	29	61	58	3	162	139	23	20	17	3
50—60	102	91	11	16	15	1	67	59	8	19	17	2
60 and over	57	49	8	7	7	...	25	23	2	25	19	6
Hindu ...	*10,995*	*7,434*	*3,561*	*5,063*	*3,579*	*1,484*	*4,767*	*3,292*	*1,475*	*1,165*	*563*	*602*
0	165	77	88	165	77	88	...	...	...	...	...	...
1—5	704	342	362	704	342	362	...	...	...	...	...	...
5—10	794	392	402	794	392	402	...	..	...	...	...	...
10—15	704	387	317	700	385	315	3	1	2	1	1	...
15—20	892	538	354	583	438	145	293	96	197	16	4	12
20—30	3,136	2,382	754	1,266	1,159	107	1,697	1,118	579	173	105	68
30—40	2,244	1,726	518	597	561	36	1,435	1,056	379	212	109	103
40—50	1,281	922	359	161	147	14	837	635	202	283	140	143
50—60	686	437	249	56	49	7	367	273	94	263	115	148
60 and over	389	231	158	37	29	8	135	113	22	217	89	128
Hindus born in Burma	*4,582*	*2,112*	*2,470*	*2,440*	*1,277*	*1,163*	*1,476*	*664*	*812*	*666*	*171*	*495*
0	146	69	77	146	69	77	...	...	...	...	...	...
1—5	559	256	303	559	256	303	...	...	...	...	...	...
5—10	639	304	335	639	304	335	...	...	...	...	...	...
10—15	518	259	259	518	259	259	..	...	...	...	...	...
15—20	429	185	244	265	159	106	149	23	126	15	3	12
20—30	821	400	421	217	167	50	508	202	306	96	31	65
30—40	534	256	278	59	45	14	363	181	182	112	30	82
40—50	431	179	252	22	13	9	265	137	128	144	29	115
50—60	292	115	177	7	2	5	133	75	58	152	38	114
60 and over	213	89	124	8	3	5	58	46	12	147	40	107
Mahomedan ...	*16,373*	*9,638*	*6,735*	*8,243*	*4,946*	*3,297*	*6,580*	*4,082*	*2,498*	*1,550*	*610*	*940*
0	295	152	143	295	152	143	...	...	...	...	...	...
1—5	1,199	611	588	1,199	611	588	...	...	...	...	...	...
5—10	1,518	775	743	1,518	775	743	...	...	...	...	...	...
10—15	1,471	746	725	1,471	746	725	...	...	...	...	...	...
15—20	1,552	819	733	1,255	744	511	282	71	211	15	4	11
20—30	3,989	2,667	1,322	1,714	1,374	340	2,120	1,207	913	155	86	69
30—40	2,864	1,883	981	510	371	139	2,131	1,403	728	223	109	114
40—50	1,705	1,018	687	180	115	65	1,176	759	417	349	144	205
50—60	1,006	581	425	65	41	24	597	423	174	344	117	227
60 and over	774	386	388	36	17	19	274	219	55	464	150	314
Mahomedans born in Burma.	*11,546*	*5,335*	*6,211*	*6,374*	*3,213*	*3,161*	*3,959*	*1,801*	*2,158*	*1,213*	*321*	*892*
0	285	146	139	285	146	139	...	...	...	...	...	...
1—5	1,138	575	563	1,138	575	563	...	...	...	...	...	...
5—10	1,432	727	705	1,432	727	705	...	...	...	...	...	...
10—15	1,359	657	702	1,359	657	702	...	...	...	...	...	...
15—20	1,203	523	680	980	485	495	212	38	174	11	...	11
20—30	2,126	964	1,162	769	446	323	1,259	484	775	98	34	64
30—40	1,620	754	866	251	118	133	1,216	591	625	153	45	108
40—50	1,081	457	624	95	36	59	725	351	374	261	70	191
50—60	703	300	403	41	17	24	375	216	159	287	67	220
60 and over	599	232	367	24	6	18	172	121	51	403	105	298
Christian ...	*4,160*	*2,083*	*2,077*	*2,598*	*1,288*	*1,310*	*1,272*	*693*	*579*	*290*	*102*	*188*
0	78	35	43	78	35	43	...	...	...	...	...	...
1—5	297	160	137	297	160	137	...	...	...	...	...	...
5—10	493	218	275	493	218	275	...	...	...	...	...	...
10—15	537	237	300	537	237	300	...	...	...	...	...	...
15—20	494	190	304	443	178	265	49	11	38	2	1	1
20—30	861	484	377	470	328	142	365	145	220	26	11	15
30—40	633	335	298	160	79	81	411	233	178	62	23	39
40—50	391	208	183	69	38	31	252	150	102	70	20	50
50—60	237	144	93	41	14	27	130	106	24	66	24	42
60 and over	139	72	67	10	1	9	65	48	17	64	23	41

Imperial Table VIIb.—*Age, Sex, and Civil Condition by Religion.*

District	District, Religion, and Age	Population: Persons	Population: Males	Population: Females	Unmarried: Persons	Unmarried: Males	Unmarried: Females	Married: Persons	Married: Males	Married: Females	Widowed: Persons	Widowed: Males	Widowed: Females
	1	2	3	4	5	6	7	8	9	10	11	12	13
MANDALAY CITY—*concld.*	***Others*** ...	*623*	*477*	*146*	*320*	*250*	*70*	*247*	*180*	*67*	*56*	*47*	*9*
	0	13	8	5	13	8	5	...	...	...	...	...	...
	1—5	43	21	22	43	21	22	...	...	...	...	...	...
	5—10	56	35	21	56	35	21	...	...	...	...	...	...
	10—15	35	24	11	35	24	11	...	...	...	...	...	...
	15—20	39	31	8	30	27	3	9	4	5	...	...	...
	20—30	146	115	31	71	68	3	68	42	26	7	5	2
	30—40	165	132	33	52	48	4	102	74	28	11	10	1
	40—50	82	72	10	17	16	1	45	38	7	20	18	2
	50—60	26	23	3	2	2	...	14	13	1	10	8	2
	60 and over	18	16	2	1	1	...	9	9	...	8	6	2
BHAMO.	***All Religions*** ...	*112,960*	*56,888*	*56,072*	*57,188*	*30,895*	*26,293*	*45,143*	*23,397*	*21,746*	*10,629*	*2,596*	*8,033*
	0	2,369	1,073	1,296	2,369	1,073	1,296	...	...	...	...	...	...
	1—5	9,423	4,590	4,833	9,423	4,590	4,833	...	...	...	...	...	...
	5—10	12,813	6,464	6,349	12,813	6,464	6,349	...	...	...	...	...	...
	10—15	12,309	6,319	5,990	12,275	6,319	5,956	34	...	34	...	...	...
	15—20	11,087	5,574	5,513	9,171	5,087	4,084	1,860	477	1,383	56	10	46
	20—30	20,712	10,827	9,885	7,929	5,377	2,552	11,893	5,128	6,765	890	322	568
	30—40	17,074	8,847	8,227	2,043	1,331	712	13,395	6,978	6,417	1,636	538	1,098
	40—50	12,485	6,381	6,104	637	393	244	9,635	5,404	4,231	2,213	584	1,629
	50—60	7,882	3,954	3,928	262	152	110	5,284	3,332	1,952	2,336	470	1,866
	60 and over	6,806	2,859	3,947	266	109	157	3,042	2,078	964	3,498	672	2,826
	Buddhist ...	*55,822*	*28,193*	*27,629*	*28,633*	*15,316*	*13,317*	*22,110*	*11,346*	*10,764*	*5,079*	*1,531*	*3,548*
	0	1,404	632	772	1,404	632	772	...	...	...	...	...	...
	1—5	5,273	2,558	2,715	5,273	2,558	2,715	...	...	...	...	...	...
	5—10	6,818	3,433	3,385	6,818	3,433	3,385	...	...	...	...	...	...
	10—15	6,597	3,298	3,299	6,597	3,298	3,299	...	...	...	...	...	...
	15—20	5,491	2,751	2,740	4,561	2,544	2,017	880	199	681	50	8	42
	20—30	9,493	4,896	4,597	2,984	2,181	803	5,965	2,504	3,461	544	211	333
	30—40	7,459	3,999	3,460	536	379	157	6,206	3,328	2,878	717	292	425
	40—50	5,765	3,043	2,722	222	143	59	4,698	2,605	2,093	865	295	570
	50—60	4,057	2,026	2,031	116	77	39	2,811	1,659	1,152	1,130	290	840
	60 and over	3,465	1,557	1,908	142	71	71	1,550	1,051	499	1,773	435	1,338
	Animist ...	*48,359*	*22,850*	*25,509*	*24,206*	*12,542*	*11,664*	*19,199*	*9,511*	*9,688*	*4,954*	*797*	*4,157*
	0	788	34	441	788	347	441	...	...	...	...	...	...
	1—5	3,606	1,764	1,842	3,606	1,764	1,842	...	...	...	...	...	...
	5—10	5,271	2,657	2,614	5,271	2,657	2,614	...	...	...	...	...	...
	10—15	5,031	2,637	2,394	4,998	2,637	2,361	33	...	33	...	...	...
	15—20	4,734	2,242	2,492	3,911	2,015	1,896	822	227	595	1	...	1
	20—30	8,801	4,105	4,696	3,849	2,194	1,655	4,674	1,841	2,833	278	70	208
	30—40	7,886	3,610	4,276	1,208	680	528	5,881	2,769	3,112	797	161	636
	40—50	5,792	2,691	3,101	341	166	175	4,271	2,311	1,960	1,180	214	966
	50—60	3,396	1,644	1,752	124	55	69	2,172	1,446	726	1,100	143	957
	60 and over	3,054	1,153	1,901	110	27	83	1,346	917	429	1,598	209	1,389
	Hindu ...	*1,897*	*1,097*	*800*	*593*	*462*	*131*	*728*	*579*	*149*	*76*	*56*	*20*
	0	26	13	13	26	13	13	...	...	...	...	...	...
	1—5	93	49	44	93	49	44	...	...	...	...	...	...
	5—10	73	40	33	73	40	33	...	...	...	...	...	...
	10—15	53	28	25	53	28	25	...	...	...	...	...	...
	15—20	94	60	34	60	48	12	33	11	22	1	1	...
	20—30	526	454	72	195	191	4	318	254	64	13	9	4
	30—40	300	260	40	68	68	...	213	175	38	19	17	2
	40—50	152	126	26	20	20	...	107	88	19	25	18	7
	50—60	56	47	9	3	3	...	40	35	5	13	9	4
	60 and over	24	20	4	2	2	...	17	16	1	5	2	3
	Hindus born in Burma	*315*	*183*	*132*	*242*	*146*	*96*	*67*	*33*	*34*	*6*	*4*	*2*
	0	26	13	13	26	13	13	...	...	...	...	...	...
	1—5	77	42	35	77	42	35	...	...	...	...	...	...
	5—10	52	32	20	52	32	20	...	...	...	...	...	...
	10—15	37	18	19	37	18	19	...	...	...	...	...	...
	15—20	36	17	19	26	17	9	10	...	10	...	...	...
	20—30	43	27	16	15	15	...	27	12	15	1	...	1
	30—40	26	19	7	6	6	...	18	11	7	2	2	...
	40—50	13	10	3	2	2	...	9	7	2	2	1	1
	50—60	3	3	...	1	1	...	1	1	...	1	1	...
	60 and over	2	2	...	...	...	...	2	2	...	...	...	...

IMPERIAL TABLE VIIB.—*Age, Sex, and Civil Condition by Religion.*

District	Religion, and Age	Population. Persons.	Population. Males.	Population. Females.	Unmarried. Persons.	Unmarried. Males.	Unmarried. Females.	Married. Persons.	Married. Males.	Married. Females.	Widowed. Persons.	Widowed. Males.	Widowed. Females.
1		2	3	4	5	6	7	8	9	10	11	12	13
BHAMO—*concluded.*	***Mahomedan*** ...	*1,960*	*1,541*	*419*	*908*	*728*	*180*	*950*	*780*	*220*	*107*	*88*	*19*
	0	42	22	20	42	22	20	...	...	...	...	...	...
	1—5	93	44	49	93	44	49	...	...	...	...	...	...
	5—10	110	62	48	110	62	48	...	...	...	...	...	...
	10—15	102	64	38	101	64	37	1	...	1	...	...	...
	15—20	203	151	52	156	139	17	46	12	34	1	...	1
	20—30	658	567	91	310	304	6	327	246	81	21	17	4
	30—40	431	368	63	64	63	1	333	272	61	34	33	1
	40—50	188	154	34	16	14	2	148	120	28	24	20	4
	50—60	86	72	14	7	7	...	65	54	11	14	11	3
	60 and over	47	37	10	4	4	..	30	26	4	13	7	6
	Mahomedans born in Burma.	*581*	*292*	*289*	*865*	*208*	*157*	*195*	*79*	*116*	*21*	*5*	*16*
	0	35	16	19	35	16	19	...	...	...	...	...	...
	1—5	76	33	43	76	33	43	...	...	...	...	...	...
	5—10	95	54	41	95	54	41	...	...	...	...	...	...
	10—15	74	42	32	74	42	32	...	...	..	...	...	...
	15—20	64	32	32	46	31	15	17	1	16	1	...	1
	20—30	92	45	47	30	25	5	57	19	38	5	1	4
	30—40	65	32	33	6	6	...	57	25	32	2	1	1
	40—50	47	23	24	3	1	2	39	21	18	5	1	4
	50—60	19	9	10	...	...	...	15	7	8	4	2	2
	60 and over	14	6	8	..	...	...	10	6	4	4	...	4
	Christian ...	*4,052*	*2,056*	*1,996*	*2,078*	*1,177*	*901*	*1,687*	*824*	*818*	*837*	*55*	*282*
	0	72	37	35	72	37	35	...	...	...	...	...	...
	1—5	282	132	150	282	132	150	...	...	...	...	...	...
	5—10	473	232	241	473	232	241	...	...	...	...	...	...
	10—15	486	267	219	486	267	219	...	...	..	...	...	...
	15—20	421	240	181	361	225	136	57	14	43	3	1	2
	20—30	779	403	376	307	225	82	444	169	275	28	9	19
	30—40	695	350	345	64	39	25	582	296	286	49	15	34
	40—50	418	207	211	22	14	8	304	180	124	92	13	79
	50—60	233	114	119	5	3	2	162	106	56	66	5	61
	60 and over	193	74	119	6	3	3	88	59	29	99	12	87
	Others (all ages)	*1,870*	*1,151*	*219*	*775*	*675*	*100*	*519*	*407*	*112*	*76*	*69*	*7*
MYITKYINA.	***All Religions*** ...	*118,882*	*63,419*	*64,968*	*60,977*	*85,221*	*25,756*	*46,541*	*24,745*	*21,796*	*10,884*	*8,458*	*7,411*
	0	23,70	1,154	1,216	2,370	1,154	1,216	...	...	...	...	...	...
	1—5	9,838	4,772	5,066	9,838	4,772	5,066	...	...	...	...	...	...
	5—10	12,752	6,425	6,327	12,752	6,425	6,327	...	...	...	...	...	...
	10—15	11,857	6,050	5,807	11,598	6,019	5,579	257	31	226	2	...	2
	15—20	12,087	6,175	5,912	10,016	5,779	4,237	1,980	384	1,596	91	12	79
	20—30	23,690	13,292	10,398	10,048	7,734	2,314	12,764	5,200	7,564	878	358	520
	30—40	19,166	10,943	8,223	2,927	2,324	603	14,400	7,909	6,491	1,839	710	1,129
	40—50	13,176	7,468	5,708	972	719	253	9,729	5,971	3,758	2,475	778	1,697
	50—60	7,716	4,345	3,371	275	193	82	4,931	3,417	1,514	2,510	735	1,775
	60 and over	5,730	2,795	2,935	181	102	79	2,480	1,833	647	3,069	860	2,209
	Buddhist ...	*39,960*	*21,587*	*18,373*	*20,885*	*11,687*	*8,648*	*16,895*	*8,539*	*7,856*	*8,280*	*1861*	*1,869*
	0	927	453	474	927	453	474	...	...	...	...	...	...
	1—5	3,947	1,954	1,993	3,947	1,954	1,993	...	...	...	...	...	...
	5—10	4,546	2,255	2,291	4,546	2,255	2,291	...	...	...	...	...	...
	10—15	4,204	2,107	2,097	4,004	2,107	1,897	200	...	200	...	...	...
	15—20	4,032	2,003	2,029	3,422	1,993	1,429	547	9	538	63	1	62
	20—30	7,358	4,130	3,228	2,472	2,101	371	4,645	1,902	2,744	241	128	113
	30—40	5,719	3,446	2,273	552	499	53	4,729	2,673	2,056	438	274	164
	40—50	4,380	2,548	1,832	293	209	84	3,419	2,078	1,341	668	261	407
	50—60	2,897	1,717	1,180	98	74	24	2,065	1,338	727	734	305	429
	60 and over	1,950	974	976	74	42	32	790	540	250	1,086	392	694
	Animist ...	*66,927*	*34,135*	*32,792*	*35,133*	*19,742*	*15,391*	*24,877*	*12,734*	*12,143*	*6,917*	*1,659*	*5,258*
	0	1,149	554	595	1,149	554	595	...	...	...	...	...	...
	1—5	4,881	2,318	2,563	4,881	2,318	2,563	...	...	...	...	...	...
	5—10	7,149	3,620	3,529	7,149	3,620	3,529	...	...	...	...	...	...
	10—15	6,710	3,394	3,316	6,710	3,394	3,316	...	...	...	...	...	...
	15—20	7,162	3,672	3,490	6,082	3,387	2,695	1,065	277	788	15	8	7
	20—30	13,208	6,817	6,391	6,357	4,471	1,886	6,328	2,203	4,125	523	143	380
	30—40	11,355	5,916	5,439	2,009	1,471	538	8,116	4,126	3,990	1,230	319	911
	40—50	7,569	4,017	3,552	555	391	164	5,385	3,215	2,170	1,629	411	1,218
	50—60	4,250	2,201	2,049	146	88	58	2,445	1,746	699	1,659	367	1,292
	60 and over	3,494	1,626	1,868	95	48	47	1,538	1,167	371	1,861	411	1,450

Imperial Table VIIb.—*Age, Sex, and Civil Condition by Religion.*

District, Religion, and Age.	Population. Persons.	Population. Males.	Population. Females.	Unmarried. Persons.	Unmarried. Males.	Unmarried. Females.	Married. Persons.	Married. Males.	Married. Females.	Widowed. Persons.	Widowed. Males.	Widowed. Females.
1	2	3	4	5	6	7	8	9	10	11	12	13
MYITKYINA—concluded.												
Hindu ...	***8,829***	***5,980***	***2,849***	***4,236***	***2,931***	***1,305***	***4,072***	***2,709***	***1,363***	***521***	***340***	***181***
0	241	119	122	241	119	122	...	...	...	...	...	...
1—5	814	407	407	814	407	407	...	...	...	...	...	...
5—10	820	422	398	820	422	398	...	...	...	...	...	...
10—15	718	401	317	663	374	289	53	27	26	2	...	2
15—20	673	379	294	348	287	61	314	90	224	11	2	9
20—30	2,458	1,893	565	955	935	20	1,413	886	527	90	72	18
30—40	1,537	1,179	358	265	260	5	1,148	829	319	124	90	34
40—50	933	703	230	98	95	3	710	528	182	125	80	45
50—60	433	336	97	23	23	...	328	262	66	82	51	31
60 and over	202	141	61	9	9	...	106	87	19	87	45	42
Hindus born in Burma	***2,606***	***1,330***	***1,276***	***2,227***	***1,212***	***1,015***	***352***	***109***	***248***	***27***	***9***	***18***
0	217	107	110	217	107	110	...	...	...	...	...	...
1—5	708	356	352	708	356	352	...	...	...	...	...	...
5—10	637	323	314	637	323	314	...	...	...	...	...	...
10—15	498	282	216	443	255	188	53	27	26	2	...	2
15—20	279	139	140	164	122	42	109	16	93	6	1	5
20—30	176	87	89	52	45	7	116	39	77	8	3	5
30—40	44	13	31	1	1	...	41	12	29	2	...	2
40—50	31	15	16	3	1	2	24	11	13	4	3	1
50—60	12	5	7	1	1	...	8	3	5	3	1	2
60 and over	4	3	1	1	1	...	1	1	...	2	1	1
Mahomedan ...	***1,283***	***899***	***384***	***603***	***435***	***168***	***610***	***414***	***196***	***70***	***50***	***20***
0	25	13	12	25	13	12	...	...	...	...	...	...
1—5	99	50	49	99	50	49	...	...	...	...	...	...
5—10	117	64	53	117	64	53	...	...	...	...	...	...
10—15	101	66	35	101	66	35	...	...	...	...	...	...
15—20	79	47	32	54	44	10	25	3	22	...	...	...
20—30	340	254	86	139	130	9	192	117	75	9	7	2
30—40	244	194	50	48	48	...	177	127	50	19	19	...
40—50	151	111	39	12	12	...	121	89	32	18	11	7
50—60	81	62	19	5	5	...	63	50	13	13	7	6
60 and over	46	37	9	3	3	...	32	28	4	11	6	5
Mahomedans born in Burma.	***548***	***262***	***286***	***360***	***207***	***153***	***169***	***51***	***118***	***19***	***4***	***15***
0	24	12	12	24	12	12	...	...	...	...	...	...
1—5	91	45	46	91	45	46	...	...	...	...	...	...
5—10	100	54	46	100	54	46	...	...	...	...	...	...
10—15	81	50	31	81	50	31	...	...	...	...	...	...
15—20	46	20	26	29	19	10	17	1	16	...	...	...
20—30	95	39	56	30	22	8	63	17	46	2	...	2
30—40	50	23	27	5	5	...	41	14	27	4	4	...
40—50	37	14	23	...	...	...	32	14	18	5	...	5
50—60	13	2	11	...	...	...	9	2	7	4	...	4
60 and over	11	3	8	...	...	...	7	3	4	4	...	4
Christian (all ages)	***995***	***536***	***459***	***485***	***287***	***198***	***419***	***228***	***191***	***91***	***21***	***70***
Others (all ages) ...	***388***	***282***	***106***	***185***	***139***	***46***	***168***	***121***	***47***	***35***	***22***	***13***
KATHA.												
All Religions ...	***253,725***	***128,444***	***125,281***	***132,346***	***70,536***	***61,810***	***101,024***	***51,103***	***49,921***	***20,355***	***6,805***	***13,550***
0	7,032	3,419	3,613	7,032	3,419	3,613	...	...	...	...	...	...
1—5	24,582	12,032	12,550	24,582	12,032	12,550	...	...	...	...	...	...
5—10	31,746	15,644	16,102	31,746	15,644	16,102	...	...	...	...	...	...
10—15	28,638	14,390	14,248	28,624	14,390	14,234	14	...	14	...	...	...
15—20	25,228	12,130	13,098	20,607	11,212	9,395	4,374	861	3,513	247	57	190
20—30	43,538	21,949	21,589	12,974	9,275	3,699	28,549	11,879	16,670	2,015	795	1,220
30—40	34,128	18,345	15,783	3,369	2,448	921	28,252	14,817	13,435	2,507	1,080	1,427
40—50	26,687	14,505	12,182	1,504	1,094	410	21,584	12,044	9,540	3,599	1,367	2,232
50—60	17,604	9,266	8,338	939	639	330	12,014	7,223	4,791	4,651	1,434	3,217
60 and over	14,542	6,764	7,778	969	413	556	6,237	4,279	1,958	7,336	2,072	5,264
Buddhist ...	***236,886***	***117,983***	***118,903***	***123,610***	***64,910***	***58,700***	***94,363***	***46,956***	***47,407***	***18,913***	***6,117***	***12,796***
0	6,620	3,209	3,411	6,620	3,209	3,411	...	...	...	...	...	...
1—5	23,094	11,302	11,792	23,094	11,302	11,792	...	...	...	...	...	...
5—10	30,044	14,794	15,250	30,044	14,794	15,250	...	...	...	...	...	...
10—15	27,260	13,653	13,607	27,246	13,653	13,593	14	...	14	...	...	...
15—20	23,821	11,299	12,522	19,491	10,454	9,037	4,100	795	3,305	230	50	180
20—30	39,858	19,515	20,343	11,365	7,894	3,471	26,627	10,905	15,722	1,866	716	1,150
30—40	30,884	16,047	14,837	2,674	1,797	877	25,989	13,350	12,639	2,221	900	1,321
40—50	24,793	13,163	11,630	1,283	882	401	20,254	11,091	9,163	3,256	1,190	2,066
50—60	16,618	8,585	8,033	857	536	321	11,409	6,746	4,663	4,352	1,303	3,049
60 and over	13,894	6,416	7,478	936	389	547	5,970	4,069	1,901	6,988	1,958	5,030

IMPERIAL TABLE VIIB.—*Age, Sex, and Civil Condition by Religion.*

District	Religion, and Age	Population: Persons	Population: Males	Population: Females	Unmarried: Persons	Unmarried: Males	Unmarried: Females	Married: Persons	Married: Males	Married: Females	Widowed: Persons	Widowed: Males	Widowed: Females
1		2	3	4	5	6	7	8	9	10	11	12	13
KATHA—*concluded.*	***Animist*** ...	*9,620*	*5,862*	*4,258*	*5,178*	*3,094*	*2,079*	*3,448*	*1,888*	*1,565*	*999*	*885*	*614*
	0	261	131	130	261	131	130	...	...	...	...	...	...
	1—5	901	437	464	901	437	464	...	...	...	...	...	...
	5—10	1,070	551	519	1,070	551	519	...	...	...	...	...	...
	10—15	906	464	442	906	464	442	...	...	...	...	...	...
	15—20	838	468	370	718	442	276	113	24	89	7	2	5
	20—30	1,847	1,041	806	829	638	191	929	366	563	89	37	52
	30—40	1,742	1,086	656	348	311	37	1,214	681	533	180	94	86
	40—50	1,047	654	393	96	90	6	714	460	254	237	104	133
	50—60	548	325	223	30	23	7	305	224	81	213	78	135
	60 and over	460	205	255	14	7	7	173	128	45	273	70	203
	Hindu ...	*3,990*	*2.935*	*1,055*	*1,918*	*1.432*	*486*	*1,834*	*1,330*	*504*	*238*	*173*	*65*
	0	81	44	37	81	44	37	...	...	...	...	...	...
	1—5	323	170	153	323	170	153	...	...	...	...	...	...
	5—10	353	169	184	353	169	184	...	...	...	...	...	...
	10—15	221	135	86	221	135	86	...	...	...	...	...	...
	15—20	254	165	88	149	138	11	99	25	74	6	3	3
	20—30	1,054	816	238	421	411	10	601	381	220	32	24	8
	30—40	913	766	147	237	235	2	609	475	134	67	56	11
	40—50	482	411	71	89	88	1	330	274	56	63	49	14
	50—60	221	193	28	28	28	...	148	134	14	45	31	14
	60 and over	88	65	23	16	14	2	47	41	6	25	10	15
	Hindus born in Burma	*870*	*480*	*390*	*755*	*423*	*332*	*103*	*50*	*53*	*12*	*7*	*5*
	0	66	33	33	66	33	33	...	...	...	...	...	...
	1—5	253	135	118	253	135	118	...	...	...	...	...	...
	5—10	237	121	116	237	121	116	...	...	...	...	...	...
	10—15	124	69	55	124	69	55	...	...	...	...	...	...
	15—20	53	32	21	37	30	7	15	1	14	1	1	...
	20—30	62	38	24	21	18	3	39	20	19	2	...	2
	30—40	39	28	11	11	11	...	26	16	10	2	1	1
	40—50	22	13	9	3	3	...	15	7	8	4	3	1
	50—60	8	6	2	2	2	...	6	4	2	...	...	...
	60 and over	6	5	1	1	1	...	2	2	...	3	2	1
	Mahomedan ..	*2,478*	*1,620*	*858*	*1,211*	*763*	*448*	*1,080*	*729*	*351*	*187*	*123*	*64*
	0	60	30	30	60	30	30	...	...	...	...	...	...
	1—5	213	99	114	213	99	114	...	...	...	...	...	...
	5—10	229	105	124	229	105	124	...	...	...	...	...	...
	10—15	202	105	97	202	105	97	...	...	...	...	...	...
	15—20	216	124	92	160	109	51	53	13	40	3	2	1
	20—30	558	395	163	220	200	20	310	177	133	28	18	10
	30—40	460	348	112	79	74	5	344	246	98	37	28	9
	40—50	283	215	68	25	23	2	221	171	50	37	21	16
	50—60	165	126	39	20	20	...	110	85	25	35	21	14
	60 and over	92	73	19	3	3	...	42	37	5	47	33	14
	Mahomedans born in Burma.	*1,382*	*624*	*758*	*837*	*415*	*422*	*478*	*190*	*288*	*72*	*19*	*58*
	0	50	24	26	50	24	26	...	...	...	...	...	...
	1—5	203	92	111	203	92	111	...	...	...	...	...	...
	5—10	208	89	119	208	89	119	...	...	...	...	...	...
	10—15	177	84	93	177	84	93	...	...	...	...	...	...
	15—20	160	78	82	121	73	48	37	4	33	2	1	1
	20—30	235	94	141	54	36	18	169	56	113	12	2	10
	30—40	159	75	84	19	14	5	130	58	72	10	3	7
	40—50	105	48	57	4	2	2	82	42	40	19	4	15
	50—60	65	31	34	1	1	...	45	24	21	19	6	13
	60 and over	20	9	11	...	...	...	10	6	4	10	3	7
	Christian (all ages)	*744*	*537*	*207*	*430*	*328*	*102*	*296*	*202*	*94*	*18*	*7*	*11*
	Others (all ages) ...	7	7	...	*4*	*4*	...	*3*	*3*	...	...	...	...
PUTAO.	***All Religions*** ...	*7,673*	*4,144*	*3,529*	*3,580*	*2,209*	*1,371*	*3,283*	*1,771*	*1,512*	*810*	*164*	*646*
	0	196	106	90	196	106	90	...	...	...	...	...	...
	1—5	665	334	331	665	334	331	...	...	...	...	...	...
	5—10	623	331	292	623	331	292	...	...	...	...	...	...
	10—15	775	422	353	767	420	347	7	2	5	1	...	1
	15—20	762	392	370	556	347	209	201	44	157	5	1	4
	20—30	1,753	1,104	649	600	537	63	1,089	542	547	64	25	39
	30—40	1,225	693	532	116	101	15	978	548	430	131	44	87
	40—50	776	403	373	36	27	9	573	344	229	167	32	135
	50—60	480	207	273	9	3	6	278	172	106	193	32	161
	60 and over	418	152	266	12	3	9	157	119	38	249	30	219

IMPERIAL TABLE VIIB.—*Age, Sex, and Civil Condition by Religion.*

DISTRICT, RELIGION, AND AGE.	POPULATION.			UNMARRIED.			MARRIED.			WIDOWED.		
	Persons.	Males.	Females.	Persons.	Males.	Females.	Persons.	Males.	Females.	Persons.	Males.	Females.
1	2	3	4	5	6	7	8	9	10	11	12	13
PUTAO—*concluded.*												
Buddhist ...	*6,128*	*2,892*	*3,231*	*2,826*	*1,564*	*1,262*	*2,563*	*1,223*	*1,340*	*734*	*105*	*629*
0	170	90	80	170	90	80	...	...	...	...	...	..
1—5	574	293	281	574	293	281	...	...	...	...	...	...
5—10	575	306	269	575	306	269	...	...	...	...	...	...
10—15	713	384	329	709	382	327	3	2	1	1	...	1
15—20	647	313	334	479	274	205	165	39	126	3	...	3
20—30	1,067	505	562	240	178	62	779	316	463	48	11	37
30—40	887	399	488	42	27	15	741	347	394	104	25	79
40—50	636	278	358	18	9	9	473	256	217	145	13	132
50—60	446	178	268	8	3	5	251	149	102	187	26	161
60 and over	408	146	262	11	2	9	151	114	37	246	30	216
Animists (all ages)	*463*	*401*	*62*	*295*	*274*	*21*	*153*	*124*	*29*	*15*	*3*	*12*
Hindu (all ages) ...	*997*	*779*	*218*	*425*	*345*	*80*	*517*	*384*	*133*	*55*	*50*	*5*
Mahomedan (all ages)	*31*	*27*	*4*	*8*	*7*	*1*	*19*	*16*	*3*	*4*	*4*	...
Christian (all ages)	*32*	*24*	*8*	*17*	*12*	*5*	*13*	*10*	*3*	*2*	*2*	..
Others (all ages) ...	*27*	*21*	*6*	*9*	*7*	*2*	*18*	*14*	*4*	..	..	..
SHWEBO.												
All Religions ...	*391,284*	*184,708*	*206,576*	*203,174*	*100,763*	*102,411*	*152,744*	*75,219*	*77,525*	*35,366*	*8,726*	*26,640*
0	11,335	5,329	6,006	11,335	5,329	6,006	...	...	...	...	...	...
1—5	37,989	17,984	20,005	37,989	17,984	20,005	...	...	...	...	...	...
5—10	46,910	22,500	24,410	46,910	22,500	24,410	...	...	...	...	...	...
10—15	45,763	22,454	23,309	45,759	22,454	23,305	4	...	4	...	...	...
15—20	40,657	18,966	21,691	33,249	16,824	16,425	7,103	2,092	5,011	305	50	255
20—30	63,665	29,656	34,009	17,654	10,090	7,564	43,008	18,760	24,248	3,003	806	2,197
30—40	45,067	21,790	23,277	4,480	2,581	1,899	36,657	18,150	18,507	3,930	1,059	2,871
40—50	39,008	18,457	20,551	2,166	1,079	1,087	31,453	16,041	15,412	5,389	1,337	4,052
50—60	29,506	13,596	15,910	1,612	808	804	20,493	11,203	9,290	7,401	1,585	5,816
60 and over	31,384	13,976	17,408	2,020	1,114	906	14,026	8,973	5,053	15,338	3,889	11,449
Buddhist ...	*378,464*	*177,347*	*201,117*	*196,557*	*96,969*	*99,588*	*147,409*	*72,002*	*75,407*	*34,498*	*8,376*	*26,122*
0	11,007	5,195	5,812	11,007	5,195	5,812	...	...	...	...	...	...
1—5	36,650	17,308	19,342	36,650	17,308	19,342	...	...	...	...	...	...
5—10	45,494	21,811	23,683	45,494	21,811	23,683	...	...	...	...	...	...
10—15	44,406	21,736	22,670	44,406	21,736	22,670	...	...	...	...	...	...
15—20	39,504	18,378	21,126	32,376	16,324	16,052	6,834	2,005	4,829	294	49	245
20—30	61,070	28,047	33,023	16,823	9,417	7,406	41,344	17,877	23,467	2,903	753	2,150
30—40	43,172	20,510	22,662	4,187	2,323	1,864	35,182	17,204	17,978	3,803	983	2,820
40—50	37,722	17,628	20,094	2,055	994	1,061	30,429	15,360	15,069	5,238	1,274	3,964
50—60	28,747	13,124	15,623	1,561	765	796	19,952	10,844	9,108	7,234	1,515	5,719
60 and over	30,692	13,610	17,082	1,998	1,096	902	13,668	8,712	4,956	15,026	3,802	11,224
Animist (all ages) ...	*888*	*805*	*83*	*161*	*126*	*35*	*204*	*164*	*40*	*23*	*15*	*8*
Hindu * ...	*2,538*	*1,925*	*613*	*1,151*	*846*	*305*	*1,226*	*948*	*278*	*161*	*131*	*30*
*Hindus born in Burma**	*603*	*331*	*272*	*496*	*266*	*230*	*98*	*60*	*38*	*9*	*5*	*4*
Mahomedan ...	*7,610*	*3,922*	*3,688*	*4,083*	*2,159*	*1,924*	*2,984*	*1,601*	*1,383*	*543*	*162*	*381*
0	197	86	111	197	86	111	...	...	...	...	...	...
1—5	874	442	432	874	442	432	...	...	...	...	...	...
5—10	954	453	501	954	453	501	...	...	...	...	...	...
10—15	964	497	467	961	497	464	3	...	3	...	...	...
15—20	771	372	399	590	315	275	173	57	116	8	...	8
20—30	1,348	727	621	359	261	98	920	432	488	69	34	35
30—40	875	493	382	83	65	18	739	408	331	53	20	33
40—50	720	392	328	38	22	16	588	342	246	94	28	66
50—60	437	239	198	14	9	5	325	200	125	98	30	68
60 and over	470	221	249	13	9	4	236	162	74	221	50	171
Mahomedans born in Burma.	*3,592*	*3,023*	*3,569*	*3,709*	*1,804*	*1,905*	*2,394*	*1,105*	*1,289*	*489*	*114*	*375*
0	192	81	111	192	81	111	...	...	...	...	...	...
1—5	851	423	428	851	423	428	...	...	...	...	...	...
5—10	915	419	496	915	419	496	...	...	...	...	...	...
10—15	928	465	463	926	465	461	2	...	2	...	...	...
15—20	696	308	388	541	269	272	147	39	108	8	...	8
20—30	1,058	476	582	214	118	96	782	331	451	62	27	35
30—40	622	271	351	34	17	17	544	243	301	44	11	33
40—50	560	250	310	21	6	15	457	228	229	82	16	66
50—60	356	162	194	8	3	5	261	137	124	87	22	65
60 and over	414	168	246	7	3	4	201	127	74	206	38	168
Christian (all ages)	*2,009*	*1,016*	*993*	*1,103*	*581*	*522*	*780*	*405*	*375*	*126*	*30*	*96*
Others (all ages) ...	*275*	*193*	*82*	*119*	*82*	*37*	*141*	*99*	*42*	*15*	*12*	*3*

* Details by age-groups omitted by mistake in this place are given on the last page of this table.

IMPERIAL TABLE VIIB.—*Age, Sex, and Civil Condition by Religion.*

	DISTRICT, RELIGION, AND AGE.	POPULATION.			UNMARRIED.			MARRIED.			WIDOWED.		
		Persons.	Males.	Females.	Persons.	Males.	Females.	Persons.	Males.	Females.	Persons.	Males.	Females.
	1	2	3	4	5	6	7	8	9	10	11	12	13
SAGAING.	*All Religions* ...	*326,908*	*155,054*	*171,854*	*177,742*	*88,744*	*88,998*	*118,054*	*57,674*	*60,380*	*31,112*	*8,636*	*22,476*
	0	10,179	4,854	5,325	10,179	4,854	5,325	...	...	...	...	...	...
	1— 5	33,387	16,174	17,213	33,387	16,174	17,213	...	...	...	...	...	...
	5—10	40,951	20,395	20,556	40,951	20,395	20,556	...	...	...	...	...	...
	10—15	38,133	18,934	19,199	38,130	18,934	19,196	3	...	3	...	...	...
	15—20	33,508	15,407	18,161	28,640	14,325	14,315	4,627	1,043	3,584	301	39	262
	20—30	53,546	24,882	28,664	17,254	9,814	7,440	33,340	14,316	19,024	2,952	752	2,200
	30—40	37,216	17,923	19,293	3,985	1,932	2,053	29,802	14,988	14,814	3,429	1,003	2,426
	40—50	30,981	14,389	16,592	2,090	925	1,165	23,693	12,057	11,636	5,198	1,407	3,791
	50—60	24,045	11,158	12,887	1,590	679	911	15,975	8,764	7,211	6,480	1,715	4,765
	60 and over	24,902	10,938	13,964	1,536	712	824	10,614	6,506	4,108	12,752	3,720	9,032
	Buddhist ...	*321,016*	*151,524*	*169,492*	*174,810*	*87,080*	*87,780*	*115,514*	*56,035*	*59,479*	*30,692*	*8,459*	*22,288*
	0	10,035	4,784	5,251	10,035	4,784	5,251	...	..	...	...	...	...
	1— 5	32,813	15,904	16,909	32,813	15,904	16,909	...	...	...	...	...	...
	5—10	40,282	20,045	20,237	40,282	20,045	20,237	...	...	...	...	...	...
	10—15	37,629	18,669	18,960	37,629	18,669	18,960	...	...	...	...	...	...
	15—20	33,036	15,127	17,909	28,239	14,076	14,163	4,498	1,013	3,485	299	38	261
	20—30	52,291	24,067	28,224	16,828	9,462	7,366	32,562	13,873	18,689	2,901	732	2,169
	30—40	36,238	17,225	19,013	3,844	1,819	2,025	29,046	14,453	14,593	3,348	953	2,395
	40—50	30,383	13,992	16,391	2,051	895	1,156	23,226	11,721	11,505	5,106	1,376	3,730
	50—60	23,666	10,924	12,742	1,507	670	897	15,702	8,575	7,127	6,397	1,679	4,718
	60 and over	24,643	10,787	13,856	1,522	706	816	10,480	6,400	4,080	12,641	3,681	8,960
	Animist (all ages) ...	*97*	*84*	*13*	*43*	*35*	*8*	*47*	*44*	*3*	*7*	*5*	*2*
	Hindu (all ages) ...	*1,956*	*1,382*	*574*	*830*	*560*	*270*	*1,001*	*747*	*254*	*125*	*75*	*50*
	Mahomedan ...	*2,811*	*1,563*	*1,248*	*1,482*	*831*	*651*	*1,114*	*651*	*463*	*215*	*81*	*314*
	0	77	31	46	77	31	46	...	...	...	...	...	...
	1— 5	276	120	156	276	120	156	...	...	...	...	...	...
	5—10	345	182	163	345	182	163	...	...	...	...	...	...
	10—15	274	148	126	274	148	126	...	...	...	...	...	...
	15—20	301	158	143	231	142	89	69	15	54	1	1	...
	20—30	589	362	227	206	163	43	355	189	166	28	10	18
	30—40	399	260	139	42	31	11	314	203	111	43	26	17
	40—50	253	137	116	19	13	6	186	114	72	48	10	38
	50—60	179	103	76	7	1	6	128	85	43	44	17	27
	60 and over	118	62	56	5	...	5	62	45	17	51	17	34
	Mahomsdans born in Burma.	*2,272*	*1,079*	*1,193*	*1,275*	*634*	*641*	*812*	*389*	*423*	*185*	*56*	*129*
	0	77	31	46	77	31	46	...	...	...	...	...	...
	1— 5	267	113	154	267	113	154	...	...	...	...	...	...
	5—10	338	177	161	338	177	161	...	...	...	...	...	...
	10—15	250	126	124	250	126	124	...	...	...	...	...	...
	15—20	254	118	136	194	106	88	59	11	48	1	1	...
	20—30	387	178	209	106	65	41	254	103	151	27	10	17
	30—40	271	147	124	23	13	10	219	121	98	29	13	16
	40—50	186	76	110	8	2	6	133	66	67	45	8	37
	50—60	144	68	76	7	1	6	97	54	43	40	13	27
	60 and over	98	45	53	5	...	5	50	34	16	43	11	32
	Ohristian (all ages)	*948*	*446*	*502*	*537*	*260*	*277*	*340*	*172*	*168*	*71*	*14*	*57*
	Others (all ages) ...	*80*	*55*	*25*	*40*	*28*	*12*	*38*	*25*	*13*	*2*	*2*	...
LOWER CHINDWIN.	*All Religions* ...	*342,880*	*156,693*	*186,187*	*176,072*	*85,968*	*90,104*	*130,693*	*63,853*	*67,840*	*36,115*	*7,872*	*28,743*
	0	10,722	5,064	5,658	10,722	5,064	5,658	...	...	...	...	...	...
	1— 5	33,525	15,908	17,617	33,525	15,908	17,617	...	...	...	...	...	...
	5—10	42,863	21,264	21,599	42,863	21,264	21,599	...	...	...	...	...	...
	10—15	39,390	19,711	19,679	39,353	19,710	19,643	37	1	36	...	...	...
	15—20	33,070	14,792	18,278	26,781	13,220	13,561	5,947	1,548	4,399	342	24	318
	20—30	52,504	22,792	29,712	13,521	6,858	6,663	35,771	15,298	20,473	3,212	636	2,576
	30—40	41,018	18,715	22,303	3,780	1,582	2,198	33,108	16,293	16,815	4,130	840	3,290
	40—50	33,018	14,818	18,200	2,008	926	1,082	25,513	12,827	12,686	5,497	1,065	4,432
	50—60	25,880	11,298	14,582	1,570	626	944	17,035	9,212	7,823	7,275	1,460	5,815
	60 and over	30,890	12,331	18,559	1,949	810	1,139	13,282	8,174	5,108	15,659	3,347	12,312

IMPERIAL TABLE VIIB.—*Age, Sex, and Civil Condition by Religion.*

DISTRICT, RELIGION, AND AGE.	POPULATION.			UNMARRIED.			MARRIED.			WIDOWED.		
	Persons.	Males.	Females.	Persons.	Males.	Females.	Persons.	Males.	Females.	Persons.	Males.	Females.
1	2	3	4	5	6	7	8	9	10	11	12	13
LOWER CHINDWIN—*concluded.*												
Buddhist ...	*840,065*	*154.657*	*185,608*	*174,867*	*85,101*	*89,766*	*129,221*	*62,196*	*67,025*	*35,977*	*7,260*	*28,717*
0	10,684	5,045	5,639	10,684	5,045	5,639	...	...	...	...	...	...
1—5	33,304	15,793	17,511	33,304	15,793	17,511	...	...	...	...	...	...
5—10	42,641	21,130	21,511	42,641	21,130	21,511	...	...	...	...	...	...
10—15	39,234	19,617	19,617	39,198	19,617	19,581	36	...	36	...	...	...
15—20	32,873	14,668	18,205	26,652	13,124	13.528	5,880	1,521	4,359	341	23	318
20—30	51,747	22,189	29,558	13,260	6,612	6,648	35,287	14,949	20,338	3,200	628	2,572
30—40	40,392	18,191	22,201	3,671	1,482	2,189	32,616	15,890	16,726	4,105	819	3,286
40—50	32,663	14,503	18,160	1,962	883	1,079	25,242	12,587	12,655	5.459	1,033	4,426
50—60	25,721	11,162	14,559	1,553	612	941	16,925	9,119	7,806	7,243	1,431	5,812
60 and over	30,806	12,259	18,547	1,942	803	1,139	13,235	8,130	5,105	15,629	3,326	12,303
Animist *(all ages)* ...	*141*	*126*	*15*	*59*	*53*	*6*	*76*	*70*	*6*	*6*	*3*	*3*
Hindu *(all ages)* ...	*1,299*	*1,006*	*293*	*521*	*390*	*131*	*721*	*567*	*154*	*57*	*49*	*8*
Mahomedan *(all ages)*	*1,025*	*794*	*231*	*449*	*329*	*120*	*515*	*412*	*103*	*61*	*53*	*8*
Christian *(all ages)*	*334*	*194*	*140*	*174*	*93*	*81*	*146*	*94*	*52*	*14*	*7*	*7*
Others *(all ages)* ...	*16*	*16*	...	*2*	*2*	...	*14*	*14*	...	...	...	...
UPPER CHINDWIN.												
All Religions ...	*179,245*	*90,713*	*88,532*	*92,593*	*43,749*	*48,844*	*70,684*	*36,882*	*33,802*	*15,968*	*5,082*	*10,886*
0	5,017	2,413	2,604	5,017	2,413	2,604	...	...	...	...	...	...
1—5	17,140	8,286	8,854	17,140	8,286	8,854	...	...	...	...	...	...
5—10	22,051	10,857	11,194	22,051	10,857	11,194	...	...	...	...	...	...
10—15	19,549	9,846	9,703	19,526	9,846	9,680	18	...	18	5	...	5
15—20	17,631	8,493	9,138	14,529	7,873	6,656	2,842	582	2,260	260	38	222
20—30	31,863	16,219	15,644	10,578	6,776	3,802	19.273	8,727	10,546	2,012	716	1,296
30—40	24,021	13,193	10,828	2,101	1,587	514	19,745	10,667	9,078	2,175	939	1,236
40—50	19,380	10,148	9,232	826	581	245	15,721	8,589	7,132	2,833	978	1,855
50—60	13,174	6,908	6,266	460	319	141	9,244	5,597	3,647	3,470	992	2,478
60 and over	9,419	4,350	5,069	365	211	154	3,841	2,720	1,121	5,213	1,419	3,794
Buddhist ...	*170,822*	*84,914*	*85,408*	*88,586*	*46,016*	*42,570*	*66,618*	*34,239*	*32,374*	*15,128*	*4,659*	*10,464*
0	4,874	2,347	2,527	4,874	2,347	2,527	...	...	...	...	...	...
1—5	16,607	7,992	8,615	16,607	7,992	8,615	...	...	...	...	...	...
5—10	21,280	10,463	10,817	21,280	10,463	10,817	...	...	...	...	...	...
10—15	18,847	9,447	9.400	18,826	9,447	9,379	16	...	16	5	...	5
15—20	16,801	8,017	8,784	13,920	7,144	6,476	2,635	539	2,096	246	34	212
20—30	29,554	14,601	14,953	9,750	6,015	3,735	17,902	7,925	9,977	1,902	661	1,241
30—40	22,222	11,912	10,310	1,790	1,297	493	18,457	9,801	8,656	1,975	814	1,161
40—50	18,311	9,396	8,915	752	515	237	14,969	8,026	6,943	2,590	855	1,735
50—60	12,631	6,529	6,102	435	296	139	8,893	5,315	3,578	3,303	918	2,385
60 and over	9,195	4,210	4,985	352	200	152	3,741	2,633	1,108	5,102	1,377	3,725
Animist ...	*3,665*	*1,982*	*1,733*	*1,699*	*1,002*	*697*	*1,646*	*790*	*756*	*420*	*140*	*280*
0	60	27	33	60	27	33	...	...	...	...	...	...
1—5	218	117	101	218	117	101	...	...	...	...	...	...
5—10	375	177	198	375	177	198	...	...	...	...	...	...
10—15	364	204	160	364	204	160	...	...	...	...	...	...
15—20	433	237	196	352	221	131	74	14	60	7	2	5
20—30	772	394	378	251	200	51	476	180	296	45	14	31
30—40	637	343	294	57	42	15	481	255	226	99	46	53
40—50	402	205	197	11	7	4	281	167	114	110	31	79
50—60	283	165	118	7	5	2	177	127	50	99	33	66
60 and over	121	63	58	4	2	2	57	47	10	60	14	46
Hindu ...	*3,223*	*2,472*	*751*	*1,370*	*1,087*	*283*	*1,583*	*1,192*	*391*	*270*	*193*	*77*
0	43	19	24	43	19	24	...	...	...	...	...	...
1—5	176	106	70	176	106	70	...	...	...	...	...	...
5—10	217	122	95	217	122	95	...	...	...	...	...	...
10—15	172	107	65	172	107	65	...	...	...	...	...	...
15—20	227	143	84	129	115	14	92	27	65	6	1	5
20—30	1,002	827	175	392	385	7	571	417	154	39	25	14
30—40	743	616	127	176	172	4	497	387	110	70	57	13
40—50	422	349	73	47	43	4	288	241	47	87	65	22
50—60	159	136	23	11	11	...	109	96	13	39	29	10
60 and over	60	47	15	7	7	...	26	24	2	29	16	13

IMPERIAL TABLE VIIB.—*Age, Sex, and Civil Condition by Religion.*

DISTRICT, RELIGION, AND AGE.	POPULATION. Persons.	POPULATION. Males.	POPULATION. Females.	UNMARRIED. Persons.	UNMARRIED. Males.	UNMARRIED. Females.	MARRIED. Persons.	MARRIED. Males.	MARRIED. Females.	WIDOWED. Persons.	WIDOWED. Males.	WIDOWED. Females.
1	2	3	4	5	6	7	8	9	10	11	12	13
UPPER CHINDWIN—concluded.												
Hindus born in Burma	*618*	*414*	*199*	*465*	*290*	*165*	*187*	*105*	*82*	*21*	*19*	*2*
0	39	18	21	39	18	21	...	...	...	...	...	...
1—5	131	81	50	131	81	50	...	...	...	...	...	...
5—10	133	74	59	133	74	59	...	...	...	...	...	...
10—15	67	41	26	67	41	26	...	...	...	...	...	...
15—20	39	25	14	30	23	7	9	2	7	...	...	...
20—30	83	64	19	37	36	1	41	25	16	5	3	2
30—40	60	53	7	13	12	1	38	32	6	9	9	...
40—50	39	36	3	5	5	...	29	26	3	5	5	...
50—60	13	13	...	...	...	...	12	12	...	1	1	...
60 and over	9	9	...	...	...	...	8	8	...	1	1	...
Mahomedan (all ages)	*1,023*	*758*	*265*	*441*	*309*	*132*	*526*	*411*	*115*	*56*	*38*	*18*
Christian (all ages)	*695*	*397*	*298*	*344*	*209*	*135*	*281*	*159*	*122*	*70*	*29*	*41*
Others (all ages) ...	*317*	*240*	*77*	*153*	*126*	*27*	*135*	*91*	*44*	*29*	*23*	*6*
CHIN HILLS.												
All Religions ...	*110,079*	*54,122*	*55,957*	*62,899*	*32,060*	*30,839*	*39,909*	*20,054*	*19,855*	*7,771*	*2,008*	*5 763*
0	1,515	730	785	1,515	730	785	...	...	...	...	...	...
1—5	12,198	5,942	6,256	12,198	5,942	6,256	...	...	...	...	...	...
5—10	15,435	7,718	7,717	15,435	7,718	7,717	...	...	...	...	...	...
10—15	12,170	6,290	5,880	12,143	6,282	5,861	27	8	19	...	...	...
15—20	10,848	5,313	5,535	9,548	5,071	4,477	1,221	199	1,022	79	43	36
20—30	18,793	8,587	10,206	8,032	4,759	3,273	10,197	3,587	6,610	544	241	323
30—40	16,294	7,947	8,347	2,059	1,058	1,001	12,850	6,454	6,396	1,385	435	950
40—50	10,719	5,354	5,365	769	323	446	8,100	4,589	3,511	1,850	442	1,408
50—60	7,012	3,592	3,420	379	107	272	4,707	3,084	1,623	1,926	401	1,525
60 and over	5,095	2,649	2,446	321	70	251	2,807	2,133	674	1,987	446	1,521
Buddhist (all ages)	*134*	*89*	*45*	*87*	*54*	*33*	*43*	*31*	*12*	*4*	*4*	..
Animist ...	*107,407*	*52,426*	*54,981*	*60,910*	*31,119*	*29,791*	*38,814*	*19,343*	*19,471*	*7,683*	*1,964*	*5,719*
0	1,453	701	752	1,453	701	752	...	...	...	...	...	...
1—5	11,913	5,811	6,102	11,913	5,811	6,102	...	...	...	...	...	...
5—10	15,089	7,545	7,544	15,089	7,545	7,544	...	...	...	...	...	...
10—15	11,904	6,131	5,773	11,877	6,123	5,754	27	8	19	...	...	...
15—20	10,593	5,168	5,425	9,363	4,933	4,430	1,151	192	959	79	43	36
20—30	18,173	8,127	10,046	7,794	4,542	3,252	9,819	3,347	6,472	560	238	322
30—40	15,935	7,700	8,235	1,998	1,002	996	12,566	6,270	6,296	1,371	428	943
40—50	10,426	5,135	5,291	744	302	442	7,855	4,407	3,448	1,827	426	1,401
50—60	6,894	3,500	3,394	367	98	269	4,620	3,011	1,609	1,907	391	1,516
60 and over	5,027	2,608	2,419	312	62	250	2,776	2,108	668	1,939	438	1,501
Hindu ...	*1,642*	*1,110*	*532*	*854*	*569*	*285*	*750*	*515*	*235*	*38*	*26*	*12*
0	36	17	19	36	17	19	...	...	...	...	...	...
1—5	190	87	103	190	87	103	...	...	...	...	...	...
5—10	200	103	97	200	103	97	...	...	...	...	...	...
10—15	128	78	50	128	78	50	...	...	...	...	...	...
15—20	128	61	67	72	56	16	56	5	51	...	...	...
20—30	459	371	88	163	163	...	293	205	88	3	3	...
30—40	216	162	54	36	36	...	174	121	53	6	5	1
40—50	183	149	34	17	17	...	157	125	32	9	7	2
50—60	66	54	12	5	5	...	53	44	9	8	5	3
60 and over	36	28	8	7	7	...	17	15	2	12	6	6
Hindus born in Burma	*659*	*324*	*335*	*579*	*315*	*264*	*79*	*9*	*70*	*1*	..	*1*
0	33	14	19	33	14	19	...	...	...	...	...	...
1—5	175	83	92	175	83	92	...	...	...	...	...	...
5—10	185	94	91	185	94	91	...	...	...	...	...	...
10—15	115	69	46	115	69	46	...	...	...	...	...	...
15—20	90	41	49	55	39	16	35	2	33	...	...	...
20—30	48	17	31	13	13	...	35	4	31	...	...	...
30—40	8	3	5	3	3	...	5	...	5	...	...	...
40—50	3	2	1	...	...	...	3	2	1	...	...	...
50—60	...	...	...	...	...	...	...	...	...	...	...	...
60 and over	2	1	1	...	...	...	1	1	...	1	...	1
Mahomedan (all ages)	*48*	*31*	*17*	*25*	*15*	*10*	*23*	*16*	*7*	..	..	..
Christian (all ages)	*826*	*450*	*376*	*514*	*297*	*217*	*267*	*140*	*127*	*45*	*13*	*32*
Others (all ages) ...	*22*	*16*	*6*	*9*	*6*	*3*	*12*	*9*	*3*	*1*	*1*	..

Imperial Table VIIb.—*Age, Sex, and Civil Condition by Religion.*

District, Religion, and Age.	Population. Persons.	Population. Males.	Population. Females.	Unmarried. Persons.	Unmarried. Males.	Unmarried. Females.	Married. Persons.	Married. Males.	Married. Females.	Widowed. Persons.	Widowed. Males.	Widowed. Females.
1	2	3	4	5	6	7	8	9	10	11	12	13
KYAUKSE.												
All Religions ...	*142,677*	*70,449*	*72,228*	*67,806*	*35,483*	*32,323*	*59,491*	*29,976*	*29,515*	*15,380*	*4,990*	*10,890*
0	4,140	2,040	2,100	4,140	2,040	2,100	...	...	...	...	...	...
1—5	12,667	6,301	6,366	12,667	6,301	6,366	...	...	...	...	...	...
5—10	14,680	7,164	7,516	14,680	7,164	7,516	...	...	...	...	...	...
10—15	15,096	7,633	7,463	15,039	7,619	7,420	57	14	43	...	...	...
15—20	14,648	6,863	7,785	11,557	6,202	5,355	2,876	614	2,262	215	47	168
20—30	25,706	12,457	13,249	6,509	4,083	2,426	17,638	7,797	9,841	1,559	577	982
30—40	16,756	8,605	8,151	1,254	825	429	13,862	7,092	6,770	1,640	688	952
40—50	16,768	8,608	8,160	787	509	278	13,182	7,083	6,099	2,799	1,016	1,783
50—60	11,619	5,815	5,804	564	361	203	7,613	4,465	3,148	3,442	989	2,453
60 and over	10,597	4,963	5,634	609	379	230	4,263	2,911	1,352	5,725	1,673	4,052
Buddhist ...	*135,082*	*66,277*	*68,805*	*63,968*	*33,350*	*30,618*	*56,381*	*28,173*	*28,208*	*14,733*	*4,754*	*9,979*
0	3,916	1,926	1,990	3,916	1,926	1,990	...	...	...	...	...	...
1—5	11,832	5,889	5,943	11,832	5,889	5,943	...	...	...	...	...	...
5—10	13,810	6,741	7,069	13,810	6,741	7,069	...	...	...	...	...	...
10—15	14,293	7,214	7,079	14,240	7,204	7,036	53	10	43	...	...	...
15—20	13,971	6,531	7,440	11,042	5,908	5,134	2,723	578	2,145	206	45	161
20—30	24,242	11,610	12,632	6,119	3,775	2,344	16,667	7,300	9,367	1,456	535	921
30—40	15,701	7,933	7,768	1,138	726	412	13,007	6,561	6,446	1,556	646	910
40—50	15,976	8,138	7,838	739	470	269	12,565	6,709	5,856	2,672	959	1,713
50—60	11,152	5,535	5,617	541	342	199	7,290	4,242	3,048	3,321	951	2,370
60 and over	10,189	4,760	5,429	591	369	222	4,076	2,773	1,303	5,522	1,618	3,904
Animist (all ages) ...	*157*	*110*	*47*	*67*	*48*	*19*	*84*	*59*	*25*	*6*	*3*	*3*
Hindu (all ages) ...	*1,028*	*821*	*207*	*416*	*318*	*98*	*538*	*447*	*91*	*74*	*56*	*18*
Mahomedan ...	*5,740*	*2,896*	*2,844*	*2,990*	*1,582*	*1,408*	*2,217*	*1,149*	*1,068*	*533*	*165*	*368*
0	171	92	79	171	92	79	...	...	...	...	...	...
1—5	691	350	341	691	350	341	...	...	...	...	...	...
5—10	730	349	381	730	349	381	...	...	...	...	...	...
10—15	662	332	330	662	332	330	...	...	...	...	...	...
15—20	532	255	277	413	236	177	111	17	94	8	2	6
20—30	1,029	522	507	227	160	67	709	326	383	93	36	57
30—40	674	363	311	42	27	15	567	310	257	65	26	39
40—50	565	293	272	26	19	7	445	240	205	94	34	60
50—60	342	182	160	12	8	4	238	152	86	92	22	70
60 and over	344	158	186	16	9	7	147	104	43	181	45	136
Mahomedans born in Burma.	*5,517*	*2,720*	*2,797*	*2,929*	*1,536*	*1,393*	*2,090*	*1,050*	*1,040*	*498*	*134*	*364*
0	171	92	79	171	92	79	...	...	...	...	...	...
1—5	690	350	340	690	350	340	...	...	...	...	...	...
5—10	725	347	378	725	347	378	...	...	...	...	...	...
10—15	650	326	324	650	326	324	...	...	...	...	...	...
15—20	528	253	275	409	234	175	111	17	94	8	2	6
20—30	949	458	491	208	143	65	664	295	369	77	20	57
30—40	620	318	302	29	15	14	531	281	250	60	22	38
40—50	531	262	269	21	14	7	422	220	202	88	28	60
50—60	324	169	155	12	8	4	223	140	83	89	21	68
60 and over	329	145	184	14	7	7	139	97	42	176	41	135
Christian (all ages)	*592*	*292*	*300*	*323*	*157*	*166*	*237*	*125*	*112*	*32*	*10*	*22*
Others (all ages) ...	*78*	*53*	*25*	*42*	*28*	*14*	*34*	*23*	*11*	*2*	*2*	..
MEIKTILA.												
All Religions ...	*289,897*	*137,573*	*152,324*	*158,213*	*79,397*	*78,816*	*106,621*	*51,911*	*54,710*	*25,063*	*6,265*	*18,798*
0	7,827	3,795	4,032	7,827	3,795	4,032	...	...	...	...	...	...
1—5	25,070	11,706	13,364	25,070	11,706	13,364	...	...	...	...	...	...
5—10	35,015	17,032	17,983	35,015	17,032	17,983	...	...	...	...	...	...
10—15	35,090	17,468	17,622	34,977	17,364	17,613	113	104	9	...	...	...
15—20	31,409	14,582	16,827	27,116	13,777	13,339	4,092	784	3,308	201	21	180
20—30	48,378	22,783	25,595	17,357	9,764	7,593	28,753	12,460	16,293	2,268	559	1,709
30—40	33,518	16,150	17,368	3,986	2,101	1,885	26,689	13,191	13,498	2,843	858	1,985
40—50	29,099	13,860	15,239	3,347	2,140	1,207	21,649	10,667	10,982	4,103	1,053	3,050
50—60	21,255	10,070	11,185	1,731	850	881	14,475	7,980	6,495	5,049	1,240	3,809
60 and over	23,236	10,127	13,109	1,787	868	919	10,850	6,725	4,125	10,599	2,534	8,065

Imperial Table VIIb.—*Age, Sex, and Civil Condition by Religion.*

District, Religion, and Age.	Population. Persons.	Population. Males.	Population. Females.	Unmarried. Persons.	Unmarried. Males.	Unmarried. Females.	Married. Persons.	Married. Males.	Married. Females.	Widowed. Persons.	Widowed. Males.	Widowed. Females.
1	2	3	4	5	6	7	8	9	10	11	12	13
MEIKTILA—concluded.												
Buddhist ...	*281,618*	*132,184*	*149,434*	*154,127*	*76,733*	*77,394*	*102,922*	*49,491*	*58,431*	*24,569*	*5,960*	*18,609*
0	7,587	3,681	3,906	7,587	3,681	3,906	...	...	...	...	...	...
1—5	24,419	11,379	13,040	24,419	11,379	13,040	...	...	...	...	...	..
5—10	34,212	16,637	17,575	34,212	16,637	17,575	...	...	...	...	...	...
10—15	34,377	17,071	17,306	34,274	16,968	17,306	103	103	...	...	..	...
15—20	30,646	14,138	16,508	26,580	13,395	13,185	3,875	724	3,151	191	19	172
20—30	46,354	21,367	24,987	16,612	9,086	7,526	27,557	11,783	15,774	2,185	498	1,687
30—40	31,965	14,967	16,998	3,721	1,850	1,871	25,517	12,352	13,165	2,727	765	1,962
40—50	28,265	13,246	15,019	3,269	2,074	1,195	21,009	10,195	10,814	3,987	977	3,010
50—60	20,817	9,747	11,070	1,684	812	872	14,164	7,730	6,434	4,969	1,205	3,764
60 and over	22,976	9,951	13,025	1,769	851	918	10,697	6,604	4,093	10,510	2,496	8,014
Animist ...	*849*	*805*	*44*	*110*	*94*	*16*	*174*	*148*	*26*	*65*	*63*	*2*
Hindu (all ages) ...	*2,644*	*2,005*	*639*	*1,190*	*895*	*295*	*1,277*	*971*	*306*	*177*	*139*	*38*
Mahomedan ...	*4,283*	*2,369*	*1,914*	*2,221*	*1,242*	*979*	*1,853*	*1,046*	*807*	*209*	*81*	*128*
0	166	75	91	166	75	91	...	...	...	...	...	...
1—5	397	190	207	397	190	207	...	...	...	...	...	...
1—10	561	262	299	561	262	299	..	...	...	...	...	...
10—15	483	273	210	483	273	210	...	...	...	...	...	...
15—20	449	219	230	308	190	118	134	28	106	7	1	6
20—30	833	459	374	202	164	38	600	279	321	31	16	15
30—40	599	384	215	58	53	5	507	313	194	34	18	16
40—50	402	252	150	22	16	6	334	217	117	46	19	27
50—60	235	159	76	20	15	5	177	133	44	38	11	27
60 and over	158	96	62	4	4	...	101	76	25	53	16	37
Mahomedans born in Burma.	*3,232*	*1,472*	*1,760*	*1,944*	*991*	*953*	*1,143*	*448*	*695*	*145*	*33*	*112*
0	166	75	91	166	75	91	...	...	...	...	...	...
1—5	377	178	199	377	178	199	...	...	...	...	...	...
5—10	543	253	290	543	253	290	...	...	...	...	...	...
10—15	449	243	206	449	243	206	...	...	...	...	...	...
15—20	382	173	209	269	153	116	107	20	87	6	...	6
20—30	564	242	322	108	72	36	432	160	272	24	10	14
30—40	322	135	187	15	11	4	287	117	170	20	7	13
40—50	218	85	133	8	2	6	182	77	105	28	6	22
50—60	121	53	68	7	2	5	84	45	39	30	6	24
60 and over	90	35	55	2	2	...	51	29	22	37	4	33
Christian ...	*772*	*532*	*240*	*475*	*368*	*107*	*265*	*153*	*112*	*32*	*11*	*21*
Others (all ages) ...	*231*	*178*	*53*	*90*	*65*	*25*	*130*	*102*	*28*	*11*	*11*	..
YAMÈTHIN.												
All Religions ...	*323,189*	*160,913*	*162,276*	*171,054*	*89,177*	*81,877*	*128,752*	*65,349*	*63,403*	*23,383*	*6,387*	*16,996*
0	8,010	3,871	4,139	8,010	3,871	4,139	...	...	...	...	...	...
1—5	29,380	14,196	15,184	29,380	14,196	15,184	...	...	...	...	...	...
5—10	42,328	20,325	22,003	42,326	20,323	22,003	2	2	...	...	...	...
10—15	38,915	19,686	19,229	38,862	19,647	19,215	53	39	14	...	...	...
15—20	32,201	15,900	16,301	26,517	14,871	11,646	5,430	997	4,433	354	32	322
20—30	55,174	27,192	27,982	17,427	11,154	6,273	35,545	15,371	20,174	2,202	667	1,535
30—40	40,026	21,126	18,900	3,854	2,509	1,345	33,506	17,651	15,855	2,666	966	1,700
40—50	34,101	17,683	16,418	2,070	1,212	858	27,859	15,185	12,674	4,172	1,286	2,886
50—60	21,217	10,732	10,485	1,218	707	511	15,242	8,871	6,371	4,757	1,154	3,603
60 and over	21,837	10,202	11,635	1,390	687	703	11,115	7,233	3,882	9,332	2,282	7,050
Buddhist ...	*298,565*	*146,086*	*152,479*	*158,402*	*81,521*	*76,881*	*118,336*	*58,808*	*59,528*	*21,827*	*5,757*	*16,070*
0	7,496	3,650	3,846	7,496	3,650	3,846	...	...	...	...	...	...
1—5	27,079	13,039	14,040	27,079	13,039	14,040	...	...	...	...	...	...
5—10	39,525	18,901	20,624	39,525	18,901	20,624	...	...	...	...	...	...
10—15	36,661	18,449	18,212	36,623	18,419	18,204	38	30	8	...	...	...
15—20	29,976	14,688	15,288	24,800	13,814	10,986	4,927	843	4,084	249	31	218
20—30	49,861	23,761	26,100	15,524	9,578	5,946	32,311	13,607	18,704	2,026	576	1,450
30—40	35,770	18,117	17,653	3,130	1,866	1,264	30,243	15,431	14,812	2,397	820	1,577
40—50	31,519	15,968	15,551	1,781	977	804	25,893	13,847	12,046	3,845	1,144	2,701
50—60	19,906	9,907	9,999	1,114	631	483	14,347	8,221	6,126	4,445	1,055	3,390
60 and over	20,772	9,606	11,166	1,330	646	684	10,577	6,829	3,748	8,865	2,131	6,734
Animist (all ages) ...	*2,719*	*1,577*	*1,142*	*1,505*	*868*	*637*	*1,098*	*654*	*444*	*116*	*55*	*61*

IMPERIAL TABLE VIIB.—*Age, Sex, and Civil Condition by Religion.*

District	Religion and Age	Population: Persons	Population: Males	Population: Females	Unmarried: Persons	Unmarried: Males	Unmarried: Females	Married: Persons	Married: Males	Married: Females	Widowed: Persons	Widowed: Males	Widowed: Females
1		2	3	4	5	6	7	8	9	10	11	12	13
YAMÈTHIN—*concluded.*	***Hindu*** ...	***6,220***	***4,797***	***1,428***	***2,782***	***2,098***	***689***	***3,225***	***2,521***	***704***	***263***	***188***	***80***
	0	97	49	48	97	49	48	...	...	...	...	...	...
	1—5	358	169	189	358	169	189	...	...	...	...	...	...
	5—10	413	210	203	411	208	203	2	2	...	...	...	...
	10—15	316	207	109	307	202	105	9	5	4	...	...	...
	15—20	435	317	118	261	233	28	173	83	90	1	1	...
	20—30	1,848	1,510	338	751	707	44	1,062	775	287	35	28	7
	30—40	1,564	1,321	243	359	346	13	1,130	908	222	75	67	8
	40—50	752	657	95	133	128	5	557	486	71	62	43	19
	50—60	282	234	48	38	36	2	202	178	24	42	20	22
	60 and over	155	123	32	17	15	2	90	84	6	48	24	24
	Hindus born in Burma	***941***	***470***	***471***	***765***	***389***	***376***	***164***	***77***	***87***	***12***	***4***	***8***
	0	79	43	36	79	43	36	...	...	...	...	...	...
	1—5	247	118	129	247	118	129	...	...	...	...	...	...
	5—10	225	100	125	223	98	125	2	2	...	...	...	...
	10—15	115	56	59	111	56	55	4	...	4	...	...	...
	15—20	81	41	40	49	30	19	32	11	21	...	...	...
	20—30	99	50	49	38	27	11	60	23	37	1	...	1
	30—40	55	36	19	12	11	1	41	24	17	2	1	1
	40—50	21	13	8	5	5	...	13	7	6	3	1	2
	50—60	10	9	1	1	1	...	7	7	...	2	1	1
	60 and over	9	4	5	...	...	...	5	3	2	4	1	3
	Mahomedan ...	***12,908***	***6,896***	***6,012***	***6,888***	***3,769***	***3,069***	***5,049***	***2,792***	***2,257***	***1,021***	***885***	***686***
	0	339	130	209	339	130	209	...	...	...	...	...	...
	1—5	1,337	675	662	1,337	675	662	...	...	...	...	...	...
	5—10	1,653	842	811	1,653	842	811	...	...	...	...	...	...
	10—15	1,375	719	656	1,370	715	655	5	4	1	...	...	...
	15—20	1,286	643	643	1,041	590	451	241	53	188	4	...	4
	20—30	2,427	1,308	1,119	709	526	183	1,607	733	874	111	49	62
	30—40	1,807	1,126	681	224	182	42	1,434	886	548	149	58	91
	40—50	1,244	696	548	86	58	28	954	571	383	204	67	137
	50—60	718	391	327	49	31	18	471	306	165	198	54	144
	60 and over	722	366	356	30	20	10	337	239	98	355	107	248
	Mahomedans born in Burma.	***10,813***	***5,110***	***5,703***	***6,176***	***3,162***	***3,014***	***3,766***	***1,745***	***2,021***	***871***	***203***	***668***
	0	334	126	208	334	126	208	...	...	...	...	...	...
	1—5	1,303	662	641	1,303	662	641	...	...	...	...	...	...
	5—10	1,631	820	801	1,631	820	801	...	...	...	...	...	...
	10—15	1,319	671	648	1,315	667	648	4	4	...	...	...	...
	15—20	1,158	530	628	936	491	445	218	39	179	4	...	4
	20—30	1,791	778	1,013	452	275	177	1,249	474	775	90	29	61
	30—40	1,213	607	606	111	71	40	996	513	483	106	23	83
	40—50	884	389	495	50	24	26	669	332	337	165	33	132
	50—60	567	256	311	33	15	18	362	210	152	172	31	141
	60 and over	623	271	352	21	11	10	268	173	95	334	87	247
	Christian (all ages)	***2,416***	***1,285***	***1,131***	***1,388***	***774***	***614***	***886***	***467***	***419***	***142***	***44***	***98***
	0	38	18	20	38	18	20	...	...	...	...	...	...
	1—5	305	152	153	305	152	153	...	...	...	...	...	...
	5—10	339	159	180	339	159	180	...	...	...	...	...	...
	10—15	265	152	113	265	152	113	...	...	...	...	...	...
	15—20	256	116	140	200	108	92	56	8	48	...	...	...
	20—30	469	270	199	177	138	39	269	122	147	23	10	13
	30—40	329	188	141	39	31	8	263	147	116	27	10	17
	40—50	218	121	97	17	11	6	177	103	74	24	7	17
	50—60	116	62	54	4	1	3	76	51	25	36	10	26
	60 and over	81	47	34	4	4	...	45	36	9	32	7	25
	Other (all ages) ...	***361***	***272***	***89***	***189***	***152***	***37***	***158***	***107***	***51***	***14***	***13***	***1***
MYINGYAN.	***All Religions*** ...	***442,008***	***213,294***	***228,714***	***239,714***	***119,195***	***120,519***	***168,147***	***84,935***	***83,212***	***34,147***	***9,164***	***24,983***
	0	10,180	4,914	5,266	10,180	4,914	5,266	...	...	...	...	...	...
	1—5	44,771	21,831	22,940	44,771	21,831	22,940	...	...	...	...	...	...
	5—10	54,079	26,187	27,892	54,079	26,187	27,892	...	...	...	...	...	...
	10—15	53,640	26,707	26,933	53,636	26,706	26,930	4	1	3	...	...	...
	15—20	46,301	21,445	24,856	39,500	19,562	19,938	6,477	1,839	4,638	324	44	280
	20—30	72,504	34,742	37,762	23,529	13,099	10,430	46,082	20,923	25,159	2,893	720	2,173
	30—40	52,944	26,887	26,057	5,504	2,981	2,523	43,542	22,740	20,802	3,898	1,166	2,732
	40—50	43,497	20,806	22,691	3,232	1,475	1,757	34,436	17,784	16,652	5,829	1,547	4,282
	50—60	31,898	15,138	16,760	2,529	1,107	1,422	28,024	12,134	9,890	7,345	1,897	5,448
	60 and over	32,194	14,637	17,557	2,754	1,333	1,421	15,582	9,514	6,068	13,858	3,790	10,068

Imperial Table VIIb.—*Age, Sex, and Civil Condition by Religion.*

District, Religion, and Age.	Population. Persons.	Population. Males.	Population. Females.	Unmarried. Persons.	Unmarried. Males.	Unmarried. Females.	Married. Persons.	Married. Males.	Married. Females.	Widowed. Persons.	Widowed. Males.	Widowed. Females.
1	2	3	4	5	6	7	8	9	10	11	12	13
MYINGYAN—concluded.												
Buddhist ..	*488,874*	*210,540*	*227,834*	*238,079*	*118,012*	*120,067*	*166,294*	*83,468*	*82,831*	*34,001*	*9,065*	*24,936*
0	10,101	4,878	5,223	10,101	4,878	5,223	...	...	...	...	...	...
1—5	44,513	21,704	22,809	44,513	21,704	22,809	...	...	...	...	...	...
5—10	53,803	26,030	27,773	53,803	26,030	27,773	...	...	...	...	...	...
10—15	53,448	26,596	26,852	53,448	26,596	26,852	...	...	...	...	...	...
15—20	46,031	21,270	24,761	39,328	19,435	19,893	6,382	1,792	4,590	321	43	278
20—30	71,409	33,834	37,575	23,110	12,700	10,410	45,431	20,432	24,999	2,868	702	2,166
30—40	52,112	26,169	25,943	5,337	2,823	2,514	42,908	22,206	20,702	3,867	1140	2,727
40—50	43,147	20,518	22,629	3,188	1,433	1,755	34,169	17,562	16,607	5,790	1,523	4,267
50—60	31,720	14,991	16,729	2,508	1,089	1,419	21,895	12,023	9,872	7,317	1,879	5,438
60 and over	32,090	14,550	17,540	2,743	1,324	1,419	15,509	9,448	6,061	13,838	3,778	10,060
Animist (all ages) ..	*382*	*295*	*87*	*179*	*134*	*45*	*190*	*151*	*39*	*13*	*10*	*8*
Hi (all ages) ..	*1,724*	*1,399*	*325*	*700*	*559*	*141*	*953*	*786*	*167*	*71*	*54*	*17*
Mahomedan (all ages)	*1,156*	*833*	*323*	*565*	*380*	*185*	*551*	*429*	*122*	*40*	*24*	*16*
Christian (all ages) ..	*342*	*202*	*140*	*184*	*106*	*78*	*136*	*85*	*51*	*22*	*11*	*11*
Others (all ages) ..	*30*	*25*	*5*	*7*	*4*	*3*	*23*	*21*	*2*	...	...	...
NORTHERN SHAN STATES.												
Religions ..	*559,223*	*285,700*	*273,523*	*286,762*	*156,506*	*130,256*	*215,993*	*111,303*	*104,690*	*56,468*	*17,891*	*38,577*
0	12,743	6,200	6,543	12,743	6,200	6,543	...	...	...	...	...	...
1—5	55,432	27,089	28,343	55,432	27,089	28,343	...	...	...	...	...	...
5—10	70,986	35,795	35,191	70,986	35,795	35,191	...	...	...	...	...	...
10—15	55,932	29,087	26,845	55,822	29,063	26,759	103	24	79	7	...	7
15—20	54,547	26,694	27,853	44,217	24,760	19,457	9,401	1,794	7,607	929	140	789
20—30	101,280	51,513	49,767	34,585	24,625	9,960	60,386	24,189	36,197	6,309	2,699	3,610
30—40	74,992	40,857	34,135	7,670	5,795	1,875	59,448	31,479	27,969	7,874	3,583	4,291
40—50	55,767	30.836	24,931	2,382	1,650	732	43,875	25,633	18,242	9,510	3,553	5,957
50—60	38,722	20,924	17,798	1,434	879	555	26,171	16,764	9,407	11,117	3,281	7,836
60 and over	38,822	16,705	22,117	1,491	650	841	16,609	11,420	5,189	20,722	4,635	16,087
Buddhist ..	*415,893*	*208,446*	*207,447*	*216,755*	*116,440*	*100,315*	*155,314*	*77,733*	*77,581*	*43,824*	*14,273*	*29,551*
0	10,398	5,072	5,326	10,398	5,072	5,326	...	...	...	...	...	...
1—5	41,500	20,181	21,319	41,500	20,181	21,319	...	...	...	...	...	...
5—10	53,570	26,740	26,830	53,570	26,740	26,830	...	...	...	...	...	...
10—15	43,709	22,397	21,312	43,635	22,389	21,246	67	8	59	7	...	7
15—20	41,616	19,754	21,862	33,896	18,576	15,320	6,855	1,063	5,792	865	115	750
20—30	72,583	35,100	37,483	24,439	17,078	7,361	42,805	15,838	26,967	5,339	2,184	3,155
30—40	51,126	26,924	24,202	5,172	3,891	1,281	40,040	20,345	19,695	5,914	2,688	3,226
40—50	40,790	22,415	18,375	1,731	1,210	521	32,003	18.457	13,546	7,056	2,748	4,308
50—60	30,261	16,377	13,884	1,138	727	411	20,492	12,999	7,493	8,631	2,651	5,980
60 and over	30,340	13,486	16,854	1,276	576	700	13,052	9,023	4,029	16,012	3,887	12,125
Animists ..	*131,057*	*67,495*	*63,562*	[illegible]	*36,490*	*28,838*	*53,798*	*27,923*	*25,875*	*11,981*	*3,082*	*8,849*
0	2,200	1,050	1,150	2,200	1,050	1,150	...	...	...	...	...	...
1—5	13,289	6,593	6,696	13,289	6,593	6,696	...	...	...	...	...	...
5—10	16,779	8,707	8,072	16,779	8,707	8,072	...	...	...	...	...	...
10—15	11,692	6,367	5,325	11,666	6,355	5,311	26	12	14	...	...	...
15—20	12,082	6,344	5,738	9,739	5,704	4,035	2,286	619	1,667	57	21	36
20—30	24,435	12,764	11,671	8,671	6,133	2,538	14,944	6,252	8,692	820	379	441
30—40	20,734	11,197	9,537	2,029	1,464	565	16,924	8,992	7,932	1,781	741	1,040
40—50	13,623	7,244	6,379	500	301	199	10,818	6,258	4,560	2,305	685	1,620
50—60	7,991	4,172	3,819	255	120	135	5,359	3,494	1,865	2,377	558	1,819
60 and over	8,232	3,057	5,175	200	63	137	3,441	2,296	1,145	4,591	698	3,893
Hindu ...	*7,804*	*6,686*	*1,118*	*2,702*	*2,240*	*462*	*4,698*	*4,092*	*606*	*404*	*354*	*50*
0	74	39	35	74	39	35	...	...	...	...	...	...
1—5	342	158	184	342	158	184	...	...	...	...	...	...
5—10	296	168	128	296	168	128	...	...	...	...	...	...
10—15	237	152	85	229	148	81	8	4	4	...	...	...
15—20	526	401	125	324	301	23	198	98	100	4	2	2
20—30	3,052	2,770	282	1,007	1,002	5	1,940	1,667	273	105	101	4
30—40	2,079	1,909	170	305	302	3	1,671	1,511	160	103	96	7
40—50	853	788	65	95	92	3	674	622	52	84	74	10
50—60	247	222	25	23	23	...	165	149	16	59	50	9
60 and over	98	79	19	7	7	...	42	41	1	49	31	18

IMPERIAL TABLE VIIB.—*Age, Sex, and Civil Condition by Religion.*

District, Religion, and Age.	Population. Persons.	Population. Males.	Population. Females.	Unmarried. Persons.	Unmarried. Males.	Unmarried. Females.	Married. Persons.	Married. Males.	Married. Females.	Widowed. Persons.	Widowed. Males.	Widowed. Females.
1	2	3	4	5	6	7	8	9	10	11	12	13
NORTHERN SHAN STATES—concld.												
Hindus born in Burma.	*801*	*402*	*399*	*707*	*370*	*337*	*86*	*28*	*58*	*8*	*4*	*4*
0	64	31	33	64	31	33	...	...	...	...	...	...
1—5	279	127	152	279	127	152	...	...	...	...	...	...
5—10	200	108	92	200	108	92	..	...	...	...	...	...
10—15	109	59	50	104	58	46	5	1	4	...	...	...
15—20	54	22	32	31	19	12	23	3	20	...	...	...
20—30	58	31	27	18	17	1	39	13	26	1	1	...
30—40	17	13	4	6	5	1	11	8	3	...	...	...
40—50	14	9	5	5	5	...	4	1	3	5	3	2
50—60	3	...	3	...	...	...	2	...	2	1	...	1
60 and over	3	2	1	...	...	...	2	2	...	1	...	1
Mahomedan (all ages)	*2,286*	*1,815*	*471*	*927*	*781*	*196*	*1,198*	*949*	*249*	*161*	*135*	*26*
Christian (all ages)	*1,929*	*1,050*	*879*	*983*	*557*	*426*	*811*	*459*	*352*	*135*	*34*	*101*
Others (all ages) ...	*254*	*208*	*46*	*67*	*48*	*19*	*174*	*147*	*27*	*18*	*18*	...
SOUTHERN SHAN STATES.												
All Religions ..	*847,618*	*427,064*	*420,554*	*427,116*	*232,445*	*194,671*	*326,741*	*163,753*	*162,988*	*93,761*	*30,866*	*62,895*
0	19,318	9,425	9,893	19,318	9,425	9,893	...	...	...	...	...	...
1—5	80,711	39,954	40,757	80,711	39,954	40,757	...	...	...	..	...	...
5—10	104,848	52,585	52,263	104,848	52,585	52,263	...	...	...	...	...	...
10—15	88,885	46,861	42,024	88,627	46,859	41,768	258	2	256	...	..	...
15—20	90,040	43,405	46,635	71,137	40,461	30,676	16,534	2,559	13,975	2,369	385	1,984
20—30	149,565	72,518	77,047	45,599	31,885	13,714	91,186	35,676	55,510	12,780	4,957	7,823
30—40	111,503	59,158	52,345	9,607	6,809	2,798	88,060	46,306	41,754	13,836	6,043	7,793
40—50	87,863	45,383	42,480	3,526	2,293	1,233	67,904	37,431	30,473	16,433	5,659	10,774
50—60	60,527	32,167	28,360	2,047	1,263	784	40,009	25,272	14,737	18,471	5,632	12,839
60 and over	54,358	25,608	28,750	1,696	911	785	22,790	16,507	6,283	29,872	8,190	21,682
Buddhist ..	*748,051*	*373,450*	*374,601*	*379,559*	*205,212*	*174,347*	*282,167*	*140,511*	*141,656*	*86,325*	*27,727*	*58,598*
0	17,819	8,636	9,183	17,819	8,636	9,183	...	...	...	...	...	...
1—5	69,618	34,520	35,098	69,618	34,520	35,098	...	...	...	...	...	...
5—10	92,636	46,007	46,629	92,636	46,007	46,629	...	...	...	...	...	...
10—15	79,868	41,994	37,874	79,689	41,994	37,695	179	...	179	...	...	...
15—20	80,009	38,085	41,924	63,773	35,884	27,889	13,975	1,873	12,102	2,261	328	1,933
20—30	129,569	62,141	67,428	40,868	28,286	12,582	76,735	29,317	47,418	11,966	4,538	7,428
30—40	96,251	50,221	46,030	8,479	5,873	2,606	75,277	39,083	36,194	12,495	5,265	7,230
40—50	78,067	39,949	38,118	3,201	2,026	1,175	59,841	32,853	26,988	15,025	5,070	9,955
50—60	54,774	28,886	25,888	1,892	1,152	740	35,898	22,628	13,270	16,984	5,106	11,878
60 and over	49,440	23,011	26,429	1,584	834	750	20,262	14,757	5,505	27,594	7,420	20,174
Animist ..	*81,211*	*42,672*	*38,539*	*38,256*	*21,598*	*16,668*	*36,631*	*18,521*	*18,110*	*6,324*	*2,558*	*3,766*
0	1,042	557	485	1,042	557	485	...	...	...	...	...	...
1—5	8,933	4,331	4,602	8,933	4,331	4,602	...	..	...	...	...	...
5—10	10,112	5,474	4,638	10,112	5,474	4,638	...	...	...	...	...	...
10—15	7,285	3,894	3,391	7,214	[illegible]	3,320	71	...	71	...	...	...
15—20	8,326	4,447	3,879	6,244	3,855	2,389	1,993	541	1,452	89	51	38
20—30	16,053	7,940	8,113	3,574	2,609	965	11,793	4,978	6,815	686	353	333
30—40	12,301	6,909	5,392	749	598	151	10,481	5,719	4,762	1,071	592	479
40—50	8,065	4,258	3,807	204	156	48	6,666	3,627	3,039	1,195	475	720
50—60	4,824	2,665	2,159	106	66	40	3,450	2,173	1,277	1,268	426	842
60 and over	4,270	2,197	2,073	78	53	25	2,177	1,483	694	2,015	661	1,354
Hindu (all ages) ...	*4,908*	*3,721*	*1,187*	*2,240*	*1,701*	*539*	*2,348*	*1,757*	*591*	*320*	*263*	*57*
Hindus born in Burma (all ages).	*1,235*	*662*	*573*	*1,069*	*612*	*457*	*157*	*47*	*110*	*9*	*3*	*6*
Mahomedan (all ages)	*2,310*	*1,467*	*843*	*1,104*	*693*	*411*	*1,057*	*674*	*383*	*149*	*100*	*49*
Christian ..	*11,137*	*5,754*	*5,383*	*5,957*	*3,246*	*2,711*	*4,537*	*2,290*	*2,247*	*643*	*218*	*425*
0	262	127	135	262	127	135	...	...	...	...	...	...
1—5	1,527	769	758	1,527	769	758	...	...	...	...	...	...
5—10	1,449	741	708	1,449	741	708	...	...	...	...	...	...
10—15	1,288	718	570	1,288	718	570	...	...	...	...	...	...
15—20	1,182	568	614	818	484	334	351	81	270	13	3	10
20—30	2,037	987	1,050	452	303	149	1,501	654	847	84	30	54
30—40	1,426	765	661	90	56	34	1,218	661	557	118	48	70
40—50	886	477	409	24	15	9	770	435	335	92	27	65
50—60	583	319	264	23	19	4	425	261	164	135	39	96
60 and over	497	283	214	24	14	10	272	198	74	201	71	130
Others (all ages) ...	*1*	...	*1*	...	...	...	*1*	...	*1*	...	...	...

Imperial Table VIIb.—*Age, Sex, and Civil Condition by Religion.*

DISTRICT, RELIGION, AND AGE.	POPULATION.			UNMARRIED.			MARRIED.			WIDOWED.		
	Persons.	Males.	Females.	Persons.	Males.	Females.	Persons.	Males.	Females.	Persons.	Males.	Females.
1	2	3	4	5	6	7	8	9	10	11	12	13
KARENNI.												
All Religions ..	*63,850*	*31,129*	*32,721*	*32,002*	*16,622*	*15,380*	*23,893*	*11,985*	*11,908*	*7,955*	*2,522*	*5,488*
0	1,676	804	872	1,676	804	872	...	...	...	...	...	...
1—5	7,149	3,563	3,586	7,149	3,563	3,586	...	...	...	...	...	..
5—10	8,122	4,082	4,040	8,122	4,082	4,040	...	...	...	...	...	...
10—15	6,566	3,396	3,170	6,544	3,375	3,169	22	21	1	...	...	...
15—20	5,375	2,372	3,003	4,168	2,148	2,020	1,028	186	842	179	38	141
20—30	10,900	4,756	6,144	3,161	1,894	1,267	6,685	2,475	4,210	1,054	387	667
30—40	10,200	5,242	4,958	707	485	222	7,914	4,162	3,752	1,579	595	984
40—50	7,091	3,597	3,494	262	162	100	4,914	2,867	2,047	1,915	568	1,347
50—60	3,933	1,992	1,941	122	63	59	2,235	1,467	768	1,576	462	1,114
60 and over	2,838	1,325	1,513	91	46	45	1,095	807	288	1,652	472	1,180
Buddhist ..	*19,502*	*10,414*	*9,088*	*8,371*	*4,880*	*3,491*	*8,023*	*4,015*	*4,008*	*3,108*	*1,519*	*1,589*
0	418	210	208	418	210	208	...	...	...	...	...	...
1—5	1,547	774	773	1,547	774	773	...	...	...	...	...	...
5—10	2,051	1,039	1,012	2,051	1,039	1,012	...	...	...	...	...	...
10—15	1,960	1,067	893	1,939	1,046	893	21	21	...	...	...	...
15—20	1,732	848	884	1,179	780	399	426	48	378	127	20	107
20—30	3,211	1,575	1,636	804	656	148	1,934	682	1,252	473	237	236
30—40	3,014	1,713	1,301	248	224	24	2,226	1,136	1,090	540	353	187
40—50	2,606	1,489	1,117	105	90	15	1,873	1,047	826	628	352	276
50—60	1,579	956	623	43	36	7	977	653	324	559	267	292
60 and over	1,384	743	641	37	25	12	566	428	138	781	290	491
Animist ..	*34,215*	*15,595*	*18,620*	*18,245*	*8,936*	*9,309*	*11,865*	*5,876*	*5,989*	*4,105*	*788*	*3,322*
0	842	398	444	842	398	444	...	...	...	...	...	...
1—5	4,402	2,186	2,216	4,402	2,186	2,216	...	...	...	...	...	...
5—10	4,706	2,353	2,353	4,706	2,353	2,353	...	...	...	...	...	...
10—15	3,494	1,759	1,735	3,494	1,759	1,735	...	...	...	...	...	...
15—20	2,727	1,100	1,627	2,315	1,010	1,305	364	76	288	48	14	34
20—30	5,893	2,293	3,600	1,928	962	966	3,459	1,209	2,250	506	122	384
30—40	5,772	2,774	2,998	339	181	158	4,541	2,398	2,143	892	195	697
40—50	3,531	1,621	1,910	126	55	71	2,298	1,393	905	1,107	173	934
50—60	1,803	744	1,059	56	17	39	895	579	316	852	148	704
60 and over	1,045	367	678	37	15	22	308	221	87	700	131	569
Hindu (all ages) ..	*298*	*254*	*89*	*100*	*87*	*13*	*177*	*151*	*26*	*16*	*16*	..
Mahomedan (all ages)	*238*	*147*	*91*	*102*	*59*	*43*	*114*	*71*	*43*	*22*	*17*	*5*
Christian ..	*9,602*	*4,719*	*4,888*	*5,184*	*2,660*	*2,524*	*3,714*	*1,872*	*1,842*	*704*	*187*	*517*
0	410	193	217	410	193	217	...	...	...	...	...	...
1—5	1,167	586	581	1,167	586	581	...	...	...	...	...	...
5—10	1,325	672	653	1,325	672	653	...	...	..	...	...	...
10—15	1,092	561	531	1,092	561	531	...	...	...	...	...	...
15—20	883	409	474	661	348	313	219	58	161	3	3	...
20—30	1,639	757	882	374	222	152	1,195	512	683	70	23	47
30—40	1,276	636	640	95	55	40	1,046	545	501	135	36	99
40—50	895	438	457	26	12	14	700	390	310	169	36	133
50—60	522	268	254	19	7	12	343	219	124	160	42	118
60 and over	393	199	194	15	4	11	211	148	63	167	47	120

ADDENDUM FOR HINDUS IN SHWEBO DISTRICT (Page 82).

CLASS AND AGE.	POPULATION.			UNMARRIED.			MARRIED.			WIDOWED.		
	Persons.	Males.	Females.	Persons.	Males.	Females.	Persons.	Males.	Females.	Persons.	Males.	Females.
1	2	3	4	5	6	7	8	9	10	11	12	13
Total Hindus ...	***2,538***	***1,925***	***613***	***1,151***	***846***	***305***	***1,226***	***948***	***278***	***161***	***181***	***80***
0	59	28	31	59	28	31	...	...	...	...	...	...
1—5	193	94	99	193	94	99	...	...	...	...	...	...
5—10	211	108	103	211	108	103	...	...	...	...	...	...
10—15	127	80	47	126	80	46	1	...	1	...	...	...
15—20	132	93	39	80	75	5	50	18	32	2	..	2
20—30	667	531	136	266	252	14	386	266	120	15	13	2
30—40	604	513	91	144	140	4	409	328	81	51	45	6
40—50	298	262	36	43	41	2	225	197	28	30	24	6
50—60	164	145	19	22	21	1	105	94	11	37	30	7
60 and over	83	71	12	7	7	...	50	45	5	26	19	7
Hindus born in Burma ...	***608***	***331***	***272***	***496***	***266***	***230***	***98***	***60***	***38***	***9***	***5***	***4***
0	54	26	28	54	26	28	...	...	...	...	...	...
1—5	146	65	81	146	65	81	...	...	...	...	...	...
5—10	156	77	79	156	77	79	...	...	...	...	...	...
10—15	81	44	37	81	44	37	...	...	...	...	...	...
15—20	38	25	13	21	20	1	15	5	10	2	...	2
20—30	54	38	16	22	19	3	32	19	13	...	...	...
30—40	37	28	9	9	8	1	26	18	8	2	2	...
40—50	20	15	5	6	6	...	13	9	4	1	...	1
50—60	12	9	3	1	1	..	8	6	2	3	2	1
60 and over	5	4	1	...	...	...	4	3	1	1	1	...

IMPERIAL TABLE VIII-A.

Literacy by Religion and Age.

NOTE 1.—This table is in four parts. Subject to Note 4 below, Part I divides into five age-groups and also into literate and illiterate the totals of each religion tabulated in Table VIA; further, the number included amongst the literate in each age-group who are literate in English is shown. Parts II and III give similar statistics for Divisional Burma and for the Eastern States respectively, the religions with few adherents being collected in these parts under the description *Others*; the *Eastern States* include the Northern and Southern Shan States and Karenni; *Divisional Burma* includes all the remainder of the province. Part IV gives for the whole province an analysis by age and race of the Christian population literate in English.

NOTE 2.—For all four parts of the table the areas and populations excluded are those excluded from Table VIA, namely those in which the census was by estimate only.

NOTE 3.—The age recorded was the number of completed years. The age-group represented by 5—10 in the table includes all who had completed five but had not yet completed ten years of age; and the other age-groups have a parallel interpretation. Persons whose age had not been clearly specified in the record of the enumeration have been assigned to the same age-group as for Imperial Table VIIA—See Note 4 on the title-page of that Table.

NOTE 4.—In this table all persons belonging to Christian races as well as all professing the Christian religion are included under the description *Christian.* (See Note 3 of Table VIA.)

NOTE 5.—Separate figures are given for Hindus born in Burma and for Hindus born outside Burma; both of these are included in the figures given for *Total Hindus.* Similarly for Mahomedans.

NOTE 6.—The term *Literate* means able both to read and to write "a letter to or from a friend" in the language with regard to which the term is used. The figures for *Literate* in columns 6, 7 and 8 include all literate in any one or more languages whatsoever, and in particular include those literate in English who are shown separately in columns 12 to 14.

NOTE 7.—Imperial Table IX gives similar statistics by races instead of by religions. Table VIIIB, which follows this table immediately, gives for each district and for the three parts of the Eastern States statistics similar to those of Parts II and III of this table. Similar statistics for the larger towns are given in Provincial Table VIII; for Buddhists alone similar statistics for the separate townships into which each district is divided are given in Provincial Table VI; and similar statistics for selected races are given for some townships or districts in Provincial Table VII. Imperial Tables VIB, XIII, XV and XVI show relationships between religion and race.

IMPERIAL TABLE VIIIA.—*Literacy by Religion and Age.*

PART I.—THE WHOLE PROVINCE.

RELIGION.	AGE.	POPULATION.											
		Total.			Literate.			Illiterate.			Literate in English.		
		Persons.	Males.	Females.	Persons.	Males.	Females.	Persons.	Males.	Females.	Persons.	Males.	Females.
1	2	3	4	5	6	7	8	9	10	11	12	13	14
ALL RELIGIONS.	TOTAL ...	*13,169,099*	*6,735,516*	*6,433,583*	*3,652,043*	*3,026,337*	*625,706*	*9,517,056*	*3,709,179*	*5,807,877*	*113,413*	*92,207*	*21,206*
	0—10	3,269,387	1,615,599	1,653,788	115,130	78,139	36,991	3,154,257	1,537,460	1,616,797	4,656	2,930	1,726
	10—15	1,504,298	776,040	728,258	373,508	289,530	83,978	1,130,790	486,510	644,280	12,241	8,890	3,351
	15—20	1,347,245	658,235	689,010	481,823	374,420	107,403	865,422	283,815	581,607	16,964	13,038	3,926
	20—30	2,332,914	1,196,041	1,136,873	894,369	727,040	167,329	1,438,545	469,001	969,544	34,908	29,549	5,359
	30 and over	4,715,255	2,489,601	2,225,654	1,787,213	1,557,208	230,005	2,928,042	932,393	1,995,649	44,644	37,800	6,844
BUDDHISTS.	TOTAL ..	*11,201,912*	*5,525,144*	*5,676,768*	*3,301,807*	*2,741,283*	*560,524*	*7,900,105*	*2,783,861*	*5,116,244*	*51,856*	*45,541*	*6,315*
	0—10	2,847,136	1,401,482	1,445,654	102,592	70,740	31,852	2,744,544	1,330,742	1,413,802	1,703	1,318	385
	10—15	1,326,097	675,679	650,418	346,484	271,598	74,886	979,613	404,081	575,532	6,375	5,131	1,244
	15—20	1,167,644	553,361	614,283	445,127	348,326	96,801	722,517	205,035	517,482	9,490	7,911	1,579
	20—30	1,893,871	905,369	988,502	788,055	638,800	149,255	1,105,816	266,569	839,247	16,055	14,678	1,377
	30 and over	3,967,164	1,989,253	1,977,911	1,619,549	1,411,819	207,730	2,347,615	577,434	1,770,181	18,233	16,503	1,730
ANIMISTS.	TOTAL ...	*702,587*	*369,188*	*333,399*	*26,816*	*25,216*	*1,600*	*675,771*	*343,972*	*331,799*	*587*	*548*	*39*
	0—10	168,429	85,318	83,111	465	352	113	167,964	84,966	82,998	14	10	4
	10—15	68,927	36,723	32,204	1,336	1,079	257	67,591	35,644	31,947	51	46	5
	15—20	66,084	33,752	32,332	1,996	1,759	237	64,088	31,993	32,095	92	81	11
	20—30	130,400	66,934	63,466	6,861	6,439	422	123,539	60,495	63,044	182	169	13
	30 and over	268,747	146,461	122,286	16,158	15,587	571	252,589	130,874	121,715	248	242	6
TOTAL HINDUS.	TOTAL ...	*484,432*	*378,177*	*106,255*	*112,016*	*104,259*	*7,757*	*372,416*	*273,918*	*98,498*	*13,710*	*12,889*	*821*
	0—10	63,521	32,989	30,532	2,453	1,702	751	61,068	31,287	29,781	317	229	88
	10—15	27,575	18,601	8,974	5,120	4,206	914	22,455	14,395	8,060	1,006	846	160
	15—20	37,782	29,160	8,622	9,041	7,886	1,155	28,741	21,274	7,467	1,360	1,207	153
	20—30	142,629	118,012	24,617	39,402	36,769	2,633	103,227	81,243	21,984	4981	4,704	277
	30 and over	212,925	179,415	33,510	56,000	53,696	2,304	156,925	125,719	31,206	6,046	5,903	143
HINDUS BORN IN BURMA.	TOTAL ..	*97,505*	*52,635*	*44,870*	*13,411*	*10,868*	*2,543*	*84,094*	*41,767*	*42,327*	*2,508*	*2,190*	*318*
	0—10	48,529	24,381	24,148	1,497	1,028	469	47,032	23,353	23,679	199	141	58
	10—15	13,502	7,506	5,996	2,387	1,830	557	11,115	5,676	5,439	547	444	103
	15—20	8,552	4,711	3,841	2,126	1,682	444	6,426	3,029	3,397	502	444	58
	20—30	12,927	7,250	5,677	3,587	2,946	641	9,340	4,304	5,036	762	688	74
	30 and over	13,995	8,787	5,208	3,814	3,382	432	10,181	5,405	4,776	498	473	25
HINDUS BORN OUTSIDE BURMA.	TOTAL ...	*386,927*	*325,542*	*61,385*	*98,605*	*93,391*	*5,214*	*288,322*	*232,151*	*56,171*	*11,202*	*10,699*	*503*
	0—10	14,992	8,608	6,384	956	674	282	14,036	7,934	6,102	118	88	30
	10—15	14,073	11,095	2,978	2,733	2,376	357	11,340	8,719	2,621	459	402	57
	15—20	29,230	24,449	4,781	6,915	6,204	711	22,315	18,245	4,070	858	763	95
	20—30	129,702	110,762	18,940	35,815	33,823	1,992	93,887	76,939	16,948	4,219	4,016	203
	30 and over	198,930	170,628	28,302	52,186	50,314	1,872	146,744	120,314	26,430	5,548	5,430	118
TOTAL MAHOMEDANS.	TOTAL ...	*500,592*	*314,527*	*186,065*	*99,122*	*85,653*	*13,469*	*401,470*	*228,874*	*172,596*	*9,656*	*9,244*	*412*
	0—10	122,516	62,022	60,494	2,868	1,942	926	119,648	60,080	59,568	179	151	28
	10—15	49,914	28,528	21,386	7,300	5,398	1,902	42,614	23,130	19,484	759	688	71
	15—20	47,349	28,033	19,316	10,601	8,422	2,179	36,748	19,611	17,137	1,247	1,148	99
	20—30	111,966	77,059	34,907	30,704	26,891	3,813	81,262	50,168	31,094	3,125	3,018	107
	30 and over	168,847	118,885	49,962	47,649	43,000	4,649	121,198	75,885	45,313	4,346	4,239	107
MAHOMEDANS BORN IN BURMA.	TOTAL ...	*335,860*	*167,529*	*168,331*	*44,267*	*32,287*	*11,980*	*291,593*	*135,242*	*156,351*	*5,101*	*4,787*	*314*
	0—10	117,386	59,032	58,354	2,529	1,673	856	114,857	57,359	57,498	156	134	22
	10—15	43,913	23,616	20,297	5,757	3,963	1,794	38,156	19,653	18,503	599	537	62
	15—20	33,076	15,227	17,849	6,297	4,287	2,010	26,779	10,940	15,839	895	806	89
	20—30	55,386	25,059	30,327	11,256	7,939	3,317	44,130	17,120	27,010	1,552	1,481	71
	30 and over	86,099	44,595	41,504	18,428	14,425	4,003	67,671	30,170	37,501	1,899	1,829	70
MAHOMEDANS BORN OUTSIDE BURMA.	TOTAL ...	*164,732*	*146,998*	*17,734*	*54,855*	*53,366*	*1,489*	*109,877*	*93,632*	*16,245*	*4,555*	*4,457*	*98*
	0—10	5,130	2,990	2,140	339	269	70	4,791	2,721	2,070	23	17	6
	10—15	6,001	4,912	1,089	1,543	1,435	108	4,458	3,477	981	160	151	9
	15—20	14,273	12,806	1,467	4,304	4,135	169	9,969	8,671	1,298	352	342	10
	20—30	56,580	52,000	4,580	19,448	18,952	496	37,132	33,048	4,084	1,573	1,537	36
	30 and over	82,748	74,290	8,458	29,221	28,575	646	53,527	45,715	7,812	2,447	2,410	37
CHRISTIANS.	TOTAL ...	*257,171*	*132,543*	*124,628*	*102,066*	*61,090*	*40,976*	*155,105*	*71,453*	*83,652*	*35,706*	*22,547*	*13,159*
	0—10	64,031	31,717	32,314	6,319	3,140	3,179	57,712	28,577	29,135	2,325	1,156	1,169
	10—15	30,115	15,556	14,559	12,562	6,768	5,794	17,553	8,788	8,765	3,819	2,035	1,784
	15—20	26,540	12,672	13,868	14,129	7,310	6,819	12,411	5,362	7,049	4,507	2,501	2,006
	20—30	48,777	24,727	24,050	26,560	15,722	10,838	22.217	9,005	13,212	10,048	6,574	3,474
	30 and over	87,708	47,871	39,837	42,496	28,150	14,346	45,212	19,721	25,491	15,007	10,281	4,726

IMPERIAL TABLE VIIIA.—*Literacy by Religion and Age.*

PART I.—THE WHOLE PROVINCE.

RELIGION.	AGE.	POPULATION. Total. Persons.	Total. Males.	Total. Females.	Literate. Persons.	Literate. Males.	Literate. Females.	Illiterate. Persons.	Illiterate. Males.	Illiterate. Females.	Literate in English. Persons.	Literate in English. Males.	Literate in English. Females.
1	2	3	4	5	6	7	8	9	10	11	12	13	14
ARYAS.	TOTAL ...	*270*	*190*	*80*	*120*	*101*	*19*	*150*	*89*	*61*	*51*	*49*	*2*
	0—10	53	22	31	3	1	2	50	21	29	1	1	...
	10—15	15	8	7	6	3	3	9	5	4	2	1	1
	15—20	19	15	4	10	9	1	9	6	3	5	5	...
	20—30	75	57	18	46	37	9	29	20	9	18	17	1
	30 and over	108	88	20	55	51	4	53	37	16	25	25	...
BRAHMOS.	TOTAL ...	*448*	*355*	*93*	*309*	*270*	*39*	*139*	*85*	*54*	*67*	*51*	*16*
	0—10	41	19	22	9	4	5	32	15	17	2	1	1
	10—15	23	7	16	14	5	9	9	2	7	10	3	7
	15—20	36	28	8	28	24	4	8	4	4	6	5	1
	20—30	146	124	22	118	109	9	28	15	13	17	15	2
	30 and over	202	177	25	140	128	12	62	49	13	32	27	5
CONFUCIANS.	TOTAL ...	*14,131*	*9,964*	*4,167*	*5,834*	*5,297*	*537*	*8,297*	*4,667*	*3,630*	*451*	*398*	*53*
	0—10	2,283	1,280	1,003	193	126	67	2,090	1,154	936	9	4	5
	10—15	1,156	663	493	403	312	91	753	351	402	56	48	8
	15—20	1,215	822	393	536	443	93	679	379	300	85	68	17
	20—30	3,082	2,329	753	1,478	1,344	134	1,604	985	619	139	120	19
	30 and over	6,395	4,870	1,525	3,224	3,072	152	3,171	1,798	1,373	162	158	4
JAINS.	TOTAL ...	*1,135*	*866*	*269*	*510*	*436*	*74*	*625*	*430*	*195*	*117*	*111*	*6*
	0—10	181	112	69	22	16	6	159	96	63	2	1	1
	10—15	62	42	20	26	17	9	36	25	11	5	5	...
	15—20	107	76	31	57	42	15	50	34	16	16	15	1
	20—30	328	253	75	184	156	28	144	97	47	56	52	4
	30 and over	457	383	74	221	205	16	236	178	58	38	38	...
JEWS.	TOTAL ...	*1,135*	*587*	*548*	*753*	*434*	*319*	*382*	*153*	*229*	*620*	*352*	*268*
	0—10	294	148	146	77	42	35	217	106	111	62	34	28
	10—15	141	65	76	113	55	58	28	10	18	103	48	55
	15—20	121	61	60	104	53	51	17	8	9	95	48	47
	24—30	210	102	108	168	87	81	42	15	27	137	69	68
	30 and over	369	211	158	291	197	94	78	14	64	223	153	70
SHINTOISTS.	TOTAL ...	*45*	*31*	*14*	*35*	*29*	*6*	*10*	*2*	*8*	*7*	*4*	*3*
	0—10	2	2	...	2	2	...	...	...	...	...	...	...
	10—15	...	...	...	...	...	...	...	...	...	...	...	...
	15—20	6	4	2	5	3	2	1	1	...	1	...	1
	20—30	21	14	7	14	13	1	7	1	6	3	3	...
	30 and over	16	11	5	14	11	3	2	...	2	3	1	2
SIKHS.	TOTAL ...	*4,843*	*3,704*	*1,139*	*2,327*	*2,070*	*257*	*2,516*	*1,634*	*882*	*312*	*296*	*16*
	0—10	817	449	368	84	54	30	733	395	338	13	10	3
	10—15	240	149	91	112	70	42	128	79	49	25	20	5
	15—20	318	239	79	165	131	34	153	108	45	38	37	1
	20—30	1,341	1,015	326	725	637	88	616	378	238	105	101	4
	30 and over	2,127	1,852	275	1,241	1,178	63	886	674	212	131	128	3
ZOROASTRIANS.	TOTAL ...	*380*	*229*	*151*	*314*	*191*	*123*	*66*	*38*	*28*	*260*	*169*	*91*
	0—10	80	39	41	40	18	22	40	21	19	27	15	12
	10—15	33	19	14	32	19	13	1	...	1	30	19	11
	15—20	23	11	12	23	11	12	...	...	...	21	11	10
	20—30	61	41	20	49	33	16	12	8	4	37	26	11
	30 and over	183	119	64	170	110	60	13	9	4	145	98	47
AGNOSTICS, ATHEISTS, FREETHINKERS AND THEOSOPHISTS.	TOTAL ...	*18*	*11*	*7*	*14*	*8*	*6*	*4*	*3*	*1*	*13*	*8*	*5*
	0—10	3	...	3	3	...	3	...	...	...	2	...	2
	10—15	...	...	...	...	...	...	...	...	...	...	...	...
	15—20	1	1	...	1	1	...	...	...	...	1	1	...
	20—30	7	5	2	5	3	2	2	2	...	5	3	2
	30 and over	7	5	2	5	4	1	2	1	1	5	4	1

IMPERIAL TABLE VIIIA.—*Literacy by Religion and Age.*

PART II.—DIVISIONAL BURMA.

Religion.	Age.	Population: Total: Persons.	Total: Males.	Total: Females.	Literate: Persons.	Literate: Males.	Literate: Females.	Illiterate: Persons.	Illiterate: Males.	Illiterate: Females.	Literate in English: Persons.	Literate in English: Males.	Literate in English: Females.
1	2	3	4	5	6	7	8	9	10	11	12	13	14
ALL RELIGIONS.	TOTAL ...	*11,698,408*	*5,991,623*	*5,706,785*	*3,546,470*	*2,926,725*	*619,745*	*8,151,938*	*3,064,898*	*5,087,040*	*111,209*	*90,360*	*20,849*
	0—10	2,908,402	1,436,102	1,472,300	113,990	77,264	36,726	2,794,412	1,358,838	1,435,574	4,620	2,916	1,713
	10—15	1,352,915	696,696	656,219	364,436	281,149	83,287	988,479	415,547	572,932	12,148	8,824	3,324
	15—20	1,197,283	585,764	611,519	468,402	362,040	106,362	728,881	223,724	505,157	16,752	12,871	3,881
	20—30	2,071,169	1,067,254	1,003,915	868,949	703,233	165 716	1,202,220	364,021	838,199	34,132	28,882	5,250
	30 and over	4,168,639	2,205,807	1,962,832	1,730,693	1,503,039	227,654	2,437,946	702,768	1,735,178	43,548	36,867	6,681
BUDDHISTS.	TOTAL ...	*10,018,466*	*4,932,834*	*5,085,632*	*3,207,156*	*2,651,251*	*555,905*	*6,811,310*	*2,281,583*	*4,529,727*	*51,249*	*44,986*	*6,263*
	0—10	2,557,579	1,258,303	1,299,276	101,785	70,112	31,673	2,455,794	1,188,191	1,267,603	1,699	1,316	383
	10—15	1,200,560	610,221	590,339	338,111	263,724	74.387	862,449	346,497	515,952	6,350	5,109	1,241
	15—20	1,044,287	494,674	549,613	432,739	336,740	95,999	611,548	157,934	453,614	9,466	7,839	1,567
	20—30	1,688,508	806,553	881,955	766,369	618,336	148,033	922,139	188,217	733,922	15,811	14,455	1,356
	30 and over	3,527,532	1,763,083	1,764,449	1,568,152	1,362,339	205,813	1,959,380	400,744	1,558,636	17,983	16,267	1,716
ANIMISTS.	TOTAL ...	*456,104*	*243,426*	*212,678*	*24,830*	*23,237*	*1,593*	*431,274*	*220,189*	*211,085*	*546*	*508*	*38*
	0—10	106,124	53,669	52,455	443	330	113	105,681	53,339	52,342	14	10	4
	10—15	46,456	24,703	21,753	1,264	1,007	257	45,192	23,696	21,496	43	38	5
	15—20	42,949	21,861	21,088	1,847	1,611	236	41,102	20,250	20,852	88	77	11
	20—30	84,019	43,937	40,082	6,320	5,900	420	77,699	38,037	39,662	169	156	13
	30 and over	176,556	99,256	77,300	14,956	14,389	567	161,600	84,867	76,733	232	227	5
TOTAL HINDUS.	TOTAL ...	*471,427*	*367,516*	*103,911*	*107,575*	*99,975*	*7,600*	*363,852*	*267,541*	*96,311*	*13,212*	*12,402*	*810*
	0—10	61,903	32,135	29,768	2,423	1,678	745	59,480	30,457	29,023	315	228	87
	10—15	27,088	18,298	8,790	5,027	4,120	907	22,061	14,178	7,883	998	840	158
	15—20	36,902	28,547	8,355	8,765	7.645	1,120	28,137	20,902	7,235	1,323	1,172	151
	20—30	138,028	113,964	24,064	37,526	34,957	2,569	100,502	79,007	21,495	4,759	4,487	272
	30 and over	207,506	174,572	32,934	53,834	51,575	2,259	153,672	122,997	30,675	5,817	5,675	142
HINDUS BORN IN BURMA.	TOTAL ...	*95,442*	*51,559*	*43,883*	*13,205*	*10,685*	*2,520*	*82,237*	*40,874*	*41,363*	*2,470*	*2,154*	*316*
	0—10	47,176	23,679	23,497	1,480	1,013	467	45,696	22,666	23,030	199	141	58
	10—15	13,215	7,342	5,873	2,349	1,797	552	10,866	5,545	5,321	543	442	101
	15—20	8,374	4,629	3,745	2,063	1,627	436	6,311	3,002	3,309	486	428	58
	20—30	12,784	7,180	5,604	3,537	2,901	636	9,247	4,279	4,968	753	679	74
	30 and over	13,893	8,729	5,164	3,776	3,347	429	10,117	5,382	4,735	489	464	25
HINDUS BORN OUTSIDE BURMA.	TOTAL ...	*375,985*	*315,957*	*60,028*	*94,370*	*89,290*	*5,080*	*281,615*	*226,667*	*54,948*	*10,742*	*10,248*	*494*
	0—9	14,727	8,456	6,271	943	665	278	13,784	7,791	5,993	116	87	29
	10—14	13,873	10,956	2,917	2,678	2,323	355	11,195	8,633	2,562	455	398	57
	15—19	28,528	23,918	4,610	6,702	6,018	684	21,826	17,900	3,926	837	744	93
	20—29	125,244	106,784	18,460	33,989	32,056	1,933	91,255	74,728	16,527	4,006	3,808	198
	30 and over	193,613	165,843	27,770	50,058	48,228	1,830	143,555	117,615	25,940	5,328	5.211	117
TOTAL MAHOMEDANS.	TOTAL ...	*495,758*	*311,098*	*184,660*	*97,728*	*84,388*	*13,340*	*398,030*	*226,710*	*171,320*	*9,504*	*9,101*	*403*
	0—10	121,595	61,522	60,073	2,841	1,920	921	118,754	59,602	59,152	179	151	28
	10—15	49,579	28,339	21,240	7,233	5,347	1,886	42,346	22,992	19,354	757	686	71
	15—20	46,996	27,815	19,181	10,488	8,324	2,164	36,508	19,491	17,017	1,231	1,134	97
	20—30	110,726	76,156	34,570	30,218	26,443	3,775	80,508	49,713	30,795	3,063	2,958	105
	30 and over	166,862	117,266	49,596	46,948	42,354	4,594	119,914	74,912	45,002	4,274	4,172	102
MAHOMEDANS BORN IN BURMA.	TOTAL ...	*333,761*	*166,529*	*167,232*	*43,936*	*32,032*	*11,904*	*289,825*	*134,497*	*155,328*	*5,053*	*4,743*	*310*
	0—10	116,532	58,565	57,967	2,507	1,655	852	114,025	56,910	57,115	156	134	22
	10—15	43,639	23,470	20,169	5,708	3,926	1,782	37,931	19,544	18,387	597	535	62
	15—20	32,878	15,134	17,744	6,243	4,246	1,997	26,635	10,888	15,747	883	796	87
	20—30	55,003	24,921	30,082	11,164	7,869	3,295	43,839	17,052	26,787	1,536	1,465	71
	30 and over	85,709	44,439	41,270	18,314	14,336	3,978	67,395	30,103	37,292	1,881	1,813	68
MAHOMEDANS BORN OUTSIDE BURMA.	TOTAL ..	*161,997*	*144,569*	*17,428*	*53,792*	*52,356*	*1,436*	*108,205*	*92,213*	*15,992*	*4,451*	*4,358*	*93*
	0—9	5,063	2,957	2,106	334	265	69	4,729	2,692	2,037	23	17	6
	10—14	5,940	4,869	1,071	1,525	1,421	104	4,415	3,448	967	160	151	9
	15—19	14,118	12,681	1,437	4,245	4,078	167	9,873	8,603	1,270	348	338	10
	20—29	55,723	51,235	4,488	19,054	18,594	480	36,669	32,661	4,008	1,527	1,493	34
	30 and over	81,153	72,827	8,326	28,634	28,018	616	52,519	44,809	7,710	2,393	2,359	34
CHRISTIANS.	TOTAL ...	*234,803*	*121,020*	*113,483*	*99,074*	*59,133*	*39,941*	*135,429*	*61,887*	*73,542*	*34,816*	*21,940*	*12,876*
	0—10	57,479	28.421	29,058	6,068	2,962	3,106	51,411	25,459	25,952	2,304	1,145	1,159
	10—15	27,573	14,187	13,386	12,100	6,471	5,629	15,473	7,716	7,757	3,769	2,007	1,762
	15—20	24,311	11,613	12,698	13,638	7,006	6,632	10,673	4,607	6,066	4.438	2,460	1,978
	20—30	44,679	22,756	21,923	25,749	15,197	10,552	18,930	7,559	11,371	9,817	6,424	3.393
	30 and over	80,461	44,043	36,418	41,519	27,497	14,022	38,942	16,546	22,396	14.488	9,904	4,584
OTHERS.	TOTAL ...	*22,150*	*15,729*	*6,421*	*10,107*	*8,741*	*1,366*	*12,043*	*6,988*	*5,055*	*1,882*	*1,423*	*459*
	0—9	3,722	2,052	1,670	430	262	168	3,292	1,790	1,502	118	66	52
	10—14	1,659	948	711	701	480	221	958	468	490	231	144	87
	15—19	1,838	1,254	584	925	714	211	913	540	373	266	189	77
	20—29	5,209	3,888	1,321	2,767	2,400	367	2,442	1,488	954	513	402	111
	30 and over	9,722	7,587	2,135	5,284	4,885	399	4,438	2,702	1,736	754	622	132

IMPERIAL TABLE VIIIA.—*Literacy by Religion and Age.*

PART III—THE EASTERN STATES.

RELIGION.	AGE.	POPULATION. Total. Persons.	Total. Males.	Total. Females.	Literate. Persons.	Literate. Males.	Literate. Females.	Illiterate. Persons.	Illiterate. Males.	Illiterate. Females.	Literate in English. Persons.	Literate in English. Males.	Literate in English. Females.
1	2	3	4	5	6	7	8	9	10	11	12	13	14
ALL RELIGIONS.	TOTAL ...	*1,470,691*	*743,893*	*726,798*	*105,573*	*99,612*	*5,961*	*1,365,118*	*644,281*	*720,837*	*2,204*	*1,847*	*357*
	0—10	360,985	179,497	181,488	1,140	875	265	359,845	178,622	181,223	27	14	13
	10—15	151,383	79,344	72,039	9,072	8,381	691	142,311	70,963	71,348	93	66	27
	15—20	149,962	72,471	77,491	13,421	12,380	1,041	136,541	60,091	76,450	212	167	45
	20—30	261,745	128,787	132,958	25,420	23,807	1,613	236,325	104,980	131,345	776	667	109
	30 and over	546,616	283,794	262,822	56,520	54,169	2,351	490,096	229,625	260,471	1,096	933	163
BUDDHISTS.	TOTAL ...	*1,183,446*	*592,310*	*591,136*	*94,651*	*90,032*	*4,619*	*1,088,795*	*502,278*	*586,517*	*607*	*555*	*52*
	0—10	289,557	143,179	146,378	807	628	179	288,750	142,551	146,199	4	2	2
	10—15	125,537	65,458	60,079	8,373	7,874	499	117,164	57,584	59,580	25	22	3
	15—20	123,357	58,687	64,670	12,388	11,586	802	110,969	47,101	63,868	84	72	12
	20—30	205,363	98,816	106,547	21,686	20,464	1,222	183,677	78,252	105,325	244	223	21
	30 and over	439,632	226,170	213,462	51,397	49,480	1,917	388,235	176,690	211,545	250	236	14
ANIMISTS.	TOTAL ...	*246,483*	*125,762*	*120,721*	*1,986*	*1,979*	7	*244,497*	*123,783*	*120,714*	*41*	*40*	*1*
	0—10	62,305	31,649	30,656	22	22	...	62,283	31,627	30,656	...	...	...
	10—15	22,471	12,020	10,451	72	72	...	22,399	11,948	10,451	8	8	...
	15—20	23,135	11,891	11,244	149	148	1	22,986	11,743	11,243	4	4	...
	20—30	46,381	22,997	23,384	541	539	2	45,840	22,458	23,382	13	13	...
	30 and over	92,191	47,205	44,986	1,202	1,198	4	90,989	46,007	44,982	16	15	1
TOTAL HINDUS.	TOTAL ...	*13,005*	*10,661*	*2,344*	*4,441*	*4,284*	*157*	*8,564*	*6,377*	*2,187*	*498*	*487*	*11*
	0—10	1,618	854	764	30	24	6	1,588	830	758	2	1	1
	10—15	487	303	184	93	86	7	394	217	177	8	6	2
	15—20	880	613	267	276	241	35	604	372	232	37	35	2
	20—30	4,601	4,048	553	1,876	1,812	64	2,725	2,236	489	222	217	5
	30 and over	5,419	4,843	576	2,166	2,121	45	3,253	2,722	531	219	228	1
HINDUS BORN IN BURMA.	TOTAL ...	*2,063*	*1,076*	*987*	*206*	*183*	*23*	*1,857*	*893*	*964*	*38*	*36*	*2*
	0—10	1,353	702	651	17	15	2	1,336	687	649	...	...	...
	10—15	287	164	123	38	33	5	249	131	118	4	2	2
	15—20	178	82	96	63	55	8	115	27	88	16	16	...
	20—30	143	70	73	50	45	5	93	25	68	9	9	...
	30 and over	102	58	44	38	35	3	64	23	41	9	9	...
TOTAL MAHOMEDANS.	TOTAL ...	*4,834*	*3,429*	*1,405*	*1,394*	*1,265*	*129*	*3,440*	*2,164*	*1,276*	*152*	*143*	*9*
	0—10	921	500	421	27	22	5	894	478	416	...	...	...
	10—15	335	189	146	67	51	16	268	138	130	2	2	...
	15—20	353	218	135	113	98	15	240	120	120	16	14	2
	20—30	1,240	903	337	486	448	38	754	455	299	62	60	2
	30 and over	1,985	1,619	366	701	646	55	1,284	973	311	72	67	5
MAHOMEDANS BORN IN BURMA.	TOTAL ...	*2,099*	*1,000*	*1,099*	*331*	*255*	*76*	*1,768*	*745*	*1,023*	*48*	*44*	*4*
	0—10	854	467	387	22	18	4	832	449	383	...	...	...
	10—15	274	146	128	49	37	12	225	109	116	2	2	...
	15—20	198	93	105	54	41	13	144	52	92	12	10	2
	20—30	383	138	245	92	70	22	291	68	223	16	16	...
	30 and over	390	156	234	114	89	25	276	67	209	18	16	2
CHRISTIANS.	TOTAL ...	*22,668*	*11,523*	*11,145*	*2,992*	*1,957*	*1,035*	*19,676*	*9,566*	*10,110*	*890*	*607*	*283*
	0—10	6,552	3,296	3,256	251	178	73	6,301	3,118	3,183	21	11	10
	10—15	2,542	1,369	1,173	462	297	165	2,080	1,072	1,008	50	28	22
	15—20	2,229	1,059	1,170	491	304	187	1,738	755	983	69	41	28
	20—30	4,098	1,971	2,127	811	525	286	3,287	1,446	1,841	231	150	81
	30 and over	7,247	3,828	3,419	977	653	324	6,270	3,175	3,095	519	377	142
OTHERS.	TOTAL ...	*255*	*208*	*47*	*109*	*95*	*14*	*146*	*113*	*33*	*16*	*15*	*1*
	0—9	32	19	13	3	1	2	29	18	11	...	...	...
	10—14	11	5	6	5	1	4	6	4	2	...	...	...
	15—19	8	3	5	4	3	1	4	..	4	2	1	1
	20—29	62	52	10	20	19	1	42	33	9	4	4	...
	30 and over	142	129	13	77	71	6	65	58	7	10	10	...

TABLE VIII-A, PART IV.—CHRISTIANS LITERATE IN ENGLISH CLASSIFIED BY AGE IN FOUR RACE-GROUPS.

In this table Christians are divided by race into four classes which are denoted in the column-headings by the symbols AOS, X, Y, RZ, taken from the notation of the system of classification used in Imperial Table XIII. The meanings of the symbols in the terms of that notation are as follows :—

AOS.—Indigenous races (that is, all races of Groups A to O inclusive) and also the Indo-Burman races (which form Group S and include Zerbadis).

X.—Indian and allied races ; that is, all races of Group X.

Y.—Christian races ; that is, all races of Group Y, namely, European and allied races, Anglo-Indians and Armenians.

RZ.—All others ; that is, Chinese (Group R) and the races of Group Z.

NOTE.—The terms *Indian*, etc., above have not the meanings assigned to them in the electoral scheme of 1922.

	Age-Group.	The whole Province.				Rangoon Town.				Mandalay City.				Remainder of Divisional Burma.				Eastern States.			
		AOS.	X.	Y	RZ.	AOS	X	Y	RZ.	AOS	X	Y	RZ	AOS.	X	Y.	RZ	AOS.	X.	Y.	RZ.
MALES	TOTAL	*6,114*	*3,705*	*12,482*	*246*	*877*	*2,876*	*5,908*	*118*	*259*	*140*	*788*	*30*	*4,784*	*1,125*	*5,448*	*97*	*194*	*64*	*848*	*6*
	0—10	183	121	842	10	26	87	337	4	20	5	80	3	134	29	417	3	3	..	8	..
	10—15	715	301	981	38	83	195	461	19	39	16	92	6	581	87	4 7	11	12	3	11	2
	15—20	1,035	354	1,082	30	217	249	560	13	49	9	66	9	745	93	444	6	24	3	12	2
	20—30	1,850	1,070	3,584	70	304	717	1,829	28	81	38	229	7	1,396	302	1,458	35	69	13	68	..
	30 and over.	2,331	1,859	5,993	98	247	1,128	2,721	49	70	72	321	5	1,928	614	2.707	42	86	45	244	2
FEMALES	TOTAL	*3,608*	*1,022*	*8,442*	*87*	*780*	*680*	*4,095*	*51*	*178*	*46*	*641*	*3*	*2,683*	*290*	*3,502*	*82*	*72*	*6*	*204*	*1*
	0—10	153	76	932	8	24	47	410	4	7	3	101	..	119	26	414	4	3	..	7	..
	10—15	530	180	1,056	18	88	121	417	11	20	13	117	..	417	45	506	7	5	1	16	..
	15—20	803	176	1,016	11	186	120	509	4	41	9	102	..	562	46	392	7	14	1	13	..
	20—30	1,124	307	2,016	27	268	202	1,082	17	52	9	118	2	781	92	762	8	23	4	54	..
	30 and over.	998	283	3,422	23	214	190	1,677	15	53	12	203	1	704	81	1,428	6	27	..	114	1

IMPERIAL TABLE VIII-B.

Literacy in each District by Religion and Age.

NOTE 1.—This table gives for each district and for the three parts of the Eastern States statistics similar to those of Parts II and III of Imperial Table VIIIA. In every district it relates to the same area and population as that table, thus excluding all areas in which the census was by estimate only, but no others.

NOTE 2.—Rangoon Town constitutes a district and statistics are given for it accordingly as for other districts.

NOTE 3.—The figures given for Mandalay District include those of Mandalay City which are given separately immediately below them.

NOTE 4.—The age recorded was the number of completed years. The age-group represented by 5—10 in the table includes all who had completed five but had not yet completed ten years of age; and the other age-groups have a parallel interpretation.

NOTE 5.—In this table all persons belonging to Christian races as well as all professing the Christian religion are included under the description *Christian.* (See Note 3 of Table VIA.)

NOTE 6.—The figures given in each district for Hindus or Mahomedans born in Burma are included in those given for the descriptions *Hindu* and *Mahomedan* respectively. Separate figures are not given for Hindus or Mahomedans born outside Burma.

NOTE 7.—In some cases in which only few persons are concerned the length of the table has been reduced by omitting the details for separate age-groups of a religion and showing only the totals for all ages of each sex.

NOTE 8.—The term *Literate* means able both to read and to write "a letter to or from a friend" in the language with regard to which the term is used. The figures for *Literate* in columns 5, 6 and 7 include all literate in any one or more languages whatsoever, and in particular include those literate in English who are shown separately in columns 11 to 13.

NOTE 9.—Similar statistics for the larger towns are given in Provincial Table VIII; for Buddhists alone similar statistics for the separate townships into which each district is divided are given in Provincial Table VI; and similar statistics for selected races are given for some townships or districts in Provincial Table VII. Imperial Tables VIB, XIII, XV and XVI show relationships between religion and race.

IMPERIAL TABLE VIIIB.—*Literacy by Religion and Age.*

DISTRICT, RELIGION AND AGE.	POPULATION.									Literate in English.		
	Total.			Literate.			Illiterate.					
	Persons.	Males.	Females.	Persons.	Males.	Females.	Persons.	Males.	Females.	Persons.	Males.	Females.
1	2	3	4	5	6	7	8	9	10	11	12	13
AKYAB.												
ALL RELIGIONS ...	*576,430*	*309,564*	*266,866*	*107,778*	*95,559*	*12,219*	*468,652*	*214,005*	*254,647*	*3,041*	*2,680*	*361*
0—10	155,209	77,951	77,2[illegible]8	2,171	1,640	531	153,038	76,311	76,727	77	44	33
10—15	66,335	35,700	30,635	9,263	7,879	1,384	57,072	27,821	29,251	276	192	84
15—20	55,982	28,723	27,259	12,974	11,095	1,879	43,008	17,628	25,380	457	385	72
20—30	102,536	55,503	47 0[illegible]3	25 988	23,206	2,782	76,548	32,297	44,251	891	814	77
30 and over	196,[illegible]68	111,687	84,681	57,382	51,739	5,643	138,986	59,948	79,038	1,340	1,245	95
BUDDHIST ...	*315,140*	*159,722*	*155,418*	*92,008*	*80,678*	*11,330*	*223,132*	*79,044*	*144,088*	*1,635*	*1,449*	*186*
0—10	76,936	[illegible]8 497	38,439	1,842	1,420	422	75,094	37,077	38,017	18	13	5
10—15	36,927	19,122	17,805	8,424	7,219	1,205	28,503	11 903	16,600	185	135	50
15—20	31,515	15,5[illegible]	1[illegible],964	11,575	9,825	1,750	19,940	5,726	14,214	309	258	51
20—30	54,077	25,[illegible]27	27,450	21,495	18,919	2,576	32,582	7,708	24,874	461	417	44
30 and over	11[illegible],685	59,925	55,760	48,672	43,295	5,377	67,013	16,630	50,383	662	626	36
ANIMIST ...	*36,806*	*19,124*	*17,682*	*648*	*632*	*16*	*36,158*	*18,492*	*17,666*	*14*	*14*	...
0—10	9,535	4,813	4,722	9	8	1	9,526	4,805	4,721	...	...	...
10—15	4,037	2,197	1,840	32	28	4	4,005	2,169	1,836	...	...	...
15—20	3,3[illegible]4	1,[illegible]09	1,755	42	40	2	3,322	1,569	1,753	4	4	..
20—30	6,408	3,152	3,256	161	159	2	6,247	2,993	3,254	3	3	...
30 and over	13,462	7,353	6,109	404	397	7	13,058	6,956	6,102	7	7	...
HINDU ...	*14,719*	*13,401*	*1,318*	*5,642*	*5,552*	*90*	*9,077*	*7,849*	*1,228*	*392*	*378*	*14*
0—10	852	439	413	35	26	9	817	413	404	6	4	2
10—15	603	493	110	130	121	9	473	372	101	11	7	4
15—20	1,394	1,265	129	466	451	15	928	814	114	30	28	2
20—30	4,751	4,458	293	1,951	1,920	31	2,800	2,538	262	158	155	3
30 and over	7,119	6,746	373	3,060	3,034	26	4,059	3,712	347	187	184	3
HINDUS BORN IN BURMA.	*1,559*	*834*	*725*	*131*	*117*	*14*	*1,428*	*717*	*711*	*6*	*3*	*3*
0—10	589	281	308	11	7	4	578	274	304	2	1	1
10—15	165	96	69	10	8	2	155	88	67	2	...	2
15—20	143	64	79	11	8	3	132	56	76	...	...	...
20—30	238	124	114	27	24	3	211	100	111	1	1	...
30 and over	424	269	155	72	70	2	352	199	153	1	1	...
MAHOMEDAN ...	*208,961*	*116,736*	*92,225*	*8,893*	*8,261*	*632*	*200,068*	*108,475*	*91,593*	*557*	*537*	*20*
0—10	67,760	34,142	33,618	236	164	72	67,524	33,978	33,546	8	7	1
10—15	24,706	13,857	10,849	626	487	139	24,080	13,370	10,710	31	28	3
15—20	19,641	10,250	9,391	832	738	94	18,809	9,512	9,297	69	67	2
20—30	37,091	21,100	15,991	2,226	2,082	144	34,865	19,018	15,847	163	157	6
30 and over	59,763	37,387	22,376	4,973	4,790	183	54,790	32,597	22,193	286	278	8
MAHOMEDANS BORN IN BURMA.	*177,277*	*90,494*	*86,783*	*4,912*	*4,331*	*581*	*172,365*	*86,163*	*86,202*	*335*	*317*	*18*
0—10	66,359	33,369	32 990	218	148	70	66,141	33,221	32,920	8	7	1
10—15	23,334	12,889	10,445	534	400	134	22,800	12,489	10,311	28	26	2
15—20	16,630	7,662	8,968	526	439	87	16,104	7 223	8,881	50	48	2
20—30	27,637	12,640	14,997	956	821	135	26,681	11,819	14,862	85	79	6
30 and over	43,317	23,934	19,383	2,678	2,523	155	40,639	21,411	19,228	164	157	7
CHRISTIAN (ALL AGES)	*618*	*428*	*190*	*496*	*356*	*140*	*122*	*72*	*50*	*413*	*276*	*137*
OTHERS (ALL AGES)	*186*	*153*	*33*	*91*	*80*	*11*	*95*	*73*	*22*	*30*	*26*	*4*
HILL DISTRICT OF ARAKAN.												
ALL RELIGIONS ...	*20,914*	*10,790*	*10,124*	*895*	*802*	*93*	*20,019*	*9,988*	*10,031*	*50*	*49*	*1*
0—10	4,539	2,307	2,232	19	11	8	4,520	2,296	2,224	...	...	...
10—15	2,291	1,218	1,073	63	47	16	2,228	1,171	1,057	...	...	...
15—20	2,083	984	1,[illegible]99	106	93	13	1,977	891	1,086	1	1	...
20—30	3,797	1,924	1,873	315	283	32	3,482	1,641	1,841	29	28	1
30 and over	8,204	4,357	3,847	392	368	24	7,812	3,989	3,823	20	20	...
BUDDHIST ...	*2,225*	*1,220*	*1,005*	*676*	*594*	*82*	*1,549*	*626*	*923*	*34*	*34*	...
0—10	539	275	264	16	8	8	523	267	256	...	...	..
10—15	225	112	113	53	37	16	172	75	97	...	...	...
15—20	243	130	113	86	74	12	157	56	101	...	...	...
20—30	400	239	161	199	171	28	201	68	133	22	22	...
30 and over	818	464	354	322	304	18	496	160	336	12	12	...
ANIMIST ...	*18,054*	*9,109*	*8,945*	*20*	*20*	...	*18,034*	*9,089*	*8,945*	...	...	...
0—10	3,879	1,962	1,917	...	...	...	3,879	1,962	1,917	...	...	...
10—15	2,020	1,081	939	...	...	..	2,020	1,081	939	...	...	...
15—20	1,791	824	967	4	4	...	1,787	820	967	...	...	...
23—30	3,219	1,544	1,675	2	2	..	3,217	1,542	1,675	...	...	...
30 and over	7,145	3,698	3,447	14	14	...	7,131	3,684	3,447	...	...	...
HINDU (ALL AGES)	*575*	*407*	*168*	*176*	*169*	7	*399*	*238*	*161*	*8*	*8*	...
MAHOMEDAN (ALL AGES).	*46*	*43*	*3*	*11*	*10*	*1*	*35*	*33*	*2*	...	...	...
CHRISTIAN (ALL AGES)	*14*	*11*	*3*	*12*	*9*	*3*	*2*	*2*	...	*8*	*7*	*1*

IMPERIAL TABLE VIIIB.—*Literacy by Religion and Age.*

District	District, Religion and Age.	Population. Total. Persons.	Total. Males.	Total. Females.	Literate. Persons.	Literate. Males.	Literate. Females.	Illiterate. Persons.	Illiterate. Males.	Illiterate. Females.	Literate in English. Persons.	Literate in English. Males.	Literate in English. Females.
1		2	3	4	5	6	7	8	9	10	11	12	13
KYAUKPYU.	ALL RELIGIONS ...	*199,873*	*96,569*	*103,304*	*39,643*	*35,897*	*3,746*	*160,230*	*60,672*	*99,558*	*473*	*444*	*29*
	0—10	50,609	25,153	25,456	550	427	123	50,059	24,726	25,333	2	1	1
	10—15	22,689	11,763	10,926	3,220	2,812	408	19,469	8,951	10,518	60	54	6
	15—20	19,961	9,405	10,556	4,939	4,359	580	15,022	5,046	9,976	89	80	9
	20—30	30,281	13,569	16,712	8,299	7,470	829	21,982	6,099	15,883	101	95	6
	30 and over	76,333	36,679	39,654	22,635	20,829	1,806	53,698	15,850	37,848	221	214	7
	BUDDHIST ...	*178,451*	*84,901*	*93,550*	*38,101*	*34,555*	*3,546*	*140,350*	*50,346*	*90,004*	*374*	*354*	*20*
	0—10	45,090	22,416	22,684	514	402	112	44,576	22,004	2,572	2	1	1
	10—15	20,266	10,471	9,795	3,091	2,712	379	17,175	7,759	9,416	51	45	6
	15—20	17,986	8,415	9,571	4,760	4,215	545	13,226	4,200	9,026	76	70	6
	20—30	26,406	11,471	14,935	7,864	7,086	778	18,542	4,385	14,157	78	74	4
	30 and over	68,703	32,138	36,565	21,872	20,140	1,732	46,831	11,998	34,833	167	164	3
	ANIMIST (ALL AGES)	*16,173*	*8,414*	*7,759*	*124*	*123*	*1*	*16,049*	*8,291*	*7,758*	*4*	*4*	...
	HINDU ...	*634*	*609*	*25*	*352*	*349*	*3*	*282*	*260*	*22*	*22*	*22*	...
	0—10	8	7	1	...	...	...	8	7	1	...	...	...
	10—15	21	20	1	10	10	...	11	10	1	...	...	...
	15—20	53	49	4	33	31	2	20	18	2	1	1	...
	20—30	229	218	11	137	136	1	92	82	10	8	8	...
	30 and over	323	315	8	172	172	...	151	143	8	13	13	...
	HINDUS BORN IN BURMA.	*28*	*25*	*3*	*10*	*10*	...	*18*	*15*	*3*	*1*	*1*	...
	0—10	5	4	1	...	...	...	5	4	1	...	...	...
	10—15	...	...	...	...	...	...	...	...	...	...	...	...
	15—20	3	3	...	1	1	...	2	2	...	...	...	...
	20—30	9	7	2	3	3	...	6	4	2	1	1	...
	30 and over	11	11	...	6	6	...	5	5	...	...	...	...
	MAHOMEDAN ...	*4,479*	*2,580*	*1,899*	*1,004*	*833*	*171*	*3,475*	*1,747*	*1,728*	*56*	*53*	*3*
	0—10	919	445	474	34	24	10	885	421	464	...	...	...
	10—15	497	269	228	107	82	25	390	187	203	8	8	...
	15—20	454	246	208	122	97	25	332	149	183	8	8	...
	20—30	900	566	334	251	211	40	649	355	294	12	12	...
	30 and over	1,709	1,054	655	490	419	71	1,219	635	584	28	25	3
	MAHOMEDANS BORN IN BURMA.	*3,150*	*1,485*	*1,665*	*656*	*489*	*167*	*2,494*	*996*	*1,498*	*51*	*49*	*2*
	0—10	771	379	392	31	21	10	740	358	382	...	...	...
	10—15	394	204	190	91	66	25	303	138	165	8	8	...
	15—20	336	149	187	96	71	25	240	78	162	8	8	...
	20—30	513	217	296	135	95	40	378	122	256	11	11	...
	30 and over	1,136	536	600	303	236	67	833	300	533	24	22	2
	CHRISTIAN (ALL AGES)	*136*	*65*	*71*	*62*	*37*	*25*	*74*	*28*	*46*	*17*	*11*	*6*
SANDOWAY.	ALL RELIGIONS ..	*112,029*	*55,304*	*56,725*	*27,655*	*23,851*	*3,804*	*84,374*	*31,453*	*52,921*	*602*	*511*	*91*
	0—10	29,645	14,835	14,810	671	472	199	28,974	14,363	14,611	17	13	4
	10—15	14,098	7,267	6,831	2,968	2,348	620	11,130	4,919	6,211	71	47	24
	15—20	11,629	5,644	5,985	3,946	3,179	767	7,683	2,465	5,218	139	120	19
	20—30	17,723	8,303	9,420	6,329	5,447	882	11,394	2,856	8,538	155	135	20
	30 and over	38,934	19,255	19,679	13,741	12,405	1,336	25,193	6,850	18,343	220	196	24
	BUDDHIST ...	*100,878*	*49,415*	*51,463*	*25,415*	*22,119*	*3,296*	*75,463*	*27,296*	*48,167*	*317*	*267*	*50*
	0—10	26,952	13,461	13,491	596	426	170	26,356	13,035	13,321	12	10	2
	10—15	12,778	6,581	6,197	2,693	2,172	521	10,085	4,409	5,676	44	29	15
	15—20	10,431	5,064	5,367	3,588	2,947	641	6,843	2,117	4,726	72	65	7
	20—30	15,758	7,229	8,529	5,772	4,980	792	9,986	2,249	7,737	68	58	10
	30 and over	34,959	17,080	17,879	12,766	11,594	1,172	22,193	5,486	16,707	121	105	16
	ANIMIST (ALL AGES)	*4,568*	*2,321*	*2,247*	*202*	*174*	*28*	*4,366*	*2,147*	*2,219*	*7*	*5*	*2*
	HINDU (ALL AGES)	*376*	*331*	*45*	*206*	*197*	*9*	*170*	*134*	*36*	*19*	*18*	*1*
	MAHOMEDAN ..	*5,251*	*2,749*	*2,502*	*1,428*	*1121*	*307*	*3,823*	*1,628*	*2,195*	*188*	*172*	*16*
	0—10	1,305	682	623	60	38	22	1,245	644	601	3	3	...
	10—15	642	328	314	199	141	58	443	187	256	17	11	6
	15—20	603	297	306	240	165	75	363	132	231	49	44	5
	20—30	922	502	420	329	270	59	593	232	361	53	49	4
	30 and over	1,779	940	839	600	507	93	1,179	433	746	66	65	1
	MAHOMEDANS BORN IN BURMA.	*4,698*	*2,229*	*2,469*	*1,160*	*855*	*305*	*3,538*	*1,374*	*2,164*	*175*	*159*	*16*
	0—10	1.290	675	615	60	38	22	1,230	637	593	3	3	...
	10—15	621	308	313	194	136	58	427	172	255	17	11	6
	15—20	527	223	304	207	132	75	320	91	229	48	43	5
	20—30	748	334	414	246	187	59	502	147	355	50	46	4
	30 and over	1,512	689	823	453	362	91	1,059	327	732	57	56	1
	CHRISTIAN (ALL AGES)	*956*	*488*	*468*	*404*	*240*	*164*	*552*	*248*	*304*	*71*	*49*	*22*

IMPERIAL TABLE VIIIB.—*Literacy by Religion and Age.*

	DISTRICT, RELIGION AND AGE.	POPULATION. Total. Persons.	Total. Males.	Total. Females.	Literate. Persons.	Literate. Males.	Literate. Females.	Illiterate. Persons.	Illiterate. Males.	Illiterate. Females.	Literate in English. Persons.	Literate in English. Males.	Literate in English. Females.
	1	2	3	4	5	6	7	8	9	10	11	12	13
RANGOON TOWN.	ALL RELIGIONS ...	*341,962*	*236,689*	*105,273*	*151,070*	*112,204*	*38,866*	*190,892*	*124,485*	*66,407*	*40,551*	*32,436*	*8,115*
	0—10	46,032	23,537	22,495	5,957	3,546	2,411	40,075	19,991	20,084	1,596	919	677
	10—15	25,390	14,913	10,477	12,968	8,424	4,544	12,422	6,489	5,933	3,898	2,757	1,141
	15—20	32,480	21,377	11,103	17,939	12,140	5,799	14,541	9,237	5,304	5,623	4,258	1,365
	20—30	95,831	72,107	23,724	46,205	35,367	10,838	49,626	36,740	12,886	13,211	10,965	2,246
	30 and over	142,229	104,755	37,474	68,001	52,727	15,274	74,228	52,028	22,200	16,223	13,537	2,686
	BUDDHIST ...	*111,550*	*58,077*	*53,473*	*68,465*	*43,814*	*24,651*	*43,085*	*14,263*	*28,822*	*12,965*	*11,407*	*1,558*
	0—10	20,580	10,272	10,308	2,961	1,786	1,175	17,619	8,486	9,133	324	226	98
	10—15	11,598	5,877	5,721	7,192	4,448	2,744	4,406	1,429	2,977	1,354	1,040	314
	15—20	12,354	6,154	6,200	9,160	5,508	3,652	3,194	646	2,548	2,187	1,833	354
	20—30	24,242	13,405	10,837	18,723	12,106	6,617	5,519	1,299	4,220	4,410	4,007	403
	30 and over	42,776	22,369	20,407	30,429	19,966	10,463	12,347	2,403	9,944	4,690	4,301	389
	ANIMIST ...	*2,883*	*2,136*	*747*	*1,127*	*1,008*	*119*	*1,756*	*1,128*	*628*	*105*	*100*	*5*
	0—10	441	248	193	13	11	2	428	237	191	3	2	1
	10—15	222	131	91	81	60	21	141	71	70	12	12	...
	15—20	244	190	54	145	112	33	99	78	21	27	25	2
	20—30	687	549	138	268	235	33	419	314	105	27	25	2
	30 and over	1,289	1,018	271	620	590	30	669	428	241	36	36	...
	HINDU ...	*125,002*	*102,313*	*22,689*	*30,297*	*27,396*	*2,901*	*94,705*	*74,917*	*19,788*	*6,889*	*6,497*	*392*
	0—10	10,816	5,640	5,176	823	528	295	9,993	5,112	4,881	164	121	43
	10—15	5,801	4,168	1,633	1,655	1,280	375	4,146	2,888	1,258	578	491	87
	15—20	9,824	7,966	1,858	2,847	2,408	439	6,977	5,558	1,419	762	682	80
	20—30	41,454	35,109	6,345	11,055	10,028	1,027	30,399	25,081	5,318	2,563	2,438	125
	30 and over	57,107	49,430	7,677	13,917	13,152	765	43,190	36,278	6,912	2,822	2,765	57
	HINDUS BORN IN BURMA.	*12,630*	*6,721*	*5,909*	*2,813*	*2,062*	*751*	*9,817*	*4,659*	*5,158*	*1,177*	*1,017*	*160*
	0—10	6,769	3,382	3,387	433	264	169	6,336	3,118	3,218	97	71	26
	10—15	1,774	970	804	662	454	208	1,112	516	596	290	236	54
	15—20	1,034	560	474	476	352	124	558	208	350	251	218	33
	20—30	1,781	1,011	770	743	580	163	1,038	431	607	343	304	39
	30 and over	1,272	798	474	499	412	87	773	386	387	196	188	8
CITY OF RANGOON.	MAHOMEDAN ...	*61,954*	*49,520*	*12,434*	*25,775*	*23,052*	*2,723*	*36,179*	*26,468*	*9,711*	*4,263*	*4,102*	*161*
	0—10	6,576	3,454	3,122	612	430	182	5,964	3,024	2,940	77	65	12
	10—15	4,083	2,821	1,262	1,655	1,290	365	2,428	1,531	897	357	333	24
	15—20	6,166	4,865	1,301	2,805	2,361	444	3,361	2,504	857	566	524	42
	20—30	19,764	16,867	2,897	8,870	8,112	758	10,894	8,755	2,139	1,371	1,325	46
	30 and over	25,365	21,513	3,852	11,833	10,859	974	13,532	10,654	2,878	1,892	1,855	37
	MAHOMEDANS BORN IN BURMA.	*16,468*	*8,270*	*8,198*	*6,386*	*4,237*	*2,149*	*10,082*	*4,033*	*6,049*	*1,972*	*1,836*	*136*
	0—10	5,324	2,712	2,612	487	329	158	4,837	2,383	2,454	65	54	11
	10—15	2,206	1,202	1,004	969	655	314	1,237	547	690	243	224	19
	15—20	1,749	8,805	944	967	595	372	782	210	572	354	315	39
	20—30	3,138	1,507	1,631	1,693	1,133	560	1,445	374	1,071	609	571	38
	30 and over	4,051	2,044	2,007	2,270	1,525	745	1,781	519	1,262	701	672	29
	CHRISTIAN ...	*25,315*	*14,236*	*11,079*	*18,320*	*10,876*	*7,444*	*6,995*	*3,360*	*3,635*	*14,880*	*9,274*	*5,606*
	0—10	5,029	2,506	2,523	1,228	595	633	3,801	1,911	1,890	939	454	485
	10—15	2,357	1,171	1,186	1,813	949	864	544	222	322	1,395	758	637
	15—20	2,553	1,325	1,228	2,307	1,236	1,071	246	89	157	1,858	1,039	819
	20—30	6,277	3,688	2,589	5,446	3,306	2,140	831	382	449	4,447	2,878	1,569
	30 and over	9,099	5,546	3,553	7,526	4,790	2,736	1,573	756	817	6,241	4,145	2,096
	OTHERS ...	*15,258*	*10,407*	*4,851*	*7,086*	*6,058*	*1,028*	*8,172*	*4,349*	*3,823*	*1,449*	*1,056*	*393*
	0—10	2,590	1,417	1,173	380	196	124	2,270	1,221	1,049	89	51	38
	10—15	1,329	745	584	572	397	175	757	348	409	202	123	79
	15—20	1,339	877	462	675	515	160	664	362	302	223	155	68
	20—30	3,407	2,489	918	1,843	1,580	263	1,564	909	655	393	292	101
	30 and over	6,593	4,879	1,714	3,676	3,370	306	2,917	1,509	1,408	548	435	107

Imperial Table VIIIb.—*Literacy by Religion and Age.*

District.	Religion and Age.	Population. Total. Persons.	Total. Males.	Total. Females.	Literate. Persons.	Literate. Males.	Literate. Females.	Illiterate. Persons.	Illiterate. Males.	Illiterate. Females.	Literate in English. Persons.	Literate in English. Males.	Literate in English. Females.
	1	2	3	4	5	6	7	8	9	10	11	12	13
INSEIN.	**All Religions** ...	*293,083*	*156,794*	*136,289*	*102,643*	*79,895*	*22,748*	*190,440*	*76,899*	*113,541*	*4,066*	*3,183*	*883*
	0—10	72,991	36,518	36,473	3,437	2,311	1,126	69,554	34,207	35,347	188	107	81
	10—15	33,587	17,671	15,916	10,865	7,863	3,002	22,722	9,808	12,914	509	382	127
	15—20	29,135	14,619	14,516	13,328	9,552	3,776	15,807	5,067	10,740	532	410	122
	20—30	52,894	28,458	24,436	25,748	19,086	6,662	27,146	9,372	17,774	1,148	922	226
	30 and over	104,476	59,528	44,948	49,265	41,083	8,182	55,211	18,445	36,766	1,689	1,362	327
	Buddhist ...	*241,481*	*122,368*	*119,113*	*87,639*	*68,503*	*19,136*	*153,842*	*53,865*	*99,977*	*1,377*	*1,257*	*120*
	0—10	63,195	31,505	31,690	2,771	1,917	854	60,424	29,588	30,836	24	16	8
	10—15	29,427	15,270	14,157	9,575	7,060	2,515	19,852	8,210	11,642	224	208	16
	15—20	24,861	11,984	12,877	11,732	8,510	3,222	13,129	3,474	9,655	215	193	22
	20—30	41,262	20,220	21,042	21,721	16,072	5,649	19,541	4,148	15,393	446	403	43
	30 and over	82,736	43,389	39,347	41,840	34,944	6,896	40,896	8,445	32,451	468	437	31
	Animist ...	*3,211*	*2,358*	*853*	*1,007*	*945*	*62*	*2,204*	*1,413*	*791*	*11*	*11*	...
	0—10	607	342	265	20	15	5	587	327	260	...	...	...
	10—15	248	169	79	52	43	9	196	126	70	...	...	...
	15—20	208	143	65	68	58	10	140	85	55	3	3	...
	20—30	575	425	150	232	214	18	343	211	132	1	1	...
	30 and over	1,573	1,279	294	635	615	20	938	664	274	7	7	...
	Hindu ...	*24,658*	*18,872*	*5,786*	*4,985*	*4,465*	*520*	*19,673*	*14,407*	*5,266*	*740*	*678*	*62*
	0—10	3,638	1,920	1,718	175	121	54	3,463	1,799	1,664	24	18	6
	10—15	1,443	949	494	296	221	75	1,147	728	419	68	54	14
	15—20	1,789	1,318	471	435	367	68	1,354	951	403	83	74	9
	20—30	6,356	5,136	1,220	1,430	1,275	155	4,926	3,861	1,065	217	201	16
	30 and over	11,432	9,549	1,883	2,649	2,481	168	8,783	7,068	1,715	348	331	17
	Hindus born in Burma.	*5,383*	*3,016*	*2,367*	*790*	*645*	*145*	*4,593*	*2,371*	*2,222*	*152*	*130*	*22*
	0—10	2,669	1,360	1,309	116	84	32	2,553	1,276	1,277	17	11	6
	10—15	750	441	309	166	122	44	584	319	265	38	28	10
	15—20	458	281	177	143	120	23	315	161	154	26	24	2
	20—30	717	411	306	183	154	29	534	257	277	41	39	2
	30 and over	789	523	266	182	165	17	607	358	249	30	28	2
	Mahomedan ...	*7,990*	*5,391*	*2,599*	*2,507*	*2,196*	*311*	*5,483*	*3,195*	*2,288*	*243*	*235*	*8*
	0—10	1,706	861	845	100	73	27	1,606	788	818	6	6	...
	10—15	717	426	291	211	168	43	506	258	248	22	21	1
	15—20	663	434	229	241	195	46	422	239	183	21	20	1
	20—30	1,832	1,341	491	724	637	87	1,108	704	404	80	76	4
	30 and over	3,072	2,329	743	1,231	1,123	108	1,841	1,206	635	114	112	2
	Mahomedans born in Burma.	*3,906*	*1,950*	*1,956*	*937*	*698*	*239*	*2,969*	*1,252*	*1,717*	*98*	*95*	*3*
	0—10	1,517	741	776	76	50	26	1,441	691	750	3	3	...
	10—15	514	267	247	143	104	39	371	163	208	12	11	1
	15—20	355	173	182	128	95	33	227	78	149	16	16	...
	20—30	622	293	329	235	171	64	387	122	265	28	27	1
	30 and over	898	476	422	355	278	77	543	198	345	39	38	1
	Christian ...	*15,579*	*7,688*	*7,891*	*6,448*	*3,740*	*2,708*	*9,131*	*3,948*	*5,183*	*1,677*	*985*	*692*
	0—10	3,804	1,866	1,938	367	182	185	3,437	1,684	1,753	132	65	67
	10—15	1,749	855	894	729	370	359	1,020	485	535	193	98	95
	15—20	1,608	735	873	848	419	429	760	316	444	207	117	90
	20—30	2,830	1,311	1,519	1,628	879	749	1,202	432	770	399	236	163
	30 and over	5,588	2,921	2,667	2,876	1,890	986	2,712	1,031	1,681	746	469	277
	Others (all ages)	*164*	*117*	*47*	*57*	*46*	*11*	*107*	*71*	*36*	*18*	*17*	*1*
HANTHAWADDY.	**All Religions** ...	*364,624*	*201,043*	*163,581*	*147,388*	*108,801*	*38,587*	*217,236*	*92,242*	*124,994*	*2,137*	*1,832*	*305*
	0—10	90,164	44,878	45,286	6,340	4,467	1,873	83,824	40,411	43,413	76	49	27
	10—15	41,472	22,048	19,424	16,343	11,296	5,047	25,129	10,752	14,377	186	151	35
	15—20	36,040	18,737	17,303	18,856	12,313	6,543	17,184	6,424	10,760	276	237	39
	20—30	67,766	38,724	29,042	36,146	25,940	10,206	31,620	12,784	18,836	710	630	86
	30 and over	129,182	76,656	52,526	69,703	54,785	14,918	59,479	21,871	37,608	889	765	124
	Buddhist ...	*293,759*	*148,754*	*145,005*	*130,638*	*93,441*	*37,197*	*163,121*	*55,313*	*107,808*	*1,070*	*992*	*78*
	0—10	77,964	38,482	39,482	5,967	4,201	1,766	71,997	34,281	37,716	18	16	2
	10—15	36,285	18,661	17,624	15,375	10,493	4,882	20,910	8,168	12,742	110	98	12
	15—20	30,099	14,283	15,816	17,444	11,106	6,338	12,655	3,177	9,478	201	182	19
	20—30	49,371	24,096	25,275	30,879	21,060	9,819	18,492	3,036	15,456	376	356	20
	30 and over	100,040	53,232	46,808	60,973	46,[illegible]81	14,392	39,067	6,651	32,416	365	340	25

Imperial Table VIIIb.—*Literacy by Religion and Age.*

District, Religion and Age.	Population. Total. Persons.	Total. Males.	Total. Females.	Literate. Persons.	Literate. Males.	Literate. Females.	Illiterate. Persons.	Illiterate. Males.	Illiterate. Females.	Literate in English. Persons.	Literate in English. Males.	Literate in English. Females.
1	2	3	4	5	6	7	8	9	10	11	12	13
HANTHAWADDY—*concluded.*												
Animist ...	*5,202*	*3,997*	*1,205*	*1,619*	*1,513*	*106*	*3,583*	*2,484*	*1,099*	*22*	*20*	*2*
0—10	931	545	386	7	...	7	924	545	379	...	...	...
10—15	332	224	108	58	44	14	274	180	94	...	...	...
15—20	311	246	65	102	89	13	209	157	52	3	3	...
20—30	1,119	885	234	426	402	24	693	483	210	9	8	1
30 and over	2,509	2,097	412	1,026	978	48	1,483	1,119	364	10	9	1
Hindu ...	*47,326*	*35,365*	*11,961*	*9,224*	*8,799*	*425*	*38,102*	*26,566*	*11,536*	*202*	*201*	*1*
0—10	7,812	4,073	3,739	163	127	36	7,649	3,946	3,703	1	1	...
10—15	3,361	2,245	1,116	449	412	37	2,912	1,833	1,079	9	9	...
15—20	3,859	2,965	894	706	649	57	3,153	2,316	837	17	17	...
20—30	12,461	9,949	2,512	2,987	2,851	136	9,474	7,098	2,376	83	83	...
30 and over	19,833	16,133	3,700	4,919	4,760	159	14,914	11,373	3,541	92	91	1
Hindus born in Burma.	*12,029*	*6,498*	*5,531*	*1,224*	*1,084*	*140*	*10,805*	*5,414*	*5,391*	*30*	*29*	*1*
0—10	6,301	3,198	3,103	112	88	24	6,189	3,110	3,079	1	1	...
10—15	1,924	1,102	822	230	206	24	1,694	896	798	6	6	...
15—20	1,073	598	475	183	156	27	890	442	448	5	5	...
20—30	1,546	848	698	372	332	40	1,174	516	658	12	12	...
30 and over	1,185	752	433	327	302	25	858	450	408	6	5	1
Mahomedan ..	*12,811*	*9,551*	*3,260*	*3,900*	*3,588*	*312*	*8,911*	*5,963*	*2,948*	*105*	*104*	*1*
0—10	2,056	1,042	1,014	69	54	15	1,987	988	999	...	...	...
10—15	977	598	379	264	213	51	713	385	328	2	2	...
15—20	1,306	965	341	400	336	64	906	629	277	7	6	1
20—30	3,744	3,134	610	1,372	1,288	84	2,372	1,846	526	45	45	...
30 and over	4,728	3,812	916	1,795	1,697	98	2,933	2,115	818	51	51	...
Mahomedans born in Burma.	*5,184*	*2,541*	*2,643*	*1,065*	*809*	*256*	*4,119*	*1,732*	*2,387*	*52*	*51*	*1*
0—10	1,881	938	943	56	43	13	1,825	895	930	...	...	...
10—15	759	406	353	193	143	50	566	263	303	1	1	...
15—20	550	260	290	197	140	57	353	120	233	2	1	1
20—30	834	384	450	296	228	68	538	156	382	22	22	...
30 and over	1,160	553	607	323	255	68	837	298	539	27	27	...
Christian ...	*5,086*	*3,028*	*2,058*	*1,862*	*1,339*	*523*	*3,224*	*1,689*	*1,535*	*720*	*499*	*221*
0—10	1,350	710	640	127	80	47	1,223	630	593	56	31	25
10—15	495	307	188	192	131	61	303	176	127	64	41	23
15—20	442	265	177	199	131	68	243	134	109	48	29	19
20—30	954	561	393	447	308	139	507	253	254	188	130	58
30 and over	1,845	1,185	660	897	689	208	948	496	452	364	268	96
Others (all ages)	*440*	*348*	*92*	*145*	*121*	*24*	*295*	*227*	*68*	*18*	*16*	*2*
THARRAWADDY.												
All Religions ...	*492,429*	*246,261*	*246,168*	*180,908*	*145,972*	*34,936*	*311,521*	*100,289*	*211,232*	*2,725*	*2,380*	*345*
0—10	128,516	63,330	65,186	6,756	4,648	2,108	121,760	58,682	63,078	93	65	28
10—15	59,647	30,402	29,245	22,079	16,917	5,162	37,568	13,485	24,083	420	339	81
15—20	52,371	25,139	27,232	26,255	19,747	6,508	26,116	5,392	20,724	542	457	85
20—30	83,866	41,476	42,390	43,653	34,099	9,554	40,213	7,377	32,836	834	746	88
30 and over	168,029	85,914	82,115	82,165	70,561	11,604	85,864	15,353	70,511	836	773	63
Buddhist ..	*467,558*	*229,477*	*238,081*	*172,945*	*139,804*	*33,141*	*294,613*	*89,673*	*204,940*	*1,834*	*1,698*	*136*
0—10	124,049	61,018	63,031	6,454	4,473	1,981	117,595	56,545	61,050	49	42	7
10—15	57,673	29,249	28,424	21,308	16,472	4,836	36,365	12,777	23,588	306	265	41
15—20	50,170	23,748	26,422	25,357	19,171	6,186	24,813	4,577	20,236	408	365	43
20—30	78,100	37,329	40,771	41,442	32,414	9,028	36,658	4,915	31,743	590	561	29
30 and over	157,566	78,133	79,433	78,384	67,274	11,110	79,182	10,859	68,323	481	465	16
Animist ...	*2,129*	*1,600*	*529*	*796*	*764*	*32*	*1,333*	*836*	*497*	*16*	*16*	...
0—10	398	244	154	18	17	1	380	227	153	...	...	...
10—15	175	116	59	49	35	14	126	81	45	...	...	...
15—20	124	89	35	47	41	6	77	48	29	2	2	...
20—30	367	267	100	167	163	4	200	104	96	11	11	...
30 and over	1,065	884	181	515	508	7	550	376	174	3	3	...

Imperial Table VIIIb.—*Literacy by Religion and Age.*

District, Religion and Age.	Population. Total. Persons.	Total. Males.	Total. Females.	Literate. Persons.	Literate. Males.	Literate. Females.	Illiterate. Persons.	Illiterate. Males.	Illiterate. Females.	Literate in English. Persons.	Literate in English. Males.	Literate in English. Females.
1	2	3	4	5	6	7	8	9	10	11	12	13
THARRAWADDY—concluded.												
Hindu ..	*9,179*	*7,422*	*1,757*	*1,896*	*1,809*	*87*	*7,283*	*5,613*	*1,670*	*176*	*170*	*6*
0—10	1,073	549	524	31	24	7	1,042	525	517	4	4	...
10—15	474	323	151	70	61	9	404	262	142	11	11	...
15—20	675	557	118	149	137	12	526	420	106	15	13	2
20—30	2,606	2,231	375	657	625	32	1,949	1,606	343	51	49	2
30 and over	4,351	3,762	589	989	962	27	3,362	2,800	562	95	93	2
Hindus born in Burma.	*1,477*	*805*	*672*	*163*	*137*	*26*	*1,314*	*668*	*646*	*37*	*37*	...
0—10	820	409	411	16	9	7	804	400	404		...	...
10—15	216	119	97	30	24	6	186	95	91	10	10	...
15—20	106	64	42	28	24	4	78	40	38	8	8	...
20—30	177	102	75	44	37	7	133	65	68	8	8	...
30 and over	158	111	47	45	43	2	113	68	45	11	11	..
Mahomedan .	*5,421*	*3,736*	*1,685*	*1,672*	*1,442*	*230*	*3,749*	*2,294*	*1,455*	*125*	*124*	*1*
0—10	1,093	571	522	56	36	20	1,[illegible]37	535	5[illegible]2	2	2	...
10—15	428	253	175	136	98	38	292	155	137	12	12	.
15—20	546	356	190	174	137	37	37[illegible]	219	153	15	15	...
20—30	1,327	971	356	486	414	72	841	557	284	39	38	1
30 and over	2,027	1,585	442	820	757	63	1,[illegible]07	828	379	57	57	..
Mahomedans born in Burma.	*2,594*	*1,224*	*1,370*	*625*	*417*	*208*	*1,969*	*807*	*1,162*	*73*	*73*	..
0—10	1,014	529	485	43	25	18	971	504	467	2	2	
10—15	324	106	158	101	68	33	223	9[illegible]	125	12	12	...
15—20	278	108	170	92	57	35	186	51	135	11	11	...
20—30	429	170	259	171	105	66	258	65	193	5	25	...
30 and over	549	251	298	218	162	56	331	89	242	23	23	...
Christian ...	*8,074*	*3,970*	*4,104*	*3,568*	*2,122*	*1,446*	*4,506*	*1,848*	*2,658*	*569*	*367*	*202*
0—10	1,898	946	952	197	98	99	1,701	848	853	38	17	21
10—15	897	461	436	516	251	265	381	210	171	91	51	40
15—20	854	387	467	528	261	267	326	126	200	102	62	40
20—30	1,440	657	783	887	469	418	553	188	365	141	85	56
30 and over	2,985	1,519	1,466	1,440	1,043	397	1,545	476	1,069	197	152	45
Others (all ages)	*68*	*56*	*12*	*31*	*31*	..	*37*	*25*	*12*	*5*	*5*	...
PEGU.												
All Religions .	*445,620*	*235,324*	*210,296*	*161,883*	*123,571*	*38,312*	*283,737*	*111,753*	*171,984*	*2,614*	*2,241*	*373*
0—10	114,045	56,342	57,703	6,469	4,205	2,264	107,576	52,137	55,439	79	62	17
10—15	52,611	27,679	24,932	18,559	13,543	5,016	34,052	14,136	19,916	278	222	56
15—20	44,237	21,768	22,469	21,342	14,851	6,491	22,895	6,917	15,9[illegible]8	377	316	61
20—30	80,274	42,116	38,158	39,979	29,421	10,558	40,295	12,695	27,600	838	716	122
30 and over	154,453	87,419	67,034	75,534	61,551	13,983	78,9[illegible]9	25,868	53,051	1,042	925	117
Buddhist ...	*378,337*	*191,185*	*187,152*	*147,966*	*112,003*	*35,963*	*230,371*	*79,182*	*151,189*	*1,446*	*1,318*	*128*
0—10	99,796	49,082	50,714	6,008	3,890	2,118	93,788	45,192	48,596	37	33	4
10—15	47,023	24,293	22,730	17,452	12,761	4,691	29,571	11,532	18,039	187	161	26
15—20	39,006	18,445	20,561	19,928	13,862	6,066	19,078	4,583	14,495	231	214	17
20—30	65,379	31,875	33,504	36,228	26,332	9,896	29,151	5,543	23,608	469	431	38
30 and over	127,133	67,490	59,643	68,350	55,158	13,192	58,783	12,332	46,451	522	479	43
Animist ...	*6,707*	*4,533*	*2,174*	*1,778*	*1,658*	*120*	*4,929*	*2,875*	*2,054*	*12*	*9*	*3*
0—10	1,415	763	652	21	16	5	1,394	747	647	...	...	...
10—15	590	348	242	93	71	22	497	277	220	1	...	1
15—20	501	320	181	131	112	19	370	208	162	2	1	1
20—30	1,245	851	394	460	419	41	785	432	353	2	1	1
30 and over	2,956	2,251	705	1,073	1,040	33	1,883	1,211	672	7	7	...
Hindu ...	*40,856*	*27,554*	*13,302*	*5,755*	*5,343*	*412*	*35,101*	*22,211*	*12,890*	*275*	*260*	*15*
0—10	8,621	4,448	4,173	202	158	44	8,419	4,290	4,129	15	12	3
10—15	3,037	1,913	1,124	340	305	35	2,697	1,608	1,089	18	17	1
15—20	2,801	1,903	898	424	369	55	2,377	1,534	843	19	17	2
20—30	9,218	6,452	2,766	1,567	1,447	120	7,651	5,005	2,646	101	95	6
30 and over	17,179	12,838	4,341	3,222	3,064	158	13,957	9,774	4,183	122	119	3
Hindus born in Burma.	*13,483*	*7,442*	*6,041*	*1,091*	*945*	*146*	*12,392*	*6,497*	*5,895*	*76*	*68*	*8*
0—10	7,249	3,677	3,572	142	111	31	7,107	3,566	3,541	12	9	3
10—15	1,962	1,124	838	197	170	27	1,765	954	811	9	8	1
15—20	1,085	628	457	134	114	20	951	514	437	12	10	2
20—30	1,553	917	636	291	255	36	1,262	662	600	24	22	2
30 and over	1,634	1,096	538	327	295	32	1,307	801	506	19	19	...

IMPERIAL TABLE VIIIB.—*Literacy by Religion and Age.*

DISTRICT, RELIGION AND AGE.	POPULATION.									Literate in English.		
	Total.			Literate.			Illiterate.					
	Persons.	Males.	Females.	Persons.	Males.	Females.	Persons.	Males.	Females.	Persons.	Males.	Females.
1	2	3	4	5	6	7	8	9	10	11	12	13
PEGU—concluded.												
MAHOMEDAN ...	9,745	6,996	2,749	2,710	2,347	363	7,035	4,649	2,386	285	263	22
0—10	1,779	871	908	80	59	21	1,699	812	887	7	4	3
10—15	821	520	301	234	168	66	587	352	235	16	15	1
15—20	894	618	276	308	248	60	586	370	216	41	39	2
20—30	2,621	2,057	564	748	648	100	1,873	1,409	464	83	75	8
30 and over	3,630	2,930	700	1,340	1,224	116	2,290	1,706	584	138	130	8
MAHOMEDANS BORN IN BURMA.	4,002	1,959	2,043	896	604	292	3,106	1,355	1,751	111	103	8
0—10	1,566	753	813	62	52	10	1,504	701	803	4	4	...
10—15	558	298	260	155	93	62	403	205	198	9	8	1
15—20	418	198	220	151	97	54	267	101	166	18	17	1
20—30	647	279	368	213	131	82	434	148	286	34	31	3
30 and over	813	431	382	315	231	84	498	200	298	46	43	3
CHRISTIAN ...	9,791	4,919	4,872	3,592	2,153	1,439	6,199	2,766	3,433	582	380	202
0—10	2,398	1,155	1,243	155	81	74	2,243	1,074	1,169	18	12	6
10—15	1,129	599	530	440	238	202	689	361	328	56	29	27
15—20	1,020	475	545	540	255	285	480	220	260	83	45	38
20—30	1,776	856	920	954	557	397	822	299	523	180	111	69
30 and over	3,468	1,834	1,634	1,503	1,022	481	1,965	812	1,153	245	183	62
OTHERS (ALL AGES)	184	137	47	82	67	15	102	70	32	14	11	3
PROME.												
ALL RELIGIONS ...	371,575	182,803	188,772	126,582	103,451	23,131	244,993	79,352	165,641	1,919	1,691	228
0—10	89,378	44,028	45,350	4,306	2,762	1,544	85,072	41,266	43,806	50	34	16
10—15	43,350	21,902	21,448	14,077	10,539	3,538	29,273	11,363	17,910	212	169	43
15—20	40,587	19,403	21,184	18,353	14,162	4,191	22,234	5,241	16,993	370	308	62
20—30	66,116	32,095	34,021	30,897	24,732	6,165	35,219	7,363	27,856	604	545	59
30 and over	132,144	65,375	66,769	58,949	51,256	7,693	73,195	14,119	59,076	683	635	48
BUDDHIST ...	356,283	172,327	183,956	122,074	99,719	22,355	234,209	72,608	161,601	1,368	1,243	125
0—10	86,771	42,709	44,062	4,110	2,640	1,470	82,661	40,069	42,592	30	22	8
10—15	42,301	21,252	21,049	13,777	10,319	3,458	28,524	10,933	17,591	156	121	35
15—20	39,346	18,640	20,706	17,887	13,835	4,052	21,459	4,805	16,654	285	248	37
20—30	62,149	29,177	32,972	29,504	23,577	5,927	32,645	5,600	27,045	454	426	28
30 and over	125,716	60,549	65,167	56,796	49,348	7,448	68,920	11,201	57,719	443	426	17
ANIMIST ...	4,274	2,649	1,625	889	798	91	3,385	1,851	1,534	15	14	1
0—10	836	427	409	34	24	10	802	403	399	...	...	...
10—15	319	180	139	32	23	9	287	157	130	2	2	...
15—20	321	176	145	75	61	14	246	115	131	3	2	1
20—30	918	583	335	237	204	33	681	379	302	4	4	...
30 and over	1,880	1,283	597	511	486	25	1,369	797	572	6	6	...
HINDU ...	5,509	4,427	1,082	1,364	1,284	80	4,145	3,143	1,002	115	112	3
0—10	618	313	305	30	22	8	588	291	297	4	3	1
10—15	239	180	59	54	47	7	185	133	52	13	13	...
15—20	393	315	78	117	102	15	276	213	63	11	11	...
20—30	1,751	1,471	280	508	482	26	1,243	989	254	28	27	1
30 and over	2,508	2,148	360	655	631	24	1,853	1,517	336	59	58	1
HINDUS BORN IN BURMA.	774	429	345	144	116	28	630	313	317	25	23	2
0—10	379	171	208	14	9	5	365	162	203	3	2	1
10—15	87	53	34	20	16	4	67	37	30	5	5	...
15—20	62	39	23	24	19	5	38	20	18	6	6	...
20—30	102	65	37	36	28	8	66	37	29	5	5	...
30 and over	144	101	43	50	44	6	94	57	37	6	5	1
MAHOMEDAN ...	4,174	2,687	1,487	1,559	1,195	364	2,615	1,492	1,123	178	162	16
0—10	872	447	425	82	46	36	790	401	389	5	3	2
10—15	360	222	138	148	110	38	212	112	100	26	24	2
15—20	393	208	185	184	116	68	209	92	117	41	32	9
20—30	1,025	728	297	468	361	107	557	367	190	42	41	1
30 and over	1,524	1,082	442	677	562	115	847	520	327	64	62	2
MAHOMEDANS BORN IN BURMA.	2,464	1,158	1,306	870	536	334	1,594	622	972	147	131	16
0—10	818	409	409	74	39	35	744	370	374	5	3	2
10—15	297	172	125	133	96	37	164	76	88	26	24	2
15—20	290	122	168	145	82	63	145	40	105	41	32	9
20—30	410	172	238	219	122	97	191	50	141	31	30	1
30 and over	649	283	366	299	197	102	350	86	264	44	42	2

Imperial Table VIIIb.—*Literacy by Religion and Age.*

District, Religion and Age.	Population. Total. Persons.	Males.	Females.	Literate. Persons.	Males.	Females.	Illiterate. Persons.	Males.	Females.	Literate in English. Persons.	Males.	Females.
1	2	3	4	5	6	7	8	9	10	11	12	13
PROME—*concluded.*												
Christian ...	*1,246*	*657*	*589*	*656*	*422*	*234*	*590*	*235*	*355*	*234*	*151*	*83*
0—10	266	122	144	49	29	20	217	93	124	11	6	5
10—15	123	67	56	65	39	26	58	28	30	15	9	6
15—20	130	60	70	88	46	42	42	14	28	30	15	15
20—30	254	128	126	168	100	68	86	28	58	73	44	29
30 and over	473	280	193	286	208	78	187	72	115	105	77	28
Others (all ages)	*89*	*56*	*33*	*40*	*33*	*7*	*49*	*23*	*26*	*9*	*9*	...
BASSEIN.												
All Religions ...	*489,473*	*252,947*	*236,526*	*167,082*	*127,928*	*39,154*	*322,391*	*125,019*	*197,372*	*3,804*	*3,037*	*767*
0—10	121,037	59,602	61,435	4,928	3,065	1,863	116,109	56,537	59,572	111	65	46
10—15	59,333	30,787	28,546	17,775	12,599	5,176	41,558	18,188	23,370	379	275	104
15—20	51,067	24,837	26,230	22,228	15,473	6,755	28,839	9,364	19,475	632	479	153
20—30	89,989	46,312	43,677	42,850	31,676	11,174	47,139	14,636	32,503	1,244	1,029	215
30 and over	168,047	91,409	76,638	79,301	65,115	14,186	88,746	26,294	62,452	1,438	1,189	249
Buddhist ...	*428,546*	*213,811*	*214,735*	*145,603*	*113,224*	*32,379*	*282,943*	*100,587*	*182,356*	*1,851*	*1,602*	*149*
0—10	109,730	53,868	55,862	4,214	2,686	1,528	105,516	51,182	54,334	51	38	13
10—15	53,626	27,633	25,993	15,599	11,394	4,205	38,027	16,239	21,788	229	190	39
15—20	45,464	21,640	23,824	19,572	13,976	5,596	25,892	7,664	18,228	325	295	30
20—30	75,596	36,181	39,415	36,812	27,490	9,322	38,784	8,691	30,093	576	544	32
30 and over	144,130	74,489	69,641	69,406	57,678	11,728	74,724	16,811	57,913	570	535	35
Animist ...	*3,356*	*2,696*	*660*	*1,307*	*1,233*	*74*	*2,049*	*1,463*	*586*	*33*	*30*	*3*
0—10	466	306	160	27	22	5	439	284	155	...	...	...
10—15	198	139	59	54	40	14	144	99	45	...	...	...
15—20	196	145	51	92	80	12	104	65	39	6	3	3
20—30	674	538	146	278	258	20	396	270	126	8	8	...
30 and over	1,822	1,578	244	856	833	23	966	745	221	19	19	...
Hindu ...	*14,947*	*13,151*	*1,796*	*2,903*	*2,775*	*128*	*12,044*	*10,376*	*1,668*	*215*	*184*	*31*
0—10	941	533	408	54	35	19	887	498	389	11	6	5
10—15	620	501	119	132	115	17	488	386	102	15	9	6
15—20	1,078	934	144	174	157	17	904	777	127	18	17	1
20—30	5,071	4,553	518	1,089	1,055	34	3,982	3,498	484	87	78	9
30 and over	7,237	6,630	607	1,454	1,413	41	5,783	5,217	566	84	74	10
Hindus born in Burma.	*1,394*	*805*	*589*	*195*	*151*	*44*	*1,199*	*654*	*545*	*37*	*29*	*8*
0—10	683	370	313	36	21	15	647	349	298	10	6	4
10—15	163	98	65	21	12	9	142	86	56	5	3	2
15—20	114	55	59	34	26	8	80	29	51	10	9	1
20—30	242	151	91	58	54	4	184	97	87	11	10	1
30 and over	192	131	61	46	38	8	146	93	53	1	1	...
Mahomedan ...	*9,994*	*7,082*	*2,912*	*2,977*	*2,610*	*367*	*7,017*	*4,472*	*2,545*	*217*	*217*	...
0—10	1,543	824	719	44	32	12	1,499	792	707	...	...	...
10—15	832	427	405	184	127	57	648	300	348	1	1	...
15—20	864	544	330	284	231	53	580	313	267	31	31	...
20—30	2,894	2,242	652	1,051	924	127	1,843	1,318	525	88	88	...
30 and over	3,861	3,045	816	1,414	1,296	118	2,447	1,749	698	97	97	...
Mahomedans born in Burma.	*5,393*	*2,701*	*2,692*	*1,283*	*932*	*351*	*4,110*	*1,769*	*2,341*	*152*	*152*	...
0—10	1,484	786	698	42	32	10	1,442	754	688	...	...	..
10—15	725	333	392	149	92	57	576	241	335	1	1	...
15—20	522	225	297	160	110	50	362	115	247	28	28	...
20—30	1,070	488	582	387	265	122	683	223	460	66	66	...
30 and over	1,592	869	723	545	433	112	1,047	436	611	57	57	...
Christian ...	*32,630*	*16,207*	*16,423*	*14,292*	*8,086*	*6,206*	*18,338*	*8,121*	*10,217*	*1,588*	*1,004*	*584*
0—10	8,357	4,071	4,286	589	290	299	7,768	3,781	3,987	49	21	28
10—15	4,057	2,087	1,970	1,806	923	883	2,251	1,164	1,087	134	75	59
15—20	3,465	1,574	1,891	2,106	1,029	1,077	1,359	545	814	252	133	119
20—30	5,754	2,808	2,946	3,620	1,949	1,671	2,134	859	1,275	485	311	174
30 and over	10,997	5,667	5,330	6,171	3,895	2,276	4,826	1,772	3,054	668	464	204
Others (all ages)	...	...	...	...	...	...	...	...	...	...	...	...

Imperial Table VIIIb.—*Literacy by Religion and Age.*

District, Religion and Age.	Population. Total. Persons.	Total. Males.	Total. Females.	Literate. Persons.	Literate. Males.	Literate. Females.	Illiterate. Persons.	Illiterate. Males.	Illiterate. Females.	Literate in English. Persons.	Literate in English. Males.	Literate in English. Females.
1	2	3	4	5	6	7	8	9	10	11	12	13
HENZADA.												
All Religions ...	*550,920*	*273,439*	*277,481*	*210,296*	*161,837*	*48,459*	*340,624*	*111,602*	*229,022*	*6,836*	*5,193*	*1,643*
0—10	139,826	68,664	71,162	9,763	6,210	3,553	130,063	62,454	67,609	606	582	24
10—15	67,375	34,822	32,553	24,551	18,426	6,125	42,824	16,396	26,428	1,288	1,055	233
15—20	58,362	27,758	30,604	29,008	20,811	8,197	29,354	6,947	22,407	1,387	875	512
20—30	95,621	45,279	50,342	48,357	36,800	11,557	47,264	8,479	38,785	1,259	1,022	237
30 and over	189,736	96,916	92,820	98,617	79,590	19,027	91,119	17,326	73,793	2,296	1,659	637
Buddhist ..	*525,231*	*257,027*	*268,204*	*200,807*	*155,096*	*45,711*	*324,424*	*101,931*	*222,493*	*6,004*	*4,584*	*1,420*
0—10	134,683	65,975	68,708	9,118	5,960	3,158	125,565	60,015	65,550	584	567	17
10—15	64,998	33,486	31,512	23,738	17,849	5,889	41,260	15,637	25,623	1,158	969	189
15—20	55,995	6,381	29,614	27,852	20,121	7,731	28,143	6,260	21,883	1,240	777	463
20—30	89,965	41,376	48,589	45,913	35,035	10,878	44,052	6,341	37,711	1,061	887	174
30 and over	179,590	89,809	89,781	94,186	76,131	18,055	85,404	13,678	71,726	1,961	1,384	577
Animist (all ages)	*1,970*	*1,632*	*338*	*715*	*673*	*42*	*1,255*	*959*	*296*	*3*	*3*	.
Hindu ...	*6,703*	*5,712*	*991*	*1,746*	*1,633*	*113*	*4,957*	*4,079*	*878*	*130*	*120*	*10*
0—10	670	391	279	26	16	10	644	375	269	3	2	1
10—15	368	289	79	80	63	17	288	226	62	3	2	1
15—20	540	458	82	138	122	16	402	336	66	1	..	1
20—30	2,105	1,862	243	608	580	28	1,497	1,282	215	13	10	3
30 and over	3,020	2,712	308	894	852	42	2,126	1,860	266	36	34	2
										77	74	3
Hindus born in Burma.	*1,023*	*622*	*401*	*202*	*160*	*42*	*821*	*462*	*359*	*22*	*20*	*2*
0—10	437	244	193	16	12	4	421	232	189	3	2	1
10—15	104	61	43	29	18	11	75	43	32	..	...	...
15—20	81	44	37	22	14	8	59	30	29	2	2	...
20—30	147	88	59	47	39	8	100	49	51	4	3	1
30 and over	254	185	69	88	77	11	166	108	58	13	13	...
Mahomedan ...	*5,211*	*3,323*	*1,888*	*1,616*	*1,324*	*292*	*3,595*	*1,999*	*1,596*	*72*	*69*	*3*
0—10	1,220	635	585	57	31	26	1,163	604	559	...	...	...
10—15	498	263	235	106	60	46	392	203	189	4	3	1
15—20	451	264	187	194	158	36	257	106	151	14	14	...
20—30	1,167	791	376	474	386	88	693	405	288	18	16	2
30 and over	1,875	1,370	505	785	689	96	1,090	681	409	36	36	...
Mahomedans born in Burma.	*3,055*	*1,441*	*1,614*	*760*	*501*	*259*	*2,295*	*940*	*1,355*	*43*	*42*	*1*
0—10	1,127	573	554	49	26	23	1,078	547	531	...	...	...
10—15	416	199	217	83	40	43	333	159	174	3	3	...
15—20	295	132	163	141	109	32	154	23	131	10	10	...
20—30	502	204	298	199	125	74	303	79	224	7	6	1
30 and over	715	333	382	288	201	87	427	132	295	23	23	...
Christian ...	*11,742*	*5,711*	*6,031*	*5,381*	*3,089*	*2,292*	*6,361*	*2,622*	*3,736*	*621*	*411*	*210*
0—10	2,983	1,492	1,491	542	191	351	2,441	1,301	1,140	19	13	6
10—15	1,408	708	700	593	426	167	815	282	533	125	83	42
15—20	1,246	552	694	781	372	409	465	180	285	119	73	46
20—30	1,969	896	1,075	1,209	656	553	760	240	520	141	82	59
30 and over	4,136	2,063	2,073	2,156	1,444	812	1,880	619	1,261	217	160	57
Others (all ages)	*63*	*34*	*29*	*31*	*22*	*9*	*32*	*12*	*20*	*6*	*6*	...
MYAUNGMYA.												
All Religions ...	*370,551*	*196,757*	*173,794*	*128,218*	*97,282*	*30,936*	*242,333*	*99,475*	*142,858*	*1,947*	*1,567*	*380*
0—10	94,489	46,729	47,760	4,736	2,906	1,830	89,753	43,823	45,930	59	36	23
10—15	44,387	23,390	20,997	13,574	9,620	3,954	30,813	13,770	17,043	263	175	88
15—20	39,021	19,479	19,542	16,927	11,451	5,476	22,094	8,028	14,066	294	234	60
20—30	67,373	36,165	31,208	31,713	23,163	8,550	35,660	13,002	22,658	602	502	100
30 and over	125,281	70,994	54,287	61,268	50,142	11,126	64,013	20,852	43,161	729	620	109
Buddhist ...	*324,315*	*165,260*	*159,055*	*112,727*	*85,773*	*26,954*	*211,588*	*79,487*	*132,101*	*994*	*905*	*89*
0—10	86,009	42,495	43,514	4,118	2,564	1,554	81,891	39,931	41,960	23	12	11
10—15	40,132	20,916	19,216	12,131	8,807	3,324	28,001	12,109	15,892	137	114	23
15—20	34,515	16,490	18,025	15,180	10,335	4,845	19,335	6,155	13,180	180	162	18
20—30	55,665	27,335	28,330	27,371	19,863	7,508	28,294	7,472	20,822	319	300	19
30 and over	107,994	58,024	49,970	53,927	44,204	9,723	54,067	13,820	40,247	335	317	18

IMPERIAL TABLE VIIIB.—*Literacy by Religion and Age.*

District, Religion and Age.	Population. Total. Persons.	Total. Males.	Total. Females.	Literate. Persons.	Literate. Males.	Literate. Females.	Illiterate. Persons.	Illiterate. Males.	Illiterate. Females.	Literate in English. Persons.	Literate in English. Males.	Literate in English. Females.
1	2	3	4	5	6	7	8	9	10	11	12	13
MYAUNGMYA—concluded.												
ANIMIST ...	*4,027*	*3,292*	*785*	*1,726*	*1,624*	*102*	*2,301*	*1,668*	*633*	*18*	*18*	...
0—10	566	327	239	39	34	5	527	293	234	...	...	...
10—15	216	144	72	61	50	11	155	94	61	4	4	...
15—20	224	183	41	78	69	9	146	114	32	...	...	...
20—30	883	732	151	391	362	29	492	370	122	5	5	...
30 and over	2,138	1,906	232	1,157	1,109	48	981	797	184	9	9	...
HINDU ...	*9,533*	*8,544*	*989*	*2,624*	*2,551*	*73*	*6,909*	*5,993*	*916*	*79*	*75*	*4*
0—10	541	279	262	30	23	7	511	256	255	1	1	...
10—15	569	483	86	27	22	5	542	461	81	5	4	1
15—20	942	830	112	226	208	18	716	622	94	4	4	...
20—30	3,440	3,205	235	1,030	1,007	23	2,410	2,198	212	32	30	2
30 and over	4,041	3,747	294	1,311	1,291	20	2,730	2,456	274	37	36	1
HINDUS BORN IN BURMA.	*863*	*484*	*379*	*96*	*68*	*28*	*767*	*416*	*351*	*7*	*7*	...
0—10	312	118	194	7	4	3	305	114	191	...	...	...
10—15	185	134	51	10	8	2	175	126	49	...	..	...
15—20	66	33	33	23	13	10	43	20	23	1	1	...
20—30	144	99	45	26	21	5	118	78	40	2	2	...
30 and over	156	100	56	30	22	8	126	78	48	4	4	...
MAHOMEDAN ...	*11,451*	*8,990*	*2,461*	*2,716*	*2,481*	*235*	*8,735*	*6,509*	*2,226*	*89*	*85*	*4*
0—10	1,644	860	784	68	44	24	1,576	816	760	1	...	1
10—15	808	507	301	148	117	31	660	390	270	8	7	1
15—20	1,202	924	278	273	242	31	929	682	247	7	6	1
20—30	3,635	3,123	512	927	864	63	2,708	2,259	449	36	35	1
30 and over	4,162	3,576	586	1,300	1,214	86	2,862	2,362	500	37	37	...
MAHOMEDANS BORN IN BURMA.	*4,021*	*1,863*	*2,158*	*628*	*428*	*200*	*3,393*	*1,435*	*1,958*	*34*	*33*	*1*
0—10	1,505	762	743	64	41	23	1,441	721	720	...	...	...
10—15	565	280	285	101	71	30	464	209	255	8	7	1
15—20	437	187	250	101	75	26	336	112	224	6	6	...
20—30	690	285	405	162	109	53	528	176	352	7	7	...
30 and over	824	349	475	200	132	68	624	217	407	13	13	...
CHRISTIAN ...	*21,198*	*10,645*	*10,553*	*8,417*	*4,845*	*3,572*	*12,781*	*5,800*	*6,981*	*761*	*478*	*283*
0—10	5,727	2,766	2,961	481	241	240	5,246	2,525	2,721	34	23	11
10—15	2,662	1,340	1,322	1,207	624	583	1,455	716	739	109	46	63
15—20	2,136	1,050	1,086	1,169	596	573	967	454	513	102	61	41
20—30	3,743	1,763	1,980	1,992	1,065	927	1,751	698	1,053	208	130	78
30 and over	6,930	3,726	3,204	3,568	2,319	1,249	3,362	1,407	1,955	308	218	90
OTHERS (ALL AGES)	*27*	*26*	*1*	*8*	*8*	...	*19*	*18*	*1*	*6*	*6*	...
MA-UBIN.												
ALL RELIGIONS ...	*330,106*	*168,513*	*161,593*	*119,629*	*93,261*	*26,368*	*210,477*	*75,252*	*135,225*	*1,561*	*1,313*	*248*
0—10	85,711	42,633	43,078	4,391	2,941	1,450	81,320	39,692	41,628	32	23	9
10—15	39,946	20,550	19,396	13,629	10,308	3,321	26,317	10,242	16,075	170	139	31
15—20	34,026	16,306	17,720	17,482	11,748	5,734	16,544	4,558	11,986	302	229	73
20—30	57,169	28,337	28,832	29,792	22,060	7,732	27,377	6,277	21,100	488	433	55
30 and over	113,254	60,687	52,567	54,335	46,204	8,131	58,919	14,483	44,436	569	489	80
BUDDHIST ...	*302,862*	*150,413*	*152,449*	*111,163*	*86,808*	*24,355*	*191,699*	*63,605*	*128,094*	*1,084*	*940*	*144*
0—10	80,569	39,988	40,581	4,061	2,730	1,331	76,508	37,258	39,250	25	21	4
10—15	37,454	19,083	18,371	12,782	9,793	2,989	24,672	9,290	15,382	135	108	27
15—20	31,396	14,670	16,726	16,423	11,087	5,336	14,973	3,583	11,390	228	190	38
20—30	50,860	23,736	27,124	27,386	20,206	7,180	23,474	3,530	19,944	341	313	28
30 and over	102,583	52,936	49,647	50,511	42,992	7,519	52,072	9,944	42,128	355	308	47
ANIMIST (ALL AGES)	*1,736*	*1,244*	*492*	*431*	*399*	*32*	*1,305*	*845*	*460*	*7*	*7*	...
HINDU ...	*6,833*	*5,954*	*879*	*1,344*	*1,300*	*44*	*5,489*	*4,654*	*835*	*64*	*62*	*2*
0—10	553	294	259	13	11	2	540	283	257	...	...	...
10—15	383	306	77	57	50	7	326	256	70	3	3	...
15—20	640	577	63	112	106	6	528	471	57	4	3	1
20—30	2,130	1,928	202	484	471	13	1,646	1,457	189	16	16	...
30 and over	3,127	2,849	278	678	662	16	2,449	2,187	262	41	40	1
HINDUS BORN IN BURMA.	*810*	*457*	*353*	*99*	*89*	*10*	*711*	*368*	*343*	*6*	*6*	...
0—10	397	197	200	8	7	1	389	190	199	...	...	...
10—15	102	50	52	15	11	4	87	39	48	3	3	...
15—20	67	37	30	15	13	2	52	24	28	1	1	...
20—30	96	61	35	20	18	2	76	43	33	...	...	...
30 and over	148	112	36	41	40	1	107	72	35	2	2	...

IMPERIAL TABLE VIIIB.—*Literacy by Religion and Age.*

District, Religion and Age.	Population. Total. Persons.	Total. Males.	Total. Females.	Literate. Persons.	Literate. Males.	Literate. Females.	Illiterate. Persons.	Illiterate. Males.	Illiterate. Females.	Literate in English. Persons.	Literate in English. Males.	Literate in English. Females.
1	2	3	4	5	6	7	8	9	10	11	12	13
MA-UBIN—*concluded.*												
MAHOMEDAN ...	*6,001*	*4,350*	*1,651*	*1,788*	*1,597*	*191*	*4,213*	*2,753*	*1,460*	*69*	*66*	*3*
0—10	1,109	558	551	75	57	18	1,034	501	533	1	...	1
10—15	505	313	192	111	76	35	394	237	157	4	4	...
15—20	546	378	168	173	139	34	373	239	134	10	8	2
20—30	1,605	1,296	309	572	522	50	1,033	774	259	25	25	...
30 and over	2,236	1,805	431	857	803	54	1,379	1,002	377	29	29	...
MAHOMEDANS BORN IN BURMA.	*2,775*	*1,331*	*1,444*	*630*	*451*	*179*	*2,145*	*880*	*1,265*	*31*	*29*	*2*
0—10	1,024	506	518	70	52	18	954	454	500	1	...	1
10—15	391	212	179	86	54	32	305	158	147	4	4	...
15—20	292	140	152	99	68	31	193	72	121	8	7	1
20—30	449	191	258	158	110	48	291	81	210	10	10	...
30 and over	619	282	337	217	167	50	402	115	287	8	8	...
CHRISTIAN ...	*11,984*	*5,976*	*6,008*	*4,621*	*2,891*	*1,730*	*7,363*	*3,085*	*4,278*	*324*	*225*	*99*
0—10	3,033	1,530	1,503	216	122	94	2,817	1,408	1,409	6	2	4
10—15	1,425	737	688	640	363	277	785	374	411	27	23	4
15—20	1,264	554	710	717	365	352	547	189	358	58	26	32
20—30	2,108	1,022	1,086	1,174	701	473	934	321	613	101	74	27
30 and over	4,154	2,133	2,021	1,874	1,340	534	2,280	793	1,487	132	100	32
OTHERS (ALL AGES)	*690*	*576*	*114*	*282*	*266*	*16*	*408*	*310*	*98*	*13*	*13*	...
PYAPÔN.												
ALL RELIGIONS ...	*288,994*	*156,721*	*132,273*	*121,944*	*90,925*	*31,019*	*167,050*	*65,796*	*101,254*	*1,891*	*1,340*	*551*
0—10	74,080	36,838	37,242	5,278	3,052	2,226	68,802	33,786	35,016	48	24	24
10—15	32,468	17,030	15,438	13,409	9,434	3,975	19,059	7,596	11,463	288	169	119
15—20	29,347	14,950	14,397	16,085	10,930	5,155	13,262	4,020	9,242	315	201	114
20—30	54,071	30,073	23,998	30,339	21,714	8,625	23,732	8,359	15,373	547	417	130
30 and over	99,028	57,830	41,198	56,833	45,795	11,038	42,195	12,035	30,160	693	529	164
BUDHDIST ...	*254,072*	*131,225*	*122,847*	*112,179*	*82,794*	*29,385*	*141,893*	*48,431*	*93,462*	*1,269*	*898*	*371*
1—10	67,956	33,549	34,407	4,970	2,874	2,096	62,986	30,675	32,311	40	19	21
10—15	29,793	15,322	14,471	12,686	8,943	3,743	17,107	6,379	10,728	215	126	89
15—20	26,280	12,739	13,541	15,149	10,263	4,886	11,131	2,476	8,655	227	160	67
20—30	44,601	22,617	21,984	27,493	19,300	8,193	17,108	3,317	13,791	368	283	85
30 and over	85,442	46,998	38,444	51,881	41,414	10,467	33,561	5,584	27,977	419	310	109
ANIMIST ...	*3,771*	*2,898*	*873*	*1,529*	*1,434*	*95*	*2,242*	*1,464*	*778*	*13*	*12*	*1*
0—10	627	378	249	32	25	7	595	353	242	2	2	...
10—15	252	163	89	54	44	10	198	119	79	...	...	...
15—20	226	158	68	74	67	7	152	91	61	...	...	...
20—30	872	717	155	416	391	25	456	326	130	3	3	...
30 and over	1,794	1,482	312	953	907	46	841	575	266	8	7	1
HINDU ...	*16,431*	*12,804*	*3,627*	*2,962*	*2,810*	*152*	*13,469*	*9,994*	*3,475*	*94*	*85*	*9*
0—10	2,483	1,375	1,108	53	33	20	2,430	1,342	1,088	4	2	2
10—15	1,132	806	326	154	140	14	978	666	312	4	4	...
15—20	1,451	1,169	282	265	243	22	1,186	926	260	8	7	1
20—30	4,820	3,940	880	906	870	36	3,914	3,070	844	30	26	4
30 and over	6,545	5,514	1,031	1,584	1,524	60	4,961	3,990	971	48	46	2
HINDUS BORN IN BURMA.	*3,279*	*1,966*	*1,313*	*314*	*266*	*48*	*2,965*	*1,700*	*1,265*	*11*	*9*	*2*
0—10	1,777	972	805	25	16	9	1,752	956	796	3	2	1
10—15	464	267	197	52	43	9	412	224	188	2	2	...
15—20	261	163	98	55	44	11	206	119	87	...	...	...
20—30	384	258	126	68	62	6	316	196	120	1	1	...
30 and over	393	306	87	114	101	13	279	205	74	5	4	1
MAHOMEDAN ...	*5,640*	*4,843*	*797*	*1,795*	*1,690*	*105*	*3,845*	*3,153*	*692*	*47*	*47*	...
0—10	546	297	249	37	29	8	509	268	241	1	1	...
10—15	258	186	72	71	61	10	187	125	62	4	4	...
15—20	518	431	87	146	129	17	372	302	70	4	4	...
20—30	2,054	1,861	193	648	609	39	1,406	1,252	154	16	16	...
30 and over	2,264	2,068	196	893	862	31	1,371	1,206	165	22	22	...
MAHOMEDANS BORN IN BURMA.	*1,348*	*757*	*591*	*364*	*283*	*81*	*984*	*474*	*510*	*15*	*15*	...
0—10	451	230	221	23	16	7	428	214	214	1	1	...
10—15	141	74	67	39	29	10	102	45	57	1	1	...
15—20	149	85	64	50	34	16	99	51	48	4	4	...
20—30	282	163	119	107	80	27	175	83	92	5	5	...
30 and over	325	205	120	145	124	21	180	81	99	4	4	...

IMPERIAL TABLE VIIIB.—*Literacy by Religion and Age.*

District, Religion and Age.	Population. Total. Persons.	Total. Males.	Total. Females.	Literate. Persons.	Literate. Males.	Literate. Females.	Illiterate. Persons.	Illiterate. Males.	Illiterate. Females.	Literate in English. Persons.	Literate in English. Males.	Literate in English. Females.
1	2	3	4	5	6	7	8	9	10	11	12	13
PYAPÔN—*concld.*												
CHRISTIAN ..	*9,054*	*4,925*	*4,129*	*3,462*	*2,180*	*1,282*	*5,592*	*2,745*	*2,847*	*468*	*298*	*170*
0—10	2,468	1,239	1,229	186	91	95	2,282	1,148	1,134	1	...	1
10—15	1,033	553	480	444	246	198	589	307	282	65	35	30
15—20	869	450	419	450	227	223	419	223	196	76	30	46
20—30	1,707	921	786	862	530	332	845	391	454	130	89	41
30 and over	2,977	1,762	1,215	1,520	1,086	434	1,457	676	781	196	144	52
OTHERS (ALL AGES)	*26*	*26*	...	*17*	*17*	...	*9*	*9*	...	...	...	...
TOUNGOO.												
ALL RELIGIONS ...	*381,883*	*197,505*	*184,378*	*106,798*	*86,635*	*20,163*	*275,085*	*110,870*	*164,215*	*3,104*	*2,414*	*690*
0—10	93,691	46,096	47,595	3,942	2,627	1,315	89,749	43,469	46,280	177	91	86
10—15	46,258	24,253	22,005	11,776	8,983	2,793	34,482	15,270	19,212	405	250	155
15—20	38,736	18,403	20,333	13,228	9,865	3,363	25,508	8,538	16,970	436	328	108
20—30	67,763	34,316	33,447	25,786	20,380	5,406	41,977	13,956	28,041	866	707	159
30 and over	135,435	74,437	60,998	52,066	44,780	7,286	83,369	29,657	53,712	1,220	1,038	182
BUDDHIST ...	*297,980*	*149,783*	*148,197*	*92,784*	*76,497*	*16,287*	*205,196*	*73,286*	*131,910*	*1,337*	*1,221*	*116*
0—10	74,260	36,446	37,814	3,261	2,291	970	70,999	34,155	36,844	38	32	6
10—15	37,376	19,602	17,774	10,301	8,107	2,194	27,075	11,495	15,580	160	135	25
15—20	30,577	14,074	16,503	11,520	8,826	2,694	19,057	5,248	13,809	239	219	20
20—30	50,750	24,337	26,413	21,942	17,481	4,461	28,808	6,856	21,952	408	370	38
30 and over	105,017	55,324	49,693	45,760	39,792	5,968	59,257	15,532	43,725	492	465	27
ANIMIST ..	*20,699*	*11,268*	*9,431*	*1,300*	*1,204*	*96*	*19,399*	*10,064*	*9,335*	*23*	*21*	*2*
0—10	4,881	2,502	2,379	36	21	15	4,845	2,481	2,364	...	...	...
10—15	2,289	1,224	1,065	90	74	16	2,199	1,150	1,049	3	2	1
15—20	2,025	972	1,053	103	88	15	1,922	884	1,038	3	3	...
20—30	3,926	2,072	1,864	331	306	25	3,605	1,766	1,839	8	7	1
30 and over	7,568	4,498	3,070	740	715	25	6,828	3,783	3,045	9	9	...
HINDU ...	*19,575*	*13,316*	*6,259*	*2,825*	*2,647*	*178*	*16,750*	*10,669*	*6,081*	*254*	*232*	*22*
0—10	4,078	1,936	2,142	54	37	17	4,024	1,899	2,125	5	3	2
10—15	1,348	658	690	113	95	18	1,235	563	672	14	9	5
15—20	1,604	1,183	421	280	243	37	1,324	940	384	19	15	4
20—30	4,630	3,543	1,087	1,089	1,029	60	3,541	2,514	1,027	85	78	7
30 and over	7,915	5,996	1,919	1,289	1,243	46	6,626	4,753	1,873	131	127	4
HINDUS BORN IN BURMA.	*5,995*	*3,088*	*2,907*	*384*	*316*	*68*	*5,611*	*2,772*	*2,839*	*57*	*46*	*11*
0—10	3,454	1,577	1,877	42	28	14	3,412	1,549	1,863	3	1	2
10—15	785	285	500	44	32	12	741	253	488	10	7	3
15—20	555	371	184	63	49	14	492	322	170	7	6	1
20—30	568	368	200	122	102	20	446	266	180	20	16	4
30 and over	633	487	146	113	105	8	520	382	138	17	16	1
MAHOMEDAN ...	*8,163*	*5,498*	*2,665*	*2,076*	*1,767*	*309*	*6,087*	*3,731*	*2,356*	*228*	*215*	*13*
0—10	1,475	724	751	70	39	31	1,405	685	720	2	2	...
10—15	726	421	305	171	123	48	555	298	257	15	12	3
15—20	816	537	279	232	178	54	584	359	225	29	26	3
20—30	2,137	1,596	541	655	566	89	1,482	1,030	452	79	77	2
30 and over	3,009	2,220	789	948	861	87	2,061	1,359	702	103	98	5
MAHOMEDANS BORN IN BURMA.	*4,476*	*2,152*	*2,324*	*1,066*	*782*	*284*	*3,410*	*1,370*	*2,040*	*137*	*129*	*8*
0—10	1,417	719	698	66	37	29	1,351	682	669	2	2	...
10—15	602	316	286	149	104	45	453	212	241	13	10	3
15—20	451	209	242	162	110	52	289	99	190	25	22	3
20—30	811	369	442	306	226	80	505	143	362	53	51	2
30 and over	1,195	539	656	383	305	78	812	234	578	44	44	...
CHRISTIAN ...	*35,442*	*17,624*	*17,818*	*7,795*	*4,509*	*3,286*	*27,647*	*13,115*	*14,532*	*1,250*	*717*	*533*
0—10	8,993	4,484	4,509	520	238	282	8,473	4,246	4,227	132	54	78
10—15	4,516	2,347	2,169	1,098	583	515	3,418	1,764	1,654	212	92	120
15—20	3,712	1,636	2,076	1,091	529	562	2,621	1,107	1,514	144	64	80
20—30	6,306	2,766	3,540	1,766	996	770	4,540	1,770	2,770	284	173	111
30 and over	11,915	6,391	5,524	3,320	2,163	1,157	8,595	4,228	4,367	478	334	144
OTHERS (ALL AGES)	*24*	*16*	*8*	*18*	*11*	*7*	*6*	*5*	*1*	*12*	*8*	*4*
SALWEEN.												
ALL RELIGIONS ...	*50,379*	*26,811*	*23,568*	*2,724*	*2,328*	*396*	*47,655*	*24,483*	*23,172*	*205*	*182*	*23*
0—10	13,626	7,106	6,520	72	52	20	13,554	7,054	6,500	7	6	1
10—15	5,149	2,797	2,352	308	233	75	4,841	2,564	2,277	18	14	4
15—20	5,106	2,497	2,609	334	261	73	4,772	2,236	2,536	19	13	6
20—30	9,529	4,652	4,877	742	618	124	8,787	4,034	4,753	68	61	7
30 and over	16,969	9,759	7,210	1,268	1,164	104	15,701	8,595	7,106	93	88	5

IMPERIAL TABLE VIIIB.—*Literacy by Religion and Age.*

District, religion and age.		Population. Total. Persons.	Total. Males.	Total. Females.	Literate. Persons.	Literate. Males.	Literate. Females.	Illiterate. Persons.	Illiterate. Males.	Illiterate. Females.	Literate in English. Persons.	Literate in English. Males.	Literate in English. Females.
1		2	3	4	5	6	7	8	9	10	11	12	13
SALWEEN—*concld.*	BUDDHIST ..	*26,327*	*14,413*	*11,914*	*2,102*	*1,805*	*297*	*24,225*	*12,608*	*11,617*	*68*	*66*	*2*
	0—10	7,255	3,769	3,486	58	44	14	7,197	3,725	3,472	2	2	...
	10—15	2,770	1,536	1,234	261	202	59	2,509	1,334	1,175	6	6	...
	15—20	2,723	1,355	1,368	280	226	54	2,443	1,129	1,314	7	6	1
	20—30	4,800	2,412	2,388	539	449	90	4,261	1,963	2,298	25	25	..
	30 and over	8,779	5,341	3,438	964	884	80	7,815	4,457	3,358	28	27	1
	ANIMIST (ALL AGES)	*22,407*	*11,200*	*11,207*	*63*	*63*	...	*22,344*	*11,137*	*11,207*	*7*	*7*	...
	HINDU (ALL AGES)	*355*	*307*	*48*	*96*	*94*	*2*	*259*	*213*	*46*	*14*	*14*	...
	MAHOMEDAN (ALL AGES).	*532*	*449*	*83*	*171*	*163*	*8*	*361*	*286*	*75*	*3*	*3*	...
	CHRISTIAN (ALL AGES)	*758*	*442*	*316*	*292*	*203*	*89*	*456*	*239*	*227*	*113*	*92*	*21*
THATÔN.	ALL RELIGIONS ...	*471,100*	*245,909*	*225,191*	*91,980*	*72,777*	*19,203*	*379,120*	*173,132*	*205,988*	*1,677*	*1,452*	*225*
	0—10	130,500	65,852	64,648	3,028	2,021	1,007	127,472	63,831	63,641	30	19	11
	10—15	56,243	29,386	26,857	9,912	7,358	2,554	46,331	22,028	24,303	119	90	29
	15—20	48,789	23,801	24,988	12,702	9,202	3,500	36,087	14,599	21,488	268	219	49
	20—30	80,568	40,006	40,562	22,792	17,373	5,419	57,776	22,633	35,143	560	497	63
	30 and over	155,000	86,864	68,136	43,546	36,823	6,723	111,454	50,041	61,413	700	627	73
	BUDDHIST ...	*430,329*	*218,580*	*211,749*	*84,182*	*66,063*	*18,119*	*346,147*	*152,517*	*193,630*	*1,123*	*996*	*127*
	0—10	121,904	61,467	60,437	2,815	1,870	945	119,089	59,597	59,492	21	12	9
	10—15	52,722	27,297	25,425	9,321	6,914	2,407	43,401	20,383	23,018	88	64	24
	15—20	45,569	21,788	23,781	11,953	8,648	3,305	33,616	13,140	20,476	210	184	26
	20—30	71,673	33,878	37,795	20,579	15,500	5,079	51,094	18,378	32,716	363	338	25
	30 and over	138,461	74,150	64,311	39,514	33,131	6,383	98,947	41,019	57,928	441	398	43
	ANIMIST (ALL AGES)	*2,303*	*1,615*	*688*	*674*	*605*	*69*	*1,629*	*1,010*	*619*	*24*	*23*	*1*
	HINDU ...	*21,112*	*14,794*	*6,318*	*2,989*	*2,828*	*161*	*18,123*	*11,966*	*6,157*	*144*	*136*	*8*
	0—10	4,008	2,062	1,946	84	69	15	3,924	1,993	1,931	1	1	...
	10—15	1,606	1,007	599	162	154	8	1,444	853	591	8	8	...
	15—20	1,571	1,102	469	237	220	17	1,334	882	452	7	5	2
	20—30	4,776	3,435	1,341	854	786	68	3,922	2,649	1,273	59	55	4
	30 and over	9,151	7,188	1,963	1,652	1,599	53	7,499	5,589	1,910	69	67	2
	HINDUS BORN IN BURMA.	*7,921*	*4,196*	*3,725*	*792*	*713*	*79*	*7,129*	*3,483*	*3,646*	*41*	*37*	*4*
	0—10	3,434	1,704	1,730	72	58	14	3,362	1,646	1,716	1	1	...
	10—25	1,068	597	471	105	99	6	963	498	465	4	4	...
	15—20	783	423	360	129	116	13	654	307	347	4	3	1
	20—30	1,265	640	625	226	194	32	1,039	446	593	19	17	2
	30 and over	1,371	832	539	260	246	14	1,111	586	525	13	12	1
	MAHOMEDAN ...	*13,405*	*8,912*	*4,493*	*2,957*	*2,598*	*359*	*10,448*	*6,314*	*4,134*	*151*	*141*	*10*
	0—10	3,058	1,557	1,501	66	48	18	2,992	1,509	1,483	1	1	...
	10—15	1,193	687	506	218	164	54	975	523	452	11	9	2
	15—20	1,128	672	456	281	220	61	847	452	395	14	10	4
	20—30	3,117	2,151	966	931	817	114	2,186	1,334	852	58	57	1
	30 and over	4,909	3,845	1,064	1,461	1,349	112	3,448	2,496	952	67	64	3
	MAHOMEDANS BORN IN BURMA.	*8,201*	*3,997*	*4,204*	*1,306*	*974*	*332*	*6,895*	*3,023*	*3,872*	*89*	*81*	*8*
	0—10	2,963	1,494	1,469	56	38	18	2,907	1,456	1,451	1	1	...
	10—15	1,044	559	485	175	124	51	869	435	434	10	8	2
	15—20	797	370	427	179	122	57	618	248	370	9	6	3
	20—30	1,495	612	883	386	279	107	1,109	333	776	32	32	...
	30 and over	1,902	962	940	510	411	99	1,392	551	841	37	34	3
	CHRISTIAN ...	*3,811*	*1,920*	*1,891*	*1,120*	*636*	*484*	*2,691*	*1,284*	*1,407*	*231*	*153*	*78*
	0—10	1,049	499	550	47	22	25	1,002	477	525	3	1	2
	10—15	503	268	235	155	86	69	348	182	166	12	9	3
	15—20	360	139	221	172	69	103	188	70	118	33	17	16
	20—30	613	268	345	262	123	139	351	145	206	70	37	33
	30 and over	1,286	746	540	484	336	148	802	410	392	113	89	24
	OTHERS (ALL AGES)	*140*	*88*	*52*	*58*	*47*	*11*	*82*	*41*	*41*	*4*	*3*	*1*
AMHERST.	ALL RELIGIONS ...	*417,910*	*223,348*	*194,562*	*87,989*	*71,011*	*16,978*	*329,921*	*152,337*	*177,584*	*6,004*	*4,653*	*1,351*
	0—10	116,456	58,805	57,651	2,700	1,743	957	113,756	57,062	56,694	252	113	139
	10—15	49,213	25,614	23,599	8,622	6,215	2,407	40,591	19,399	21,192	788	492	296
	15—20	43,481	21,901	21,580	11,461	8,373	3,088	32,020	13,528	18,492	1,043	761	282
	20—30	72,821	38,447	34,374	21,973	17,509	4,464	50,848	20,938	29,910	1,618	1,314	304
	30 and over	135,939	78,581	57,358	43,233	37,171	6,062	92,706	41,410	51,296	2,303	1,973	330

IMPERIAL TABLE VIIIB.—*Literacy by Religion and Age.*

DISTRICT, RELIGION AND AGE.	POPULATION.									Literate in English.		
	Total.			Literate.			Illiterate.					
	Persons.	Males.	Females.	Persons.	Males.	Females.	Persons.	Males.	Females.	Persons.	Males.	Females.
1	2	3	4	5	6	7	8	9	10	11	12	13
AMHERST—*concluded.*												
BUDDHIST ...	*355,175*	*181,489*	*173,686*	*74,210*	*60,081*	*14,129*	*280,965*	*121,408*	*159,557*	*2,966*	*2,577*	*389*
0—10	103,644	52,122	51,522	2,123	1,403	720	101,521	50,719	50,802	76	26	50
10—15	43,442	22,214	21,228	7,359	5,420	1,939	36,083	16,794	19,289	314	234	80
15—20	37,957	18,498	19,459	9,919	7,290	2,629	28,038	11,208	16,830	589	485	104
20—30	58,953	28,714	30,239	18,200	14,454	3,746	40,753	14,260	26,493	842	733	109
30 and over	111,179	59,941	51,238	36,609	31,514	5,095	74,570	28,427	46,143	1,145	1,099	46
ANIMIST ...	*3,442*	*2,446*	*996*	*1,043*	*947*	*96*	*2,399*	*1,499*	*900*	*67*	*57*	*10*
0—10	773	455	318	20	14	6	753	441	312	3	1	2
10—15	305	194	111	79	59	20	226	135	91	10	9	1
15—20	258	146	112	106	85	21	152	61	91	13	12	1
20—30	519	374	145	233	209	24	286	165	121	21	17	4
30 and over	1,587	1,277	310	605	580	25	982	697	285	20	18	2
HINDU ...	*25,415*	*19,468*	*5,947*	*4,304*	*3,924*	*380*	*21,111*	*15,544*	*5,567*	*482*	*439*	*43*
0—10	3,296	1,747	1,549	126	84	42	3,170	1,663	1,507	13	7	6
10—15	1,489	1,029	460	204	167	37	1,285	862	423	32	26	6
15—20	1,976	1,464	512	361	312	49	1,615	1,152	463	60	51	9
20—30	6,647	5,285	1,362	1,354	1,234	120	5,293	4,051	1,242	167	155	12
30 and over	12,007	9,943	2,064	2,259	2,127	132	9,748	7,816	1,932	210	200	10
HINDUS BORN IN BURMA.	*8,083*	*4,466*	*3,617*	*1,195*	*978*	*217*	*6,888*	*3,488*	*3,400*	*197*	*175*	*22*
0—10	2,799	1,452	1,347	103	69	34	2,696	1,383	1,313	9	7	2
10—15	970	582	388	129	100	29	841	482	359	21	17	4
15—20	820	448	372	159	127	32	661	321	340	37	31	6
20—30	1,462	764	698	330	267	63	1,132	497	635	70	64	6
30 and over	2,032	1,220	812	474	415	59	1,558	805	753	60	56	4
MAHOMEDAN ...	*26,678*	*16,261*	*10,417*	*5,213*	*4,302*	*911*	*21,465*	*11,959*	*9,506*	*552*	*515*	*37*
0—10	6,919	3,551	3,368	211	132	79	6,708	3,419	3,289	12	8	4
10—15	2,929	1,648	1,281	428	304	124	2,501	1,344	1,157	53	45	8
15—20	2,496	1,397	1,099	595	431	164	1,901	966	935	69	58	11
20—30	5,479	3,465	2,014	1,485	1,234	251	3,994	2,231	1,763	188	180	8
30 and over	8,855	6,200	2,655	2,494	2,201	293	6,361	3,999	2,362	230	224	6
MAHOMEDANS BORN IN BURMA.	*19,915*	*9,995*	*9,920*	*3,141*	*2,296*	*845*	*16,774*	*7,699*	*9,075*	*413*	*381*	*32*
0—10	6,795	3,476	3,319	205	127	78	6,590	3,349	3,241	12	8	4
10—15	2,751	1,492	1,259	379	260	119	2,372	1,232	1,140	52	45	7
15—20	2,024	952	1,072	448	288	160	1,576	664	912	58	48	10
20—30	3,359	1,464	1,895	763	538	225	2,596	926	1,670	106	101	5
30 and over	4,986	2,611	2,375	1,346	1,083	263	3,640	1,528	2,112	185	179	6
CHRISTIAN ...	*7,074*	*3,596*	*3,478*	*3,175*	*1,724*	*1,451*	*3,899*	*1,872*	*2,027*	*1,919*	*1,053*	*866*
0—10	1,793	910	883	216	108	108	1,577	802	775	147	71	76
10—15	1,043	528	515	549	265	284	494	263	231	376	178	198
15—20	783	390	393	475	252	223	308	138	170	308	153	155
20—30	1,192	588	604	690	371	319	502	217	285	397	226	171
30 and over	2,263	1,180	1,083	1,245	728	517	1,018	452	566	691	425	266
OTHERS (ALL AGES)	*126*	*88*	*38*	*44*	*33*	*11*	*82*	*55*	*27*	*18*	*12*	*6*
TAVOY.												
ALL RELIGIONS ...	*156,786*	*80,994*	*75,792*	*43,180*	*35,114*	*8,066*	*113,606*	*45,880*	*67,726*	*1,399*	*1,202*	*197*
0—10	41,620	20,830	20,790	1,134	723	411	40,486	20,107	20,379	26	13	13
10—15	19,773	10,347	9,426	4,447	3,077	1,370	15,326	7,270	8,056	119	89	30
15—20	15,511	7,733	7,778	5,693	4,164	1,529	9,818	3,569	6,249	201	164	37
20—30	26,412	13,388	13,024	9,635	7,459	2,176	16,777	5,929	10,848	328	267	61
30 and over	53,470	28,696	24,774	22,271	19,691	2,580	31 199	9,005	22,194	725	669	56
BUDDHIST ...	*145,146*	*72,612*	*72,534*	*39,353*	*31,926*	*7,427*	*105,793*	*40,686*	*65,107*	*813*	*749*	*64*
0—10	39,832	19,934	19,898	1,048	676	372	38,784	19,258	19,526	9	6	3
10—15	18,972	9,929	9,043	4,272	2,972	1,300	14,700	6,957	7,743	81	65	16
15—20	14,679	7,229	7,450	5,425	3,997	1,428	9,254	3,232	6,022	151	133	18
20—30	23,311	10,980	12,331	8,474	6,476	1,998	14,837	4,504	10,333	154	134	20
30 and over	48,352	24,540	23,812	20,134	17,805	2,329	28,218	6,735	21,483	418	411	7
ANIMIST ...	*2,773*	*2,194*	*579*	*962*	*947*	*15*	*1,811*	*1,247*	*564*	*21*	*19*	*2*
0—10	342	180	162	2	...	2	340	180	160	...	...	...
10—15	133	58	75	10	7	3	123	51	72	...	...	...
15—20	114	58	56	15	14	1	99	44	55	1	...	1
20—30	607	522	85	258	256	2	349	266	83	8	7	1
30 and over	1,577	1,376	201	677	670	7	900	706	194	12	12	...

Imperial Table VIIIb.—*Literacy by Religion and Age.*

District, Religion and Age.	Population. Total. Persons.	Total. Males.	Total. Females.	Literate. Persons.	Literate. Males.	Literate. Females.	Illiterate. Persons.	Illiterate. Males.	Illiterate. Females.	Literate in English. Persons.	Literate in English. Males.	Literate in English. Females.
1	2	3	4	5	6	7	8	9	10	11	12	13
TAVOY—concluded.												
Hindu ...	*3,319*	*2,953*	*366*	*867*	*820*	*47*	*2,452*	*2,133*	*319*	*96*	*92*	*4*
0—10	206	97	109	12	3	9	194	94	100	...	...	...
10—15	104	84	20	18	9	9	86	75	11	2	1	1
15—20	217	185	32	37	33	4	180	152	28	5	5	...
20—30	1,272	1,156	116	336	320	16	936	836	100	37	34	3
30 and over	1,520	1,431	89	464	455	9	1,056	976	80	52	52	...
Hindus born in Burma.	*284*	*164*	*120*	*54*	*39*	*15*	*230*	*125*	*105*	*16*	*13*	*3*
0—10	134	69	65	8	3	5	126	66	60	...	...	...
10—15	38	24	14	6	3	3	32	21	11	2	1	1
15—20	11	6	5	4	4	...	7	2	5	1	1	...
20—30	45	22	23	14	8	6	31	14	17	5	3	2
30 and over	56	43	13	22	21	1	34	22	12	8	8	...
Mahomedan ...	*2,873*	*1,844*	*1,029*	*1,043*	*844*	*199*	*1,830*	*1,000*	*830*	*86*	*86*	...
0—10	609	314	295	26	20	6	583	294	289	...	...	...
10—15	211	105	106	55	35	20	156	70	86	2	2	...
15—20	234	139	95	104	74	30	130	65	65	6	6	...
20—30	725	478	247	349	277	72	376	201	175	32	32	...
30 and over	1,094	808	286	509	438	71	585	370	215	46	46	...
Mahomedans born in Burma.	*1,878*	*888*	*990*	*554*	*362*	*192*	*1,324*	*526*	*798*	*59*	*59*	...
0—10	591	302	289	24	18	6	567	284	283	...	...	...
10—15	197	94	103	50	30	20	147	64	83	2	2	...
15—20	176	81	95	75	45	30	101	36	65	6	6	...
20—30	371	141	230	160	92	68	211	49	162	21	21	...
30 and over	543	270	273	245	177	68	298	93	205	30	30	...
Christian ...	*2,645*	*1,371*	*1,274*	*940*	*565*	*375*	*1,705*	*806*	*899*	*376*	*250*	*126*
0—10	623	300	323	46	24	22	577	276	301	17	7	10
10—15	351	170	181	92	54	38	259	116	143	34	21	13
15—20	266	121	145	111	45	66	155	76	79	38	20	18
20—30	491	249	242	214	128	86	277	121	156	96	59	37
30 and over	914	531	383	477	314	163	437	217	220	191	143	48
Others (all ages)	*30*	*20*	*10*	*15*	*12*	*3*	*15*	*8*	*7*	*7*	*6*	*1*
MERGUI.												
All Religions ...	*135,465*	*72,878*	*62,587*	*34,958*	*28,192*	*6,766*	*100,507*	*44,686*	*55,821*	*924*	*851*	*73*
0—10	35,488	17,648	17,840	622	375	247	34,866	17,273	17,593	6	4	2
10—15	16,049	8,464	7,585	2,656	1,896	760	13,393	6,568	6,825	25	19	7
15—20	13,471	6 985	6,486	4,368	3,237	1,131	9,103	3,748	5,355	109	99	10
20—30	25,694	13,826	11,868	9,452	7,391	2,060	16,242	6,434	9,808	312	287	25
30 and over	44,763	25,955	18,808	17,860	15,292	2,568	26,903	10,663	16,240	471	442	29
Buddhist ...	*104,617*	*53,200*	*51,417*	*29,459*	*23,798*	*5,661*	*75,158*	*29,402*	*45,756*	*542*	*538*	*4*
0—10	29,072	14,336	14,736	557	334	223	28,515	14,002	14,513	1	1	...
10—15	12 982	6,659	6,323	2,341	1,699	642	10,641	4,960	5,681	13	12	1
15—20	10,506	5,190	5,316	3,825	2,877	948	6,681	2,313	4,368	87	87	...
20—30	18,681	9,159	9,522	7,819	6,115	1,704	10,862	3,044	7,818	189	189	...
30 and over	33,376	17,856	15,520	14,917	12,773	2,144	18,459	5,083	13,376	252	249	3
Animist ...	*6,426*	*4,258*	*2,168*	*823*	*787*	*36*	*5,603*	*3,471*	*2,132*	*15*	*15*	...
0—10	1,322	649	673	4	3	1	1,318	646	672	...	...	...
10—15	507	290	217	23	17	6	484	273	211	...	...	...
15—20	411	215	196	25	24	1	386	191	195	1	1	...
20—30	1,147	693	454	132	123	9	1,015	570	445	7	7	...
30 and over	3,039	2,411	628	639	620	19	2,400	1,791	609	7	7	...
Hindu ...	*6,613*	*5,842*	*771*	*856*	*831*	*25*	*5,757*	*5,011*	*746*	*49*	*43*	*6*
0—10	454	277	177	9	7	2	445	270	175	...	...	...
10—15	431	386	45	28	26	2	403	360	43	3	1	2
15—20	773	703	70	81	78	3	692	625	67	3	2	1
20—30	2,416	2,160	256	378	365	13	2,038	1,795	243	12	10	2
30 and over	2,539	2,316	223	360	355	5	2,179	1,961	218	31	30	1
Hindus born in Burma.	*296*	*166*	*130*	*21*	*17*	*4*	*275*	*149*	*126*	*3*	*1*	*2*
0—10	168	70	98	1	...	1	167	70	97	...	...	...
10—15	27	15	12	3	2	1	24	13	11	1	...	1
15—20	10	4	6	...	...	...	10	4	6	...	...	...
20—30	51	39	12	9	7	2	42	32	10	1	...	1
30 and over	40	38	2	8	8	...	32	30	2	1	1	...

IMPERIAL TABLE VIIIB.—*Literacy by Religion and Age.*

District.	Religion and Age.	Population. Total. Persons.	Total. Males.	Total. Females.	Literate. Persons.	Literate. Males.	Literate. Females.	Illiterate. Persons.	Illiterate. Males.	Illiterate. Females.	Literate in English. Persons.	Literate in English. Males.	Literate in English. Females.
	1	2	3	4	5	6	7	8	9	10	11	12	13
MERGUI—*concluded.*	MAHOMEDAN ...	*11,645*	*6,270*	*5,375*	*2,149*	*1,734*	*415*	*9,496*	*4,536*	*4,960*	*1*	...	*1*
	0—10	2,923	1,515	1,408	16	15	1	2,907	1,500	1,407	...	...	...
	10—15	1,330	689	641	118	76	42	1,212	613	599	...	...	...
	15—20	1,215	593	622	241	155	86	974	438	536	1	...	1
	20—30	2,252	1,208	1,044	606	487	119	1,646	721	925	...	...	...
	30 and over	3,925	2,265	1,660	1,168	1,001	167	2,757	1,254	1,493	...	...	...
	MAHOMEDANS BORN IN BURMA.	*10,086*	*5,057*	*5,029*	*1,677*	*1,262*	*415*	*8,409*	*3,795*	*4,614*	*1*	...	*1*
	0—10	2,887	1,497	1,390	16	15	1	2,871	1,482	1,389	...	...	...
	10—15	1,277	649	628	115	73	42	1,162	576	586	...	...	...
	15—20	1,111	524	587	219	133	86	892	391	501	1	...	1
	20—30	1,792	831	961	449	330	119	1,343	501	842	...	...	...
	30 and over	3,019	1,556	1,463	878	711	167	2,141	845	1,296	...	...	...
	CHRISTIAN ...	*6,153*	*3,297*	*2,856*	*1,666*	*1,037*	*629*	*4,487*	*2,260*	*2,227*	*316*	*254*	*62*
	0—10	1,717	871	846	36	16	20	1,681	855	826	5	3	2
	10—15	799	440	359	146	78	68	653	362	291	10	6	4
	15—20	564	282	282	195	102	93	369	180	189	17	9	8
	20—30	1,195	603	592	515	300	215	680	303	377	103	80	23
	30 and over	1,878	1,101	777	774	541	233	1,104	560	544	181	156	25
	OTHERS (ALL AGES)	*11*	*11*	...	*5*	*5*	...	*6*	*6*	...	*1*	*1*	...
THAYETMYO.	ALL RELIGIONS ...	*255,406*	*125,283*	*130,123*	*78,302*	*68,248*	*10,054*	*177,104*	*57,035*	*120,069*	*822*	*733*	*89*
	0—10	63,574	31,141	32,433	2,165	1,519	646	61,409	29,622	31,787	24	15	9
	10—15	30,801	15,446	15,355	7,978	6,635	1,343	22,823	8,811	14,012	116	94	22
	15—20	26,793	12,766	14,032	10,481	8,867	1,614	16,317	3,899	12,418	146	115	31
	20—30	41,612	19,841	21,771	17,899	15,416	2,483	23,713	4,425	19,288	223	207	16
	30 and over	92,621	46,089	46,532	39,779	35,811	3,968	52,842	10,278	42,564	313	302	11
	BUDDHIST ...	*239,726*	*116,712*	*123,014*	*75,937*	*66,281*	*9,656*	*163,789*	*50,431*	*113,358*	*524*	*494*	*30*
	0—10	60,043	29,395	30,648	2,088	1,475	613	57,955	27,920	30,035	12	10	2
	10—15	29,153	14,577	14,576	7,770	6,486	1,284	21,383	8,091	13,292	71	63	8
	15—20	25,299	12,005	13,294	10,260	8,705	1,555	15,039	3,300	11,739	111	92	19
	20—30	38,702	18,208	20,494	17,224	14,857	2,367	21,478	3,351	18,127	145	144	1
	30 and over	86,529	42,527	44,002	38,595	34,758	3,837	47,934	7,769	40,165	185	185	...
	ANIMIST ...	*11,269*	*5,725*	*5,544*	*783*	*713*	*70*	*10,486*	*5,012*	*5,474*	*5*	*4*	*1*
	0—10	2,653	1,317	1,336	10	6	4	2,643	1,311	1,332	...	...	...
	10—15	1,292	657	635	63	50	13	1,229	607	622	1	1	...
	15—20	1,145	553	592	69	59	10	1,076	494	582	...	...	...
	20—30	1,882	922	960	174	154	20	1,708	768	940	2	1	1
	30 and over	4,297	2,276	2,021	467	444	23	3,830	1,832	1,998	2	2	...
	HINDU ...	*1,946*	*1,405*	*541*	*469*	*436*	*33*	*1,477*	*969*	*508*	*52*	*43*	*9*
	0—10	346	169	177	5	5	...	341	164	177	3	3	...
	10—15	124	83	41	28	21	7	96	62	34	7	2	5
	15—20	132	85	47	27	25	2	105	60	45	4	3	1
	20—30	460	355	105	153	140	13	307	215	92	16	13	3
	30 and over	884	713	171	256	245	11	628	468	160	22	22	...
	HINDUS BORN IN BURMA (ALL AGES).	*667*	*365*	*302*	*81*	*68*	*13*	*586*	*297*	*289*	*18*	*12*	*6*
	MAHOMEDAN ...	*1,994*	*1,177*	*817*	*841*	*630*	*211*	*1,153*	*547*	*606*	*100*	*99*	*1*
	0—10	447	224	223	46	29	17	401	195	206	1	1	...
	10—15	181	103	78	85	58	27	96	45	51	14	14	...
	15—20	168	93	75	87	56	31	81	37	44	7	7	...
	20—30	471	297	174	276	216	60	195	81	114	26	25	1
	30 and over	727	460	267	347	271	76	380	189	191	52	52	...
	MAHOMEDANS BORN IN BURMA.	*1,461*	*679*	*782*	*543*	*339*	*204*	*918*	*340*	*578*	*79*	*79*	...
	0—10	432	211	221	45	28	17	387	183	204	1	1	...
	10—15	169	94	75	81	54	27	88	40	48	14	14	...
	15—20	140	65	75	72	41	31	68	24	44	7	7	...
	25—80	282	117	165	150	91	59	132	26	106	22	22	...
	30 and over	438	192	246	195	125	70	243	67	176	35	35	...
	CHRISTIAN (ALL AGES)	*465*	*261*	*204*	*270*	*186*	*84*	*195*	*75*	*120*	*139*	*91*	*48*
	OTHERS (ALL AGES)	*6*	*3*	*3*	*2*	*2*	...	*4*	*1*	*3*	*2*	*2*	...

Imperial Table VIIIb.—*Literacy by Religion and Age.*

District.	Religion and Age.	Population. Total. Persons.	Population. Total. Males.	Population. Total. Females.	Population. Literate. Persons.	Population. Literate. Males.	Population. Literate. Females.	Population. Illiterate. Persons.	Population. Illiterate. Males.	Population. Illiterate. Females.	Literate in English. Persons.	Literate in English. Males.	Literate in English. Females.
1		2	3	4	5	6	7	8	9	10	11	12	13
PAKÔKKU.	All Religions ...	465,771	223,943	241,828	123,464	111,458	12,006	342,307	112,485	229,822	948	898	50
	0—10	124,637	61,458	63,179	2,950	2,210	740	121,687	59,248	62,439	50	49	1
	10—15	52,744	26,854	25,890	11,584	9,711	1,873	41,160	17,143	24,017	67	62	5
	15—20	46,986	21,592	25,394	16,048	13,750	2,298	30,938	7,842	23,096	135	126	9
	20—30	74,650	35,238	39,412	28,858	26,063	2,795	45,792	9,175	36,617	282	258	24
	30 and over	166,754	78,801	87,953	64,024	59,724	4,300	102,730	19,077	83,653	414	403	11
	Buddhist ...	460,158	220,495	239,663	122,296	110,434	11,862	337,862	110,061	227,801	781	759	22
	0—10	123,518	60,878	62,640	2,927	2,198	729	20,591	58,680	61,911	48	48	...
	10—15	52,250	26,577	25,673	11,534	9,677	1,857	40,716	16,900	23,816	63	60	3
	15—20	46,557	21,356	25,201	15,949	13,676	2,273	30,608	7,680	22,928	121	117	4
	20—30	73,502	34,491	39,011	28,492	25,741	2,751	45,010	8,750	36,260	237	226	11
	30 and over	164,331	77,193	87,138	63,394	59,142	4,252	100,937	18,051	82,886	312	308	4
	Animist (all ages)	3,345	1,756	1,589	164	161	3	3,181	1,595	1,586	6	5	1
	Hindu (all ages)	842	702	140	361	331	30	481	371	110	37	35	2
	Mahomedan (all ages).	1,022	701	321	389	346	43	633	355	278	27	27	...
	Christian (all ages).	308	211	97	211	148	63	97	63	34	93	68	25
	Others (all ages)	96	78	18	43	38	5	53	40	13	4	4	...
MINBU.	All Religions ...	274,302	134,495	139,807	86,157	76,659	9,498	188,145	57,836	130,309	708	659	49
	0—10	65,056	31,887	33,169	1,870	1,421	449	63,186	30,466	32,720	9	9	...
	10—15	31,851	15,971	15,880	8,735	7,234	1,501	23,116	8,737	14,379	95	81	14
	15—20	29,233	14,101	15,132	11,923	10,318	1,605	17,310	3,783	13,527	136	123	13
	20—30	46,713	22,809	23,904	20,582	18,231	2,351	26,131	4,578	21,553	232	222	10
	30 and over	101,449	49,727	51,722	43,047	39,455	3,592	58,402	10,272	48,130	236	224	12
	Buddhist ...	265,885	129,039	136,846	84,537	75,195	9,342	181,348	53,844	127,504	535	507	28
	0—10	63,253	30,950	32,303	1,836	1,406	430	61,417	29,544	31,873	6	6	..
	10—15	31,086	15,543	15,543	8,641	7,168	1,473	22,445	8,375	14,070	87	75	12
	15—20	28,489	13,671	14,818	11,782	10,200	1,582	16,707	3,471	13,236	120	110	10
	20—30	44,881	21,488	23,393	20,067	17,755	2,312	24,814	3,733	21,081	174	172	2
	30 and over	98,176	47,387	50,789	42,211	38,666	3,545	55,965	8,721	47,244	148	144	4
	Animist ...	4,860	2,620	2,240	312	288	24	4,548	2,332	2,216	6	6	...
	0—10	1,305	685	620	5	3	2	1,300	682	618	...	...	...
	10—15	553	281	272	16	10	6	537	271	266	...	...	...
	15—20	488	248	240	42	39	3	446	209	237	3	3	...
	20—30	828	468	360	86	83	3	742	385	357	2	2	...
	30 and over	1,686	938	748	163	153	10	1,523	785	738	1	1	...
	Hindu ...	1,995	1,752	243	669	652	17	1,326	1,100	226	34	34	...
	0—10	187	104	83	...	...	...	187	104	83	...	...	...
	10—15	83	61	22	22	18	4	61	43	18	...	...	...
	15—20	134	110	24	39	37	2	95	73	22	3	3	...
	20—30	625	573	52	227	221	6	398	352	46	13	13	...
	30 and over	966	904	62	381	376	5	585	528	57	18	18	...
	Hindus born in Burma (all ages).	270	161	109	31	27	4	239	134	105	...	...	...
	Mahomedan ...	1,223	842	381	455	384	71	768	458	310	42	37	5
	0—10	246	108	138	22	8	14	224	100	124	...	...	...
	10—15	100	67	33	38	27	11	62	40	22	4	3	1
	15—20	101	60	41	46	35	11	55	25	30	7	5	2
	20—30	286	216	70	139	123	16	147	93	54	10	10	...
	30 and over	490	391	99	210	191	19	280	200	80	21	19	2
	Mahomedans born in Burma.	684	345	339	217	158	59	467	187	280	28	23	5
	0—10	235	103	132	20	8	12	215	95	120	..	...	...
	10—15	85	54	31	36	25	11	49	29	20	4	3	1
	15—20	76	38	38	35	24	11	41	14	27	7	5	2
	20—30	125	67	58	58	45	13	67	22	45	5	5	...
	30 and over	163	83	80	68	56	12	95	27	68	12	10	2
	Christian (all ages).	174	118	56	130	91	39	44	27	17	78	62	16
	Others (all ages)	165	124	41	54	49	5	111	75	36	13	13	...

Imperial Table VIIIb.—*Literacy by Religion and Age.*

District	Religion and Age	Total Persons	Total Males	Total Females	Literate Persons	Literate Males	Literate Females	Illiterate Persons	Illiterate Males	Illiterate Females	Literate in English Persons	Literate in English Males	Literate in English Females
	1	2	3	4	5	6	7	8	9	10	11	12	13
MAGWE.	ALL RELIGIONS ...	*423,252*	*211,686*	*211,566*	*134,475*	*124,809*	*9,666*	*288,777*	*86,877*	*201,900*	*2,141*	*1,908*	*233*
	0—10	104,681	52,310	52,371	3,023	2,442	581	101,658	49 868	51,790	60	30	30
	10—15	49,449	24,961	24,488	11,185	9,854	1,331	38,264	15,107	23,157	82	69	13
	15—20	44,850	21,355	23,495	18,844	17,141	1,703	26,006	4 214	21,792	213	190	23
	20—30	73,533	37,286	36,247	33,507	30,961	2,546	40,026	6,325	33,701	748	690	58
	30 and over	150,739	75,774	74,965	67,916	64,411	3,505	82,823	11,363	71,460	1,038	929	109
	BUDDHIST ..	*410,548*	*200,865*	*209,683*	*128,681*	*119,496*	*9,185*	*281,867*	*81,369*	*200,498*	*1,225*	*1,146*	*79*
	0—10	103,488	51,666	51,822	2,887	2.349	538	100,601	49.317	51,284	25	10	15
	10—15	48,984	24,650	24.334	11,034	9,748	1,286	37 950	14,902	23,048	60	53	7
	15—20	43,806	20,504	23,302	18,443	16,802	1,641	25,363	3,702	21,661	172	157	15
	20—30	69,217	33,453	35,764	31,490	29,105	2,385	37,727	4,348	33,379	492	486	9
	30 and over	145,053	70,592	74,461	64,827	61,492	3,335	80,226	9,100	71,120	476	440	36
	ANIMIST (ALL AGES)	*629*	*533*	*96*	*315*	*304*	*11*	*314*	*229*	*85*	*9*	*8*	*1*
	HINDU ...	*7,243*	*6,669*	*574*	*2,902*	*2,826*	*76*	*4,341*	*3,843*	*498*	*146*	*138*	*8*
	0—10	410	242	168	34	29	5	376	213	163	2	...	2
	10—15	206	163	43	62	52	10	144	111	33	5	5	...
	15—20	647	585	62	207	196	11	440	389	51	8	8	...
	20—30	2,634	2,476	158	1,049	1,023	26	1,585	1,453	132	45	40	5
	30 and over	3,346	3,203	143	1,550	1,526	24	1,796	1,677	119	86	85	1
	HINDUS BORN IN BURMA.	*607*	*362*	*245*	*167*	*137*	*30*	*440*	*225*	*215*	*20*	*17*	*3*
	0—10	269	147	122	12	10	2	257	137	120	1	..	1
	10—15	61	34	27	21	13	8	40	21	19	3	3	...
	15—20	53	24	29	23	16	7	30	8	22	3	3	...
	20—30	114	72	42	57	49	8	57	23	34	7	6	1
	30 and over	110	85	25	54	49	5	56	36	20	6	5	1
	MAHOMEDAN ..	*3,521*	*2,748*	*773*	*1,639*	*1,495*	*144*	*1,882*	*1,253*	*629*	*105*	*100*	*5*
	0—10	505	267	238	41	33	8	464	234	230	...	...	...
	10—15	174	105	69	49	33	16	125	72	53	2	1	1
	15—20	290	202	88	131	108	23	159	94	65	17	16	1
	20—30	1,179	995	184	623	569	54	556	426	130	30	27	3
	30 and over	1,373	1,179	194	795	752	43	578	427	151	56	56	...
	MAHOMEDANS BORN IN BURMA.	*1,268*	*687*	*581*	*437*	*330*	*107*	*831*	*357*	*474*	*60*	*59*	*1*
	0—10	428	223	205	33	26	7	395	797	198	...	...	...
	10—15	135	73	62	35	21	14	100	52	48	1	1	...
	15—20	135	62	73	57	39	18	78	23	55	8	7	1
	20—30	256	134	122	135	97	38	121	37	84	23	23	...
	30 and over	314	195	119	177	147	30	137	48	89	28	38	...
	CHRISTIAN ..	*1,153*	*746*	*407*	*866*	*621*	*245*	*287*	*125*	*162*	*647*	*508*	*139*
	0—10	186	93	93	53	25	28	133	68	65	32	20	12
	10—15	51	22	29	29	13	16	22	9	13	14	9	5
	15—20	64	26	38	46	19	27	18	7	11	15	8	7
	20—30	300	185	115	247	169	78	53	16	37	174	130	44
	30 and over	552	420	132	491	395	96	61	25	36	412	341	71
	OTHERS (ALL AGES)	*158*	*125*	*33*	*72*	*67*	*5*	*86*	*58*	*28*	*9*	*8*	*1*
PAKÔKKU HILL TRACTS.	ALL RELIGIONS ...	*20,043*	*9 840*	*10,203*	*243*	*231*	*12*	*19.800*	*9,609*	*10,191*	*13*	*12*	*1*
	0—10	6,209	3,114	3,095	1	1	..	6,208	3,113	3,095	...	...	...
	10—15	1,920	1,060	860	32	30	2	1,888	1,030	858	...	...	...
	15—20	1,705	889	816	30	27	3	1,675	862	813	...	...	...
	20—30	3,765	1,659	2,106	108	105	3	3,657	1,554	2,103	6	5	1
	30 and over	6,444	3,118	3,326	72	68	4	6,372	3,050	3,322	7	7	...
	ANIMIST (ALL AGES)	*19,712*	*9,599*	*10,113*	*78*	*78*	...	*19,634*	*9,521*	*10,113*	...	..	...
	HINDU ...	*183*	*143*	*40*	*75*	*75*	...	*108*	*68*	*40*	*3*	*3*	...
	0—10	39	18	21	...	...	...	39	18	21	...	...	...
	10—15	9	7	2	...	...	...	9	7	2	...	...	...
	15—20	1	1	..	1	1	...	...	...	...	...	...	...
	20—30	68	61	7	42	42	...	26	19	7	2	2	...
	30 and over	66	56	10	32	32	...	34	24	10	1	1	...
	HINDU (ALL AGES)	*183*	*143*	*40*	*75*	*75*	...	*108*	*68*	*40*	*3*	*3*	...
	MAHOMEDAN (ALL AGES).	*8*	*5*	*3*	*3*	*3*	..	*5*	*2*	*3*	*3*	*3*	...
	CHRISTIAN (ALL AGES).	*11*	*7*	*4*	*7*	*5*	*2*	*4*	*2*	*2*	*4*	*3*	*1*

IMPERIAL TABLE VIIIB.—*Literacy by Religion and Age.*

District, Religion and Age.	Population. Total. Persons.	Total. Males.	Total. Females.	Literate. Persons.	Literate. Males.	Literate. Females.	Illiterate. Persons.	Illiterate. Males.	Illiterate. Females.	Literate in English. Persons.	Literate in English. Males.	Literate in English. Females.
1	2	3	4	5	6	7	8	9	10	11	12	13
MANDALAY.												
ALL RELIGIONS ...	*356,621*	*182,999*	*173,622*	*146,271*	*115,832*	*30,439*	*210,350*	*67,167*	*143,183*	*9,354*	*7,054*	*2,300*
0—10	72,820	35,386	37,434	4,897	3,120	1,777	67,923	32,266	35,657	645	363	282
10—15	37,161	18,491	18,670	14,052	10,349	3,703	23,109	8,142	14,967	1,115	729	386
15—20	36,792	18,580	18,212	18,375	13,863	4,512	18,447	4,717	13,700	1,328	970	358
20—30	70,976	38,863	32,113	38,691	30,758	7,933	32,285	8,105	24,180	2,979	2,474	505
30 and over	138,872	71,679	67,193	70,256	57,742	12,514	68,616	13,937	54,679	3,287	2,518	769
BUDDHIST ...	*299,327*	*146,205*	*153,122*	*123,001*	*98,122*	*24,879*	*176,326*	*48,083*	*128,243*	*2,618*	*2,311*	*307*
0—10	62,462	30,170	32,292	3,771	2,499	1,272	58,691	27,671	31,020	61	39	22
10—15	32,628	16,058	16,570	12,160	9,196	2,964	20,486	6,862	13,606	319	252	67
15—20	31,605	15,469	16,136	15,903	12,191	3,712	15,702	3,278	12,424	471	395	76
20—30	55,832	27,943	27,889	31,301	24,849	6,452	24,531	3,094	21,437	948	883	65
30 and over	116,800	56,565	60,235	59,866	49,387	10,479	56,934	7,178	49,756	819	742	77
ANIMIST ...	*2,698*	*2,301*	*397*	*1,231*	*1,156*	*75*	*1,467*	*1,145*	*322*	*30*	*28*	*2*
0—10	251	127	124	13	10	3	238	117	121	...	...	..
10—15	79	58	21	24	20	4	55	38	17	1	1	...
15—20	277	240	37	91	83	8	186	157	29	4	3	1
20—30	1,074	984	90	490	466	24	584	518	66	14	13	1
30 and over	1,017	892	125	613	577	36	404	315	89	11	11	...
HINDU ...	*22,061*	*15,591*	*6,470*	*7,435*	*6,634*	*801*	*14,626*	*8,957*	*5,669*	*1,174*	*1,103*	*71*
0—10	3,476	1,745	1,731	167	114	53	3,309	1,631	1,678	30	21	9
10—15	1,310	751	559	402	306	96	908	445	463	106	98	8
15—20	1,752	1,147	605	609	484	125	1,143	663	480	113	101	12
10—20	6,479	5,031	1,448	2,740	2,445	295	3,739	2,586	1,153	408	381	27
30 and over	9,044	6,917	2,127	3,517	3,285	232	5,527	3,632	1,895	517	502	15
HINDUS BORN IN BURMA.	*7,261*	*3,499*	*3,762*	*1,802*	*1,397*	*405*	*5,459*	*2,102*	*3,357*	*266*	*244*	*22*
0—10	2,811	1,375	1,436	120	82	38	2,691	1,293	1,398	15	9	6
10—15	868	458	410	269	206	63	599	252	347	73	69	4
15—20	670	314	356	257	190	67	413	124	289	45	43	2
20—30	1,102	543	559	490	345	145	612	198	414	88	80	8
30 and over	1,810	809	1,001	666	574	92	1,144	235	909	45	43	2
MAHOMEDAN ...	*23,209*	*13,665*	*9,544*	*8,211*	*6,062*	*2,149*	*14,998*	*7,603*	*7,395*	*681*	*640*	*41*
0—10	4,663	2,356	2,307	296	174	122	4,367	2,182	2,185	39	38	1
10—15	2,131	1,145	986	667	440	227	1,464	705	759	69	55	14
15—20	2,104	1,162	942	902	625	277	1,202	537	665	78	73	5
20—30	5,415	3,509	1,906	2,411	1,798	613	3,004	1,711	1,293	224	215	9
30 and over	8,896	5,493	3,403	3,935	3,025	910	4,961	2,468	2,493	271	259	12
MAHOMEDANS BORN IN BURMA.	*16,571*	*7,815*	*8,756*	*5,685*	*3,643*	*2,042*	*10,886*	*4,172*	*6,714*	*445*	*412*	*33*
0—10	4,427	2,218	2,209	276	160	116	4,151	2,058	2,093	39	38	1
10—15	1,965	1,010	955	608	388	220	1,357	622	735	62	48	14
15—20	1,645	776	869	733	469	264	912	307	605	65	61	4
20—30	3,047	1,379	1,668	1,490	911	579	1,557	468	1,089	145	138	7
30 and over	5,487	2,432	3,055	2,578	1,715	863	2,909	717	2,192	134	127	7
CHRISTIAN ..	*8,329*	*4,506*	*3,823*	*5,967*	*3,498*	*2,469*	*2,362*	*1,008*	*1,354*	*4,730*	*2,886*	*1,844*
0—10	1,769	882	887	615	303	312	1,154	579	575	496	256	240
10—15	962	444	518	780	371	409	182	73	109	608	313	295
15—20	992	515	477	838	457	381	154	58	96	649	389	260
20—30	1,948	1,231	717	1,653	1,117	536	295	114	181	1,368	969	399
30 and over	2,658	1,434	1,224	2,081	1,250	831	577	184	393	1,609	959	650
OTHERS ..	*997*	*731*	*266*	*426*	*360*	*66*	*571*	*371*	*200*	*121*	*86*	*35*
0—10	199	106	93	35	20	15	164	86	78	19	9	10
10—15	51	35	16	19	16	3	32	19	13	12	10	2
15—20	62	47	15	32	23	9	30	24	6	13	9	4
20—30	228	165	63	96	83	13	132	82	50	17	13	4
30 and over	457	378	79	244	218	26	213	160	53	60	45	15
MANDALAY CITY.												
ALL RELIGIONS ...	*148,917*	*77,763*	*71,154*	*72,697*	*53,200*	*19,497*	*76,220*	*24,563*	*51,657*	*5,202*	*4,032*	*1,170*
0—10	26,754	12,743	14,011	2,339	1,393	946	24,415	11,350	13,065	319	181	138
10—15	14,081	6,818	7,263	6,633	4,493	2,140	7,448	2,325	5,123	643	433	210
15—20	15,019	7,944	7,075	9,034	6,296	2,738	5,985	1,648	4,337	757	540	217
20—30	32,098	18,471	13,627	20,009	14,921	5,088	12,089	3,550	8,539	1,630	1,376	254
30 and over	60,965	31,787	29,178	34,682	26,097	8,585	26,283	5,690	20,593	1,853	1,502	351

Imperial Table VIIIB.—*Literacy by Religion and Age.*

District, Religion and Age.	Population: Total. Persons.	Males.	Females.	Literate. Persons.	Males.	Females.	Illiterate. Persons.	Males.	Females.	Literate in English. Persons.	Males.	Females.
1	2	3	4	5	6	7	8	9	10	11	12	13
MANDALAY CITY—*concluded.*												
Buddhist ...	*115,154*	*56,811*	*58,343*	*58,766*	*42,830*	*15,936*	*56,388*	*13,981*	*42,407*	*2,024*	*1,808*	*216*
0—10	20,907	9,819	11,088	1,738	1,066	672	19,169	8,753	10,416	42	29	13
10—15	11,272	5,377	5,895	5,502	3,824	1,678	5,770	1,553	4,217	242	199	43
15—20	11,913	6,266	5,647	7,569	5,391	2,178	4,344	875	3,469	370	314	56
20—30	23,555	12,464	11,091	15,822	11,677	4,145	7,733	787	6,946	733	686	47
30 and over	47,507	22,885	24,622	28,135	20,872	7,263	19,372	2,013	17,359	637	580	57
Animist ..	*1,612*	*1,320*	*292*	*879*	*815*	*64*	*733*	*505*	*228*	*22*	*20*	*2*
0—10	192	98	94	12	9	3	180	89	91	...	...	...
10—15	62	47	15	21	17	4	41	30	11	1	1	...
15—20	129	100	29	60	53	7	69	47	22	4	3	1
20—30	411	359	52	263	245	18	148	114	34	9	8	1
30 and over	818	716	102	523	491	32	295	225	70	8	8	...
Hindu ...	*10,995*	*7,434*	*3,561*	*3,710*	*3,269*	*441*	*7,285*	*4,165*	*3,120*	*517*	*481*	*36*
0—10	1,663	811	852	66	49	17	1,597	762	835	12	7	5
10—15	704	387	317	221	167	54	483	220	263	43	38	5
15—20	892	538	354	315	247	68	577	291	286	40	35	5
20—30	3,136	2,382	754	1,334	1,154	180	1,802	1,228	574	181	167	14
30 and over	4,600	3,316	1,284	1,774	1,652	122	2,826	1,664	1,162	241	234	7
Hindus born in Burma.	*4,582*	*2,112*	*2,470*	*1,249*	*981*	*268*	*3,333*	*1,131*	*2,202*	*129*	*118*	*11*
0—10	1,344	629	715	43	34	9	1,301	595	706	5	2	3
10—15	518	259	259	153	112	41	365	147	218	29	26	3
15—20	429	185	244	151	112	39	278	73	205	19	18	1
20—30	821	400	421	363	250	113	458	150	308	49	46	3
30 and over	1,470	639	831	539	473	66	931	166	765	27	26	1
Mahomedan .	*16,373*	*9,638*	*6,735*	*6,218*	*4,523*	*1,695*	*10,155*	*5,115*	*5,040*	*494*	*462*	*32*
0—10	3,012	1,538	1,474	197	120	77	2,815	1,418	1,397	36	35	1
10—15	1,471	746	725	449	288	161	1,022	458	564	46	36	10
15—20	1,552	819	733	664	432	232	888	387	501	54	51	3
20—30	3,989	2,667	1,322	1,836	1,374	462	2,153	1,293	860	162	155	7
30 and over	6,349	3,868	2,481	3,072	2,309	763	3,277	1,559	1,718	196	185	11
Mahomedans born in Burma	*11,546*	*5,335*	*6,211*	*4,243*	*2,618*	*1,625*	*7,303*	*2,717*	*4,586*	*345*	*317*	*28*
0—10	2,855	1,448	1,407	188	112	76	2,667	1,336	1,331	36	35	1
10—15	1,359	657	702	410	254	156	949	403	546	42	32	10
15—20	1,203	523	680	537	313	224	666	210	456	48	45	3
20—35	2,126	964	1,162	1,096	653	443	1,030	311	719	112	105	7
30 and over	4,003	1,743	2,260	2,012	1,286	726	1,991	457	1,534	107	100	7
Christian ...	*4,160*	*2,083*	*2,077*	*2,877*	*1,560*	*1,317*	*1,283*	*523*	*760*	*2,080*	*1,217*	*863*
0—10	868	413	455	302	137	165	566	276	290	219	108	111
10—15	537	237	300	427	187	240	110	50	60	303	153	150
15—20	494	190	304	413	164	249	81	26	55	285	133	152
20—30	861	484	377	697	422	275	164	62	102	536	355	181
30 and over	1,400	759	641	1,038	650	388	362	109	253	737	468	269
Others ...	*623*	*477*	*146*	*247*	*203*	*44*	*376*	*274*	*102*	*65*	*44*	*21*
0—10	112	64	48	24	12	12	88	52	36	10	2	8
10—15	35	24	11	13	10	3	22	14	8	8	6	2
15—20	39	31	8	13	9	4	26	22	4	4	4	...
20—30	146	115	31	57	49	8	89	66	23	9	5	4
30 and over	291	243	48	140	123	17	151	120	31	34	27	7
BHAMO.												
All Religions	*112,960*	*56,888*	*56,072*	*16,849*	*14,661*	*2,188*	*96,111*	*42,227*	*53,884*	*431*	*385*	*46*
0—10	24,605	12,127	12,478	361	256	105	24,244	11,871	12,373	8	5	3
10—15	12,309	6,319	5,990	1,539	1,200	339	10,770	5,119	5,651	29	22	7
15—20	11,087	5,574	5,513	2,212	1,834	378	8,875	3,740	5,135	61	55	6
20—30	20,712	10,827	9,885	4,457	3,821	636	16,255	7,006	9,249	147	131	16
30 and over	44,247	22,041	22,206	8,280	7,550	730	35,967	14,491	21,476	186	172	14
Buddhist ...	*55,822*	*28,193*	*27,629*	*13,876*	*12,091*	*1,785*	*41,946*	*16,102*	*25,844*	*151*	*142*	*9*
0—10	13,495	6,623	6,872	257	183	74	13,238	6,440	6,798	1	...	1
10—15	6,597	3,298	3,299	1,236	987	249	5,361	2,311	3,050	15	10	5
15—20	5,491	2,751	2,740	1,783	1,483	300	3,708	1,268	2,440	30	27	3
20—30	9,493	4,896	4,597	3,498	2,977	521	5,995	1,919	4,076	51	51	...
30 and over	20,746	10,625	10,121	7,102	6,461	641	13,644	4,164	9,480	54	54	...

Imperial Table VIIIb.—*Literacy by Religion and Age.*

District, Religion and Age.	Population. Total. Persons.	Total. Males.	Total. Females.	Literate. Persons.	Literate. Males.	Literate. Females.	Illiterate. Persons.	Illiterate. Males.	Illiterate. Females.	Literate in English. Persons.	Literate in English. Males.	Literate in English. Females.
1	2	3	4	5	6	7	8	9	10	11	12	13
BHAMO—*concluded*.												
Animist ...	*48,359*	*22,850*	*25,509*	*396*	*360*	*36*	*47,963*	*22,490*	*25,473*	...	...	...
0—10	9,665	4,768	4,897	23	17	6	9,642	4,751	4,891	...	...	...
10—15	5,031	2,637	2,394	92	85	7	4,939	2,552	2,387	...	..	
15—20	4,734	2,242	2,492	67	61	6	4,667	2,181	2,486	..	...	...
20—30	8,801	4,105	4,696	106	93	13	8,695	4,012	4,683	...	...	...
30 and over	20,128	9,098	11,030	108	104	4	20,020	8,994	11,026	...	...	..
Hindu ...	*1,397*	*1,097*	*300*	*577*	*525*	*52*	*820*	*572*	*248*	*72*	*71*	*1*
0—10	192	102	90	8	7	1	184	95	89	...	...	...
10—15	53	28	25	23	15	8	30	13	17	4	4	...
15—20	94	60	34	41	29	12	53	31	22	5	5	
20—30	526	454	72	183	167	16	343	287	56	29	28	1
30 and over	532	453	79	322	307	15	210	146	64	34	34	...
Hindus born in Burma.	*315*	*183*	*132*	*75*	*53*	*22*	*240*	*130*	*110*	*15*	*15*	*15*
0—10	155	87	68	4	4	...	151	83	68	...	...	...
10—15	37	18	19	18	11	7	19	7	12	2	2	...
15—20	36	17	19	19	11	8	17	6	11	3	3	...
20—30	43	27	16	15	12	3	28	15	13	6	6	...
30 and over	44	34	10	19	15	4	25	19	6	4	4	...
Mahomedan ...	*1,960*	*1,541*	*419*	*567*	*496*	*71*	*1,393*	*1,045*	*348*	*30*	*29*	*1*
0—10	245	128	117	7	4	3	238	124	114	...	...	...
10—15	102	64	38	29	16	13	73	48	25	1	1	...
15—20	203	151	52	92	75	17	111	76	35	8	8	...
20—30	658	567	91	164	146	18	494	421	73	4	4	...
30 and over	752	631	121	275	255	20	477	376	101	17	16	1
Mahomedans born in Burma.	*581*	*292*	*289*	*164*	*110*	*54*	*417*	*182*	*235*	*18*	*18*	...
0—10	206	103	103	6	4	2	200	99	101	...	...	...
10—15	74	42	32	21	11	10	53	31	22	1	1	...
15—20	64	32	32	38	24	14	26	8	18	8	8	...
20—30	92	45	47	40	27	13	52	18	34	4	4	...
30 and over	145	70	75	59	44	15	86	26	60	5	5	...
Christian ...	*4,052*	*2,056*	*1996*	*775*	*571*	*204*	*3,277*	*1,485*	*1,792*	*151*	*119*	*32*
0—10	827	401	426	61	42	19	766	359	407	7	5	2
10—15	486	267	219	141	83	58	345	184	161	6	4	2
15—20	421	240	181	152	113	39	269	127	142	17	11	3
20—30	779	403	376	234	185	49	545	218	327	54	40	14
30 and over	1,539	745	794	187	148	39	1,352	597	755	67	56	11
Others (all ages)	*1,370*	*1,151*	*219*	*658*	*618*	*40*	*712*	*533*	*179*	*27*	*24*	*3*
MYITKYINA.												
All Religions ...	*118,382*	*63,419*	*54,963*	*16,811*	*15,404*	*1,407*	*101,571*	*48,015*	*53,556*	*557*	*500*	*57*
0—10	24,960	12,351	12,609	370	273	97	24,590	12,078	12,512	16	12	4
10—15	11,857	6,050	5,807	1,178	1,016	162	10,679	5,034	5,645	29	20	9
15—20	12,087	6,175	5,912	1,775	1,582	193	10,312	4,593	5,719	59	54	5
20—30	23,690	13,292	10,398	4,584	4,228	356	19,106	9,064	10,042	202	188	14
30 and over	45,788	25,551	20,237	8,904	8,305	599	36,884	17,246	19,638	251	226	25
Buddhist ...	*39,960*	*21,587*	*18,373*	*12,623*	*11,505*	*1,118*	*27,337*	*10,082*	*17,255*	*131*	*129*	*2*
0—10	9,420	4,662	4,758	274	198	76	9,146	4,464	4,682	...	...	...
10—15	4,204	2,107	2,097	940	820	120	3,264	1,287	1,977	1	...	1
15—20	4,032	2,003	2,029	1,493	1,336	157	2,539	667	1,872	14	14	...
20—30	7,358	4,130	3,228	3,082	2,814	268	4,276	1,316	2,960	54	54	...
30 and over	14,946	8,685	6,261	6,834	6,337	497	8,112	2,348	5,764	62	61	1
Animist ...	*66,927*	*34,135*	*32,792*	*516*	*501*	*15*	*66,411*	*33,634*	*32,777*	*1*	*1*	...
0—10	13,179	6,492	6,687	1	...	1	13,178	6,492	6,686	...	...	...
10—15	6,710	3,394	3,316	10	10	...	6,700	3,384	3,316	...	...	...
15—20	7,162	3,672	3,490	30	29	1	7,132	3,643	3,489	...	...	...
20—30	13,208	6,817	6,391	153	147	6	13,055	6,670	6,385	1	1	...
30 and over	26,668	13,760	12,908	322	315	7	26,346	13,445	12,901	...	...	...
Hindu ..	*8,829*	*5,980*	*2,849*	*2,811*	*2,699*	*132*	*5,998*	*3,281*	*2,717*	*224*	*215*	*9*
0—10	1,875	948	927	69	58	11	1,806	890	916	7	7	...
10—15	718	401	317	139	118	21	579	283	296	17	14	3
15—20	673	379	394	179	160	19	494	219	275	34	33	1
20—30	2,458	1,893	565	1,101	1,062	39	1,357	831	526	90	86	4
30 and over	3,105	2,359	746	1,343	1,301	42	1,762	1,058	704	76	75	1

IMPERIAL TABLE VIIIB.—*Literacy by Religion and Age.*

District, Religion and Age.	Population. Total. Persons.	Total. Males.	Total. Females.	Literate. Persons.	Literate. Males.	Literate. Females.	Illiterate. Persons.	Illiterate. Males.	Illiterate. Females.	Literate in English. Persons.	Literate in English. Males.	Literate in English. Females.
1	2	3	4	5	6	7	8	9	10	11	12	13
MYITKYINA—*concluded.*												
HINDUS BORN IN BURMA.	*2,606*	*1,330*	*1,276*	*336*	*290*	*46*	*2,270*	*1,040*	*1,230*	*70*	*64*	*6*
0—10	1,562	786	776	52	46	6	1,510	740	770	5	5	...
10—15	498	282	216	105	91	14	393	191	202	14	11	3
15—20	279	139	140	88	75	13	191	64	127	26	25	1
20—30	176	87	89	71	62	9	105	25	80	23	22	1
30 and over	91	36	55	20	16	4	71	20	51	2	1	1
MAHOMEDAN ...	*1,283*	*899*	*384*	*407*	*357*	*50*	*876*	*542*	*334*	*59*	*59*	...
0—10	241	127	114	7	6	1	234	121	113	...	...	...
10—15	101	66	35	23	19	4	78	47	31	4	4	...
15—20	79	47	32	27	23	4	52	24	28	5	5	...
20—30	340	254	86	131	110	21	209	144	65	22	22	...
30 and over	522	405	117	219	199	20	303	206	97	28	28	...
MAHOMEDANS BORN IN BURMA.	*548*	*262*	*286*	*134*	*89*	*45*	*414*	*173*	*241*	*27*	*27*	...
0—10	215	111	104	5	4	1	210	107	103	...	...	...
10—15	81	50	31	18	14	4	63	36	27	3	3	...
15—20	46	20	26	15	11	4	31	9	22	4	4	...
20—30	95	39	56	44	25	19	51	14	37	10	10	...
30 and over	111	42	69	52	35	17	59	7	52	10	10	...
CHRISTIAN (ALL AGES)	*995*	*536*	*459*	*318*	*234*	*84*	*677*	*302*	*375*	*132*	*86*	*46*
OTHERS (ALL AGES)	*388*	*282*	*106*	*116*	*108*	*8*	*272*	*174*	*98*	*10*	*10*	...
KATHA.												
ALL RELIGIONS ...	*253,725*	*128,444*	*125,281*	*74,649*	*66,630*	*8,019*	*179,076*	*61,814*	*117,262*	*840*	*729*	*111*
0—10	63,360	31,095	32,265	1,647	1,301	346	61,713	29,794	31,919	19	12	7
10—15	28,638	14,390	14,248	7,595	6,542	1,053	21,043	7,848	13,195	40	33	7
15—20	25,228	12,130	13,098	9,528	8,058	1,470	15,700	4,072	11,628	98	80	18
20—30	43,538	21,949	21,589	18,039	15,830	2,209	25,499	6,119	19,380	271	236	35
30 and over	92,961	48,880	44,081	37,840	34,899	2,941	55,121	13,981	41,140	412	368	44
BUDDHIST ...	*236,886*	*117,983*	*118,903*	*71,407*	*63,784*	*7,623*	*165,479*	*54,199*	*111,280*	*431*	*400*	*31*
0—10	59,758	29,305	30,453	1,584	1,265	319	58,174	28,040	30,134	10	8	2
10—15	27,260	13,653	13,607	7,437	6,434	1,003	19,823	7,219	12,604	21	17	4
15—20	23,821	11,299	12,522	9,236	7,823	1,413	14,585	3,476	11,109	59	55	4
20—30	39,858	19,515	20,343	17,032	14,938	2,094	22,826	4,577	18,249	156	143	13
30 and over	86,189	44,211	41,978	36,118	33,324	2,794	50,071	10,887	39,184	185	177	8
ANIMIST ...	*9,620*	*5,362*	*4,258*	*598*	*570*	*28*	*9,022*	*4,792*	*4,230*	*10*	*10*	...
0—10	2,232	1,119	1,113	11	9	2	2,221	1,110	1,111	...	...	...
10—15	906	464	442	12	9	3	894	455	439	...	...	...
15—20	838	468	370	58	54	4	780	414	366	3	3	...
20—30	1,847	1,041	806	172	165	7	1,675	876	799		...	...
30 and over	3,797	2,270	1,527	345	333	12	3,452	1,937	1,515	7	7	...
HINDU ...	*3,990*	*2,935*	*1,055*	*1,267*	*1,161*	*106*	*2,723*	*1,774*	*949*	*115*	*108*	*7*
0—10	757	383	374	17	4	13	740	379	361	1	...	1
10—15	221	135	86	47	34	13	174	101	73	3	3	...
15—20	254	166	88	78	63	15	176	103	73	10	7	3
20—30	1,054	816	238	423	387	36	631	429	202	41	39	2
30 and over	1,704	1,435	269	702	673	29	1,002	762	240	60	59	1
HINDUS BORN IN BURMA.	*870*	*480*	*390*	*105*	*75*	*30*	*765*	*405*	*360*	*19*	*16*	*3*
0—10	556	289	267	14	4	10	542	285	257	1	...	1
10—15	124	69	55	25	15	10	99	54	45	1	1	...
15—20	53	32	21	18	11	7	35	21	14	7	5	2
20—30	62	38	24	22	20	2	40	18	22	7	7	...
30 and over	75	52	23	26	25	1	49	27	22	3	3	...
MAHOMEDAN ...	*2,478*	*1,620*	*858*	*941*	*773*	*168*	*1,537*	*847*	*690*	*65*	*57*	*8*
0—10	502	234	268	21	15	6	481	219	262	1	...	1
10—15	202	105	97	80	50	30	122	55	67	6	6	...
15—20	216	124	92	102	79	23	114	45	69	8	7	1
20—30	558	395	163	264	218	46	294	177	117	12	12	...
30 and over	1,000	762	238	474	411	63	526	351	175	38	32	6
MAHOMEDANS BORN IN BURMA.	*1,382*	*624*	*758*	*467*	*304*	*163*	*915*	*320*	*595*	*35*	*32*	*3*
0—10	461	205	256	20	14	6	441	191	250	1	...	1
10—15	177	84	93	74	44	30	103	40	63	6	6	...
15—20	160	78	82	77	54	23	83	24	59	8	7	1
20—30	235	94	141	113	67	46	122	27	95	8	8	...
30 and over	349	163	186	183	125	58	166	38	128	12	11	1
CHRISTIAN (ALL AGES)	*744*	*537*	*207*	*432*	*338*	*94*	*312*	*199*	*113*	*218*	*153*	*65*
OTHERS (ALL AGES)	*7*	*7*	...	*4*	*4*	...	*3*	*3*	...	*1*	*1*	...

Imperial Table VIIIb.—*Literacy by Religion and Age.*

District	Religion and Age	Population: Total: Persons	Population: Total: Males	Population: Total: Females	Population: Literate: Persons	Population: Literate: Males	Population: Literate: Females	Population: Illiterate: Persons	Population: Illiterate: Males	Population: Illiterate: Females	Literate in English: Persons	Literate in English: Males	Literate in English: Females
1		2	3	4	5	6	7	8	9	10	11	12	13
PUTAO.	All Religions ...	7,673	4,144	3,529	1,760	1,664	96	5,913	2,480	3,433	70	66	4
	0—10	1,484	771	713	14	12	2	1,470	759	711	...	...	...
	10—15	775	422	353	134	131	3	641	291	350	1	1	...
	15—20	762	392	370	188	184	4	574	208	366	4	3	1
	20—30	1,753	1,104	649	578	543	35	1,175	561	614	40	38	2
	30 and over	2,899	1,455	1,444	846	794	52	2,053	661	1,392	25	24	1
	Buddhist ...	6,123	2,892	3,231	1,095	1,029	66	5,028	1,863	3,165	14	14	...
	0—10	1,319	689	630	5	5	...	1,314	684	630	...	...	...
	10—15	713	384	329	115	114	1	598	270	328	..	...	...
	15—20	647	313	334	171	171	...	476	142	334	2	2	...
	20—30	1,067	505	562	268	248	20	799	257	542	5	5	...
	30 and over	2,377	1,001	1,376	536	491	45	1,841	510	1,331	7	7	...
	Animist (all ages)	463	401	62	28	28	..	435	373	62	...	...	...
	Hindu (all ages)	997	779	218	583	561	22	414	218	196	26	24	2
	Mahomedan (all ages).	31	27	4	10	9	1	21	18	3	5	5	...
	Christian (all ages).	32	24	8	23	20	3	9	4	5	16	14	2
	Others (all ages)	27	21	6	21	17	4	6	4	2	9	9	...
SHWEBO.	All Religions ...	391,284	184,708	206,576	114,669	105,890	8,779	276,615	78,818	197,797	1,043	880	163
	0—10	96,234	45,813	50,421	3,021	2,510	511	93,213	43,303	49,910	15	11	4
	10—15	45,763	22,454	23,309	11,255	9,918	1,337	34,508	12,536	21,972	100	74	26
	15—20	40,657	18,966	21,691	15,096	13,597	1,499	25,561	5,369	20,192	157	126	31
	20—30	63,665	29,656	34,009	26,507	24,206	2,301	37,158	5,450	31,708	352	284	68
	30 and over	144,965	67,819	77,146	58,790	55,659	3,131	86,175	12,160	74,015	419	385	34
	Buddhist ...	378,464	177,347	201,117	110,595	102,413	8,182	267,869	74,934	192,935	603	515	88
	0—10	93,151	44,314	48,137	2,879	2,399	480	90,272	41,915	48,357	7	6	1
	10—15	44,406	21,736	22,670	10,826	9,600	1,226	33,580	12,136	21,444	69	49	20
	15—20	39,504	18,378	21,126	14,670	13,281	1,389	24,834	5,097	19,737	125	105	20
	20—30	61,070	28,047	33,023	25,383	23,246	2,137	35,687	4,801	30,886	211	176	35
	30 and over	140,333	64,872	75,461	56,837	53,887	2,950	83,496	10,985	72,511	191	179	12
	Animist (all ages)	388	305	83	162	156	6	226	149	77	1	1	...
	Hindu ...	2,538	1,925	613	824	769	55	1,714	1,156	558	141	134	7
	0—10	463	230	233	24	15	9	439	215	224	2	2	...
	10—15	127	80	47	30	21	9	97	59	38	12	10	2
	15—20	132	93	39	36	34	2	96	59	37	8	8	...
	20—30	667	531	136	263	245	18	404	286	118	38	33	5
	30 and over	1,149	991	158	471	454	17	678	537	141	81	81	...
	Hindus born in Burma.	603	331	272	91	77	14	512	254	258	24	23	1
	0—10	356	168	188	16	11	5	340	157	183	2	2	...
	10—15	81	44	37	17	10	7	64	34	30	8	7	1
	15—20	38	25	13	10	10	...	28	15	13	5	5	...
	20—30	54	38	16	22	22	...	32	16	16	5	5	...
	30 and over	74	56	18	26	24	2	48	32	16	4	4	...
	Mahomedan ...	7,610	3,922	3,688	2,083	1,863	220	5,527	2,059	3,468	62	59	3
	0—10	2,025	981	1,044	81	73	8	1,944	908	1,036	...	...	...
	10—15	964	497	467	270	224	46	694	273	421	2	2	...
	15—20	771	372	399	250	206	44	521	166	355	5	4	...
	20—30	1,348	727	621	513	461	52	835	266	569	19	18	1
	30 and over	2,502	1,345	1,157	969	899	70	1,533	446	1,087	36	35	1
	Mahomedans born in Burma.	6,592	3,023	3,569	1,671	1,460	211	4,921	1,563	3,358	26	23	3
	0—10	1,958	923	1,035	80	72	8	1,878	851	1,027	...	...	...
	10—15	928	465	463	262	216	46	666	249	417	2	2	...
	15—20	696	308	388	225	183	42	471	125	346	4	3	1
	20—30	1,058	476	582	395	345	50	663	131	532	12	11	1
	30 and over	1,952	851	1,101	709	644	65	1,243	207	1,036	8	7	1
	Christian ...	2,009	1,016	993	855	560	295	1,154	456	698	209	145	64
	0—10	491	237	254	33	20	13	458	217	241	6	3	3
	10—15	236	122	114	117	64	53	119	58	61	14	10	4
	15—20	201	84	117	115	55	60	86	29	57	17	7	10
	20—30	404	220	184	255	172	83	149	48	101	74	48	26
	30 and over	677	353	324	335	249	86	342	104	238	98	77	21
	Others (all ages)	275	193	82	150	129	21	125	64	61	27	26	1

IMPERIAL TABLE VIIIB.—*Literacy by Religion and Age.*

District, Religion and Age.		Population. Total. Persons.	Total. Males.	Total. Females.	Literate. Persons.	Literate. Males.	Literate. Females.	Illiterate. Persons.	Illiterate. Males.	Illiterate. Females.	Literate in English. Persons.	Literate in English. Males.	Literate in English. Females.
1		2	3	4	5	6	7	8	9	10	11	12	13
SAGAING.	ALL RELIGIONS ...	326,908	155,054	171,854	95,193	82,278	12,915	231,715	72,776	158,939	944	803	141
	0—10	84,517	41,423	43,094	2,820	2,100	720	81,697	39,323	42,374	36	21	15
	10—15	38,133	18,934	19,199	10,850	8,805	2,045	27,283	10,129	17,154	126	94	32
	15—20	33,568	15,407	18,161	13,543	11,116	2,427	20,025	4,291	15,734	169	142	27
	20—30	53,546	24,882	28,664	22,032	18,654	3,378	31,514	6,228	25,286	266	224	42
	30 and over	117,144	54,408	62,736	45,948	41,603	4,345	71,196	12,805	58,391	347	322	25
	BUDDHIST ...	321,016	151,524	169,492	93,109	80,746	12,363	227,907	70,778	157,129	614	540	74
	0—10	83,130	40,733	42,397	2,746	2,059	687	80,384	38,674	41,710	22	13	9
	10—15	37,629	18,669	18,960	10,678	8,699	1,979	26,951	9,970	16,981	108	85	23
	15—20	33,036	15,127	17,909	13,291	10,964	2,327	19,745	4,163	15,582	126	112	14
	20—30	52,291	24,067	28,224	21,434	18,211	3,223	30,857	5,856	25,001	166	148	18
	30 and over	114,930	52,928	62,002	44,960	40,813	4,147	69,970	12,115	57,855	192	182	10
	ANIMIST ...	97	84	13	45	43	2	52	41	11	3	2	1
	HINDU (ALL AGES)	1,956	1,382	574	540	485	55	1,416	897	519	111	96	15
	HINDUS BORN IN BURMA (ALL AGES)	674	355	319	138	107	31	536	248	288	27	17	10
	MAHOMEDAN ...	2,811	1,563	1,248	1,008	726	282	1,803	837	966	78	78	...
	0—10	698	333	365	34	17	17	664	316	348	2	2	...
	10—15	274	148	126	99	71	28	175	77	98	4	4	...
	15—20	301	158	143	149	93	56	152	65	87	18	18	...
	20—30	589	362	227	293	213	80	296	149	147	24	24	...
	30 and over	949	562	387	433	332	101	516	230	286	30	30	...
	MAHOMEDANS BORN IN BURMA.	2,272	1,079	1,193	802	524	278	1,470	555	915	55	55	...
	0—10	682	321	361	34	17	17	648	304	344	2	2	...
	10—15	250	126	124	91	64	27	159	62	97	4	4	...
	15—20	254	118	136	129	73	56	125	45	80	16	16	...
	20—30	387	178	209	211	133	78	176	45	131	17	17	...
	30 and over	699	336	363	337	237	100	362	99	263	16	16	...
	CHRISTIAN (ALL AGES).	948	446	502	456	248	208	492	198	294	131	81	50
	OTHERS (ALL AGES)	80	55	25	35	30	5	45	25	20	7	6	1
LOWER CHINDWIN.	ALL RELIGIONS ...	342,880	156,693	186,187	92,693	83,914	8,779	250,187	72,779	177,408	576	491	85
	0—10	87,110	42,236	44,874	2,651	2,032	619	84,459	40,204	44,255	45	12	33
	10—15	39,390	19,711	19,679	10,587	9,127	1,460	28,803	10,584	18,219	67	58	9
	15—20	33,070	14,792	18,278	11,767	10,373	1,394	21,303	14,419	16,884	88	79	9
	20—30	52,504	22,792	29,712	19,722	17,294	2,428	32,782	5,498	27,284	166	147	19
	30 and over	130,806	57,162	73,644	47,966	45,088	2,878	82,840	12,074	70,766	210	195	15
	BUDDHIST ...	340,065	154,557	185,508	91,476	82,877	8,599	248,589	71,680	176,909	411	365	46
	0—10	86,629	41,968	44,661	2,596	2,000	596	84,033	39,968	44,065	38	8	30
	10—15	39,234	19,617	19,617	10,522	9,086	1,436	28,712	10,531	18,181	52	47	5
	15—20	32,873	14,668	18,205	11,672	10,308	1,364	21,201	4,360	16,841	73	71	2
	20—30	51,747	22,189	29,558	19,345	16,970	2,375	32,402	5,219	27,183	125	118	7
	30 and over	129,582	56,115	73,467	47,341	44,513	2,828	82,241	11,602	70,639	123	121	2
	ANIMIST (ALL AGES)	141	126	15	81	76	5	60	50	10	2	2	...
	HINDU (ALL AGES)	1,299	1,006	293	503	454	49	796	552	244	56	52	4
	MAHOMEDAN (ALL AGES).	1,025	794	231	427	376	51	598	418	180	2	...	2
	CHRISTIAN (ALL AGES).	334	194	140	205	130	75	129	64	65	105	72	33
	OTHERS (ALL AGES)	16	16	...	1	1	...	15	15	...	...	...	...
UPPER CHINDWIN.	ALL RELIGIONS ...	179,245	90,713	88,532	54,009	50,888	3,121	125,336	39,825	85,411	541	476	65
	0—10	44,208	21,556	22,652	593	470	123	43,615	21,086	22,529	20	2	18
	10—15	19,549	9,846	9,703	3,818	3,481	337	15,731	6,365	9,366	33	26	7
	15—20	17,631	8,493	9,138	6,224	5,717	507	11,407	2,776	8,631	75	65	10
	20—30	31,863	16,219	15,644	13,925	12,959	966	17,938	3,260	14,678	177	160	17
	30 and over	65,994	34,599	31,395	29,449	28,261	1,188	36,545	6,338	30,207	236	223	13
	BUDDHIST ..	170,322	84,914	85,408	52,042	49,018	3,024	118,280	35,896	82,384	354	307	47
	0—10	42,761	20,802	21,959	576	455	121	42,185	20,347	21,838	20	2	18
	10—15	18.847	9,447	9,400	3,762	3,440	322	15,085	6,007	9,078	30	23	7
	15—20	16,801	8,017	8,784	6,085	5,597	488	10,716	2,420	8,296	58	50	8
	20—30	29,554	14,601	14,953	13,160	12,222	938	16,394	2,379	14,015	110	102	8
	30 and over	62,359	32,047	30,312	28,459	27,304	1,155	33,900	4,743	29,157	136	130	6

IMPERIAL TABLE VIIIB.—*Literacy by Religion and Age.*

DISTRICT, RELIGION AND AGE.	POPULATION.									Literate in English.		
	Total.			Literate.			Illiterate.					
	Persons.	Males.	Females.	Persons.	Males.	Females.	Persons.	Males.	Females.	Persons.	Males.	Females.
1	2	3	4	5	6	7	8	9	10	11	12	13
UPPER CHINDWIN—*concluded.*												
ANIMIST ...	3,665	1,932	1,733	132	125	7	3,533	1,807	1,726	4	4	...
0—10	653	321	332	...	...	...	653	321	332	...	...	.
10—15	364	204	160	5	5	...	359	199	160	1	1	...
15—20	433	237	196	24	21	3	409	216	193	2	2	...
20—30	772	394	378	49	49	...	723	345	378	...	...	..
30 and over	1,443	776	667	54	50	4	1,389	726	663	1	1	...
HINDU ...	3,223	2,472	751	1,087	1,056	31	2,136	1,416	720	69	66	3
0—10	436	247	189	7	7	...	429	240	189	...	...	...
10—15	172	107	65	27	17	10	145	90	55	...	...	...
15—20	227	143	84	61	56	5	166	87	79	7	5	2
20—30	1,002	827	175	444	436	8	558	391	167	22	21	1
30 and over	1,386	1,148	238	548	540	8	838	608	230	40	40	..
HINDUS BORN IN BURMA.	613	414	199	92	92	...	521	322	199	6	6	...
0—10	303	173	130	5	5	...	298	168	130	..	...	...
10—15	67	41	26	6	6	...	61	35	26	...	...	...
15—20	39	25	14	13	13	...	26	12	14	1	1	...
20—30	83	64	19	25	25	...	58	39	19	4	4	..
30 and over	121	111	10	43	43	...	78	68	10	1	1	...
MAHOMEDAN (ALL AGES).	1,023	758	265	431	405	26	592	353	239	20	19	1
CHRISTIAN (ALL AGES).	695	397	298	174	149	25	521	248	273	86	72	14
OTHERS (ALL AGES)	317	240	77	143	135	8	174	105	69	8	8	...
CHIN HILLS.												
ALL RELIGIONS ...	110,079	54,122	55,957	1,286	1,220	66	108,793	52,902	55,891	115	98	17
0—10	29,148	14,390	14,758	42	30	12	29,106	14,360	14,746	3	1	2
10—15	12,170	6,290	5,880	126	115	11	12,044	6,175	5,869	2	1	1
15—20	10,848	5,313	5,535	147	134	13	10,701	5,179	5,522	9	7	2
20—30	18,793	8,587	10,206	520	505	15	18,273	8,082	10,191	44	40	4
30 and over	39,120	19,542	19,578	451	436	15	38,669	19,106	19,563	57	49	8
BUDDHIST (ALL AGES)	134	89	45	74	64	10	60	25	35	8	8	...
ANIMIST ...	107,407	52,426	54,981	416	406	10	106,991	52,020	54,971	3	3	...
0—10	28,455	14,057	14,398	11	9	2	28,444	14,048	14,396	..	...	...
10—15	11,904	6,131	5,773	66	61	5	11,838	6,070	5,768	...	...	...
15—20	10,593	5,168	5,425	75	72	3	10,518	5,096	5,422	...	...	...
20—30	18,173	8,127	10,046	176	176	...	17,997	7,951	10,046	3	3	...
30 and over	38,282	18,943	19,339	88	88	...	38,194	18,855	19,339	...	...	...
HINDUS (ALL AGES)	1,642	1,110	532	609	593	16	1,033	517	516	58	57	1
HINDUS BORN IN BURMA (ALL AGES).	659	324	335	61	53	8	598	271	327	8	7	1
MAHOMEDAN (ALL AGES).	48	31	17	23	23	...	25	8	17	2	2	...
CHRISTIAN (ALL AGES).	826	450	376	151	122	29	675	328	347	44	28	16
OTHERS (ALL AGES)	22	16	6	13	12	1	9	4	5	...	...	...
KYAUKSÈ.												
ALL RELIGIONS ..	142,677	70,449	72,228	42,546	36,306	6,240	100,131	34,143	65,988	429	386	43
0—10	31,487	15,505	15,982	1,229	778	451	30,258	14,727	15,531	11	9	2
10—15	15,096	7,633	7,463	3,846	2,934	912	11,250	4,699	6,551	59	53	6
15—20	14,648	6,863	7,785	5,084	4,067	1,017	9,564	2,796	6,768	60	50	10
20—30	25,706	12,457	13,249	10,626	8,983	1,643	15,080	3,474	11,606	151	141	10
30 and over	55,740	27,991	27,749	21,761	19,544	2,217	33,979	8,147	25,532	148	133	15
BUDDHIST ...	135,082	66,277	68,805	40,647	34,772	5,875	94,435	31,505	62,930	264	246	18
0—10	29,558	14,556	15,002	1,148	736	412	28,410	13,820	14,590	3	2	1
10—15	14,293	7,214	7,079	3,636	2,786	850	10,657	4,428	6,229	45	41	4
15—20	13,971	6,531	7,440	4,874	3,922	952	9,097	2,609	6,488	47	41	6
20—30	24,242	11,610	12,632	10,108	8,575	1,533	14,134	3,035	11,099	93	92	1
30 and over	53,018	26,366	26,652	20,881	18,753	2,128	32,137	7,613	24,524	76	70	6
ANIMIST (ALL AGES)	157	110	47	58	55	3	99	55	44	1	1	...
HINDU (ALL AGES)	1,028	821	207	321	299	22	707	522	185	38	36	2
MAHOMEDAN ...	5,740	2,896	2,844	1,233	971	262	4,507	1,925	2,582	41	38	3
0—10	1,592	791	801	56	28	28	1,536	763	773	2	2	...
10—15	662	332	330	154	106	48	508	226	282	...	...	...
15—20	532	255	277	149	109	40	383	146	237	2	2	...
20—30	1,029	522	507	338	256	82	691	266	425	21	18	3
30 and over	1,925	996	929	536	472	64	1,389	524	865	16	16	...

Imperial Table VIIIb.—*Literacy by Religion and Age.*

District, Religion and Age.	Population. Total. Persons.	Total. Males.	Total. Females.	Literate. Persons.	Literate. Males.	Literate. Females.	Illiterate. Persons.	Illiterate. Males.	Illiterate. Females.	Literate in English. Persons.	Literate in English. Males.	Literate in English. Females.
1	2	3	4	5	6	7	8	9	10	11	12	13
KYAUKSÊ—*concld.*												
Mahomedans born in Burma.	*5,517*	*2,720*	*2,797*	*1,128*	*883*	*245*	*4,389*	*1,837*	*2,552*	*20*	*20*	...
0—10	1,586	789	797	55	27	28	1,531	762	769	1	1	...
10—15	650	326	324	152	104	48	498	222	276	...	...	...
15—20	528	253	275	148	108	40	380	145	235	2	2	...
20—30	949	458	491	287	213	74	662	245	417	9	9	...
30 and over	1,804	894	910	486	431	55	1,318	463	855	8	8	...
Christian (all ages).	*592*	*292*	*300*	*259*	*182*	*77*	*333*	*110*	*223*	*83*	*63*	*20*
Others (all ages)	*78*	*53*	*25*	*28*	*27*	*1*	*50*	*26*	*24*	*2*	*2*	...
MEIKTILA.												
All Religions ...	*289,897*	*137,573*	*152,324*	*82,224*	*75,005*	*7,219*	*207,673*	*62,568*	*145,105*	*1,207*	*1,054*	*153*
0—10	67,912	32,533	35,379	1,831	1,384	447	66,081	31,149	34,932	35	27	8
10—15	35,090	17,468	17,622	7,703	6,718	985	27,387	10,750	16,637	107	88	19
15— 0	31,409	14,582	16,827	10,868	9,662	1,206	20,541	4,920	15,621	139	121	18
20—30	48,378	22,783	25,595	19,634	17,648	1,986	28,744	5,135	23,609	450	407	43
30 and over	107,108	50,207	56,901	42,188	39,593	2,595	64,920	10,614	54,306	476	411	65
Buddhist ...	*281,618*	*132,184*	*149,434*	*79,476*	*72,656*	*6,820*	*202,142*	*59,528*	*142,614*	*570*	*547*	*23*
0—10	66,218	31,697	34,521	1,729	1,310	419	64,489	30,387	34,102	18	16	2
10—15	34,377	17,071	17,306	7,527	6,596	931	26,850	40,475	16,375	65	55	10
15—20	30,646	14,138	16,508	10,600	9,445	1,155	20,046	4,693	15,353	83	80	3
20—30	46,354	21,367	24,987	18,770	16,912	1,858	27,584	4,455	23,129	244	241	3
30 and over	104,023	47,911	56,112	40,850	38,393	2,457	63,173	9,518	53,655	160	155	5
Animist (all ages)	*349*	*305*	*44*	*107*	*99*	*8*	*242*	*206*	*36*	*3*	*3*	...
Hindu ...	*2,644*	*2,005*	*639*	*916*	*820*	*96*	*1,728*	*1,185*	*543*	*172*	*154*	*18*
0—10	386	202	184	30	23	7	356	179	177	2	2	...
10—15	158	86	72	47	35	12	111	51	60	16	13	3
15—20	156	96	60	50	35	15	106	61	45	5	2	3
20—30	756	606	150	297	259	38	459	347	112	69	59	10
30 and over	1,188	1,015	173	492	468	24	696	547	149	80	78	2
Hindus born in Burma.	*536*	*258*	*278*	*102*	*75*	*27*	*434*	*183*	*251*	*27*	*22*	*5*
0—10	282	138	144	19	14	5	263	124	139	2	2	...
10—15	76	31	45	19	12	7	57	19	38	5	3	2
15—20	42	17	25	13	8	5	29	9	20	2	1	1
20—30	70	35	35	26	21	5	44	14	30	11	9	2
30 and over	66	37	29	25	20	5	41	17	24	7	7	...
Mahomedan ..	*4,283*	*2,369*	*1,914*	*1,024*	*905*	*119*	*3,259*	*1,464*	*1,795*	*104*	*104*	...
0—10	1,124	527	597	43	35	8	1,081	492	589	...	...	...
10—15	483	273	210	80	61	19	403	212	191	6	6	...
15—20	449	219	230	111	95	16	338	124	214	12	12	...
20—30	833	459	374	268	224	44	565	235	330	30	30	...
30 and over	1,394	891	503	522	490	32	872	401	471	56	56	...
Mahomedans born in Burma.	*3,232*	*1,472*	*1,760*	*538*	*436*	*102*	*2,694*	*1,036*	*1,658*	*48*	*48*	...
0—10	1,086	506	580	40	32	8	1,046	474	572	...	...	...
10—15	449	243	206	66	48	18	383	195	188	4	4	...
15—20	382	173	209	84	71	13	298	102	196	10	10	...
20—30	564	242	322	155	117	38	409	125	284	16	16	...
30 and over	751	308	443	193	168	25	558	140	418	18	18	...
Christian ...	*772*	*532*	*240*	*561*	*403*	*158*	*211*	*129*	*82*	*349*	*238*	*111*
0—10	119	72	47	21	12	9	98	60	38	13	8	5
10—15	49	27	22	33	18	15	16	9	7	20	14	6
15—20	120	99	21	93	76	17	27	23	4	39	27	12
20—30	247	192	55	205	165	40	42	27	15	104	74	30
30 and over	237	142	95	209	132	77	28	10	18	173	115	58
Others (all ages)	*231*	*178*	*53*	*140*	*122*	*18*	*91*	*56*	*35*	*9*	*8*	*1*
YAMÈTHIN.												
All Religions ...	*323,189*	*160,913*	*162,276*	*100,415*	*88,785*	*11,630*	*222,774*	*72,128*	*150,646*	*1,845*	*1,593*	*252*
0—10	79,718	38,392	41,326	3,519	2,440	1,079	76,199	35,952	40,247	73	46	27
10—15	38,915	19,686	19,229	9,230	7,550	1,680	29,685	12,136	17,549	231	183	48
15—20	32,201	15,900	16,301	13,028	11,228	1,800	19,173	4,672	14,501	280	229	51
20—30	55,174	27,192	27,982	23,709	20,889	2,820	31,465	6,303	25,162	587	531	56
30 and over	117,181	59,743	57,438	50,929	46,678	4,251	66,252	13,065	53,187	674	604	70

IMPERIAL TABLE VIIIB.—*Literacy by Religion and Age.*

District	Religion and Age.	Population. Total. Persons.	Total. Males.	Total. Females.	Literate. Persons.	Literate. Males.	Literate. Females.	Illiterate. Persons.	Illiterate. Males.	Illiterate. Females.	Literate in English. Persons.	Literate in English. Males.	Literate in English. Females.
1		2	3	4	5	6	7	8	9	10	11	12	13
YAMETHIN—*concluded.*	BUDDHIST ...	*298,565*	*146,086*	*152,479*	*94,022*	*83,373*	*10,649*	*204,543*	*62,713*	*141,830*	*1,019*	*917*	*102*
	0—10	74,100	35,590	38,510	3,254	2,271	983	70,846	33,319	37,527	35	25	10
	10—15	36,661	18,449	18,212	8,682	7,155	1,527	27,979	11,294	16,685	130	108	22
	15—20	29,976	14,688	15,288	12,320	10,687	1,633	17,656	4,001	13,655	178	152	26
	20—30	49,861	23,761	26,100	21,853	19,305	2,548	28,008	4,456	23,552	348	330	18
	30 and over	107,967	53,598	54,369	47,913	43,955	3,958	60,054	9,643	50,411	328	302	26
	ANIMIST (ALL AGES)	*2,719*	*1,577*	*1,142*	*411*	*382*	*29*	*2,308*	*1,195*	*1,113*	*14*	*14*	...
	HINDU ...	*6,220*	*4,797*	*1,423*	*1,598*	*1,469*	*129*	*4,622*	*3,328*	*1,294*	*176*	*161*	*15*
	0—10	868	428	440	39	23	16	829	405	424	2	2	...
	10—15	316	207	109	75	59	16	241	148	93	13	9	4
	15—20	435	317	118	124	102	22	311	215	96	17	12	5
	20—30	1,848	1,510	338	574	533	41	1,274	977	297	59	55	4
	30 and over	2,753	2,335	418	786	752	34	1,967	1,583	384	85	83	2
	HINDUS BORN IN BURMA.	*941*	*470*	*471*	*118*	*80*	*38*	*823*	*390*	*433*	*30*	*24*	*6*
	0—10	551	261	290	13	6	7	538	255	283	2	2	...
	10—15	115	56	59	28	17	11	87	39	48	8	4	4
	15—20	81	41	40	20	14	6	61	27	34	6	5	1
	20—30	99	50	49	31	22	9	68	28	40	9	9	...
	30 and over	95	62	33	26	21	5	69	41	28	5	4	1
	MAHOMEDAN ...	*12,908*	*6,896*	*6,012*	*3,596*	*3,002*	*594*	*9,312*	*3,894*	*5,418*	*262*	*250*	*12*
	0—10	3,329	1,647	1,682	153	105	48	3,176	1,542	1,634	5	4	1
	10—15	1,375	719	656	381	283	98	994	436	558	46	43	3
	15—20	1,286	643	643	468	362	106	818	281	537	38	36	2
	20—30	2,427	1,308	1,119	964	793	171	1,463	515	948	76	73	3
	30 and over	4,491	2,579	1,912	1,630	1,459	171	2,861	1,120	1,741	97	94	3
	MAHOMEDANS BORN IN BURMA.	*10,813*	*5,110*	*5,703*	*2,747*	*2,192*	*555*	*8,066*	*2,918*	*5,148*	*189*	*179*	*10*
	0—10	3,258	1,608	1,650	146	102	44	3,112	1,506	1,606	5	4	1
	10—15	1,319	671	648	362	265	97	957	406	551	46	43	3
	15—20	1,158	530	628	411	306	105	747	224	523	35	33	2
	20—30	1,791	778	1,013	693	539	154	1,098	239	859	52	50	2
	30 and over	3,287	1,523	1,764	1,135	980	155	2,152	543	1,609	51	49	2
	CHRISTIAN ...	*2,416*	*1,285*	*1,131*	*612*	*407*	*205*	*1,804*	*878*	*926*	*351*	*230*	*121*
	0—10	682	329	353	50	26	24	632	303	329	30	14	16
	10—15	265	152	113	60	28	32	205	124	81	37	19	18
	15—20	256	116	140	82	47	35	174	169	105	42	25	17
	20—30	469	270	199	174	126	48	295	144	151	94	63	31
	30 and over	744	418	326	246	180	66	498	238	260	148	109	39
	OTHERS (ALL AGES)	*361*	*272*	*89*	*176*	*152*	*24*	*185*	*120*	*65*	*23*	*21*	*2*
MYINGYAN.	ALL RELIGIONS ...	*442,008*	*213,294*	*228,714*	*123,211*	*109,550*	*13,661*	*318,797*	*103,744*	*215,053*	*1,095*	*984*	*111*
	0—10	109,030	52,932	56,098	3,716	2,761	955	105,314	50,171	55,143	28	22	6
	10—15	53,640	26,707	26,933	11,945	9,982	1,963	41,695	16,725	24,970	76	56	20
	15—20	46,301	21,445	24,856	15,687	13,516	2,171	30,614	7,929	22,685	183	162	21
	20—30	72,504	34,742	37,762	27,981	24,944	3,037	44,523	9,798	34,725	396	367	29
	30 and over	160,533	77,468	83,065	63,882	58,347	5,535	96,651	19,121	77,530	412	377	35
	BUDDHIST ...	*438,374*	*210,540*	*227,834*	*121,686*	*108,230*	*13,456*	*316,688*	*102,310*	*214,378*	*622*	*541*	*81*
	0—10	108,417	52,612	55,805	3,637	2,703	934	104,780	49,909	54,871	9	8	1
	10—15	53,448	26,596	26,852	11,869	9,932	1,937	41,579	16,664	24,915	61	46	15
	15—20	46,031	21,270	24,761	15,570	13,433	2,137	30,461	7,837	22,624	149	133	16
	20—30	71,409	33,834	37,575	27,449	24,471	2,978	43,960	9,363	34,597	227	208	19
	30 and over	159,069	76,228	82,841	63,161	57,691	5,470	95,908	18,537	77,371	176	146	30
	ANIMIST (ALL AGES)	*382*	*295*	*87*	*214*	*185*	*29*	*168*	*110*	*58*	*11*	*11*	...
	HINDUS ...	*1,724*	*1,399*	*325*	*595*	*554*	*41*	*1,129*	*845*	*284*	*49*	*46*	*3*
	0—10	239	135	104	21	17	4	218	118	100	1	1	...
	10—15	66	42	24	20	19	1	46	23	23	4	3	1
	15—20	114	86	28	40	32	8	74	54	20	3	3	...
	20—30	602	516	86	243	228	15	359	288	71	22	20	2
	30 and over	703	620	83	271	258	13	432	362	70	19	19	...

Imperial Table VIIIb.—*Literacy by Religion and Age.*

District, Religion and Age.	Population. Total. Persons.	Total. Males.	Total. Females.	Literate. Persons.	Literate. Males.	Literate. Females.	Illiterate. Persons.	Illiterate. Males.	Illiterate. Females.	Literate in English. Persons.	Literate in English. Males.	Literate in English. Females.
1	2	3	4	5	6	7	8	9	10	11	12	13
MYINGYAN—*concluded*.												
Hindus born in Burma.	342	212	130	55	47	8	287	165	122	9	9	...
0—10	146	81	65	6	3	3	140	78	62	1	1	...
10—15	26	17	9	7	7	...	19	10	9	1	1	...
15—20	22	12	10	5	4	1	17	8	9	...	...	...
20—30	55	34	21	16	16	...	39	18	21	3	3	...
30 and over	93	68	25	21	17	4	72	51	21	4	4	...
Mahomedan (all ages).	1,156	833	323	480	407	73	676	426	250	301	299	2
Mahomedans born in Burma (all ages)	521	258	263	148	99	49	373	159	214	9	9	...
Christian (all ages).	342	202	140	221	161	60	121	41	80	112	87	25
Others (all ages)	30	25	5	15	13	2	15	12	3	..	...	...
NORTHERN SHAN STATES.												
All Religions ...	559,223	285,700	273,523	41,100	38,815	2,285	518,123	246,885	271,238	1,322	1,146	176
0—10	139,161	69,084	70,077	544	417	127	138,617	68,667	69,950	14	8	6
10—15	55,932	29,087	26,845	3,374	3,112	262	52,558	25,975	26,583	42	34	8
15—20	54,547	26,694	27,853	4,772	4,387	385	49,775	22,307	27,468	98	81	17
20—30	101,280	51,513	49,767	10,698	10,065	633	90,582	41,448	49,134	507	445	62
30 and over	208,303	109,322	98,981	21,712	20,834	878	186,591	88,488	98,103	661	578	83
Buddhist ...	415,893	208,446	207,447	35,212	33,323	1,889	380,681	175,123	205,558	337	313	24
0—10	105,468	51,993	53,475	470	365	105	104,998	51,628	53,370	2	2	...
10—15	43,709	22,397	21,312	3,166	2,939	227	40,543	19,458	21,085	11	11	...
15—20	41,616	19,754	21,862	4,335	4,010	325	37,281	15,744	21,537	43	38	5
20—30	72,583	35,100	37,483	8,451	7,943	508	64,132	27,157	36,975	140	130	10
30 and over	152,517	79,202	73,315	18,790	18,066	724	133,727	61,136	72,591	141	132	9
Animist ...	131,057	67,495	63,562	1,594	1,590	4	129,463	65,905	63,558	31	30	1
0—10	32,268	16,350	15,918	20	20	...	32,248	16,330	15,918	...	...	...
10—15	11,692	6,367	5,325	63	63	...	11,629	6,304	5,325	6	6	...
15—20	12,082	6,344	5,738	130	129	1	11,952	6,215	5,737	1	1	...
20—30	24,435	12,764	11,671	479	478	1	23,956	12,286	11,670	13	13	...
30 and over	50,580	25,670	24,910	902	900	2	49,678	24,770	24,908	11	10	1
Hindu ...	7,804	6,686	1,118	2,594	2,520	74	5,210	4,166	1,044	338	329	9
0—10	712	365	347	14	10	4	698	355	343	1	...	1
10—15	237	152	85	44	41	3	193	111	82	2	2	...
15—20	526	401	125	152	139	13	374	262	112	19	17	2
20—30	3,052	2,770	282	1,195	1,163	32	1,857	1,607	250	164	159	5
30 and over	3,277	2,998	279	1,189	1,167	22	2,088	1,831	257	152	151	1
Hindus born in Burma.	801	402	399	66	58	8	735	344	391	11	11	...
0—10	543	266	277	8	7	1	535	259	276	...	...	...
10—15	109	59	50	6	5	1	103	54	49	..	...	...
15—20	54	22	32	13	11	2	41	11	30	2	2	...
20—30	58	31	27	23	20	3	35	11	24	5	5	...
30 and over	37	24	13	16	15	1	21	9	12	4	4	...
Mahomedan ...	2,286	1,815	471	809	754	55	1,477	1,061	416	95	89	6
0—10	269	149	120	8	6	2	261	143	118	...	...	...
10—15	121	76	45	30	24	6	91	52	39	...	...	...
15—20	151	110	41	60	57	3	91	53	38	6	6	...
20—30	726	600	126	334	317	17	392	283	109	48	46	2
30 and over	1,019	880	139	377	350	27	642	530	112	41	37	4
Mahomedans born in Burma.	714	389	325	155	133	22	559	256	303	20	19	1
0—10	243	136	107	4	3	1	239	133	106	...	...	...
10—15	94	59	35	20	18	2	74	41	33	...	...	...
15—20	64	37	27	24	23	1	40	14	26	...	...	...
20—30	153	72	81	45	38	7	108	34	74	3	3	...
30 and over	160	85	75	62	51	11	98	34	64	10	10	...
										7	6	1
Christian ...	1,929	1,050	879	782	533	249	1,147	517	630	505	370	135
0—10	412	208	204	29	15	14	383	193	190	11	6	5
10—15	162	90	72	66	44	22	96	46	50	23	15	8
15—20	164	82	82	91	49	42	73	33	40	27	18	9
20—30	422	227	195	219	145	74	203	82	121	138	93	45
30 and over	769	443	326	377	280	97	392	163	229	306	238	68
Others (all ages)	254	208	46	109	95	14	145	113	32	16	15	1

IMPERIAL TABLE VIIIB.—*Literacy by Religion and Age.*

District	Religion and Age	Population: Total: Persons	Total: Males	Total: Females	Literate: Persons	Literate: Males	Literate: Females	Illiterate: Persons	Illiterate: Males	Illiterate: Females	Literate in English: Persons	Literate in English: Males	Literate in English: Females
1		2	3	4	5	6	7	8	9	10	11	12	13
SOUTHERN SHAN STATES.	ALL RELIGIONS ...	*847,618*	*427,064*	*420,554*	*60,388*	*57,440*	*2,948*	*787,230*	*369,624*	*417,606*	799	*626*	*173*
	0—10	204,877	101,964	102,913	506	413	93	204,371	101,551	102,820	9	4	5
	10—15	88,885	46,861	42,024	5,284	4,971	313	83,601	41,890	41,711	49	30	19
	15—20	90,040	43,405	46,635	8,183	7,645	538	81,857	35,760	46,097	107	79	28
	20—30	149,565	72,518	77,047	13,764	12,983	781	135,801	59,535	76,266	239	196	43
	30 and over	314,251	162,316	151,935	32,651	31,428	1,223	281,600	130,888	150,712	395	317	78
	BUDDHIST ...	*748,051*	*373,450*	*374,601*	*56,612*	*54,234*	*2,378*	*691,439*	*319,216*	*372,223*	*239*	*212*	*27*
	0—10	180,073	89,163	90,910	311	251	60	179,762	88,912	90,850	1	...	1
	10—15	79,868	41,994	37,874	4,976	4,749	227	74,892	37,245	37,647	14	11	3
	15—20	80,009	38,085	41,924	7,753	7,332	421	72,256	30,753	41,503	28	31	7
	20—30	129,569	62,141	67,428	12,673	12,045	628	116,896	50,096	66,800	94	83	11
	30 and over	278,532	142,067	136,465	30,899	29,857	1,042	247,633	112,210	135,423	92	87	5
	ANIMIST ...	*81,211*	*42,672*	*38,539*	*276*	*276*	...	*80,935*	*42,396*	*38,539*	*3*	*3*	...
	0—10	20,087	10,362	9,725	...	...	...	20,087	10,362	9,725	...	...	...
	10—15	7,285	3,894	3,391	...	...	...	7,285	3,894	3,391	...	...	...
	15—20	8,326	4,447	3,879	12	12	...	8,314	4,435	3,879	1	1	...
	20—30	16,053	7,940	8,113	31	31	...	16,022	7,909	8,113	...	..	...
	30 and over	29,460	16,029	13,431	233	233	...	29,227	15,796	13,431	2	2	...
	HINDU ...	*4,908*	*3,721*	*1,187*	*1,742*	*1,663*	79	*3,166*	*2,058*	*1,108*	*157*	*155*	2
	0—10	885	479	406	16	14	2	869	465	404	1	1	...
	10—15	245	149	96	46	43	3	199	106	93	6	4	2
	15—20	341	205	136	119	98	21	222	107	115	18	18	...
	20—30	1,432	1,172	260	623	592	31	809	580	229	55	55	...
	30 and over	2,005	1,716	289	938	916	22	1,067	800	267	77	77	...
	HINDUS BORN IN BURMA.	*1,235*	*662*	*573*	*137*	*123*	*14*	*1,098*	*539*	*559*	*27*	*25*	2
	0—10	793	428	365	9	8	1	784	420	364	...	...	..
	10—15	175	103	72	29	26	3	146	77	69	4	2	2
	15—20	122	60	62	50	44	6	72	16	56	14	14	...
	20—30	84	39	45	27	25	2	57	14	43	4	4	...
	30 and over	61	32	29	22	20	2	39	12	27	5	5	...
	MAHOMEDAN (ALL AGES).	*2,310*	*1,467*	*843*	*530*	*459*	*71*	*1,780*	*1,008*	*772*	*57*	*54*	*3*
	MAHOMEDANS BORN IN BURMA.	*1,255*	*563*	*692*	*166*	*112*	*54*	*1,089*	*451*	*638*	*28*	*25*	*3*
	CHRISTIAN ...	*11,137*	*5,754*	*5,383*	*1,228*	*808*	*420*	*9,909*	*4,946*	*4,963*	*343*	*202*	*141*
	0—10	3,238	1,637	1,601	161	133	28	3,077	1,504	1,573	7	3	4
	10—15	1,288	718	570	225	152	73	1,063	566	497	27	13	14
	15—20	1,182	568	614	247	163	84	935	405	530	40	21	19
	20—30	2,037	987	1,050	300	198	102	1,737	789	948	76	44	32
	30 and over	3,392	1,844	1,548	295	162	133	3,097	1,682	1,415	193	121	72
	OTHER (ALL AGES)	*1*	...	*1*	..	..	...	*1*	...	*1*	...	...	...
KARENNI.	ALL RELIGIONS ...	*63,850*	*31,129*	*32,721*	*4,085*	*3,357*	*728*	*59,765*	*27,772*	*31,993*	*83*	*75*	*8*
	0—10	16,947	8,449	8,498	90	45	45	16,857	8,404	8,453	4	2	2
	10—15	6,566	3,396	3,170	414	298	116	6,152	3,098	3,054	2	2	...
	15—20	5,375	2,372	3,003	466	348	118	4,909	2,024	2,885	7	7	...
	20—30	10,900	4,756	6,144	958	759	199	9,942	3,997	5,945	30	26	4
	30 and over	24,062	12,156	11,906	2,157	1,907	250	21,905	10,249	11,656	40	38	2
	BUDDHIST ...	*19,502*	*10,414*	*9,088*	*2,827*	*2,475*	*352*	*16,675*	*7,939*	*8,736*	*31*	*30*	*1*
	0—10	4,016	2,023	1,993	26	12	14	3,990	2,011	1,979	1	...	1
	10—15	1,960	1,067	893	231	186	45	1,729	881	848	...	...	...
	15—20	1,732	848	884	300	244	56	1,432	604	828	3	3	...
	20—30	3,211	1,575	1,636	562	476	86	2,649	1,099	1,550	10	10	...
	30 and over	8,583	4,901	3,682	1,708	1,557	151	6,875	3,344	3,531	17	17	...
	ANIMIST ...	*34,215*	*15,595*	*18,620*	*116*	*113*	*3*	*34,099*	*15,482*	*18,617*	*7*	*7*	...
	0—10	9,950	4,937	5,013	2	2	...	9,948	4,935	5,013	...	...	...
	10—15	3,494	1,759	1,735	9	9	...	3,485	1,750	1,735	2	2	..
	15—20	2,727	1,100	1,627	7	7	...	2,720	1,093	1,627	2	2	...
	20—30	5,893	2,293	3,600	31	30	1	5,862	2,263	3,599	...	...	...
	30 and over	12,151	5,506	6,645	67	65	2	12,084	5,441	6,643	3	3	...
	HINDU (ALL AGES)	*293*	*254*	*39*	*105*	*101*	*4*	*188*	*153*	*35*	*3*	*3*	...
	MAHOMEDAN (ALL AGES).	*238*	*147*	*91*	*55*	*52*	*3*	*183*	*95*	*88*	...	...	...
	CHRISTIAN ...	*9,602*	*4,719*	*4,883*	*982*	*616*	*366*	*8,620*	*4,103*	*4,517*	*42*	*35*	*7*
	0—10	2,902	1,451	1,451	61	30	31	2,841	1,421	1,420	3	2	1
	10—15	1,092	561	531	171	101	70	921	460	461	...	...	...
	15—20	883	409	474	153	92	61	730	317	413	2	2	...
	20—30	1,639	757	882	292	182	110	1,347	575	772	17	13	4
	30 and over	3,086	1,541	1,545	305	211	94	2,781	1,330	1,451	20	18	2

IMPERIAL TABLE IX.

Literacy by Race.

NOTE 1.—This table supplements Imperial Tables VIIIA and VIIIB which show literacy by religion, and is presented in three parts:—

Part I shews for each sex of certain classes defined by race and religion the total numbers enumerated in the province and the numbers included therein who were literate in any language whatsoever or were literate in English.

Part II shows the number of persons literate in any language whatsoever in separate age-groups of certain classes defined by race and religion and place of enumeration.

Part III gives statistics similar to those of Parts I and II for samples of the six Indian races most largely represented in Burma.

NOTE 2.—The classes shown in Parts I and II of the table are not necessarily the most literate; some less literate classes have also been chosen for which the statistics were likely to be of use. In Part II the districts selected for each class are such as would give a representative sample of that class; in the case of the Karens twelve districts shown in the table have been selected in which one or other kind of Karen is numerous, and statistics have been given for each kind throughout all those districts. In Part III the samples represented are those for whom statistics of birth-place are given in Imperial Table XIB, and the title-page of that table should be consulted for particulars.

NOTE 3.—The term *Literate* means, as in Imperial Tables VIIIA and VIIIB, able both to read and to write "a letter to or from a friend" in the language with regard to which the term is used. In Parts I and III the persons shown as *Literate in English* are also included amongst those shown as *Literate in any language*.

NOTE 4.—The letters and numbers prefixed to the names of race-groups and races in the first column of the table are the group-letters and numbers assigned to each in Imperial Table XIII and serve to identify them in that table.

NOTE 5.—The age recorded was the number of completed years. The age-group represented by 5—10 in the table includes all who had completed five but had not yet completed ten years of age; and the other age-groups have a parallel interpretation.

NOTE 6.—Neither for the total nor for the illiterate in each age-group are statistics given in this table; but for every sample tabulated in Parts II and III the total number of persons in any age-group is shown in Imperial Table XIV, in which all samples are identical with samples in this table similarly described as to race, religion and district of enumeration, and the illiterate or the proportion of literate in each age-group can thus be calculated when required.

NOTE 7.—Similar statistics are given for certain races in some districts separately in Provincial Table VII. Imperial Tables VIA, VIB and XIII show also that in some districts one or other religion is almost confined to one race, so that the statistics given in Imperial Table VIIIB for those districts and that religion may be regarded with sufficient accuracy as proportional statistics for that race.

IMPERIAL TABLE IX, PART I.—*Literacy amongst Selected Race-groups and Races.*

[NOTE.—The figures of this part of the table in all cases cover the whole province.]

	Race.	Males.			Females.		
		Total.	Literate in any language.	Literate in English.	Total.	Literate in any language.	Literate in English.
	1	2	3	4	5	6	7
A	Burma Group * ...	4,247,900	24,21,181	42,690	4,426,539	512,195	6,861
A1	Burmese * ..	3,828,482	2,245,850	40,198	4,000,907	487,764	6,545
A2	Arakanese ...	151,190	83,383	1,580	149,510	11,807	218
A3	Yanbye ...	80,234	31,379	293	87,951	2,963	18
A4	Chaungtha ..	23,396	7,340	19	22,757	830	...
A5	Tavoyan ..	64,329	30,968	567	64,958	7,283	56
A9	Danu ...	37,382	11,816	10	37,260	745	2
A10	Intha ...	27,093	8,1[illegible]9	14	28,482	656	21
A11	Taungyo ...	11,984	1,278	1	11,693	1	...
B	Lolo-Muso Group ..	39,494	209	3	36,351	71	...
	Christian ...	*2,284*	*188*	*3*	*2,150*	*71*	...
C	Kuki-Chin Group † ...	140,638	14,279	130	141,236	1,115	62
E	Kachin Group ...	70,611	1,497	37	76,234	266	2
F	Sak Group ...	24,497	12,021	2	25,229	428	...
I	Tai Group ..	508,975	114,924	399	509,012	9,093	103
I1	Shan (unspecified race)§	142,237	35,753	157	146,747	2,349	24
I2	Shangale ...	293,747	65,29[illegible]	184	294,658	5,544	68
I3	Shangyi ...	15,100	4,141	35	13,904	712	6
I4	Shan-Tayok ...	15,885	942	1	12,816	72	...
I6	Siamese ..	7,245	2,283	16	6,041	283	5
I7	Khun ...	16,350	3,364	5	17,044	53	...
I8	Lu ..	12,086	1,881	...	13,184	8	...
K	Mon Group ...	163,830	65,877	485	159,679	16,147	107
L	Palaung-Wa Group ...	78,674	6,889	25	78,029	95	1
N	Karen Group ...	612,116	136,003	5,243	608,240	47,680	2,464
	Buddhists ...	*475,514*	*100,187*	*813*	*468,364*	*22,796*	*248*
	Animists ...	*47,723*	*870*	*14*	*50,530*	*161*	*5*
	Christians ..	*88,879*	*34,946*	*4,416*	*89,346*	*24,723*	*2,211*
N1	Karen (unspecified kind)‡	32,010	6,440	595	30,617	2,421	267
	Buddhists ...	*13,158*	*2,836*	*51*	*12,365*	*468*	*3*
	Christians ...	*11,457*	*3,226*	*541*	*10,961*	*1,899*	*263*
N2	Sgaw ...	218,609	55,696	3,329	218,501	25,935	1,734
	Buddhists ...	*155,530*	*32,788*	*405*	*154,300*	*8,924*	*155*
	Christians ...	*48,295*	*22,578*	*2,921*	*49,554*	*16,932*	*1,575*
N8	Karenbyu ...	9,[illegible]74	1,428	95	8,696	840	21
	Christians ...	*5,409*	*1,245*	*94*	*5,176*	*827*	*21*
N9	Pwo ...	208,2[illegible]5	53,401	937	203,606	15,674	404
	Buddhists ...	*193,778*	*47,050*	*295*	*189,028*	*11,523*	*77*
	Christians ...	*13,887*	*6,291*	*641*	*13,807*	*4,134*	*327*
N11	Taungthu ...	108,746	17,225	158	109,491	1,879	15
	Buddhists ...	*108,603*	*17,075*	*59*	*109,372*	*1,853*	*12*
R	Yünnanese and other Chinese of all religions.	101,877	37,157	3,250	47,183	4,969	379
R1	*Chinese Mahomedans (Panthays).*	*1,076*	*335*	*24*	*441*	*60*	*2*
S1	Arakan-Mahomedans ...	12,740	1,150	47	11,035	133	2
S2	Mahomedan Zerbadis ...	45,129	18,107	3,032	48,353	7,894	160
	Mahomedans (*other than Zerbadis, Arakan Mahomedans and Panthays*).						
	(i) Born in Burma ...	109,382	12,943	1,687	108,664	3,917	151
	(ii) Born outside Burma	146,200	52,524	4,454	17,572	1,465	97
	Hindus { Born in Burma ..	52,635	10,868	2,190	44,870	2,543	318
	Hindus { Born outside Burma	385,542	93,391	10,699	61,385	5,214	503
	All Indian Races—						
	Buddhists ...	5,822	2,452	540	1,333	216	40
	Animists ...	5,005	676	22	1,420	31	1
	Christians ...	13,674	6,785	3,651	8,928	2,646	1,039

* Mahomedans omitted.
† Hindus and Mahomedans omitted.

§‡ That is, described only as *Shan* (*or Karen*) in the enumeration-record without specification of a particular kind of Shan (or Karen).

IMPERIAL TABLE IX, PART II.—*Literacy by Age amongst samples of Selected Races.*

[NOTE.—Each sample tabulated includes all of the specified race and religion enumerated in the districts indicated.]

	Description of Sample.					Literate in any language classified by age.					
	Race.	Religion.	Districts.	Sex.	Total persons	All ages.	0–10	10–15	15–20	20–30	30 and over.
	1	2	3a	3b	4	5	6	7	8	9	10
A2, 3, 4	Arakanese, Yanbye and Chaungtha.	Buddhist ...	Akyab, Kyaukpyu and Sandoway.	M	246,579	117,615	1,032	10,110	14,534	26,358	64,381
				F	254,351	15,109	559	1,672	2,373	3,396	7,109
A 9	Danu ...	Buddhist ...	North and South Shan States.	M	35,904	11,237	99	727	1,412	2,617	6,382
				F	36,190	724	29	77	166	212	240
A10	Intha ...	Buddhist ...	Southern Shan States.	M	26,088	7,662	64	428	929	2,116	4,125
				F	27,03[illegible]	598	22	73	116	169	218
B7	Akha ...	Animist ...	Southern Shan States.	M	18,225	1	...	...	1	...	...
				F	15,848	...	...	...	...	...	...
E1	Kachin ...	Buddhist ...	Northern Shan States.	M	69	17	...	2	4	5	6
				F	88	27	...	6	4	5	12
	Do. ...	Animist ...	Do.	M	27,158	131	16	16	22	43	34
				F	29,544	...	...	...	...	...	...
I	Tai (Shan) Group	Buddhist ...	Bhamo, Myitkyina Katha and Upper Chindwin.	M	112,979	64,137	725	5,314	7,238	15,611	35,248
				F	115,555	4,777	256	563	947	1,285	1,726
I	Tai (Shan) Group other than Khun.	Buddhist ...	North and South Shan States.	M	324,481	43,039	258	3,737	5,504	9,476	24,064
				F	326,849	1,493	38	148	244	350	713
I7	Khun ...	Buddhist ...	Southern Shan States.	M	16,329	3,363	9	571	547	624	1,612
				F	17,014	53	2	4	5	11	31
K1	Talaing ...	Buddhist ...	Amherst and Thatôn.	M	129,577	45,505	869	4,008	5,631	11,193	23,804
				F	120,090	7,801	344	1,198	1,661	2,154	2,444
L16	Palaung and Pale	Buddhist ...	Northern Shan States.	M	52,322	4,459	26	682	745	1,185	1,821
				F	52,019	25	1	5	...	4	15
N1	Karen (unspecified kind*).	Buddhist ...	(As in Imperial Table XIV) Rangoon, Insein, Hanthawaddy, Tharrawaddy, Pegu, Bassein, Henzada, Myaungmya Ma-ubin, Toungoo, Amherst and Thatôn.	M	11,141	1,537	49	157	193	385	753
				F	10,871	308	15	34	71	85	103
		Christian ...		M	10,404	2,606	132	333	314	596	1,231
				F	10,525	1,757	108	234	315	522	578
		Anglican ...		*M*	*1,023*	*169*	*4*	*33*	*22*	*29*	*81*
				F	*989*	*79*	*2*	*9*	*20*	*25*	*23*
		Baptist ...		*M*	*5,653*	*1,797*	*90*	*210*	*230*	*421*	*846*
				F	*5,735*	*1,416*	*80*	*199*	*247*	*409*	*481*
		Roman Catholic		*M*	*3,727*	*639*	*38*	*90*	*62*	*146*	*303*
				F	*3,795*	*261*	*26*	*26*	*48*	*88*	*73*
		Other Sects ...		*M*	*1*	*1*	...	...	...	...	*1*
				F	*6*	*1*	...	...	...	...	*1*
N2	Sgaw ...	Buddhist ...		M	133,234	28,999	748	2,658	3,710	7,489	14,394
				F	132,093	6,977	352	1,113	1,413	2,088	2,011
		Christian ...		M	41,387	19,683	825	2,365	2,519	4,621	9,353
				F	43,146	15,058	792	2,173	2,693	4,155	5,245
		Anglican ...		*M*	*398*	*179*	*15*	*28*	*23*	*45*	*68*
				F	*443*	*128*	*11*	*29*	*34*	*29*	*25*
		Baptist ...		*M*	*36,674*	*17,542*	*718*	*2,101*	*2,242*	*4,137*	*8,344*
				F	*38,399*	*13,632*	*688*	*1,921*	*2,410*	*3,789*	*4,824*
		Roman Catholic		*M*	*4,229*	*1,918*	*91*	*230*	*251*	*424*	*922*
				F	*4,270*	*1,291*	*92*	*222*	*247*	*336*	*394*
		Other Sects ...		*M*	*86*	*44*	*1*	*6*	*3*	*15*	*19*
				F	*34*	*7*	*1*	*1*	*2*	*1*	*2*
N9	Pwo ...	Buddhist ..		M	187,779	42,655	758	3,735	5,311	10,726	22,125
				F	183,114	8,081	436	1,127	1,680	2,443	2,395
		Christian ...		M	12,900	5,808	250	777	790	1,266	2,725
				F	12,996	3,810	235	642	747	973	1,213
		Anglican ...		*M*	*481*	*241*	*11*	*57*	*34*	*26*	*113*
				F	*450*	*141*	*12*	*21*	*28*	*39*	*41*
		Baptist ...		*M*	*9,422*	*4,374*	*189*	*564*	*593*	*976*	*2,052*
				F	*9,316*	*2,846*	*181*	*472*	*549*	*720*	*924*
		Roman Catholic		*M*	*2,990*	*1,189*	*50*	*155*	*163*	*263*	*558*
				F	*3,214*	*818*	*41*	*149*	*170*	*211*	*247*
		Other Sects ...		*M*	*7*	*4*	...	*1*	...	*1*	*2*
				F	*16*	*5*	*1*	...	...	*3*	*1*

* That is, described only as *Karen* in the enumeration-record without specification of a particular kind of Karen.

IMPERIAL TABLE IX, PART II.—*Literacy by Age amongst samples of Selected Races*—concld.

	Description of Sample.					Literate in any language classified by age.					
	Race.	Religion.	Districts.	Sex.	Total persons	All ages.	0–10	10–15	15–20	20–30	30 and over.
	1	2	3a	3b	4	5	6	7	8	9	10
N various	Other Karens ...	Buddhist (see note in column 3a).	(As in Imperial Table XIV) Rangoon, Insein, Hanthawaddy, Tharrawaddy, Pegu, Bassein, Henzada, Myaungmya, Ma-ubin, Toungoo, Amherst & Thatôn. NOTE.—But the figures for *Buddhists* exclude the Taungthu Buddhists of Thatôn district for whom separate figures are given below.	M	7,759	2,077	42	162	233	526	1,114
				F	7,438	77	6	10	18	21	22
		Christian ...		M	7,016	1,813	75	227	229	425	857
				F	6,967	1,292	87	178	226	378	423
		Anglican ...		*M*	*1,215*	*333*	*18*	*55*	*33*	*60*	*167*
				F	*1,266*	*224*	*24*	*32*	*35*	*52*	*81*
		Baptist ..		*M*	*4,485*	*1,284*	*54*	*147*	*165*	*311*	*607*
				F	*4,311*	*990*	*57*	*140*	*168*	*304*	*321*
		Roman Catholic		*M*	*1,316*	*196*	*3*	*25*	*31*	*54*	*83*
				F	*1,390*	*78*	*6*	*6*	*23*	*22*	*21*
		Other Sects ...		*M*	*0*	...	..	...	...	...	...
				F	*0*	...	...	...	...	...	...
N11	Taungthu ...	Buddhist ...	Thatôn ...	M	26,813	8,689	295	858	1,010	2,022	4,504
				F	25,845	1,496	114	171	290	433	488
	Do. ...	Do. ...	Southern Shan States.	M	73,408	6,034	27	810	924	1,220	3,053
				F	75,122	56	5	2	6	9	34
N15	Karenni ...	Animist ...	Karenni States ...	M	12,043	28	2	14	8	...	4
				F	14,976	2	...	...	...	...	2
S2	Zerbadi ...	Mahomedan ...	The whole Province.	M	45,129	18,107	877	2,196	2,455	4,608	7,971
				F	48,353	7,894	479	1,088	1,320	2,255	2,752
S1	Arakan-Mahomedan ...		The whole Province.	M	12,740	1,150	48	105	110	245	642
				F	11,035	133	11	28	17	37	40

IMPERIAL TABLE IX, PART III.—*Literacy by Age amongst Males of certain Indian Races in Selected Districts.*

[NOTE 1.—The selected districts are the same as in Imperial Tables XIB and XIV, namely:—Akyab, Rangoon, Insein, Hanthawaddy, Pegu, Bassein, Myaungmya, Pyapôn, Toungoo, Thatôn, Amherst, Mandalay and Yamèthin.

NOTE 2.—The entries *In* and *Out* in column 3 indicate respectively persons born *in* and persons born *outside* Burma.

Race.	Religion.	Birth-place (See Note 2 above.)	Total literate and illiterate.	Literate in any language classified by age.						Literate in English (all ages)
				All ages.	0—10	10—15	15—20	20—30	30 and over.	
1	2	3	4	5	6	7	8	9	10	11
Bengali ...	Hindus and Animists.	In	900	303	90	57	31	71	54	168
		Out	9,155	5,607	64	153	428	2,210	2,752	2,337
	Mahomedans ...	In	11,919	1,330	74	139	167	368	582	157
		Out	28,393	7,981	17	129	524	3,051	4,260	811
Chittagonian	Hindus and Animists.	In	195	30	1	1	2	11	15	4
		Out	4,677	2,194	3	32	187	844	1,198	190
	Mahomedans ...	In	71,843	2,699	75	207	251	622	1,544	80
		Out	44,330	12,156	18	127	943	5,129	5,939	837
Hindustani ...	Hindus and Animists.	In	10,509	1,491	141	207	204	405	534	140
		Out.	53,606	17,841	95	350	956	6,242	10,188	987
	Mahomedans ...	In	2,311	794	61	116	104	204	309	176
		Out	14,974	5,080	33	146	309	1,517	3,075	498
Oriya ...	Hindus and Animists.	In	1,000	179	15	18	42	37	67	34
		Out	31,314	7,296	20	132	563	3,144	3,432	85
Tamil ...	Hindus and Animists.	In	18,339	4,042	349	776	652	1,142	1,123	953
		Out	44,828	17,452	207	845	1,393	5,028	9,979	2,471
	Mahomedans ...	In	4,177	1,304	87	236	199	335	447	304
		Out	14,183	8,058	66	454	870	2,554	4,114	351
Telegu ...	Hindus and Animists.	In	9,743	1,505	144	240	213	466	442	344
		Out	98,865	10,375	85	311	767	3,445	5,767	1,071

IMPERIAL TABLE X.

Language.

NOTE 1.—The area and population covered by this table are the same as those covered by Imperial Table VI-A, so that the areas (indicated in Note 1 of that table) in which the population was only estimated have been omitted from it.

NOTE 2.—Persons who speak more than one language have been entered only as speakers of that language which they returned in the enumeration schedules as the language they ordinarily used in their homes.

NOTE 3.—The languages returned have been collected into four classes as *Indigenous*, *Indian*, *European* and *Other* Languages.

NOTE 4.—No attempt has been made to classify in accordance with any accepted linguistic scheme the languages included under the last three names, the meanings of which are defined by Part IB of the table which gives a list of the separate languages included under each and the numbers of their speakers.

NOTE 5.—The indigenous languages have been arranged according to the best available information into groups, branches, sub-families and families as shown in Parts IA and IB of the table, which also show the number of speakers of each language and the total number of speakers of languages of each group or higher class.

For convenience in reference and indexing the letters A to O inclusive have been used to represent the groups of indigenous languages other than Chinese which is represented by R. The *Indian*, *European* and *Other* classes are similarly treated for convenience as artificial groups and represented by the letters X, Y and Z respectively. The letter corresponding to each group is shown in Part IA of the table. S is used in Imperial Table XIII to include the Zerbadis, the Arakan-Mahomedans and the Arakan-Kamans, but it does not appear in this table as these races have not separate languages.

For further information with regard to the classification scheme the Report Volume should be consulted.

NOTE 6.—Part IB shows in its *Remarks* column the districts in which are found speakers of some indigenous languages which are spoken over only a small area and for which more detailed information is not given in Part III of the table. In addition it gives, in italics, for some languages, other names which are in some cases alternative names of the same language and in other cases names of dialects of that language; further study may in some cases require some dialects to be regarded as separate languages, but generally such division has been avoided where not particularly required. The addition of * or † to a name has the same meaning as in Part IC (See Note 7).

NOTE 7.—Part IC is an alphabetical index of the various names of languages and dialects designed to show where in Part IB the speakers of each indigenous language or dialect are tabulated. To make this index serve the purposes of Imperial Table XIII also, some names are included which are used only for races and not for languages. Such names are marked with an *, while names which are used for languages but not for races are marked with a †. Some names however which are properly used only to designate a race or tribe have been used by some people to designate a language or *vice versâ*.

NOTE 8.—Part II gives the distribution by districts of the total speakers of languages of each class and of each indigenous group and also of speakers of English, and at the same time classifies the whole population of each district according to the group to which their languages belong.

NOTE 9.—Part III gives the distribution by districts of the speakers of the most important and widely spread languages of the indigenous class.

NOTE 10.—The form of Imperial Table XIII has been made parallel to that of this table to facilitate the extraction of corresponding figures for race and language. It should however be noted that, while Chinese (R) has been regarded as an indigenous language-group, none of the races of the Chinese group has been treated as an indigenous race.

IMPERIAL TABLE X.—*Language*. PART IA.—*Classification System for Languages.*

	Family.	Sub-Family.	Branch.	Group.	Speakers. Males.	Speakers. Females.
Indigenous (or Indo-Chinese) Languages—Groups A to O and Group R.	Tibeto-Chinese M. 5,342,247 F. 5,463,913	Tibeto-Burmese M. 4,796,806 F. 4,965,685	Assam-Burmese M. 4,789,543 F. 4,958,624	A. Burma ...	4,533,501	4,699,135
				B. Lolo-Muhso	39,413	36,273
				C. Kuki-Chin	134,025	134,355
				D. Naga ...	197	205
				E. Kachin ...	70,110	75,808
				F. Sak (Lui) ..	12,297	12,848
			North-Assam	G. Mishmi ...	...	...
			Unclassed ...	H Mro ...	7,263	7,061
		Tai-Chinese M. 545,441 F. 498,228	Tai ..	I. Tai ...	461,325	460,182
			Chinese ...	R. Chinese ...	84,116	38,046
	Austric M. 173,998 F. 168,483	Austronesian	Indonesian ...	J. Malay ...	2,739	2,638
		Austroasiatic M. 171,259 F. 165,845	Mon-Khmer	K. Mon ...	97,020	92,243
				L. Palaung-Wa	74,239	73,602
				M. Khasi ...	...	...
	Karen			N. Karen ...	557,995	556,021
	Man			O. Man ...	331	260
Non-Indigenous Languages.	Artificial Groups formed for the purposes of this Table.			X. Indian Languages	646,168	234,238
				Y. European Languages	14,178	10,263
				Z. Other Languages ...	599	405
Total speakers of Indigenous Languages (Groups A to O and Group R) ...					6,074,571	6,188,677
Total speakers of Non-Indigenous Languages (Groups X, Y, Z) ...					660,945	244,906
Grand Total ..					6,735,516	6,433,583

IMPERIAL TABLE X.—*Language.* PART IB.—*Provincial Totals of Speakers of each Language.*

	Language.		Males.	Females.	Remarks. (See Note 6 on page 133.)
	1		2	3	4
	GRAND TOTAL	...	6,735,516	6,433,583	Omits only estimated areas and those entirely omitted from the census.
A	**Burma group**	...	4,533,501	4,699,135	
A1	Burmese	...	4,192,314	4,277,780	*Bama, Mranma, Myamma.* Throughout the Province. See Part III of this Table.
A2	Arakanese	...	195,283	129,408	*Rakhaing, Yakaing.* See Part III of this Table.
A3	Yanbye	...	119,790	130,228	*Ramree.* Kyaukpyu: M. 78,763, F. 87,894; Akyab: M. 41,025, F. 42,332.
A4	Chaungtha	...	4,632	4,420	Akyab: M. 3,631, F. 3,501; Hill District of Arakan: M. 1,001, F. 919.
A5	Tavoyan	...	65,511	66,235	*Dawè.* Tavoy: M. 65,301, F. 65,125.
A6	Merguese	...	98	79	*Myeik, Beik.* Tavoy only.
A7	Yabein	...	...	...	*Zabein, Labein.* This language is still remembered on the Pegu Yomas, though it may have dropped out of every-day use.
A8	Yaw	...	...	2	Bhamo.
A9	Danu	...	36,311	36,614	Southern Shan States: M. 29,001, F. 29,684; Northern Shan States: M. 7,200, F. 6,900.
A10	Intha	...	26,981	28,026	*Angsa, Tai Nawng, Man Nawng.* Southern Shan States: M. 26,224, F. 27,245; Karenni: M. 729, F. 780.
A11	Taungyo	...	10,967	11,565	*Töru.* Southern Shan States.
A12	P'un	...	121	122	*Hpon, Hpö, Hpye, Megyaw, Samong.* Myitkyina only.
A13	Atsi	...	3,034	2,629	*Tsi, Ssi.* Myitkyina: M. 1,192, F. 1,439; Bhamo: M. 1,539, F. 873; Northern Shan States: M. 303, F. 317.
A14	Lashi	...	8,356	8,214	Myitkyina: M. 6,452, F. 6,193; Northern Shan States: M. 1,599, F. 1,703; Bhamo: M. 300, F. 318; also Putao: M. 5.
A15	Maru	...	9,827	10,750	*Lawngwaw.* Myitkyina: M. 5,132, F. 5,557; Northern Shan States: M. 4,468, F. 4,966; Bhamo: M. 209, F. 222; and Putao: M. 18, F. 5.
A16	Maingtha	...	276	63	*Achang, Ngachang, Mongsa, Lahsa Shan, Hohsa Shan, Khe-hsa.* Bhamo, Myitkyina and Katha.
B	**Lolo-Mus'o group**	...	39,413	36,273	
B1	Lis'aw	...	6,638	6,514	*Yawyin, Lisu.* Northern Shan States: M. 3,577, F. 3,535; Southern Shan States: M. 1,568, F. 1,[illegible]9; Katha: M. 823, F. 649; Myitkyina: M. 670, F. 723.
B2	Lolo	...	380	389	*Lawlaw.* Northern Shan States only.
B3	Lahu	...	11,630	11,112	*Mus'o, Manghtam.* Southern Shan States only.
B4	Akō	...	30	21	Southern Shan States only.
B5	Pyin	...	506	421	*Hpin.* Southern Shan States only.
B6	Kwi	...	1,851	1,825	*Lahu-hsi.* Southern Shan States only.
B7	Akha	...	18,335	15,930	*Kaw, I-kaw, Kha-kaw, Kao.* Southern Shan States only.
B8	Nung	...	25	39	*Anung, Khanung, Kioutse, Lutse.* Putao only.
B9	Tangsir	...	...	...	*Kwinpang.* Spoken in Putao outside the census area.
B10	Hop'a	...	...	...	Spoken in Putao District outside the census area.
B11	Wat'ao-khum	...	18	22	Myitkyina
C	**Kuki-Chin group**	...	184,025	184,855	
C1	Meit'ei	...	1,794	610	*Manipuri, Kathè.* Distribution is shown in Part III of this Table.
C2	T'ado	..	1,831	1,112	Chin Hills: M. 922, F. 910; Kyaukpyu: M. 209; F. 202.
C3	Siyin	...	1,512	1,631	*Htaote.* Chin Hills: M. 1,494, F. 1,623; Upper Chindwin: M. 18, F. 8.
C4	Sokte	...	8,597	8,766	Chin Hills: M. 8,404, F. 8,579; Upper Chindwin: M. 193, F. 187.
C5	Kamhow	...	4,361	4,303	Chin Hill: M. 3,626, F. 3,596; Upper Chindwin: M. 468, F. 425; Hill District of Arakan: M. 267, F. 282.
C6	Paite	...	580	574	*Vuite.* Chin Hills only.
C7	Yo	...	2,746	2,703	Chin Hills only.

IMPERIAL TABLE X.—*Language.* PART I B.—*Provincial Totals of Speakers of each Language*—contd.

	Language.	Males.	Females.	Remarks. (See Note 6 on page 133.)
	1	2	3	4
C8	Tashon ...	3,500	4,059	*Shunkla, Falam Chin.* Chin Hills: M. 3,306, F. 3880; Upper Chindwin: M. 194, F. 179.
C9	Yahow ...	4,588	5,457	*Zahow.* Chin Hills only.
C10	Laiyo ...	4,472	4,805	*Laizau, Hlunseo.* Chin Hills: M. 4,406, F. 4,766; Upper Chindwin: M. 66, F. 39.
C11	Kwangli ..	1,655	1,949	Chin Hills only.
C12	Ngorn ...	1,908	1,924	*Bwelkwa, Tapong.* Chin Hills.
C13	Kwelshim ...	1,163	1,295	*I, Mi Err.* Chin Hills only.
C14	Lai ..	9,700	9,738	*Haka Chin.* Chin Hills: M. 9,396, F. 9,433; Upper Chindwin: M. 304, F. 305.
C15	Tlantlang ...	...	...	Reported to be a dialect of Lai. The speakers however have all been returned as speaking Lai.
C16	Yokwa ...	97	115	Chin Hills.
C17	Lakher ...	...	6	Hill District of Arakan.
C18	Lawt'u ...	1,619	1,424	*Lohtaw.* Chin Hills only.
C19	Yotun ...	2,559	2,550	Chin Hills only.
C20	Shentang ...	2,862	2,858	Chin Hills only.
C21	Lushei ...	159	147	*Ngente.* Upper Chindwin: M. 128, F. 122; Chin Hills: M. 31, F. 25.
C22	Hualngo ...	1,490	1,660	*Whenoh.* Chin Hills only.
C23	Kyaw ...	183	168	*Chaw.* Hill District of Arakan only.
C24	Anu ...	349	363	Hill District of Arakan only.
C25	Chinbok ...	...	...	*Yawdwin, Twi-li-chang.* Pakôkku Hill Tracts. Returned as Chin (unknown).
C26	Chinbon ...	345	338	*Ur-per, Twi-sheep, Num-lan.* Recorded as such only in Akyab. It is more plentiful in Pakôkku and the Pakôkku Hill Tracts where it has been recorded as Chin (unspecified).
C27	Chinmè ...	...	...	*Rawvan.* Pakôkku. It has probably been returned as Chin (unspecified).
C28	Khami ...	13,599	12,972	*Ayaing Khami, Awa Khami, Kwe myi.* Akyab: M. 7,500, F. 6,920; Hill District of Arakan: M. 6,099, F. 6,052.
C29	Taungtha ...	2,836	3,417	*Rongtu.* Pakôkku only.
C30	Yindu ...	51	54	*Ni-du, Hniyun, Ka-dhak, Ka-chak.* Recorded in Hill District of Arakan. It is also spoken in the Pakôkku Hill Tracts where it has been recorded as Chin (unspecified).
C31	Sho ...	...	...	*Southern Chin, Asho-so.* Spoken in Thayetmyo, Minbu, Prome and Sandoway. Unfortunately it has been entered in the schedules as Chin (unspecified).
C32	Chin (unspecified kind)‡	52,864	52,626	Distribution is shown in Part III of this Table.
C33	Chaunggyi Chin ...	349	317	Akyab only.
C34	Kaukadan ...	6	3	Akyab.
C35	Kaungtso	33	24	Hill District of Arakan.
C36	Ledu ...	1,016	595	Kyaukpyu: M. 680, F. 707; Akyab: M. 336, F. 288.
C37	Matu ...	23	28	Kyaukpyu only.
C38	Saingbaung ...	3,814	3,418	Kyaukpyu: M. 3,773, F. 3,418; Akyab: M. 48.
C39	Sittu ..	2,032	1,886	Kyaukpyu only.
C40	Taman ...	32	60	Upper Chindwin only.
D	**Naga Group** ...	197	205	
D1	Naga (unspecified kind)§	80	86	Upper Chindwin only.
D2	Tangkul	117	119	Upper Chindwin only.
D3	Senkadong ...	...	...	Upper Chindwin only. This language has probably been returned as Naga (unspecified).
E	**Kachin Group** ...	70,110	75,808	
E1	Kachin	69,969	75,649	*Chingpaw, Singpho, Shingpraw, Theinbaw, Ka-hang, Khaku,*† *Kawri,*† *Maran,*† *Marip,** *Laktawng,** *Laphai,** *Nkum,**. For distribution, *see* Part II of this table.
E2	Nogmung	77	91	Putao only.
E3	Ntit	...	...	Spoken in Putao Dist. outside the census area.
E4	Pangsu	...	...	Spoken in Putao Dist. outside the census area.

*† See Note 7 on page 133.

‡ § That is, persons for whom the racial description given in the enumeration-record was only *Chin* (or *Naga*).

IMPERIAL TABLE X.—*Language*. PART IB.—*Provincial Totals of Speakers of each Language*—contd.

	Language.	Males.	Females.	Remarks. (See Note 6 on page 133.)
	1	2	3	4
E5	Kang	...	...	Spoken in Putao Dist. outside the census area.
E6	Langkhai	...	...	Spoken in Putao Dist. outside the census area.
E7	Nokkyo	64	68	Putao District only.
E8	Yoya	...	...	Spoken in Putao Dist. outside the census area.
E9	Tawhawng ...	...	...	Spoken in Putao Dist. outside the census area.
F	**Sak (Lui) Group** ...	**12,297**	**12,848**	
F1	Kadu	8,935	9,659	*A-sak.* Katha: M. 8,409, F. 9,137.
F2	Ganan	509	513	Katha; M. 205, F. 228, Upper Chindwin; M. 272, F. 285.
F3	Sak	321	293	*Thet.* Akyab District only.
F4	Daingnet	2,532	2,383	Akyab District only.
G	**Mishmi Group** ...	...	...	
G1	Khaman-Mishmi ...	...	...	Spoken in Putao Dist. outside the census area.
H	**Mro Group** ...	**7,263**	**7,061**	
H1	Mro	7,263	7,061	*Mru.* *See* Part II of this table.
I	**Tai Group**	**461,325**	**460,182**	
I1	Shan (unspecified kind)‡	162,264	164,251	For distribution, *see* Part III of this table.
I2	Shangale	237,964	236,914	*Tai-awn, Mong Leng, Tai-chaung, Shweli Shan, see* Part III of this table.
I3	Shangyi ...	9,117	8,957	*Tai-long.* See Part III of this table.
I4	Shan-Tayok ...	12,685	10,788	*Shan-Chinese, Tai-khe, Tai-khawng, Tai-Nō.* Bhamo; M. 5,212, F. 5,018; Myitkyina: M. 3,023, F. 2,427; Southern Shan States: M. 2,532, F. 2,147; Northern Shan States; M. 1,483, F. 1,028; and scattered.
I5	Daye	414	332	Southern Shan States only.
I6	Siamese	4,729	4,014	*Yodaya Shan, Htai.* Amherst: M. 2,598, F. 2,029; Mergui: M. 2,074, F. 1,954; and few scattered.
I7	Khun	16,243	16,967	Southern Shan States only.
I8	Lu	12,834	13,274	Southern Shan States only.
I9	Lao	2,307	1,544	*Yun.* Southern Shan States, M. 1,411, F. 1,458; Amherst: M. 458; Salween; M. 182, F. 44; Karenni: M. 112, F. 41; and a few scattered.
I10	Shan-Bama ...	2	3	*Tai-man.* Myitkyina.
I11	Kamti	2,766	3,138	Putao: M. 2,658, F. 2,997; Myitkyina: M. 108, F. 147.
I12	Annamese ...	...	...	*Kiao.* There are few speakers in the Southern Shan States, they have probably been returned as Shan (unspecified).
I13	Tai-Lem	...	...	
I14	Tai-Loi	...	...	
J	**Malay Group** ...	**2,739**	**2,638**	
J1	Malay	1,813	1,633	*Pashu.* Mergui: M. 1,801, F. 1,619; also a few scattered.
J2	Salon	926	1,005	*Mawken.* Mergui only.
K	**Mon Group** ...	**97,020**	**92,243**	
K1	Talaing	97,020	92,243	*Daleng, Mon, Peguan, Martabanese.* For distribution, *see* Part II of this table.
L	**Palaung-Wa Group** ...	**74,289**	**73,602**	
L1	Wa	7,211	6,537	*La, Lawa, Sawn, Son, Hsen, Khalam, Hsensum*; Northern Shan States: M. 3,600, F. 3,309; Southern Shan States; M. 3,509, F. 3,226; Mandalay: M. 2.
L2	Danaw	679	754	*Ganaw.* Southern Shan States only.
L3	En	...	...	*In.*

‡ That is, persons for whom the racial description given in the enumeration-record was only *Shan*.

IMPERIAL TABLE X.—*Language.* PART IB.—*Provincial Totals of Speakers of each Language*—contd.

	Language.	Males	Females.	Remarks. (See note 6 on page 133.)
	1	2	3	4
L4	Khamuk	195	8	*Khamu.* Southern Shan States; M. 133, F. 8. Remainder in Northern Shan States, Salween and Karenni.
L5	Lem	400	382	Southern Shan States only.
L6	Tai-Loi	...	...	*Wekut.*
L7	Yang (unspecified kind)‡	576	621	*Yin, Riang.* Southern Shan States only.
L8	Yanglam	6,374	6,479	*Karennet, Yang-wan-kun, Yang-kaw-leng.* Southern Shan States; M. 5,834, F. 5,913; Northern Shan States; M. 540, F. 566.
L9	Yangsek	...	...	*Riangleng.* Probably returned as Yang (unspecified).
L10	Palaung and Pale ...	58,904	58,821	*Katurr, Kunloi, Kwanhai, Manloi, Ngawnhawt, Rumai, Sawpana, Tawngma, Ta-ang.* Northern Shan States: M. 50,208, F. 50,884; Southern Shan States: M. 6,502, F. 5,834; Katha: M. 2,054, F. 1,993; also a few scattered.
M	**Khasi Group** ...	...	...	
M1	Khasi	...	...	Spoken in Putao District outside the census area.
N	**Karen Group¶** ...	**557,995**	**556,021**	
N1	Karen (unspecified kind)§	50,852	47,861	For distribution, *see* Part III of this table.
N2	Sgaw	183,269	185,013	*Bama-Kayin, Pahti.* For distribution, *see* Part III of this table.
N3	Paku	613	593	*Bugu.* Karenni: M. 487, F. 491; Toungoo: M. 103, F. 102; rest scattered.
N4	Wewaw	123	133	*Wewa.* Karenni: M. 116, F. 132; Tavoy: M. 7, F. 1.
N5	Monnepwa ...	35	37	*Monnepga* Toungoo only.
N6	Bwè	5,168	5,459	*Brè, Bge, Manö.* Karenni: M. 2,263, F. 2,647; Toungoo: M. 2,461, 2,390; Southern Shan States: M. 419, F. 413; also a few scattered.
N7	Brek	309	307	*Prè.* Karenni.
N8	Karenbyu	5,604	5,556	*Geba, Kunni, Konni, Tabara, Tayang.* Toungoo: M. 4,368, F. 4,495; Karenni: M. 662, F. 610; Southern Shan States: M. 322, F. 288; Yamèthin: M. 127, F. 141; remainder in Bhamo and Myaungmya.
N9	Pwo ¶	178,609	173,857	*Talaing-Kayin, Mohti, Mohteik, Shu, Blaimaw.* For distribution, *see* Part III of this table.
N10	Mopwa	...	...	*Mopga,* Spoken in Toungoo. The language has probably been returned as Karen (unspecified).
N11	Taungthu	104,637	105,898	*Pa-O, Titauk, Kunlong, Balah, Nakrai, Tawthu*: Southern Shan States: M. 71,935, F. 74,182; Thatôn: M. 25,447, F. 24,322. Others mostly in Toungoo, Pegu, Amherst, and Karenni.
N12	Padaung	7,060	6,683	*Padaw.* Southern Shan States: M. 6,732, F. 6,351; Karenni: M. 312, F. 326; and a few scattered.
N13	Yinbaw	2,632	2,730	*Yeinbaw, Gunga, Kekawngdu, Lawi.* Karenni: M. 2,288, F. 2,430; Southern Shan States: M. 328, F. 300; Myitkyina: M. 16.
N14	Gheko	1,278	1,301	*Gaku.* Toungoo: M. 650, F. 696; Southern Shan States: M. 627, F. 605.
N15	Karenni	15,803	18,685	*Kaya, Lakan, Mite, Manu-Manaw, Taru, Yintalai, Yangtalai.* Karenni: M. 12,687, F. 15,624; Southern Shan States: M. 1,665, F. 1,894; Toungoo: M. 923, F. 841; Amherst: M. 245, F. 166; rest scattered.
N16	Zayein	2,003	1,908	*Banpa, Banyang, Banyin, Banyok, Gaungto, Kalasi, Kawng-Sawng, Loilong, Hohta, Lahta, Tabaing, Zayein,* Southern Shan States: M. 1995, F. 1,899; Karenni: M. 8, F. 9.
N17	T'alaing-Kalasi ...	...	...	Spoken in Yamèthin. This language has probably been returned as Karen (unspecified) or Zayein.

‡ § That is, persons for whom the racial description given in the enumeration-record was only *Karen* (or *Yang*).

¶ See Chapter IX of the Report Volume concerning a probable defect of about 4,000 Pwo females wrongly tabulated as speakers of Burmese.

IMPERIAL TABLE X.—*Language.* PART IB.—*Provincial Totals of Speakers of each Language*—contd.

	Language.	Males.	Females.	Remarks. (See Note 6 on page 133.)
	1	2	3	4
O	**Man Group** ...	331	260	
O1	Miao	226	168	*Miao-tsu, Miaobyu. Pe Miao, Hmeng, Mung, Khe-pok.* Southern Shan States only.
O2	Yao	105	92	*Lanten.* Southern Shan States only.
R	**Chinese Group** ...	84,116	38,046	For distribution of Chinese Languages as a whole, *see* Part II of this Table.
R1	Yunnanese ...	32,675	22,941	*Anya Tayok, Momyin Tayok, Khe-long.* Northern Shan States: M. 28,232, F. 21,733. Rest in Southern Shan States, Myitkyina, Bhamo and scattered.
R2	Other Chinese Languages.	51,441	15,105	*Tayok, Tarok, Talok, Khe.* Paukpaw.*
X	**Indian Languages** ...	646,168	234,238	For distribution of Indian Languages as a whole, *see* Part II of this Table. The distribution of separate languages is not given.
	Arabic	162	67	
	Persian	388	92	
	Pashto	1,057	47	
	Baluchi	6	5	
	Kashmiri	34	22	
	Sindhi	152	15	
	Marathi	997	306	
	Oriya	45,800	1,745	
	Bihari	61	26	
	Bengali	195,041	105,098	
	Assamese	247	91	
	Hindi	14,188	5,629	
	Hindustani ...	103,905	24,723	
	Urdu	7,695	2,259	
	Punjabi	13,806	4,039	
	Gujarati	9,410	3,730	
	Rajasthani ...	953	214	
	Naipali	15,277	6,629	
	Garhwali	240	23	
	Goanese	244	26	
	Tamil	101,392	50,866	
	Malayalam ...	5,327	599	
	Kanarese	756	59	
	Kodagu	1	...	
	Telugu	127,591	27,928	
	Unspecified ...	538	...	
Y	**European Languages**	14,178	10,263	For distribution of European Languages as a whole, *see* Part II of this Table. With the exception of English the distribution of separate languages is not given.
	English	13,955	10,130	
	Danish	1	...	
	Dutch	17	7	
	Flemish	1	...	
	French	53	61	
	German	1	...	
	Greek	7	3	
	Italian	20	25	
	Portuguese ...	116	32	
	Russian	1	1	
	Spanish	2	3	
	Swedish	2	1	
	Swiss	2	...	
Z	**Other Languages** ...	599	405	For distribution of "Other Languages" as a whole, *see* Part II of this Table. The distribution of separate languages is not given.
	Hebrew	207	128	
	Armenian	48	34	
	Singhalese ...	72	12	
	Turkish	1	...	
	Japanese	224	227	
	Tagalog and other Philippine languages.	42	3	
	Nicobarese ...	5	1	

* See Note 7 on page 133.

IMPERIAL TABLE X.—*Language.*] PART IC.—*Alphabetical Index for Indigenous Races and Languages.*

NOTE.—*The letter against each name indicates the Group to which it belongs and the number is its serial number in that Group in Part IB of this Table or Part I of Imperial Table XIII.*

Group	Name
A18	Achang
B7	Akha
B4	Akö
A10	Angsa
I12	Annamese
B8	Anung
C24	Anu
R1	Anya Tayok
A2	Arakanese
S3	Arakan-Kaman*
S1	Arakan-Mahomedan*
F1	Asak
C31	Asho-zo
A13	Atsi
C28	Awa Khami
C28	Ayaing Khami
N11	Balah
A1	Bama
N2	Bama-kayin
N16	Banpa
N16	Banyang
N16	Banyin
N16	Banyok
A6	Beik
N6	Bge
L8	Black-Riang
L8	Black-yin
N9	Blaimaw
N6	Brè
N7	Brek
A1	Burmese
N6	Bwè
C12	Bwelkwa
C33	Chaunggyi Chin
A4	Chaungtha
C23	Chaw
C32	Chin (unspecified kind).
C25	Chinbok
C26	Chinbon
R2	Chinese (other than Yünnanese).
C27	Chinmè
E1	Chingpaw
F4	Daingnet
K1	Daleng
L2	Danaw
A9	Danu
A5	Dawè
I5	Daye
L3	En
C8	Falam Chin
N14	Gaku
F2	Ganan
L2	Ganaw
N16	Gaungto
N8	Geba
N14	Gheko
N13	Gunnga
C14	Haka Chin
C10	Hlunseo
O1	Hmeng
C30	Hniyun
B10	Hop'a
A16	Hohsa-Shan
N16	Hohta
B5	Hpin
A12	Hpö
A12	Hpon
A12	Hpye
L1	Hsen
L1	Hsensum
I6	Htai
C3	Htaote
C22	Hualngo
C13	I
B7	I-Kaw
L3	In
A10	Intha
C30	Ka-chak
E1	Kachin
C30	Ka-dhak
F1	Kadu
E1	Kahang
N16	Kalasi
S3	Kaman* (Arakan-Kaman).
C5	Kamhow
I11	Kamti-Shan
E5	Kang
B7	Kao
N1	Karen (unspecified kind).
N8	Karenbyu
L8	Karennet
N15	Karenni
C1	Kathè
C34	Kaukadan
C35	Kaungtso
B7	Kaw
N16	Kawng-Sawng
E1	Kawri†
N13	Kekawngdu
B7	Kha-kaw
E1	Khaku†
L1	Khalam
G1	Khaman-Mishmi
C28	Khami
I11	Khamti
L4	Khamu
L4	Khamuk
B8	Khanung
M1	Khasi
R2	Khe
A16	Khe-hsa
R1	Khe-long
O1	Khe-pok
I7	Khun
I12	Kiao
B8	Kioutze
N8	Konni
N11	Kunlong
N8	Kunni
C11	Kwangli
L10	Kwanhai
C13	Kwelshim
C28	Kwe-myi
B6	Kwi
B10	Kwinpang
C23	Kyaw
L1	La
A7	Labein
A16	Lahsa-Shan
N16	Lahta
E1	Lahtawng*
B3	Lahu
B6	Lahu-hsi
C14	Lai
C10	Laiyo
C10	Laizau
C17	Lakher
N15	Lakan
O2	Lanten
E6	Langkhai
I9	Lao
E1	Laphai*
A14	Lashi
A15	Lawngwaw
L1	Lawa
N13	Lawi
B2	Lawlaw
C18	Lawt'u
C36	Ledu
L5	Lem
B1	Lis'aw
B1	Lisu
N16	Loilong
N15	Lokan
B2	Lolo
C18	Lohtaw
I8	Lu
C21	Lushei
B8	Lutze
A16	Maingtha
J1	Malay
B3	Manghtam
C1	Manipuri
L10	Manloi
A10	Man-Nawng
N6	Manö
N15	Manu-Manaw
E1	Marant†
E1	Marip*
K1	Martabanese
A15	Maru
C37	Matu
J2	Mawken
A12	Megyaw
C30	Men
C1	Meit'ei
A6	Merguese
O1	Miao
O1	Miaobyu
O1	Miaotsu
C13	Mi-err
G1	Mishmi
N15	Mite
N9	Mohteik
N9	Mohti
R1	Momyin-Tayok
K1	Mon
I2	Mong Leng
A16	Mongsa
N5	Monnepga
N5	Monnepwa
N10	Mopga
N10	Mopwa
A1	Mranma
H1	Mro
H1	Mru
B3	Mus'o
N9	Muhteik
N9	Muhti
O1	Mung

IMPERIAL TABLE X.—*Language*. PART IC.—*Alphabetical Index for Indigenous Races and Languages*—concld.

NOTE.—*The letter against each name indicates the Group to which it belongs and the number is its serial number in that Group in Part IB of this Table or Part I of Imperial Table XIII.*

Group	Name
A1	Myanma
A6	Myeik
D1	Naga (unspecified kind)
N11	Nakrai
A16	Ngachang
L10	Ngawnhawt
C21	Ngente
C12	Ngorn
C30	Ni-du
E1	Nkum*
E2	Nogmung
E7	Nokkyo
E3	Ntit
C26	Num-Lan
B8	Nung
N12	Padaung
N12	Padaw
C6	Paite
N2	Pahti
N3	Paku
L10	Palaung
L10	Pale
E4	Pangsu
N11	Pa-o
J1	Pashu
R2	Paukpaw*
K1	Peguan
O1	Pe-Miao
N7	Pre
N9	Pwo
A12	P'un
B5	Pyin
A2	Rakhaing
A3	Ramree
C27	Rawvan
L9	Red-Riang
L9	Red-Yin
L7	Riang
L9	Riangleng
C29	Rongtu
L10	Rumai
C38	Saingbaung
F3	Sak
J2	Salon
A12	Samong
L1	Sawn
D3	Senkadong
N2	Sgaw
I1	Shan (unspecified kind)
I10	Shan-Bama
I4	Shan-Chinese
I2	Shangale
I3	Shangyi
I4	Shan-Tayok
C20	Shentang
E1	Shingpraw
C31	Sho
N9	Shu
C8	Shunkla
I2	Shweli-Shan
I6	Siamese
E1	Singpho
C39	Sittu
C3	Siyin
C4	Sokte
L1	Son
C31	Southern Chin
A13	Szi
L10	Ta-ang
N16	Tabaing
N8	Tabara
C2	T'ado
I2	Tai-awn
I2	Tai-chaung
I4	Taikhawng
I4	Tai-khe
I13	Tai-Lem
I14	Tai-Loi (of Mogôk)
L6	Tai-Loi (Southern Shan States)
I3	Tai Long
I10	Tai-Man
A10	Tai-Nawng
I4	Tai-Nō
I2	Tai-on
K1	Talaing
N9	Talaing-kayin
N17	T'alaing Kalasi
R2	Talok
C40	Taman
D1	Tangkul
B9	Tangsir
C12	Tapong
R2	Tarok
N15	Taru
C8	Tashon
C29	Taungtha
N11	Taungthu
A11	Taungyo
A5	Tavoyan
E9	Tawhawng
L10	Tawngma
N11	Tawthu
R2	Tayok
E1	Theinbaw
F3	Thet
N11	Titauk
A11	Töru
A13	Tsi
C25	Twi-li-chang
C26	Twi-sheep
C26	Ur-per
C6	Vuite
L1	Wa
B11	Wat'ao-khum
L6	Wekut
N4	Wewa
N4	Wewaw
C22	Whenoh
A7	Yabein
C9	Yahow
A2	Yakaing
A3	Yanbye
L7	Yang (unspecified kind)
L8	Yang-kaw-Leng
L8	Yang Lam
L9	Yang-Sek
N15	Yangtalai
L8	Yang-wan-kun
O2	Yao
A8	Yaw
C25	Yawdwin
B1	Yawyin
L7	Yin
N13	Yinbaw
C30	Yindu
N15	Yintalai
C7	Yo
I6	Yodaya
C16	Yokwa
C19	Yotun
E8	Yoya
I9	Yun
R1	Yünnanese
A7	Zabein
C9	Zahow
N16	Zarein
N16	Zayein
S2	Zerbadi*

* † See Note 7 on page 133 for the meanings of these marks.

Serial No.	District or State.	Total Population.		A.—Burma Group.		B.—Lolo-Mus'o Group.		C.—Kuki-Chin Group.	
		Males.	Females.	Males.	Females.	Males.	Females.	Males.	Females.
	1	2	3	4	5	6	7	8	9
	PROVINCIAL TOTAL ...	**6,735,516**	**6,433,583**	**4,533,501**	**4,699,135**	**39,413**	**36,273**	**134,025**	**134,355**
	DIVISIONAL BURMA ...	**5,991,623**	**5,706,785**	**4,432,263**	**4,599,830**	**1,537**	**1,451**	**133,936**	**134,333**
	Arakan Division	*472,227*	*437,019*	*292,098*	*300,021*	..	..	*32,941*	*31,674*
1	Akyab	309,564	266,866	154,995	152,262	...	...	12,891	12,120
2	Hill District of Arakan ...	10,790	10,124	1,135	988	...	...	8,006	7,897
3	Kyaukpyu	96,569	103,304	85,478	94,158	...	...	8,325	7,750
4	Sandoway	55,304	56,725	50,490	52,613	...	...	3,719	3,907
	Pegu Division	*1,258,914*	*1,050,879*	*886,291*	*889,470*	*1*	...	*5,983*	*5,622*
5	Rangoon Town ...	236,689	105,273	60,796	58,216	...	...	55	52
6	Insein	156,794	136,289	122,311	107,985	...	...	88	86
7	Hanthawaddy ...	201,043	163,581	142 703	138,157	...	...	52	...
8	Tharrawaddy	246,261	246,168	220,856	229,010	...	...	694	525
9	Pegu	235,324	210,296	180,148	175,682	1	...	818	636
10	Prome	182,803	188,772	169,477	180,420	...	...	4,276	4,323
	Irrawaddy Division ..	*1,048,877*	*981,667*	*804,932*	*804,294*	..	..	*1,397*	*1,456*
11	Bassein	252,947	236,526	185,492	185,143	...	..	115	111
12	Henzada	273,439	277,481	244,264	253,118	...	...	1,243	1,342
13	Myaungmya	196,757	173,794	126,570	121,210	...	...	12	1
14	Ma-ubin	168,513	161,593	121,095	126,047	..	...	22	...
15	Pyapôn	156,721	132,273	127,581	118,776	...	...	5	1
	Tenasserim Division ..	*847,445*	*766,078*	*401,646*	*395,635*	..	..	*294*	*268*
16	Toungoo	197,505	184,378	134,790	134,716	...	...	292	263
17	Salween	26,811	23,568	1,562	900	...	...	...	...
18	Thatôn	245,909	225,191	85,536	82,854	...	...	...	...
19	Amherst	223,348	194,562	65,303	63354	...	...	2	...
20	Tavoy	80,994	75,792	69,439	69,705	...	...	...	...
21	Mergui	72,878	62,587	44,956	44,106	...	...	...	...
	Magwe Division	*705,247*	*738,627*	*652,878*	*693,697*	..	..	*36,225*	*37,088*
22	Thayetmyo	125,283	130,123	113,779	119,786	..	...	9,226	9,508
23	Pakôkku	223,943	241,828	214,742	233,093	...	...	7,717	8,426
24	Minbu	134,495	139,807	122,884	131,340	...	...	8,923	8,023
25	Magwe	211,686	211,566	201,381	209,432	...	..	760	1,013
26	Pakôkku Hill Tracts ...	9,840	10,203	92	46	...	...	9,599	10,113
	Mandalay Division ..	*485,894*	*418,467*	*279,667*	*285,811*	*1,536*	*1,451*	*1,181*	*284*
27	Mandalay	182,999	173,622	152,861	168,936	...	...	1,066	191
	Mandalay City ...	*77,763*	*71,154*	*62,866*	*67,299*	...	...	*726*	*6*
28	Bhamo	56,688	56,072	15,628	14,444	...	18	8	...
29	Myitkyina	63,419	54,963	21,414	18,925	688	745	46	40
30	Katha	128,444	125,281	89,711	88,925	823	649	60	3
31	Putao	4,144	3,529	53	21	25	39	1	...
	Sagaing Division	*641,290*	*709,106*	*550,631*	*622,747*	..	..	*55,288*	*57,860*
32	Shwebo	184,[illegible]08	206,576	181,510	205,630	...	...	11	...
33	Sagaing	155,054	171,854	153,032	171,116	...	...	107	107
34	Lower Chindwin ...	156,693	186,187	154,842	185,726	...	...	6	1
35	Upper Chindwin ...	90,713	88,532	61,184	60,241	...	...	2,262	1,930
36	Chin Hills	54,122	55,957	63	34	...	...	52,847	55,322
	Meiktila Division	*582,229*	*615,542*	*564,120*	*608,655*	..	..	*682*	*642*
37	Kyauksè	70,449	72,228	69,182	71,800	...	...	2	4
38	Meiktila	137,573	152,324	133,652	151,127	...	...	1	...
39	Yamèthin	160,913	162,276	150,140	157,522	...	...	668	638
40	Myingyan	213,294	228,714	211,146	228,206	...	...	11	...
	EASTERN STATES ...	**743,893**	**726,798**	**101,238**	**99,305**	**37,876**	**34,822**	**89**	**22**
41	Northern Shan States ...	285,700	273,523	26,495	24,157	3,957	3,924	23	...
42	Southern Shan States ...	427,064	420,554	73,350	73,974	33,919	30,898	66	22
43	Karenni	31,129	32,721	1,393	1,174	...	...	...	...

PART II.—*Language-Groups in each District.*

[*Continued on next page.*

D.—Naga Group.		E.—Kachin Group.		F.—Sak (Lui) Group.		H.—Mro Group.		I.—Tai (Shan) Group.		J.—Malay Group.		Serial No. of District, etc. (See column 1).
Males.	Females.	Males.	Females.	Males.	Females.	Males.	Females.	Males.	Females.	Males.	Females.	
10	11	12	13	14	15	16	17	18	19	20	21	
197	**205**	**70,110**	**75,808**	**12,297**	**12,848**	**7,263**	**7,061**	**461,325**	**460,182**	**2,739**	**2,638**	
197	**205**	**42,244**	**45,292**	**12,200**	**12,825**	**7,263**	**7,061**	**107,528**	**106,423**	**2,739**	**2,638**	
..	..	..	..	*2,858*	*2,676*	*7,263*	*7,061*	*22*	*1*	..	..	
...	...	...	...	2,853	2,676	6,218	6,014	13	1	...	...	1
...	...	...	...	...	...	1,045	1,047	...	...	..	...	2
...	...	...	...	..	...	...	...	3	...	...	...	3
...	...	...	...	..	...	...	...	6	...	...	...	4
..	..	*18*	*6*	..	..	..	..	*7,686*	*7,864*	*7*	*7*	
...	...	15	...	...	...	...	...	69	77	2	...	5
...	...	1	..	...	...	...	...	2,333	2,308	...	...	6
...	...	...	...	...	...	...	...	1,151	1,264	5	7	7
...	...	...	...	...	...	...	...	1,456	1,644	...	...	8
...	...	...	...	...	.	...	...	2,190	2,105	...	...	9
...	...	2	6	...	...	...	...	387	456	...	...	10
..	..	..	..	..	..	..	..	*844*	*299*	..	*8*	
...	...	...	...	...	...	..	...	125	101	...	...	11
...	..	...	...	...	...	...	...	124	68	...	...	12
...	...	...	...	...	...	...	..	66	82	...	...	13
...	...	...	...	...	...	...	...	21	23	...	3	14
...	...	...	...	..	...	...	...	8	5	...	...	15
..	..	*1*	..	..	..	..	..	*22,271*	*19,178*	*2,731*	*2,628*	
...	...	...	...	...	...	...	...	5,624	5,000	..	...	16
...	...	...	...	...	...	...	...	2,301	1,597	...	...	17
...	...	...	...	...	...	...	...	2,709	2,280	4	...	18
...	...	1	..	...	...	...	...	5,503	4,725	...	4	19
...	...	...	...	...	...	...	...	35	18	...	...	20
...	...	...	...	...	...	..	..	6,099	5,558	2,727	2,624	21
..	..	..	..	..	..	..	..	*23*	*21*	..	..	
...	...	...	...	...	...	...	...	2	1	...	...	22
...	...	...	...	...	...	...	...	1	1	...	...	23
...	...	...	...	...	...	..	...	13	14	...	...	24
...	...	...	...	...	...	...	...	7	5	...	...	25
...	...	...	...	..	...	...	...	...	...	...	...	26
..	..	*42,186*	*45,257*	*9,007*	*9,789*	..	..	*58,872*	*58,921*	*1*	..	
...	...	698	63	...	...	...	...	1,787	1,739	1	...	27
...	..	*61*	*6*	...	..	...	...	*49*	*4*	*1*	...	
...	...	20,493	24,283	142	170	...	..	16,093	15,927	...	...	28
...	...	17,505	17,644	251	254	...	...	14,600	13,913	...	...	29
...	...	3,089	3,074	8,614	9,365	...	...	18,196	19,313	...	...	30
...	...	351	193	...	...	...	...	2,696	3,029	...	..	31
197	*205*	*88*	*28*	*340*	*360*	..	..	*28,696*	*25,019*	..	..	
..	...	45	2	3	6	...	...	5	6	...	...	32
...	...	...	...	...	...	...	...	6	2	...	...	33
...	...	...	...	..	...	...	...	17	7	...	...	34
197	205	43	26	337	354	...	...	23,668	25,004	...	...	35
..	...	...	...	...	...	...	...	..	...	...	...	36
..	..	*1*	*1*	..	..	..	..	*214*	*180*	..	..	
...	...	...	...	...	...	...	...	28	27	...	...	37
..	...	...	...	...	...	...	...	43	11	...	...	38
...	...	1	1	..	...	...	...	143	90	.	...	39
...	...	...	...	...	...	...	...	...	2	...	...	40
...	...	**27,866**	**30,516**	**97**	**23**	...	...	**353,797**	**353,759**	...	...	
...	...	27,796	30,422	97	23	...	...	135,044	136,798	...	...	41
..	...	70	94	...	...	...	...	211,144	210,446	...	...	42
...	...	...	...	...	...	...	...	7,609	6,515	...	...	43

Serial No.	District or State.		K.—Mon Group. Males.	K.—Mon Group. Females.	L.—Palaung-Wa Group. Males.	L.—Palaung-Wa Group. Females.	M.—Khasi Group. Males.	M.—Khasi Group. Females.	N.—Karen Group. Males.	N.—Karen Group. Females.
	1		22	23	24	25	26	27	28	29
	PROVINCIAL TOTAL	...	**97,020**	**92,243**	**74,239**	**73,602**	..	...	**557,995**	***556,021**
	DIVISIONAL BURMA	...	**96,978**	**92,236**	**2,238**	**2,103**	...	...	**451,657**	***444,771**
	Arakan Division	..	..	..	..	..	..	..	*67*	*7*
1	Akyab ...	...	...	...	...	...	...	...	1	1
2	Hill District of Arakan	...	...	...	...	...	...	...	1	...
3	Kyaukpyu ...	...	...	...	...	...	...	...	...	...
4	Sandoway ...	...	...	...	...	...	...	...	65	6
	Pegu Division	..	*820*	*276*	..	..	..	..	*54,188*	*55,918*
5	Rangoon Town	...	26	10	...	...	...	...	844	679
6	Insein ...	...	49	37	...	...	...	...	16,679	17,407
7	Hanthawaddy	...	6	6	.	...	...	...	8,003	8,496
8	Tharrawaddy	...	..	...	...	...	...	...	11,746	12,118
9	Pegu ...	...	239	223	...	...	...	...	15,353	15,500
10	Prome ...	...	...	...	...	..	...	...	1,558	1,718
	Irrawaddy Division	..	*150*	*134*	..	..	..	..	*159,425*	**160,898*
11	Bassein ...	...	34	53	...	...	...	...	46,746	48,116
12	Henzada ...	...	...	...	...	...	...	...	18,871	21,080
13	Myaungmya	...	13	26	..	...	...	...	49,984	49,718
14	Ma-ubin ...	...	...	...	...	...	...	...	36,808	*33,819
15	Pyapôn ...	..	103	55	...	...	...	...	7,016	7,660
	Tenasserim Division	..	*96,600*	*91,821*	*66*	*17*	..	..	*284,887*	*226,861*
16	Toungoo ...	...	176	169	20	...	...	...	38,584	36,853
17	Salween ...	...	8	...	21	...	...	...	22,149	20,957
18	Thatôn ...	...	18,342	17,859	13	...	...	...	117,307	114,197
19	Amherst ...	...	77,574	73,454	12	17	...	...	42,265	40,180
20	Tavoy ..	...	348	284	...	...	...	...	5,061	5,193
21	Mergui ...	...	52	55	...	...	...	...	9,021	8,979
	Magwe Division	..	*8*	*2*	..	..	..	..	*222*	*88*
22	Thayetmyo ...	...	...	...	...	...	...	...	54	17
23	Pakôkku ...	...	...	...	...	...	...	...	74	1
24	Minbu ...	...	3	...	...	..	...	...	46	11
25	Magwe ...	...	...	2	...	...	...	...	48	9
26	Pakôkku Hill Tracts	...	...	...	...	...	...	..	...	...
	Mandalay Division	..	..	*1*	*2,172*	*2,086*	..	..	*611*	*122*
27	Mandalay ...	...	...	...	2	...	...	...	34	52
	Mandalay City	...	...	...	...	...	...	...	*15*	*35*
28	Bhamo ...	...	...	1	116	93	...	...	194	32
29	Myitkyina ...	...	...	...	...	...	...	...	37	14
30	Katha ...	...	...	...	2,054	1,993	..	...	346	24
31	Putao ...	...	...	...	...	...	...	...	...	...
	Sagaing Division	..	..	..	..	..	..	..	*224*	*78*
32	Shwebo ...	...	...	...	...	...	...	...	134	42
33	Sagaing ...	...	...	...	...	...	...	...	14	5
34	Lower Chindwin	...	...	...	...	...	...	...	32	10
35	Upper Chindwin	...	...	...	...	...	...	...	34	4
36	Chin Hills ...	...	...	...	...	...	...	...	10	6
	Meiktila Division	..	*5*	*2*	..	..	..	..	*2,588*	*1,859*
37	Kyauksè ...	...	...	...	...	...	...	...	13	18
38	Meiktila ...	...	1	...	...	...	...	...	238	10
39	Yamèthin ...	...	4	...	...	...	...	...	2,328	1,825
40	Myingyan ...	...	...	2	...	...	...	...	9	6
	EASTERN STATES	...	**42**	**7**	**72,001**	**71,499**	..	...	**106,338**	**111,250**
41	Northern Shan States	...	1	...	54,348	54,761	...	...	392	25
42	Southern Shan States	...	6	...	17,633	16,738	...	...	84,385	86,266
43	Karenni ...	...	35	7	20	...	...	...	21,561	24,959

* See footnote ¶ on page 138.

PART II.—*Language-Groups in each District*—concld.

O.—Man Group.		R.—Chinese Group.		X.—Indian Languages.		Y.—European Languages.				Z.—Other Languages.		Serial No. of District, etc. (See column 1).
						English.		Other European Languages.				
Males.	Females.	Males.	Females.	Males.	Females.	Males.	Females.	Males.	Females.	Males.	Females.	
30	31	32	33	34	35	36	37	38	39	40	41	
331	**260**	**84,116**	**38,046**	**646,168**	**234,238**	**13,955**	**10,130**	**223**	**133**	**599**	**405**	
...	...	**53,438**	**15,858**	**633,039**	**231,359**	**13,549**	**9,869**	**221**	**126**	**596**	**405**	
..	..	*587*	*184*	*186,152*	*95,286*	*292*	*156*	*2*	*1*	..	*8*	
...	...	423	113	131,900	93,537	268	138	2	1	...	3	1
...	...	...	...	595	191	8	1	...	...	...	...	2
...	...	67	15	2,691	1,379	5	2	...	...	..	...	3
...	...	47	6	966	179	11	14	...	..	...	...	4
..	..	*23,808*	*8,550*	*272,626*	*76,217*	*7,977*	*6,059*	*158*	*71*	*466*	*329*	
...	...	13,110	5,644	154,430	35,062	6,755	5,160	147	61	440	312	5
...	...	1,990	587	22,812	7,373	522	485	...	10	9	11	6
...	...	2,711	710	46,012	14,716	394	225	2	...	4	...	7
...	...	1,317	350	10,112	2,466	73	55	3	...	4	...	8
...	...	3,403	1,039	33,004	15,008	162	98	...	...	6	5	9
...	...	772	220	6,256	1,592	71	36	1	...	3	1	10
..	..	*10,688*	*2,660*	*71,060*	*12,197*	*861*	*221*	*6*	*4*	*19*	*17*	
...	...	2,274	584	17,946	2,273	205	132	3	3	7	10	11
...	...	1,145	348	7,717	1,454	72	49	3	1	...	1	12
...	...	3,270	702	16,814	2,029	25	20	...	...	3	6	13
...	...	1,255	245	9,352	1,443	30	13	...	...	...	...	14
...	...	2,739	771	19,238	4,998	29	7	...	...	9	...	15
..	..	*9,747*	*2,159*	*78,467*	*26,820*	*1,218*	*1,146*	*27*	*17*	*90*	*83*	
...	...	1,358	403	16,365	6,581	279	373	15	17	2	3	16
...	...	73	4	686	108	11	2	...	...	...	...	17
...	...	1,456	525	20,496	7,456	46	20	...	...	...	...	18
...	...	2,054	715	29,942	11,450	620	656	4	...	8	5	19
...	...	2,041	102	3,928	408	134	73	...	...	8	9	20
...	...	2,765	410	7,050	817	128	22	8	...	72	16	21
..	..	*911*	*205*	*14,448*	*2,801*	*589*	*174*	*2*	..	*1*	*6*	
...	...	208	69	1,972	737	42	5	...	...	...	...	22
...	...	149	28	1,226	265	34	14	...	...	...	...	23
...	...	250	60	2,331	354	44	5	1	...	...	...	24
...	...	304	48	8,767	901	417	150	1	...	1	6	25
...	...	...	...	147	44	2	...	...	...	...	...	26
..	..	*6,603*	*1,779*	*86,970*	*11,709*	*2,598*	*1,762*	*25*	*80*	*15*	*15*	
...	...	1,511	305	22,639	6,602	2,366	1,630	21	30	13	14	27
...	...	*1,170*	*218*	*12,022*	*2,900*	*824*	*653*	*20*	*29*	*9*	*4*	
...	...	1,160	513	2,981	563	68	27	4		1	1	28
...	...	1,929	288	6,881	3,093	67	47	...	...	1	...	29
...	...	1,830	661	3,631	1,221	90	53	...	...	...	...	30
...	...	173	12	838	230	7	5	...	...	...	...	31
..	..	*552*	*112*	*10,119*	*8,088*	*206*	*117*	*4*	*2*	..	..	
...	...	240	55	2,693	799	63	34	4	2	...	...	32
...	...	77	13	1,775	583	43	28	...	...	...	...	33
...	...	118	26	1,643	391	35	20	...	...	...	...	34
...	...	90	9	2,855	744	43	15	...	...	...	...	35
...	...	27	9	1,153	566	22	20	...	...	...	...	36
..	..	*1,102*	*269*	*18,202*	*8,746*	*858*	*235*	*2*	*1*	*5*	*2*	
...	...	133	54	1,064	312	26	13	1	...	...	...	37
...	..	273	28	3,215	1,044	147	104	...	...	3	...	38
...	...	499	129	7,092	1,959	157	112	...	...	1	...	39
...	...	197	58	1,901	431	28	6	1	1	1	2	40
331	**260**	**30,678**	**22,188**	**13,129**	**2,879**	**406**	**261**	**2**	**7**	**3**	...	
...	...	28,863	21,838	8,403	1,427	278	148	...	...	3	..	41
331	260	1,696	339	4,345	1,400	119	110	...	7	...	...	42
...	...	119	11	381	52	9	3	2	...	...	...	43

Serial No.	District or State.	A1.—Burmese.		A2 and A3.—Arakanese and Yanbye.*		A4.—Other Burmese dialects.		C1.—Meit'ei (Manipuri).	
		Males.	Females.	Males.	Females.	Males.	Females.	Males.	Females.
	1	2	3	4	5	6	7	8	9
	PROVINCIAL TOTAL ...	**4,122,314**	**4,277,780**	**245,073**	**252,636**	**166,114**	**168,719**	**1,794**	**610**
	DIVISIONAL BURMA ...	**4,101,626**	**4,261,666**	**245,061**	**252,633**	**85,576**	**85,531**	**1,778**	**607**
	Arakan Division	*45,821*	*45,445*	*242,145*	*250,154*	*4,632*	*4,422*	*88*	*26*
1	Akyab	2,772	2,413	148,592	146,346	3,631	3,503	31	26
2	Hill District of Arakan ...	9	15	125	54	1,001	919	...	...
3	Kyaukpyu	5,372	5,087	80,106	89,071	...	...	...	...
4	Sandoway	37,168	37,930	13,322	14,683	...	...	2	...
	Pegu Division	*886,159*	*889,409*	*129*	*57*	*8*	*4*	*125*	*48*
5	Rangoon Town ...	60,674	58,165	120	50	2	1	49	48
6	Insein	112,305	107,982	6	3	...	...	...	...
7	Hanthawaddy ...	142,702	138,152	...	2	1	3	49	...
8	Tharrawaddy ...	220,856	219,010	...	...	...	...	6	...
9	Pegu	180,147	175,680	1	2	...	...	...	...
10	Prome	169,475	180,420	2	..	...	...	21	...
	Irrawaddy Division ..	*802,182*	*† 801,999*	*2,744*	*2,295*	*6*	...	*47*	...
11	Bassein	182,828	182,872	2,661	2,271	3	...	2	...
12	Henzada	244,260	253,118	4	...	...	...	8	
13	Myaungmya	126,493	121,186	77	24	...	...	10	...
14	Ma-ubin	121,024	† 126,047	...	...	1	...	22	...
15	Pyapôn	127,577	118,776	2	...	2	...	5	...
	Tenasserim Division ..	*835,925*	*829,312*	*20*	*12*	*65,701*	*66,311*	*6*	...
16	Toungoo	134,730	134,716	1	...	59	...	4	...
17	Salween	1,556	900	...	...	6	...	...	...
18	Thatôn	85,497	82,851	1	...	38	3	...	...
19	Amherst	65,161	63,249	4	3	198	102	2	...
20	Tavoy	4,029	3,494	11	7	65,399	66,204	...	...
21	Mergui	44,952	44,102	3	2	1	2	...	...
	Magwe Division	*652,878*	*693,695*	*5*	*2*	...	...	*3*	...
22	Thayetmyo	113,779	119,786	...	...	...	...	...	...
23	Pakôkku	214,742	233,092	...	1	...	...	1	...
24	Minbu	122,880	131,339	4	1	...	...	...	...
25	Magwe ...	201,380	209,432	1	...	...	...	2	...
26	Pakôkku Hill Tracts ...	92	46	...	...	..	...	...	...
	Mandalay Division ..	*264,426*	*270,409*	*8*	*108*	*15,288*	*14,794*	*962*	*209*
27	Mandalay	152,855	162,888	6	108	...	...	850	189
	Mandalay City ...	*62,860*	*67,191*	*6*	*108*	.	..	*724*	*4*
28	Bhamo	13,477	13,007	...	...	2,151	1,437	8	...
29	Myitkyina	8,450	5,614	...	.	12,964	13,311	44	17
30	Katha	89,614	88,884	2	...	95	41	60	3
31	Putao	30	16	..	...	23	5	...	...
	Sagaing Division	*550,627*	*622,747*	*8*	...	*1*	...	*597*	*320*
32	Shwebo	181,510	205,630	...	...	...	...	11	...
33	Sagaing	153,032	171,116	...	...	...	...	107	107
34	Lower Chindwin ...	154,842	185,726	...	...	...	...	1	1
35	Upper Chindwin ...	61,180	60,241	3	...	1	...	471	212
36	Chin Hills	63	34	...	...	...	...	7	...
	Meiktila Division	*564,118*	*608,650*	*7*	*5*	...	...	*5*	*4*
37	Kyauksè	69,181	71,800	1	...	...	...	2	4
38	Meiktila	133,651	151,127	1	...	...	...	...	...
39	Yamèthin	150,135	157,520	5	2	...	...	...	...
40	Myingyan	211,146	228,203	...	3	...	...	3	...
	EASTERN STATES ...	**20,688**	**16,114**	**12**	**3**	**80,538**	**83,188**	**16**	**3**
41	Northern Shan States ...	12,933	10,267	12	3	13,580	13,887	...	...
42	Southern Shan States ...	7,172	5,483	...	...	66,178	68,491	16	3
43	Karenni	613	364	...	...	780	810	...	...

* Part IB of the table gives the location for Yanbye alone; other figures in this column are for Arakanese.

† Probably roughly 4,000 in excess; see footnote ¶ on page 138.

Distribution by Districts of Selected Languages. [*Continued on next page.*

C8.—Chin (unspecified).		C.—Other Chin dialects.		11.—Shan (unspecified).		12.—Shangale.		13.—Shangyi.		I.—Other Shan dialects		Serial No. of District, etc. (See column 1).
Males.	Females.	Males.	Females.	Males.	Females.	Males.	Females.	Males.	Females.	Males.	Females.	
10	11	12	13	14	15	16	17	18	19	20	21	
52,864	**52,626**	**79,367**	**81,119**	**162,264**	**164,251**	**237,964**	**236,914**	**9,117**	**8,957**	**51,980**	**50,060**	
52,791	**52,607**	**79,367**	**81,119**	**32,530**	**32,578**	**49,833**	**50,544**	**8,430**	**8,492**	**16,735**	**14,809**	
10,634	***10,593***	***22,274***	***21,055***	***10***	***1***	***12***	..	..	..	..	..	
4,284	4,228	8,576	7,866	1	1	12	...	...	..	..	...	1
1,025	949	6,981	6,948	...	...	...	...	...	..	...	...	2
1,608	1,509	6,717	6,241	3	...	...	...	...	...	...	...	3
3,717	3,907	...	...	6	...	...	...	...	...	...	...	4
5,858	***5,574***	..	..	***4,369***	***4,646***	***263***	***252***	***2,768***	***2,877***	***186***	***79***	
6	4	...	...	65	71	...	...	...	...	4	6	5
28	86	...	...	178	173	244	237	1,779	1,826	132	72	6
3	...	...	...	1,151	1,264	...	...	...	..	...	...	7
688	525	...	...	1,456	1,642		2	...	...	...	...	8
818	636	...	...	1,135	1,043	19	13	988	1,048	48	1	9
4,255	4,323	...	...	384	453	...	...	1	3	2	...	10
1,350	***1,455***	..	..	***162***	***148***	***36***	***63***	***146***	***88***	..	..	
113	111	...	...	1	11	32	18	92	72	...	...	11
1,235	1,342	...	...	107	72	4	..	13	16	...	...	12
2	1	...	...	25	37	...	45	41	...	...	...	13
...	...	...	...	21	23	...	...	...	...	...	...	14
...	1	...	...	8	5	...	...	...	...	...	...	15
288	***263***	..	..	***12,311***	***11,212***	***3,596***	***3,057***	***1,018***	***867***	***5,346***	***4,042***	
288	263	...	...	4,433	3,781	818	873	369	346	4	...	16
...	...	...	...	7	7	1,989	1,543	99	...	200	47	17
...	...	...	...	1,411	1,180	748	596	550	500	...	4	18
...	...	...	...	2,406	2,630	41	45	...	21	3,056	2,029	19
...	...	...	...	29	10	...	...	...	...	6	8	20
...	...	...	...	4,025	3,604	...	...	...	...	2,074	1,954	21
33,385	***33,666***	***2,837***	***3,417***	***23***	***19***	...	***1***	..	***1***	..	..	
9,226	9,508	...	...	2	1	...	...	...	...	...	...	22
4,879	5,009	2,837	3,417	1	...	...	...	...	1	...	...	23
8,923	8,023	...	...	13	13	...	1	...	...	...	...	24
758	1,013	...	...	7	5	.	...	...	...	...	...	25
9,599	10,113	...	...	...	...	...	...	...	...	...	...	26
219	***25***	..	..	***14,889***	***15,741***	***22,818***	***22,841***	***4,476***	***4,655***	***11,194***	***10,684***	
216	2	...	...	1,783	1,736	4	3	...	...	...	...	27
2	2	...	...	45	4	4	...	...	...	...	...	
...	...	...	...	149	143	7,561	7,975	3,171	3,491	5,212	5,018	28
2	23	...	...	609	666	9,907	9,809	951	861	3,133	2,577	29
...	...	...	.	12,313	13,158	5,341	5,754	351	303	191	98	30
1	...	...	...	35	38	...	...	3	..	2,658	2,991	31
380	***393***	***54,256***	***56,647***	***593***	***697***	***23,100***	***24,318***	..	..	***3***	***4***	
...	...	...	...	5	6	...	...	...	...	...	...	32
...	...	...	...	6	2	...	...	...	...	...	...	33
5	...	...	...	14	3	...	...	...	...	3	4	34
375	393	1,416	1,325	568	686	23,100	24,318	...	...	...	...	35
...	...	52,840	55,322	...	...	...	..	...	...	...	..	36
677	***638***	..	..	***178***	***114***	***13***	***12***	***22***	***4***	***6***	..	
...	...	...	...	28	27	...	...	...	...	...	...	37
1	...	..	...	43	11	...	...	...	...	...	...	38
668	638	...	...	108	74	13	12	22	4	6	...	39
8	...	..	...	...	2	...	...	...	...	...	...	40
73	**19**	...	...	**129,734**	**131,673**	**188,131**	**186,370**	**687**	**465**	**35,245**	**35,251**	
23	...	...	...	128,951	131,494	4,185	3,985	317	291	1,591	1,028	41
50	19	...	...	775	148	176,817	176,057	109	62	33,443	34,179	42
...	...	...	...	8	31	7,129	6,328	261	112	211	44	43

IMPERIAL TABLE X.—*Language*. PART III.—*Distribution by Districts of Selected Languages*.

Serial No.	District or State.		N1.—Karen (unspecified). Males.	Females.	N2.—Sgaw. Males.	Females.	N3.—Pwo. Males.	Females.	Other Karen dialects. Males.	Females.	Serial No. of District, etc. (See column 1).
	1		22	23	24	25	26	27	28	29	
	PROVINCIAL TOTAL	...	50,852	47,861	183,269	185,013	178,609	*173,857	145,265	149,290	
	DIVISIONAL BURMA	...	49,964	47,343	182,549	184,344	178,413	*173,655	40,731	39,429	
	Arakan Division	...	*35*	*1*	*26*	*5*	*5*	*1*	*1*	..	
1	Akyab ...	...	1	1	...	...	...	...	...	...	1
2	Hill District of Arakan	...	...	...	...	...	...	...	1	...	2
3	Kyaukpyu ...	...	...	...	...	...	...	...	...	...	3
4	Sandoway ...	..	34	..	26	5	5	1	...	...	4
	Pegu Division	...	*13,255*	*12,467*	*33,789*	*35,742*	*6,155*	*6,478*	*984*	*1,231*	
5	Rangoon Town	...	468	356	318	268	57	55	1	...	5
6	Insein ...	...	89	96	14,758	15,379	1,832	1,932	...	...	6
7	Hanthawaddy	...	1,350	1,215	2,983	3,468	3,659	3,799	11	14	7
8	Tharrawaddy	...	3,338	3,186	8,290	8,856	118	76	...	...	8
9	Pegu ...	...	6,561	6,300	7,332	7,367	488	616	972	1,217	9
10	Prome ...	...	1,449	1,314	108	404	1	...	...	...	10
	Irrawaddy Division	...	*7,827*	*7,776*	*48,011*	*52,645*	*103,488*	**99,926*	*99*	*47*	
11	Bassein ...	...	3,187	3,266	13,953	14,578	29,606	30,272	...	...	11
12	Henzada ...	...	3,521	3,382	11,118	13,155	4,232	4,543	...	...	12
13	Myaungmya ..	...	784	841	5,992	6,284	43,192	42,571	16	22	13
14	Ma-ubin ...	...	5	18	11,851	12,848	24,933	*20,946	19	7	14
15	Pyapôn ...	..	330	268	5,097	5,780	1,525	1,594	64	18	15
	Tenasserim Division	...	*26,249*	*25,439*	*100,345*	*95,888*	*68,720*	*67,241*	*39,073*	*37,793*	
16	Toungoo ..	...	21,821	21,428	5,013	3,889	...	2	11,747	11,534	16
17	Salween ...	...	1	...	22,032	20,862	25	...	91	95	17
18	Thatôn ...	...	2,055	1,989	45,958	44,435	43,806	43,425	25,488	24,348	18
19	Amherst ...	...	2,226	1,650	17,286	16,672	21,019	20,045	1,734	1,815	19
20	Tavoy ...	...	2	2	3,083	3,152	1,965	2,038	11	1	20
21	Mergui ...	...	141	370	6,973	6,878	1,905	1,731	2	...	21
	Magwe Division	...	*137*	*87*	*81*	*1*	*2*	..	*2*	..	
22	Thayetmyo ...	...	40	16	14	1	...	...	...	...	22
23	Pakôkku ...	...	71	1	1	...	...	...	2	...	23
24	Minbu ...	...	15	11	30	...	1	...	...	...	24
25	Magwe ...	...	11	9	36	...	1	...	...	...	25
26	Pakôkku Hill Tracts	...	...	...	...	...	...	...	...	...	26
	Mandalay Division	..	*221*	*68*	*223*	*32*	*11*	*9*	*151*	*18*	
27	Mandalay ...	...	33	50	...	...	1	...	...	2	27
	Mandalay City	...	*15*	*34*	...	...	...	...	...	*1*	
28	Bhamo ...	...	...	...	64	16	...	...	123	10	28
29	Myitkyina ...	...	2	4	7	9	7	6	28	1	29
30	Katha ...	...	186	14	157	7	...	...	..	...	30
31	Putao ...	...	...	...	...	...	3	3	...	...	31
	Sagaing Division	..	*168*	*64*	*27*	*8*	*15*	..	*19*	*1*	
32	Shwebo ...	...	126	42	4	...	...	...	4	...	32
33	Sagaing ..	...	5	5	..	...	9	...	...	...	33
34	Lower Chindwin	...	28	15	3	1	1	...	...	...	34
35	Upper Chindwin	...	4	2	10	1	5	...	15	1	35
36	Chin Hills ...	...	...	...	10	6	...	...	...	...	36
	Meiktila Division	..	*2,077*	*1,492*	*42*	*23*	*17*	..	*402*	*344*	
37	Kyauksè ...	...	4	4	9	14	...	...	...	...	37
38	Meiktila ...	...	228	7	1	3	...	...	9	...	38
39	Yamèthin ...	...	1,838	1,475	32	6	17	...	391	344	39
40	Myingyan ...	...	7	6	...	...	...	...	2	...	40
	EASTERN STATES	...	888	518	720	669	196	202	104,534	109,861	
41	Northern Shan States	...	364	19	...	...	...	...	28	6	41
42	Southern Shan States	...	273	245	36	47	53	42	84,023	85,932	42
43	Karenni ...	...	251	254	684	622	143	160	20,483	23,923	43

* See footnote ¶ on page 138.

IMPERIAL TABLE XI-A.

Birth-places.

NOTE 1.—This table classifies by birth-place the whole population actually enumerated throughout the province, and omits only the population excluded from Imperial Table VIA, namely the areas entirely omitted from the census and those in which the population was by estimate only. The total estimated population of the latter areas was 43,093; further details of them are given in Note 1 of Imperial Table VIA.

NOTE 2.—The table is in three parts; Part I constitutes the main table to which Parts II and III are appendices.

Part I.—In constructing Part I the whole tabulated population of the province and of each district has been divided by birth-place into eight classes, of which the first seven, lettered A to G in column 1, correspond to the seven parts into which the whole world has been divided for this purpose and the eighth class (H) includes persons whose birth-place was not recorded or could not be identified. Class A, which includes all born in India or Burma, has been divided further to correspond to parts of India according to the following scheme:—

A-I.—Burma,

A-II.—Other British Provinces and Indian States,

(*a*) Contiguous Provinces and associated states—
(i) Provinces; (ii) States;

(*b*) Non-contiguous Provinces and all other states—
(i) Provinces; (ii) States.

A-III.—French and Portuguese Settlements:

A-IV.—India (without further specification in the record).

In sub-class A-II (*b*) details have been separately shown only for those provinces and states to which considerable figures correspond, and the totals of these entries do not make up the total of the sub-class; the balances are accounted for in Section A of Part II of the table. For some provinces in both parts of Class A-II separate figures are given in italics for the districts which make the largest contributions to the figures given for the province; these also do not make up the totals for the provinces, but the balances are accounted for in Section B of Part II. Similarly in Classes B, C, E the details given in ordinary type for certain areas do not make up the totals of the classes; the balances are accounted for in Section A of Part II. Corresponding to each birth-place tabulated in Part I are shown in successive columns the number of persons enumerated in the whole province, Divisional Burma, the Eastern States and in each separate district (or other ordinary unit of tabulation). The figures given in the columns for Mandalay District include those for persons enumerated in Mandalay City which are given in the columns immediately following them. For the purposes of this table the town of Rangoon is the same as the Rangoon Town District.

In *Part II* are given some miscellaneous statistics supplementing those given in Part I for Classes A-II, B, C and E.

In *Part III* the persons of each area of enumeration shown in Part I as born in Burma are classified according to the district (or other ordinary unit of tabulation) of birth.

NOTE 3.—Imperial Table XIB gives statistics of the birth-places of Indians of certain races.

DISTRICT

Birth-place.	The Whole Province.			Divisional Burma.			The Eastern States.		
	Persons.	Males.	Females.	Persons.	Males.	Females.	Persons.	Males.	Females.
1	2	3	4	5	6	7	8	9	10
TOTAL POPULATION ...	13,169,099	6,735,516	6,433,583	11,698,408	5,991,623	5,706,785	1,470,691	743,893	726,798
A. INDIA (including Burma)	**13,034,880**	**6,635,448**	**6,399,432**	**11,599,570**	**5,915,336**	**5,684,234**	**1,435,310**	**720,112**	**715,198**
A-I Burma	12,462,350	6,148,649	6,313,701	11,037,795	5,438,158	5,599,637	1,424,555	710,491	714,064
A-II British Provinces and Indian States.	568,460	479,016	84,444	552,717	469,407	83,310	10,743	9,609	1,184
(*a*) *Contiguous Provinces*	*422,144*	*358,435*	*63,709*	*418,256*	*354,913*	*63,343*	*3,888*	*3,522*	*366*
(i) British Territory	420,082	357,122	62,960	416,239	353,640	62,599	3,843	3,482	361
Assam	1,513	1,294	219	1,506	1,288	218	7	6	1
Bengal	146,058	129,960	16,098	144,229	128,348	15,881	1,829	1,612	217
Calcutta	*11,254*	*9,005*	*2,249*	*11,111*	*8,887*	*2,224*	*143*	*118*	*25*
Chittagong	*88,345*	*80,698*	*7,647*	*87,559*	*79,947*	*7,612*	*786*	*751*	*35*
Dacca	*2,720*	*2,209*	*511*	*2,646*	*2,153*	*493*	*74*	*56*	*18*
Noakhali	*3,977*	*3,925*	*52*	*3,927*	*3,875*	*52*	*50*	*50*	...
Madras	272,511	225,868	46,643	270,504	224,004	46,500	2,007	1,864	143
Ganjam	*49,115*	*46,851*	*2,264*	*48,145*	*45,885*	*2,260*	*970*	*966*	*4*
Godavari	*25,686*	*22,260*	*3,426*	*25,675*	*22,251*	*3,424*	*11*	*9*	*2*
Kistna	*8,663*	*7,703*	*960*	*8,658*	*7,698*	*960*	*5*	*5*	...
Malabar	*4,547*	*4,242*	*305*	*4,408*	*4,118*	*290*	*139*	*124*	*15*
Ramnad	*13,171*	*10,695*	*2,476*	*13,155*	*10,679*	*2,476*	*16*	*16*	...
Tanjore	*14,386*	*11,196*	*3,190*	*14,368*	*11,178*	*3,190*	*18*	*18*	...
Visagapatam	*36,255*	*30,585*	*5,670*	*36,240*	*30,573*	*5,667*	*15*	*12*	3
(ii) Indian States	2,062	1,313	749	2,017	1,273	744	45	40	5
Bengal States	29	19	10	1,462	846	616	43	38	5
Madras States	528	410	118	27	17	10	2	2	...
Manipur	1,505	884	621	528	410	118	...	...	...
(*b*) *Non-Contiguous Provinces*	*141,816*	*120,581*	*20,735*	*134,461*	*114,494*	*19,967*	*6,855*	*6,087*	*768*
(i) British Territory	126,613	108,620	17,993	120,208	102,887	17,321	6,405	5,733	672
Bihar and Orissa	20,189	17,574	2,615	18,658	16,057	2,601	1,531	1,517	14
Chapra	*2,239*	*2,103*	*136*	*2,226*	*2,092*	*134*	*13*	*11*	*2*
Patna	*1,288*	*989*	*299*	*1,273*	*979*	*294*	*15*	*10*	*5*
Puri	*4,142*	*4,055*	*87*	*4,029*	*3,944*	*85*	*113*	*111*	*2*
Bombay and Aden	12,816	10,098	2,718	12,376	9,735	2,641	440	363	77
Punjab	19,804	16,460	3,344	17,787	14,760	3,027	2,017	1,700	317
United Provinces	70,767	61,953	8,814	68,493	59,927	8,566	2,274	2,026	248
Azamgarh	*4,975*	*4,567*	*408*	*4,897*	*4,491*	*406*	*78*	*76*	*2*
Fyzabad	*18,171*	*15,879*	*2,292*	*17,871*	*15,619*	*2,252*	*300*	*260*	*40*
Gorakhpur	*5,046*	*4,910*	*136*	*4,944*	*4,808*	*136*	*102*	*102*	...
Sultanpur	*11,738*	*10,419*	*1,319*	*11,389*	*10,115*	*1,274*	*349*	*304*	*45*
(ii) States and Agencies	14,703	11,961	2,742	14,253	11,607	2,646	450	354	96
Bombay States	5,655	4,560	1,095	5,426	4,353	1,073	229	207	22
Rajputana Agency	3,418	2,818	600	3,306	2,757	549	112	61	51
A-III French and Portuguese Settlements.	651	563	88	644	556	88	7	7	...
A-IV India (part unspecified)	8,419	7,220	1,199	8,414	7,215	1,199	5	5	...
B. OTHER ASIATIC COUNTRIES	**126,793**	**94,454**	**32,339**	**91,722**	**70,874**	**20,848**	**35,071**	**23,580**	**11,491**
China	102,344	76,301	26,043	74,416	57,845	16,571	27,928	18,456	9,472
Japan	449	223	226	448	222	226	1	1	...
Nepal	13,712	10,720	2,992	10,276	7,940	2,336	3,436	2,780	656
Siam	7,645	5,090	2,555	4,326	3,057	1,269	3,319	2,033	1,286
C. EUROPE	**6,553**	**5,040**	**1,513**	**6,339**	**4,896**	**1,443**	**214**	**144**	**70**
United Kingdom	6,097	4,735	1,362	5,923	4,623	1,300	174	112	62
England and Wales *	*4,211*	*3,223*	*988*	*4,086*	*3,143*	*943*	*125*	*80*	*45*
Scotland	*1,531*	*1,275*	*256*	*1,494*	*1,254*	*240*	*37*	*21*	*16*
Ireland	*355*	*237*	*118*	*343*	*226*	*117*	*12*	*11*	*1*
France	204	139	65	184	119	65	20	20	...
D. AFRICA	**70**	**52**	**18**	**70**	**52**	**18**	...	...	...
E. AMERICA	**559**	**355**	**204**	**524**	**339**	**185**	**35**	**16**	**19**
Canada	43	22	21	42	21	21	1	1	...
United States	254	163	91	244	158	86	10	5	5
F. AUSTRALASIA	**214**	**139**	**75**	**153**	**98**	**55**	**61**	**41**	**20**
G. AT SEA	**6**	**4**	**2**	**6**	**4**	**2**	...	...	...
H. NOT RECORDED	**24**	**24**	...	**24**	**24**	...	...	...	...

* One male born in the Channel Islands is included in columns 2, 3, 5 and 6 for *England and Wales.*

PART I.—*General Statement.*

IN WHICH ENUMERATED.

Akyab.			Hill District of Arakan.			Kyaukpyu.			Sandoway.		
Persons.	Males.	Females.	Persons.	Males.	Females.	Persons.	Males.	Females.	Persons.	Males.	Females.
11	12	13	14	15	16	17	18	19	20	21	22
576,430	309,564	266.866	20,914	10.790	10,124	199,873	96,569	103,304	112,029	55,304	56,725
575,360	308,594	266,766	20,668	10,587	10,081	199,728	96,438	103,290	111,825	55,124	56,701
527,239	267,492	259,747	20,183	10,235	9,948	197,789	94,754	103,035	111,006	54,351	56,655
48,047	41,029	7,018	485	352	183	1,934	1,679	255	819	773	46
45,496	*88,751*	*6,745*	*464*	*883*	*131*	*1,865*	*1,628*	*242*	*716*	*679*	*37*
45,453	38,718	6,735	463	332	131	1,861	1,619	242	713	679	34
129	124	5	...	...	...	1	1	...	4	2	2
42,903	36,217	6,686	447	316	131	1,778	1,537	241	651	620	31
227	*181*	*46*	...	...	...	*123*	*1*	*122*	*7*	*7*	...
39,816	*33,501*	*6,315*	*398*	*293*	*105*	*1,001*	*996*	*5*	*537*	*513*	*24*
113	*91*	*22*	...	...	...	*6*	*6*	...	*15*	*11*	*4*
381	*371*	*10*	*2*	*2*	...	*45*	*41*	*4*	*20*	*20*	...
2,421	2,377	44	16	16	...	82	81	1	58	57	1
842	*842*	...	*7*	*7*	...	*14*	*14*	...	*4*	*4*	...
3	*2*	*1*	...	...	...	..	...	...	*3*	*3*	...
3	*3*	...	...	...	...	...	...	...	...	...	...
28	*28*	...	...	...	...	5	5	...	...	...	...
42	*42*	...	...	...	...	...	...	...	...	...	...
12	*8*	4	...	...	...	*1*	*1*	..	...	...	...
24	*16*	8	...	...	...	*1*	*1*	...	...	...	...
43	33	10	1	1	...	4	4	...	3	...	3
5	...	5	...	...	...	...	...	...	3	...	3
6	6	...	...	...	...	3	3	...	...	...	...
32	27	5	1	1	...	1	1	...	...	...	...
2,551	*2,278*	*273*	*21*	*19*	*2*	*69*	*56*	*13*	*103*	*94*	*9*
2,084	1,881	203	20	18	2	47	37	10	84	75	9
935	884	51	1	1	...	6	5	1	5	5	...
17	*17*	...	...		..	..	..	...	...	...	...
17	*17*	...	...	...	...	...	...	...	...	...	...
...	...	...	...	...	...	*1*	*1*	...	...	...	...
183	156	27	...	...	...	4	4	...	7	5	2
144	114	30	9	7	2	6	5	1	37	36	1
806	711	95	10	10	...	3	3	...	30	28	2
15	*15*	...	...	...	...	...	..	...	*4*	*3*	1
121	*105*	*16*	...	...	...	...	...	...	*6*	*6*	...
23	*23*	...	...	...	...	...	...	...	..	...	...
83	*77*	*6*	...	...	...	.	...	...	*9*	*8*	*1*
467	397	70	1	1	...	22	19	3	19	19	...
165	159	6	...	...	...	7	7	...	16	16	...
233	180	53	...	...	..	3	2	1	3	3	...
25	24	1	...	...	...	...	...	...	...	...	...
49	49	...	...	...	...	5	5	...	...	...	...
939	857	82	241	199	42	143	129	14	198	178	20
439	368	71	...	...	...	79	67	12	67	62	5
3	...	3	...	...	...	...	..	..	...	...	...
35	27	8	241	199	42	57	55	2	128	113	15
...	...	...	...	...	...	...	...	...	3	3	...
125	110	15	5	4	1	2	2	...	1	1	...
121	108	13	4	4	...	2	2	...	1	1	...
73	*67*	*6*	*3*	*3*	...	*1*	*1*	...	*1*	*1*	...
33	*31*	*2*	...	...	...	...	...	...	...	...	...
15	*10*	*5*	*1*	*1*	...	*1*	*1*	...	...	...	...
1	1	...	...	...	..	...	...	...	...	...	...
...	...	...	...	...	...	...	...	...	..	...	...
1	1	...	...	...	...	...	..	...	4	1	3
1	1	...	...	...	...	...	...	...	2	1	1
...	...	...	..	...	...	...	...	...	...	...	...
4	1	3	...	...	...	...	...	...	...	...	...
1	1	...	...	...	...	...	...	...	1	...	1
...	...	...	...	...	...	...	...	..	...	...	...

DISTRICT IN

Birth-place.	Rangoon Town.			Insein.			Hanthawaddy.		
	Persons.	Males.	Females.	Persons.	Males.	Females.	Persons.	Males.	Females.
1	23	24	25	26	27	28	29	30	31
TOTAL POPULATION ...	341,962	236,689	105,273	293,083	156,794	136,289	364,624	201,043	163,581
A. INDIA (including Burma)	322,623	222,026	100,597	290,621	154,790	135,831	361,430	198,384	163,046
A-I Burma	155,086	78,977	76,109	266,390	134,909	131,481	315,116	159,964	156,152
A-II Other British Provinces and Indian States.	166,891	142,509	24,382	23,658	19,353	4,305	46,196	38,330	7,866
(*a*) *Contiguous Provinces*	*127,381*	*108,228*	*19,163*	*16,994*	*12,844*	*3,150*	*41,004*	*33,419*	*7,586*
(i) British Territory	127,054	107,977	19,077	15,951	12,801	3,150	41,000	33,415	7,585
Assam	155	132	23	43	39	4	22	21	1
Bengal	26,932	25,053	1,879	4,127	3,384	743	7,866	7,176	690
Calcutta	3,583	2,623	960	698	486	212	356	298	58
Chittagong	16,665	16,333	332	765	714	51	5,080	4,991	89
Dacca	1,138	996	142	76	47	29	3	3	...
Noakhali	1,910	1,891	19	...	...	...	50	50	...
Madras	99,967	82,792	17,175	11,781	9,378	2,403	33,112	26,118	6,894
Ganjam	20,819	19,741	1,078	3,385	3,226	159	2,843	2,743	100
Godavari	16,174	14,189	1,985	195	159	36	1,209	1,035	174
Kistna	5,848	5,252	596	75	59	16	1,146	1,031	115
Malabar	1,558	1,411	147	244	227	17	87	87	...
Ramnad	5,735	4,651	1,084	209	114	95	1,946	1,547	399
Tanjore	3,958	3,242	716	776	498	278	3,230	3,057	1,173
Vizagapatam	15,930	13,422	2,508	364	314	50	1,118	985	133
(ii) Indian States	327	251	76	43	43	...	4	4	...
Bengal States	...	...	...	...	...	...	...	...	.
Madras States	312	236	76	13	13	...	3	3	...
Manipur	15	15	..	30	30	...	1	1	...
(*b*) *Non-Contiguous Provinces*	*39,610*	*34,281*	*5,229*	*7,664*	*6,509*	*1,155*	*5,192*	*4,911*	*281*
(i) British Territory	34,415	30,539	3,876	7,138	6,078	1,060	5,080	4,808	272
Bihar and Orissa	3,429	3,162	267	390	345	45	321	308	13
Chapra	1,193	1,135	58	124	106	18	55	55	...
Patna	376	297	79	23	15	8	115	105	10
Puri	370	367	3	40	39	1	...	...	...
Bombay and Aden	4,751	3,575	1,176	1,104	817	287	243	194	49
Punjab	2,556	2,123	433	817	630	187	517	402	115
United Provinces	22,776	20,900	1,876	4,682	4,160	522	3,834	3,759	75
Azamgarh	2,059	1,950	109	262	208	54	161	160	1
Fyzabad	6,496	5,906	590	2,053	1,874	179	573	567	6
Gorakhpur	2,204	2,144	60	233	215	18	1,883	1,881	2
Sultanpur	3,833	3,556	277	466	405	61	178	168	10
(ii) States and Agencies	5,095	3,742	1,353	526	431	95	112	103	9
Bombay States	2,626	1,918	708	259	218	41	...	...	...
Rajputana Agency	869	652	217	25	21	4	50	45	5
A-III French and Portuguese Settlements.	487	417	70	4	4	...	16	15	1
A-IV India (part unspecified)	159	123	36	569	524	45	102	75	27
B. OTHER ASIATIC COUNTRIES	15,988	12,044	3,944	2,325	1,931	394	2,966	2,481	485
China	14,175	10,792	3,383	2,156	1,794	362	2,921	2,445	476
Japan	307	144	163	8	7	1	2	...	2
Nepal	545	489	56	90	75	15	...	...	...
Siam	45	29	16	21	13	8	11	8	3
C. EUROPE	3,103	2,457	646	111	62	49	213	167	46
United Kingdom	2,930	2,330	600	98	60	38	207	161	46
England and Wales *	1,744	1,304	440	81	47	34	97	79	18
Scotland	1,020	903	117	13	12	1	101	75	26
Ireland	166	123	43	4	1	3	9	7	2
France	68	47	21	5	...	5	4	4	...
D. AFRICA	33	24	9	9	3	6	...	...	...
E. AMERICA	126	72	54	16	8	8	11	8	3
Canada	2	2	...	3	...	3	...	...	...
United States	75	34	41	4	3	1	2	...	2
F. AUSTRALASIA	65	42	23	...	...	...	3	2	1
G. AT SEA	...	...	...	1	...	1	1	1	...
H. NOT RECORDED	24	24	...	...	..	...	...	...	...

* One male born in the Channel Islands is included in columns 23 and 24 for *England and Wales.*

WHICH ENUMERATED.

Tharrawaddy.			Pegu.			Prome.			Bassein.		
Persons.	Males.	Females.	Persons.	Males.	Females.	Persons.	Males.	Females.	Persons.	Males.	Females.
32	33	34	35	36	37	38	39	40	41	42	43
492,429	246,261	246,168	445,620	235,824	210,296	371,575	182,803	188,772	489,478	252,947	236,528
490,758	**244,837**	**245,921**	**441,645**	**232,039**	**209,606**	**370,487**	**181,883**	**188,604**	**486,485**	**250,448**	**236,037**
479,988	235,534	244,455	407,519	206,089	201,430	363,063	175,669	187,397	467,659	233,131	234,528
10,652	9,199	1,453	33,890	25,760	8,130	7,320	6,117	1,203	18,761	17,279	1,482
7,141	*6,205*	*936*	*26,292*	*20,504*	*5,788*	*4,958*	*4,081*	*877*	*13,776*	*12,587*	*1,189*
7,139	6,203	936	26,250	20,486	5,764	4,958	4,081	877	13,763	12,580	1,183
...	...	...	151	151	...	1	...	1	393	393	...
1,560	1,431	129	6,167	5,201	966	1,136	996	140	5,253	4,991	262
198	*182*	*16*	*562*	*424*	*138*	*120*	*101*	*19*	*466*	*422*	*44*
759	*747*	*12*	*2,042*	*1,934*	*108*	*400*	*370*	*30*	*2,679*	*2,619*	*60*
53	*35*	*18*	*42*	*8*	*34*	*5*	*4*	*1*	*138*	*104*	*34*
...	...	...	..	...	...	...	...	..	*195*	*195*	...
5,579	4,772	807	19,932	15,134	4,798	3,821	3,085	736	8,122	7,196	926
1,420	*1,319*	*101*	*2,414*	*2,268*	*146*	*358*	*316*	*42*	*1,583*	*1,505*	*78*
463	*366*	*97*	*1,005*	*730*	*275*	*88*	*81*	*7*	*1,225*	*1,047*	*178*
113	*108*	*5*	*234*	*187*	*47*	*51*	*44*	*7*	*298*	*264*	*34*
115	*115*	...	*234*	*214*	*20*	*105*	*103*	*2*	*138*	*137*	*1*
554	*509*	*45*	*1,122*	*836*	*286*	*43*	*37*	*6*	*150*	*138*	*12*
159	*140*	*19*	*794*	*512*	*282*	*113*	*110*	*3*	*131*	*127*	*4*
1,107	*892*	*215*	*1,635*	*1,210*	*425*	*596*	*537*	*59*	*1,928*	*1,658*	*270*
2	2	...	42	18	24	...	...	...	8	7	1
...	...	...	...	...	...	...	...	...	...	...	...
...	...	...	42	18	24	...	..	...	8	7	1
2	2	...	...	...	...	...	...	...	...	...	...
3,611	*2,994*	*617*	*7,598*	*5,256*	*2,342*	*2,862*	*2,036*	*826*	*4,985*	*4,692*	*293*
3,088	2,607	481	7,256	4,967	2,289	2,246	1,943	303	3,470	3,227	253
236	213	23	533	452	81	98	90	8	573	568	5
146	*140*	*6*	*2*	...	*2*	*42*	*39*	*3*	*39*	*38*	*1*
47	*37*	*10*	*82*	*60*	*22*	*7*	*7*	..	*12*	*9*	*3*
..	...	...	*204*	*178*	*26*	*12*	*12*	...	*162*	*161*	*1*
374	335	39	573	349	224	395	322	73	393	353	40
262	220	42	371	294	77	282	222	60	312	279	33
2,188	1,811	377	5,726	3,845	1,881	1,449	1,287	162	2,137	1,962	175
159	*124*	*35*	*96*	*81*	*15*	*45*	*45*	..	*230*	*204*	*26*
991	*796*	*195*	*933*	*761*	*172*	*448*	*377*	*71*	*432*	*403*	*29*
56	*54*	*2*	*40*	*33*	*7*	*34*	*34*	..	...	...	...
256	*224*	*32*	*429*	*368*	*61*	*295*	*275*	*20*	*765*	*688*	*77*
423	387	36	342	289	53	116	93	23	1,505	1,465	40
277	277	...	106	91	15	69	54	15	69	64	5
81	55	26	28	28	...	12	7	5	864	835	29
...	...	...	6	1	5	8	8	...	20	17	3
117	104	13	230	189	41	93	89	4	45	21	24
1,643	**1,405**	**238**	**3,950**	**3,269**	**681**	**1,048**	**891**	**157**	**2,877**	**2,415**	**462**
1,637	1,399	238	3,817	3,165	652	1,038	881	157	2,828	2,377	451
...	...	..	1	...	1	1	1	..	11	2	9
1	1	...	16	16	...	7	7	...	8	8	...
3	3	...	45	42	3	...	...	...	10	10	...
24	**18**	**6**	**16**	**12**	**4**	**36**	**27**	**9**	**99**	**79**	**20**
20	15	5	15	11	4	30	27	9	90	73	17
17	*14*	*3*	*12*	*9*	*3*	*18*	*15*	*3*	*60*	*52*	*8*
2	*1*	*2*	*3*	*2*	*1*	*16*	*11*	*5*	*20*	*14*	*6*
...	...	...	...	...	...	*2*	*1*	*1*	*10*	*7*	*3*
3	3	...	1	1	...	...	...	...	6	3	3
...	...	...	...	...	..	...	...	...	...	...	...
4	**1**	**3**	**7**	**2**	**5**	**3**	**2**	**1**	**12**	**5**	**7**
...	...	...	...	...	...	...	...	...	1	...	1
3	1	2	...	...	...	2	1	1	3	2	1
...	...	...	**2**	**2**	...	**1**	...	**1**	...	...	...
...	...	...	...	...	...	...	...	...	...	...	...
...	...	...	...	...	..	...	...	...	..	...	...

Birth-place.	DISTRICT IN								
	HENZADA.			MYAUNGMYA.			MA-UBIN.		
	Persons.	Males.	Females.	Persons.	Males.	Females.	Persons.	Males.	Females.
1	44	45	46	47	48	49	50	51	52
TOTAL POPULATION ...	550,920	273,439	277,481	370,551	196,757	173,794	330,103	168,518	161,593
A. INDIA (including Burma)	**549,533**	**272,296**	**277,237**	**366,889**	**193,568**	**173,321**	**328,367**	**166,952**	**161,415**
A-I Burma	540,995	264,698	276,297	349,810	177,544	172,266	318,681	158,057	160,624
A-II Other British Provinces and Indian States.	8,437	7,499	938	15,255	14,287	968	9,673	8,882	791
(a) *Contiguous Provinces*	*6,584*	*5,894*	*690*	*12,981*	*12,167*	*814*	*7,918*	*7,318*	*600*
(i) British Territory	6,562	5,872	690	12,970	12,157	813	7,915	7,315	600
Assam	1	...	1	13	13	...	3	3	...
Bengal	1,898	1,756	142	7,509	7,235	274	3,405	3,258	147
Calcutta	287	256	31	712	661	51	1,041	969	72
Chittagong	691	671	20	1,785	1,748	37	1,494	1,452	42
Dacca	15	13	2	108	98	10	42	39	3
Noakhali	13	11	2	181	181	...	46	46	...
Madras	4,663	4,116	547	5,449	4,910	539	4,507	4,054	453
Ganjam	853	827	26	773	760	13	826	804	22
Godavari	113	101	12	125	122	3	356	309	47
Kistna	38	24	14	68	59	9	229	188	41
Malabar	161	152	9	69	68	1	69	67	2
Ramnad	72	61	11	575	554	21	38	37	1
Tanjore	20	17	3	81	69	12	144	130	14
Visagapatam	811	679	132	196	184	12	452	408	44
(ii) Indian States	22	22	...	11	10	1	3	3	...
Bengal States	...	...	..	...	...	...	...	...	...
Madras States	16	16	..	1	...	1	...	...	...
Manipur	6	6	...	10	10	...	3	3	...
(b) *Non-Contiguous Provinces*	*1,858*	*1,605*	*248*	*2,274*	*2,120*	*164*	*1,765*	*1,664*	*191*
(i) British Territory	1,712	1,476	236	1,842	1,705	137	1,555	1,384	171
Bihar and Orissa	580	559	21	605	587	18	178	169	9
Chapra	58	58	...	14	14	...	...	...	...
Patna	61	56	5	21	21	...	11	11	...
Puri	17	15	2	227	227	...	60	57	3
Bombay and Aden	66	37	29	208	174	34	217	196	21
Punjab	265	213	52	176	133	43	170	140	30
United Provinces	782	650	132	847	805	42	874	763	111
Azamgarh	36	34	2	56	56	..	51	48	3
Fyzabad	197	160	37	114	104	10	397	336	61
Gorakhpur	6	5	1	...	...	...	1	1	...
Sultanpur	159	135	24	164	151	13	206	178	28
(ii) States and Agencies	141	129	12	432	415	17	200	180	20
Bombay States	7	7	...	328	328	...	...	...	...
Rajputana Agency	86	80	6	44	44	...	51	50	1
A-III French and Portuguese Settlements.	...	...	...	...	...	...	13	13	..
A-IV India (part unspecified)	101	99	2	1,824	1,737	87	...	...	...
B. OTHER ASIATIC COUNTRIES	**1,354**	**1,123**	**231**	**3,655**	**3,184**	**471**	**1,715**	**1,542**	**173**
China	1,330	1,103	227	3,579	3,118	461	1,690	1,519	171
Japan	..	...	...	6	2	4	...	...	...
Nepal	12	12	...	...	...	...	3	2	1
Siam	...	...	...	1	...	1	1	...	1
C. EUROPE	**20**	**14**	**6**	**7**	**5**	**2**	**20**	**18**	**2**
United Kingdom	11	9	2	5	3	2	18	16	2
England and Wales	10	8	2	3	1	2	10	9	1
Scotland	1	1	...	1	1	...	8	7	1
Ireland	...	...	...	1	1	...	...	...	...
France	3	3	...	1	1	...	1	1	...
D. AFRICA	**2**	**1**	**1**	...	...	...	...	...	...
E. AMERICA	**8**	**2**	**6**	...	...	...	**4**	**1**	**3**
Canada	...	...	..	...	...	...	...	...	...
United States	...	...	...	...	...	...	...	...	...
F. AUSTRALASIA	**3**	**3**	...	...	...	...	...	...	..
G. AT SEA	..	...	...	...	...	...	...	...	..
H. NOT RECORDED	...	...	..	...	...	...	...	...	...

PART I.—*General Statement*—continued.

WHICH ENUMERATED.

Pyapon.			Toungoo.			Salween.			Thaton.		
Persons.	Males.	Females.	Persons.	Males.	Females.	Persons.	Males.	Females.	Persons.	Males.	Females.
53	54	55	56	57	58	59	60	61	62	63	64
288,994	156,721	132,273	381,883	197,505	184,378	50,379	26,811	23,568	471,100	245,909	225,191
285,913	**154,128**	**131,785**	**379,722**	**195,707**	**184,015**	**49,177**	**25,812**	**23,365**	**469,153**	**244,334**	**224,819**
266,227	137,627	128,600	361,764	181,622	180,142	48,592	25,253	23,339	450,431	228,550	221,881
19,564	16,397	3,167	15,196	11,843	8,353	585	559	26	18,692	15,769	2,923
17,160	*14,250*	*2,910*	*7,030*	*6,084*	*946*	*522*	*500*	*22*	*15,869*	*12,848*	*2,626*
17,160	14,250	2,910	7,014	6,069	945	514	492	22	15,369	12,843	2,526
...	...	...	5	2	3	1	...	1	79	71	8
4,348	4,076	272	1,684	1,453	231	393	375	18	5,570	5,035	535
603	*531*	*72*	*336*	*260*	*76*	*16*	*15*	*1*	*124*	*106*	*18*
2,266	*2,223*	*43*	*1,017*	953	*64*	*79*	*78*	*1*	*1,669*	*1,603*	*66*
69	*66*	*3*	*27*	*22*	*5*	*2*	*2*	...	*115*	*112*	*3*
139	*139*	...	68	*64*	*4*	*219*	*218*	*1*	*218*	*214*	*4*
12,812	10,174	2,638	5,325	4,614	711	120	117	3	9,720	7,737	1,983
476	*436*	*40*	*1,584*	*1,493*	*91*	*50*	*49*	*1*	*805*	*644*	*161*
333	*292*	*41*	*224*	*178*	*46*	*19*	*17*	*2*	*495*	*417*	*78*
49	*44*	*5*	*87*	*80*	*7*	...	...	...	*58*	*54*	*4*
78	*78*	..	*108*	*107*	*1*	*7*	*7*	...	*206*	*202*	*4*
721	*469*	*252*	*160*	*160*	...	...	...	...	*807*	*635*	*172*
837	*685*	*152*	*212*	*200*	*12*	...	...	...	*968*	*768*	*200*
559	*451*	*108*	*897*	*701*	*196*	...	...	...	*1,303*	*1,104*	*199*
...	...	...	16	15	1	8	8	...	...	...	...
...	...	..	...	...	...	7	7	...	...	...	..
...	...	...	4	3	1	...	...	...	...	...	...
...	...	...	12	12	...	1	1	...	...	...	...
2,404	*2,147*	*257*	*8,166*	*5,759*	*2,407*	*63*	*59*	*4*	*3,323*	*2,926*	*397*
1,726	1,552	174	7,758	5,377	2,381	56	54	2	3,010	2,618	392
752	665	87	4,171	2,458	1,713	35	35	...	1,054	930	124
...	...	...	*110*	*92*	*18*	...	...	...	*51*	*28*	*23*
29	*10*	*19*	*108*	*60*	*48*	...	...	...	*83*	*31*	*52*
1	...	*1*	*219*	*215*	*4*	*22*	*22*	...	*227*	*199*	*28*
192	162	30	378	350	28	6	6	...	281	226	55
210	184	26	622	512	110	9	8	1	509	440	69
510	479	31	2,496	1,972	524	5	4	1	1,109	967	142
...	...	...	*275*	*239*	*36*	*1*	...	*1*	*35*	*31*	*4*
148	*132*	*16*	*593*	*486*	*107*	...	...	...	*248*	*199*	*49*
...	...	...	*28*	*23*	*5*	...	...	...	*31*	*26*	*5*
125	*119*	*6*	*327*	*287*	*40*	...	...	...	*165*	*145*	*20*
678	595	83	408	382	26	7	5	2	313	308	5
14	9	5	161	159	2	...	...	...	61	61	...
169	162	7	17	8	9	4	3	1	49	45	4
...	...	...	15	11	4	...	...	...	2	1	1
122	104	18	2,747	2,231	516	...	...	...	28	14	14
3,086	**2,580**	**486**	**2,035**	**1,729**	**306**	**1,181**	**979**	**202**	**1,941**	**1,570**	**371**
2,904	2,451	453	1,773	1,484	289	111	105	6	1,826	1,485	341
...	...	...	5	2	3	...	...	...	1	...	1
1	...	1	77	77	...	117	99	18	3	...	3
...	...	...	168	154	14	953	775	178	87	64	23
13	**12**	**1**	**110**	**62**	**48**	**18**	**18**	...	**6**	**5**	**1**
13	12	1	78	47	31	5	5	..	5	4	1
7	*6*	*1*	*61*	*37*	*24*	*4*	*4*	...	*4*	*3*	*1*
6	*6*	...	*15*	*9*	*6*	...	...	...	*1*	*1*	...
...	...	...	*2*	*1*	*1*	*1*	*1*	...	...	...	...
...	...	...	...	...	...	13	13	...	...	..	...
...	...	...	**1**	**1**	...	...	...	...	...	...	...
2	**1**	**1**	**15**	**6**	**9**	...	...	...	...	...	...
...	...	...	1	...	1	...	...	...	...	...	..
...	...	...	11		7	—	...	...	...	...	...
...	...	...	...	...	...	**3**	**2**	**1**	...	...	...
...	...	...	...	...	...	...	...	...	...	...	...
...	...	...	...	...	...	...	...	...	...	...	...

DISTRICT IN

Birth-place.	AMHERST.			TAVOY.			MERGUI.		
	Persons.	Males.	Females.	Persons.	Males.	Females.	Persons.	Males.	Females.
1	65	66	67	68	69	70	71	72	73
TOTAL POPULATION ...	417,910	228,848	194,562	156,786	80,994	75,792	135,465	72,878	62,587
A. INDIA (including Burma)	**413,357**	**219,913**	**193,444**	**154,064**	**78,529**	**75,535**	**131,301**	**69,435**	**61,866**
A-I Burma	888,642	198,180	190,462	150,174	74,924	75,270	128,980	62,796	61,184
A-II Other British Provinces and Indian States.	23,908	21,030	2,876	8,886	8,621	265	7,280	6,568	667
(a) *Contiguous Provinces*	*19,977*	*17,588*	*2,394*	*2,449*	*2,274*	*175*	*6,808*	*5,690*	*618*
(i) **British Territory**	19,939	17,548	2,391	2,449	2,274	175	6,306	5,690	616
Assam	1	1	...	4	4	...	2	...	2
Bengal	4,461	4,273	188	821	743	78	661	647	14
Calcutta	*294*	*231*	*63*	*185*	*157*	*28*	*53*	*51*	*2*
Chittagong	*3,316*	*3,237*	*79*	*259*	*253*	*6*	*321*	*318*	*3*
Dacca	*106*	*90*	*16*	*39*	*29*	*10*	...	...	...
Noakhali	*296*	*296*	...	*32*	*30*	*2*	...	...	...
Madras	15,477	13,274	2,203	1,624	1,527	97	5,643	5,043	600
Ganjam	*1,859*	*1,787*	*72*	*298*	*297*	*1*	*108*	*104*	*4*
Godavari	*2,855*	*2,636*	*219*	*246*	*231*	*15*	*147*	*88*	*59*
Kistna	*200*	*171*	*29*	*5*	*4*	*1*	*73*	*60*	*13*
Malabar	*186*	*160*	*26*	*187*	*185*	*2*	*57*	*55*	*2*
Ramnad	*435*	*376*	*59*	*18*	*18*	...	*4*	*4*	...
Tanjore	*1,467*	*1,246*	*221*	*47*	*45*	*2*	*42*	*38*	*4*
Visagapatam	*2,980*	*2,410*	*570*	*352*	*325*	*27*	*4,679*	*4,238*	*441*
(ii) **Indian States**	38	35	3	...	...	...	...	...	...
Bengal States	...	...	...	...	...	...	...	...	...
Madras States	38	35	3	...	...	...	...	..	...
Manipur	...	...	...	...	...	...	...	...	...
(b) *Non-Contiguous Provinces*	*8,929*	*8,447*	*482*	*1,487*	*1,847*	*90*	*924*	*878*	*51*
(i) **British Territory**	3,265	2,979	286	1,410	1,325	85	870	831	39
Bihar and Orissa	1,233	1,215	18	543	541	2	412	424	18
Chapra	*10*	*10*	...	*6*	*6*	..	*4*	*4*	...
Patna	*25*	*18*	*7*	*29*	*28*	*1*	*62*	*44*	*18*
Puri	*1,017*	*1,008*	*9*	*472*	*472*	...	*137*	*136*	*1*
Bombay and Aden	406	336	70	143	137	6	66	63	3
Punjab	394	340	54	258	224	34	136	130	6
United Provinces	1,181	1,046	135	407	365	42	203	191	12
Azamgarh	*12*	*12*	..	...	...	...	*76*	*76*	...
Fyzabad	*385*	*350*	*35*	*86*	*76*	*10*	*39*	*36*	*3*
Gorakhpur	*12*	*12*	...	...	...	...	*10*	*10*	..
Sultanpur	*380*	*337*	*43*	*147*	*124*	*23*	*32*	*31*	*1*
(ii) **States and Agencies**	664	468	196	27	22	5	54	42	12
Bombay States	442	286	156	9	8	1	30	26	4
Rajputana Agency	107	81	26	2	2	...	11	6	5
A-III French and Portuguese Settlements.	25	24	1	1	1	...	12	12	...
A-IV India (part unspecified)	784	679	105	8	8	...	79	64	15
B. OTHER ASIATIC COUNTRIES	4,376	3,316	1,060	2,629	2,401	228	4,098	3,389	707
China	2,384	1,968	416	2,253	2,088	165	2,890	2,578	302
Japan	14	9	5	9	4	5	56	40	16
Nepal	35	21	14	271	223	48	106	163	3
Siam	1,699	1,080	619	40	35	5	1,008	622	386
C. EUROPE	150	109	41	72	50	22	54	44	10
United Kingdom	128	98	30	71	49	22	52	42	10
England and Wales	*80*	*64*	*16*	*50*	*35*	*15*	*46*	*36*	*10*
Scotland	*29*	*21*	*8*	*14*	*11*	*3*	*6*	*6*	...
Ireland	*19*	*13*	*6*	*7*	*3*	*4*	...	...	...
France	13	8	5	1	1	...	...	...	...
D. AFRICA	2	1	1	2	2	...	...	...	...
E. AMERICA	18	6	12	5	2	3	...	...	...
Canada	2	1	1	...	...	...	...	...	...
United States	2	...	2	...	...	...	...	..	...
F. AUSTRALASIA	7	3	4	14	10	4	14	10	4
G. AT SEA	...	...	...	...	...	...	...	...	...
H. NOT RECORDED	...	...	...	...	...	...	...	...	...

WHICH ENUMERATED.

Thayetmyo.			Pakokku.			Minbu.			Magwe.		
Persons.	Males.	Females.	Persons.	Males.	Females.	Persons.	Males.	Females.	Persons.	Males.	Females.
74	75	76	77	78	79	80	81	82	83	84	85
255,406	125,283	130,123	465,771	223,948	241,823	274,002	134,495	139,807	423,252	211,686	211,566
255,096	125,027	130,069	465,509	223,705	241,804	273,953	134,192	139,761	422,201	210,778	211,423
253,192	123,413	129,779	464,188	222,542	241,646	271,533	131,984	139,549	412,983	202,185	210,798
1,900	1,610	290	1,298	1,145	153	2,286	2,074	212	9,109	8,506	603
919	*779*	*140*	*717*	*632*	*85*	*987*	*941*	*46*	*5,928*	*5,587*	*336*
915	779	136	697	612	85	987	941	46	5,922	5,586	336
3	3	...	9	9	...	...	...	...	...	...	...
493	425	68	366	324	42	263	251	12	1,569	1,455	114
43	*35*	*8*	*34*	*28*	*6*	*15*	*14*	*1*	*90*	*73*	*17*
194	*192*	*2*	*162*	*155*	*7*	*76*	*76*	...	*860*	*839*	*21*
16	*14*	*2*	*19*	*19*	...	*5*	*4*	*1*	*69*	*56*	*13*
13	*13*	...	*1*	*1*	...	...	...	...	*38*	*38*	...
419	351	68	322	279	43	724	690	34	4,353	4,131	222
83	*81*	*2*	*66*	*66*	...	*419*	*410*	*9*	*3,293*	*3,256*	*37*
34	*31*	*3*	...	...	...	*8*	*8*	...	...	...	...
2	...	*2*	...	...	...	...	...	...	*6*	*3*	*3*
7	*5*	*2*	*5*	*4*	*1*	*25*	*25*	...	*145*	*133*	*12*
7	*6*	*1*	*27*	*24*	*3*	*52*	*52*	...	*80*	*75*	*5*
15	*8*	*7*	...	...	...	*21*	*19*	*2*	*4*	...	*4*
5	*1*	*4*	*4*	*4*	...	*11*	*11*	...	*80*	*80*	...
4	...	4	20	20	...	...	...	...	1	1	...
...	...	...	1	1	...	...	...	...	...	...	...
...	...	...	1	1	...	...	...	...	1	1	...
4	...	4	18	18	...	...	...	...	...	...	...
981	*831*	*150*	*581*	*513*	*68*	*1,299*	*1,133*	*166*	*3,186*	*2,919*	*267*
896	773	123	545	482	63	1,069	929	140	3,042	2,784	258
133	121	12	37	37	...	181	180	1	454	444	10
36	*35*	*1*	*3*	*3*	...	*45*	*45*	...	*58*	*58*	...
12	*10*	*2*	*6*	*6*	...	...	...	...	*36*	*32*	*4*
66	*63*	*3*	*2*	*2*	...	*87*	*86*	*1*	*329*	*329*	...
78	67	11	46	39	7	45	36	9	174	154	20
238	198	40	180	149	31	324	274	50	602	514	88
420	370	50	272	247	25	512	439	73	1,732	1,592	140
59	*58*	*1*	*5*	*3*	*2*	*23*	*16*	*7*	*74*	*74*	...
170	*135*	*35*	*75*	*66*	*9*	*162*	*141*	*21*	*423*	*399*	*24*
...	...	...	...	...	...	...	...	...	*116*	*116*	...
118	*105*	*13*	*77*	*66*	*11*	*109*	*95*	*14*	*503*	*446*	*57*
85	58	27	36	31	5	230	204	26	144	135	9
11	11	...	19	19	...	160	160	...	50	50	...
43	21	22	8	3	5	23	2	21	...	...	...
...	...	...	1	1	...	...	...	...	...	...	...
4	4	...	22	17	5	184	184	...	109	87	22
275	230	45	235	216	19	330	288	42	620	563	57
270	225	45	197	180	17	329	287	42	477	429	48
...	...	...	...	...	...	...	..	...	5	...	5
...	...	...	...	...	...	...	...	...	60	60	...
2	2	...	39	37	2	...	...	...	1	1	...
...	...	...	...	...	...	...	...	...			
25	19	6	20	16	4	12	10	2	212	163	49
25	19	6	19	15	4	12	10	2	202	157	45
17	*11*	*6*	*12*	*10*	*2*	*11*	*9*	*2*	*140*	*102*	*38*
8	*8*	...	*7*	*5*	*2*	...	..	...	*52*	*46*	*6*
...	...	...	...	...	...	*1*	*1*	...	*10*	*9*	*1*
...	...	...	...	..	...	...	...	...	1	1	...
1	1	...	...	...	...	...	...	...	...	...	...
7	4	3	7	6	1	7	5	2	213	179	34
1	...	1	...	...	...	...	...	...	21	13	8
2	1	1	1	1	...	...	...	...	121	104	17
2	2	...	...	...	...	...	...	...	6	3	3
...	...	...	...	...	...	...	...	...	...	...	...
...	...	...	...	...	...	...	...	...	...	...	...

Birth-place.	DISTRICT IN								
	PAKÔKKU HILL TRACTS.			MANDALAY (INCLUDING MANDALAY CITY).			MANDALAY CITY.		
	Persons.	Males.	Females.	Persons.	Males.	Females.	Persons.	Males.	Females.
1	86	87	88	89	90	91	92	93	94
TOTAL POPULATION ...	20,048	9,840	10,208	356,621	182,999	173,622	148,917	77,763	71,154
A. INDIA (including Burma)	**19,995**	**9,801**	**10,194**	**352,121**	**179,366**	**172,755**	**147,071**	**76,220**	**70,851**
A-I Burma	19,898	9,714	10,184	329,509	160,710	168,799	134,792	65 849	68,943
A-II Other British Provinces and Indian States.	97	87	10	22,855	18,469	3,886	12,043	10,200	1,843
(*a*) *Contiguous Provinces*	*16*	*11*	*5*	*11,291*	*9,170*	*2,121*	*6,087*	*5,127*	*960*
(i) British Territory	16	11	5	11,257	9,144	2,113	6,078	5,118	960
Assam	2	2	..	19	13	6	8	5	3
Bengal	12	7	5	5,112	4,276	836	3,584	3,079	505
Calcutta	...	...	...	449	362	87	303	257	46
Chittagong	1	1	...	1,141	1,119	22	781	772	9
Dacca	...	..	...	154	76	78	68	42	26
Noakhali	...	...	...	8	8	...	...	..	...
Madras	2	2	...	6,126	4,855	1,271	2,486	2,034	452
Ganjam	...	...	...	886	862	24	181	181	..
Godavari	...	...	...	66	58	8	40	38	2
Kistna	...	...	...	55	45	9	24	24	...
Malabar	2	2	...	131	123	8	29	29	...
Ramnad	...	...	...	60	60	...	56	56	...
Tanjore	...	..	...	162	135	27	78	75	3
Vizagapatam	.	...	...	614	493	122	189	171	18
(ii) Indian States	..	...	...	34	26	8	9	9	...
Bengal States	...	...	...	10	8	2	...	...	..
Madras States	...	...	...	19	13	6	9	9	...
Manipur	...	...	...	5	5	...	...	...	...
(*b*) *Non-Contiguous Provinces*	*81*	*76*	*5*	*11,064*	*9,299*	*1,765*	*5,956*	*5,078*	*883*
(i) British Territory	80	75	5	10,017	8,569	1,448	5,195	4,483	712
Bihar and Orissa	1	1	...	519	482	37	154	154	...
Chapra	..	...	...	105	108	...	44	44	...
Patna	...	...	...	36	36	...	22	22	...
Puri	...	...	...	102	102	...	10	10	...
Bombay and Aden	.	...	...	1,017	763	254	726	545	181
Punjab	8	7	1	2,677	2,208	469	1,653	1,382	271
United Provinces	71	67	4	5,358	4,718	640	2,335	2,113	222
Azamgarh	...	...	...	450	432	18	177	175	2
Fyzabad	...	...	...	1,210	1,002	208	440	397	43
Gorakhpur	...	...	...	154	130	24	41	41	...
Sultanpur	...	...	...	896	804	92	448	410	38
(ii) States and Agencies	1	1	...	1,047	730	317	761	590	171
Bombay States	...	...	...	277	209	68	246	186	60
Rajputana Agency	...	.	...	247	164	83	210	164	46
A-III French and Portuguese Settlements.	...	...	...	1	1	...	...	...	...
A-IV India (part unspecified)	...	...	...	256	186	70	236	171	65
B. OTHER ASIATIC COUNTRIES	**47**	**38**	**9**	**2,943**	**2,445**	**498**	**1,413**	**1,226**	**187**
China	...	...	...	1,692	1,461	231	1,271	1,104	167
Japan	...	...	...	13	8	5	12	8	4
Nepal	47	38	9	1,140	890	250	97	83	14
Siam	..	...	...	...	...	..	...	...	...
C. EUROPE	**1**	**1**	...	**1,499**	**1,155**	**344**	**417**	**310**	**107**
United Kingdom	1	1	...	1,437	1,128	309	371	293	78
England and Wales	1	1	...	1,286	1,056	230	317	255	62
Scotland	...	...	...	83	43	40	32	24	8
Ireland	...	...	...	68	29	39	22	14	8
France	...	...	...	43	18	25	36	15	21
D. AFRICA	...	...	...	**15**	**14**	**1**	...	...	...
E. AMERICA	...	...	...	**20**	**6**	**14**	**11**	**4**	**7**
Canada	...	...	...	5	1	4	3	...	3
United States	...	...	...	6	3	3	6	3	3
F. AUSTRALASIA	...	...	...	**23**	**13**	**10**	**5**	**3**	**2**
G. AT SEA	...	...	...	...	...	...	...	...	...
H. NOT RECORDED	...	...	...	...	...	...	...	..	...

WHICH ENUMERATED.

Bhamo.			Myitkyina.			Katha.			Putao.			Shwebo.		
Persons.	Males.	Females.	Persons.	Males.	Females.	Persons.	Males.	Females.	Persons.	Males.	Females.	Persons.	Mal s.	Females.
95	96	97	98	99	100	101	102	103	104	105	106	107	108	109
112,960	56,888	56,072	118,382	63,419	54,963	253,725	128,444	125,281	7,678	4,144	3,529	391,284	184,708	206,576
101,584	**50,670**	**50,914**	**109,607**	**57,081**	**52,526**	**249,506**	**125,380**	**124,126**	**6,885**	**3,436**	**3,449**	**390,842**	**184,344**	**206,498**
98,629	48,079	50 550	103,008	54,141	51,867	243,249	122,532	123,717	6,638	3,230	3,408	387,635	181,668	205,967
2,954	2,591	363	3,594	2,935	659	3,092	2,772	320	247	206	41	3,034	2,542	522
499	*482*	*67*	*1,468*	*1,145*	*318*	*1,661*	*1,569*	*92*	*115*	*91*	*24*	*1,466*	*1,290*	*176*
464	399	65	1,406	1,097	309	1,661	1,569	92	112	88	24	1,463	1,290	173
1	1	...	70	47	23	79	70	9	19	18	1	1	...	1
297	273	24	681	467	214	881	846	35	82	60	22	872	772	100
19	18	1	37	31	6	105	99	6	...	...	...	50	42	8
212	205	7	164	155	9	236	232	4	12	11	1	223	216	7
33	22	11	19	17	2	21	18	3	3	2	1	26	13	13
...	...	...	...	...	...	...	...	...	...	..	...	18	12	6
166	125	41	655	583	72	701	653	48	11	10	1	590	518	72
9	9	...	420	401	19	147	147	...	2	2	...	81	79	2
1	...	1	...	...	...	8	8	...	...	...	...	2	1	1
...	...	...	...	...	...	...	...	...	...	...	...	1	1	...
18	18	...	23	23	...	37	36	1	2	1	1	40	40	...
12	12	...	...	...	...	42	42	...	.	...	...	4	1	3
2	2	...	4	3	1	14	14	..	.	...	...	17	17	...
8	8	...	9	7	2	55	41	14	2	2	...	11	3	8
35	33	2	57	48	9	...	...	...	3	3	...	3	...	3
...	...	...	...	...	...	..	...	...	...	...	...	...	...	...
8	8	...	1	..	1	...	...	...	1	1	...	...	...	...
27	25	2	56	48	8	...	...	...	2	2	...	3	...	3
2,455	*2,159*	*296*	*2,131*	*1,790*	*341*	*1,481*	*1,208*	*228*	*132*	*115*	*17*	*1,598*	*1,252*	*346*
2,293	2,032	261	1,994	1,685	309	1,291	1,068	223	123	107	16	1,544	1,212	332
35	35	...	324	320	4	64	64	...	1	1	...	109	102	7
...	...	...	8	7	1	4	4	...	...	...	...	14	14	...
...	..	...	4	3	1	4	4	...	...	...	...	11	11	...
...	...	...	83	83	...	8	8	...	...	...	...	...	...	...
138	134	4	38	30	8	52	44	8	1	1	...	83	68	15
1,366	1,218	148	812	689	123	492	380	112	70	57	13	514	404	110
685	501	94	799	626	173	678	576	102	48	45	3	805	626	179
170	151	19	85	66	19	16	15	1	4	4	...	47	32	15
30	30	...	224	163	61	150	132	18	8	8	...	157	102	55
...	..	...	57	42	15	4	4	...	...	...	...	13	12	1
87	46	41	192	145	47	121	108	13	14	13	1	214	155	59
162	127	35	137	105	32	140	135	5	9	8	1	54	40	14
...	...	...	27	22	5	45	42	3	...	...	...	13	13	...
3	2	1	34	28	6	36	36	...	1	1	...	5	1	4
...	...	...	...	...	...	...	...	...	...	...	...	8	2	1
1	...	1	5	5	...	165	76	89	...	...	...	140	132	8
11,332	**6,181**	**5,151**	**8,742**	**6,316**	**2,426**	**4,200**	**3,052**	**1,148**	**786**	**706**	**80**	**390**	**331**	**59**
10,928	5,795	5,133	5,060	3,708	1,352	3,229	2,444	785	167	163	4	362	306	56
153	152	1	..	.	...	..	..	...	...	...	...	...	...	...
251	234	17	3,667	2,594	1,073	958	598	360	618	542	76	27	24	3
...	...	...	3	3	..	3	1	2	...	...	...	...	...	...
40	**35**	**5**	**29**	**19**	**10**	**19**	**12**	**7**	**2**	**2**	...	**42**	**26**	**16**
35	30	5	12	2	10	19	12	7	1	1	...	34	22	12
22	20	2	9	...	9	15	9	6	...	...	...	21	13	8
5	3	2	2	2	...	3	2	1	1	1	...	8	7	1
8	7	1	1	...	1	1	1	...	...	...	...	5	2	3
4	4	...	1	1	...	...	...	...	...	...	...	5	2	3
1	**1**	...	**2**	**2**	...	...	...	...	...	...	...	**1**	**1**	...
3	**1**	**2**	**1**	...	**1**	...	...	...	...	...	...	**5**	**2**	**3**
...	...	...	...	...	...	...	...	...	...	...	...	1	...	1
...	...	...	1	...	1	...	...	...	...	...	...	3	1	2
...	...	...	**1**	**1**	...	...	...	...	...	...	...	**2**	**2**	...
...	...	...	...	...	..	...	...	...	...	...	...	**2**	**2**	...
...	...	...	...	...	...	...	...	...	...	...	...	...	...	...

DISTRICT IN

Birth-place.	Sagaing.			Lower Chindwin.			Upper Chindwin.		
	Persons.	Males.	Females.	Persons.	Males.	Females.	Persons.	Males.	Females.
1	110	111	112	113	114	115	116	117	118
TOTAL POPULATION ...	326,908	155,054	171,854	342,880	156,693	186,187	179,245	90,713	88,532
A. INDIA (including Burma)	**326,783**	**154,942**	**171,841**	**342,613**	**156,475**	**186,138**	**178,035**	**89,749**	**88,286**
A-I Burma	324,840	153,347	171,493	340,925	155,018	185,907	174,600	87,244	87,356
A-II Other British Provinces and Indian States.	1,926	1,578	348	1,604	1,379	225	3,434	2,505	929
(a) *Contiguous Provinces*	*988*	*831*	*157*	*655*	*554*	*101*	*2,268*	*1,481*	*782*
(i) British Territory	987	830	157	648	548	100	1,061	869	192
Assam	2	2	...	..	..	--	277	153	124
Bengal	509	461	48	432	381	51	521	484	37
Calcutta	*12*	*6*	*6*	*30*	*28*	*2*	*16*	*14*	*2*
Chittagong	*269*	*264*	*5*	*161*	*156*	*5*	*333*	*327*	*6*
Dacca	*21*	*19*	*2*	*10*	*5*	*5*	*24*	*19*	*5*
Noakhali	*3*	*3*	...	...	...	...	*2*	*2*	...
Madras	476	367	109	216	167	49	263	232	31
Ganjam	*55*	*55*	...	*44*	*42*	*2*	*87*	*75*	*12*
Godavari	..	...	...	*5*	*3*	*2*	*4*	*4*	...
Kistna	...	...	...	..	...	...	...	..	...
Malabar	*22*	*18*	*4*	*41*	*39*	*2*	*13*	*10*	*3*
Ramnad	*25*	*25*	...	..	...	..	...	...	...
Tanjore	*16*	*7*	*9*	*1*	*1*	...	*1*	*1*	...
Vizagapatam	*112*	*88*	*24*	*9*	*6*	*3*	...	...	...
(ii) Indian States	1	1	...	7	6	1	1,202	612	590
Bengal States	1	1	...	7	6	1	...	...	...
Madras States	...	...	...	...	...	...	...	...	...
Manipur	...	...	...	7	6	1	1,202	612	590
(b) *Non-Contiguous Provinces*	*938*	*747*	*191*	*949*	*825*	*124*	*1,171*	*1,024*	*147*
(i) British Territory	891	707	184	902	781	121	1,113	970	143
Bihar and Orissa	34	29	5	46	42	4	161	161	...
Chapra	...	...	...	*6*	*5*	*1*	*2*	*2*	...
Patna	...	...	...	*4*	*4*	...	*5*	*5*	...
Puri	*1*	...	*1*	*2*	*2*	...	*14*	*14*	...
Bombay and Aden	37	33	4	36	31	5	111	110	1
Punjab	183	147	36	300	252	48	421	336	85
United Provinces	633	494	139	510	446	64	384	354	30
Azamgarh	*27*	*27*	..	*17*	*15*	*2*	*8*	...	*8*
Fyzabad	*215*	*166*	*49*	*53*	*40*	*13*	*5*	*5*	...
Gorakhpur	*12*	*6*	*6*	..	...	...	..	...	...
Sultanpur	*149*	*124*	*25*	*159*	*130*	*29*	*14*	*14*	...
(ii) States and Agencies	47	40	7	47	44	3	58	54	4
Bombay States	11	10	1	28	27	...	...	...	...
Rajputana Agency	22	21	1	2	1	1	20	20	...
A-III French and Portuguese Settlements.	1	1	...	1	1	...	...	...	...
A-IV India (part unspecified)	16	16	...	88	77	6	1	...	1
B. OTHER ASIATIC COUNTRIES	**115**	**104**	**11**	**251**	**207**	**44**	**1,176**	**939**	**237**
China	100	92	8	153	131	22	99	94	5
Japan	...	...	...	...	...	...	...	...	...
Nepal	7	7	...	64	53	11	1,074	842	232
Siam	3	2	1	14	6	8	2	2	...
C. EUROPE	**9**	**8**	**1**	**16**	**11**	**5**	**32**	**23**	**9**
United Kingdom	6	5	1	16	11	5	32	23	9
England and Wales	*5*	*4*	*1*	*15*	*10*	*5*	*26*	*19*	*7*
Scotland	*1*	*1*	...	*1*	*1*	...	*5*	*4*	*1*
Ireland	...	...	...	...	...	...	*1*	...	*1*
France	2	2	...	...	...	...	...	...	...
D. AFRICA	...	...	...	...	...	...	...	...	...
E. AMERICA	**1**	...	**1**	...	...	...	**2**	**2**	...
Canada	...	...	...	...	...	...	...	...	...
United States	...	...	...	...	...	...	...	...	...
F. AUSTRALASIA	...	...	...	...	...	...	...	...	...
G. AT SEA	...	...	...	...	...	...	...	...	...
H. NOT RECORDED	...	...	...	...	...	...	...	...	...

WHICH ENUMERATED.

Chin Hills.			Kyauksè.			Meiktila.			Yamèthin.			Myingyan.		
Persons.	Males.	Females.	Persons.	Males.	Females.	Persons.	Males.	Females.	Persons.	Males.	Females.	Persons.	Males.	Females.
119	120	121	122	123	124	125	126	127	128	129	130	131	132	133
110,079	54,122	55,957	142,677	70,449	72,228	289,897	137,573	152,324	323,189	160,913	162,276	442,008	213,294	228,714
109,821	53,877	55,944	142 533	70,329	72,204	289,365	137,122	152,243	322,303	160,183	162,120	441,712	213,055	228,657
109,002	53,265	55,737	141,348	69,317	72,031	285,942	134,277	151,665	314,749	153,933	160,816	439,589	211,223	228,366
816	609	207	1,153	986	167	3,166	2,613	553	7,526	6,233	1,293	2,019	1,737	282
121	*71*	*50*	*665*	*593*	*72*	*1,441*	*1,121*	*320*	*4,535*	*3,764*	*771*	*1,148*	*994*	*154*
113	64	49	658	590	68	1,429	1,109	320	4,487	3,719	768	1,148	994	154
7	4	3	...	...	...	9	9	..	1	1	...	...	..	...
86	48	38	212	189	23	556	428	128	1,324	1,103	321	391	325	66
4	*4*	...	*33*	*26*	*7*	*84*	*70*	*14*	*68*	*50*	*18*	*31*	*25*	*6*
8	*7*	1	*32*	*29*	*3*	*81*	*73*	*8*	*184*	*179*	*5*	*171*	*164*	*7*
10	*6*	*4*	*1*	*1*	..	*39*	*35*	*4*	*57*	*45*	*12*	*7*	*6*	*1*
...	...	...	...	..	.	*26*	*26*	...	...	...	...	*3*	*3*	...
20	12	8	446	401	45	864	672	192	3,162	2,615	547	757	669	88
...	...	...	*148*	*146*	*2*	*123*	*118*	*5*	*776*	*765*	*11*	*135*	*135*	...
...	...	...	*1*	*1*	...	*33*	*33*	...	*224*	*90*	*134*	*11*	*11*	...
...	...	...	*7*	*7*	.	*4*	*1*	*3*		...	..	*8*	*8*	...
...	-	...	*31*	*31*	..	*79*	*66*	*13*	*117*	*112*	*5*	*28*	*24*	*4*
...	...	...	*21*	*21*	...	*34*	*30*	*4*	*80*	*72*	*8*	*80*	*71*	*9*
...	...	...	*3*	*3*	...	*21*	*15*	*6*	*43*	*8*	*35*	*52*	*52*	...
...	...	...	*11*	*11*	.	*12*	*12*	...	*360*	*260*	*100*	*5*	*5*	...
8	7	1	7	3	4	12	12	...	48	45	3	...	...	...
...	...	...	...	...	...	...	...	-	..	..	...	...	...	..
...	...	...	3	1	2	...	...	...	45	45	...	..	...	...
8	7	1	4	2	2	12	12	..	3	...	3	...	...	...
695	*538*	*157*	*488*	*393*	*95*	*1,725*	*1,492*	*233*	*2,991*	*2,469*	*522*	*871*	*743*	*128*
680	533	147	463	380	3	1,526	1,329	197	2,745	2,259	486	852	731	121
2	2	...	27	23	4	162	154	8	219	214	5	29	29	...
...	...	...	...	...	...	*24*	*22*	*2*	*22*	*22*	...	*14*	*14*	...
...	...	...	*4*	...	*4*	*21*	*20*	*1*	...	...	..	*12*	*12*	...
...	...	..	*8*	*8*	...	*27*	*27*	...	*1*	...	1	...	...	...
1	...	1	41	39	2	145	123	22	256	203	53	87	63	24
110	93	17	178	145	33	408	338	70	693	577	116	149	118	31
458	437	21	207	169	38	751	659	92	1,541	1,239	302	574	514	60
..	...	...	*10*	*4*	*6*	*73*	*61*	*12*	*244*	*235*	*9*	*12*	*12*	...
9	*9*	...	*52*	*43*	*9*	*178*	*143*	*35*	*395*	*292*	*103*	*95*	*69*	*26*
...	...	...	*4*	*2*	*2*	*15*	*15*	...	*11*	*11*	...	*9*	*9*	...
6	*4*	*2*	*84*	*72*	*12*	*196*	*166*	*30*	*256*	*191*	*65*	*175*	*155*	*20*
15	5	10	25	13	12	199	163	36	246	210	36	19	12	7
...	...	...	4	4	...	60	48	12	75	55	20	6	..	6
2	2	...	...	...	...	25	21	4	119	117	2	8	8	...
...	...	...	...	...	...	...	...	...	1	1	...	2	1	1
8	8	...	32	26	6	257	232	25	27	16	11	102	94	8
238	237	1	127	107	20	439	395	44	833	685	148	277	222	55
23	22	1	118	102	16	316	297	19	578	482	96	272	219	53
...	...	...	...	...	...		...	..	...	...	...	2	...	2
215	215	...	...	...	...	114	89	25	247	195	52	3	3	...
...	...	...	1	...	1	...	...	...	4	4	...	...	...	...
19	7	12	16	12	4	77	46	31	51	43	8	13	12	1
19	*7*	12	12	9	3	72	44	28	50	42	8	9	8	1
18	*7*	*11*	*9*	*6*	*3*	*54*	*32*	*22*	*37*	*33*	*4*	*6*	*6*	...
1	...	1	*3*	*3*	..	*14*	*8*	*6*	*7*	*6*	*1*	*3*	*2*	*1*
...	...	...	...	..	..	*4*	4	...	*6*	*3*	*3*	...	...	...
...	...	...	3	3	...	4	1	3	...	...		1	1	...
...	...	...	...	...	...	...	...	...	...	...	...	1	1	...
1	1	...	...	...	...	16	10	6	2	2	...	3	3	...
...	...	...	...	...	...	3	2	1	...	...	...	1	1	...
...	...	...	...	...	...	6	2	4	...	...	...	...	...	...
...	...	...	1	1	...	...	...	...	...	...	...	2	1	1
...	...	...	...	...	...	...	...	...	...	...	...	...	...	...
...	...	...	...	...	...	...	...	...	...	...	...	...	...	...

IMPERIAL TABLE XIA.—*Birth-place.* PART I.—*General Statement*—concluded.

Birth-place.	AREA IN WHICH ENUMERATED.								
	NORTHERN SHAN STATES.			SOUTHERN SHAN STATES.			KARENNI.		
	Persons.	Males.	Females.	Persons.	Males.	Females.	Persons.	Males.	Females.
1	134	135	136	137	138	139	140	141	142
TOTAL POPULATION ...	559,223	285,700	273,523	847,618	427,064	420,554	63,850	31,129	32,721
A. INDIA (including Burma)	**532,604**	**268,118**	**264,486**	**840,387**	**421,958**	**418,429**	**62,319**	**30,036**	**32,283**
A-I Burma	525,417	261,588	263,829	837,093	419,115	417,978	62,045	29,788	32,257
A-II Other British Provinces and Indian States.	7,180	6,523	657	3,289	2,838	451	274	248	26
(a) *Contiguous Provinces*	*2 627*	*2,418*	*209*	*1,147*	*995*	*152*	*114*	*109*	*5*
(i) **British Territory**	2,582	2,378	204	1,147	995	152	114	109	5
Assam	4	4	...	3	2	1	...	...	...
Bengal	1,170	1,066	104	609	499	110	50	47	3
Calcutta	75	65	10	68	53	15	...	...	...
Chittagong	590	573	17	164	148	16	32	30	2
Dacca	58	45	13	16	11	5	...	...	...
Noakhali	39	39	...	11	11	...	...	...	...
Madras	1,408	1,308	100	535	494	41	64	62	2
Ganjam	799	795	4	129	129	...	42	42	...
Godavari	2	1	1	1	...	1	8	8	...
Kistna	5	5	...	..	...	..	...	...	...
Malabar	132	119	13	3	2	1	4	3	1
Ramnad	10	10	...	5	5	..	1	1	...
Tanjore	16	16	...	2	2	...	...	...	...
Vizagapatam	15	12	3	...	...	...	...	...	...
(ii) **Indian States**	45	40	5	...	...	...	...	...	...
Bengal States	2	2	...	...	.	...	...	...	...
Madras States	...	...	...	...	...	...	...	...	...
Manipur	43	38	5	...	...	...	...	...	..
(b) *Non-Contiguous Provinces*	*4,553*	*4,105*	*448*	*2,142*	*1,843*	*299*	*160*	*139*	*21*
(i) **British Territory**	4,260	3,870	390	2,004	1,738	266	141	125	16
Bihar and Orissa	1,437	1,423	14	84	84	...	10	10	...
Chapra	13	11	2	...	...	...	...	...	...
Patna	15	10	5	...	...	...	...	...	...
Puri	110	108	2	3	3	...	.	...	...
Bombay and Aden	262	219	43	173	139	34	5	5	...
Punjab	991	843	148	940	783	157	86	74	12
United Provinces	1,492	1,319	173	742	671	71	40	36	4
Azamgarh	35	33	2	43	43	..	...	...	...
Fyzabad	192	167	25	108	93	15	...	...	...
Gorakhpur	47	47	...	68	55	13	...	...	...
Sultanpur	297	256	41	47	43	4	5	5	...
(ii) **States and Agencies**	293	235	58	138	105	33	19	14	5
Bombay States	130	129	1	81	65	16	18	13	5
Rajputana Agency	107	57	50	5	4	1	...	...	...
A-III French and Portuguese Settlements.	4	4		3	3	...	...	...	...
A-IV India (part unspecified)	8	8	...	2	2	...	...	...	...
B. OTHER ASIATIC COUNTRIES	**26,429**	**17,452**	**8,977**	**7,136**	**5,060**	**2,076**	**1,506**	**1,068**	**438**
China	24,514	15,860	8,654	3,095	2,290	805	319	306	13
Japan	1	1	..	.	..		...	...	...
Nepal	1,865	1,546	319	1,465	1,135	330	106	99	7
Siam	13	10	3	2,226	1,361	865	1,080	662	418
C. EUROPE	**108**	**77**	**31**	**81**	**42**	**39**	**25**	**25**	...
United Kingdom	102	71	31	66	35	31	6	6	...
England and Wales	76	53	23	44	22	22	5	5	...
Scotland	16	9	7	20	11	9	1	1	...
Ireland	10	9	1	2	2	...	...	...	...
France	...	..	.	3	3	...	17	17	...
D. AFRICA	...	..	...	...	.	...	...	...	...
E. AMERICA	**21**	**12**	**9**	**14**	**4**	**10**	...	...	...
Canada	1	1	...	..	...	...	...	...	...
United States	7	4	3	3	1	2	...	...	...
F. AUSTRALASIA	**61**	**41**	**20**	...	...	...	...	...	...
G. AT SEA	...	...	...	...	...	...	...	...	...
H. NOT RECORDED	...	...	...	...	...	...	...	...	...

SECTION A.—*Details by Provinces and Countries not separately shown in Part I.*

(Figures are totals enumerated in the whole of Burma.)

Birth-places.	Males.	Females.
A-II (b). Details of Non-Contiguous Provinces of India.	120,581	20,735
(i) BRITISH TERRITORY ...	*108,620*	*17,993*
Details in Part I	106,085	17,491
Ajmer-Merwara	38	2
Andaman and Nicobar Islands	102	26
Baluchistan	24	5
Central Provinces and Berar	797	268
Coorg	3	...
Delhi	635	92
North-West Frontier Province	936	109
(ii) INDIAN STATES AND AGENCIES	*11,961*	*2,742*
Details in Part I	7,378	1,695
Baluchistan States ...	...	2
Baroda State	578	84
Bihar and Orissa States ...	349	78
Central Indian Agency ...	459	46
Central Province States ...	318	42
Gwalior State	122	7
Hyderabad State	376	118
Kashmir	136	13
Mysore	1,192	448
North-West Frontier Province, Tribal Area and Agencies.	11	1
Punjab States	963	171
Sikkhim	10	5
States of the United Provinces ..	69	32
A-III. French and Portuguese Settlements.	563	88
Goa	533	82
Pondicherry	30	6
B. Other Asiatic Countries ...	94,454	32,339
Details in Part I	92,334	31,816
Afghanistan	76	1
Arabia	43	...
Armenia	8	4
Asia Minor	4	...
Ceylon	1,065	126
French Indo-China	277	76
Hongkong	7	...
Mesopotamia	124	103
Persia	90	35
Straits Settlements and Federated Malay States.	408	178
Tibet	18	...

Birth-places.	Males.	Females.
C. Europe ...	5,040	1,513
Details in Part I	4,874	1,437
Belgium	16	4
Czeko-Slovakia ...	2	...
Denmark	6	1
Germany	11	2
Gibraltar ...	1	1
Greece	11	2
Holland	24	6
Italy	33	38
Malta	3	4
Rumania	1	1
Russia	16	6
Servia	2	...
Spain	4	6
Sweden	4	3
Switzerland	13	7
Turkey in Europe	3	3
Europe (country unspecified)	16	2
D. Africa	52	18
Cape Verde	1	...
Egypt	5	...
Mauritius	1	...
St. Helena	11	...
South Africa	2	13
Africa (part unspecified) ...	32	5
E. America	355	204
Details in Part I	185	112
British Guiana	1	...
Jamaica	1	...
Mexico	1	...
North America (unspecified part)	...	1
South America (unspecified part)	4	1
West Indies (unspecified part) ..	1	...
America (country unspecified)	162	90
F. Australasia	139	75
Australia	108	58
Borneo	1	...
Celebes	...	1
Fiji Islands	4	...
Java	...	4
New Zealand	13	7
Philippine Islands	13	5

SECTION B.—*Details by districts for certain Indian Provinces.*

(Figures are totals enumerated in the whole of Burma.)

Province and District of Birth-place.	Males.	Females.
Bengal ..	129,960	16,098
Details in Part I ...	95,837	10,459
Darjeeling ...	682	464
Hoogly ...	492	95
Murshidabad ...	446	8
Mymensingh ...	1,743	23
Tipperrah ...	587	35
Other Districts ...	2,218	314
District unspecified*	27,955	4,700
Madras ...	225,868	46,643
Details in Part I ...	133,532	18,291
Madura ...	4,681	1,522
Guntur ...	1,235	173
Tinnavelly ...	3,678	766
Trichinopoly ...	1,433	396
Other Districts ...	5,102	1,196
District unspecified †	76,207	24,299

Province and District of Birth-place.	Males.	Females.
Bihar and Orissa ..	17,574	2,615
Details in Part I ..	7,147	522
Arrah ..	2,837	1,693
Cuttack ...	1,184	56
Other Districts .	2,762	174
District unspecified	3,644	170
Bombay and Aden ..	10,098	2,718
Aden ...	7	4
Hyderabad (Scind)	2,720	687
Surat ...	2,395	801
Other Districts	1,881	295
District unspecified	3,095	931
Punjab	16,460	3,344
Amritsar .	2,009	379
Lahore ...	1,371	288
Other Districts	5,652	1,131
District unspecified	7,428	1,546

Province and District of Birth-place.	Males.	Females.
United Provinces .	61,953	8,814
Details in Part I ...	35,775	4,155
Agra ...	3,705	1,803
Allahabad ...	1,266	256
Almora ...	1,450	84
Barabanki ..	1,125	139
Basti ...	1,269	117
Benares ...	1,253	252
Garhwal ...	1,155	109
Ghazipur ...	1,016	136
Gonda ...	3,359	435
Jaunpur ...	2,603	174
Partabgarh ...	1,128	229
Other Districts ...	3,471	658
District unspecified	3,078	267

SECTION C.—*District of enumeration in Burma of persons born in unspecified districts of Madras or Bengal.*

MADRAS.

District of Enumeration.	Males.	Females.
Total	76,207	24,299
Akyab ...	1,399	31
Rangoon ...	12,111	6,498
Insein	4,692	1,706
Hanthawaddy ...	14,371	4,479
Tharrawaddy ...	1,028	297
Pegu	8,039	2,949
Prome ...	1,748	593
Bassein ...	1,970	341
Henzada ...	2,173	293
Myaungmya ...	2,599	381
Ma-ubin ...	1,796	259
Pyapôn ..	7,030	1,027
Toungoo ...	1,621	325
Thatôn ...	3,458	1,045
Amherst ...	3,688	915
Mandalay ...	1,569	565
Yamèthin ...	1,107	250

BENGAL.

District of Enumeration.	Males.	Females.
Total	27,955	4,700
Akyab ...	1,989	279
Insein ...	2,127	440
Hanthawaddy ..	1,828	532
Pegu ..	2,282	686
Bassein ...	1,402	115
Myaungmya ...	3,745	154
Pyapôn ...	1,106	146
Thatôn ...	2,450	431
Mandalay ...	2,557	113

DISTRICT OR OTHER AREA

	District, etc., of Birth-place.	THE WHOLE PROVINCE.			DIVISIONAL BURMA.			EASTERN STATES.		
		Persons.	Males.	Females.	Persons.	Males.	Females.	Persons.	Males.	Females.
	1	2	3	4	5	6	7	8	9	10
	ALL BURMA ...	12,462,350	6,148,649	6,313,701	11,037,795	5,438,158	5,599,637	1,424,555	710,491	714,064
	Divisional Burma ...	11,030,563	5,434,945	5,595,618	11,013,677	5,424,620	5,589,057	16,886	10,325	6,561
	Arakan Division ...	*864,250*	*431,698*	*432,552*	*864,066*	*431,592*	*432,474*	*184*	*106*	*78*
1	Akyab .	525,150	265,974	259,176	525,141	265,969	259,172	9	5	4
2	Hill District of Arakan ...	20,251	10,310	9,941	20,186	10,303	9,883	65	7	58
3	Kyaukpyu ...	205,306	99,900	105,406	205,233	99,834	105,399	73	66	7
4	Sandoway ...	113,543	55,514	58,029	113,506	55,486	58,020	37	28	9
	Pegu Division ...	*1,898,420*	*940,815*	*957,605*	*1,897,412*	*940,182*	*957,280*	*1,008*	*633*	*375*
5	Rangoon Town ...	145,055	73,065	71,990	144,407	72,662	71,745	648	403	245
6	Insein ...	234,310	116,957	117,353	234,276	116,931	117,345	34	26	8
7	Hanthawaddy ...	321,706	162,102	159,604	321,675	162,081	159,594	31	21	10
8	Tharrawaddy ...	462,106	225,330	236,776	462,026	225,281	236,745	80	49	31
9	Pegu ..	342,502	171,396	171,106	342,389	171,330	171,059	113	66	47
10	Prome ...	392,741	191,965	200,776	392,639	191,897	200,742	102	68	34
	Irrawaddy Division ...	*1,856,864*	*920,717*	*936,147*	*1,856,242*	*920,284*	*935,958*	*622*	*433*	*189*
11	Bassein ...	465,577	230,980	234,597	465,480	230,919	234,561	97	61	36
12	Henzada ...	569,406	280,001	289,405	569,332	279,963	289,369	74	38	36
13	Myaungmya ...	296,700	147,634	149,066	296,299	147,336	148,963	401	298	103
14	Ma-ubin ...	318,394	158,561	159,833	318,368	158,546	159,822	26	15	11
15	Pyapôn ...	206,787	103,541	103,246	206,763	103,520	103,243	24	21	3
	Tenasserim Division ...	*1,495,548*	*755,227*	*740,316*	*1,494,386*	*754,458*	*739,928*	*1,157*	*769*	*388*
16	Toungoo ...	317,579	158,508	159,071	316,966	158,119	158,847	613	389	224
17	Salween ...	46,314	23,744	22,570	46,192	23,674	22,518	122	70	52
18	Thatôn ...	456,096	230,963	225,133	456,036	230,925	225,111	60	38	22
19	Amherst ...	399,164	203,267	195,897	398,823	203,013	195,810	341	254	87
20	Tavoy ...	153,749	77,049	76,700	153,730	77,033	76,697	19	16	3
21	Mergui ...	122,641	61,696	60,945	122,639	61,694	60,945	2	2	...
	Magwe Division ...	*1,493,358*	*731,076*	*762,282*	*1,493,185*	*730,973*	*762,212*	*173*	*103*	*70*
22	Thayetmyo ...	279,586	137,587	141,999	279,555	137,573	141,982	31	14	17
23	Pakôkku	486,515	236,331	250,184	486,450	236,284	250,166	65	47	18
24	Minbu ...	276,092	135,412	140,680	276,050	135,392	140,658	42	20	22
25	Magwe ...	431,051	211,874	219,177	431,016	211,852	219,164	35	22	13
26	Pakôkku Hill Tracts ...	20,114	9,872	10,242	20,114	9,872	10,242	...	...	...
	Mandalay Division ...	*783,495*	*385,798*	*397,697*	*774,163*	*380,447*	*393,716*	*9,332*	*5,351*	*3,981*
27	Mandalay ...	345,839	169,995	175,844	339,976	166,748	173,228	5,863	3,247	2,616
28	Bhamo ...	97,708	47,455	50,253	96,911	47,105	49,806	797	350	447
29	Myitkyina ...	89,736	44,297	45,439	89,563	44,210	45,354	172	87	85
30	Katha ...	241,781	119,859	121,922	239,301	118,206	121,095	2,480	1,653	827
31	Putao ...	8,431	4,192	4,239	8,411	4,178	4,233	20	14	6
	Sagaing Division ...	*1,397,944*	*667,539*	*730,405*	*1,396,222*	*666,264*	*729,958*	*1,722*	*1,275*	*447*
32	Shwebo ...	405,471	192,807	212,664	404,353	192,019	212,334	1,118	788	330
33	Sagaing ..	344,817	164,983	179,834	344,637	164,860	179,777	180	123	57
34	Lower Chindwin ...	366,624	170,756	195,868	366,534	170,692	195,842	90	64	26
35	Upper Chindwin ...	167,232	83,087	84,145	166,976	82,843	84,133	256	244	12
36	Chin Hills ...	113,800	55,906	57,894	113,722	55,850	57,872	78	56	22
	Meiktila Division ...	*1,289,174*	*601,282*	*687,892*	*1,286,486*	*599,627*	*686,859*	*2,688*	*1,655*	*1,033*
37	Kyauksè ...	131,511	64,337	67,174	130,427	63,688	66,739	1,084	649	435
38	Meiktila ...	321,861	153,952	167,909	320,994	153,431	167,563	867	521	346
39	Yamèthin ...	311,099	152,078	159,021	310,438	151,647	158,791	661	431	230
40	Myingyan ...	474,703	230,915	243,788	474,627	230,861	243,766	76	54	22
	*Unadministered Territory ** ...	*1,515*	*793*	*722*	*1,515*	*793*	*722*	...	...	...
	Eastern States ...	1,431,787	713,704	718,083	24,118	13,538	10,580	1,407,669	700,166	707,503
41	Northern Shan States ...	522,224	258,963	263,261	11,413	6,288	5,125	510,811	252,675	258,136
42	Southern Shan States ...	847,283	424,934	422,349	11,581	6,560	5,021	835,702	418,374	417,328
43	Karenni ...	62,280	29,807	32,473	1,124	690	434	116,156	29,117	32,039

* Reckoned as part of Divisional Burma in the second line of this table.

IN WHICH ENUMERATED.

Akyab.			Hill District of Arakan.			Kyaukpyu.			Sandoway.			
Persons.	Males.	Females.	Persons.	Males.	Females.	Persons.	Males.	Females.	Persons.	Males.	Females.	
11	12	13	14	15	16	17	18	19	20	21	22	
527,239	**267,492**	**259,747**	**20,183**	**10,235**	**9,948**	**197,789**	**94,754**	**103,035**	**111,006**	**54,351**	**56,655**	
527,229	**267,489**	**259,740**	**20,179**	**10,234**	**9,945**	**197,779**	**94,745**	**103,034**	**111,001**	**54,347**	**56,654**	
526,617	*267,045*	*259,572*	*20,128*	*10,215*	*9,913*	*197,156*	*94,334*	*102,822*	*110,093*	*53,697*	*56,396*	
522,773	264,381	258,392	330	194	136	790	481	309	65	53	12	1
81	57	24	19,780	10,011	9,769	5	4	1	75	57	18	2
3,475	2,374	1,101	13	7	6	195,933	93,580	102,353	1,552	1,289	263	3
288	233	55	5	3	2	428	269	159	108,401	52,298	56,103	4
290	*190*	*100*	*3*	*2*	*1*	*36*	*26*	*10*	*242*	*170*	*72*	
226	143	83	3	2	1	16	7	9	27	12	15	5
6	6	...	..	...	...	...	...	...	3	2	1	6
13	8	5	...	...	...	...	...	...	7	5	2	7
13	9	4	...	...	...	4	4	...	7	5	2	8
7	5	2	...	...	...	2	2	...	4	2	2	9
25	19	6	...	...	...	14	13	1	194	144	50	10
39	*27*	*12*	...	...	...	*43*	*40*	*3*	*438*	*332*	*106*	
19	12	7	...	...	...	22	19	3	204	149	55	11
17	13	4	...	...	...	18	18	...	216	170	46	12
1	1	...	...	...	...	3	3	...	15	10	5	13
2	1	1	..	...	...	...	...	...	2	2	...	14
...	...	...	...	...	...	...	...	...	1	1	...	15
60	*37*	*23*	...	...	...	*5*	*4*	*1*	*66*	*52*	*14*	
7	4	3	...	...	...	1	...	1	1	...	1	16
2	...	2	...	...	...	...	...	...	...	...	...	17
4	3	1	...	...	...	2	2	...	25	25	...	18
26	12	14	...	...	...	1	1	..	18	15	3	19
16	16	...	...	...	...	...	...	...	20	10	10	20
5	2	3	...	...	...	1	1	...	2	2	...	21
60	*57*	*3*	*3*	*1*	*2*	*516*	*322*	*194*	*95*	*58*	*37*	
27	25	2	...	...	...	92	58	34	72	45	27	22
11	11	...	1	1	...	10	7	3	12	5	7	23
21	21	...	...	...	...	411	255	156	4	4	...	24
1	...	1	2	...	2	3	2	1	7	4	3	25
...	...	...	...	...	...	...	...	...	...	...	...	26
37	*29*	*8*	*2*	*1*	*1*	*13*	*10*	*3*	*46*	*27*	*19*	
34	28	6	1	1	...	12	9	3	39	22	17	27
...	...	...	1	...	1	...	...	...	2	2	...	28
1	...	1	...	...	...	...	...	...	3	1	2	29
2	1	1	...	...	...	1	1	...	...	...	...	30
...	...	...	...	...	...	...	...	...	2	2	...	31
109	*92*	*17*	*3*	*3*	...	*7*	*6*	*1*	*14*	*10*	*4*	
5	2	3	2	2	...	1	...	1	4	3	1	32
4	2	2	...	...	...	4	4	...	7	5	2	33
12	12	...	...	...	...	1	1	...	2	2	..	34
75	69	6	...	...	...	1	1	...	...	...	...	35
13	7	6	1	1	...	...	...	...	1	...	1	36
17	*12*	*5*	...	...	...	*3*	*3*	...	*7*	*1*	*6*	
2	2	...	...	...	..	...	...	...	3	1	2	37
11	9	2	...	...	...	2	2	...	2	..	2	38
1	...	1	...	...	...	...	...	...	2	...	2	39
3	1	2	...	...	...	1	1	...	...	...	...	40
...	...	...	*40*	*12*	*28*	...	...	...	...	...	..	
10	**3**	**7**	**4**	**1**	**3**	**10**	**9**	**1**	**5**	**4**	**1**	
6	3	3	...	...	...	10	9	1	1	1	...	41
4	...	4	4	1	3	...	...	...	4	3	1	42
...	...	...	...	...	...	...	...	...	...	...	...	43

DISTRICT IN

	District, etc., of Birth-place.	Rangoon Town.			Insein.			Hanthawaddy.		
		Persons.	Males.	Females.	Persons.	Males.	Females.	Persons.	Males.	Females.
	1	23	24	25	26	27	28	29	30	3
	ALL BURMA ...	155,086	78,977	76,109	266,390	134,909	131,481	315,116	159,984	155,152
	Divisional Burma ...	154,797	78,847	75,950	265,448	134,514	130,934	314,934	159,861	155,073
	Arakan Division ..	*758*	*582*	*221*	*176*	*124*	*52*	*71*	*62*	*9*
1	Akyab ...	512	347	165	82	67	15	40	35	5
2	Hill District of Arakan	65	53	12	24	11	13	5	5	...
3	Kyaukpyu ...	58	50	8	11	10	1	10	9	1
4	Sandoway ...	118	82	36	59	36	23	16	13	3
	Pegu Division ..	*125,614*	*62,015*	*63,599*	*246,082*	*128,503*	*122,579*	*296,882*	*148,360*	*148,522*
5	Rangoon Town ...	110,315	53,492	56,823	4,516	2,415	2,101	3,278	1,818	1,460
6	Insein ...	2,933	1,505	1,428	220,539	109,617	110,922	1,746	950	796
7	Hanthawaddy ...	5,490	2,995	2,495	3,166	1,775	1,391	289,069	143,995	145,074
8	Tharrawaddy ...	2,042	1,129	913	9,202	5,225	3,977	290	169	121
9	Pegu ...	2,561	1,629	932	3,189	1,614	1,575	2,012	1,116	896
10	Prome ...	2,273	1,265	1,008	5,470	2,857	2,613	487	312	175
	Irrawaddy Division ..	*8,678*	*4,916*	*3,757*	*6,727*	*3,581*	*3,196*	*3,514*	*2,020*	*1,494*
11	Bassein ...	1,672	876	796	455	279	176	309	161	148
12	Henzada ...	2,410	1,451	959	2,880	1,514	1,366	311	198	113
13	Myaungmya ...	690	393	297	82	51	31	151	93	58
14	Ma-ubin ...	2,287	1,283	1,004	2,915	1,471	1,444	1,456	835	621
15	Pyapôn ...	1,614	913	701	395	216	179	1,287	733	554
	Tenasserim Division ..	*8,941*	*4,629*	*4,812*	*1,469*	*942*	*527*	*1,061*	*635*	*426*
16	Toungoo ...	1,240	690	550	373	214	159	170	81	89
17	Salween ...	5	4	1	6	1	5	4	3	1
18	Thatôn ...	693	413	280	191	119	72	204	124	80
19	Amherst ...	5,441	2,798	2,643	593	386	207	488	305	183
20	Tavoy ...	1,199	529	670	224	160	64	163	105	58
21	Mergui ...	363	195	168	82	62	20	32	17	15
	Magwe Division ..	*2,047*	*1,381*	*666*	*4,361*	*2,472*	*1,889*	*3,268*	*2,020*	*1,248*
22	Thayetmyo ...	576	338	238	816	447	369	152	89	63
23	Pakôkku ...	580	431	149	607	370	237	1,758	1,083	675
24	Minbu ...	399	241	158	754	470	284	1,020	614	406
25	Magwe ...	489	371	118	2,184	1,185	999	326	222	104
26	Pakôkku Hill Tracts	3	...	3	...	...	...	12	12	...
	Mandalay Division ..	*5,226*	*2,977*	*2,249*	*1,649*	*960*	*689*	*1,216*	*758*	*463*
27	Mandalay ...	5,023	2,864	2,159	1,562	915	647	1,174	729	445
28	Bhamo ...	95	54	41	11	5	6	15	12	3
29	Myitkyina ...	35	21	14	38	14	24	10	6	4
30	Katha ...	72	37	35	36	24	12	17	6	11
31	Putao ...	1	1	...	2	2	...	...	...	...
	Sagaing Division ..	*1,924*	*1,331*	*593*	*2,969*	*1,797*	*1,172*	*5,718*	*3,858*	*1,855*
32	Shwebo ...	510	403	107	1,530	920	610	2,483	1,703	780
33	Sagaing ...	531	337	194	869	533	336	1,232	833	399
34	Lower Chindwin ..	798	537	261	473	336	137	1,888	1,227	661
35	Upper Chindwin ...	69	47	22	93	8	85	110	95	15
36	Chin Hills ...	16	7	9	4	...	4	...	...	...
	Meiktila Division ..	*1,619*	*1,066*	*553*	*2,015*	*1,185*	*830*	*3,209*	*2,153*	*1,056*
37	Kyauksè ...	79	51	28	67	37	30	49	37	12
38	Meiktila ...	442	277	165	497	318	179	1,148	840	308
39	Yamèthin ...	305	177	128	75	40	35	85	46	39
40	Myingyan ...	793	561	232	1,376	790	586	1,927	1,230	697
	Unadministered Territory	...	...	...	...	...	...	...	...	...
	Eastern States ...	289	130	159	942	395	547	182	103	79
41	Northern Shan States	159	84	75	506	291	215	81	40	41
42	Southern Shan States	128	44	84	436	104	332	100	63	37
43	Karenni ...	2	2	...	...	...	...	1	...	1

PART III.—*Birth-places in Burma*—continued.

WHICH ENUMERATED.

Tharrawaddy			Pegu			Prome			Bassein			
Persons.	Males.	Females.	Persons.	Males.	Females.	Persons.	Males.	Females.	Persons.	Males.	Females.	
32	33	34	35	36	37	38	39	40	41	42	43	
479,989	**235,534**	**244,455**	**407,519**	**206,089**	**201,430**	**363,066**	**175,669**	**187,397**	**467,659**	**233,131**	**234,528**	
479,477	**235,204**	**244,273**	**405,245**	**204,760**	**200,485**	**362,846**	**175,572**	**187,274**	**467,575**	**233,082**	**234,493**	
56	*41*	*15*	*124*	*96*	*28*	*102*	*78*	*24*	*6,818*	*3,921*	*2,897*	
19	12	7	31	20	11	15	11	4	54	51	3	1
2	2	...	21	15	6	3	2	1	4	...	4	2
12	9	3	30	30	...	10	10	...	3,398	1,937	1,461	3
23	18	5	42	31	11	74	55	19	3,362	1,933	1,429	4
452,107	*219,856*	*232,251*	*351,157*	*175,327*	*175,830*	*351,929*	*169,329*	*182,600*	*2,202*	*1,360*	*842*	
591	335	256	3,990	2,197	1,793	520	280	240	838	517	331	5
935	541	394	3,973	2,072	1,901	115	45	70	59	38	31	6
782	449	333	7,754	4,113	3,641	75	35	40	83	47	36	7
429,608	207,507	222,101	10,598	5,515	5,083	2,781	1,441	1,340	239	153	86	8
674	432	242	321,312	159,568	161,744	67	39	28	55	36	19	9
19,517	10,5[illegible]2	8,925	3,530	1,862	1,668	348,371	167,489	180,882	928	569	359	10
10,988	*5,801*	*5,182*	*2,603*	*1,317*	*1,286*	*1,802*	*746*	*557*	*453,475*	*224,641*	*228,834*	
551	310	241	368	172	196	147	91	56	438,345	216,415	221,930	11
9,561	5,053	4,508	1,209	650	559	914	516	398	11,834	6,466	5,368	12
111	51	60	78	32	46	74	48	26	1,538	858	680	13
572	312	260	623	322	301	109	56	53	1,618	823	795	14
138	75	63	325	141	184	58	34	24	140	79	61	15
656	*397*	*259*	*21,746*	*11,168*	*10,578*	*399*	*267*	*182*	*323*	*199*	*124*	
299	168	131	8,005	4,026	3,979	129	73	56	52	27	25	16
4	4	...	134	79	55	12	10	2	1	...	1	17
92	59	33	12,280	6,249	6,031	51	44	7	23	11	12	18
196	136	60	1,123	682	441	161	106	55	148	81	67	19
55	24	31	127	67	60	41	39	11	87	75	12	20
10	6	4	77	65	12	5	4	1	12	5	7	21
10,727	*6,094*	*4,633*	*4,052*	*2,430*	*1,622*	*7,672*	*4,235*	*3,437*	*1,781*	*1,103*	*678*	
3,306	1,898	1,408	610	328	282	6,099	3,395	2,704	179	117	62	22
1,074	606	468	1,055	605	450	171	118	53	1,059	642	417	23
558	262	296	551	434	117	132	78	54	331	205	126	24
5,789	3,328	2,461	1,836	1,063	773	1,270	644	626	210	139	71	25
...	...	...	...	...	...	...	...	...	2	..	2	26
1,250	*716*	*534*	*1,867*	*1,054*	*813*	*792*	*475*	*317*	*752*	*484*	*268*	
1,207	695	512	1,778	988	790	748	448	300	708	452	256	27
7	3	4	16	14	2	12	7	5	4	1	3	28
15	6	9	21	16	5	6	4	2	6	3	3	29
16	12	4	52	36	16	26	16	10	34	28	6	30
5	...	5	...	...	...	...	...	...	...	...	...	31
2,416	*1,463*	*953*	*5,565*	*3,293*	*2,272*	*392*	*254*	*138*	*1,414*	*855*	*559*	
996	593	403	2,289	1,377	912	185	136	49	483	306	177	32
426	264	162	1,069	616	453	87	49	38	511	308	203	33
911	562	349	2,182	1,282	900	104	65	39	317	201	116	34
81	43	38	25	18	7	16	4	12	102	40	62	35
2	1	1	...	...	...	..	...	...	1	...	1	36
1,382	*886*	*496*	*18,131*	*10,075*	*8,056*	*258*	*189*	*69*	*810*	*519*	*291*	
48	23	25	186	112	74	15	12	3	24	14	10	37
184	136	48	11,706	6,524	5,182	52	39	13	48	34	14	38
84	60	24	2,749	1,172	1,577	14	8	6	11	5	6	39
1,016	617	399	3,490	1,967	1,523	177	130	47	727	466	261	40
...	...	...	..	...	...	...	...	...	...	...	...	
512	**338**	**182**	**2,274**	**1,329**	**945**	**226**	**97**	**123**	**84**	**49**	**35**	
337	211	126	1,083	619	464	150	75	75	60	31	29	41
175	119	56	1,176	695	481	70	22	48	24	18	6	42
...	...	...	15	15	...	...	...	...	...	...	...	43

	District, etc., of Birth-place.	DISTRICT IN								
		HENZADA.			MYAUNGMYA.			MA-UBIN.		
		Persons.	Males.	Females.	Persons.	Males.	Females.	Persons.	Males.	Females.
	1	44	45	46	47	48	49	50	51	52
	ALL BURMA ...	**540,995**	**264,698**	**276,297**	**349,810**	**177,544**	**172,266**	**318,681**	**158,057**	**160,624**
	Divisional Burma ...	**540,971**	**264,679**	**276,292**	**349,723**	**177,487**	**172,236**	**318,613**	**158,013**	**160,600**
	Arakan Division ...	*88*	*60*	*88*	*762*	*599*	*163*	*89*	*82*	*7*
1	Akyab ...	9	7	2	56	45	11	10	9	1
2	Hill District of Arakan	3	3	...	7	7	...	7	5	2
3	Kyaukpyu ...	14	5	9	361	266	95	10	8	2
4	Sandoway ...	62	35	27	338	281	57	12	10	2
	Pegu Division ..	*5,501*	*2,981*	*2,520*	*5,697*	*3,350*	*2,347*	*5,519*	*3,021*	*2,498*
5	Rangoon Town ...	709	447	262	2,345	1,368	977	1,395	812	583
6	Insein ...	448	197	251	160	91	69	879	511	368
7	Hanthawaddy ...	151	87	64	534	287	247	1,611	876	735
8	Tharrawaddy ...	2,245	1,204	1,041	558	325	233	274	191	83
9	Pegu ...	140	83	57	526	300	226	185	109	76
10	Prome ..	1,808	963	845	1,574	979	595	1,175	522	653
	Irrawaddy Division ..	*523,290*	*254,872*	*268,418*	*322 815*	*161,538*	*161,277*	*298,051*	*147,093*	*150,958*
11	Bassein ...	2,545	1,303	1,242	14,230	7,558	6,672	3,061	1,395	1,666
12	Henzada ...	518,560	252,463	266,097	7,275	3,964	3,311	6,833	3,456	3,377
13	Myaungmya ...	172	77	95	287,346	142,455	144,891	1,150	725	425
14	Ma-ubin ...	1,893	984	909	10,979	5,978	5,001	284,958	140,420	144,538
15	Pyapôn ...	120	45	75	2,985	1,583	1,402	2,049	1,097	952
	Tenasserim Division ..	*324*	*209*	*115*	*416*	*246*	*170*	*418*	*201*	*217*
16	Toungoo ...	43	21	22	162	81	81	103	65	38
17	Salween ...	18	18	...	7	5	2	4	4	...
18	Thatôn ...	36	16	20	67	47	20	40	27	13
19	Amherst ...	130	86	44	140	86	54	102	65	36
20	Tavoy ...	11	9	2	26	19	7	51	34	17
21	Mergui ...	86	59	27	13	7	6	119	6	113
	Magwe Division ..	*5,654*	*3,045*	*2,609*	*12,895*	*6,993*	*5,402*	*5,613*	*3,155*	*2,458*
22	Thayetmyo ...	2,593	1,322	1,271	2,701	1,474	1,227	920	504	416
23	Pakôkku ...	2,184	1,256	928	2,997	1,820	1,177	2,131	1,263	868
24	Minbu ...	590	319	271	3,170	1,736	1,434	1,897	999	898
25	Magwe ...	287	148	139	3,527	1,963	1,564	665	389	276
26	Pakôkku Hill Tracts .	...	...	...	...	...	...	...	...	...
	Mandalay Division ..	*1,264*	*747*	*517*	*1,891*	*845*	*546*	*1,849*	*771*	*1,078*
27	Mandalay ..	1,209	732	477	1,344	805	539	1,821	753	1,068
28	Bhamo ...	34	9	25	16	14	2	15	12	3
29	Myitkyina ...	11	...	11	7	6	1	4	...	4
30	Katha ...	10	6	4	24	20	4	9	6	3
31	Putao ...	...	...	...	...	...	...	...	...	...
	Sagaing Division ..	*3,402*	*1,980*	*1,422*	*3,361*	*2,383*	*1,248*	*4,842*	*2,457*	*2,385*
32	Shwebo ...	797	474	323	1,076	723	353	1,504	625	879
33	Sagaing ...	1,179	677	502	973	601	372	2,282	1,240	1,042
34	Lower Chindwin ...	1,163	815	348	1,466	567	499	1,044	583	461
35	Upper Chindwin ...	258	13	245	64	40	24	11	8	3
36	Chin Hills ...	5	1	4	2	2	...	1	1	...
	Meiktila Division ..	*1,448*	*795*	*653*	*2,667*	*1,584*	*1,083*	*2,282*	*1,283*	*999*
37	Kyauksè ...	35	25	10	80	47	33	53	27	26
38	Meiktila .	121	64	57	68	56	12	94	80	14
39	Yamèthin ...	29	20	9	16	15	1	17	15	2
40	Myingyan ...	1,263	686	577	2,503	1,466	1,037	2,118	1,161	957
	Unadministered Territory	...	...	...	...	...	...	...	...	..
	Eastern States ...	**24**	**19**	**5**	**87**	**57**	**30**	**68**	**44**	**24**
41	Northern Shan States	16	11	5	27	20	7	32	17	15
42	Southern Shan States	6	6	...	58	35	23	33	24	9
43	Karenni ...	2	2	...	2	2	...	3	3	...

PART III.—*Birth-places in Burma*—continued.

WHICH ENUMERATED.

Pyapon.			Toungoo.			Salween.			Thaton.			
Persons.	Males.	Females.	Persons.	Males.	Females.	Persons.	Males.	Females.	Persons.	Males.	Females.	
53	54	55	56	57	58	59	60	61	62	63	64	
266,227	**137,627**	**128,600**	**361,764**	**181,622**	**180,142**	**48,592**	**25,253**	**23,339**	**450,431**	**228,550**	**221,881**	
266,135	**137,567**	**128,568**	**355,459**	**178,184**	**177,275**	**47,408**	**24,448**	**22,960**	**448,705**	**227,449**	**221,256**	
62	*44*	*18*	*64*	*39*	*25*	*6*	*6*	...	*48*	*36*	*12*	
18	11	7	35	22	13	4	4	...	13	10	3	1
11	11	...	10	9	1	...	...	...	9	8	1	2
24	16	8	10	4	6	...	...	...	6	3	3	3
9	6	3	9	4	5	2	2	...	20	15	5	4
21,038	*11,885*	*9,153*	*12,047*	*6,401*	*5,646*	*95*	*63*	*32*	*3,983*	*2,299*	*1,684*	
5,731	3,181	2,550	1,719	863	856	20	12	8	787	478	309	5
1,260	670	590	324	181	143	12	11	1	105	58	47	6
10,304	5,824	4,480	627	322	305	18	8	10	605	423	182	7
824	457	367	1,354	745	609	6	6	...	188	119	69	8
1,423	805	618	6,144	3,290	2,854	36	23	13	2,064	1,074	990	9
1,496	948	548	1,879	1,000	879	3	3	...	234	147	87	10
214,760	*107,842*	*106,918*	*992*	*534*	*458*	*79*	*56*	*23*	*656*	*369*	*287*	
1,354	776	578	219	129	90	21	18	3	82	58	24	11
4,109	2,137	1,972	341	177	164	27	17	10	309	189	120	12
3,923	2,017	1,906	50	32	18	14	13	1	38	18	20	13
9,059	5,046	4,013	258	132	126	14	5	9	168	69	99	14
196,315	97,866	98,449	124	64	60	3	3	...	59	35	24	15
1,081	*530*	*551*	*304,891*	*151,050*	*153,841*	*47,098*	*24,214*	*22,884*	*441,902*	*223,254*	*218,648*	
186	138	48	300,463	148,871	151,592	246	162	84	654	359	295	16
42	35	7	187	117	70	45,627	23,297	22,330	73	48	25	17
336	101	235	2,813	1,558	1,255	1,021	632	389	432,349	218,006	214,343	18
350	199	151	800	436	364	195	118	77	8,545	4,626	3,919	19
111	46	65	101	56	45	4	3	1	233	181	52	20
56	11	45	27	12	15	5	2	3	48	34	14	21
14,916	*8,260*	*6,656*	*3,927*	*2,192*	*1,735*	*7*	*7*	...	*520*	*359*	*161*	
2,766	1,519	1,247	2,439	1,333	1,106	...	...	...	21	14	7	22
3,417	2,012	1,405	256	164	92	3	3	...	279	261	18	23
5,833	3,113	2,720	126	65	61	3	3	...	20	16	4	24
2,896	1,612	1,284	1,105	629	476	1	1	...	119	29	90	25
4	4	...	1	1	...	...	...	...	81	39	42	26
1,952	*1,202*	*750*	*1,412*	*797*	*615*	*32*	*26*	*6*	*540*	*345*	*195*	
1,845	1,126	719	1,325	746	579	30	25	5	454	295	159	27
33	20	13	15	9	6	...	...	...	29	28	1	28
24	13	11	16	7	9	1	1	...	10	2	8	29
48	41	7	56	35	21	1	...	1	29	20	9	30
2	2	...	...	...	...	...	...	...	18	...	18	31
7,822	*4,993*	*2,829*	*4,872*	*2,849*	*2,023*	*67*	*56*	*11*	*478*	*360*	*118*	
2,286	1,514	772	3,338	1,755	1,583	38	28	10	223	166	57	32
3,697	2,169	1,528	521	291	230	1	1	...	98	76	22	33
1,598	1,080	518	381	203	178	17	17	...	109	86	23	34
241	230	11	131	100	31	10	10	...	32	27	5	35
...	...	...	1	...	1	1	...	1	11	5	6	36
4,504	*2,811*	*1,693*	*28,254*	*14,822*	*13,432*	*24*	*20*	*4*	*583*	*427*	*156*	
101	76	25	235	128	107	...	...	...	29	19	10	37
819	594	225	10,064	5,291	4,773	10	9	1	285	218	67	38
61	42	19	15,346	7,980	7,366	7	6	1	122	77	45	39
3,523	2,099	1,424	2,609	1,423	1,186	7	5	2	147	113	34	40
...	...	...	...	...	...	...	...	...	...	...	...	
92	**60**	**32**	**6,305**	**3,438**	**2,867**	**1,184**	**805**	**379**	**1,726**	**1,101**	**625**	
24	13	11	2,028	1,118	910	321	217	104	552	319	233	41
47	35	12	3,604	1,937	1,667	680	481	199	1,167	776	391	42
21	12	9	673	383	290	183	107	76	7	6	1	43

	District, etc., of Birth-place.	DISTRICT IN								
		AMHERST.			TAVOY.			MERGUI.		
		Persons.	Males.	Females.	Persons.	Males.	Females.	Persons.	Males.	Females.
	1	65	66	67	68	69	70	71	72	73
	ALL BURMA ...	**388,642**	**198,180**	**190,462**	**150,174**	**74,904**	**75,270**	**123,980**	**62,796**	**61,184**
	Divisional Burma ...	**387,826**	**197,598**	**190,228**	**150,136**	**74,874**	**75,262**	**123,874**	**62,698**	**61,176**
	Arakan Division ...	*57*	*35*	*22*	*49*	*32*	*17*	*17*	*14*	*3*
1	Akyab ...	45	32	13	27	17	10	8	5	3
2	Hill District of Arakan	6	...	6	11	6	5	...	...	...
3	Kyaukpyu ...	...	...	...	1	1	...	6	6	...
4	Sandoway ...	6	3	3	10	8	2	3	3	...
	Pegu Division ...	*1,531*	*930*	*601*	*518*	*331*	*187*	*322*	*233*	*89*
5	Rangoon Town ...	705	384	321	362	222	140	219	150	69
6	Insein ...	52	37	15	18	14	4	16	11	5
7	Hanthawaddy ...	266	162	104	4	4	...	13	8	5
8	Tharrawaddy ...	76	46	30	33	15	18	25	22	3
9	Pegu ...	225	156	69	39	25	14	21	20	1
10	Prome ...	207	145	62	62	51	11	28	22	6
	Irrawaddy Division ...	*391*	*254*	*137*	*91*	*63*	*28*	*184*	*129*	*55*
11	Bassein ...	193	110	83	35	28	7	69	48	21
12	Henzada ...	103	78	25	32	23	9	43	32	11
13	Myaungmya ...	25	18	7	3	3	...	37	24	13
14	Ma-ubin ...	42	28	14	4	1	3	32	22	10
15	Pyapôn ...	28	20	8	17	13	4	3	3	...
	Tenasserim Division ...	*384,477*	*195,366*	*189,111*	*149,212*	*74,257*	*74,955*	*123,036*	*62,059*	*60,977*
16	Toungoo ...	175	95	80	49	41	8	58	39	19
17	Salween ...	29	23	6	1	1	...	2	2	...
18	Thatôn ...	5,228	3,078	2,150	53	40	13	38	22	16
19	Amherst ...	377,478	191,093	186,385	933	588	345	338	239	99
20	Tavoy ...	1,301	896	405	147,731	73,318	74,413	1,874	1,190	684
21	Mergui ...	266	181	85	445	269	176	120,726	60,567	60,159
	Magwe Division ...	*253*	*196*	*57*	*43*	*31*	*12*	*163*	*157*	*6*
22	Thayetmyo ...	39	23	16	12	9	3	14	12	2
23	Pakôkku ...	151	121	30	10	9	1	15	12	3
24	Minbu ...	36	31	5	15	7	8	10	9	1
25	Magwe ...	26	21	5	6	6	...	124	124	...
26	Pakôkku Hill Tracts	1	...	1	...	...	...	...	...	...
	Mandalay Division ...	*569*	*411*	*158*	*116*	*87*	*29*	*80*	*50*	*30*
27	Mandalay ...	511	384	127	104	79	25	79	49	30
28	Bhamo ...	17	6	11	5	3	2	...	...	...
29	Myitkyina ...	7	2	5	5	4	1	1	1	...
30	Katha ...	34	19	15	2	1	1	...	...	...
31	Putao ...	...	...	...	...	...	...	...	...	...
	Sagaing Division ...	*300*	*236*	*64*	*63*	*42*	*21*	*35*	*26*	*9*
32	Shwebo ...	74	56	18	12	11	1	10	9	1
33	Sagaing ...	86	63	23	17	13	4	23	15	8
34	Lower Chindwin ...	106	88	18	33	17	16	2	2	...
35	Upper Chindwin ...	34	29	5	1	1	...	...	...	...
36	Chin Hills ...	...	...	...	...	...	...	...	...	...
	Meiktila Division ...	*248*	*170*	*78*	*44*	*26*	*18*	*37*	*30*	*7*
37	Kyauksè ...	20	19	1	6	2	4	9	8	1
38	Meiktila ...	74	56	18	8	6	2	17	14	3
39	Yamèthin ...	41	21	20	21	9	12	5	3	2
40	Myingyan ...	113	74	39	9	9	...	6	5	1
	Unadministered Territory	...	...	...	...	...	...	...	...	...
	Eastern States ...	**816**	**582**	**234**	**38**	**30**	**8**	**106**	**98**	**8**
41	Northern Shan States	187	113	74	13	8	5	...	...	...
42	Southern Shan States	430	319	111	25	22	3	105	97	8
43	Karenni ...	199	150	49	...	...	...	1	1	...

PART III.—*Birth-places in Burma*—continued.

WHICH ENUMERATED.

Thayetmyo.			Pakokku.			Minbu.			Magwe.			
Persons.	Males.	Females.	Persons.	Males.	Females.	Persons.	Males.	Females.	Persons.	Males.	Females.	
74	75	76	77	78	79	80	81	82	83	84	85	
253,192	**123,413**	**129,779**	**464,188**	**222,542**	**241,646**	**271,533**	**131,984**	**139,549**	**412,983**	**202,185**	**210,798**	
253,186	**123,409**	**129,777**	**464,157**	**222,521**	**241,636**	**271,510**	**131,965**	**139,545**	**412,957**	**202,175**	**210,782**	
54	*42*	*12*	*85*	*80*	*5*	*189*	*135*	*54*	*47*	*35*	*12*	
12	9	3	9	9	...	...	...	...	17	16	1	1
2	1	1	...	...	...	1	1	...	6	4	2	2
27	22	5	16	14	2	185	131	54	6	4	2	3
13	10	3	10	7	3	3	3	...	18	11	7	4
1,204	*827*	*377*	*414*	*265*	*149*	*1,129*	*556*	*573*	*1,941*	*1,067*	*874*	
175	122	53	203	138	65	220	142	78	393	230	163	5
25	14	11	32	9	23	66	29	37	8	5	3	6
24	15	9	24	16	8	99	44	55	543	327	216	7
135	92	43	29	19	10	231	99	132	238	126	112	8
34	24	10	43	25	18	128	53	75	48	23	25	9
811	560	251	83	58	25	385	189	196	711	356	355	10
338	*203*	*135*	*446*	*293*	*153*	*1,272*	*547*	*725*	*781*	*444*	*337*	
39	25	14	79	49	30	182	85	97	166	95	71	11
142	84	58	131	122	59	301	99	202	234	145	89	12
24	6	18	66	47	19	202	92	110	106	58	48	13
62	43	19	77	55	22	252	114	138	157	89	68	14
71	45	26	43	20	23	335	157	178	118	57	61	15
154	*103*	*51*	*135*	*103*	*82*	*211*	*132*	*79*	*280*	*140*	*90*	
68	43	25	79	66	13	63	49	14	73	49	24	16
...	...	...	1	1	...	...	...	...	1	...	1	17
28	20	8	17	11	6	26	10	16	9	7	2	18
41	28	13	29	17	12	102	59	43	93	52	41	19
7	5	2	8	7	1	18	12	6	21	7	14	20
10	7	3	1	1	...	2	2	...	33	25	8	21
250,929	*121,894*	*129,035*	*455,465*	*217,448*	*238,022*	*267,108*	*129,718*	*137,895*	*403,606*	*196,698*	*206,918*	
248,470	120,475	127,995	174	133	41	2,084	1,085	999	2,984	1,593	1,391	22
111	59	52	453,863	216,418	237,445	4,631	2,453	2,178	3,408	2,225	1,183	23
1,030	583	447	1,166	698	468	255,238	123,530	131,708	1,815	1,091	724	24
1,318	777	541	230	194	36	5,155	2,645	2,510	395,397	191,784	203,613	25
...	...	...	32	...	32	...	...	...	2	...	2	26
149	*109*	*40*	*367*	*211*	*156*	*467*	*254*	*213*	*859*	*460*	*399*	
136	99	37	345	197	148	442	244	198	807	441	366	27
4	3	1	10	6	4	1	1	...	7	2	5	28
7	5	2	8	5	3	5	5	...	29	8	21	29
2	2	...	3	2	1	15	4	11	13	9	4	30
...	...	...	1	1	...	4	...	4	3	...	3	31
160	*115*	*45*	*4,803*	*2,875*	*1,928*	*283*	*169*	*64*	*298*	*212*	*86*	
17	10	7	55	44	11	37	26	11	40	31	9	32
53	32	21	617	344	273	118	85	33	122	88	34	33
82	66	16	1,341	777	564	62	49	13	107	72	35	34
6	5	1	95	77	18	13	7	6	19	16	3	35
2	2	..	2,195	1,133	1,062	3	2	1	10	5	5	36
198	*116*	*82*	*2,992*	*1,801*	*1,191*	*901*	*459*	*442*	*5,195*	*3,124*	*2,071*	
1	1	...	13	12	1	19	10	9	13	6	7	37
18	14	4	81	57	24	91	43	48	231	126	105	38
34	19	15	42	30	12	31	14	17	219	91	128	39
145	82	63	2,856	1,708	1,154	760	392	368	4,732	2,901	1,831	40
...	...	...	...	...	...	...	...	...	...	...	...	
6	**4**	**2**	**31**	**21**	**10**	**23**	**19**	**4**	**26**	**10**	**6**	
5	3	2	13	4	9	19	17	2	13	6	7	41
1	1	...	18	17	1	4	2	2	11	2	9	42
...	...	...	..	...	...	...	...	...	2	2	...	43

	District, etc., of Birth-place.	DISTRICT IN								
		PAKOKKU HILL TRACTS.			MANDALAY, including City.			MANDALAY CITY.		
		Persons.	Males.	Females.	Persons.	Males.	Females.	Persons.	Males.	Females.
	1	86	87	88	89	90	91	92	93	94
	ALL BURMA ...	**19,898**	**9,714**	**10,184**	**329,509**	**160,710**	**168,799**	**134,792**	**65,849**	**68,943**
	Divisional Burma ...	**19,898**	**9,714**	**10,184**	**328,695**	**160,168**	**168,527**	**134,495**	**65,642**	**68,853**
	Arakan Division ..	...	...	...	*157*	*111*	*46*	*116*	*85*	*31*
1	Akyab ...	...	...	...	76	54	22	49	38	11
2	Hill District of Arakan	...	...	..	16	14	2	16	14	2
3	Kyaukpyu ...	...	...	...	12	11	1	7	6	1
4	Sandoway ...	...	...	...	53	32	21	44	27	17
	Pegu Division ..	*3*	*1*	*2*	*3,621*	*2,126*	*1,495*	*2,298*	*1,441*	*852*
5	Rangoon Town ...	...	...	...	2,242	1,203	1,039	1,407	794	613
6	Insein ...	...	...	...	238	136	102	61	34	27
7	Hanthawaddy ...	3	1	2	103	56	47	61	39	22
8	Tharrawaddy ...	...	...	...	277	198	79	210	160	50
9	Pegu ...	...	...	...	335	241	94	250	200	50
10	Prome ...	...	...	...	426	292	134	304	214	90
	Irrawaddy Division ..	...	...	...	*1,055*	*715*	*340*	*894*	*634*	*260*
11	Bassein ...	...	...	..	357	234	123	305	210	95
12	Henzada ...	...	...	...	408	297	111	337	264	73
13	Myaungmya ...	...	...	...	49	26	23	30	15	15
14	Ma-ubin ...	...	...	...	182	106	76	169	97	72
15	Pyapôn ...	...	...	...	59	52	7	53	48	5
	Tenasserim Division ..	*1*	...	*1*	*1,482*	*930*	*552*	*1,068*	*700*	*368*
16	Toungoo ...	...	...	...	553	323	230	399	250	149
17	Salween ...	...	...	..	4	...	4	...	..	...
18	Thatôn ...	...	...	...	128	109	19	101	91	10
19	Amherst ...	1	...	1	607	342	265	440	250	190
20	Tavoy ...	...	...	...	148	125	23	96	83	13
21	Mergui ...	...	...	...	42	31	11	32	26	6
	Magwe Division ..	*19,876*	*9,700*	*10,176*	*1,608*	*1,238*	*365*	*1,052*	*843*	*209*
22	Thayetmyo ...	...	..	...	376	248	128	281	202	79
23	Pakôkku ...	109	62	47	462	346	116	295	256	39
24	Minbu ...	46	36	10	192	124	68	145	93	52
25	Magwe ...	1	1	...	361	308	53	328	289	39
26	Pakôkku Hill Tracts	19,720	9,601	10,119	212	212	...	3	3	...
	Mandalay Division ..	*14*	*10*	*4*	*303,162*	*145,965*	*157,197*	*118,278*	*56,257*	*62,021*
27	Mandalay ...	5	3	2	301,870	144,968	156,902	117,812	55,931	61,881
28	Bhamo ...	1	1	...	689	546	143	122	62	60
29	Myitkyina ...	2	...	2	215	164	51	108	83	25
30	Katha ...	6	6	...	342	242	100	190	136	54
31	Putao ...	..	...	...	46	45	1	46	45	1
	Sagaing Division ..	*2*	*2*	...	*13,176*	*6,270*	*6,906*	*8,025*	*3,798*	*4,227*
32	Shwebo ...	...	...	...	4,738	2,444	2,294	2,193	1,235	958
33	Sagaing ..	...	...	...	5,785	2,414	3,371	3,506	1,362	2,144
34	Lower Chindwin ...	...	...	...	2,457	1,241	1,216	2,209	1,093	1,116
35	Upper Chindwin ...	2	2	...	49	30	19	25	19	6
36	Chin Hills ...	...	...	...	147	141	6	92	89	3
	Meiktila Division ...	*2*	*1*	*1*	*4,439*	*2,813*	*1,626*	*2,769*	*1,884*	*885*
37	Kyauksè ...	...	...	...	1,930	1,094	836	808	507	301
38	Meiktila ...	...	...	...	688	361	327	447	223	224
39	Yamèthin ...	1	1	...	950	759	191	804	665	139
40	Myingyan ...	1	...	1	871	599	272	710	489	221
	Unadministered Territory*	...	...	...	...	...	...	...	...	..
	Eastern States ...	...	...	...	**814**	**542**	**272**	**297**	**207**	**90**
41	Northern Shan States	...	...	...	561	342	219	192	147	45
42	Southern Shan States	...	...	...	253	200	53	105	60	45
43	Karenni ...	..	...	...	...	...	..	...	...	...

* Reckoned as part of Divisional Burma in the second line of this table.

PART III.—*Birth-places in Burma*—continued.

WHICH ENUMERATED.

Bhamo.			Myitkyina.			Katha.			Putao.			Shwebo.			
Persons.	Males.	Females.	Persons.	Males	Females.	Persons.	Males.	Females.	Persons	Males.	Females	Persons.	Males	Females.	
95	96	97	98	99	100	101	102	103	104	105	106	107	108	109	
98,629	**48,079**	**50,550**	**106,008**	**54,141**	**51,867**	**246,249**	**122,532**	**123,717**	**6,638**	**3,230**	**3,408**	**387,635**	**181,668**	**205,967**	
97,131	**47,506**	**49,625**	**104,942**	**53,412**	**51,530**	**243,153**	**120,787**	**122,366**	**6,614**	**3,220**	**3,394**	**387,595**	**181,638**	**205,957**	
10	*6*	*4*	*22*	*16*	*6*	*47*	*26*	*21*	...	...	..	*4*	*4*	...	
3	...	3	5	5	...	15	8	7	...	...	...	3	3	...	1
2	1	1	3	3	...	3	1	2	...	...	...	...	...	...	2
1	1	...	2	1	1	9	4	5	...	...	...	...	...	...	3
4	4	...	12	7	5	20	13	7	..	...	...	1	1	..	4
219	*176*	*43*	*152*	*91*	*61*	*604*	*403*	*201*	*3*	*3*	...	*730*	*402*	*328*	
124	100	24	73	37	36	291	190	102	2	2	...	293	163	130	5
10	8	2	2	1	1	19	10	9	...	...	...	84	45	39	6
9	6	3	4	1	3	20	18	2	...	...	...	53	31	22	7
39	38	1	22	15	7	97	68	29	1	1	...	101	53	48	8
26	17	9	26	21	5	101	68	33	...	...		143	84	59	9
11	7	4	25	16	9	75	49	26	...	...	...	56	26	30	10
135	*101*	*34*	*80*	*38*	*42*	*146*	*94*	*52*	*7*	*3*	*4*	*426*	*193*	*233*	
29	17	12	27	15	12	50	33	17	1	1	...	68	46	22	11
43	38	5	39	18	21	54	36	18	5	2	3	94	55	39	12
41	28	13	2	...	2	6	3	3	...	...	...	125	23	102	13
12	8	4	9	4	5	27	19	8	1	...	1	96	46	50	14
10	10	...	3	1	2	9	3	6	...	...	...	43	23	20	15
243	*209*	*34*	*139*	*91*	*48*	*540*	*439*	*101*		*1*	...	*327*	*204*	*123*	
181	160	21	75	48	27	364	304	60	...	...	...	200	133	67	16
1	...	1	...	...	...	...	...	...	...	...	...	...	...	...	17
11	7	4	9	7	2	46	42	4	1	1	...	31	13	18	18
26	21	5	49	33	16	84	56	28	...	...	..	83	48	35	19
21	19	2	4	3	1	40	33	7	...	...	..	13	10	3	20
3	2	1	2	...	2	6	4	2	...	...	...	...	...	...	21
166	*151*	*15*	*1,096*	*778*	*318*	*253*	*179*	*74*	*4*	*4*	...	*329*	*175*	*154*	
24	16	8	78	54	24	31	20	11	.	...	...	64	22	42	22
130	126	4	951	675	276	160	118	42	2	2	...	186	115	71	23
7	6	1	35	26	9	50	34	16	...	..	..	60	28	32	24
5	3	2	31	22	9	11	6	5	2	2	...	19	10	9	25
...	...	...	1	1	...	1	1	...	...	...	...	...	...	...	26
95,819	*46,455*	*49,364*	*99,038*	*49,660*	*49,378*	*233,774*	*115,049*	*118,725*	*6,486*	*3,122*	*3,364*	*2,567*	*1,420*	*1,147*	
730	449	281	702	431	271	3,936	2,538	1,398	13	7	6	1,930	1,028	892	27
93,173	44,834	48,339	1,508	940	568	1,005	458	547	12	9	3	85	59	26	28
212	79	133	87,602	43,114	44,488	771	419	352	135	74	61	89	50	39	29
1,697	1,087	610	9,110	5,061	4,049	226,173	110,651	115,522	24	15	9	473	283	190	30
7	6	1	116	114	2	1,889	983	906	6,302	3,017	3,285	...	...	...	31
425	*318*	*107*	*2,940*	*1,981*	*959*	*7,467*	*4,388*	*3,079*	*4*	*4*	...	*382,532*	*178,890*	*203,642*	
302	237	65	619	464	155	6,357	3,580	2,777	1	1	...	372,231	173,253	198,978	32
89	64	25	122	84	38	431	286	145	...	...	...	5,888	3,212	2,676	33
16	7	9	293	247	46	378	311	67	1	1	...	4,372	2,390	1,976	34
16	9	7	1,895	1,178	717	56	25	31	1	1	...	31	24	7	35
2	1	1	11	8	3	245	186	59	1	1	...	10	5	5	36
114	*90*	*24*	*105*	*57*	*48*	*322*	*209*	*113*	*4*	*2*	*2*	*680*	*350*	*330*	
15	12	3	37	21	16	42	27	15	1	...	1	67	31	36	37
15	9	6	16	13	3	63	37	26	...	...	...	146	87	59	38
53	44	9	38	15	23	151	102	49	2	2	...	135	38	97	39
31	25	6	14	8	6	66	43	23	1	...	1	332	194	138	40
...	...	...	*1,870*	*700*	*670*	...	...	...	*105*	*81*	*24*	...	...	...	
1,498	**573**	**925**	**1,066**	**729**	**337**	**3,096**	**1,745**	**1,351**	**24**	**10**	**14**	**40**	**30**	**10**	
1,450	558	892	748	577	171	2,421	1,341	1,080	12	10	2	22	18	4	41
48	15	33	317	151	166	674	403	271	12	...	12	15	9	6	42
...	...	...	1	1	...	1	1	...	...	...	...	3	3	...	43

DISTRICT IN

	District, etc., of Birth-place.	Sagaing.			Lower Chindwin.			Upper Chindwin.		
		Persons.	Males.	Females.	Persons.	Males.	Females.	Persons.	Males.	Females.
	1	110	111	112	113	114	115	116	117	118
	ALL BURMA ...	**324,840**	**153,347**	**171,493**	**340,925**	**155,018**	**185,907**	**174,600**	**87,244**	**87,356**
	Divisional Burma ...	**324,786**	**153,332**	**171,464**	**340,893**	**155,000**	**185,893**	**174,577**	**87,244**	**87,353**
	Arakan Division ...	*33*	*22*	*11*	*14*	*9*	*5*	*19*	*18*	*1*
1	Akyab ...	5	5	...	1	...	1	9	9	...
2	Hill District of Arakan	6	3	3	...	...	...	...	...	...
3	Kyaukpyu ...	3	2	1	4	4	..	3	2	1
4	Sandoway ...	19	12	7	9	5	4	7	7	...
	Pegu Division ...	*787*	*400*	*387*	*361*	*235*	*126*	*139*	*91*	*48*
5	Rangoon Town ...	365	186	179	202	132	70	56	36	20
6	Insein ...	45	21	24	20	14	6	3	2	1
7	Hanthawaddy ...	52	30	22	26	15	11	13	8	5
8	Tharrawaddy ...	78	42	36	35	24	11	15	9	6
9	Pegu ...	130	58	72	46	24	22	27	15	12
10	Prome ...	117	63	54	32	26	6	25	21	4
	Irrawaddy Division ...	*995*	*464*	*531*	*158*	*107*	*51*	*64*	*50*	*14*
11	Bassein ...	123	65	58	52	34	18	21	18	3
12	Henzada ...	370	183	187	52	35	17	27	19	8
13	Myaungmya ...	53	23	30	9	5	4	2	2	...
14	Ma-ubin ...	256	114	142	22	15	7	9	6	3
15	Pyapôn ...	193	79	114	23	18	5	5	5	...
	Tenasserim Division ..	*240*	*115*	*125*	*91*	*50*	*41*	*111*	*74*	*37*
16	Toungoo ...	130	60	70	47	29	18	69	48	21
17	Salween ...	...	...	...	...	...	...	2	1	1
18	Thatôn ...	17	9	8	17	4	13	1	1	...
19	Amherst ...	72	34	38	26	17	9	27	19	8
20	Tavoy ...	10	5	5	...	...	...	7	4	3
21	Mergui ...	11	7	4	1	...	1	5	1	4
	Magwe Division ..	*1,295*	*700*	*595*	*536*	*317*	*219*	*2,193*	*1,323*	*870*
22	Thayetmyo ...	52	21	31	42	25	17	75	52	23
23	Pakôkku ...	1,101	592	509	464	272	192	1,834	1,107	727
24	Minbu ...	44	35	9	16	9	7	225	129	96
25	Magwe ...	97	52	45	14	11	3	44	35	9
26	Pakôkku Hill Tracts	1	...	1	...	...	...	15	...	15
	Mandalay Division ..	*2,515*	*1,170*	*1,345*	*435*	*242*	*193*	*1,092*	*618*	*474*
27	Mandalay ...	2,419	1,127	1,292	384	215	169	181	107	74
28	Bhamo ...	17	6	11	10	7	3	5	5	...
29	Myitkyina ...	20	12	8	18	9	9	97	49	48
30	Katha ...	59	25	34	21	11	10	809	457	352
31	Putao ...	...	...	...	2	...	2	...	...	...
	Sagaing Division .	*315,129*	*148,732*	*166,397*	*339,094*	*153,954*	*185,140*	*170,887*	*85,004*	*85,883*
32	Shwebo ...	963	431	532	61	38	23	403	244	159
33	Sagaing ...	312,750	147,513	165,237	975	489	486	142	123	19
34	Lower Chindwin ...	1,379	760	619	338,034	153,409	184,625	4,915	2,907	2,008
35	Upper Chindwin ...	37	28	9	21	16	5	163,325	80,613	82,712
36	Chin Hills ...	...	...	.	3	2	1	2,102	1,117	985
	Meiktila Division ...	*3,792*	*1,719*	*2,073*	*204*	*86*	*118*	*72*	*46*	*26*
37	Kyauksè ...	582	221	361	5	3	2	...	...	...
38	Meiktila ...	542	309	233	23	15	8	20	8	12
39	Yamèthin ...	59	34	25	80	32	48	11	11	...
40	Myingyan ...	2,609	1,155	1,454	96	36	60	41	27	14
	Unadministered Territory	...	...	...	...	...	...	...	...	...
	Eastern States ...	**54**	**25**	**29**	**32**	**18**	**14**	**23**	**20**	**3**
41	Northern Shan States	24	14	10	16	14	2	9	8	1
42	Southern Shan States	30	11	19	16	4	12	14	12	2
43	Karenni ...	...	...	...	...	...	...	...	...	...

PART III.—*Birth-places in Burma*—continued.

WHICH ENUMERATED.

Chin Hills.			Kyaukse.			Meiktila.			Yamethin.			Myingyan.			
Persons.	Males.	Females.	Persons.	Males.	Females.	Persons.	Males.	Females.	Persons.	Males.	Females.	Persons.	Males.	Females.	
119	120	121	122	123	124	125	126	127	128	129	130	131	132	133	
109,002	**53,265**	**55,737**	**141,348**	**69,317**	**72,031**	**285,942**	**134,277**	**151,665**	**314,749**	**153,933**	**160,816**	**439,589**	**211,223**	**228,366**	
108,998	**53,265**	**55,733**	**140,874**	**69,064**	**71,810**	**285,210**	**133,923**	**151,287**	**313,701**	**153,576**	**160,125**	**439,440**	**211,079**	**228,361**	
...	...	...	*8*	*8*	...	*50*	*35*	*15*	*53*	*34*	*19*	*38*	*29*	*9*	
...	...	...	4	4	...	12	10	2	33	23	10	1	...	1	1
...	...	...	1	1	.	4	1	3	12	7	5	1	...	1	2
...	...	...	1	1	...	6	5	1	5	1	4	19	17	2	3
...	...	..	2	2	...	28	19	9	3	3	...	17	12	5	4
11	*7*	*4*	*429*	*208*	*221*	*747*	*459*	*288*	*1,652*	*886*	*766*	*471*	*347*	*124*	
4	3	1	195	104	91	358	219	139	705	385	320	193	135	58	5
1	...	1	19	7	12	41	36	5	58	19	39	22	18	4	6
...	...	.	6	3	3	47	32	15	33	23	10	44	32	12	7
1	1	...	74	34	40	65	35	30	158	85	73	63	55	8	8
...	...	...	80	34	46	154	79	75	324	193	131	58	43	15	9
5	3	2	55	26	29	82	58	24	374	181	193	91	64	27	10
11	*7*	*4*	*164*	*87*	*77*	*366*	*297*	*69*	*333*	*199*	*134*	*409*	*317*	*92*	
11	7	4	48	21	27	136	125	11	64	34	30	126	108	18	11
...	...	...	43	26	17	82	55	27	147	75	72	108	89	19	12
...	...	...	12	7	5	56	54	2	18	14	4	27	26	1	13
...	..	...	21	15	6	53	39	14	59	37	22	82	46	36	14
...	...	...	40	18	22	39	24	15	45	39	6	66	48	18	15
16	*4*	*12*	*184*	*98*	*86*	*518*	*351*	*167*	*2,418*	*1,498*	*920*	*265*	*201*	*64*	
8	4	4	108	59	49	348	225	123	2,098	1,318	780	86	46	40	16
...	...	...	2	2	...	2	2	...	21	17	4	...	...	...	17
...	...	...	23	12	11	43	38	5	58	33	25	25	25	...	18
8	...	8	35	16	19	96	73	23	184	105	79	55	35	20	19
...	...	.	12	7	5	14	7	7	24	15	9	8	6	2	20
...	...	...	4	2	2	15	6	9	33	10	23	91	89	2	21
18	*15*	*3*	*133*	*81*	*52*	*277*	*175*	*102*	*8,741*	*4,770*	*3,971*	*1,484*	*1,056*	*428*	
1	1	...	25	16	9	53	34	19	1,554	807	747	34	21	13	22
15	14	1	18	18	...	81	49	32	101	68	33	1,042	765	277	23
...	...	..	23	15	8	61	30	31	32	15	17	129	121	8	24
...	...		47	32	15	78	61	17	7,054	3,880	3,174	279	149	130	25
2	..	2	20	...	20	4	1	3	...	...	...	...	...	...	26
5	*4*	*1*	*2,685*	*1,452*	*1,233*	*885*	*497*	*388*	*1,309*	*704*	*605*	*480*	*278*	*202*	
5	4	1	2,572	1,371	1,201	845	482	363	1,209	645	564	447	247	200	27
...	...	...	8	...	8	20	7	13	23	16	7	7	6	1	28
..	...	...	78	74	4	3	...	3	25	11	14	26	25	1	29
...	...	...	27	7	20	17	8	9	41	27	14	...	...	..	30
...	...	...	...	...	...	...	...	...	11	5	6	...	...	...	31
108,934	*53,225*	*55,709*	*3,551*	*1,870*	*1,681*	*519*	*356*	*163*	*505*	*314*	*191*	*580*	*291*	*289*	
...	...	...	239	142	97	181	113	68	195	128	67	68	27	41	32
4	2	2	3,203	1,662	1,541	184	115	69	134	75	59	403	175	228	33
12	7	5	95	63	32	145	119	26	142	97	45	96	80	16	34
14	7	7	13	3	10	9	9	...	12	6	6	8	4	4	35
108,904	53,209	55,695	1	...	1	...	...	...	22	8	14	5	5	...	36
8	*8*	...	*133,720*	*65,260*	*68,460*	*281,848*	*131,753*	*150,095*	*298,690*	*145,171*	*153,519*	*435,713*	*208,560*	*227,153*	
...	...	...	125,678	61,133	64,545	425	205	220	521	255	266	37	17	20	37
...	...	...	5,198	2,673	2,595	279,126	130,281	148,845	8,203	4,302	3,901	881	529	352	38
2	2	...	257	145	112	1,037	601	436	288,234	139,638	148,596	111	73	38	39
1	1	...	2,587	1,309	1,278	1,260	666	594	1,732	976	756	434,684	207,941	226,743	40
...	...	...	...	...	...	...	...	...	...	...	...	...	...	...	
4	...	**4**	**474**	**253**	**221**	**732**	**354**	**378**	**1,048**	**357**	**691**	**149**	**144**	**5**	
1	...	1	147	64	83	176	49	127	161	44	117	22	19	3	41
3	...	3	[illegible]27	189	138	556	305	251	879	313	566	127	125	2	42
...	.	..	...	...	...	...	...	...	8	..	8	...	...	...	43

IMPERIAL TABLE XIA.—*Birth-place.* PART III.—*Birth-places in Burma*—concluded.

	District, etc., of Birth-place.	AREA IN WHICH ENUMERATED.								
		NORTHERN SHAN STATES.			SOUTHERN SHAN STATES.			KARENNI.		
		Persons.	Males.	Females.	Persons.	Males.	Females.	Persons.	Males.	Females.
	1	134	135	136	137	138	139	140	141	142
	ALL BURMA ...	**525,417**	**261.588**	**263,829**	**837.093**	**419,115**	**417,978**	**62.045**	**29.788**	**32,257**
	Divisional Burma ...	**12,356**	**7,345**	**5,011**	**3,449**	**2,204**	**1,245**	**1,081**	**776**	**305**
	Arakan Division ...	*162*	*89*	*73*	*20*	*15*	*5*	*2*	*2*	...
1	Akyab ...	4	...	4	5	5	...	...	...	...
2	Hill District of Arakan	61	3	58	3	3	...	1	1	...
3	Kyaukpyu ...	71	64	7	1	1	...	1	1	...
4	Sandoway ...	26	22	4	11	6	5	...	...	—
	Pegu Division ...	*650*	*394*	*256*	*323*	*213*	*110*	*35*	*26*	*9*
5	Rangoon Town ...	440	267	173	192	125	67	16	11	5
6	Insein ...	26	20	6	8	6	2	...	...	...
7	Hanthawaddy ...	21	12	9	5	5	...	5	4	1
8	Tharrawaddy ...	45	26	19	33	22	11	2	1	1
9	Pegu ...	64	35	29	44	26	18	5	5	...
10	Prome ...	54	34	20	41	29	12	7	5	2
	Irrawaddy Division ...	*120*	*80*	*40*	*131*	*64*	*67*	*371*	*289*	*82*
11	Bassein ...	55	38	17	40	21	19	2	2	...
12	Henzada ...	22	14	8	49	21	28	3	3	...
13	Myaungmya ...	15	6	9	26	14	12	360	278	82
14	Ma-ubin ...	8	4	4	12	5	7	6	6	...
15	Pyapôn ...	20	18	2	4	3	1	...	...	..
	Tenasserim Division ...	*303*	*207*	*96*	*358*	*235*	*123*	*496*	*327*	*169*
16	Toungoo ...	170	116	54	201	126	75	242	147	95
17	Salween ...	...	...	...	..	...	...	122	70	52
18	Thatôn ...	15	10	5	38	22	16	7	6	1
19	Amherst ...	108	72	36	108	78	30	125	104	21
20	Tavoy ...	8	7	1	11	9	2	...	...	...
21	Mergui ...	2	2	...	...	..	...	...	...	...
	Magwe Division ...	*89*	*56*	*33*	*69*	*39*	*30*	*15*	*8*	*7*
22	Thayetmyo ...	16	8	8	15	6	9	...	...	...
23	Pakôkku ...	43	36	7	16	8	8	6	3	3
24	Minbu ...	17	4	13	18	12	6	7	4	3
25	Magwe ...	13	8	5	20	13	7	2	1	1
26	Pakôkku Hill Tracts	...	...	...	...	...	..	...	...	...
	Mandalay Division	*8,619*	*4,869*	*3,750*	*642*	*431*	*211*	*71*	*51*	*20*
27	Mandalay ...	5,275	2,841	2,434	527	360	167	61	46	15
28	Bhamo ...	776	338	438	15	9	6	6	3	3
29	Myitkyina ...	131	61	70	40	25	15	1	1	...
30	Katha ...	2,417	1,615	802	60	37	23	3	1	2
31	Putao ...	20	14	6	..	...	...	...	...	...
	Sagaing Division ...	*1,587*	*1,184*	*403*	*170*	*129*	*41*	*15*	*12*	*3*
32	Shwebo ...	1,045	733	312	65	48	17	8	7	1
33	Sagaing ...	149	101	48	29	20	9	2	2	...
34	Lower Chindwin ...	43	26	17	42	35	7	5	3	2
35	Upper Chindwin ...	247	236	11	9	8	1	...	...	...
36	Chin Hills ...	53	38	15	25	18	7	...	...	...
	Meiktila Division ...	*876*	*516*	*360*	*1,736*	*1,078*	*658*	*76*	*61*	*15*
37	Kyauksè ...	600	345	255	480	300	180	4	4	...
38	Meiktila ...	70	53	17	768	446	322	29	22	7
39	Yamèthin ...	167	89	78	456	312	144	38	30	8
40	Myingyan ...	39	29	10	32	20	12	5	5	...
	Unadministered Territory	...	...	...	...	...	..	...	...	...
	Eastern States ...	**513,061**	**254,243**	**258.818**	**833,644**	**416,911**	**416,733**	**60.964**	**29,012**	**31,952**
41	Northern Shan States	507,271	250,664	256,607	3,464	1,950	1,514	76	61	15
42	Southern Shan States	5,790	3,579	2,211	829,868	414,757	415,111	44	38	6
43	Karenni ...	...	...	...	312	204	108	60,844	28,913	31,931

IMPERIAL TABLE XI-B.

Birth-places of Indians of Selected Races.

NOTE 1.—Part I of this table shows by provinces the birth-places of (i) all Hindus and Animists and (ii) all Mahomedans of the six Indian races most numerously represented in Burma who were enumerated in the following thirteen districts: Akyab, Rangoon, Insein, Hanthawaddy, Pegu, Bassein, Myaungmya, Pyapôn, Toungoo, Thatôn, Amherst, Mandalay and Yamèthin. The six selected Indian races are shown in Note 3 below.

NOTE 2.—Parts II, III, IV and V expand to show details for separate districts of birth the statistics given for some classes in Part I. The classes treated in each part are as follows:—

II. Persons of each selected race born in Burma.
III. Bengalis and Chittagonians born in Bengal.
IV. Hindustanis born in the United Provinces.
V. (i) Oriyas born in Madras or in Bihar and Orissa.
(ii) Tamils and Telugus born in Madras.

NOTE 3.—The total numbers in the province of all Indian races and of the six selected races are shown in Imperial Table XIII as follows:—

RACE.	All Religions.		Hindus and Animists.		Mahomedans.	
	Males.	Females.	Males.	Females	Males.	Females.
1	2	3	4	5	6	7
All Indian Races	653,980	233,097	379,529	104,428	249,600	1[illegible]6,671
Bengali	60,117	27,871	12,172	3,002	46,651	14,632
Chittagonian	129,854	76,534	5,110	286	122,870	75,682
Hindustani	107,557	26,090	8[illegible],482	19,657	23,400	5,984
Oriya	49,993	2,482	4[illegible],017	1,973	823	212
Tamil	100,315	51,749	[illegible],192	36,761	21,328	7,196
Telugu	129,566	28,621	12[illegible],413	27,095	2,047	818
Other Indian Races	70,578	29,820	3[illegible],143	15,654	32,449	12,147

NOTE 4.—The total numbers of all races (including non-Indians) born in each province of India and enumerated in Burma are shown in Imperial Table XIA.

NOTE 5.—Imperial Tables IX and XIV give statistics of literacy and civil condition respectively by age and sex for the persons represented in this table.

IMPERIAL TABLE XIB.—*Birth-places of Indians of Selected Races.*

PART I.—PROVINCES OF BIRTH

BIRTH-PLACE.	Total for Selected Races.		Bengali.		Chittagonian.		Hindustani.		Oriya.		Tamil.		Telugu.	
	Males.	Females.	Males.	Females	Males.	Females	Males.	Females	Males.	Females	Males.	Females	Males.	Females
1	2	3	4	5	6	7	8	9	10	11	12	13	14	15
Population tabulated:—														
Total	477,842	176,824	50,367	14,726	121,046	75,223	81,400	19,515	32,902	1,777	81,547	41,095	110,580	24,488
Hindus and Animists	283,152	78,184	10,055	2,258	4,873	248	64,115	15,370	32,314	1,602	63,187	34,929	108,608	23,777
Mahomedans ...	194,690	98,640	40,312	12,468	116,173	74,975	17,285	4,145	588	175	18,360	6,166	1,972	711
Burma	131,674	119,433	12,819	10,858	72,039	70,833	12,820	8,857	1,076	598	22,536	20,194	10,384	8,093
Hindus and Animists	40,707	32,294	900	698	196	128	10,509	6,779	1,000	512	18,359	16,494	9,743	7,683
Mahomedans .	90,967	8[illegible],139	11,919	10,160	71,843	70,705	2,311	2,078	76	86	4,177	3,700	641	410
Assam	909	34	437	7	203	..	101	21	27	...	24	4	117	2
Hindus and Animists	338	33	73	7	32	...	66	21	27	...	24	3	116	2
Mahomedans ...	571	1	364	..	171	...	35	...	..	..	..	1	1	...
Bengal	102,180	11,543	33,859	3,485	47,246	4,291	10,810	1,646	3,160	142	3,072	1,094	4,033	885
Hindus and Animists	29,974	4,579	8,140	1,293	4,493	110	8,291	1,288	3,004	137	2,232	904	3,814	847
Mahomedans .	72,206	6,964	25,719	2,192	42,753	4,181	2,519	358	156	5	840	190	219	38
Madras	176,109	37,320	1,176	114	573	51	11,172	2,535	19,121	779	52,602	18,876	91,465	14,515
Hindus and Animists	159,594	34,055	312	81	38	2	9,665	2,230	18,890	704	40,192	16,746	90,497	14,292
Mahomedans ...	16,515	2,815	864	33	535	49	1,507	305	231	75	12,410	2,130	968	223
Bihar and Orissa ..	9,715	787	213	46	30	1	3,115	314	5,008	110	479	170	870	146
Hindus and Animists	9,086	698	111	42	7	...	2,695	244	4,975	109	431	163	867	140
Mahomedans ..	629	89	102	4	23	1	420	70	33	1	48	7	3	6
Bombay	4,244	1,013	182	40	171	9	2,306	556	608	28	368	188	609	192
Hindus and Animists	3,210	856	57	21	11	6	1,742	461	599	26	211	160	590	182
Mahomedans .	1,034	157	125	19	160	3	564	95	9	2	157	28	19	10
Punjab	2,496	410	132	31	135	5	1,319	240	402	11	186	65	322	58
Hindus and Animists	1,782	313	34	16	2	1	909	183	387	11	142	47	308	55
Mahomedans ...	714	97	98	15	133	4	410	57	15	...	44	18	14	3
United Provinces ...	41,246	5,457	651	87	218	17	36,802	4,871	1,406	45	792	158	1,377	279
Hindus and Animists	31,806	4,268	286	64	9	1	28,185	3,800	1,367	41	623	95	1,336	267
Mahomedans ...	9,440	1,189	365	23	209	16	8,617	1,071	39	4	169	63	41	12
Rajputana Agency ...	1,493	138	69	...	14	...	406	73	721	17	37	25	246	23
Hindus and Animists	1,351	132	17	..	4	...	338	69	721	17	25	23	246	23
Mahomedans ..	142	6	52	..	10	..	68	4	...	..	12	2	...	..
Other Parts of India ...	2,614	409	86	5	50	10	971	133	545	15	531	187	431	59
Hindus and Animists	1,950	321	30	3	4	...	716	72	543	15	236	176	421	55
Mahomedans	664	88	56	2	46	10	255	61	2	...	295	11	10	4
India (locality unspecified)	4,324	640	731	49	318	5	1,368	249	803	26	420	90	684	221
Hindus and Animists	2,572	553	88	30	48	...	800	206	776	24	232	77	628	216
Mahomedans ..	1,752	87	643	19	270	5	568	43	27	2	188	13	56	5
Outside India ..	838	90	12	4	49	1	210	20	25	6	500	44	42	15
Hindus and Animists	782	82	7	3	29	...	199	17	25	6	480	41	42	15
Mahomedans ...	56	8	5	1	20	1	11	3	...	...	20	3	...	...

IMPERIAL TABLE XIB.—*Birth-places of Indians of Selected Races.*

PART II.—BIRTH-DISTRICTS IN BURMA.

District of Birth-place.	Total for Selected Races.		Bengali.		Chittagonian.		Hindustani.		Oriya.		Tamil.		Telugu	
	Males.	Females.	Males.	Females	Males.	Females	Males.	Females	Males.	Females	Males.	Females	Males.	Females
1	2	3	4	5	6	7	8	9	10	11	12	13	14	15
Hindus and Animists ...	40,707	32,294	900	698	196	128	10,509	6,779	1,000	512	18,359	16,494	9,743	7,683
Akyab	851	716	35	43	159	103	626	556	10	2	8	7	13	5
Rangoon Town ...	7,097	6,107	392	276	6	1	747	545	213	143	3,348	3,182	2,391	1,960
Insein	2,007	1,884	53	51	...	...	371	568	94	50	887	772	602	443
Hanthawaddy ...	7,064	5,510	24	14	2	..	737	425	54	25	5,089	4,571	1,128	675
Pegu	7,093	5,600	56	36	1	...	3,302	2,577	194	117	1,942	1,656	1,598	1,214
Bassein ...	748	569	32	34	...	...	239	160	52	15	133	121	292	233
Myaungmya ...	399	259	17	15	1	...	172	74	55	28	91	90	63	52
Pyapôn ...	1,481	1,142	22	18	8	6	142	104	74	32	890	719	345	263
Toungoo ...	2,934	1,522	50	40	2	6	2,397	1,018	53	11	160	195	272	252
Thatôn ...	3,969	3,524	18	17	3	3	421	323	56	38	2,625	2,287	846	856
Amherst ...	4,657	3,806	73	35	9	5	214	88	41	23	2,592	2,315	1,728	1,339
Mandalay ...	1,512	939	72	57	...	..	792	280	40	22	367	401	241	179
Yamèthin ..	334	346	10	12	...	1	184	106	6	1	46	53	88	113
Other Districts and the Shan States.	561	370	46	49	5	3	165	89	28	5	181	125	136	99
Mahomedans ...	90,967	87,139	11,919	10,160	71,843	70,705	2,311	2,078	76	86	4,177	3,700	641	410
Akyab	77,161	75,266	7,378	6,277	69,768	68,983	4	4	...	...	11	2	...	...
Rangoon Town ...	2,043	1,632	323	232	233	194	656	519	11	8	783	642	37	37
Insein	868	780	109	100	85	74	161	112	8	9	402	378	103	107
Hanthawaddy ...	916	922	112	105	137	128	48	83	5	25	608	580	6	1
Pegu	1,056	855	76	63	207	184	190	198	1	1	444	339	138	70
Bassein ...	628	573	420	414	44	31	70	41	1	..	76	77	17	10
Myaungmya ...	641	632	337	342	36	31	53	78	4	4	202	171	9	6
Pyapôn	304	211	109	57	83	80	17	14	19	5	59	45	17	10
Toungoo ...	682	478	110	56	207	182	144	194	7	1	152	34	62	11
Thatôn	1,497	1,314	970	831	116	46	90	81	6	9	286	338	29	9
Amherst ...	3,636	3,120	1,665	1,534	848	703	124	64	5	...	961	794	33	25
Mandalay ...	899	730	209	45	21	25	473	475	..	9	76	102	120	74
Yamèthin ...	358	255	47	18	30	1	185	105	5	8	47	84	44	39
Other Districts and the Shan States.	278	371	54	86	28	43	96	110	4	7	70	114	26	11

PART III.—BIRTH-DISTRICTS OF BENGALIS AND CHITTAGONIANS BORN IN BENGAL.

District of Birth-place.	Bengalis.						Chittagonians.					
	Males.			Females.			Males.			Females.		
	Total.	Hindus and Animists	Maho-medans.	Total	Hindus and Animists	Maho-medans.	Total.	Hindus and Animists	Maho-medans.	Total.	Hindus and Animists	Maho-medans.
1	2	3	4	5	6	7	8	9	10	11	12	13
Bengal Province	33,859	8,140	25,719	3,485	1,293	2,192	47,246	4,493	42,753	4,291	110	4,181
Burdwan ...	249	53	196	30	14	16	19	...	19	...	...	..
Calcutta ...	2,395	788	1,607	589	357	232	262	6	256	17	2	15
Chittagong ...	20,019	4,706	15,313	1,970	248	1,722	43,835	4,291	39,544	3,969	100	3,869
Dacca ...	1,343	495	848	279	250	29	77	7	70	...	...	...
Faridpur ...	99	88	11	37	37	...	1	1	...	...	...	...
Hooghly ...	368	84	284	29	27	2	7	...	7	2	...	2
Howrah ...	126	75	51	46	46	...	3	...	3	...	...	...
Mymensingh ..	1,323	22	1,301	15	...	15	109	...	109	4	...	4
Nadia ...	100	40	60	25	17	8	..	...	...	...	...	...
Noakhali ...	2,445	493	1,952	32	19	13	670	14	656	1	...	1
24-Parganas ...	78	6	72	4	4	...	...	...	...	...	...	...
Tippera ...	227	163	64	23	23	...	26	3	23	...	...	...
Other Districts	176	104	72	28	24	4	45	1	44	...	..	...
Dist. not recorded	4,911	1,023	3,888	378	227	151	2,192	170	2,022	298	8	290

IMPERIAL TABLE XIB.—*Birth-places of Indians of Selected Races.*

PART IV.—BIRTH-DISTRICTS OF HINDUSTANIS BORN IN THE UNITED PROVINCES.

NOTE.—*H. and A.* indicates Hindus and Animists and *M.* indicates Mahomedans.

DISTRICT OF BIRTH-PLACE.	Males.			Females.			DISTRICT OF BIRTH-PLACE.	Males.			Females.		
	Total.	H. and A.	M.	Total.	H. and A.	M.		Total.	H. and A.	M.	Total.	H. and A.	M.
1	2	3	4	5	6	7	1	2	3	4	5	6	7
United Provinces	36,802	28,185	8,617	4,871	3,800	1,071							
							Gonda ...	1,178	923	255	138	92	46
Agra ...	2,670	2,576	94	1,480	1,451	29	Gorakpur ...	4,210	4,112	98	94	85	9
Allahabad ..	634	371	263	104	69	35	Jaunpur ...	1,725	1,175	550	111	83	28
Azamgarh ...	2,8[illegible]9	1,6[illegible]	1,269	177	143	34	Lucknow ...	404	176	228	122	84	38
Barabanki ..	567	273	294	72	39	33	Partabgarh ...	783	312	471	129	44	85
Basti .	765	600	159	68	45	23	Sultanpur ..	6,150	4,448	1,702	597	391	206
Benares .	499	364	135	136	121	15	Other Districts ...	1,177	834	343	191	144	47
Fyzabad ...	10,734	8,310	2,422	1,106	802	394	Dist. not specified	1,839	1,533	306	166	135	31
Ghazipur ..	446	418	28	83	65	18	Indian States ...	134	134	...	7	7	...

PART V.—BIRTH-DISTRICTS OF (*i*) ORIYAS BORN IN MADRAS OR IN BIHAR AND ORISSA AND OF (*ii*) TAMILS AND TELUGUS BORN IN MADRAS.

NOTE.—*H. and A.* indicates Hindus and Animists and *M.* indicates Mahomedans.

DISTRICT OF BIRTH-PLACE.	ORIYAS.						TAMILS.						TELUGUS.					
	Males.			Females.			Males.			Females.			Males.			Females.		
	Total.	H. & A.	M.	Total	H. & A.	M.	Total.	H. & A.	M.	Total.	H. & A.	M.	Total.	H. & A.	M.	Total.	H. & A.	M.
1	2	3	4	5	6	7	8	9	10	11	12	13	14	15	16	17	18	19
Madras Province.	19,121	18,890	231	779	704	75	52,602	40,192	12,410	18,876	16,746	2,130	91,465	90,497	968	14,515	14,292	223
Anantapur	...	...	.	...	...	..	68	57	11	9	8	1	448	423	25	33	27	6
Chingleput	...	..	..	...	.	..	209	191	18	97	92	5	290	284	6	40	40	...
Ganjam ...	12,387	12,341	46	316	309	7	528	490	38	122	115	7	21,907	21,873	34	1,366	1,357	9
Godavari ...	359	333	26	33	30	3	748	650	98	226	202	24	18,539	18,388	151	2,576	2,525	51
Guntur ..	125	125	...	4	4		276	250	26	38	36	2	342	342	...	49	49	...
Kistna	84	84	...	10	10	...	395	328	67	115	97	18	5,941	5,916	25	550	546	4
Madras ...	...		...		...	.	246	2[illegible]5	1	113	93	20	231	231	...	26	26	..
Madura	182	180	2	4	4	...	3,122	2,377	745	1,177	1,029	148	311	308	3	98	95	2
Malabar ...	66	65	1	..	..	...	395	199	196	72	60	12	156	143	13	32	32	...
Nellore ...	16	16	...	.	...	...	112	96	16	44	43	1	721	707	14	80	80	...
Ramnad ...	119	104	15	21	19	2	8,037	5,322	2,715	1,988	1,635	353	616	572	44	120	117	3
Salem ...	.	...	.		...	...	307	219	88	108	96	12	131	126	5	9	9	...
Tanjore ..	175	174	1	36	36	..	7,596	5,433	2,163	2,277	2,103	174	1,507	1,472	35	423	419	4
Tinnevelly	8	8	..	...	...	..	2,525	1,046	1,479	458	352	106	216	216	...	89	88	1
Trichinopoly	12	12	...	..	...	...	803	631	172	271	245	26	161	144	17	54	54	...
Vizagapatam	311	309	2	74	74	...	670	539	131	180	164	16	21,113	20,906	207	4,175	4,129	46
Other Districts.	119	119	...	4	4	..	456	409	47	187	180	7	660	660	...	119	118	1
District not specified.	5,158	5,020	138	277	214	63	26,000	21,639	4,361	11,130	9,947	1,183	18,076	17,689	387	4,668	4,573	95
States ...	...	..	..	..	..	..	109	71	38	264	249	15	99	97	2	8	7	1
Bihar and Orissa.	5,008	4,975	33	110	109	1	479	431	48	170	163	7	870	867	3	146	140	6
Bhagalpur	198	198	...	...	...	...	Figures not available for Tamils and Telugus by separate districts.											
Cuttack ...	654	654	...	16	16	...												
Gaya ...	56	56		7	6	1												
Nilgiri ...	65	65	.	...	...	...												
Puri ...	1,915	1,904	11	36	36													
Other Districts.	155	146	9	4	4	...												
District not specified.	1,965	1,952	13	47	47	..												

IMPERIAL TABLE XII.

Infirmities.

NOTE 1.—This table is arranged in three parts as follows :—
Part I, Distribution by Age.
Part II, Distribution by Districts.
Part III, Distribution by Race-groups and Races.

NOTE 2.—Cognisance was taken in the enumeration of only the four infirmities specified in the tables; but for every person enumerated, whether in a synchronous or non-synchronous area, a record was made whether any or none of these infirmities was present. The population in which the tabulated infirmities appeared is therefore the whole of that shown in Imperial Tables VIIA, VIA and XIII which thus provide a basis of comparison for the several parts of this table. The areas for which no record of infirmities was made are the estimated areas and the areas omitted entirely from the census; these are shown in Notes 13 and 12 respectively of Imperial Table II.

NOTE 3.—Subsidiary tables on page 186 show particulars relating to persons afflicted with more than one of the tabulated infirmities. Such persons are counted once for each infirmity in all three Parts of the table except in the columns of Parts I and II which show *Persons Afflicted*; in those columns each such person is shown only once.

NOTE 4.—The age recorded was the number of completed years. The age-group represented by 5–10 in Part I of the table includes all who had completed five but had not yet completed ten years of age; and the other age-groups have a parallel interpretation.

NOTE 5.—Deductions drawn from the figures of Part II of the table must allow for the fact that the numbers shown in that table for certain districts include persons enumerated in asylums and special schools related to the enumerated infirmities and situated in those districts, some of whom may have been born and may previously have been ordinarily resident in some other district. The numbers of such persons are shown in Note 9 of this table on page 186.

NOTE 6.—The boundary of the Rangoon Town and Insein Districts passes through the Leper Asylum at Kemmendine, but the main portion of the asylum is in Rangoon and the institution is properly associated with that district. Accordingly 18 female inmates included in the Insein District record have been transferred in Part II of the table and in Note 9 to be shown as if enumerated in Rangoon. The new Rangoon Lunatic Asylum, situated in the Insein District, was still vacant on the date of the census.

NOTE 7.—The system of race-groups in Part III is that adopted for Table XIII and described in Note 3 of that table. Records for race-groups are printed in the table in distinctive type; entries in ordinary type below those are for separate races included in the group. Races which are not represented amongst the infirm persons are not mentioned in the table. Thus although the figures in columns 5 to 16 for each race-group are the sum of the details given below them, this is not necessarily the case for the figures in columns 2 to 4.

IMPERIAL TABLE XII.—*Infirmities.*

PART I.—DISTRIBUTION BY AGE.

Age.	Population afflicted.			Insane.			Deaf Mutes.			Blind.			Lepers.		
	Persons.	Males.	Females.	Persons.	Males.	Females.	Persons.	Males.	Females.	Persons.	Males.	Females.	Persons.	Males.	Females.
1	2	3	4	5	6	7	8	9	10	11	12	13	14	15	16
Provincial Total	57,824	30.445	26,879	11,573	6,285	5,288	11,877	6,447	5,430	24,523	11,325	13,198	9,765	6,589	3,176
0	37	22	15	3	2	1	6	4	2	29	14	15	3	3	...
1	72	44	28	7	4	3	20	12	8	42	26	16	4	3	1
2	141	67	74	20	8	12	49	30	19	65	26	39	8	4	4
3	230	123	107	53	26	27	103	60	43	67	34	33	9	4	5
4	311	179	132	41	24	17	156	87	69	108	66	42	11	5	6
Total 0—5	791	435	356	124	64	60	334	193	141	311	166	145	35	19	16
5—10	2,313	1,289	1,024	434	222	212	1,208	674	534	584	335	249	105	69	36
10—15	3.127	1,706	1,421	608	301	307	1,424	762	662	761	437	324	369	221	148
15—20	3,993	2,198	1,795	929	486	413	1,407	722	685	945	547	398	754	462	292
20—25	4,804	2,739	2,065	1,209	678	531	1,576	847	729	994	526	468	1,089	717	372
25—30	4,483	2,640	1,843	1,151	675	476	1,098	596	502	1,109	606	503	1,162	785	377
30—35	5,303	3,156	2,147	1,496	863	633	1,291	713	578	1,228	651	577	1,350	960	390
35—40	3,910	2,430	1,480	1,082	655	427	614	375	269	1,120	600	520	1,091	811	280
40—45	5,012	2,800	2,212	1,362	720	642	854	472	382	1,697	828	869	1,137	799	338
45—50	3,613	2,003	1,610	841	435	406	389	215	174	1,638	834	804	757	525	232
50—55	4,527	2,279	2,248	861	446	415	501	271	230	2,416	1,041	1,375	765	528	237
55—60	2,828	1,355	1,473	452	240	212	211	110	101	1,794	769	1,025	380	238	142
60—65	4,110	1,904	2,206	480	243	237	318	170	148	2,922	1,249	1,673	400	246	154
65—70	2,425	1,077	1,348	201	100	101	190	103	87	1,899	786	1,113	144	93	51
70 and over	6,085	2,434	3,651	343	157	186	432	224	208	5,105	1,950	3,155	227	116	111

IMPERIAL TABLE XII.—*Infirmities.*

PART II.—DISTRIBUTION BY DISTRICTS.

Serial No.	District or State.	Population afflicted.			Insane.			Deaf Mutes.			Blind.			Lepers.		
		Persons.	Males.	Females.	Persons.	Males.	Females.	Persons.	Males.	Females.	Persons.	Males.	Females.	Persons.	Males.	Females.
	1	2	3	4	5	6	7	8	9	10	11	12	13	14	15	16
	Provincial Total ...	57.324	30,445	26,879	11.573	6,285	5,288	11,877	6,447	5,430	24,523	11,325	13,198	9,765	6.589	3,176
	Divisional Burma	47.000	25,169	21,831	9,356	5,129	4,227	8,340	4,606	3,734	21,073	9,754	11,319	8,513	5,823	2,690
	Arakan Division ...	*2,886*	*1,312*	*1,074*	*906*	*484*	*422*	*570*	*342*	*228*	*691*	*355*	*336*	*230*	*139*	*91*
1	Akyab ..	1,484	826	658	606	316	290	379	238	141	390	214	176	117	65	52
2	Hill District of Arakan.	205	109	96	43	18	25	10	4	6	68	29	39	84	58	26
3	Kyaukpyu ...	400	212	188	160	90	70	105	58	47	116	55	61	19	9	10
4	Sandoway .	297	165	132	97	60	37	76	42	34	117	57	60	10	7	3
	Pegu Division ...	*6,041*	*3,713*	*2,328*	*1,652*	*1,132*	*520*	*714*	*417*	*297*	*2,387*	*1,199*	*1,188*	*1,306*	*975*	*331*
5	Rangoon City	1,361	1,015	346	826	658	168	68	41	27	249	147	102	222	172	50
6	Insein ..	506	314	192	93	63	30	67	41	26	211	105	106	136	106	30
7	Hanthawaddy	927	569	358	158	93	65	144	89	55	372	196	176	261	194	67
8	Tharrawaddy	1,346	743	603	230	127	103	144	80	64	643	293	350	329	243	86
9	Pegu ...	958	572	386	163	85	78	128	74	54	435	237	198	235	177	58
10	Prome .	943	500	443	182	106	76	163	92	71	477	221	256	123	83	40
	Irrawaddy Division	*5,106*	*3,116*	*1,990*	*938*	*524*	*414*	*887*	*492*	*395*	*1831*	*996*	*835*	*1,464*	*1,111*	*358*
11	Bassein .	875	550	325	172	99	73	152	82	70	242	133	109	309	236	73
12	Henzada ...	1,730	1,042	688	331	184	147	321	180	141	667	354	313	413	324	89
13	Myaungmya	779	485	294	145	86	59	123	70	53	266	143	123	248	187	61
14	Ma-ubin ..	1,135	696	439	206	107	99	182	107	75	394	222	172	361	266	95
15	Pyapôn	587	343	244	84	48	36	109	53	56	262	144	118	133	98	35
	Tenasserim Division	*3,826*	*2,256*	*1,570*	*1,007*	*544*	*463*	*797*	*485*	*312*	*1,483*	*824*	*659*	*562*	*416*	*146*
16	Toungoo ..	1,399	828	571	268	143	125	283	181	102	674	376	298	187	133	54
17	Salween ..	108	56	52	42	19	23	24	13	11	32	15	17	10	9	1
18	Thatôn ...	820	503	317	222	114	108	166	101	65	272	158	114	160	130	30
19	Amherst ..	759	464	295	214	130	84	169	103	66	228	124	104	155	113	42
20	Tavoy .	388	207	181	155	86	69	54	29	25	152	77	75	28	15	13
21	Mergui	352	198	154	106	52	54	101	58	43	125	74	51	22	16	6
	Magwe Division ...	*7,626*	*3,837*	*3,789*	*1,206*	*664*	*542*	*1,183*	*670*	*513*	*4,069*	*1,731*	*2,338*	*1,197*	*790*	*407*
22	Thayetmyo ...	743	420	323	148	93	55	38	23	15	431	219	212	126	85	41
23	Pakôkku ...	3,308	1,540	1,768	506	246	260	608	340	268	1,860	747	1,113	348	214	134
24	Minbu ..	1,778	929	849	369	235	134	200	107	93	879	373	506	343	224	119
25	Magwe ...	1,596	825	771	171	84	87	178	102	76	884	388	496	303	251	112
26	Pakôkku Hill Tracts	201	123	78	12	6	6	159	98	61	15	4	11	17	16	1
	Mandalay Division	*5,650*	*2.952*	*2,698*	*1,022*	*528*	*494*	*1,658*	*872*	*786*	*2,222*	*1,054*	*1,168*	*862*	*555*	*307*
27	Mandalay ..	2,036	1,107	929	234	121	113	155	89	66	1,026	493	533	631	408	223
	Mandalay City	*1,024*	*561*	*463*	*96*	*54*	*42*	*63*	*35*	*28*	*395*	*168*	*227*	*474*	*305*	*169*
28	Bhamo ...	1,327	645	681	336	171	165	771	379	392	262	116	146	25	11	14
29	Myitkyina ..	1,091	577	514	283	145	138	559	309	250	240	112	128	36	28	8
30	Katha ..	1,161	605	556	153	81	72	169	92	77	681	329	352	168	107	61
31	Putao .	35	18	17	16	10	6	4	3	1	13	4	9	2	1	1
	Sagaing Division	*10,552*	*5,091*	*5,461*	*1,950*	*913*	*1,037*	*1,868*	*986*	*882*	*4,993*	*2,094*	*2,899*	*1,801*	*1,121*	*680*
32	Shwebo	2,097	985	1,112	254	131	123	214	116	98	1,357	557	800	280	184	96
33	Sagaing .	2,522	1,228	1,294	286	149	137	174	97	77	1,342	543	799	734	444	290
34	L. Chindwin	2,328	1,064	1,264	241	109	132	164	76	88	1,506	631	875	423	251	172
35	U. Chindwin	1,613	769	844	403	187	216	439	229	210	670	288	382	133	77	56
36	Chin Hills ...	1,992	1,045	947	766	337	429	877	468	409	118	75	43	231	165	66
	Meiktila Division	*5,813*	*2,892*	*2,921*	*675*	*340*	*335*	*663*	*342*	*321*	*3,397*	*1,501*	*1,896*	*1,091*	*716*	*375*
37	Kyauksè .	813	423	390	128	63	65	97	47	50	513	250	263	79	65	14
38	Meiktila .	1,204	551	653	150	70	80	141	63	78	685	283	402	228	135	93
39	Yamèthin .	1,314	649	665	169	85	84	161	90	71	808	363	445	181	115	66
40	Myingyan ...	2,482	1,269	1,213	228	122	106	264	142	122	1,391	605	786	603	401	202
	Eastern States ...	10,324	5,276	5,048	2.217	1,156	1,061	3,537	1,841	1,696	3,450	1,571	1,879	1,252	766	486
41	N. Shan States	4,029	2,044	1,985	809	418	391	1,864	951	913	1,306	610	696	182	123	59
42	S. Shan States	5,816	2,980	2,836	1,330	692	638	1,506	794	712	1,963	888	1,075	1,017	606	411
43	Karenni ...	479	252	227	78	46	32	167	96	71	181	73	108	53	37	16

Imperial Table XII.—*Infirmities.*

PART III.—DISTRIBUTION BY RACE-GROUPS AND RACES.

Race-group, Race or Tribe.	Population dealt with.			Insane.			Deaf Mutes.			Blind.			Lepers.		
	Persons.	Males.	Females.	Persons.	Males.	Females.	Persons.	Males.	Females.	Persons.	Males.	Females.	Persons.	Males.	Females.
1	2	3	4	5	6	7	8	9	10	11	12	13	14	15	16
Provincial Total for All Races.	13,169.099	6,735,516	6,433,583	11,573	6.285	5,288	11,877	6,447	5,430	24,523	11,325	13,198	9,765	6,589	3,176
A. Burma Group * ..	*8.706,809*	*4263,828*	*4443,487*	*6,479*	*3,551*	*2,928*	*5,020*	*2,774*	*2,246*	*18,696*	*8,505*	*10,191*	*6,958*	*4,692*	*2;266*
1 Burmese ..	7,837,985	3,831,165	4,006,820	5,265	2,922	2,343	4,107	2,250	1,857	17,680	8,021	9,659	6,677	4,517	2,160
2 Arakanese *	324 475	163,930	160,545	610	332	278	346	.02	144	385	195	190	69	33	36
4 Chaungtha	46,153	23,396	22,757	61	27	34	23	13	10	42	23	19	12	9	3
5 Tavoyan ..	129,287	64,329	64,958	143	76	67	47	26	21	135	65	7(	24	11	13
9 Danu ...	64,642	37,382	27,260	128	67	61	69	43	26	239	119	120	26	21	5
10 Intha ...	56,175	27,693	28,482	79	36	43	37	26	11	86	34	52	143	96	47
13 Atsi ...	4,857	2,677	2,180	54	28	26	84	49	35	15	8	7	2	2	...
14 Lashi ...	17,010	8,567	.8,443	76	38	38	129	59	70	35	13	22	1	1	...
15 Maru ...	21,425	10,315	11,110	60	24	36	177	105	72	78	26	52	4	2	2
Yaw, Taung-yo and Maingtha.	24,297	12,479	11,818	3	1	2	1	1	...	1	1	...	...	...	..
B. Lolo Mus'o Group	*76,845*	*39,494*	*36,351*	*32*	*23*	*9*	*97*	*49*	*48*	*96*	*37*	*59*	*4*	*2*	*2*
1 Lisaw ..	13.260	6,703	6,557	19	11	8	33	11	22	23	6	17	...	...	...
7 Akha ...	34,265	18,335	15,930	13	12	1	64	38	26	73	31	42	4	2	2
C. Kuki-Chin Group ...	*288,847*	*144,318*	*144,529*	*983*	*435*	*548*	*1,229*	*661*	*568*	*371*	*186*	*185*	*397*	*277*	*120*
32 Chin (unspecified).	116,591	58,319	58,272	977	433	544	1,225	660	565	343	176	167	388	275	113
1 Meit'ei ...	9,407	5,555	3,852	6	2	4	4	1	3	28	10	18	9	2	7
D. Naga Group ...	*406*	*197*	*209*	*1*	...	*1*	..	...	...	*1*	*1*	...	...	...	...
E. Kachin Group ...	*146,845*	*70,611*	*76,234*	*623*	*318*	*305*	*1,647*	*836*	*811*	*341*	*147*	*194*	*39*	*25*	*14*
F. Sak (Lui) Group ...	*49,726*	*24,497*	*25,229*	*30*	*11*	*19*	*42*	*28*	*14*	*127*	*63*	*64*	*45*	*26*	*19*
1 Kadu ...	37,710	18,625	1 ,085	25	9	16	40	26	14	126	62	64	45	26	19
4 Daingnet .	4,928	2,535	2,393	5	2	3	2	2	..	1	1	. .	...	...	...
H. Mro ...	*14,771*	*7,520*	*7,251*	*26*	*21*	*5*	*12*	*7*	*5*	*19*	*13*	*6*	*24*	*19*	*5*
I. Tai Group ...	*1,017,987*	*508,975*	*509,012*	*1,876*	*751*	*625*	*1,870*	*974*	*896*	*2,958*	*1,347*	*1,611*	*1,140*	*699*	*441*
1 Shan unspecified.	288,984	142,237	146,747	308	158	150	359	195	164	765	353	412	156	111	45
2 Shangale ...	588,405	293,747	294,658	956	526	430	1,290	674	616	1,894	893	1,001	868	522	346
3 Shangyi ...	29,004	15,100	13,904	21	13	8	27	17	10	166	28	138	16	12	4
4 Shan Tayok	28,701	15,885	12,816	20	12	8	31	20	11	25	18	7	4	4	...
6 Siamese .	13,286	7,245	6,041	8	6	2	5	2	3	10	7	3	4	3	1
7 Khun ..	33,394	16,350	17,044	38	19	19	101	47	54	57	28	29.	47	20	27
8 Lü ...	25,870	12,686	13,184	12	9	3	55	17	38	34	17	17	43	26	17
11 Kamti ...	4,83	2,256	2,595	13	8	5	2	2	...	7	3	4	2	1	1
J. Malay Group ...	*6,658*	*3,144*	*3,509*	*7*	*2*	*5*	*9*	*5*	*4*	*6*	*2*	*4*	*2*	*2*	...

* For this table Arakan-Mahomedans (Race S1) numbering 12,740 males and 11,035 females have been added to the Arakanese Race A2 and the Burma Group.

IMPERIAL TABLE XII.—*Infirmities.*

PART III.—DISTRIBUTION BY RACE-GROUPS AND RACES.

Race-group, Race or Tribe.	Population dealt with.			Insane.			Deaf-Mutes.			Blind.			Lepers.		
	Persons.	Males.	Females.	Persons.	Males.	Females.	Persons.	Males.	Females.	Persons.	Males.	Females.	Persons.	Males.	Females.
1	2	3	4	5	6	7	8	9	10	11	12	13	14	15	16
K. Talaing ...	*323,509*	*163,830*	*159,679*	*157*	*95*	*62*	*123*	*83*	*40*	*179*	*88*	*91*	*99*	*77*	*22*
L. Palaung-Wa Group	*156,708*	*78,674*	*78,029*	*202*	*111*	*91*	*443*	*228*	*215*	*247*	*131*	*116*	*27*	*16*	*11*
1 Wa ...	14,762	7,695	7,067	4	3	1	11	6	5	106	105	1	...	...	...
8 Yanglam ...	13,879	6,622	7,257	27	12	15	16	13	3	32	16	16	6	3	3
10 Palaung and Pale.	122,257	61,315	60,942	171	96	75	416	209	207	109	10	99	21	13	8
N. Karen Group ...	*1,220,356*	*612,116*	*608,240*	*987*	*503*	*484*	*861*	*478*	*383*	*1,007*	*499*	*508*	*710*	*500*	*210*
1 Karen unspecified.	62,627	32,010	30,617	84	54	30	87	55	32	92	55	37	23	15	8
2 Sgaw ...	437,110	218,609	218,501	268	134	134	176	95	81	232	114	118	167	123	44
3 Paku ...	1,986	1,021	965	...	...	...	6	4	2	1	1	...	...	..	...
6 Bwè ...	7,467	3,553	3,914	5	4	1	22	18	4	17	7	10	7	2	5
8 Karenbyu ...	18,370	9,674	8,696	13	4	9	20	14	6	7	6	1	4	...	4
9 Pwo ...	411,891	208,285	203,606	247	143	104	159	92	67	263	149	114	363	272	91
11 Taungthu ..	218,237	108,746	109,491	331	145	186	280	145	135	286	130	156	125	74	51
14 Gheko ...	2,663	1,317	1,346	2	...	2	...	...	...	...	...	...	...	...	...
15 Karenni .	35,391	16,364	19,027	37	19	18	111	55	56	109	37	72	21	14	7
R. Chinese Group ...	*149,060*	*101,877*	*47,183*	*167*	*128*	*39*	*233*	*122*	*111*	*118*	*69*	*49*	*88*	*84*	*4*
1 Yünnanese	59,232	35,752	23,480	9	7	2	5	3	2	2	2	...	1	1	...
2 Other Chinese	89,828	66,125	23,703	158	121	37	228	119	109	116	67	49	37	33	4
S2. Zerbadi † ...	*94,316*	*45,648*	*48,668*	*68*	*34*	*34*	*40*	*23*	*17*	*79*	*41*	*38*	*70*	*48*	*22*
X. Indian Races ...	*887,077*	*653,980*	*233,097*	*381*	*270*	*111*	*246*	*177*	*69*	*271*	*191*	*80*	*187*	*157*	*30*
3 Bengali ...	77,988	60,117	17,871	18	13	5	25	15	11	21	19	2	5	4	1
8 Chittagonian	206,388	129,854	76,534	100	57	43	86	59	27	69	45	24	24	14	10
14 Gurkha ...	22,251	15,506	6,745	9	7	2	6	4	2	10	7	3	8	8	...
15 Hindustani	133,577	107,557	26,020	87	66	21	31	23	8	46	35	11	28	23	5
31 Oriya ...	52,475	49,993	2,482	19	17	2	8	8	...	22	17	5	14	14	...
35 Punjabi ...	21,041	16,307	4,734	6	6	...	7	7	...	10	9	1	5	5	...
39 Tamil ...	152,064	100,315	51,749	68	49	19	45	33	12	44	25	19	41	32	9
40 Telugu ...	158,187	129,566	28,621	61	45	16	28	20	8	33	24	9	59	54	5
Other Indians	63,106	44,765	18,341	13	10	3	9	8	1	16	10	6	3	3	...
Anglo-Indian ...	*16,688*	*8,458*	*8,230*	*31*	*17*	*14*	*3*	*1*	*2*	*3*	*2*	*1*	*20*	*11*	*9*
English ...	*4,896*	*3,657*	*1,239*	*7*	*7*	...	...	...	...	*1*	*1*	...	*2*	*2*	...
Other British ‡ ...	*2,449*	*1,874*	*575*	...	...	...	...	...	...	...	...	...	...	...	...
Other Europeans ...	*972*	*584*	*388*	*2*	*2*	...	...	...	...	...	...	...	*3*	*2*	*1*
Others ...	*5,183*	*2,739*	*2,444*	*14*	*6*	*8*	*2*	*1*	*1*	*3*	*2*	*1*	..	...	...

† For S1 Arakan-Mahomedans see A2 and note * on opposite page; S3 Arakan-Kamans are in *Others.*
‡ That is, other European races of the British Empire; see Part A1 of Imperial Table XVI.
§ *Others* includes Groups G, M, O, and Races S 3 and Y3.

NOTE 7.—The following is a statement of the returns of persons suffering from two or more of the tabulated infirmities :—

	Divisional Burma.		Provincial Total.	
	Males.	Females.	Males.	Females.
Insane deaf-mutes	97	92	146	152
Insane and blind	11	20	13	22
Insane lepers	2	1	2	1
Blind deaf-mutes	14	10	22	21
Leprous deaf-mutes ...	3	5	3	5
Blind lepers	9	4	9	4
* Insane and blind deaf-mutes ...	1	3	1	4
* Blind and leprous deaf mutes	1	...	1	...
* Insane and blind lepers .	1	...	1	...
Total ...	139	135	198	209

* Persons with three infirmities are not included in the figures given above for persons with two infirmities.

NOTE 8.—The racial distribution of insane deaf-mutes (including those who were also blind) is as follows :—

District.		Total.		Burmese.		Kachins.		Races of the Karen Group.		Races of the Shan Group.		Chinese and Yünnanese.		Others.	
Serial No.	Name.	Males.	Females.	Males.	Females.	Males.	Females.	Males.	Females.	Males.	Females.	Males.	Females.	Males.	Females.
28	Bhamo	31	31	...	...	24	24	...	...	..	2	...	...	7	7
29	Myitkyina	15	10	...	...	10	8	...	...	...	..	...	...	5	2
35	Upper Chindwin ...	10	14	5	6	...	.	...	...	2	6	...	...	3	2
41	Northern Shan States	48	61	...	...	24	36	...	...	6	9	8	7	10	9
42	Southern Shan States	...	...	...	...	...	..	...	...	...	...	...	.	..	...
43	Karenni	..	...	...	...	...	...	...	...	...	...	...	...	...	...
	Remainder ...	43	40	27	26	1	...	4	6	2	2	.	1	9	5
	Total ...	147	156	32	32	59	66	4	6	10	19	8	8	34	25

NOTE 9.—The following is the table classifying by birth-place infirm persons in asylums and schools to which reference is made in Note 5 on page 181 :—

Infirmity.	District.	Total.		Classification by Birth-place.					
				District of Enumeration.		Other Districts of Burma.		Outside Burma.	
		Males.	Females.	Males.	Females.	Males.	Females.	Males.	Females.
1	2	3	4	5	6	7	8	9	10
Insanity ...	Rangoon ...	604	139	42	59	377	64	185	16
	Minbu ...	128	...	10	...	117	...	1	...
Deaf-mutism ...	Rangoon ...	5	3	...	1	5	2	...	...
Blindness ...	Rangoon ...	30	5	...	...	29	5	1	...
	Amherst ...	4	...	1	...	2	...	1	...
Leprosy ...	Rangoon ...	122	20	23	3	52	11	47	6
	Amherst ..	40	14	13	5	15	6	12	3
	Mandalay ...	200	102	72	66	81	34	47	2

IMPERIAL TABLE XIII.

Race.

NOTE 1.—The area and population covered by this table are the same as those covered by Imperial Tables VIA and X, so that the areas (indicated in Note 1 of Table VIA) in which the population was only estimated have been omitted from it.

NOTE 2.—The term *Race* is discussed in the Report Volume; in these notes and in the table, it is used as the generic name of the lowest classes tabulated in Part I of the table.

NOTE 3.—The races corresponding to each of the indigenous language-groups of Imperial Table X have been regarded as forming a racial *Group* to which the same index-letter has been assigned. Race-groups A to O have been regarded as *Indigenous Races* and the remainder as *Non-indigenous*. [*Note*.—Chinese (R) is an indigenous language but not an indigenous race.] No attempt has been made to classify the non-indigenous races according to any accepted anthropological scheme; but they have been divided into five artificial groups with index-letters as follows:—R, Chinese; S, Indo-Burman; X, Indian; Y, European, etc.; Z, Others. Indians have not been classified by caste; certain clearly distinguished races have been separately tabulated and the remaining Indians have been classified in quasi-national classes, each of which includes all those races which are particularly associated with a certain territory roughly indicated by the name of the class. A list of the races included in each group is given in Part I of the table; for further information with regard to the classification scheme, the Report Volume should be consulted.

NOTE 4.—Part I of this table corresponds to Part IB of Imperial Table X, and, besides exhibiting the classification-scheme, classifies the whole population described in Note 1 and further classifies each race by sex and religion. In Group Y details are not given for the separate European and allied races; they are given in Imperial Table XVI. Some races are shown with *nil* entries because although not recorded in the area covered by this table they are known to exist in the other parts of the province.

NOTE 5.—Alternative names of some Races and many of the names of Clans will be found in Parts IB and IC of Imperial Table X. (See Notes 6 and 7 of that table.)

NOTE 6.—Part II of this table, which corresponds to Part II of Imperial Table X, shows the distribution of each race-group by districts and at the same time classifies the population of each district by race-groups. For selected race-groups a further classification is given in each district by religion.

NOTE 7.—Part III is divided into three parts. Part IIIA shows the distribution by districts of certain selected indigenous races for some of which a classification by religion is also given. Part IIIB supplements Part IIIA by giving the distribution of all other indigenous races. Part IIIC shows similarly the distribution by districts and religion of the more numerously represented Indian races.

NOTE 8.—For Parts IV and V of this table the classification of races by groups has been exchanged for a classification, depending chiefly upon race but taking account also of religion and birthplace, which divides the whole population of each sex into 13 *Peoples* distinguished by Roman serial numbers, and is used in Imperial Table XX. The constitution of each people is shown in Note 9 below Part V of this table and in the Appendix to Imperial Table XX. Part IV of the table gives at the same time the distribution of each people by districts and the classification of the population of each district by sex and people; Part V classifies the population of the whole province by sex, people and religion. Details for Peoples XI and XII and for the Armenians of People XIII, which are not given in this table, are given in Imperial Table XVI.

NOTE 9.—Note 9 is printed below Part V of the table.

IMPERIAL TABLE XIII—*Race.* PART I.—*Provincial Totals of Races by Religion.*

	Race-group and Race.	Religion.	Males.	Females.
	GRAND TOTAL	......	**6,735,516**	**6,433,583**
A	**Burma Group**	......	**4,250,583**	**4,432,452**
A1	Burmese ...	Total ..	3,831,165	4,006,820
		Buddhist ...	*3,821,833*	*3,992,953*
		Animist ...	*367*	*442*
		Mahomedan ...	*2,683*	*5,913*
		Christian ...	*6,282*	*7,512*
A2	Arakanese ...	Total ...	151,190	149,510
		Buddhist ...	*151,104*	*149,444*
		Animist ...	*38*	*42*
		Christian ...	*48*	*24*
A3	Yanbye ..	Total ...	80,234	87,951
		Buddhist ...	*80,228*	*87,944*
		Animist ...	*3*	*3*
		Christian ...	*3*	*4*
A4	Chaungtha	Total ...	23,396	22,757
		Buddhist ...	*23,358*	*22,742*
		Animist ...	*24*	*11*
		Christian ...	*14*	*4*
A5	Tavoyan ...	Total ...	64,329	64,958
		Buddhist ...	*64,300*	*64,924*
		Animist ...	*8*	*7*
		Christian ..	*21*	*27*
A6	Merguese ...	Total ...	102	76
		Buddhist ...	*101*	*75*
		Christian ...	*1*	*1*
A7	Yabein ...	Buddhist ...	882	892
A8	Yaw ..	Total ...	75	14
		Buddhist ...	*75*	*12*
		Christian ...	...	*2*
A9	Danu ...	Total ...	37,382	37,260
		Buddhist ...	*37,376*	*37,257*
		Animist ...	*4*	...
		Christian ...	*2*	*3*
A10	Intha ...	Total ...	27,693	28,482
		Buddhist ...	*27,094*	*27,878*
		Animist ...	*599*	*603*
		Christian ...	...	*1*
A11	Taungyo ...	Buddhist ...	11,984	11,693
A12	P'un ...	Buddhist ...	172	195
A13	Atsi ...	Total ...	2,677	2,180
		Animist ...	*2,546*	*2,018*
		Christian ...	*131*	*162*
A14	Lashi ...	Total ...	8,567	8,443
		Buddhist ...	...	*1*
		Animist ...	*8,466*	*8,352*
		Christian ...	*101*	*90*
A15	Maru ...	Total ...	10,315	11,110
		Buddhist ...	*84*	*17*
		Animist ...	*10,198*	*10,998*
		Christian ...	*83*	*95*
A16	Maingtha ...	Total ...	420	111
		Buddhist ...	*346*	*77*
		Animist ...	*74*	*34*

	Race-group and Race.	Religion.	Males.	Females.
B	**Lolo-Mus'o Group.**	......	**39,494**	**36,851**
B1	Lisaw ...	Total ...	6,703	6,557
		Buddhist ...	*5*	...
		Animist ...	*6,698*	*6,554*
		Christian ...	...	*3*
B2	Lolo ...	Animist ...	380	389
B3	Lahu ...	Total ...	11,597	11,099
		Buddhist ...	*1*	*59*
		Animist ...	*10,333*	*9,873*
		Christian ...	*1,263*	*1,167*
B4	Ako ...	Animist ...	30	21
B5	Pyin ...	Total ...	515	421
		Buddhist ...	*294*	*231*
		Animist ...	*221*	*190*
B6	Kwi ...	Total ...	1,877	1,836
		Animist ...	*966*	*938*
		Christian ...	*911*	*898*
B7	Akha ..	Total ..	18,335	15,930
		Animist ...	*18,225*	*15,848*
		Christian ...	*110*	*82*
B8	Nung ...	Total ...	42	76
		Buddhist ...	*31*	*61*
		Animist ...	*11*	*15*
B9	Tangsir ...	......	...	...
B10	Hop'a ...	......	...	...
B11	Wat'ao-khum	Animist ...	15	22
C	**Kuki-Chin Group.**	......	**144,818**	**144,529**
C1	Meit'ei (also called Kathè).	Total ...	5,555	3,852
		Buddhist ...	*1,759*	*451*
		Animist ...	*116*	*104*
		Hindu ...	*3,644*	*3,245*
		Mahomedan .	*36*	*48*
		Christian ...	...	*4*
C2	T'ado ...	Animist ..	1,138	1,143
C3	Siyin ...	Total ...	1,562	1,681
		Animist ...	*1,386*	*1,499*
		Christian ...	*176*	*182*
C4	Sokte ...	Total ...	8,641	8,828
		Animist ...	*8,605*	*8,798*
		Christian ...	*36*	*30*
C5	Kamhow ...	Total ...	4,399	4,269
		Buddhist ...	...	*1*
		Animist ...	*4,259*	*4,139*
		Christian ...	*140*	*129*
C6	Paite ...	Total ...	668	659
		Animist ...	*655*	*653*
		Christian ...	*13*	*6*
C7	Yo ...	Animist ...	2,801	2,758
C8	Tashon ...	Total ...	3,803	4,467
		Buddhist ...	*8*	*2*
		Animist ...	*3,767*	*4,434*
		Christian ...	*28*	*31*
C9	Yahow ...	Total ...	2,481	2,927
		Animist ...	*2,451*	*2,903*
		Christian ...	*30*	*24*
C10	Laiyo ...	Total ...	5,316	5,770
		Animist ...	*5,198*	*5,692*
		Christian ...	*118*	*78*

IMPERIAL TABLE XIII—*Race.* PART I.—*Provincial Totals of Races by Religion* (contd.).

	Race-group and Race.	Religion.	Males.	Females.
C11	Kwangli ...	Animist ...	2,143	2,499
C12	Ngorn ...	Total ...	1,930	2,021
		Buddhist ...	*3*	...
		Animist ...	*1,927*	*2,021*
C13	Kwelshim ..	Animist ...	961	1,101
C14	Lai ...	Total ...	4,632	4,720
		Animist ...	*4,598*	*4,670*
		Christian ...	*34*	*50*
C15	Tlantlang ...	Total ...	4,057	4,001
		Animist ...	*4,036*	*3,994*
		Christian ...	*21*	*7*
C16	Yokwa ...	Total ...	1,195	1,310
		Animist ..	*1,187*	*1,308*
		Christian ..	*8*	*2*
C17	Lakher ...	Animist ..	...	12
C18	Lawt'u ...	Animist ...	1,619	1,424
C19	Yotun ..	Animist ...	2,562	2,550
C20	Shentang ...	Total ...	3,067	3,025
		Animist ...	*3,039*	*3,005*
		Christian ...	*28*	*20*
C21	Lushei ..	Total ...	161	156
		Animist ...	*112*	*111*
		Christian ...	*49*	*45*
C22	Hualngo ...	Total ...	1,555	1,745
		Animist ...	*1,554*	*1,745*
		Christian ...	*1*	...
C23	Kyaw ...	Animist ...	183	168
C24	Anu ...	Animist ...	199	213
C25	Chinbok ...	Buddhist ...	1	...
C26	Chinbon ...	Animist ...	345	338
C27	Chinmè ...	......	...	...
C28	Khami ...	Total ...	13,329	12,775
		Buddhist ...	*438*	*410*
		Animist ...	*12,891*	*12,365*
C29	Taungtha ...	Buddhist ..	3,470	4,100
C30	Yindu ...	Total ...	51	54
		Buddhist ...	*1*	..
		Animist ...	*50*	*54*
C31	Sho ...	......	...	...
C32	Chin (unspecified kind†‡).	Total ...	58,319	58,272
		Buddhist ...	*27,564*	*27,603*
		Animist ...	*29,420*	*29,248*
		Christian ...	*1,335*	*1,421*
C33	Chaunggyi	Animist ...	349	317
C34	Kaukadan	Total ..	126	167
		Buddhist ...	*125*	*167*
		Animist ...	*1*	...
C35	Kaungtso ...	Animist ...	185	185
C36	Ledu ...	Animist ...	1,118	1,116
C37	Matu ...	Animist ...	23	28
C38	Saingbaung	Total ...	3,956	3,563
		Buddhist ...	*3*	*2*
		Animist ...	*3,953*	*3,561*
C39	Sittu ...	Animist ...	2,032	1,886
C40	Taman ...	Buddhist ...	386	429
D	**Naga Group**	......	**197**	**209**
D1	Naga (unspecified kind†).	Total ...	80	89
		Buddhist ...	...	*2*
		Animist ...	*80*	*87*
D2	Tangkul ...	Total ...	117	120
		Buddhist ...	...	*1*
		Animist ...	*117*	*119*
D3	Senkadong	......	...	...
E	**Kachin Group**	......	**70,611**	**76,234**
E1	Kachin ..	Total ...	70,245	75,834
		Buddhist ...	*411*	*371*
		Animist ...	*67,591*	*73,155*
		Christian ...	*2,243*	*2,308*
E2	Nogmung ...	Buddhist ...	78	91
E3	Ntit ...	Buddhist ..	5	5
E4	Pangsu ...	Buddhist ..	84	89
E5	Kang ...	Buddhist ...	42	39
E6	Langkhai ...	Buddhist ...	49	53
E7	Nokkyo ...	Buddhist ...	64	68
E8	Yoya	Buddhist ...	16	16
E9	Tawhawng	Buddhist ...	28	39
F	**Sak * Group**	... ..	**24,497**	**25,229**
F1	Kadu ...	Total ...	18,625	19,085
		Buddhist ...	*18,621*	*19,081*
		Animist ...	*2*	...
		Christian ...	*2*	*4*
F2	Ganan ...	Buddhist ..	3,016	3,458
F3	Sak ...	Buddhist ..	321	293
F4	Daingnet ...	Buddhist ...	2,535	2,393
G	**Mishmi Group**	.. ...	**9**	**4**
G1	Khaman-Mishmi.	Buddhist ...	9	4
H	**Mro Group**	......	**7,520**	**7,251**
H1	Mro ...	Total ...	7,520	7,251
		Buddhist ...	*48*	*40*
		Animist ...	*7,472*	*7,211*
I	**Tai Group**	......	**508,975**	**509,012**
I1	Shan (unspecified kind†).	Total ...	142,237	146,747
		Buddhist	*141,870*	*146,209*
		Animist ...	*107*	*250*
		Christian ...	*260*	*288*
I2	Shangale	Total ...	293,747	294,658
		Buddhist ...	*293,404*	*294,334*
		Animist ...	*161*	*153*
		Christian ...	*182*	*170*
		Atheist .	..	*1*
I3	Shangyi ...	Total ...	15,100	13,904
		Buddhist ...	*15,018*	*13,857*
		Animist ...	*78*	*31*
		Christian ...	*4*	*16*
I4	Shan-Tayok	Total ...	15,885	12,816
		Buddhist ...	*12,531*	*10,135*
		Animist ...	*3,332*	*2,655*
		Christian ...	*22*	*26*
I5	Daye ...	Buddhist ...	551	417
I6	Siamese ...	Total ...	7,245	6,041
		Buddhist ...	*7,233*	*6,029*
		Animist ...	*4*	*4*
		Christian ...	*8*	*8*

* Formerly called the Lui Group.

† That is, shown in the enumeration-record only as *Chin* (or *Naga* or *Shan*) without specification of a particular kind.

‡ See the footnote † on page 199.

IMPERIAL TABLE XIII—*Race.* PART I.—*Provincial Totals of Races by Religion* (contd.).

Race-group and Race.		Religion.	Males.	Females
I 7	Khun ...	Total ...	16,350	17,044
		Buddhist ...	16,333	17,014
		Animist ...	17	24
		Christian ...	...	6
I 8	Lu ...	Total ...	12,686	13,184
		Buddhist ...	12,674	13,163
		Christian ...	12	21
I 9	Lao ...	Total ...	2,911	1,595
		Buddhist ...	2,711	1,407
		Animist ...	200	188
I 10	Shan-Bama	Total ...	6	10
		Buddhist ...	5	8
		Animist ...	1	2
I 11	Kamti ...	Total ...	2,256	2,595
		Buddhist ...	2,253	2,594
		Animist ...	3	...
		Christian ...	...	1
I 12	Annamese ...	Christian ...	1	1
I 13	Tai Lem ...	......	...	...
I 14	Tai Loi ...	......	...	...
J	**Malay Group**	......	**8,144**	**8,509**
J1	Malay ..	Total ...	2,215	2,497
		Buddhist ...	9	11
		Animist ..	..	1
		Mahomedan ...	2,202	2,484
		Christian ...	4	1
J2	Salon ...	Total ...	929	1,012
		Buddhist ...	3	7
		Animist ...	926	1,005
K	**Mon Group**	......	**163,830**	**159,679**
K1	Talaing ...	Total ...	163,830	159,679
		Buddhist ..	163,451	159,238
		Animist ...	16	34
		Christian ...	363	407
L	**Palaung-Wa Group.**	... ..	**78,674**	**78,029**
L1	Wa ...	Total ...	7,695	7,067
		Buddhist ...	6,664	5,941
		Animist ...	984	1,125
		Christian ...	47	1
L2	Danaw ...	Buddhist ...	816	853
L3	En ...	Buddhist ...	17	...
L4	Khamuk ...	Total ...	390	12
		Buddhist ...	180	4
		Animist ...	210	8
L5	Lem ...	Buddhist ...	406	385
L6	Tai-Loi ...	Buddhist ...	2	...
L7	Yang (unspecified kind†).	Buddhist ...	1,411	1,513
L8	Yanglam ...	Total ...	6,622	7,257
		Buddhist ...	6,601	7,247
		Animist ...	...	1
		Christian ..	21	9
L9	Yangsek ...	......	...	...
L10	Palaung and Pale.	Total ...	61,315	60,942
		Buddhist ...	61,222	60,844
		Animist ...	91	95
		Christian ...	2	3

Race-group and Race.		Religion.	Males	Females.
M	**Khasi Group**	... ..	2	1
M1	Khasi ...	Christian ...	[illegible]	1
N	**Karen Group**	......	612,116	608,240
N1	Karen (unspecified kind*).	Total ...	32,010	30,617
		Buddhist ...	13,158	12,365
		Animist ...	7,395	7,291
		Christian ...	11,457	10,961
N2	Sgaw ..	Total ...	218,609	218,501
		Buddhist ...	155,530	154,300
		Animist ...	14,784	14,647
		Christian ...	48,295	49,554
N3	Paku ...	Total ...	1,021	965
		Buddhist ...	4	...
		Animist ...	196	179
		Christian ..	821	786
N4	Wewaw ..	Total ...	163	172
		Buddhist ...	6	...
		Christian ...	157	172
N5	Monnepwa	.....	...	...
N6	Bwè ...	Total ...	3,553	3,914
		Buddhist ..	1	1
		Animist ...	1,386	1,646
		Christian ...	2,166	2,267
N7	Brek ...	Total ...	311	307
		Animist ...	167	160
		Christian ...	144	147
N8	Karenbyu ...	Total ..	9,674	8,696
		Buddhist ...	1,851	1,277
		Animist ...	2,414	2,243
		Christian ...	5,409	5,176
N9	Pwo ...	Total ...	208,285	203,606
		Buddhist ...	193,778	189,028
		Animist ...	620	771
		Christian ...	13,887	13,807
N10	Mopwa ...	Christian ...	1	4
N11	Taungthu ..	Total ...	108,746	109,491
		Buddhist ...	108,603	109,372
		Animist ..	15	6
		Christian ...	128	113
N12	Padaung ...	Total ...	7,077	6,678
		Buddhist ...	191	211
		Animist ...	4,808	4,462
		Christian ...	2,078	2,005
N13	Yinbaw ...	Total ...	2,837	2,914
		Buddhist ...	384	326
		Animist ...	502	619
		Christian ...	1,951	1,969
N14	Gheko ...	Total ...	1,317	1,346
		Animist ...	160	156
		Christian ...	1,157	1,190
N15	Karenni ...	Total ...	16,364	19,027
		Buddhist ...	1,413	936
		Animist ...	13,726	16,896
		Christian ...	1,225	1,195
N16	Zayein ...	Total ...	2,145	2,002
		Buddhist ...	595	548
		Animist ..	1,550	1,454
N17	Htalaing-Kalasi.	Christian ...	3	...

*† That is, entered in the enumeration-record only as *Karen* (or *Yang*) without specification of any particular kind of Karen (or Yang).

IMPERIAL TABLE XIII—*Race.* PART I.—*Provincial Totals of Races by Religion* (concld.).

Race-group and Race.		Religion.	Males.	Females.
O	**Man Group**	......	**338**	**259**
O1	Miao ...	Total ...	229	167
		Buddhist ...	*58*	...
		Animist ...	*171*	*167*
O2	Yao ...	Total ...	109	92
		Buddhist ...	*5*	...
		Animist ...	*104*	*92*
R	**Chinese Group.**	.. ...	**101,877**	**47,183**
R1	Yünnanese ..	Total ...	35,752	23,480
		Mahomedan	*1,076*	*441*
		Christian ...	*12*	*2*
		Others ...	*34,664*	*23,037*
R2	Other Chinese	Total ...	66,125	23,703
		Christian ...	*827*	*272*
		Others ...	*65,298*	*23,431*
S	**Indo-Burman Races.**	......	**59,442**	**60,829**
S1	Arakan-Mahomedans.	Mahomedan	12,740	11,035
S2	Zerbadi * ..	Total ...	45,648	48,668
		Buddhist ...	*484*	*280*
		Animist ...	*8*	*16*
		Mahomedan	*45,129*	*48,353*
		Christian ...	*27*	*19*
S3	Arakan-Kaman.	Total ...	1,054	1,126
		Buddhist ..	*10*	*7*
		Mahomedan	*1,044*	*1,119*
X	**Indian Races**	......	**658,980**	**283,097**
X1	Arab ...	......	80	26
X2	Assamese ...	......	183	123
X3	Bengali ...	Total ...	60,117	17,871
		Hindu and Animist.	*12,172*	*3,002*
		Mahomedan ...	*46,651*	*14,632*
		Others ...	*1,294*	*237*
X4	Bhotya ...	......	348	16
X5	Bihari ...	......	3,264	2,301
X6	Bondili ...	......	53	5
X7	Bora ...	......	141	32
X8	Chittagonian	Total ...	129,854	76,534
		Hindu and Animist.	*5,110*	*286*
		Mahomedan	*122,872*	*75,682*
		Others ...	*1,872*	*566*
X9	Deccani † ...	......	1,866	787
X10	Dogra ..	......	198	64
X11	Garhwali ...	......	1,484	278
X12	Goanese ...	......	503	89
X13	Gujarati ...	......	3,310	1,330
X14	Gurkha ...	......	15,506	6,745
X15	Hindustani	Total ...	107,557	26,020
		Hindu and Animist.	*82,482*	*19,657*
		Mahomedan	*23,400*	*5,984*
		Others ...	*1,675*	*379*
X16	Jat ...	......	119	19
X17	Kachchhi ...	......	516	330
X18	Kanarese ...	......	143	44
X19	Kashmiri ...	......	147	4
X20	Khoja ...	......	393	160
X21	Komati ...	......	44	14
X22	Kumauni ...	......	932	551
X23	Madras-Mahomedans	......	1,908	625
X24	Mahratta ...	......	739	143
X25	Malabari ..	Total ...	1,682	306
		Hindu ...	*1,109*	*192*
		Mahomedan	*539*	*100*
		Christian ...	*34*	*14*
X26	Marwari ...	......	1,417	699
X27	Memon ...	......	3,537	854
X28	Moghul ...	......	1,073	613
X29	Mopla (Mappila).	......	4,542	257
X30	Myedu ...	......	2,309	2,682
X9	Nursapuri	......	†	†
X31	Oriya ...	Total ...	49,993	2,482
		Hindu and Animist.	*48,017*	*1,973*
		Others ...	*1,976*	*509*
X32	Parsi ...	......	229	151
X33	Pathan ...	......	5,148	1,160
X34	Persian ...	......	471	152
X35	Punjabi ...	Total ...	16,307	4,734
		Hindu and Animist.	*7,064*	*2,096*
		Mahomedan	*5,465*	*1,493*
		Sikh, Arya, Brahmo.	*3,661*	*1,127*
		Others ...	*117*	*18*
X36	Rajput ...	......	1,317	138
X37	Sindhi ...	......	196	17
X38	Surati ...	......	3,690	2,158
X39	Tamil ...	Total ..	100,315	51,749
		Hindu and Animist.	*68,192*	*36,761*
		Mahomedan	*21,328*	*7,196*
		Christian ..	*10,146*	*7,591*
		Others ...	*649*	*201*
X40	Telugu	Total ...	129,566	28,681
		Hindu and Animist.	*125,413*	*27,095*
		Christian ...	*1,521*	*603*
		Mahomedan †	*2,047*	*818*
		Others ...	*585*	*105*
X41	Indians of unspecified race.	Total ...	2,783	2,219
		Buddhist ..	*444*	*93*
		Hindu ...	*968*	*967*
		Mahomedan	*1,202*	*1,081*
		Others ..	*169*	*78*
Y	**European, etc.**	......	**14,758**	**10,595**
	European and allied races.	... ...	6,115	2,208
	Anglo-Indian.	......	8,458	8,230
	Armenian	......	185	163
Z	**Other races**	......	**1,151**	**891**
	Goa-Portuguese.	......	47	17
	Japanese .	......	269	261
	Jew ...	......	632	570
	Mauritian ...	......	1	2
	Negro ...	......	19	4
	Nicobarese ...	......	6	4
	Philippino ...	......	53	15
	Singhalese ...	......	131	14
	Turk ...	......	3	4

* See Note * on page 210.

† Nursapuri are tabulated above under *Deccani* by which name they are more commonly known in Burma. As in Burma they are also called *Coringhi Mahomedans* a small number may have been included wrongly amongst the Mahomedan Telugus.

Serial No.	DISTRICT OR STATE.	TOTAL POPULATION.		A.—BURMA.									
				Total.		Buddhist.		Animist.		Mahomedan.		Christian.	
		Males.	Females.	Males.	Females.	Males.	Females.	Males.	Females.	Males.	Females.	Males.	Females.
	1	2	3	4	5	6	7	8	9	10	11	12	13
	PROVINCIAL TOTAL ...	**6,735,516**	**6,433,583**	**4,250,583**	**4,432,452**	**4,218,887**	**4,396,104**	**22,327**	**22,510**	**2,683**	**5,913**	**6,686**	**7,925**
	DIVISIONAL BURMA ...	**5,991,623**	**5.706,785**	**4,153,984**	**4,338,078**	**4,129,656**	**4,309,772**	**15,078**	**14,692**	**2,668**	**5,817**	**6,582**	**7,797**
	Arakan Division ...	**472,227**	**437,019**	**288,558**	**296,349**	**288,882**	**296,062**	**68**	**59**	**95**	**159**	**68**	**69**
1	Akyab ...	309,564	266,866	154,486	151,485	154,386	151,386	65	54	1	5	34	40
2	Hill Dist. of Arakan	10,790	10,124	1,079	985	1,076	985	...	...	...	...	3	...
3	Kyaukpyu ...	96,569	103,304	84,825	93,521	84,816	93,504	3	3	..	1	6	13
4	Sandoway ...	55,304	56,725	48,168	50,358	48,054	50,187	...	2	94	153	20	16
	Pegu Division ..	**1,258,914**	**1,050,379**	**820,799**	**831,501**	**817,926**	**827,554**	**146**	**176**	**655**	**1,341**	**2,072**	**2,430**
5	Rangoon Town ...	236,689	105,273	52,398	50,827	51,781	49,442	...	8	65	345	552	1,032
6	Insein ...	156,794	136,289	107,602	104,325	106,736	103,623	22	41	440	176	404	485
7	Hanthawaddy ..	201,043	163,581	128,451	125,315	128,289	124,806	17	25	..	321	145	163
8	Tharrawaddy ...	246,261	246,168	217,025	226,064	216,486	225,550	23	14	...	153	516	347
9	Pegu ...	235,324	210,196	149,406	147,230	149,096	146,679	25	60	150	346	135	145
10	Prome ...	182,803	188,772	165,917	177,740	165,538	177,154	59	28	...	...	320	258
	Irrawaddy Division ...	**1,048,377**	**981,667**	**760,568**	**765,863**	**758,455**	**763,274**	**67**	**94**	**1,048**	**1,514**	**998**	**981**
11	Bassein ...	252,947	236,526	170,909	171,202	170,709	170,993	34	36	...	...	166	173
12	Henzada ...	273,439	277,181	236,413	247,716	235,774	247,133	18	27	403	356	218	200
13	Myaungmya ...	196,757	173,794	122,867	117,687	122,217	116,695	15	11	352	740	283	241
14	Ma-ubin ...	168,513	161,593	109,596	116,174	109,348	115,751	...	20	56	217	192	186
15	Pyapôn ..	156,721	132,273	120,783	113,084	120,407	112,702	...	...	237	201	139	181
	Tenasserim Division	**847,445**	**766,078**	**327,39[illegible]**	**324,864**	**326,487**	**323,391**	**77**	**119**	**294**	**574**	**591**	**780**
16	Toungoo ...	197,505	184,378	124,857	126,405	124,439	125,842	...	..	222	327	196	236
17	Salween ...	26,811	23,568	1,072	803	1,072	799	...	...	...	4	...	...
18	Thatôn ...	245,909	225,191	56,175	55,156	56,103	55,074	19	35	...	...	53	47
19	Amherst ...	223,348	194,562	36,637	34,195	36,356	33,579	23	57	54	224	204	335
20	Tavoy ...	80,994	75,792	67,252	67,826	67,191	67,764	6	8	5	2	50	52
21	Mergui ...	72,878	62,587	41,406	40,479	41,276	40,333	29	19	13	17	88	110
	Magwe Division ...	**705,247**	**733,527**	**645,569**	**686,776**	**645,285**	**686,216**	**37**	**27**	**101**	**333**	**146**	**200**
22	Thayetmyo ...	125,283	130,123	111,830	118,178	111,722	118,041	31	26	52	89	25	22
23	Pakôkku ...	223,943	241,828	212,744	231,574	212,653	231,462	5	...	37	60	49	52
24	Minbu ...	134,495	139,807	120,876	128,112	120,847	128,021	...	...	12	68	17	23
25	Magwe ...	211,686	211,566	200,031	208,869	199,977	208,649	1	1	...	116	53	103
26	Pakôkku Hill Tracts	9,840	10,203	88	43	86	43	...	...	...	..	2	...
	Mandalay Division ...	**435,894**	**413,467**	**229,686**	**234,772**	**213,705**	**218,281**	**14,665**	**14,210**	**219**	**812**	**1,097**	**1,469**
27	Mandalay ...	182,999	173,622	143,563	152,861	142,706	151,204	9	7	139	588	709	1,062
	Mandalay City ...	*77,763*	*71,154*	*57,096*	*59,590*	*56,442*	*58,211*	*6*	*4*	*66*	*498*	*582*	*877*
28	Bhamo ...	56,888	56,072	13,273	11,957	11,302	10,610	1,788	1,110	41	68	142	169
29	Myitkyina ...	63,119	54,963	17,791	16,170	4,743	2,889	12,845	13,078	...	7	203	196
30	Katha ...	128,444	125,281	54,991	53,761	54,910	53,560	...	10	39	149	42	42
31	Putao ...	4,144	3,529	68	23	44	18	23	5	...	...	1	...
	Sagaing Division ...	**641,290**	**709,106**	**527,551**	**599,288**	**526,855**	**597,854**	**4**	**...**	**50**	**60**	**1,142**	**1,374**
32	Shwebo ...	184,708	206,576	177,973	201,961	177,226	201,082	...	...	...	...	747	879
33	Sagaing ...	155,054	171,854	151,414	169,528	151,092	169,110	..	...	...	...	322	418
34	Lower Chindwin .	156,693	186,187	154,558	185,548	154,457	185,445	...	...	41	42	60	61
35	Upper Chindwin ...	90,713	88,532	43,550	42,220	43,525	42,191	4	...	9	18	12	11
36	Chin Hills ...	54,122	55,957	56	31	55	26	..	...	..	...	1	5
	Meiktila Division ...	**582,229**	**615,542**	**553,854**	**598,665**	**553,161**	**597,140**	**14**	**7**	**206**	**1,024**	**478**	**494**
37	Kyauksè ...	70,449	72,228	66,352	68,962	66,119	68,723	1	2	12	...	220	237
38	Meiktila ...	137,573	152,324	132,145	149,527	131,981	149,202	..	5	110	267	54	53
39	Yamèthin ...	160,913	162,276	144,726	152,281	144,529	151,407	13	...	84	757	100	117
40	Myingyan ...	213,294	228,714	210,631	227,895	210,532	227,808	...	...	...	...	99	87
	EASTERN STATES ...	**743,893**	**726,798**	**96,599**	**94,374**	**89,231**	**86,332**	**7,249**	**7,818**	**15**	**96**	**104**	**128**
41	Northern Shan States	285,700	273,523	24,142	22,287	17,424	14,964	6,631	7,202	11	24	76	97
42	Southern Shan States	427,064	420,554	71,185	71,043	70,547	70,333	610	614	...	66	28	30
43	Karenni ...	31,129	32,721	1,272	1,044	1,260	1,035	8	2	4	6	...	1

Race-groups by Religion and District.

[Continued on next page.

B.—LOLO-MUS'O.						C.—KUKI-CHIN.										D.—NAGA		Serial No. of District or State (col. 1).
Total.		Animist.		Others.		Total.		Buddhist.		Animist.		Hindu.		Others.		All religions*		
Males.	Females.	Males.	Females.	Males.	Females.	Males.	Females.	Males.	Females.	Males.	Females.	Males.	Females.	Males.	Females.	Males.	Females.	
14	15	16	17	18	19	20	21	22	23	24	25	26	27	28	29	30	31	
[illegible],494	36,351	36,879	33,850	2,615	2,501	144,318	144,529	33,758	33,165	104,863	106,042	3,644	3,245	2,053	2;077	197	209	
1,456	1,397	1,423	1,333	33	64	144,188	144,498	33,712	33,157	104,821	106,026	3,603	3,242	2,052	2,073	197	209	
...	...	..	...	...	...	33,250	31,748	2,156	2,049	30,593	29,172	30	27	471	500	...	..	
...	...	...	...	...	...	12,839	12,090	841	758	11,964	11,296	26	26	8	10	...	...	1
...	...	...	...	...	...	8,066	7,899	9	3	8,056	7,895	1	1	...	...	...	...	2
.	...	...	...	..	..	8,402	7,825	34	29	8,314	7,740	1	...	53	56	...	...	3
...	...	...	..	...	...	3,943	3,934	1,272	1,259	2,259	2,241	2	...	410	434	...	...	4
1	...	...	...	1	...	7,873	6,691	5,947	5,212	1,048	1,038	618	142	260	299	...	...	
...	...	.	..	...	...	189	152	24	17	...	1	155	123	10	11	...	...	5
...	...	..	..	...	...	349	83	65	55	.	...	256	...	28	28	...	...	6
...	...	...	...	...	...	50	2	29	2	3	...	18	...	.	...		...	7
...	...	...	...	..	...	755	537	607	420	137	111	2	...	9	6	...	...	8
1	..	...	...	1	..	1,028	673	755	570	5	2	180	13	88	88	...	..	9
...	...	...	..	...	...	5,502	5,244	4,467	4,148	903	924	7	6	125	166	.	...	10
...	...	...	...	...	.	2,079	1,856	1,560	1,527	8	2	274	78	242	249	...	..	
...	...		.	...	...	216	152	171	129	..	...	12	...	33	23	...	..	11
...	...	...	...	...	...	1,735	1,687	1,366	1,393	...	2	160	70	209	222	..	...	12
...	...	...	...	..	...	22	5	17	1	3	...	2	..	...	4	...	...	13
...	...	...	...	..	..	81	6	...	...	..	...	81	6	...	...	...	.	14
...	...	...	...	..	...	25	6	6	4	...	...	19	2		...	..	...	15
...	...	..	...	...	..	606	616	170	153	102	94	298	331	41	38	...	...	
..	.	...	...	...	...	463	591	163	149	98	93	166	312	36	37	...	...	16
...	...	...	...	...	...	4	...	...	..	...	...	4	...	.	..	...	...	17
...	...	...	...	...	...	12	...	.	...	...	...	9	...	3	...	...	..	18
...	...	...	..	...	...	115	22	4	3	4	1	105	18	2	.	...	..	19
...	...	...	..	...	...	9	2	...		...	...	9	1	...	1	...	...	20
...	...	...	..	...	..	3	1	3	1	..		...	...	...	...	...	...	21
...	...	...	...	...	...	40,422	42,295	21,464	22,925	18,785	19,217	39	8	134	150	...	...	
...	...	...	...	...	...	10,395	10,452	4,877	4,945	5,401	5,391	12	1	105	115	...	...	22
...	...	...	...	...	...	9,314	9,750	7,730	8,194	1,556	1,554	27	2	1	..	...	...	23
...	...	...		...	..	10,340	10,935	8,111	8,777	2,229	2,158	...	...	..	...	.	...	24
...	...	...	..	...	...	774	1,045	746	1,009	...	1	...	..	28	35	...	...	25
...	...	...	...	...	...	9,599	10,113	...	...	9,599	10,113	..	...	...	...	...	...	26
1,454	1,397	1,423	1,333	31	64	3,136	2,485	1,221	78	238	28	1,677	2,320	...	9	..		
...	...	...	...	...	...	2,906	2,353	1,123	43	235	25	1,548	2,279	...	6	...	...	27
...	...	...	...	...	...	*1,413*	*2,046*	70	*35*	*15*	*10*	*1,328*	*1,996*	..	5	...	...	
...	18	...	18	...	..	35	9	8	..	..	...	27	6	...	3	...	...	28
563	645	563	642		3	80	52	37	31	2		41	21	...	...	..	...	29
849	658	849	658	...	...	114	21	53	4	...	3	61	14	...	..	...	...	30
42	76	11	15	31	61	1	...	...	...	1	...	...	...	...	...	...	...	31
1	...	..	...	1	..	56,016	58,160	746	789	54,001	56,447	554	305	715	619	197	209	
...	..	...	...	...	...	14	...	9	..	...	...	5	..	...	...	...	...	32
1	...	...	...	1	...	441	468	328	352	...	...	113	116	...	...	..	...	33
...	...	...	...	...	..	13	8	1	1	5	...	7	3	...	4	...	...	34
...	...	...	...	.	...	2,703	2,362	408	436	1,570	1,466	423	185	302	275	197	209	35
..	...	...	...	...	...	52,845	55,322	...	...	52,426	54,981	6	1	413	340	...	...	36
...	...	...	...	...	...	806	697	448	424	51	28	118	36	189	209	...	...	
...	...	...	...	...	...	26	5	4	5	...	...	22	...	...	...	..	...	37
...	...	...	...	...	...	22	23	1	...	...	...	21	10	...	13	...	...	38
...	...	...	...	...	...	747	669	440	419	43	28	75	26	189	196	..	...	39
...	...	...	..	...	.	11	...	3	...	8	...	...	...	...	...	...	..	40
38,038	34,954	35,456	32,517	2,582	2,437	130	31	46	8	42	16	41	3	1	4	.	...	
4,095	4,061	4,090	4,061	5	...	64	2	15	...	10	...	38	1	1	1	...	...	41
3,943	30,893	31,366	28,456	2,577	2,437	61	28	29	7	32	16	...	2	...	3	...	...	42
...	...	...	...	...	...	5	1	2	1	...	...	3	..	..	...	...	...	43

* All Nagas are Animists with the exception of three Buddhist females.

Serial No.	DISTRICT OR STATE.	E.—Kachin. All religions. Males.	Females.	F.—Sak (Lui). All religions. Males.	Females.	G.—Mishmi. Buddhist. Males.	Females.	H.—Mro. All religions. Males.	Females.	I.—Tai. Total. Males.	Females.	Buddhist. Males.	Females.	Others. Males.	Females.
	1	32	33	34	35	36	37	38	39	40	41	42	43	44	45
	PROVINCIAL TOTAL ...	**70,611**	**76,234**	**24,497**	**25,229**	**9**	**4**	**7,520**	**7,251**	**508,975**	**509,012**	**504,583**	**505,167**	**4,392**	**3,845**
	DIVISIONAL BURMA ...	**42,891**	**46,047**	**24,214**	**25,186**	**9**	**4**	**7,520**	**7,251**	**160,025**	**157,821**	**156,707**	**155,011**	**3,318**	**2,810**
	Arakan Division ..	...	...	**2,856**	**2,686**	..		**7,520**	**7,251**	**45**	**18**	**45**	**16**	...	**2**
1	Akyab ...	...	...	2,856	2,686	...	.	6,475	6,204	26	11	26	11	...	...
2	Hill Dist. of Arakan	..	...	...	...	...	...	1,045	1,047	.	2	...	..	...	2
3	Kyaukpyu ...	...	...	...	...	...	...	...	...	5	...	5	...	...	...
4	Sandoway ..	..	...	..	...	...	...	...	...	14	5	14	5	...	...
	Pegu Division ...	**21**	**4**	.	..	...	..	...	...	**11,424**	**11,189**	**11,899**	**11,189**	**25**	**50**
5	Rangoon Town ...	15	..	...	.	...	...	..	..	202	250	194	236	8	14
6	Insein	3	...	...	..	...	...	...	...	2,791	2,780	2,784	2,756	7	24
7	Hanthawaddy ...	...	..	...	...	..	...	...	...	2,990	3,073	2,988	3,070	2	3
8	Tharrawaddy ...	1	1	...	...	...	.	...	...	1,710	1,712	1,707	1,712	3	...
9	Pegu	...	...	...	...	..	...	...	...	3,289	2,882	3,285	2,877	4	5
10	Prome	2	3	..	...	...	..		..	442	492	441	488	1	4
	Irrawaddy Division .	..	...		...	.	...	...	...	**1,142**	**785**	**1,184**	**729**	**8**	**6**
11	Bassein ...	...	...	...	...	...	...	...	...	390	300	389	298	1	2
12	Henzada ...	...	...	...	...	...	...	...	...	374	113	373	110	1	3
13	Myaungmya ...	...	...	..	...	...	...	...	...	89	98	84	97	5	1
14	Ma-ubin ...	...	.	...	...	...	...	...	..	40	48	39	48	1	...
15	Pyapôn ...	...	...	...	.	...	...	...	..	249	176	249	176	...	...
	Tenasserim Division	**1**	**2**	..	.		...	...	...	**26,707**	**22,952**	**26,682**	**22,922**	**75**	**30**
16	Toungoo ..	...	2	...	...			...	..	7,997	6,967	7,976	6,958	21	9
17	Salween ...	..	...	...	.	..	...	...	...	2,469	1,583	2,448	1,581	21	2
18	Thatôn ...	...		...	...	...	...	...	...	4,103	3,435	4,100	3,431	3	4
19	Amherst ...	1	..	...	...	...	...	...	...	6,835	6,182	6,821	6,176	14	6
20	Tavoy ...	...	...	...	...	...	...	...	..	50	20	50	20	...	...
21	Mergui ...	...	...	...	...			...	..	5,253	4,765	5,237	4,756	16	9
	Magwe Division ...	...	..	...	...	...	..	..	.	**50**	**29**	**45**	**24**	**5**	**5**
22	Thayetmyo ...	...	...	...	...	...	...	...	...	7	5	2	1	5	4
23	Pakôkku ..	...	..	...		...	...	...	..	17	5	17	4	...	1
24	Minbu ..	...	...	...	...	...	...	...	..	18	14	18	14	...	...
25	Magwe ...	...	...	...	...	...	...	...	...	8	5	8	5	..	...
26	Pakôkku Hill Tracts	..	...	...	...	...	...	...	...	...	...	...	...	...	...
	Mandalay Division .	**42,762**	**45,998**	**20,770**	**21,794**	**9**	**4**	..	...	**79,821**	**80,450**	**76,632**	**77,746**	**3,189**	**2,704**
27	Mandalay ...	709	63	9	...	...	...	...	..	1,873	1,802	1,857	1,780	16	22
	Mandalay City ...	67	6	9		...		..	..	111	64	99	51	12	13
28	Bhamo ...	20,693	24,467	247	236	...	.	...	..	17,699	17,788	16,356	16,517	1,343	1,271
29	Myitkyina ...	17,432	17,673	471	502	...	.	...	..	17,838	16,258	16,118	14,923	1,720	1,335
30	Katha .	3,108	3,099	20,043	21,056	...	..	...	...	40,231	42,116	40,123	42,041	108	75
31	Putao ...	820	691	..	..	9	4	...	...	2,180	2,486	2,178	2,485	2	1
	Sagaing Division ...	**106**	**47**	**588**	**706**	...	...	...	...	**40,488**	**42,117**	**40,426**	**42,111**	**7**	**6**
32	Shwebo ...	45	2	5	6	...	...	..	..	9	8	8	8	1	...
33	Sagaing ...	1	...	6	...	...	...	...	...	18	21	18	21	...	...
34	Lower Chindwin ..	...	...	...	...	...	...	...	...	23	14	18	8	5	6
35	Upper Chindwin ...	60	45	577	700	...	.	...	...	40,383	42,074	40,382	42,074	1	...
36	Chin Hills ...	...	..	..	...	...	...	...	...	...	...	...	...	...	...
	Meiktila Division ..	**1**	**1**	...	...	..	...	...	...	**408**	**331**	**394**	**324**	**9**	**7**
37	Kyauksè ..	...	..	...	...	...	...	...	...	71	55	71	53	...	2
38	Meiktila .	...	...	...	...	...	...	...	...	64	27	63	22	1	5
39	Yamèthin ..	1	1	...	...	...	...	...	...	268	246	260	246	8	...
40	Myingyan .	...	..	...	...	.	...	...	...	...	3	...	3	...	...
	EASTERN STATES ...	**27,720**	**30,187**	**283**	**43**	...	..	...	...	**348,950**	**351,191**	**347,876**	**350,156**	**1,074**	**1,035**
41	Northern Shan States	27,649	30,093	283	43	...	...		...	133,483	135,685	133,071	135,236	412	449
42	Southern Shan States	70	94	..	...	.	...	...	...	208,334	209,184	207,739	208,627	595	557
43	Karenni ...	1	...	...	...	.	...	...	...	7,133	6,322	7,066	6,293	67	29

Race-groups by Religion and District (continued). [*Continued on next page.*

J.—Malay.		K.—Mon.		L.—Palaung-wa.		M.—Khasi.		N.—Karen.								O.—Man.		Serial No. of Dist. or State (col. 1).
All religions.		All religions.*		All religions.		Christian.		Total.		Buddhist.		Animist.		Christian.		Animist and Buddhist.		
Males.	Females.	Males.	Females.	Males.	Females.	Males.	Females.	Males.	Females.	Males.	Females.	Males.	Females.	Males.	Females.	Males.	Females.	
46	47	48	49	50	51	52	53	54	55	56	57	58	59	60	61	62	63	
3,144	3,509	163,830	159,679	78,674	78,029	2	1	612,116	608,240	475,514	468,364	47,723	50,530	88,879	89,346	338	259	
3,144	3,509	163,724	159,651	2,483	2,179	2	1	502,394	494,511	397,057	388,985	24,144	23,858	81,193	81,668	4	...	
...	...	...	...	...	...	...	...	69	8	20	2	1	...	48	6	...	...	
...	...	...	...	...	...	...	...	1	2	...	...	...	...	1	2	...	...	1
...	...	...	...	...	...	...	...	1	...	...	...	1	...	...	...	...	...	2
...	...	...	...	...	...	...	...	...	...	...	...	...	...	...	...	...	...	3
...	...	...	...	...	...	...	...	67	6	20	2	...	...	47	4	...	...	4
20	7	27,540	27,672	2	...	...	...	66,417	67,814	49,537	50,491	1,452	1,371	15,428	15,952	4	...	
14	3	151	135	...	...	...	...	1,008	915	165	144	...	...	843	771	...	...	5
3	3	373	319	...	...	...	...	18,159	18,940	11,692	12,225	195	217	6,272	6,498	...	...	6
3	...	3,592	3,613	...	...	...	...	13,875	14,006	13,098	13,296	35	30	742	680	4	...	7
...	...	8	...	...	...	...	...	13,419	13,898	10,135	10,233	1	12	3,283	3,653	...	...	8
...	1	23,413	23,605	2	...	...	...	18,112	18,084	12,734	12,748	1,151	1,038	4,227	4,298	...	...	9
...	...	3	...	...	...	...	...	1,844	1,971	1,713	1,845	70	74	61	52	...	...	10
...	1	4,755	4,206	...	...	...	...	187,032	187,171	147,831	146,659	239	279	38,962	40,233	...	...	
...	...	2,406	2,138	...	...	...	...	54,731	56,932	39,210	40,968	20	24	15,501	15,940	...	...	11
...	...	34	...	...	...	...	...	23,996	24,933	18,899	19,423	4	4	5,093	5,506	...	...	12
...	1	22	31	...	...	...	...	51,941	52,175	42,075	42,068	4	4	9,862	10,103	...	...	13
...	...	233	5	...	...	...	...	45,855	42,538	40,091	36,545	210	236	5,554	5,757	...	...	14
...	...	2,060	2,032	...	...	...	...	10,509	10,593	7,556	7,655	1	11	2,952	2,927	...	...	15
3,121	3,500	131,398	127,758	132	10	...	...	244,868	236,996	198,644	191,253	21,519	21,223	24,705	24,520	...	...	
...	...	417	334	40	...	...	...	42,116	40,439	16,028	14,710	9,255	8,761	16,833	16,968	...	...	16
...	...	44	...	65	...	...	...	22,283	21,028	10,722	9,510	11,131	11,204	430	314	...	...	17
6	44	35,059	33,957	...	...	...	...	123,426	120,193	121,781	118,445	8	13	1,637	1,735	...	...	18
21	17	94,805	92,454	27	10	...	...	42,712	40,930	40,818	39,156	34	49	1,860	1,725	...	...	19
5	...	976	942	...	...	...	...	5,131	5,251	3,727	3,655	346	508	1,058	1,088	...	...	20
3,089	3,439	97	66	...	...	...	...	9,200	9,155	5,568	5,777	745	688	2,887	2,690	...	...	21
1	...	7	4	...	...	...	...	254	53	58	23	1	1	195	29	...	...	
...	...	1	...	...	...	...	...	58	18	20	11	1	1	37	6	...	...	22
1	...	...	1	...	...	...	...	91	3	10	...	...	...	81	3	...	...	23
...	...	4	2	...	...	...	...	46	16	16	12	...	...	30	4	...	...	24
...	...	2	1	...	...	...	...	56	13	12	...	...	...	44	13	...	...	25
...	...	...	...	...	...	...	...	3	3	...	...	...	...	3	3	...	...	26
1	1	14	7	2,349	2,169	2	1	760	186	134	23	...	...	626	163	...	...	
1	...	8	1	4	...	...	...	79	78	7	11	...	...	72	67	...	...	27
1	...	*6*	*1*	*2*	...	...	...	*50*	*55*	*6*	*11*	...	...	*44*	*44*	...	...	
...	...	...	...	188	121	...	...	206	41	11	...	...	...	195	41	...	...	28
...	...	...	1	...	...	...	...	48	19	20	2	...	...	28	17	...	...	29
...	1	6	5	2,157	2,048	...	...	427	48	96	10	...	...	331	38	...	...	30
...	...	...	...	...	...	2	1	...	...	...	...	...	...	...	...	...	...	31
...	...	4	4	...	...	...	...	284	92	60	19	6	1	218	72	...	...	
...	...	2	...	...	...	...	...	141	42	29	16	...	...	112	26	...	...	32
...	...	2	4	...	...	...	...	37	14	27	...	...	...	10	14	...	...	33
...	...	...	...	...	...	...	...	44	23	...	2	1	...	43	21	...	...	34
...	...	...	...	...	...	...	...	52	7	4	1	5	1	43	5	...	...	35
...	...	...	...	...	...	...	...	10	6	...	...	...	...	10	6	...	...	36
1	...	6	5	...	...	...	...	2,710	2,191	773	516	926	983	1,011	693	...	...	
...	...	...	...	...	...	...	...	17	22	1	...	...	...	16	22	...	...	37
...	...	...	2	...	...	...	...	282	208	61	191	...	...	221	17	...	...	38
1	...	6	3	...	...	...	...	2,397	1,950	711	322	924	983	762	645	...	...	39
...	...	...	...	...	...	...	...	14	11	...	2	2	...	12	9	...	...	40
...	...	106	28	76,191	75,850	...	...	109,722	113,729	78,457	79,379	23,579	26,672	7,686	7,678	334	259	
...	...	6	9	57,222	57,411	...	...	750	399	685	380	...	...	65	19	...	...	41
...	...	32	6	18,889	18,434	...	...	87,012	88,139	75,865	77,259	8,227	8,100	2,920	2,780	334	259	42
...	...	68	13	80	5	...	...	21,960	25,191	1,907	1,740	15,352	18,572	4,701	4,879	...	...	43

* Most of the Christians and Animists shown in Part I are in Amherst District, the remainders being scattered in numerous districts.

Serial No.	DISTRICT OR STATE.	R.—CHINESE.*						S.—INDO-BURMAN.									
		Mahomedan.		Yünnanese other than Mahomedans.		Other Chinese.		Arakan Mahomedan and Arakan-Kamao.†		Zerbadi.				Total.		Hindu and	
										Mahomedan.		Others.		Indians.		Born in Burma.	
		Males.	Females.	Males.	Females.	Males.	Females.	Males.	Females.	Males.	Females.	Males.	Females.	Males.	Females.	Males.	Females.
	1	64	65	66	67	68	69	70	71	72	73	74	75	76	77	78	79
	PROVINCIAL TOTAL.	1,076	441	34,676	23,039	66,125	23,703	13,794	12,161	45,129	48,353	519	315	653,980	233,097	51,328	42,397
	DIVISIONAL BURMA ...	860	296	5,445	1,274	64,672	23,479	13,792	12,161	44,601	47,971	473	289	640,081	229,762	50,245	41,412
	Arakan Division ...	..	...	1	...	632	178	13,768	12,161	2,243	2,456	12	12	122,990	84,000	1,010	850
1	Akyab ...	...	...	1	...	479	152	13,244	11,562	33	14	1	1	118,864	82,524	857	730
2	Hill Dt. of Arakan	...		...	..	...	...	...	...	..	...	...	...	591	190	120	100
3	Kyaukpyu ..	...	..	...	...	88	17	515	599	213	179	5	6	2,511	1,155	25	3
4	Sandoway ...	...	..	...	..	65	9	9	...	1,997	2,263	6	5	1,024	131	8	17
	Pegu Division ...	224	46	211	85	28,859	11,756	14	...	8,238	8,509	167	108	277,888	78,133	25,206	21,024
5	Rangoon Town ...	135	28	...	...	15,793	7,863	14	..	4,212	4,338	63	64	154,537	34,797	6,608	5,801
6	Insein ...	6	...	86	41	2,522	668	.	...	524	510	15	...	23,828	8,101	3,024	2,369
7	Hanthawaddy ..	..	...	79	33	3,193	908	...	..	1,558	1,248	45	23	46,741	15,129	6,712	5,645
8	Tharrawaddy ...	13	...	...	..	1,875	508	...	...	786	737	13	2	10,576	2,654	822	688
9	Pegu ...	56	12	46	11	4,365	1,490	...		600	623	25	18	34,828	15,551	7,553	6,124
10	Prome ...	14	6	...	...	1,111	319	..	...	558	1,053	6	1	7,328	1,901	487	397
	Irrawaddy Division	77	11	1,172	197	12,642	3,261	..		3,504	3,561	78	30	74,885	14,518	4,335	3,025
11	Bassein ...	34	10	1,170	184	1,942	618	...	...	2,008	2,016	17	..	18,874	2,823	800	589
12	Henzada ..	10	...	2	5	1,582	404	..	.	388	446	21	5	8,810	2,114	566	343
13	Myaungmya ...	16	...	..	...	3,641	834	..	...	640	585	35	6	17,442	2,348	501	386
14	Ma-ubin ...	13	1	...	..	2,002	371	...	...	386	391	5	16	10,263	2,028	471	360
15	Pyapôn ...	4	...	...	8	3,475	1,034	..	...	82	123	...	3	19,496	5,205	1,997	1,347
	Tenasserim Division	194	49	116	6	15,898	6,491	2	...	12 371	13,659	138	70	82,953	27,726	12,196	10,315
16	Toungoo ...	65	29	...	...	2,042	624	...	...	882	1,406	73	5	18,251	7,181	3,109	2,643
17	Salween ...	40	4	...	..	72	1	...	..	20	25	...	...	731	122	29	21
18	Thatôn ...	41	5	10		2,951	1,418	...	...	2,114	2,697	5	5	21,964	8,258	4,264	3,788
19	Amherst ...	25	8	11	1	5,055	3,333	...	...	5,818	5,803	57	58	30,438	10,742	4,460	3,613
20	Tavoy ...	9	...	63	2	2,421	220	2	...	725	873	1	...	4,190	568	164	120
21	Mergui ..	14	3	32	3	3,352	895	.	..	2,812	2,855	2	2	7,379	855	170	130
	Magwe Division ..	26	1	284	36	1,141	270	...	...	1,188	1,262	28	28	15,700	2,565	1,039	754
22	Thayetmyo ...	3	...	2	..	277	79	..	...	437	551	4	12	2,219	803	392	331
23	Pakôkku ...	3	...	194	27	33	9	..	..	123	133	8	...	1,373	309	94	46
24	Minbu ...	...	1	81	9	336	80	...	...	250	230	2	13	2,497	384	161	109
25	Magwe ...	20	...	7	...	495	102	...	...	373	348	14	3	9,463	1,025	368	246
26	Pakôkku H. Trcts.	...	..	...	...	...	...	..	...	...	.	...	...	148	44	24	2[illegible]
	Mandalay Division	272	188	3,469	927	3,487	952	1	.	7,026	7,908	16	12	38,182	12,310	4,171	3,389
27	Mandalay ...	48	30	150	...	1,648	390	.	...	6,436	7,297	12	6	23,117	6,959	2,081	1,485
	Mandalay City ...	*39*	*24*	*150*	...	*1,255*	*303*		..	*4,626*	*5,363*	*9*	*6*	*12,032*	*2,928*	*908*	*476*
28	Bhamo ...	.	17	1,050	554	157	51		...	175	145	..	3	3,076	628	182	132
29	Myitkyina ...	4	1	1,649	183	346	110	1	...	148	186	2	...	6,974	3,114	1,320	1,266
30	Katha ...	220	140	451	179	1,281	400	...	...	266	280	2	3	4,174	1,375	492	393
31	Putao ...	...	...	169	11	5	1	...		1	..		...	841	234	96	113
	Sagaing Division ..	29	.	88	20	688	178	3		1,846	2,098	21	13	18,206	6,041	1,240	1,082
32	Shwebo ...	19	...	68	17	271	66	...	...	681	742	2	6	5,399	3,677	333	273
33	Sagaing ..	10	...	11	3	97	16	3	...	1,006	1,136	8	1	1,950	631	242	203
34	Lower Chindwin	...	...	5	...	163	61	...	...	61	91	5	5	1,760	420	131	107
35	Upper Chindwin ..	.	..	4	...	103	16	...	...	96	129	6	1	2,939	753	210	164
36	Chin Hills ...	..	..	..	..	34	19	...	...	2	...	...	...	1,158	560	384	335
	Meiktila Division ..	38	1	104	3	1,380	393	4	...	8,190	8,518	13	16	14,827	4,469	1,048	97[illegible]
37	Kyauksè ...	6	..	3	...	163	64	4	..	2,596	2,759	5	...	1,176	348	117	110
38	Meiktila ...	6		76	...	264	41	...	...	856	1,046	3	2	3,696	1,347	255	276
39	Yamèthin ...	13	1	25	3	667	191	...	..	4,583	4,464	5	13	7,312	2,332	464	454
40	Myingyan ...	13	...	...	..	286	97	...	...	155	249	...	1	2,143	442	212	133
	EASTERN STATES ...	216	145	29,231	21,765	1,453	224	2	...	528	382	46	26	13,899	3,335	1,083	985
41	N. Shan States ..	42	34	28,394	21,637	492	83	...	...	191	149	13	2	8,573	1,478	402	399
42	S. Shan States ...	174	111	791	127	805	124	2	...	316	205	33	24	4,947	1,761	669	571
43	Karenni ...	...	...	43	1	156	17	...	...	21	28	...	.	379	96	12	15

* The total Chinese in any district is most conveniently taken from columns 12 and 13 of Part IV below.

† For the distribution of these races separately compare columns 72 and 73 of this page with columns 14 and 15 of Part IV of the table: see also footnotes on pages 98 and 30.

Race-groups by Religion and District (concluded).

X.—INDIAN RACES.																Y. EUROPEAN, ETC.		Z. OTHER RACES.	
Animist.		Buddhist.		Mahomedan.				Sikh, Arya and Brahmo.				Christian.		Others.		All religions.		All religions.	
Born outside Burma.				Born in Burma.		Born outside Burma.		Born in Burma.		Born outside Burma.									
Males.	Females.	Males.	Females.	Males.	Females.	Males.	Females.	Males.	Females.	Males.	Females.	Males.	Females.	Males.	Females.	Males.	Females.	Males.	Females.
80	81	82	83	84	85	86	87	88	89	90	91	92	93	94	95	96	97	98	99
328,201	**62,030**	**5,822**	**1,333**	**103,461**	**99,429**	**146,139**	**17,242**	**506**	**455**	**3,743**	**857**	**13,674**	**8,928**	**1,106**	**426**	**14,758**	**10,595**	**1,151**	**891**
318,619	**60,861**	**5,642**	**1,293**	**103,069**	**98,888**	**143,865**	**17,002**	**497**	**445**	**3,547**	**823**	**13,492**	**8,812**	**1,105**	**426**	**14,320**	**10,327**	**1,144**	**884**
14,038	**714**	**1,680**	**540**	**78,109**	**76,150**	**27,894**	**5,710**	**14**	**12**	**24**	**4**	**130**	**10**	**91**	**10**	**274**	**142**	**9**	**10**
12,802	594	1,489	520	77,216	75,202	26,242	5,442	14	12	24	4	129	10	91	10	250	125	9	10
293	70	135	17	6	2	37	1	...	.	...	...	...	...	...	...	8	1	...	...
599	22	33	3	758	893	1,095	234	...	...	...	...	1	...	...	...	5	2	...	...
344	28	23	.	129	53	520	33	...	..	...	...	...	...	...	...	11	14	...	...
172,674	**36,318**	**1,414**	**235**	**8,157**	**7,634**	**60,564**	**6,674**	**184**	**109**	**1,176**	**320**	**7,887**	**5,512**	**626**	**307**	**8,372**	**6,139**	**890**	**725**
95,565	16,778	509	86	3,963	3,493	41,109	4,223	78	59	829	183	5,405	3,895	471	279	7,096	5,194	862	707
15,634	3,420	220	22	984	1,270	3,433	640	19	12	71	29	416	333	27	0	530	517	3	2
29,857	6,663	269	57	980	1,074	7,010	617	12	13	142	60	1,675	986	84	14	454	224	8	7
6,685	1,113	30	5	433	480	2,504	315	...	5	34	7	60	41	8	...	76	55	4	..
20,375	7,368	340	62	1,199	1,068	4,991	700	17	14	63	20	265	193	25	2	146	112	7	4
4,558	976	46	3	598	249	1,517	179	8	6	37	21	66	64	11	6	70	37	6	5
42,803	**5,350**	**1,156**	**155**	**3,528**	**3,411**	**20,434**	**1,207**	**6**	**11**	**28**	**14**	**2,536**	**1,837**	**64**	**8**	**412**	**231**	**31**	**26**
12,559	1,224	300	34	685	669	4,355	217	...	.	...		175	90	...	..	234	137	16	14
5,458	605	132	11	645	811	1,875	274	6	10	23	12	100	44	5	4	72	54	2	4
8,361	636	219	33	871	829	7,111	303	...	...	...	...	363	161	16	...	38	16	4	8
5,504	540	219	39	888	835	3,007	207	.	1	4	2	143	40	27	4	39	15	...	...
10,921	2,345	286	38	434	267	4,086	206	...	...	1	.	1,755	1,002	16	...	29	9	9	...
44,721	**9,257**	**746**	**247**	**7,249**	**6,097**	**16,936**	**1,201**	**7**	**2**	**60**	**22**	**995**	**569**	**48**	**16**	**1,418**	**1,328**	**128**	**56**
10,280	3,398	288	62	1,019	571	3,310	331	1	..	8	6	233	168	3	2	294	391	8	4
274	27	38	24	31	37	358	13	.	..	..	...	1	...	...	...	11	2	...	...
10,672	2,613	95	36	1,874	1,460	4,880	287	...	...	3	2	175	71	1	1	42	22	1	1
14,967	2,329	195	115	4,102	3,871	6,242	497	3	1	31	11	401	293	37	12	759	783	32	24
2,781	245	63	10	153	115	945	39	3	1	10	3	69	34	2	1	152	77	8	11
5,747	645	67	..	70	43	1,201	34	...	.	8	..	116	3	...	...	160	53	79	16
9,740	**826**	**158**	**18**	**668**	**385**	**3,494**	**314**	**37**	**27**	**203**	**58**	**272**	**177**	**89**	**6**	**569**	**192**	**18**	**16**
1,044	247	55	11	190	142	495	35	.	...	2	3	40	34	1	...	42	20	8	5
585	92	42	1	81	84	456	44	4	6	65	10	37	24	9	2	42	17	...	..
1,591	134	15	..	83	40	497	42	28	13	76	28	26	18	20	...	45	11	...	...
6,401	335	46	6	314	117	2,041	192	5	8	60	17	169	100	59	4	438	144	5	11
119	18	...	.	...	2	5	1	...	..	...	...	...	1	...	...	2	...	...	...
20,658	**5,229**	**353**	**57**	**1,661**	**1,235**	**8,572**	**1,059**	**146**	**158**	**1,342**	**229**	**1,221**	**926**	**58**	**28**	**2,666**	**1,915**	**61**	**46**
11,998	2,724	159	11	1,213	846	5,828	779	100	96	547	109	1,150	888	41	21	2,395	1,741	41	41
5,214	*1,103*	*45*	*8*	*620*	*331*	*4,286*	*516*	*50*	*42*	*381*	*78*	*497*	*368*	*31*	*11*	*873*	*753*	*24*	*15*
892	162	20	27	76	66	1,249	120	42	37	580	72	19	5	16	7	70	32	19	5
4,632	1,562	53	12	112	93	634	97	1	24	195	43	26	17	1	...	71	49	1	...
2,453	676	113	5	259	229	836	60	...	...	2	...	19	12	...	..	124	91	...	...
683	105	8	2	1	1	25	3	3	1	18	5	7	4	...	...	6	2	...	...
6,104	**1,377**	**58**	**4**	**2,569**	**3,008**	**2,549**	**268**	**84**	**67**	**346**	**92**	**211**	**121**	**50**	**22**	**227**	**181**	**2**	**2**
1,589	341	16	...	2,337	2,827	885	119	30	26	133	47	72	40	4	4	77	47	2	2
1,028	255	23	1	72	57	475	55	8	14	36	7	64	38	2	1	49	32	...	...
868	183	8	1	100	46	592	48	1	...	15	...	45	35	...	...	41	17	..	...
1,839	402	6	2	49	64	579	43	42	24	149	35	21	2	44	17	43	16	...	...
780	196	..	...	11	14	18	3	3	3	13	3	9	6	...	..	17	19	...	...
7,881	**1,590**	**82**	**37**	**1,133**	**968**	**3,422**	**569**	**69**	**59**	**368**	**84**	**240**	**160**	**84**	**29**	**382**	**249**	**10**	**8**
682	97	20	5	102	38	176	47	13	16	40	9	26	26	...	...	30	13	...	...
1,735	353	35	13	506	434	891	154	12	22	157	31	101	64	4	...	154	101	5	...
4,274	943	26	16	429	482	1,786	308	41	21	171	41	63	40	58	27	160	122	2	...
1,190	197	1	3	96	14	569	60	3	...	...	3	50	30	22	2	38	13	3	3
9,582	**1,369**	**180**	**40**	**392**	**541**	**2,274**	**240**	**9**	**10**	**196**	**34**	**182**	**116**	**1**	...	**438**	**268**	**7**	**7**
6,256	718	51	10	172	123	1,397	140	9	10	196	34	89	44	1	..	299	149	2	1
3,087	627	126	30	197	370	778	91	...	..	...	...	90	72	...	...	128	116	5	6
239	24	3	...	23	48	99	9	...	...	...	...	3	...	...	...	11	3	...	...

Serial No.	DISTRICT OR STATE.	A1.—Burmese.*						C1.—Meit'ei.	
		Total.		Buddhist.		Christian.		Total.	
		Males.	Females.	Males.	Females.	Males.	Females.	Males.	Females.
	1	2	3	4	5	6	7	8	9
	PROVINCIAL TOTAL ...	3,831,165	4,006,820	3,821,833	3,992,953	6,282	7,512	5,555	3,852
	DIVISIONAL BURMA ...	3,816,552	3,996,074	3,807,340	3,982,423	6,192	7,405	5,499	3,843
	Arakan Division ...	40,804	40,955	40,683	40,788	28	55	128	31
1	Akyab ...	2,253	1,919	2,245	1,877	4	36	122	26
2	Hill District of Arakan ...	6	12	6	12	...	...	1	1
3	Kyaukpyu ...	5,176	4,981	5,176	4,917	...	3	3	4
4	Sandoway ...	33,369	34,103	33,256	33,932	19	16	2	..
	Pegu Division ...	819,478	830,471	816,618	826,581	2,059	2,423	697	169
5	Rangoon Town ...	52,167	50,758	51,553	49,?73	549	1,032	179	146
6	Insein ...	107,517	104,282	106,655	103,586	400	479	258	2
7	Hanthawaddy ...	128,395	125,302	128,235	124,793	143	163	47	2
8	Tharrawaddy ...	217,006	226,060	216,407	225,546	516	347	7	...
9	Pegu ...	148,496	146,330	148,190	145,780	131	244	184	12
10	Prome ...	165,897	177,739	165,518	177,453	320	258	92	6
	Irrawaddy Division ...	754,153	761,334	752,041	758,745	997	981	311	86
11	Bassein ...	164,809	166,712	164,609	166,503	166	173	13	...
12	Henzada ...	236,409	247,715	235,770	247,130	218	200	174	71
13	Myaungmya ...	122,582	117,653	121,933	116,661	182	241	18	4
14	Ma-ubin ...	109,583	116,172	109,335	115,749	192	186	21	6
15	Pyapôn ...	120,770	113,082	120,394	112,700	139	181	25	5
	Tenasserim Division ...	262,517	259,828	261,582	258,888	570	754	307	340
16	Toungoo ...	124,596	126,400	124,178	125,837	196	236	170	317
17	Salween ...	990	803	990	799	...	...	4	...
18	Thatôn ...	55,960	55,105	55,888	55,024	53	46	12	...
19	Amherst ...	35,728	33,618	35,447	33,002	204	335	109	21
20	Tavoy ...	3,847	3,428	3,813	3,398	29	27	9	1
21	Mergui ...	41,396	40,474	41,266	40,328	88	110	3	1
	Magwe Division ...	645,528	686,768	645,246	686,211	144	197	43	7
22	Thayetmyo ...	111,824	118,177	111,716	118,040	25	22	12	2
23	Pakôkku ...	212,728	231,571	212,637	231,459	49	52	29	5
24	Minbu ...	120,872	128,111	120,843	128,020	17	23	...	...
25	Magwe ...	200,016	208,866	199,964	208,649	51	100	2	...
26	Pakôkku Hill Tracts ...	88	43	86	43	2	...	..	...
	Mandalay Division ...	218,947	219,780	212,934	217,831	784	1,127	2,860	2,403
27	Mandalay ...	143,449	152,749	142,594	151,094	709	1,060	2,683	2,351
	Mandalay City ...	*56,986*	*59,480*	*56,354*	*58,102*	*582*	*876*	*1,405*	*2,044*
28	Bhamo ...	11,275	10,692	11,212	10,605	22	19	35	9
29	Myitkyina ...	4,542	2,699	4,529	2,686	10	6	45	24
30	Katha ...	54,657	53,628	54,576	53,434	42	42	97	19
31	Putao ...	24	12	23	12	1	...	..	...
	Sagaing Division ...	527,542	599,285	526,346	597,851	1,142	1,874	1,027	758
32	Shwebo ...	177,973	201,961	177,225	201,082	747	879	14	..
33	Sagaing ...	151,405	169,525	151,083	169,107	322	418	441	466
34	Lower Chindwin ...	154,558	185,548	154,457	185,145	60	61	8	4
35	Upper Chindwin ...	43,550	42,220	43,525	42,191	12	11	517	251
36	Chin Hills ...	56	31	55	26	1	5	47	32
	Meiktila Division ...	552,583	597,658	551,890	596,128	473	494	126	54
37	Kyauksè ...	66,3?2	68,954	66,119	68,715	220	237	26	5
38	Meiktila ...	130,895	148,543	130,731	148,218	54	53	21	23
39	Yamèthin ...	144,705	152,268	144,508	151,394	100	117	76	26
40	Myingyan ...	210,531	227,888	210,532	227,801	99	87	3	...
	EASTERN STATES ...	14,613	10,746	14,493	10,530	90	107	56	9
41	Northern Shan States ...	9,610	7,660	9,537	7,559	62	77	41	2
42	Southern Shan States ...	4,688	2,920	4,646	2,812	28	29	11	7
43	Karenní ...	315	166	310	159	...	1	4	...

* Arakanese, Tavoyans, etc., are shown in Part IIIB and are not included in the figures on this page.

—Selected Indigenous Races by Districts.

[Continued on next page.

Hindus and Mahomedans. Males.	Hindus and Mahomedans. Females.	C30—Chin (unspecified).† Total. Males.	C30—Chin (unspecified).† Total. Females.	I-1.—Shan (unspecified). Total. Males.	I-1.—Shan (unspecified). Total. Females.	I-2.—Shangale. Total. Males.	I-2.—Shangale. Total. Females.	I-3.—Shangyi. Total. Males.	I-3.—Shangyi. Total. Females.	Other Shans. Total. Males.	Other Shans. Total. Females.	Serial No. of District or State (col. 1).
10	11	12	13	14	15	16	17	18	19	20	21	
3,680	3,293	58,319	58,272	142,237	146,747	293,747	294,658	15,100	13,904	57,891	53,703	
3,638	3,289	58,245	58,250	19,392	19,710	107,344	108,264	13,528	13,016	19,761	16,831	
30	27	10,746	10,418	42	18	...	...	8	..	...	...	
26	26	4,044	3,471	26	11	...	...	...	...	...	...	1
1	1	1,379	928	...	2	...	...	...	...	...	...	2
1	...	1,682	1,580	2	...	...	...	3	...	...	..	3
2	...	3,941	3,934	14	5	...	...	...	...	...	...	4
624	149	7,176	6,622	4,920	4,801	944	909	5,095	5,857	465	122	
160	130	10	6	197	236	...	...	...	..	5	14	5
257	..	91	81	72	83	378	394	2,171	2,200	170	103	6
18	..	3	...	2,279	2,374	509	490	48	209	154	...	7
2	...	748	537	1,719	1,351	...	3	...	358	...	..	8
180	13	844	660	298	432	57	20	2,800	2,425	134	5	9
7	6	5,480	5,238	364	325	...	2	76	165	2	...	10
274	82	1,768	1,770	617	419	160	122	865	194	..	..	
12	...	203	152	174	149	50	44	166	107	..	...	11
160	70	1,561	1,616	213	61	39	23	122	89	...	...	12
2	4	4	1	45	21	...	39	44	38	...	...	13
81	6	..	...	31	48	4	...	5	...	...	...	14
19	2	...	1	154	140	67	16	28	90	...	...	15
296	332	299	276	10,539	11,189	5,973	4,356	2,215	1,878	7,980	6,079	
166	313	293	274	5,299	5,653	1,973	927	705	387	20	...	16
4	...	...	...	34	2	1,924	1,534	109	...	402	47	17
12	...	...	...	1,042	972	1,829	1,534	1,221	925	11	4	18
105	18	6	1	3,147	3,551	247	361	180	66	3,261	2,204	19
9	1	...	1	46	12	...	...	...	...	4	8	20
...	...	...	...	971	949	...	...	...	...	4,280	3,816	21
40	3	86,908	88,188	34	22	16	5	..	2	...	...	
12	1	10,383	10,450	7	5	...	...	..	..	...	...	22
28	2	5,814	5,945	17	3	..	...	...	2	...	...	23
...	...	10,340	10,935	9	13	9	1	...	...	...	...	24
...	...	772	1,945	1	1	7	4	...	...	...	...	25
...	...	† 9,599	† 10,113	...	...	...	...	...	...	...	..	26
1,677	2,327	258	82	2,929	3,060	59,808	60,876	5,787	5,900	11,297	10,614	
1,548	2,283	222	2	1,830	1,793	27	7	13	2	3	...	27
1,328	*1,999*	*2*	*2*	*78*	*63*	*21*	...	*9*	*1*	*3*	...	
27	9	1	...	133	143	9,328	9,135	3,121	3,503	5,112	5,007	28
41	21	34	28	...	...	13,255	12,543	1,095	869	3,488	2,846	29
61	14	...	2	931	1,079	37,197	39,189	1,554	1,525	549	323	30
...	...	1	...	35	45	1	2	4	1	2,140	2,438	31
579	320	410	406	31	25	40,378	41,928	16	158	8	16	
5	...	...	...	9	8	...	...	...	...	...	...	32
113	116	...	2	15	12	2	6	1	3	...	...	33
7	7	5	...	7	5	8	...	...	...	8	9	34
448	196	405	404	...	...	40,368	41,917	15	150	...	7	35
6	1	...	...	...	...	...	...	...	...	...	...	36
118	49	680	643	280	226	65	78	47	82	11	...	
22	...	...	..	71	55	...	..	...	...	...	...	37
21	23	1	1	49	15	9	8	6	4	..	...	38
75	26	671	643	160	153	56	65	41	28	11	...	39
...	...	8	...	...	3	...	...	...	...	...	...	40
42	4	74	22	122,845	127,037	186,403	186,394	1,572	888	38,130	38,872	
39	2	23	...	122,845	127,015	5,738	5,521	1,059	798	3,841	3,441	41
...	2	50	21	..	22	174,314	174,782	213	67	33,807	34,313	42
3	...	1	1	...	...	6,351	6,091	300	113	482	118	43

† Details of the figures in columns 12 and 13 for the Pakôkku Hill Tracts have since been obtained; see Appendix B of Volume I of this Report.

Serial No.	DISTRICT OR STATE.	1.—Karen (unspecified). Total. Males.	Total. Females.	Buddhist. Males.	Buddhist. Females.	Christian. Males.	Christian. Females.	2.—Sgaw. Total. Males.	Total. Females.	Buddhist. Males.	Buddhist. Females.	Christian. Males.	Christian. Females.
	1	22	23	24	25	26	27	28	29	30	31	32	33
	PROVINCIAL TOTAL ...	**32,010**	**30,617**	**13,158**	**12,365**	**11,457**	**10,961**	**218,609**	**218,501**	**155,530**	**154,300**	**48,295**	**49,554**
	DIVISIONAL BURMA ...	**30,877**	**29,925**	**12,340**	**11,966**	**11,397**	**10,938**	**217,816**	**217,802**	**155,521**	**154,294**	**48,088**	**49,406**
	Arakan Division ...	**36**	**2**	**1**	...	**35**	**2**	**27**	**5**	**14**	**2**	**13**	**3**
1	Akyab ..	1	2	...	...	1	2	...	...	...	..	...	..
2	Hill District of Arakan	...	...	..	...	...	...	...	...	...	...	..	...
3	Kyaukpyu ...	...	...	...	...	...	...	...	...	...	..	.	...
4	Sandoway ..	35	.	1	...	34	...	27	5	14	2	13	3
	Pegu Division ..	**2,387**	**2,483**	**1,977**	**2,014**	**334**	**385**	**49,332**	**50,920**	**34,240**	**35,265**	**13,762**	**14,397**
5	Rangoon Town ...	170	237	82	59	88	178	614	537	43	42	571	495
6	Insein ...	102	111	89	103	12	8	15,583	16,434	9,544	10,137	5,845	6,081
7	Hanthawaddy ...	250	366	219	340	31	26	4,741	4,959	4,281	4,518	427	411
8	Tharrawaddy ...	345	293	255	230	90	63	12,867	13,498	9,719	9,941	3,147	3,545
9	Pegu ...	622	542	522	428	75	85	14,620	14,455	9,788	9,636	3,750	3,838
10	Prome ...	898	934	810	854	38	25	907	1,037	865	991	22	27
	Irrawaddy Division ...	**1,958**	**1,931**	**1,196**	**1,182**	**762**	**748**	**59,872**	**63,058**	**32,908**	**34,947**	**26,911**	**28,087**
11	Bassein ...	38	51	4	14	34	37	16,808	17,547	4,766	5,344	12,028	12,184
12	Henzada ..	1,087	1,002	763	636	324	365	15,797	17,087	11,802	12,734	3,991	4,350
13	Myaungmya ...	608	685	279	380	329	305	6,237	6,521	1,077	1,050	5,157	5,471
14	Ma-ubin ..	1	10	1	10	...	...	13,802	14,661	10,449	11,040	3,322	3,583
15	Pyapôn ...	224	183	149	142	75	41	7,228	7,237	4,814	4,779	2,413	2,449
	Tenasserim Division ...	**25,827**	**24,826**	**8,960**	**8,715**	**9,541**	**9,558**	**108,018**	**103,480**	**88,274**	**83,881**	**6,929**	**6,825**
16	Toungoo ...	22,875	22,943	6,851	7,085	9,200	9,310	6,264	5,090	4,759	3,677	733	748
17	Salween ...	1	...	...	...	1	...	22,074	20,924	10,556	9,417	392	305
18	Thatôn ...	1,368	1,340	1,324	1,323	42	12	51,103	49,309	49,960	48,048	1,140	1,257
19	Amherst ...	931	399	752	263	179	136	18,356	17,758	17,046	16,526	1,276	1,183
20	Tavoy ...	1	...	1	...	...	...	3,093	3,172	1,816	1,825	986	1,032
21	Mergui .	151	144	32	44	119	100	7,128	7,227	4,137	4,388	2,402	2,300
	Magwe Division ...	**115**	**34**	**27**	**22**	**87**	**11**	**128**	**16**	**21**	...	**102**	**16**
22	Thayetmyo ...	34	14	15	11	18	2	15	2	...	..	15	2
23	Pakôkku ..	71	1	5	...	66	1	16	2	1	...	15	2
24	Minbu ...	4	11	4	11	...	...	41	4	11	...	30	4
25	Magwe ...	3	8	3	.	...	8	51	5	9	...	42	5
26	Pakôkku Hill Tracts	3	...	...	...	3	...	...	3	...	...	...	3
	Mandalay Division ...	**248**	**89**	**39**	**6**	**204**	**83**	**276**	**54**	**59**	**7**	**217**	**47**
27	Mandalay ...	60	51	7	2	53	49	7	11	...	...	7	11
	Mandalay City ...	*45*	*28*	*6*	*2*	*39*	*26*	*5*	*11*	...	..	*5*	*11*
28	Bhamo ...	...	...	...	...	...	...	70	21	...	...	70	21
29	Myitkyina ...	11	9	.	...	11	9	7	8	...	1	7	7
30	Katha ...	172	29	32	4	140	25	192	14	59	6	133	8
31	Putao ...	...	...	...	...	...	..	...	...	...	...	...	...
	Sagaing Division ...	**160**	**60**	**28**	**18**	**181**	**42**	**64**	**31**	**4**	**1**	**59**	**30**
32	Shwebo ...	131	42	28	16	103	26	6	...	1	...	5	...
33	Sagaing ...	...	1	...	...	...	1	8	13	...	...	8	13
34	Lower Chindwin ...	25	15	..	2	24	13	19	8	...	...	19	8
35	Upper Chindwin ...	4	2	...	...	4	2	21	4	3	1	17	3
36	Chin Hills ...	...	...	...	...	...	...	10	6	...	...	10	6
	Meiktila Division ...	**651**	**500**	**112**	**9**	**308**	**109**	**104**	**243**	**1**	**191**	**95**	**51**
37	Kyauksè ...	4	8	1	...	3	8	13	14	...	...	13	14
38	Meiktila ...	215	8	24	...	191	8	29	200	...	191	29	9
39	Yamèthin ...	420	473	87	7	97	84	62	29	1	...	53	28
40	Myingyan ...	12	11	...	2	12	9	...	...	...	..	...	..
	EASTERN STATES ...	**1,133**	**692**	**818**	**399**	**60**	**23**	**793**	**699**	**9**	**6**	**207**	**148**
41	Northern Shan States	366	23	309	8	57	15	9	4	2	...	7	4
42	Southern Shan States	512	415	509	391	3	8	75	69	...	1	75	62
43	Karenni ..	255	254	...	..	...	...	709	626	7	5	125	82

Selected Indigenous Races by Districts (concluded).

N°.—Pwo.						Other Karens.						Serial No. of District or State (col. 1).
Total.		Buddhist.		Christian.		Total.		Buddhist.		Christian.		
Males.	Females.	Males.	Females.	Males.	Females.	Males.	Females.	Males.	Females.	Males.	Females.	
34	35	36	37	38	39	40	41	42	43	44	45	
208,285	203,606	193,778	189,028	13,887	13,807	153,212	155,516	113,048	112,671	15,240	15,024	
208,074	203,387	193,762	189,014	13,874	13,793	45,627	43,397	35,434	33,711	7,834	7,531	
5	1	5	...	...	1	1	...	...	...	...	...	
...	...	...	...	...	...	...	...	...	...	...	...	1
...	...	..	..	...	...	1	..	...	...	...	...	2
...	...	..	..	...	...	...	...	...	..	..	...	3
5	1	5	...	...	1	...	...	...	...	...	...	4
13,473	12,987	12 151	11,808	1,285	1,153	1,225	1,424	1,169	1,404	47	17	
217	140	38	42	179	98	7	1	2	1	5	...	5
2,464	2,391	2,059	1,984	405	406	10	4	...	1	10	3	6
8,872	8,667	8,586	8,424	284	243	12	14	12	14	..	...	7
207	107	161	62	46	45	...	...	...	..	..	...	8
1,674	1,682	1,269	1,296	370	361	1,196	1,405	1,155	1,388	32	14	9
39	...	38	...	1	...	...		...	...	...	...	10
125,067	122,151	113,641	110,515	11,240	11,428	135	36	86	15	49	20	
37,885	39,334	34,440	35,610	3,439	3,719	...	...	...	.	...	...	11
7,112	6,844	6,334	6,053	778	791	..	..	...	...	..	...	12
45,088	44,967	40,716	40,638	4,371	4,325	8	2	3	...	5	2	13
32,009	27,853	29,619	25,490	2,211	2,165	43	14	22	5	21	9	14
2,973	3,153	2,532	2,724	441	428	84	20	61	10	23	9	15
69,403	68,228	67,927	66,690	1,262	1,192	42,120	40,462	33,483	31,967	6,973	6,945	
12	5	12	...	...	5	12,965	12,401	4,406	3,948	6,900	6,905	16
86	4	67	...	19	4	122	100	99	93	18	5	17
43,967	43,614	43,549	43,170	415	440	26,988	25,930	26,948	25,904	40	26	18
21,398	20,743	20,996	20,345	402	398	2,027	2,030	2,024	2,022	3	8	19
2,021	2,078	1,906	1,830	60	55	16	1	4	...	12	1	20
1,919	1,784	1,397	1,345	366	290	2	...	2	...	...	...	21
12	3	6	1	6	2	4	...	4	...	...	...	
9	2	5	...	4	2	...	...	...	...	...	...	22
...	...	...	...	...	...	4	...	4	...	...	...	23
1	1	1	1	...	...	...	...	...	...	...	...	24
2	...	...	...	[illegible]	...	...	..	...	...	...	...	25
...	..	...	...	...	...	..	..	...	...	...	...	26
60	17	5	...	55	17	181	26	31	10	150	16	
3	6	...	...	3	6	9	10	...	9	9	1	27
...	*6*	...	...	...	*6*	...	*10*	...	*9*	...	*1*	
8	6	...	...	8	6	128	14	11	...	117	14	28
2	...	...	...	2	...	28	2	20	1	8	1	29
47	5	5	...	42	5	16	...	...	...	16	...	30
...	...	...	...	...	...	...	...	...	...	...	..	31
37	...	27	...	9	...	28	1	1	...	19	...	
...	..	...	...	.	...	4	...	...	...	4	...	32
29	...	27	...	2	...	...	...	...	...	...	...	33
...	...	-	...	...	...	..	...	...	..	...	...	34
8	...	...	...	7	..	19	1	1	..	15	...	35
...	...	..	.	..	...	...	...	...	...	...	...	36
17	...	...	...	17	...	1,938	1,448	660	315	596	533	
...	...	...	...	...	...	...	..	...	...	...	...	37
...	...	...	...	...	...	38	..	37	...	1	...	38
17	...	...	..	17	...	1,898	1,448	623	315	595	533	39
...	...	...	...	...	...	2	...	...	...	...	...	40
211	219	16	14	13	14	107,585	112,119	77,614	78,960	7,406	7,493	
2	...	1	...	1	...	373	372	373	372	...	...	41
64	56	...	...	12	14	86,361	87,599	75,356	76,867	2,830	2,696	42
145	163	15	14	...	...	20,851	24,148	1,885	1,721	4,576	4,797	43

IMPERIAL TABLE XIII—*Race*. PART IIIB.—*Other Indigenous Races by Districts.*

A.—Burma Group.

Race.	District or State.	Males.	Females.
A2 Arakanese	Total ...	151,190	149,510
	Akyab ...	127,815	127,312
	Kyaukpyu ...	1,388	1,067
	Sandoway ...	14,799	16,255
	Bassein ...	6,097	4,489
	Elsewhere ..	1,091	387
A3 Yanbye	Total ..	80,234	87,951
	Akyab ...	1,970	416
	Kyaukpyu ...	78,261	87,533
	Elsewhere ...	3	2
A4 Chaungtha	Total ...	23,396	22,757
	Akyab ..	22,448	21,838
	Hill District of Arakan.	948	919
A5 Tavoyan	Total ...	64,329	64,958
	Amherst ..	897	572
	Tavoy ..	63,280	64,309
	Elsewhere .	152	77
A6 Merguese	Total ...	102	76
	Tavoy ..	102	74
	Elsewhere ...	...	2
A7 Yabein	Total ...	882	892
	Insein .	21	18
	Pegu ...	861	874
A8 Yaw ...	Total ...	75	14
	Katha ...	73	10
	Elsewhere ..	2	2
A9 Danu ...	Total ...	37,382	37,260
	Meiktila ...	1,037	984
	N. S. States	7,867	7,397
	S. S. States	28,037	28,795
	Elsewhere ...	441	84
A10 Intha ...	Total ..	27,693	28,482
	S. S. States	26,684	27,638
	Karenni ...	880	844
	Elsewhere ..	129	...
A11 Taungyo	Total ...	11,984	11,693
	S. S. States	11,762	11,689
	Elsewhere ...	222	4
A12 P'un ...	Myitkyina .	172	195
A13 Atsi ...	Total ...	2,677	2,180
	Bhamo ...	1,163	449
	Myitkyina ..	1,181	1,383
	N. S. States	333	348
A14 Lashi ...	Total ...	8,567	8,443
	Bhamo ...	353	410
	Myitkyina ...	6,612	6,304
	N S. States	1,597	1,728
	Elsewhere ...	5	1
A15 Maru ...	Total ...	10,315	11,110
	Bhamo .	357	372
	Myitkyina ..	5,215	5,583
	N. S. States	4,704	5,145
	Elsewhere ...	39	10
A16 Maingtha	Total ...	420	111
	Bhamo ...	125	32
	Myitkyina ..	64	...
	Katha ...	204	78
	Elsewhere ...	27	1

B.—Lolo-Mus'o Group.

Race.	District or State.	Males.	Females.
B1 Lisaw	Total ...	6,703	6,557
	Myitkyina	548	623
	Katha ...	849	658
	N. S. States	3,715	3,672
	S. S. States	1,591	1,586
	Elsewhere	..	18
B2 Lolo ..	N. S. States	380	389
B3 Lahu	Total ...	11,597	11,099
	S. S. States	11,595	11,099
	Elsewhere	2	...
B4 Ako ...	S. S. States	30	21
B5 Pyin ...	S. S. States	515	421
B6 Kwi ...	S. S. States	1,877	1,836
B7 Akha ...	S. S. States	18,335	15,930
B8 Nung	Putao ...	42	76
B11 Wat'-aokhum.	Myitkyina	15	22

B9 Tangsir and B10 Hop'a are to be found in the parts of Putao District which were omitted from the Census.

C.—Kuki-Chin Group.

List I below this shows the distribution by districts of some races of the Kuki-Chin Group. Details for C1 (*Meit'ei*) and C32 (*Chins whose tribe was not specified*) are given in Part IIIA of the table. All other Chins enumerated are shown in List II to the right of this. For each race in List II only the number enumerated in the district specified for it is given; but for all except the races marked* these make up the provincial total shown in Part I of the table, while for no race marked* does the total enumerated outside the districts specified for it exceed 19 males and 8 females. For all the races marked* together the number of persons omitted from List II is 56 males and 10 females.

Kuki-Chin, List II—See the note on Group C in the centre of the page.

District.	Race.	Males.	Females.
Akyab ...	C26 Chinbon	345	338
	C33 Chaunggyi Chin.	349	317
	C34 Kaukadan.	125*	167
Hill District of Arakan.	C17 Lakher	...	12
	C23 Kyaw	183	168
	C24 Anu ...	199	213
	C30 Yindu	50*	54
	C35 Kaungtso	185	183*
Kyaukpyu	C37 Matu ...	23	28
	C39 Sittu ...	2,032	1,886
Pakôkku	C25 Chinbok	1	..
	C29 Taungtha.	3,470	4,100
U. Chindwin	C40 Taman	369*	429
Chin Hills	C3 Siyin ..	1,543*	1,673*
	C6 Paite ...	668	659
	C7 Yo ...	2,801	2,758
	C9 Yahow...	2,481	2,927
	C11 Kwangli	2,143	2,499
	C12 Ngorn	1,916*	2,021
	C13 Kwelshim.	961	1,101
	C15 Tlantlang	4,057	4,001
	C16 Yokwa	1,194*	1,310
	C18 Lawt'u	1,619	1,494
	C19 Yotun	2,559*	2,550
	C20 Shentang	3,067	3,025
	C22 Hualngo	1,555	1,745

Kuki-Chin, List I—See the note above.

Race.	Total.		Akyab.		Hill District of Arakan.		Kyaukpyu.		Upper Chindwin.		Chin Hills.	
	M.	F.	M.	F.	M.	F.	M.	F.	M.	F.	M.	F.
C2 T'ado ...	1,138	1,148	...	...	...	...	209	202	...	...	929	941
C4 Sokte ...	8,641	8,828	...	...	...	...	...	...	194	187	8,447	8,641
C5 Kamhow ...	4,399	4,269	...	...	267	282	...	...	474	426	3,658	3,561
C8 Tashon ...	3,803	4,467	...	...	...	...	...	...	209	190	3,594	4,277
C10 Laiyo ...	5,316	5,770	...	...	...	...	...	...	66	39	5,250	5,731
C14 Lai ...	4,632	4,720	...	...	...	...	..	...	307	309	4,325	4,411
C21 Lushei ...	161	156	...	...	...	...	...	...	130	123	31	33
C28 Khami ...	13,329	12,775	7,233	6,726	6,096	6,049	...	...	...	...	...	...
C36 Ledu ...	1,118	1,116	438	400	...	9	680	707	...	...	...	...
C38 Saingbaung ...	3,956	3,568	188	148	..	...	3,773	3,418	...	...	...	...

D.—Naga Group.

Races of the Naga Group have been recorded in the Upper Chindwin District only. For their numbers see Part I of the table.

E.—Kachin Group.

Races classed as E2 to E9, for which detailed figures are given in Part I, were recorded in the Putao District only. These, together with 454 male and 291 female Kachins make up the numbers shown for males and females of the Kachin group for the Putao District in Part II of the table. For other districts the numbers given in Part II for the Kachin group represent E1 Kachins only.

G.—Mishmi Group.

G1 Khaman-Mishmi is the only race of this group represented in the area of this census and it was recorded only in the Putao District. Its numbers are given in Part I of the table.

F.—Sak Group.

Sak (F3) and Daingnet (F4) were recorded in the Akyab District only. Their numbers are given in Part I of the table. The Kadus and Ganan are distributed as follows:—

District or State.	F1 Kadu.		F2 Ganan.	
	Males.	Females.	Males.	Females.
Bhamo ...	242	236	5	...
Myitkyina	471	502	...	...
Katha ...	17,346	17,906	2,697	3,150
U. Chindwin	305	392	272	308
N. S. States	241	43	42	...
Elsewhere	20	6	...	...
Total ...	18,625	19,085	3,016	3,458

H.—Mro Group.

H1 Mro is the only race included in this group. Its numbers are therefore the same as those given for the Mro group in Part II of the table.

IMPERIAL TABLE XIII—*Race*. PART IIIB.—*Other Indigenous Races by Districts* (concluded).

I.—Tai Group.

DISTRICT OR STATE.	Total of races shown here.*		I-5 Shan-Tayok.		I-6 Siamese.		I-7 Khun.		I-8 Lu.		I-9 Lao.		I-10 Shan Bama.		I-11 Kamti.	
	M.	F.	M.	F.	M.	F.	M.	F.	M.	F.	M.	F.	M.	F.	M.	F.
Insein ...	170	103	155	96	15	7	...	...	...	...	...	...	...	...	...	...
Hanthawaddy ...	154	...	...	...	...	...	...	...	...	...	154	...	...	...	...	...
Pegu ...	134	5	2	..	94	4	...	...	...	...	38	1	.	...	...	...
Salween ...	402	47	39	...	11	3	...	...	...	...	352	44	...	...	...	...
Amherst ...	3,260	2,204	1	1	2,794	2,183	...	...	...	...	465	20	...	...	...	...
Mergui ...	4,282	3,816	...	...	4,282	3,816	...	...	...	.	...	...	...	...	...	...
Bhamo ...	5,117	5,007	5,117	5,007	...	...	...	...	...	...	...	...	...	...	...	...
Myitkyina ...	3,488	2,846	3,369	2,686	...	...	...	..	...	...	...	...	3	3	116	157
Katha ...	549	323	547	323	1	...	...	..	...	...	...	...	...	...	1	...
Putao ...	2,140	2,438	1	...	...	...	...	...	...	...	...	...	...	...	2,139	2,438
N. Shan States	3,841	2,441	3,718	2,441	2	.	...	...	...	...	121	...	...	...	...	...
S. Shan States	33,807*	34,313*	2,745	2,253	9	1	16,346	17,044	12,679	13,183	1,476	1,414	...	...	...	...
Karenni ...	482	118	178	4	1	..	4	...	7	1	292	113	...	...	...	...
Elsewhere ...	65	42	13	5	36	27	...	..	...	...	13	3	3	7	...	...
Total ...	57,891*	53,703*	15,885	12,816	7,245	6,041	16,350	17,044	12,686	13,184	2,911	1,595	6	10	2,256	2,595

* The totals given for the Southern Shan States and the Province include 551 male and 417 female I5 Dayes and 1 male and 1 female I12 Annamese besides those shown in the subsequent columns.

J.—Malay Group.—J2 Salons, 929 males and 1,012 females, are found in the Mergui District only. If these be deducted from the group figures given in Part II of the Table, the balance will represent the Malay race only.

K.—Mon Group.—K1 Talaing is the only member of this group found in Burma. The distribution of Talaing is therefore identical with that of Mon given in Part II of the Table.

L.—Palaung-Wa Group.

Race.	Total.		Salween.		Katha.		N. Shan States.		S. Shan States.		Karenni.		Elsewhere.	
	M.	F.	M.	F.	M.	F.	M.	F.	M.	F.	M.	F.	M.	F.
L1 Wa ...	7,695	7,067	...	...	...	...	4,165	3,841	3,528	3,226	...	...	2	...
L2 Danaw ...	816	853	...	..	...	.	...	...	816	853	...	...	...	...
L3 En ...	17	...	...	..	.	...	...	...	...	...	...	...	17	...
L4 Khamuk ...	390	12	65	...	...	...	...	...	218	8	78	4	29	...
L5 Lem ...	406	385	...	...	...	...	...	...	406	385	...	...	...	...
L6 Tai-loi ...	2	...	...	...	...	...	2	...	...	...	...	...	...	...
L7 Yang (unspecified)	1,411	1,513	.	...	...	...	...	...	1,411	1,513	..	...	...	...
L8 Yanglam ...	6,622	7,257	...	...	..	...	641	659	5,980	6,597	1	1	...	...
L10 Palaung and Pale	61,315	60,942	...	...	2,157	2,048	52,414	52,911	6,530	5,852	1	...	213	131
Total ...	78,674	78,029	65	...	2,157	2,048	57,222	57,411	18,889	18,434	80	5	261	131

M.—Khasi Group.—M1 Khasi, the only member of this group, was recorded only in the Putao District. Its numbers are given in Part I of the table.

N.—Karen Group.

Race.	Total.		Toungoo.		Thatôn.		Yamèthin.		S. Shan States.		Karenni.		Elsewhere.	
	M.	F.	M.	F.	M.	F.	M.	F.	M.	F.	M.	F.	M.	F.
N3 Paku ...	1,021	965	498	474	...	...	7	...	...	..	487	490	29	1
N4 Wewaw ..	163	172	35	39	...	...	...	...	...	...	121	132	7	1
N6 Bwè ...	3,553	3,914	24	841	...	...	3	...	419	414	2,264	2,647	43	12
N7 Brek ...	311	307	...	...	..	...	..	...	...	...	308	307	3	..
N8 Karenbyu	9,674	8,696	6,557	6,323	..	...	1,555	1,135	729	617	686	615	147	6
N10 Mopwa ...	1	4	...	4	...	...	...	...	...	...	...	...	1	...
N11 Taungthu	108,746	109,491	3,350	3,063	26,849	25,871	324	312	73,486	75,201	1,546	1,484	3,191*	3,560*
N12 Padaung ...	7,077	6,678	11	7	...	...	9	...	6,738	6,344	316	327	3	..
N13 Yinbaw ...	2,837	2,914	...	...	...	...	...	...	527	484	2,294	2,430	16	...
N14 Gheko ...	1,317	1,346	689	740	...	...	...	...	628	606	...	...	...	...
N15 Karenni ...	16,364	19,027	1,001	910	139	59	...	1	1,698	1,940	12,821	15,707	705†	410†
N16 Zarein ...	2,145	2,002	...	...	...	...	...	...	2,136	1,993	8	9	1	...
N17 T'laing-Kalasi.	3	...	...	...	...	...	...	...	...	...	...	...	3	...
Total of races shown here.	153,212	155,516	12,965	12,401	26,988	25,930	1,898	1,448	86,361	87,599	20,851	24,148	4,149	3,990

* Of these numbers 1,635 males and 1,780 females were recorded in the Amherst District, 1,136 males and 1,388 females in the Pegu District and 357 males and 372 females in the Northern Shan States; the rest are scattered.

† Of these numbers 392 males and 250 females were recorded in the Amherst District and 96 males and 95 females in the Salween District; the rest are scattered.

O.—Man Group.—The two races of this group were recorded only in the Southern Shan States. Their numbers are given in Part I of the table.

Serial No.	DISTRICT OR STATE.	BENGALI. Total. Males.	Total. Females.	Hindu and Animist. Males.	Hindu and Animist. Females.	Mahomedan. Males.	Mahomedan. Females.	Others. Males.	Others. Females.	CHITTA… Total. Males.	Total. Females.	Hindu and Animist. Males.	Hindu and Animist. Females.
	1	2	3	4	5	6	7	8	9	10	11	12	13
	PROVINCIAL TOTAL ...	**60,117**	**17,871**	**12,172**	**3,002**	**46,651**	**14,632**	**1,294**	**237**	**129,854**	**76,534**	**5,110**	**286**
	DIVISIONAL BURMA ...	**59,160**	**17,717**	**11,825**	**2,906**	**46,089**	**14,583**	**1,246**	**228**	**129,592**	**76,529**	**5,086**	**286**
	Arakan Division ...	**19,389**	**9,083**	**2,868**	**167**	**16,957**	**8,910**	**64**	**6**	**93,381**	**73,496**	**3,715**	**196**
1	Akyab ...	16,838	7,954	1,959	148	14,837	7,806	42	...	93,000	73,451	3,687	191
2	Hill District of Arakan	7	3	7	...	...	...	...	3	198	17	23	...
3	Kyaukpyu ...	1,923	1,065	311	6	1,595	1,056	17	3	139	24	...	5
4	Sandoway ...	621	61	91	13	525	48	5	...	44	4	5	...
	Pegu Division ...	**15,605**	**2,503**	**5,674**	**1,497**	**9,363**	**923**	**568**	**83**	**20,981**	**1,091**	**652**	**12**
5	Rangoon Town ...	11,233	1,578	4,304	1,036	6,549	473	380	69	12,625	313	405	4
6	Insein ...	1,291	342	507	190	729	148	55	4	614	103	53	...
7	Hanthawaddy ...	1,631	197	381	61	1,148	129	102	7	4,410	212	137	...
8	Tharrawaddy ...	437	89	131	63	300	26	6	...	714	80	...	4
9	Pegu ...	641	200	262	94	357	105	22	1	2,312	353	36	3
10	Prome ...	372	97	89	53	280	42	3	2	306	30	21	1
	Irrawaddy Division ..	**11,098**	**2,009**	**1,441**	**282**	**9,494**	**1,701**	**163**	**26**	**5,962**	**605**	**335**	**22**
11	Bassein ...	3,092	633	754	106	2,331	526	7	1	1,050	40	156	5
12	Henzada ...	789	354	120	50	663	303	6	1	590	199	22	5
13	Myaungmya ...	4,560	499	236	29	4,204	458	120	12	1,297	78	42	1
14	Ma-ubin ...	1,021	367	114	46	899	321	8	...	1,313	166	39	1
15	Pyapôn ...	1,636	156	217	51	1,397	93	22	12	1,712	122	76	10
	Tenasserim Division	**9,472**	**3,026**	**964**	**305**	**8,366**	**2,676**	**142**	**45**	**4,926**	**1,080**	**237**	**33**
16	Toungoo ...	931	206	230	110	658	80	43	16	1,121	200	23	10
17	Salween ...	383	37	34	6	345	31	4	...	5	...	...	...
18	Thatôn ...	3,805	990	172	48	3,617	937	16	5	495	58	28	3
19	Amherst ...	4,009	1,702	422	93	3,516	1,587	71	22	2,862	759	172	18
20	Tavoy ...	207	65	56	32	143	31	8	2	201	12	8	2
21	Mergui ...	137	26	50	16	87	10	...	...	242	1	6	...
	Magwe Division ...	**437**	**120**	**204**	**76**	**164**	**33**	**69**	**11**	**1,291**	**38**	**45**	...
22	Thayetmyo ...	95	27	40	21	48	6	7	...	201	9	2	...
23	Pakôkku ...	70	21	39	17	22	...	9	4	141	9	1	...
24	Minbu ...	30	5	15	4	12	1	3	...	62	...	...	...
25	Magwe ...	241	67	109	34	82	26	50	7	887	20	42	...
26	Pakôkku Hill Tracts	1	..	1	...	...	...	...	...	...	...	...	...
	Mandalay Division ...	**1,849**	**443**	**719**	**306**	**996**	**112**	**134**	**25**	**1,608**	**99**	**62**	...
27	Mandalay ...	1,396	323	523	219	792	97	81	7	1,026	54	38	...
	Mandalay City ...	*740*	*179*	*254*	*109*	*465*	*63*	*21*	*7*	*932*	*32*	*38*	...
28	Bhamo ...	90	38	51	30	27	...	12	8	174	...	...	...
29	Myitkyina ...	110	35	71	28	26	1	13	6	137	21	6	...
30	Katha ...	234	41	64	26	151	14	19	1	271	24	18	...
31	Putao ...	19	6	10	3	...	...	9	3	...	...	...	...
	Sagaing Division ...	**576**	**248**	**227**	**127**	**323**	**111**	**26**	**10**	**905**	**41**	**15**	**16**
32	Shwebo ...	216	130	71	47	132	77	13	6	182	8	...	1
33	Sagaing ...	108	43	49	26	55	17	4	...	235	4	8	3
34	Lower Chindwin ...	116	30	31	19	77	7	8	4	182	16	6	12
35	Upper Chindwin ..	106	20	51	17	54	3	1	...	305	13	...	...
36	Chin Hills ...	30	25	25	18	5	7	...	...	1	...	1	...
	Meiktila Division ...	**734**	**285**	**228**	**146**	**426**	**117**	**80**	**22**	**538**	**129**	**25**	**7**
37	Kyauksè ...	120	12	30	6	90	6	...	...	3	3	...	...
38	Meiktila ...	189	134	79	52	99	80	11	2	157	99	5	4
39	Yamèthin ..	311	117	88	73	177	29	46	15	207	27	20	3
40	Myingyan ...	114	22	31	15	60	2	23	5	171	..	...	...
	EASTERN STATES ...	**957**	**154**	**347**	**96**	**562**	**49**	**48**	**9**	**262**	**5**	**24**	...
41	Northern Shan States	705	88	270	64	406	22	29	2	146	4	24	...
42	Southern Shan States	213	59	75	28	121	24	17	7	92	1	...	...
43	Karenni ...	39	7	2	4	35	3	2	...	24	...	...	...

Selected Indian Races by Districts.

[*Continued on next page*

GONIAN.				HINDUSTANI.								
Mahomedan.		Others.		Total.		Hindu and Animist.		Mahomedan.		Others.		Serial No. of Dist. or State (col. 1).
Males.	Females.	Males.	Females.	Males.	Females.	Males.	Females.	Males.	Females.	Males.	Females.	
14	15	16	17	18	19	20	21	22	23	24	25	
122,872	75,682	1,872	566	107,557	26,020	82,482	19,657	23,400	5,984	1,675	379	
122,644	75,680	1,862	563	105,816	25,571	81,252	19,351	22,898	5,845	1,666	375	
88,075	72,768	1,591	532	4,634	862	4,338	822	268	38	28	2	
87,865	72,742	1,448	518	4,375	851	4,111	816	240	33	24	2	1
40	3	135	14	33	...	33	...	...	..	..	...	2
133	19	6	..	162	7	146	4	15	3	1	...	3
37	4	2	...	64	4	48	2	13	2	3	...	4
20,164	1,060	165	19	54,383	13,626	42,148	10,650	11,520	2,823	715	153	
12,107	297	113	12	23,609	3,072	15,795	1,740	7,513	1,286	301	46	5
552	101	9	2	7,553	2,346	6,416	1,791	1,074	549	63	6	6
4,245	208	28	4	6,366	762	5,816	560	334	133	216	69	7
714	76	...	...	2,918	913	2,160	561	727	350	31	2	8
2,262	349	14	1	11,754	6,077	10,464	5,656	1,206	394	84	27	9
284	29	1	...	2,183	456	1,497	342	666	111	20	3	10
5,615	581	12	2	11,859	2,137	9,142	1,475	2,262	546	455	116	
892	35	2	...	3,948	522	3,113	413	690	88	145	21	11
567	194	1	..	1,529	411	1,161	209	310	196	58	6	12
1,246	76	9	1	2,978	434	2,110	252	764	157	104	25	13
1,274	164	...	1	1,554	298	1,231	234	272	60	51	4	14
1,636	112	...	...	1,850	472	1,527	367	226	45	97	60	15
4,642	994	47	3	10,982	3,106	8,735	2,463	2,059	596	188	47	
1,060	188	38	2	5,723	1,954	4,851	1,585	812	354	60	15	16
5	...	...	...	26	6	15	1	11	5	..	...	17
466	55	1	..	2,334	749	1,798	592	492	137	44	23	18
2,686	740	4	1	1,800	265	1,376	179	404	76	20	10	19
189	10	4	...	648	83	461	70	165	11	22	2	20
236	1	...	...	451	49	234	36	175	13	48	...	21
1,230	87	16	1	4,765	833	3,617	604	1,061	211	87	18	
196	9	3	...	796	305	670	262	105	36	21	7	22
129	8	11	1	467	108	312	69	141	39	14	...	23
60	...	2	...	845	127	624	77	210	48	11	2	24
845	20	...	...	2,655	293	2,009	196	605	88	41	9	25
...	...	...	...	2	...	2	...	...	..	...	...	26
1,523	93	23	6	10,854	2,441	7,309	1,518	3,405	892	140	31	
969	48	19	6	8,107	1,643	5,424	963	2,581	655	102	25	27
893	*32*	*1*	...	*3,966*	*652*	*2,542*	*384*	*1,359*	*253*	*65*	*15*	
174	...	...	..	596	123	301	82	289	37	6	4	28
131	21	...	...	1,096	397	805	313	280	84	11	..	29
249	24	4	...	1,003	273	735	155	249	116	19	2	30
...	...	...	...	52	5	44	5	6	...	2	...	31
885	25	5	...	3,333	1,151	2,734	896	581	255	18	...	
180	7	2	...	1,455	528	1,195	391	252	137	8	...	32
225	1	2	...	875	335	736	281	134	54	5	..	33
175	4	1	...	499	134	375	102	120	32	2	...	34
305	13	...	...	425	105	351	73	71	32	3	...	35
...	...	...	...	79	49	77	49	2	...	...	...	36
510	122	3	...	5,006	1,415	3,229	923	1,742	484	85	8	
1	3	2	...	435	143	326	94	100	44	9	5	37
151	95	1	...	1,338	344	804	167	522	174	12	3	38
187	24	...	...	2,276	694	1,314	456	949	238	13	.	39
171	...	...	...	957	234	785	206	171	28	1	..	40
228	2	10	3	1,741	449	1,230	306	502	139	9	4	
122	2	...	2	976	223	684	133	290	89	2	1	41
83	...	9	1	734	219	536	168	191	48	7	3	42
23	...	1	...	31	7	10	5	21	2	...	...	43

Serial No.	DISTRICT OR STATE.	ORIYA.						TAMIL.						
		Total.		Hindu and Animist.		Others.		Total.		Hindu and Animist.		Mahomedan.		Chris
		Males.	Females.	Males.	Females.	Males.	Females.	Males.	Females.	Males.	Females.	Males.	Females.	Males.
	1	26	27	28	29	30	31	32	33	34	35	36	37	38
	PROVINCIAL TOTAL ...	**49,993**	**2,482**	**48,017**	**1,973**	**1,976**	**509**	**100,315**	**51.749**	**68,192**	**36,761**	**21,328**	**7,196**	**10,146**
	DIVISIONAL BURMA ...	**47,081**	**2,456**	**45,155**	**1,951**	**1,926**	**505**	**99,902**	**51,608**	**67,942**	**36,696**	**21,287**	**7,191**	**10,053**
	Arakan Division ...	**2.140**	**28**	**2,051**	**23**	**89**	**5**	**798**	**18**	**610**	**8**	**107**	**4**	**67**
1	Akyab ...	2,004	26	1,973	22	31	4	782	18	602	8	107	4	67
2	Hill District of Arakan	8	...	5	...	3	...	1	...	1	...	...	...	...
3	Kyaukpyu ...	95	2	45	1	50	1	4	...	4	...	...	...	...
4	Sandoway ...	33	...	28	...	5	.	6	...	3	...	...	...	...
	Pegu Division	**17,451**	**1,089**	**17,088**	**1,016**	**368**	**73**	**62,618**	**33,818**	**43,381**	**24,704**	**12,758**	**4,121**	**6,182**
5	Rangoon Town ...	5,557	404	5,435	396	122	8	27,763	14,283	15,742	9,175	7,770	1,571	4,168
6	Insein ...	3,210	166	3,132	148	78	18	5,218	3,015	3,781	2,081	1,038	611	334
7	Hanthawaddy .	3,105	105	3,051	77	54	28	19,872	11,450	16,592	9,555	1,792	1,004	1,399
8	Tharrawaddy ...	1,668	53	1,666	47	2	6	1,454	437	952	247	453	149	47
9	Pegu ...	3,502	341	3,408	328	94	13	7,281	4,136	5,589	3,296	1,455	679	182
10	Prome ...	409	20	396	20	13	..	1,030	497	725	350	250	87	52
	Irrawaddy Division ...	**13,098**	**779**	**11,975**	**470**	**1,123**	**309**	**12,848**	**4,796**	**8,081**	**2,921**	**3,180**	**1,009**	**1,469**
11	Bassein ...	2,599	76	2,475	67	124	9	1,479	421	952	232	411	111	109
12	Henzada ...	2,283	79	2,193	75	85	4	1,052	404	511	131	449	232	89
13	Myaungmya ..	3,458	174	3,174	102	284	72	2,259	653	1,201	522	944	288	104
14	Ma-ubin ..	2,145	109	1,999	79	146	30	1,460	486	614	178	789	275	34
15	Pyapôn .	2,613	341	2,129	147	484	194	6,598	2,832	4,803	2,058	587	103	1,133
	Tenasserim Division	**6,808**	**258**	**6,605**	**229**	**203**	**29**	**16,933**	**9,031**	**12,249**	**6.975**	**3,825**	**1,500**	**721**
16	Toungoo ..	1,892	80	1,779	74	113	6	1,534	521	817	285	479	73	205
17	Salween ...	92	...	91	...	1	...	13	..	9	...	3	...	1
18	Thatôn ...	1,570	109	1,517	93	53	16	7,687	4,385	6,522	3,860	985	468	142
19	Amherst ..	1,810	53	1,788	50	22	3	7,205	4,011	4,597	2,764	2,242	956	308
20	Tavoy ..	884	13	882	9	2	4	392	91	258	53	83	4	42
21	Mergui ...	560	3	548	3	12	...	102	23	46	13	33	7	23
	Magwe Division ..	**2,840**	**48**	**2,809**	**48**	**31**	...	**1,126**	**567**	**532**	**309**	**358**	**94**	**228**
22	Thayetmyo ...	156	13	143	13	7	...	261	199	208	166	16	2	32
23	Pakôkku ...	38	...	33	...	5	...	129	46	83	13	32	10	22
24	Minbu ...	703	19	687	19	16	.	97	51	29	18	46	15	22
25	Magwe ...	1,949	16	1,946	16	3	...	689	270	212	112	264	67	147
26	Pakôkku Hill Tracts	...	..	...	...	...	...	...	1	...	..	...	.	...
	Mandalay Division ..	**2,245**	**121**	**2,204**	**104**	**41**	**17**	**3,334**	**2,214**	**1,852**	**1,187**	**481**	**168**	**1,021**
27	Mandalay ...	1,232	102	1,216	89	16	13	2,925	2,107	1,580	1,132	360	142	964
	Mandalay City ...	*970*	*56*	*958*	*54*	*12*	*2*	*1,486*	*890*	*756*	*488*	*337*	*57*	*382*
28	Bhamo ..	14	4	13	..	1	4	62	23	43	17	5	2	14
29	Myitkyina ..	625	7	617	7	8		102	32	71	20	6	...	24
30	Katha ...	370	8	354	8	16	..	240	49	156	18	60	19	16
31	Putao ...	4	..	4	...	...	...	5	3	2	...	...	...	3
	Sagaing Division ...	**619**	**35**	**603**	**32**	**16**	**3**	**534**	**259**	**219**	**118**	**139**	**86**	**169**
32	Shwebo ...	197	23	185	20	12	3	209	77	68	27	89	14	52
33	Sagaing ...	145	10	144	10	1	...	189	100	85	46	41	17	57
34	Lower Chindwin ...	54	.	51	..	3	...	65	38	25	12	9	2	30
35	Upper Chindwin ...	223	2	223	2	...	.	54	31	33	26	...	3	21
36	Chin Hills ...	...	...	...	...	...	...	17	13	8	7	...	...	9
	Meiktila Division ...	**1,880**	**98**	**1,820**	**29**	**60**	**69**	**1,716**	**905**	**1,018**	**474**	**489**	**264**	**201**
37	Kyauksè ...	219	16	211	9	8	7	124	70	58	30	42	14	24
38	Meiktila ...	260	11	248	11	12	...	649	398	355	240	204	91	85
39	Yamèthin ..	1,268	71	1,237	9	31	62	650	351	409	161	190	144	43
40	Myingyan ...	133	...	124		9	...	293	86	196	43	53	15	44
	EASTERN STATES ..	**2,912**	**26**	**2,862**	**22**	**50**	**4**	**413**	**141**	**250**	**65**	**41**	**5**	**93**
41	Northern Shan States	2,328	22	2,312	19	16	3	267	95	181	57	24	5	59
42	Southern Shan States	525	4	491	3	34	1	141	46	69	8	13	...	33
43	Karenni ...	59	...	59	...	...	...	5	...	...	...	4	...	1

Selected Indian Races by Districts (concluded).

...tian.	Others.		TELUGU. Total.		Hindu and Animist.		Christian.		Others.		OTHER INDIAN RACES. Total.		Hindu and Animist.		Mahomedan.		Others.		Serial No. of Dist. or State (col. 1).
Females.	Males.	Females.	Males.	Females.	Males.	Females.	Males.	Females.	Males.	Females.	Males.	Females.	Males.	Females.	Males.	Females.	Males.	Females.	
39	40	41	42	43	44	45	46	47	48	49	50	51	52	53	54	55	56	57	
7,591	**649**	**201**	**129,566**	**28,621**	**125,413**	**27,095**	**1,521**	**603**	**2,632**	**923**	**76,578**	**29,820**	**38,143**	**15,653**	**32,449**	**12,147**	**5,986**	**2,020**	
7,530	**620**	**191**	**129,455**	**28,592**	**125,312**	**27,075**	**1,513**	**594**	**2,630**	**923**	**69,075**	**27,289**	**32,292**	**13,808**	**31,137**	**11,561**	**5,646**	**1,920**	
6	**9**	...	**865**	**24**	**839**	**23**	**2**	**1**	**24**	..	**1,788**	**489**	**1,127**	**825**	**517**	**187**	**144**	**27**	
6	6	...	787	19	770	18	2	1	15	...	1,078	205	557	121	378	57	143	27	1
...	...	...	6	..	6	..	...	...	...	..	338	170	338	170	...	...	...	...	2
...	...	...	43	1	38	1	.	...	5	...	145	56	80	8	65	48	...	.	3
...	3	.	29	4	25	4	..	.	4		227	58	152	26	74	32	1	..	4
4,903	**297**	**90**	**82,911**	**17,609**	**81,041**	**16,805**	**878**	**381**	**992**	**423**	**23,889**	**8,397**	**7,896**	**2,658**	**13,996**	**4,930**	**1,997**	**809**	
3,490	83	17	56,884	9,192	55,704	8,776	726	289	454	127	16,866	5,955	4,788	1,452	10,725	3,969	1,353	534	5
290	65	13	3,662	1,401	3,568	1,226	28	23	66	152	2,280	728	1,201	353	935	316	144	59	6
872	89	19	10,450	2,031	10,337	1,994	53	26	60	11	907	372	255	61	417	192	235	119	7
37	2	4	2,337	793	2,293	790	12	3	32	.	1,048	289	305	89	712	188	31	12	8
154	55	7	7,490	3,657	7,162	3,490	57	39	331	128	1,848	787	1,067	625	623	111	158	51	9
60	3		2,088	535	2,037	529	2	1	49	5	940	266	280	78	584	154	76	34	10
833	**118**	**33**	**15,826**	**3,215**	**14,625**	**2 891**	**379**	**143**	**822**	**181**	**4 194**	**977**	**1,539**	**314**	**2,369**	**589**	**286**	**74**	
78	7	.	5,967	1,028	5,714	978	34	12	119	38	839	103	195	12	610	90	34	1	11
39	3	2	1,711	439	1,624	396	5	1	82	42	856	228	388	82	402	114	66	32	12
37	10	6	2,203	298	1,913	236	63	43	227	19	687	212	186	80	480	129	21	3	13
18	23	15	1,992	349	1,817	316	90	9	85	24	778	253	161	46	540	193	77	14	14
661	75	10	4,053	1,101	3,557	965	187	78	309	58	1,034	181	609	94	337	63	88	24	15
515	**138**	**41**	**23,399**	**5,998**	**22,681**	**5,843**	**170**	**28**	**548**	**127**	**10,488**	**5,277**	**5,446**	**3,724**	**4,700**	**1,424**	**287**	**129**	
160	33	3	2,501	822	2,328	772	18	...	155	50	4,549	3,398	3,361	3,205	1,107	170	81	23	16
...	...	-	42	10	37	10	.	..	5	...	170	69	117	31	24	14	29	24	17
60	38	5	4,673	1,812	4,557	1,780	16	4	100	23	1,400	155	342	25	1,053	127	5	3	18
258	58	33	10,538	2,560	10,330	2,494	47	24	161	42	2,214	1,392	742	344	1,373	976	99	72	19
34	9	...	858	98	817	98	13	..	28		1,000	206	463	101	503	98	34	7	20
3	...	...	4,787	696	4,612	689	76	...	99	7	1,100	57	421	18	640	39	39	...	21
163	**13**	**1**	**2,496**	**182**	**2,426**	**165**	**13**	**5**	**57**	**12**	**2,745**	**777**	**1,146**	**378**	**1,313**	**312**	**286**	**87**	
31	5	..	215	48	195	45	8	1	12	2	501	202	178	71	305	122	18	9	22
23	2	...	102	15	86	15	.	...	16	.	416	110	135	24	212	71	79	15	23
18	...	...	42	14	36	14	2	...	4	.	718	168	361	111	239	18	118	39	24
90	6	1	2,137	105	2,109	91	3	4	25	10	965	254	342	132	552	98	71	24	25
1	...	..	...	...	...	...	...	...	...	...	145	43	140	40	5	3	...	...	26
856	**30**	**8**	**2,132**	**751**	**1,963**	**632**	**48**	**23**	**121**	**96**	**16,160**	**6,241**	**10,720**	**4,871**	**3,751**	**928**	**1,689**	**447**	
825	21	8	1,833	679	1,715	561	48	23	70	95	6,598	2,051	3,583	1,245	2,267	577	748	229	27
339	*11*	*6*	*827*	*263*	*737*	*231*	*35*	*10*	*55*	*21*	*3,111*	*856*	*837*	*312*	*1,789*	*421*	*485*	*123*	
4	...	...	19	13	17	12	...	...	2	1	2,121	427	649	153	828	142	644	132	28
12	1	...	23	22	22	22	...	...	1	...	4,881	2,600	4,360	2,438	299	84	2.2	78	29
12	8	.	256	37	208	37	...	...	48	...	1,800	943	1,410	825	337	116	53	2	30
3	...	...	1	..	1	...	...		...	..	760	220	718	210	20	4	22	6	31
104	**7**	**1**	**411**	**165**	**398**	**148**	**7**	**8**	**6**	**9**	**6,828**	**4,142**	**3,148**	**1,122**	**3,188**	**2,838**	**492**	**182**	
36	...	...	95	56	95	48	..	-	..	8	3,045	2,855	308	80	2,569	2,700	168	75	32
36	6	1	149	59	146	58	2	1	1	...	249	80	102	34	92	23	55	23	33
24	1	...	131	44	124	36	5	7	2	1	713	158	387	109	307	49	19	...	34
2	...	..	36	6	33	6	...	...	3	...	1,790	576	1,358	442	198	56	234	78	35
6	...	..	...	...	...	...	...	...	...	...	1,031	473	993	457	22	10	16	6	36
150	**8**	**17**	**1,415**	**648**	**1,339**	**568**	**16**	**5**	**60**	**75**	**3,038**	**989**	**1,270**	**416**	**1 808**	**408**	**465**	**165**	
26	...	...	56	25	46	25	1	...	9	.	219	79	128	43	45	11	46	25	37
61	5	6	196	71	173	45	8	...	15	26	907	290	326	110	401	124	180	56	38
35	3	11	1,048	541	1,013	487	7	5	28	49	1,552	531	657	208	664	244	231	79	39
28	...	...	115	11	107	11	.	...	8	...	360	89	159	55	193	29	8	5	40
61	**29**	**10**	**111**	**29**	**101**	**20**	**8**	**9**	**2**	...	**7 503**	**2,531**	**5,851**	**1,845**	**1,312**	**586**	**340**	**100**	
31	3	2	51	14	49	12	1	2	1	-	4,100	1,032	3,138	832	720	145	242	55	41
30	26	8	54	15	46	8	7	7	1	..	3,188	1,417	2,539	983	553	389	96	45	42
...	...	...	6	...	6	...	...	..	...	...	215	82	174	30	39	52	2	...	43

NOTE.—The title given in the heading below the serial number of each people is only an approximate description

Serial No.	DISTRICT OR STATE.	TOTAL POPULATION.		PEOPLE I. Burma and Mon Groups.		PEOPLE II. Christian Karens.		PEOPLE III. Non-Christian Karens.		PEOPLE IV. Other Indigenous Races.	
		Males.	Females.	Males.	Females.	Males.	Females.	Males.	Females.	Males.	Females.
	1	2	3	4	5	6	7	8	9	10	11
	PROVINCIAL TOTAL ...	**6,735,516**	**6,433,583**	**4,412,232**	**4,586,521**	**88,879**	**89,346**	**523,237**	**518,894**	**871,897**	**874,840**
	DIVISIONAL BURMA ...	**5,991,623**	**5,706,785**	**4,315,496**	**4,492,189**	**81,193**	**81,668**	**421,201**	**412,843**	**380,293**	**382,329**
	Arakan Division ...	**472,227**	**437,019**	**288,476**	**296,209**	**48**	**6**	**21**	**2**	**43,641**	**41,676**
1	Akyab	309,564	266,866	154,486	151,481	1	2	...	...	22,170	20,965
2	Hill District of Arakan ...	10,790	10,124	1,079	985	...	...	1	...	9,110	8,947
3	Kyaukpyu	96,569	103,304	84,831	93,533	...	...	...	...	8,406	7,825
4	Sandoway	55,304	56,725	48,080	50,210	47	4	20	2	3,955	3,939
	Pegu Division ...	**1,258,914**	**1,050,379**	**847,844**	**857,934**	**15,428**	**15,952**	**50,989**	**51,862**	**18,706**	**17,789**
5	Rangoon Town ..	236,689	105,273	52,543	50,675	843	771	165	144	251	275
6	Insein	156,794	1[illegible]6,289	107,550	104,168	6,272	6,498	11,887	12,442	2,886	2,863
7	Hanthawaddy ...	201,043	163,581	132,088	128,630	742	680	13,133	13,326	3,026	3,075
8	Tharrawaddy ...	246,261	246,168	217,043	225,913	3,283	3,653	10,136	10,245	2,464	2,250
9	Pegu	235,324	210,296	172,694	170,507	4 227	4,298	13,885	13,786	4,140	3,543
10	Prome	182,803	188,772	165,926	177,741	61	52	1,783	1,919	5,939	5,733
	Irrawaddy Division ...	**1,048,377**	**981,667**	**764,353**	**768,585**	**38,962**	**40,233**	**148,070**	**146,938**	**2,947**	**2,510**
11	Bassein	252,947	236,526	173,332	173,340	15,501	15,940	39,230	40,992	594	452
12	Henzada	273,439	277,481	236,065	247,365	5,093	5,506	18,903	19,427	1,949	1,730
13	Myaungmya	196,757	1[illegible]3,794	122,572	116,984	9,862	10,103	42,079	42,072	109	100
14	Ma-ubin	168,513	161,593	109,778	115,978	5,554	5,757	40,301	36,781	40	48
15	Pyapôn	156,721	132,273	122,606	114,915	2,952	2,927	7,557	7,666	255	180
	Tenasserim Division ...	**847,445**	**766,078**	**458 635**	**452,113**	**24,705**	**24,520**	**220,163**	**212,476**	**28,086**	**24,267**
16	Toungoo	197,505	184,378	125,124	126,417	16,833	16,968	25,283	23,471	8,334	7,247
17	Salween	26,811	23,568	1,116	799	430	314	21,853	20,714	2,534	1,583
18	Thatôn	245,909	225,191	91,239	89,118	1,637	1,735	121,789	118,458	4,109	3,435
19	Amherst	223,348	194,562	131,440	126,483	1,860	1,725	40,852	39,205	6,874	6,199
20	Tavoy	80,994	75,792	68,224	68,766	1,058	1,088	4,073	4,163	50	21
21	Mergui	72,878	62,587	41,492	40,530	2,887	2,690	6,313	6,465	6,185	5,782
	Magwe Division ...	**705,247**	**733,527**	**645,497**	**686,473**	**195**	**29**	**59**	**24**	**40,433**	**42,321**
22	Thayetmyo	125,283	130,123	111,783	118,101	37	6	21	12	10,390	10,456
23	Pakôkku	223,943	241,828	212,715	231,515	81	3	10	...	9,304	9,753
24	Minbu	134,495	139,807	120,870	128,059	30	4	16	12	10,358	10,949
25	Magwe	211,686	211,566	200,041	208,755	44	13	12	...	782	1,050
26	Pakôkku Hill Tracts ...	9,840	10,2[illegible]3	88	43	3	3	...	...	9,599	10,113
	Mandalay Division ...	**435,894**	**413,467**	**229,495**	**233,978**	**626**	**163**	**134**	**23**	**148,626**	**151,917**
27	Mandalay	182,999	173,622	143,442	152,280	72	67	7	11	3,953	1,935
	Mandalay City ...	*77,763*	*71,154*	*57,043*	*59,099*	*44*	*44*	*6*	*11*	*274*	*117*
28	Bhamo	56,888	56,072	13,232	11,891	195	41	11	...	38,835	42,630
29	Myitkyina	63,419	54,963	17,793	16,164	28	17	20	2	36,343	35,109
30	Katha	128,444	125,281	54,960	53,620	331	38	96	10	66,441	68,985
31	Putao	4,144	3,529	68	23	...	...	.	...	3,054	3,258
	Sagaing Division ...	**641,290**	**709,106**	**527,529**	**599,245**	**218**	**72**	**66**	**20**	**96,762**	**100,919**
32	Shwebo	184,708	206,576	177,977	201,967	112	26	29	16	68	16
33	Sagaing	155,054	171,854	151,427	169,533	10	14	27	...	354	373
34	Lower Chindwin ...	156,693	186,187	154,522	185,511	43	21	1	2	29	15
35	Upper Chindwin ...	90,713	88,532	43,547	42,203	43	5	9	2	43,472	45,194
36	Chin Hills	54,122	55,957	56	31	10	6	...	..	52,839	55,321
	Meiktila Division ...	**582,229**	**615,542**	**553,667**	**597,652**	**1,011**	**693**	**1,699**	**1,498**	**1,092**	**980**
37	Kyauksè	70,449	72,228	66,345	68,962	16	22	1	...	75	60
38	Meiktila	137,573	152,324	132,038	149,264	221	17	61	191	65	27
39	Yamèthin	160,913	162,276	144,653	151,530	762	645	1,635	1,305	941	890
40	Myingyan	213,294	228,714	210,631	227,896	12	9	2	2	11	3
	EASTERN STATES ...	**743,893**	**726,798**	**96,736**	**94,332**	**7,686**	**7,678**	**102,036**	**106,051**	**491,604**	**492,511**
41	Northern Shan States ...	285,700	273,523	24,150	22,274	65	19	685	380	222,757	227,293
42	Southern Shan States ...	427,004	420,554	71,250	71,007	2,920	2,780	84,092	85,359	261,631	258,890
43	Karenni	31,129	32,721	1,336	1,051	4,701	4,879	17,259	20,312	7,216	6,328

PART IV.—*Peoples.*

of the persons included in that people. For a more precise description see the lower part of the next page.

PEOPLE V.		PEOPLE VI.		PEOPLES VII AND VIII.				PEOPLES IX AND X.				PEOPLES XI AND XII.		PEOPLE XIII.		Serial No. of District or State (col. 1).
Chinese.		Burma Moslems.		Other Mahomedans (*i.e.*, all not in People V or VI).				Hindus, Indian Animists, Sikhs, Aryas and Brahmos.				European and allied races and Anglo-Indians.		Others.		
				VII—Born in Burma.		VIII—Born outside Burma.		IX—Born in Burma.		X—Born outside Burma.						
Males.	Females.	Males.	Females.	Males.	Females.	Males.	Females.	Males.	Females.	Males.	Females.	Males.	Females.	Males.	Females.	
12	13	14	15	16	17	18	19	20	21	22	23	24	25	26	27	
101,877	**47,183**	**57,869**	**59 388**	**109,382**	**108,664**	**146,200**	**17,572**	**53,892**	**45,871**	**333,539**	**63,116**	**14,573**	**10,432**	**21,939**	**11,756**	
70,977	**25,049**	**57,339**	**59,006**	**108,975**	**108,027**	**143,924**	**17,331**	**52,800**	**44,874**	**323,720**	**61,712**	**14,144**	**10,167**	**21,561**	**11,590**	
633	**178**	**14,966**	**13,491**	**79,248**	**77,428**	**7,894**	**5, 0**	**1,044**	**887**	**14,072**	**720**	**274**	**142**	**1,910**	**570**	
480	152	12,721	11,035	77,773	75,748	26,242	5,442	888	767	12,835	599	250	125	1,718	550	1
...	...	...	...	6	2	37	1	121	100	293	71	8	1	135	17	2
88	17	243	193	1,242	1,472	1,095	234	25	3	600	22	5	2	34	3	3
65	9	2,002	2,263	227	206	520	33	10	17	344	28	11	14	23	...	4
29,294	**11,887**	**8,246**	**8,509**	**8,822**	**8,980**	**60,589**	**6,679**	**25,469**	**21,269**	**174,344**	**36,644**	**8,225**	**6,017**	**10,958**	**6,907**	
15,928	7,891	4,220	4,338	4,033	3,843	41,132	4,225	6,805	5,977	96,435	16,967	6,957	5,081	7,377	5,086	5
2,614	709	524	510	1,426	1,446	3,435	643	3 043	2,381	15,961	3,449	524	508	672	372	6
3,272	941	1,558	1,248	983	1,395	7,010	617	6,727	5,658	30,014	6,723	453	224	2,037	1,064	7
1,888	508	786	737	433	633	2,504	315	822	693	6,721	1,120	76	55	105	46	8
4,467	1,513	600	623	1,349	1,414	4,991	700	7,571	6,151	20,617	7,388	146	112	637	261	9
1,125	325	558	1,053	598	249	1,517	179	501	409	4,596	997	69	37	130	78	10
18,891	**3,469**	**3,504**	**3,561**	**4,573**	**4,930**	**20,434**	**1,207**	**4,430**	**3,102**	**43,016**	**5,376**	**412**	**231**	**3,785**	**1,525**	
3,146	812	2,008	2,016	685	669	4,355	217	807	589	12,561	1,224	234	137	491	138	11
1,594	409	388	446	1,050	1,168	1,875	274	636	419	5,577	621	72	54	237	62	12
3,657	834	640	585	1,223	1,573	7,111	303	503	386	8,361	636	38	16	602	202	13
2,015	372	386	391	944	1,052	3,007	207	487	361	5,573	548	39	15	389	83	14
3,479	1,042	82	123	671	468	4,086	206	1,997	1,347	10,941	2,347	29	9	2,066	1,040	15
16,203	**6,546**	**12,378**	**13,659**	**9,724**	**8,841**	**16,943**	**1,513**	**12,229**	**10,638**	**45,048**	**9,289**	**1,411**	**1,324**	**1,925**	**892**	
2,107	653	882	1,406	1,241	899	3,310	331	3,110	2,049	10,451	3,410	293	391	534	236	16
112	5	20	25	31	41	358	13	30	21	277	27	11	2	39	24	17
3,002	1,423	2,114	2,697	1,874	1,504	4,883	287	4,264	3,738	10,684	2.615	40	22	274	109	18
5,091	3,342	5,818	5,803	4,174	4,109	6,244	497	4,488	3,629	15,078	2,343	757	780	672	447	19
2,493	222	727	873	161	117	947	39	167	121	2,800	249	150	76	144	57	20
3,398	901	2,812	2,855	2,243	2,171	1,231	346	170	130	5,755	645	160	53	262	19	21
1,451	**307**	**1,183**	**1,262**	**769**	**718**	**3,495**	**314**	**1,089**	**785**	**9,973**	**886**	**569**	**192**	**534**	**216**	
282	79	437	551	242	231	495	35	402	335	1,052	250	42	20	100	47	22
230	36	123	133	118	144	457	44	101	52	674	104	42	17	88	27	23
417	90	250	230	95	108	497	42	189	122	1,667	162	45	11	61	18	24
522	102	373	348	314	233	2,041	192	373	254	6,461	352	438	144	285	123	25
...	...	...	...	...	2	5	1	24	22	119	18	2	...	...	1	26
7,178	**2,067**	**7,027**	**7,908**	**1,880**	**2,053**	**8,573**	**1,060**	**5,761**	**5,840**	**22,233**	**5,485**	**2,651**	**1,882**	**1,710**	**1,091**	
1,846	420	6,436	7,297	1,352	1,438	5,829	779	3,604	3,860	12,670	2,833	2.380	1,708	1,408	994	27
1,448	*327*	*4,626*	*5,363*	*686*	*832*	*4,287*	*516*	*2,166*	*2,514*	*5,715*	*1,181*	*867*	*744*	*601*	*406*	
1,207	622	175	145	117	136	1,249	121	229	169	1,494	240	70	32	74	45	28
1,999	294	149	186	112	100	634	97	1,332	1,300	4,857	1,616	71	49	81	29	29
1,952	719	266	280	298	378	836	60	497	397	2,511	686	124	91	132	17	30
174	12	1		1	1	25	3	99	114	701	110	6	2	15	6	31
805	**198**	**1,846**	**2,098**	**2,619**	**3,072**	**2,574**	**279**	**1,641**	**1,302**	**6,687**	**1,621**	**223**	**131**	**320**	**149**	
358	83	681	742	2 337	2,827	885	119	363	299	1,727	388	77	47	94	47	32
118	19	1,006	1,136	72	57	475	55	363	333	1,054	262	49	32	89	40	33
188	61	61	91	141	92	592	48	132	109	890	184	37	17	57	36	34
107	16	96	129	58	82	604	54	456	223	2,207	587	43	16	71	21	35
34	19	2	...	11	14	18	3	387	338	799	200	17	19	9	6	36
1,522	**397**	**8,194**	**8,518**	**1,340**	**2,005**	**3,422**	**569**	**1,137**	**1,051**	**8,347**	**1,691**	**379**	**248**	**419**	**240**	
172	64	2,600	2,759	114	38	176	47	140	126	734	106	29	13	47	31	37
346	41	856	1,046	616	714	891	154	270	300	1,910	392	154	101	145	77	38
705	195	4,583	4,464	514	1,239	1,786	308	512	492	4,513	993	158	121	151	94	39
299	97	155	249	96	14	569	60	215	133	1,190	200	38	13	76	38	40
30,900	**22,134**	**530**	**382**	**407**	**637**	**2.276**	**241**	**1,092**	**997**	**9,819**	**1,404**	**429**	**265**	**378**	**166**	
28,928	21,754	191	149	183	147	1,399	141	411	409	6,490	753	299	149	142	55	41
1,773	362	318	205	197	436	778	91	669	573	3,087	627	119	113	230	111	42
199	18	21	28	27	54	99	9	12	15	242	24	11	3	6	...	43

IMPERIAL TABLE XIII—*Race.* PART V.—*Classification by People and Religion.*

The titles of Peoples in column 2 are approximately correct abbreviations of the full descriptions given in Note 9 which is printed below the table. The upper line of figures for each people represents males; the lower line (in italics) females.

People.		Total for all religions.	Buddhists.	Animists.	Hindus.	Mahomedans.	Christians.	Others.
No.	Title.							
1	2	3	4	5	6	7	8	9
	Total ...	6,735,516 *6,433,583*	5,525,159 *5,676,784*	369,188 *333,399*	378,177 *106,255*	314,587 *186,065*	132,498 *124,608*	15,967 *6,472*
I	Burma and Môn Groups	4,412,232 *4,586,521*	4,382,832 *4,555,629*	22,351 *22,560*	... ...	... ...	7,049 *8,332*	... ...
II	Christian Karens ...	88,879 *89,346*	... ...	... ...	... ...	... ..	88,879 *89,346*	... ...
III	Non-Christian Karens ...	523,237 *518,894*	475,514 *468,364*	47,723 *50,530*	... ...	... ..	... ...	... ...
IV	Other Indigenous Races ...	871,897 *874,840*	641,393 *641,531*	223,393 *226,265*	.. ..	.. ...	7,111 *7,043*	... *1*
V	Chinese	101,877 *47,183*	19,282 *9,677*	70,716 *32,624*	.. ...	1,076 *441*	839 *274*	9,964 *4,167*
VI	Burma Moslems ...	57,869 *59,388*	...	.. ...	... ...	57,869 *59,388*	... ...	. ...
VII	Other Mahomedans — Born in Burma.	109,382 *108,664*	... ..	... ...	. ...	109,382 *108,664*	... ...	... ...
VIII	Other Mahomedans — Born outside Burma.	146,200 *17,572*	... .	... ...	... ...	146,200 *17,572*	... .	... ...
IX	Hindus, Indian Animists, etc. — Born in Burma.	53,892 *45,871*	... ..	751 *546*	52,635 *44,870*	.. ..	... ...	506 *455*
X	Hindus, Indian Animists, etc. — Born outside Burma.	333,539 *63,116*	.. ...	4,254 *874*	325,542 *61,385*	... ..	... ..	3,743 *857*
XI	European and allied races	6,115 *2,202*	4 ...	... ...	... ..	... ...	6,084 *2,198*	27 *4*
XII	Anglo-Indians ...	8,458 *8,230*	11 *16*	... ...	... ...	... ...	8,444 *8,214*	3 ...
XIII	Others	21,939 *11,756*	6,123 *1,567*	... ...	... ...	.. .	14,092 *9,201*	1,724 *988*

NOTE 9.—The titles of the peoples in Parts IV and V give a short approximate description of their constitutions. More precise descriptions are given below, and the racial composition of each people is shown numerically in the Appendix to Imperial Table XX :—

I.—All Buddhists, Animists and Christians of the Burma and Mon Groups (A and K) and also Buddhists and Animists of all races in Group S. (Christians of Group S are in People XIV).

II.—Christian Karens (Christians of Group N).

III.—All non-Christian Karens, except Hindus and Mahomedans. (No Hindu or Mahomedan Karens were recorded.)

IV.—All persons of indigenous races (*i.e.*, Groups A to O) except Hindus, Mahomedans and persons included in Peoples I to III.

V.—Yunnanese and all other Chinese of whatever religion.

VI.—Mahomedan Zerbadis * and Arakan-Mahomedans.

VII. } VIII. } Mahomedans other than Chinese, Zerbadis and Arakan Mahomedans { VII Born in Burma †. VIII Born outside Burma †.

IX. } X. } Hindus, Animists of an Indian race, Sikhs, Aryas and Brahmos { IX Born in Burma †. X Born outside Burma †.

XI.—European and allied races as defined in Imperial Table XVI.

XII.—Anglo-Indians, including all persons descended partly from persons of Peoples I to X or of Indian races of People XIII and partly from persons of People XI.

XIII.—All others. In particular this people includes all Armenians and all Indian and Zerbadi * Christians and the Goa-Portuguese described in the note to Part A of Imperial Table XVI, as well as all Jains, Jews and Parsis, and all other races of Group Z.

* This term Zerbadi is used to represent the persons of mixed Indian and indigenous descent who are often called Burma Muslims or Pathis but are more commonly known by this description, which has the advantage of including those of similar descent who are not Mahomedans.

† *Burma* here represents, as everywhere in this report, the whole province, including the Shan States and Karenni.

IMPERIAL TABLE XIV.

Age and Civil Condition by Sex amongst Selected Races.

NOTE 1.—This table supplements Imperial Tables VIIA and VIIB which shew age, sex and civil condition by religion, and it is presented in two parts. Part I gives the statistics for samples of the indigenous race-groups or races and of the Yünnanese, Other Chinese, Mahomedan Zerbadis and Arakan-Mahomedans respectively; while Part II gives them for samples of the six Indian races most largely represented in Burma.

NOTE 2.—In both parts of the table the statistics relate to a representative sample of each race defined by an area of enumeration consisting of whole districts. In Part I the districts selected for each race are generally those in which the principal part of that race was enumerated, and in some cases separate statistics are given for one race in two or more areas in which the statistics indicate that for the subject of this table conditions are different; in the case of the Karens twelve districts shown in the table have been selected in which one or other kind of Karen is numerous, and statistics have been given for each kind throughout all those districts. In Part II the samples represented are those for whom statistics of birth-places are given in Imperial Table XIB, and the title-page of that table should be consulted for particulars.

NOTE 3.—The letters and numbers prefixed to the names of race-groups and races in the first column of the table are the group-letters and numbers assigned to each in Imperial Table XIII and serve to identify them in that table.

NOTE 4.—The age recorded was the number of completed years. The age-group represented by 5–10 in the table includes all who had completed five but had not yet completed ten years of age; and the other age-groups have a parallel interpretation.

NOTE 5.—Similar statistics are given for certain races in some districts separately in Provincial Table IV and for certain races in some towns in Provincial Table V. Imperial Tables VIA or VIB and XIII show also that in some districts one or other religion is almost confined to one race, so that the statistics given in Imperial Table VIIB for those districts and that religion may be regarded with sufficient accuracy as proportional statistics for that race. Statistics for age, but not for civil condition, are given for Europeans, Anglo-Indians and Armenians in Imperial Table XVI.

Imperial Table XIV.—*Age, Sex and Civil Condition for*

Description of Sample.						Unmarried.					
	Race.	Religion.	Districts.	Sex.	Total persons.	All ages.	Age 0	1–5	5–10	10–12	12–15
	1	2	3	4	5	6	7	8	9	10	11
A2 A3 A4	Arakanese, and Yanbye and Chaungtha.	Buddhist ...	Akyab, Kyaukpyu, and Sandoway.	M F	246,579 254,351	127,235 111,527	5,626 6,077	23,707 24,076	32,658 32,214	13,297 12,460	16,773 15,486
A9	Danu ...	Buddhist ...	N. and S. Shan States.	M F	35,904 36,190	21,019 18,383	1,108 1,187	3,533 3,643	4,732 4,762	1,683 1,724	2,503 2,409
A10	Intha ...	Buddhist ...	Southern Shan States	M F	26,088 27,036	15,247 13,919	573 622	2,427 2,391	3,615 3,624	1,467 1,295	1,780 1,705
A11	Taungyo ...	Buddhist ...	Southern Shan States.	M F	11,762 11,689	6,816 6,083	563 580	810 869	1,681 1,524	650 628	755 833
B7	Akha ...	Animist ...	Southern Shan States.	M F	18,225 15,848	8,784 6,066	100 102	1,413 1,420	2,364 1,954	812 549	935 707
							0—5				
C	Kuki-Chin Group	Animist ...	Ten districts shown in the three following entries.	M F	102,707 104,293	57,922 52,154	13,261 13,526		14,014 14,067	6,280 5,795	5,653 4,990
			Chin Hills, Pakôkku Hill Tracts and the Hill District of Arakan.	M F	70,081 72,989	40,501 37,674	9,009 9,401		9,844 9,746	4,477 4,160	3,658 3,270
			Akyab, Kyaukpyu, Pakôkku and Minbu.	M F	24,063 22,748	13,062 10,534	3,252 3,073		3,157 3,309	1,353 1,186	1,413 1,231
			Sandoway, Prome and Thayetmyo.	M F	8,563 8,556	4,359 3,946	1,000 1,052		1,013 1,012	450 449	582 489
E	Kachin Group ..	Animist ...	Bhamo, Myitkyina and Northern Shan States.	M F	63,520 69,868	35,645 31,233	6,132 6,695		7,727 7,440	3,292 3,210	3,186 2,938
	Do. ...	Do. ...	Northern Shan States.	M F	27,158 29,544	14,773 12,933	415 480	2,624 2,663	3,687 3,240	1,426 1,306	1,141 961
I	Tai Group (Shans, etc.).	Buddhist ...	Bhamo, Myitkyina, Katha and Upper Chindwin.	M F	112,979 115,555	62,123 57,162	2,897 3,438	11,182 11,908	14,486 15,269	5,734 5,641	7,191 7,318
I	Tai Group (Shans, etc.) other than Khun.	Buddhist ...	N. and S. Shan States.	M F	324,481 326,849	174,780 146,448	7,559 8,004	30,082 31,162	40,009 40,455	14,308 14,455	19,631 16,816
I7	Khun ...	Buddhist ...	Southern Shan States.	M F	16,329 17,014	8,429 7,309	285 309	1,478 1,568	1,768 1,945	709 630	1,212 847
K1	Talaing ...	Buddhist ...	Amherst and Thatôn.	M F	129,577 126,090	79,812 71,399	3,994 4,015	16,129 15,706	19,078 18,144	6,980 6,288	9,299 9,082
L10	Palaung and Pale	Buddhist ...	Northern Shan States.	M F	52,322 52,819	30,408 27,360	1,135 1,191	5,418 5,782	6,556 6,466	3,037 2,973	2,779 2,677

Selected Races. PART I.—*Indigenous and closely related races.*

[*Continued on next page.*

				Married.							Widowed or divorced.					
15–20	20–40	40–60	60 and over.	All ages.	Age 10–12	12–15	15–20	20–40	40–60	60 and over.	All ages.	Age 12–15	15–20	20–40	40–60	60 and over.
12	13	14	15	16	17	18	19	20	21	22	23	24	25	26	27	28
22,282	11,191	1,252	449	101,365	...	21	1,836	54,707	35,052	9,749	17,979	...	231	7,409	6,250	4,079
14,577	5,546	728	363	102,371	140	209	9,795	60,292	27,770	4,165	40,453	42	1,723	11,453	15,051	12,184
3,647	3,288	426	99	12,374	...	...	150	5,835	5,037	1,352	2,511	...	20	695	1,037	759
2,985	1,429	182	62	12,769	...	...	935	7,436	3,861	537	5,038	...	135	1,213	1,917	1,773
2,556	2,505	257	67	9,157	...	...	147	4,877	3,394	739	1,684	...	10	478	719	477
2,187	1,652	322	121	9,246	..	...	874	5,562	2,479	331	3,871	...	76	927	1,690	1,178
1,148	1,059	119	31	4,154	...	...	56	2,070	1,661	367	792	...	7	240	361	184
1,041	529	60	19	3,699	...	...	282	2,337	1,133	147	1,707	...	17	351	752	587
1,976	1,117	53	14	8,133	...	...	266	4,877	2,412	578	1,308	...	29	511	464	304
1,006	296	24	8	7,958	...	...	508	5,081	2,025	344	1,824	...	1	326	813	684
		40 and over.							40 and over.						40 and over.	
8,916	9,134	664		40,107	...	8	673	20,823	18,603		4,678	..	85	1,668	2,925	
7,265	5,397	1,114		41,372	...	53	2,849	26,785	11,685		10,767	...	124	2,390	8,253	
6,361	6,648	504		26,738	...	8	358	13,809	12,563		2,842	...	57	987	1,798	
5,397	4,708	992		27,514	...	19	1,616	18,135	7,744		7,801	...	66	1,798	5,937	
1,791	1,984	112		9,690	...	...	248	5,064	4,378		1,311	...	22	519	770	
1,218	446	71		10,214	...	27	986	6,452	2,749		2,000	...	42	392	1,566	
764	502	48		3,679	...	...	67	1,950	1,662		525	...	6	162	357	
650	243	51		3,644	...	7	247	2,198	1,192		966	...	16	200	750	
5,863	8,908	537		25,547	...	...	459	12,453	12,635		2,328	...	11	727	1,590	
5,167	5,138	645		27,126	...	25	1,679	17,652	7,770		11,509	...	22	2,347	9,140	
2,210	3,014	224	32	11,517	...	...	180	5,638	4,433	1,266	868	...	4	296	425	143
1,969	2,046	201	67	11,704	...	...	679	7,324	3,109	592	4 907	...	20	876	1,892	2,119
9,722	9,599	1,016	296	45,002	...	...	763	23,073	17,474	3,692	5,854	...	45	1,815	2,292	1,702
8,784	3,894	575	335	45,382	...	26	3,109	27,038	13,620	1,589	13,011	..	209	2,613	5,306	4,883
29,491	30,362	2,612	726	124,227	...	2	1,730	58,241	50,467	13,787	25,474	...	301	9,642	9,202	6,329
22,154	11,441	1,225	736	126,662	...	170	11,377	74,505	35,783	4,827	53,739	4	1,882	12,708	18,874	20,271
1,400	1,410	133	34	6,798	...	...	69	3,455	2,757	517	1,102	...	6	424	367	305
1,416	496	64	34	7,151	...	...	407	4,483	2,041	220	2,554	...	40	634	927	953
13,048	9,848	1,065	371	44,091	...	...	489	24,209	14,794	4,599	5,674	...	28	1,499	2,075	2,072
11,767	5,674	494	229	45,583	...	5	2.454	28,017	12,907	2,200	9,108	...	185	2,360	3,373	3,190
5,036	5,748	508	191	18,958	...	2	165	9,236	7,035	2,520	2,956	...	17	863	1,111	965
4,669	3,052	334	216	19,211	...	22	1,070	11,718	4,600	1,801	6,248	...	70	1,403	2,304	2,471

IMPERIAL TABLE XIV.—*Age, Sex and Civil Condition for*

Description of Sample.						Unmarried.					
	Race.	Religion.	Districts.	Sex.	Total persons.	All ages.	Age 0	1–5	5–10	10–12	12–15
	1	2	3	4	5	6	7	8	9	10	11
N1	Karen (unspecified kind*).	Buddhist ...	(As in Imperial Table IX) Rangoon, Insein, Hanthawaddy, Tharrawaddy, Pegu, Bassein, Henzada, Myaungmya, Ma-ubin, Toungoo, Amherst and Thatôn. NOTE.—But the figures for *Other Karens, Buddhists*, exclude the Taungthu Buddhists of Thatôn District for which separate figures are given below.	M F	11,141 10,871	7,130 6,347	225 226	1,390 1,405	1,563 1,520	688 659	722 692
	Do. ...	Christian †		M F	10,404 10,525	6,117 5,724	252 257	1,058 1,048	1,377 1,336	584 525	791 661
N2	Sgaw ...	Buddhist ...		M F	133,234 132,693	82,358 74,225	3,159 3,420	15,413 15,476	17,626 17,052	7,242 7,055	8,810 7,842
	Do. ..	Christian †		M F	41,387 43,146	24,565 24,827	947 937	4,372 4,600	5,100 5,389	2,177 2,104	2,999 2,959
N9	Pwo ...	Buddhist		M F	187,779 183,114	114,157 99,995	4,465 4,390	21,082 21,081	25,593 22,609	10,355 9,335	12,743 11,949
	Do ...	Christian †		M F	12,900 12,996	7,683 7,442	295 291	1,407 1,407	1,709 1,792	712 644	1,011 916
N various.	Other Karens ...	Buddhist ... (*See note in column* 3.)		M F	7,759 7,438	4,340 3,768	187 167	772 579	919 884	323 335	439 439
	Do. ...	Christian †		M F	7,016 6,967	4,257 3,899	137 138	684 684	934 914	394 391	552 471
N11	Taungthu ...	Buddhist ..	Thatôn ...	M F	26,813 25,845	15,658 13,592	760 773	2,935 2,856	3,381 3,031	1,503 1,237	1,827 1,739
	Do. ...	Do. ...	Southern Shan States.	M F	73,408 75,122	43,101 38,557	1,824 2,077	7,204 7,187	9,893 10,273	4,138 3,935	5,481 4,654
N15	Karenni ...	Animist ...	Karenni States ..	M F	12,043 14,976	7,112 7,542	317 361	1,718 1,772	1,968 1,981	706 646	742 769
R1	Yünnanese ..	All except Mahomedans	Northern Shan States.	M F	28,394 21,637	15,097 10,047	0–5 2,943 3,031		3,505 3,167	1,251 956	1,368 1,050
R2	Other Chinese .	All ...	The whole province	M F	66,125 23,703	34,708 13,104	4,561 3,565		4,604 3,443	1,752 1,221	2,554 1,663
S2	Zerbadi ...	Mahomedan	The whole province	M F	45,129 48,353	29,103 26,529	0 1,402 1,465	1–4 5,832 5,624	6,882 6,916	2,590 2,173	3,650 3,766
S1	Arakan-Mahomedans		The whole province	M F	12,740 11,035	7,240 5,586	299 314	1,329 1,479	1,798 1,921	703 683	945 720

* That is, described only as *Karen* in the enumeration-record without specification of a particular kind of Karen.
† See the appendix to this table for tabulation by sect.

Selected Races. PART I.—*Indigenous and closely related races*—concluded.

				Married.							Widowed or divorced.					
15–20	20–40	40–60	60 and over.	All ages.	Age 10–12	12–15	15–20	20–40	40–60	60 and over.	All ages.	Age 12–15	15–20	20–40	40–60	60 and over.
12	13	14	15	16	17	18	19	20	21	22	23	24	25	26	27	28
1,012	1,391	121	18	3,332	...	...	36	1,680	1,348	268	679	...	1	179	325	174
1,057	667	93	28	3,597	...	...	180	2,385	925	107	927	...	5	170	455	297
948	1,036	67	10	3,867	...	...	37	2,140	1,365	325	420	...	...	138	168	124
978	813	81	25	3,854	...	...	266	2,606	908	74	947	...	16	204	499	228
12,600	15,767	1,380	351	44,295	1	5	372	23,064	15,899	4,954	6,581	.	10	1,686	2,773	2,172
11,883	10,106	1,063	328	46,667	...	10	2,364	29,410	12,928	1,955	11,801	2	76	2,707	5,155	3,861
4,026	4,532	327	85	14,934	...	2	117	7,529	5,714	1,572	1,888	...	...	493	769	626
4,349	3,705	631	103	14,725	...	...	536	9,143	4,273	773	3,594	...	23	750	1,645	1,170
18,713	18,755	1,973	479	65,158	...	4	1,029	35,802	21,920	6,403	8,464	2	31	2,200	3,437	2,704
17,186	11,818	1,234	393	68,544	...	7	3,189	42,503	19,642	3,203	14,575	...	135	3,379	6,036	5,085
1,233	1,185	98	33	4,565	...	...	44	2,462	1,591	468	652	...	1	148	290	213
1,310	952	106	21	4,641	...	...	189	2,851	1,389	212	913	...	15	213	382	303
668	910	93	29	2,979	...	...	46	1,563	1,031	339	440	...	4	137	179	120
641	639	65	19	2,770	...	...	208	1,722	736	104	900	...	6	280	394	220
643	843	55	15	2,027	...	...	26	1,179	714	108	732	.	...	119	382	231
680	511	68	18	2,310	...	3	128	1,585	548	40	758	...	3	215	391	149
2,471	2,468	250	63	9,431	...	...	116	5,172	3,173	970	1,724	...	3	484	697	540
2,326	1,388	154	88	9,519	...	11	644	6,000	2,551	313	2,734	...	42	697	1,169	826
7,167	6,587	653	154	25,670	..	...	330	12,503	10,082	2,755	4,637	.	45	1,576	1,623	1,387
6,082	3,691	494	154	25,827	...	44	1,870	15,332	7,496	1,085	10,738	...	262	2,703	4,084	3,689
809	791	49	12	4,107	...	...	83	2,770	1,441	171	524	..	13	193	210	168
1,043	941	67	22	4,583	...		221	3,373	920	69	2,851	...	30	924	1,404	493
		40 and over.							40 and over.						40 and over.	
2,522	2,694	814		11,548	...	6	328	2,920	8,310		1,749	...	15	227	1,507	
1,345	417	81		9,348	.	14	653	6,335	2,346		2,242	...	...	340	1,902	
4,318	13,547	3,372		28,198	...	14	230	15,278	12,676		3,219	...	4	990	2,285	
1,659	1,286	267		8,832	...	29	449	6,089	2,265		1,767	...	17	427	1,323	
4,204	4,092	352	99	14,208	...	10	289	8,309	4,478	1,122	1,818	...	17	598	652	551
3,534	2,523	420	108	16,900	...	11	1,671	10,987	3,739	492	4,924	...	84	1,278	2,053	1,509
1,074	1,008	57	27	4,538	...	1	96	2,616	1,428	397	952	...	6	374	387	195
985	133	34	17	4,267	3	68	857	2,618	650	71	1,182	13	61	325	512	271

IMPERIAL TABLE XIV.—*Age, Sex and Civil Condition*

NOTE 1.—The statistics in this table represent the total of the specified races in the following districts: Akyab

NOTE 2.—The entries *In* and *Out* in column 3 relate to persons

Selected Indian Races in the districts noted above.				Total persons.	Unmarried.					
Race	Religion.	Birth-place (see note 2 above).	Sex.		All ages.	Age 0	1–5	5–10	10–12	12–15
1	2	3	4	5	6	7	8	9	10	11
Bengali	Hindus and Animists	In	M	900	759	80	227	226	59	43
			F	698	576	73	208	199	44	32
		Out	M	9,155	3,671	24	101	139	99	152
			F	1,560	413	20	96	127	45	43
	Mahomedans ...	In	M	11,919	7,680	310	1,651	2,135	772	838
			F	10,160	5,666	315	1,496	1,946	612	659
		Out	M	28,393	11,891	28	171	268	193	515
			F	2,308	633	17	114	189	90	82
Chittagonian	Hindus and Animists	In	M	196	114	6	31	26	12	14
			F	128	75	5	26	26	3	5
		Out	M	4,677	1,660	5	18	27	26	59
			F	120	28	2	12	10	2	1
	Mahomedans ...	In	M	71,843	46,421	2,145	12,174	13,694	4,763	5,589
			F	70,705	38,082	1,931	12,059	13,564	4,020	3,802
		Out	M	44,330	16,912	30	221	340	271	747
			F	4,270	812	13	146	265	110	123
Hindustani	Hindus and Animists	In	M	10,509	8,117	351	2,303	2,389	643	589
			F	6,779	5,266	344	1,802	1,832	508	381
		Out	M	53,606	20,089	64	435	660	477	783
			F	8,591	1,753	46	328	457	196	134
	Mahomedans ...	In	M	2,311	1,704	96	356	407	159	154
			F	2,078	1,330	94	410	394	121	125
		Out	M	14,974	4,900	10	106	212	171	317
			F	2,067	424	11	84	135	47	30
Oriya	Hindus and Animists	In	M	1,000	808	37	177	183	65	63
			F	512	393	24	143	121	39	36
		Out	M	31,314	16,292	5	71	166	297	815
			F	1,090	262	9	37	62	25	24
Tamil	Hindus and Animists	In	M	18,359	15,110	712	3,494	4,053	1,331	1,622
			F	16,494	11,777	801	3,592	4,054	1,158	1,130
		Out	M	44,828	21,134	75	771	1,268	794	1,379
			F	18,435	3,754	114	652	1,006	418	446
	Mahomedans ...	In	M	4,177	3,125	166	692	788	279	399
			F	3,700	2,335	138	669	741	220	257
		Out	M	14,183	6,193	9	120	300	343	800
			F	2,466	568	12	95	163	64	76
Telugu	Hindus and Animists	In	M	9,743	7,697	455	1,835	1,999	633	700
			F	7,683	5,539	459	1,843	1,845	497	408
		Out	M	98,865	32,657	75	681	1,578	1,280	2,222
			F	16,094	3,216	81	649	905	311	307

for Selected Races. PART II.—*Indian Races.*

Rangoon, Insein, Hanthawaddy, Pegu, Bassein, Myaungmya, Pyapôn, Toungoo, Thatôn, Amherst, Mandalay and Yamèthin. born in Burma and persons born outside Burma respectively.

				Married.							Widowed or divorced.					
15–20	20–40	40–60	60 and over.	All ages.	Age 10-12	12–15	15–20	20–40	40–60	60 and over.	All ages	Age 12–15	15–20	20 40	40–60	60 and over.
12	13	14	15	16	17	18	19	20	21	22	23	24	25	26	27	28
47	71	5	1	124	2	...	...	86	32	4	17	...	...	8	5	4
7	9	3	1	99	...	4	24	66	5	..	23	...	...	11	8	4
658	2,297	180	21	5,110	1	4	68	3,519	1,364	164	374	...	1	190	138	45
27	50	3	2	1,007	3	17	163	695	119	10	140	...	2	44	66	28
962	894	94	24	3,721	...	6	100	2,403	924	288	518	..	9	257	159	93
405	188	33	12	3,689	...	42	704	2,321	559	63	805	3	55	259	329	159
2,015	7,817	754	130	14,655	...	9	258	9,785	3,880	723	1,847	2	24	915	588	318
53	68	16	4	1,284	...	9	168	807	276	24	391	1	13	84	158	135
9	14	2	...	69	...	...	...	43	19	7	13	...	...	5	6	2
6	4	...	...	44	...	4	7	24	9	...	9	...	...	3	2	4
410	1,043	61	11	2,783	..	...	35	1,851	786	111	234	...	2	108	90	34
...	1	...	...	78	...	...	16	56	6	..	14	...	1	7	4	2
5,320	2,575	114	47	23,537	...	28	622	14,617	6,144	2,126	1,885	...	43	827	531	484
1,804	714	100	48	25,901	...	531	5,056	15,897	4,048	369	6,722	9	262	2,040	2,615	1,796
3,908	10,548	723	124	25,644	2	13	506	17,066	6,704	1,353	1,774	1	13	844	576	340
63	73	16	3	2,374	6	36	237	1,290	698	107	1,084	2	13	168	487	414
620	1,053	148	21	2,152	...	1	364	1,184	498	105	240	...	1	121	76	42
907	172	17	3	1,330	7	14	288	847	156	18	183	...	10	68	61	44
2,274	12,922	2,197	277	30,026	8	41	913	19,969	7,868	1,227	3,491	2	42	1,601	1,364	482
138	353	80	21	6,006	7	16	411	4,163	1,101	208	832	...	16	174	346	296
213	280	34	5	543	...	2	25	349	137	30	64	...	1	26	24	13
112	73	1	...	662	..	3	98	458	93	10	86	...	...	37	34	15
736	2,836	436	76	9,220	...	14	284	5,845	2,652	425	854	...	5	375	312	162
33	67	14	3	1,464	1	9	105	1,048	267	34	179	...	...	39	84	56
90	170	20	3	169	...	...	9	110	41	9	23	...	...	12	7	4
17	13	...	...	106	...	...	28	67	11	...	13	...	1	5	5	2
2,930	10,550	1,343	115	13,406	3	24	419	9,370	3,321	269	1,616	...	38	884	561	133
38	55	11	1	745	...	5	60	547	121	12	83	...	1	28	42	12
1,675	1,975	211	37	2,823	2	5	99	2,007	613	97	426	...	6	172	177	71
686	311	29	16	4,130	8	37	766	2,904	367	48	587	1	40	262	211	73
2,937	11,594	1,969	347	20,708	12	14	275	11,806	7,173	1,428	2,986	...	13	911	1,452	610
391	512	174	41	12,267	6	49	937	8,724	2,307	244	2,414	50	19	524	1,204	617
399	372	24	6	950	...	...	17	641	236	56	102	...	...	50	30	22
201	97	8	4	1,177	1	13	205	792	143	23	188	..	5	77	66	40
1,486	2,749	315	71	7,430	2	7	103	4,636	2,195	487	560	...	2	199	203	156
72	68	13	5	1,577	2	12	128	1,085	303	47	321	1	2	62	142	114
709	1,210	125	31	1,800	3	...	92	1,278	368	59	246	..	1	121	88	36
328	140	14	5	1,881	11	19	319	1,328	168	36	263	1	12	110	107	33
5,715	18,046	2,764	296	62,628	19	77	1,703	43,831	15,319	1,679	3,580	1	39	1,467	1,498	575
246	580	117	20	11,180	39	51	838	8,319	1,721	212	1,698	1	17	425	852	403

Appendix.—*Karen Christians by Sect and Sex and Age.*

Note.—This table relates to the Christian Karens shown in Part I of the table.

Race.		Sect.	Sex.	All ages.	0–10	10–15	15–20	20–30	30 and over.
1	2	3	4	5	6	7	8	9	10
N1	Karen (unspecified kind).	All ...	M	10,404	2,687	1,375	979	1,684	3,679
			F	10,525	2,641	1,186	1,260	2,135	3,303
		Anglican ...	M	1,023	260	155	95	146	367
			F	989	269	108	103	168	341
		Baptist ...	M	5,653	1,247	735	592	977	2,102
			F	5,735	1,273	669	762	1,199	1,832
		Roman Catholic	M	3,727	1,180	485	292	561	1,209
			F	3,795	1,098	407	395	767	1,128
		Other Sects ..	M	1	...	...	...	..	1
			F	6	1	2	...	1	2
N2	Sgaw ...	All ...	M	41,387	10,410	5,178	4,143	6,878	14,769
			F	43,146	10,926	5,063	4,908	8,145	14,104
		Anglican ...	M	398	102	48	39	75	134
			F	443	109	58	56	85	135
		Baptist ...	M	36,674	9,179	4,582	3,691	6,147	13,075
			F	38,399	9,742	4,497	4,353	7,262	12,545
		Roman Catholic	M	4,229	1,116	535	406	640	1,532
			F	4,270	1,065	504	493	794	1,414
		Other Sects ..	M	86	22	13	7	16	28
			F	34	10	4	6	4	10
N9	Pwo ...	All ...	M	12,900	3,411	1,723	1,278	2,059	4,429
			F	12,996	3,490	1,560	1,514	2,328	4,104
		Anglican ...	M	481	133	85	42	50	171
			F	450	113	49	54	82	152
		Baptist ...	M	9,422	2,445	1,248	921	1,520	3,288
			F	9,316	2,517	1,115	1,079	1,656	2,949
		Roman Catholic	M	2,990	833	389	314	487	967
			F	3,214	853	396	378	587	1,000
		Other Sects ..	M	7	...	1	1	2	3
			F	16	7	...	3	3	3
...	Other Karens	All ...	M	7,016	1,755	946	669	1,068	2,578
			F	6,967	1,760	865	811	1,391	2,140
		Anglican ...	M	1,215	336	167	100	162	450
			F	1,266	332	157	143	244	390
		Baptist ...	M	4,485	1,088	589	432	707	1,669
			F	4,311	1,047	529	495	901	1,339
		Roman Catholic	M	1,316	331	190	137	199	459
			F	1,390	381	179	173	246	411
		Other Sects ...	M	0	...	...	...	...	...
			F	0	...	...	...	...	...

IMPERIAL TABLE XV.

Christians classified by Sect and Race.

NOTE 1.—This table consists of two parts. In Part I Christians are divided by race into the four classes: (A) Indigenous races, (B) Europeans and allied races and Armenians, (C) Anglo-Indians, (D) Others; and each class is classified by sect in every district. In Part II of the table the totals for the province for the more numerous sects are classified in greater detail by race, and the term *Christian Races* is used to include both classes B and C of Part I. The term *Indigenous Races* includes all the races included in groups A to O in the system adopted for Table XIII and described in the preface to that table; it does not include Zerbadis. The term *European and Allied Races* and the term *Anglo-Indian* are explained in Notes 1, 3 and 4 of Table XVI.

NOTE 2.—The table relates to the same area as Table VI, and to the persons tabulated as Christians in that table; the discrepancy between it and Tables VII, VIII and XVI is explained by Note 3 of Table VIA and Notes 3 and 4 of Table XVI.

NOTE 3.—The term *Sect* is used in this table as a generic name for the religious classes of the tabulation. The Methodist sect includes Wesleyans and Episcopal Methodists; the Baptist sect includes both English and American Baptists; the Protestant sect consists of those who described themselves only as Protestants without further particularisation; in other cases *Sect* is synonymous with *Church* or *Denomination*.

NOTE 4.—The sects included under *Others* are shown in the following sub-table in the notes to which are given details for the larger contributions to the figures by districts other than Rangoon Town. A similar table for Rangoon Town is given in Note 5. (The letters M and F represent the sexes and A, B, C, D the four classes mentioned in Note 1 above.)

Sect.	Total, all races.		Indigenous races.		Europeans, etc., and Armenians.		Anglo-Indians.		Other races.		See Note.
	M.	F.	M.	F.	M.	F.	M.	F.	M.	F.	
Total ...	723	444	106	58	200	121	45	69	372	196	
Armenian ...	129	99	...	5	110	88	9	6	10	...	a
Congregationalist ...	2	1	...	...	2	1	...	...	...	...	
Greek ...	41	6	...	...	21	...	4	2	16	4	b
Lutheran ...	236	157	...	...	10	1	...	1	226	155	c
Minor Protestant Denominations.	235	134	99	50	11	13	22	49	103	22	
Seventh Day Adventist	*155*	*112*	*20*	*28*	*11*	*13*	*22*	*49*	*102*	*22*	d
Silein ...	*80*	*22*	*79*	*22*	...	...	...	...	*1*	...	e
Protestant ...	74	32	5	2	44	17	10	8	15	5	f
Salvation Army ...	6	15	2	1	2	1	...	3	2	10	

(*a*) Insein, M: 6B, 1C; F: 9B. Tavoy, M: 9B; F: 4B. Mandalay, M: 5B; F: 1A, 12B.
(*b*) Mandalay, M: 1B, 4C; F: 2C. Shwebo, M: 12D.
(*c*) The few who are not in Rangoon are widely scattered.
(*d*) Hanthawaddy, M: 3B, 14D; F: 10D. Myaungmya, M: 77D; F: 12D. Salween, M: 6A, 2B; F: 12A, 2B. Meiktila, M: 7A, 3C, 2D; F: 6A, 1B, 8C.
(*e*) Hanthawaddy, M: 27. Insein, M: 43, F: 4. Tharrawaddy, M: 5, F: 14. Ma-ubin, M 5, F 4. All are Sgaw Karens with the exception of one Bengali male in Hanthawaddy. The sect is of local origin.
(*f*) Hanthawaddy, M: 7B, 2C. Magwe, M: 11B, 2C; F: 8B.

NOTE 5.—The details of sects included under *Others* for Rangoon Town are as follows:—

Sect.	Total, all races.		Indigenous races.		Europeans, etc., and Armenians.		Anglo-Indians.		Other races.	
	M.	F.	M.	F.	M.	F.	M.	F.	M.	F.
Total ...	424	307	10	15	139	81	29	41	246	170
Armenian	95	71	...	3	88	63	7	5	...	...
Greek	22	3	...	...	18	...	...	...	4	3
Lutheran	221	153	...	...	5	...	...	1	216	152
Seventh Day Adventist ...	36	47	7	9	4	10	16	28	9	...
Protestant	44	18	1	2	22	7	6	4	15	5
Salvation Army	6	15	2	1	2	1	...	3	2	10

NOTE 6.—Further particulars for Christians of some races will be found in Imperial Table XIII and in Part A-1 of Imperial Table XVI.

Serial No.	District or State.	ALL DENOMINATIONS. Total. Persons.	Total. Males.	Total. Females.	Distribution by Race. Indigenous Races. Males.	Indigenous Races. Females.	European and Allied Races and Armenians. Males.	European and Allied Races and Armenians. Females.	Anglo-Indians. Males.	Anglo-Indians. Females.	Others. Males.	Others. Females.
	1	2	3	4	5	6	7	8	9	10	11	12
	Provincial Total ...	**257,108**	**132,498**	**124,608**	**103,039**	**104,721**	**8,269**	**2,361**	**8,444**	**8,214**	**14,746**	**9,312**
	Divisional Burma ...	**234,438**	**120,975**	**113,463**	**92,177**	**93,971**	**8,045**	**2,228**	**8,230**	**8,079**	**14,523**	**9,185**
	Arakan Division ...	*1,724*	*992*	*732*	*582*	*577*	*133*	*27*	*141*	*116*	*136*	*13*
1	Akyab ...	618	428	190	43	52	121	22	129	103	135	13
2	Hill Dist. of Arakan	14	11	3	3	2	5	1	3	...	.	...
3	Kyaukpyu ...	136	65	71	59	69	3	...	2	2	1	...
4	Sandoway ...	956	488	468	477	454	4	4	7	10	...	..
	Pegu Division ...	*65,030*	*34,457*	*30,573*	*17,816*	*18,743*	*3,297*	*1,201*	*5,034*	*4,918*	*8,310*	*5,711*
5	Rangoon City ...	25,275	14,208	11,067	1,429	1,833	2,924	1,004	4,144	4,178	5,711	4,052
6	Insein ...	15,579	7,688	7,891	6,727	7,040	93	94	437	423	431	334
7	Hanthawaddy ...	5,074	3,022	2,052	889	846	209	70	239	148	1,685	988
8	Tharrawaddy ...	8,074	3,970	4,104	3,811	4,007	24	11	52	44	83	42
9	Pegu ...	9,790	4,918	4,872	4,451	4,534	18	15	127	97	322	226
10	Prome ...	1,238	651	587	509	483	29	7	35	28	78	69
	Irrawaddy Division ...	*86,608*	*43,464*	*43,144*	*40,242*	*41,525*	*150*	*54*	*262*	*177*	*2,810*	*1,388*
11	Bassein ...	32,630	16,207	16,423	15,733	16,185	89	31	145	105	240	102
12	Henzada ...	11,742	5,711	6,031	5,521	5,931	23	14	49	40	118	46
13	Myaungmya ...	21,198	10,645	10,553	10,150	10,348	5	2	33	14	457	189
14	Ma-ubin ...	11,984	5,976	6,008	5,747	5,945	19	5	20	10	190	50
15	Pyapôn ...	9,054	4,925	4,129	3,091	3,118	14	2	15	7	1,805	1,002
	Tenasserim Division ...	*55,883*	*28,250*	*27,633*	*25,658*	*25,669*	*375*	*193*	*1,043*	*1,135*	*1,174*	*636*
16	Toungoo ...	35,442	17,624	17,818	17,075	17,250	78	66	216	325	255	177
17	Salween ...	758	442	316	430	314	11	2	...	...	1	...
18	Thatôn ...	3,811	1,920	1,891	1,697	1,796	7	1	35	21	181	73
19	Amherst ...	7,074	3,596	3,478	2,349	2,351	134	80	625	703	488	344
20	Tavoy ...	2,645	1,371	1,274	1,132	1,158	80	35	72	42	87	39
21	Mergui ...	6,153	3,297	2,856	2,975	2,800	65	9	95	44	162	3
	Magwe Division ...	*2,110*	*1,342*	*768*	*480*	*384*	*432*	*120*	*736*	*72*	*294*	*192*
22	Thayetmyo ...	465	261	204	172	147	31	6	11	24	47	37
23	Pakôkku ...	307	210	97	131	56	25	7	16	10	38	24
24	Minbu ...	174	118	56	47	27	16	4	29	7	26	18
25	Magwe ...	1,153	746	407	125	151	358	103	80	42	183	112
26	Pakôkku Hill Tracts	11	7	4	5	3	2	...	...	...	...	1
	Mandalay Division ...	*14,151*	*7,658*	*6,493*	*3,661*	*3,626*	*1,412*	*513*	*1,253*	*1,402*	*1,332*	*952*
27	Mandalay ...	8,329	4,506	3,823	861	1,169	1,323	481	1,072	1,260	1,250	913
	Mandalay City ...	*4,160*	*2,083*	*2,077*	*644*	*941*	*356*	*150*	*517*	*603*	*566*	*383*
28	Bhamo ...	4,052	2,056	1,996	1,964	1,958	44	9	26	23	22	6
29	Myitkyina ...	994	535	459	437	393	28	15	42	33	28	17
30	Katha ...	744	537	207	390	104	12	7	112	84	23	12
31	Putao ...	32	24	8	9	2	5	...	1	2	9	4
	Sagaing Division ...	*4,810*	*2,501*	*2,309*	*2,063*	*2,056*	*95*	*56*	*130*	*75*	*213*	*122*
32	Shwebo ...	2,008	1,015	993	865	905	32	19	44	28	74	41
33	Sagaing ...	948	446	502	335	432	8	2	41	30	64	38
34	Lower Chindwin ...	334	194	140	108	88	16	8	25	9	45	35
35	Upper Chindwin ...	695	397	298	333	280	29	11	14	5	21	2
36	Chin Hills ...	825	449	376	424	351	10	16	6	3	9	6
	Meiktila Division ...	*4,122*	*2,311*	*1,811*	*1,675*	*1,391*	*151*	*64*	*231*	*185*	*254*	*171*
37	Kyauksè ...	592	292	300	236	261	15	5	15	8	26	26
38	Meiktila ...	772	532	240	376	75	70	44	84	57	102	64
39	Yamèthin ...	2,416	1,285	1,131	1,052	959	47	12	113	110	73	49
40	Myingyan ...	342	202	140	111	96	19	3	19	10	53	32
	Eastern States ...	*22,668*	*11,523*	*11,145*	*10,862*	*10,760*	*224*	*133*	*214*	*135*	*228*	*127*
41	Northern Shan States	1,929	1,050	879	655	685	151	72	148	77	96	45
42	Southern Shan States	11,137	5,754	5,383	5,502	5,185	65	60	63	56	124	82
43	Karenni ...	9,602	4,719	4,883	4,705	4,880	8	1	3	2	3	...

Christians in Four Race-Classes by Sect.

ANGLICAN.											METHODIST.											
Total.			Distribution by Race.								Total.			Distribution by Races.								Serial No. of District, etc. (column 1).
			Indigenous Races.		European and Allied Races, and Armenians.		Anglo-Indians.		Others.					Indigenous Races.		Europeans, etc		Anglo-Indians.		Others.		
Persons.	Males.	Females.	Males.	Females.	Males.	Females.	Males.	Females.	Males.	Females.	Persons.	Males.	Females.	Males.	Females.	Males.	Females.	Males.	Females.	Males.	Females.	
13	14	15	16	17	18	19	20	21	22	23	24	25	26	27	28	29	30	31	32	33	34	
20,410	**11,489**	**8,921**	**3,976**	**4,078**	**3,315**	**1,246**	**2,771**	**2,612**	**1,427**	**985**	**1,424**	**723**	**701**	**200**	**324**	**179**	**67**	**143**	**174**	**201**	**136**	
20,044	**11,259**	**8,785**	**3,963**	**4,064**	**3,187**	**1,171**	**2,703**	**2,575**	**1,406**	**975**	**1,393**	**702**	**691**	**189**	**318**	**176**	**64**	**139**	**174**	**198**	**135**	
216	*162*	*54*	*4*	*1*	*86*	*15*	*50*	*36*	*22*	*2*	*3*	*3*	...	...	...	*1*	...	*2*	...	..	...	
198	148	50	1	1	82	15	43	32	22	2	...	...	..	...	...	...	...	...	...	...	...	1
2	2	...	...	...	1	...	1	...	...	...	3	3	...	...	...	1	...	2	...	...	...	2
3	3	...	...	...	2	...	1	...	...	...	...	...	.	...	...	...	...	...	...	...	...	3
13	9	4	3	..	1	...	5	4	...	...	...	...	...	...	...	...	...	...	...	...	...	4
8,287	*4,723*	*3,564*	*565*	*656*	*1,566*	*599*	*1,663*	*1,634*	*929*	*675*	*771*	*373*	*398*	*65*	*114*	*55*	*42*	*103*	*129*	*160*	*113*	
6,572	3,773	2,799	215	314	1,406	530	1,344	1,358	808	507	585	280	305	21	61	42	27	87	115	130	102	5
886	460	426	149	163	44	27	202	194	65	42	48	21	27	8	6	3	8	7	10	3	3	6
287	187	100	27	21	79	26	59	37	22	16	105	51	54	30	43	10	7	9	4	2	...	7
174	101	73	52	42	17	5	17	24	15	2	1	1	...	...	...	...	...	...	..	1	..	8
92	47	45	8	13	9	8	24	17	6	7	30	18	12	4	4	..	...	...	...	14	8	9
276	155	121	114	103	11	3	17	4	13	11	2	2	...	2	...	...	...	...	...	...	...	10
1,882	*990*	*892*	*775*	*772*	*59*	*15*	*42*	*27*	*114*	*78*	*18*	*10*	*8*	*1*	*3*	*4*	...	*1*	...	*4*	*5*	
177	119	58	40	29	45	8	23	18	11	3	8	5	3	...	3	4	...	1	...	...	...	11
272	153	119	138	112	1	1	3	4	11	2	...	...	..	...	...	...	...	...	...	...	...	12
940	483	457	390	397	3	2	10	1	80	57	10	5	5	1	...	...	...	...	...	4	5	13
377	179	198	167	191	8	2	3	4	1	1	...	...	...	...	...	...	...	...	...	...	..	14
116	56	60	40	43	2	2	3	...	11	15	...	...	...	...	...	...	...	...	...	...	...	15
6,638	*2,935*	*2,703*	*2,306*	*2,320*	*196*	*80*	*316*	*232*	*117*	*71*	*71*	*37*	*34*	*1*	*14*	*9*	*6*	*12*	*13*	*15*	*1*	
4,764	2,392	2,372	2,233	2,239	38	30	91	85	40	18	37	13	24	...	5	2	6	11	13	...	...	16
4	4	...	..	...	4	...	...	...	...	...	...	...	.	...	...	...	...	...	...	...	...	17
54	40	14	17	7	5	1	0	...	9	6	...	...	..	...	...	...	...	...	...	.	...	18
585	341	244	36	52	79	27	167	119	59	46	25	18	7	...	7	5	...	...	...	13	...	19
95	60	35	5	4	34	16	26	15	5	...	...	...	..	..	...	...	...	...	..	...	...	20
136	98	38	25	18	36	6	33	13	4	1	9	6	3	1	2	2	...	1	...	2	1	21
323	*209*	*114*	*16*	*49*	*133*	*49*	*32*	*9*	*28*	*7*	*94*	*79*	*15*	*5*	*1*	*68*	*7*	...	...	*6*	*7*	
39	30	9	1	2	13	3	5	1	11	3	...	..	...	...	...	...	...	...	...	...	...	22
51	31	20	10	13	10	4	5	3	6	...	9	6	3	...	...	2	...	...	...	4	3	23
13	12	1	1	1	7	...	2	...	2	...	5	4	1	4	1	...	...	...	...	...	...	24
218	134	84	4	33	101	42	20	5	9	4	80	69	11	1	...	66	7	...	...	2	4	25
2	1	...	...	...	2	...	...	..	...	...	...	...	...	...	...	...	...	...	...	...	...	26
2,945	*1,808*	*1,137*	*143*	*130*	*1,021*	*346*	*489*	*562*	*155*	*105*	*239*	*120*	*119*	*48*	*83*	*35*	*3*	*20*	*30*	*17*	*3*	
2,621	1,592	1,029	73	96	955	315	419	523	145	95	238	119	119	48	83	35	3	19	30	17	3	27
844	*507*	*337*	*49*	*63*	*257*	*73*	*147*	*165*	*54*	*36*	*164*	*68*	*96*	*45*	*74*	*2*	*2*	*10*	*17*	*11*	*2*	
83	52	31	9	14	30	5	12	12	1	...	1	1	...	...	...	...	...	1	...	...	...	28
75	48	27	6	1	23	15	18	11	1	...	...	..	...	...	...	...	...	...	...	...	...	29
156	108	48	55	19	10	5	39	15	4	9	...	...	...	...	...	...	...	..	...	...	...	30
10	8	2	...	...	3	...	1	1	4	1	...	...	...	...	..	...	...	...	...	...	...	31
293	*175*	*118*	*40*	*33*	*58*	*40*	*53*	*33*	*24*	*12*	*107*	*54*	*53*	*47*	*45*	*3*	*3*	*1*	...	*3*	*5*	
115	77	38	30	14	18	9	19	10	10	5	...	...	...	...	...	...	...	...	...	...	...	32
66	35	31	4	8	3	1	19	15	9	7	15	10	5	10	5	...	...	...	...	...	...	33
41	20	21	4	9	9	5	6	7	1	...	90	42	48	35	40	3	3	1	...	3	5	34
43	30	13	2	2	21	10	5	1	2	...	2	2	...	2	..	...	...	...	...	...	...	35
38	15	15	...	...	7	15	4	...	2	...	...	...	...	...	...	-	...	...	...	...	...	36
460	*257*	*203*	*114*	*103*	*68*	*33*	*58*	*42*	*17*	*25*	*90*	*26*	*64*	*22*	*58*	*1*	*8*	...	*2*	*3*	*1*	
40	19	21	6	11	4	2	6	3	3	5	41	2	39	2	37	...	2	..	...	...	...	37
88	34	54	4	10	20	23	10	16	...	5	3	1	2	...	1	1	1	...	.	..	...	38
272	156	116	78	77	37	8	36	23	5	8	46	23	23	20	20	...	...	...	2	3	1	39
60	48	12	26	5	7	...	6	...	9	7	...	...	...	...	...	...	...	...	...	...	...	40
366	*230*	*136*	*13*	*14*	*128*	*75*	*68*	*37*	*21*	*10*	*31*	*21*	*10*	*11*	*6*	*3*	*3*	*4*	...	*3*	*1*	
226	152	74	7	8	95	49	37	14	13	3	3	2	1	1	1	...	...	1	...	...	...	41
134	74	60	2	4	33	26	31	23	8	7	38	19	9	10	8	3	3	3	...	3	1	42
6	4	2	4	2	...	...	...	...	...	...	...	...	...	...	...	...	...	...	...	...	...	43

	District or State.	BAPTIST.											PRESBYTERIAN.										
		Total.			Distribution by Race.								Total.			Distribution by Race.							
					Indigenous Races.		Europeans, etc.		Anglo-Indians.		Others.					Indigenous Races.		Europeans, etc.		Anglo-Indians.		Others.	
Serial No.		Persons.	Males.	Females.	Males.	Females.	Males.	Females.	Males.	Females.	Males.	Females.	Persons.	Males.	Females.	Males.	Females.	Males.	Females.	Males.	Females.	Males.	Females.
	1	35	36	37	38	39	40	41	42	43	44	45	46	47	48	49	50	51	52	53	54	55	56
	Provincial Total ...	**160,656**	**80,705**	**79,951**	**78,790**	**77,526**	**508**	**273**	**889**	**780**	**2,518**	**1,372**	**1,508**	**1,171**	**337**	**24**	**15**	**1,027**	**223**	**71**	**68**	**49**	**31**
	Divisional Burma ...	**148,893**	**74,765**	**74,128**	**71,017**	**71,792**	**483**	**257**	**858**	**771**	**2,407**	**1,308**	**1,474**	**1,149**	**325**	**24**	**15**	**1,005**	**211**	**71**	**68**	**49**	**31**
	Arakan Division ...	*923*	*456*	*467*	*441*	*451*	*7*	*4*	*4*	*10*	*4*	*2*	...	...	...	...	...	...	...	...	...	...	...
1	Akyab ...	45	18	27	8	17	4	...	2	8	4	2	...	...	...	...	...	...	...	...	...	...	...
2	Hill Dist. of Arakan	6	4	2	3	2	...	...	1	...	...	...	...	...	...	...	...	...	...	...	...	...	...
3	Kyaukpyu ...	122	55	67	53	65	1	...	1	2	...	...	...	...	...	...	...	...	...	...	...	...	...
4	Sandoway ...	750	379	371	377	367	2	4	...	...	...	...	...	...	...	...	...	...	...	...	...	...	...
	Pegu Division ...	*33,673*	*16,869*	*16,804*	*15,175*	*15,625*	*171*	*107*	*409*	*400*	*1,114*	*672*	*1,186*	*939*	*247*	*4*	*3*	*840*	*161*	*51*	*55*	*44*	*28*
5	Rangoon City ...	3,795	2,043	1,752	1,033	1,071	102	66	261	244	647	371	1,071	868	203	3	2	782	126	43	52	40	33
6	Insein ...	13,235	6,477	6,758	6,275	6,595	21	22	73	63	108	72	17	11	6	...	...	4	5	7	5	...	...
7	Hanthawaddy ...	1,427	760	667	509	472	32	8	43	71	176	116	76	47	29	...	...	47	29	...	...	...	...
8	Tharrawaddy ...	6,130	2,976	3,154	2,937	3,134	1	4	6	1	32	15	15	7	8	...	1	3	2	...	...	4	5
9	Pegu ...	8,425	4,275	4,150	4,128	4,062	4	5	21	11	122	72	2	2	...	...	...	1	...	1	...	...	...
10	Prome ...	661	338	323	293	290	11	2	5	5	29	26	5	4	1	1	...	3	1	...	...	...	...
	Irrawaddy Division ...	*68.028*	*33,571*	*34,457*	*32,946*	*34,122*	*31*	*23*	*76*	*50*	*518*	*262*	*42*	*31*	*11*	*3*	*3*	*20*	*6*	*5*	...	*3*	*2*
11	Bassein ...	29,778	14,806	14,972	14,644	14,907	11	13	36	22	115	30	28	20	8	1	...	13	6	3	...	3	2
12	Henzada ...	7,182	3,366	3,816	3,278	3,765	10	7	24	19	54	25	...	...	...	...	...	...	...	...	...	...	...
13	Myaungmya ...	15,629	7,721	7,908	7,594	7,844	1	...	2	1	124	63	5	2	3	2	3	...	...	...	...	...	...
14	Ma-ubin ...	9,492	4,704	4,788	4,651	4,775	1	3	8	2	44	8	9	9	...	...	...	7	...	2	...	...	...
15	Pyapôn ...	5,947	2,974	2,973	2,779	2,831	8	...	6	6	181	136	...	...	...	...	...	...	...	...	...	...	...
	Tenasserim Division ...	*36,650*	*18,528*	*18,122*	*17,980*	*17,768*	*43*	*36*	*123*	*140*	*382*	*178*	*73*	*45*	*28*	*3*	*4*	*35*	*17*	*5*	*6*	*2*	*7*
16	Toungoo ...	20,006	10,020	9,986	9,935	9,898	11	7	20	34	54	47	19	9	10	...	...	9	5	...	4	...	1
17	Salween ...	692	408	284	405	284	3	...	...	...	...	...	...	...	...	...	...	...	...	...	...	...	...
18	Thatôn ...	3,442	1,682	1,760	1,599	1,720	1	...	6	11	76	29	...	...	...	...	...	...	...	...	...	...	...
19	Amherst ...	4,733	2,372	2,366	2,182	2,176	9	18	78	86	103	86	44	28	16	3	4	20	10	3	2	2	...
20	Tavoy ...	2,360	1,187	1,173	1,112	1,143	13	11	12	4	50	15	...	...	...	...	...	...	...	...	...	...	...
21	Mergui ...	5,412	2,859	2,553	2,747	2,547	6	...	7	5	99	1	10	8	2	...	...	6	2	2	...	...	...
	Magwe Division ...	*970*	*607*	*363*	*343*	*249*	*110*	*24*	*54*	*24*	*100*	*66*	*83*	*66*	*17*	...	*1*	*62*	*14*	*4*	*2*	...	...
22	Thayetmyo ...	309	171	138	139	122	5	...	2	6	25	10	9	9	...	...	...	9	...	...	...	...	...
23	Pakôkku ...	94	72	22	61	16	5	3	3	...	3	3	2	2	...	...	...	2	...	...	...	...	...
24	Minbu ...	96	64	32	38	21	6	3	13	4	7	4	...	...	...	...	...	...	...	...	...	...	...
25	Magwe ...	463	295	168	100	87	94	18	36	14	65	49	72	55	17	...	1	51	14	4	2	...	...
26	Pakôkku Hill Tracts	8	5	3	5	3	...	...	...	...	...	...	...	...	...	...	...	...	...	...	...	...	...
	Mandalay Division ...	*5,291*	*2,740*	*2,551*	*2,429*	*2,346*	*45*	*39*	*105*	*99*	*161*	*67*	*69*	*51*	*18*	*14*	*2*	*36*	*11*	*1*	*5*	...	...
27	Mandalay ...	909	453	456	223	282	36	36	61	81	133	57	62	46	16	12	...	33	11	1	5	...	...
	Mandalay City ...	*500*	*245*	*255*	*127*	*168*	*17*	*12*	*29*	*40*	*72*	*35*	*25*	*17*	*8*	...	...	*17*	*6*	*1*	*2*	...	...
28	Bhamo ...	3,204	1,583	1,621	1,567	1,615	6	2	3	...	7	4	1	1	...	...	...	1	...	...	...	...	...
29	Myitkyina ...	846	443	403	427	388	3	1	8	8	5	6	1	1	...	...	...	1	...	...	...	...	...
30	Katha ...	322	251	71	206	61	...	...	33	10	12	...	...	...	...	...	...	...	...	...	...	...	...
31	Putao ...	10	10	...	6	...	...	...	...	...	4	...	5	3	2	2	2	1	...	...	...	...	...
	Sagaing Division ...	*1,691*	*951*	*740*	*896*	*706*	*13*	*6*	*15*	*9*	*27*	*19*	*12*	*10*	*2*	...	...	*8*	*2*	*2*	...	...	...
32	Shwebo ...	157	121	36	96	17	6	6	5	3	14	10	6	5	1	...	...	4	1	1	...	...	...
33	Sagaing ...	108	48	60	30	51	1	...	7	5	10	4	...	...	...	...	...	...	...	...	...	...	...
34	Lower Chindwin ...	65	44	21	39	18	1	...	2	...	2	3	1	1	...	...	...	1	...	...	...	...	...
35	Upper Chindwin ...	592	317	275	312	274	4	...	1	1	...	...	5	4	1	...	...	3	1	1	...	...	...
36	Chin Hills ...	769	421	348	419	346	1	...	...	...	1	2	...	...	...	...	...	...	...	...	...	...	...
	Meiktila Division ...	*1,667*	*1,043*	*624*	*807*	*525*	*63*	*18*	*72*	*39*	*101*	*42*	*9*	*7*	*2*	...	*2*	*4*	...	*3*	...	...	...
37	Kyauksè ...	57	25	32	16	29	1	1	1	...	7	2	4	4	...	...	...	3	...	1	...	...	...
38	Meiktila ...	469	392	77	249	43	43	14	52	13	48	7	...	...	...	...	...	...	...	...	...	...	...
39	Yamèthin ...	989	528	461	481	423	9	2	13	20	25	16	...	...	...	...	...	...	...	...	...	...	...
40	Myingyan ...	152	98	54	61	30	10	1	6	6	21	17	5	3	2	...	2	1	...	2	...	...	...
	Eastern States ...	*11,763*	*5,940*	*5,823*	*5,773*	*5,734*	*25*	*16*	*31*	*9*	*111*	*64*	*34*	*22*	*12*	...	...	*22*	*12*	...	...	...	...
41	Northern Shan States	1,340	677	663	618	645	8	2	24	5	27	11	32	20	12	...	...	20	12	...	...	...	...
42	Southern Shan States	5,231	2,700	2,531	2,596	2,461	15	13	7	4	82	53	2	2	...	...	...	2	...	...	...	...	...
43	Karenni ...	5,192	2,563	2,629	2,559	2,628	2	1	...	...	2	...	...	...	...	...	...	...	...	...	...	...	...

Christians in Four Race-Classes by Sect.

ROMAN CATHOLIC.											OTHER SECTS.											
Total.			Distribution by Race.								Total.			Distribution by Race.								
			Indigenous Races.		Europeans and Allied Races, and Armenians.		Anglo-Indians.		Others.					Indigenous Races.		Europeans, etc.		Anglo-Indians.		Others.		
Persons.	Males.	Females.	Males.	Females.	Males.	Females.	Males.	Females.	Males.	Females.	Persons.	Males.	Females.	Males.	Females.	Males.	Females.	Males.	Females.	Males.	Females.	Serial No.
57	58	59	60	61	62	63	64	65	66	67	68	69	70	71	72	73	74	75	76	77	78	
71,941	**37,687**	**34,254**	**21,943**	**22,720**	**1,046**	**431**	**4,525**	**4,511**	**10,179**	**6,592**	**1,167**	**723**	**444**	**106**	**58**	**200**	**121**	**45**	**69**	**372**	**196**	
61,477	**32,380**	**29,097**	**16,878**	**17,724**	**996**	**405**	**4,415**	**4,428**	**10,091**	**6,540**	**1,157**	**720**	**437**	**106**	**58**	**198**	**120**	**44**	**63**	**372**	**196**	
578	*368*	*210*	*137*	*125*	*36*	*7*	*85*	*69*	*110*	*9*	*4*	*3*	*1*	...	...	*3*	*1*	...	...	...	...	
372	259	113	34	34	34	7	82	63	109	9	...	...	...	...	...	...	...	...	...	...	...	1
2	2	...	...	...	1	...	1	...	...	...	4	3	1	...	...	3	1	...	...	...	...	2
11	7	4	6	4	...	...	...	...	1	...	...	...	...	...	...	...	...	...	...	...	...	3
193	100	93	97	87	1	...	2	6	...	...	...	...	...	...	...	...	...	...	...	...	...	4
20,230	*11,016*	*9,214*	*1,919*	*2,311*	*509*	*202*	*2,776*	*2,659*	*5,812*	*4,042*	*883*	*537*	*346*	*88*	*34*	*156*	*90*	*32*	*41*	*261*	*181*	
12,521	6,820	5,701	147	370	453	174	2,380	2,368	3,840	2,789	731	424	307	10	15	139	81	29	41	246	170	5
1,330	669	661	252	271	15	25	147	148	255	217	163	50	13	43	4	6	9	1	...	...	...	6
3,115	1,923	1,192	297	310	30	...	126	36	1,470	846	64	54	10	26	...	11	...	2	...	25	10	7
1,729	876	853	813	815	3	...	29	19	31	19	25	9	16	9	15	...	...	...	...	...	1	8
1,241	576	665	311	455	4	2	81	69	180	139	...	...	...	...	...	...	...	...	...	...	...	9
294	152	142	99	90	4	1	13	19	36	32	...	...	...	...	...	...	...	...	...	...	...	10
16,638	*8,778*	*7,760*	*6,512*	*6,621*	*34*	*10*	*138*	*100*	*2,094*	*1,029*	*100*	*84*	*16*	*5*	*4*	*2*	...	...	...	*77*	*12*	
2,637	1,255	1,382	1,048	1,246	14	4	82	66	111	66	...	2	...	...	...	2	...	...	...	...	...	11
4,288	2,192	2,096	2,105	2,054	12	6	22	17	53	19	...	...	...	...	...	...	...	...	...	...	...	12
4,525	2,357	2,168	2,163	2,104	1	...	21	12	172	52	89	77	12	...	...	...	...	...	...	77	12	13
2,097	1,079	1,018	924	973	3	...	7	4	145	41	9	5	4	5	4	...	...	...	...	...	...	14
2,991	1,895	1,096	272	244	4	...	6	1	1,613	851	...	...	...	...	...	...	...	...	...	...	...	15
13,406	*6,682*	*6,724*	*5,362*	*5,550*	*80*	*48*	*585*	*741*	*655*	*385*	*58*	*36*	*22*	*6*	*13*	*23*	*6*	*4*	*3*	*3*	...	
10,614	5,189	5,425	4,917	5,107	17	18	94	189	161	111	2	1	1	...	1	1	...	...	...	...	...	16
40	22	18	19	18	2	...	...	...	1	...	22	8	14	6	12	2	2	...	...	...	...	17
215	198	117	81	69	1	...	20	10	96	38	...	...	...	...	...	...	...	...	...	...	...	18
1,679	834	845	128	112	21	25	377	496	308	212	3	3	...	...	...	...	...	...	...	3	...	19
177	115	62	15	11	24	4	44	23	32	24	13	9	4	...	...	9	4	...	...	...	...	20
581	324	257	202	233	15	1	50	23	57	...	18	15	3	...	...	11	...	4	3	...	...	21
596	*351*	*245*	*116*	*84*	*43*	*16*	*44*	*33*	*148*	*112*	*31*	*17*	*14*	...	...	*5*	*10*	...	*4*	*12*	...	
92	40	52	32	25	4	2	4	3	...	24	16	11	5	...	...	...	1	...	4	11	...	22
151	99	52	60	27	6	...	8	7	25	18	...	...	...	...	...	...	...	...	...	...	...	23
59	37	22	4	4	3	1	14	3	16	14	1	1	...	...	...	...	...	...	...	1	...	24
393	175	118	20	30	30	13	18	20	107	55	14	5	9	...	...	5	9	...	...	...	...	25
1	...	1	...	...	...	...	...	...	...	1	...	...	...	...	...	...	...	...	...	...	...	26
5,569	*2,923*	*2,646*	*1,027*	*1,064*	*268*	*108*	*634*	*700*	*994*	*774*	*38*	*16*	*22*	...	*1*	*7*	*12*	*4*		*5*	*3*	
4,461	2,280	2,181	505	707	257	104	568	615	950	755	38	16	22	...	1	7	12	4	6	5	3	27
2,614	*1,239*	*1,375*	*423*	*635*	*57*	*52*	*330*	*379*	*429*	*309*	*13*	*7*	*6*	...	*1*	*6*	*5*	*1*	...	...	...	
763	419	344	388	329	7	2	10	11	14	3	...	...	...	...	...	...	...	...	...	...	...	28
72	43	29	4	4	1	...	16	14	22	11	...	...	...	...	...	...	...	...	...	...	...	29
266	178	88	129	24	2	2	40	59	7	3	...	...	...	...	...	...	...	...	...	...	...	30
7	3	4	1	...	1	...	...	1	1	3	...	...	...	...	...	...	...	...	...	...	...	31
2,691	*1,296*	*1,395*	*1,080*	*1,272*	*11*	*5*	*58*	*32*	*147*	*86*	*16*	*15*	*1*	...	...	*2*	...	*1*	*1*	*12*	...	
1,717	799	918	739	874	3	3	19	15	38	26	13	13	...	...	...	1	...	...	...	12	...	32
759	353	406	289	368	4	1	15	10	45	27	...	...	...	...	...	...	...	...	...	...	...	33
134	85	49	30	21	1	...	15	1	39	27	3	2	1	...	...	1	...	1	1	...	...	34
53	44	9	17	4	1	...	7	3	19	2	...	...	...	...	...	...	...	...	...	...	...	35
28	15	13	5	5	2	1	2	3	6	4	...	...	...	...	...	...	...	...	...	...	...	36
1,869	*966*	*903*	*725*	*697*	*15*	*9*	*95*	*94*	*131*	*103*	*27*	*12*	*15*	*7*	*6*	...	*1*		*8*	*2*	...	
450	242	208	212	184	7	...	7	5	16	19	...	...	...	...	...	...	...	...	...	...	...	37
185	93	92	16	15	6	5	19	20	52	52	27	12	15	7	6	...	1	3	8	2	...	38
1,109	578	531	473	439	1	2	64	65	40	25	...	...	...	...	...	...	...	...	...	...	...	39
128	53	72	24	59	1	2	5	4	25	7	...	...	...	...	...	...	...	...	...	...	...	40
10,464	*5,307*	*5,157*	*5,065*	*4,996*	*44*	*26*	*110*	*83*	*88*	*52*	*10*		*7*	...	...	*2*	*1*	*1*	*6*	...	...	
328	199	129	29	31	28	9	86	58	56	31	...	...	...	...	...	...	...	...	...	...	...	41
5,732	2,956	2,776	2,894	2,718	10	17	21	23	31	21	10	3	7	...	...	2	1	1	6	...	...	42
4,404	2,152	2,252	2,142	2,250	6	...	3	2	1	...	...	...	...	...	...	...	...	...	...	...	...	43

IMPERIAL TABLE XV, PART II.—*Christians classified by Sect and Race.*

Race-group or Race.	All Sects.		Anglican.		Baptist.		Roman Catholic.		Methodist.		Presbyterian.		Unspecified and Other specified sects. ‡	
	Males.	Females.	Males.	Females.	Males.	Females.	Males.	Females.	Males.	Females.	Males.	Females.	Males.	Females.
1	2	3	4	5	6	7	8	9	10	11	12	13	14	15
Total for all Races ..	132,498	124,608	11,489	8,921	80,705	79,951	37,887	34,254	723	701	1,171	337	723	444
Indigenous Races	*108,039*	*104,721*	*8,976*	*4,078*	*76,790*	*77,526*	*21,948*	*22,720*	*200*	*324*	*24*	*15*	*106*	*58*
Burma group and Talaings* ...	7,049	8,332	588	705	3,489	3,776	2,783	3,552	162	272	6	7	21	20
Karen group	88,879	89,346	3,306	3,276	67,208	67,716	18,241	18,265	35	47	4	6	85	36
Karen (unspecified races †) ...	*11,457*	*10,961*	*1,070*	*1,020*	*6,477*	*6,067*	*3,909*	*3,866*	..	*7*	...	...	*1*	*1*
Sgaw	*48,295*	*49,554*	*470*	*479*	*43,001*	*44,410*	*4,727*	*4,618*	*11*	*12*	*2*	*2*	*84*	*33*
Pwo	*13,887*	*13,807*	*486*	*453*	*10,342*	*10,066*	*3,052*	*3,270*	*5*	*12*	*2*	*4*	...	*2*
Taungthu	*128*	*113*	*1*	*6*	*113*	*96*	*8*	*9*	*6*	*2*	...	...	...	...
Other Karens (specified races)	*15,112*	*14,911*	*1,279*	*1,318*	*7,275*	*7,077*	*6,545*	*6,502*	*13*	*14*	...	..	...	...
Other indigenous races ...	7,111	7,043	82	97	6,093	6,034	919	903	3	5	14	2	..	2
Christian Races	*14,718*	*10,575*	*6,086*	*8,858*	*1,387*	*1,058*	*5,565*	*4,942*	*822*	*241*	*1,098*	*291*	*245*	*190*
European and allied races ...	6,084	2,198	3,283	1,204	475	240	1,030	426	175	66	1,024	223	97	39
Armenians	185	163	32	42	33	33	10	5	4	1	3	...	103	82
Anglo-Indians	8,444	8,214	2,771	7,612	889	780	4,525	4,511	143	174	71	68	45	69
Others	*14,746*	*9,812*	*1,427*	*985*	*2,518*	*1,872*	*10,179*	*6,692*	*201*	*136*	*49*	*81*	*872*	*196*
Chinese	839	274	35	15	378	129	373	102	51	28	1	...	1	...
Tamils and Telegus	11,667	8,194	1,163	865	1,789	1,079	8,281	5,935	118	105	42	30	274	180
Zerbadis	27	19	3	3	10	10	13	5	...	1	1	...	...	...
All others §	2,213	825	226	102	341	154	1,512	550	32	2	5	1	97	16
Total excluding Christian Races. 1921	117,785	114,033	5,403	5,063	79,308	78,898	32,322	29,312	401	460	73	46	478	254
Total excluding Christian Races. 1911	94,980	90,562	5,209	4,790	60,745	59,804	26,746	24,024	670	509	36	31	1,574‡	1,404‡
*Talaings in Amherst and Thatôn Districts, 1921.	274	296	17	18	238	166	19	112	...	...	...	...	...	...

* The total number of Talaing Christians was 363 males and 407 females, of whom 270 males and 286 females were in Amherst District, 4 males and 10 females in Thatôn District and *nil* in Pegu District. Classification by Sect is given for these Districts in the bottom line of the table and is not available for other districts.

† These are persons who described themselves as *Karen* without specifying any particular Karen race.

‡ The figures for *Other Sects* in 1911 include 1,190 males and 1,168 females described as Protestants and 221 males and 127 females described only as Christians. The corresponding figures for 1921 are 74 males and 32 females described as Protestants and *nil* described only as Christians.

§ Includes 2,007 males and 734 females of Indian races.

IMPERIAL TABLE XVI.

European and Allied Races, Anglo-Indians and Armenians Classified by Nationality, Race, Sex and Age.

NOTE 1.—This table has been prepared in three parts A, B and C. Part A relates to European and Allied Races and is itself divided into three sections distinguished as I, II and III, of which Part A-I may be regarded as the definition of the term *European and Allied Races* for the purposes of this Census. In the three sections of Part A persons of European and Allied Races are classified as follows:—

Part A-I.—By race, nationality and sex for the whole province.

Part A-II.—By nationality and sex for each district.

Part A-III.—By nationality, sex and age for each district.

Parts B and C classify Anglo-Indians and Armenians respectively by sex and age in each district. The term *Anglo-Indian* includes all those who were described as such (or as Anglo-Burmans or Euro-Burmans or by other names indicating similar mixed descent) in 1921 before a new definition of *Anglo-Indian* was given in connection with the electoral scheme of 1922.

NOTE 2.—The table covers the whole province except those areas in which the census was only by estimation and those entirely omitted from the census. (*See* Notes 11 and 12 of Imperial Table II.)

NOTE 3.—The numbers given for some districts in columns 7 and 8 of Imperial Table XV for European and allied races and Armenians differ from the corresponding figures of this table because Table XV is confined to Christians, whereas the present table includes some of European and allied races who are not Christians. The number of these in each district is shown at the foot of Part A-I on the next page.

NOTE 4.—Similarly the numbers of Anglo-Indians shown in Part B of this table differ from the numbers shown in columns 9 and 10 of Imperial Table XV because the latter exclude Anglo-Indians who were not Christians. The number of these also in each district is shown at the foot of Part A-I on the next page.

NOTE 5.—The age recorded was the number of completed years. The age-group represented by 30–40 in the table includes all who had completed 30 but had not yet completed 40 years of age; and the other age-groups have a parallel interpretation.

NOTE 6.—All figures given for Mandalay District include the corresponding figures for Mandalay City which are given immediately below them.

Imperial Table XVI, Part A-I.—*European and Allied Races by Nationality and Race.*

Races of the British Empire.			Other Races.				
Race and Important Districts.	British Subjects.		Race and Important Districts.	British Subjects.		Foreign Subjects	
	Males.	Females.		Males.	Females.	Males.	Females.
English ...	3,657	1,239	American ...	50	48	292	167
Rangoon ...	*1,505*	*511*	*Rangoon* ...	22	11	48	54
Mandalay ...	*1,155*	*318*	*Magwe* ...	2	7	165	22
Scotch ...	1,376	299	Austrian ...	...	...	...	2
Rangoon ...	*940*	*153*	Belgian ...	...	1	6	4
Mandalay ...	*62*	*28*	Caucasian ...	2	1	2	3
Irish ...	277	174	Danish ...	1	...	5	1
Rangoon ...	*132*	*82*	Dutch ...	6	8	19	7
Mandalay ..	*36*	*35*	French ...	20	22	70	44
Welsh ...	33	8	*Rangoon* ...	15	13	19	12
Rangoon ...	*13*	*3*	*Mandalay* ...	3	4	16	12
Mandalay ...	*5*	...	German ...	4	2	6	..
British ...	99	28	Greek ...	4	1	14	5
Rangoon ...	*19*	...	Italian ...	5	6	30	34
Mandalay ...	*18*	*8*	*Rangoon* ...	4	3	3	...
Canadian ...	24	20	*Toungoo* ..	...	...	15	17
Magwe ...	*13*	*8*	*Mandalay* ..	...	...	1	8
Australian ..	61	37	Mexican .	...	...	1	...
Rangoon ...	*14*	*10*	Norwegian ..	1	3	...	...
Northern Shan States.	*30*	*19*	Pole ...	1	...	...	...
New Zealander ..	...	1	Portugese* ...	6	2	13	...
Ceylon Burgher ...	3	4	Rumanian ...	1	...	1	...
Maltese ...	1	4	Russian ...	...	...	1	1
			Servian ...	...	...	2	..
			Spanish ...	1	5	2	4
			Swedish ...	...	..	3	...
			Swiss ...	3	2	7	4
			European (Race not specified).	5	1	...	11
Total ..	5,531	1,814	Total ...	110	101	474	287
			Grand Total † ...	5,641	1,915	474	287

* Note.—47 males and 17 females who described themselves as Portugese born in Goa, but speaking the Portugese language have been tabulated as Goa-Portugese and regarded as non-Europeans and included amongst "*Others*" in Imperial Table XV and in People XIV for Imperial Tables XVII, etc.

† See the Explanation below.

Explanation of the Difference between the Numbers of Imperial Tables XV and XVI.

The numbers of persons of European and allied races and Armenians and the numbers of Anglo-Indians shown in columns 7 to 10 of Imperial Table XV are less for certain districts than the corresponding numbers in Imperial Table XVI because the former include only Christians while the latter include also persons of these races who do not follow the Christian religion. If the numbers of Armenians shown in Part C of Table XVI (all of whom are Christians) are subtracted from the numbers in columns 7 and 8 of Table XV the the number of Christians of European and allied races of each sex in each district will be found. The discrepancies then found between Tables XV and XVI in each district arise from the inclusion in Table XVI of the persons represented in the following table :—

European and Allied Races.				Anglo-Indian.			
District.	Religion.	Males.	Females.	District.	Religion.	Males.	Females.
5 Rangoon ...	Agnostic ...	8	...	5 Rangoon ..	Agnostic ...	2	...
	Buddhist ...	2	...		Buddhist ...	9	10
	Freethinker ...	7	2				
7 Hanthawaddy	Atheist ...	1	...	7 Hanthawaddy	Buddhist ...	2	6
	Buddhist ..	1	...		Freethinker ..	1	...
	Freethinker ...	1	...				
Others ...	As in Note 3 of Imperial Table VIA.	11	2	Others ...	......	...	...
Total for the Province ...		31	4	Total for the Province ..		14	16
Total, Christians in Table XV (less Armenians).		6,084	2,198	Total, Christian Anglo-Indians in Table XV.		8,444	8,214
Total, agreeing with Table XVI ...		6,115	2,202	Total, agreeing with Table XVI ...		8,458	8,230

IMPERIAL TABLE XVI, PART A-II.—*European and Allied Races in each District by Nationality.*

Serial No.	District or State.	TOTAL.			RACES OF THE BRITISH EMPIRE.		OTHER RACES.			
							British Subjects.		Foreign Subjects.	
		Persons.	Males.	Females.	Males.	Females.	Males.	Females.	Males.	Females.
	1	2	3	4	5	6	7	8	9	10
	Provincial Total ...	8,317	6,115	2,202	5,531	1,814	110	101	474	287
	Divisional Burma ...	7,972	5,900	2,072	5,346	1,710	104	98	450	264
	Arakan Division ...	*160*	*133*	*27*	*129*	*28*	*2*	...	*2*	*4*
1	Akyab	143	121	22	120	21	...	...	1	...
2	Hill District of Arakan	6	5	1	5	1	...	..	...	...
3	Kyaukpyu	3	3	..	3	..	...	...	...	...
4	Sandoway	8	4	4	1	...	2	...	1	4
	Pegu Division	*4,260*	*3,177*	*1,083*	*2,969*	*920*	*68*	*58*	*145*	*105*
5	Rangoon Town ...	3,695	2,802	893	2,629	766	56	45	117	82
6	Insein	172	87	85	77	63	2	11	8	11
7	Hanthawaddy ..	281	211	70	196	65	4	1	11	4
8	Tharrawaddy ..	35	24	11	20	9	...	...	4	2
9	Pegu	34	19	15	15	9	1	1	3	5
10	Prome	43	34	9	32	8	...	...	2	1
	Irrawaddy Division ...	*204*	*150*	*54*	*130*	*33*	*1*	...	*19*	*21*
11	Bassein	120	89	31	80	22	...	...	9	9
12	Henzada	37	23	14	17	6	1	...	5	8
13	Myaungmya ...	[illegible]	5	2	4	2	[illegible]	...	1	...
14	Ma-ubin	24	19	5	16	2	...	...	3	3
15	Pyapôn	16	14	2	13	1	...	...	1	1
	Tenasserim Division ...	*557*	*368*	*189*	*315*	*129*	*10*	*14*	*43*	*46*
16	Toungoo ...	143	77	66	53	36	4	4	20	26
17	Salween	13	11	2	11	2	..	..	..	...
18	Thatôn	6	5	1	5	1	...	...	...	...
19	Amherst	209	132	77	116	53	3	7	13	17
20	Tavoy	112	78	34	77	28	..	3	1	3
21	Mergui	74	65	9	53	9	3	...	9	...
	Magwe Division ..	*558*	*438*	*120*	*240*	*78*	*9*	*9*	*184*	*33*
22	Thayetmyo ...	37	31	6	25	5	3	...	3	1
23	Pakôkku	33	26	7	21	6	..	..	5	1
24	Minbu	20	16	4	10	2	...	...	6	2
25	Magwe	461	358	103	182	65	6	9	170	29
26	Pakôkku Hill Tracts ...	2	2	...	2	...	...	...	...	...
	Mandalay Division ...	*1,878*	*1,398*	*480*	*1,359*	*428*	*8*	*12*	*31*	*40*
27	Mandalay	1,756	1,308	448	1,280	400	4	11	24	37
	Mandalay City ...	*491*	*350*	*141*	*328*	*105*	*4*	*5*	*18*	*31*
28	Bhamo	53	44	9	36	6	2	1	6	2
29	Myitkyina	45	29	16	26	15	2	...	1	1
30	Katha	19	12	7	12	7	..	...	...	...
31	Putao	5	5	...	5	...	...	...	...	...
	Sagaing Division ..	*149*	*93*	*56*	*82*	*49*	*1*	...	*10*	*7*
32	Shwebo	52	33	19	28	13	1	...	4	6
33	Sagaing	10	8	2	5	1	...	...	3	1
34	Lower Chindwin ...	20	12	8	12	8	...	...	...	...
35	Upper Chindwin ..	40	29	11	27	11	...	...	2	...
36	Chin Hills	27	11	16	10	16	..	..	1	...
	Meiktila Division ...	*211*	*148*	*63*	*122*	*50*	*10*	*5*	*16*	*8*
37	Kyauksè	19	14	5	11	5	...	...	3	...
38	Meiktila ...	114	70	44	55	32	9	4	6	8
39	Yamèthin	56	45	11	44	10	...	1	1	...
40	Myingyan	22	19	3	12	3	1	...	6	..
	Eastern States	345	215	130	185	104	6	3	24	23
41	Northern Shan States	223	151	72	131	65	5	1	15	6
42	Southern Shan States	113	56	57	48	39	1	1	7	17
43	Karenni	9	8	1	6	...	...	1	2	..

Serial No.	District or State.	Total.			BRITISH SUBJECTS.												
					All Ages.			0—10		10—16		16—18		18—30			
		Total.	Males.	Females.	Total.	Males.	Females.	Males.	Females.	Males.	Females.	Males.	Females.	Males.	Females.		
	1	2	3	4	5	6	7	8	9	10	11	12	13	14	15		
	Provincial Total ...	8,317	6,115	2,202	7,556	5,641	1,915	390	357	135	88	42	20	2,294	457		
	Divisional Burma ...	7,972	5,900	2,072	7,258	5,450	1,808	371	333	129	80	42	18	2,256	433		
	Arakan Division ...	*160*	*133*	*27*	*154*	*131*	*23*	*7*	*3*	*3*	*1*	...	...	*52*	*5*		
1	Akyab	143	121	22	142	120	22	4	3	3	1	...	..	51	4		
2	Hill District of Arakan	6	5	1	6	5	1	2	...	...	...	...	...	1	1		
3	Kyaukpyu ...	3	3	...	3	3	...	...	...	...	...	...	...	...	...		
4	Sandoway	8	4	4	3	3	...	1	...	...	...	...	...	...	...		
	Pegu Division ...	*4,260*	*3,177*	*1,083*	*4,010*	*3,032*	*978*	*188*	*174*	*72*	*44*	*27*	*9*	*1,188*	*233*		
5	Rangoon Town ...	3,695	2,802	893	3,496	2,685	811	154	138	67	37	26	9	1,101	202		
6	Insein	172	87	85	153	79	74	5	16	2	5	1	.	18	14		
7	Hanthawaddy ...	281	211	70	266	200	66	25	13	3	2	.	...	52	11		
8	Tharrawaddy ..	35	24	11	29	20	9	3	2	...	...	...	...	4	1		
9	Pegu	34	19	15	26	16	10	1	4	...	...	...	...	1	2		
10	Prome . ..	43	34	9	40	32	8	..	1	...	...	..	...	12	3		
	Irrawaddy Division ...	*204*	*150*	*54*	*164*	*131*	*33*	*10*	*6*	..	...	*1*	...	*42*	*10*		
11	Bassein ...	120	89	31	102	80	22	4	3	...	...	1	...	32	8		
12	Henzada	37	23	14	24	18	6	6	3	...	...	...	...	2	1		
13	Myaungmya ...	7	5	2	6	4	2		...	...	...	...	...	1	...		
14	Ma-ubin	24	19	5	18	16	2	...	...	...	...	...	...	5	...		
15	Pyapôn	16	14	2	14	13	1	...	..	...	...	...	...	2	1		
	Tenasserim Division ...	*557*	*368*	*189*	*468*	*325*	*143*	*24*	*28*	*4*	*7*	*3*	*1*	*68*	*28*		
16	Toungoo	143	77	66	97	57	40	6	7	2	5	...	..	9	9		
17	Salween	13	11	2	13	11	2	...	1	..	...	...	...	1	1		
18	Thatôn	6	5	1	6	5	1	...	...	..	...	...	..	...	...		
19	Amherst	209	132	77	179	119	60	5	14	1	2	2	1	32	10		
20	Tavoy	112	78	34	108	77	31	11	5	1	.	1	...	10	6		
21	Mergui	74	65	9	65	56	9	2	1	...	...	...	...	14	2		
	Magwe Division ...	*553*	*433*	*120*	*336*	*249*	*87*	*15*	*23*	*3*	*1*	...	...	*64*	*32*		
22	Thayetmyo ..	37	31	5	33	28	5	1	1	...	...	...	...	9	2		
23	Pakôkku	33	26	7	27	21	6	2	1	...	...	...	...	1	4		
24	Minbu	20	16	4	12	10	2	...	...	...	...	...	...	4	2		
25	Magwe	401	358	103	262	188	74	12	21	3	1	..	...	50	24		
26	Pakôkku Hill Tracts ...	2	2	...	2	2	..	...	...	...	...	..	...	...	...		
	Mandalay Division ...	*1,878*	*1,398*	*480*	*1,807*	*1,367*	*440*	*106*	*84*	*44*	*25*	*11*	*7*	*787*	*101*		
27	Mandalay	1,756	1,308	448	1,695	1,284	411	101	79	44	25	11	6	765	91		
	Mandalay City .	*491*	*350*	*141*	*442*	*332*	*110*	*25*	*18*	*9*	*5*	*1*	*3*	*160*	*27*		
28	Bhamo	53	44	9	45	38	7	4	...	...	...	...	...	14	4		
29	Myitkyina	45	29	16	43	28	15	1	4	...	...	...	...	6	4		
30	Katha	19	12	7	19	12	7	...	1	...	.	..	1	...	2		
31	Putao	5	5	..	5	5	...	...	...	...	...	..	...	2	...		
	Sagaing Division ...	*149*	*93*	*56*	*132*	*83*	*49*	*2*	*9*	*1*	*1*	...	...	*22*	*12*		
32	Shwebo	52	33	19	42	29	13	...	1	...	...	...	...	8	3		
33	Sagaing	10	8	2	6	5	1	...	...	...	...	...	...	1	1		
34	Lower Chindwin ..	20	12	8	20	12	8	1	2	1	...	...	...	2	1		
35	Upper Chindwin ..	40	29	11	38	27	11	...	2	...	...	...	...	9	4		
36	Chin Hills	27	11	16	26	10	16	1	4	..	1	...	...	2	3		
	Meiktila Division ...	*211*	*143*	*68*	*187*	*132*	*55*	*19*	*6*	*2*	*1*	...	*1*	*35*	*12*		
37	Kyauksè	19	14	5	16	11	5	...	1	...	...	...	...	3	1		
38	Meiktila	114	70	44	100	64	36	16	2	2	...	...	1	14	7		
39	Yamèthin	56	45	11	55	44	11	3	2	...	1	...	...	13	3		
40	Myingyan	22	19	3	16	13	3	...	1	...	...	...	...	5	1		
	Eastern States	345	215	130	298	191	107	19	24	6	8	...	2	38	24		
41	Northern Shan States ..	223	151	72	202	136	66	17	15	...	4	..	1	31	16		
42	Southern Shan States ...	113	56	57	89	49	40	2	9	6	4	...	1	5	8		
43	Karenni	9	8	1	7	6	1	...	...	...	...	...	...	2	...		

European and Allied Races by Nationality, Sex and Age.

30—40		40—50		50 and over.		OTHERS. All Ages.			0—10		10—16		16—18		18—30		30—40		40—50		50 and over.		Serial No. of District, etc. (column 1).
Males.	Females.	Males.	Females.	Males.	Females.	Total.	Males.	Females.	Males.	Females.	Males.	Females.	Males.	Females.	Males.	Females.	Males.	Females.	Males.	Females.	Males.	Females.	
16	17	18	19	20	21	22	23	24	25	26	27	28	29	30	31	32	33	34	35	36	37	38	
1,509	577	869	254	402	162	761	474	287	11	16	6	8	...	2	64	57	164	92	143	60	86	57	
1,439	544	834	244	379	156	714	450	264	11	16	6	3	...	2	62	53	151	85	137	55	83	50	
38	*8*	*18*	*6*	*13*	...	*6*	*2*	*4*	...	*1*	...	...	...	...	...	...	*1*	*2*	*1*	*1*	...	...	
35	8	17	6	10	...	1	1	...	...	...	...	...	...	...	...	...	1	...	...	...	...	...	1
1	...	...	...	1	...	...	...	...	...	...	...	...	...	...	...	...	...	...	...	...	...	...	2
1	...	...	...	2	...	...	...	...	...	...	...	...	...	...	...	...	...	...	...	...	...	...	3
1	...	1	...	...	...	5	1	4	...	1	...	...	...	...	...	...	...	2	1	1	...	...	4
828	*292*	*496*	*148*	*233*	*83*	*250*	*145*	*105*	*5*	*12*	*5*	*1*	...	*1*	*31*	*31*	*44*	*20*	*35*	*19*	*25*	*21*	
710	239	433	119	194	67	199	117	82	3	12	3	1	...	1	29	27	38	16	29	8	15	17	5
22	14	13	13	18	12	19	8	11	1	...	2	...	...	...	...	...	...	...	1	7	4	4	6
68	29	37	9	15	2	15	11	4	1	...	...	...	...	...	1	1	3	3	4	...	2	...	7
9	5	4	1	...	...	6	4	2	...	...	...	...	...	...	...	...	1	1	...	1	3		8
7	3	5	...	2	1	8	3	5	...	...	...	...	...	...	1	3	...	...	1	2	1	...	9
12	2	4	1	4	1	3	2	1	...	...	...	...	...	...	...	...	2	...	...	1	...	...	10
36	*6*	*33*	*6*	*9*	*5*	*40*	*19*	*21*	...	*3*	*1*	...	...	*1*	...	*1*	*1*	*8*	*9*	*4*	*8*	*4*	
21	4	18	4	4	3	18	9	9	...	1	...	...	...	1	...	...	...	4	4	2	5	1	11
4	...	2	1	4	1	13	5	8	...	2	1	...	...	...	...	1	1	2	2	2	1	1	12
1	1	2	1	...	...	1	1	...	...	...	...	...	...	...	...	...	...	...	1	...	...	...	13
6	1	4	...	1	1	6	3	3	...	...	...	...	...	...	...	...	...	2	2	...	1	1	14
4	...	7	...	...	...	2	1	1	...	...	...	...	...	...	...	...	...	...	...	...	1	1	15
109	*46*	*79*	*11*	*40*	*22*	*89*	*43*	*46*	*3*	...	...	...	...	...	*4*	*4*	*14*	*25*	*9*	*10*	*13*	*7*	
21	10	14	3	5	6	46	20	26	3	...	...	...	...	...	1	2	4	14	6	4	6	6	16
7	...	1	...	2	...	...	...	...	...	...	...	...	...	...	...	...	...	...	...	...	...	...	17
2	1	3	...	...	...	...	...	...	...	...	...	...	...	...	...	...	...	...	...	...	...	...	18
33	15	27	7	19	11	30	13	17	...	...	...	...	...	...	2	1	3	10	2	6	6	...	19
24	17	21	...	9	3	4	1	3	...	...	...	...	...	...	...	1	1	1	...	...	...	1	20
22	3	13	1	5	2	9	9	...	...	...	...	...	...	...	1	...	6	...	1	...	1	...	21
102	*23*	*49*	*8*	*16*	...	*217*	*184*	*33*	*2*	...	...	*1*	...	...	*24*	*10*	*73*	*14*	*67*	*8*	*18*	...	
6	1	5	1	7	...	4	3	1	...	...	...	...	...	...	1	1	...	...	2	...	...	...	22
12	1	5	...	1	...	6	5	1	...	...	...	...	...	...	1	1	2	...	2	...	...	...	23
6	...	...	...	...	...	8	6	2	...	...	...	...	...	...	...	...	4	2	2	...	...	...	24
76	21	39	7	8	...	199	170	29	2	...	...	1	...	...	22	8	67	12	61	8	18	...	25
2	...	...	...	...	...	...	...	...	...	...	...	...	...	...	...	...	...	...	...	...	...	...	26
239	*129*	*132*	*60*	*48*	*34*	*71*	*31*	*40*	...	...	...	...	...	...	*2*	*3*	*11*	*12*	*11*	*9*	*7*	*16*	
214	124	109	54	40	32	61	24	37	...	...	...	...	...	...	2	3	8	10	8	9	6	15	27
85	*32*	*46*	*19*	*16*	*6*	*49*	*18*	*31*	...	...	...	...	...	...	...	*3*	*6*	*8*	*7*	*8*	*5*	*12*	
9	2	7	1	4	...	8	6	2	...	...	...	...	...	...	...	...	2	1	3	...	1	1	28
10	3	9	3	2	1	2	1	1	...	...	...	...	...	...	...	...	1	1	...	...	...	...	29
5	...	5	2	2	1	...	...	...	...	...	...	...	...	...	...	...	...	...	...	...	...	...	30
1	...	2	...	...	...	...	...	...	...	...	...	...	...	...	...	...	...	...	...	...	...	...	31
41	*19*	*10*	*5*	*7*	*8*	*17*	*10*	*7*	...	...	...	...	...	...	...	*2*	*3*	*1*	*1*	*2*	*6*	*2*	
12	8	6	1	3	...	10	4	6	...	...	...	...	...	...	...	2	1	1	...	2	3	1	32
3	...	...	...	1	...	4	3	1	...	...	...	...	...	...	...	...	...	...	...	...	3	1	33
7	2	...	1	1	2	...	...	...	...	...	...	...	...	...	...	...	...	...	...	...	...	...	34
13	4	3	1	2	...	2	2	...	...	...	...	...	...	...	...	...	1	...	1	...	...	...	35
6	5	1	2	...	1	1	1	...	...	...	...	...	...	...	...	...	1	...	...		...	...	36
46	*21*	*17*	*5*	*13*	*9*	*24*	*16*	*8*	*1*	...	...	*1*	...	...	*1*	*2*	*4*	*3*	*4*	*2*	*6*	...	
5	1	1	1	2	1	3	3	...	...	...	...	...	...	...	...	...	...	...	...	...	3	...	37
18	15	7	4	7	7	14	6	8	1	...	...	1	...	...	...	2	3	3	2	2	...	...	38
19	4	6	...	3	1	1	1	...	...	...	...	...	...	...	...	...	...	...	1	...	...	...	39
4	1	3	...	1	...	6	6	...	...	...	...	...	...	...	1	...	1	...	1	...	3	...	40
70	33	35	10	23	6	47	24	23	...	...	...	...	...	...	2	4	13	7	6	5	3	7	
51	22	29	4	8	4	21	15	6	...	...	...	...	...	...	2	3	9	1	4	2	...	...	41
17	11	4	6	15	1	24	7	17	...	...	...	...	...	...	...	1	3	6	1	3	3	7	42
2	...	2	...	...	1	2	2	...	...	...	...	...	...	...	...	...	1	...	1	...	...	...	43

Serial No.	District or State.	All Ages. Total.	All Ages. Males.	All Ages. Females.	0—1 Males.	0—1 Females.	1—5 Males.	1—5 Females.	5—10 Males.	5—10 Females.	10—15 Males.	10—15 Females.	15—20 (See also columns 25 to 30.) Males.	15—20 Females.
	1	2	3	4	5	6	7	8	9	10	11	12	13	14
	Provincial Total ...	16,688	8,458	8,230	229	211	834	864	1,157	1,235	941	1,142	842	944
	Divisional Burma ...	16,339	8,244	8,095	222	207	804	845	1,130	1,216	929	1,131	832	935
	Arakan Division ...	*256*	*141*	*116*	*8*	*8*	*18*	*17*	*17*	*28*	*12*	*13*	*16*	*14*
1	Akyab	232	129	103	3	2	9	15	17	21	12	13	16	12
2	Hill District of Arakan	3	3	...		...	...	...	...	...	...	...	...	...
3	Kyaukpyu	4	2	2	...	...	...	...	...	..	...	..	...	1
4	Sandoway	17	7	10	...	1	4	2	...	2	...	...	...	1
	Pegu Division ...	*9,982*	*5,048*	*4,934*	*156*	*142*	*478*	*512*	*652*	*647*	*517*	*583*	*642*	*554*
5	Rangoon Town ...	8,343	4,155	4,188	124	116	79	424	530	536	434	508	466	480
6	Insein	860	437	423	14	13	48	45	60	50	32	48	50	47
7	Hanthawaddy ...	396	242	154	8	7	18	24	41	32	37	18	19	10
8	Tharrawaddy ...	96	52	44	.	4	4	5	4	8	2	2	2	3
9	Pegu	224	127	97	10	2	23	10	15	15	10	5	5	13
10	Prome	63	35	28	...	...	1	4	2	6	2	2	...	1
	Irrawaddy Division ...	*439*	*262*	*177*	*8*	*6*	*46*	*22*	*40*	*31*	*7*	*10*	*7*	*10*
11	Bassein	251	145	106	7	4	27	8	24	26	5	5	7	8
12	Henzada	89	49	40	...	...	13	11	8	3	1	1	...	2
13	Myaungmya ...	47	33	14	...	1	6	2	3	...	...	1	...	...
14	Ma-ubin	30	20	10	1	1	...	1	5	1	1	2	...	...
15	Pyapôn .. .	22	15	7	...	...	...	...	..	1	..	1	...	...
	Tenasserim Division ...	*2,178*	*1,043*	*– 1,135*	*15*	*20*	*89*	*103*	*180*	*216*	*163*	*261*	*79*	*142*
16	Toungoo	541	216	325	...	4	24	22	46	64	35	89	7	43
17	Salween	...	...	...	...	...	...	...	...	...	...	...	...	...
18	Thatôn	56	35	21	1	3	1	6	..	...	...	1	3	1
19	Amherst	1,328	625	703	9	9	50	56	122	136	122	164	64	93
20	Tavoy	114	72	42	..	1	4	5	5	9	3	5	4	3
21	Mergui	139	95	44	5	3	10	14	7	7	3	2	1	2
	Magwe Division ...	*208*	*136*	*72*	*3*	*3*	*18*	*13*	*13*	*11*	*5*	*5*	*6*	*5*
22	Thayetmyo ..	25	11	14	...	1	1	3	...	2	...	1	...	1
23	Pakôkku	26	16	10	...	1	...	3	...	...	..	...	..	2
24	Minbu	36	29	7	...	...	2	2	8	...	1	1	2	...
25	Magwe	121	80	41	3	1	15	5	5	9	4	3	4	2
26	Pakôkku Hill Tracts ...	...	...	...	...	..	...	...	...	...	...	...	...	...
	Mandalay Division ...	*2,655*	*1,253*	*1,402*	*23*	*24*	*127*	*134*	*192*	*247*	*209*	*241*	*161*	*179*
27	Mandalay	2,332	1,072	1,260	22	22	119	107	171	226	200	227	155	164
	Mandalay City ...	*1,120*	*517*	*603*	*11*	*12*	*60*	*54*	*64*	*116*	*88*	*111*	*61*	*94*
28	Bhamo	49	26	23	...	...	...	8	3	2	1	1	...	1
29	Myitkyina	75	42	33	1	1	6	4	8	8	1	5	...	3
30	Katha	196	112	84	..	1	2	15	10	11	7	8	6	10
31	Putao	3	1	2	...	...		...	...	...	..	...	...	1
	Sagaing Division ...	*205*	*130*	*75*	*5*	*2*	*15*	*9*	*8*	*12*	*3*	*6*	*5*	*11*
32	Shwebo	72	44	28	2	1	8	4	1	3	2	4	2	5
33	Sagaing	71	41	30	3	1	6	3	4	5	.	1	1	4
34	Lower Chindwin ...	34	25	9	...	...	.	1	3	2	1	1	2	2
35	Upper Chindwin ...	19	14	5	...	...	.	...	...	...	...	..	...	...
36	Chin Hills	9	6	3	...	..	1	1	..	2	...	..	...	...
	Meiktila Division ...	*416*	*231*	*185*	*9*	*7*	*23*	*35*	*28*	*29*	*18*	*12*	*16*	*20*
37	Kyauksè	23	15	8	...	..	1	2	2	1	...	1	...	.
38	Meiktila	141	84	57	4	2	10	9	9	6	5	3	6	8
39	Yamèthin	223	113	110	4	5	11	21	13	20	8	8	10	10
40	Myingyan	29	19	10	1	...	1	3	4	2	..	..	...	2
	Eastern States ...	349	214	135	7	4	30	19	27	19	12	11	10	9
41	Northern Shan States .	225	148	77	5	2	19	13	19	13	11	7	8	4
42	Southern Shan States ...	119	63	56	2	2	10	6	8	5	1	4	2	5
43	Karenni	5	3	2	..	...	1		..	1	..	...	...	...

—Anglo-Indians.

20—30 Males	20—30 Females	30—40 Males	30—40 Females	40—50 Males	40—50 Females	50—60 Males	50—60 Females	60 and over Males	60 and over Females	Expansion of columns 13 and 14: 15 Males	15 Females	16—18 Males	16—18 Females	18—20 Males	18—20 Females	Serial No. of District, etc. (column 1).
15	16	17	18	19	20	21	22	23	24	25	26	27	28	29	30	
1,443	1,551	1,306	1,028	919	621	507	387	280	247	182	221	368	375	292	348	
1,413	1,523	1,259	1,005	892	614	488	376	275	243	180	219	363	373	289	343	
18	*18*	*29*	*17*	*17*	*7*	*9*	*2*	*7*	*1*	*4*	*5*	*7*	*4*	*5*	*5*	
17	15	25	16	16	6	8	2	6	1	4	5	7	4	5	3	1
1	...	1	..	1	...	...	..	...	..	...	...	...	...	..	...	2
...	...	2	1	...	...	...	...	..	...	...	...	...	...	...	1	3
...	3	1	..	...	1	1	...	1	...	...	...	...	..	...	1	4
926	*1,014*	*798*	*653*	*552*	*407*	*265*	*262*	*167*	*160*	*106*	*113*	*233*	*220*	*203*	*221*	
769	882	652	543	457	357	209	209	135	133	88	102	194	179	184	199	5
69	70	66	64	47	33	32	33	19	20	13	10	18	21	19	16	6
44	25	30	26	25	4	14	6	6	2	...	1	19	4	...	5	7
10	7	13	7	9	2	4	4	4	2	1	...	1	2	.	1	8
22	25	27	9	10	9	3	7	2	2	4	...	1	13	...	...	9
12	5	10	4	4	2	3	3	1	1	...	...	...	1	...	...	10
57	*44*	*38*	*25*	*29*	*17*	*23*	*8*	*7*	*4*	...	*1*	*4*	*4*	*3*	*5*	
23	29	20	14	16	6	12	3	4	3	...	1	4	2	3	5	11
9	8	5	6	8	4	5	4	...	1	...	...	...	2	...	...	12
11	3	7	2	...	5	3	...	3	...	...	...	...	...	...	...	13
7	3	3	1	2	...	1	1	.	..	...	...	...	...	...	...	14
7	1	3	2	3	2	2	...	...	...	...	...	...	..	...	...	15
168	*155*	*148*	*93*	*93*	*69*	*65*	*31*	*43*	*45*	*20*	*48*	*41*	*56*	*18*	*38*	
41	50	29	24	16	10	12	10	6	9	2	10	3	23	2	10	16
...	...	...	...	...	.	..	...	..	...	...	...	...	...	...	...	17
7	5	11	1	5	2	4	2	3	...	...	...	2	1	1	...	18
79	84	68	58	45	53	37	17	29	33	17	37	33	29	14	27	19
15	9	22	6	12	3	4	1	3	..	1	...	2	2	1	1	20
26	7	18	4	15	1	8	1	2	3	...	1	1	1	..	...	21
32	*15*	*28*	*14*	*19*	*3*	*10*	*3*	*2*	...	...	...	*2*	*4*	*4*	*1*	
...	3	4	1	1	...	4	2	1	...	...	...	...	1	..	...	22
6	2	3	2	4	.	2	..	1	...	...	.	...	2	...	...	23
6	3	7	1	3	...	..	...	..	...	..	...	1	...	1	...	24
20	7	14	10	11	3	4	1	...	..	...	...	1	1	3	1	25
...	...	.	...	...	...	...	...	...	...	...	...	...	...	...	...	26
151	*230*	*141*	*176*	*132*	*87*	*82*	*57*	*35*	*27*	*43*	*45*	*72*	*73*	*46*	*61*	
111	208	109	151	90	82	63	47	32	26	40	43	71	68	44	53	27
68	*94*	*66*	*67*	*47*	*31*	*37*	*19*	*15*	*5*	*11*	*28*	*34*	*42*	*16*	*24*	
7	5	4	4	6	1	5	...	...	1	...	...	...	1	...	...	28
4	4	9	5	12	...	...	3	1	...	..	...	..	1	...	2	29
28	13	19	15	24	4	14	7	2	...	3	2	1	3	2	5	30
1	...	...	1	...	...	...	...	...	...	...	...	...	...	...	1	31
26	*16*	*24*	*7*	*23*	*6*	*16*	*5*	*5*	*1*	*2*	*1*	*1*	*6*	*2*	*4*	
11	4	7	3	6	2	4	2	1	...	1	..	...	3	1	2	32
8	6	7	3	5	3	5	3	2	1	...	...	1	2	...	2	33
1	2	5	...	6	1	5	...	2	...	1	1	..	1	1	...	34
5	4	3	1	5	...	1	...	...	...	...	...	...	...	...	...	35
1	...	2	...	1	...	1	...	...	...	..	...	...	...	...	...	36
35	*31*	*53*	*20*	*27*	*18*	*18*	*8*	*9*	*5*	*5*	*6*	*3*	*6*	*8*	*8*	
6	2	4	1	2	...	...	1	...	...	...	...	...	...	...	...	37
8	7	22	11	8	7	8	2	4	2	...	4	1	...	5	4	38
16	20	22	8	15	11	9	4	5	3	5	1	2	5	3	4	39
5	2	5	...	2	...	1	1	...	...	...	1	...	1	...	...	40
30	28	47	23	27	7	19	11	5	4	2	2	5	2	3	5	
21	16	36	15	19	2	8	4	2	1	2	2	3	1	3	1	41
9	11	9	8	8	5	11	7	3	3	..	...	2	1	...	4	42
...	1	2	...	...	...	...	...	...	...	...	...	...	...	...	...	43

IMPERIAL TABLE XVI.—PART C.—*Armenians*.

Nationality and District.	Total.			Ages.													
				0—10		10—16		16—18		18—30		30—40		40—50		50 and over.	
	Persons.	Males.	Females.	Males.	Females.	Males.	Females.	Males.	Females.	Males.	Females.	Males.	Females.	Males.	Females.	Males.	Females.
1	2	3	4	5	6	7	8	9	10	11	12	13	14	15	16	17	18
Grand Total ...	348	185	163	37	35	14	23	6	8	39	37	36	24	24	18	29	18
Total British Subjects	272	130	142	35	31	10	21	4	7	26	34	20	19	17	12	18	18
Rangoon Town	183	91	92	22	20	5	12	4	7	24	21	14	13	12	9	10	10
Insein ...	14	5	9	1	...	1	1	.	...	...	1	1	2	1	1	1	4
Mandalay ...	45	12	33	5	10	...	5	...	...	...	11	3	2	2	2	2	3
Other Districts†	30	22	8	7	1	4	3	...	..	2	1	2	2	2	...	5	1
Mandalay City *	*15*	*6*	*9*	*3*	*4*	...	...	...	...	...	*2*	*1*	...	*2*	*1*	...	*2*
Total Foreign Subjects	76	55	21	2	4	4	2	2	1	13	3	16	5	7	6	11	...
Rangoon Town	69	48	21	2	4	4	2	1	1	11	3	14	5	7	6	9	.
Insein ...	1	1	...	...	...	...	...	...	...	...	...	..	...	..	..	1	..
Mandalay ...	3	3	...	...	...	...	...	1	...	...	...	1	...	...	..	1	...
Other Districts ‡	3	3	...	...	...	...	...	...	...	2	...	1	...	...	...	...	...
Mandalay City	*Nil*	...	...	...	...	...	...	...	...	..	...	...	...	...	...	...	...

* These figures are included in those for Mandalay District just above.

† British subjects in other districts:—Males: Hanthawaddy 1, Prome 1, Toungoo 1, Thatôn 1, Tavoy 2, Lower Chindwin 4, Kyauksè 1, Yamèthin 2, Southern Shan States 9; Females: Amherst 3, Tavoy 1, Yamèthin 1, Southern Shan States 3.

‡ Foreign subjects in other districts: 1 male in Thatôn and 2 males in Amherst District.

IMPERIAL TABLE XVII.

Occupations.

NOTE 1.—The area and population covered by this table are the same as for Imperial Table VIA and thus represent the whole province except those areas described in the Notes to Imperial Table II which were omitted from the census or were censused only by estimate.

NOTE 2.—The population is classified by this table into 225 *Groups*, each of which is in two parts corresponding to *Workers* and *Dependents*, and the groups are further classified in 60 *Orders* which are themselves classified in 14 *Sub-classes* of 4 *Classes*. For further information about these categories Part I of the table should be consulted.

NOTE 3.—The Table has been prepared in three parts :—

PART I defines the special terms and describes the system of classification used in the table and exhibits the relationship of the latter to the system used in other provinces of India at this census and to the system used in Burma as well as in other provinces at the census of 1911. Section B of this Part should always be consulted with reference to any figures of Part II or III which it is proposed to use.

PART II gives statistics of occupations for the province as a whole.

PART III elaborates Part II by showing the contribution by each district to the provincial totals for each class, sub-class, order and group, each of these grades of the occupational classification being completed in turn. In this part of the table the figures given for the Rangoon Town District represent also Rangoon Town, which, for the purposes of the Imperial Census Tables, is conterminous with the district. The figures given for the Mandalay District include the separate figures given in italics immediately below them for Mandalay City.

NOTE 4.—Throughout Parts II and III of the table the statistics show the number of workers of each group or higher category classified by sex and also the number of dependents and the number of workers and dependents taken together without classification by sex. Workers of each sex who have a subsidiary occupation are included in the numbers shown for *Total Workers* but are also separately tabulated in two classes according as the subsidiary occupation is *Agricultural* or not.

NOTE 5.—*Occupation*, *Principal Occupation*, *Subsidiary Occupation*, and *Agricultural Occupation* are amongst the special terms defined in Section A of Part I of the table.

NOTE 6.—Further statistics for Principal Occupations by racial groups and races are given in Imperial Table XX, and further statistics for Subsidiary Occupations in Imperial Tables XVIII and XIX, while various statistics for persons employed in industrial establishments are given in Imperial Tables XXIIA and XXIIB.

IMPERIAL TABLE XVII.—*Occupations.*

PART I.—The System of Classification.

This part of the table is presented in five sections named A to E as follows :—

A.—Definitions.
B.—The Contents of the Categories.
C.—Alphabetical Index of Occupations (abridged).
D.—Variations in Burma from the Standard Scheme of 1921.
E.—Comparison of the Classification-schemes of 1921 and 1911.

SECTION A.—DEFINITIONS.

1. The whole population is first divided into the two classes of *Workers* and *Dependents*. The term *Dependents* includes all (except a few classes conventionally treated as workers) who have not their own direct incomes but are supported by another who does not stand to them in the relation of an employer; all others are *Workers*. The term *Workers* thus includes those whose income is derived directly from such sources as begging, pensions, rent, dividends or profit of trading as well as those whose income or maintenance is received as payment for their labour or other services; and it is conventionally extended to include priests and Buddhist monks even if they have no income, and also prisoners in jails and inmates of asylums and some other special classes. Wives of workers who do not assist directly in the work for which their husbands receive remuneration are regarded as dependents upon their husbands unless they obtain an income either by their own labour or in their own right.

As persons who partake of the characters of both workers and dependents are classified according to the description given in the enumeration-schedules, many wives and children who earn a small amount occasionally or have a small private income have been tabulated as workers, although they are principally supported as dependents and others under the same conditions have been tabulated as such.

2. Every Worker is assigned to one or other of 225 *Groups* according to either his occupation, trade, profession, office or other source of income or economic support or the industry, profession, branch of commerce or of public service in connection with which he practises that occupation or trade, follows that profession, fills that office or derives that income. For convenience the groups are called *Occupational Groups* and the character which determines the group to which each worker is assigned is called his *Occupation*, although many of these characters are not occupations in the ordinary sense of that word.

3. For a worker who has the occupational characters of more than one group the principal character (*i.e.* generally that with which the greater part of his income is associated) is called his *Principal Occupation*, and the next most important his *Subsidiary Occupation*; any still less important occupational character is ignored. An *Agricultural Occupation* is any occupation belonging to one of the six groups 1, 2*a*, 3*a*, 3*b*, 3*c*, and 4; the distinction between this term and *Agriculture Proper* should be noticed, the latter covering only Groups 3*a*, 3*b* and 3*c*. Occupations of Groups 5, 6 or 7 are not regarded as agricultural. The subsidiary occupation of a worker whose principal occupation is agricultural is ignored if it belongs to the same occupational group as that principal occupation (Note : 3*a*, 3*b* and 3*c* are different groups, not subdivisions of a group).

4. The occupational group to which each dependent is assigned is that of the person on whom he principally depends for maintenance.

5. The 225 groups are numbered serially with Arabic figures from 1 to 191 inclusive, each of the following 17 numbers being used for two or more groups distinguished by letters affixed to their numbers:—2, 3, 6, 9, 22, 45, 64, 83, 98, 107, 110, 113, 123, 125, 127, 136, 177.

6. The 225 groups have also been further classified into 60 *Orders* numbered serially in Roman notation from I to LVI, the number II being used for 5 separate orders distinguished as IIA, IIB ... IIE.

7. The 60 Orders have been classified into 14 *Sub-classes* numbered serially in Roman notation in italics from *I* to *XII*, the number *I* being used for Sub-classes *Ia*, *Ib* and *Ic*.

8. The 14 Sub-classes are associated in 4 *Classes* distinguished as A, B, C and D.

9. The groups, orders and sub-classes respectively which are included in any higher category of the classification are shown by Part II of this table.

10. In the following notes the term *Standard Scheme of 1911* means the scheme used in 1911 for the classification of occupations in all provinces, including Burma; while the term *Standard Scheme of 1921* means the scheme used in all provinces other than Burma in the census of 1921, and the plural *Standard Schemes* includes these two standard schemes and no others. Section D of this Part of the table indicates, with the aid of the group-titles, the correspondence between the Burma scheme of 1921 and the standard scheme of that year, and, in conjunction with Section E, indicates similarly the correspondence between the Burma schemes of 1921 and 1911.

Section B.—The Contents of the Categories.

1. The principal part of this section has been cast in the form of a note on Class B followed by notes on selected groups in order; but certain general notes applying throughout are given in these prefatory paragraphs.

2. Generally the occupations included in each category (class, sub-class, order or group) are indicated approximately by its title in Parts II and III of the table, if that is read with reference to the titles of the higher categories which include it and the lower categories which it includes. Some titles which had to be abbreviated in Parts II and III of the table are given more fully in this section of Part I, and various notes which give further help in showing the meaning of the titles and the corresponding figures are also included; it is always desirable to refer to the relevant notes of this Section before any of the figures of Parts II and III are used. In association with Section C this Section is also intended to assist in discovering the group or higher category in which any specified occupation is included.

3. In all cases persons who repair any articles are classified in the same group as those who make those articles. The term *occupied with* includes making or repairing or using but not mere buying and selling by persons who take no part in the manufacture or preparation of the article concerned. The terms *dealer* and *trade in* include the hiring as well as the selling of the articles mentioned, but do not include the making of those articles. Persons who make, extract or grow as well as sell or lend or refine any article or substance are classified as makers, extractors or growers as the case may be.

4. The articles with the manufacture or sale of which any group of Sub-classes *III* and *V* is concerned are generally characterised either by being finally determined for similar or related uses or by being made of the same or similar materials

5. Clerks, messengers and all unskilled workers are classified in the same group as the majority of the persons to whose work theirs is auxiliary; *e.g.*, the clerks, peons and coolies in a rice-mill or its office are all assigned to Group 65 together with the managing rice-miller. Generally this rule applies to all the skilled and unskilled workers who co-operate in the same industrial or commercial undertaking, except those (such as factory-doctors and railway-police) who do not assist in the specific industrial or commercial work of the undertaking, but apply a special technique which is independent of the nature of that work. This exception does not apply to artisans who make articles which are used in such an undertaking; thus carpenters employed in railway-works are classified in Group 118, those in motor-car workshops in Group 90, those in shipbuilding-yards in Group 92. For most skilled artisans however the enumeration-schedules did not give sufficient information for this classification to be made; in such cases the artisan was assigned to the same class as those who practise the same trade in an independent or general way.

6. Government or municipal officers are assigned to the groups which correspond to their specific occupations (*e.g.*, professor, forest-officer, settlement officer); only those officers (*e.g.*, magistrates) for whom no other group is provided are assigned to Group 161, 162 or 163. The whole establishments of such officers, including peons and chaprasis, are assigned to the same groups as the officers themselves.

7. Domestic and other private servants except sweepers are all shown in Groups 181, 182 and 183 and excluded from all other groups.

8. No person is regarded as taking part in an industry or business merely because he is a shareholder in a company which is engaged in that industry or business, or lives without working on the savings from the income or profits formerly obtained by practising that industry or business. If dividends on shares, interest on savings and the like are the principal immediate source of his income he is assigned to Group 180 without regard to the origin of his fortune.

9. Groups 184 to 187 inclusive (constituting Order LIII) have been provided for persons engaged in productive occupations which were not described in the enumeration-schedules with sufficient clearness for proper classification; they thus imply improper diminutions of the numbers tabulated for other orders and groups. Some others for which the description given was not even clear enough for tabulation in these groups are in Group 191.

10. As it cannot be hoped that the notes below are complete, no conclusions can generally be drawn from omissions. The intention however has been to omit from them mention of those categories which seem to call for no special remark. For any class, sub-class or order the notes on the groups included in it should be consulted; for Class B there is a special note in addition immediately below this paragraph. In the notes on groups the number in antique type prefixed to each note indicates the group to which the note relates.

Classes.

Class B.—This class includes the same occupations as Class B of the standard schemes although the title *Industry and Commerce* has been adopted instead of *Preparation and supply of material substances.* The class includes however some groups which are not covered even by the new title—*e.g.*, Groups 101, 102, 103—but were included to reduce the variations in Burma from the standard scheme to a minimum.

Groups.

1. This group, although its title has been changed, is equivalent to Group 1 of the standard schemes. In 1911 the designation *Rent-receiver* was used in Imperial Table XVB, for persons of this group to contrast them with persons of Group 2 of that year who were called *Rent-payers*; and the same terms have been used by the Government of India with the same meanings in 1921. See also Note (ii) on Groups 3*a*, 3*b*, 3*c*, below. Persons supported by the ownership of, or rights over, land or water used for purposes excluded by the title of this group are in Group 180.

(ii) Workers of Groups 1, 2*a*, 3*b*, 3*c*, or 4 are said to have an agricultural subsidiary occupation only if they have a subsidiary occupation which does not belong to the same group as their principal occupation.

2a, 2b.—(i) Group 2*b* includes all belonging to the Settlement, Land Records and Agricultural Departments of Government. The Irrigation Branch of the Public Works Department however is included not in this group, but in Groups 108 and 109.

(ii) The two groups 2*a* and 2*b* together correspond approximately to Group 3 of the standard schemes, but a few persons have been somewhat arbitrarily classified by those schemes in different groups, and in 1911 the subordinate land-records staff was divided between Groups 144 and 158 corresponding to Groups 161 and 176 of 1921.

(iii) Note (ii) of Group 1 applies to Group 2*a*. Probably no occupations of Group 2*b* are practised as subsidiary occupations. See also the note below on Group 6.

3a, 3b, 3c.—(i) The sum of the three Groups 3*a*, 3*b*, 3*c*, is *Agriculture Proper* as defined and distinguished from *Agriculture* in Article 3 of Section A above.

(ii) Groups 3*a*, 3*b* and 4 taken together correspond to the term *Rent-payer* as used in Imperial Table XVB of 1911 for Burma. [See also Note (i) of Group 1.]

(iii) Note (ii) of Group 1 also applies to these three groups.

4. *Taungya* cultivation is a system of temporary cultivation practised by primitive tribes and people. A patch of jungle on a hill-side is cleared by fire and various seeds sown, chiefly or solely with a view to providing household requirements directly. A fresh patch is taken each year, but in some parts a return is made to each after a cycle of years. Notes (ii) and (iii) for Group 3*a* also apply to this group.

5. Market-gardening means the intensive cultivation of vegetables for regular supplies to an urban market. The group was intended to include Chinese vegetable growers and those Shans and Indians who practise similar intensive methods; but, as the records were generally not sufficiently precise to identify these, they have generally been included in Group 3*a*, 3*b* or 3*c*. The correct number however cannot be large.

6. Some rubber estates have labour organised on the typical *Plantation* system; but apart from these there is no general distinction between persons in this group and those in Groups 3*a*, 3*b* and 3*c* beyond the difference of the crop cultivated. Indeed most cultivators of betel-vine or sugar-cane grow these crops only as subsidiaries to some other kind of cultivation, and have been tabulated in the group corresponding to the latter (generally 3*a*, 3*b* or 3*c*); and the same may be true of some cultivators of the other crops with which this group is concerned. Some cultivators of sugar-cane have been tabulated in Group 71; see the note for that group. The cultivation of opium or ganja is illegal except in certain Shan states east of the Salween. (See the notes on Groups 75 and 137.)

8. Assistants of timber firms have been classified under sawyers in Group 43.

9b. Most elephant drivers are included in this group instead of Group 182 to which they are assigned in the standard schemes, because in Burma they are chiefly employed in collecting timber.

9c. In Burma cutch is always boiled in the camp of its collectors, and it is not possible to distinguish collectors and boilers. Cutch boilers are therefore included in this group and not in Group 64*c*.

9d. Grass-cutters are in this group. Collectors of edible birds' nests are also included in this group, but are few and confined to the Tavoy and Mergui districts.

10. The figures for this group are *nil* because lac-collecting is always regarded as a subsidiary industry.

11. Probably some in this group are carters or keep pack-cattle and have been wrongly classified through incomplete information. Some are dairymen with exactly the same occupation as others who are tabulated in Groups 70 and 133. See the notes on those groups.

16. Probably many who breed silk-worms have been tabulated as silk-spinners. The figures of Groups 16 and 34 should be taken together and not used separately.

19. See the note on Group 21.

21. The metals concerned in Burma are copper, gold, lead, molybdenum, platinum, silver, tin, wolfram and some others in minute quantities. (Some of those mentioned are also extracted only in very small quantities.) Silver and lead are found together and their smelters are included in this group as well as their miners. (See note on Group 50.) This group also includes coal-miners who get coal for use in smelting silver-lead ore. Many who recover gold from the refuse of goldsmiths' shops or from pagoda platforms were returned as gold-washers and included in this group.

27. As in some cases the record failed to state whether the weaver used silk or cotton it is probable that some weavers using cotton have been tabulated as silk-weavers in Group 35 and *vice versâ*.

34. See the note on Group 16.

35. See the note on Group 27.

36. Brush-makers and persons occupied with bristles are now included in Group 41; but in the census of 1911 they were associated in Group 28 with the textile workers using hair who now form Group 36 without them. See note on Group 41.

38. This group includes the making of lace, crepe, embroideries, fringes, etc., and also all textile industries insufficiently described for classification in the preceding groups.

40. This group includes the makers of such leathern articles as trunks, water-bags, saddlery and harness. It includes also the makers of all kinds of saddles, even Burmese saddles which may have no leather in them. Makers of leathern articles of dress or of the toilet are in the groups of Order XIII. See item 3 in Section E.

41. This group includes the furriers and persons occupied with feathers who in 1911 constituted the whole of Groups 34 and 29 respectively, and also the brush-makers and persons occupied with bristles who in 1911 formed part of Group 28. See note on Group 36.

42. Button-makers are in Group 79.

43. See note on Group 8.

44. This group includes all described as carpenters, turners, joiners or other workers in wood without the specification of any particular industry. In particular it includes all erectors of wooden (but not bamboo) buildings. See also the notes for Groups 45*c*, 83, 84, 89 and 177*d*. Many carpenters and other workers in wood are tabulated in the groups which relate to the industries in connection with which they are employed.

45a. This group includes makers of baskets, sieves, fish-traps and other cages of bamboo, cane and similar materials. Lacquer workers are also included because they usually make the basket foundations of their work and could not be accurately distinguished from others of this group.

45b. This group includes makers of thinbyu, nigyaw-pya and hlè-paung-mo (which are three kinds of reed matting of varying degrees of fineness) and makers of all similar matting.

45c. This group includes makers of thatch and of wa-tayan, kyu-tayan and other matting used for walls of floors and also builders using bamboo, reeds or similar substances. Thatchers and erectors of bamboo houses, now in this group, were included in Group 79 in 1911; see note on Groups 86 to 89.

46. The ordinary blacksmith is assigned to Group 48, not to this group.

47. Makers of dahs or spears have been assigned to Group 48 and not to this group because they make chiefly dahs used as agricultural and household implements. (*Dah* is a generic name in Burmese for knife, cutlass, sword, dagger.)

48. Fitters and other mechanics for whom the records did not show the industry in which they were employed are included in Group 186. See also note on Groups 46 and 47.

49. This group would include smelters and refiners of copper, but none were recorded in Burma. Makers of brass images should have been separately tabulated in Group 177*d* but have been included in Group 49 by mistake. See note on Group 177*d*.

50. It was intended that smelters of silver-lead ore should be regarded as workers in lead and tabulated in this group. But, as the records for workers in the silver-lead mines and refineries of the Northern Shan States did not distinguish persons employed in the mines from those employed in smelting and refining, all these have been tabulated in Group 21 (see note on Group 21 above). Electro-platers are in Group 50.

52. Workers in glass mosaic are also included in this group.

57. In Burma workers in alabaster are almost entirely engaged in making representations of Gotama and his disciples; they are accordingly classified as sculptors in Group 177*c*. Workers in glass mosaic have been tabulated in Group 52.

59. In 1911 ice-makers who are now included in this group were in Group 83 which corresponds otherwise to Group 93 of 1921.

62. Many persons in the Hanthawaddy district employed in mineral-oil refineries have been tabulated in Groups 185, 186 and 187 through deficiencies in the record.

64c. Lac, cutch, candles and tallow are amongst the substances included in this group, but the figures corresponding to them are *nil*. Lac is not manufactured in Burma but exported raw. Cutch is cut and boiled by the same group of persons, and in fact the occupation of collecting cutch is known as cutch-boiling; all such persons are entered in Group 9*c*. Candles are made only of mineral wax in the petroleum refineries represented in Group 62. There is no industry connected with tallow in Burma.

68. This group includes all concerned in the slaughter of animals for food; those who only trade in meat are assigned to Group 138.

69. Many fish curers are also fishermen and tabulated as such in Group 17.

70. Persons tabulated in this group were returned as butter-makers, etc., but probably all are cow-keepers and not differentiated from others tabulated in Group 11 or 133. See the notes on those groups.

71. *Jaggery* is the product of evaporation of the juice of the palmyra palm (*Borassus flabellifer*) and is generally prepared by the palm-climber or his family or other assistants, although some preparers buy their palm-juice. Some preparers of jaggery were recorded as such and tabulated in Group 71, while some were recorded as toddy-drawers and tabulated in Group 74; many of the latter class are really preparers of jaggery but in the tabulation-office there was no way of distinguishing them from those who collect the palm-juice to sell it as toddy.

Dhani-th'gya is a product similar to jaggery derived from the dhani palm (*Nipa fruticans*), and the conditions for tabulation were essentially the same as noted above for jaggery.

Kyantaga is obtained by evaporating the juice of the sugar-cane and is generally prepared by the cultivator of the sugar-cane or by his family or other assistants. Some preparers of kyantaga were recorded as such and tabulated in Group 71, while some were recorded as cultivators of sugar-cane and tabulated in Group 6*c*, or (because sugar-cane was not their main crop) were recorded as cultivators of paddy, etc., and tabulated in Group 3*a*, 3*b* or 3*c*; there is no difference between these two classes, but in the tabulation-office there was no way of distinguishing the latter from other cultivators of sugar-cane who do not prepare kyantaga at all.

72. Although jaggery, dhani-th'gya and kyantaga are used as sweetmeats preparers of them are tabulated in Group 71. See the note upon that group.

74. See the note of Group 71. All Upper Burma and some Lower Burma figures of this group represent preparers of jaggery; and some palm-climbers are in Group 71. Some females are shown as toddy-drawers although females never climb the trees; the whole family assisting the toddy-drawer is customarily regarded as engaged in palm-climbing and is shown accordingly in the enumeration-schedules.

75. In Burma tobacco is always cured by the growers who are included in Groups 3*a*, 3*b* and 3*c*. Cigar-makers are included in this group. In the standard schemes manufacturers of opium and ganja are included in this group, but in Burma these manufactures are illegal except in certain Shan States east of the Salween, where however the persons who manufacture opium are the cultivators who are tabulated as such in Group 6*f* unless they have other more important cultivation which causes them to be classified otherwise. See also the note on Group 137.

79. This group is provided in the standard schemes for industries relating to gloves, socks, gaiters, belts, buttons, umbrellas, walking-sticks and canes, etc. In Burma the umbrella-makers are practically the only class represented; the numbers making other articles concerned in this group are very small.

82. The title of this group in the standard schemes is "Other industries connected with the toilet (tattooers, shampooers, workers in bath-houses, etc.)"; but in Burma the *a-hneik-thè*, who massage sometimes to promote a feeling of health and well-being but generally for the removal of rheumatic or other pains, constitute nearly the whole of the group. Besides them there are only tattooers, the number of whom is both small and diminishing.

83a. } 83b. } Group 83 was divided into two parts at the request of the Industries Department; but it was always doubtful whether the division could really be made, because it was expected that polishers would be described in the same way as cabinet-makers. Experience in tabulation suggested that probably cabinet-makers and polishers have been returned as a rule as carpenters (Group 44) as the Burmese word *let-thama* (carpenter) is often used for a cabinet-maker instead of the long term *ein-daung pari-bawga lok-thama*. Tabulation has necessarily followed the entries in the schedules and thus included cabinet-makers in Group 44.

84. Many upholsterers are probably included in Group 44 through being described by the Burmese term for carpenter (see note to Group 83). Those employed in motor or carriage workshops are in Groups 90 and 91. Probably the persons tabulated in Group 84 are really makers of mattresses, pillows, etc., rather than upholsterers.

85. Surki-pounders are not included in this group but in Group 89.

86, 87. } 88, 89. } These four groups, together with thatchers and erectors of bamboo houses, who are now in Group 45*c*, are equivalent to Groups 77, 78 and 79 of 1911. A more complete title for Group 89 is "Painters and decorators of buildings, tilers, roofers (not using thatch), plumbers and all builders other than bricklayers, masons, carpenters or erectors of buildings principally made of bamboo or similar materials." Pounders of bricks for making *surki*, white-washers and sign-board painters are also in Group 89. See too the notes on Groups 111 and 176.

90. Makers and repairers of all kinds of cycles, whether motor-cycles or not, are included in this group. Also makers and repairers of motor cars and other motor land vehicles. Makers of motor-boats or air-ships would be in Group 92, but none were recorded in Burma. See also the note on Group 113*b* in which also some engaged in repairs of motor-vehicles are included.

91. This group includes makers and repairers of carts, carriages, rickshaws and all other vehicles used on land except (i) cycles (see note on Group 90) and (ii) vehicles used on railways (see note on Groups 118 and 119).

92. Aeroplane builders belong also to this group, but none were recorded in Burma.

99. Makers of paper flowers have been included in this group in accordance with the standard schemes although Group 100 seems more appropriate and does include the makers of paper lanterns.

100. This group includes makers of kites, of dolls and marionettes and of fishing tackle, but not makers of fish-cages and fish-traps for whom Group 45*a* provides. Making paper lanterns and taxidermy would also belong to this group; but, because they are not practised as principal but only as occasional occupations, none returned them. See also the note for Group 99.

101. This group includes the management and service of racecourses, football-grounds, etc., huntsmen, billiard-markers, the managers and other employees (except performers) of theatres, cinemas and other places of public entertainment and the staffs of public societies. Actors, singers and dancers are included in Group 178; boxers, conjurers, etc., in Group 179.

105. Pilot and light-house services are included in this group.

106. Persons belonging to this group have not been tabulated correctly because their returns failed to indicate the place of their employment. Probably most are included in Groups 186 and 187. Coolies on wharves and jetties are included in Group 117.

107a. } Clerks, peons, etc., working for persons of these groups are included in Group
107b. } 107*a*. (But see the note on Group 117 for coolies at wharves)—*Ship* includes (i) all vessels propelled by mechanical power otherwise than by an outboard motor, and (ii) sea-going vessels which are not of those types which are generally associated with some particular point on the shore from which they make short excursions to sea. (See the note on Group 110*a* below.)

108. (i) The whole of the Irrigation Branch of the Public Works Department is included in these two groups although only a small part of it is concerned strictly with transport (*e g.*, the staffs of the Twante and Pegu-Sittang canals) and the greater part is really assisting in agriculture. (ii) Clerks, peons, etc., employed in association with occupations properly of this group are included in it (iii) Probably some persons of this group have been tabulated in Group 111 through insufficient information in their returns.

109. The records for persons of this group do not indicate the place of their employment. Probably most are included in Groups 186 and 187, and some may be in Group 112.

110a. Clerks, peons and all others working for boat-owners except boatmen and towmen are included in this group. *Boat* includes (i) small sea-going vessels of the types which are generally associated with some particular point on the shore from which they make short excursions to sea, and (ii) inland vessels which are either not propelled by mechanical power or are propelled by an outboard motor. (See the definition of *ship* in the note on Group 107*a*.)

110b. See the definition of boat for Group 110*a* above. See also the note on Group 117 for coolies at wharves and other landing-places.

111. } The whole of the Roads and Buildings Branch of the Public Works Department
112. } is included in these groups; some of its members have little to do with means of transport and are chiefly occupied with the construction of residential buildings and of offices not concerned with transport, but it is impossible to classify them more minutely. The Public Works Departments of Municipal Committees and other local authorities should be classified here if specialised in work on roads and described accordingly in the schedules; but in most cases one or both of these conditions was not satisfied, and classification in Group 163 was given accordingly.

113a. } These two groups exclude all private servants but include all others who
113b. } are occupied in connection with transport by mechanically driven vehicles of any kind, including taxis, lorries, trams, etc. Managers for companies or persons owning such vehicles, and owners of such vehicles who manage the transport business, are included and also all their mechanics, drivers, cleaners, clerks, messengers and all other employees whether in the garage, works office or elsewhere Of these, drivers and engine-cleaners have been tabulated separately in Group 113*a* and all others in Group 113*b*. Makers or repairers of motor-vehicles who are not principally engaged in the actual transportation business together with all their employees, are in Group 90 See also the note on Group 114.

114 Occupations associated with transport on land are divided amongst Groups 111 to 119 inclusive. Groups 111 and 112 deal with the construction of roads; Groups 118 and 119 deals with railway construction and working; Group 116 deals with direct carriage by animals without the aid of vehicles, and Groups 113*a*, 113*b*, 114. 115 and 117 deal with transport by vehicles or by human labour as explained below.

Persons employed as private servants in connection with animals or vehicles having been separately classified in Groups 182 and 183, all others whose occupations are associated with vehicles are classified according to the motive power of the vehicle: Groups 113*a* and 113*b* taken together, Group 114 and Group 115 respectively thus correspond to vehicles propelled by mechanical power, by animals and by human labour. An exception is made however in the case of hand-carts which are regarded rather as contrivances assisting porters to carry goods than as vehicles, so that persons whose occupations are related to transport by hand-carts are assigned to Group 117. (See note on Group 117.)

The notes on the separate Groups 111 to 119 should also be consulted.

115. The vehicles concerned in this group are rickshaws, sedan-chairs and other vehicles drawn or carried by human labour and intended for the conveyance of human passengers. Hand-carts are not included; see note on Group 114.

116. This group is concerned only with actual carriage by animals, without the use of vehicles. See also the note on Group 114.

117. See also the note on Group 114. Group 117 was intended to include only porters and messengers employed in general transport on land otherwise than by rail. Coolies at jetties or wharves or goods stations loading or unloading boats or railway trucks have been regarded as belonging to this group when so identified in the records; and this applies also to coolies carrying luggage at railway stations but not on the railway staff. Hand-cart coolies have also been included in this group. So too have owners of hand-carts, who only hire the carts to coolies, although the title of the group does not cover them. Many belonging to this group have doubtlessly been included in Group 187, the note on which should be consulted. In accordance with the general rule peons or porters engaged for a particular industry or business or office are included not in Group 117 but in the group to which that industry, etc., belongs; *e.g.* peons in the employ of a wholesale dealer in piece-goods are in Group 123*a*; peons in a settlement office in Group 2; postal and telegraph peons in Group 120; porters on the railway staff in Group 119.

118.} These groups include all persons (except those mentioned below) engaged in
119.} railway offices and workshops and on railway construction as well as those engaged in working the railways. Railway doctors are in Group 171, railway police in Group 159, sweepers on railways in Group 103, the railway postal service in Group 120. Probably a number of persons of these two groups are included in Groups 185, 186 or 187. See also for coolies the note on Group 117.

121. A more complete title for either Group 121 or Order XXIV would be as follows: "All employed in connection with banking, money-lending, pawnbroking, foreign exchange, money changing and all occupations concerned solely with finance, credit and insurance—except stock and share brokers and jobbers and auditors, who are included in Group 122."

122. A more complete title for either Group 122 or Order XXV would be: "(i) Stock and share brokers and jobbers, auditors and labour agents; (ii) all such brokers (other than stock or share brokers), commission agents, auctioneers, appraisers (other than Government servants), commercial travellers or warehouse-owners as are not confined to a specified particular kind of trade, and (iii) all employees of the foregoing."

127. This group includes trade in pottery which constituted Group 112 of 1911 and also trade in bricks and tiles which formed part of Group 128 of 1911. See note on Group 143 below.

128. The term *chemical products* includes drugs, dyes, paints, petrol, kerosene, candles and all other products of petroleum refineries, medicines (patent or not), explosives, etc. But there is the difficulty that as the Burmese word *hse* for tobacco is often used for medicines without the distinguishing prefix *bara*, some persons belonging to this group may have been tabulated in Group 137 or *vice-versa*. Many traders tabulated in other groups sell articles concerned in this group but are not tabulated here because they are either general dealers or trade principally in some other kind of goods.

129. This group includes the same occupations as the corresponding Group 114 of the census of 1911 although the title in 1911 did not mention trade in ice.

133. Most of this group are cattle-keepers who sell milk; and some people of the same kind have probably been returned as cattle-keepers and included in Group 11. There is confusion in the tabulation of Groups 11, 70 and 133 owing to incomplete descriptions in the schedules. See the notes on those groups.

137. The number of opium dealers in any district of Divisional Burma is small; the total number of opium shops in the province in 1921, excluding the Shan States, Chin Hills and some other areas under special administration, was only 125, and the total number of this group in the whole province who are concerned with opium is probably under 1,000. The remainder of the group are tobacco-dealers. Many of the cigar-makers of Group 75 also are sellers of the cigars they make. See the notes on Groups 75 and 128.

139. Sellers of oil-cake are in this group.

140. This group includes trade in hats, socks, ready-made shoes and ready-made clothing of all kinds and also in umbrellas, walking-sticks or canes, perfumes, etc.

141. "Woven furnishings" include carpets, curtains, bedding and mats made of reeds, bamboos, etc., which are not used for building. Tent-sellers are also in this group.

142. The goods with which this group is concerned include all household goods not in Group 141, such as hardware, cooking-utensils, porcelain, crockery, glassware, bottles, gardening tools.

143. This group includes trade in building-stone, plaster, cement, sand, etc. The corresponding group in 1911 was Group 128, which however included also trade in bricks and tiles which has been transferred to Group 127 of 1921. See note on Group 127.

144.} Group 144 relates to all kinds of cycles whether with motors or not, and also
145.} to all kinds of mechanical transport whether on land or water. Group 145 relates to all kinds of transport without mechanical power except cycles. Hirers of hackney carriages are in Groups 113*b* and 114.

147. Fuel includes wood, charcoal, coal; cow-dung is not commonly used as fuel in Burma and there are none who live by selling it for use in this (or any other) way.

149. Sellers of images of all kinds are included in this group.

151. There is no trade in stable refuse or cow-dung in Burma. See note on Group 147. Trade in bats' guano is covered by this group.

154. Stamp-vendors are included in this group.

155. In this group are included 319 Mahomedan and 130 Hindu male workers, all born outside Burma, who although in military service reported an agricultural subsidiary occupation; it seems probable that some of them were merely taking advantage of being far from their homes to pretend to have the status of landowners, or that their wish was father to their thought. The Mahomedans were Pathans or Punjabis while the Hindus were Mahrattas.

159. There are 448 female workers recorded in this group; probably all are dependents of this group for whom the enumeration-record was written in the wrong column. The numbers are distributed through most of the districts and the matter was noticed too late for correction. The Excise Department is included in Group 161, not associated with police in this group.

161.} Soldiers, sailors and police belong to Sub-class VI; engineers, doctors,
162.} sweepers and others, the character of whose occupation is not affected by the
163.} fact that they are employed in the public service, are not included in this group but in the group assigned to their specific occupation. The Official Assignee and his staff are in Group 161, and so are all the Excise Department. Health Officers have all been assigned to Group 171. See Article 6 of the preface to this section of the table.

165.} *Methilayin*, *pothudaw* and *yathe* have been treated as workers of Group 166
166.} and *koyin* as dependents in the same group. *Tayahaw* and other lay preachers
167.} have been assigned to Group 167, but *kappiya* have been assigned to Group 181 as domestic servants.

169. This group includes solicitors and conveyancers, notaries public, receivers for courts, *kazis*. The Official Assignee and his staff are in Group 161.

170. Interpreters in courts of justice are included here.

171. This group includes all practising principally as doctors, dentists, oculists or veterinary surgeons, etc., whether with European or orthodox qualifications or not; also all health officers.

172. This group includes all hospital and asylum establishments except those in Group 171.

173. All grades of the Education Department are included in this group.

176. Civil engineers of the Public Works Department and their staffs are in Groups 108, 109, 111, 112; while those of the railways, with their staffs are in Groups 118 and 119. The Land Records Department was included partly in Group 159 of 1911 which corresponds to Group 176 of 1921, but in 1921 it is in Group 2*b*; see items 1 and 10 of Section E below. The figures for Group 176 are obviously inaccurate.

177b. There is no distinction between many included in this group and the *bedin-saya* of Group 179, as many shown in each might be described with equal reason so as to belong to either group. Neither the figures shown for this group nor those shown for Group 179 should ever be used alone, but only the sum of those for the two groups. See also the note on Group 179.

177c. See the note on Group 57.

177d. It was originally intended to include all makers of images in Groups 177*c* and 177*d*, those who worked in stone being separated in Group 177*c* while those who worked in other materials formed Group 177*d*. But owing to an entry in the index for *wood-carvers* ("Group 83 if not cabinet-maker") and another for *Carver in wood and ebony* ("Group 44 if not for furniture") those of Group 177*d* were wrongly classified in Groups 44 or 49 according as the material was wood or metal.

177e. Adult scholarship-holders studying for a particular profession stated in the enumeration-schedules are included in the group corresponding to that profession; all others are in Group 177*e*. Juvenile scholarship-holders are classified as dependents in the group of their parents or guardians, but if that is not known they are classified as dependents in Group 177*e*.

179. Practically all in this group were described as *bedin-saya* (fortune teller). See the notes on Groups 101 and 177*b*.

180. The workers of this group include all who derive the principal part of their incomes from such sources as pensions, dividends or royalties, or the ownership of rights-of-way or of buildings or of land used for building, mining or any other purpose than the occupations of Sub-classes 1*b* and 1*c*. See also the note for Group 1, and Article 8 of Section B of this Part.

181. } 182. } 183. } These three groups include all domestic servants except sweepers. In particular they include all the private servants excluded from Groups 113 to 116 inclusive—see particularly the note of Group 114. Group 182 includes coachmen, grooms (or syces), private rickshaw-pullers, dog-boys, private milch-cow tenders and the like. Group 183 includes drivers and cleaners of private motor-cars; all other domestic servants clearly described as such are included in Group 181, except sweepers. (All sweepers are in Group 103 wherever employed.) In agreement with the standard schemes all except sweepers and punkha-pullers who have designations generally representing domestic servants (*e.g.* waterman) but are employed in offices, factories, shops, etc., are classified, in accordance with Article 3 of the preface to this Section, in the same group as clerks or messengers employed in the same office, factory, shop, etc.; but they have been regarded as domestic servants if the place of employment was not indicated. The standard schemes follow this rule for punkha-pullers also; but in Burma punkha-pullers whose place of employment was not indicated have been assigned to Group 187 as there are very few domestic servants specifically employed as punkha-pullers. Group 183 corresponds to a part of Group 166 of 1911, the remainder of that group forming now Group 186.

184, 185 } 186, 187 } See Articles 4, 5 and 6 of the preface to this Section and the note on Group 117. Groups 183 and 186 together correspond to Group 166 of 1911.

188. Prisoners under trial as well as convicted prisoners are included in this group.

191. Only a few persons with definitely described occupations had to be tabulated as "other non-productive" A few described as *gambler* are included; they are probably persons who set up booths for games of chance at pagoda festivals The group consists chiefly of persons for whom the record was so defective that they could not be classified even in Groups 184 to 187. A number of persons shown in the schedules only as *Dependents* have been tabulated as dependents in this group for lack of further information; a particular instance of this is afforded by approximately 2,400 persons in Toungoo district, almost entirely Indians of Peoples IX and X.

SECTION C.—ALPHABETICAL INDEX OF OCCUPATIONS (*Abridged*).

The index below shows only a few occupations for which the discovery of the group containing them is likely to be difficult. A complete index of all occupations recorded in the schedules would occupy about fifteen or twenty of these pages in double columns, and even more if all the various names given to some occupations were separately shown. It is believed that with the aid of the explanations of Sections A and B the group-titles themselves will give a sufficiently clear indication of the group which includes almost any occupation other than those shown below unless the numbers concerned are negligeably small.

In all cases the note in Section B on any group mentioned in this index should be consulted.

Occupation.	Group.	Occupation.	Group.
Appraiser (not Government service)	122	Interpreter in courts of justice	170
Auctioneer	122	Jemadar	*
Auditor (commercial)	122	Jetty-cooly	117
Asylum service	172	Knife-grinder	48
Bat's guano seller	151	Koyin	166†
Birds' nests, collector of	9*d*	Life-assurance	121
Boat painter	92	Light-house service	105
Boxer	179	Milkman	11, 70, 133
Brick pounder	89	Oil-cake seller	139
Carver of images	177*c* and 177*d*	Paper flowers, maker of	99
Castrator of cattle	172	Paper lanterns, maker of	100
Cloth saddles, maker of	40	Picture-frame maker	100
Cooly recruiting-agent	122	Pilot	105
Cutch-boiler	9*c*	Sail-maker	92
Dah-maker	48	Scene-painter	101
Dairyman	11, 70, 133	Scholarship-holder	177*e*
Education service	173	Sign-board painter	89
Electroplater	50	Spear-maker	48
Elephant-driver	9*b*	Stamp-vendor	154
Export agent (general)	122	Steamer-cooly	117
Flower (artificial) maker	99	Stone-images, seller of	149
Gambler	191	Story-teller	179
Glass-mosaic worker	52	Tent-maker	184
Grass-cutter	9*d*	Tent-seller	141
Hand-cart cooly	117	Type-founder	50
Health officer	171	Upasin	165
Hospital service	172	Whitewasher	89

SECTION D.—VARIATIONS IN BURMA FROM THE STANDARD SCHEME OF 1921.

Some occupations are assigned to different groups in different provinces because they are practised under different conditions which alter their essential nature; *e.g.* elephant-drivers are assigned to Group 182 in the standard scheme, but in Burma they are assigned

* According to service in which employed; if a sweeper, 103.
† Koyin are tabulated in Group 166 as *dependents.*

to Group 9*b* because they are employed not as private servants but in connection with the timber industry. Such variations which really aim at maintaining essential uniformity, and also variations of titles without change of content, are ignored in this Section, which takes account only of differences in the system of the classification. Subject to this reservation each category of the Burma system is equivalent to the category of the standard scheme of the same grade and serial number unless the contrary is stated below.

Sub-class I of the standard scheme, with the title *Exploitation of Animals and Vegetation*, is represented in Burma by the three Sub-classes *Ia, Ib* and *Ic*.

Order I of the standard scheme with the title *Pasture and Agriculture* is represented by Orders I, IIA, IIB, IIC and IID of the Burma Scheme (Burma Order IIE corresponds to Standard Order II). For the separate parts into which Order I is divided in the standard scheme the relationships are as follows:—Groups 1 and 3 of Order I (*a*), *Ordinary Cultivation*, are equivalent to Burma Order I; while the remainder of Standard Order I (*a*)—that is Groups 2, 4 and 5—and Standard Order I (*b*) together constitute Burma Order IIA; Standard Orders I (*c*), I (*d*) and I (*e*) are equivalent to Burma Orders IIB, IIC and IID respectively.

Order II of the standard scheme, *Fishing and Hunting*, corresponds to Order IIE of the Burma Scheme.

Groups.—Each group of the standard scheme of 1921, except Nos. 1 to 7 inclusive, is equivalent to the Burma group of the same serial number, or in cases where two or more Burma groups have the same serial number with different letters affixed, to the sum of all those groups. For Groups 1 to 7 the relationship is as follows:—

Group of the Standard Scheme.		Equivalent in the Burma Scheme.
No.	Title.	
1	Income from rent of agricultural land	Group 1.
2	Ordinary cultivators	Groups 3*a*, 3*b* and 4.
3	Agents, managers of landed estates (*not planters*), clerks, rent collectors, etc.	Groups 2*a* and 2*b*.
4	Farm servants	} Group 3*c*.
5	Field labourers	
6	Tea, coffee, cinchona, rubber and indigo plantations ...	Groups 6*b*, 6*e*, 6*g*, 6*h* and 6*j*.
7	Growers of fruit, flowers, vegetables, betel-vine, areca-nut, etc.	Groups 5, 6*a*, 6*c*, 6*d*, 6*f* and 7.

Section E.—Comparison of the Classification-Schemes of 1921 and 1911.

1. The principal variations of the classification-scheme of 1921 from that of 1911 are:—

(*a*) All the variations from the standard scheme of 1921 which are shown in Section D above.

(*b*) Changes in the content of the following categories as detailed in the schedule at the end of this section:—

Classes—All.
Sub-classes—*Ia* and *III* to *XI* inclusive.
Orders *—1, 2, 6, 7, 8, 9, 11, 15, 16, 17, 18, 20, 21, 24, 25, 30, 35, 40 (equal to 41 of 1911), 49, 50, 52 and 53.
Groups—See the schedule below.

(*c*) The subdivision of certain groups—see paragraph 3 below.

(*d*) Changes in the serial numbers of some groups—see paragraph 3 below.

(*e*) Changes in the titles of some categories without other change of their content besides that (if any) noted in items (*a*) and (*b*) above—see paragraph 4 below.

2. Minor changes besides the above have been caused by the association of some occupations with different groups, in some cases by direction in the index of occupation-names used in classification, in others unwittingly as a result of the recognition at the time of classification of different aspects of one and the same occupation. Only cases of no numerical significance can fall into the latter class; and it is hoped that all of the former class which have such significance have been included in the schedule below.

* The numbers of Orders are here given in Arabic type for clearness although properly Roman numerals should be used for Orders.

3. Apart from a few cases noted in the schedule below, the groups are ranged in the same serial order in the standard schemes of 1921 and 1911, the parts of each group which has been subdivided being arranged consecutively in the place of the group they replace. As these subdivisions have been separately numbered in the series the numbers of corresponding groups in the standard scheme of 1911 and 1921 are not identical ; but as *Orders* of the same serial number in the two schemes are approximately identical, and as the serial order of groups in each *Order* is generally the same, there is no difficulty in identifying corresponding groups by their titles. Those groups which are distinguished by letters added to the same serial number represent subdivisions made in Burma alone of the group of that serial number in the standard scheme, and should be taken together as one unit for such a comparison.

4. Those cases in which the change of the title of a category corresponds to a change of its content (other than a minor change of the kind noted in paragraph 2 above) are noted in the schedule below. Notes on some other cases of a change of title are included in Section B ; in other cases the equality will generally be obvious.

Item No.	Orders, Sub-classes and Classes affected, 1921 and 1911.	Groups affected. 1921.	Groups affected. 1911.	Remarks. (*Title* means the title of the group of 1911 shown in column 4.)
1	2	3	4	5
1	Orders I, IIA, XLIX. Sub-classes *Ia*, *VIII*. Classes A, C.	1 to 7 inclusive and 176.	1 to 7 inclusive, 144 and 158.	Groups 1 to 7 inclusive include nominally the same occupations in 1921 as in 1911 although the distribution between the groups differs as shown in Section D. But in 1911 the Land Records staffs were divided between Groups 144 and 158 as government servants or surveyors, while in 1921 they have been tabulated in Group 2*b* (corresponding to Group 3 of 1911) as assistants of Government in its aspect of landowner. See also item 10 of this list and Section B.
2	Orders VI, VII.	36 and 41	28	*Title*.—Textile work with hair or bristles, brush-makers, etc.
			29	*Title*—Persons occupied with feathers.
			34	*Title*—Furriers.
3	Orders VII, XVI.	40	33	*Title*—Makers of leather articles, such as trunks, water-bags, etc.
			81	*Title*—Saddlers, harness-makers, whip and lash-makers.
4	Orders VIII, XV.	45*a*, 45*b* and 45*c*.	37	*Title*—Basket makers and other industries of wooden material, including leaves (except Group 44 of 1921).
			79	The thatchers and builders using bamboo and similar materials are taken from this group to be associated with Group 37 of 1911 in the three groups 45*a*, 45*b* and 45*c* ; the remainder of the group forms new Group 89 for which see below.
5	Orders IX, XV	48	39	*Title*—Plough and agricultural implement makers.
			41	*Title*—Iron workers not in Groups 46 and 47 of 1921, and makers of implements and tools principally or exclusively of iron.
			79	Only the locksmiths of Group 79 of 1911 have been transferred to Group 48 of 1921 ; for the remainder of Group 79 see below.
6	Orders XI, XVII.	59	51	*Title*—Manufacture of aerated and mineral waters.
			83	The ice-makers of Group 83 of 1911 have been taken to Group 59 of 1921 leaving the balance to form Group 93 of 1921.
7	Orders VIII, XV	86 to 89	77, 78 and 79.	These three groups of 1911 included all building industries other than lime-burning and cement-working, and together equal the three groups of 1921, save that thatchers and builders of bamboo houses who were included in Group 79 have been transferred to Group 45*c*.
8	Order XVII	93	83	Group 83 of 1911 included Group 93 of 1921 and also ice-makers who have been transferred to Group 59 of 1921. (See above.)
9	...	104	...	No corresponding group or order in 1911.

Item No.	Orders, Sub-classes and Classes affected, 1921 and 1911.	Groups affected. 1921.	Groups affected. 1911.	Remarks. (*Title* means the title of the group of 1911 shown in column 4.)
1	2	3	4	5
10	Orders XX, XXI, XLV, Sub-classes *IV*, *VII*, *VIII*. Classes B, C.	108 109 111 112 161 176	96 98 144 158	The scheme of 1911 required "Public Works Department officers, etc." to be assigned to Group 158 which corresponds in title to Group 176 of 1921, while their labourers and their contractors and the employees of those contractors were assigned to Groups 96 or 98. The instruction of 1911 was vague and the exact manner of its application is not known; probably the Public Works Department (including engineers, overseers, clerks and peons) was divided in practice between Groups 144 and 158 which correspond to Groups 161 and 176 of 1921. See also item 1 of this list for Groups 144 and 158 of 1911.
11	Orders XXIV, XXV.	121	107	Pawnbrokers have been transferred from Group 122 (otherwise equivalent to Group 107 of 1911) to Group 121.
12	Orders XXX, XXXVI.	127	112 128	*Title*—Trade in pottery. *Title*—Trade in building materials. But only trade in bricks and tiles has been transferred to Group 127 of 1921 and the remainder constitutes Group 143 of 1921.
13	Orders XXX, XXXVI.	143	128	See above note on Group 127 of 1921.
14	...	158	..	No corresponding group or order in 1911.
15	...	165, 166, 167	148, 149, 150	The three groups of 1921 are equivalent to the three of 1911, but the distribution amongst the three has changed.
16	Orders XLIX and L.	173 174	156	Nominally the content of Group 156 of 1911 was the sum of Groups 173 and 174 of 1921; but in fact *Drawing-masters* (and their peons, etc.) were placed in Group 159 and *Music Teachers* (and their peons, etc.) in Group 160. For 1921 these have been included in Groups 173, 174 under Order XLIX, *Instruction*.
17	See Column 5 for this entry.	176	158	See items 1 and 10 of this schedule.
18	Orders XVIII, L. Sub-classes III, V. Classes B, C.	177*a* to *e*	85 159	*Title*—Newspaper and magazine managers and editors, journalists, etc. The remainder of Groups 177*a* to *e* inclusive, and also Drawing-masters and their clerks, peons, etc., for which see preceding note on Groups 173 and 174.
19	Orders XLIX and L.	178	160	Group 178 of 1921 differs from Group 160 of 1911 by the exclusion of music teachers and their peons, etc. See note on Groups 173 and 174 above.
20	* Orders XL, L. Sub-classes V, VIII. Classes B, C.	179	137	The group has been displaced as a whole without change of content.
21	Order LI. Sub-class IX. Classes C, D.	181	161	(*a*) Group 161 of 1911 included the occupations of Group 181 of 1921 and also the scholarship-holders who in 1921 are classified as described in the note on Group 177*e* in Section B above. (*b*) The group so amended, has been transferred from Class C in which it was included in 1911 to Class D. (*c*) Classes C and D are affected both by the amendment (*a*) and the transfer (*b*); but Order LI and Sub-class IX are affected only by (*a*).
22	Orders III, LIII Sub-classes X, XI.	184 186	166	Group 186 of 1921 differs from Group 166 of 1911 by the exclusion of private motor-drivers and cleaners separately tabulated in Group 183 of 1921.

* XL of 1921, corresponding to XLI of 1911.

Imperial Table XVII.—*Occupations.* Part II.—*Provincial Summary.*

Class.	Sub-Class.	TITLE OF CLASS OR SUB-CLASS OF OCCUPATIONS.	WHOLE PROVINCE. Total Workers and Dependents.	Workers. Total Workers. Males.	Workers. Total Workers. Females.	Workers with an agricultural or other subsidiary occupation. Agricultural. Males.	Agricultural. F'm'l's	Other. Males.	Other. F'm'l's.	Dependents.
1a	1b	1d	2	3	4	5	6	7	8	9
		All Occupations (Total Population) ...	13,169,099	4,060,921	2,734,517	104,566	64,700	405,320	210,295	6,373,661
A	...	**Production of raw materials** ..	9,675,097	2,843,137	2,016,572	71,282	44,533	364,313	179,607	4,815,388
	I	*Exploitation of animals or vegetation* ...	*9,632,212*	*2,816,117*	*2,013,577*	*71,079*	*44,512*	*364,106*	*179,556*	*4,802,518*
	Ia	Control of land or water used for the exploitation of animals or vegetation.	157,135	36,596	40,732	1,069	1,089	5,888	4,570	79,807
	Ib	Cultivated and wild plants	9,239,997	2,689,311	1,945,333	67,810	42,748	352,877	173,253	4,605,353
	Ic	Domestic and wild animals	235,080	90,210	27,512	2,200	675	5,341	1,733	117,358
	II	Exploitation of minerals	42,885	27,020	2,995	203	21	207	51	12,870
B	..	**Industry and commerce**	2,321,919	727,093	530,819	18,619	12,012	30,417	22,961	1,064,007
	III	Industry	870,827	280,631	203,317	8,662	6,464	10,423	10,521	386,879
	IV	Transport	354,274	177,404	15,938	4,119	315	5,088	964	160,932
	V	Trade, finance and insurance ...	1,096,818	269,058	311,564	5,838	5,133	14,906	11,476	516,196
C	..	**Public service and the professions and liberal arts.**	462,007	214,983	17,760	11,152	171	4,345	293	229,264
	VI	Public force	76,400	37,628	469	779	1	155	39	38,303
	VII	Public administration	103,041	33,242	992	9,102	90	1,763	42	68,807
	VIII	The professions and liberal arts ...	282,566	144,113	16,299	1,271	80	2,427	212	122,154
D	...	**Miscellaneous**	710,076	275,708	169,366	3,513	7,984	6,245	7,434	265,002
	IX	Persons (not in Sub-class I*a*) without an occupation but receiving an income.	13,800	3,230	1,175	153	10	344	41	9,395
	X	Domestic service ...	73,669	43,059	8,001	807	87	637	115	22,609
	XI	Insufficiently described occupations ...	573,641	202,629	149,294	2,533	7,855	5,117	7,172	221,718
	XII	Unproductive and unclassified ...	48,966	26,790	10,896	20	32	147	106	11,280

ORDER AND GROUP.

Class / Sub-class	Ser. No.	Title.	2	3	4	5	6	7	8	9
A.—PRODUCTION OF RAW MATERIALS. *Ia.—Control of land or water used for the exploitation of animals or vegetation.*	1	**Control by persons not principally practising an occupation of Sub-class I*b* or I*c* of land or water used for such an occupation.**	157,135	36,596	40,732	1,069	1,089	5,888	4,570	79,807
	1	Ownership and rights over land or water used for occupations of Sub-class I*b* or I*c*.	147,764	33,419	40,732	999	1,089	5,831	4,570	73,613
	2*a*	Agents, managers, clerks, rent-collectors, etc., for land or water belonging to persons of Group I.	5	1	...	..	...	...	...	4
	2*b*	Agents, managers, clerks, rent-collectors, etc., for land or water similarly used but belonging to Government.	9,366	3,176	...	70	...	57	...	6,190

IMPERIAL TABLE XVII.—*Occupations.* PART II.—*Provincial Summary*—continued.

Class.	Sub-Class.	Serial No.	ORDER AND GROUP. TITLE.	WHOLE PROVINCE. Total Workers and Dependents.	WORKERS. Total Workers. Males.	Females.	Workers with an agricultural or other subsidiary occupation. Agricultural. Males.	F'm'l's	Other. Males.	F'm'l's.	DEPENDENTS.
1a	1b	1c	1d	2	3	4	5	6	7	8	9
A.—PRODUCTION OF RAW MATERIALS.	Ib.—CULTIVATED AND WILD PLANTS.	IIA	**Cultivation**	9,158,932	2,657,681	1,937,779	67,012	42,574	350,823	172,926	4,563,472
		3	*Agriculture proper*	7,954,012	2,300,084	1,639,878	50,889	30,269	308,844	149,922	4,024,050
			(a) Cultivating owners ...	4,064,042	1,165,537	903,295	32,366	18,371	183,783	93,923	1,995,210
			(b) Cultivating tenants ...	1,814,164	512,362	331,178	14,641	9,055	74,184	27,513	970,624
			(c) Agricultural labourers ...	2,085,806	622,185	405,405	3,882	2,843	50,877	28,486	1,058,216
		4	Taungya	942,285	278,011	246,833	10,264	8,884	36,366	20,185	417,441
		5	Market gardening	162	71	1	...	..	...	...	90
		6	*Cultivation of certain crops (planters, managers and labourers).*	90,682	28,756	19,932	3,002	2,010	1,938	845	41,994
			(a) Betel-vine	19,412	5,616	3,701	567	136	739	175	10,095
			(b) Rubber	9,129	5,620	807	14	9	48	17	2,702
			(c) Sugarcane	16,809	5,336	1,969	312	77	320	83	9,504
			(d) Citronella ...	344	218	6	29	..	..	...	120
			(e) Tea	38,115	10,305	11,423	1,745	1,670	511	154	16,387
			(f) Opium and Ganja ...	6,867	1,658	2,024	335	118	320	416	3,185
			(g) Coffee	2	1	..	...	...	...	...	1
			(h) Indigo	2	...	2	...	...	...	...	...
			(j) Cinchona	2	2	...	...	...	...	..	...
		7	Orchard gardens and all other horticulture not included in Groups 5 and 6.	161,791	50,759	31,135	2,857	1,411	3,675	1,974	79,897
		IIB	**Forestry**	81,065	31,630	7,554	798	174	2,054	327	41,881
		8	Forest officers, rangers, guards, etc.	12,168	4,189	189	43	...	34	12	7,790
		9a	Charcoal burners	3,584	1,214	365	34	28	37	21	2,005
		9b	Wood and bamboo-cutters and fuel-collectors.	51,322	21,278	3,745	589	91	1,617	176	26,296
		9c	Cutch collectors	2,482	747	506	20	19	61	40	1,229
		9d	All other collectors of forest produce except lac-collectors.	11,493	4,196	2,741	112	36	305	78	4,556
		10	Lac collectors	16	6	5	...	...	...	...	5
	Ic.—DOMESTIC AND WILD ANIMALS.	IIC	**Raising of farm stock** ...	72,611	34,985	10,205	799	361	2,672	1,058	27,421
		11	Cattle and buffalo breeders and keepers.	26,214	11,786	3,204	192	62	1,391	313	11,224
		12	Sheep, goat and pig breeders ...	14,505	3,809	3,762	240	233	615	565	6,934
		13	Breeders of other animals (horses, mules, asses, etc.).	636	382	42	10	3	12	...	212
		14	Herdsmen, shepherds, goatherds, etc.	31,256	19,008	3,197	357	63	654	180	9,051
		IID	**Raising of other animals** ...	1,660	768	382	7	3	13	8	510
		15	Birds, bees, etc	748	197	177	...	...	3	2	374
		16	Silk-worms	912	571	205	7	3	10	6	136
		IIE	**Exploitation of wild animals** ...	160,809	54,457	16,925	1,394	311	2,656	667	89,427
		17	Fishing and pearling ...	157,855	52,462	16,790	1,384	311	2,642	665	88,603
		18	Hunting	2,954	1,995	135	10	...	14	2	824

IMPERIAL TABLE XVII.—*Occupations.* PART II.—*Provincial Summary*—continued.

Class.	Sub-Class.	Serial No.	ORDER AND GROUP. TITLE.	WHOLE PROVINCE. Total Workers and Dependents.	Workers. Total Workers. Males.	Total Workers. Females.	Workers with an agricultural or other subsidiary occupation. Agricultural. Males.	Agricultural. F'm'l's.	Other. Males.	Other. F'm'l's.	Dependents.
1a	1b	1c	1d	2	3	4	5	6	7	8	9
A.—PRODUCTION OF RAW MATERIALS—*contd.*	*II.—EXPLOITATION OF MINERALS.*	III	**Coal, petroleum and metals** .	**28,136**	**19,486**	**856**	**69**	**8**	**71**	**11**	**7,794**
		19	Coal mines	54	23	1	..	...	...	...	30
		20	Petroleum wells ..	13,229	9,487	309	34	2	27	6	3,433
		21	Metals and minerals from which metals are extracted.	14,853	9,976	546	35	6	44	5	4,331
		IV	**Minerals not of Order III or V** ...	**10,787**	**5,989**	**1,720**	**51**	**4**	**89**	**20**	**3,078**
		22a	Jade	2,251	1,865	33	11	...	12	...	353
		22b	Rubies, spinels and associated stones and all precious stones.	2,412	756	938	2	...	24	8	718
		22c	Other minerals not soluble in water (limestone, laterite, etc.).	6,124	3,368	749	38	4	53	12	2,007
		V	**Minerals soluble in water**	**3,962**	**1,545**	**419**	**83**	**9**	**47**	**20**	**1,998**
		23	Rock, sea and marsh salt	3,962	1,545	419	83	9	47	20	1,998
		24	Saltpetre, alum and other substances soluble in water.	...	...	...	...	...	...	...	...
B.—INDUSTRY AND COMMERCE.	*III.—INDUSTRY.*	VI	**Textiles**	**115,338**	**8,859**	**75,018**	**81**	**2,810**	**370**	**4,287**	**31,461**
		25	Cotton ginning, cleaning and pressing	5,278	1,039	2,872	16	85	24	120	1,367
		26	Cotton spinning	5,144	508	3,490	2	14	1	64	1,146
		27	Cotton sizing and weaving ...	65,913	1,846	46,863	22	2,155	52	3,194	17,204
		28	Jute spinning, pressing and weaving ...	360	39	250	...	...	...	..	71
		29	Rope, twine, or string making ...	4,261	1,353	994	15	...	74	21	1,914
		30	Work with other fibres	61	23	1	...	...	1	...	37
		31	Wool-carding and spinning ...	...	...	...	...	...	...	...	...
		32	Weaving of woollen blankets ...	...	...	...	...	...	...	...	...
		33	Weaving of woollen carpets .	...	...	...	...	...	...	...	...
		34	Silk spinning	926	83	490	...	...	1	3	353
		35	Silk weaving	29,436	2,936	18,041	20	510	185	764	8,459
		36	Textile work using hair	2	2	...	...	...	...	...	...
		37	Dyeing, bleaching, printing, preparation and sponging of textiles.	3,956	1,029	2,017	6	46	32	121	910
		38	Other textile industries	1	1	...	...	...	...	...	...
		VII	**Hides, feathers, bristles and hard materials from the animal kingdom.**	**1,067**	**537**	**53**	**1**	..	...	**5**	**477**
		39	Tanners, curriers, leather-dressers, leather-dyers, etc.	193	118	2	...	...	...	...	73
		40	Makers of leather articles other than articles of dress.	750	349	50	1	.	...	5	351
		41	Furriers and persons occupied with feathers or bristles; brush makers.	...	...	...	...	...	..	...	...
		42	Workers in bone, ivory, horn, shell, etc. (except button-makers).	124	70	1	...	...	...	...	53
		VIII	**Wood**	**214,170**	**79,498**	**24,870**	**1,489**	**777**	**3,255**	**1,049**	**109,802**
		43	Sawyers	60,040	25,737	1,685	487	21	899	38	32,618
		44	Carpenters, turners and joiners, etc. ...	90,969	36,399	2,283	612	46	1,235	76	52,287
		45a	Lacquer-workers and makers of basket-work, sieves and cages of bamboo, cane, etc.	16,525	6,343	3,263	120	38	372	149	6,919
		45b	Makers with woody material of mats not used for walls or floors.	24,712	5,131	10,386	138	407	390	462	9,195
		45c	All others working with leaves or other woody materials.	21,924	5,888	7,253	132	265	359	324	8,783

IMPERIAL TABLE XVII.—*Occupations.* PART II.—*Provincial Summary*—continued.

Class.	Sub-Class.	Serial No.	ORDER AND GROUP. TITLE.	WHOLE PROVINCE. Total Workers and Dependents.	Workers. Total Workers. Males.	Total Workers. Females.	Workers with an agricultural or other subsidiary occupation. Agricultural. Males.	Agricultural. F'm'l's.	Other. Males.	Other. F'm'l's.	Dependents.
1a	1b	1c	1d	2	3	4	5	6	7	8	9
B.—INDUSTRY AND COMMERCE—*continued.*	III.—*INDUSTRY*—continued.	IX	**Metals**	41,776	16,690	1,037	321	27	640	46	24,049
		46	Smelting, casting, forging and rolling of iron.	798	442	10	...	.	...	2	346
		47	Makers of guns and other arms ...	150	84	...	..	...	1	...	66
		48	Other workers in iron and makers of articles consisting principally or exclusively of iron.	32,053	12,394	745	278	25	562	44	18,914
		49	All workers in brass, copper and bell-metal.	2,508	1,120	143	25	...	17	..	1,245
		50	All workers in other metals except precious metals.	6,233	2,648	137	18	2	60	...	3,448
		51	Workers in mints, die-sinkers, etc. ..	34	2	2	...	...	..	..	30
		X	**Ceramics**	30,602	9,901	9,771	150	192	272	405	10,930
		52	Makers of glass and crystal ware .	844	239	256	4	4	10	5	349
		53	Makers of bangles, beads, necklaces, ear-studs, etc., made of glass.	52	11	9	..	...		...	32
		54	Makers of porcelain and crockery ...	22	5	6	1	..	...	...	11
		55	Potters and earthen pipe and bowl makers.	17,035	3,129	7,628	83	173	154	370	6,298
		56	Brick and tile makers ...	12,629	6,517	1,872	62	15	108	30	4,240
		57	Workers in mosaic, talc, mica, etc., and workers in alabaster other than sculptors.	...	..	...	...	...	..	.	...
		XI	**Manufacture or refining of chemical products and analogous substances.**	20,324	9,021	1,778	166	18	146	70	9,525
		58	Matches and explosive materials .	24	18	..	...		1	..	6
		59	Aerated and mineral waters and ice .	363	164	10		...	1	...	189
		60	Dyes, paints, ink and pencils ...	33	7	9	..	...	...	..	17
		61	Vegetable oils	7,345	3,130	1,174	42	15	122	54	3,041
		62	Mineral oils	11,455	4,957	427	5	2	21	1	6,071
		63	Paper, cardboard and papier maché ...	332	114	129	2	1	1	13	89
		64a	Soap	114	30	25	...	...		2	59
		64b	Perfumes	616	567	4	117	...	...	...	45
		64c	Drugs, resin, celluloid and chemical or analogous products not included in other groups of Order XI.	42	34	...	..	...	...	...	8
		XII	**Food**	223,528	68,293	60,807	5,486	2,238	3,256	3,717	94,428
		65	Rice huskers and pounders; and flour-grinders.	97,416	36,527	24,402	142	560	453	1,448	36,487
		66	Bakers and biscuit makers .	2,037	1,361	130	.		16	3	546
		67	Grain parchers	...	...	...	...	...	...	...	...
		68	Butchers	2,041	737	70	4	...	30	8	1,234
		69	Fish curers	930	212	287	9	10	12	11	431
		70	Butter, cheese and ghee makers	86	45	7	2	...	2	...	34
		71	Sugar, jaggery and kyantaga-makers	8,040	748	5,686	13	550	20	563	1,606
		72	Sweetmeat makers, preparers of jam and condiments, etc.	20,562	3,287	8,795	44	231	189	453	8,550
		73	Brewers and distillers	231	76	43	2	1	...	...	112
		74	Toddy-drawers	70,645	23,958	8,331	5,249	862	2,492	1,036	38,356
		75	Tobacco manufacturers .	21,540	1,412	13,056	21	24	42	195	7,072
		XIII	**Dress and the toilet**	114,864	41,144	26,057	293	277	1,188	861	47,663
		76	Hat, cap and turban makers ...	513	119	101	12	.	9	1	293
		77	Tailors, milliners, dressmakers, darners and embroiderers on linen.	64,971	19,166	17,635	215	221	873	652	27,870
		78	Shoe, boot and sandal makers ...	11,776	5,539	1,162	18	9	76	23	5,075
		79	Makers of umbrellas and of other articles pertaining to dress.	4,796	2,121	720	4	...	36	10	1,955
		80	Washing, cleaning and dyeing articles of dress.	17,233	8,078	4,311	6	9	47	24	6,844
		81	Barbers, hairdressers and wig-makers	5,006	3,324	192	1		23	...	1,490
		82	Massagers (*ahnetkthè*) and tattooers ..	10,569	2,497	3,936	37	38	194	151	4,136

IMPERIAL TABLE XVII.—*Occupations.* PART II.—*Provincial Summary*—continued.

Class.	Sub-Class.	Serial No.	ORDER AND GROUP. TITLE.	Total Workers and Dependents.	WHOLE PROVINCE. Workers. Total Workers. Males.	Females.	Workers with an agricultural or other subsidiary occupation. Agricultural. Males.	F'm'l's.	Other. Males.	F'm'l's.	DEPENDENTS.
1a	1b	1c	1d	2	3	4	5	6	7	8	9
B.—INDUSTRY AND COMMERCE—*continued.*	*III.—INDUSTRY—concluded.*	XIV	**Furniture**	860	374	97	...	1	4	...	389
		83*a*	Cabinet-makers, etc.	471	237	28	..	...	2	...	206
		83*b*	Polishers, carriage-painters, etc. ...	322	134	27		1	2	...	161
		84	Upholsterers, tent-makers, etc. ...	67	3	42	...	..	...	...	22
		XV	**Building**	22,022	9,526	1,236	165	13	278	25	11,260
		85	Lime-burners, cement-workers ...	3,137	889	260	22	5	61	4	1,988
		86	Excavators and well-sinkers ...	192	118	8	..		2	...	66
		87	Stone-cutters and dressers ...	188	21	80	...	...	...	1	87
		88	Bricklayers and masons ...	14,741	6,511	792	137	5	189	20	7,438
		89	Builders (not using wood, bamboo, etc.), house-painters, plumbers, etc.	3,764	1,987	96	6	3	26	..	1,681
		XVI	**Construction of means of transport** ...	9,097	4,359	274	33	2	168	16	4,464
		90	Making, assembling or repairing cycles or motor land-vehicles.	1,596	800	17	1	...	24	.	779
		91	Makers and repairers of other land vehicles, and wheelwrights.	3,891	1,372	155	25	2	10[illegible]	14	2,364
		92	Ship or boat builders ...	3,610	2,187	102	7	...	41	2	1,321
		XVII 93	**Production and transmission of physical forces. (Gas-works, electric light and power and water-power.)**	577	177	5	2	...	2	...	395
		XVIII	**Other industries**	76,602	32,252	2 314	475	109	844	40	42,036
		94	Printers, lithographers, engravers, etc.	4,441	1,787	38		...	8	..	2,616
		95	Bookbinders and stitchers, envelope makers, etc.	684	353	6	..	...	2	..	325
		96	Makers of musical instruments ..	197	101	6	4	...	1	...	90
		97	Makers of watches and clocks and optical, photographic, mathematical and surgical instruments.	1,388	421	19	1	...	6	...	948
		98*a*	Makers of imitation jewellery ...	174	112	...	..	...	...	...	62
		98*b*	Gilders	1,091	718	..	1	...	24	...	373
		98*c*	Jewellers, workers in gold, silver and other precious metals, enamellers, etc.	53,365	20,862	1,110	402	106	719	35	31,393
		99	Makers of bangles or beads or necklaces of other material than glass and makers of spangles, lingams, sacred threads or artificial flowers.	625	245	235	1	...	5	3	145
		100	Makers of toys and miscellaneous small articles.	1,028	507	90	8	2	6	1	431
		101	Persons other than performers employed in places of entertainment and persons engaged in connection with sports and games.	3,040	1,302	72	48	1	36	1	1,666
		102	Contractors for the disposal of refuse, dust, etc.	...	.	...	...	...	...	.	...
		103	Scavengers and sweepers	10,569	5,844	738	10	...	37	..	3,987

IMPERIAL TABLE XVII.—*Occupations.* PART II.—*Provincial Summary*—continued.

Class.	Sub-Class.	Serial No.	ORDER AND GROUP. TITLE.	WHOLE PROVINCE. Total Workers and Dependents.	Workers. Total Workers. Males.	Total Workers. Females.	Workers with an agricultural or other subsidiary occupation. Agricultural. Males.	Agricultural. F'm'l's.	Other. Males.	Other. F'm'l's.	DEPENDENTS.
1a	1b	1c	1d	2	3	4	5	6	7	8	9
B.—INDUSTRY AND COMMERCE—*continued.*	IV.—*TRANSPORT.*	XIX 104	**Transport by air (aeroplanes, etc., and aerodromes).**	..	...	...	...	...	...	...	...
		XX	**Transport by water ... ...**	118,083	64,920	2,350	2,307	22	1,951	195	50,813
		105	Persons (other than persons of Group 108 and labourers) employed in harbours and docks.	1,475	662	13	...	..	6	...	800
		106	Labourers in harbours and docks not of Group 109.	17	2	...	...	..	...	...	15
		107a	Shipowners, shipbrokers and shipping agents and all their employees not in Group 107*b*.	16,881	13,971	121	40	...	70	...	2,789
		107b	Ships' officers and engineers	5,225	4,128	2	18	...	59	...	1,095
		108	Persons (other than labourers) employed on the construction and maintenance of harbours, docks, streams, rivers and canals.	2,084	942	98	31		98	2	1,044
		109	Labourers associated with the work of persons of Group 108.	25	3	...	..	...	...	...	22
		110a	Boat-owners and their employees other than Group 110*b*.	15,733	7,081	405	153	...	272	19	8,247
		110b	Boatmen and towmen	76,643	38,131	1,711	2,065	22	1,446	174	36,801
		XXI	**Transport on land otherwise than by rail.**	199,089	92,105	12,615	1,772	293	3,008	766	94,369
		111	Persons (other than labourers) employed on the construction and maintenance of roads and bridges.	4,869	1,703	212	6	4	22	12	2,954
		112	Labourers associated with persons of Group 111.	50,210	26,247	6,137	521	139	850	475	17,826
		113a	Drivers and engine-cleaners (excluding private servants) connected with mechanically driven land-vehicles (including trams and taxis).	3,421	1,655	8	3	...	114	...	1,758
		113b	All others (excluding private servants) connected with such vehicles.	3,272	2,859	2	...	.	3	..	411
		114	All (except private servants) connected with transport by vehicles drawn by animals.	114,413	45,905	5,164	1,128	147	1,860	256	63,344
		115	Owners and pullers of rickshaws, etc. (excluding private servants).	2,236	1,751	15	...		5	...	470
		116	Owners and drivers of pack-elephants, mules, bullocks, etc.	1,412	769	141	25	...	46	1	502
		117	Porters and messengers	19,256	11,216	936	89	3	109	22	7,104
		XXII	**Transport by rail ... ...**	27,774	15,876	828	14	..	58	2	11,070
		118	Railway employees of all kinds other than labourers, doctors, police, sweepers and postal service.	18,000	9,716	322	10	...	36	...	7,962
		119	Labourers of all kinds associated with railways (excluding sweepers).	9,774	6,160	506	4	...	22	2	3,108
		XXIII 120	**Postal, telegraph and telephone services**	9,328	4,503	145	26	...	71	1	4,680

Class.	Sub-Class.	Serial No.	ORDER AND GROUP. TITLE.	Total Workers and Dependents.	WHOLE PROVINCE. Workers. Total Workers. Males.	Females.	Workers with an agricultural or other subsidiary occupation. Agricultural Males.	Agricultural F'm'l's.	Other. Males.	Other. F'ml's.	DEPENDENTS.
1a	1b	1c	1d	2	3	4	5	6	7	8	9
B.—INDUSTRY AND COMMERCE—*continued*.	V.—TRADE, FINANCE AND INSURANCE.	XXIV 121	**Credit, finance and insurance** ...	22,210	8,706	2 909	362	140	518	246	10,595
		XXV 122	**Brokerage, commission, auditing** ...	16,409	6,940	586	44	7	108	21	8,883
		XXVI	**Trade in cotton, silk, hair or other textiles or in piece-goods.**	55,306	14,881	17,194	197	278	708	909	23,231
		123a	Wholesale dealers and brokers ...	10,762	4,669	932	83	3	12[illegible]	35	5,161
		123b	Retail dealers and hawkers ...	44,544	10,212	16,262	114	275	579	874	18,070
		XXVII 124	**Trade in skins, leather, furs, feathers, horn, etc., and articles made from these not included in Order XXXIV or other orders.**	2 811	962	342	27	8	52	10	1,507
		XXVIII	**Trade in wood (not firewood), cork, bark, bamboo, thatch, etc., and articles made from these.**	34,519	11,325	4,328	552	78	960	176	18,866
		125a	Wholesale dealers and brokers ...	9,197	3,191	426	99	4	173	19	5,880
		125b	Retail dealers and hawkers ...	25,[illegible]22	8,134	3,902	453	74	787	157	12,986
		XXIX 126	**Trade in metals, machinery, knives, tools, etc.**	4,795	1,240	954	3	13	24	6	2,601
		XXX	**Trade in pottery, bricks and tiles** ...	1,603	445	336	35	...	15	19	822
		127a	Trade in pottery not for domestic use nor for gardening.	8[illegible]1	268	201	2	...	7	1	402
		127b	Trade in bricks or tiles	732	177	135	33	...	8	18	420
		XXXI 128	**Trade in chemical products** ...	9,941	2,717	1,982	38	27	195	90	5,242
		XXXII	**Hotels, cafés, restaurants, etc.** ...	49,662	17,567	9 822	119	126	671	349	22,273
		129	Dealers in wine, liquors, aerated waters and ice.	8,685	4,156	672	30	2	134	50	3,857
		130	Owners and managers of hotels, cook-shops, dâk-bungalows, etc., and their employees.	40,977	13,411	9,150	89	124	537	299	18,416
		XXXIII	**Other trade in foodstuffs**	357,040	75,839	111,743	1,444	1,559	4,373	4,039	169,458
		131	Fish	60,565	10,509	22,388	158	286	570	933	27,668
		132	Grocery, vegetable oil, salt, and other condiments.	23,591	5,995	6,262	195	67	479	243	11,334
		133	Milk, butter, ghee, poultry, eggs, etc. ...	5,165	1,870	749	7	18	49	18	2,546
		134	Sugar, jaggery and sweetmeats ...	65,060	11,233	27,925	267	482	533	756	25,902
		135	Cardamom, betel-leaf, vegetables, fruit and areca nut.	64,326	11,432	24,631	186	325	548	8[illegible]7	28,263
		36	Grain, pulse, flour and bran—								
			(a) Wholesale dealers and brokers	59,590	15,645	7,648	295	95	972	454	36,297
			(b) Retail dealers and hawkers ...	34,391	9,890	9,177	174	157	653	417	15,324
		137	Tobacco and opium ...	28,271	4,702	10,153	80	94	310	307	13,416
		138	Meat, sheep, goats and pigs ...	14,648	3,950	2,531	81	31	245	74	8,167
		139	Hay, grass and fodder	1,433	613	279	1	4	14	20	541
		X XIV 140	**Trade in ready-made clothing and other articles of dress and the toilet.**	8,410	2,681	1,597	17	9	111	76	4,132

Class.	Sub-Class.	Serial No.	ORDER AND GROUP. TITLE.	WHOLE PROVINCE. Total Workers and Dependents.	Workers. Total Workers. Males.	Total Workers. Females.	Workers with an agricultural or other subsidiary occupation. Agricultural. Males.	Agricultural. F'm'l's.	Other. Males.	Other. F'm'l's.	Dependents.
1a	1b	1c	1d	2	3	4	5	6	7	8	9
B.—INDUSTRY AND COMMERCE—*concluded*.	V.—*TRADE, FINANCE AND INSURANCE*—concluded.	XXXV	**Trade in household goods ... ...**	17,907	4,154	6,651	82	102	233	352	7,102
		141	Furniture and woven furnishings ...	8,691	1,521	4,349	30	73	127	246	2,821
		142	Hardware, glass, gardening tools, etc. ..	9,216	2,633	2,302	52	29	106	106	4,281
		XXXVI 143	**Trade in building materials (other than bricks, tiles, thatch and woody materials).**	11,865	2,205	5,827	49	229	161	311	3,833
		XXXVII	**Trade in means of transport ...**	23,739	7,338	3,028	240	100	742	377	13,373
		144	Dealers in, and hirers of, cycles and all kinds of mechanical transport (not hirers of hackney carriages).	330	87	8	.	...	1	...	235
		145	Dealers in, and hirers of, other carriages, carts, boats, etc. (not hirers of hackney carriages).	2,456	803	231	8	5	80	25	1,422
		146	Dealers and hirers of elephants, horses, cattle, mules, etc.	20,953	6,448	2,789	232	95	661	35[illegible]	11,716
		XXXVIII 147	**Trade in fuel ... ...**	11,568	3,732	1,832	59	40	223	114	6,004
		XXXIX	**Trade in articles of luxury and articles pertaining to letters or to the arts or sciences.**	14,176	4,189	2,170	15	8	179	55	7,817
		148	Dealers in precious stones, jewellery (real and imitation), clocks, optical instruments, etc.	10,216	3,064	1,167	11	6	161	34	5,985
		149	Dealers in common bangles, bead necklaces, fans, small articles, toys, hunting and fishing tackle, flowers, etc.	2,883	672	924	3	2	10	20	1,287
		150	Publishers, booksellers, stationers, dealers in music, pictures, musical instruments and curiosities.	1,077	453	79	1	...	8	1	545
		XL	**Trade of other sorts ... ..**	454,857	104,137	140,263	2,555	2,509	5,633	4,326	210,457
		151	Dealers in rags or refuse ...	29	20	5	...	...	1	...	4
		152	General store-keepers and shop-keepers, otherwise unspecified.	452,916	103,629	139,856	2,545	2,490	5,612	4,294	209,431
		153	Itinerant traders in miscellaneous or unspecified goods.	1,216	351	193	3	3	10	8	672
		154	Other kinds of trade not in the foregoing groups.	696	137	209	7	16	10	24	350
C.—PUBLIC SERVICE, AND THE PROFESSIONS AND LIBERAL ARTS.	VI.—*PUBLIC FORCE*.	XLI	**Army ... ...**	11,026	7,839	21	567	...	4	...	3,166
		155	Imperial army	11,025	7,838	21	567	...	4	...	3,166
		156	Indian State or foreign armies ...	1	1	.	...	...	...	...	...
		XLII 157	**Navy ... ...**	...	...	...	...	...	...	...	...
		XLIII 158	**Air-force ... ...**	...	...	...	...	..	...	...	...
		XLIV	**Police and professional village-watchmen**	65,374	29,789	448	2[illegible]	1	151	39	35,137
		159	Police	65,327	29,767	448	211	1	151	39	35,112
		160	Professional village-watchmen ..	47	22	...	...	...	...	...	25

IMPERIAL TABLE XVII.—*Occupations.* PART II.—*Provincial Summary*—continued.

Class.	Sub-Class.	Serial No.	ORDER AND GROUP. TITLE.	WHOLE PROVINCE. Total Workers and Dependents.	Workers. Total Workers. Males.	Total Workers. Females.	Workers with an agricultural or other subsidiary occupation. Agricultural. Males.	Agricultural. F'm'l's.	Other. Males.	Other. F'm'l's	DEPENDENTS.
1a	1b	1c	1d	2	3	4	5	6	7	8	9
C.—PUBLIC SERVICE AND THE PROFESSIONS AND LIBERAL ARTS.	VII.—PUBLIC ADMINISTRATION.	XLV	**Public administration ... ...**	103,041	33,242	992	9,102	90	1,763	42	68,807
		161	General service of the Government of India or a provincial government.	35,364	12,071	341	204	2	87	6	22,952
		162	General service of a Shan, Indian or foreign state.	11,913	5,446	78	3,500	2	421	1	6,389
		163	Municipal and other local (not village) service.	6,479	2,806	132	11	2	67	2	3,541
		164	Village officials and village servants other than watchmen.	49,285	12,919	441	5,387	84	1,188	33	35,925
	VIII.—THE PROFESSIONS AND LIBERAL ARTS.	XLVI	**Religion ... ...**	1,55,310	97,077	8,024	71	10	318	14	50,209
		165	Pôngyis, upazins, priests, ministers, etc.	1,06,429	69,593	224	56	9	203	1	36,612
		166	Nuns, religious mendicants, inmates of monasteries.	47,342	26,830	7,745	2	1	110	13	12,767
		167	Lay preachers, catechists, readers, church and mission service.	478	190	7	13	...	3	...	281
		168	Temple, burial or burning ground service, circumcisers.	1,061	464	48	...	...	2	...	549
		XLVII	**Law ... .**	10,936	2,779	93	64	...	95	2	8,064
		169	Lawyers of all kinds	6,413	1,472	41	45	...	63	...	4,900
		170	Lawyers' clerks, petition writers, etc. ...	4,523	1,307	52	19	...	32	2	3,164
		XLVIII	**Medicine ... .**	56,258	20,564	3,332	719	26	1,205	78	32,362
		171	Medical practitioners of all kinds ...	49,491	18,883	1,767	710	22	1,168	57	28,841
		172	Nurses, midwives, vaccinators, compounders.	6,767	1,681	1,565	9	4	37	21	3,521
		XLIX	**Instruction ... ...**	33,794	11,940	2,955	267	22	391	77	18,899
		173	Professors and teachers of all kinds ...	32,801	11,442	2,950	257	22	361	77	18,409
		174	Clerks and servants connected with education.	993	498	5	10	...	30	...	490
		L	**Letters and the arts and sciences ...**	26,268	11,753	1,895	150	22	418	41	12,620
		175	Public scribes, stenographers, etc. ...	631	349	...	...	...	...	...	282
		176	Architects, surveyors, civil engineers who are not of the Public Works Department; and their employees.	190	2	17	...	...	...	...	171
		177a	Photographers	844	277	9	...	...	8	...	558
		177b	Horoscope casters, astrologers and almanac makers.	676	258	8	9	..	54	...	410
		177c	Sculptors in stone	1,761	780	22	24	8	49	1	959
		177d	Sculptors and image-makers in wood, brass and other materials than stone.	...	...	...	...	...	...	...	.
		177e	Authors, editors, journalists, poets, artists, and all scientists not in Group 177b.	2,779	1,618	49	3	...	26	...	1,112
		178	Music composers, band-masters, players on all kinds of musical instruments (not military), singers, actors and dancers.	15,851	7,132	1,302	91	12	218	29	7,417
		179	Conjurors, acrobats, fortune-tellers, reciters, exhibitors of curiosities and wild animals.	3,536	1,337	488	20	2	63	11	1,711

IMPERIAL TABLE XVII.—*Occupations.* PART II.—*Provincial Summary*—concluded.

Class.	Sub-Class.	Serial No.	ORDER AND GROUP. TITLE.	Total Workers and Dependents.	WHOLE PROVINCE. Workers. Total Workers. Males.	Total Workers. Females.	Workers with an agricultural or other subsidiary occupation. Agricultural. Males.	Agricultural. F'm'l's	Other. Males.	Other. F'm'l's.	DEPENDENTS.
1a	1b	1c	1d	2	3	4	5	6	7	8	9
D.—MISCELLANEOUS.	IX.	LI 180	All persons without an occupation but receiving an income who are not included in Group I.	13,800	3,230	1,175	153	10	344	41	9,395
	X—DOMESTIC SERVICE.	LII	**Domestic service**	73,669	43,059	8,001	807	87	637	115	22,609
		181	Domestic servants (excluding sweepers and all employed on account of animals or vehicles).	58,739	33,421	7,772	210	81	332	104	17,546
		182	Domestic servants employed on account of animals or of vehicles moved by animals or by human labour.	13,397	8,751	225	597	6	300	11	4,421
		183	Private motor-drivers and cleaners ...	1,533	887	4	..	.	5	...	642
	XI—INSUFFICIENTLY DESCRIBED OCCUPATIONS.	LIII	**Insufficiently described occupations** ...	573,641	202,629	149,294	2,533	7,855	5,117	7,172	221,718
		184	Manufacturers, business men and contractors otherwise unspecified.	110,554	13,323	68,653	793	6,086	869	3,893	28,578
		185	Cashiers, accountants, book-keepers, and other clerical employees in unspecified industries or trades.	71,478	35,505	1,015	272	...	417	1	34,958
		186	Mechanics otherwise unspecified ..	13,374	7,118	700	19	9	45	29	5,556
		187	Labourers and workmen otherwise unspecified.	378,235	146,683	78,925	1,449	1,760	3,780	3,249	152,626
	XII—UNPRODUCTIVE AND UNCLASSIFIED.	LIV 188	**Prisoners in jails, etc., and inmates of asylums and almshouses.**	16,324	15,827	497	2	2	1	.	...
		LV	**Beggars, vagrants, prostitutes, etc.** ...	28,787	10,516	10,360	17	30	117	98	7,911
		189	Beggars, vagrants, wizards, witches, etc.	27,190	10,239	9,323	17	30	108	98	7,628
		190	Procurers and prostitutes	1,597	277	1,037	...	...	9	...	283
		LVI 191	**Other unproductive occupations and unclassified.**	3,855	447	39	1	...	29	8	3,369

Serial No.	District or State.	TOTAL FOR ALL OCCUPATIONS.							
		Total Workers and Dependents.	WORKERS.						DEPENDENTS.
			Total Workers.		Workers with an agricultural or other subsidiary occupation.				
					Agricultural.		Other.		
			Males.	Females.	Males.	Females.	Males.	Females.	
	1	2	3	4	5	6	7	8	9
	Provincial Total	13,169,099	4,060,921	2,734,517	104,566	64,700	405,320	210,295	6,373,661
	Divisional Burma ...	11,698,408	3,585,013	2,342,125	72,712	39,681	326,162	157,916	5,771,270
	Arakan Division	909,246	275,548	142,086	9,751	3,309	23,096	8,351	491,612
1	Akyab ...	576,430	183,619	61,829	4,895	343	10,786	1,939	330,982
2	Hill Dist. of Arakan ..	20,914	7,179	6,305	40	47	43	3	7,430
3	Kyaukpyu	199,873	54,110	47,354	2,940	1,659	7,313	3,909	98,409
4	Sandoway ...	112,029	30,640	26,598	1,876	1,260	4,954	2,500	54,791
	Pegu Division ..	2,309,293	779,657	340,826	8,925	4,236	49,044	20,463	1,188,810
5	Rangoon Town	341,962	188,507	21,907	111	5	535	62	171,548
6	Insein	293,083	93,599	45,432	477	297	5,210	1,995	153,982
7	Hanthawaddy ...	364,624	122,364	37,113	991	350	5,563	1,023	205,147
8	Tharrawaddy ..	492,429	135,611	91,986	3,291	1,552	16,168	6,592	264,832
9	Pegu	445,620	137,220	67,448	1,357	899	8,568	2,700	240,952
10	Prome	371,575	102,286	76,940	2,698	1,133	13,000	8,091	192,349
	Irrawaddy Division ...	2,030,044	634,505	448,895	9,585	4,813	30,019	16,529	946,644
11	Bassein	489,473	157,677	107,572	1,975	862	6,985	4,176	224,224
12	Henzada ...	550,920	162,502	142,633	3,544	2,806	12,133	7,144	245,785
13	Myaungmya ...	370,551	119,128	75,424	2,045	275	4,959	1,842	175,999
14	Ma-ubin	330,106	101,098	83,378	1,579	758	4,170	2,600	145,630
15	Pyapôn	288,994	94,100	39,888	442	112	1,772	767	155,006
	Tenasserim Division	1,613,523	484,269	265,226	6,418	2,009	31,224	12,836	864,028
16	Toungoo	381,883	113,725	63,756	1,081	455	7,023	2,586	204,402
17	Salween ...	50,379	14,834	7,258	256	62	702	298	28,287
18	Thatôn ..	471,100	139,839	82,712	1,889	634	7,385	3,800	248,549
19	Amherst ..	417,910	130,203	67,955	1,359	378	7,265	3,764	219,752
20	Tavoy ..	156,786	47,120	31,991	1,358	322	6,683	2,219	77,675
21	Mergui ...	135,465	38,548	11,554	475	158	2,166	169	85,363
	Magwe Division ...	1,438,774	419,643	363,196	13,900	8,790	60,856	28,015	655,935
22	Thayetmyo ...	255,406	70,993	57,296	2,979	1,668	8,241	3,740	127,117
23	Pakôkku	465,771	129,730	111,822	4,893	2,344	25,193	12,722	224,219
24	Minbu ...	274,302	80,904	77,035	4,479	3,374	16,167	7,123	116,363
25	Magwe ..	423,252	132,358	110,942	1,549	1,404	11,217	4,430	179,952
26	Pakôkku Hill Tracts ...	20,043	5,658	6,101	...	...	18	...	8,284
	Mandalay Division ..	849,361	273,810	175,187	5,518	4,416	28,903	10,386	400,364
27	Mandalay	356,621	120,750	78,290	1,124	1,164	5,936	3,308	157,581
	Mandalay City	*148,917*	*53,614*	*31,229*	*463*	*9*	*228*	*139*	*64,074*
28	Bhamo	112,960	34,286	26,206	1,631	1,679	4,660	1,206	52,468
29	Myitkyina	118,382	41,532	22,244	877	607	3,643	637	54,606
30	Katha ...	253,725	74,453	46,547	1,762	857	14,298	5,142	132,725
31	Putao ...	7,673	2,789	1,900	124	109	366	93	2,984
	Sagaing Division ..	1,350,396	390,572	377,914	12,727	8,222	71,163	41,835	581,910
32	Shwebo	391,284	113,137	123,952	1,243	824	26,808	15,516	154,195
33	Sagaing	326,908	92,198	81,392	4,937	2,875	17,612	14,832	153,318
34	Lower Chindwin ...	342,880	91,908	91,430	3,430	2,564	14,170	6,951	159,542
35	Upper Chindwin	179,245	56,003	42,530	2,782	1,959	13,127	4,453	80,712
36	Chin Hills ...	110,079	37,326	38,610	335	...	46	83	34,143
	Meiktila Division ..	1,197,771	327,009	228,795	5,888	5,886	31,877	19,501	641,967
37	Kyauksè	142,677	41,556	26,026	808	1,204	3,900	1,920	75,095
38	Meiktila	289,897	77,693	51,783	1,275	724	9,512	6,112	160,421
39	Yamèthin	323,189	89,089	44,122	1,525	333	8,384	2,820	189,978
40	Myingyan	442,008	118,671	106,864	2,280	1,625	10,081	8,649	216,473
	Eastern States ...	1,470,691	475,908	392,392	31,854	25,019	79,158	52,379	602,391
41	Northern Shan States ...	559,223	183,664	145,094	13,577	7,877	34,072	25,630	230,465
42	Southern Shan States	847,618	273,873	230,899	17,843	16,646	44,032	26,348	342,846
43	Karenni ...	63,850	18,371	16,399	434	496	1,054	401	29,080

PART III.—*Details by districts.*

Class A.—Production of Raw Materials. (Sub-Classes *Ia, Ib, Ic, II.*)								Class B.—Industry and Commerce. (Sub-Classes *III, IV, V.*)								Serial No. of District, etc. (column 1)
Total Workers and Dependents.	Workers.						Dependents.	Total Workers and Dependents.	Workers.						Dependents.	
	Total Workers.		Workers with an agricultural or other subsidiary occupation.						Total Workers.		Workers with an agricultural or other subsidiary occupation.					
			Agricultural.		Other.						Agricultural.		Other.			
	Males.	Females.	Males.	Females.	Males.	Females.			Males.	Females.	Males.	Females.	Males.	Females.		
10	11	12	13	14	15	16	17	18	19	20	21	22	23	24	25	
9,675,097	2,843,137	2,016,572	71,282	44,533	364,313	179,607	4,815,388	2,321,919	727,093	530,819	18,619	12,012	30,417	22,961	1,064,007	
8,528,259	2,475,772	1,732,072	48,253	27,685	291,277	134,449	4,320,415	2,220,365	692,687	507,277	16,188	10,438	27,389	20,697	1,020,401	
733,546	211,672	109,748	6,406	2,750	20,925	7,072	412,126	112,932	40,373	23,252	2,557	310	1,567	1,013	49,308	
458,243	135,644	42,760	2,342	278	9,568	1,334	279,839	86,638	34,060	16,221	2,293	61	1,049	571	36,350	1
19,636	6,536	6,261	29	47	39	3	6,839	401	215	32	2	..	...	...	154	2
163,410	44,142	38,226	2,379	1,294	6,777	3,526	81,042	14,102	3,410	3,884	177	143	234	208	6,808	3
92,257	25,350	22,501	1,656	1,131	4,541	2,209	44,406	11,791	2,688	3,115	85	106	284	234	5,988	4
1,480,496	426,175	232,538	6,417	2,466	43,601	18,319	821,783	576,685	227,564	89,486	1,545	1,644	4,079	1,812	259,635	
11,600	5,400	845	10	..	30	15	5,355	226,992	126,121	16,034	70	5	355	36	84,837	5
216,021	63,229	34,581	303	155	4,459	1,738	118,141	50,712	18,255	8,675	100	132	621	229	23,782	6
245,703	74,964	20,536	499	193	4,380	725	150,203	72,573	22,671	12,158	271	140	846	218	37,744	7
396,948	106,193	74,636	2,754	1,161	15,016	6,154	216,119	67,835	18,658	14,614	411	360	779	320	34,563	8
340,120	102,472	50,841	673	382	7,471	2,371	186,807	79,895	22,758	14,764	386	465	893	311	42,373	9
270,104	73,847	51,099	2,178	575	12,245	7,316	145,158	78,678	19,101	23,241	307	542	585	698	36,336	10
1,563,647	477,475	354,818	6,745	3,582	24,736	13,998	731,354	346,094	104,362	80,567	1,501	1,111	4,195	2,238	161,165	
375,161	114,275	87,030	1,197	540	5,436	3,588	173,856	89,362	30,541	19,214	501	295	1,278	572	39,607	11
428,505	126,584	114,532	2,676	2,243	10,754	6,153	187,389	85,415	22,507	21,615	472	491	1,086	775	41,293	12
282,607	89,072	58,148	1,478	182	3,783	1,393	135,387	61,170	18,374	14,035	239	84	928	423	28,761	13
252,437	77,582	64,419	1,228	572	3,375	2,197	110,436	62,202	16,345	17,712	155	183	591	378	28,145	14
224,937	69,962	30,689	166	45	1,388	667	124,286	47,945	16,595	7,991	134	58	312	90	23,359	15
1,223,416	354,167	196,096	4,723	1,435	28,165	10,563	673,153	274,474	80,440	60,186	1,051	549	2,285	2,041	133,848	
286,080	82,776	48,960	768	314	6,193	2,260	154,344	63,659	18,186	11,974	147	132	637	264	33,499	16
45,958	12,826	6,890	225	53	659	269	26,242	2,493	938	281	13	9	31	11	1,274	17
370,329	108,442	62,951	1,421	488	6,397	2,959	198,936	66,794	17,414	16,737	227	135	646	731	32,643	18
299,147	85,762	50,596	912	231	6,766	3,202	162,789	89,552	30,353	15,400	373	145	449	541	43,799	19
114,846	35,093	19,176	992	192	6,215	1,743	60,577	33,206	8,175	12,234	274	127	374	455	12,797	20
107,056	29,268	7,523	405	157	1,935	130	70,265	18,776	5,374	3,566	17	1	148	39	9,836	21
1,092,516	319,040	277,514	8,899	6,202	54,137	22,902	495,962	271,561	68,159	77,302	4,017	2,495	5,879	4,829	126,100	
198,132	55,738	45,465	2,725	1,538	7,702	3,396	96,929	40,461	9,211	10,096	79	118	463	310	21,154	22
320,012	91,405	72,011	1,611	1,041	21,277	9,564	156,596	124,288	28,729	37,974	2,860	1,295	3,596	3,084	57,585	23
199,861	60,259	55,110	3,487	2,466	14,755	5,892	84,192	53,237	13,169	17,883	710	847	1,195	1,071	22,185	24
354,762	106,195	98,828	1,076	1,157	10,335	4,050	149,739	53,515	17,002	11,349	368	235	625	364	25,164	25
19,749	5,443	6,100	...		18	...	8,206	60	48	..	...	...	...	...	12	26
527,460	156,678	111,429	3,729	3,893	25,610	8,605	259,353	207,347	63,609	53,536	541	471	2,347	1,584	90,202	
140,656	44,279	28,474	450	188	4,804	2,368	67,903	155,156	46,692	43,524	138	362	881	917	64,940	27
10,533	*4,153*	*1,431*	...	..	*64*	*73*	*4,949*	*100,516*	*30,440*	*25,849*	7	9	82	*60*	44,227	
91,733	25,831	22,669	1,503	1,668	4,113	1,017	43,233	14,617	4,711	3,267	44	10	486	185	6,639	28
101,584	33,531	20,625	615	596	3,220	563	47,378	8,787	3,874	1,269	143	10	346	71	3,644	29
187,237	51,237	37,729	1,048	733	13,112	4,564	98,271	28,597	8,189	5,470	215	89	630	411	14,938	30
6,250	1,800	1,882	113	108	361	93	2,568	190	143	6	1	..	4		41	31
1,051,171	298,237	305,181	7,422	5,628	65,541	36,790	447,753	218,894	58,322	61,469	3,783	2,444	4,608	4,693	99,103	
312,089	87,340	104,951	432	182	25,559	14,767	119,798	44,861	12,182	12,322	383	457	838	509	20,357	32
234,225	66,858	54,650	2,979	1,136	15,578	12,249	112,717	74,849	18,394	24,179	1,743	1,137	1,294	2,541	32,276	33
255,527	65,019	70,834	1,935	1,959	12,595	5,805	119,674	73,861	19,312	19,762	1,242	585	1,410	1,152	34,787	34
142,017	43,151	36,152	2,075	1,641	11,769	3,888	62,714	24,860	8,241	5,202	411	265	1,062	460	11,417	35
107,313	35,859	38,594	1	...	30	81	32,850	463	193	4	4	.	4	1	266	36
856,007	232,328	144,748	3,912	1,729	28,562	16,200	478,931	212,385	49,858	61,479	1,193	1,414	2,429	2,487	101,048	
93,887	27,836	14,293	380	225	3,303	1,504	51,758	26,070	6,620	7,132	168	388	383	213	12,318	37
209,541	56,574	30,516	778	191	8,709	5,215	122,451	60,353	12,555	18,552	388	516	669	834	29,246	38
235,182	62,853	29,105	1,096	192	7,556	2,132	143,224	58,676	15,085	12,012	247	130	633	312	31,579	39
317,397	85,065	71,034	1,658	1,121	8,994	7,049	161,198	67,276	15,598	23,773	390	380	744	1,128	27,905	40
1,146,838	367,365	284,500	23,029	16,848	73,036	45,158	494,973	101,554	34,406	23,542	2,431	1,574	3,028	2,264	43,606	
487,010	153,793	130,919	12,515	7,208	32,293	24,359	202,298	44,339	15,704	10,357	504	665	1,360	1,117	18,278	41
607,898	99,984	139,332	10,193	9,201	39,864	20,437	268,582	52,076	17,009	12,211	1,868	879	1,662	1,125	22,856	42
51,930	13,588	14,249	321	445	879	362	24,093	5,149	1,693	984	59	30	106	22	2,472	43

CLASS C.—PUBLIC SERVICE AND THE PROFESSIONS AND LIBERAL ARTS. (Sub-Classes *VI, VII, VIII.*)

Serial No.	DISTRICT OR STATE.	Total Workers and Dependents.	WORKERS.						DEPENDENTS.
			Total Workers.		Workers with an agricultural or other subsidiary occupation.				
					Agricultural.		Other.		
			Males.	Females.	Males.	Females.	Males.	Females.	
	1	2	3	4	5	6	7	8	9
	Provincial Total ...	462,007	214,983	17,760	11,152	171	4,345	293	229,264
	Divisional Burma ..	401,496	180,780	16,163	6,805	151	3,324	257	204,553
	Arakan Division ...	22,522	8,153	633	458	4	193	7	13,736
1	Akyab ...	13,622	5,011	398	215	...	83	5	8,213
2	Hill Dist. of Arakan ...	682	294	2	9	...	2	...	386
3	Kyaukpyu ...	4,641	1,594	175	123	4	65	1	2,872
4	Sandoway ...	3,577	1,254	58	111	...	43	1	2,265
	Pegu Division ...	91,945	38,504	3,767	785	6	640	20	49,674
5	Rangoon Town ...	33,341	13,819	1,596	12	...	63	5	17,896
6	Insein ...	9,739	3,634	449	50	1	62	7	5,656
7	Hanthawaddy ...	10,212	4,573	380	173	...	73	...	5,259
8	Tharrawaddy ..	13,581	5,481	388	66	2	241	4	7,712
9	Pegu ...	13,870	6,276	548	293	2	114	2	7,046
10	Prome ...	11,202	4,691	406	191	1	87	2	6,105
	Irrawaddy Division ...	54,883	23,235	2,392	1,093	43	543	48	29,256
11	Bassein ...	14,488	6,585	513	264	8	182	7	7,390
12	Henzada ...	14,158	5,935	658	330	27	130	23	7,565
13	Myaungmya ...	9,217	3,704	430	263	2	96	1	5,083
14	Ma-ubin ...	8,917	3,549	490	102	2	81	12	4,878
15	Pyapôn ...	8,103	3,462	301	134	4	54	5	4,340
	Tenasserim Division ...	49,461	20,885	2,333	539	8	314	50	26,243
16	Toungoo ...	12,631	5,850	426	152	6	108	1	6,355
17	Salween ...	950	447	31	16	...	7	18	472
18	Thatôn ...	11,815	4,783	527	184	2	89	11	6,505
19	Amherst ...	14,207	5,988	854	55	...	10	9	7,365
20	Tavoy ...	5,550	2,323	326	88	..	52	11	2,901
21	Mergui ...	4,308	1,494	169	44	...	48	...	2,645
	Magwe Division ...	42,667	19,974	1,114	928	18	525	45	21,579
22	Thayetmyo ...	8,344	2,747	185	175	6	47	6	5,412
23	Pakôkku ...	14,398	7,304	459	411	1	199	27	6,635
24	Minbu ...	10,571	4,061	328	238	5	99	11	6,182
25	Magwe ...	9,166	5,718	142	104	6	180	1	3,306
26	Pakôkku Hill Tracts ..	188	144	...	..	..	...	...	44
	Mandalay Division ...	51,577	27,085	1,790	1,047	25	376	26	22,702
27	Mandalay ...	29,541	16,851	1,108	524	...	164	4	11,582
	Mandalay City ..	18,878	10,759	702	456	...	74	4	7,417
28	Bhamo ...	4,961	2,799	140	79	1	49	2	2,022
29	Myitkyina ...	5,736	2,942	60	98	1	44	..	2,734
30	Katha ...	10,280	3,788	478	336	23	119	20	6,014
31	Putao ...	1,059	705	4	10	...	...	...	350
	Sagaing Division ..	47,227	23,902	2,305	1,335	29	507	32	21,020
32	Shwebo ...	13,466	7,432	633	313	20	100	13	5,401
33	Sagaing ..	13,573	5,670	1,255	208	1	93	4	6,648
34	Lower Chindwin ..	10,091	6,156	180	237	..	112	3	3,755
35	Upper Chindwin ..	8,280	3,574	235	277	8	94	12	4,471
36	Chin Hills ..	1,817	1,070	2	300	...	8	..	745
	Meiktila Division ...	41,214	19,042	1,829	620	18	226	29	20,343
37	Kyauksè ...	6,451	2,636	325	192	2	49	1	3,490
38	Meiktila ...	10,475	5,611	609	83	8	68	8	4,255
39	Yamèthin ..	11,943	5,277	354	171	7	70	9	6,312
40	Myingyan ..	12,345	5,518	541	174	1	39	11	6,286
	Eastern States ...	60,511	34,203	1,597	4,347	20	1,021	36	24,711
41	Northern Shan States ...	15,944	8,869	965	502	4	368	27	6,110
42	Southern Shan States ...	42,958	24,684	567	3,818	12	640	7	17,717
43	Karenni ...	1,599	650	65	27	4	13	2	884

PART III.—*Details by districts*—contd.

Class D.—MISCELLANEOUS. (Sub-Classes *IX, X, XI, XII.*) Total Workers and Dependents.	Workers. Total Workers. Males.	Workers. Total Workers. Females.	Workers with an agricultural or other subsidiary occupation. Agricultural. Males.	Agricultural. Females.	Other. Males.	Other. Females.	Dependents.	Sub-Class *Ia*—Control of land or water used for the exploitation of animals or vegetation. (Order I.) Total Workers and Dependents.	Workers. Total Workers. Males.	Total Workers. Females.	Workers with an agricultural or other subsidiary occupation. Agricultural. Males.	Agricultural. Females.	Other. Males.	Other. Females.	Dependents.	Serial No. of District, etc. (column 1).
10	11	12	13	14	15	16	17	18	19	20	21	22	23	24	25	
710,076	275,708	169,366	3,513	7,984	6,245	7,434	265,002	157,135	36,596	40,732	1,069	1,089	5,888	4,570	79,807	
548,288	235,774	86,613	1,466	1,407	4,172	2,513	225,901	151,026	34,227	39,487	860	896	5,391	4,340	77,312	
40,253	15,350	8,453	330	245	411	259	16,450	17,421	3,562	4,228	189	105	515	337	9,631	
17,934	8,904	2,450	45	4	86	29	6,580	10,568	1,978	2,086	87	14	169	109	6,504	1
195	134	10	...	...	2		51	19	...	15	...	...	...	..	4	2
17,720	4,964	5,069	261	218	237	174	7,687	3,170	711	967	35	37	176	91	1,492	3
4,404	1,348	924	24	23	86	56	2,132	3,664	873	1,160	67	54	170	137	1,631	4
160,167	87,414	15,035	178	120	724	312	57,718	28,700	6,132	6,140	134	89	944	532	16,428	
70,029	43,137	3,432	19	...	87	6	23,460	1,313	274	134	...	...	2	6	905	5
16,611	8,481	1,727	24	9	68	21	6,403	3,216	695	666	7	7	97	37	1,854	6
36,136	20,156	4,039	48	17	264	80	11,941	2,147	459	254	14	1	95	15	1,434	7
14,065	5,279	2,348	60	29	132	114	6,438	7,785	1,597	1,697	38	46	336	122	4,491	8
11,735	5,714	1,295	5	50	90	16	4,726	6,872	1,634	1,111	48	23	177	68	4,127	9
11,591	4,647	2,194	22	15	83	75	4,750	7,367	1,472	2,278	27	12	237	284	3,617	10
65,420	29,433	11,118	246	77	545	245	24,869	30,287	7,455	7,396	140	136	1,122	706	15,436	
10,462	6,276	815	13	19	89	9	3,371	6,779	1,900	1,656	39	17	276	190	3,223	11
22,842	7,476	5,888	66	45	163	193	9,538	7,88[illegible]	1,885	2,595	27	81	26	203	3,401	12
17,557	7,978	2,811	65	7	152	25	6,768	7,293	1,837	1,592	38	10	349	182	3,864	13
6,550	3,622	757	94	1	123	13	2,171	5,514	1,035	1,073	31	26	135	85	3,406	14
8,009	4,081	907	8	5	18	5	3,021	2,820	798	48[illegible]	5	2	102	46	1,542	15
66,172	28,777	6,611	105	17	460	182	30,784	14,173	3,316	2,928	96	24	442	268	7,929	
19,513	6,913	2,396	14	3	85	61	10,204	4,834	789	951	24	10	137	56	3,094	16
978	623	56	2	...	5	...	299	84	20	23	6	...	4	3	41	17
22,162	9,200	2,497	57	9	253	99	10,465	3,583	917	826	14	6	89	70	1,840	18
15,004	8,100	1,105	19	2	40	12	5,799	3,314	853	643	38	2	94	57	1,838	19
3,181	1,529	255	4	3	42	10	1,400	1,833	491	463	9	3	111	76	879	20
5,331	2,412	302	9	..	35	...	2,617	525	246	42	5	3	7	6	237	21
32,030	12,470	7,266	56	75	295	239	12,294	21,168	4,864	7,331	146	162	1,000	829	8,973	
8,469	3,297	1,550	.	6	29	28	3,622	4,258	912	1,546	45	51	128	125	1,800	22
7,073	2,292	1,378	11	7	121	47	3,403	6,097	1,421	2,150	25	31	351	359	2,526	23
10,633	3,415	3,714	44	56	118	149	3,504	6,325	1,433	2,009	65	63	293	167	2,883	24
5,809	3,443	623	1	6	27	15	1,743	4,488	1,093	1,626	11	17	228	178	1,764	25
46	23	1	...	..	...	...	22	...	...	...	...	...	..	...	...	26
62,977	26,438	8,432	201	27	570	171	28,107	2,483	673	569	14	13	95	68	1,241	
31,268	12,928	5,184	12	14	87	19	13,156	1,433	408	355	7	4	34	40	670	27
18,990	*8,262*	*3,247*	...	...	*8*	*2*	*7,481*	*406*	*90*	*59*	...	...	...	*1*	*257*	
1,649	945	130	5	...	12	2	574	141	37	25	2	...	3	5	79	28
2,275	1,185	240	21	...	33	3	850	81	35	7	...	...	5	...	39	29
27,611	11,239	2,870	163	12	437	147	13,502	828	193	182	5	9	53	23	453	30
174	141	8	...	1	1	...	25	...	..	..	...	...	...	...	...	31
33,104	10,111	8,959	187	121	507	320	14,034	20,261	4,513	6,340	94	272	814	1,070	9,408	
20,868	6,183	6,046	115	65	301	167	8,639	4,337	1,044	1,629	7	16	37	282	1,664	32
4,261	1,276	1,308	7	1	47	38	1,677	6,28[illegible]	1,518	[illegible]	30	17	338	396	2,706	33
8,401	1,481	654	16	10	53	21	1,326	7,904	1,560	2,197	38	216	311	297	4,147	34
4,088	1,037	941	19	45	102	93	2,110	1,792	391	510	19	23	128	95	891	35
486	194	10	30	...	4	1	281	...	...	...	...	..	...	...	...	36
88,165	25,781	20,739	163	725	660	785	41,645	16,533	3,712	4,555	47	95	459	530	8,266	
16,469	4,464	4,476	68	589	165	202	7,529	1,569	302	422	4	12	79	50	845	37
9,518	2,953	2,096	26	9	66	55	4,469	4,104	913	117	12	5	171	173	2,019	38
17,388	5,874	2,651	11	4	125	67	8,863	4,925	1,071	845	1	16	46	77	3,009	39
44,790	12,490	11,516	58	123	304	461	20,784	5,935	1,426	2,116	30	62	163	230	2,393	40
161,788	39,934	82,753	2,047	6,577	2,073	4,921	39,101	6,109	2,369	1,245	209	193	497	230	2,495	
11,940	5,298	2,8[illegible]3	56	6	151	127	3,779	1,637	401	412	[illegible]	7	85	110	824	41
144,676	32,196	78,789	1,964	6,554	1,866	4,779	33,691	4,453	1,966	824	18	180	411	120	1,663	42
5,172	2,440	1,101	27	17	56	15	1,631	19	2	9	...	...	1	...	8	43

Sub-Class *Ib.*—Cultivated and wild plants. (Orders IIA, IIB.)

Serial No.	District or State.	Total Workers and Dependents.	Workers. Total Workers. Males.	Workers. Total Workers. Females.	Workers with an agricultural or other subsidiary occupation. Agricultural. Males.	Workers with an agricultural or other subsidiary occupation. Agricultural. Females.	Workers with an agricultural or other subsidiary occupation. Other. Males.	Workers with an agricultural or other subsidiary occupation. Other. Females.	Dependents.
	1	2	3	4	5	6	7	8	9
	Provincial, Total ...	9,239,997	2,689,311	1,945,333	67,810	42,748	352,877	173,253	4,605,353
	Divisional Burma ...	8,121,753	2,336,932	1,664,621	45,395	26,335	281,023	128,642	4,120,200
	Arakan Division ...	701,908	202,035	104,257	5,922	2,540	20,026	6,685	3,95,616
1	Akyab ...	441,869	130,470	40,173	2,161	245	9,326	1,209	271,226
2	Hill Dist. of Arakan ...	19,598	6,528	6,246	29	47	39	3	6,824
3	Kyaukpyu ...	151,907	41,849	36,733	2,226	1,217	6,399	3,411	76,325
4	Sandoway ...	85,534	23,188	21,105	1,506	1,031	4,262	2,062	41,241
	Pegu Division ...	1,419,747	405,042	223,388	6,012	2,324	41,853	17,663	791,317
5	Rangoon Town ...	8,336	3,873	572	10	...	27	4	3,891
6	Insein ...	205,984	59,022	33,324	274	146	4,211	1,678	113,638
7	Hanthawaddy ...	238,980	72,252	19,822	461	188	4,194	698	146,906
8	Tharrawaddy ...	380,708	101,292	71,973	2,544	1,074	14,332	5,995	207,443
9	Pegu ...	326,203	97,601	49,167	581	354	7,160	2,279	179,435
10	Prome ...	259,[illegible]36	71,002	48,530	2,142	562	11,929	7,009	140,004
	Irrawaddy Division ...	1,474,979	449,736	337,987	6,271	3,358	23,008	13,010	687,256
11	Bassein ...	358,352	108,823	84,088	1,080	511	4,966	3,268	165,441
12	Henzada ...	413,001	121,924	111,085	2,578	2,146	10,373	5,911	179,992
13	Myaungmya ...	267,949	84,613	55,365	1,343	156	3,321	1,194	127,971
14	Ma-ubin ...	222,461	68,332	58,534	1,149	515	3,105	2,024	95,595
15	Pyapôn ...	213,216	66,044	28,915	121	30	1,243	613	118,257
	Tenasserim Division ...	1,149,436	328,087	189,275	4,285	1,388	27,170	10,217	632,074
16	Toungoo ...	276,874	80,178	47,601	722	303	5,931	2,186	149,095
17	Salween ...	45,591	12,672	6,845	215	52	650	266	26,074
18	Thatôn ...	360,062	104,958	61,297	1,382	482	6,235	2,864	193,807
19	Amherst ...	287,214	80,954	49,432	849	227	6,631	3,131	156,818
20	Tavoy ...	99,141	29,045	17,393	798	174	5,927	1,646	52,703
21	Mergui ...	80,554	20,270	6,707	319	150	1,796	124	53,577
	Magwe Division ...	1,041,930	298,930	267,289	8,624	5,950	52,796	21,794	475,711
22	Thayetmyo ...	190,802	53,636	43,636	2,673	1,485	7,489	3,251	93,530
23	Pakôkku ...	306,725	87,746	68,598	1,535	955	20,810	9,034	150,381
24	Minbu ...	189,610	57,236	52,398	3,389	2,374	14,351	5,652	80,006
25	Magwe ...	335,016	94,869	96,557	1,027	1,136	10,128	3,857	143,590
26	Pakôkku Hill Tracts ...	19,747	5,443	6,100	...	...	18	...	8,204
	Mandalay Division ...	498,305	144,138	107,916	3,560	3,871	24,670	8,374	246,251
27	Mandalay ...	127,648	39,278	26,804	378	779	4,605	2,283	61,566
	Mandalay City ...	*6,969*	*2,897*	*791*	...	...	*38*	*72*	*3,281*
28	Bhamo ...	88,910	24,459	22,469	1,466	1,668	3,957	958	41,982
29	Myitkyina ...	95,396	29,445	20,404	591	595	2,824	522	45,547
30	Katha ...	180,223	49,259	36,362	1,012	721	12,923	4,518	94,602
31	Putao ...	6,128	1,697	1,877	113	108	361	93	2,554
	Sagaing Division ...	1,011,330	285,803	296,596	6,949	5,294	63,733	35,366	428,931
32	Shwebo ...	305,213	85,422	102,774	394	256	25,376	14,387	117,017
33	Sagaing ...	219,468	61,829	51,901	2,737	1,701	14,989	11,769	105,738
34	Lower Chindwin ...	243,457	61,850	68,131	1,851	1,753	12,133	5,439	113,476
35	Upper Chindwin ...	136,064	40,905	35,212	1,967	1,584	11,206	3,690	59,947
36	Chin Hills ...	107,128	35,797	38,578	...	...	29	81	32,753
	Meiktila Division ...	824,128	223,161	137,913	3,772	1,610	27,767	15,533	463,044
37	Kyauksè ...	89,116	26,533	13,357	341	210	3,136	1,432	49,226
38	Meiktila ...	202,234	54,427	28,905	739	174	8,448	5,017	118,902
39	Yamèthin ...	227,002	60,449	27,700	1,083	174	7,444	2,335	138,853
40	Myingyan ...	305,766	81,752	67,951	1,609	1,052	8,739	6,749	156,063
	Eastern States ...	1,118,244	352,379	280,712	22,415	16,413	71,854	44,611	485,153
41	Northern Shan States ...	473,007	144,590	129,751	12,444	7,167	31,954	24,194	198,666
42	Southern Shan States ...	593,415	194,243	136,726	9,650	8,801	39,025	20,055	262,446
43	Karenni ...	51,822	13,546	14,235	321	445	875	362	24,041

PART III.—*Details by districts*—contd.

Sub-Class Ie.—Domestic and wild animals. (Orders IIc, IId, IIe)								Sub-Class II.—Exploitation of Minerals. (Orders III, IV, V)								
Total Workers and Dependents.	WORKERS. Total Workers. Males.	WORKERS. Total Workers. Females.	Workers with an agricultural or other subsidiary occupation. Agricultural. Males.	Agricultural. Females.	Other. Males.	Other. Females.	DEPENDENTS.	Total Workers and Dependents.	WORKERS. Total Workers. Males.	WORKERS. Total Workers. Females.	Workers with an agricultural or other subsidiary occupation. Agricultural. Males.	Agricultural. Females.	Other. Males.	Other. Females.	DEPENDENTS.	Serial No. of District, etc. (column 1).
10	11	12	13	14	15	16	17	18	19	20	21	22	23	24	25	
235,080	90,210	27,512	2,299	675	5,341	1,733	117,358	42,885	27,020	2,985	203	21	207	51	12,870	
219,670	83,725	25,005	1,795	435	4,656	1,416	110,940	35,810	20,888	2,959	203	19	207	51	11,963	
14,138	6,058	1,240	294	105	380	48	6,840	79	17	23	1	...	4	2	39	
5,792	3,194	501	93	19	73	16	2,097	14	2	...	1	...	...	...	12	1
19	8	...	...	...	...	...	11	..	..	...	...	...	...	..	...	2
5,298	1,570	513	118	40	198	22	3,215	35	12	13	...	...	4	2	10	3
3,029	1,286	226	83	46	109	10	1,517	30	3	10	...	...	...	...	17	4
31,201	14,550	2,996	270	53	804	124	13,655	848	451	14	1	...	...	...	383	
1,758	1,184	139	...	..	1	5	435	193	69	...	...	...	...	...	124	5
6,546	3,431	580	22	2	151	23	2,535	275	150	11	...	...	...	...	114	6
4,440	2,182	459	23	4	91	12	1,799	136	71	1	1	...	...	...	64	7
8,426	3,288	966	172	41	348	37	4,172	29	16	...	...	..	...	...	13	8
7,047	3,246	563	44	5	134	24	3,238	8	1	...	..	...	...	..	7	9
2,984	1,219	289	9	1	79	23	1,476	207	144	2	...	...	..	...	61	10
57,483	19,919	9,370	309	86	599	282	28,194	898	365	65	25	2	7	...	468	
9,337	3,262	1,231	53	19	190	130	4,844	693	290	55	25	2	4	..	348	11
7,572	2,738	850	71	16	121	39	3,984	51	37	2	...	...	...	...	12	12
7,212	2,584	1,183	97	16	110	17	3,445	153	38	8	...	.	3	...	107	13
24,461	8,215	4,812	48	31	135	85	11,434	1	..	...	...	...	...	...	1	14
8,901	3,120	1,294	40	13	43	8	4,487		...	...	...	..	..	...	...	15
48,571	16,886	3,361	368	16	497	71	28,324	11,236	5,878	532	74	7	56	7	4,826	
4,269	1,797	376	22	1	123	17	2,117	112	42	32	...	..	2	1	38	16
276	128	21	4	1	4	...	127	7	6	1	...	..	1	...	...	17
5,919	2,176	759	23	...	71	25	2,984	765	391	69	2	..	2	.	305	18
6,669	3,072	447	2	2	35	12	3,150	1,950	873	94	23	...	6	2	983	19
9,213	2,912	1,066	145	8	149	17	5,235	4,059	2,635	954	40	7	28	4	1,770	20
22,234	6,821	692	72	4	115	...	14,721	3,743	1,931	82	9	..	17	...	1,730	21
15,856	5,633	2,532	97	88	293	272	7,691	13,562	9,613	362	32	2	48	7	3,587	
2,764	1,048	238	7	2	64	20	1,478	308	142	45	...	...	21	...	121	22
6,248	1,853	1,224	40	55	110	171	3,171	942	385	39	11	...	6		518	23
3,244	1,345	648	32	27	101	72	1,251	652	245	55	1	2	10	1	352	24
3,598	1,387	422	18	4	18	9	1,789	11,660	8,841	223	20	...	11	6	2,596	25
2	...	...	...	..	...	...	2	...	...	...	...	...		...	...	26
19,261	7,989	1,415	128	6	776	143	9,857	7,411	3,878	1,529	27	3	69	20	2,004	
9,319	3,748	774	53	2	155	41	4,797	2,256	845	541	12	3	10	4	870	27
2,187	704	194		...	26	...	1,289	961	372	387	...	...		..	202	
2,624	1,302	175	35	..	153	54	1,170	8	6	...	...	...	...	...	2	28
2,893	1,294	214	10	1	356	39	1,385	3,214	2,757	50	14	...	35	2	407	29
4,253	1,515	247	30	3	112	9	2,491	1,933	270	954	1	..	24	14	795	30
122	103	5	...	...	...	..	14	...	...	...	...	...	...	...	...	31
18,466	7,580	1,961	336	57	974	342	8,925	1,114	341	284	43	5	20	12	489	
3,350	899	519	9	10	149	93	1,932	189	65	29	22	...	7	5	95	32
8,013	3,370	606	200	13	247	84	4,037	516	141	139	12	5	4	..	236	33
3,819	1,495	399	41	...	144	62	1,918	354	114	107	5	...	7	7	133	34
4,106	1,834	421	85	34	433	103	1,851	55	21	9	4	...	2	...	25	35
185	72	16	1	...	1	...	97	...	...	...	...	...	...	...	...	36
14,694	5,110	2,130	93	24	333	134	7,454	662	345	150	...	...	3	3	167	
3,091	1,091	313	35	3	88	22	1,687	1	...	1	...	...	...	..	...	37
3,152	1,183	439	27	12	89	25	1,530	51	51	...		...	1	...	...	38
2,690	1,050	434	12	2	65	20	1,206	565	283	126	..	...	1	...	156	39
5,848	1,876	941	19	7	91	67	3,031	45	11	23	...	...	1	3	11	40
15,410	6,485	2,507	405	240	685	317	6,418	7,075	6,132	36	...	2	...	...	907	
5,295	2,671	720	49	26	254	55	1,904	7,071	6,131	36	...	2	...	...	904	41
10,026	3,774	1,782	356	214	428	262	4,470	4	1	...	...	...	...	...	3	42
89	40	5	...	...	3	...	44	...	...	...	...	...	...	...	...	43

Serial No.	District or State.	Total Workers and Dependents.	Total Workers. Males.	Total Workers. Females.	Workers with an agricultural or other subsidiary occupation. Agricultural. Males.	Agricultural. Females.	Other. Males.	Other. Females.	Dependents.
		Sub-Class *III.*—Industry. (Orders VI to XVIII.)							
	1	2	3	4	5	6	7	8	9
	Provincial Total ...	870,827	280,631	203,317	8,662	6,464	10,423	10,521	386,879
	Divisional Burma ...	344,504	271,885	197,378	8,189	5,924	9,871	10,122	375,241
	Arakan Division	33,943	9,870	9,240	153	64	325	356	14,833
1	Akyab	26,714	7,975	7,623	86	11	176	206	11,116
2	Hill Dist. of Arakan ...	89	47	2	...	...	...	...	40
3	Kyaukpyu	2,252	737	219	40	10	46	29	1,296
4	Sandoway	4,888	1,111	1,396	27	43	103	121	2,381
	Pegu Division ...	207,686	92,828	29,900	463	655	961	772	84,958
5	Rangoon Town ...	99,666	57,514	6,520	17	...	105	9	35,632
6	Insein	13,698	6,168	1,976	25	61	114	113	5,554
7	Hanthawaddy ...	18,694	7,636	1,956	57	46	101	39	9,102
8	Tharrawaddy ..	23,066	7,314	4,649	66	144	226	153	11,103
9	Pegu	18,680	6,009	3,103	92	76	156	81	9,568
10	Prome	33,882	8,187	11,696	206	328	259	377	13,099
	Irrawaddy Division ...	87,736	29,464	17,196	533	303	980	557	41,076
11	Bassein	21,949	9,140	3,035	198	47	273	100	9,774
12	Henzada	26,172	7,954	5,665	213	143	351	262	12,553
13	Myaungmya ...	13,380	4,510	2,456	51	5	189	79	6,114
14	Ma-ubin	16,028	4,112	5,259	42	106	127	100	6,657
15	Pyapôn	10,207	3,748	781	29	2	40	16	5,678
	Tenasserim Division ...	94,823	27,800	20,878	378	279	699	1,072	46,145
16	Toungoo	17,946	5,462	3,076	26	69	172	73	9,408
17	Salween	705	227	113	2	6	14	9	365
18	Thatôn	19,622	4,958	4,953	48	41	198	454	9,711
19	Amherst	36,154	11,906	7,076	151	116	103	287	17,172
20	Tavoy	13,113	3,174	4,600	145	47	163	227	5,339
21	Mergui	7,283	2,073	1,060	6	...	49	22	4,150
	Magwe Division ...	129,619	34,002	33,640	3,068	1,561	3,159	2,566	61,977
22	Thayetmyo	15,912	4,136	3,624	43	56	219	129	8,152
23	Pakôkku	70,072	16,913	20,081	2,490	1,016	2,315	1,884	33,078
24	Minbu	21,970	5,579	6,919	413	408	453	442	9,472
25	Magwe	21,620	7,334	3,016	122	81	172	111	11,270
26	Pakôkku Hill Tracts ..	45	40	...	...	...	...	...	5
	Mandalay Division ...	86,813	26,726	25,572	124	267	717	742	34,515
27	Mandalay ...	74,923	22,259	23,590	56	235	408	635	29,074
	Mandalay City ...	*46,523*	*14,215*	*13,303*	...	*8*	*17*	*24*	*19,005*
28	Bhamo	3,517	1,279	669	9	...	102	15	1,569
29	Myitkyina	2,329	1,109	243	20	3	59	13	977
30	Katha	5,945	1,989	1,069	39	29	145	79	2,887
31	Putao	99	90	1	...	...	3	...	8
	Sagaing Division ...	114,249	29,246	34,174	2,835	1,990	2,033	2,807	50,829
32	Shwebo	19,226	5,332	6,008	282	408	338	363	7,886
33	Sagaing	38,351	9,528	12,532	1,406	979	662	1,626	16,291
34	Lower Chindwin ..	47,312	11,600	13,439	977	436	729	653	22,273
35	Upper Chindwin ...	9,104	2,671	2,191	166	167	304	164	4,242
36	Chin Hills	256	115	4	4	...	...	1	137
	Meiktila Division ...	89,635	21,949	26,778	635	805	997	1,250	40,908
37	Kyauksè	10,251	2,751	2,542	54	167	143	106	4,958
38	Meiktila	29,860	6,299	9,612	260	383	313	467	13,949
39	Yamèthin	21,664	5,353	4,543	80	63	220	146	11,768
40	Myingyan	27,860	7,546	10,081	241	192	321	531	10,233
	Eastern States ...	26,323	8,746	5,939	473	540	552	399	11,638
41	Northern Shan States ...	13,996	4,281	4,319	129	496	247	322	5,396
42	Southern Shan States ...	11,630	4,208	1,543	344	44	303	77	5,879
43	Karenni	697	257	77	...	...	2	...	363

PART III.—*Details by districts*—contd.

Sub-Class *IV*.—Transport. (Orders XIX to XXIII.) Total Workers and Dependents.	Workers. Total Workers. Males.	Workers. Total Workers. Females.	Workers with an agricultural or other subsidiary occupation. Agricultural. Males.	Agricultural. Females.	Other. Males.	Other. Females.	Dependents.	Sub-Class *V*.—Trade, finance and insurance. (Orders XXIV to XL.) Total Workers and Dependents.	Workers. Total Workers. Males.	Workers. Total Workers. Females.	Workers with an agricultural or other subsidiary occupation. Agricultural. Males.	Agricultural. Females.	Other. Males.	Other. Females.	Dependents.	Serial No. of District, etc. (column 1).
10	11	12	13	14	15	16	17	18	19	20	21	22	23	24	25	
354,274	177,404	15,938	4,119	315	5,088	964	160,932	1,096,818	269,058	311,564	5,838	5,233	14,906	11,476	516,196	
339,906	170,625	14,862	3,805	253	4,476	875	154,419	1,035,955	250,177	295,037	4,194	4,261	13,042	9,700	490,741	
16,448	12,436	206	1,759	3	239	10	3,806	62,534	18,067	13,806	645	243	1,003	647	30,661	
13,639	11,333	98	1,741	...	160	4	2,208	46,278	14,752	8,500	466	50	713	361	23,026	1
49	29	...	...	...	...	...	20	263	139	30	2	.	...	...	94	2
1,128	592	36	8	2	29	2	500	10,722	2,081	3,629	129	131	159	177	5,012	3
1,632	482	72	10	1	50	4	1,078	5,271	1,095	1,647	48	62	131	109	2,529	4
111,472	64,383	2,063	443	14	753	32	45,025	257,528	70,353	57,523	639	975	2,365	1,008	129,652	
50,961	37,660	458	35		94	..	12,843	76,365	30,947	9,056	18	5	156	27	36,362	5
12,501	6,173	451	28	1	122	2	5,877	24,513	5,914	6,248	47	70	385	114	12,3[illegible]1	6
15,403	6,865	139	105	3	116	9	8,799	38,476	8,170	10,063	108	91	629	170	20,243	7
8,666	3,926	196	101	1	101	...	4,544	36,103	7,418	9,769	244	215	452	167	18,916	8
14,614	5,638	305	108	6	191	4	8,671	36,601	11,111	11,356	186	383	546	226	24,134	9
9,326	4,121	514	65	3	129	17	4,691	35,470	6,793	11,031	36	211	197	304	1[illegible],646	10
38,246	20,520	1,527	190	5	513	93	16,199	220,112	54,378	61,844	778	803	2,702	1,588	103,890	
8,762	5,433	233	74	4	116	11	3,096	5[illegible],651	15,968	15,946	229	244	889	461	26,737	11
10,869	5,036	531	55	...	195	69	5,302	48,374	9,517	15,419	204	348	540	444	23,438	12
3,496	2,108	209	12	...	78	1	1,179	44,294	11,756	11,370	1[illegible]6	79	661	343	21,168	13
6,711	3,287	340	11	...	75	4	3,084	39,463	8,916	12,113	102	77	389	274	18,404	14
8,408	4,656	214	38	1	49	8	3,538	29,330	8,191	6,996	67	55	223	66	14,143	15
49,424	23,923	1,209	320	11	367	43	24,292	130,227	28,717	38,099	353	259	1,219	926	63,411	
9,397	4,185	322	57	3	113	7	4,890	36,3[illegible]6	8,539	8,5[illegible]6	64	60	3[illegible]	184	19,201	16
466	278	1	2	...	2	...	187	1,322	433	167	9	3	15	2	722	17
9,761	3,900	230	82	8	106	14	5,631	37,411	8,556	11,554	97	86	342	263	17,301	18
20,534	10,416	542	102	...	52	17	9,576	32,864	8,031	7,782	120	29	294	237	17,051	19
5,570	2,917	69	72	...	65	2	2,584	14,523	2,084	7,565	57	[illegible]0	146	226	4,874	20
3,[illegible]96	2,227	45	5	...	29	3	1,424	[illegible],791	1,074	2,455	6	1	70	14	4,2[illegible]2	21
35,574	13,323	3,241	388	106	770	172	19,010	106,368	20,834	40,421	561	828	1,950	2,091	45,113	
5,859	2,125	261	5	2	114	28	3,473	18,690	2,950	6,211	31	60	130	153	9,529	22
11,801	4,209	934	130	15	349	60	6,658	[illegible]2,415	7,607	6,950	240	264	[illegible]32	1,110	17,849	23
6,875	2,772	558	146	54	183	27	3,515	24,392	4,818	10,406	151	385	559	602	9,168	24
11,027	4,210	1,488	107	35	124	57	5,329	20,868	5,458	6,845	139	1[illegible]9	329	196	8,[illegible]65	25
12	7	...	...	...	...	...	5	3	1	...	...	...	...	...	2	26
29,168	14,475	939	185	3	425	24	13,754	91,366	22,408	27,025	232	201	1,205	818	41,933	
22,587	10,936	763	42	2	241	15	10,888	57,646	13,497	19,171	40	125	232	267	24,978	27
12,871	*5,978*	*271*	*3*	...	*3*	*2*	*6,622*	*41,122*	*10,247*	*12,275*	*4*	*1*	*52*	*34*	*18,600*	
2,663	1,359	72	6	..	105	1	1,232	8,437	2,073	2,526	29	10	279	69	3,838	28
1,854	1,238	28	111	...	28	5	588	4,604	1,527	998	12	7	259	53	2,079	29
2,020	914	76	25	1	50	3	1,030	20,632	5,286	4,325	151	59	435	329	11,021	30
44	28	...	1	...	1	..	16	47	25	5	...	..	...	..	17	31
33,268	12,699	3,142	342	76	1,025	386	17,427	71,377	16,377	24,153	606	378	1,550	1,500	30,847	
5,950	2,205	645	16	9	123	31	3,100	19,685	4,645	5,669	85	40	377	175	9,371	32
13,845	4,497	1,569	166	35	307	247	7,779	22,653	4,369	10,078	171	123	325	668	8,206	33
8,670	3,263	798	102	25	301	86	4,609	17,879	4,449	5,525	163	124	380	383	7,905	34
4,708	2,689	130	58	7	292	22	1,889	11,048	2,881	2,881	187	91	406	274	5,286	35
95	45	..	...	...	2	.	50	112	33	...	...	...	2	...	79	36
26,307	8,866	2,535	178	35	384	115	14,906	96,443	19,043	32,166	380	574	1,048	1,122	45,234	
3,754	1,535	145	43	8	67	6	2,074	12,065	2,334	4,445	71	213	173	101	5,286	37
6,412	2,009	636	27	7	50	11	3,767	24,091	4,247	8,314	101	126	306	356	11,530	38
11,253	3,758	1,292	88	12	151	37	6,203	25,759	5,974	6,177	79	55	262	129	13,608	39
4,888	1,564	462	20	8	116	61	2,962	34,528	6,188	13,230	129	180	307	536	14,810	40
14,368	6,779	1,076	314	62	612	89	6,513	60,863	18,881	16,527	1,644	972	1,864	1,776	25,455	
6,970	3,540	672	74	9	150	57	2,758	23,363	7,883	5,3[illegible]6	301	60	863	738	10,124	41
7,165	3,148	382	235	53	[illegible]62	31	3,635	33,281	9,653	10,286	1,289	782	897	1,017	13,312	42
233	91	22	5	...	...	1	120	4,219	1,345	885	54	30	104	21	1,989	43

Serial No.	DISTRICT OR STATE.	Sub-Class VI.—Public force. (Orders XLI to XLIV.)							
		Total Workers and Dependents.	WORKERS.						DEPENDENTS.
			Total Workers.		Workers with an agricultural or other subsidiary occupation.				
					Agricultural.		Other.		
			Males.	Females.	Males.	Females.	Males.	Females.	
	1	2	3	4	5	6	7	8	9
	Provincial Total ...	76,400	37,628	469	779	1	155	39	38,303
	Divisional Burma ...	70,712	34,787	322	664	...	138	28	35,603
	Arakan Division ...	3,993	1,461	62	4	...	6	...	2,470
1	Akyab ...	1,537	707	1	3	...	...	...	829
2	Hill Dist. of Arakan ...	521	249	...	1	...	2	...	272
3	Kyaukpyu ...	867	121	61	...	...	...	...	685
4	Sandoway ...	1,068	384	...	...	...	4	...	684
	Pegu Division ...	15,082	7,352	77	102	...	20	...	7,653
5	Rangoon Town ...	5,376	3,302	5	4	...	2	...	2,069
6	Insein ...	1,520	625	47	...	...	...	...	848
7	Hanthawaddy ...	1,933	875	21	...	...	1	...	1,037
8	Tharrawaddy ...	2,286	846	...	...		1	...	1,440
9	Pegu ...	2,158	911	2	95	...	14	...	1,245
10	Prome ...	1,809	793	2	3	...	2	...	1,014
	Irrawaddy Division ...	7,226	2,956	10	2	...	1	...	4,260
11	Bassein ...	2,189	904	...	...	...	...	...	1,285
12	Henzada ...	1,877	696	...	...	...	1	...	1,181
13	Myaungmya ...	1,178	518	6	...	...	...	...	654
14	Ma-ubin ...	1,019	424	4	1	...	...	...	591
15	Pyapon ...	963	414	...	1	...	...	...	549
	Tenasserim Division ...	7,424	3,493	43	3	...	11	19	3,888
16	Toungoo ...	1,847	985	13	...	...	4	...	849
17	Salween ...	362	238	18	1	...	1	18	106
18	Thaton ...	1,802	648	8	1	...	2	1	1,146
19	Amherst ...	1,754	842	3	...	...	3	...	909
20	Tavoy ...	923	455	1	1	...	...	...	467
21	Mergui ...	736	345	...	...	...	1	...	391
	Magwe Division ...	6,007	2,415	7	1	...	...	...	3,585
22	Thayetmyo ...	1,472	431	2	...	...	...	...	1,039
23	Pakokku ...	1,763	611	...	1	...	...	...	1,152
24	Minbu ...	1,448	585	1	...	...	...	...	862
25	Magwe ...	1,175	658	4	...	...	...	...	513
26	Pakokku Hill Tracts ...	149	130	...	...	...	...	...	19
	Mandalay Division ...	17,242	10,796	71	458	...	12	8	6,375
27	Mandalay ...	8,369	5,331	15	449	...	2	...	3,023
	Mandalay City ...	*4,330*	*2,843*	*5*	*449*	...	*1*	...	*1,482*
28	Bhamo ...	2,558	1,986	1	...	...	...	...	571
29	Myitkyina ...	3,644	2,056	3	9	...	3	...	1,585
30	Katha ...	1,848	849	52	...	...	7	8	947
31	Putao ...	823	574	...	...	...	...	...	249
	Sagaing Division ...	6,762	3,395	35	94	...	85	1	3,332
32	Shwebo ...	1,966	823	32	...	...	1	...	1,111
33	Sagaing ...	914	394	1	...	...	...	1	519
34	Lower Chindwin ...	1,372	716	1	...	...	1	...	655
35	Upper Chindwin ...	1,357	777	1	...	...	82	...	579
36	Chin Hills ...	1,153	691	...	94	...	1	...	462
	Meiktila Division ...	6,976	2,919	17	...	...	3	...	4,040
37	Kyaukse ...	1,127	348	...	...	...	1	...	779
38	Meiktila ...	1,867	935	12	...	...	2	...	920
39	Yamethin ...	2,400	1,085	5	...	...	...	...	1,310
40	Myingyan ...	1,582	551	...	...	...	...	...	1,031
	Eastern States ...	5,688	2,841	147	115	1	17	11	2,700
41	Northern Shan States ...	2,441	1,638	134	77	1	11	11	669
42	Southern Shan States ...	3,060	1,119	13	38	...	6	...	1,928
43	Karenni ...	187	84	...	...	...	...	...	103

PART III.—*Details by districts*—contd.

Sub-Class *VII.*—Public administration. (Order XLV.)								Sub-Class *VIII.*—The professions and liberal arts. (Orders XLVI to L.)								
Total Workers and Dependents.	WORKERS.						DEPENDENTS.	Total Workers and Dependents.	WORKERS.						DEPENDENTS.	Serial No. of District, etc. (column 1).
	Total Workers.		Workers with an agricultural or other subsidiary occupation.						Total Workers.		Workers with an agricultural or other subsidiary occupation.					
			Agricultural.		Other.						Agricultural.		Other.			
	Males.	Females.	Males.	Females.	Males.	Females.			Males.	Females.	Males.	Females.	Males.	Females		
10	11	12	13	14	15	16	17	18	19	20	21	22	23	24	25	
103,041	33,242	992	9,102	90	1,763	42	68,807	282,566	144,113	16,299	1,271	80	2,427	212	122,134	
83,598	26,418	795	5,181	84	1,227	38	56,385	247,186	119,575	15,046	960	67	1,959	191	112,585	
5,343	1,259	25	374	2	43	...	4,059	13,186	5,433	546	80	2	144	7	7,207	
3,330	793	4	170	...	21	...	2,533	8,755	3,511	393	42	...	62	5	4,851	1
115	25	...	8	.	..	..	90	46	20	2	...	..	...	...	24	2
1,024	235	20	101	2	14	...	769	2,750	1,238	94	22	2	51	1	1,418	3
874	206	1	95	...	8	...	667	1,635	664	57	16	...	31	1	914	4
21,338	6,997	247	556	...	259	...	14,094	55,525	24,155	3,443	127	6	361	20	27,927	
10,262	3,742	174	4	...	13	...	6,346	17,703	6,805	1,417	4	...	48	5	9,481	5
2,614	640	26	34	...	17	..	1,948	5,605	2,369	376	16	1	45	7	1,860	6
1,159	463	2	147	...	23	...	694	7,120	3,235	357	26	...	44	...	3,528	7
2,762	713	6	42	...	127	..	2,043	8,533	3,922	382	24	2	113	4	4,229	8
2,560	696	11	164	...	53	..	1,853	9,152	4,669	535	34	2	47	2	3,948	9
1,981	743	28	165	...	21	...	1,210	7,412	3,155	376	23	1	64	2	3,881	10
12,039	3,607	112	889	20	228	13	8,320	35,618	16,672	2,270	202	23	314	35	16,676	
3,366	1,104	8	231	2	85	...	2,254	8,933	4,577	505	33	6	97	7	3,851	11
2,867	910	47	239	14	45	6	1,910	9,414	4,329	611	91	13	84	17	4,474	12
2,433	708	40	230	...	44	...	1,685	5,606	2,478	384	33	2	52	1	2,744	13
1,754	486	12	72	1	28	7	1,256	6,144	2,639	474	29	1	53	5	3,031	14
1,619	399	5	117	3	26	.	1,215	5,521	2,649	295	16	1	28	5	2,576	15
11,313	3,970	43	423	2	90	6	7,300	30,724	13,422	2,247	113	6	213	25	15,055	
3,266	1,311	5	112	...	29	...	1,950	7,518	3,554	408	40	6	75	1	3,556	16
208	55	...	10	...	2	...	153	380	154	13	5	...	4	...	213	17
2,235	725	17	149	2	19	1	1,493	7,778	3,410	502	34	..	68	9	3,866	18
3,015	1,031	11	39	...	3	3	1,973	9,438	4,135	840	16	...	4	6	4,463	19
1,200	459	8	72	...	16	2	733	3,427	1,409	317	15	...	36	9	1,701	20
1,389	389	2	41	...	21	...	998	2,183	760	167	3	...	26	...	1,256	21
8,940	2,503	82	838	13	243	4	6,355	27,720	15,056	1,025	89	5	282	41	11,639	
2,207	602	14	172	6	31	1	1,591	4,665	1,714	169	3	...	16	5	2,782	22
2,791	787	4	377	...	53	2	2,000	9,844	5,906	455	33	1	146	25	3,483	23
2,217	517	16	191	1	38	1	1,684	6,906	2,959	311	47	4	67	10	3,636	24
1,705	593	48	98	6	127	...	1,064	6,286	4,467	90	6	...	53	1	1,729	25
20	4	...	..	...	...	...	16	19	10	...	...	...	...	...	9	26
7,735	2,712	106	514	23	157	6	4,917	26,600	13,577	1,613	75	2	207	12	11,410	
3,039	1,436	29	47	...	53	..	2,174	17,533	10,084	1,064	28	..	109	4	6,385	27
1,870	*813*	*6*	*6*	...	*12*	...	*1,051*	*12,478*	*7,103*	*691*	*1*	...	*61*	*4*	*2,684*	
762	191	2	69	...	26	1	569	1,641	622	137	10	1	23	1	882	28
893	284	5	88	1	19	...	604	1,199	602	52	1	...	22	...	545	29
2,294	726	70	302	22	59	5	1,498	6,138	2,313	356	34	1	53	7	3,569	30
147	75	...	8	...	...	...	72	89	56	4	2	...	...	...	29	31
8,382	2,878	98	1,064	11	143	3	5,406	32,083	17,629	2,172	177	18	279	28	12,282	
2,352	738	86	270	10	29	1	1,528	9,148	5,871	515	43	10	70	12	2,762	32
1,990	650	3	153	1	29	1	1,337	10,669	4,626	1,251	55	...	64	2	4,792	33
1,298	549	...	194	...	33	...	749	7,421	4,897	179	43	..	78	3	2,345	34
2,303	636	9	242	...	45	1	1,658	4,620	2,161	225	35	8	67	11	2,234	35
439	305	...	205	...	7	...	134	225	74	2	1	...	...	..	149	36
8,508	2,492	82	523	13	64	6	5,934	25,730	13,631	1,730	97	5	159	23	10,369	
1,746	550	...	176	...	7	...	1,196	3,578	1,738	325	16	2	41	1	1,515	37
1,913	507	43	36	8	20	3	1,363	6,695	4,169	554	47		46	5	1,972	38
2,787	743	39	148	5	25	3	2,005	6,756	3,449	310	23	2	45	6	2,997	39
2,062	692	...	163	...	12	...	1,370	8,701	4,275	541	11	1	27	11	3,885	40
19,443	6,824	197	3,921	6	536	4	12,422	35,380	24,538	1,253	311	13	468	21	9,589	
4,019	1,163	81	403	2	108	3	2,775	9,484	6,068	750	22	1	249	13	2,666	41
14,948	5,507	105	3,501	2	427	1	9,336	24,960	18,058	449	279	10	207	6	6,453	42
476	154	11	17	2	1	...	311	936	412	54	10	2	12	2	470	43

Serial No.	DISTRICT OR STATE.	Sub-Class *IX.*—Persons (not in Sub-Class I-A) without an occupation but receiving an income. (Order LI.)							
		Total Workers and Dependents.	WORKERS.						DEPENDENTS.
			Total Workers.		Workers with an agricultural or other subsidiary occupation.				
					Agricultural.		Other.		
			Males.	Females.	Males.	Females.	Males.	Females.	
	1	2	3	4	5	6	7	8	9
	Provincial Total ...	13,800	3,230	1,175	153	10	344	41	9,395
	Divisional Burma ...	13,168	3,110	1,105	136	8	312	39	8,953
	Arakan Division ..	603	133	18	12	...	27	4	452
1	Akyab	284	53	10	4	...	7	1	221
2	Hill Dist. of Arakan ...	27	8	...	..	...	...	...	19
3	Kyaukpyu	126	36	7	4	...	10	3	83
4	Sandoway	166	36	1	4	...	10	...	129
	Pegu Division	4,575	842	458	6	..	56	10	3,275
5	Rangoon Town ...	2,859	528	253	1	...	37	6	2,078
6	Insein	326	80	29	2	...	2	3	217
7	Hanthawaddy ...	153	57	22		...	...	...	74
8	Tharrawaddy ...	458	63	56	3	...	7	...	339
9	Pegu	452	57	55	...	...	8	1	340
10	Prome	327	57	43	...	...	2	...	227
	Irrawaddy Division .	1,130	265	97	10	...	11	3	768
11	Bassein	342	85	28	1	...	2	1	229
12	Henzada	267	66	18	6	...	4	...	183
13	Myaungmya ...	200	45	15	2	...	3	1	140
14	Ma-ubin	199	33	19	1	..	2	1	147
15	Pyapôn	122	36	17	...	...	...	...	69
	Tenasserim Division ...	1,912	413	286	22	3	32	11	1,213
16	Toungoo	393	87	20	4	...	4	2	286
17	Salween	19	4	...	1	...	1	...	15
18	Thatôn	266	29	37	2	1	...	5	200
19	Amherst	754	149	169	7	...	1	2	436
20	Tavoy	211	74	33	2	2	19	2	104
21	Mergui	269	70	27	6	...	7	...	172
	Magwe Division ...	921	367	26	11	2	12	1	528
22	Thayetmyo	453	205	9	...	1	3	...	239
23	Pakôkku	205	66	...	4	...	7	...	139
24	Minbu	152	37	9	7	1	2	...	106
25	Magwe	111	59	8	...	...	...	1	44
26	Pakôkku Hill Tracts ...	..	...	..	...	...	...	...	...
	Mandalay Division ...	2,165	533	127	21	1	71	3	1,505
27	Mandalay ...	1,602	366	111	7	1	46	2	1,125
	Mandalay City ...	*934*	*160*	*106*	...	...	*1*	...	*668*
28	Bhamo	104	31	4	3	...	2	1	69
29	Myitkyina	290	95	3	11	...	17	...	192
30	Katha	157	39	8	...	...	6	...	110
31	Putao	12	2	1	...	...	...	..	9
	Sagaing Division ...	982	339	33	47	1	72	4	610
32	Shwebo	328	99	17	16	...	17	...	212
33	Sagaing	257	70	6	6	...	11	1	181
34	Lower Chindwin ...	170	92	1	11	...	18	...	77
35	Upper Cnindwin ...	158	56	8	9	1	22	2	94
36	Chin Hills	69	22	1	5	...	4	1	46
	Meiktila Division .	880	218	60	7	1	31	3	602
37	Kyauksè	179	58	3	..	...	12	...	118
38	Meiktila	227	55	34	1	...	11	...	138
39	Yamèthin	327	51	12	4	1	5	2	264
40	Myingyan	147	54	11	2	...	3	1	82
	Eastern States ...	632	120	70	17	2	32	2	442
41	Northern Shan States	235	28	44	5	2	10	2	163
42	Southern Shan States ..	387	90	26	12	...	22	...	271
43	Karenni	10	2	...	...	...	...	...	8

PART III.—*Details by districts*—contd.

Sub-Class *X.*—Domestic service. (Order LII.)								Sub-Class *XI.*—Insufficiently described occupations. (Order LIII.)								Serial No. of District, etc. (column 1).
Total Workers and Dependents.	WORKERS.						DEPENDENTS.	Total Workers and Dependents.	WORKERS.						DEPENDENTS.	
	Total Workers.		Workers with an agricultural or other subsidiary occupation.						Total Workers.		Workers with an agricultural or other subsidiary occupation.					
			Agricultural.		Other.						Agricultural.		Other.			
	Males.	Females.	Males.	Females.	Males.	Females.			Males.	Females.	Males.	Females.	Males.	Females.		
10	11	12	13	14	15	16	17	18	19	20	21	22	23	24	25	
73,669	43,059	8,001	807	87	637	115	22,609	573,641	202,629	149,294	2,533	7,855	5,117	71,72	221,718	
58,743	33,785	6,854	45	67	273	94	18,104	431,608	173,667	69,715	1,275	1,327	3,476	2,311	188,226	
2,465	1,725	405	5		6	3	335	32,792	11,881	6,665	307	242	369	234	14,246	
2,231	1,580	375	5	...	5	3	266	11,486	5,893	808	30	1	65	7	4,785	1
30	26	3	...	...	...	...	1	130	96	3	...	...	2	..	31	2
74	46	10	...	..	1	...	18	17,180	4,724	4,964	257	218	226	171	7,492	3
140	73	17	...	..	...	..	50	3,996	1,168	890	20	23	76	56	1,938	4
24,105	14,705	2,588	10	46	36	12	6,812	121,436	64,346	10,431	161	74	619	290	46,659	
17,930	10,959	1,769	5	...	11	...	5,202	44,395	28,001	590	13	...	39		15,804	5
1,170	623	194	3	...	3	...	353	12,569	5,371	1,471	19	9	63	14	5,727	6
1,289	833	174	1	...	3	...	282	34,332	19,093	3,769	46	17	261	73	11,470	7
1,028	692	112	...	...	6	4	224	12,253	4,330	2,099	57	29	118	114	5,824	8
1,361	778	249	1	45	10	7	334	9,243	4,502	772	4	5	60	15	3,969	9
1,327	820	90	...	1	3	1	417	8,644	3,049	1,730	22	14	78	74	3,865	10
4,812	3,066	641	4	4	50	5	1,105	54,378	22,272	9,801	232	71	478	233	22,305	
1,823	1,277	130	..	..	31	1	416	6,854	3,648	518	12	19	56	7	2,688	11
961	511	240	.	1	12	3	210	20,240	6,044	5,421	60	42	147	190	8,775	12
778	440	90	2	...	4	1	248	15,052	6,195	2,591	61	7	145	23	6,266	13
634	432	72	...	...	2	..	130	5,208	2,844	574	93	1	113	8	1,790	14
616	406	109	2	3	1	...	101	7,084	3,541	697	6	2	17	5	2,786	15
6,503	4,037	656	4	1	99	7	1,810	52,653	22,506	5,297	79	13	329	149	24,850	
1,284	801	95		...	8	...	388	15,027	5,791	2,214	10	3	73	59	7,022	16
49	35	3	..	...	...	...	11	902	578	51	1	...	4		273	17
882	409	111	...	..	62	...	362	20,511	8,549	2,231	55	8	191	85	9,731	18
2,974	1,946	261	3	...	17	...	767	9,841	4,951	500	9	2	22	4	4,390	19
650	360	135	...	1	9	7	155	2,146	922	83	2	...	14	1	1,141	20
664	486	51	1	...	3	...	127	4,226	1,715	218	2	...	25	...	2,293	21
4,550	2,307	530	...	6	32	5	1,713	21,600	7,014	5,591	45	67	223	223	8,995	
681	311	41	...	...	3	3	329	5,832	1,544	1,437	...	5	23	25	2,854	22
1,265	539	210	..	2	6	2	516	4,116	1,099	787	7	5	87	44	2,230	23
871	388	192		2	13	..	291	8,154	2,359	2,968	37	53	95	140	2,807	24
1,705	1,032	86	...	2	10	...	567	3,480	2,006	399	1	4	17	14	1,075	25
28	17	1	...	...	...	...	10	18	6	...	...	...	...	...	12	26
9,019	4,682	911	4	1	11	1	3,426	45,682	18,153	6,081	175	25	472	166	21,448	
7,265	3,479	852	..		4	1	2,934	18,213	6,709	3,213	5	13	33	16	8,291	27
4,386	*2,081*	*634*	...	...	..	...	*1,671*	*11,308*	*4,235*	*2,057*	...	...	7	2	*5,016*	
553	363	18	...	..	4	...	172	770	470	18	2	..	6	1	282	28
540	383	15	4	...	...	..	142	1,331	695	129	6	...	16	3	507	29
580	390	23	...	...	2	..	167	25,294	10,211	2,720	162	12	417	146	12,363	30
81	67	3	...	1	1	...	11	74	68	1	...	...	...	...	5	31
2,866	1,346	430	18	6	17	11	1,090	25,694	6,998	7,048	121	114	414	302	11,648	
979	424	102	1	...	1	...	453	18,182	5,107	5,481	97	65	281	167	7,594	32
626	350	70	1	...	6		206	2,347	585	561	...	1	28	37	1,201	33
701	235	220	...	6	4	11	246	1,555	584	166	5	4	31	8	805	34
379	227	36	3	...	6	..	116	3,384	663	837	7	44	74	90	1,884	35
181	110	2	13	...	.	...	69	226	59	3	12	...	...	...	164	36
4,423	1,937	693	...	3	22	50	1,813	77,373	20,497	18,801	155	721	572	714	38,075	
434	231	30	...	...	4	1	167	14,948	3,672	4,265	68	589	149	200	7,011	37
1,500	564	237	..	...	...	14	699	6,975	1,943	1,521	25	9	55	41	3,511	38
1,341	693	114	...	3	3	2	534	14,900	4,697	2,299	7	...	100	63	7,904	39
1,148	429	306	...	...	15	33	413	40,550	10,185	10,716	55	123	268	410	19,649	40
14,926	9,274	1,147	762	20	364	21	4,505	142,033	28,962	79,579	1,258	6,528	1,641	4,861	33,492	
1,975	836	858	13	...	35	11	281	7,954	3,846	1,113	33	2	74	94	2,995	41
12,872	8,404	261	749	10	329	10	4,207	129,154	22,777	77,465	1,198	6,519	1,511	4,752	28,912	42
79	34	28	...	10	...	...	17	4,925	2,339	1,001	27	7	56	15	1,585	43

Serial No.	DISTRICT OR STATE.	Sub-Class *XII.*—Unproductive and unclassified. (Orders LIV to LVI.)							
		Total Workers and Dependents.	WORKERS.						DEPENDENTS.
			Total Workers.		Workers with an agricultural or other subsidiary occupation.				
					Agricultural.		Other.		
			Males.	Females.	Males.	Females.	Males.	Females.	
	1	2	3	4	5	6	7	8	9
	Provincial Total ...	48,966	26,790	10,896	20	32	147	106	11,280
	Divisional Burma	44,769	25,212	8,939	10	5	111	69	10,618
	Arakan Division	4,393	1,611	1,365	6	3	9	18	1,417
1	Akyab ...	3,913	1,378	1,257	6	3	9	18	1,308
2	Hill Dist. of Arakan ...	8	4	4	...	...	...	...	...
3	Kyaukpyu	340	158	88	...	...	...	...	94
4	Sandoway	102	71	16	...	...	...	...	15
	Pegu Division ..	10,051	7,521	1,558	1	...	13	...	972
5	Rangoon Town ...	4,845	3,649	820	...	...	...	..	378
6	Insein	2,546	2,407	33	...	...	...	...	106
7	Hanthawaddy .	362	173	74	1	..	...	...	115
8	Tharrawaddy ...	326	194	81	...	...	1	...	51
9	Pegu	679	377	219	...	...	12	...	83
10	Prome	1,293	781	331	...	...	...	...	241
	Irrawaddy Division	5,100	3,830	579	...	2	6	4	691
11	Bassein	1,443	1,266	139	...	...	...	...	38
12	Henzada	1,374	855	149	...	2	...	...	370
13	Myaungmya ...	1,527	1,298	115	...	...	...	...	114
14	Ma-ubin	509	313	92	...	...	6	4	104
15	Pyapôn	247	98	84	...	...	...	...	65
	Tenasserim Division ...	5,104	1,821	372	..	...	...	15	2,911
16	Toungoo	2,809	234	67	...	...	...	...	2,508
17	Salween	8	6	2	...	...	...	...	...
18	Thatôn	503	213	118	...	..	...	9	172
19	Amherst	1,435	1,054	175	...	...	...	6	206
20	Tavoy	177	173	4	..	...	...	...	...
21	Mergui	172	141	6	...	...	...	...	25
	Magwe Division ...	4,959	2,782	1,119	...	...	28	10	1,058
22	Thayetmyo	1,503	1,237	63	..	...	...	...	203
23	Pakôkku	1,487	588	381	...	...	21	1	518
24	Minbu	1,456	631	545	...	...	7	9	280
25	Magwe	513	326	130	...	...	...	...	57
26	Pakôkku Hill Tracts ...	...	...	...	...	...	...	...	...
	Mandalay Division ...	6,111	3,070	1,313	1	...	16	1	1,728
27	Mandalay	4,188	2,374	1,008	...	...	4	...	808
	Mandalay City ...	2,362	1,786	450	...	...	...	...	126
28	Bhamo	222	81	90	...	...	...	...	51
29	Myitkyina	114	12	93	...	...	...	...	9
30	Katha.	1,580	599	119	1	...	12	1	862
31	Putao	7	4	3	...	..	...	...	..
	Sagaing Division. ...	3,562	1,428	1,448	1	...	4	3	686
32	Shwebo	1,379	553	446	1	...	2	.	380
33	Sagaing	1,031	271	671	...	...	2	...	89
34	Lower Chindwin ...	975	510	257	...	...	...	2	198
35	Upper Chindwin ...	167	91	60	...	...	...	1	16
36	Chin Hills	10	3	4	...	...	...	...	3
	Meiktila Division ...	5,489	3,149	1,185	1	...	35	18	1,155
37	Kyauksè	908	503	172	...	...	...	1	233
38	Meiktila	816	391	304	...	...	...	...	121
39	Yamèthin	820	433	226	...	...	17	...	161
40	Myingyan	2,945	1,802	483	1	...	18	17	640
	Eastern States ...	4,197	1,578	1,957	10	27	36	37	662
41	Northern Shan States ...	1,776	588	848	5	2	32	20	340
42	Southern Shan States ...	2,263	925	1,037	5	25	4	17	301
43	Karenni	158	65	72	...	...	...	...	21

PART III.—*Details by districts*—contd.

Sub-Class Ia.—Control of land or water used for the exploitation of animals or vegetation. Order I.—Control by persons not principally practising an occupation of Sub-Class Ib or Ic of land or water used for such an occupation. (Groups 1, 2a, 2b.) Total Workers and Dependents.	Workers. Total Workers. Males.	Workers. Total Workers. Females.	Workers with an agricultural or other subsidiary occupation. Agricultural. Males.	Agricultural. Females.	Other. Males.	Other. Females.	Dependents.	Sub-Class Ib—Cultivated and wild plants. Order IIa.—Cultivation. (Groups 3 to 7.) Total Workers and Dependents.	Workers. Total Workers. Males.	Workers. Total Workers. Females.	Workers with an agricultural or other subsidiary occupation. Agricultural. Males.	Agricultural. Females.	Other. Males.	Other. Females.	Dependents.	Serial No. of District, etc. (column 1).
10	11	12	13	14	15	16	17	18	19	20	21	22	23	24	25	
157,135	36,596	40,732	1,069	1,089	5,888	4,570	79,807	9,158,932	2,657,681	1,937,779	67,012	42,574	350,823	172,926	4,563,472	
151,026	34,227	39,487	860	896	5,391	4,340	77,312	8,043,634	2,306,524	1,657,226	44,688	26,177	279,052	128,321	4,079,884	
17,421	3,562	4,228	189	105	515	337	9,631	699,888	201,607	104,167	5,915	2,540	20,011	6,674	394,114	
10,968	1,978	2,086	87	14	169	109	6,504	440,304	130,210	40,132	2,159	245	9,324	1,199	269,962	1
19	...	15	...	...	...	...	4	19,578	6,519	6,240	29	47	39	3	6,813	2
3,170	711	967	35	37	176	91	1,492	154,704	41,783	36,704	2,223	1,217	6,396	3,410	76,217	3
3,664	873	1,160	67	54	170	137	1,631	85,302	23,095	21,085	1,504	1,031	4,252	2,062	41,122	4
28,700	6,132	6,140	134	89	944	532	16,428	1,408,272	400,573	222,556	5,973	2,317	41,778	17,657	785,143	
1,313	274	134	...	...	2	6	905	7,486	3,511	537	10	...	26	4	3,438	5
3,216	696	666	7	7	97	37	1,854	203,700	58,116	33,074	261	141	4,196	1,678	112,510	6
2,147	459	254	14	1	95	15	1,434	238,733	72,182	19,802	459	188	4,193	698	146,749	7
7,785	1,597	1,697	38	46	336	122	4,491	377,615	99,993	71,925	2,537	1,074	14,319	5,995	205,697	8
6,872	1,634	1,111	48	23	177	68	4,127	323,535	96,673	48,902	565	352	7,130	2,277	177,960	9
7,367	1,472	2,278	27	12	237	284	3,617	257,203	70,098	48,316	2,141	562	11,914	7,005	138,789	10
30,287	7,455	7,396	140	136	1,122	706	15,436	1,467,016	446,978	337,169	6,229	3,352	22,926	13,001	682,869	
6,779	1,900	1,656	39	17	276	190	3,223	354,816	107,781	83,684	1,058	505	4,923	3,260	163,351	11
7,881	1,885	2,595	27	81	260	203	3,401	411,959	121,487	110,958	2,570	2,146	10,361	5,911	179,514	12
7,293	1,837	1,592	38	10	349	182	3,864	266,101	83,876	55,170	1,334	156	3,300	1,194	127,055	13
5,514	1,035	1,073	31	26	135	85	3,406	221,962	68,135	58,478	1,149	515	3,102	2,023	95,349	14
2,820	798	480	5	2	102	46	1,542	212,178	65,699	28,879	118	30	1,240	613	117,600	15
14,173	3,316	2,928	96	24	442	268	7,929	1,132,744	322,416	187,570	4,166	1,350	26,947	10,145	622,758	
4,834	789	951	24	10	137	56	3,094	270,461	77,512	47,428	695	303	5,822	2,177	145,521	16
84	20	23	6	...	4	3	41	45,200	12,495	6,823	214	49	648	264	25,882	17
3,583	917	826	14	6	89	70	1,840	357,362	104,147	61,048	1,370	464	6,218	2,847	192,167	18
3,314	853	623	38	2	94	57	1,838	233,443	79,776	49,100	814	219	6,631	3,120	154,567	19
1,833	491	463	9	3	111	76	879	96,873	28,570	16,551	754	165	5,848	1,619	51,752	20
525	246	42	5	3	7	6	237	79,405	19,916	6,620	319	150	1,780	118	52,869	21
21,168	4,864	7,331	146	162	1,000	829	8,973	1,035,418	296,111	266,466	8,570	5,932	52,537	21,730	472,841	
4,258	912	1,546	45	51	128	125	1,800	188,983	53,027	43,185	2,673	1,478	7,453	3,200	92,771	22
6,097	1,421	2,150	25	31	351	359	2,526	303,742	86,264	68,432	1,490	955	20,618	9,026	149,046	23
6,325	1,433	2,009	65	63	293	167	2,883	188,548	56,799	52,294	3,382	2,363	14,327	5,647	79,455	24
4,488	1,098	1,626	11	17	228	178	1,764	334,457	94,614	96,455	1,025	1,136	10,121	3,857	143,388	25
...	...	...	...	...	...	...	...	19,688	5,407	6,100	...	...	18		8,181	26
2,483	673	569	14	13	95	68	1,241	486,327	138,677	106,895	3,454	3,850	24,354	8,328	240,755	
1,433	408	355	7	4	34	40	670	122,197	36,911	26,302	330	772	4,461	2,280	58,984	27
406	90	59	..	...	...	1	257	6,058	2,562	722	..	...	38	71	2,774	
141	37	25	2	..	3	5	79	86,417	23,134	22,319	1,428	1,668	3,827	950	40,964	28
81	35	7	...	..	5	...	39	94,571	28,865	20,382	588	595	2,817	520	45,324	29
828	193	182	5	9	53	23	453	177,014	48,070	36,015	995	707	12,888	4,485	92,929	30
...	...	...	...	...	...	...	...	6,128	1,697	1,877	113	108	361	93	2,554	31
20,261	4,513	6,340	94	272	814	1,070	9,408	998,996	280,350	295,405	6,730	5,227	63,013	35,270	423,241	
4,337	1,044	1,629	7	16	37	282	1,664	303,717	84,913	102,490	377	231	25,316	14,347	111,314	32
6,228	1,518	2,004	30	17	338	396	2,706	217,265	61,090	51,661	2,693	1,695	14,851	11,753	104,514	33
7,904	1,560	2,197	38	216	311	297	4,147	241,013	60,458	68,083	1,815	1,752	11,930	5,436	112,472	34
1,792	391	510	19	23	128	95	891	129,880	38,095	34,593	1,845	1,549	10,887	3,653	57,192	35
...	...	...	...	...	...	...	...	107,121	35,794	38,578	...	...	29	81	32,749	36
16,533	3,712	4,555	47	95	459	530	8,266	814,973	219,812	136,998	3,651	1,609	27,486	15,516	458,163	
1,569	302	422	4	12	79	50	845	88,662	26,380	13,335	335	210	3,123	1,432	48,947	37
4,104	913	1,172	12	5	171	173	2,019	200,744	54,007	28,356	738	173	8,422	5,013	118,381	38
4,925	1,071	845	1	16	46	77	3,009	220,205	57,787	27,478	969	174	7,202	2,330	134,940	39
5,935	1,426	2,116	30	62	103	230	2,393	305,362	81,638	67,829	1,609	1,052	8,739	6,741	155,895	40
6,109	2,369	1,245	209	193	497	230	2,495	1,115,298	351,157	280,553	22,324	16,397	71,771	44,605	483,588	
1,637	401	412	22	7	85	110	824	470,665	143,642	129,621	12,377	7,155	31,884	24,189	197,402	41
4,453	1,966	824	187	186	411	120	1,663	592,904	194,018	136,700	9,626	8,797	39,012	20,054	262,186	42
19	2	9	...	...	1	...	8	51,729	13,497	14,232	321	445	875	362	24,000	43

Serial No.	DISTRICT OR STATE.	Sub-Class *Ib.*—Cultivated and wild plants—*concld.* Order IIB.—Forestry. (Groups 8 to 10.) Total Workers and Dependents.	WORKERS. Total Workers. Males.	Total Workers. Females.	Workers with an agricultural or other subsidiary occupation. Agricultural. Males.	Agricultural. Females.	Other. Males.	Other. Females.	DEPENDENTS.
	1	2	3	4	5	6	7	8	9
	Provincial Total ...	81,065	31,630	7,554	798	174	2,054	327	41,881
	Divisional Burma ...	78,119	30,408	7,395	707	158	1,971	321	40,316
	Arakan Division ...	2,020	428	90	7	...	15	11	1,502
1	Akyab	1,565	260	41	2	...	2	10	1,264
2	Hill Dist. of Arakan ..	20	9	...	...	...	..	...	11
3	Kyaukpyu	203	66	29	3	...	3	1	108
4	Sandoway ...	232	93	20	2	...	10	..	119
	Pegu Division	11,475	4,469	832	39	7	75	6	6,174
5	Rangoon Town ..	850	362	35			1	...	453
6	Insein ..	2,284	906	250	13	5	15	...	1,128
7	Hanthawaddy ...	247	70	20	2	...	1	...	157
8	Tharrawaddy ...	3,093	1,299	48	7	...	13	...	1,746
9	Pegu	2,668	928	265	16	2	30	2	1,475
10	Prome	2,333	904	214	1	..	15	4	1,215
	Irrawaddy Division ...	7,963	2,758	818	42	6	82	9	4,387
11	Bassein	3,536	1,042	404	22	6	43	8	2,090
12	Henzada	1,042	437	127	8	...	12	...	478
13	Myaungmya ...	1,848	737	195	9	..	21	...	916
14	Ma-ubin	499	197	56	...	..	3	1	246
15	Pyapôn	1,038	345	36	3	...	3	...	657
	Tenasserim Division ...	16,692	5,671	1,705	119	38	223	72	9,316
16	Toungoo	6,413	2,666	173	27	...	109	9	3,574
17	Salween	391	177	22	1	3	2	2	192
18	Thatôn	2,700	811	249	12	18	17	17	1,640
19	Amherst	3,771	1,188	332	35	8	...	11	2,251
20	Tavoy	2,268	475	842	44	9	79	27	951
21	Mergui	1,149	354	87	...	...	16	6	708
	Magwe Division ...	6,512	2,819	823	54	18	259	64	2,870
22	Thayetmyo ...	1,819	609	451	...	7	36	51	759
23	Pakôkku	2,983	1,482	166	45	...	192	8	1,335
24	Minbu	1,092	437	104	7	11	24	5	551
25	Magwe	559	255	102	2	...	7	...	202
26	Pakôkku Hill Tracts ...	59	36	...	...	..	...	...	23
	Mandalay Division ...	11,978	5,461	1,021	106	21	316	46	5,496
27	Mandalay	5,451	2,367	502	48	7	144	3	2,582
	Mandalay City ...	*911*	*335*	*69*	...	...		*1*	*507*
28	Bhamo	2,493	1,325	150	38	...	130	8	1,018
29	Myitkyina	825	580	22	3	...	7	2	223
30	Katha	3,209	1,189	347	17	14	35	33	1,673
31	Putao	...	...	...	...	...	...	...	..
	Sagaing Division ...	12,334	5,453	1,191	219	67	720	96	5,690
32	Shwebo ...	1,496	509	284	17	25	60	40	703
33	Sagaing	2,203	739	240	44	6	138	16	1,224
34	Lower Chindwin ...	2,444	1,392	48	36	1	203	3	1,004
35	Upper Chindwin ...	6,184	2,810	619	122	35	319	37	2,755
36	Chin Hills	7	3	...	...	...	...	...	4
	Meiktila Division ...	9,145	3,349	915	121	1	281	17	4,881
37	Kyauksè	454	153	22	6	...	13	...	279
34	Meiktila	1,490	420	549	1	1	26	4	521
39	Yamèthin	6,797	2,662	222	114	...	242	5	3,913
40	Myingyan	404	114	122	...	...	..	8	168
	Eastern States ...	2,946	1,222	159	91	16	83	6	1,565
41	Northern Shan States ..	2,342	948	130	67	12	70	5	1,264
42	Southern Shan States ..	511	225	26	24	4	13	1	260
43	Karenni	93	49	3	...	...	...	...	41

PART III.—*Details by districts*—contd.

Sub-Class Ic.—Domestic and wild animals.

Order IIc.—Raising of farm stock. (Groups 11 to 14.)								Order IID.—Raising of other animals. (Groups 15, 16.)								
Total Workers and Dependents.	WORKERS.						DEPENDENTS.	Total Workers and Dependents.	WORKERS.						DEPENDENTS.	Serial No. of District, etc. (column 1).
	Total Workers.		Workers with an agricultural or other subsidiary occupation.						Total Workers.		Workers with an agricultural or other subsidiary occupation.					
			Agricultural.		Other.						Agricultural.		Other.			
	Males.	Females.	Males.	Females.	Males.	Females.			Males.	Females.	Males.	Females.	Males.	Females.		
10	11	12	13	14	15	16	17	18	19	20	21	22	23	24	25	
72,611	34,985	19,205	799	361	2,672	1,058	27,421	1,660	768	382	7	3	13	8	510	
62,617	30,517	7,968	510	142	2,195	757	24,132	1,581	726	353	2	..	13	8	502	
3,228	2,368	213	48	4	51	5	647	2	...	2	...	...	...	...	...	
2,622	1,904	159	44	2	31	2	559	...	...	...	...	...	...	.	..	1
18	8	...	...	..	...	...	10	...	...	...	...	...	...	...	...	2
19	7	7	1	...	1	..	5	...	...	...	...	...	...	...	...	3
569	419	47	3	2	19	3	73	2	...	2	...	..	...	...	...	4
14,423	8,312	1,124	59	2	381	41	4,987	342	103	37	...	...	2	...	202	
1,293	852	121	...	...	1	5	320	74	34	5	...	...	...	...	35	5
4,847	2,861	386	22	...	101	18	1,600	65	15	20	...	...	...	...	30	6
1,940	996	137	9	1	54	1	807	157	47	4	...	..	2	...	106	7
1,836	1,195	87	9	...	90	2	554	1	...	...	...	...	...	...	1	8
3,113	1,759	263	15	1	85	11	1,091	31	7	3	...	...	.	...	21	9
1,394	649	130	4	...	50	4	615	14	...	5	...	...	...	...	9	10
4,778	2,606	493	31	6	131	17	1,679	24	10	8	...	...	...	...	6	
1,241	622	136	6	2	29	6	483	8	..	7	...	...	...	...	1	11
1,323	810	104	10	...	31	2	409	5	...	1	..	...	...	..	4	12
826	427	101	13	4	49	7	298	2	2	...	...	...	...	...	...	13
695	381	81	2	...	22	..	233	...	...	...	...	...	..	..	...	14
693	366	71	...	...	...	2	256	9	8	...	..	...	...	...	1	15
8,509	4,095	987	40	4	149	42	3,427	239	27	96	...	...	...	2	116	
1,914	976	125	20	1	45	9	813	156	3	82	...	...	..	2	71	16
244	106	21	4	1	4		117	...	...		...	...	...	...	...	17
2,252	797	393	7	...	47	18	1,062	21	5	12	...	.	...	...	4	18
3,117	1,667	294	2	...	30	8	1,156	32	19	1	...	...	...	...	12	19
709	384	138	7	2	15	7	187	25	...	...	...	...	...	...	25	20
273	165	16	...	...	8	...	92	5	...	1	...	...	...	...	4	21
5,953	2,179	1,398	62	79	177	235	2,376	25	7	2		...	...	.	16	
866	348	136	5	2	33	16	382	7	3	2	...	...	..	...	2	22
2,692	781	827	37	55	71	165	1,084	2	...	...	...	.	...	...	2	23
1,301	568	278	11	20	59	46	455	...	...	...	...	...	...	...	...	24
1,092	482	157	9	2	14	8	453	16	4	..	...	...	...	...	12	25
2	...	...	...	...	...	...	2	...	...	...	...	...	...	...	...	26
7,213	3,099	601	32	2	420	81	3,513	865	571	194	2	...	11	3	100	
3,177	1,386	291	7	2	78	7	1,500	848	563	187	2	...	10	3	98	27
1,355	*544*	*146*	...	..	*11*	...	*665*	*87*	*5*	*28*	..	...	...	...	*54*	
738	271	95	...	...	19	36	372	1	...	1	...	...	...	...	...	28
1,971	916	144	10	...	284	33	911	16	8	6	...	...	1	...	2	29
1,205	423	66	15	..	39	5	716	..	...	...	...	...	...		...	30
122	103	5	...	...	...	...	14	...	...	...	...	..	...	...	...	31
8,923	4,267	1,487	164	22	605	218	3,169	7	3	2	...	...	...	...	2	
1,611	567	412	6	10	116	54	632	3	1	..	...	...	...	...	2	32
3,275	1,719	504	84	8	121	24	1,052	...	...	..	...	...	...	...	...	33
1,884	826	320	30	...	69	52	738	4	2	2	..	...	...	...	.	34
1,968	1,083	235	43	4	298	88	650	...	...	...	..	.	...	...	...	35
185	72	16	1	...	1	...	97	...	...	...	..	...	..	...	...	36
9,590	3,591	1,665	74	23	281	118	4,334	77	5	12	...	...	...	3	60	
2,315	792	264	27	3	69	19	1,259	..	..	...	..	...	...	...	...	37
2,351	1,009	357	25	11	75	24	985	14	2	2	..	...	...	...	10	38
2,054	850	271	12	2	60	14	933	62	3	9		...	...	3	50	39
2,870	940	773	10	7	77	61	1,157	1	...	1	...	...	...	...	...	40
9,994	4,468	2,237	289	219	477	301	3,289	79	42	29	5	3	..	...	8	
4,417	2,366	591	43	26	234	52	1,460	17	8	4	...	...	...	...	5	41
5,536	2,082	1,646	246	193	240	249	1,808	62	34	25	5	3	...	...	3	42
41	20	...	..	...	3	...	21	...	...	...	...	...	...	...	..	43

Serial No.	DISTRICT OR STATE.	Sub-Class Ic.—Domestic and wild animals—*contd.* Order IIb.—Exploitation of wild animals. (Groups 17, 18.) Total Workers and Dependents.	WORKERS. Total Workers. Males.	Total Workers. Females.	Workers with an agricultural or other subsidiary occupation. Agricultural. Males.	Agricultural. Females.	Other. Males.	Other. Females.	DEPENDENTS.
	1	2	3	4	5	6	7	8	9
	Provincial Total ...	160,809	54,457	16,925	1,394	311	2,656	667	89,427
	Divisional Burma ..	155,472	52,482	16,684	1,283	293	2,448	651	86,306
	Arakan Division ...	10,908	3,690	1,025	246	101	329	43	6,193
1	Akyab ..	3,170	1,290	342	49	17	42	14	1,538
2	Hill Dist. of Arakan ...	1	..		...	...	...	...	1
3	Kyaukpyu	5,279	1,563	506	117	40	197	22	3,210
4	Sandoway	2,458	837	177	80	44	90	7	1,444
	Pegu Division	16,436	6,135	1,835	211	51	421	83	8,466
5	Rangoon Town ...	391	298	13	..	...		...	80
6	Insein	1,634	555	174	...	2	50	5	905
7	Hanthawaddy ..	2,343	1,139	318	14	3	35	11	886
8	Tharrawaddy ...	6,589	2,093	879	163	41	258	35	3,617
9	Pegu	3,893	1,470	297	29	4	49	13	2,126
10	Prome	1,586	580	154	5	1	29	19	852
	Irrawaddy Division ..	52,681	17,303	8,869	278	80	468	265	26,509
11	Bassein	8,088	2,640	1,088	47	8	161	124	4,360
12	Henzada	6,244	1,928	745	61	16	90	37	3,571
13	Myaungmya ...	6,384	2,155	1,082	84	12	61	10	3,147
14	Ma-ubin	23,766	7,834	4,731	46	31	113	88	11,201
15	Pyapôn	8,199	2,746	1,223	40	13	43	6	4,230
	Tenasserim Division ..	39,823	12,764	2,278	228	12	348	27	24,781
16	Toungoo	2,190	788	169	2	...	78	6	1,233
17	Salween	32	22	..	...	...	..	...	10
18	Thatôn	3,646	1,374	354	16	..	24	7	1,918
19	Amherst	3,520	1,386	152	...	2	5	4	1,982
20	Tavoy	8,479	2,538	928	138	6	134	10	5,013
21	Mergui	21,956	6,656	675	72	4	107	..	14,625
	Magwe Division ...	9,878	3,447	1,132	35	9	116	37	5,299
22	Thayetmyo	1,891	697	100	2	...	31	4	1,094
23	Pakôkku	3,554	1,072	397	3	...	39	6	2,085
24	Minbu	1,943	777	370	21	7	42	26	796
25	Magwe	2,490	901	265	9	2	4	1	1,324
26	Pakôkku Hill Tracts ...	...	...	...	...		...	...	...
	Mandalay Division ...	11,183	4,319	620	94	4	345	59	6,244
27	Mandalay	5,294	1,799	296	44	...	67	31	3,199
	Mandalay City ...	755	245	20	..	...	15	...	490
28	Bhamo ..	1,935	1,058	79	35	...	134	18	798
29	Myitkyina ...	906	370	64	...	1	71	6	472
30	Katha	3,048	1,092	181	15	3	73	4	1,775
31	Putao	...	...	...	...	...	...	...	...
	Sagaing Division ..	9,536	3,310	472	172	35	369	124	5,754
32	Shwebo	736	241	107	3	...	33	39	388
33	Sagaing .	4,738	1,651	102	116	5	126	60	2,985
34	Lower Chindwin ...	1,924	667	77	11	...	75	10	1,180
35	Upper Chindwin ...	2,138	751	186	42	30	135	15	1,201
36	Chin Hills	...	...	...	...	...	..	...	...
	Meiktila Division ...	5,027	1,514	453	19	1	52	13	3,060
37	Kyaukse	686	209	49	8	...	19	3	428
38	Meiktila	787	172	80	2	1	14	1	535
39	Yamèthin .	574	197	154	...	...	5	3	223
40	Myingyan	2,980	936	170	9	...	14	6	1,874
	Eastern States ...	5,337	1,975	241	111	18	208	16	3,121
41	Northern Shan States ...	861	297	125	6	...	20	3	439
42	Southern Shan States ...	4,428	1,658	111	105	18	188	13	2,659
43	Karenni	48	20	5	...	...	...	...	23

PART III.—*Details by districts*—contd.

Sub-Class *II*.—Exploitation of minerals.

Order III.—Coal, petroleum and metals. (Groups 19, 20, 21.)								Order IV.—Minerals not of Order III or V. (Group 22.)								
Total Workers and Dependents.	WORKERS. Total Workers.		Workers with an agricultural or other subsidiary occupation. Agricultural.		Other.		DEPENDENTS.	Total Workers and Dependents.	WORKERS. Total Workers.		Workers with an agricultural or other subsidiary occupation. Agricultural.		Other.		DEPENDENTS.	Serial No. of District, etc. (column 1).
	Males.	Females.	Males.	Females	Males.	Females.			Males.	Females.	Males.	Females.	Males.	Females.		
10	11	12	13	14	15	16	17	18	19	20	21	22	23	24	25	
28,136	19,486	856	69	8	71	11	7,794	10,787	5,989	1,720	51	4	89	20	3,078	
21,615	13,877	820	69	6	71	11	6,918	10,234	5,466	1,720	51	4	89	20	3,048	
15	2	3	1	...	...	1	10	5	..	...	...	...	...	...	5	
9	2	...	1	...	...	...	7	5	...	...	..	...	...	..	5	1
...	...	...	...	...	...	...	...	...	...	...	...	...	...	...	...	2
5	...	3	...	...	...	1	2	...	...	...	...	...	...	...	...	3
1	...	...	...	...	...	...	1	...	...	...	..	...	...	...	...	4
276	109	1	...	...	..	...	166	455	283	13	..	..	...	...	159	
189	69	...	...	...	..	...	120	...	...	...	...	...	...	...	...	5
7	2	...	..	...	...	...	5	268	148	11	...	...	...	...	109	6
19	11	1	...	...	...	...	7	4	1	...	...	...	...	...	3	7
12	1	...	...	...	...	.	11	17	15	...	..	...	...	...	2	8
8	1	...	...	...	...	...	7		...	...	...	...	...	...	...	9
41	25	...	...	...	...		16	166	119	2	...	...	...	...	45	10
54	28	...	...	...	...	...	26	158	115	22	...	...	...	...	21	
29	5	...	...	...	...	...	24	131	101	20	...	...	...	...	10	11
24	23	...	...	..	...	..	1	27	14	2	...	...	...	...	11	12
...	...	...	...	..	...	...	,	.	...	..	...	...	...	...	..	13
1	...	...	...	...	...	...	1	...	...	...	...	..	...	...	...	14
...	...	...	...	...	...		.	...	...	...	...	...	...	...	...	15
7,610	4,225	248	35	4	35	4	3,137	1,134	537	149	5	1	3	1	448	
4		...	...	.	...	...	4	108	42	32	...	...	2	1	34	16
7	6	1	...	...	1	...	...	.	...	...	.	...	...	...	..	17
28	8	7	...	...	1	...	13	731	383	62	2	...	1	...	286	18
151	52	7	...	...	...	...	92	178	61	7	3	...	...	...	110	19
4,125	2,452	188	29	4	19	4	1,485	116	51	48	...	1	...	...	17	20
3,295	1,707	45	6	...	14	...	1,543	1	...	...	...		...	...	1	21
13,168	9,418	308	31	2	27	6	3,442	385	193	51	1	..	21	1	141	
65	59	...	...	.	...	...	6	243	63	45	...	...	21	.	115	22
929	383	32	11	...	6	.	514	4	...	4	...	...	...	...	...	23
595	216	53	1	2	10	...	326	57	29	2	..	...	..	1	26	24
11,579	8,760	223	19	...	11	6	2,596	81	81	...	1	...	...	...	...	25
...	...	...	...	...	...	...	..	...	...	..	...	...	...	...	...	26
408	53	260	...	...	8	.	95	6,899	3,797	1,243	27	3	55	12	1,859	
356	30	251	...	...	...	...	75	1,896	814	290	12	3	10	4	792	27
325	*26*	*251*	...	...	.	...	*48*	*632*	*345*	*136*	...	..	..	...	*151*	
3	3	...	...	.	...	...	...	5	3	...	...	...	...	...	2	28
46	19	7	...	...	8	...	20	3,142	2,725	33	14	...	23	...	384	29
3	1	2	...	...	...	...	..	1,856	255	920	1	...	22	8	681	30
...	...	...	...	...	...	...	...	...	...	...	...	...	..	...	...	31
63	33	..	2	...	1	...	30	577	205	107	18		7	6	265	
42	19	...	2	...	...	...	23	83	20	24	1	...	2	5	39	32
4	3	...	...	...	...	...	1	309	115	61	8	...	2	...	133	33
9	9	...	...	. .	1	...	...	147	51	22	5	...	1	1	74	34
8	2	...	...	..	...	...	6	38	19	...	4	...	2	...	19	35
...	...	...	...	...	...	...	...	...	...	...	...	...	...	..	...	36
21	9	...	...	...	..	...	12	621	336	135	.	...	3	...	150	
...	...	...	...	...	...	...	..	1	...	1	...	...	...	...	...	37
2	2	...	...	...	...	..	...	49	49	...	...	...	1	...	...	38
9	2	...	...	..	..	...	7	556	281	126	...	..	1	...	149	39
10	5	...	...	...	..	...	5	15	6	8	...	...	1	...	1	40
6,521	5,609	36	...	2	...	...	876	553	523		...	...	...	...	30	
6,519	5,609	36	...	2	...	...	874	552	522	..	...	...	...	...	30	41
2	...	...	...	...	...	...	2	1	1	...	...	...	...	...	...	42
...	...	...	...	...	...	...	...	...	...	...	...	...	...	...	...	43

Serial No.	DISTRICT OR STATE.	Total Workers and Dependents.	WORKERS. Total Workers. Males.	Females.	Workers with an agricultural or other subsidiary occupation. Agricultural. Males.	Females.	Other. Males.	Females.	DEPENDENTS.
	Sub-Class II.—Exploitation of minerals—concluded. Order V.—Minerals soluble in water. (Groups 23, 24.)								
	1	2	3	4	5	6	7	8	9
	Provincial Total ...	3,962	1,545	419	83	9	47	20	1,998
	Divisional Burma ...	3,961	1,545	419	83	9	47	20	1,997
	Arakan Division ...	59	15	20	...	...	4	1	24
1	Akyab ...	...	...	...	...	...	...	...	...
2	Hill Dist. of Arakan ...	...	...	...	...	...	...	...	...
3	Kyaukpyu ...	30	12	10	...	...	4	1	8
4	Sandoway ...	29	3	10	...	...	...	...	16
	Pegu Division ...	117	59	...	1	...	...	...	58
5	Rangoon Town ...	4	...	...	...	...	...	...	4
6	Insein ...	...	...	...	...	...	...	...	...
7	Hanthawaddy ...	113	59	...	1	...	...	...	54
8	Tharrawaddy ...	...	...	...	...	...	...	...	...
9	Pegu ...	...	...	...	...	...	...	...	...
10	Prome ...	...	...	...	...	...	...	...	...
	Irrawaddy Division ...	686	222	43	25	2	7	...	421
11	Bassein ...	533	184	35	25	2	4	...	314
12	Henzada ...	...	...	...	...	...	...	...	...
13	Myaungmya ...	153	38	8	...	...	3	...	107
14	Ma-ubin ...	...	...	...	...	...	...	...	...
15	Pyapôn ...	...	...	...	...	...	...	...	...
	Tenasserim Division ...	2,492	1,116	135	34	2	18	2	1,241
16	Toungoo ...	...	...	...	...	...	...	...	...
17	Salween ...	...	...	...	...	...	...	...	...
18	Thatôn ...	6	...	...	...	...	...	...	6
19	Amherst ...	1,621	760	80	20	...	6	2	781
20	Tavoy ...	418	132	18	11	2	9	...	268
21	Mergui ...	447	224	37	3	...	3	...	186
	Magwe Division ...	9	2	3	...	...	...	...	4
22	Thayetmyo ...	...	...	...	...	...	...	...	...
23	Pakôkku ...	9	2	3	...	...	...	...	4
24	Minbu ...	...	...	...	...	...	...	...	...
25	Magwe ...	...	...	...	...	...	...	...	...
26	Pakôkku Hill Tracts ...	...	...	...	...	...	...	...	...
	Mandalay Division ...	104	28	26	...	...	6	8	50
27	Mandalay ...	4	1	...	...	...	...	...	3
	Mandalay City ...	*4*	*1*	...	...	...	...	...	*3*
28	Bhamo ...	...	...	...	...	...	...	...	...
29	Myitkyina ...	26	13	10	...	...	...	...	3
30	Katha ...	74	14	16	...	...	4	2	44
31	Putao ...	...	...	...	...	...	2	6	...
	Sagaing Division ...	474	103	177	23	5	12	6	194
32	Shwebo ...	64	26	5	19	...	5	...	33
33	Sagaing ...	203	23	78	4	5	2	...	102
34	Lower Chindwin ...	198	54	85	...	...	5	6	59
35	Upper Chindwin ...	9	...	9	...	...	...	...	...
36	Chin Hills ...	...	...	...	...	...	...	...	...
	Meiktila Division ...	20	...	15	...	...	...	3	5
37	Kyauksè ...	...	...	...	...	...	...	...	...
38	Meiktila ...	...	...	...	...	...	...	...	...
39	Yamèthin ...	...	...	...	...	...	...	...	...
40	Myingyan ...	20	...	15	...	...	...	3	5
	Eastern States ...	1	...	...	...	...	...	...	1
41	Northern Shan States ...	...	...	...	...	...	...	...	...
42	Southern Shan States ...	1	...	...	...	...	...	...	1
43	Karenni ...	...	...	...	...	...	...	...	...

PART III.—*Details by districts*—contd.

Sub-Class *III.*—Industry.																
Order VI.—Textiles. (Groups 25 to 38.)								Order VII.—Hides, feathers, bristles and hard materials from the animal kingdom. (Groups 39 to 42.)								
Total Workers and Dependents.	WORKERS.						DEPENDENTS.	Total Workers and Dependents.	WORKERS.						DEPENDENTS.	Serial No. of District, etc. (column 1).
	Total Workers.		Workers with an agricultural or other subsidiary occupation.						Total Workers.		Workers with an agricultural or other subsidiary occupation.					
			Agricultural.		Other.						Agricultural.		Other.			
	Males.	Females.	Males.	Females.	Males.	Females.			Males.	Females	Males.	Females.	Males.	Females.		
10	11	12	13	14	15	16	17	18	19	20	21	22	23	24	25	
115,338	8,859	75,018	81	2,810	370	4,287	31,461	1,067	537	53	1	...	...	5	477	
111,045	8,531	71,708	74	2,357	365	4,091	30,806	1,009	484	53	1	...	...	5	472	
4,175	233	1,976	3	14	11	52	1,966	2	...	1	...	...	...	...	1	
3,850	211	1,753	2	2	7	20	1,886	...	...	...	...	...	...	...	...	1
4	..	1	...	...	...	...	3	...	...	...	...	...	...	...	...	2
135	20	84	1	6	4	20	31	2	...	1	...	...	...	...	1	3
186	2	138	...	6	...	12	46	...	...	...	...	...	...	...	...	4
14,122	1,005	8,844	11	419	20	338	4,273	168	103	11	...	...	..	...	54	
312	153	56	...	...	..	...	103	91	41	2	.	...	...	...	48	5
663	132	309	2	40	3	73	222	70	58	9	...	...	...	...	3	6
646	48	263	...	...	...	4	335	...	...	...	...	...	...	...	...	7
1,176	97	806	...	67	2	69	273	3	...	...	..	...	...	...	3	8
513	64	315	...	23	...	12	134	2	2	..	...	...	...	...	...	9
10,812	511	7,095	9	289	15	180	3,206	2	2	...	..	.	...	...	...	10
2,937	384	1,446	6	28	21	56	1,107	...	...	...	...	...	...	...	...	
510	51	310	...	10	3	5	149	...	...	...	...	...	...	...	...	11
1,127	94	613	6	17	..	37	420	...	...	...	..	...	...	...	...	12
146	2	82	...	...	1	12	62	...	...	...	...	...	...	...	...	13
1,072	220	419	...	1	17	2	433	...	...	...	...	...	...	...	...	14
82	17	22	...	..	...	...	43	...	...	...	...	...	...	...	..	15
9,949	206	7,591	5	147	3	526	2,152	46	6	3	...	...	...	1	37	
208	7	39	...	8	...	1	162	...	...	...	...	...	...	...	...	16
...	...	..	...	...	...	...	...	...	...	...	...	...	...	..	...	17
2,901	104	2,132	...	17	3	186	665	...	...	...	...	...	...	..	...	18
3,984	79	3,249	5	99	...	207	656	28	2	...	...	...	...	...	26	19
2,389	15	1,995	...	23	...	132	370	15	4	3	...	...	...	1	8	20
467	1	176	...	..	...	...	290	3	..	...	...	...	...	...	3	21
16,933	696	12,139	...	395	38	830	4,098	18	6	...	...	...	...	...	12	
2,526	312	1,566	...	12	...	53	648	...	..	...	...	...	...	...	...	22
9,995	253	7,243	...	161	38	526	2,499	9	1	...	...	...	...	...	8	23
3,897	102	2,500	...	175	...	182	695	9	5	...	...	...	...	...	4	24
1,115	29	830	...	47	..	69	256	...	...	...	...	...	...	...	...	25
...	...	...	...	...	...	...	...	...	...	...	...	...	...	...	...	26
21,321	3,654	11,861	12	102	189	488	5,806	230	125	1	...	...	...	...	104	
20,861	3,627	11,594	12	89	189	471	5,650	221	117	..	...	...	...	...	104	27
6,661	*648*	*4,218*	...	*2*	*3*	*1*	*1,795*	*206*	*102*	...	...	...	...	...	*104*	
173	17	57	...	...	...	5	99	9	8	1	...	...	...	...	..	28
32	1	19	...	...	...	4	12	...	...	...	...	...	...	...	...	29
255	19	191	..	13	...	8	45	...	...	...	...	...	...	...	...	30
...	...	...	...	...	...	...	...	...	...	...	...	...	...	...	...	31
22,930	1,010	14,564	26	892	61	1,145	7,356	495	203	36	1	...	...	4	256	
2,906	112	2,177	4	178	10	165	617	...	...	...	...	...	...	...	...	32
9,215	511	4,878	13	368	22	650	3,826	7	3	..	...	...	...	...	4	33
10,193	372	6,933	9	328	28	313	2,818	488	200	36	1	...	...	4	252	34
679	12	574	...	18	1	17	93	...	...	..	...	...	...	...	...	35
7	3	2	...	...	...	...	2	...	...	...	...	...	...	...	...	36
18,678	1,343	13,287	11	360	22	656	4,048	50	41	1	...	...	...	...	8	
472	18	253	...	16	3	19	201	28	25	...	...	...	...	...	3	37
7,645	281	5,551	7	210	11	285	1,813	16	10	1	...	...	...	...	5	38
2,797	30	2,046	3	18	2	80	721	6	6	...	...	...	...	...	..	39
7,764	1,014	5,437	1	126	6	272	1,313	...	...	...	...	...	...	...	...	40
4,293	328	3,310	7	453	5	196	655	58	53	..	...	...	...	...	5	
3,134	327	2,403	7	422	5	141	404	56	53	...	...	...	...	...	3	41
1,150	...	902	...	31	...	55	248	2	...	...	...	...	...	...	2	42
9	1	5	...	..	...	...	3	..	...	...	...	...	...	..	...	43

Sub-Class *III.*—

Order VIII.—Wood. (Groups 43, 44, 45.)

Serial No.	District or State.	Total Workers and Dependents.	Workers: Total Workers: Males.	Workers: Total Workers: Females.	Workers with an agricultural or other subsidiary occupation: Agricultural: Males.	Agricultural: Females.	Other: Males.	Other: Females.	Dependents.
	1	2	3	4	5	6	7	8	9
	Provincial Total ...	214,170	79,498	24,870	1,489	777	3,255	1,049	109,802
	Divisional Burma ...	205,283	75,495	24,445	1,316	753	3,084	1,019	105,343
	Arakan Division ...	6,838	2,756	599	58	3	109	25	3,483
1	Akyab ...	4,451	1,914	469	27	...	41	13	2,068
2	Hill Dist. of Arakan ...	36	18	...	...	...	...	...	18
3	Kyaukpyu ...	744	254	20	10	3	16	1	470
4	Sandoway ...	1,607	570	110	21	...	52	11	927
	Pegu Division ...	49,046	22,513	3,004	145	90	310	90	23,529
5	Rangoon Town ...	23,200	13,860	190	12	...	15	..	9,150
6	Insein ...	3,669	1,453	305	12	15	28	18	1,911
7	Hanthawaddy ...	4,895	1,577	386	16	..	22	6	2,932
8	Tharrawaddy ...	7,586	2,181	1,231	49	46	83	27	4,174
9	Pegu ...	5,150	1,840	302	31	17	75	22	3,008
10	Prome ...	4,546	1,602	590	25	12	87	17	2,354
	Irrawaddy Division ...	27,215	8,614	4,862	186	172	442	148	13,739
11	Bassein ...	5,420	2,026	462	27	10	119	25	2,932
12	Henzada ...	8,228	2,911	1,278	111	70	197	63	4,039
13	Myaungmya ...	3,684	1,224	386	18	..	72	6	2,074
14	Ma-ubin ...	6,601	1,313	2,636	15	92	39	53	2,652
15	Pyapôn ...	3,282	1,140	100	15	...	15	1	2,042
	Tenasserim Division ...	35,589	12,611	3,407	233	43	350	168	19,571
16	Toungoo ...	7,665	2,470	783	13	19	90	27	4,412
17	Salween ...	323	118	26	2	...	3	...	179
18	Thatôn ...	5,465	1,515	951	25	6	95	70	2,999
19	Amherst ...	13,071	5,897	451	85	2	20	21	7,323
20	Tavoy ...	5,084	1,594	875	106	16	105	28	2,615
21	Mergui ...	3,381	1,017	321	2	...	37	22	2,043
	Magwe Division ...	23,409	7,986	2,275	171	74	612	151	13,148
22	Thayetmyo ...	4,842	1,025	328	21	26	117	19	2,889
23	Pakôkku ...	9,643	2,746	737	24	16	328	90	6,160
24	Minbu ...	4,409	1,408	925	91	30	125	38	2,015
25	Magwe ...	4,510	2,143	284	35	2	42	4	2,083
26	Pakôkku Hill Tracts ..	5	4	...	...	...	...	...	1
	Mandalay Division ...	16,835	6,230	2,128	58	48	247	43	8,477
27	Mandalay ...	12,769	4,521	1,814	21	48	98	21	6,434
	Mandalay City ...	8,531	3,061	1,111	..	...	2	...	4,359
28	Bhamo ...	1,383	617	119	9	...	69	4	647
29	Myitkyina ...	815	420	31	9	...	19	...	364
30	Katha ...	1,854	659	164	19	...	61	18	1,031
31	Putao ...	14	13	...	...	...	...	...	1
	Sagaing Division ...	25,940	8,306	4,893	380	235	647	297	12,741
32	Shwebo ...	4,599	1,688	649	90	90	118	30	2,262
33	Sagaing ...	7,847	2,178	2,400	135	114	166	198	3,269
34	Lower Chindwin ...	10,072	3,371	1,747	117	27	227	57	5,554
35	Upper Chindwin ...	2,749	1,039	97	38	4	136	12	1,613
36	Chin Hills ...	73	30	...	..	...	...	...	43
	Meiktila Division ...	20,411	6,479	3,277	85	88	367	97	10,655
37	Kyauksè ...	2,440	838	341	29	49	61	11	1,273
38	Meiktila ...	5,250	1,445	1,132	8	30	95	42	2,673
39	Yamèthin ...	7,438	2,338	658	40	5	120	9	4,442
40	Myingyan ...	5,277	1,864	1,146	8	4	91	35	2,267
	Eastern States ...	8,887	4,003	425	173	24	171	30	4,459
41	Northern Shan States ...	3,963	1,574	334	57	24	99	27	2,055
42	Southern Shan States ...	4,622	2,322	86	116	...	72	3	2,214
43	Karenni ...	302	107	5	...	...	...	...	190

Part III.—*Details by districts*—contd.

Industry—*continued.*

Order IX.—Metals. (Groups 46 to 51.)								Order X.—Ceramics. (Groups 52 to 57.)								
Total Workers and Dependents.	WORKERS.						DEPENDENTS.	Total Workers and Dependents.	WORKERS.						DEPENDENTS.	Serial No. of District, etc. (column 1).
	Total Workers.		Workers with an agricultural or other subsidiary occupation.						Total Workers.		Workers with an agricultural or or other subsidiary occupation.					
			Agricultural.		Other.						Agricultural.		Other.			
	Males.	Females.	Males.	Females.	Males.	Females.			Males.	Females.	Males.	Females.	Males.	Females.		
10	11	12	13	14	15	16	17	18	19	20	21	22	23	24	25	
41,776	16,690	1,037	321	27	640	46	24,049	30,602	9,901	9,771	150	192	272	405	10,930	
38,977	15,556	977	247	24	469	43	22,444	30,363	9,764	9,711	137	192	267	401	10,888	
1,145	628	14	6	...	13	1	503	1,733	519	518	24	3	17	12	696	
733	494	.	...	...	6	..	239	1,505	449	449	21	...	11	...	607	1
6	6	...	...	...	...	..	...	...	...	...	...	...	...	...	...	2
209	59	13	6	...	4	1	137	36	20	1	1	...	1	...	15	3
197	69	1	...	...	3	...	127	192	50	68	2	3	5	12	74	4
10,575	4,858	136	55	2	100	6	5,581	8,727	4,187	1,476	38	17	79	37	3,064	
4,486	2,450	16	2	...	4	...	2,020	1,074	791	79	...	...	1	...	204	5
982	401	50	3	...	18	...	531	2,404	1,678	182	...	...	29	...	544	6
1,194	637	3	7	1	20	3	534	1,121	454	131	5	...	2	...	536	7
1,232	403	25	5	...	20	...	804	1,074	412	243	...	1	11	2	419	8
1,395	482	5	17	...	16	...	908	1,754	484	431	16	3	14	4	839	9
1,286	485	37	21	1	22	3	764	1,300	368	410	17	13	22	31	522	10
5,375	1,872	159	29	6	48	11	3,344	3,858	914	1,313	16	19	16	32	1,631	
1,180	433	35	4	..	15	3	712	1,312	176	562	...	3	1	16	574	11
1,613	484	33	6	4	11	6	1,096	998	211	317	15	16	10	15	470	12
1,144	457	50	9	1	15	2	637	393	160	103	1	...	4	...	130	13
755	267	41	8	1	4	...	447	1,056	324	321	..	...	1	1	411	14
683	231	..	2	...	3	...	452	99	43	10	...	...	...	...	46	15
6,329	2,307	68	49	2	70	3	3,954	2,903	808	906	5	14	11	155	1,189	
1,111	445	11	1	1	20	1	655	596	201	143	2	4	2	6	252	16
62	23	2	...	...	4	..	37	14	5	...	...	...	...	...	9	17
1,825	538	8	12	...	16	1	1,279	976	142	488	2	4	2	144	346	18
2,384	927	32	24	1	20	1	1,425	656	289	83	...	6	2	1	284	19
643	269	7	11	...	10	...	367	335	91	144	1	...	5	4	100	20
304	105	8	1	...	...	...	191	326	80	48	...	...	...	...	198	21
4,490	1,704	142	35	5	96	9	2,644	3,663	864	1,574	26	70	59	45	1,225	
769	264	29	6	2	22	4	476	754	173	280	2	3	3	5	301	22
1,959	695	32	9	...	50	...	1,232	1,290	213	670	5	53	30	25	407	23
863	309	42	13	2	17	4	512	1,192	326	529	14	9	18	12	337	24
897	434	39	7	1	7	1	424	427	152	95	5	5	8	3	180	25
2	2	..	...	...	...	...	...	...	...	...	...	...	...	...	...	26
3,535	1,674	106	14	1	29	1	1,755	3,032	861	1,365	...	10	7	29	806	
2,662	1,236	64	8	..	5	..	1,362	2,459	686	1,103	...	6	5	21	670	27
2,016	*880*	*25*	...	...	*1*	...	*1,111*	*1,257*	*441*	*463*	...	*6*	...	*19*	*353*	
182	113	4	...	...	3	...	65	366	102	165	...	...	...	...	99	28
175	123	2	3	...	10	...	50	22	4	7	...	...	...	..	11	29
514	201	36	3	1	11	1	277	160	44	90	..	4	2	8	26	30
2	1	...	...	...	...	...	1	25	25	...	...	...	...	...	...	31
2,672	1,025	72	34	5	57	2	1,575	3,095	1,011	1,053	20	22	57	57	1,031	
773	294	44	13	4	12	...	435	1,381	400	585	2	17	12	25	396	32
411	57	4	...	...	2	.	350	563	327	89	13	...	16	...	147	33
1,136	545	20	12	1	28	1	571	824	184	237	2	4	14	11	403	34
332	123	3	5	...	15	..	206	327	100	142	3	1	15	21	85	35
20	6	1	4	...	...	1	13	—	...	...	...	...	...	...	...	36
4,856	1,488	280	25	3	56	10	3,088	3,352	600	1,506	8	37	21	34	1,246	
539	189	24	5	...	10	...	326	696	79	388	3	2	4	4	229	37
714	233	8	...	..	7	...	473	977	165	530	...	6	8	9	282	38
2,308	670	113	3	1	22	1	1,525	834	150	248	...	29	...	3	436	39
1,295	396	135	17	2	17	9	764	845	206	340	5	...	9	18	299	40
2,799	1,134	60	74	3	171	3	1,605	239	137	60	13	..	5	4	42	
929	458	29	6	1	19	...	442	217	115	60	13	...	5	4	42	41
1,806	644	29	68	2	152	3	1,133	6	6	...	...	...	...	...	...	42
64	32	2	...	...	...	...	30	16	16	...	...	..	...	...	...	43

Sub-Class *III.*—

Order XI.—Manufacture or refining of chemical products and analogous substances. (Groups 58 to 64.)

Serial No.	DISTRICT OR STATE.	Total Workers and Dependents.	WORKERS. Total Workers. Males.	Females.	Workers with an agricultural or other subsidiary occupation. Agricultural. Males.	Agricultural. Females.	Other. Males.	Other. Females.	DEPENDENTS.
	1	2	3	4	5	6	7	8	9
	Provincial Total ...	20.324	9,021	1,778	166	18	146	70	9,525
	Divisional Burma ...	19,923	8,891	1,681	160	17	128	57	9,351
	Arakan Division ...	105	61	3	3	...	1	...	41
1	Akyab	93	55	3	...	...	...	...	35
2	Hill Dist. of Arakan ...	...	...	...	...	..	...	...	...
3	Kyaukpyu	5	3	...	2	...	...	...	2
4	Sandoway	7	3	...	1	...	1	...	4
	Pegu Division ...	6,411	4,192	121	3	...	10	6	2,098
5	Rangoon Town ...	3,819	2,676	16	...	...	1	...	1,127
6	Insein	125	74	20	...		...	...	31
7	Hanthawaddy ...	1,698	1,074	24	3	...	4	...	603
8	Tharrawaddy .	192	111	7	..	...	5	3	74
9	Pegu	55	7	10	...	...	...	...	38
10	Prome	522	250	44	..	...	..	3	228
	Irrawaddy Division ...	795	635	6	118	...	7	...	64
11	Bassein	559	544	3	117	..	...	...	12
12	Henzada	129	87	2	1	...	7	...	40
13	Myaungmya ...	...	...	...	...	...	...	...	...
14	Ma-ubin	5	...	1	...	...	...	...	4
15	Pyapôn	12	4	...	...	...	...	...	8
	Tenasserim Division ...	763	354	27	8	5	9	3	382
16	Toungoo	248	93	12	...	1	4	1	143
17	Salween	7	4	..	...	...	1	...	3
18	Thatôn	48	23	12	..	4	3	2	13
19	Amherst	331	180	3	4	...	1	...	148
20	Tavoy	82	39	...	4	...	...	...	43
21	Mergui	47	15	...	...	...	...	...	32
	Magwe Division ...	8,414	2,403	740	7	3	44	11	5,271
22	Thayetmyo	807	313	163	...	...	4	1	331
23	Pakôkku	1,160	428	136	7	...	32	4	596
24	Minbu	267	79	72	...	1	3	6	116
25	Magwe	6,180	1,583	369	...	2	5	...	4,228
26	Pakôkku Hill Tracts ...	...	...	...	...	...	..	...	...
	Mandalay Division ...	1,027	277	310	2	..	9	...	440
27	Mandalay ...	938	242	302	2	...	4	...	394
	Mandalay City .	*483*	*180*	*105*	..	...	*1*	...	*198*
28	Bhamo	49	21	5	...	...	2	...	23
29	Myitkyina ...	36	13	3	...	...	3	...	20
30	Katha	4	1	...	...	...	...	...	3
31	Putao	...	...	...	...	...	...	...	...
	Sagaing Division ...	1,874	740	303	15	1	30	16	831
32	Shwebo	16	10	...	1	...	...	...	6
33	Sagaing ..	284	91	33	5	1	7	5	160
34	Lower Chindwin ...	1,202	403	232	9	...	23	11	567
35	Upper Chindwin ...	372	236	38	...	...	...	...	98
36	Chin Hills	...	...	...	...	...	...	...	...
	Meiktila Division ...	624	229	171	4	8	18	21	224
37	Kyauksè	10	3	...	...	...	...	...	7
38	Meiktila	55	38	...	1	...	2	...	17
39	Yamèthin	24	4	8	...	...	...	...	12
40	Myingyan	535	184	163	3	8	16	21	188
	Eastern States ...	401	130	97	6	1	18	13	174
41	Northern Shan States ..	347	101	94	4	1	15	13	152
42	Southern Shan States ..	54	29	3	2	...	3	...	22
43	Karenni	...	...	...	...	...	...	...	...

Industry—*continued.*

Order XII.—Food. (Groups 65 to 75.)								Order XIII.—Dress and the toilet. (Groups 76 to 82.)								Serial No. of District, etc. (column 1).
Total Workers and Dependents.	WORKERS.						DEPENDENTS.	Total Workers and Dependents.	WORKERS.						DEPENDENTS.	
	Total Workers.		Workers with an agricultural or other subsidiary occupation.						Total Workers.		Workers with an agricultural or other subsidiary occupation.					
			Agricultural.		Other.						Agricultural.		Other.			
	Males.	Females.	Males.	Females.	Males.	Females.			Males.	Females.	Males.	Females.	Males.	Females.		
10	11	12	13	14	15	16	17	18	19	20	21	22	23	24	25	
223,528	68,293	60,807	5,486	2,238	3,256	3,717	94,428	114,864	41,144	26,057	293	277	1,188	861	47,663	
220,501	67,424	59,974	5,464	2,208	3,200	3,624	93,103	112,299	40,445	25,023	284	254	1,164	806	46,831	
11,216	1,494	5,755	13	42	25	245	3,967	3,070	1,737	208	15	2	48	18	1,134	
9,427	1,418	4,736	13	9	19	173	3,273	2,229	1,427	81	7	..	15	...	731	1
...	...	...	...	...	...	...	...	13	6	1	...	...	...	..	6	2
35	2	18	...	...	...	1	15	315	124	49	5	1	12	4	142	3
1,754	74	1,001	...	33	6	71	679	522	180	77	3	1	21	14	265	4
54,640	26,927	9,639	145	56	144	159	18,074	29,409	12,454	5,825	17	71	91	132	11,130	
31,875	18,928	4,048	1	...	18	...	8,899	14,458	7,903	1,616	..	...	8	9	4,939	5
1,648	910	245	...	1	4	...	493	1,782	508	734	...	5	14	19	540	6
3,488	1,978	502	4	...	1	7	1,008	3,189	845	629	12	45	18	20	1,715	7
5,689	1,869	1,500	1	18	46	29	2,320	2,930	921	712	...	12	6	23	1,297	8
3,588	1,129	900	8	25	14	11	1,559	2,967	744	1,120	4	8	11	32	1,103	9
8,352	2,113	2,444	131	12	61	112	3,795	6,083	1,533	1,014	1	1	34	29	1,536	10
18,097	5,278	5,830	49	44	70	155	6,989	17,362	6,414	3,244	60	30	222	142	7,704	
5,200	2,546	800	8	13	9	13	1,854	4,688	1,905	788	14	11	78	37	1,995	11
6,620	1,385	2,511	37	24	48	101	2,724	4,628	1,633	889	29	9	60	33	2,106	12
2,627	493	1,149	3	3	9	30	985	2,988	1,089	561	5	1	41	26	1,338	13
1,631	106	1,016	1	4	2	11	509	2,910	1,009	720	6	7	33	31	1,181	14
2,019	748	354	...	...	2	...	917	2,148	778	286	6	2	10	15	1,084	15
14,991	3,575	4,954	27	50	57	123	6,462	11,207	3,169	3,562	6	18	62	92	4,476	
3,076	442	1,305	3	32	11	24	1,329	2,401	761	731	..	4	10	12	910	16
131	19	60	...	5	2	6	52	74	16	23	...	1	2	3	35	17
1,644	563	322	1	.	12	8	759	2,695	749	857	2	10	29	43	1,089	18
7,423	2,109	2,084	23	8	21	44	3,230	3,523	1,006	1,106	...	...	7	13	1,411	19
1,819	286	949	...	5	10	41	584	1,578	343	602	2	3	11	21	633	20
898	156	234	...	...	1	...	508	935	294	243	2	...	3	...	398	21
53,359	13,661	14,164	2,717	981	1,903	1,396	25,534	9,646	2,990	2,250	47	29	219	107	4,406	
2,139	327	732	8	9	16	26	1,080	2,017	547	480	..	4	11	19	990	22
40,288	10,771	10,495	2,414	784	1,689	1,193	19,022	2,571	725	641	12	1	81	36	1,205	23
6,893	1,475	2,188	248	171	159	162	3,230	2,615	821	591	24	18	84	36	1,203	24
4,007	1,060	749	47	17	39	15	2,198	2,441	895	538	11	6	43	16	1,008	25
32	28	...	...	...	...	...	4	2	2	...	...	...	...	...	...	26
9,581	2,240	3,725	6	86	51	124	3,616	17,548	5,633	5,153	5	10	70	53	6,762	
8,426	1,964	3,307	5	85	40	96	3,155	15,420	5,010	4,529	3	6	37	22	5,881	27
5,675	*1,159*	*2,419*	...	...	...	...	*2,097*	*13,294*	*4,219*	*4,176*	..	...	*10*	*3*	*4,899*	
369	75	149	...	...	1	3	145	412	117	163	...	...	2	3	132	28
281	54	90	...	1	1	4	77	421	147	74	...	2	6	5	200	29
551	134	179	1	...	8	21	238	1,278	343	387	2	11	31	23	548	30
14	13	...	...	...	1	...	1	17	16	...	...	...	2	...	1	31
35,837	8,602	9,977	2,069	665	699	1,096	17,258	13,352	4,738	2,653	102	62	293	172	5,961	
4,413	963	1,623	136	87	95	100	1,827	3,171	1,046	701	21	32	47	32	1,424	32
11,440	3,522	3,831	1,150	477	318	686	5,087	4,830	1,577	1,132	40	15	89	83	2,121	33
16,493	3,753	3,461	774	65	235	208	9,279	4,308	1,739	711	24	8	109	47	1,855	34
2,491	364	1,062	9	36	51	102	1,065	962	346	108	17	7	48	10	508	35
...	..	..	...	...	...	..	...	81	30	1	...	...	...	...	50	36
22,780	5,647	5,930	438	284	251	326	11,203	10,696	3,310	2,128	32	23	151	90	5,258	
3,590	844	1,253	1	90	14	58	1,493	1,282	383	243	6	10	26	9	656	37
9,828	2,338	1,767	227	127	107	112	5,723	3,246	1,048	610	14	10	56	19	1,588	38
3,263	613	1,007	20	7	31	40	1,643	2,625	819	435	6	2	24	13	1,371	39
6,099	1,852	1,903	190	60	99	116	2,344	3,543	1,060	840	6	1	45	49	1,643	40
3,027	869	833	22	30	56	93	1,325	2,565	699	1,034	9	23	24	55	832	
2,851	825	805	20	30	56	93	1,221	1,296	336	491	4	12	12	39	469	41
161	31	28	2	...	...	...	102	1,167	348	486	5	11	11	16	333	42
15	13	...	...	...	...	...	2	109	15	57	...	...	1	...	30	43

Sub-Class *III.*—

Serial No.	District or State.		Order XIV.—Furniture. (Groups 83, 84.)							
			Total Workers and Dependents.	Workers.						Dependents.
				Total Workers.		Workers with an agricultural or other subsidiary occupation.				
						Agricultural.		Other.		
				Males.	Females.	Males.	Females.	Males.	Females.	
	1		2	3	4	5	6	7	8	9
	Provincial Total	...	860	374	97	...	1	4	...	389
	Divisional Burma	...	860	374	97	...	1	4	...	389
	Arakan Division	...	...	...	...	...	...	...	...	...
1	Akyab ...	.	..	...	...	...	...	...	...	...
2	Hill Dist. of Arakan	...	..	...	...	...	...	...	...	...
3	Kyaukpyu ..	...	...	...	...	...	...	...	...	...
4	Sandoway ...	...	...	...	...	...	...	...	...	...
	Pegu Division	...	196	59	1	...	...	2	...	136
5	Rangoon Town	...	176	59	1	...	...	2	...	116
6	Insein ...	...	...	...	...	...	...	...	...	...
7	Hanthawaddy	...	...	...	...	...	...	...	...	...
8	Tharrawaddy	...	12	...	...	...	...	...	...	12
9	Pegu ...	...	8	...	...	...	...	...	...	8
10	Prome ...	...	..	...	...	...	...	...	...	...
	Irrawaddy Division	...	54	15	5	...	...	1	...	34
11	Bassein ...	...	1	...	...	...	...	...	...	1
12	Henzada ...	...	43	15	...	...	...	1	...	28
13	Myaungmya	...	...	...	...	...	...	...	...	...
14	Ma-ubin ...	...	10	...	5	..	...	...	...	5
15	Pyapôn ...	...	...	...	...	...	...	...	...	...
	Tenasserim Division	...	42	9	17	...	...	...	...	16
16	Toungoo .	...	4	...	...	...	...	...	...	4
17	Salween ...	...	...	...	...	...	...	...	...	...
18	Thatôn ...	...	...	...	...	...	...	...	...	...
19	Amherst ...	...	15	3	...	...	...	...	...	12
20	Tavoy ...	...	23	6	17	...	...	...	...	...
21	Mergui ...	...	...	...	...	...	...	...	...	...
	Magwe Division	...	52	...	33	...	...	...	...	19
22	Thayetmyo ...	...	10	...	1	...	...	...	..	9
23	Pakôkku ...	...	4	...	2	...	...	...	...	2
24	Minbu ...	...	...	...	...	...	...	...	...	...
25	Magwe ...	...	38	...	30	...	...	...	...	8
26	Pakôkku Hill Tracts	...	...	...	...	...	...	...	...	...
	Mandalay Division	...	285	209	4	...	...	...	...	72
27	Mandalay .	...	285	209	4	...	..	...	...	72
	Mandalay City	..	*141*	*71*	*4*	...	...	...	...	*66*
28	Bhamo ...	...	...	...	...	...	...	...	...	...
29	Myitkyina ..	...	..	...	...	...	...	...	...	...
30	Katha ..	...	...	...	...	...	...	..	...	...
31	Putao ...	...	...	...	...	...	...	...	...	...
	Sagaing Division	...	211	79	27	...	1	1	...	105
32	Shwebo ...	...	7	...	5	...	...	...	...	2
33	Sagaing	...	161	55	22	..	1	1	...	84
34	Lower Chindwin	...	43	24	...	...	...	...	...	19
35	Upper Chindwin	...	...	...	...	...	...	...	...	...
36	Chin Hills ...	...	...	...	...	...	...	...	...	...
	Meiktila Division	...	20	3	10	...	...	...	...	7
37	Kyauksè ...	...	5	...	5	...	...	...	...	...
38	Meiktila ..	...	7	...	5	...	...	...	...	2
39	Yamèthin ...	...	1	1	...	...	...	...	...	...
40	Myingyan ...	...	7	2	...	...	...	...	...	5
	Eastern States	...	...	...	...	...	...	...	...	...
41	Northern Shan States	...	...	...	...	...	...	...	...	...
42	Southern Shan States	...	...	...	...	...	...	...	...	...
43	Karenni ...	...	...	...	...	...	...	...	...	...

PART III.—*Details by districts*—contd.

Industry—*continued.*

Order XV.—Building. (Groups 85 to 89.)								Order XVI.—Construction of means of transport. (Groups 90, 91, 92.)								
Total Workers and Dependents.	WORKERS.						DEPENDENTS.	Total Workers and Dependents.	WORKERS.						DEPENDENTS.	Serial No. of District, etc. (column 1).
	Total Workers.		Workers with an agricultural or other subsidiary occupation.						Total Workers.		Workers with an agricultural or other subsidiary occupation.					
			Agricultural.		Other.						Agricultural.		Other.			
	Males.	Females.	Males.	Females.	Males.	Females.			Males.	Females.	Males.	Females.	Males.	Females.		
10	11	12	13	14	15	16	17	18	19	20	21	22	23	24	25	
22,022	9,526	1,236	165	13	278	25	11,260	9,097	4,359	274	33	2	168	16	4,464	
21,410	9,235	1,197	142	9	255	21	10,978	8,972	4,313	267	32	2	166	15	4,392	
421	195	2	9	...	2	...	224	555	235	79	1	...	17	1	241	
242	123	1	.	...	..	..	118	502	212	76	1	...	15		214	1
...	...	...	..	...	...	...	...	...		...	...	...	...	...	...	2
117	43	1	9	...	...	...	73	34	18	2	...	...	...	...	14	3
62	29	...	...	..	2	.	33	19	5	1	...	...	2	1	13	4
5,465	3,214	98	6	...	28	3	2,153	3,849	2,414	32	3	..	53	...	1,403	
3,375	2,204	13	...	...	15	..	1,158	3,165	2,137	21	...	...	19	...	1,007	5
375	204	7	1	...	2	...	164	67	9	4	...	...	2	...	54	6
306	180	3	2	...	2	2	123	82	50	3	1	...	6	..	29	7
478	204	56	...	...	4	...	218	145	86	...	...	..	17	...	59	8
475	203	3	3	..	4	...	269	214	64	...	2	...	2	...	150	9
456	219	16	...	...	1	1	221	176	68	4	..	...	7	...	104	10
1,588	834	51	15	1	17	1	703	482	149	21	5	1	9	1	312	
349	207	7	2	...	2	...	135	213	47	12	4	1	4	...	154	11
436	188	2	5	1	3	1	246	64	25	..	1	...	1	...	39	12
464	270	31	8	...	12	...	163	57	33	3	...	..	1	1	21	13
240	104	11	...	..	...	...	125	106	40	4	...	...	3	...	62	14
99	65	..	..	...	...	...	34	42	4	2	...	...	...	...	36	15
3,273	1,151	173	13	...	20	..	1,949	1,410	540	23	3	...	14	1	847	
303	113	13	1	...	3	...	177	615	212	9	...	...	8	1	394	16
19	16	...	...	...	..	...	3	14	1	...	.	...	...	...	13	17
1,598	483	132	...	...	5	..	983	256	114	3	2	...	1	...	139	18
848	320	20	3	.	1	...	508	367	147	11	1	...	3	...	209	19
303	116	2	9	...	9	..	185	114	27	...	.		1	...	87	20
202	103	6	...	...	2	...	93	44	39	...			1		5	21
2,401	839	96	37	2	68	...	1,466	707	208	82	4	...	16	8	417	
655	151	19	...		30	...	485	28	6	1	..	...	...	...	21	22
792	244	28	4	...	22	...	520	393	90	75	2	...	9	8	228	23
469	128	21	16	2	10	...	320	158	47	6	2	...	4	...	105	24
485	316	28	17	...	6	...	141	128	65	...	..	...	3	...	63	25
...	...	...	...	.	...	...	...	...	...	...	...	...	...		..	26
3,901	1,311	480	10	1	50	3	2,110	496	190	18	1	..	9	...	288	
3,435	1,043	479	2	1	25	3	1,913	394	151	14	...		3	...	229	27
2,060	*495*	*400*	...	...	.	*1*	*1,165*	*320*	*119*	*14*	..	...	--	...	*187*	
213	65	1	...	...	20	..	147	17	7	1		...	3	..	9	28
90	73	...	1	..	...	...	17	4	3	...	...	...	...	...	1	29
163	130	..	7	..	5	...	33	79	29	3	1		3	--	47	30
...	...	...	...	...	...	...	.	2	..	..	...	..	...	..	2	31
2,470	1,067	230	41	4	50	9	1,173	588	274	2	13		25	1	312	
480	187	89	5	..	9	6	204	229	104	...	3	...	10	...	125	32
1,128	447	97	18	1	12	2	584	123	61	...	7	...	6		62	33
737	353	43	18	3	26	1	341	222	105	1	2		8	..	116	34
108	64	1	...	...	3	...	43	14	4	1	1	...	1	1	9	35
17	16	..	...	...	...	...	1	.	...	...	.	..	...	..	...	36
1,891	624	67	11	1	20	5	1,200	885	303	10	2	1	23	3	572	
484	121	19	6	...	11	.	344	38	14	3	1		1	3	21	37
348	138	4	..	..	3	...	206	243	108	...	..	...	5	.	135	38
332	100	6	.	...	...	...	226	483	138	3	1	1	10		342	39
727	265	38	5	1	6	5	424	121	43	4	...	...	7		74	40
612	291	39	23	4	23	4	282	125	46	7	1		2	1	72	
321	154	38	3	4	5	4	129	115	43	7	1	...	2	1	65	41
270	134	...	20	...	18	...	136	9	3	..	.	.	.	..	6	42
21	3	1	...	...	.	...	17	1	...	...	...		---	...	1	43

Sub-Class *III.*—Industry

Order XVII.—Production and transmission of physical forces. (Group 93.)

Serial No.	DISTRICT OR STATE.	Total Workers and Dependents.	WORKERS. Total Workers. Males.	Females.	Workers with an agricultural or other subsidiary occupation. Agricultural. Males.	Females.	Other. Males.	Females.	DEPENDENTS.
	1	2	3	4	5	6	7	8	9
	Provincial Total ...	577	177	5	2	...	2	...	395
	Divisional Burma ...	565	177	4	2	...	2	...	384
	Arakan Division ...	...	...	...	...	...	...	...	...
1	Akyab ...	...	...	...	...	...	...	...	...
2	Hill Dist. of Arakan ...	...	...	...	...	...	...	...	...
3	Kyaukpyu ...	...	...	...	...	...	...	...	...
4	Sandoway ...	...	...	...	...	...	...	...	...
	Pegu Division ...	429	103	1	2	...	2	...	325
5	Rangoon Town ...	327	71	1	2	...	2	...	255
6	Insein ...	67	18	...	...	...	...	...	49
7	Hanthawaddy ...	20	4	...	...	...	...	...	16
8	Tharrawaddy ...	3	...	...	...	...	...	...	3
9	Pegu ...	3	2	...	...	...	...	...	1
10	Prome ...	9	8	...	...	...	...	...	1
	Irrawaddy Division ...	22	9	...	...	...	...	...	13
11	Bassein ...	3	2	...	...	...	...	...	1
12	Henzada ...	3	...	...	...	...	...	...	3
13	Myaungmya ...	...	...	...	...	...	...	...	...
14	Ma-ubin ...	1	1	...	...	...	...	...	...
15	Pyapôn ...	15	6	...	...	...	...	...	9
	Tenasserim Division ...	40	18	...	...	...	...	...	22
16	Toungoo ...	15	6	...	...	...	...	...	9
17	Salween ...	...	...	...	...	...	...	...	...
18	Thatôn ...	15	7	...	...	...	...	...	8
19	Amherst ...	4	1	...	...	...	...	...	3
20	Tavoy ...	4	2	...	...	...	...	...	2
21	Mergui ...	2	2	...	...	...	...	...	...
	Magwe Division ...	3	2	...	...	...	...	...	1
22	Thayetmyo ...	...	...	...	...	...	...	...	...
23	Pakôkku ...	...	...	...	...	...	...	...	...
24	Minbu ...	...	...	...	...	...	...	...	...
25	Magwe ...	3	2	...	...	...	...	...	1
26	Pakôkku Hill Tracts ...	...	...	...	...	...	...	...	...
	Mandalay Division ...	62	40	3	...	...	...	...	19
27	Mandalay ...	60	38	3	...	...	...	...	19
	Mandalay City ...	*56*	*37*	*3*	...	...	...	...	*16*
28	Bhamo ...	...	...	...	...	...	...	...	...
29	Myitkyina ...	...	...	...	...	...	...	...	...
30	Katha ...	2	2	...	...	...	...	...	...
31	Putao ...	...	...	...	...	...	...	...	...
	Sagaing Division ...	2	2	...	...	...	...	...	...
32	Shwebo ...	2	2	...	...	...	...	...	...
33	Sagaing ...	...	...	...	...	...	...	...	...
34	Lower Chindwin ...	...	...	...	...	...	...	...	...
35	Upper Chindwin ...	...	...	...	...	...	...	...	...
36	Chin Hills ...	...	...	...	...	...	...	...	...
	Meiktila Division ...	7	3	...	...	...	...	...	4
37	Kyauksè ...	...	...	...	...	...	...	...	...
38	Meiktila ...	...	...	...	...	...	...	...	...
39	Yamèthin ...	3	3	...	...	...	...	...	...
40	Myingyan ...	4	...	...	...	...	...	...	4
	Eastern States ...	12	...	1	...	...	...	...	11
41	Northern Shan States ...	12	...	1	...	...	...	...	11
42	Southern Shan States ...	...	...	...	...	...	...	...	...
43	Karenni ...	...	...	...	...	...	...	...	...

PART III.—*Details by districts*—contd.

—*concluded.* | Sub-Class *IV.*—Transport.

Order XVIII.—Other industries. (Groups 94 to 103.) Total Workers and Dependents.	WORKERS. Total Workers. Males.	WORKERS. Total Workers. Females.	Workers with an agricultural or other subsidiary occupation. Agricultural. Males.	Agricultural. Females.	Other. Males.	Other. Females.	DEPENDENTS.	* Order XIX. Total.	Order XX.—Transport by water. (Groups 105 to 110.) Total Workers and Dependents.	WORKERS. Total Workers. Males.	WORKERS. Total Workers. Females.	Workers with an agricultural or other subsidiary occupation. Agricultural. Males.	Agricultural. Females.	Other. Males.	Other. Females.	DEPENDENTS.	Serial No. of District, etc. (column 1).
10	11	12	13	14	15	16	17	18	19	20	21	22	23	24	25	26	
76,602	32,252	2,314	475	109	844	40	42,036	.	118,083	64,920	2,350	2,307	22	1,951	195	50,813	
73,297	31,196	2,241	330	107	767	40	39,860	...	117,251	64,641	2,179	2,287	18	1,935	160	50,431	
4,674	2,012	85	21	...	82	2	2,577	..	10,354	8,115	113	1,722	2	209	6	2,126	
3,682	1,672	55	15	...	62	...	1,955	...	9,168	7,747	71	1,710	..	141	4	1,350	1
30	17	...	...	...	...	...	13	.	15	15	...	...	...	...	...	...	2
620	194	30	6	...	9	2	396	.	310	88	31	5	2	24	2	191	3
342	129	...	...	...	11	...	213	...	861	265	11	7	...	44	...	585	4
24,649	10,799	712	38	...	122	1	13,138	..	44,039	25,994	263	152	6	328	10	17,782	
13,308	6,241	461	2	...	20	...	6,606	.	21,736	17,011	23	30	...	70		4,709	5
1,846	723	111	7	...	14	...	1,012	...	3,020	1,049	121	12	...	19	2	1,850	6
2,055	789	12	7	...	26	...	1,254	..	11,910	5,348	68	59	2	76	7	6,494	7
2,546	1,030	69	11	...	32	...	1,447	...	928	415	...	1		9	...	513	8
2,556	988	17	11	...	20	..	1,551		4,868	1,293	7	12	1	81	...	3,568	9
2,338	1,028	42	...	...	10	1	1,268	.	1,577	878	44	38	3	73	1	655	10
10,041	4,346	259	49	2	127	11	5,436	.	20,451	10,540	697	88	1	316	54	9,214	
2,514	1,203	56	22	1	42	1	1,255	..	4,064	2,391	67	12	...	70	8	1,606	11
2,283	921	20	2	...	13	6	1,342	...	3,005	1,271	138	22	...	122	35	1,596	12
1,877	782	91	7	...	34	2	1,004	..	2,017	1,268	83	10	...	41	...	666	13
1,641	728	85	12	1	28	2	828	..	4,157	1,801	220	6	...	36	3	2,136	14
1,726	712	7	6	...	10	...	1,007	...	7,208	3,809	189	38	1	47	8	3,210	15
8,281	3,046	147	29	...	103	...	5,088	...	16,446	8,287	323	111	5	110	18	7,836	
1,703	712	30	6	...	24	...	961	..	1,330	465	50	..	...	21	3	815	16
61	25	2	...	...	2	...	34	...	101	33	...	...	...	2	...	68	17
2,199	720	48	4	...	32	...	1,431	..	2,869	1,068	65	45	5	39	6	1,736	18
2,920	946	37	6	...	28	...	1,937	...	8,745	4,895	181	43	...	7	8	3,669	19
724	382	6	12	...	12	...	336	.	1,300	501	18	21	.	24	1	721	20
674	261	24	1	...	5	.	389	..	2,101	1,265	9	2	...	17	...	827	21
6,524	2,643	145	24	2	104	9	3,736	...	10,451	4,039	478	51	4	327	42	5,934	
1,365	418	25	6	..	16	2	922	..	2,858	1,017	119	3	...	93	20	1,722	22
1,968	747	22	13	1	36	2	1,199	...	3,953	1,510	169	39	4	144	13	2,274	23
1,798	819	44	5	...	33	2	935	...	1,481	475	71	7	...	41	2	865	24
1,389	655	54	...	1	19	3	680	..	2,229	1,037	119	2	...	49	7	1,073	25
4	4	...	...	...	...	...	...	.	...	...	..	...	...	...	...	..	26
8,960	4,282	418	16	...	48	1	4,260	.	4,407	2,335	109	26		100	.	1,963	
6,993	3,425	377	3	...	2	1	3,191	.	3,336	1,753	96	20	...	61	...	1,487	27
5,823	*2,803*	*365*	...	...	...	...	*2,655*	...	*1,053*	*767*	...	...	...		...	286	
344	137	4	...	...	2	...	203	..	559	294	8	1	...	26	...	257	28
513	271	17	7	...	20	...	225	...	278	180	2	5	...	8	...	96	29
1,085	427	19	6	...	24	...	639	...	234	108	3	...	...	5	...	123	30
25	22	1	..	...	...	...	2	...	..	...	...	...	...	...	...	...	31
4,783	2,189	364	134	103	113	8	2,230	...	10,005	4,889	158	134	...	505	22	4,958	
1,249	526	135	7	...	25	5	588	..	1,137	593	26	10	...	45	3	518	32
1,342	699	46	25	2	23	2	597	...	3,660	1,591	88	60	.	102	10	1,987	33
1,064	551	18	9	...	31	...	495	...	2,349	976	18	14	...	123	3	1,355	34
1,070	383	165	93	101	34	1	522	...	2,853	1,729	26	50	...	235	6	1,098	35
58	30	...	...	...	...	..	28	...	...	.	..	...	...	...	...	...	36
5,385	1,879	111	19	...	68	8	3,395	...	1,098	442	38	3	..	40	8	618	
661	243	13	3	...	13	2	405	..	291	67	7	1	...	7	...	217	37
1,531	495	4	3	...	19	...	1,032	...	45	18	...	1	...	..	...	27	38
1,550	481	19	7	...	11	...	1,050	...	170	89	2	...	...	1	..	79	39
1,643	660	75	6	...	25	6	908	...	592	268	29	1	...	32	8	295	40
3,305	1,056	73	145	2	77	...	2,176	...	832	279	171	20	4	16	35	382	
755	295	57	14	2	29	...	403	...	374	103	171	6	4	10	35	100	41
2,383	691	9	131	...	47	...	1,683	..	456	176	...	14	...	6	...	280	42
167	70	7	...	...	1	...	90	...	2	...	...	--	...	..	...	2	43

* [illegible]port by air (aeroplanes, etc., and aerodromes).

Sub-Class *IV.*—

Order XXI.—Transport on land otherwise than by rail. (Groups 111 to 117.)

Serial No.	District or State.	Total Workers and Dependents.	Workers. Total Workers. Males.	Total Workers. Females.	Workers with an agricultural or other subsidiary occupation. Agricultural. Males.	Agricultural. Females.	Other. Males.	Other. Females.	Dependents.
	1	2	3	4	5	6	7	8	9
	Provincial Total ...	199,089	92,105	12,615	1,772	293	3,008	766	94,369
	Divisional Burma ..	186,807	86,299	11,755	1,481	235	2,414	712	88,753
	Arakan Division ...	5,399	3,977	80	26	1	23	4	1,342
1	Akyab	3,879	3,290	17	20	...	12	..	572
2	Hill Dist. of Arakan ...	34	14	...	...	...	...	...	20
3	Kyaukpyu ...	787	480	3	3	...	5	...	304
4	Sandoway	699	193	60	3	1	6	4	446
	Pegu Division ..	49,672	28,025	1,362	285	8	380	22	20,285
5	Rangoon Town ...	19,280	14,743	144	5	...	20	...	4,393
6	Insein	6,098	3,128	253	16	1	96	...	2,717
7	Hanthawaddy ...	3,047	1,231	69	47	1	38	2	1,747
8	Tharrawaddy ...	6,531	2,859	190	99	1	65	...	3,482
9	Pegu ... –	7,650	3,310	237	91	5	106	4	4,103
10	Prome	7,066	2,754	469	27	...	55	16	3,843
	Irrawaddy Division ...	16,188	9,142	815	102	4	188	39	6,231
11	Bassein	4,126	2,702	155	62	4	46	3	1,269
12	Henzada	7,095	3,397	389	33	...	67	34	3,309
13	Myaungmya ...	1,365	785	126	2	...	34	1	454
14	Ma-ubin	2,447	1,431	120	5	...	39	1	896
15	Pyapôn	1,155	827	25	...	...	2	...	303
	Tenasserim Division ...	28,628	13,250	813	200	6	234	25	14,565
16	Toungoo ...	6,338	2,959	242	57	3	80	4	3,137
17	Salween	335	225	1	2	..	...	...	109
18	Thatôn	6,119	2,418	151	31	3	61	8	3,559
19	Amherst	10,343	4,534	333	59	..	45	9	5,476
20	Tavoy ...	3,924	2,208	50	48	...	37	1	1,736
21	Mergui	1,499	906	36	3	..	11	3	557
	Magwe Division ...	24,387	8,873	2,752	332	102	435	130	12,762
22	Thayetmyo	2,891	1,056	142	2	2	21	8	1,693
23	Pakôkku	7,630	2,586	765	87	11	204	47	4,279
24	Minbu	5,337	2,248	486	138	54	140	25	2,603
25	Magwe	8,522	2,980	1,359	105	35	70	50	4,183
26	Pakôkku Hill Tracts ...	7	3	...	..	...	..	...	4
	Mandalay Division ..	19,616	9,195	680	155	3	309	23	9,741
27	Mandalay ...	15,926	6,884	531	22	2	180	15	7,811
	Mandalay City ...	*10,141*	4,415	240	3	...	*13*	2	5,486
28	Bhamo	1,966	1,005	64	5	...	79	1	897
29	Myitkyina	1,085	731	24	105	...	16	5	330
30	Katha	1,308	554	61	22	1	33	2	693
31	Putao	31	21	...	1	...	1	...	10
	Sagaing Division ...	21,034	6,792	2,952	207	76	508	364	11,290
32	Shwebo	4,030	1,240	601	6	9	74	28	2,189
33	Sagaing ...	9,242	2,478	1,467	106	35	203	237	5,297
34	Lower Chindwin .	6,052	2,157	780	87	25	177	83	3,115
35	Upper Chindwin	1,644	891	104	8	7	53	16	649
36	Chin Hills ...	66	26	...	.	...	1	..	40
	Meiktila Division ...	21,883	7,045	2,301	174	35	337	105	12,537
37	Kyaukse	3,251	1,399	122	42	8	60	6	1,730
38	Meiktila ...	5,199	1,526	583	25	7	47	11	3,080
39	Yamèthin	9,475	1,905	1,245	88	12	146	35	5,325
40	Myingyan	3,958	1,205	351	19	8	84	53	2,403
	Eastern States ...	12,282	5,806	860	291	58	594	54	5,616
41	Northern Shan States ...	5,624	2,838	456	68	5	139	22	2,330
42	Southern Shan States ..	6,436	2,879	382	218	53	455	31	3,175
43	Karenni	222	89	22	5	...	...	1	111

PART III.—*Details by districts*—*contd.*

Transport—*concluded.*

Order XXII.—Transport by rail. (Groups 118, 119.)								Order XXIII.—Postal, telegraph and telephone services. (Group 120.)								Serial No. of District, etc. (column 1).
Total Workers and Dependents.	WORKERS.						DEPENDENTS.	Total Workers and Dependents.	WORKERS.						DEPENDENTS.	
	Total Workers.		Workers with an agricultural or other subsidiary occupation.						Total Workers.		Workers with an agricultural or other subsidiary occupation.					
			Agricultural.		Other.						Agricultural.		Other.			
	Males.	Females.	Males.	Females.	Males.	Females.			Males.	Females.	Males.	Females.	Males.	Females.		
10	11	12	13	14	15	16	17	18	19	20	21	22	23	24	25	
27,774	15,876	828	14	...	58	2	11,070	9,328	4,503	145	26	...	71	1	4,680	
26,877	15,361	783	14	...	58	2	10,833	8,871	4,324	145	23	...	69	1	4,402	
164	98	8	...	...	...	...	58	531	246	5	11	...	7	...	280	
164	98	8	...	...	...	...	58	428	198	2	11	...	7	...	228	1
...	...	...	...	...	...	...	...	...	...	...	...	...	...	...	...	2
...	...	...	...	...	...	..	..	31	24	2	...	...	..	...	5	3
...	...	...	...	..	...	...	...	72	24	1	...	...	...	...	47	4
14,379	8,541	370	4	...	18	...	5,468	3,381	1,823	8	2	..	27	...	1,490	
7,738	4,715	244	...	.	2	...	2,779	2,207	1,191	47	...	...	2	..	969	5
3,295	1,932	59	..	...	7	...	1,204	188	64	18		...	..	..	106	6
150	147	...	...	...	...	..	3	296	139	2	...	...	2	..	155	7
992	537	6	1	...	4	...	449	215	115	...	...		23	...	100	8
1,929	936	61	3	...	4		932	167	99	...	2	...	...	..	68	9
375	274	...	..	...	1	...	101	308	215	1	...	...	...	...	92	10
1,068	599	13	...	..	6	..	456	539	239	2	...	...	3	...	298	
429	288	10	..	...	...	...	131	143	52	1	...	...	...	...	90	11
635	308	3	...	...	6	...	324	134	60	1	...	...	.	...	73	12
4	3	...	...	...	...	...	1	110	52	...	...	...	3	..	58	13
...		...	...	...	..	...	...	107	55	...	...	...	...	...	52	14
..	...	...	...	...	...	...	...	45	20	...	...	.	...	...	25	15
3,129	1,874	67	6	...	16	..	1,188	1,221	512	6	3	...	7		703	
1,474	670	30	..	...	10	..	774	255	91		...	...	2	...	164	16
...	..	...	..	...	...	...	...	30	20	...	...	...	..	..	10	17
631	344	13	6	...	6	...	274	142	70	1	.	.	...	...	71	18
1,023	859	24	...	...		...	140	423	128	4	...	...	...	...	291	19
	..	...	...	...	...	...	...	276	148	1	3	...	4	..	127	20
1	1	...	...	...	..	...	...	95	55	..	..	...	1	...	40	21
51	40	9	..	..	...	...	2	685	371	2	5	...	8	...	312	
1	1	...		...	...	...	...	109	51	...	..	...	...	..	58	22
...	...	...		...	...	...	...	218	113	...	4	...	1	...	105	23
2	2		...	...	..	...	...	125	47	1	1	...	2		77	24
48	37	9	...	...	...	...	2	228	156	1	...	..	5	...	71	25
..	...	...	...	...	...	...	...	5	4	..	...	...	..	...	1	26
3,834	2,312	143	4	..	6	...	1,379	1,311	633	7	...	...	10	1	671	
3,132	1,864	131	...	...	...	...	1,137	893	435	5	...	...	...	...	453	27
959	444	28	...	...	...	...	487	718	352	3	.	...	...	..	303	
17	3	...	..	...	...	..	14	121	57	.	...	...	...	..	64	28
357	262	2	1	...	1	...	93	134	65	...	...	...	3	...	69	29
385	181	10	3	...	5	...	134	153	71	2	...	...	7	1	80	30
3	2	...	...	.	..	...	1	10	5	...	...	...	..	...	5	31
1,545	724	27	...	..	5	...	794	684	294	5	1	...	7	...	385	
566	254	13	...	...	4	...	299	217	118	5	...	...	...	...	91	32
835	392	14	..	...	1	...	429	102	36	...	...	.	1	.	66	33
144	78	..	.	..	...	...	66	125	52	...	1	...	1	...	73	34
...	...	...	...	...	...	...	..	211	69	...	...	..	4	..	142	35
...	...	...	..	...	...	...	.	29	19	...	...	...	1	..	10	36
2,807	1,173	146	...	...	7	2	1,488	519	206	50	1	.	...	...	263	
162	53	..	...	...	...	...	109	50	16	16	...	...	.	...	18	37
987	372	53	...	...	3	...	562	181	83	..	1	...	...	...	98	38
1,438	694	45	..	...	4	2	699	170	70	...	...		...	..	100	39
220	54	48	...	..	...	..	118	118	37	34		...	...	...	47	40
797	515	45	..	...	..	...	237	457	179	...	3	...	2	...	278	
763	497	45	..	...	..	...	221	209	102	...	...	...	1	...	107	41
34	18	...	...	...	..	...	16	239	75	..	3	...	1	...	164	42
...	...	...	...	...	...	.	...	9	2	...	...	...	...	...	7	43

Sub-Class V.—Trade,

Order XXIV.—Credit, finance and insurance. (Group 121.)

Serial No.	DISTRICT OR STATE.	Total Workers and Dependents.	WORKERS. Total Workers. Males.	Females.	Workers with an agricultural or other subsidiary occupation. Agricultural. Males.	Females.	Other. Males.	Females.	DEPENDENTS.
	1	2	3	4	5	6	7	8	9
	Provincial Total ...	22,210	8,706	2,909	362	140	518	246	10,595
	Divisional Burma ...	21,881	8,618	2,877	346	136	502	242	10,386
	Arakan Division ...	1,465	380	202	35	11	64	20	883
1	Akyab	815	228	58	10	..	22	10	529
2	Hill Dist. of Arakan ...	...	...	...	...	...	...	...	...
3	Kyaukpyu	338	81	71	15	6	21	4	186
4	Sandoway	312	71	73	10	5	21	6	168
	Pegu Division ...	6,185	3,048	512	42	26	27	25	2,625
5	Rangoon Town ...	2,795	1,640	108	...	2	7	4	1,047
6	Insein	475	138	75		1	...	6	262
7	Hanthawaddy ..	485	224	48	17	..	11	...	213
8	Tharrawaddy ...	880	390	87	2	6	2	7	403
9	Pegu	761	331	80	21	...	...	...	350
10	Prome	789	325	114	2	17	7	8	350
	Irrawaddy Division ...	4,850	1,836	671	77	27	136	64	2,343
11	Bassein	1,496	564	219	19	16	39	25	713
12	Henzada	928	363	114	17	5	21	4	451
13	Myaungmya ...	1,128	403	156	26	...	48	22	569
14	Ma-ubin	723	273	126	3	1	28	12	324
15	Pyapôn	575	233	56	12	5	...	1	286
	Tenasserim Division ...	2,013	731	260	30	4	40	17	1,022
16	Toungoo	672	252	88	7	1	18	9	332
17	Salween	9	4	1	...	...	...	...	4
18	Thatôn	435	185	52	10	...	6	4	198
19	Amherst	565	199	46	3	...	2	...	320
20	Tavoy	187	41	49	10	3	10	4	97
21	Mergui	145	50	24	...	...	4	...	71
	Magwe Division ...	2,165	641	497	46	29	87	48	1,027
22	Thayetmyo	494	137	107	7	4	9	7	250
23	Pakôkku	720	202	147	29	12	38	29	371
24	Minbu	400	120	113	10	6	11	9	167
25	Magwe	551	182	130	...	7	28	3	239
26	Pakôkku Hill Tracts ...	...	...	...	...	...	...	...	...
	Mandalay Division ...	1,176	394	238	3	3	35	11	544
27	Mandalay	819	258	195	2	3	12	5	366
	Mandalay City ..	*538*	*172*	*116*	...	...	*1*	...	*250*
28	Bhamo	37	12	6	..	...	2	2	19
29	Myitkyina	65	20	2	...	...	2	...	43
30	Katha	255	104	35	1	...	19	4	116
31	Putao	...	...	...	...	...	...	...	...
	Sagaing Division ...	1,948	908	170	65	20	66	35	870
32	Shwebo	396	108	85	12	12	13	7	203
33	Sagaing	820	472	26	19	6	22	16	322
34	Lower Chindwin ...	503	276	25	29	...	20	4	202
35	Upper Chindwin ...	229	52	34	5	2	11	8	143
36	Chin Hills	...	...	...	...	...	...	...	...
	Meiktila Division ...	2,079	680	327	48	16	47	22	1,072
37	Kyauksè	199	39	50	...	...	...	...	110
38	Meiktila	582	213	76	13	7	24	5	293
39	Yamèthin	573	158	64	5	...	11	4	351
40	Myingyan	725	270	137	30	9	12	13	318
	Eastern States ...	329	88	32	16	4	16	4	209
41	Northern Shan States ...	202	48	19	4	3	14	2	135
42	Southern Shan States ...	114	38	9	12	1	2	1	67
43	Karenni	13	2	4	...	...	...	1	7

finance and insurance.

Order XXV.—Brokerage, commission, auditing. (Group 122.)								Order XXVI.—Trade in cotton, silk, hair or other textiles or in piece-goods. (Groups 123a and 123b.)								
Total Workers and Dependents.	WORKERS. Total Workers. Males.	Total Workers. Females.	Workers with an agricultural or other subsidiary occupation. Agricultural. Males.	Agricultural. Females.	Other. Males.	Other. Females.	DEPENDENTS.	Total Workers and Dependents.	WORKERS. Total Workers. Males.	Total Workers. Females.	Workers with an agricultural or other subsidiary occupation. Agricultural. Males.	Agricultural. Females.	Other. Males.	Other. Females.	DEPENDENTS.	Serial No. of District, etc. (column 1).
10	11	12	13	14	15	16	17	18	19	20	21	22	23	24	25	
16,409	6,940	586	44	7	108	21	8,883	55,306	14,881	17,194	197	278	708	909	23,231	
15,790	6,726	522	41	7	93	18	8,542	52,750	13,972	16,658	119	251	615	775	22,120	
564	191	23	3		4	3	350	1,901	990	294	9	6	41	8	617	
427	151	...	1	...	...	...	276	1,597	839	259	5	2	33	4	499	1
...	...	...	...	...	...	...	...	18	13	...	...	...	...	...	5	2
103	22	23	2	...	4	3	58	1	1	...	...	...	...	...	...	3
34	18	...	...	...	...	...	16	285	137	35	4	4	8	4	113	4
6,296	2,832	131	5	.	31	4	3,333	13,499	4,549	1,579	4	16	64	42	7,371	
3,649	1,686	31	1	.	3	...	1,932	5,694	2,641	449	..	...	11	3	2,604	5
443	175	20	...	...	2	2	248	474	130	112	...	...	7	...	232	6
1,026	537	18	2	...	15	...	471	1,912	429	116			5	23	1,367	7
89	48	3	...	...	...	...	38	1,379	348	203	3	3	9	3	828	8
611	234	16	2	..	11	2	361	1,248	381	235	1	9	26	5	630	9
478	152	43	...	...	...	...	283	2,792	618	464	..	4	6	8	1,710	10
1,677	546	55	2	...	9	1	1,076	4,743	1,633	1,231	5	4	81	48	1,879	
683	278	7	...	...	...	...	398	1,984	806	506	2	1	44	14	672	11
198	58	18	1	...	...	...	122	1,029	216	296	2	2	11	15	517	12
469	194	2	1	...	8	...	273	525	239	90	...	...	14	10	196	13
143	4	10	...	...	...	1	129	482	41	208	.	1	5	6	233	14
184	12	18	...	...	1	...	154	723	331	131	1	.	7	3	261	15
1,807	906	26	3	...	6	...	875	5,351	1,733	1,363	9	2	48	23	2,255	
402	263	4	1	...	...	...	135	1,204	372	278	2	1	15	6	554	16
4	2	...	...	...	..	...	2	26	24	1	..	...	...	..	1	17
848	374	17	1	...	6	..	457	1,264	534	263	2	...	10	1	467	18
507	242	2	1	...	...	..	263	2,002	658	530	5	1	14	8	814	19
18	9	...	...	...	...	...	9	574	91	238	...	..	4	8	245	20
28	16	3	...	...	...	...	9	281	54	53	...	...	5	..	174	21
1,821	549	71	24	7	24	2	1,201	11,086	1,263	6,462	29	125	116	478	3,361	
439	68	37	...	7	5		334	820	157	344	8	5	15	6	319	22
983	275	22	7	..	17	...	686	8,241	606	5,424	16	109	70	445	2,211	23
265	131	9	17	..	...	2	125	1,306	265	525	3	11	19	24	516	24
134	75	3	...	...	2	...	56	719	235	169	2	...	12	3	315	25
..	...	...	...	..	...	...	.	...	...	...	.	...	...	...	...	26
1,768	1,022	30	2	...	6	...	716	4,432	1,288	1,169	5	10	70	32	1,974	
1,598	973	23	...	...	1	...	602	3,303	805	970	1	7	26	16	1,528	27
1,517	956	15	...	...	1	...	546	2,287	600	587	.	...	4	...	1,100	
7	3	...	...	..	...	...	4	441	187	99	3	1	6	7	155	28
33	11	...	...	...	3	...	22	388	170	64	...	1	23	2	154	29
129	34	7	2	...	2	...	88	299	126	36	1	1	15	7	137	30
1	1	...	...	...	...	...	...	...	...	...	...	...	...	...	...	31
403	142	20	1	.	4	...	241	6,347	1,515	2,443	45	53	145	81	2,389	
186	58	19	1	...	3	...	109	1,074	296	269	...	8	28	20	509	32
140	42	1	...	...	...	...	97	2,633	430	1,554	17	8	39	9	649	33
75	42	...	...	...	1	...	33	1,861	525	490	21	32	43	42	846	34
2	...	...	...	...	...	...	2	774	264	130	7	5	35	10	380	35
..	...	...	...	...	...	...	...	5	...	...	...	...	...	...	5	36
1,454	538	166	1	..	9	8	750	5,392	1,001	2,117	13	35	50	63	2,274	
24	13	...	...		...	...	11	364	90	118	2	2	7	...	156	37
257	68	74	.	...	7	...	115	2,579	371	1,200	4	27	23	42	1,008	38
431	213	9	1	..	2	..	209	1,304	341	334	6	3	8	6	629	39
742	244	83	...	...	...	8	415	1,145	199	465	1	3	12	15	481	40
619	214	64	3	...	15	3	341	2,556	909	536	78	27	93	134	1,111	
328	115	27	1	...	6	...	186	2,294	778	464	60	13	87	117	982	41
283	97	35	2	.	9	3	151	331	131	72	18	14	6	17	128	42
8	2	2	...	...	...	...	4	1	...	...	..	...	...	...	1	43

Sub-Class V.—Trade, finance

Order XXVII.—Trade in skins, leather, furs, feathers, horn, etc., and articles made from these not included in Order XXXIV or other orders. (Group 124.)

	DISTRICT OR STATE.	Total Workers and Dependents.	WORKERS.						DEPENDENTS.
			Total Workers.		Workers with an agricultural or other subsidiary occupation.				
					Agricultural		Other.		
			Males.	Females.	Males.	Females.	Males.	Females.	
	1	2	3	4	5	6	7	8	9
	Provincial Total ..	2,811	962	342	27	8	52	10	1,507
	Divisional Burma ...	2,711	932	296	27	7	49	9	1,483
	Arakan Division ...	24	12	...	...	...	1	...	12
1	Akyab	23	11	...	...	...	1	...	12
2	Hill Dist. of Arakan .	...	...	...	...	...	...	...	...
3	Kyaukpyu	..		...	...	...	...	...	...
4	Sandoway	1	1	...	...	...	...	...	.
	Pegu Division .	536	157	147	...	...	...	...	232
5	Rangoon Town ...	207	92	7	...	...	...	...	108
6	Insein	41	38	...	...	...	...	...	3
7	Hanthawaddy ...	3	...	1	...	...	...	...	2
8	Tharrawaddy ...	220	8	136	...	...	...	...	76
9	Pegu	16	2	...	...	...	...	...	14
10	Prome	49	17	3	...	...	...	...	29
	Irrawaddy Division ...	54	9	5	1	...	1	...	40
11	Bassein	8	...	1	...	...	...	...	7
12	Henzada	40	8	4	1	...	1	...	28
13	Myaungmya ...	1	...	...	...	...	...	...	1
14	Ma-ubin ...	5	1	...	...	...	...	...	4
15	Pyapôn ...	...	...	...	...	...	...	...	...
	Tenasserim Division ...	92	37	7	...	...	1	..	48
16	Toungoo	42	15	7	...	...	...	...	20
17	Salween	...	...	...	...	...	...	...	..
18	Thatôn	9	2	...	..	...	...	...	7
19	Amherst	33	13	...	...	...	...	...	20
20	Tavoy	8	7	...	...	...	1	...	1
21	Mergui	...	...	...	...	...	...	...	...
	Magwe Division ...	632	215	26	2	...	17	4	391
22	Thayetmyo ...	32	12	4	...	...	...	.	16
23	Pakôkku	416	139	18	..	...	8	3	259
24	Minbu	122	34	4	...	...	4	1	84
25	Magwe	62	30	...	2	...	5	.	32
26	Pakôkku Hill Tracts ...	...	...	...	...	...	...	...	...
	Mandalay Division ...	304	87	21	...	...	5	...	196
27	Mandalay	294	80	21	...	..	4	...	193
	Mandalay City ...	*231*	*63*	*20*	...	...	...	...	148
28	Bhamo	4	1	...	...	...	1	...	3
29	Myitkyina	...	...		...	...	...	...	...
30	Katha	6	6	...	...	...	..	...	...
31	Putao	...	...	...	...	...	..	...	...
	Sagaing Division ...	591	276	79	17	7	20	5	236
32	Shwebo	72	41	5	...	...	4	...	26
33	Sagaing	329	153	39	6	7	4	5	137
34	Lower Chindwin ...	175	77	34	11	...	12	...	64
35	Upper Chindwin ...	15	5	1	...	...	...	...	9
36	Chin Hills	...	...	...	...	...	...	..	...
	Meiktila Division ..	478	139	11	7	...	4	...	328
37	Kyauksè	49	8	...	...	...	...	...	41
38	Meiktila	159	46	7	...	...	2	...	106
39	Yamèthin ...	139	37	...	4	...	1	...	102
40	Myingyan	131	48	4	3	...	1		79
	Eastern States ...	100	30	46	...	1	3	1	24
41	Northern Shan States ...	95	28	46	...	1	3	1	21
42	Southern Shan States ...	5	2	...	...	...	...	...	3
43	Karenni	...	...	...	...	...	...	...	...

and insurance—*continued*.

Order XXVIII.—Trade in wood (not firewood), cork, bark, bamboo, thatch, etc., and articles made from these. (Groups 125a and 125b.)								Order XXIX.—Trade in metals, machinery, knives, tools, etc. (Group 126.)								Serial No. of District, etc (column 1).
Total Workers and Dependents.	WORKERS. Total Workers.		Workers with an agricultural or other subsidiary occupation. Agricultural.		Other.		DEPENDENTS.	Total Workers and Dependents.	WORKERS. Total Workers.		Workers with an agricultural or other subsidiary occupation. Agricultural.		Other.		DEPENDENTS.	
	Males.	Females.	Males.	Females.	Males.	Females.			Males.	Females.	Males.	Females.	Males.	Females.		
10	11	12	13	14	15	16	17	18	19	20	21	22	23	24	25	
34,519	11,325	4,328	552	78	960	176	18,866	4,795	1,240	954	3	13	24	6	2,601	
33,421	10,895	4,196	536	72	916	1	18,330	4,753	1,230	951	3	13	21	6	2,572	
2,038	923	89	225	...	177	1	1,026	81	55	...	...	...	...	...	26	
1,821	868	60	222	...	172	1	893	74	53	...	...	...	...	...	21	1
5	2	...	1	...	...	...	3	...	...	...	...	...	...	...	...	2
43	...	21	...	...	...	...	22	...	..	...	...	...	...	...	...	3
169	53	8	2	..	5	..	108	7	2	...	...	...	...	...	5	4
7,588	2,994	827	41	12	143	20	3,767	1,997	453	322	..	12	2	3	1,222	
1,666	710	80	...	..	4	...	876	882	315	20	...	..	...	...	547	5
887	425	97	5	...	48	..	365	27	6	2	...	...	...	...	19	6
1,488	698	279	23		33	4	511	85	19	18	...	...	...	...	48	7
579	196	79	5	6	17	1	304	759	24	273	...	12	...	3	462	8
1,677	530	142	8	6	35	8	1,005	96	40	1	..	...	...	...	55	9
1,291	435	150	...	...	6	7	706	148	49	8	...	...	2	...	91	10
4,193	1,290	538	34	6	100	26	2,365	397	103	17	..	...	2	..	187	
2,468	817	231	23	3	57	15	1,420	96	34	6	...	..	1	...	56	11
710	130	134	3	2	18	7	446	82	22	9	...	...	...	...	51	12
261	69	18	7	...	7	..	174	23	5	2	...	..	...	...	16	13
531	195	138	1	1	7	2	198	78	24	...	...	...	...	...	54	14
223	79	17	...	...	11	2	127	28	18	..	...	...	1	...	10	15
4,180	1,101	441	14	1	45	12	2,638	908	185	431	...	..	2	...	292	
1,224	351	73	4	1	13	...	800	64	13	7	...	.	...	...	44	16
75	22	13	2	...	1	..	40	4	1	1	...	..	...	...	2	17
1,105	436	118	3	...	16	3	551	49	27	...	...	...	..	...	22	18
1,612	245	216	5	...	13	6	1,151	333	106	25	...	...	2	...	202	19
124	31	20	..	...	1	3	73	449	34	396	...	...	...	...	19	20
40	16	1	...	...	1	...	23	9	4	2	...	.	..	...	3	21
3,901	1,211	720	33	13	181	37	1,970	349	109	24	1		5	2	216	
135	77	2	1	..	...	...	56	61	18	5	...	.	.	...	38	22
2,810	791	558	17	...	119	20	1,461	230	67	10	1	...	4	...	153	23
789	244	157	12	13	56	17	388	41	14	9	...	...	1	2	18	24
167	99	3	3	...	6	...	65	17	10	...	...	...	...	...	7	25
...	...	...	...	...	...	...	...	...	...	...	...	...	...	...	...	26
4,892	1,292	595	41	11	110	29	3,005	680	172	120	2	..	3	1	388	
1,989	569	325	8	10	12	2	1,095	611	148	111	2	...	2	1	352	27
1,294	*392*	*180*	..	...	*2*	..	*722*	*528*	*96*	*111*	...	...	..	*1*	*321*	
1,257	318	132	8	...	48	9	807	30	17	2	.	...	...	...	11	28
176	54	8	2	..	8	...	114	21	4	7	...	...	...	...	10	29
1,470	351	130	23	1	42	18	989	18	3	...	...	...	1	...	15	30
...	...	...	...	...	...	...	...	...	...	...	...	...	...	...	...	31
2,767	954	201	124	3	78	8	1,612	168	62	6	...	...	4	...	100	
537	177	63	3	...	14	1	297	84	16	3	...	...	2	...	65	32
233	73	62	1	1	5	4	98	38	28	1	...	...	...	...	9	33
935	338	49	15	...	32	...	548	39	15	2	...	...	1	...	22	34
1,057	364	27	105	2	27	3	666	7	3	...	...	...	1	...	4	35
5	2	...	...	...	...	...	3	...	...	...	...	...	...	...	...	36
3,862	1,130	785	24	26	82	25	1,947	263	91	31	...	1	3	...	141	
738	176	359	1	22	9	9	203	21	9	1	...	...	...	...	11	37
1,084	250	145	11	2	24	13	689	47	17	3	...	...	1	...	27	38
1,224	447	208	8	2	19	3	569	141	43	23	...	1	2	...	75	39
816	257	73	4	...	30	...	486	54	22	4	...	...	...	...	28	40
1,098	430	132	16	6	44	18	536	42	10	3	...	...	3	...	29	
909	372	113	14	5	30	18	424	33	4	3	...	...	2	...	26	41
182	56	16	2	1	14	...	110	9	6	...	...	...	1	...	3	42
7	2	3	...	...	...	...	2	...	...	...	...	...	...	...	...	43

Sub-Class V.—Trade, finance

DISTRICT OR STATE.	Order XXX.—Trade in pottery, bricks and tiles. (Groups 127a and 127b.)							
	Total Workers and Dependents.	WORKERS. Total Workers. Males.	WORKERS. Total Workers. Females.	Workers with an agricultural or other subsidiary occupation. Agricultural. Males.	Agricultural. Females.	Other. Males.	Other. Females.	DEPENDENTS.
1	2	3	4	5	6	7	8	9
Provincial Total	1,603	445	336	35	...	15	19	822
Divisional Burma	1,602	444	336	35	...	15	19	822
Arakan Division	...	...	...	...	...	...	...	...
1 Akyab	...	...	...	...	...	...	...	...
2 Hill Dist. of Arakan	...	...	...	...	...	...	...	...
3 Kyaukpyu	...	...	...	...	...	...	...	...
4 Sandoway	...	...	...	...	...	...	...	...
Pegu Division	171	78	3	1	...	1	...	90
5 Rangoon Town	28	18	...	...	...	...	...	10
6 Insein	58	29	...	...	...	...	...	29
7 Hanthawaddy	41	11	2	...	...	...	...	28
8 Tharrawaddy	21	8	...	1	...	1	...	13
9 Pegu	9	1	1	...	...	...	...	7
10 Prome	14	11	...	...	...	...	...	3
Irrawaddy Division	148	95	10	1	...	...	...	43
11 Bassein	127	86	8	...	...	...	...	33
12 Henzada	3	1	...	...	...	...	...	2
13 Myaungmya	14	6	1	1	...	...	...	7
14 Ma-ubin	4	2	1	...	...	...	...	1
15 Pyapôn	...	...	...	...	...	...	...	...
Tenasserim Division	759	183	144	33	...	8	18	432
16 Toungoo	16	4	...	...	...	...	...	12
17 Salween	1	...	...	...	...	...	...	1
18 Thatôn	18	4	9	...	...	...	...	5
19 Amherst	720	175	135	33	...	8	18	410
20 Tavoy	...	...	...	...	...	...	...	...
21 Mergui	4	...	...	...	...	...	...	4
Magwe Division	226	20	127	...	...	...	1	79
22 Thayetmyo	3	1	1	...	...	...	...	1
23 Pakôkku	1	1	...	...	...	...	...	...
24 Minbu	200	7	126	...	...	...	1	67
25 Magwe	22	11	...	...	...	...	...	11
26 Pakôkku Hill Tracts	...	...	...	...	...	...	...	...
Mandalay Division	46	24	...	...	...	...	...	22
27 Mandalay	46	24	...	...	...	...	...	22
Mandalay City	42	20	...	...	...	...	...	22
28 Bhamo	...	...	...	...	...	...	...	...
29 Myitkyina	...	...	...	...	...	...	...	...
30 Katha	...	...	...	...	...	...	...	...
31 Putao	...	...	...	...	...	...	...	...
Sagaing Division	35	14	3	...	...	5	...	18
32 Shwebo	8	3	2	...	...	...	...	3
33 Sagaing	5	3	1	...	...	...	...	1
34 Lower Chindwin	17	5	-	...	...	...	...	12
35 Upper Chindwin	5	3	...	...	...	5	...	2
36 Chin Hills	...	...	...	...	...	...	...	...
Meiktila Division	217	30	49	...	...	1	...	138
37 Kyauksè	4	...	...	...	...	...	...	4
38 Meiktila	3	1	1	...	...	...	...	1
39 Yamèthin	129	28	15	...	...	1	...	86
40 Myingyan	81	1	33	...	...	...	...	47
Eastern States	1	1	...	...	...	...	...	...
41 Northern Shan States	1	1	...	...	...	...	...	...
42 Southern Shan States	...	...	...	...	...	...	...	...
43 Karenni	...	...	...	...	...	...	...	...

and insurance—*continued.*

Order XXXI.—Trade in chemical products. (Group 128.)								Order XXXII.—Hotels, cafés, restaurants, etc. (Groups 129, 130.)								Serial No. of District, etc. (column 1).
Total Workers and Dependents.	WORKERS.						DEPENDENTS.	Total Workers and Dependents.	WORKERS.						DEPENDENTS.	
	Total Workers.		Workers with an agricultural or other subsidiary occupation.						Total Workers.		Workers with an agricultural or other subsidiary occupation.					
			Agricultural.		Other.						Agricultural.		Other.			
	Males.	Females.	Males.	Females.	Males.	Females.			Males.	Females.	Males.	Females	Males.	Females.		
10	11	12	13	14	15	16	17	18	19	20	21	22	23	24	25	
9,941	2,717	1,982	38	27	195	90	5,242	49,662	17,567	9,822	119	126	671	349	22,273	
9,454	2,596	1,867	33	22	170	72	4,991	46,892	16,567	9,073	97	114	546	246	21,252	
144	50	28	1	1	4	2	66	3,006	775	682	10	3	37	23	1,549	
75	36	...	...	...	2	...	39	2,645	663	608	5	2	16	21	1,374	1
1	...	..	...	...	...	...	1	1	...	1	...	...	...	...	...	2
18	5	8	1	...	...	..	5	27	16	2	1	...	2	...	9	3
50	9	20	...	1	2	2	21	333	96	71	4	1	19	2	166	4
2,389	697	373	4	1	32	5	1,319	12,215	5,848	1,372	17	32	112	23	4,995	
559	193	40	...	...	1	...	326	4,712	3,080	144	...	...	5	2	1,488	5
197	63	15	...	...	4	...	119	832	348	93	3	...	31	...	391	6
104	22	26	1	...	2	1	56	666	316	45	1	...	5	...	305	7
608	151	159	...	..	9	1	298	1,787	500	315	2	9	20	2	972	8
391	80	46	...	...	5	2	265	2,129	840	293	10	10	38	5	996	9
530	188	87	3	1	11	1	255	2,089	764	482	1	13	13	14	843	10
1,726	447	311	2	2	29	6	968	6,906	2,479	1,137	12	14	55	23	3,290	
628	95	172	...	1	6	5	361	2,083	784	371	3	4	16	5	928	11
192	88	8	1	...	1	...	96	1,381	407	267	2	5	10	7	707	12
178	55	25	...	1	3	..	98	1,140	402	217	4	1	15	5	521	13
526	161	83	1	...	8	...	282	1,478	468	188	3	4	9	4	822	14
202	48	23	...	...	1	1	131	824	418	94	...	...	5	2	312	15
1,029	233	127	4	9	14	9	669	6,222	2,264	1,173	3	6	67	14	2,785	
357	104	21	3	2	6	...	232	1,714	667	313	..	...	23	1	734	16
...	...	..	...	...	...	...	...	51	24	...	...	...	2	...	27	17
274	65	58	1	6	2	5	151	1,666	468	410	...	...	12	4	788	18
299	42	32	...	1	6	3	225	2,080	744	382	3	...	21	9	954	19
69	7	12	...	...	...	1	50	394	215	48	...	6	4	...	131	20
30	15	4	...	...	...	...	11	317	146	20	...	...	5	...	151	21
1,174	353	268	7	4	32	18	553	1,956	1,321	1,419	15	16	74	54	2,216	
91	21	24	...	...	1	...	46	848	204	246	...	7	..	4	398	22
290	77	75	...	...	13	2	138	1,439	417	338	4	3	32	24	684	23
505	129	141	1	4	6	16	235	1,022	273	267	4	5	16	12	482	24
288	126	28	6	...	12	...	134	1,645	427	568	7	1	26	14	650	25
...	...	...	...	...	...	...	...	2	...	...	...	...	...	...	2	26
704	220	159	...	1	1	1	325	5,606	1,677	1,359	7	5	64	25	2,570	
550	187	129	...	...	1	1	234	4,362	1,214	1,157	6	...	16	2	1,991	27
453	*154*	*115*	...	...	...	...	*184*	*3,486*	*930*	*967*	...	...	*3*	*1*	*1,589*	
67	15	12	...	...	...	...	40	472	157	72	1	...	14	17	243	28
24	8	3		...	...	...	13	293	132	56	...	3	23	2	105	29
63	10	15	...	1	...	...	38	479	174	74	...	2	11	4	231	30
...	...	...	...	...	...	...	...	...	...	...	...	...	...	...	...	31
1,146	337	297	9	3	42	19	512	3,075	892	693	17	16	64	38	1,490	
525	133	154	3	2	26	8	238	921	342	65	6	...	17	1	514	32
280	82	62	..	1	5	11	136	1,005	254	266	4	11	15	24	485	33
288	93	81	6	...	7	..	114	806	243	179	7	5	30	5	384	34
53	29	...	...	...	4	...	24	338	52	183	...	...	2	8	103	35
...	...	...	...	...	...	...	...	5	1	...	...	...	...	...	4	36
1,142	259	304	6	1	16	12	579	4,906	2,311	1,238	16	22	73	46	2,357	
398	53	166	2	1	4	6	179	895	282	163	8	10	25	3	450	37
299	68	59	3	..	7	3	172	1,438	351	371	2	5	25	25	716	38
260	98	21	1	...	5	3	141	1,669	463	401	3	...	13	5	805	39
185	40	58	...	...	...	...	87	904	215	303	3	7	10	13	386	40
487	121	115	5	5	25	18	251	2,770	1,000	749	22	12	125	103	1,021	
344	88	68	4	...	15	18	188	2,396	895	648	18	12	115	99	853	41
137	31	47	1	5	10	...	59	333	92	86	4	...	10	4	155	42
6	2	...	...	...	...	...	4	41	13	15	...	...	...	...	13	43

Sub-Class V.—Trade, finance

Order XXXIII.—Other trade in foodstuffs. (Groups 131 to 139.)

Serial No.	DISTRICT OR STATE.	Total Workers and Dependents.	WORKERS. Total Workers. Males.	Total Workers. Females.	Workers with an agricultural or other subsidiary occupation. Agricultural. Males.	Agricultural. Females.	Other. Males.	Other. Females.	DEPENDENTS.
	1	2	3	4	5	6	7	8	9
	Provincial Total ...	357,040	75,839	111,743	1,444	1,559	4,373	4,039	169,458
	Divisional Burma ...	348,087	73,271	109,337	1,324	1,427	4,038	3,778	165,479
	Arakan Division ...	23,414	6,596	5,117	143	55	297	259	11,701
1	Akyab	21,506	6,261	4,353	112	18	257	189	10,892
2	Hill District of Arakan	30	7	6	...	...	...	...	17
3	Kyaukpyu	125	39	31	19	1	1	...	55
4	Sandoway	1,753	289	727	12	36	39	70	737
	Pegu Division ...	88,390	20,617	22,324	275	315	542	343	45,449
5	Rangoon Town ...	30,668	10,005	5,541	6	3	68	14	15,142
6	Insein	5,098	1,148	1,248	22	15	57	23	2,702
7	Hanthawaddy ...	13,445	1,647	4,442	22	36	62	48	7,356
8	Tharrawaddy ...	12,327	2,662	2,898	141	43	183	64	6,767
9	Pegu	14,069	3,028	3,779	58	131	130	61	7,262
10	Prome	12,763	2,127	4,416	26	84	52	133	6,220
	Irrawaddy Division ...	62,532	14,241	17,580	219	250	797	535	30,711
11	Bassein	21,806	5,514	6,521	90	126	302	231	9,771
12	Henzada	11,745	2,258	2,760	79	78	154	77	6,727
13	Myaungmya ...	7,319	2,037	1,492	16	9	143	86	3,790
14	Ma-ubin	15,291	2,898	5,218	27	28	138	127	7,175
15	Pyapôn	6,371	1,534	1,589	7	9	60	14	3,248
	Tenasserim Division ...	45,362	7,246	16,266	92	125	292	365	21,850
16	Toungoo	12,575	2,438	3,133	21	21	88	82	7,004
17	Salween	106	32	25	2	...	1	...	49
18	Thatôn	8,922	1,432	3,277	15	35	82	62	4,213
19	Amherst	12,739	2,458	3,601	34	14	70	89	6,680
20	Tavoy	8,413	658	5,306	20	55	41	132	2,449
21	Mergui - ...	2,607	228	924	...	...	10	...	1,455
	Magwe Division ...	43,279	8,131	17,177	248	333	911	824	17,971
22	Thayetmyo ...	7,346	1,086	2,961	11	11	59	71	3,299
23	Pakôkku	16,646	2,651	7,123	106	104	367	384	6,872
24	Minbu	9,329	1,809	4,090	56	154	284	249	3,430
25	Magwe	9,958	2,585	3,003	75	64	201	120	4,370
26	Pakôkku Hill Tracts ...	...	...	...	...	...	...	...	...
	Mandalay Division ...	27,221	5,139	10,528	34	53	284	304	11,554
27	Mandalay ...	19,226	3,124	7,991	3	44	45	145	7,811
	Mandalay City ...	*14,253*	*2,590*	*5,566*	*1*	...	*6*	*19*	*6,097*
28	Bhamo	3,757	774	1,535	8	5	134	102	1,448
29	Myitkyina	1,098	296	349	3	3	39	11	453
30	Katha	3,140	645	653	20	1	66	46	1,842
31	Putao	...	...	...	...	...	...	...	...
	Sagaing Division ...	25,291	5,310	9,713	197	147	577	779	10,268
32	Shwebo	5,469	1,236	1,523	28	14	101	53	2,710
33	Sagaing	9,343	1,744	4,354	77	53	146	384	3,245
34	Lower Chindwin ...	7,865	1,552	3,068	60	42	185	253	3,245
35	Upper Chindwin ...	2,610	776	768	32	38	145	89	1,066
36	Chin Hills	4	2	...	...	...	...	...	2
	Meiktila Division ...	32,598	5,991	10,632	116	149	338	369	15,975
37	Kyauksè	5,098	1,049	1,698	28	66	71	44	2,351
38	Meiktila	8,629	1,393	2,952	47	16	96	126	4,284
39	Yamèthin	10,505	2,017	2,845	19	27	98	65	5,643
40	Myingyan	8,366	1,532	3,137	22	40	73	134	3,697
	Eastern States ...	8,953	2,568	2,406	120	132	335	261	3,979
41	Northern Shan States ...	7,133	2,211	1,605	90	48	295	178	3,317
42	Southern Shan States ...	1,743	343	774	30	84	39	83	626
43	Karenni	77	4	27	...	...	1	...	36

and insurance—*continued.*

Order XXXIV.—Trade in ready-made clothing and other articles of dress and the toilet). (Group 140.)								Order XXXV.—Trade in household goods. (Groups 141, 142.)								Serial No. of District, etc. (column 1).
Total Workers and Dependents.	WORKERS. Total Workers.		Workers with an agricultural or other subsidiary occupation. Agricultural.		Other.		DEPENDENTS.	Total Workers and Dependents.	WORKERS. Total Workers.		Workers with an agricultural or other subsidiary occupation. Agricultural.		Other.		DEPENDENTS.	
	Males.	Females.	Males.	Females.	Males.	Females.			Males.	Females.	Males.	Females.	Males.	Females.		
10	11	12	13	14	15	16	17	18	19	20	21	22	23	24	25	
8,410	2,681	1,597	17	9	111	76	4,132	17,907	4,154	6,651	82	102	233	352	7,102	
8,135	2,606	1,479	12	5	107	55	4,050	17,512	3,947	6,609	63	102	213	349	6,956	
52	19	...	...	...	1	...	33	592	236	140	3	...	3	...	216	
51	18	...	...	...	1	...	33	584	236	132	3	...	3	...	216	1
...	...	...	...	...	...	...	...	...	...	...	...	...	...	...	..	2
...	...	...	...	...	...	...	...	8	...	8	...	...	...	...	...	3
1	1	.	..	...	...	...	..	...	...	...	...	...	...	...	...	4
1,805	640	265	...	...	16	...	900	3,439	764	839	9	46	17	10	1,836	
1,084	460	126	..	..	7	...	498	1,172	375	74	...	...	...	...	723	5
116	27	20	...	...	7	...	69	398	48	279	...	6	...	...	71	6
85	12	2	...	...	...	...	71	371	79	113	1	...	1	...	179	7
149	28	34	...	...	2	...	87	766	85	178	4	29	7	7	503	8
98	21	21	...	...	...	...	56	551	108	159	3	6	9	1	284	9
273	92	62	..	...	...	..	119	181	69	36	1	5	...	2	70	10
513	116	56	..	...	8	1	341	4,005	1,055	1,204	12	10	37	38	1,746	
209	54	15	...	...	4	1	140	1,372	647	132	8	4	31	3	593	11
111	24	7	...	...	...	...	80	601	54	324	2	4	5	7	223	12
85	16	6	...	...	4	...	63	532	49	381	...	...	...	5	102	13
75	15	22	...	...	...	...	38	1,397	265	340	2	2	1	23	792	14
33	7	6	...	...	...	...	20	103	40	27	...	...	...	...	36	15
652	191	131	2	...	8	5	330	1,143	132	548	...	6	5	16	463	
217	84	10	2	...	4	...	123	204	50	42	...	...	4	4	112	16
...	...	...	...	...	...	...	...	...	...	...	...	...	...	...	...	17
182	48	52		...	2	1	82	414	25	260	...	6	...	11	129	18
156	12	61	..	...	..	4	83	326	52	96	...	...	...	1	178	19
91	45	8	...	...	1	...	38	181	4	146	...	...	1	...	31	20
6	2	...	...	...	1	...	4	18	1	4	...	...	...	...	13	21
965	292	161	...	5	19	12	512	2,416	617	988	16	17	107	61	811	
142	33	30	...	5	...	...	79	85	24	21	...	1	...	...	40	22
615	205	75	...	...	15	12	335	1,182	315	567	16	3	87	48	300	23
197	45	56	..	...	2	..	96	436	84	171	...	11	9	9	181	24
11	9	..	...	...	2	...	2	713	194	229	...	2	11	4	290	25
...	...	...	..	...	...	...	...	...	...	...	...	...	...	...	...	26
1,951	775	257	2	...	17	...	919	1,639	386	641	2	4	8	26	612	
1,874	729	250	1	...	14	...	895	1,349	307	512	2	3	5	15	530	27
1,821	*704*	*250*	...	.	*14*	...	*867*	*627*	*185*	*118*	...	...	...	...	*324*	
63	35	5	1	..	1	...	23	78	39	4	...	...	...	...	35	28
5	4	1	...	...	1	...	...	29	6	10	...	...	1	...	13	29
9	7	1	...	...	1	...	1	183	34	115	...	1	2	11	34	30
...	...	...	...	...	...	...	...	...	...	...	...	...	...	...	...	31
888	316	155	5	...	21	9	417	1,970	307	974	3	6	17	63	689	
227	120	41	...	...	4	8	60	653	165	255	...	2	8	14	233	32
394	96	76	4	...	7	1	222	854	68	531	1	2	5	37	255	33
251	86	38	1	...	8	...	127	440	68	183	2	2	4	12	189	34
16	14	..	...	...	2	...	2	23	6	5	...	...	...	...	12	35
...	...	...	...	...	...	...	...	...	...	...	...	...	...	...	...	36
1,309	257	454	3	...	17	28	598	2,308	450	1,275	18	13	19	135	583	
105	35	12	2	...	2	1	58	67	44	1	1	.	3	..	22	37
354	98	76	...	...	8	6	180	199	60	64	...	1	1	...	75	38
174	28	25	...	..	2	...	121	708	240	193	12	9	6	3	275	39
676	96	341	1	..	5	21	239	1,334	106	1,017	5	3	9	132	211	40
275	75	118	5	4	4	21	82	395	207	42	19	...	20	3	146	
255	65	115	5	1	4	21	74	103	49	18	...	..	...	3	36	41
20	9	3	...	3	...	...	8	298	158	24	19	...	20	...	110	42
...	...	...	...	...	...	...	...	...	...	...	...	...	...	...	...	43

Sub-Class *V.*—Trade, finance

Order XXXVI.—Trade in building-materials other than bricks, tiles, thatch and woody materials. (Group 143.)

Serial No.	DISTRICT OR STATE.	Total Workers and Dependents.	WORKERS.						DEPENDENTS.
			Total Workers.		Workers with an agricultural or other subsidiary occupation.				
					Agricultural.		Other.		
			Males.	Females.	Males.	Females.	Males.	Females.	
	1	2	3	4	5	6	7	8	9
	Provincial Total ...	11,865	2,205	5,827	49	229	161	311	3,833
	Divisional Burma ...	11,420	2,152	5,568	47	204	149	258	3,700
	Arakan Division ...	249	91	43	2	4	4	...	115
1	Akyab	247	90	43	2	4	4	...	114
2	Hill Dist. of Arakan ...	...	...	...	...	...	...	...	...
3	Kyaukpyu	2	1	...	...	...	...	...	1
4	Sandoway	...	...	...	...	...	...	...	...
	Pegu Division ...	2,583	697	904	7	11	25	24	982
5	Rangoon Town ...	109	77	7	...	...	1	...	25
6	Insein	104	20	36	...	...	4	...	48
7	Hanthawaddy ...	1,484	312	679	5	9	16	20	493
8	Tharrawaddy ...	470	180	122	...	...	...	3	168
9	Pegu	357	99	40	1	2	4	1	218
10	Prome	59	9	20	1	...	...	...	30
	Irrawaddy Division ...	1,693	382	675	13	...	47	20	636
11	Bassein	280	180	32	12	...	15	...	140
12	Henzada	470	136	160	1	...	18	11	174
13	Myaungmya ...	233	62	54	...	...	11	6	117
14	Ma-ubin	235	48	95	...	...	...	3	92
15	Pyapôn	475	28	334	...	...	3	...	113
	Tenasserim Division ...	721	188	105	1	3	9	4	428
16	Toungoo	[illegible]91	127	27	...	2	7	1	137
17	Salween	...	...	...	...	...	...	...	...
18	Thatôn	262	47	38	...	...	1	...	177
19	Amherst	132	3	29	...	1	...	3	100
20	Tavoy	16	...	9	...	...	...	...	7
21	Mergui	20	11	2	1	...	1	...	7
	Magwe Division ...	2,665	211	2,006	6	81	7	125	448
22	Thayetmyo	269	78	86	...	1	...	...	105
23	Pakôkku	490	50	276	5	3	1	21	164
24	Minbu	1,845	61	1,640	...	77	5	104	144
25	Magwe	61	22	4	1	...	1	...	35
26	Pakôkku Hill Tracts ...	...	...	...	...	...	...	...	...
	Mandalay Division ...	1,268	273	536	9	3	20	25	459
27	Mandalay	458	185	30	5	...	8	...	243
	Mandalay City ...	*195*	*104*	*15*	...	...	...	...	*76*
28	Bhamo	423	54	252	1	...	6	5	117
29	Myitkyina	26	...	22	...	...	...	...	4
30	Katha	361	34	232	3	3	6	20	95
31	Putao	...	...	...	...	...	...	...	...
	Sagaing Division ...	534	118	230	8	15	19	29	186
32	Shwebo	149	24	77	3	...	...	9	48
33	Sagaing	168	64	40	1	...	17	3	64
34	Lower Chindwin ...	80	5	48	...	15	...	5	27
35	Upper Chindwin ...	137	25	65	4	...	2	12	47
36	Chin Hills	...	...	...	...	...	...	...	...
	Meiktila Division ...	1,707	192	1,069	1	87	18	31	446
37	Kyauksè	803	73	602	1	87	13	14	128
38	Meiktila	56	3	34	...	...	...	3	19
39	Yamèthin	536	79	284	...	...	1	7	173
40	Myingyan	312	37	149	...	...	4	7	126
	Eastern States ...	445	53	259	2	25	12	53	133
41	Northern Shan States ...	348	52	169	2	14	12	46	127
42	Southern Shan States ...	97	1	90	...	11	...	7	6
43	Karenni	...	...	...	...	...	...	...	...

and insurance—*continued.*

Order XXXVII.—Trade in means of transport. (Groups 144, 145, 146.) Total Workers and Dependents.	Workers. Total Workers. Males.	Workers. Total Workers. Females.	Workers with an agricultural or other subsidiary occupation. Agricultural. Males.	Agricultural. Females.	Other. Males.	Other. Females.	Dependents.	Order XXXVIII.—Trade in fuel. (Group 147.) Total Workers and Dependents.	Workers. Total Workers. Males.	Workers. Total Workers. Females.	Workers with an agricultural or other subsidiary occupation. Agricultural. Males.	Agricultural. Females.	Other. Males.	Other. Females.	Dependents.	Serial No. of District, etc. (column 1).
10	11	12	13	14	15	16	17	18	19	20	21	22	23	24	25	
23,739	7,338	3,028	240	100	742	377	13,373	11,568	3,732	1,832	59	40	223	114	6,004	
21,787	6,736	2,663	183	94	640	274	12,388	11,174	3,568	1,738	59	3	193	100	5,868	
3,523	722	612	47	15	87	70	2,189	394	144	45	2	...	1	4	205	
3,017	565	525	30	7	63	57	1,927	332	136	34	2	...	1	4	162	1
...	...	...	...	...	...	...	...	...	...	...	...	...	...	...	...	2
242	79	41	10	...	12	4	122	9	4	1	...	...	...	...	4	3
264	78	46	7	8	12	9	140	53	4	10	...	...	...	...	39	4
5,008	1,709	558	54	21	161	33	2,741	3,318	1,277	479	2	1	64	15	1,562	
398	170	2	...	...	...	...	226	1,234	638	125	...	...	6	...	471	5
591	220	91	4	5	24	5	280	622	220	57	2	..	30	...	345	6
365	211	21	3	...	25	...	133	141	43	20	...	...	1	...	78	7
1,642	441	239	33	11	54	18	962	86	13	...	...	.	2	...	73	8
1,245	442	141	14	...	56	1	662	831	275	110	...	1	25	13	446	9
767	225	64	..	5	2	9	478	404	88	167	...	...	...	2	149	10
3,360	1,015	388	24	22	102	29	1,957	1,818	705	212	10		22	12	901	
973	312	56	7	3	38	4	605	632	264	73	3	...	5	2	295	11
940	246	192	5	17	37	15	502	202	87	17	4	...	1	4	98	12
143	79	20	1	1	5	...	44	551	212	98	...	...	11	4	241	13
1,123	262	109	11	1	22	10	752	266	72	24	3	...	2	2	170	14
181	116	11	...	...	...	..	54	167	70	...	...	...	3	...	97	15
3,213	1,202	273	25	5	93	25	1,738	1,428	309	196	3	2	18	6	923	
1,247	408	154	5	4	56	18	665	118	30	33	...	...	4	...	55	16
60	25	...	2	...	2	...	35	...	...	...	...	...	...	...	...	17
839	298	74	6	...	19	1	467	622	169	37	3	...	7	...	416	18
834	363	33	3	...	3	...	438	571	106	51	...	...	6	2	414	19
199	69	12	9	1	12	6	118	113	2	75	...	2	1	4	36	20
34	19	...	...	...	1	...	15	4	2	..	...	...	...	...	2	21
1,382	485	187	4	5	49	12	710	1,067	224	268	. .	9	15	35	575	
319	43	77	..	2	3	2	199	197	31	64	...	4	2	4	102	22
769	354	14	3	...	37	...	401	691	143	140	...	5	10	31	408	23
165	47	57	...	2	7	10	61	115	7	64	...	...	2	...	44	24
129	41	39	1	1	2	...	49	64	43	...	...	...	1	.	21	25
...	...	...	...	...	...	...	...	..	...	...	...	...	...	...	..	26
1,865	637	194	11	10	74	54	1,034	1,318	378	285	11	18	20	16	655	
819	265	16	...	...	3	...	538	861	207	221	4	18	10	10	433	27
653	*212*	*8*	...	..	...	...	*433*	*518*	*188*	*95*	*3*	..	*9*	*3*	*235*	
161	59	14	2	...	14	10	88	104	44	11	...	...	3	...	49	28
201	62	53	3	...	9	12	86	9	2	...	1	..	...	...	7	29
679	250	111	6	10	48	32	318	344	125	53	6	...	7	6	166	30
5	1	..	...	..	...	...	4	...	...	...	...	...	...	...	...	31
1,463	350	276	7	15	17	38	837	987	239	161	3	...	26	9	587	
382	101	55	1	...	2	2	226	511	199	3	3		18	...	309	32
263	108	2	..	...	6	1	153	240	6	109	...	.	...	...	185	33
428	133	40	5	...	6	...	249	142	26	33	...	...	7	9	83	34
396	8	179	1	15	3	35	209	94	8	16	...	...	1	...	70	35
...	...	.	...	...	...	...	...	...	...	...	...	...	...	...	...	36
1,973	616	175	11	1	57	13	1,182	844	292	92	28	3	27	3	460	
224	64	29	3	..	5	...	131	240	97	23	16	3	7	2	120	37
666	168	55	2	1	17	11	443	86	15	24	...	.	1	1	47	38
804	262	64	3	...	34	2	478	356	98	31	10	...	15	...	287	39
279	122	27	3	...	1	...	130	162	82	14	2	...	4		66	40
1,952	602	365	57	6	102	103	985	394	164	94	...	7	30	14	136	
899	286	179	27	3	35	54	434	283	139	55	...	1	17	2	89	41
1,015	297	185	28	3	66	49	533	111	25	39	...	6	13	12	47	42
38	19	1	2	...	1	...	18	...	...	...	...	.	...	...	...	43

Sub-Class V.—Trade, finance

Order XXXIX.—Trade in articles of luxury and articles pertaining to letters or to the arts or sciences. (Groups 148, 149, 150.)

Serial No.	District or State.	Total Workers and Dependents.	Workers. Total Workers. Males.	Females.	Workers with an agricultural or other subsidiary occupation. Agricultural. Males.	Females.	Other. Males.	Females.	Dependents.
	1	2	3	4	5	6	7	8	9
	Provincial Total ...	14,176	4,189	2,170	15	8	179	55	7,817
	Divisional Burma ...	13,844	4,059	2,094	12	7	172	53	7,691
	Arakan Division ...	116	80	4	...	...	1	2	32
1	Akyab ...	91	68	...	...	...	...	...	23
2	Hill Dist. of Arakan ...	...	...	...	...	...	...	...	...
3	Kyaukpyu ...	3	3	...	...	...	...	...	...
4	Sandoway ...	22	9	4	...	...	1	2	9
	Pegu Division ...	3,176	892	555	2	...	11	1	1,729
5	Rangoon Town ...	2,100	587	426	...	...	4	...	1,087
6	Insein ...	206	63	15	1	...	1	...	128
7	Hanthawaddy ...	86	17	25	1	...	...	...	44
8	Tharrawaddy ...	158	48	7	...	...	5	...	103
9	Pegu ...	227	64	10	...	...	...	1	153
10	Prome ...	399	113	72	...	...	1	...	214
	Irrawaddy Division ...	1,029	232	158	...	1	15	9	639
11	Bassein ...	283	81	11	...	...	9	1	191
12	Henzada ...	337	64	88	...	1	5	7	185
13	Myaungmya ...	102	32	11	...	...	1	1	59
14	Ma-ubin ...	244	46	40	...	...	...	...	158
15	Pyapôn ...	63	9	8	...	...	...	...	46
	Tenasserim Division ...	1,275	375	142	1	...	15	1	758
16	Toungoo ...	148	54	9	...	...	5	...	85
17	Salween ...	...	...	...	...	...	...	...	...
18	Thatôn ...	287	109	34	...	...	1	...	144
19	Amherst ...	537	161	64	1	...	8	...	312
20	Tavoy ...	153	17	29	...	...	1	1	107
21	Mergui ...	150	34	6	...	...	...	...	110
	Magwe Division ...	763	108	150	1	1	...	4	505
22	Thayetmyo ...	66	13	30	...	...	...	...	23
23	Pakôkku ...	543	42	99	...	1	...	3	402
24	Minbu ...	118	34	18	...	...	...	1	66
25	Magwe ...	36	19	3	1	...	...	...	14
26	Pakôkku Hill Tracts ...	...	...	...	...	...	...	...	...
	Mandalay Division ...	6,226	1,958	862	3	2	114	12	3,406
27	Mandalay ...	3,009	856	710	...	...	12	4	1,443
	Mandalay City ...	2,927	822	698	...	...	11	4	1,407
28	Bhamo ...	67	26	14	...	2	1	...	27
29	Myitkyina ...	572	206	31	2	...	65	3	335
30	Katha ...	2,578	870	107	1	...	36	5	1,601
31	Putao ...	...	...	...	...	...	...	...	...
	Sagaing Division ...	642	182	125	3	1	9	20	335
32	Shwebo ...	323	85	76	1	...	4	12	162
33	Sagaing ...	141	51	29	1	1	3	3	61
34	Lower Chindwin ...	123	31	12	1	...	1	...	80
35	Upper Chindwin ...	55	15	8	...	...	1	5	32
36	Chin Hills ...	...	...	...	...	...	...	...	...
	Meiktila Division ...	617	232	98	2	2	7	4	287
37	Kyauksè ...	57	25	8	1	...	2	...	24
38	Meiktila ...	171	88	19	1	...	4	...	64
39	Yamèthin ...	224	65	23	...	...	1	...	136
40	Myingyan ...	165	54	48	...	2	...	4	63
	Eastern States ...	332	130	76	3	1	7	2	126
41	Northern Shan States ...	298	112	74	3	1	7	2	112
42	Southern Shan States ...	28	17	1	...	...	...	...	10
43	Karenni ...	6	1	1	...	...	...	...	4

Part III.—Details by districts—contd.

and insurance—*continued.*								Sub-Class *VI*.—Public force.								
Order XL.—Trade of other sorts. (Groups 151 to 154.)								Order XLI.—Army, XLII.—Navy, and XLIII.—Air-force.* (Groups 155 to 158 inclusive.)								Serial No. of District, etc. (column 1).
Total Workers and Dependents.	Workers. Total Workers.		Workers with an agricultural or other subsidiary occupation. Agricultural.		Other.		Dependents.	Total Workers and Dependents.	Workers. Total Workers.		Workers with an agricultural or other subsidiary occupation. Agricultural.		Other.		Dependents.	
	Males.	Females.	Males.	Females.	Males.	Females.			Males.	Females.	Males.	Females.	Males.	Females.		
10	11	12	13	14	15	16	17	18	19	20	21	22	23	24	25	
454,857	104,137	140,263	2,555	2,509	5,633	4,326	210,457	11,026	7,839	21	567	...	4	...	3,166	
414,742	91,858	128,773	1,257	1,767	4,603	3,288	194,111	9,611	7,132	19	499	...	3	...	2,460	
24,971	6,803	6,527	65	148	281	255	11,641	133	116	...	1	...	...	...	17	
12,973	4,529	2,428	74	17	138	75	6,016	130	116	...	1	...	...	...	14	1
208	117	23	1	...	...	...	68	2	...	...	...	...	...	...	2	2
9,803	1,830	3,423	81	124	119	166	4,550	...	...	...	...	...	...	...	...	3
1,987	327	653	9	7	24	14	1,007	1	...	...	...	...	...	...	1	4
98,933	23,101	26,333	176	482	1,117	460	49,499	1,717	1,284	1	3	...	...	...	432	
19,388	8,260	1,876	11	...	39	4	9,252	1,422	1,026	1	...	...	...	...	395	5
13,944	2,816	4,088	10	43	170	78	7,040	12	2	...	...	...	...	...	10	6
16,689	3,593	4,208	32	46	453	74	8,888	35	32	...	...	...	...	...	3	7
14,183	2,288	5,016	53	96	141	58	6,859	25	9	...	...	...	...	...	16	8
22,285	4,683	6,282	68	215	207	126	11,370	48	46	...	...	...	...	...	2	9
12,444	1,511	4,843	2	82	107	120	6,090	175	169	...	3	...	...	...	6	10
120,558	28,294	37,596	366	467	1,261	776	54,768	155	92	...	1	...	...	...	63	
23,523	5,504	7,585	62	86	322	155	10,414	57	9	...	...	...	...	...	48	11
29,405	5,355	11,021	86	234	248	290	13,029	29	25	...	...	...	...	...	4	12
31,590	7,896	8,797	120	67	391	204	14,897	15	6	...	...	...	...	...	9	13
16,862	4,171	5,511	51	39	169	84	7,180	4	4	...	1	...	...	...	...	14
19,178	5,248	4,682	47	41	131	43	9,248	50	48	...	...	...	...	...	2	15
54,072	11,701	16,466	133	96	548	411	25,905	275	194	...	...	...	...	...	81	
15,821	3,287	4,377	19	28	109	63	8,157	26	5	...	...	...	...	...	21	16
986	299	126	3	3	9	2	561	...	...	...	...	...	...	...	...	17
20,215	4,383	6,855	56	39	178	171	9,027	7	...	...	...	...	...	...	7	18
9,418	2,452	2,479	32	12	141	94	4,487	149	115	...	...	...	...	...	34	19
3,534	854	1,217	18	13	69	67	1,463	13	1	...	...	...	...	...	12	20
4,098	476	1,412	5	1	42	14	2,210	80	73	...	...	...	...	...	7	21
27,521	5,084	9,870	129	183	306	374	12,567	162	148	2	...	...	...	...	12	
7,343	947	2,172	4	13	36	59	4,224	6	3	2	...	...	...	...	1	22
6,349	1,272	2,073	36	24	114	118	3,004	145	137	...	...	...	...	...	8	23
7,537	1,514	2,959	48	102	136	145	3,064	5	5	...	...	...	...	...	...	24
6,291	1,350	2,666	41	44	20	52	2,275	4	3	...	...	...	...	...	1	25
1	1	...	...	...	...	...	...	2	...	...	...	...	...	...	2	26
30,271	6,686	10,031	100	81	374	282	13,554	5,690	4,234	8	453	...	2	...	1,448	
16,478	3,266	6,510	6	40	61	66	6,702	4,229	2,989	7	449	...	1	...	1,233	27
9,752	*2,059*	*3,414*	...	*1*	*1*	*6*	*4,279*	*2,680*	*1,935*	*5*	*449*	...	*1*	...	*740*	
1,469	382	368	5	2	49	17	769	1,090	939	1	...	...	...	...	150	28
1,664	552	392	1	...	85	23	720	127	80	...	4	...	1	...	47	29
10,619	2,513	2,756	88	39	179	176	5,350	241	223	...	...	...	...	...	18	30
41	23	5	...	...	...	...	13	3	3	...	...	...	...	...	...	31
23,122	4,455	8,607	102	92	436	367	10,060	598	468	...	41	...	1	...	130	
8,168	1,541	2,974	24	2	133	40	3,653	296	219	...	...	...	...	...	77	32
5,767	695	2,925	40	33	51	170	2,147	107	92	...	...	...	...	...	15	33
3,857	934	1,243	5	28	18	53	1,680	13	12	...	...	...	1	...	1	34
5,237	1,257	1,465	33	29	232	104	2,515	33	30	...	...	...	...	...	3	35
93	28	...	...	...	2	...	65	149	115	...	41	...	...	...	34	36
35,294	5,884	13,343	86	218	280	363	16,117	881	596	8	...	...	...	...	277	
2,779	277	1,215	6	22	25	22	1,287	2	2	...	...	...	...	...	...	37
7,480	1,037	3,154	18	67	66	121	3,291	591	415	8	...	...	...	...	168	38
6,584	1,357	1,637	7	13	43	31	3,588	278	174	...	...	...	...	...	104	39
18,451	3,163	7,337	55	116	146	189	7,951	10	5	...	...	...	...	...	5	40
40,115	12,279	11,490	1,298	742	1,030	1,038	16,346	1,415	707	2	68	...	1	...	706	
7,512	2,639	1,753	73	58	221	177	3,120	377	213	2	67	...	...	...	162	41
28,581	8,350	8,905	1,173	654	707	841	11,326	974	439	...	1	...	1	...	535	42
4,022	1,290	832	52	30	102	20	1,900	64	55	...	...	...	...	...	9	43

* All the figures under this heading belonged to Group 155 of Order XLI, Imperial Army, except one male worker in Meiktila district who belonged to Group 156 of the same Order (Indian State or foreign armies). The entries for Orders XLII and XLIII were *nil*.

Sub-Class *VI*.—Public force—*concluded*.

Order XLIV.—Police and professional village-watchmen. (Groups 159, 160.)

Serial No.	DISTRICT OR STATE.	Total Workers and Dependents.	WORKERS. Total Workers. Males.	Females.	Workers with an agricultural or other subsidiary occupation. Agricultural. Males.	Females.	Other. Males.	Females.	DEPENDENTS.
	1	2	3	4	5	6	7	8	9
	Provincial Total ...	65,374	29,789	448	212	1	151	39	35,137
	Divisional Burma ...	61,101	27,655	303	165	...	135	28	33,143
	Arakan Division ...	3,860	1,345	62	3	...	6	...	2,453
1	Akyab	1,407	591	1	2	...	..	...	815
2	Hill Dist. of Arakan ...	519	249	...	1	...	2	...	270
3	Kyaukpyu	807	121	61	...	...	...	...	685
4	Sandoway ...	1,067	384	...	...	...	4	...	683
	Pegu Division	13,365	6,068	76	99	...	20	...	7,221
5	Rangoon Town ...	3,954	2,276	4	4	...	2	...	1,674
6	Insein	1,508	623	47	..	...	...	...	838
7	Hanthawaddy ...	1,898	843	21	..	...	1	...	1,034
8	Tharrawaddy ..	2,261	837	...	...	...	1	...	1,424
9	Pegu	2,110	865	2	95	...	14	...	1,243
10	Prome	1,634	624	2	...	...	2	...	1,008
	Irrawaddy Division ...	7,071	2,864	10	1	...	1	...	4,197
11	Bassein	2,132	895	...	...	...	...	...	1,237
12	Henzada	1,848	671	..	...	...	1	...	1,177
13	Myaungmya ...	1,163	512	6	...	...	...	...	645
14	Ma-ubin	1,015	420	4	..	...	...	...	591
15	Pyapôn	913	366	..	1	...	...	...	547
	Tenasserim Division ...	7,149	3,299	43	3	...	11	19	3,807
16	Toungoo	1,801	980	13	...	...	4	...	808
17	Salween	362	238	18	1	...	1	18	106
18	Thatôn	1,795	648	8	1	...	2	1	1,139
19	Amherst	1,605	707	3	...	...	3	...	895
20	Tavoy	910	454	1	1	...	...	...	455
21	Mergui	656	272	...	...	...	1	...	384
	Magwe Division ...	5,845	2,267	5	1	...	...	...	3,573
22	Thayetmyo	1,466	428	...	...	...	...	...	1,038
23	Pakôkku	1,618	474	...	1	...	...	...	1,144
24	Minbu	1,443	580	1	...	...	...	...	862
25	Magwe ...	1,171	655	4	...	...	...	...	512
26	Pakôkku Hill Tracts ..	147	130	...	...	...	...	...	17
	Mandalay Division ...	11,552	6,562	63	5	...	10	8	4,927
27	Mandalay	4,140	2,342	8	...	...	1	...	1,790
	Mandalay City ...	*1,850*	*908*	...	...	...	...	...	*942*
28	Bhamo	1,468	1,047	...	...	...	...	...	421
29	Myitkyina	3,517	1,976	3	5	...	2	..	1,538
30	Katha	1,607	626	52	...	...	7	8	929
31	Putao	820	571	...	...	...	...	...	249
	Sagaing Division ...	6,164	2,927	35	53	...	84	1	3,202
32	Shwebo	1,670	604	32	...	...	1	...	1,034
33	Sagaing	807	302	1	...	...	...	1	504
34	Lower Chindwin ...	1,359	698	1	...	...	...	...	660
35	Upper Chindwin ..	1,324	747	1	...	...	82	...	576
36	Chin Hills	1,004	576	...	53	...	1	...	428
	Meiktila Division ..	6,095	2,323	9	...	...	3	...	3,763
37	Kyauksè	1,125	346	...	...	...	1	..	779
38	Meiktila	1,276	520	4	...	...	2	...	752
39	Yamèthin	2,122	911	5	...	...	...	...	1,206
40	Myingyan	1,572	546	...	...	...	...	...	1,026
	Eastern States ...	4,273	2,134	145	47	1	16	11	1,994
41	Northern Shan States ...	2,064	1,425	132	10	1	11	11	507
42	Southern Shan States ...	2,086	680	13	37	.	5	...	1,393
43	Karenni	123	29	...	...	...	...	...	94

PART III.—*Details by districts*—*contd.*

Sub-Class *VII.*—Public administration. Order XLV.—Public administration. (Groups 161 to 164.) Total Workers and Dependents.	Workers. Total Workers. Males.	Workers. Total Workers. Females.	Workers with an agricultural or other subsidiary occupation. Agricultural. Males.	Agricultural. Females.	Other. Males.	Other. Females.	Dependents.	Sub-Class *VIII.*—The professions and liberal arts. Order XLVI.—Religion. (Groups 165 to 168.) Total Workers and Dependents.	Workers. Total Workers. Males.	Workers. Total Workers. Females.	Workers with an agricultural or other subsidiary occupation. Agricultural. Males.	Agricultural. Females.	Other. Males.	Other. Females.	Dependents.	Serial No. of District, etc. (column 1).
10	11	12	13	14	15	16	17	18	19	20	21	22	23	24	25	
103,041	33,242	992	9,102	90	1,763	42	68,807	155,310	97,077	8,024	71	10	318	14	50,209	
83,598	26,418	795	5,181	84	1,227	38	56,385	126,987	75,398	7,032	54	5	97	2	44,557	
5,343	1,259	25	374	2	43	...	4,059	5,782	2,541	217	12	...	26	1	3,024	
3,330	793	4	170	...	21	...	2,533	3,628	1,432	195	10	...	18	...	2,001	1
115	25	...	8	...	...	...	90	17	10	2	...	...	...	...	5	2
1,024	235	20	101	2	14	...	769	1,429	752	3	...	...	2	..	674	3
874	206	1	95	...	8	..	667	708	347	17	2	...	6	1	344	4
21,338	6,997	247	556	...	259	...	14,094	23,003	12,625	1,482	7	1	4	...	8,896	
10,262	3,742	174	4	...	13	...	6,346	5,988	2,702	518	..	...	...	...	2,768	5
2,614	640	26	34	...	17	...	1,948	2,226	1,211	141	2	1	2	...	874	6
1,159	463	2	147	...	28	...	694	3,691	1,950	217	...	...	..	...	1,524	7
2,762	713	6	42	...	127	...	2,043	3,378	2,117	191	4	...	2	...	1,070	8
2,560	696	11	164	...	53	...	1,853	4,231	2,956	326	1	...	...	...	949	9
1,981	743	28	165	...	21	...	1,210	3,489	1,689	89	...	...	...	..	1,711	10
12,039	3,607	112	889	20	228	13	8,320	14,566	8,945	721	12	...	9	...	4,900	
3,366	1,104	8	231	2	85	...	2,254	3,701	2,640	148	...	...	...	...	913	11
2.867	910	47	239	14	45	6	1,910	3,894	2,447	194	11	...	3	...	1,253	12
2,433	708	40	230	...	44	...	1,685	1,994	1,069	108	...	...	2	...	817	13
1,754	486	12	72	1	28	7	1,256	2,505	1,313	141	1	...	1	...	10,51	14
1,619	399	5	117	3	26	...	1,115	2,472	1,476	130	...	...	3	...	866	15
11,313	3,970	43	423	2	90	6	7,300	14,442	7,830	1,017	17	2	18	..	5,595	
3,266	1,311	5	112	...	29	..	1,950	3,321	2,035	199	12	2	10	...	1,087	16
208	55	...	10	...	2	...	153	196	76	3	...	...	1	...	117	17
2,235	725	17	149	2	19	1	1,493	3,593	1,904	249	2	..	...	...	1,440	18
3,015	1,031	11	39	...	3	3	1,973	4,485	2,551	349	...	...	...	...	1,585	19
1,200	459	8	72	...	16	2	733	1,906	877	205	1	...	4	...	824	20
1,389	389	2	41	...	21	...	998	941	387	12	2	...	3	...	542	21
8,940	2,503	82	838	13	243	4	6,355	17,485	10,809	440	...	...	3	..	6,231	
2,207	602	14	172	6	31	1	1,591	2,632	1,015	102	..	...	1	..	1,515	22
2,791	787	4	377	...	53	2	2,000	6,186	4,271	211	.	..	...	...	1,704	23
2,217	517	16	191	1	32	1	1,684	4,105	1,922	110	...	...	2	...	2,073	24
1,705	593	48	98	6	127	...	1,064	4,562	3,601	17	...	...	...	...	944	25
20	4	...	...	...	...	...	16	...	...	...	...	...	...	...	...	26
7,735	2,712	106	514	23	157	6	4,917	14,912	8,966	646	2	...	15	1	5,300	
3,639	1,436	29	47	...	53	...	2,174	8,912	6,769	262	...	...	3	...	1,881	27
1,870	813	6	6	...	12	...	1,051	6,293	4,644	143	...	.	...	...	1,506	
762	191	2	69	...	26	1	569	912	346	93	1	...	1	...	473	28
893	284	5	88	1	19	...	604	565	347	25	-	...	6	...	193	29
2,294	726	70	302	22	59	5	1,498	4,475	1,471	262	1	...	5	1	2,742	30
147	75	...	8	...	...	...	72	48	33	4	...	...	...	...	11	31
8,382	2,878	98	1,064	11	143	3	5,406	21,834	13,760	1,595	2	...	5	...	6,479	
2,352	738	86	270	10	29	1	1,528	6,167	4,742	241	1	...	2	..	1,184	32
1,990	650	3	153	1	29	1	1,337	7,276	3,457	1,080	1	...	...	...	2,739	33
1,298	549	...	194	...	33	...	749	5,335	3,926	116	...	..	3	...	1,293	34
2,303	636	9	242	..	45	1	1,658	3,013	1,623	158	...	...	...	...	1,232	35
439	305	...	205	...	7	...	134	43	12	...	...	...	...	.	31	36
8,508	2,492	82	523	13	64	6	5,934	14,963	9,922	914	2	2	17	...	4,127	
1,746	550	..	176	...	7	...	1,196	1,599	1,022	181	1	1	..	...	396	37
1,913	507	43	36	8	20	3	1,363	4,034	3,299	387	...	...	1	...	348	38
2,787	743	39	148	5	25	3	2,005	3,840	2,519	156	1	1	15	...	1,165	39
2,062	692	...	163	...	12	...	1,370	5,490	3,082	190	...	.	1	...	2,218	40
19,443	6,824	197	3,921	6	536	4	12,422	28,323	21,679	992	17	5	221	12	5,652	
4,019	1,163	81	.403	2	108	3	2,775	7,725	5,326	687	1	1	214	12	1,712	41
14,948	5,507	105	3,501	2	427	1	9,336	20,040	16,131	296	16	4	7	...	3,813	42
476	154	11	17	2	1	...	311	358	282	9	...	...	...	...	127	43

Sub-Class *VIII.*—The

Order XLVII.—Law. (Groups 169, 170.)

Serial No.	DISTRICT OR STATE.	Total Workers and Dependents.	WORKERS. Total Workers. Males.	Total Workers. Females.	Workers with an agricultural or other subsidiary occupation. Agricultural. Males.	Agricultural. Females.	Other. Males.	Other. Females.	DEPENDENTS.
	1	2	3	4	5	6	7	8	9
	Provincial Total ...	10,936	2,779	93	64	...	95	2	8,064
	Divisional Burma ...	10,847	27,55	84	64	...	95	2	8,008
	Arakan Division ...	610	124	...	4	...	4	...	486
1	Akyab	476	108	...	2	...	3	...	368
2	Hill Dist. of Arakan ...	...	...	...	...	...	...	...	...
3	Kyaukpyu	88	7	...	1	...	...	...	81
4	Sandoway	46	9	...	1	...	1	...	37
	Pegu Division ...	3,298	806	40	9	..	14	1	2,452
5	Rangoon Town ...	1,318	371	...	3	...	10	...	947
6	Insein	344	86	7	...	...	1	...	251
7	Hanthawaddy ...	233	44	...	2	...	...	...	189
8	Tharrawaddy ...	411	84	...	...	...	..	...	327
9	Pegu	731	154	32	4	...	1	1	545
10	Prome	261	67	1	...	...	2	...	193
	Irrawaddy Division ...	1,774	429	...	5	...	10	...	1,345
11	Bassein	436	136	...	..	...	...	...	300
12	Henzada	363	81	...	1	...	3	...	282
13	Myaungmya ...	428	98	...	3	...	3	...	330
14	Ma-ubin	350	84	...	1	...	3	...	266
15	Pyapôn	197	30	...	...	...	1	...	167
	Tenasserim Division ...	1,228	258	1	7	...	7	..	969
16	Toungoo	225	38	...	...	...	1	...	187
17	Salween	23	5	...	...	...	1	...	18
18	Thatôn	345	74	...	2	...	...	...	271
19	Amherst	393	86	1	5	..	...	...	306
20	Tavoy	131	30	...	...	...	2	...	101
21	Mergui	111	25	...	...	...	3	...	86
	Magwe Division ...	964	292	15	9	...	20	1	657
22	Thayetmyo ...	282	61	15	..	...	...	1	206
23	Pakôkku	158	81	...	3	...	7	...	77
24	Minbu	251	58	...	6	...	3	...	193
25	Magwe	272	91	...	...	...	10	...	181
26	Pakôkku Hill Tracts ...	1	1	...	...	.	...	...	...
	Mandalay Division ...	880	304	4	6	...	11	...	572
27	Mandalay	646	240	3	4	...	9	...	403
	Mandalay City ...	*464*	*171*	*3*	...	...	...	...	*290*
28	Bhamo	38	8	...	...	...	...	...	30
29	Myitkyina	95	28	1	...	...	1	...	66
30	Katha	82	19	...	...	...	1	...	63
31	Putao	19	9	...	2	..	...	...	10
	Sagaing Division ...	913	272	21	18	...	9	...	620
32	Shwebo	254	47	21	-	...	...	...	186
33	Sagaing	303	114	...	10	...	...	...	189
34	Lower Chindwin ...	196	74	...	6	...	8	...	122
35	Upper Chindwin ...	90	19	...	1	...	1	...	71
36	Chin Hills	70	18	...	1	...	...	...	52
	Meiktila Division ...	1,180	270	3	6	...	20	...	907
37	Kyauksè	148	33	...	...	..	11	...	115
38	Meiktila	340	74	...	4	...	5	...	266
39	Yamèthin	404	88	3	2	...	4	.	313
40	Myingyan	288	75	...	...	...	...	...	213
	Eastern States ...	89	24	9	...	...	...	...	56
41	Northern Shan States ...	37	8	...	...	...	...	...	29
42	Southern Shan States ...	32	13	9	...	...	...	...	10
43	Karenni	20	3	...	...	...	...	...	17

professions and liberal arts—*continued.*

Order XLVIII.—Medicine. (Groups 171, 172.)								Order XLIX.—Instruction. (Groups 173, 174.)								Serial No. of District, etc. (column 1).
Total Workers and Dependents.	WORKERS.						DEPENDENTS.	Total Workers and Dependents.	WORKERS.						DEPENDENTS.	
	Total Workers.		Workers with an agricultural or other subsidiary occupation.						Total Workers.		Workers with an agricultural or other subsidiary occupation.					
			Agricultural.		Other.						Agricultural.		Other.			
	Males.	Females.	Males.	Females.	Males.	Females.			Males.	Females.	Males.	Females.	Males.	Females.		
10	11	12	13	14	15	16	17	18	19	20	21	22	23	24	25	
56,258	20,564	3,332	719	26	1,205	78	32,362	33,794	11,940	2,955	267	22	391	77	18,899	
51,794	18,697	3,241	500	22	1,012	76	29,856	32,237	11,336	2,869	206	21	358	76	18,032	
3,975	1,562	103	43	...	48	1	2,310	1,721	726	73	9	...	34	...	922	
2,844	1,170	61	16	..	17	1	1,613	1,098	496	36	7	...	20	...	566	1
24	10	...	...	...	...	..	14	5	...	...	...	...	...	...	5	2
705	238	32	18	...	20	...	435	280	119	17	...	...	6	...	144	3
402	144	10	9	...	11	.	248	338	111	20	2	...	8	...	207	4
12,257	4,499	659	51	1	215	3	7,099	11,071	3,641	854	46	1	95	13	6,576	
3,565	1,085	290	1	...	19	...	2,190	4,227	1,581	431	...	...	10	5	2,215	5
1,523	526	78	11	...	18	3	919	1,258	425	130	3	...	22	4	703	6
1,746	639	67	13	..	31	...	1,040	1,123	423	68	8	...	11	...	632	7
2,280	773	43	3	...	82	...	1,464	1,653	540	108	15	1	29	2	1,005	8
788	1,000	63	16	1	34	...	725	1,899	361	50	13	...	10	...	1,488	9
1,355	476	118	7	...	31	...	761	911	311	67	7	...	13	2	533	10
9,730	3,532	582	117	10	199	16	5,616	6,154	2,156	694	53	13	68	18	3,304	
2,239	828	111	16	2	66	2	1,300	1,778	603	187	17	4	31	4	988	11
2,810	961	176	57	6	48	10	1,673	1,391	500	178	13	7	12	7	713	12
1,533	613	81	14	1	40	1	839	1,020	349	121	11	1	5	...	550	13
1,676	589	170	17	1	28	...	917	1,121	386	135	9	...	14	5	600	14
1,472	541	44	13	...	17	3	887	844	318	73	3	1	6	2	453	15
7,796	2,536	593	44	2	118	13	4,667	4,561	1,509	480	34	2	43	11	2,572	
2,298	756	77	8	2	48	1	1,465	1,173	511	93	20	2	12	...	569	16
75	32	5	2	...	2	...	38	67	28	2	1	...	...	...	37	17
2,047	712	108	18	...	45	3	1,227	1,234	456	92	12	...	12	6	686	18
1,928	579	205	2	...	...	4	1,144	1,318	269	228	...	..	4	2	821	19
773	260	58	14	..	12	5	455	415	126	53	..	...	6	3	236	20
675	197	140	...	...	11	...	338	354	119	12	1	...	9	...	223	21
4,202	1,612	244	59	4	129	10	2,346	1,922	871	127	9	1	48	24	924	
740	276	38	2	...	10	4	432	416	132	11	...	...	2	..	273	22
1,425	490	63	23	...	58	2	872	811	419	77	7	1	33	20	315	23
1,311	489	104	30	4	32	4	718	418	132	35	2	...	5	4	251	24
709	348	39	4	...	29	...	322	270	188	4	...	...	8	...	78	25
11	9	...	...	...	...	...	2	7	...	...	...	...	..	...	7	26
4,616	1,638	486	51	1	89	5	2,492	2,310	767	244	9	1	9	3	1,299	
2,888	898	400	14	...	28	4	1,590	1,644	536	199	3	...	3	..	909	27
1,816	*520*	*282*	...	...	*6*	*4*	*1,014*	*1,015*	*307*	*115*	...	...	...	...	*593*	
423	162	19	4	...	20	...	242	180	57	16	5	1	1	1	107	28
339	154	18	...	...	11	...	167	165	50	8	1	...	1	..	107	29
946	412	49	33	1	30	1	485	319	122	21	...	...	4	2	170	30
20	12	...	...	...	...	...	8	2	2	...	...	...	...	..	...	31
3,966	1,527	190	71	3	124	10	2,249	2,372	817	173	37	1	44	3	1,382	
1,158	411	80	16	3	37	8	667	686	267	77	10	1	14	1	342	33
1,215	469	87	21	...	29	...	659	991	283	53	13	..	17	...	655	33
696	335	2	10	...	17	..	359	392	164	38	7	...	7	2	190	34
833	285	19	24	...	41	2	529	255	86	5	7	..	6	...	104	35
64	27	2	...	...	...	...	35	48	17	...	...	...	...	...	31	36
5,252	1,791	384	64	1	90	18	3,077	2,126	849	224	9	2	17	4	1,053	
927	347	64	10	1	21	...	516	413	146	35	...	...	7	1	232	37
1,326	429	98	30	...	31	4	799	542	204	31	4	...	4	1	307	38
1,589	504	82	15	...	17	5	1,003	469	223	37	5	1	6	...	209	39
1,410	511	140	9	...	21	9	759	702	276	121	...	1	...	2	305	40
4,464	1,867	91	219	4	193	2	2,506	1,557	604	86	61	1	33	1	867	
790	412	6	18	...	29	...	372	376	138	20	...	...	2	...	218	41
3,309	1,282	76	191	3	152	1	1,971	982	456	33	61	...	31	...	493	42
345	173	9	10	1	12	1	163	199	10	33	...	1	...	1	156	43

Serial No.	DISTRICT OR STATE.	Sub-Class *VIII.*—The professions and liberal arts—*concluded.* Order L.—Letters and the arts and sciences. (Groups 175 to 179.)							
		Total Workers and Dependents.	WORKERS. Total Workers.		Workers with an agricultural or other subsidiary occupation. Agricultural.		Other.		DEPENDENTS.
			Males.	Females.	Males.	Females.	Males.	Females.	
	1	2	3	4	5	6	7	8	9
	Provincial Total ...	26,268	11,753	1,895	150	22	418	41	12,620
	Divisional Burma ...	25,321	11,389	1,820	136	19	397	35	12,112
	Arakan Division ...	1,098	480	153	12	2	32	5	465
1	Akyab	709	305	101	7	...	4	4	303
2	Hill Dist. of Arakan ...	...	...	...	...	...	.	...	..
3	Kyaukpyu	248	122	42	3	2	23	1	84
4	Sandoway	141	53	10	2	...	5	...	78
	Pegu Division ...	5,986	2,584	408	14	3	33	3	2,904
5	Rangoon	2,605	1,066	178	...	...	9	...	1,361
6	Insein	254	121	20	...	...	2	...	113
7	Hanthawaddy ...	327	179	5	3	...	2	...	143
8	Tharrawaddy ...	811	408	40	2	1	...	2	363
9	Pegu	503	198	64	...	1	2	1	241
10	Prome	1,396	612	101	9	1	18	...	683
	Irrawaddy Division ...	3,394	1,610	273	15	...	28	1	1,511
11	Bassein	779	370	59	...	...	...	1	350
12	Henzada	956	340	63	9	...	18	...	553
13	Myaungmya ...	631	349	74	5	...	2	...	208
14	Ma-ubin	492	267	28	1	...	7	...	197
15	Pyapôn	536	284	49	...	...	1	...	203
	Tenasserim Division ...	2,697	1,289	156	11	...	27	1	1,252
16	Toungoo	501	214	39	...	...	4	...	248
17	Salween	19	13	3	2	...	...	...	3
18	Thatôn	559	264	53	...	...	11	...	242
19	Amherst	1,314	650	57	9	...	...	...	607
20	Tavoy	202	116	1	...	...	12	1	85
21	Mergui	102	32	3	...	...	...	...	67
	Magwe Division ...	3,147	1,472	199	12	...	82	6	1,476
22	Thayetmyo	589	230	3	1	...	3	...	356
23	Pakôkku	1,264	645	104	...	...	48	3	515
24	Minbu	821	358	62	9	...	25	2	401
25	Magwe	473	239	30	2	...	6	1	264
26	Pakôkku Hill Tracts ...	...		...	...	...	...	...	...
	Mandalay Division ...	3,882	1,902	233	7	...	83	3	1,747
27	Mandalay	3,443	1,641	200	7	...	66	...	1,602
	Mandalay City ...	*2,890*	*1,461*	*148*	*1*	...	*55*	...	*1,281*
28	Bhamo	88	49	9	...	...	1	...	30
29	Myitkyina	35	23	...	...	...	3	...	12
30	Katha	316	189	24	...	...	13	3	103
31	Putao	...	...	...	...	...	...	...	...
	Sagaing Division ...	2,998	1,253	193	49	14	97	15	1,552
32	Shwebo	883	404	96	16	6	17	3	383
33	Sagaing	884	303	31	10	...	18	2	550
34	Lower Chindwin ...	802	398	23	20	...	43	1	381
35	Upper Chindwin ...	429	148	43	3	8	19	9	238
36	Chin Hills	...	...	...	...	...	...	...	...
	Meiktila Division ...	2,209	799	205	16	...	15	1	1,205
37	Kyauksè	491	190	45	5	...	2	...	256
38	Meiktila	453	163	38	9	...	5	...	252
39	Yamèthin	454	115	32	...	...	3	1	307
40	Myingyan	811	331	90	2	...	5	...	390
	Eastern States ...	947	364	75	14	3	21	6	508
41	Northern Shan States ...	556	184	37	3	...	4	1	335
42	Southern Shan States ...	377	176	35	11	3	17	5	166
43	Karenni	14	4	3	...	...	...	...	7

PART III.—*Details by districts*—contd.

Total Workers and Dependents.	Sub-Class *IX*.—Persons (not in Sub-Class *Ia*) without an occupation but receiving an income. Order LI.—All persons without an occupation but receiving an income who are not included in Group I. (Group 180.) WORKERS. Total Workers. Males.	Total Workers. Females.	Workers with an agricultural or other subsidiary occupation. Agricultural. Males.	Agricultural. Females.	Other. Males.	Other. Females.	DEPENDENTS.	Sub-Class *X*.—Domestic service. Order LII.—Domestic service. (Groups 181, 182, 183.) Total Workers and Dependents.	WORKERS. Total Workers. Males.	Total Workers. Females.	Workers with an agricultural or other subsidiary occupation. Agricultural. Males.	Agricultural. Females.	Other. Males.	Other. Females.	DEPENDENTS.	Serial No. of District, etc (column 1).
10	11	12	13	14	15	16	17	18	19	20	21	22	23	24	25	
13,800	3,230	1,175	153	10	344	41	9,395	73,669	43,059	8,001	807	87	637	115	22,609	
13,168	3,110	1,105	136	8	312	39	8,953	58,743	33,785	6,854	45	67	273	94	18,104	
603	133	18	12	...	27	4	452	2,465	1,725	405	5	...	6	3	335	
284	53	10	4	...	7	1	221	2,221	1,580	375	5	...	5	3	266	1
27	8	...	...	...	...	...	19	30	26	3	...	...	...	...	1	2
126	36	7	4	..	10	3	83	74	46	10	...	...	1	...	18	3
166	36	1	4	...	10	...	129	140	73	17	...	...	...	...	50	4
4,575	842	458	6	...	56	10	3,275	24,105	14,705	2,588	10	46	36	12	6,812	
2,859	528	253	1		37	6	2,078	17,930	10,959	1,769	5	...	11	...	5,202	5
326	80	29	2	...	2	3	217	1,170	623	194	3	...	3	4	353	6
153	57	22	...	...	...	...	74	1,289	833	174	1	...	3	7	282	7
458	63	56	3	...	7	...	339	1,098	692	112	...	...	6	...	224	8
452	57	55	...	...	8	1	340	1,361	778	249	1	45	10	...	334	9
327	57	43	...	...	2	...	227	1,327	820	90	...	1	3	1	417	10
1,130	265	97	10	...	11	3	768	4,812	3,866	641	4	4	50	5	1,105	
342	85	28	1	...	2	1	229	1,823	1,277	130	...	...	31	1	416	11
267	66	18	6	..	4	...	183	961	511	240	...	1	12	3	210	12
200	45	15	2	...	3	1	140	778	440	90	2	...	4	1	248	13
199	33	19	1	..	2	1	147	634	432	72	...	...	2	...	130	14
122	36	17	...	...	...	...	69	616	406	109	2	3	1	...	101	15
1,912	413	286	22	3	32	11	1,213	6,503	4,037	656	4	1	99	7	1,810	
393	87	20	4	...	4	2	286	1,284	801	95	..	...	8	...	388	16
19	4	...	1	...	1	...	15	49	35	3	...	...	..	...	11	17
266	29	37	2	1	...	5	200	882	409	111	...	...	62	..	362	18
754	149	169	7	...	1	2	436	2,974	1,946	261	3	...	17	...	707	19
211	74	33	2	2	19	2	104	650	360	135	...	1	9	7	155	20
269	70	27	6	...	7	...	172	664	486	51	1	...	3	...	127	21
921	367	26	11	2	12	1	528	4,550	2,307	530	...	6	32	5	1,713	
453	205	9	...	1	3	...	239	681	311	41		.	3	3	329	22
205	66	...	4	...	7	...	139	1,265	539	210	..	2	6	2	516	23
152	37	9	7	1	2	...	106	871	388	192	..	2	13	...	291	24
111	59	8	...	...	...	1	44	1,705	1,052	86	..	2	10	...	567	25
...	...	...	...	...	...	...	...	28	17	1	...	...	...	...	10	26
2,165	533	127	21	1	71	3	1,505	9,019	4682	911	4	1	11	1	3,426	
1,602	366	111	7	1	46	2	1,125	7,265	3,479	842	..	...	4	1	2,934	27
934	*160*	*106*	...	...	*1*	...	*668*	*4,386*	*2,081*	*634*	..	...	..	.	*1,671*	
104	31	4	3	...	2	1	69	553	363	18	...	...	4	...	172	28
290	95	3	11	...	17	...	192	540	383	15	4	..	...	..	142	29
157	39	8	...	...	6	...	110	580	390	23	...	...	2	...	167	30
12	2	1	...	...	...	...	9	81	67	3	...	1	1	...	11	31
982	339	33	47	1	72	4	610	2,866	1,346	430	18	6	17	11	1,090	
328	99	17	16	...	17	...	212	979	424	102	1	...	1	...	453	32
257	70	6	6	...	11	1	181	626	350	70	1	...	6	...	206	33
170	92	1	11	...	18	.	77	701	235	220	...	6	4	11	246	34
158	56	8	9	1	22	2	94	379	227	36	3	...	6	...	116	35
69	22	1	5	...	4	1	46	181	110	2	13	...	...	...	69	36
880	218	60	7	1	31	3	602	4,423	1,917	693	...	3	22	50	1,813	
179	58	3	...	...	12	...	118	431	331	36	...	...	4	1	167	37
227	55	34	1	...	11	...	138	1,500	564	237	...	...	...	14	699	38
327	51	12	4	1	5	2	264	1,341	693	114	...	3	3	2	534	39
147	54	11	2	...	3	1	80	1,148	429	306	...	...	15	33	413	40
632	120	70	17	2	32	2	442	14,926	9,274	1,147	762	20	364	21	4,505	
235	28	44	5	2	10	2	163	1,975	836	858	13	..	35	11	281	41
387	90	26	12	..	20	...	271	12,872	8,404	261	749	10	329	10	4,207	42
10	2	...	...	...	...	...	8	79	34	28	...	10	...	...	17	43

Serial No.	DISTRICT OR STATE.	Sub-Class *XI.*—Insufficiently described occupations. Order LIII.—Insufficiently described occupations. (Groups 184 to 187.) Total Workers and Dependents.	WORKERS. Total Workers. Males.	Females.	Workers with an agricultural or other subsidiary occupation. Agricultural. Males.	Females.	Other. Males.	Females.	DEPENDENTS.	Sub-Class *XII.*— Order LIV.—Prisoners in jails, etc., and inmates of asylums and almshouses. (Group 188.) Total Workers and Dependents.	WORKERS.* Males.	Females.
	1	2	3	4	5	6	7	8	9	10	11	12
	Provincial Total ...	**573,641**	**202,629**	**149,294**	**2,533**	**7,855**	**5,117**	**7,172**	**221,718**	**16,324**	**15,827**	**497**
	Divisional Burma ..	**431,608**	**173,667**	**69,715**	**1,275**	**1,327**	**3,476**	**2,311**	**188,226**	**16,124**	**15,627**	**497**
	Arakan Division ...	**32,792**	**11,881**	**6,665**	**307**	**242**	**369**	**234**	**14,246**	**700**	**668**	**32**
1	Akyab ...	11,486	5,893	808	30	1	65	7	4,785	537	505	32
2	Hill Dist. of Arakan ...	130	96	3	...	...	2	...	31	...	...	...
3	Kyaukpyu ...	17,180	4,724	4,964	257	218	226	171	7,492	114	114	...
4	Sandoway ...	3,995	1,168	890	20	23	76	56	1,938	49	49	...
	Pegu Division ...	**121,436**	**64,346**	**10,431**	**161**	**74**	**619**	**290**	**46,659**	***6,202**	***6,054**	**148**
5	Rangoon Town ...	44,395	28,001	590	13	..	39	...	15,804	3,093	2,973	120
6	Insein ...	12,569	5,371	1,471	19	9	63	14	5,727	2,321	2,321	...
7	Hanthawaddy ...	34,332	19,093	3,769	46	17	261	73	11,470	*4	*4	...
8	Tharrawaddy ...	12,253	4,330	2,099	57	29	118	114	5,824	63	57	6
9	Pegu ...	9,243	4,502	772	4	5	60	15	3,969	79	76	3
10	Prome ...	8,644	3,049	1,730	22	14	78	74	3,865	642	623	19
	Irrawaddy Division ..	**54,378**	**22,272**	**9,801**	**232**	**71**	**478**	**233**	**22,305**	***3,090**	**3,016**	***74**
11	Bassein ..	6,854	3,648	518	12	19	56	7	2,688	1,141	1,123	18
12	Henzada ...	20,240	6,044	5,421	60	42	147	193	8,775	* 604	552	* 52
13	Myaungmya ...	15,052	6,195	2,591	61	7	145	23	6,266	1,144	1,142	2
14	Ma-ubin ..	5,208	2,844	574	93	1	113	8	1,790	168	166	2
15	Pyapôn ...	7,024	3,541	697	6	2	17	5	2,786	33	33	...
	Tenasserim Division ...	**52,653**	**22,506**	**5,297**	**79**	**13**	**329**	**149**	**24,850**	**1,153**	**1,141**	**12**
16	Toungoo ...	15,027	5,791	2,214	10	3	73	59	7,022	...	...	...
17	Salween ..	902	578	51	1	...	4	...	273	2	2	...
18	Thatôn ...	20,511	8,549	2,231	55	8	191	85	9,731	51	51	...
19	Amherst ...	9,841	4,951	500	9	2	22	4	4,390	805	796	9
20	Tavoy ...	2,146	922	83	2	...	14	1	1,141	160	160	...
21	Mergui ...	4,226	1,715	218	2	...	25	..	2,293	135	132	3
	Magwe Division ...	**21,600**	**7,014**	**5,591**	**45**	**67**	**223**	**223**	**8,995**	**1,552**	**1,521**	**31**
22	Thayetmyo ...	5,832	1,544	1,437	...	5	23	25	2,851	1,061	1,032	29
23	Pakôkku ...	4,116	1,099	787	7	5	87	44	2,230	27	27	...
24	Minbu ...	8,154	2,359	2,968	37	53	96	140	2,827	165	163	2
25	Magwe ...	3,480	2,006	399	1	4	17	14	1,075	299	299	...
26	Pakôkku Hill Tracts ...	18	6	...	...	...	...	...	12	...	...	...
	Mandalay Division ...	**45,682**	**18,153**	**6,081**	**175**	**25**	**472**	**166**	**21,448**	**1,860**	**1,664**	**196**
27	Mandalay ...	18,213	6,709	3,213	5	13	33	16	8,291	1,634	1,497	137
	Mandalay City ...	*11,308*	*4,235*	*2,057*	..	...	*7*	*2*	*5,016*	*1,604*	*1,474*	*130*
28	Bhamo ...	770	470	18	2	...	6	1	282	30	30	..
29	Myitkyina ...	1,331	695	129	6	...	16	3	507	59	..	59
30	Katha ...	25,294	10,211	2,720	162	12	417	146	12,363	137	137	...
31	Putao ..	74	68	1	...	...	...	..	5	...	...	...
	Sagaing Division ...	**25,694**	**6,998**	**7,048**	**121**	**114**	**414**	**302**	**11,648**	**173**	**173**	..
32	Shwebo ...	18,182	5,107	5,481	97	65	281	167	7,594	1	1	...
33	Sagaing ...	2,347	585	561	..	1	28	37	1,201	1	1	...
34	Lower Chindwin ..	1,555	584	166	5	4	31	8	805	170	170	...
35	Upper Chindwin ...	3,384	663	837	7	44	74	90	1,884	1	1	...
36	Chin Hills ...	226	59	3	12	...	...	...	164	...	...	...
	Meiktila Division ...	**77,373**	**20,497**	**18,801**	**155**	**721**	**572**	**714**	**38,075**	**1,394**	**1,390**	**4**
37	Kyauksè ...	14,948	3,672	4,265	68	589	149	200	7,011	1	...	1
38	Meiktila ...	6,975	1,943	1,521	25	9	55	41	3,511	157	155	2
39	Yamèthin ...	14,900	4,697	2,299	7	...	100	63	7,904	107	106	1
40	Myingyan ...	40,550	10,185	10,716	55	123	268	410	19,649	1,129	1,129	...
	Eastern States ...	**142,033**	**28,962**	**79,579**	**1,258**	**6,528**	**1,641**	**4,861**	**33,498**	**200**	**200**	...
41	Northern Shan States ...	7,954	3,846	1,113	33	2	74	94	2,995	34	34	...
42	Southern Shan States ...	129,154	22,777	77,465	1,198	6,519	1,511	4,752	28,912	142	142	...
43	Karenni ...	4,925	2,339	1,001	27	7	56	15	1,585	24	24	...

* One male in Hanthawaddy district and one in the Northern Shan States and two females in Henzada district had agricultural subsidiary occupations; one male in Tharrawaddy district had a non-agricultural subsidiary occupation.

PART III.—*Details by districts*—contd.

Unproductive and unclassified.

Order LV.—Beggars, vagrants, prostitutes, etc. (Groups 189, 190.)								Order LVI.—Other unproductive occupations and unclassified. (Group 191.)								
Total Workers and Dependents.	WORKERS. Total Workers.		WORKERS. Workers with an agricultural or other subsidiary occupation. Agricultural.		Other.		DEPENDENTS.	Total Workers and Dependents.	WORKERS. Total Workers.		WORKERS. Workers with an agricultural or other subsidiary occupation. Agricultural.		Other.		DEPENDENTS.	Serial No. of District, etc. (column 1).
	Males.	Females.	Males.	Females.	Males.	Females.			Males.	Females.	Males.	Females	Males.	Females.		
12	14	15	16	17	18	19	20	21	22	23	24	25	26	27	28	
28,787	10,516	10,360	17	30	117	98	7,911	3,855	447	39	1	...	29	8	3,369	
24,849	9,174	8,411	8	3	98	62	7,264	3,796	411	31	1	...	12	7	3,354	
3,690	941	1,333	6	3	9	18	1,416	3	2	...	...	...	...	...	1	
3,406	873	1,225	6	3	9	18	1,308	...	...	...	...	...	...	...	...	1
8	4	4	...	...	...	...	...	...	...	...	...	...	...	...	...	2
224	42	88	...	...	...	...	94	2	2	...	...	...	...	...	...	3
52	22	16	...	...	...	...	14	1	...	...	...	...	...	...	1	4
3,690	1,411	1,396	...	...	12	...	883	159	56	14	...	...	...	...	89	
1,657	666	689	...	...	...	...	302	95	10	11	...	...	...		74	5
219	80	33	...	...	...	...	106	6	6	...	...	...	...	...	...	6
357	168	74	...	...	...	...	115	1	1	...	...	...	...	...	...	7
247	136	75	...	...	...	...	36	16	1	...	...	...	...	...	15	8
568	272	213	...	...	12	...	83	32	29	3	...	...	...	...	...	9
642	89	312	...	...	...	...	241	9	9	...	...	...	...	...	...	10
1,792	806	504	...	...	6	4	482	218	8	1	...	...	...	...	209	
302	143	121	...	...	...	...	38	...	...	...	...	...	...	...	...	11
567	299	96	...	...	...	...	172	203	4	1	...	...	...	...	198	12
383	156	113	...	...	...	...	114	...	...	...	...	...	...	...	...	13
308	145	90	...	...	6	4	93	13	2	...	...	...	...	...	11	14
212	63	84	...	...	...	...	65	2	2	...	...	...	...	...	...	15
1,454	660	353	...	...	...	9	441	2,497	20	7	...	...	...	6	2,470	
406	233	66	...	...	...	...	107	2,403	1	1	...	...	...	...	2,401	16
5	3	2	...	...	...	...		1	1		...	...	...	...	...	17
429	152	118	...	...	...	9	159	23	10	...	...	...	...	...	13	18
560	250	160	...	...	...	...	150	70	8	6	...	...	...	6	56	19
17	13	4	...	...	...	...	...	...	...	...	...	...	...	...	...	20
37	9	3	...	...	...	...	25	...	...	...	...	...	...	...	...	21
3,366	1,260	1,086	...	...	27	9	1,020	41	1	2	...	...	1	1	38	
442	205	34	...	...	...	...	203	...	...		...	...	...	...	...	22
1,460	561	381	...	...	21	1	518	...	...	...	...	...	...	...	...	23
1,273	467	548	...	...	6	8	264	18	1	1	...	...	1	1	16	24
191	27	129	...	...	...	...	35	23	...	1	...	...	...		22	25
...	...	...	...	...	...	...	...	...		...	...			...	...	26
3,567	1,211	1,110	...	...	6	1	1,246	684	195	7	1	...	10	...	482	
2,458	877	871	...	...	4	...	710	96		...	...	...	...	...	96	27
733	*312*	*320*	...	...	...	...	*101*	*25*	...	...	...	...	...	...	*25*	
187	49	87	...	...	...	...	51	5	2	3	...	...	...	...	...	28
51	12	31	...	...	...		8	4	...	3	...	...	...	...	1	29
864	269	118	...	...	2	1	477	579	193	1	1	...	10	...	385	30
7	4	3	...	...	...	...	...		...	...	...	...	...		...	31
3,375	1,249	1,448	1	...	3	3	678	14	6		...	...	1	...	8	
1,378	552	446	1	...	2	...	380		...	...	...	...	...	...	...	32
1,021	264	671	...	...	1	...	86	9	6	...	...	...	1	...	3	33
805	340	267	...	...	...	2	198	...	...	...	...	...	...	...	...	34
161	90	60	...	...	...	1	11	5	...	...	...	...	...	...	5	35
10	3	4	...	...	...	...	3	...	...	...	...	...	...	...	...	36
3,915	1,636	1,181	1	...	35	18	1,098	180	123	...	...		...	...	57	
907	503	171	...	...	...	1	233	...	...	...	...	...	...	...	...	37
562	143	302	...	...	...	...	117	97	93	...	...	...	...	...	4	38
692	315	225	...	...	17	...	152	21	12	...		...	...	...	9	39
1,754	675	483	1	...	18	17	596	62	18	...	...	...	...	...	44	40
3,938	1,342	1,949	9	27	19	36	647	59	36	8	...	...	17	1	15	
1,698	519	846	4	2	15	19	333	44	35	2	...	...	17	1	7	41
2,108	782	1,032	5	25	4	17	294	13	1	5	...	...	...	...	7	42
132	41	71	...	...	...	...	20	2	...	1	...	...	...	...	1	43

Serial No.	District or State.	Total Workers and Dependents.	Total Workers. Males.	Total Workers. Females.	Agricultural. Males.	Agricultural. Females.	Other. Males.	Other. Females.	Dependents.	Total Workers and Dependents.	Workers (All without subsidiary occupation.) Males.	Workers (All without subsidiary occupation.) Females.	Dependents.
		Order I.—Control by persons not principally practising an occupation of Sub-Class *Ib*											
		Group 1.—Ownership and rights over land or water used for occupations of Sub-Class *Ib* or *Ic*.								Group 2a.—Agents, managers, clerks, rent-collectors, etc., for land or water belonging to persons of Group 1.			
			Workers.		Workers with an agricultural or other subsidiary occupation.								
	1	2	3	4	5	6	7	8	9	10	11	12	13
	Provincial Total ...	147,764	33,419	40,732	999	1,089	5,831	4,570	73,613	5	1	...	4
	Divisional Burma ..	141,717	31,074	39,487	797	896	5,337	4,340	71,156	5	1	...	4
	Arakan Division ...	16,930	3,426	4,228	188	105	514	337	9,276	...	...	...	...
1	Akyab	10,176	1,850	2,086	86	14	168	109	6,240	...	...	...	...
2	Hill Dist. of Arakan ...	19	...	15	...	..	...	...	4	...	...	...	...
3	Kyaukpyu	3,097	707	967	35	37	176	91	1,423	...	...	...	...
4	Sandoway ...	3,638	869	1,160	67	54	70	137	1,609	...	...	...	...
	Pegu Division	27,104	5,711	6,140	130	89	943	532	15,253	2	...	...	2
5	Rangoon Town ...	1,170	221	134	...	.	2	6	815	2	...	...	2
6	Insein ..	2,827	632	666	5	7	97	37	1,529	...	...	...	...
7	Hanthawaddy ..	1,910	391	254	12	1	95	15	1,265	...	...	...	...
8	Tharrawaddy ..	7,524	1,525	1,697	38	46	336	122	4,302	...	..	...	...
9	Pegu	6,414	1,513	1,111	48	23	177	68	3,790	...	...	...	..
10	Prome	7,259	1,429	2,278	27	12	236	284	3,552	..	..	...	...
	Irrawaddy Division ..	28,588	6,821	7,396	139	136	1,113	706	14,371	2	...	...	2
11	Bassein	6,129	1,557	1,656	39	17	269	190	2,916	...	...	...	2
12	Henzada	7,480	1,816	2,595	26	81	259	203	3,069	...	...	...	...
13	Myaungmya ..	7,015	1,752	1,592	38	10	349	182	3,671	...	...	..	...
14	Ma-ubin	5,368	983	1,073	31	26	135	85	3,312	...	...	..	...
15	Pyapôn	2,596	713	480	5	2	101	46	1,403	2	..	...	2
	Tenasserim Division ...	12,774	2,742	2,928	61	24	422	268	7,104	...	...	..	...
16	Toungoo	4,648	746	951	24	10	136	56	2,951	...	...	...	...
17	Salween ..	83	20	23	6	..	4	3	40	...	...	...	..
18	Thatôn	3,310	832	826	13	6	88	70	1,652	...	...	...	...
19	Amherst ...	2,912	707	623	7	2	81	57	1,582	...	...	...	...
20	Tavoy	1,632	388	463	9	3	108	76	781	...	...	..	...
21	Mergui	189	49	42	2	3	5	6	98	..	...	...	...
	Magwe Division ...	20,224	4,494	7,331	146	162	991	829	8,399	1	1	...	...
22	Thayetmyo	4,109	858	1,546	45	51	128	125	1,705	..	..	...	...
23	Pakôkku ..	5,895	1,312	2,150	25	31	351	359	2,433	1	1	...	...
24	Minbu ...	6,088	1,365	2,009	65	63	293	167	2,714	...	..	...	...
25	Magwe	4,132	959	1,626	11	17	219	178	1,547	...	...	...	..
26	Pakôkku Hill Tracts ..	...	...	..	...		...	..	...	...	...	...	...
	Mandalay Division ...	1,872	422	569	14	13	95	68	881	...	..	...	...
27	Mandalay	990	215	355	7	4	34	40	420	...	...	...	...
	Mandalay City ...	*150*	*5*	*59*	..	...	...	*1*	*86*	..	...	...	...
28	Bhamo	121	31	25	2	...	3	5	65	--	...	...	...
29	Myitkyina	54	21	7	...	...	5	...	26	..	...	...	...
30	Katha	707	155	182	5	9	53	23	370	...	...	.	...
31	Putao	...	..	...	..		...	...	...	...	..	...	...
	Sagaing Division ...	18,908	4,084	6,340	79	272	808	1,070	8,484	...	..	...	...
32	Shwebo	3,786	839	1,629	1	16	35	282	1,318	...	...	...	...
33	Sagaing	5,728	1,422	2,004	29	17	336	396	2,302	..	...	...	...
34	Lower Chindwin ..	7,624	1,448	2,197	30	216	309	297	3,979	...	...	...	...
35	Upper Chindwin ..	1,770	375	510	19	23	128	95	885	...	...	...	...
36	Chin Hills	...	...	...	...	...	...		...	...	...	...	...
	Meiktila Division ...	15,317	3,374	4,555	40	95	451	530	7,388	...	...	...	...
37	Kyauksè	1,440	287	422	4	12	78	50	731	..	...	...	...
38	Meiktila	3,744	797	1,172	8	5	169	173	1,775	...	...	...	...
39	Yamèthin	4,433	930	845	...	16	43	77	2,658	...	...	...	...
40	Myingyan	5,700	1,360	2,216	28	62	161	230	2,224	..	...	...	..
	Eastern States ...	6,047	2,345	1,245	202	193	494	230	2,457	..	..	...	...
41	Northern Shan States ...	1,616	400	412	22	7	85	110	804	...	...	...	...
42	Southern Shan States ...	4,414	1,944	824	180	186	409	120	1,646	.	...	...	...
43	Karenni	17	1	9		..	...	...	7	...	...	...	...

PART III.—*Details by districts*—contd.

or *Ic* of land or water used for such an occupation.								Order IIA.—Cultivation.								
Group 2*b*.—Agents, managers, clerks, rent-collectors, etc., for land or water belonging to Government and used for occupations of Sub-Class *Ib* or *Ic*.								Group 3*a*.—Cultivating owners.								Serial No. of District, etc. (column 1).
Total Workers and Dependents.	WORKERS.						DEPENDENTS.	Total Workers and Dependents.	WORKERS.						DEPENDENTS.	
	Total Workers.		Workers with an agricultural or other subsidiary occupation.						Total Workers.		Workers with an agricultural or other subsidiary occupation.					
			Agricultural.		Other.						Agricultural.		Other.			
	Males.	Females.	Males.	Females.	Males.	Females.			Males.	Females.	Males.	Females.	Males.	Females.		
14	15	16	17	18	19	20	21	22	23	24	25	26	27	28	29	
9,366	3,176	..	70	...	57	...	6,190	4,064,042	1,165,537	903,295	32,366	18,371	183,783	93,923	1,995,210	
9,304	3,152	..	63	..	54	...	6,152	3,479,304	978,200	764,941	23,669	13,407	145,845	69,904	1,736,163	
491	136	...	1	...	1	...	355	269,677	74,417	48,645	2,904	1,356	8,679	3,799	146,615	
392	128	...	1	...	1	..	264	134,746	36,855	14,286	776	84	2,937	423	83,605	1
...	...	..	...	.	...	.	..	34	27	...	...	...	5	...	7	2
73	4	...	...	..	...		69	87,590	24,957	22,106	1,031	561	3,419	2,085	40,527	3
26	4	...	...	...	...	...	22	47,307	12,578	12,253	1,097	711	2,318	1,291	22,476	4
1,594	421	..	4	...	1	..	1,173	380,881	103,182	64,674	3,073	983	11,625	5,383	213,025	
141	53	...		...	...	.	83	1,640	441	126		..	11	3	1,073	5
389	64	...	2	.	...	...	325	31,769	8,367	4,760	95	51	445	130	18,642	6
237	68	...	2	...	...	.	169	27,446	5,851	4,016	210	124	544	174	17,579	7
261	72	.	...	...	...	...	189	134,578	35,215	22,645	1,326	447	3,989	1,833	76,718	8
458	121		...		...	...	337	60,623	18,390	10,055	230	107	1,135	284	32,178	9
108	43	..	...	...	1	...	65	124,825	34,918	23,072	1,211	254	5,501	2,959	66,835	10
1,697	634	.	1	...	9		1,063	414,011	122,834	104,265	2,827	1,410	7,661	4,614	186,912	
650	343	...	..	...	7	..	307	88,011	27,385	17,864	346	182	1,432	759	42,762	11
401	69	...	1	...	1	...	332	146,958	43,398	40,962	969	982	3,707	2,156	62,598	12
278	85	...	...	..	...	.	193	66,802	19,901	15,169	757	36	903	547	31,732	13
146	52	.	..	...	.		94	81,669	24,855	24,709	701	192	1,382	1,031	32,105	14
222	85	...	...	...	1		137	30,571	7,295	5,561	54	18	237	121	17,715	15
1,399	574		35	...	20		825	405,698	115,300	70,610	1,468	609	8,597	3,818	219,788	
186	43	...	..	.	1		143	73,006	25,024	6,317	193	115	1,406	253	41,665	16
1	...	...	...	..	..		1	11,454	2,995	1,399	33	18	424	90	7,060	17
273	85	...	1		1		188	143,351	39,497	32,417	601	182	2,054	1,580	71,437	18
402	146	...	31	...	1		256	120,843	34,422	23,742	360	116	2,349	1,413	62,679	19
201	103	..	...	..			98	20,453	5,966	3,680	174	54	1,260	433	10,807	20
336	197	...	3	...	:		139	36,591	7,396	3,055	107	124	1,104	49	26,140	21
943	369	.	.	.	9	.	574	643,244	185,169	171,596	4,046	2,843	30,378	12,929	286,479	
149	54	...	...	...		.	95	129,544	36,236	28,875	1,466	781	4,450	2,352	64,433	22
201	108	..	...	...	...	..	93	178,406	52,364	41,938	848	487	11,529	5,462	84,104	23
237	68	...	.	.	..		169	85,719	21,757	25,739	956	726	7,319	2,630	38,293	24
356	139	..	...	...	9	...	217	249,170	74,678	74,928	776	849	7,080	2,485	99,564	25
...	...	...	...	...	...	...	...	405	134	116	...	...	...	...	155	26
611	251	...	...	...	...	..	360	273,930	78,135	54,440	2,609	2,795	16,707	5,274	141,355	
443	193	...	..	...	...	...	250	58,466	16,726	11,075	139	341	1,945	941	30,665	27
256	*85*	.	...	...	...	...	*171*	*2,793*	*938*	*365*	...	...	...	*52*	*1,490*	
20	6	...	...	...	...	...	14	43,572	11,527	9,667	1,146	1,255	2,994	717	22,378	28
27	14	...	...	...	..	...	13	36,005	12,968	8,069	478	586	1,922	238	14,968	29
121	38	...	...	.	...	...	83	130,055	35,388	23,825	738	506	9,583	3,291	70,842	30
...	...	...	...	...	...	...	...	5,832	1,526	1,804	108	107	263	87	2,502	31
1,353	429	...	15	...	6	..	924	553,248	153,568	163,636	4,208	2,277	42,790	23,123	236,044	
551	205	...	6	...	2	...	346	239,529	67,811	83,076	310	129	20,250	11,372	88,642	32
500	96	...	1	...	2	...	404	98,445	26,989	23,556	1,507	957	8,238	6,326	47,900	33
280	112	...	8	...	2	...	168	126,147	32,160	33,387	1,055	610	6,278	2,396	60,600	34
22	16	...	...	...	...	...	6	89,126	26,607	23,617	1,336	581	8,024	3,029	38,902	35
...	...	...	.	...	...	...	..	1	1	...		...	...	...	...	36
1,216	338	...	7	..	8	..	878	538,615	145,595	87,075	2,534	1,134	19,408	10,964	305,945	
129	15	...	...	...	1	.	114	38,788	11,161	4,183	118	107	1,567	460	23,444	37
360	116	...	4	...	2	...	244	152,839	39,565	21,622	605	119	6,698	4,151	91,652	38
492	141	...	1	.	3	...	351	137,555	35,503	14,423	670	117	4,282	1,282	87,629	39
235	66	...	2	.	2	..	169	209,433	59,366	46,847	1,141	791	6,861	5,071	103,220	40
62	24	..	7	...	3	...	38	584,738	187,337	138,354	8,697	4,964	37,938	24,019	259,047	
21	1	...	...	...	..	...	20	162,072	51,726	40,708	4,459	1,524	11,417	9,366	69,638	41
39	22	...	7	...	2	...	17	404,773	130,865	93,281	4,023	3,071	25,947	14,401	180,627	42
2	1	..	...	..	1	...	1	17,893	4,746	4,365	215	369	574	252	8,782	43

Order IIA.—

Group 3*b*.—Cultivating tenants.

Serial No.	DISTRICT OR STATE.	Total Workers and Dependents.	WORKERS. Total Workers. Males.	Total Workers. Females.	Workers with an agricultural or other subsidiary occupation. Agricultural. Males.	Agricultural. Females.	Other. Males.	Other. Females.	DEPENDENTS.
	1	2	3	4	5	6	7	8	9
	Provincial Total	1,814,164	512,362	331,178	14,641	9,055	74,184	27,513	970,624
	Divisional Burma	1,750,197	491,193	320,586	12,377	7,947	67,750	25,744	938,418
	Arakan Division	185,332	47,880	23,549	1,898	700	4,545	1,456	113,903
1	Akyab	130,183	34,685	11,370	801	121	1,782	371	84,128
2	Hill Dist. of Arakan	8	6	...	...	...	2	...	2
3	Kyaukpyu	32,352	6,975	7,221	793	351	1,593	646	18,156
4	Sandoway	22,789	6,214	4,958	304	228	1,168	439	11,617
	Pegu Division	319,651	86,705	39,239	1,289	522	10,528	2,607	193,707
5	Rangoon Town	1,202	511	119	...	.	8	...	572
6	Insein	42,517	12,300	6,109	21	42	1,000	211	24,108
7	Hanthawaddy	62,773	17,065	3,655	57	17	1,125	192	42,053
8	Tharrawaddy	79,848	21,106	12,582	517	210	3,656	573	46,160
9	Pegu	85,204	23,016	10,133	129	77	1,786	391	52,055
10	Prome	48,107	12,707	6,641	565	176	2,953	1,240	28,759
	Irrawaddy Division	372,392	121,653	75,977	1,478	770	5,744	2,364	174,762
11	Bassein	92,709	33,842	20,334	291	122	918	437	38,533
12	Henzada	80,178	27,428	18,426	653	447	2,852	1,378	34,324
13	Myaungmya	87,605	26,290	16,545	273	20	982	87	44,770
14	Ma-ubin	48,608	14,844	11,132	229	176	646	319	22,632
15	Pyapôn	63,292	19,249	9,540	32	5	346	143	34,503
	Tenasserim Division	177,877	49,735	27,464	578	191	5,545	2,096	100,678
16	Toungoo	53,956	14,[illegible]96	6,523	180	46	1,487	340	32,937
17	Salween	1,320	437	206	25	...	28	22	677
18	Thatôn	52,515	16,071	8,365	79	69	973	468	28,079
19	Amherst	42,655	10,933	8,051	130	45	1,404	668	23,671
20	Tavoy	21,446	6,392	3,696	118	23	1,507	585	11,358
21	Mergui	5,985	1,406	623	46	8	146	13	3,956
	Magwe Division	259,552	69,968	58,157	4,124	2,902	18,129	6,319	131,427
22	Thayetmyo	31,1[illegible]5	8,929	7,5[illegible]8	980	626	1,327	499	14,698
23	Pakôkku	100,518	27,6[illegible]6	19,610	585	424	8,116	2,796	53,302
24	Minbu	72,752	21,068	19,913	2,316	1,572	5,968	2,003	31,771
25	Magwe	55,147	12,365	11,126	243	280	2,718	1,021	31,656
26	Pakôkku Hill Tracts	...	...	...	...	...	...	...	...
	Mandalay Division	42,499	12,968	9,630	259	290	2,659	965	19,901
27	Mandalay	22,682	7,251	4,395	138	219	1,334	491	11,036
	Mandalay City	*783*	*256*	*142*	...	...	...	*16*	*385*
28	Bhamo	1,104	198	284	8	2	113	64	622
29	Myitkyina	3,080	1,274	609	2	...	70	1	1,197
30	Katha	15,615	4,24[illegible]	4,335	111	69	1,142	409	7,040
31	Putao	18	5	7	...	...	...		6
	Sagaing Division	244,435	66,105	61,920	2,113	2,155	15,664	7,812	116,410
32	Shwebo	40,856	11,377	11,287	64	47	3,928	1,782	18,192
33	Sagaing	86,129	25,552	16,866	1,066	680	5,510	3,367	43,711
34	Lower Chindwin	96,188	23,036	28,606	594	635	4,924	2,457	44,546
35	Upper Chindwin	21,262	[illegible]	5,161	389	793	1,302	206	9,961
36	Chin Hills	...	...	...	...	...	...	...	...
	Meiktila Division	148,459	36,179	24,650	638	417	4,936	2,125	87,630
37	Kyauksè	19,502	5,944	1,909	97	95	940	191	11,649
38	Meiktila	24,234	6,474	3,322	63	45	1,018	398	14,438
39	Yamèthin	35,087	9,391	3,480	91	21	1,647	277	22,216
40	Myingyan	69,636	14,370	15,939	387	256	1,331	1,259	39,327
	Eastern States	63,967	21,169	10,592	2,264	1,108	6,434	1,769	32,206
41	Northern Shan States	9,125	2,771	1,406	94	27	824	385	4,948
42	Southern Shan States	52,973	17,816	8,774	2,154	1,066	5,513	1,371	26,383
43	Karenni	1,869	582	412	16	15	97	13	875

PART III.—*Details by districts*—contd.

Cultivation—*continued.*

Group 3c.—Agricultural labourers. Total Workers and Dependents.	Workers. Total Workers. Males.	Workers. Total Workers. Females.	Workers with an agricultural or other subsidiary occupation. Agricultural. Males.	Agricultural. Females.	Other. Males.	Other. Females.	Dependents.	Group 4.—Taungya. Total Workers and Dependents.	Workers. Total Workers. Males.	Workers. Total Workers. Females.	Workers with an agricultural or other subsidiary occupation. Agricultural. Males.	Agricultural. Females.	Other. Males.	Other. Females.	Dependents.	Serial No. of District, etc. (column 1).
10	11	12	13	14	15	16	17	18	19	20	21	22	23	24	25	
2,085,806	622,185	405,405	3,882	2,843	50,877	28,486	1,058,216	942,285	278,011	246,833	10,264	8,884	36,366	20,185	417,441	
2,059,835	612,863	398,162	3,615	2,393	49,565	27,787	1,048,810	570,010	163,895	142,054	2,300	1,392	11,976	3,321	264,061	
156,826	52,371	10,592	409	74	4,332	821	93,863	83,658	25,533	20,597	643	387	2,368	565	37,528	
139,866	47,060	6,669	324	13	3,553	196	85,537	32,486	10,008	7,388	238	27	1,003	198	15,090	1
20	3	3	.	..	...	...	14	19,497	6,473	6,240	29	47	32	3	6,784	2
13,239	3,635	2,812	81	51	567	466	6,792	20,541	5,921	4,329	285	241	787	203	10,291	3
3,701	1,073	1,108	4	10	212	159	1,520	11,134	3,131	2,640	91	72	546	161	5,363	4
644,998	192,321	108,801	1,086	579	17,940	9,060	343,876	23,592	5,977	3,325	131	77	856	238	14,290	
1,592	843	176	...	...	2	1	573	4	3	..	...	...	...	...	1	5
118,678	33,691	20,790	73	13	2,589	1,255	64,197	1,951	525	294	13	5	46	21	1,132	6
140,422	47,178	10,878	106	28	2,308	274	82,366	1,018	237	186	4	4	58	13	595	7
150,914	40,785	34,635	606	343	6,307	3,470	75,494	4,167	970	645	4	18	216	20	2,552	8
174,019	54,371	28,065	179	148	4,052	1,572	91,583	2,222	425	418	9	7	96	7	1,379	9
59,373	15,453	14,257	122	47	2,682	2,488	29,663	14,230	3,817	1,782	101	43	440	177	8,631	10
625,434	185,366	143,088	1,005	587	8,454	5,378	296,980	9,519	2,986	2,241	63	46	194	114	4,292	
150,819	39,462	39,746	124	64	2,112	1,847	71,611	5,533	1,685	1,422	22	9	107	47	2,426	11
168,582	45,573	47,286	632	477	3,418	2,037	75,723	2,703	914	606	35	36	61	52	1,183	12
103,185	34,956	21,530	126	...	1,244	515	46,699	1,178	348	201	6	1	21	15	629	13
85,883	20,597	21,015	93	42	1,026	634	38,271	37	11	3	...	...	2	...	23	14
116,965	38,778	13,511	30	4	654	345	64,676	68	28	9	...		3	..	31	15
303,960	86,862	44,816	564	90	8,236	2,785	172,282	182,995	49,377	36,770	672	243	3,600	1,137	96,848	
90,159	23,228	21,302	85	22	2,022	1,232	45,029	42,790	10,845	11,423	48	53	775	306	20,522	16
1,600	761	202	2	...	37	8	637	30,100	8,059	4,943	123	21	149	139	17,098	17
114,821	34,038	10,391	159	39	2,507	588	70,392	34,260	10,851	8,360	232	100	406	145	15,049	18
72,669	20,940	10,866	70	18	2,138	618	40,863	31,176	8,409	4,417	112	16	478	135	18,350	19
19,630	6,303	1,558	168	9	1,415	118	11,709	30,147	8,212	6,633	155	50	1,548	383	15,302	20
5,081	1,532	497	80	2	117	21	3,052	14,522	3,001	994	2	3	244	29	10,527	21
82,017	26,868	23,471	123	85	2,126	2,092	31,678	45,409	12,473	12,004	184	71	1,612	297	20,932	
6,708	1,708	1,774	56	16	194	64	[illegible],226	20,889	5,975	4,939	169	55	1,460	285	9,975	22
20,583	5,352	6,112	29	26	770	726	9,119	3,093	626	514	14	9	105	11	1,953	23
25,355	12,471	5,425	34	36	850	953	7,4[illegible]9	2,108	598	550	1	7	29	1	960	24
29,371	7,337	10,160	4	7	312	349	11,874	36	1	17	...	...	...	...	18	25
...	...	...	...	...	...	...	..	19,283	5,273	5,984	...	...	18	...	8,026	26
55,001	15,540	15,349	74	246	2,116	1,253	24,112	105,029	28,500	25,941	452	488	2,608	654	50,588	
32,037	9,665	9,382	16	165	833	652	12,990	1,350	518	181	...	21	201	62	651	27
1,898	*1,019*	*208*	...	..	*9*	*3*	*671*	*259*	*147*	...	...	..	*28*	..	*112*	
3,285	808	714	..	1	128	62	1,703	37,874	10,461	11,557	273	410	584	73	15,856	28
2,693	736	803	3	...	105	11	1,154	52,338	13,709	10,848	105	9	702	267	27,781	29
16,841	4,277	4,394	54	80	1,044	522	8,170	13,337	3,701	3,346	70	48	1,029	252	6,290	30
145	54	56	1	...	6	6	35	130	111	9	4	...	92	...	10	31
86,706	23,031	29,050	174	715	4,007	4,041	34,625	111,807	36,788	40,120	74	67	393	261	34,899	
21,933	5,606	7,396	...	53	1,123	1,170	8,931	1,063	26	590	1	2	7	21	447	32
31,982	8,280	11,160	112	55	1,053	2,052	12,542	36	7	-	...	...	6	...	29	33
17,023	4,833	5,661	16	506	642	569	6,529	92	...	16	..	...	..	2	76	34
15,722	4,304	4,833	46	101	1,189	250	6,585	3,548	972	936	73	65	351	157	1,640	35
46	8	...	...	.	...	...	38	107,068	35,783	38,578	...	...	29	81	32,707	36
104,893	30,504	22,945	180	17	2,354	2,357	51,394	[illegible],001	2,261	1,056	81	13	345	55	4,684	
27,053	8,378	6,946	31	1	536	781	11,729	1,662	434	185	64	7	41	...	1,043	37
19,369	6,600	3,102	26	6	460	438	9,667	1,229	603	120	...	3	177	25	500	38
35,951	9,758	8,157	101	10	1,104	745	18,046	3,537	774	563	...	...	77	17	2,200	39
22,510	5,768	4,790	22	...	254	393	11,952	1,573	450	182	17	3	50	13	941	40
25,971	9,322	7,243	267	450	1,312	699	9,406	372,275	114,116	104,779	7,964	7,492	24,390	16,864	153,380	
9,934	2,905	3,441	67	26	500	444	3,558	237,476	72,121	68,333	5,725	3,791	17,880	13,152	97,022	41
15,021	5,977	3,565	200	419	798	246	[illegible],479	104,026	34,328	27,261	2,156	3,645	6,325	3,624	42,443	42
1,046	440	237	...	5	14	9	369	30,773	7,673	9,1[illegible]5	83	56	185	88	13,915	43

Order IIA.—Culti

Serial No.	DISTRICT OR STATE.	Group 5.—Market gardening. Total Workers and Dependents.	Group 5.—WORKERS. (All without subsidiary occupation.) Males.	Group 5.—WORKERS. Females.	Group 5.—DEPENDENTS.	Group 6a.—Betel-vine. Total Workers and Dependents.	WORKERS. Total Workers. Males.	WORKERS. Total Workers. Females.	Workers with an agricultural or other subsidiary occupation. Agricultural. Males.	Agricultural. Females.	Other. Males.	Other. Females.	DEPENDENTS.
	1	2	3	4	5	6	7	8	9	10	11	12	13
	Provincial Total ...	162	71	1	90	19,412	5,616	3,701	567	136	739	175	10,095
	Divisional Burma ...	162	71	1	90	19,268	5,554	3,689	542	136	734	173	10,025
	Arakan Division ...	.	...	...	...	635	95	242	...	3	2	7	298
1	Akyab ...	...	...	...	...	575	95	197	...	...	2	3	283
2	Hill Dist. of Arakan ...	...	...	...	...	...	...	...	...	...	...	...	...
3	Kyaukpyu ...	...	...	...	...	...	...	...	...	...	...	.	...
4	Sandoway ...	...	...	...	...	60	...	45	...	3	...	4	15
	Pegu Division ...	86	49	...	37	1,816	495	328	75	10	95	...	993
5	Rangoon Town ...	84	47	...	37	4	4	...	...	...	...	...	...
6	Irsein ...	...	...	...	...	288	61	63	9	...	2	...	164
7	Hanthawaddy ...	...	...	...	...	4	...	1	...	...	...	...	3
8	Tharrawaddy ...	...	...	...	...	293	2	127	...	10	...		164
9	Pegu ...	2	2	...	...	1	...	...	...	...	...	...	1
10	Prome ...	...	...	...	...	1,226	428	137	66	...	93	...	661
	Irrawaddy Division ...	1	...	...	1	4,793	1,470	1,167	113	98	128	83	2,156
11	Bassein ...	...	...	...	...	1,488	430	397	25	19	31	16	661
12	Henzada ...	...	...	...	...	2,275	734	509	73	72	84	52	1,032
13	Myaungmya ...	1	...	...	1	603	200	146	15	6	13	15	257
14	Ma-ubin ...	...	...	...	...	70	12	14	...	1	...	...	44
15	Pyapôn ...	...	...	...	...	357	94	101	...	...	...	...	162
	Tenasserim Division ...	7	...	...	7	1,985	571	185	90	2	60	12	1,229
16	Toungoo ...	...	...	...	...	259	1	51	...	1	1	...	207
17	Salween ...	...	...	...	...	2	...	...	...	...	...	...	2
18	Thatôn ...	2	...	...	2	321	114	4	2	...	31	...	203
19	Amherst ...	5	...	...	5	953	314	59	54	...	10	1	580
20	Tavoy ...	...	...	...	...	447	142	71	34	1	18	11	234
21	Mergui ...	...	...	...	...	3	...	...	...	...	...	...	3
	Magwe Division ...	22	13	...	9	4,019	1,192	1,034	56	20	226	63	1,793
22	Thayetmyo ...	...	...	...	...	456	100	40	...		13	...	316
23	Pakôkku ...	22	13	...	9	993	283	242	13	8	93	28	468
24	Minbu ...	...	...	...	...	1,913	636	539	41	12	110	35	738
25	Magwe ...	...	...	...	...	657	173	213	2	...	10	...	271
26	Pakôkku Hill Tracts ...	...	...	...	...	...	...	...	...	...	...	...	...
	Mandalay Division ...	46	9	1	36	207	86	48	2	...	15	...	73
27	Mandalay ...	7	3	...	4	206	85	48	2	...	15	...	73
	Mandalay City ...	*7*	*3*	...	*4*	*16*	*7*	...	...	...	...	...	*9*
28	Bhamo ...	4	4	...	...	1	1	...	...	...	...	...	...
29	Myitkyina ...	19	2	...	17	...	...	...	...	...	...	...	...
30	Katha ...	16	...	1	15	...	...	...	...	...	...	...	...
31	Putao ...	...	...	...	...	...	...	...	...	...	...	...	...
	Sagaing Division ...	...	...	...	...	1,620	543	316	156	3	115	8	761
32	Shwebo ...	...	...	...	...	13	1	6	1	...	.	...	6
33	Sagaing ...	...	...	...	...	244	112	55	5	3	23	8	77
34	Lower Chindwin ...	...	...	...	...	1,313	405	255	150	...	80	...	653
35	Upper Chindwin ...	...	...	...	...	50	25	...	...	...	12	...	25
36	Chin Hills ...	...	...	...	...	...	...	...	...	...	.	...	...
	Meiktila Division ...	...	...	...	...	4,193	1,102	369	50	...	93	...	2,722
37	Kyauksè ...	...	...	...	...	476	167	96	4	...	17	...	313
38	Meiktila ...	...	...	...	...	2,945	732	163	43	...	66	...	2,050
39	Yamèthin ...	...	...	...	...	690	187	85	3	...	9	...	418
40	Myingyan ...	...	...	...	...	82	16	25	...	...	1	...	41
	Eastern States ...	...	...	...	...	144	62	12	25	...	5	2	70
41	Northern Shan States ...	...	...	...	...	...	...	...	...	...	...	...	...
42	Southern Shan States ...	...	...	...	...	144	62	12	25	...	5	2	70
43	Karenni ...	...	...	...	...	...	...	...	...	...	...	...	...

PART III.—*Details by districts*—contd.

vation—*continued.*

Group 6b.—Rubber.								Group 6c.—Sugar-cane.								
Total Workers and Dependents.	WORKERS.						DEPENDENTS.	Total Workers and Dependents.	WORKERS.						DEPENDENTS.	Serial No. of District, etc. (column 1).
	Total Workers.		Workers with an agricultural or other subsidiary occupation.						Total Workers.		Workers with an agricultural or other subsidiary occupation.					
			Agricultural.		Other.						Agricultural.		Other.			
	Males.	Females.	Males.	Females.	Males.	Females.			Males.	Females.	Males.	Females.	Males.	Females.		
14	15	16	17	18	19	20	21	22	23	24	25	26	27	28	29	
9,129	5,620	807	14	9	48	17	2,702	16,809	5,336	1,969	312	77	320	83	9,504	
9,129	5,620	807	14	9	48	17	2,702	16,700	5,284	1,958	293	77	320	82	9,458	
55	4	1	...	...	...	...	50	335	104	78	3	7	9	4	153	
55	4	1	...	...	...	...	50	184	52	28	...	...	5	...	104	1
...	...	...	...	...	...	...	...	...	...	...	...	...	...	...	...	2
...	...	...	...	...	...	...	...	...	...	...	...	...	...	...	...	3
...	...	...	...	...	...	...	...	151	52	50	3	7	4	4	49	4
494	177	64	1	...	...	1	253	745	197	209	26	5	5	10	339	
38	5	...	...	...	...	...	33	...	...	...	...	...	...	...	...	5
174	62	13	...	...	...	...	99	64	27	11	...	...	...	...	26	6
215	86	33	1	...	...	1	96	56	...	35	...	...	...	...	21	7
...	...	...	...	...	...	...	...	145	32	32	25	...	...	...	81	8
67	24	18	...	...	...	...	25	28	9	3	...	...	...	...	16	9
...	...	...	...	...	...	...	...	452	129	128	1	5	5	10	195	10
...	...	...	...	...	...	...	...	993	359	202	21	1	46	20	432	
...	...	...	...	...	...	...	...	715	266	157	15	1	40	20	292	11
...	...	...	...	...	...	...	...	119	50	1	6	...	5	...	68	12
...	...	...	...	...	...	...	...	68	8	23	...	...	...	...	37	13
...	...	...	...	...	...	...	...	46	24	11	...	...	1	...	11	14
...	...	...	...	...	...	...	...	45	11	10	...	...	...	...	24	15
8,397	5,399	713	13	...	46	7	2,285	6,802	2,229	668	130	39	114	31	3,905	
790	656	36	...	...	2	2	98	1,886	740	243	17	8	60	19	903	16
1	1	...	...	...	...	...	...	212	102	6	4	...	1	...	104	17
481	319	8	4	...	...	...	154	2,989	822	221	85	27	46	2	1,946	18
1,093	541	179	4	...	1	...	373	1,507	529	184	19	2	3	8	794	19
684	342	53	5	...	6	5	289	206	36	14	5	2	4	2	156	20
5,348	3,540	437	...	...	37	...	1,371	2	...	...	...	...	...	...	2	21
83	7	6	...	...	...	...	70	18	9	1	...	...	2	...	8	
...	...	...	...	...	...	...	...	18	9	1	...	...	2	...	8	22
66	...	3	...	...	...	...	63	...	...	...	...	...	...	...	...	23
17	7	3	...	...	...	...	7	...	...	...	...	...	...	...	...	24
...	...	...	...	...	...	...	...	...	...	...	...	...	...	...	...	25
...	...	...	...	...	...	...	...	...	...	...	...	...	...	...	...	26
38	26	2	...	...	1	...	10	626	318	45	13	...	64	8	263	
2	...	...	...	...	...	...	2	12	12	...	...	...	9	...	...	27
2	...	...	...	...	...	...	2	...	...	...	...	...	...	...	...	
6	5	1	...	...	...	...	...	9	9	...	...	...	...	...	...	28
12	11	1	...	...	...	...	...	40	19	9	...	...	...	...	12	29
18	10	...	...	...	1	...	8	565	278	36	13	...	55	8	251	30
...	...	...	...	...	...	...	...	...	...	...	...	...	...	...	...	31
57	2	21	...	9	...	9	34	5	2	...	...	...	2	...	3	
9	2	3	...	...	...	...	4	...	...	...	...	...	...	...	...	32
...	...	...	...	...	...	...	...	2	...	...	...	...	...	...	2	33
...	...	...	...	...	...	...	...	...	...	...	...	...	...	...	...	34
48	...	18	...	9	...	9	30	3	2	...	...	...	2	...	1	35
...	...	...	...	...	...	...	...	...	...	...	...	...	...	...	...	36
5	5	...	...	...	1	...	...	7,176	2,066	755	100	25	78	9	4,355	
...	...	...	...	...	...	...	...	5	3	...	...	...	...	...	2	37
5	5	...	...	...	1	...	...	43	...	7	...	...	...	...	36	38
...	...	...	...	...	...	...	...	7,128	2,063	748	100	25	78	9	4,317	39
...	...	...	...	...	...	...	...	...	...	...	...	...	...	...	...	40
...	...	...	...	...	...	...	...	109	52	11	19	...	...	1	46	
...	...	...	...	...	...	...	...	57	20	11	...	...	...	1	26	41
...	...	...	...	...	...	...	...	52	32	...	19	...	...	...	20	42
...	...	...	...	...	...	...	...	...	...	...	...	...	...	...	...	43

Order II.—

Groups 6*d*.—Citronella, 6*e*.—Tea, 6*f*.—Opium and Ganja, 6*g*.—Coffee, 6*h*.—Indigo, 6*j*.—Cinchona.

Serial No.	DISTRICT OR STATE.	Total Workers and Dependents.	WORKERS. Total Workers. Males.	Females.	Workers with an agricultural or other subsidiary occupation. Agricultural. Males.	Females.	Other. Males.	Females.	DEPENDENTS.
	1	2	3	4	5	6	7	8	9
	Provincial Total ...	45,332	12,184	13,455	2,109	1,788	831	570	19,693
	Divisional Burma ...	137	62	15	3	...	...	...	60
	Arakan Division ..								
1	Akyab								
2	Hill Dist of Arakan ...								
3	Kyaukpyu								
4	Sandoway								
	Pegu Division ..								
5	Rangoon Town ...								
6	Insein								
7	Hanthawaddy ...								
8	Tharrawaddy ...								
9	Pegu								
10	Prome								
	Irrawaddy Division ...								
11	Bassein								
12	Henzada ..								
13	Myaungmya ...								
14	Ma-ubin								
15	Pyapôn								
	Tenasserim Division ..								
16	Toungoo								
17	Salween								
18	Thatôn								
19	Amherst								
20	Tavoy								
21	Mergui								
	Magwe Division ...								
22	Thayetmyo ...								
23	Pakôkku								
24	Minbu								
25	Magwe ...								
26	Pakôkku Hill Tracts ...								
	Mandalay Division ...								
27	Mandalay ...								
	Mandalay City ...								
28	Bhamo								
29	Myitkyina .								
30	Katha								
31	Putao								
	Sagaing Division ...								
32	Shwebo								
33	Sagaing ...								
34	Lower Chindwin ...								
35	Upper Chindwin ...								
36	Chin Hills								
	Meiktila Division ...								
37	Kyauksè								
38	Meiktila								
39	Yamèthin ...								
40	Myingyan								
	Eastern States ..								
41	Northern Shan States ...								
42	Southern Shan States .								
43	Karenni								

Analysis of figures for Group 6*d*.—Citronella, 6*e*.—Tea, 6*f*.—Opium and Ganja, 6*g*.—Coffee, 6*h*.—Indigo, 6*j*.—Cinchona.

DISTRICT.	Total Workers and Dependents.	WORKERS. Total Workers. Males.	Females.	Workers with an agricultural or other subsidiary occupation. Agricultural. Males.	Females.	Other. Males.	Females.	DEPENDENTS.
1	2	3	4	5	6	7	8	9
	45,332	12,184	13,455	2,109	1,788	831	570	19,693
Thatôn (6*d*) ...	4	4	...	...	...	...	...	...
Amherst (6*d*) ...	118	55	6	3	...	...	...	57
Tavoy (6*j*) ...	2	2	...	...	...	...	...	...
Katha (6*e*) ...	9	...	7	...	...	...	...	2
Shwebo (6*e*) ...	2	1	...	...	...	...	...	1
Lower Chindwin (6*h*) ...	2	...	2	...	...	...	...	...
N. Shan States (6*d*) ...	222	159	...	26	...	...	...	63
N. Shan States (6*e*) ...	38,104	10,304	11,416	1,745	1,670	511	154	16,384
N. Shan States (6*f*) ...	5,298	1,200	1,621	167	38	233	287	2,477
N. Shan States (6*g*) ...	2	1	...	...	...	...	...	1
S. Shan States (6*f*) ...	1,569	458	403	168	80	87	129	708

PART III.—*Details by districts*—contd.

Cultivation—*concluded.*								Order II B.—Forestry.								
Group 7.—Orchard gardens and all other horticulture not included in Groups 5 and 6.								Group 8.—Forest officers, rangers, guards, etc.								
Total Workers and Dependents.	RKERS.						DEPENDENTS.	Total Workers and Dependents.	WORKERS.						DEPENDENTS.	Serial No. of District, etc. (column 1).
	Total Workers.		Workers with an agricultural or other subsidiary occupation.						Total Workers.		Workers with an agricultural or other subsidiary occupation.					
			Agricultural.		Other.						Agricultural.		Other.			
	Males.	Females.	Males.	Females.	Males.	Females.			Males.	Females.	Males.	Females.	Males.	Females.		
10	11	12	13	14	15	16	17	18	19	20	21	22	23	24	25	
161,791	50,759	31,135	2,857	1,411	3,675	1,974	79,897	12,168	4,189	189	43	...	34	12	7,790	
138,892	43,782	25,013	1,875	816	2,814	1,293	70,097	11,806	4,068	187	43	...	31	12	7,551	
3,370	1,203	463	58	13	76	22	1,704	460	158	14	3	...	2	..	288	
2,209	851	193	20	...	42	8	1,165	220	76	...	..	...	2	...	144	1
19	10	3	...	...	...	..	6	14	9	...	...	...	...	...	5	2
982	295	236	33	13	30	10	451	103	46	13	3	...	...	...	44	3
160	47	31	5	...	4	4	82	123	27	1	.	.	...	...	95	4
36,009	11,470	5,916	292	141	729	358	18,623	3,150	1,084	49	1	...	3	...	2,027	
2,922	1,657	116	10	...	5	...	1,149	494	68	35	..	...	..	...	391	5
8,259	3,083	1,034	49	30	114	61	4,142	315	160	.	.	...	...	...	155	6
6,799	1,765	998	81	15	158	44	4,036	33	2	10	...	...	..		21	7
7,670	1,883	1,259	59	46	151	99	4,528	1,631	587	1	...	...	...	...	1,043	8
1,369	436	210	18	13	61	23	723	298	121	2	1	...	...	.	175	9
8,990	2,646	2,299	75	37	240	131	4,045	379	146	1	...	...	3	...	232	10
39,873	12,310	10,229	722	440	699	428	17,334	601	205	5	2	...	...	...	392	
15,541	4,711	3,764	235	108	283	134	7,066	191	62	...	...	...	..	...	129	11
11,144	3,390	3,168	202	132	234	236	4,586	198	73	.	2	...	..	..	125	12
6,659	2,173	1,556	157	93	137	15	2,930	79	23	5	..	..	...	...	51	13
5,849	1,792	1,594	126	104	45	39	2,263	39	16	...	..	..	.	...	23	14
880	244	147	2	3	...	4	489	94	31	..	...	.	.	...	63	15
44,899	12,882	6,338	648	176	749	259	25,679	2,933	958	24	20	...	4	7	1,951	
7,015	2,522	1,533	172	58	69	25	3,560	1,178	423	1	17	...	4	1	754	16
511	140	67	27	10	9	5	304	124	52	1	..	...		...	71	17
8,618	2,431	1,282	208	47	201	64	4,905	381	137	3	...	...		...	241	18
12,424	3,633	1,596	62	22	248	77	2,195	920	231	1	...	...	...	..	688	19
3,858	1,115	846	95	26	90	82	1,897	220	84	...	3	...	...	..	136	20
11,873	3,041	1,014	84	13	132	6	7,818	110	31	18	...	...	.	6	61	21
1,054	412	197	37	11	64	30	445	801	354	...	2	...	...	...	447	
233	70	48	2	...	7	..	115	311	129	...	...	...	.	..	182	22
61	20	13	1	1	5	3	28	242	121	...	2	...	...	..	121	23
684	262	125	34	10	51	25	297	164	55	...	...	...	...	.	109	24
76	60	11	...	...	1	2	5	82	48	...	...		...	...	34	25
...	...	...	...	...	...	...	..	2	1	...	...	...	...	..	1	26
8,942	3,095	1,432	45	31	184	174	4,415	1,645	586	86	4	..	8	4	973	
7,435	2,651	1,221	35	26	124	134	3,563	433	201	1	1	..	5	...	231	27
300	*192*	7	...	...	*1*	...	*101*	*117*	*28*	...	...	...	...	...	89	
562	121	96	1	...	8	34	345	258	90	2	1	...	2	...	166	28
384	146	43	...	...	18	3	195	183	80	4	...	...	1	...	99	29
558	176	71	9	4	34	3	311	771	215	79	2	...	..	4	477	30
3	1	1	...	1	...	...	1	...	...	..	...	...	...	...	—	31
1,114	310	340	5	1	42	16	464	1,063	373		11	...	11	1	683	
312	89	132	1	..	8	2	91	241	78	5	...	...	...	1	158	32
427	150	24	3	.	21	...	253	96	14	...	...	...	...	...	82	33
248	24	156	...	1	6	12	68	133	69	...	...	...	3	...	64	34
121	45	28	1	...	7	2	48	586	209	2	11	...	8	...	375	35
6	2	...	...	...	...	...	4	7	3	...	...	...		...	4	36
3,631	2,100	98	68	3	271	6	1,433	1,153	350	2	...		3	...	801	
1,176	293	16	21	...	22	...	867	18	1	...	...	.	...	...	17	37
80	28	14	1	...	2	1	38	154	52	1	...	...	1	..	101	38
247	111	22	4	1	5	...	114	908	265	1	...	...	2	...	642	39
2,128	1,668	46	42	2	242	5	414	73	32	...	...	...	..	...	41	40
22,899	6,977	6,122	982	595	861	681	9,800	362	121	2	...	...	3	...	239	
8,405	2,435	2,685	94	79	519	400	3,285	191	59	2	...	...	...	.	130	41
14,346	4,486	3,404	881	516	337	281	6,456	136	53	...	...	...	3	...	83	42
148	56	33	7	...	5	...	59	35	9	...	...	...	...	...	26	43

Serial No.	DISTRICT OR STATE.	Total Workers and Dependents.	Group 9a.—Charcoal burners. WORKERS. Total Workers. Males.	Females.	Workers with an agricultural or other subsidiary occupation. Agricultural. Males.	Females.	Other. Males.	Females.	DEPENDENTS.
	1	2	3	4	5	6	7	8	9
	Provincial Total ...	3,584	1,214	365	34	28	37	21	2,005
	Divisional Burma ...	3,558	1,207	354	32	28	37	21	1,997
	Arakan Division ...	79	47	4	...	...	...	...	28
1	Akyab ...	74	46	1	...	...	...	...	27
2	Hill Dist. of Arakan ...	...	..	...	...	...	..	...	...
3	Kyaukpyu ...	1	1	...	...	...	...	...	...
4	Sandoway ...	4	...	3	...	...	...	...	1
	Pegu Division ...	903	336	127	...	...	10	...	440
5	Rangoon Town ...	...	..	...	...	...	...	...	...
6	Insein ...	609	254	57	...	...	9	...	298
7	Hanthawaddy ...	...	...	...	...	...	...	...	...
8	Tharrawaddy ...	39	23	3	-	...	...	...	13
9	Pegu ...	55	14	1	...	...	1	...	40
10	Prome ...	200	45	66	...	...	...	...	89
	Irrawaddy Division ...	99	44	7	...	...	1	...	48
11	Bassein ...	76	31	7	...	...	...	...	38
12	Henzada ...	23	13	...	...	...	1	...	10
13	Myaungmya ...	...	...	...	...	..	...	...	...
14	Ma-ubin ...	...	...	...	...	...	...	...	...
15	Pyapôn ...	..	...	...	...	...	...	...	...
	Tenasserim Division ...	1,638	400	179	23	28	9	20	1,059
16	Toungoo ...	96	31	7	...	...	2	...	58
17	Salween ...	...	...	...	...	...	...	...	...
18	Thatôn ...	1,055	272	120	3	18	7	16	663
19	Amherst ...	391	72	22	20	8	...	...	297
20	Tavoy ...	34	...	30	...	2	.	4	4
21	Mergui ...	62	25	...	...	...	.	...	37
	Magwe Division ...	121	51	6	...	...	2	...	64
22	Thayetmyo	98	37	5	...	...	2	...	56
23	Pakôkku ...	...	...	...	...	...	...	...	...
24	Minbu ...	23	14	1	...	...	...	...	8
25	Magwe ...	...	...	...	...	...	...	...	...
26	Pakôkku Hill Tracts ...	...	...	..	..	...	...	...	...
	Mandalay Division ...	413	196	25	3	...	9	1	192
27	Mandalay ...	208	69	20	2	...	6	1	119
	Mandalay City ...	*30*	*1*	*20*	..	...	..	*1*	*9*
28	Bhamo ...	159	109	1	1	...	3	...	49
29	Myitkyina ...	1	1	...	...	...	...	...	...
30	Katha ...	45	17	4	...	...	...	..	24
31	Putao ...	...	...	...	...	...	...	...	...
	Sagaing Division ..	171	80	3	5	...	3	...	88
32	Shwebo ...	...	...	...	...	...	...	...	...
33	Sagaing ...	85	8	2	3	...	1	...	75
34	Lower Chindwin ...	...	...	...	...	.	...	...	...
35	Upper Chindwin ...	86	72	1	2	...	2	...	13
36	Chin Hills ...	...	...	...	...	...	...	...	...
	Meiktila Division ...	134	53	3	1	...	3	...	78
37	Kyauksè ...	..	...	...	...	...	...	...	...
38	Meiktila ...	2	...	...	...	...	...	...	2
39	Yamèthin ...	127	52	3	1	...	3	...	72
40	Myingyan ...	5	1	..	...	...	...	...	4
	Eastern States ...	26	7	11	2	..	...	...	8
41	Northern Shan States ...	8	5	3	...	...	...	...	...
42	Southern Shan States ...	18	2	8	2	...	...	...	8
43	Karenni ...	...	...	...	...	...	...	...	...

PART III.—*Details by districts—contd.*

IIB.—Forestry—*continued.*

Group 9b.—Wood and bamboo cutters and fuel collectors.								Group 9c.—Cutch collectors.								
Total Workers and Dependents.	WORKERS.						DEPENDENTS.	Total Workers and Dependents.	WORKERS.						DEPENDENTS.	Serial No. of District, etc. (column 1).
	Total Workers.		Workers with an agricultural or other subsidiary occupation.						Total Workers.		Workers with an agricultural or other subsidiary occupation.					
			Agricultural.		Other.						Agricultural.		Other.			
	Males.	Females.	Males.	Females.	Males.	Females.			Males.	Females.	Males.	Females.	Males.	Females.		
10	11	12	13	14	15	16	17	18	19	20	21	22	23	24	25	
51,322	21,278	3,748	589	91	1,617	176	26,296	2,482	747	506	20	19	61	40	1,229	
49,058	20,280	3,638	504	76	1,541	171	25,140	2,366	724	954	20	18	61	40	1,147	
1,257	143	53	3	...	11	10	1,061	172	59	...	1	...	...	..	113	
1,086	67	39	1	...	...	10	980	172	59	...	1	...	...	...	113	1
...	...	...	...	..	...	...	..	...	...	...	...	...	...	...	...	2
77	15	2	...	...	1	...	60	...	...	..	...	...	...	...	...	3
94	61	12	2	...	10	...	21	...	...	...	...	...	...	...	...	4
5,914	2,455	410	31	1	48	5	3,049	266	35	64	...	...	11	...	167	
148	93	...	...	...	1	...	55	2	..	...	..	..	...	...	2	5
1,023	430	102	13	1	6	...	491	...	...	...	...	...	...	...	...	6
198	57	9	2	...	1	..	132	...	...	...	...	...	...	...	...	7
1,398	679	44	7	...	13	..	675	...	...	...	...	...	...	...	...	8
2,005	686	202	8	...	26	1	1,117	..	...	...	...	...	.	...	...	9
1,142	510	53	1	..	1	4	579	264	35	64	...	.	11	...	165	10
6,506	2,247	666	34	3	72	8	3,593	29	19	6	...	...	1	...	4	
3,151	949	312	22	3	43	7	1,890	...	...	..	...	...	...	...	...	11
646	284	116	6	...	9	...	246	29	19	6	...	...	1	...	4	12
1,436	525	190	3	...	14	...	721	...	...	...	.	...	...	...	...	13
373	181	15	...	...	3	1	177	...	...	...	...	...	...	...	...	14
900	308	33	3	...	3	...	559	...	...	...	...	...	...	...	...	15
8,189	3,273	221	54	4	157	11	4,695	101	38	...	...	..	1	...	63	
3,890	1,764	48	10	..	75	5	2,078	87	29	...	...	...	1	...	58	16
230	120	6	1	3	2	1	104	..	..	...	...	...	..	...	...	17
919	253	31	..	...	3	...	635	9	9	...	...	...	...	...	.	18
1,672	743	86	9	..	...	3	843	5	...	...	..	...	...		5	19
851	301	17	34	1	75	2	533	...	...	...	...	...	...	...	...	20
627	92	33	...	...	2	...	502	...	...	..	...	..	...	...	...	21
3,604	1,638	451	19	7	149	51	1,515	971	350	192	11	...	38	8	429	
1,287	419	303	...	7	34	51	505	5	5	...	..	...	...	...	...	22
1,778	958	73	15	...	94	...	747	535	181	84	9	.	34	8	270	23
446	206	13	4		21	..	227	58	36	8	1	...	1	...	14	24
36	20	2	...	...	...	...	14	373	128	100	1	.	3	...	145	25
57	35	...	...	...	..	...	22	...	.	...	...	..	...	...	...	26
7,436	3,280	626	59	15	205	28	3,530	98	61	12	...	...	...	...	25	
3,431	1,340	383	12	7	68	2	1,708	78	43	10	...	..		...	25	27
550	*189*	*37*	...	...	...		*324*	*31*	*31*	...	...	...	...	...	...	
1,540	745	91	29	...	96	6	704	...	...	...	...	...	...	...	...	28
370	291	12	3	...	6	1	67	2	..	2	..	...	...	...	...	29
2,095	904	140	15	8	35	19	1,051	18	18	..	...	..	...	...	...	30
...	...	...	...	..	...	...	...	...	...	...	..	..	...	...	...	31
9,725	4,539	846	185	46	647	58	4,340	454	108	179	7	18	6	32	167	
870	324	115	17	6	35	11	431	2.0	31	138	.	18	1	27	41	32
1,729	588	199	40	4	133	16	942	1	1	...	..	...	..	...	...	33
2,098	1,287	33	31	1	187	3	838	109	43	12	2	...	5	..	54	34
5,028	2,400	493	97	35	292	23	2,129	134	33	29	5	...	...	5	72	35
...	...	..	...	..	...	...	...		...	...	...	...	...	..	...	36
6,427	2,705	365	119	...	252	...	3,357	275	54	42	1	...	4	...	179	
417	145	19	6		13	...	253	...	...	...	...	...	...	...	...	37
796	307	318	...	.	21	...	171	173	33	5	1	...	1	...	135	38
5,083	2,213	4	113	...	218	...	2,866	59	9	23	...	...	3	...	27	39
131	40	24	..	...	...	...	67	43	12	14	...	...	...	...	17	40
2,264	998	110	85	15	76	5	1,156	116	23	11	...	1		...	82	
1,886	805	95	66	11	70	5	986	115	23	11	...	1	..	...	81	41
335	155	15	19	4	6	...	165	...	...	...	...	...	...	...	...	42
43	38	...	...	...	...	...	5	1	..	...	...	...	...	..	1	43

Serial No.	District or State.	Order IIb.—Forestry—*concluded.* Group 9d.—All other collectors of forest produce except lac collectors. Total Workers and Dependents.	Workers. Total Workers. Males.	Workers. Total Workers. Females.	Workers with an agricultural or other subsidiary occupation. Agricultural. Males.	Agricultural. Females.	Other. Males.	Other. Females.	Dependents.	Group 10.—Lac collectors. Total Workers and Dependents.	Workers. (All without subsidiary occupation.) Males.	Females.	Dependents.
	1	2	3	4	5	6	7	8	9	10	11	12	13
	Provincial Total ...	11,493	4,196	2,741	112	36	305	78	4,556	16	6	5	5
	Divisional Burma ...	11,317	4,123	2,718	108	36	301	77	4,476	14	6	3	5
	Arakan Division ...	52	21	19	...	...	2	1	12	...	...	...	...
1	Akyab ...	13	12	1	...	...	...	...	...	...	...	...	...
2	Hill Dist. of Arakan ...	6	...	...	...	...	...	...	6	...	...	...	...
3	Kyaukpyu ...	22	4	14	...	...	2	1	4	...	...	...	...
4	Sandoway ...	11	5	4	...	...	...	...	2	...	...	...	...
	Pegu Division ...	1,242	559	182	7	6	3	1	501	...	...	...	...
5	Rangoon Town ...	206	201	...	...	...	...	...	5	...	...	...	...
6	Insein ...	337	62	91	...	4	...	...	184	...	...	...	...
7	Hanthawaddy ...	16	11	1	...	...	...	...	4	...	...	...	...
8	Tharrawaddy ...	25	10	...	...	...	...	...	15	...	...	...	...
9	Pegu ...	310	107	60	7	2	3	1	143	...	...	...	...
10	Prome ...	348	168	30	...	...	...	...	150	...	...	...	...
	Irrawaddy Division ...	728	243	134	6	3	8	1	351	...	...	...	...
11	Bassein ...	118	...	85	...	3	...	1	33	...	...	...	...
12	Henzada ...	146	48	5	...	...	1	...	93	...	...	...	...
13	Myaungmya ...	333	189	...	6	...	7	...	144	...	...	...	...
14	Ma-ubin ...	87	...	41	...	...	...	...	46	...	...	...	...
15	Pyapôn ...	44	6	3	...	...	...	...	35	...	...	...	...
	Tenasserim Division ...	3,830	1,001	1,281	22	6	52	34	1,548	1	1	...	...
16	Toungoo ...	1,102	419	117	...	...	27	3	626	...	...	...	...
17	Salween ...	37	5	15	...	...	...	1	17	...	...	...	...
18	Thatôn ...	336	140	95	9	...	7	1	101	...	...	...	...
19	Amherst ...	782	141	223	6	...	...	8	418	1	1	...	...
20	Tavoy ...	1,163	90	795	7	6	4	21	278	...	...	...	...
21	Mergui ...	350	206	36	...	...	14	...	108	...	...	...	...
	Magwe Division ...	1,002	421	171	22	11	70	5	410	13	5	3	5
22	Thayetmyo ...	118	19	83	...	...	...	...	16	...	...	...	...
23	Pakôkku ...	428	222	9	19	...	64	...	197	...	...	...	...
24	Minbu ...	388	121	79	2	11	2	5	188	13	5	3	5
25	Magwe ...	68	59	...	1	...	4	...	9	...	...	...	...
26	Pakôkku Hill Tracts ...	...	...	...	...	...	...	...	...	...	...	...	...
	Mandalay Division ...	2,386	1,338	272	40	6	94	13	776	...	...	...	...
27	Mandalay ...	1,301	714	88	33	...	65	...	499	...	...	...	...
	Mandalay City ...	*183*	*86*	*12*	...	...	...	...	*85*	...	...	...	...
28	Bhamo ...	536	381	56	7	...	29	2	99	...	...	...	...
29	Myitkyina ...	269	208	4	...	...	...	1	57	...	...	...	...
30	Katha ...	280	35	124	...	6	...	10	121	...	...	...	...
31	Putao ...	...	...	...	...	...	...	...	...	...	...	...	...
	Sagaing Division ...	921	353	156	11	3	53	5	412	...	...	...	...
32	Shwebo ...	175	76	26	...	1	24	1	73	...	...	...	...
33	Sagaing ...	292	128	39	1	2	4	...	125	...	...	...	...
34	Lower Chindwin ...	104	53	3	3	...	8	...	48	...	...	...	...
35	Upper Chindwin ...	350	96	88	7	...	17	4	166	...	...	...	...
36	Chin Hills ...	...	...	...	...	...	...	...	...	...	...	...	...
	Meiktila Division ...	1,156	187	503	...	1	19	17	466	...	...	...	...
37	Kyaukse ...	19	7	3	...	...	...	...	9	...	...	...	...
38	Meiktila ...	365	28	225	...	1	3	4	112	...	...	...	...
39	Yamèthin ...	620	123	191	...	...	16	5	306	...	...	...	...
40	Myingyan ...	152	29	84	...	...	...	8	39	...	...	...	...
	Eastern States ...	176	73	23	4	...	4	1	80	2	...	2	...
41	Northern Shan States ...	140	56	17	1	...	...	...	67	2	...	2	...
42	Southern Shan States ...	22	15	3	3	...	4	1	4	...	...	...	...
43	Karenni ...	14	2	3	...	...	...	...	9	...	...	...	...

Order IIc.—Raising of farm stock.																
Group 11.—Cattle and buffalo breeders and keepers.								Group 12.—Sheep, goat and pig breeders.								Serial No. of District, etc. (column 1).
Total Workers and Dependents.	WORKERS.						DEPENDENTS.	Total Workers and Dependents.	WORKERS.						DEPENDENTS.	
	Total Workers.		Workers with an agricultural or other subsidiary occupation.						Total Workers.		Workers with an agricultural or other subsidiary occupation.					
			Agricultural.		Other.						Agricultural.		Other.			
	Males.	Females.	Males.	Females.	Males.	Females.			Males.	Females.	Males.	Females.	Males.	Females.		
14	15	16	17	18	19	20	21	22	23	24	25	26	27	28	29	
26,214	11,786	3,204	192	62	1,391	313	11,224	14,505	3,809	3,762	240	233	615	565	6,934	
23,803	10,885	2,758	156	29	1,241	252	10,160	11,364	3,042	2,512	97	76	428	347	5,810	
311	173	42	..	..	8	2	96	8	1	5	...	1	...	...	2	
153	146	36		..	6	1	71	6	1	4	...	1	...	...	1	1
18	8	..	...	...	...	...	10	...	...	...	...	...	...	...	...	2
...	...	...	...	...	...	...	...	2	...	1	...	...	...	...	1	3
40	19	6	..	...	2	1	15	...	...	...	...	...	...	...	...	4
6,089	3,610	616	20	1	211	16	2,463	1,351	363	233	2	...	27	14	755	
1,050	748	48	...	...	1	...	254	126	...	73	...	...	...	5	53	5
3,189	1,759	251	11	...	91	10	1,119	346	132	54	...	...	...	7	160	6
368	141	59	1	..	2	..	168	306	92	21	2	..	12	..	193	7
920	259	56	3	...	56	2	305	102	18	9	...	...	...	..	75	8
853	379	124	2	1	23	..	350	387	93	61	...	...	10	2	233	9
669	324	78	2	.	39	4	267	84	28	15	...	..	5	...	41	10
1,732	900	159	3	...	48	3	673	613	150	87	...	4	29	10	376	
481	298	27		...	5	1	156	169	13	33	...	1	...	4	123	11
432	177	45	..	...	10	2	210	78	40	2	...	..	4	...	36	12
214	137	17	1	...	18	...	60	236	82	26	...	3	25	4	128	13
429	194	58	2	..	15	...	177	45	14	9	...	...	...	...	22	14
176	94	12	...	...	...	...	70	85	1	17	...	...	...	2	67	15
2,192	947	293	11	1	67	18	952	1,831	528	373	2	3	56	19	930	
718	304	79	...	...	31	9	335	182	45	5	...	1	9	...	132	16
73	23	4	3	1	2	..	40	1	...	1	...		...	...	...	17
308	160	11	3	...	24	6	127	675	98	277	...	...	13	10	300	18
671	313	77	...	..	1	.	281	784	290	61	2	..	26	5	433	19
310	105	101	5	...	3	3	104	117	39	29	...	2	6	4	49	20
112	42	11	...	...	6	...	59	72	56	.	...	...	2	...	16	21
1,958	755	336	11	16	74	51	867	1,931	375	669	24	51	47	144	887	
506	185	77	4	2	17	5	244	82	39	14	...	...	2	6	29	22
676	148	200	5	14	27	44	328	1,036	98	443	15	37	31	110	495	23
364	196	28	2	...	26	...	140	393	120	123	3	13	8	24	150	24
412	226	31	...	.	4	2	155	420	118	89	6	1	6	4	213	25
...	...	...	...	...	...	...	...	...	..	...	...	...	...	...	...	26
4,070	1,975	332	19	...	344	39	2,363	961	228	184	3	2	44	36	549	
1,953	965	142	5	..	54	2	846	320	28	80	2	2	3	4	212	27
945	*413*	*85*	...	.	*11*	...	*447*	*137*	*4*	*29*	...	...	...	...	*104*	
285	105	20	...	...	2	..	160	258	46	61	...	...	10	31	151	28
1,450	576	114	3	...	262	33	760	206	105	29	...	..	21	...	72	29
943	309	51	11	...	26	4	583	177	49	14	1	...	10	1	114	30
39	20	5	...	..	...	..	14	.	...	...	...	...	...	...	...	31
3,415	1,498	550	69	8	400	106	1,367	2,291	876	443	58	7	147	62	972	
507	210	64	...	1	50	1	233	776	191	281	6	7	53	44	304	32
989	466	193	28	3	41	8	[illegible]	807	366	87	32	...	52	...	354	33
569	207	88	3	..	22	9	274	660	303	63	2	...	38	18	294	34
1,268	558	189	37	4	286	88	521	48	16	12	...	...	4	..	20	35
142	57	16	1	..	1	...	69	..	...	...	...	.	..	...	...	36
2,836	1,027	430	23	3	89	17	1,379	2,378	521	518	8	8	78	62	1,339	
818	229	125	11	3	24	10	464	356	73	57	4	..	13	9	226	37
603	235	92	6	...	7	1	276	483	141	66	3		20	...	276	38
753	324	83	1	..	31		346	408	55	86	1	2	6	11	267	39
663	239	130	5	...	27	6	293	1,131	25	309	.	6	33	42	570	40
2,411	901	446	36	33	150	61	1,064	3,141	767	1,250	143	157	187	218	1,124	
925	428	91	4	2	65	5	406	789	245	178	7	20	84	35	366	41
1,447	453	355	32	31	85	56	639	2,352	528	1,078	136	137	103	183	758	42
39	20	...	..	...	3	...	19	...	...	...	...	...	...	...	...	43

Serial No.	DISTRICT OR STATE.	Order IIc.—Raising of farm stock—*concluded.* Group 13.—Breeders of other animals (horses, mules, asses, etc.). Total Workers and Dependents.	WORKERS. Total Workers. M's.	F's.	Workers with an agricultural or other subsidiary occupation. Agricultural. M's.	F's.	Other. M's.	F's.	DEPENDENTS.	Group 14.—Herdsmen, shepherds, goatherds, etc. Total Workers and Dependents.	WORKERS. Total Workers. Males.	Females.	Workers with an agricultural or other subsidiary occupation. Agricultural. Males.	Females.	Other. Males.	Females.	DEPENDENTS.
	1	2	3	4	5	6	7	8	9	10	11	12	13	14	15	16	17
	Provincial Total ..	636	382	42	10	3	12	...	212	31,256	19,008	3,197	357	63	654	180	9,051
	Divisional Burma ...	481	335	1	8		3	..	145	26,969	16,255	2,697	249	37	523	158	8,017
	Arakan Division ...	..	...	...	...	...	...	...	..	2,909	2,194	166	48	3	43	3	549
1	Akyab ...	...	...	...	..			...	...	2,363	1,757	119	44	1	25	1	487
2	Hill Dist. of Arakan ...	...	...	...	...		...	...	...	...		...	...	...	...	...	...
3	Kyaukpyu ..	...	..	..	...	...	...	...	...	17	7	6	1	...	1	...	4
4	Sandoway ...	...	...	...	..	...	...	...	..	529	430	41	3	2	17	2	58
	Pegu Division ...	..	..	...	..	...			..	6,383	4,339	275	37	1	143	11	1,769
5	Rangoon Town ...	...		..	...	...	...	...	...	117	104	...		...	...	...	13
6	Insein ...	..	...	...	...	...	...	...	...	1,372	970	81	10	...	11	1	381
7	Hanthawaddy ...	...	...	...	...	..	...	...	..	1,266	763	57	6	1	40	1	446
8	Tharrawaddy ...	...	...	...	...	...	..	...	...	1,114	918	22	6	...	34	...	174
9	Pegu ...	...	...	...	...	...	...	...	...	1,873	1,287	78	13	...	52	9	508
10	Prome ..	...	..	...	..	...	...	...	...	641	297	37	2	..	6	...	307
	Irrawaddy Division ...	..	...	...	...	...		...	...	2,433	1,556	247	28	2	54	4	630
11	Bassein ..	...	..			...	...	...	...	591	311	76	6	1	24	1	204
12	Henzada ...	...	...	...		...			...	813	593	57	10	...	17	...	163
13	Myaungmya	...	..	...		...	...	...		376	208	58	12	1	6	3	110
14	Ma-ubin ...	...	...	..	...	...	...	..	...	221	173	14	..	..	7	...	34
15	Pyapôn ...	...	..	...	..	...	..	...	...	432	271	42	...	...	...	...	119
	Tenasserim Division ..	75	...			..	..		75	4,411	2,620	321	27	..	26	5	1,470
16	Toungoo ...	10	...		...	...	...		10	1,004	627	41	20	...	5	...	336
17	Salween ...	..	...	..	..	...	..	...	...	170	83	16	1	...	2	...	71
18	Thatôn ...		...	...	..	...			..	1,269	539	95	4	...	10	2	635
19	Amherst ...	65	...		..	...	...		65	1,597	1,064	156	...	...	3	3	377
20	Tavoy ...	...		...	...	...		..	...	282	240	8	2	...	6	...	34
21	Mergui ...	...	...	...	...	...	...	...	..	89	67	5	...	...		..	17
	Magwe Division ...	21	16	...		..	1	..	5	2,043	1,033	393	27	12	55	40	617
22	Thayetmyo ...	...	...	...	...	...	..		...	278	124	45	1	..	4	5	109
23	Pakôkku ...	15	15		...		...	..	..	965	520	184	17	4	23	11	261
24	Minbu ...	4	1	...	...	...	1	..	3	540	251	127	6	7	24	22	162
25	Magwe ...	...	...	...	..	...	...		...	260	138	37	3	1	4	2	85
26	Pakôkku Hill Tracts	2	...	...	...	..	..	...	2		...	...	...	...	...	...	...
	Mandalay Division ..	306	269	...	7	...	1	..	37	1,276	627	85	3		31	6	564
27	Mandalay ..	109	73	...	...	...	...	...	36	795	320	69	...	...	21	1	406
	Mandalay City	*78*	*42*	...	...		...		*36*	*195*	*85*	*32*	...	...	...	...	*78*
28	Bhamo ..	6	6	...		...	...	...		189	114	14	..	...	7	5	61
29	Myitkyina ...	108	108	...	7	..	1	...	...	207	127	1	...	...	...	...	79
30	Katha ..	1	...	...	...	...	...	...	1	84	65	1	3	...	3	...	18
31	Putao	82	82	...	..	...	...	..	...	1	1	...	...		...	...	...
	Sagaing Division ...	46	34	..	...		...	..	12	3,171	1,859	494	37	7	58	50	818
32	Shwebo ...	4	4	...	...	..	...	...		324	162	67	...	2	13	9	95
33	Sagaing ...	5	1	...	...	...		...	4	1,534	886	224	24	5	28	16	424
34	Lower Chindwin ..	19	14	..	..	...	...	...	5	636	302	169	7	...	9	25	165
35	Upper Chindwin ..	...	...	...	...		...		...	652	509	34	6	...	8	...	109
36	Chin Hills ...	18	15	...	...	...	...		3	25	...	...	...	...	...	...	25
	Meiktila Division ...	33	16	1	1	...	1		16	4,343	2,027	716	42	12	113	39	1,600
37	Kyauksè ..	2	1		...	...	...	...	1	1,139	489	82	12	...	32	...	568
38	Meiktila ...	2	2			...	1	..	...	1,263	631	199	16	11	41	23	433
39	Yamèthin ...	6	1	..	...	...	...	...	5	887	470	102	10	...	23	3	315
40	Myingyan ...	23	12	1	1		...	...	10	1,054	437	333	4	1	17	13	284
	Eastern States ...	155	47	41	2	3	9	..	67	4,287	2,753	500	108	26	131	22	1,034
41	Northern Shan States	97	20	17		...	8	...	60	2,606	1,673	305	32	4	77	12	628
42	Southern Shan States ...	58	27	24	2	3	1	...	7	1,679	1,080	195	76	22	54	10	404
43	Karenni ...	...	...	...	...	...	...	...	...	2	...	...	...	...		...	2

PART III.—*Details by districts*—contd.

Order IID.—Raising of other animals.

Group 15.—Birds, bees, etc.								Group 16.—Silk-worms.								
Total Workers and Dependents.	Workers. Total Workers. Males.	Workers. Total Workers. Females.	Workers with an agricultural or other subsidiary occupation. Agricultural. Males.	Agricultural. Females.	Other. Males.	Other. Females.	Dependents.	Total Workers and Dependents	Workers. Total Workers. Males.	Workers. Total Workers. Females.	Workers with an agricultural or other subsidiary occupation. Agricultural. Males.	Agricultural. Females.	Other. Males.	Other. Females.	Dependents.	Serial No. of District, etc. (column 1).
18	19	20	21	22	23	24	25	6	27	28	29	30	31		33	
748	197	177	...	...	3	2	374	912	571	205	7	3	10	6	136	
694	168	157	...		3	2	369	887	558	196	2	...	10	6	133	
...	...	...	...	...	...	...	...	2	...	2		...	...	...	...	
...	...	...	...	...	...	...	...	...	...	...	...	...		...	...	1
...	...	...	...	...	...	...	...	...	...	...	...	...	...	...	...	2
...	...	...	...	...	...	...	...	...	...	...	...	...	...	...	...	3
...	...	...	...	...	...	...	...	2	...	2	...	...	...	...	...	4
327	103	32	...	...	2	...	192	15	...	5	...	...	...	...	10	
74	34	5	...		...	...	35	...	...	...	...	...	...	...	...	5
65	15	20	...	...	...	...	30	...	...	...	...	...	...	...	...	6
157	47	4		...	2	...	106	...	...	...	...	...	...	...	...	7
...	...	...	...	...	...	...	...	1	...	...	...	...	...	...	1	8
31	7	3	...	...	...	...	21	...	...	...	...	...	...	...	...	9
...	...	...	...	...	...	...	...	14	...	5	...	...	...	...	9	10
24	10	8	...	...	...	...	6	...	...	...	...	...	...	...		
8	...	7	...	...	...	...	1	...	...	...	...	...	...	...	...	11
5	...	1	...	...	...	...	4	...	...	...	...	...	...	...	...	12
2	2	...	...	...	...	...	...	...	...	...	...	...	...	...	...	13
...	...	...	...	...	...	...	...	...	...	...	...	...	...	...	...	14
9	8	...	...	...	...	...	1	...	...	...	...	...	...	...	...	15
191	27	84	...	...	...	2	80	48	...	12	...	...	...	...	36	
137	3	70	...	...	...	2	64	19	...	12	...	...	...	...	7	16
...	...	...	...	...	...	...	...	...	...	...	...	...	...	...	...	17
21	5	12	...	...	...	...	4	...	...		...	...	...	...	...	18
28	19	1	...	...			8	4	...	...	...	...	...	...	4	19
...	...	...	...	...		...	...	25	...	...	...	...	...	...	25	20
5	...	1	...	...	...	...	4	...	...	...	...	...	...	...	...	21
11	3	2			...	...	6	14	4	...	...	...	...	...	10	
7	3	2	...	...	...	...	2	...	...	...	...	...	...	...	...	22
...	...	...	...	...	...	...	...	2		...	...	...	...	...	2	23
...	...	...	...	...	...	...		...	...	...	...	...	...	...	...	24
4	...	...	...	...	...	...	4	12	4	...	...	...	...	...	8	25
...	...	...	...	...	...	...	...	...	...	...	...	...	...	...	...	26
101	19	26	...	...	1	...	56	764	552	168	2	...	10	3	44	
84	11	19	...	...	...	...	54	764	552	168	2	...	10	3	44	27
78	5	19	...	...	...	...	54	9	...	9	...	...	...	...	...	
1	...	1	...	...	...	...	...	...	...	...	...	...	...	...	...	28
16	8	6	...	...	1	...	2	...	...	...	...	...	...	...	...	29
...	...	...	...	...	...	...	...	...	...	...	...	...	...	...	...	30
...	...	...	...	...	...	...	...	...	...	...	...	...	...	...	...	31
5	1	2	...	...	...	...	2	2	2	...	...	...	...	...	...	
3	1	...	...	...	...	...	2	...	...	...	...	...	...	...	...	32
...	...	...	...	...	...	...	...	...	...	...	...	...	...	...	...	33
2	...	2	...	...	...	...	...	2	2	...	...	...	...	...	...	34
...	...	...	...	...	...	...	...	...	...	...	...	...	...	...	...	35
...	...	...	...	...	...	...	...	...	...	...	...	...	...	...	...	36
35	5	3	...	...	...	...	27	42	...	9	...	...	...	3	33	
...	...	...	...	...	...	...	...	...	...	...	...	...	...	...	...	37
14	2	2	...	...	...	...	10	...	...	...	...	...	...	...	...	38
20	3	...	...	...	...	...	17	42	...	9	...	...	...	3	33	39
1	...	1	...	...	...	...	...	...	...	...	...	...	...	...	...	40
54	29	20	...	...	...	...	5	25	13	9	5	3	...	...	3	
17	8	4	...	...	...	...	5	...	...	...	...	...	...	...	...	41
37	21	16	...	...	...	...	...	25	13	9	5	3	...	...	3	42
...	...	...	...	...	...	...	...	...	...	...	...	...	...	...	...	43

Order II.—Exploitation

Group 17.—Fishing and pearling.

Serial No.	District or State.	Total Workers and Dependents.	Workers. Total Workers. Males.	Workers. Total Workers. Females.	Workers with an agricultural or other subsidiary occupation. Agricultural. Males.	Agricultural. Females.	Other. Males.	Other. Females.	Dependents.
	1	2	3	4	5	6	7	8	9
	Provincial Total ...	157,855	52,462	16,790	1,384	311	2,642	665	88,603
	Divisional Burma ...	153,120	50,681	16,667	1,275	293	2,442	651	85,772
	Arakan Division ...	10,842	3,638	1,025	246	101	392	43	6,179
1	Akyab ...	3,169	1,289	342	49	17	42	14	1,538
2	Hill Dist. of Arakan ...	1	...	...	...	...	...	...	1
3	Kyaukpyu ...	5,278	1,562	506	117	40	197	22	3,210
4	Sandoway ...	2,394	787	177	80	44	90	7	1,430
	Pegu Division ...	16,208	5,998	1,828	211	51	421	83	8,382
5	Rangoon Town ...	391	298	13	...	...	...	...	80
6	Insein ...	1,595	551	170	...	2	50	5	874
7	Hanthawaddy ...	2,342	1,138	318	14	3	35	11	886
8	Tharrawaddy ...	6,545	2,073	876	163	41	258	35	3,596
9	Pegu ...	3,856	1,459	297	29	4	49	13	2,100
10	Prome ...	1,479	479	154	5	1	29	19	846
	Irrawaddy Division ...	52,425	17,092	8,869	278	80	466	265	26,464
11	Bassein ...	7,850	2,431	1,088	47	8	159	124	4,308
12	Henzada ...	6,244	1,928	745	61	16	90	37	3,571
13	Myaungmya ...	6,383	2,154	1,082	84	12	61	10	3,147
14	Ma-ubin ...	23,766	7,834	4,731	46	31	113	88	11,201
15	Pyapôn ...	8,182	2,742	1,223	40	13	43	6	4,217
	Tenasserim Division ...	38,799	11,992	2,278	221	12	348	27	24,529
16	Toungoo ...	1,875	570	169	...	...	78	6	1,136
17	Salween ...	32	22	...	...	...	...	...	10
18	Thatôn ...	3,634	1,364	354	16	...	24	7	1,916
19	Amherst ...	3,490	1,378	152	...	2	5	4	1,960
20	Tavoy ...	8,287	2,429	928	133	6	134	10	4,930
21	Mergui ...	21,481	6,229	675	72	4	107	...	14,577
	Magwe Division ...	9,642	3,307	1,126	35	9	116	37	5,209
22	Thayetmyo ...	1,856	664	100	2	...	31	4	1,098
23	Pakôkku ...	3,466	1,071	392	3	...	39	6	2,003
24	Minbu ...	1,860	701	369	21	7	42	26	790
25	Magwe ...	2,460	871	265	9	2	4	1	1,324
26	Pakôkku Hill Tracts ...	...	...	...	...	...	...	...	...
	Mandalay Division ...	10,698	3,863	619	94	4	341	59	6,216
27	Mandalay ...	5,932	1,760	195	44	...	67	31	3,177
	Mandalay City ...	752	242	20	...	...	15	...	490
28	Bhamo ...	1,757	880	79	35	...	134	18	798
29	Myitkyina ...	859	325	64	...	1	71	6	470
30	Katha ...	2,850	898	181	15	3	69	4	1,771
31	Putao ...	...	...	...	...	...	...	...	...
	Sagaing Division ...	9,507	3,298	472	171	35	369	124	5,737
32	Shwebo ...	724	233	107	3	...	33	39	384
33	Sagaing ...	4,724	1,647	102	115	5	126	60	2,975
34	Lower Chindwin ...	1,924	667	77	11	...	75	10	1,180
35	Upper Chindwin ...	2,135	751	186	42	30	135	15	1,198
36	Chin Hills ...	...	...	...	...	...	...	...	...
	Meiktila Division ...	4,999	1,493	450	19	1	52	13	3,056
37	Kyaukse ...	684	207	49	8	...	19	3	428
38	Meiktila ...	780	169	86	2	1	14	1	531
39	Yamèthin ...	564	187	154	...	...	5	3	923
40	Myingyan ...	2,971	930	167	9	...	14	6	1,874
	Eastern States ...	4,735	1,781	1223	109	18	200	14	2,831
41	Northern Shan States ...	308	128	7	5	...	14	1	173
42	Southern Shan States ...	4,382	1,634	111	104	18	186	13	2,637
43	Karenni ...	45	19	5	...	...	...	...	21

Order II (contd.) — of wild animals: Group 18.—Hunting. Total Workers and Dependents	Group 18. Workers. Total Workers. Males	Group 18. Workers. Total Workers. Females	Group 18. Workers with an agricultural or other subsidiary occupation. Agricultural. Males	Agricultural. Females	Other. Males	Other. Females	Group 18. DEPENDENTS	Order III.—Coal, petroleum and metals. Group 19.—Coal mines. Total Workers and Dependents	Group 19. Workers (All without subsidiary occupation.) Males	Group 19. Workers. Females	Group 19. DEPENDENTS	Group 20.—Petroleum wells. Total Workers and Dependents	Group 20. Workers. Total Workers. Males	Total Workers. Females	Workers with an agricultural or other subsidiary occupation. Agricultural. Males	Agricultural. Females	Other. Males	Other. Females	Group 20. DEPENDENTS	Serial No. of District, etc. (column 1)
10	11	12	13	14	15	16	17	18	19	20	21	22	23	24	25	26	27	28	29	
2,954	1,995	135	10	...	14	2	824	54	23	1	30	13,229	9,487	309	34	2	27	6	3,433	
2,352	1,801	17	8	..	6	...	534	54	23	1	30	13,177	9,487	309	34	2	27	6	3,381	
66	52	...	...	...	...	...	14	...	...	...	...	2	2	...	1	...	...	...	...	
1	1	...	...	...	...	...	...	...	...	...	...	2	2	...	1	...	...	...	...	1
...	...	...	...	...	...	...	...	...	...	...	...	...	...	...	...	...	...	...	...	2
1	1	...	...	...	...	...	...	...	...	...	...	...	...	...	...	...	...	...	...	3
64	50	...	...	...	...	...	14	...	...	...	...	...	...	...	...	...	...	...	...	4
228	137	7	...	...	...	...	84	...	...	...	...	116	42	...	...	...	...	...	74	
...	...	...	...	...	...	...	...	...	...	...	...	96	34	...	...	...	...	...	62	5
39	4	4	...	...	...	...	31	...	...	...	...	3	...	...	...	...	...	...	3	6
1	1	...	...	...	...	...	...	...	...	...	...	5	5	...	...	...	...	...	...	7
44	20	3	...	...	...	...	21	...	...	...	...	...	...	...	...	...	...	...	...	8
37	11	...		...	...	...	26	...	...	...	...	...	...	...	...	...	...	...	...	9
107	101	...	...	...	...	...	6	...	...	...	...	12	3	...	...	...	...	...	9	10
256	211	...	...	...	2	...	45	41	18	...	23	3	1	...	...	...	...	...	2	
238	206	...	...	...	2	...	32	22	...	...	22	1	...	...	...	...	...	...	1	11
...	...	...	...	...	...	...	...	19	18	...	1	1	1	...	...	...	...	...	...	12
1	1	...	...	...	...	...	...	...	...	...	...	...	...	...	...	...	...	...	...	13
...	...	...	...	...	...	...	...	...	...	...	...	1	...	...	...	...	...	...	1	14
17	4	...	...	...	...	...	13	...	...	...	...	...	...	...	...	...	...	...	...	15
1,024	772	...	7	...	...	...	252	...	...	...	...	1	1	...	...	...	...	...	...	
315	218	...	2	...	...	...	97	...	...	...	...	...	...	...	...	...	...	...	...	16
...	...	...	...	...	...	...	...	...	...	...	...	...	...	...	...	...	...	...	...	17
12	10	...	...	...	...	...	2	...	...	...	...	...	...	...	...	...	...	...	...	18
30	8	...	...	...	...	...	22	...	...	...	...	1	1	...	...	...	...	...	...	19
192	109	...	5	...	...	...	83	...	...	...	...	...	...	...	...	...	...	...	...	20
475	427	...	...	...	...	...	48	...	...	...	...	...	...	...	...	...	...	...	...	21
236	140	6	...	...	...	...	90	1	...	...	1	12,978	9,415	305	31	2	27	6	3,298	
35	33	...	...	...	...	...	2	...	...	...	...	65	59	...	...	...	...	...	6	22
88	1	5	...	...	...	...	82	...	...	...	...	926	380	32	11	...	6	...	514	23
83	76	1	...	...	...	...	6	1	...	...	1	408	216	50	1	2	10	...	142	24
30	30	...	...	...	...	...	...	...	...	...	...	11,579	8,760	223	19	...	11	6	2,596	25
...	...	...	...	...	...	...	...	...	...	...	...	...	...	...	...	...	...	...	...	26
485	456	1	...		4	...	28	1	.	1	...	29	1	4	...	...	...	...	24	
62	39	1	...	...	...	...	22	...	...	...	...	28		4	...	.	...	...	24	27
3	*3*	...	...	...	...	...	...	...	...	...	...	*28*	...	4	...	...	...	...	24	
178	178	...	...	...	...	...	...	...	...	...	...	1	1	...	...	...	...	...	...	28
47	45	...	...	...	...	...	2	1	...	1	.	...	.	...	...	...	...	...	...	29
198	194	...	...	...	4	...	4	...	...	...	...	...	...	...	...	...	...	...	...	30
...	...	...	.	...	...	...	...	.	...	...	...	...	...	...	...	...	...	...	...	31
29	12	...	1	...		...	17	11	5	...	6	42	20	.	2	...	...	...	22	
12	8	...	...	...	...	...	4	...	...	...	...	39	17		2	...	...	...	22	32
14	4	...	1	...	...	...	10	...	...	...	...	...	...	...	...	...	...	...	...	33
...	...	...	...	...	...	...	...	5	5	...	...	1	1	...	...	...	...	...	...	34
3	...	...	...	...	.	...	3	6		...	6	2	2	...	...	...	...	...	...	35
...	...	...	...	...	...		...	...	...	...	...	...	...		...	...	...	...	...	36
28	21	3	.	...	...	...	4	...	...	...	...	6	5	...	...	.	...	...	1	
2	2	...	...	...	.	...	...	...	...	...	...	...	.	...	...	.	...	...	...	37
7	3	...	...	...	.	...	4	.	...	...	...	...	...	...	...	...	.	...	...	38
10	10	...	...	...	...	...	...	...	...	...	...	...	...	...	...	...	...	...	...	39
9	6	3	...		...	...	...	..	..	...		6	5	...	...	...	...	...	1	40
602	194	118	2	...	8	2	290	...	...		...	52	...	...	...	...	...	...	52	
553	169	118	1	...	6	2	266	...	...	...	...	52	...	...	...	...	...	...	52	41
46	24	...	1	...	2	...	22	...	...	...	...	...	...	...	...	...	...	...	...	42
3	1	...	...	...	...	...	2	...	...	...	...	...	...	...	...	...	...	...	...	43

Serial No.	DISTRICT OR STATE.	Order III.—Coal, petroleum and metals—*concld.* Group 21.—Metals and minerals from which metals are extracted. Total Workers and Dependents.	Workers. Total Workers. Males.	Females	Workers with an agricultural or other subsidiary occupation. Agricultural. Males.	Females	Other. Males.	Females.	DEPENDENTS.	Order IV.—Minerals. Groups 22a.—Jade, and 22b.—Rubies, spinels and associated stones and all precious stones. Total Workers and Dependents.	Workers. Total Workers. Males.	Females	Workers with an agricultural or other subsidiary occupation. Agricultural. Males.	Females	Other. Males.	Females	DEPENDENTS.
	1	2	3	4	5	6	7	8	9	10	11	12	13	14	15	16	17
	Provincial Total ...	14,853	9,976	546	35	6	44	5	4,331	4,663	2,621	971	13	...	36	8	1,071
	Divisional Burma ...	8,384	4,367	510	35	4	44	5	3,507	4,226	2,188	971	13	..	36	8	1,067
	Arakan Division ...	13	..	3	...	...	...	1	10								
1	Akyab	7	...	...	...	...	...	...	7								
2	Hill Dist. of Arakan	...	...	...	...	...	...	..	...								
3	Kyaukpyu ...	5	...	3	...	...	...	1	2								
4	Sandoway ...	1	...	..	...	...	..		1								
	Pegu Division ...	160	67	1	...	...	...	...	92								
5	Rangoon Town ...	93	35	..	...	...	...	.	58								
6	Insein	4	2	...	...	...	...		2								
7	Hanthawaddy ...	14	6	1	...	...	..	...	7								
8	Tharrawaddy ...	12	1	...	...	...	...	...	11								
9	Pegu	8	1	...	...	...	...	...	7								
10	Prome	29	22	...	...	...	...	...	7								
	Irrawaddy Division ..	10	9	...	...	...	...	..	1								
11	Bassein ...	6	5	..	...	...	...	..	1								
12	Henzada ...	4	4	...	...	...	...	...	...								
13	Myaungmya ...	...	...	...	...	...	...	...	...								
14	Ma-ubin ...	...	...	...	...	...	...	...	...								
15	Pyapôn ..	...	..	...	..	...	...	...	...								
	Tenasserim Division ...	7,609	4,224	248	35	4	35	4	3,137								
16	Toungoo	4	...	...	...	..	...	.	4								
17	Salween ...	7	6	1	...	...	1	...	...								
18	Thatôn ...	28	8	7	...	...	1	..	13								
19	Amherst ...	150	51	7	..	...	...	...	92								
20	Tavoy .	4,125	2,452	188	29	4	19	4	1,485								
21	Mergui ...	3,295	1,707	45	6	...	14	...	1,543								
	Magwe Division ...	189	3	3	...	.	...	.	183								
22	Thayetmyo ...	...	...	...	...	...	...	..	...								
23	Pakôkku ...	3	3	...	...	...	...	...	...								
24	Minbu	186	...	3	...	.	...	...	183								
25	Magwe ...	..	...	...	...	...	...	...	...								
26	Pakôkku Hill Tracts	...	...	...	...	...	...	...	...								
	Mandalay Division ...	378	52	255	...	...	8	.	71								
27	Mandalay ...	328	30	247	...	...	...	..	51								
	Mandalay City ...	297	26	247	...	..		..	24								
28	Bhamo ...	2	2	...	...	...	...	...	...								
29	Myitkyina ...	45	19	6	...	...	8	...	20								
30	Katha	3	1	2	...	...	...	...	...								
31	Putao	...	...	...	...	..	...	...	...								
	Sagaing Division ...	10	8	...	...	...	1	..	2								
32	Shwebo ...	3	2	...	...	..	...	..	1								
33	Sagaing ...	4	3	...	...	..	...	..	1								
34	Lower Chindwin ...	3	3	...	...	...	1	...	...								
35	Upper Chindwin ...	..	..	...	...	...	...	...	...								
36	Chin Hills ...	...	...	...	...	...	..	...	...								
	Meiktila Division ...	15	4	...	..	...	...	...	11								
37	Kyauksè ...	...	...	...	...	...	...	..	...								
38	Meiktila ...	2	2	...	..	...	...		...								
39	Yamèthin ...	9	2	...	...	...	...	..	7								
40	Myingyan ...	4	...	...	...	...	...	..	4								
	Eastern States ...	6,469	5,609	36	...	2	...	...	824								
41	N. Shan States ...	6,467	5,609	36	...	2	...	...	822								
42	S Shan States ...	2		..	...	..	...	...	2								
43	Karenni ...	...	...	...	...	...	...	..	...								

Analysis of Group 22a.—Jade, and 22b.—Rubies, spinels and associated stones and all precious stones.

DISTRICT.	Total Workers and Dependents.	Total Workers. Males.	Females.	Agricultural. Males.	Females.	Other. Males.	Females.	DEPENDENTS
1	2	3	4	5	6	7	8	9
	4,663	2,621	971	13	...	36	8	1,071
Hanthawaddy (22b) ...	1	...	...	...	...	...	...	1
Toungoo (22a) ...	1	1	...	...		...	...	...
Do. (22b) ...	2	...	...	..	...	...	...	2
Tavoy (22b) ...	45	43	...	...	...	...	...	2
Mandalay (22a) .	4	...	...	...	...	...	...	4
Bhamo (22a) ...	2	...	...	..	...	...	...	2
Myitkyina (22a) ...	2,240	1,864	33	11	...	12	...	343
Do. (22b) ...	7	7	...	...	...	...	...	...
Katha (22b) ...	1,856	255	920	1	...	22	8	681
Shwebo (22b) ...	33	18	..	1	...	2	...	15
Sagaing (22b) ...	35	...	18	...	...	...	...	17
Northern Shan States (22a)	4	..	...	...	...	...	...	4
Do. (22b)	433	433	...	...	...	...	...	...

not of Order III or V. — Group 22c.—Other minerals not soluble in water (lime-stone, laterite, etc.).								Order V.—Minerals soluble in water. — Group 23.—Rock, sea and marsh salt.								Group 24.*	
Total Workers and Dependents.	WORKERS. Total Workers. Males.	Total Workers. Females.	Workers with an agricultural or other subsidiary occupation. Agricultural. Males.	Agricultural. Females	Other. Males.	Other. Females.	DEPENDENTS.	Total Workers and Dependents.	WORKERS. Total Workers. Males.	Total Workers. Females.	Workers with an agricultural or other subsidiary occupation. Agricultural. Males.	Agricultural. Females	Other. Males.	Other. Females	DEPENDENTS.	Total.	Serial No. of District, etc. (column 1).
18	19	20	21	22	23	24	25	26	27	28	29	30	31	32	33	34	
6,124	3,368	749	38	4	53	12	2,007	3,962	1,545	419	83	9	47	20	1,998	..	
6,008	3,278	749	38	4	53	12	1,981	3,961	1,545	419	83	9	47	20	1,997	...	
5	...	...	...	...	...	...	5	59	15	20	...	...	4	1	24	...	
5	...	...	...	...	.	...	5	...	...	...	...	...	...	..	...	...	1
...	..	...	...	...	...	...	...	...	...	...	...	...	...	...	...	...	2
...	...	...	...	...	...	...	...	30	12	10	...	...	4	1	8	...	3
...	...	...	...	...	...	.	...	29	3	10	...	...	...	...	16	...	4
454	283	13	...	...	...	...	158	117	59	..	1	...	...	...	58	...	
...	...	...	...	...	...	...	...	4	...	...	...	...	...	...	4	...	5
268	148	11	...	...	...	...	109	...	...	...	...	...	...	...	...	...	6
3	1	...	...	...	..	...	2	113	59	..	1	...	...	...	54	...	7
17	15	...	...	...	...	...	2	...	...	...	...	...	...	...	...	...	8
...	...	...	...	..	...	..	...	...	...	...	...	...	...	...	...	...	9
166	119	2	...	...	...	...	45	...	...	...	...	...	...	...	...	...	10
158	115	22	...	...	...	...	21	686	222	43	25	2	7	...	421	...	
131	101	20	...	...	...	...	10	533	184	35	25	2	4	...	314	..	11
27	14	2	..	...	...	...	11	.	...	...	...	...	...	...	...	...	12
...	...	...	...	...	...	...	...	153	38	8	...	...	3	...	107	...	13
...	...	...	...	...	...	...	...	...	...	...	...	...	...	...	...	...	14
...	...	..	...	...	...	...	...	...	...	...	...	...	...	...	...	...	15
1,086	493	149	5	1	3	1	444	2,492	1,116	135	34	2	18	2	1,241	...	
105	41	32	.	...	2	1	32	...	...	...	...	...	...	...	...	...	16
...	...	...	...	...	...	...	...	...	...	...	...	...	...	...	...	...	17
731	383	62	2	...	1	...	286	6	...	...	...	...	...	...	6	...	18
178	61	7	3	..	...	...	110	1,621	760	80	20	...	6	2	781	...	19
71	8	48	...	1	...	...	15	418	132	18	11	2	9	...	268	...	20
1	...	...	...	...	...	...	1	447	224	37	3	...	3	...	186	...	21
385	193	51	1	...	21	1	141	9	2	3	...	...	...	...	4	...	
243	83	45	...	...	21	...	115	...	...	..	...	...	...	...	...	...	22
4	...	4	...	...	...	...	...	9	2	3	...	...	...	...	4	...	23
57	29	2	...	...	...	1	26	...	...	...	..	...	...	...	...	...	24
81	81	...	1	...	...	...	...	...	...	...	...	...	...	...	..	...	25
...	...	...	...	...	...	...	...	...	...	...	...	...	...	...	...	...	26
2790	1,671	290	15	3	21	4	829	104	28	26	...	..	6	8	50	...	
1,892	814	290	12	3	10	4	788	4	1	...	...	...	...	...	3	...	27
632	*345*	*136*	..	...	...	...	*151*	*4*	*1*	...	...	...	...	...	*3*	...	
3	3	...	...	...	...	...	...	...	...	...	...	...	...	...	...	...	28
895	854	...	3	...	11	...	41	26	13	10	...	...	4	2	3	..	29
...	...	...	...	...	...	...	...	74	14	16	...	...	2	6	44	...	30
...	...	..	...	...	...	...	...	...	.	...	...	...	...	...	...	...	31
509	187	89	17	...	5	6	233	474	103	177	23	5	12	6	194	...	
50	2	24	...	...	...	5	24	64	26	5	19	...	5	...	33	...	32
274	115	43	8	...	2	...	116	203	23	78	4	5	2	...	102	...	33
147	51	22	5	.	1	1	74	198	54	85	...	...	5	6	59	...	34
38	19	...	4	...	2	...	19	9	...	9	...	...	...	...	...	...	35
...	...	...	...	...	...	...	...	...	...	...	...	...	...	...	...	...	36
621	336	135	...	...	3	...	150	20	...	15	...	...	...	3	5	...	
1	...	1	...	...	...	...	...	...	...	...	...	...	...	..	...	...	37
49	49	...	...	...	1	...	...	...	...	...	...	...	...	...	...	...	38
556	281	126	...	...	1	...	149	...	...	...	...	...	...	...	...	...	39
15	6	8	...	...	1	...	1	20	...	15	...	...	...	3	5	...	40
116	90	...	...	...	..	...	26	1	...	...	...	...	...	...	1	...	
115	89	...	...	...	...	...	26	..	...	...	...	...	...	...	...	...	41
1	1	...	...	...	...	...	...	1	...	...	...	...	...	...	1	...	42
..	...	...	...	...	...	...	...	...	...	...	...	...	...	...	...	...	43

* Saltpetre, alum and other substances soluble in water.

Order VI.—

Serial No.	DISTRICT OR STATE.	Group 25.—Cotton ginning, cleaning and pressing.								Group 26.—Cotton spinning.							
		Total Workers and Dependents.	WORKERS.						DEPENDENTS.	Total Workers and Dependents.	WORKERS.						DEPENDENTS.
			Total Workers.		Workers with an agricultural or other subsidiary occupation.						Total Workers.		Workers with an agricultural or other subsidiary occupation.				
					Agricultural.		Other.						Agricultural.		Other.		
			Males.	Females	Males.	Females	Males.	Females			Males.	Females	Males.	Females	Males.	Females	
	1	2	3	4	5	6	7	8	9	10	11	12	13	14	15	16	17
	Provincial Total ..	5,278	1,039	2,872	16	85	24	120	1,367	5,144	508	3,490	2	14	1	64	1,146
	Divisional Burma ...	4,991	780	2,867	15	85	22	120	1,344	5,072	508	3,457	2	14	1	64	1,107
	Arakan Division ...	3	...	3	...	..	..	...	...	25	...	7	...	...	...	...	18
1	Akyab ...	3	...	3	..	...	...	...	...	17	...	7	...	...	...	...	10
2	Hill Dist. of Arakan	...	..	...	...	...	...	...	...	...	...	...	...	...	...	...	...
3	Kyaukpyu ...	...	..	...	...	...	...	...	..	...	..	...	.	..	...	..	...
4	Sandoway ...	...	...	..	.	...	.	...	...	8	...	...	...	...	...	...	8
	Pegu Division ...	4	4	..	...		3	...	.	278	178	40	...	2	1	3	60
5	Rangoon Town ...	...	...	...	..	..	...	...	...	1	1	..	...	...	...	...	...
6	Insein ...	4	4	..	..	..	3	...	.	...	...	...	..	..	...	...	...
7	Hanthawaddy ..	...	...	...	...	...	...	...	...	..	...	...	...	...	..	...	...
8	Tharrawaddy ..	...	...	...	...	..	...	...	..	23	11	..	...	...	1	...	12
9	Pegu ...	...	...	...	...	...	...	...	...	...	...	...	...	...	...	...	...
10	Prome ...	...	...	...	..	...	...	.	..	254	166	40	..	2	..	3	48
	Irrawaddy Division ...	731		547	...	16	...	37	184	28	...	15	...	..	...	...	13
11	Bassein ...	...	...	...	...	...	...	...	...	...	...	..	..	...	...	...	...
12	Henzada ...	731	...	547	...	16	...	37	184	...	...	...	...	...	...	...	.
13	Myaungmya ..	.	...	...	...	...	...	...	...	...	...	...	...	...	...	...	...
14	Ma-ubin ...	...	...	...	...	...	...	...	...	28	...	15	..	...	...	...	13
15	Pyapôn ...	...	..	..	...	...	...	...		...	...	...	...	...	...	...	...
	Tenasserim Division ..	..	..	...	...	...	...	...	..	191	35	14	..	...	...	...	142
16	Toungoo ..	...	...	...	...	...	...	...	...	...	..	...	...	...	...	...	...
17	Salween ...	..	...	...	...	...	...	...	...	...	...	..	..	...	...	...	...
18	Thatôn ..	...	...	..	...	...	...	...	...	10	2	...	...	...	...	...	8
19	Amherst ...	...	...	...	..	...	...	..	...	164	33	14	...	...	...	...	117
20	Tavoy ...	...	...	...	...	...	..	...	...	17	...	...	...	...	...	...	17
21	Mergui ...	...	...	...	...	...	...	...	...	...	..	...	...	...	...	...	...
	Magwe Division ...	612	246	123	...	...	..	...	243	707	4	576	...	4	...	10	127
22	Thayetmyo ...	487	246	75	...	..	...	...	166	248	4	165	...	4	...	2	79
23	Pakôkku ...	5	...	...	..	...	...	...	5	371	...	331	...	...	..	6	40
24	Minbu ...	120	...	48	...	..	...	...	72	61	...	59	...	...	..	2	2
25	Magwe ...	...	...	..	...	...	...	...	...	27	...	21	...	..	...	...	6
26	Pakôkku Hill Tracts	...	...	...	...	...	...	...	.	...	...	...	..	...	...	...	...
	Mandalay Division ..	28	1	19	..	...	...	7	8	1 959	250	1,367	..	2	...	...	342
27	Mandalay ...	4	1	2	...	...	..	1	1	1,946	248	1,357	...	2	...	..	341
	Mandalay City ...	4	*1*	*2*	...		...	*1*	*1*	*1,939*	*242*	*1,357*	...	*2*	..	...	340
28	Bhamo ...	3	...	3	..	..	..	3	...	..	...	...	...	...	...	...	...
29	Myitkyina ...	21	...	14	...	..	...	3	7	..	...	...	...	...	...	..	...
30	Katha ...	...	..	...	...	...	...	...	...	13	2	10	...	...	...	...	1
31	Putao ...	...	...	...	...	...	...	...	...	...	...	...	...	...	...	...	...
	Sagaing Division ...	2,742	355	1,818	9	62	16	67	569	407	31	117	2	...	...	...	259
32	Shwebo ...	...	...	...	...	...	...	...	...	44	...	44	...	..	...	...	...
33	Sagaing ...	2,637	333	1,747	9	61	16	67	557	150	17	...	...	...	...	...	133
34	Lower Chindwin .	105	22	71	...	1	...	...	12	207	11	72	2	..	...	...	124
35	Upper Chindwin ...	...	...	...		...	...	...	..	1	...	1	...	...	..	...	...
36	Chin Hills ...	...	...	..	...	...	...	...	...	5	3	...	...	...	..	...	2
	Meiktila Division ...	871	174	357	6	7	3	9	340	1,477	10	1,321	...	6	...	51	146
37	Kyauksè ...	...	...	...	...	...	..	...	...	...	...	...	...	...	...	...	...
38	Meiktila ...	674	115	262	6	7	3	7	297	210	2	186	...	2	...	11	22
39	Yamèthin ...	18	1	16	...	...	...	...	1	38	...	37	...	2	...	1	1
40	Myingyan ...	179	58	79	...	...	...	2	42	1,229	8	1,098	...	2	...	39	123
	Eastern States ...	287	259	5	1	...	2	...	23	72	...	33	...	..	.	...	39
41	Northern Shan States	279	259	...	1	...	2	...	20	...	...	...	...	...	..	...	...
42	Southern Shan States	...	...	...	...	...	...	...	...	72	...	33	...	...	..	...	39
43	Karenni ...	8	...	5	...	...	...	...	3	...	...	...	...	...	...	...	...

PART III.—*Details by districts*—contd.

Textiles.

Group 27.—Cotton sizing and weaving. Total Workers and Dependents.	Group 27. WORKERS. Total Workers. Males.	Group 27. WORKERS. Total Workers. Females.	Group 27. Workers with an agricultural or other subsidiary occupation. Agricultural. Males.	Group 27. Agricultural. Females.	Group 27. Other. Males.	Group 27. Other. Females.	Group 27. DEPENDENTS.	Group 28.—Jute spinning, pressing and weaving. Total Workers and Dependents.	Group 28. WORKERS (All without subsidiary occupation). Males.	Group 28. WORKERS. Females.	Group 28. DEPENDENTS.	Group 29.—Rope, twine or string making. Total Workers and Dependents.	Group 29. WORKERS. Total Workers. Males.	Group 29. Total Workers. Females.	Group 29. Workers with an agricultural or other subsidiary occupation. Agricultural. Males.	Group 29. Agricultural. Females.	Group 29. Other. Males.	Group 29. Other. Females.	Group 29. DEPENDENTS.	Serial No. of District, etc. (column 1).
18	19	20	21	22	23	24	25	26	27	28	29	30	31	32	33	34	35	36	37	
65,913	1,846	46,863	22	2,155	52	3,194	17,204	360	39	250	71	4,261	1,353	994	15	...	74	21	1,914	
62,079	1,798	43,659	17	1,702	49	2,998	16,622	360	39	250	71	4,204	1,343	947	14		74	21	1,914	
3,396	35	1,908	...	14	3	43	1,453	...	...	...	...	731	192	50	3	...	7	8	489	
3,163	30	1,717	...	2	1	7	1,416	...	...	...	...	664	178	26	2	...	6	3	460	1
2	...	1	...	...	...	...	1	...	...	...	...	...	...	...	...	...	...	...	...	2
86	5	72	...	6	2	19	9	...	...	...	...	34	12	4	1	...	1	...	18	3
145	...	118	...	6	...	7	27	...	...	...	...	33	2	20	...	...	...	5	11	4
2,441	124	1,623	2	130	...	158	694	41	39	...	2	776	276	159	...		...	...	341	
46	23	15	...	...	...	...	8	41	39	...	2	210	76	41	...	...	...	...	93	5
459	27	260	2	40	...	73	172	...	...	...	...	197	101	49	...	...	...	...	47	6
435	4	251	...	...	...	4	180	...		...	...	208	42	12	...	...	...	...	154	7
1,060	46	804	...	67	...	69	210	...	...	...	...	25	3	2	...	...	...	...	20	8
431	14	293	...	23	...	12	124	...	...	...	...	62	36	22	...	...	...	...	4	9
10	10	...	...	...	...	...	...	...	...	...	...	74	18	33	...	...	...	...	23	10
686	35	470	...	12	3	5	181	...	...	...	...	1,400	326	404	6	...	18	6	670	
448	21	306	...	10	3	5	121	...	...	...	...	19	8	4	...	...	...	...	7	11
91	4	66	...	1	...	...	21	...	...	...		298	90	...	6	...	...	...	208	12
52	...	35	...	...	...	...	17	...	...	...	...	80	1	38	...	...	1	4	41	13
77	7	48	...	1	...	...	22	...	...	...	...	939	213	355	...	...	17	2	371	14
18	3	15	...	...	...	...	...	...	...	...	...	64	14	7	...	...	...	...	43	15
8,655	101	6,837	5	136	...	470	1,717	...	...	...	...	69	11	22	...	...	...	...	36	
196	3	39	...	8	...	1	154	...	...	...	...	12	4	...		...	...	...	8	16
...	...	...	...	...	...	...	...	...	...	...	...	...	...	...	...	...	...	...	...	17
2,788	44	2,132	...	17	...	186	612	...	...	...	...	26	7	...	...	...	...	...	19	18
3,812	44	3,234	5	99	...	207	534	...	...	...	...	6	...	1	...	...	...	...	5	19
1,625	10	1,327	...	12	...	76	288	...	...	...	...	25		21	...	...	...	...	4	20
234	...	105	...	...	...	...	129	...	...	...	...	...	...	...	...	...	...	...	...	21
14,406	252	10,719	...	390	20	804	3,435	319	...	250	69	283	139	8	...	...	18	1	136	
1,422	20	1,076	...	8	...	51	326	319	...	250	69	11	11	...	...	...	...	...	...	22
8,876	157	6,455	...	160	20	507	2,264	...	...	...		220	96	...	...	...	18	...	124	23
3,038	55	2,379	...	175	...	177	604	...	...			40	25	8	...	...	...	1	7	24
1,070	20	809	...	47	...	69	241	...	...	...	...	10	7	...	...	...	...	...	5	25
...	...	...	...	...	...	...	...	...	...	...	...	...	...	...	...	...	...	...	...	26
373	20	218	...	12	...	10	135	...	...	...	...	183	12	143	...	...	3	...	28	
...	...		...	...	...	...	...	...	...	...	...	167	12	130	...	...	3	...	25	27
...	...	...	...	...	...	...	...	...	...	...	...	156	4	130	...	...	...	...	22	
169	16	54	...	...	...	2	99	...	...	...	...		...	...	...	...	...	...	...	28
8	...	4	...	...	...	1	4	...	...	...	...	...	...	...	...	...	...	...	...	29
196	4	160	...	12	...	7	32	...	...	...	...	16	...	13	...	...	...	...	3	30
...	...	...	...	...	...	...	...	...	...	...	...	...	...	...	...	...	...	...	...	31
16,352	227	10,370	5	661	12	915	5,755	...	...	...	...	515	266	115	5	...	22	4	134	
211	5	137	2	9	...	6	69	...	...	...	...	45	35	...	...	...	3	...	10	32
6,020	44	2,941	1	307	3	581	3,035	...	...	...	...	283	97	106	3	...	3	2	80	33
9,531	174	6,788	2	327	9	313	2,569	...	...	...	...	168	127	2	2	...	15	...	39	34
588	4	502	...	18	...	15	82	...	...	...	...	19	7	7	...	...	1	2	5	35
2	...	2	...	...	...	...	...	...	...	...	...	...	...	...	...	...	...	...	...	36
15,770	1,004	11,514	5	347	11	593	3,252	...	...	...	...	247	121	46	...	...	6	2	80	
434	15	248	...	16	3	19	171		...		...	1	1	...	...	...	...	...	...	37
6,545	92	5,065	1	201	4	267	1,388	...	...	...	...	115	40	34	...	...	2	...	41	38
2,584	29	1,955	3	16	2	78	600	...	...	...	...	2	...	...	...	...	...	...	2	39
6,207	868	4,246	1	114	2	229	1,093	...	...	...	...	129	80	12	...	...	4	2	37	40
3,834	48	3,204	5	453	3	196	582	...	...	...	...	57	10	47	1	...	...	...	...	
2,824	48	2,403	5	422	3	141	373	...	...	...	...	9	9	...	1	...	...	...	...	41
1,010	...	801	...	31	...	55	209	...	...	...	...	47	...	47	...	...	...	...	...	42
...	...	...	...	...	...	...	...	...	...	...	...	1	1	...	—	...	...	...	...	43

Order VI.—

Serial No.	DISTRICT OR STATE.	Group 30.—Work with other fibres. Total Workers and Dependents.	Group 30. WORKERS.* Males.	Group 30. WORKERS.* Females.	Group 30. DEPENDENTS.	Groups 31, 32 and 33.† Total.	Group 34.—Silk spinning. Total Workers and Dependents.	WORKERS. Total Workers. Males.	WORKERS. Total Workers. Females.	Workers with an agricultural or other subsidiary occupation. Agricultural. Males.	Agricultural. Females.	Other. Males.	Other. Females.	DEPENDENTS.
	1	2	3	4	5	6	7	8	9	10	11	12	13	14
	Provincial Total	61	23	1	37	...	926	83	490	...	...	1	3	353
	Divisional Burma	61	23	1	37	...	926	83	490	...	...	1	3	353
	Arakan Division	1	1	...	...	...	...	...	...	...	...	...	...	...
1	Akyab	...	...	...	...	...	...	...	...	...	...	...	...	...
2	Hill Dist. of Arakan	...	...	...	...	...	...	...	...	...	...	...	...	...
3	Kyaukpyu	1	1	...	...	...	...	...	...	...	...	...	...	...
4	Sandoway	...	...	...	...	...	...	...	...	...	...	...	...	...
	Pegu Division	...	...	...	...	...	523	...	298	...	...	...	3	225
5	Rangoon Town	...	...	...	...	...	...	...	...	...	...	...	...	...
6	Insein	...	...	...	...	...	...	...	...	...	...	...	...	...
7	Hanthawaddy	...	...	...	...	...	...	...	...	...	...	...	...	...
8	Tharrawaddy	...	...	...	...	...	...	...	...	...	...	...	...	...
9	Pegu	...	...	...	...	...	...	...	...	...	...	...	...	...
10	Prome	...	...	...	...	...	523	...	298	...	...	...	3	225
	Irrawaddy Division	28	...	1	27	...	...	...	...	...	...	...	...	...
11	Bassein	...	...	...	...	...	...	...	...	...	...	...	...	...
12	Henzada	...	...	...	...	...	...	...	...	...	...	...	...	...
13	Myaungmya	...	...	...	...	...	...	...	...	...	...	...	...	...
14	Ma-ubin	28	...	1	27	...	...	...	...	...	...	...	...	...
15	Pyapôn	...	...	...	...	...	...	...	...	...	...	...	...	...
	Tenasserim Division	...	...	...	...	...	2	2	...	...	...	...	...	...
16	Toungoo	...	...	...	...	...	...	...	...	...	...	...	...	...
17	Salween	...	...	...	...	...	...	...	...	...	...	...	...	...
18	Thatôn	...	...	...	...	...	...	...	...	...	...	...	...	...
19	Amherst	...	...	...	...	...	2	2	...	...	...	...	...	...
20	Tavoy	...	...	...	...	...	...	...	...	...	...	...	...	...
21	Mergui	...	...	...	...	...	...	...	...	...	...	...	...	...
	Magwe Division	32	22	...	10	...	...	...	...	...	...	...	...	...
22	Thayetmyo	...	...	...	...	...	...	...	...	...	...	...	...	...
23	Pakôkku	...	...	...	...	...	...	...	...	...	...	...	...	...
24	Minbu	32	22	...	10	...	...	...	...	...	...	...	...	...
25	Magwe	...	...	...	...	...	...	...	...	...	...	...	...	...
26	Pakôkku Hill Tracts	...	...	...	...	...	...	...	...	...	...	...	...	...
	Mandalay Division	...	...	...	...	...	323	69	136	...	...	...	...	118
27	Mandalay	...	...	...	...	...	323	69	136	...	...	...	...	118
	Mandalay City	...	...	...	...	...	*312*	*64*	*136*	...	...	...	...	*112*
28	Bhamo	...	...	...	...	...	...	...	...	...	...	...	...	...
29	Myitkyina	...	...	...	...	...	...	...	...	...	...	...	...	...
30	Katha	...	...	...	...	...	...	...	...	...	...	...	...	...
31	Putao	...	...	...	...	...	...	...	...	...	...	...	...	...
	Sagaing Division	...	...	...	...	...	77	11	56	...	...	1	...	10
32	Shwebo	...	...	...	...	...	5	5	...	...	...	1	...	...
33	Sagaing	...	...	...	...	...	72	6	56	...	...	...	...	10
34	Lower Chindwin	...	...	...	...	...	...	...	...	...	...	...	...	...
35	Upper Chindwin	...	...	...	...	...	...	...	...	...	...	...	...	...
36	Chin Hills	...	...	...	...	...	...	...	...	...	...	...	...	...
	Meiktila Division	...	...	...	...	...	1	1	...	...	...	...	...	...
37	Kyauksè	...	...	...	...	...	1	1	...	...	...	...	...	...
38	Meiktila	...	...	...	...	...	...	...	...	...	...	...	...	...
39	Yamèthin	...	...	...	...	...	...	...	...	...	...	...	...	...
40	Myingyan	...	...	...	...	...	...	...	...	...	...	...	...	...
	Eastern States	...	...	...	...	...	...	...	...	...	...	...	...	...
41	Northern Shan States	...	...	...	...	...	...	...	...	...	...	...	...	...
42	Southern Shan States	...	...	...	...	...	...	...	...	...	...	...	...	...
43	Karenni	...	...	...	...	...	...	...	...	...	...	...	...	...

* All without subsidiary occupations except one male in Kyaukpyu District with a non-agricultural subsidiary occupation.

† Groups 31, 32 and 33 relate to the carding, spinning and weaving of wool.

Textiles—*concluded.*

Group 35.—Silk weaving. Total Workers and Dependents.	Workers. Total Workers. Males.	Workers. Total Workers. Females.	Workers with an agricultural or other subsidiary occupation. Agricultural. Males.	Agricultural. Females.	Other. Males.	Other. Females.	Dependents.	Groups 36, 38.‡ Total (all Males).	Group 37.—Dyeing, bleaching, printing, preparation and sponging of textiles. Total Workers and Dependents.	Workers. Total Workers. Males.	Workers. Total Workers. Females.	Workers with an agricultural or other subsidiary occupation. Agricultural. Males.	Agricultural. Females.	Other. Males.	Other. Females.	Dependents.	Serial No. of District, etc. (column 1).
15	16	17	18	19	20	21	22	23	24	25	26	27	28	29	30	31	
29,436	2,936	18,041	20	510	185	764	8,459	3	3,956	1,029	2,017	6	46	32	121	910	
29,418	2,936	18,023	20	510	185	764	8,459	3	3,931	1,018	2,014	6	46	32	121	899	
2	...	...	...	...	...	...	2	...	17	5	8	...	...	...	1	4	
...	...	...	...	...	...	...	...	...	3	3	...	...	...	...	...	...	1
2	...	...	...	...	...	...	2	...	...	...	...	...	...	...	...	...	2
...	...	...	...	...	...	...	...	...	14	2	8	...	...	...	1	4	3
...	...	...	...	...	...	...	...	...	...	...	...	...	...	...	...	...	4
9,951	317	6,720	9	287	15	174	2,914	3	105	64	4	...	...	1	...	37	
...	...	...	...	...	...	...	...	1	13	13	...	...	...	...	...	...	5
3	...	...	...	...	...	...	3	...	...	...	...	...	...	...	...	...	6
1	...	...	...	...	...	...	1	2	...	...	...	...	...	...	...	...	7
...	...	...	...	...	...	...	...	...	68	37	...	...	...	1	...	31	8
...	...	...	...	...	...	...	...	...	20	14	...	...	...	...	...	6	9
9,947	317	6,720	9	287	15	174	2,910	...	4	...	4	...	...	...	...	...	10
13	1	9	...	...	...	8	3	...	51	22	...	...	...	...	...	29	
...	...	...	...	...	...	...	...	...	43	22	...	...	...	...	...	21	11
...	...	...	...	...	...	...	...	...	7	...	...	...	...	...	...	7	12
13	1	9	...	...	...	8	3	...	1	...	...	...	...	...	...	1	13
...	...	...	...	...	...	...	...	...	...	...	...	...	...	...	...	...	14
...	...	...	...	...	...	...	...	...	...	...	...	...	...	...	...	...	15
955	6	718	...	11	...	56	231	...	77	51	...	...	...	3	...	26	
...	...	...	...	...	...	...	...	...	...	...	...	...	...	...	...	...	16
...	...	...	...	...	...	...	...	...	...	...	...	...	...	...	...	...	17
...	...	...	...	...	...	...	...	...	77	51	...	...	...	3	...	26	18
...	...	...	...	...	...	...	...	...	...	...	...	...	...	...	...	...	19
722	5	647	...	11	...	56	70	...	...	...	...	...	...	...	...	...	20
233	1	71	...	...	...	...	161	...	...	...	...	...	...	...	...	...	21
435	...	425	...	1	...	13	10	...	139	33	38	...	...	...	2	68	
...	...	...	...	...	...	...	...	...	39	31	...	...	...	...	...	8	22
435	...	425	...	1	...	13	10	...	88	...	32	...	...	...	...	56	23
...	...	...	...	...	...	...	...	...	6	...	6	...	...	...	2	...	24
...	...	...	...	...	...	...	...	...	6	2	...	...	...	...	...	4	25
...	...	...	...	...	...	...	...	...	...	...	...	...	...	...	...	...	26
15,320	2,558	8,049	9	42	165	354	4,713	...	3,135	744	1,929	3	46	21	117	462	
15,315	2,556	8,048	9	41	165	354	4,711		3,106	731	1,921	3	46	21	116	454	27
4,025	*285*	*2,593*	...	...	*3*	...	*1,147*	.	*225*	*52*	...	...	...	...	...	*173*	
1	1	...	...	...	...	...	...	...	...	...	...	...	...	...	...	...	28
1	1	...	...	...	...	...	...	...	2	...	1	...	...	...	...	1	29
3	...	1	...	1	...	...	2	...	27	13	7	...	...	...	1	7	30
...	...	...	...	...	...	...	...	...	...	...	...	...	...	...	...	...	31
2,650	53	2,077	2	169	5	159	520	...	187	67	11	3	...	5	...	109	
2,532	39	1,988	2	169	5	159	505	...	69	28	8	...	...	1	...	33	32
50	14	25	...	...	...	...	11	...	3	...	3	...	...	...	...	...	33
...	...	...	...	...	...	...	...	...	112	38	...	3	...	4	...	74	34
68	...	64	...	...	...	...	4	...	3	1	...	...	...	...	...	2	35
...	...	...	...	...	...	...	...	...	...	...	...	...	...	...	...	...	36
92	1	25	...	...	...	...	66	...	220	32	24	...	...	2	1	164	
...	...	...	...	...	...	...	...	...	36	1	5	...	...	...	...	30	37
15	1	4	...	...	...	...	10	...	86	31	...	...	...	2	...	55	38
77	...	21	...	...	...	...	56	...	78	...	17	...	...	...	1	61	39
...	...	...	...	...	...	...	...	...	20	...	2	...	...	...	...	18	40
18	...	18	...	...	...	...	...	...	25	11	3	...	...	...	...	11	
...	...	...	...	...	...	...	...	...	22	11	...	...	...	...	...	11	41
18	...	18	...	...	...	...	...	...	3	...	3	...	...	...	...	...	42
...	...	...	...	...	...	...	...	...	...	...	...	...	...	...	...	...	43

‡ Group 36.—Textile work using hair, and Group 38.—Other textile industries. Only male workers without subsidiary occupations.

Serial No.	DISTRICT OR STATE.	Order VII.—Hides, feathers, bristles and hard materials from the animal: Group 39.—Tanners, curriers, leather dressers, leather dyers, etc.: Total Workers and Dependents.	Group 39: WORKERS. (All without subsidiary occupation.) Males.	Group 39: WORKERS. Females.	Group 39: DEPENDENTS.	Group 40.—Makers of leather articles other than articles of dress.: Total Workers and Dependents.	Group 40: WORKERS. Total Workers. Males.	Group 40: WORKERS. Total Workers. Females.	Group 40: Workers with an agricultural or other subsidiary occupation. Agricultural. Males.	Agricultural. Females.	Other. Males.	Other. Females.	Group 40: DEPENDENTS.	Group 41.*: Total.
	1	2	3	4	5	6	7	8	9	10	11	12	13	14
	Provincial Total ..	193	118	2	73	750	349	50	1	...	...	5	351	...
	Divisional Burma ...	193	118	2	73	748	349	50	1	...	...	5	349	...
	Arakan Division ...	...	.	...	...	...	...	...	...	...	...	...	...	...
1	Akyab ...	...		...	...	...	...	...	.	...	.	..	...	...
2	Hill Dist. of Arakan ...	...	...	...	...	...	...	...	...	.	.	..	...	...
3	Kyaukpyu ...	..	..	...	...	..	...	...	...	.	...	...	.	...
4	Sandoway ...	...	...	...	...	..	...	...	...	..	...	...	...	...
	Pegu Division ...	59	57	..	2	67	32	11	..	...	...	...	24	...
5	Rangoon Town .	2	...	...	2	47	27	2	...	...	...	...	18	...
6	Insein ..	57	57	...	...	13	1	9	...	...	...	...	3	...
7	Hanthawaddy ...	...	...	...	...	...	.	...	...	...	...	..	...	...
8	Tharrawaddy ...	...	...	...	...	3	...	...	...	...	...	...	3	...
9	Pegu ...	...	...	...	..	2	2	...	...	...	...	...	...	..
10	Prome ...	...	..	...	...	2	2	...	...	..	...	...	...	...
	Irrawaddy Division ...	..	...	...	...	...	...	...	...	...	..	...	..	...
11	Bassein ...	...	..	.	.	...	...	...	...	...	...	..	...	..
12	Henzada ...	.	...	...	...	.	.	..	...	...	...	...	...	...
13	Myaungmya ...	..		...	...	...	...	...	...	...	...	...	...	...
14	Ma-ubin ...	...	...	...	.	.	...	...	...	...	...	...	...	...
15	Pyapôn ..	.	...	..	...	...	...	...	...	...	...	...	...	...
	Tenasserim Division ...	18	5	...	13	7	1	3	...	...	...	1	3	...
16	Toungoo ...	...	...	...	...	...	...	...	...	...	...	...	...	...
17	Salween ...	...	...	...	...	...	...	..	...	...	...	...	...	...
18	Thatôn ...	...	...	...	...	...	...	...	...	...	...	...	...	...
19	Amherst ...	7	2	...	5	...	...	...	...	...	...	...	..	...
20	Tavoy ...	8	3	...	5	7	1	3	...	...	...	1	3	...
21	Mergui ...	3	...	...	3	...	...	...	...	...	...	...	...	...
	Magwe Division ...	1	1	...	...	17	5	...	...	...	...	...	12	..
22	Thayetmyo ...	...	...	..	...	..	...	..		..	..	...	..	...
23	Pakôkku ...	1	1	.	...	8	...	.	...	...	...	...	8	.
24	Minbu ...	..	..	...		9	5	...	...	...	...	...	4	...
25	Magwe ..	...	...	...	..	...	...	...	...	...	...	...	...	...
26	Pakôkku Hill Tracts .	..	...	...	...	...	...	...	...	.	...	..	...	...
	Mandalay Division ..	65	15	1	49	162	107	...	...	...	...	...	55	...
27	Mandalay ...	64	15	...	49	154	99	...	...	.	...	...	55	...
	Mandalay City ..	*52*	*8*	...	*49*	*151*	*96*	...	...	...	...	.	*55*	...
28	Bhamo ...	1	...	1	..	8	8	...	...	...	..	...	...	...
29	Myitkyina ..	..	..	...	...	...	...	...	...	...	...	...	..	...
30	Katha ...	...	...	...	...	...	...	...	...	...	...	...	...	...
31	Putao ...	...	...	...	...	...	...	...	...	...	.	.	...	...
	Sagaing Division ...	3	1	...	2	492	202	36	1	...	...	4	254	...
32	Shwebo ..	...	...	..	..	...	...	...	...	...	...	...	...	...
33	Sagaing ...	1	.	...	1	6	3	...	...	...	...	...	3	...
34	Lower Chindwin ...	2	1	..	1	486	199	36	1	...	..	4	251	...
35	Upper Chindwin ...	...	...	.	...	..	...	...	...	...	...	...	...	...
36	Chin Hills ...	...	...	..	...	...	...	...	...	...	...	...	...	...
	Meiktila Division ...	47	39	1	7	3	2		..	...	...	...	1	..
37	Kyaukse ..	28	25		3	...	..	...	...	...	.	...	..	...
38	Meiktila ...	15	10	1	4	1	...	..	...	...	.	...	1	...
39	Yamèthin ...	4	4	...	...	2	2	...	..	...	..	...	...	...
40	Myingyan ...	.	...	...	...	...	...	...	.	...	...	...	...	...
	Eastern States ...	..	...	...	...	2	...	...	...	...	..	...	2	..
41	Northern Shan States ...	...	...	...	...	.	...	..	...	...	...	...	...	..
42	Southern Shan States ...	...	...	...	...	2	...	...	...	...	.	.	[illegible]	...
43	Karenni ...	...	...	...	..	...	...	...	...	...	...	...	...	...

* Furriers and persons occupied with feathers or bristles; brush makers.

PART III.—*Details by districts*—contd.

kingdom. Group 42.—Workers in bone, ivory, horn, shell, etc. (except button-makers). Total Workers and Dependents.	Workers (All without subsidiary occupation). Males.	Workers (All without subsidiary occupation). Females.	Dependents.	Order VIII.—Wood. Group 43.—Sawyers. Total Workers and Dependents.	Workers. Total Workers. Males.	Workers. Total Workers. Females.	Workers with an agricultural or other subsidiary occupation. Agricultural. Males	Agricultural. Females	Other. Males	Other. Females	Dependents.	Group 44.—Carpenters, turners, joiners, etc. Total Workers and Dependents.	Workers. Total Workers. Males.	Workers. Total Workers. Females.	Workers with an agricultural or other subsidiary occupation. Agricultural. Males.	Agricultural. Females.	Other. Males.	Other. Females.	Dependents.	Serial No. of District, etc. (column 1).
15	16	17	18	19	20	21	22	23	24	25	26	27	28	29	30	31	32	33	34	
124	70	1	53	60,040	25,737	1,685	487	21	899	38	32,618	90,969	36,399	2,283	612	46	1,235	76	52,287	
68	17	1	50	58,706	25,156	1,661	467	20	865	38	31,889	84,596	33,371	2,147	486	31	1,147	65	49,078	
2	...	1	1	1,424	505	40	29	3	39	1	879	3,057	1,553	27	21	...	33	1	1,477	
	...	...	...	597	242	30	15	...	9	...	325	1,865	1,103	16	5	...	6	...	746	1
...	...	..	...	...	...	...	...		...	...	...	36	18	...	...	...	...	...	18	2
2	...	1	1	163	49	10	3	3	4	1	104	567	202	7	7	...	10	..	358	3
...	..	...	...	664	214	..	11	...	26	...	450	589	230	4	9	...	17	1	355	4
42	14	...	28	13,147	7,363	253	37	...	60	2	5,531	27,697	12,839	526	69	12	158	8	14,332	
42	14	...	28	7,207	5,348	28	9	..	5		1,831	15,414	8,191	124	3	...	8	...	7,099	5
...	...	...	...	697	303	43	6	.	5	1	351	2,353	968	76	2	1	17	...	1,309	6
...	...	.	..	1,035	198	110	4	...	1	1	727	2,886	1,159	20	8	..	19	...	1,707	7
...	...	...	...	1,788	582	19	2	...	16	...	1,187	2,306	821	1	35	...	44	...	1,484	8
...	...	...	...	1,328	496	19	13	..	18	...	813	2,680	978	2	14	...	41	...	1,700	9
.	...	...	...	1,092	436	34	3	..	15	...	622	2,058	722	303	7	11	29	8	1,033	10
..	...	...	...	6,381	2,400	237	47	...	102	13	3,744	8,373	3,009	109	60	1	139	2	5,255	
..	..	...	..	1,786	666	49	11	...	34	3	1,071	1,906	794	4	10	...	44	...	1,108	11
...	...	...	...	1,351	505	47	19	...	21	10	799	2,144	749	1	26	1	38	...	1,394	12
.	...	...	...	1,772	626	85	12	...	36	...	1,061	919	316	26	4	...	21	...	577	13
...	...	...	...	805	354	33	2	...	9	...	418	1,846	611	58	11	...	27	2	1,174	14
...	...	...	...	667	249	23	3	...	2	...	395	1,558	536	20	9	...	9	...	1,002	15
21	...	...	21	15,604	6,565	322	140	8	111	11	8,717	13,271	4,600	116	71	6	125	5	8,555	
...	...	...	..	3,231	1,118	132	6	5	24	2	1,981	2,438	881	27	7	...	24	...	1,530	16
...	..	...	...	95	36	2	1	...	1	...	57	150	60	...	1	...	2	...	90	17
..	...	...	..	1,620	411	64	...	...	14	5	1,145	1,806	596	60	7	6	36	4	1,150	18
21	...	...	21	7,635	3,959	100	53	2	3	3	3,576	5,254	1,763	21	32	...	3	1	3,470	19
...	...	...	..	1,808	664	20	80	1	55	1	1,124	1,943	744	4	24	...	39	...	1,195	20
.	...	...	...	1,215	377	4	...	...	14	...	834	1,680	556	4	...	...	21	...	1,120	21
...	...	...	...	6,459	2,266	123	57	5	189	3	4,070	8,466	3,176	300	55	5	223	14	4,990	
...	...	...	...	1,141	380	10	8	3	22	...	751	1,119	351	3	...	...	15	...	765	22
...	...	...	...	3 406	1,095	62	6	...	111	...	2,249	3,624	1,153	87	12	1	154	7	2,384	23
...	...	..	...	850	323	5	32	2	38	2	522	1,589	588	163	25	2	48	6	838	24
...	...	...	...	1,059	465	46	11	...	18	1	548	2,132	1,083	47	18	2	6	1	1,002	25
...	...	...	...	3	3	...	...	...	...	...	...	2	1	...	...	...	...	...	1	26
3	3	...	..	4,661	2,162	245	21	..	60	2	2,254	8,082	2,913	243	24	...	137	3	4,926	
3	3	...	..	3,269	1,436	227	4	..	9	...	1,606	6,138	2,131	139	9	...	60	...	3,868	27
3	*3*	...	...	*2,558*	*1,197*	*213*	..		...	...	*1,148*	*4,038*	*1,338*	*103*	...	...	2	...	2,597	
...	...	...	...	581	292	7	1	...	28	...	282	602	239	70	8	...	30	1	293	28
..	...	...	...	310	179	2	1	..	4	...	129	403	214	5	3	..	13	...	184	29
..	...	...	.	500	254	9	15		19	2	237	926	317	29	4	...	34	2	580	30
..	...	..	...	1	1	...	...	...	..		...	13	12	...	...	...	...	...	1	31
...	...	...		6,110	2,064	292	98	1	175	5	3,754	9,024	3,217	314	152	4	235	11	5,493	
...	...	...	...	1,512	624	43	47	1	56	..	845	1,349	507	49	4	...	28	...	793	32
..	...	...	...	1,199	394	12	20	...	38	...	793	2,601	1,054	33	92	1	69	8	1,514	33
...	...	...	...	2,084	610	218	15	...	42	...	1,256	4,126	1,258	230	43	3	71	3	2,638	34
...	...	...	...	1,291	426	19	16	...	39	5	846	899	378	2	13	...	67	...	519	35
.	...	...	...	24	10	...	.	...	...	...	14	49	20	...	...	...	...	...	29	36
...	...	...	...	4,920	1,831	149	38	3	129	1	2,940	6,626	2,064	512	34	3	97	21	4,050	
...	...	...	.	202	60	...	...	...	1	...	142	1,366	489	3	22	...	26	...	874	37
...	...	...	...	516	190	45	2	...	30	...	281	2,059	485	296	6	3	29	16	1,278	38
...	..	.	...	3,667	1,405	45	36	...	93	1	2,217	2,168	665	209	4	...	22	5	1,294	39
...	...	...	...	535	176	59	...	3	5	...	300	1,033	425	4	2	...	20	...	604	40
56	53	...	3	1,334	581	24	20	1	34	...	729	6,373	3,028	136	126	15	88	11	3,209	.
56	53	...	3	1,099	504	24	18	1	28	...	571	1,843	693	114	19	15	25	11	1,036	41
...	...	...	...	206	69	...	2	...	6	...	137	4,259	2,236	17	107	...	63	...	2,006	42
...	...	...	...	29	8	...	...	...	...	...	21	271	99	5	...	...	...	...	167	43

Order VIII.—

Group 45*a*.—Lacquer-workers and makers of basket-work, sieves and cages of bamboo, cane, etc.

Serial No.	DISTRICT OR STATE.		Total Workers and Dependents.	WORKERS. Total Workers. Males.	Total Workers. Females.	Workers with an agricultural or other subsidiary occupation. Agricultural. Males.	Agricultural. Females.	Other. Males.	Other. Females.	DEPENDENTS.
	1		2	3	4	5	6	7	8	9
	Provincial Total	...	16,525	6,343	3,263	120	38	372	149	6,919
	Divisional Burma	...	16,110	6,192	3,171	107	34	355	143	6,747
	Arakan Division	...	156	89	9	2	...	8	...	58
1	Akyab ...	...	133	79	7	2	..	6	...	47
2	Hill Dist. of Arakan	...	...	...	...	...	...	..	...	...
3	Kyaukpyu ...	...	6	2	...	...	...	1	...	4
4	Sandoway ...	...	17	8	2	...	...	1	...	7
	Pegu Division ...	...	2,274	987	299	12	1	32	8	988
5	Rangoon Town	...	298	155	17	...	...	2	...	126
6	Insein ...	...	144	78	10	1	.	2	...	56
7	Hanthawaddy	...	221	130	24	2	...	1	...	67
8	Tharrawaddy	...	505	242	76	3	...	10	1	187
9	Pegu ...	...	465	223	44	3	...	10	2	198
10	Prome ...	...	641	159	128	3	1	7	5	354
	Irrawaddy Division	..	1,836	816	208	8	4	47	11	812
11	Bassein ...	...	331	184	31	1	2	9	...	116
12	Henzada ...	...	751	285	100	6	2	30	9	366
13	Myaungmya	...	300	125	25	1	...	5	1	150
14	Ma-ubin ...	...	225	118	31	...	...	2	1	76
15	Pyapôn ...	...	229	104	21	...	...	1	...	104
	Tenasserim Division	...	1,155	495	221	2	8	29	4	439
16	Toungoo ...	...	452	104	158	...	8	3	2	190
17	Salween ...	...	...	...	...	...	...	...	...	...
18	Thatôn ...	...	287	162	19	2	...	9	...	106
19	Amherst ...	...	288	159	25	...	...	14	1	104
20	Tavoy ...	..	65	48	3	...	...	3	1	14
21	Mergui ...	...	63	22	16	...	...	...	...	25
	Magwe Division	...	2,412	882	466	22	9	71	44	1,064
22	Thayetmyo	...	67	65	...	...	...	...	...	2
23	Pakôkku ...	...	1,208	352	215	4	3	52	26	641
24	Minbu ...	...	725	259	191	16	6	9	17	275
25	Magwe ...	...	412	206	60	2	...	10	1	146
26	Pakôkku Hill Tracts	...	...	...	...	...	...	...	...	...
	Mandalay Division	...	624	175	172	7	...	23	3	277
27	Mandalay ...	...	523	122	168	2	...	18	3	233
	Mandalay City	..	*288*	...	*144*	...	..	...	...	*144*
28	Bhamo ...	...	30	15	...	...	...	2	...	15
29	Myitkyina ...	...	32	10	...	5	...	1	...	22
30	Katha ...	...	39	28	4	...	...	2	...	7
31	Putao ...	...	...	...	...	...	...	...	...	...
	Sagaing Division	...	3,805	1,221	1,112	49	12	61	41	1,472
32	Shwebo ...	...	390	177	76	8	...	11	4	137
33	Sagaing ...	...	1,510	338	687	13	10	29	20	485
34	Lower Chindwin	...	1,786	643	349	27	2	17	17	794
35	Upper Chindwin	..	119	63	...	1	...	4	...	56
36	Chin Hills ...	...	...	...	...	...	...	...	...	...
	Meiktila Division	...	3,848	1,527	684	5	...	84	32	1,637
37	Kyauksè ...	...	184	132	...	...	...	15	...	32
38	Meiktila ...	...	491	300	4	...	...	8	..	187
39	Yamèthin ...	...	467	68	82	...	...	4	1	317
40	Myingyan ...	...	2,706	1,027	598	5	..	57	31	1,081
	Eastern States	...	415	151	92	13	4	17	6	172
41	Northern Shan States	...	393	150	73	13	4	17	5	170
42	Southern Shan States	...	22	1	19	...	...	...	1	2
43	Karenni ...	...	...	...	...	...	...	...	...	...

PART III.—*Details by districts*—contd.

Wood—*concluded.*

Group 45*b*.—Makers with woody materials of mats not used for walls or floors.								Group 45*c*.—All others working with leaves or other woody materials.								
Total Workers and Dependents.	WORKERS.						DEPENDENTS.	Total Workers and Dependents.	WORKERS.						DEPENDENTS.	Serial No. of District, etc. (column 1).
	Total Workers.		Workers with an agricultural or other subsidiary occupation.						Total Workers.		Workers with an agricultural or other subsidiary occupation.					
			Agricultural.		Other.						Agricultural.		Other.			
	Males.	Females.	Males.	Females	Males.	Females.			Males.	Females.	Males.	Females	Males.	Females		
10	11	12	13	14	15	16	17	18	19	20	21	22	23	24	25	
24,712	5,131	10,386	138	407	390	462	9,195	21,924	5,888	7,253	132	265	359	384	8,783	
24,288	4,996	10,307	132	407	373	460	8,985	21,583	5,780	7,159	124	261	344	313	8,644	
748	202	135	5	...	10	16	411	1,453	407	388	1	...	19	7	658	
649	172	107	4	...	7	13	370	1,207	318	309	1	...	13	...	580	1
...	...	...	...	...	...	...	...	...	...	...	...	...	..	...	...	2
4	1	...	...	.	1	...	3	4	...	3	...	...	..	...	1	3
95	29	28	1	...	2	3	38	242	89	76	...	...	6	7	77	4
2,320	486	880	6	67	35	48	954	3,608	838	1,046	21	10	25	24	1,724	
121	92	10		...	...	...	19	160	74	11	...	...	...	...	75	5
121	38	43	...	5	3	8	40	354	66	133	3	9	1	9	155	6
474	35	142	1	...	1	3	297	279	55	90	1	...	...	2	134	7
1,068	162	514	5	45	4	18	392	1,919	374	621	4	1	9	8	924	8
359	41	171	...	17	...	19	147	318	102	66	1	..	6	1	150	9
177	118	.	.	...	27	...	59	578	167	125	12	.	9	4	286	10
6,228	803	3,382	14	122	24	71	2,043	4,397	1,586	926	57	45	130	51	1,885	
657	147	220	5	5	9	11	290	740	235	158	...	3	23	11	347	11
1,915	475	643	9	25	14	12	797	2,067	897	487	51	42	94	32	683	12
91	32	3	..	...	.	...	59	599	125	247	1	...	10	5	227	13
3,486	149	2,486	...	92	1	47	851	239	78	28	2	...	...	3	133	14
76	...	30	..	...	...	1	46	752	251	6	3	...	3	...	495	15
2,096	194	1,342	10	7	35	98	560	3,463	757	1,406	10	14	50	50	1,300	
183	41	73	...	...	13	4	69	1,361	326	393	...	6	26	19	642	16
9	3	1	...		...	...	5	69	19	23	..	..	...	...	27	17
767	121	443	10	...	20	58	203	985	225	365	6	...	16	3	395	18
86	3	56	...		...	2	27	408	13	249	...	.	...	14	146	19
730	15	488	...	7	1	12	227	538	123	360	2	8	7	14	55	20
321	11	281	...	..	1	21	89	102	51	16	2	...	1	...	35	21
4,172	1,383	688	26	16	117	64	2,101	1,900	279	698	11	39	12	26	923	
1,790	775	157	8	4	80	5	858	725	54	158	5	19	...	14	513	22
1,275	143	366	2	12	9	57	766	130	3	7	...	...	2	...	120	23
471	179	90	12	...	20	1	202	774	119	477	6	20	10	12	178	24
636	286	75	4	...	8	1	275	271	103	56		...	...	...	112	25
..	...	..	...	...	..	...	...	...	...	...	...	...	...	.	...	26
459	86	220	...	...	7	4	153	3,009	894	1,248	6	48	20	31	867	
303	14	195	..	...	1	...	94	2,536	818	1,085	6	48	10	18	633	27
167	*8*	*103*	...	..	...	...	*56*	*1,480*	*518*	*548*	...	..	...	...	*414*	
42	23	4	..	...	3	...	15	128	48	38	...	...	6	3	42	28
21	6	2	...	...	...	...	13	49	11	22	..	...	1	...	16	29
93	43	19	...	...	3	4	31	296	17	103	...	...	3	10	176	30
...	..	...	...	...	...	...	...	...	...	...	...	...	...	...	...	31
4,574	1,066	2,239	64	132	107	124	1,269	2,427	738	936	17	86	69	116	753	
1,007	265	408	30	89	17	16	334	341	115	73	1	...	6	10	153	32
1,231	136	880	2	28	6	72	215	1,306	256	788	8	75	24	98	262	33
1,942	498	883	24	11	61	30	561	734	362	67	8	11	36	7	305	34
394	167	68	8	4	23	6	159	46	5	8	...	...	3	1	33	35
...	...	...	.	...	...	.	..	...	...	...	...	...	...	...	...	36
3,691	776	1,421	7	63	38	35	1,494	1,326	281	511	1	29	19	8	534	
559	93	325	7	49	10	11	143	135	58	15	...	...	9	..	62	37
1,478	383	439	.	9	24	21	656	706	87	348	...	18	4	5	271	38
913	142	264		5	...	2	507	223	58	58	...	...	1	...	107	39
741	158	395	.	...	4	1	188	262	78	90	1	1	5	3	94	40
424	135	79	6	...	17	2	210	341	108	94	8	4	15	11	139	
337	131	32	5	...	16	2	174	291	96	91	2	4	13	9	104	41
87	4	47	1	...	1	...	36	48	12	3	6	...	2	2	33	42
...	...	...	...	...	...	...	...	2	...	...	...	...	-	...	2	43

Order IX.—

Serial No.	DISTRICT OR STATE.	Group 46.—Smelting, casting, forging and rolling of iron. Total Workers and Dependents.	WORKERS.* Males.	WORKERS.* Females	DEPENDENTS.	Group 47.—Makers of guns and other arms. Total Workers and Dependents.	WORKERS.† Males.	DEPENDENTS.	Group 48.—Other workers in iron and makers of articles consisting principally exclusively of iron. Total Workers and Dependents.	WORKERS. Total Workers. Males.	Total Workers. Females	Workers with an agricultural or other subsidiary occupation. Agricultural. Males.	Agricultural. Females	Other. Males.	Other. Females	DEPENDENTS.
	1	2	3	4	5	6	7	8	9	10	11	12	13	14	15	16
	Provincial Total ...	798	442	*10	346	150	84	66	32,053	12,394	745	278	25	562	44	18,914
	Divisional Burma ..	798	442	*10	346	150	84	66	29,577	11,406	689	206	22	397	41	17,482
	Arakan Division ..	...	...	...	...	..	..	...	866	505	8	6	...	8	1	353
1	Akyab	...	...	..	...	...	...	...	523	392	...	...	...	3	...	131
2	Hill Dist. of Arakan ...	...	...	...	...	...	.	...	6	6	...	...	...	..	...	...
3	Kyaukpyu	...	...	.	...	...	...	...	195	51	8	6	...	4	1	136
4	Sandoway	...	...	...	..	.	..	...	142	56	...	...	...	1	...	86
	Pegu Division	660	401	1	258	149	†84	65	6,909	2,937	103	36	1	76	6	3,869
5	Rangoon Town ..	660	401	1	258	149	†84	65	1,966	1,067	9	2	...	...	...	890
6	Insein	...	...	...	...	...	...	...	841	366	41	3	...	17	3	434
7	Hanthawaddy ...	...	...	..	...	..	...	...	774	393	...	6	...	15	...	381
8	Tharrawaddy ...	...	...	-	...	...	...	...	1,090	333	23	5	...	19	...	734
9	Pegu	...	...	...	...	...	...	...	1,230	417	1	11	...	13	...	812
10	Prome	...	...	...	...	...	...	...	1,008	361	29	9	1	12	3	618
	Irrawaddy Division ...	82	...	*9	73	...	...		4,519	1,582	123	29	5	42	9	2,814
11	Bassein	...	...	...	..	...	...	...	1,021	375	25	4	...	10	3	621
12	Henzada	82	..	*9	73	..	...	...	1,259	388	20	6	3	11	4	851
13	Myaungmya ..	...	...	..	...	...	...	...	1,022	404	42	9	1	15	2	576
14	Ma-ubin	...	...	..	..	...	...	...	644	233	36	8	1	3	...	375
15	Pyapôn	...	...	...	...	...	...	...	573	182	...	2	...	3	...	391
	Tenasserim Division ..	...	...	...	...	1	...	1	5,022	1,805	33	30	2	59	3	3,184
16	Toungoo	...	...	...	...	1	...	1	886	361	10	...	1	18	1	515
17	Salween	...	...	...	...	...	...	..	61	22	2	...	...	4	...	37
18	Thaton	...	...	...	...	...	...	...	1,633	477	5	12	...	13	1	1,151
19	Amherst	...	...	..	...	...	...	...	1,903	737	14	10	1	20	1	1,152
20	Tavoy	..	...	...	...	...	...	...	342	136	...	7	...	4	...	206
21	Mergui	...	...	...	..	...	...	..	197	72	2	1	...	...	...	123
	Magwe Division ...	3	1	...	2	...	...	...	3,865	1,416	122	34	5	88	9	2,327
22	Thayetmyo	2	...	...	2	...	...	...	698	246	28	6	2	21	4	424
23	Pakôkku	...	...	.	...	...	...	...	1,590	539	16	9	...	47	...	1,035
24	Minbu	...	...	...	..	...	.	...	787	273	39	13	2	13	4	475
25	Magwe ...	1	1	...	...	...	...	...	788	356	39	6	1	7	1	393
26	Pakôkku Hill Tracts ...	...	...	...	...	...	...		2	2	..	...	...	...	...	...
	Mandalay Division ..	51	39	...	12	...	...	...	2,645	1,268	81	14	1	27	1	1,296
27	Mandalay	49	39	...	10	...	...	...	1,900	878	42	8	...	4	...	980
	Mandalay City ...	*49*	*39*	...	*10*	...	...	...	*1,314*	*547*	*3*	...	...	*1*	..	*764*
28	Bhamo	2	...	...	2	...	...	...	152	102	3	...	...	3	...	47
29	Myitkyina	...	...	...	...	...	...	...	156	111	1	3	...	9	...	44
30	Katha	...	..	...	...	...	..	..	435	176	35	3	1	11	1	224
31	Putao	...	...	...	...	...	...	...	2	1	...	...	...	...	...	1
	Sagaing Division ..	1	1	..	...	..	...	...	1,897	711	56	33	5	47	2	1,130
32	Shwebo	1	1		...	...	...	...	665	249	44	13	4	12	...	372
33	Sagaing	...	...	...	...	...	...	...	209	9	...	..	...	...	...	200
34	Lower Chindwin ...	...	...	...	...	...	...	...	714	346	9	12	1	24	1	359
35	Upper Chindwin ...	...	..	...	...	...	...	...	289	101	2	4	...	11	...	186
36	Chin Hills	...	...	...	...	..	...	...	20	6	1	4	...	...	1	13
	Meiktila Division ...	1	...	...	1	...	...	...	3,854	1,182	163	24	3	50	10	2,509
37	Kyauksè	...	...	...	...	...	...	...	477	163	21	5	...	9	...	293
38	Meiktila	..	...	...	...	...	...	...	606	193	...	...	...	7	...	413
39	Yamèthin	...	..	...	..	...	...	...	1,634	476	12	3	1	22	1	1,140
40	Myingyan	1	...	...	1	...	...	...	1,137	350	130	16	2	12	9	657
	Eastern States ...	...	...	...	...	...	...	...	2,476	988	56	72	3	165	3	1,432
41	Northern Shan States ...	..	...	...	...	...	...	...	667	344	25	5	1	13	...	298
42	Southern Shan States ...	...	...	...	...	...	...	...	1,760	624	29	67	2	152	3	1,107
43	Karenni	...	...	...	...	...	...	...	49	20	2	...	...	...	...	2[illegible]

* Two females in Henzada district have a non-agricultural subsidiary occupation, all other workers have no subsidiary occupation.
† All males and all without subsidiary occupation except one with a non-agricultural subsidiary occupation.

PART III.—*Details by districts*—contd.

Metals.

Group 49.—All workers in brass, copper and bell-metal.								Group 50.—All workers in other metals except precious metals.								
Total Workers and Dependents.	WORKERS.						DEPENDENTS.	Total Workers and Dependents.	WORKERS.						DEPENDENTS.	Serial No. of District, etc. (column 1).
	Total Workers.		Workers with an agricultural or other subsidiary occupation.						Total Workers.		Workers with an agricultural or other subsidiary occupation.					
			Agricultural.		Other.						Agricultural.		Other.			
	Males.	Females.	Males.	Females	Males.	Females.			Males.	Females.	Males.	Females	Males.	Females		
17	18	19	20	21	22	23	24	25	26	27	28	29	30	31	32	
2,508	1,120	143	25	...	17	...	1,245	6,233	2,648	137	18	2	60	...	3,448	
2,344	1,053	140	24	...	13	...	1,151	6,075	2,570	136	17	2	58	...	3,369	
7	3	...	...	...	...	...	4	272	120	6	...	...	5	...	146	
7	3	...	...	...	...	...	4	203	99	...	...	...	3	...	104	1
...	...	...	...	...	...	...	...	...	...	...	...	...	...	...	...	2
...	...	...	...	...	...	...	...	14	8	5	...	...	...	...	1	3
...	...	...	...	...	...	...	...	55	13	1	...	...	2	...	41	4
653	344	2	12	...	7	...	307	2,204	1,092	30	7	1	16	...	1,082	
339	117	1	...	...	...	..	231	1,372	781	5	...	...	3	...	586	5
34	1	..	...	...	...	...	33	107	34	9	...	...	1	...	64	6
182	165	...	...	...	...	...	17	238	79	3	1	1	5	...	156	7
...	...	...	...	...	...	...	...	142	70	2	...	...	1	...	70	8
10	7	...	...	...	...	...	3	155	58	4	6	...	3	...	93	9
88	54	1	12	...	7	...	33	190	70	7	...	...	3	..	113	10
112	53	6	...	...	1	...	53	662	237	21	...	1	5	..	404	
49	27	2	...	..	1	..	20	110	31	8	...	...	4	..	71	11
32	8	1	...	...	..	...	23	240	88	3	..	1	...	.	149	12
23	14	2	...	...	...	...	7	99	39	6	...	...	...	..	54	13
5	2	1	...	...	...	...	2	106	32	4	...	...	1	...	70	14
3	2	...	...	...	...	..	1	107	47	...	...	-	...	...	60	15
114	90	4	12	...	...	...	20	1,159	411	29	7	...	11	...	719	
7	2	1	...	...	...	...	4	217	82	...	1	...	2	...	135	16
...	...	...	...	...	...	...	...	1	1	...	...	...	..	..	...	17
5	2	1	...	...	...	...	2	187	59	2	...	...	3	...	126	18
92	83	...	12	...	...	...	9	357	107	16	2	...	...		234	19
4	1	...	...	...	...	...	3	295	131	7	4	...	6	...	158	20
6	2	2	...	...	...	...	2	101	31	4	...	...	...	...	66	21
186	94	3	...	...	3	...	89	436	193	17	1	..	5	...	226	
14	3	1	...	...	...	...	10	55	15	...	...	...	1	..	40	22
152	72	1	...	...	3	...	79	217	84	15	..	...	...	...	118	23
1	...	1	...	...	...	...	...	75	36	2	...	...	4	.	37	24
19	19	...	...	...	...	...	...	89	58	...	1	...	...	...	31	25
...	...	...	...	...	...	...	...	...	..	...	...	...	...	...	...	26
241	116	9	...	...	...	...	116	598	251	16	...	...	2	..	331	
234	112	9	...	...	...	...	113	479	207	13	...	...	1	...	259	27
224	*109*	*9*	...	...	...	...	*106*	*429*	*185*	*13*	...	...	...	...	*231*	
1	1	...	...	...	...	...	...	27	10	1	...	.	...	..	15	28
2	2	...	...	...	...	...	...	17	10	1	...	...	1	...	6	29
4	1	...	...	...	...	...	3	75	24	1	...	...	...	...	50	30
...	...	...	..	...	...	...	...	...	...	...	..	...	...	..	...	31
475	176	15	...	..	2	...	284	299	137	1	1	...	8	...	161	
9	8	...	...	..	...	...	1	98	36	...	...	..	...	...	62	32
187	12	4	...	...	1	...	111	75	36	...	...	...	1	...	39	33
339	156	11	...	...	1	...	172	83	43	...	...	...	3	...	40	34
...	...	...	...	...	...	...	...	43	22	1	1	...	4	...	20	35
...	...	...	...	...	...	...	...	...	...	...	...	...	...	...	...	36
556	177	101	...	...	...	...	278	445	129	16	1	...	6	..	300	
...	...	...	...	...	...	...	...	62	26	3	...	...	1	...	33	37
11	9	...	...	...	...	...	2	97	31	8	...	...	...	...	58	38
540	163	101	...	...	...	..	276	134	31	...	...	...	...	...	103	39
5	5	...	...	...	...	...	...	152	41	5	1	...	5	...	106	40
164	67	3	1	..	4	...	94	158	78	1	1	...	2	...	79	
154	57	3	1	...	4	...	94	107	56	1	...	...	2	..	50	41
...	...	...	...	...	...	...	...	46	20	...	1	...	...	...	26	42
10	10	...	...	...	...	...	...	5	2	..	...	...	...	...	3	43

Serial No.	DISTRICT OR STATE.	Order IX—Metals—*concld.* Group 51.—Workers in mints, die-sinkers, etc. Total Workers and Dependents.	WORKERS. (All without subsidiary occupation.) Males.	Females.	DEPENDENTS.	Order X.— Group 52.—Makers of glass and crystal ware. Total Workers and Dependents.	WORKERS. Total Workers. Males.	Total Workers. Females	Workers with an agricultural or other subsidiary occupation. Agricultural. Males.	Agricultural. Females	Other. Males.	Other. Females.	DEPENDENTS.	Group 53.—Makers of bangles, beads, necklaces, ear-studs, etc., made of glass. Total Workers and Dependents.	WORKERS. (All without subsidiary occupation.) Males.	Females.	DEPENDENTS.
	1	2	3	4	5	6	7	8	9	10	11	12	13	14	15	16	17
	Provincial Total ...	34	2	2	30	844	239	256	4	4	10	5	349	52	11	9	32
	Divisional Burma ...	33	1	2	30	844	239	256	4	4	10	5	349	52	11	9	32
	Arakan Division ...	...	...	...	...	...	...	...	...	...	...	...	...	...	...	...	...
1	Akyab ...	...	...	...	...	...	...	...	...	...	...	...	...	...	...	...	...
2	Hill Dist. of Arakan	...	...	...	...	...	...	...	...	...	...	...	...	...	...	...	...
3	Kyaukpyu ...	...	...	...	...	...	...	...	...	...	...	...	...	...	...	...	...
4	Sandoway ...	...	...	...	...	...	...	...	...	...	...	...	...	...	...	...	...
	Pegu Division ...	...	...	...	...	225	36	49	...	...	...	...	140	15	6	2	7
5	Rangoon Town ...	...	...	...	...	130	7	48	...	...	...	...	75	12	6	...	6
6	Insein ...	...	...	...	...	45	23	1	...	...	...	...	21	3	...	2	1
7	Hanthawaddy ...	...	...	...	...	4	...	...	...	...	...	...	4	...	...	...	...
8	Tharrawaddy ...	...	...	...	...	4	4	...	...	...	...	...	...	...	...	...	...
9	Pegu ...	...	...	...	...	12	2	...	...	...	...	...	10	...	...	...	...
10	Prome ...	...	...	...	...	30	...	...	...	...	...	...	30	...	...	...	...
	Irrawaddy Division ...	...	...	...	...	47	27	...	...	...	3	...	20	...	...	...	...
11	Bassein ...	...	...	...	...	10	...	...	...	...	...	...	10	...	...	...	...
12	Henzada ...	...	...	...	...	9	7	...	...	...	1	...	2	...	...	...	...
13	Myaungmya ...	...	...	...	...	17	13	...	...	...	2	...	4	...	...	...	...
14	Ma-ubin ...	...	...	...	...	6	4	...	...	...	...	...	2	...	...	...	...
15	Pyapôn ...	...	...	...	...	5	3	...	...	...	...	...	2	...	...	...	...
	Tenasserim Division ...	33	1	2	30	63	48	...	...	...	1	...	15	...	...	...	...
16	Toungoo ...	...	...	...	...	45	41	...	...	...	...	...	4	...	...	...	...
17	Salween ...	...	...	...	...	...	...	...	...	...	...	...	...	...	...	...	...
18	Thatôn ...	...	...	...	...	3	3	...	...	...	...	...	...	...	...	...	...
19	Amherst ...	32	...	2	30	8	3	...	...	...	...	...	5	...	...	...	...
20	Tavoy ...	1	1	...	...	7	1	...	...	...	1	...	6	...	...	...	...
21	Mergui ...	...	...	...	...	...	...	...	...	...	...	...	...	...	...	...	...
	Magwe Division ...	...	...	...	...	262	11	162	...	4	...	5	89	...	...	...	...
22	Thayetmyo ...	...	...	...	...	250	4	161	...	3	...	5	85	...	...	...	...
23	Pakôkku ...	...	...	...	...	...	...	...	...	...	...	...	...	...	...	...	...
24	Minbu ...	...	...	...	...	10	5	1	...	1	...	...	4	...	...	...	...
25	Magwe ...	...	...	...	...	2	2	...	...	...	...	...	...	...	...	...	...
26	Pakôkku Hill Tracts	...	...	...	...	...	...	...	...	...	...	...	...	...	...	...	...
	Mandalay Division ...	...	...	...	...	115	36	45	...	...	...	...	34	23	3	4	16
27	Mandalay ...	...	...	...	...	115	36	45	...	...	...	...	34	23	3	4	16
	Mandalay City ...	...	...	...	...	*111*	*32*	*45*	...	...	...	...	*34*	*17*	...	*4*	*13*
28	Bhamo ...	...	...	...	...	...	...	...	...	...	...	...	...	...	...	...	...
29	Myitkyina ...	...	...	...	...	...	...	...	...	...	...	...	...	...	...	...	...
30	Katha ...	...	...	...	...	...	...	...	...	...	...	...	...	...	...	...	...
31	Putao ...	...	...	...	...	...	...	...	...	...	...	...	...	...	...	...	...
	Sagaing Division ...	...	...	...	...	105	64	...	4	...	6	...	41	14	2	3	9
32	Shwebo ...	...	...	...	...	8	8	...	...	...	...	...	...	...	...	...	...
33	Sagaing ...	...	...	...	...	62	31	...	3	...	4	...	31	11	2	...	9
34	Lower Chindwin ...	...	...	...	...	20	14	...	...	...	2	...	6	3	...	3	...
35	Upper Chindwin ...	...	...	...	...	15	11	...	1	...	...	...	4	...	...	...	...
36	Chin Hills ...	...	...	...	...	...	...	...	...	...	...	...	...	...	...	...	...
	Meiktila Division ...	...	...	...	...	27	17	...	...	...	...	...	10	...	...	...	...
37	Kyauksè ...	...	...	...	...	...	...	...	...	...	...	...	...	...	...	...	...
38	Meiktila ...	...	...	...	...	13	3	...	...	...	...	...	10	...	...	...	...
39	Yamèthin ...	...	...	...	...	...	...	...	...	...	...	...	...	...	...	...	...
40	Myingyan ...	...	...	...	...	14	14	...	...	...	...	...	...	...	...	...	...
	Eastern States ...	1	1	...	...	...	...	...	...	...	...	...	...	...	...	...	...
41	Northern Shan States	1	1	...	...	...	...	...	...	...	...	...	...	...	...	...	...
42	Southern Shan States	...	...	...	...	...	...	...	...	...	...	...	...	...	...	...	...
43	Karenni ...	...	...	...	...	...	...	...	...	...	...	...	...	...	...	...	...

PART III.—*Details by districts*—contd.

Ceramics.

Group 54.—Makers of porcelain and crockery.				Group 55.—Potters and earthen pipe and bowl makers.								Group 56.—Brick and tile makers.								Group 57.†	Serial No. of District, etc. (column 1).
Total Workers and Dependents.	WORKERS.*		DEPENDENTS.	Total Workers and Dependents.	WORKERS.						DEPENDENTS.	Total Workers and Dependents.	WORKERS.						DEPENDENTS.	Total.	
					Total Workers.		Workers with an agricultural or other subsidiary occupation.						Total Workers.		Workers with an agricultural or other subsidiary occupation.						
							Agricultural.		Other.						Agricultural.		Other.				
	Males.	Females.			Males.	Females.	Males.	Females.	Males.	Females.			Males.	Females.	Males.	Females.	Males.	Females.			
18	19	20	21	22	23	24	25	26	27	28	29	30	31	32	33	34	35	36	37	38	
22	5	6	11	17,055	3,129	7,628	83	173	154	370	6,298	12,629	6,517	1,872	62	15	108		4,240	...	
6	5	1	...	16,940	3,092	7,574	80	173	149	366	6,274	12,521	6,417	1,871	52	15	108	30	4,233	..	
...		...	...	1,514	385	516	11	3	15	12	613	219	134	2	13	...	2	...	83	.	
...	...	...	...	1,309	327	447	9	...	9	...	535	196	122	2	12	...	2	...	72	...	1
...	...	...	...	...	...	...	...	...	...	...	...	...	...	...	...	...	...	...	...	...	2
...	...	...	...	14	8	1	...	...	1	...	5	22	12	...	1	...	..	...	10	...	3
...	...	...	...	191	50	68	2	3	5	12	73	1	...	...	...	...	...	...	1	...	4
...	...	...	...	3,138	673	1,021	28	17	34	37	1,444	5,349	3,472	404	10	...	45	...	1,473	...	
..	...	..	...	102	84	7	...	...	...	...	11	830	694	24	...	...	1	...	112	...	5
...	...	..	...	47	2	21	...	...	...	...	24	2,309	1,653	158	...	...	29	...	498	..	6
...	...	..	...	512	153	95	1	...	1	...	264	605	301	36	4	...	1	...	268	...	7
...	...	...	...	501	10	237	...	1	8	2	254	569	398	6	...	...	3	...	165	...	8
...		...	...	1,305	308	336	16	3	10	4	661	437	174	95	...	...	4	..	168	...	9
...	...	...	...	671	116	325	11	13	15	31	230	599	252	85	6	...	7	...	262	...	10
...	...		..	2,812	458	1,116	10	19	10	31	1,238	999	429	197	6	...	3	1	373	..	
...	.	.	...	1,044	24	529	...	3	1	15	491	258	152	33	...	...	...	1	73	...	11
...	...	...	...	837	141	305	10	16	6	15	391	152	63	12	5	...	3	...	77	...	12
...	...	...	...	133	84	4	...	...	2	...	45	243	63	99	1	...	...	...	81	...	13
...	...	...	...	758	204	272	...	...	1	1	282	292	116	49	...	...	...	...	127	...	14
...	..	...	...	40	5	6	...	...	...	...	29	54	35	4	...	...	...	...	15	...	15
...	...	...	...	1,470	177	774	1	8	5	154	519	1,370	583	132	4	6	5	1	655	...	
...	...	...	...	227	5	116	...	4	...	6	106	324	155	27	2	...	2	...	142	...	16
...	...	...	...	14	5	...	...	...	...	..	9	...	...	...	...	...	...	...	...	...	17
...	...	...	...	699	29	463	...	4	.	144	207	274	110	25	2	..	2	...	139	...	18
...	...	...	...	257	100	54	...	...	1	...	103	391	186	29	..	6	1	1	176	...	19
...	...	...	...	249	38	141	1	...	4	4	70	79	52	3	...	...	...	...	24	...	20
...	...	...	...	24	...	...	..	...	...	...	24	302	80	48	...	...	...	...	174	...	21
...	...	...	...	2,399	305	1,313	16	66	32	39	781	1,002	548	99	10	...	27	1	355	...	
.	...	...	...	301	35	117	2	...	3	..	149	203	134	2	...	...	...	...	67	...	22
...	...	...		1,086	104	670	5	53	16	25	312	204	109	...	...	...	14	...	95	...	23
...	.	...	...	744	98	441	9	8	9	11	205	438	223	87	5	...	9	1	128	...	24
...	...	...	...	268	68	85	...	5	4	3	115	157	82	10	5	..	4	...	65	...	25
...	...	...	...	...	...	...	...	...	...	...	...	...	...	...	...	...	...	...	...	...	26
..	...	..	...	1,255	232	717	...	2	5	4	306	1,639	590	599	...	8	2	25	450	...	
...	...	...	...	856	132	532	...	...	3	..	192	1,465	515	522	...	6	2	21	428	...	27
...	..	...	...	*134*	*43*	*66*	..	...	...	...	*25*	*995*	*366*	*348*	...	*6*	...	*19*	*281*	...	
...	.	...	...	314	62	158	...	...	...	...	94	52	40	7	.	...	...	...	5	...	28
...	...	..	...	9	...	7	...	...	..	...	2	13	4	...	...	...	...	...	9	...	29
...	...	...	...	76	38	20	...	2	2	4	18	84	6	70	...	2	...	4	8	...	30
...	..	...	...	...	...	...	...	...	...	...	...	25	25	...	...	...	..	...	...	...	31
*5	5	...	...	1,984	546	868	6	21	29	55	570	987	394	182	9	1	22	2	411	...	
...	.		...	1,069	233	527	1	17	3	25	309	304	159	58	1	...	9	...	87	...	32
*2	2	...	...	250	187	...	2	...	4	...	63	238	105	89	7	..	8	...	44	...	33
3	3	...	...	388	60	201	1	3	8	9	127	410	107	33	1	1	4	2	270	...	34
...	...	..	...	277	66	140	2	1	14	21	71	35	23	2	...	...	1	...	10	...	35
..	...	...	...	...	...	...	...	...	...	...	...	...	...	...	...	..	...	...	...	...	36
1	...	1	...	2,368	316	1,249	8	37	19	34	803	956	267	256	...	...	2	...	433	...	
...	...	..	...	696	79	388	3	2	4	4	229	...	...	...	...	...	...	...	...	...	37
...	...	...	...	654	73	431	...	6	8	9	150	310	89	99	...	...	..	...	122	...	38
1	.	1	...	341	39	117	...	29	..	3	185	492	111	130	...	...	...	..	251	...	39
..	...	...	...	677	125	313	5	...	7	18	239	154	67	27	...	...	2	...	60	...	40
16	.	5	11	115	37	54	3	...	5	4	24	108	100	1	10	...	...	..	7	...	
16	...	5	11	115	37	54	3	...	5	4	24	86	78	1	10	...	...	...	7	...	41
...	...	...	...	...	...	...	...	...	...	..	...	6	6	...	..	...	...	...	...	..	42
...	...	...	...	...	...	...	..	...	.	...	...	16	16	...	...	...	...	...	...	...	43

* All without subsidiary occupation except one male in Sagaing district with an agricultural subsidiary occupation.
† Workers in mosaic, talc, mica, etc., and workers in alabaster other than sculptors.

Order XI.—Manufacture or refining of

Serial No.	DISTRICT OR STATE.	Group 58.—Matches and explosive materials. Total Workers and Dependents.	Group 58. WORKERS.* Males.	Group 58. DEPENDENTS.	Group 59.—Aerated and mineral waters and ice. Total Workers and Dependents.	Group 59. WORKERS.† Males.	Group 59. WORKERS.† Females.	Group 59. DEPENDENTS.	Group 60.—Dyes, paint, ink and pencils. Total Workers and Dependents.	Group 60. WORKERS. (All without subsidiary occupation.) Males.	Group 60. WORKERS. (All without subsidiary occupation.) Females.	Group 60. DEPENDENTS.
	1	2	3	4	5	6	7	8	9	10	11	12
	Provincial Total ...	24	18	6	363	164	10	189	33	7	9	17
	Divisional Burma ...	24	18	6	361	162	10	189	33	7	9	17
	Arakan Division ...	2	2	...	...	...	...	...	...	...	...	...
1	Akyab ...	2	2	...	...	...	...	...	...	...	...	...
2	Hill Dist. of Arakan ...	...	...	...	...	...	...	...	...	...	...	...
3	Kyaukpyu ...	...	...	...	...	...	...	...	...	...	...	...
4	Sandoway ...	...	...	...	...	...	...	...	...	...	...	...
	Pegu Division ...	10	8	2	222	88	8	126	15	6	4	5
5	Rangoon Town ...		...	...	195	80	4	111	6	4	...	2
6	Insein ...	...	...	...	16	5	4	7	2	2	...	...
7	Hanthawaddy ...	...	...	...	...	...	...	...	...	...	...	...
8	Tharrawaddy ...	...	...	...	...	...	...	...	...	...	...	...
9	Pegu ...	...	...	...	11	3	...	8	7	...	4	3
10	Prome ...	10	8	2	...	...	...	...	...	...	...	...
	Irrawaddy Division ...	8	*5	3	19	9	...	10	...	...	...	...
11	Bassein ...	...	...	...	2	1	...	1	...	...	...	...
12	Henzada ...	8	*5	3	7	6	...	1	...	...	...	...
13	Myaungmya ...	...	...	...	...	...	...	...	...	...	...	...
14	Ma-ubin ...	...	...	...	...	...	...	...	...	...	...	...
15	Pyapôn ...	...	...	...	10	2	...	8	...	...	...	...
	Tenasserim Division ...	...	...	...	28	25	...	3	2	1	...	1
16	Toungoo ...	...	...	...	5	4	...	1	...	...	...	...
17	Salween ...	...	...	...	...	...	...	...	...	...	...	...
18	Thatôn ...	...	...	...	3	3	...	...	...	...	...	...
19	Amherst ...	...	...	...	8	8	...	...	...	...	...	...
20	Tavoy ...	...	...	...	8	8	...	...	2	1	...	1
21	Mergui ...	...	...	...	4	2	...	2	...	...	...	...
	agwe Division ...	...	...	...	23	6	...	17	...	...	...	...
22	Thayetmyo ...	...	...	...	3	...	...	3	...	...	...	...
23	Pakôkku ...	...	...	...	11	...	...	11	...	...	...	...
24	Minbu ...	...	...	...	3	3	...	...	...	...	...	...
25	Magwe ...	...	...	...	6	3	...	3	...	...	...	...
26	Pakôkku Hill Tracts ...	...	...	...	...	...	...	...	...	...	...	...
	Mandalay Division ...	...	...	...	55	27	2	26	12	...	5	7
27	Mandalay ...	...	...	...	47	20	2	25	...	...	...	...
	Mandalay City ...	...	...	...	*32*	*5*	*2*	*25*	...	...	...	...
28	Bhamo ...	...	...	...	8	7	...	1	12	...	5	7
29	Myitkyina ...	...	...	...	...	...	...	...	...	...	...	...
30	Katha ...	...	...	...	...	...	...	...	...	...	...	...
31	Putao ...	...	...	...	...	...	...	...	...	...	...	...
	Sagaing Division ...	4	3	1	8	2	...	6	...	...	...	...
32	Shwebo ...	4	3	1	...	...	...	...	...	...	...	
33	Sagaing ...	...	...	...	8	2	...	6	...	...	...	...
34	Lower Chindwin ...	...	...	...	...	...	...	...	...	...	...	...
35	Upper Chindwin ...	...	...	...	...	...	...	...	...	...	...	...
36	Chin Hills ...	...	...	...	...	...	...	...	...	...	...	...
	Meiktila Division ...	...	...	...	6	5	...	1	4	...	...	4
37	Kyauksè ...	...	...	...	...	...	...	...	...	...	...	...
38	Meiktila ...	...	...	...	6	5	...	1	...	...	...	...
39	Yamèthin ...	...	...	...	...	...	...	...	...	...	...	...
40	Myingyan ...	...	...	...	...	...	...	...	4	...	...	4
	Eastern States ...	...	...	...	2	2	...	...	...	...	...	...
41	Northern Shan States ...	...	...	...	2	2	...	...	...	...	...	...
42	Southern Shan States ...	...	...	...	...	...	...	...	...	...	...	...
43	Karenni ...	...	...	...	...	...	...	...	...	...	...	...

* All males and all without subsidiary occupation except one in Henzada district with a non-agricultural occupation.
† All without subsidiary occupation except one in Mandalay district with a non-agricultural occupation.

chemical products and analogous substances—*continued.*

Group 61.—Vegetable oils.								Group 62.—Mineral oils.								
Total Workers and Dependents.	WORKERS. Total Workers.		Workers with an agricultural or other subsidiary occupation. Agricultural.		Other.		DEPENDENTS.	Total Workers and Dependents.	WORKERS. Total Workers.		Workers with an agricultural or other subsidiary occupation. Agricultural.		Other.		DEPENDENTS.	Serial No. of District, etc. (column 1).
	Males.	Females.	Males.	Females.	Males.	Females.			Males.	Females.	Males.	Females.	Males.	Females.		
13	14	15	16	17	18	19	20	21	22	23	24	25	26	27	28	
7,345	3,130	1,174	42	15	122	54	3,041	11,455	4,957	427	5	2	21	1	6,071	
7,071	3,026	1,142	36	15	105	51	2,903	11,450	4,956	427	5	2	20	1	6,067	
67	43	3	1	...	1	..	21	36	16	...	2	...	...	...	20	
61	41	3	...	...	...	...	17	30	12	...	...	...	...	...	18	1
...	...	...	...	...	...	...	...	...	...	...	...	...	...	...	...	2
...	...	...	...	...	...	...	...	5	3	...	2	...	...	...	2	3
6	2	...	1	...	1	...	4	1	1	...	...	...	...	...	...	4
1,738	1,257	45	...	...	5	6	436	4,287	2,760	60	3	...	5	...	1,467	
1,235	1,017	2	...	...	...	..	216	2,314	1,542	8	...	...	1	...	764	5
74	45	14	...	...	...	...	15	8	5	..	...	..	..	...	3	6
...	...	...	...	...	...	..	...	1,674	1,053	24	3	..	4	...	597	7
134	74	7	..	...	5	3	53	55	35	...	..	...	...	...	20	8
23	4	4	...	..	...	..	15	8	...	2	...	...	...	...	6	9
272	117	18	...	..	...	3	137	228	125	26	...	...	...	...	77	10
65	30	5	1	...	1	...	30	63	53	...	...	...	5	...	10	
3	...	3	...	...	...		...	5	5	...	...	...	...	...	...	11
55	28	1	1	...	1	...	26	58	48	...	...	...	5	..	10	12
...	...	...	...	...	...	...	...	...	...	...	...	...	...	...	...	13
5	...	1	..	...	...	...	4	...	...	...	...	...	...	...	...	14
2	2	...	...	...	...	...	...	...	...	...	...	...	...	...	...	15
650	264	25	8	5	8	3	361	74	63	...	...	..	1	...	11	
243	89	12	...	1	4	1	142	...	...	...	...	...	...	...	...	16
7	4	...	...	..	1	...	3	...	..	...	...	...	...	...	...	17
43	20	12	...	4	3	2	11	...	...	...	...	...	...	...	...	18
258	116	1	4	...	...	...	141	59	55	.	...	...	1	...	4	19
56	22	...	4	..	...		34	15	8	...	...	...	...	...	7	20
43	13	...	...	...	...	...	30	...	...	...	...	...	...	...	...	21
1,795	556	411	7	1	35	10	828	6,565	1,814	329	...	2	9	1	4,422	
438	148	151	...	...	...	...	136	366	165	9	...	...	4	1	192	22
1,056	345	136	7	...	30	4	575	62	56	..	...	...	2	...	6	23
114	21	65	...	1	3	6	28	150	55	7	...	...	...	...	88	24
187	42	56	...	...	2	...	89	5,987	1,538	313	...	2	3	..	4,136	25
...	...	...	...	..	...	...	...	...	..	..	...	...	...	...	...	26
769	175	255	2	...	8	...	339	35	9	...	...	...	...	...	26	
703	147	252	2	...	3	...	304	32	9	...	...	...	...	...	23	27
286	105	55	...	...	1	...	126	9	4	...	...	..	...	...	5	
29	14	...	...	.	2	...	15	...	...	...	...	...	..	...	...	28
36	13	3	.	...	3	...	20	.	...	...	...	..	...	...	...	29
1	1	...	.	...	...	..	...	3	...	...	...	...	...	...	3	30
...	...	...	..	...	...	...	...	...	...	...	...	...	...	..	...	31
1,395	481	235	13	1	29	11	679	381	239	38	...	...	...	...	104	
9	6	...	1	..	...	...	3	...	...	...	...	...	...		...	32
201	76	3	3	1	6	...	112	...	...	...	...	...	...		...	33
1,185	399	232	9	...	23	11	554	10	4	...	...	...	...	...	6	34
...	..	...	...	...	...	...	...	371	235	38	...	...	...	...	98	35
...	...	...	...	...	...	...	...	...	...	...	...	..	...	...	...	36
592	220	163	4	8	18	21	209	9	2	...	...	...	...	...	7	
10	3	..	...	...	...	...	7	...	...	...	...	...	...	...	...	37
46	32	...	1	...	2	...	14	2	1	...	...	...	...	...	1	38
12	3	...	...	...	...	...	9	4	1	...	...	...	...	...	3	39
521	182	163	3	8	16	21	179	3	...	...	...	...	...	...	3	40
274	104	32	6	...	17	3	138	5	1	...	...	...	1	...	4	
221	76	29	4	...	15	3	116	4		..	..	...	...	...	4	41
53	28	3	2	...	2	...	22	1	1	..	...	...	1	...	...	42
...	...	...	...	...	...	...	...	...	...	...	...	...	...	...	...	43

Order XI.—Manufacture or refining of chemical products and analogous substances

Serial No.	District or State.	Group 63.—Paper, cardboard and papier maché. Total Workers and Dependents.	Group 63. Workers. Total Workers. Males.	Group 63. Workers. Total Workers. Females.	Group 63. Workers with an agricultural or other subsidiary occupation. Agricultural. Males.	Group 63. Agricultural. Females.	Group 63. Other. Males.	Group 63. Other. Females.	Group 63. Dependents.	Group 64a.—Soap. Total Workers and Dependents.	Group 64a. Workers.* Males.	Group 64a. Workers.* Females.	Group 64a. Dependents.	Group 64b.—Perfumes. Total Workers and Dependents.	Group 64b. Workers.† Males.	Group 64b. Workers.† Females.	Group 64b. Dependents.
	1	2	3	4	5	6	7	8	9	10	11	12	13	14	15	16	17
	Provincial Total ..	332	114	129	2	1	1	13	89	114	30	25	59	616	567	4	45
	Divisional Burma ...	219	96	64	2	...	1	3	59	109	25	25	59	614	567	4	43
	Arakan Division ...	...	...	...	...	...	...	...	.	...	...	...	..	...	...		...
1	Akyab	...	...	...	...	...	...	...	...	..	...	...	...	...	...	...	...
2	Hill Dist. of Arakan	...	..	..	..	...	...	...	...	...	...	...	...	...	..	...	...
3	Kyaukpyu ...	...	...	...	...	...	...	...	...	...	...	...	...	...	...	...	...
4	Sandoway ...	...	...	..	...	...	..	...	..	...	...	...	...	...	...	...	...
	Pegu Division ..	2	2	..	...	...	...		...	42	9	2	31	59	29	2	28
5	Rangoon Town ..	2	2	...	..	...	..	...	...	14	7	...	7	53	24	2	27
6	Insein	...	...	...	...	...	...	...	...	7	...	2	5	...	...	...	...
7	Hanthawaddy ...	...	...	...	...	...	...	...	..	...	...	...	...	6	5	...	1
8	Tharrawaddy ...	...	...	...	...	...	...	...	...	3	2	...	1	...	...	...	...
9	Pegu	...	...	...	..	..	...	...	...	6	...	...	6	...	...	...	...
10	Prome	...	...	...	...	...	...	...	...	12	...	...	12	...	...	...	...
	Irrawaddy Division ...	..	...	...	...	...	...	...	...	...	...	..	..	548	†538	1	9
11	Bassein ...	...	...	...	...	...	..	...	.	...	...	...	...	547	†538	...	9
12	Henzada ...	...	...	...	...	...	..	...	..	...	...	...	...	1	...	1	...
13	Myaungmya ..	...	..	..	...	...	...	...	..	...	...	...	...	...	...	...	..
14	Ma-ubin ..	...	...	...	...	...	...	...	...	...	...	...	...	...	...	...	...
15	Pyapôn ...	..	..	...	...	..	...	...	...	...	...	...	..	...	...	...	...
	Tenasserim Division ...	...	.	..	...	...	...	...	...	5	...	2	3	...	...	...	...
16	Toungoo ...	...	...	...	...	...	...	...	..	...	...	...	...	...	..	...	...
17	Salween ...	...	..	...	.	...	...	...	...	...	...	...	...	...	...	...	...
18	Thatôn	...	...	...	...	...	...	...	..	2	...	...	2	...	...	...	...
19	Amherst ...	...	...	...	...	...	...	...	...	2	...	2	...	...	...	...	...
20	Tavoy	...	...	...	...	..	...	...	...	1	...	...	1	...	..	...	...
21	Mergui ...	...	...	...	...	...	...	...	...	...	...	...	...	.	...	...	...
	Magwe Division ...	22	22	...	...	...	...	...	...	9	5	...	4	...	...	...	...
22	Thayetmyo ...	...	...	...	...	...	...	...	...	...	...	..	...	...	...	...	...
23	Pakôkku ...	22	22	...	...	...	...	...	..	9	5	...	4	...	...	...	...
24	Minbu	...	...	..	...	...	...	...	...	...	...	...	...	...	..	...	...
25	Magwe ...	...	...	...	...	...	...	...	...	...	...	...	...	..	...	...	...
26	Pakôkku Hill Tracts	...	...	...	..	...	...	...	...	...	...	...	...	...	...	...	...
	Mandalay Division ...	141	60	47	...	...	...	...	34	8	6	...	2	7	...	1	6
27	Mandalay ...	141	60	47	...	...	...	...	34	8	6	...	2	7	...	1	6
	Mandalay City ...	*141*	*60*	*47*	...	...	...	...	*34*	*8*	*6*	...	*2*	*7*	...	*1*	*6*
28	Bhamo	...	...	...	...	...	...	...	...	..	...	...	...	..	...	...	...
29	Myitkyina ...	...	...	...	...	...	...	...	...	...	..	...	...	..	...	...	...
30	Katha	...	...	...	..	...	...	...	..	...	...	..	...	...	...	...	...
31	Putao	...	...	...	...	...	...	...	..	..	...	...	...	...	...	...	...
	Sagaing Division ...	54	12	17	2	..	1	3	25	32	3	*13	16	...	...	...	...
32	Shwebo ...	...	..	...	...	...	...	...	...	3	1	...	2	...	..	...	...
33	Sagaing ...	54	12	17	2	..	1	3	25	21	1	*13	7	...	...	...	...
34	Lower Chindwin ...	...	...	...	...	...	...	..	...	7	...	...	7	...	...	...	...
35	Upper Chindwin ...	..	...	..	...	...	...	...	..	1	1	...	...	...	...	...	...
36	Chin Hills ...	...	...	...	...	...	...	...	...	...	...	...	...	...	...	...	..
	Meiktila Division ...	...	..	..	...	...	...	..	...	13	2	8	3	...	...	...	...
37	Kyauksè ..	...	...	...	...	...	...	...	...	...	...	...	...	...	...	...	...
38	Meiktila ...	...	...	..	...	...	...	...	...	1	...	...	1	...	. .	...	...
39	Yamèthin ...	...	...	...	...	...	...	...	...	8	...	8	...	..	...	...	...
40	Myingyan ...	...	...	...	...	...	...	.	...	4	2	...	2	...	...	.	...
	Eastern States ...	113	18	65	..	1	..	10	30	5	5	...	...	2	...	...	2
41	Northern Shan States	113	18	65	...	1	...	10	30	5	5	...	.	2	...	...	2
42	Southern Shan States	...	...	...	...	...	...	...	...	...	...	...	.	...	..	...	...
43	Karenni ...	...	...	...	...	...	...	...	...	...	...	...	...	...	...	...	...

* All without subsidiary occupations except 2 females in Sagaing district with non-agricultural subsidiary occupations.

† 117 males in Bassein district had an agricultural subsidiary occupation; all others had no subsidiary occupation.

—*concluded.*			Order XII.—Food.																
Group 64*e*.—Drugs, resin, celluloid and chemicals or analogous products not included in other groups of Order XI.			Group 65.—Rice huskers and pounders and flour-grinders.								Group 66.—Bakers and biscuit makers.								Serial No. of District, etc. (column 1).
Total Workers and Dependents.	WORKERS. (All males without subsidiary occupation.)	DEPENDENTS.	Total Workers and Dependents.	WORKERS.						DEPENDENTS.	Total Workers and Dependents.	WORKERS.						DEPENDENTS.	
				Total Workers.		Workers with an agricultural or other subsidiary occupation.						Total Workers.		Workers with an agricultural or other subsidiary occupation.					
						Agricultural.		Other.						Agricultural.		Other.			
	Males.			Males.	Females.	Males.	Females.	Males.	Females			Males.	Females.	Males.	Females.	Males.	Females		
18	19	20	21	22	23	24	25	26	27	28	29	30	31	32	33	34	35	36	
42	34	8	97,416	36,527	24,402	142	560	453	1,448	36,487	2,037	1,361	130	...	...	16	3	546	
42	34	8	96,339	36,313	23,961	127	541	417	1,378	36,065	2,020	1,351	128	..	...	13	3	541	
...	...	...	7,428	1,058	4,014	9	17	9	188	2,356	28	8	2	...	...	...	...	18	
...	...	...	7,051	1,048	3.767	9	9	7	171	2,236	27	7	2	...	...	...	...	18	1
...	...	...	...	...	...	..	...		...	...		...	...	...	...	...	...	...	2
...	...	...	3	1	...	...	...	...	...	2	1	1	...	...	...	...	...	...	3
...	...	.	374	9	247	.	8	2	17	118	...	...	...	..	...	...	...	...	4
36	33	3	39,789	23,796	3,718	12	10	81	28	12,275	1,272	979	87	..	...	7	2	206	
...	...	.	25,997	17.373	1,483	1	...	16	...	7,141	967	814	38	...	...	1	...	115	5
18	17	1	1,116	702	62	...	...	...	...	352	173	118	12	...	...	4	...	43	6
18	16	2	2,564	1,849	187	1	.	1	..	518	76	7	56	...	...	...	1	33	7
...	...	...	4,444	1,650	976	...	7	36	6	1,8.8	16	8	...	...	...	2	..	8	8
...	...	...	2,544	1,043	282	8	1	12	2	1,219	16	19	1	..	...	...	1	6	9
...	...	...	3,124	1,179	728	2	2	16	20	1,217	14	13	...	...	...	...	...	1	10
2	...	2	9,095	4,132	1,482	15	7	28	82	3,481	91	14	28	...	...	...		49	
2	...	2	4,446	2,492	443	8	3	9	7	1,511	10	1	3	...	...	...	...	6	11
...	...	...	2,118	632	688	3	2	11	69	798	6	6	...	...	...	...	...	...	12
...	...	...	899	379	118	3	...	8	4	402	14	4	1	...	...	...	...	9	13
...	...	...	456	76	170	1	2	...	2	210	61	3	24	...	...	...	...	34	14
...	...	...	1,176	553	63	...	...	...	...	560	...	...	...	...	...	...	...	...	15
4	1	3	6,997	2,583	1,270	24	31	18	53	3,144	145	76	4	...	...	2	...	65	
...	...	...	1,177	244	365	1	27	8	9	568	34	21	2	...	...	...	...	11	16
...	...	...	16	6	3	...	...	...	1	7	5	2	...	...	..	1	...	3	17
..	...	...	789	349	82	1	...	5	3	358	47	28	...	...	...	...	...	19	18
4	1	3	3,732	1,695	323	22	...	...	14	1,714	17	3	...	...	...	..	...	14	19
...	...	...	798	203	351	...	4	5	26	244	18	11	2	...	...	...	.	5	20
...	...	.	485	86	146	...	...	...	...	253	24	11	...	...	...	1	...	13	21
...	...	.	13,979	2,244	6,954	39	220	169	556	4,781	115	61	3	...	...	1	..	52	
...	...	...	1,150	124	571	2	9	5	26	455	27	11	...	...	...	1	...	16	22
...	...	...	8,917	1,459	4,509	10	63	135	209	2,949	23	3	2	...	...	...	...	18	23
...	...	...	3,705	621	1,821	27	145	29	129	1,963	10	4	1	...	...	...	...	5	24
...	...	...	175	12	53	...	3	...	2	110	55	43	...	...	...	...	..	12	25
...	...	...	32	28	...	...	...	...	..	4	...	..	...	...	...	...	...	...	26
..	...	...	4,859	1,219	1,522	6	85	44	102	2,118	184	135	1	...	...	...	1	48	
...	...	...	4,242	1,069	1,287	5	85	37	96	1,886	135	112	.	...	...	...	...	23	27
...	...	...	*2,120*	*659*	*482*	...	...	...	...	*1,029*	*83*	*69*	...	...	...	...	...	*14*	
..	...	...	231	43	100	...	...	1	3	88	8	7	...	...	...	...	...	1	28
...	...	...	144	33	75	...		1	...	36	26	8	1	...	...	...	1	17	29
...	...	...	229	62	60	1	...	4	3	107	14	7	...	...	...	...	...	7	30
...	...	...	13	12	...	...	...	1	...	1	1	1	...	...	...	...	...	...	31
..	...	...	10,704	840	3,723	20	121	49	312	6,141	62	23	...	...	...	2	...	39	
..	...	..	1,672	252	796	3	60	16	53	624	25	5	...	...	...	1	...	20	32
.	...	...	1,551	173	856	1	23	12	87	582	19	9	...	...	...	...	...	10	33
...	...	...	6,369	228	1,596	12	18	8	128	4,545	8	6	...	...	...	...	...	9	34
...	...	...	1,112	187	475	4	20	13	44	450	10	3	...	...	...	1	...	7	35
...	...	...	...	...	...	...	...	...	...	...	...	...	...	...	...	...	...	...	36
...	..	...	3,488	441	1,278	2	50	19	57	1,769	123	55	3	...	...	1	...	65	
...	...	...	619	85	289		9	11	17	245	18	5	...	...	...	...	...	13	37
..	...	...	853	86	305	...	4	4	12	462	36	15	2	...	...	1	...	19	38
...	..	...	1,556	180	525	2	5	4	24	851	55	27	...	...	...	...	...	28	39
...	...	...	460	90	159	...	2	...	4	211	14	8	1	...	.	...	...	5	40
...	...	...	1,077	214	441	15	19	36	70	422	17	10	2	...	...	3	...	5	
...	...	...	1,0.9	201	430	15	19	36	70	388	17	10	2	..	...	3	...	5	41
...	...	...	58	13	11	...	...	...	...	34	...	...	...	...	...	...	...	..	42
...	...	...	...	..	..	...	...	...	...	...	...	...	...	...	...	...	...	...	43

Serial No.	DISTRICT OR STATE.	Group 67.—Grain parchers, etc.	Group 68.—Butchers.								Group 69.—Fish curers.							
		Total Workers and Dependents.	Total Workers and Dependents.	WORKERS. Total Workers.		Workers with an agricultural or other subsidiary occupation. Agricultural.		Other.		DEPENDENTS.	Total Workers and Dependents.	WORKERS. Total Workers.		Workers with an agricultural or other subsidiary occupation. Agricultural.		Other.		DEPENDENTS.
				Males.	Females.	Males	Females	Males	Females			Males	Females	Males	Females	Males	Females	
	1	2	3	4	5	6	7	8	9	10	11	12	13	14	15	16	17	18
	Provincial Total ...	...	2,041	737	70	4	.	30	8	1,234	930	212	287	9	10	12	11	431
	Divisional Burma ...	...	1,977	701	66	4	...	30	8	1,210	930	212	287	9	10	12	11	431
	Arakan Division ...	...	187	64	4	...	...	2	...	119	45	2	43	2	...	...	2	...
1	Akyab ...	...	181	62	4	...	...	2	...	115	45	2	43	2	...	...	2	...
2	Hill Dist. of Arakan	...	...	...	...	...	...	...	...	...	...	...	...	...	...	...	...	...
3	Kyaukpyu	...	...	...	...	...	...	...	...	...	...	...	...	...	...	...	...	...
4	Sandoway ...	...	6	2	...	...	...	...	...	4	...	...	...	...	...	...	...	...
	Pegu Division ...	...	392	130	11	1	...	2	...	251	64	22	12	1	...	...	...	30
5	Rangoon Town ...	...	149	44	1	...	...	...	...	104	1	...	...	...	...	...	...	1
6	Insein ...	...	64	24	6	...	...	...	...	34	1	1	...	...	...	...	...	...
7	Hanthawaddy ...	...	30	9	1	1	...	...	...	20	2	2	...	1	...	...	...	...
8	Tharrawaddy ...	...	46	20	...	...	...	...	...	26	30	16	...	...	...	...	...	14
9	Pegu ...	...	45	18	...	...	...	1	...	27	30	3	12	...	...	...	...	15
10	Prome ...	...	58	15	3	...	...	1	...	40	...	...	...	...	...	...	...	...
	Irrawaddy Division ...	...	169	95	1	...	...	3		73	598	134	163	...	10	2	7	301
11	Bassein ...	...	8	...	...	...	...	...	...	8	132	...	62	...	10	...	3	70
12	Henzada ...	...	40	7	...	...	...	...	...	33	20	13	...	...	...	...	...	7
13	Myaungmya ...	...	101	81	...	...	...	1	...	20	108	2	100	...	...	...	4	106
14	Ma-ubin ...	...	18	7	...	...	...	2	...	11	17	9	1	...	...	...	...	7
15	Pyapôn ...	...	2	...	1	...	...	...	...	1	221	110	...	...	...	2	...	111
	Tenasserim Division ...	...	262	63	4	1	...	1	...	195	90	8	32	...	...	...	...	50
16	Toungoo ...	...	58	10	4	...	...	...	...	44	9	...	5	...	...	...	...	4
17	Salween .	...	1	1	...	...	...	...	...	...	...	...	...	...	...	...	...	...
18	Thatôn ...	...	6	1	...	...	...	1	...	5	5	5	...	...	...	...	...	...
19	Amherst ...	...	169	44	...	1	...	...	...	125	2	...	...	...	...	...	...	2
20	Tavoy ...	...	24	6	...	...	...	...	...	18	20	...	20	...	...	...	...	...
21	Mergui ...	...	4	1	...	...	...	...	...	3	54	3	7	...	...	...	...	44
	Magwe Division ...	...	94	26	...	.	...	3	...	68	...	...	...	...	...	...	...	...
22	Thayetmyo ...	...	2	1	...	...	...	...	...	1	...	...	...	...	...	...	...	...
23	Pakôkku ...	...	17	6	...	...	...	...	...	11	...	...	...	...	...	...	...	...
24	Minbu ...	...	58	7	...	...	...	1	...	51	...	...	...	...	...	...	...	...
25	Magwe .	...	17	12	...	...	...	2	...	5	...	...	...	...	...	...	...	...
26	Pakôkku Hill Tracts	...	...	...	...	...	...	...	...	...	...	...	...	...	...	...	...	...
	Mandalay Division ...	...	338	127	17	...	...	...	...	194	45	26	16	...	...	1	2	3
27	Mandalay ...	...	267	114	8	...	...	...	...	145	...	...	...	...	...	...	...	...
	Mandalay City ...	...	*197*	*87*	*6*	...	...	...	...	*104*	...	...	...	...	...	...	...	...
28	Bhamo ...	...	44	5	9	...	...	...	...	30	...	...	...	...	...	...	...	...
29	Myitkyina ...	...	4	...	...	...	...	...	...	4	5	...	5	...	...	...	2	...
30	Katha ...	...	23	8	...	...	...	...	...	15	40	26	11	...	...	1	...	3
31	Putao ...	...	...	...	...	...	...	...	...	...	...	...	...	...	...	...	...	...
	Sagaing Division ...	...	200	91	11	...	...	6	...	98	83	20	21	6	...	9	...	42
32	Shwebo ...	...	127	66	10	...	...	3	...	51	...	...	...	...	...	...	...	...
33	Sagaing ...	...	36	8	1	...	...	...	...	27	23	11	...	6	...	...	...	12
34	Lower Chindwin ...	...	26	14	...	...	...	1	...	12	10	...	3	...	...	...	...	7
35	Upper Chindwin ...	...	11	3	...	...	...	2	...	8	50	9	18	...	...	9	...	23
36	Chin Hills ...	...	...	...	...	...	...	...	...	...	...	...	...	...	...	...	...	...
	Meiktila Division ...	...	335	105	18	2	...	13	8	212	5	...	...	...	...	...	...	5
37	Kyauksè ...	...	3	1	...	...	...	...	...	2	...	...	...	...	...	...	...	...
38	Meiktila ...	...	165	63	1	...	...	5	...	101	...	...	...	...	...	...	...	...
39	Yamèthin ...	...	72	18	3	...	...	2	...	51	5	...	...	...	...	...	...	5
40	Myingyan ...	...	95	23	14	2	...	6	8	58	...	...	...	...	...	...	...	...
	Eastern States ...	...	64	36	4	...	...	...	...	24	...	...	...	...	...	...	...	...
41	Northern Shan States	...	49	23	4	...	...	...	...	22	...	...	...	...	...	...	...	...
42	Southern Shan States	...	1	1	...	...	...	...	...	...	...	...	...	...	...	...	...	...
43	Karenni ...	...	14	12	...	...	...	...	...	2	...	...	...	...	...	...	...	...

Part III.—*Details by districts*—contd.

Food—*continued*.

Group 70.—Butter, cheese and ghee makers. Total Workers and Dependents.	Group 70. Workers.* Males.	Group 70. Workers.* Females.	Group 70. Dependents.	Group 71.—Sugar, jaggery and kyantaga makers. Total Workers and Dependents.	Group 71. Workers. Total Workers. Males	Group 71. Workers. Total Workers. Females	Group 71. Workers with an agricultural or other subsidiary occupation. Agricultural. Males.	Group 71. Agricultural. Females	Group 71. Other. Males.	Group 71. Other. Females	Group 71. Dependents.	Group 72.—Sweetmeat makers, preparers of jam and condiments, etc. Total Workers and Dependents.	Group 72. Workers. Total Workers. Males.	Group 72. Total Workers. Females	Group 72. Workers with an agricultural or other subsidiary occupation. Agricultural. Males.	Group 72. Agricultural. Females	Group 72. Other. Males.	Group 72. Other. Females	Group 72. Dependents.	Serial No. of District, etc. (column 1).
18	19	20	21	22	23	24	25	26	27	28	29	30	31	32	33	34	35	36	37	
86	45	7	34	8,040	748	5,686	13	550	20	563	1,606	20,562	3,217	8,795	44	231	189	453	8,550	
86	45	7	34	8,015	742	5,679	13	550	20	563	1,594	19,627	2,967	8,478	39	221	174	430	8,182	
...	...	..	..	12	3	...	...	..	...	...	9	3,108	337	1,463	2	25	14	55	1,308	
..	...	...	...	12	3	...	...	...	...	...	9	1,743	280	705	2	...	10	...	758	1
...	...	...	...	...	...	...	...	...	...	...	...	...	...	...	...	...	...	...	...	2
..	...	...	...	.	...	...	...	..	...	...	...	7	...	4	...	...	...	1	3	3
...	...	...	...	...	...	...	...	...	...	...	...	1,358	57	754	...	25	4	54	547	4
9	8	1	...	66	5	8	...	...	...	...	53	3,269	728	1,104	6	43	9	39	1,437	
8	8	..	...	..	..	...	...	...	...	...	...	896	308	136	...	...	...	...	392	5
1	...	1	...	1	..	1	...	...	...	...	.	82	65	...	...	...	...	..	17	6
..	...	...	...	..	...	.	...	...	...	...	...	453	48	161	1	...	...	...	244	7
...	...	...	...	65	5	7		...	...	...	53	876	143	378	1	11	8	23	355	8
..	...	...	...	...	...	...	...	...	...	...	...	333	13	176	...	22	1	5	144	9
...	...	...	...	...	...	...	...	...	...	...	...	629	91	253	4	10	...	11	285	10
15	15	...	...	71	10	52	...	4	...	4	9	3,117	369	1,473	6	19	9	28	1,275	
...	...	...	...	14	10	...	...	...	...	...	4	116	14	60	...	..	...	...	42	11
..	...	...	...	52	.	52	...	4	..	4	...	2,265	279	1,055	6	18	9	22	931	12
...	...	...	...	5	...	...	...	...	...	...	5	623	26	345	..	1	...	6	252	13
7	7	.	...	..	...	...	...	...	...	...	...	41	2	8	...	...	...	...	31	14
8	8	...	...	...	..	...	...	...	...	...	...	72	48	5	...	...	..	...	19	15
1	...	1	...	665	197	34	...	1	4	...	434	2,971	315	1,352	...	15	23	35	1,304	
...	...	..	...	9	5	...	...	...	...	...	4	1,088	42	580	...	4	1	14	466	16
...	...	...	...	...	...	..	...	...	...	...	...	98	10	48	...	5	1	5	40	17
...	...	...	...	170	50	...	..	...	2	...	120	152	50	1	...	...	...	...	101	18
...	...	...	.	407	125	22	..	...	...	...	260	823	111	356	...	6	18	5	356	19
...	...	..	...	73	17	9	...	1	2	...	47	538	47	304	...	...	3	11	187	20
1	...	1	...	6	..	3	...	...	...	.	3	272	55	63	...	...	...	...	154	21
...	...		.	325	39	217	...	5	...	2	69	276	72	89	...	...	4	4	115	
...	...	...	...	...	...	...	..	...	...	..	...	1	1	...	...	...	...	...	...	22
..	...	...	...	95	39	...	...	...	...	...	56	8	7	...	...	...	.	...	1	23
..	...	...	...	13	...	13	...	...	...	...	...	31	17	...	...	...	1	...	14	24
...	...	..	...	217	...	204	...	5	...	2	13	236	47	89	...	...	3	4	100	25
...	...	...	...	...	...	...	...	...	...	...	...	...	...	...	...	...	...	...	...	26
5	5	...	...	278	246	.	...	...	...	...	32	766	277	226	...	...	3	18	263	
5	5	..	...	257	233	...	...	...	...	...	24	496	240	104	...	...	...	...	152	27
3	*3*	...	...	*24*	...	...	...	...	...	..	*24*	*437*	*211*	*104*	...	...	...	..	*122*	
...	...	.	...	...	...	...	...	...	...	...	...	32	8	22	...	...	...	...	2	28
...	...	..	...	20	13	...	..	...	...	...	7	17	...	4	...	...	...	...	13	29
...	...	...	...	1	.	...	...	...	...	...	1	231	29	96	...	...	3	18	96	30
..	...	...	...	..	...	...	...	...	...	...	...	...	...	...	...	...	...	...	...	31
50	*14	4	32	3,786	33	3,176	3	400	4	453	577	4,242	775	1,739	24	61	106	208	1,728	
2	...	...	2	263	...	242	...	7	...	3	21	658	103	320	1	...	8	33	235	32
48	*14	4	30	2,077	1	2,076	..	361	...	415	...	1,092	193	389	10	35	27	96	510	33
...	...	...	..	1,446	32	858	3	32	4	35	556	1,281	317	472	8	10	45	21	492	34
.	...	...	..	...	...	..	...	...	...	...	..	1,211	162	558	5	16	26	58	491	35
...	...	...	...	..	...	...	...	...	..	...	...	...	..	...	..	...	...	...	...	36
6	*3	1	2	2,812	209	2,192	10	140	12	104	411	1,878	94	1,032	1	58	6	43	752	
4	*2	1	1	2	1	...	...	...	...	...	1	1,013	19	584	...	49	2	22	420	37
2	1	...	1	1,033	2	925	..	86	..	26	106	374	48	192	1	9	4	10	134	38
...	...	...	...	322	175	11	70	...	12	...	136	303	18	136	..	...	...	6	149	39
...	...	...	...	1,455	31	1,256	...	54	...	78	168	178	9	120	...	...	...	5	49	40
..	...	..	.	25	6	7	..	...	...	...	12	935	250	317	5	10	15	23	368	
...	...	..	.	25	6	7	...	...	...	..	12	922	245	317	5	10	15	23	360	41
...	...	...	...	...	...	...	.	...	...	...	..	12	4	...	...	...	...	...	8	42
...	...	...	...	...	...	...	...	...	...	...	...	1	1	...	...	...	...	...	..	43

* All without subsidiary occupations except 2 males in Sagaing district with an agricultural subsidiary occupation and 1 male each Sagaing and Kyauksè districts with a non-agricultural subsidiary occupation.

Order XII.—

Serial No.	DISTRICT OR STATE.	Group 73.—Brewers and distillers. Total Workers and Dependents.	WORKERS. Total Workers. Males	Total Workers. Females	Workers with an agricultural or other subsidiary occupation. Agricultural. Males	Agricultural. Females	Other. Males	Other. Females	DEPENDENTS.	Group 74.—Toddy-drawers. Total Workers and Dependents.	WORKERS. Total Workers. Males.	Total Workers. Females	Workers with an agricultural or other subsidiary occupation. Agricultural. Males.	Agricultural. Females.	Other. Males.	Other. Females	DEPENDENTS.
	1	2	3	4	5	6	7	8	9	10	11	12	13	14	15	16	17
	Provincial Total ...	231	76	43	2	1		...	112	70,645	23,958	8,331	5,249	862	2,492	1,036	38,356
	Divisional Burma ...	97	45	16	...	...	...	...	36	70,640	23,955	8,331	5,249	862	2,492	1,036	38,354
	Arakan Division ...	...	...	...	...	...	...	...	...	16	11	...	...	...	...	...	5
1	Akyab ...	...	...	...	...	...	...	...	...	5	5	...	...	...	...	...	...
2	Hill Dist. of Arakan	...	...	...	...	...	...	...	...	...	...	...	...	...	...	...	...
3	Kyaukpyu ...	...	...	...	...	...	...	...	...	...	...	...	...	...	...	...	...
4	Sandoway ...	...	...	...	...	...	...	...	...	11	6	...	...	...	...	...	5
	Pegu Division ...	22	22	...	...	...	...	...	...	2,181	808	2	125	...	41	...	1,871
5	Rangoon Town ...	...	...	...	...	...	...	...	...	1	1	...	...	...	...	...	...
6	Insein ...	...	...	...	...	...	...	...	...	...	...	...	...	...	...	...	...
7	Hanthawaddy ...	21	21	...	...	...	...	...	...	1	...	...	...	...	...	...	1
8	Tharrawaddy ...	...	...	...	...	...	...	...	...	45	27	...	...	...	...	...	18
9	Pegu ...	1	1	...	...	...	...	...	...	8	8	...	...	...	...	...	...
10	Prome ...	...	...	...	...	...	...	...	...	2,126	772	2	125	...	41	...	1,352
	Irrawaddy Division ...	...	...	...	...	...	...	...	...	1,151	413	47	26	...	28	6	691
11	Bassein ...	...	...	...	...	...	...	...	...	85	29	3	...	...	...	...	53
12	Henzada ...	...	...	...	...	...	...	...	...	1,062	380	44	26	...	28	6	638
13	Myaungmya ...	...	...	...	...	...	...	...	...	...	...	...	...	...	...	...	...
14	Ma-ubin ...	...	...	...	...	...	...	...	...	...	...	...	...	...	...	...	...
15	Pyapôn ...	...	...	...	...	...	...	...	...	4	4	...	...	...	...	...	...
	Tenasserim Division ...	8	...	...	...	...	...	...	8	440	189	1	2	...	5	...	250
16	Toungoo ...	...	...	...	...	...	...	...	...	182	109	...	2	...	2	...	73
17	Salween ...	...	...	...	...	...	...	...	...	...	...	...	...	...	...	...	...
18	Thatôn ...	1	...	...	...	...	...	...	1	84	58	...	...	...	3	...	26
19	Amherst ...	...	...	...	...	...	...	...	...	162	21	1	...	...	...	...	140
20	Tavoy ...	...	...	...	...	...	...	...	...	12	1	...	...	...	...	...	11
21	Mergui ...	7	...	...	...	...	...	...	7	...	...	...	...	...	...	...	...
	Magwe Division ...	...	...	...	...	...	...	...	...	37,998	11,181	6,580	2,678	754	1,721	833	20,237
22	Thayetmyo ...	...	...	...	...	...	...	...	...	687	174	19	6	...	8	...	494
23	Pakôkku ...	...	...	...	...	...	...	...	...	31,056	9,242	5,884	2,404	721	1,554	794	15,930
24	Minbu ...	...	...	...	...	...	...	...	...	2,980	826	280	221	24	128	32	1,874
25	Magwe ...	...	...	...	...	...	...	...	...	3,275	939	397	47	9	31	7	1,939
26	Pakôkku Hill Tracts	...	...	...	...	...	...	...	...	...	...	...	...	...	...	...	...
	Mandalay Division ...	45	12	16	...	...	...	...	17	166	94	...	...	...	3	...	72
27	Mandalay ...	...	...	...	...	...	...	...	...	165	94	...	...	...	3	...	71
	Mandalay City ...	...	...	...	...	...	...	...	...	76	63	...	...	...	...	...	13
28	Bhamo ...	45	12	16	...	...	...	...	17	1	...	...	...	...	...	...	1
29	Myitkyina ...	...	...	...	...	...	...	...	...	...	...	...	...	...	...	...	...
30	Katha ...	...	...	...	...	...	...	...	...	...	...	...	...	...	...	...	...
31	Putao ...	...	...	...	...	...	...	...	...	...	...	...	...	...	...	...	...
	Sagaing Division ...	...	...	...	...	...	...	...	...	15,684	6,629	1,002	2,003	80	500	106	8,053
32	Shwebo ...	...	...	...	...	...	...	...	...	1,556	533	196	132	19	66	8	827
33	Sagaing ...	...	...	...	...	...	...	...	...	7,329	3,106	371	1,131	58	278	62	3,852
34	Lower Chindwin ...	...	...	...	...	...	...	...	...	6,798	2,990	435	740	3	156	16	3,373
35	Upper Chindwin ...	...	...	...	...	...	...	...	...	1	...	...	...	...	...	...	1
36	Chin Hills ...	...	...	...	...	...	...	...	...	...	...	...	...	...	...	...	...
	Meiktila Division ...	22	11	...	...	...	...	...	11	13,004	4,630	699	415	28	194	91	7,675
37	Kyauksè ...	...	...	...	...	...	...	...	...	1,857	729	321	...	2	...	19	807
38	Meiktila ...	...	...	...	...	...	...	...	...	6,973	2,092	75	222	[illegible]	90	48	4,806
39	Yamèthin ...	22	11	...	...	...	...	...	11	507	172	32	8	...	13	3	303
40	Myingyan ...	...	...	...	...	...	...	...	...	3,667	1,637	271	185	4	91	21	1,759
	Eastern States ...	134	31	27	2	1	...	...	76	5	3	...	...	...	...	...	2
41	Northern Shan States	49	21	10	...	1	...	...	18	...	...	...	...	...	...	...	...
42	Southern Shan States	85	10	17	2	...	...	...	58	5	3	...	...	...	...	...	2
43	Karenni ...	...	...	...	...	...	...	...	...	...	...	...	...	...	...	...	...

Food—*concluded.* Group 75.—Tobacco manufacturers. Total Workers and Dependents.	Workers. Total Workers. Males.	Workers. Total Workers. Females.	Workers with an agricultural or other subsidiary occupation. Agricultural. Males.	Agricultural. Females.	Other. Males.	Other. Females.	Dependents.	Order XIII.—Dress and the toilet. Group 76.—Hat, cap and turban makers. Total Workers and Dependents.	Workers. Total Workers. Males.	Total Workers. Females.	Workers with an agricultural or other subsidiary occupation. Agricultural. Males.	Agricultural. Females.	Other. Males.	Other. Females.	Dependents.	Serial No. of District, etc. (column 1).
18	19	20	21	22	23	24	25	26	27	28	29	30	31	32	33	
21,540	1,412	13,056	21	24	42	195	7,072	513	119	101	12	...	9	1	293	
20,770	1,093	13,021	21	24	40	195	6,656	513	119	101	12	...	9	1	293	
392	11	229	...	...	...	...	152	...	...	...	...	...	...	...	...	
363	11	215	...	...	...	...	137	...	...	...	...	...	...	...	...	1
...	...	...	...	...	...	...	...	...	...	...	...	...	...	...	...	2
24	...	14	...	...	...	...	10	...	...	...	...	...	...	...	...	3
5	...	...	...	...	...	...	5	...	...	...	...	...	...	...	...	4
7,576	429	4,696	...	3	4	90	2,451	512	118	101	12	...	9	1	293	
3,856	320	2,390	...	...	1	...	1,146	36	24	...	...	...	...	...	12	5
210	...	163	...	1	...	...	47	7	...	...	...	...	...	...	7	6
341	42	117	...	...	...	6	182	469	94	101	12	...	9	1	274	7
167	...	139	...	...	...	...	28	...	...	...	...	...	...	...	...	8
601	24	429	...	2	...	3	148	...	...	...	...	...	...	...	...	9
2,401	43	1,458	...	...	3	81	900	...	...	...	...	...	...	...	...	10
3,790	96	2,584	2	4	...	28	1,110	...	...	...	...	...	...	...	...	
389	...	229	...	...	...	3	160	...	...	...	...	...	...	...	...	11
1,057	68	672	2	...	...	...	317	...	...	...	...	...	...	...	...	12
777	1	585	...	2	...	16	191	...	...	...	...	...	...	...	...	13
1,031	2	813	...	2	...	9	216	...	...	...	...	...	...	...	...	14
536	25	285	...	...	...	...	226	...	...	...	...	...	...	...	...	15
3,412	144	2,256	...	3	4	35	1,012	1	1	...	...	...	...	...	...	
519	11	349	...	1	...	1	159	...	...	...	...	...	...	...	...	16
11	...	9	...	...	...	...	2	...	...	...	...	...	...	...	...	17
390	22	239	...	...	1	5	129	...	...	...	...	...	...	...	...	18
2,111	110	1,382	...	2	3	25	619	...	...	...	...	...	...	...	...	19
336	1	263	...	...	...	4	72	...	...	...	...	...	...	...	...	20
45	...	14	...	...	...	...	31	1	1	...	...	...	...	...	...	21
572	38	321	...	2	5	1	213	...	...	...	...	...	...	...	...	
272	16	142	...	...	2	...	114	...	...	...	...	...	...	...	...	22
172	15	100	...	...	...	...	57	...	...	...	...	...	...	...	...	23
96	...	73	...	2	...	1	23	...	...	...	...	...	...	...	...	24
32	7	6	...	...	3	...	19	...	...	...	...	...	...	...	...	25
...	...	...	...	...	...	...	...	...	...	...	...	...	...	...	...	26
2,895	99	1,927	...	1	...	1	869	...	...	...	...	...	...	...	...	
2,859	97	1,908	...	...	...	...	854	...	...	...	...	...	...	...	...	
2,735	67	1,877	...	...	...	...	791	...	...	...	...	...	...	...	...	27
8	...	2	...	...	...	...	6	...	...	...	...	...	...	...	...	28
5	...	5	...	1	...	1	...	...	...	...	...	...	...	...	...	29
23	2	12	...	...	...	...	9	...	...	...	...	...	...	...	...	30
...	...	...	...	...	...	...	...	...	...	...	...	...	...	...	...	31
1,026	177	301	11	3	22	17	548	...	...	...	...	...	...	...	...	
110	4	59	...	1	1	3	47	...	...	...	...	...	...	...	...	32
265	7	134	...	...	...	6	124	...	...	...	...	...	...	...	...	33
555	166	97	11	2	21	8	292	...	...	...	...	...	...	...	...	34
96	...	11	...	...	...	...	85	...	...	...	...	...	...	...	...	35
...	...	...	...	...	...	...	...	...	...	...	...	...	...	...	...	36
1,107	99	707	8	8	5	23	301	...	...	...	...	...	...	...	...	
64	2	58	1	...	...	...	4	...	...	...	...	...	...	...	...	37
387	31	267	4	6	3	16	89	...	...	...	...	...	...	...	...	38
426	12	300	...	2	...	7	114	...	...	...	...	...	...	...	...	39
230	54	...	3	...	2	...	94	...	...	...	...	...	...	...	...	40
770	319	82	...	...	2	...	416	...	...	...	...	...	...	...	...	
770	319	35	...	...	2	...	416	...	...	...	...	...	...	...	...	41
...	...	...	...	...	...	...	...	...	...	...	...	...	...	...	...	42
...	...	...	...	...	...	...	...	...	...	...	...	...	...	...	...	43

Order XIII.—Dress

Group 77.—Tailors, milliners, dressmakers, darners and embroiderers on linen.

Serial No.	District or State.	Total Workers and Dependents.	Workers. Total Workers. Males.	Workers. Total Workers. Females.	Workers with an agricultural or other subsidiary occupation. Agricultural. Males.	Agricultural. Females.	Other. Males.	Other. Females.	Dependents.
	1	2	3	4	5	6	7	8	9
	Provincial Total ...	64,971	19,466	17,635	215	221	873	652	27,870
	Divisional Burma ...	63,607	19,155	16,993	213	212	863	627	27,459
	Arakan Division ...	1,985	1,090	169	14	2	33	18	726
1	Akyab	1,388	899	62	6	...	10	...	427
2	Hill Dist. of Arakan ...	9	2	1	...	..	..	...	6
3	Kyaukpyu	247	87	45	5	1	5	4	115
4	Sandoway	341	102	61	3	1	18	14	178
	Pegu Division ...	14,658	4,741	4,232	4	67	56	125	5,685
5	Rangoon Town ...	5,578	2,788	1,013	...	..	2	8	1,777
6	Insein	1,119	195	645	...	5	14	19	279
7	Hanthawaddy ...	1,717	255	375	...	43	4	18	1,087
8	Tharrawaddy ...	2,049	490	596	...	12	4	23	963
9	Pegu	1,681	223	842	3	7	7	32	616
10	Prome	2,514	790	761	1	...	25	25	963
	Irrawaddy Division ...	12,308	4,005	2,559	52	26	191	127	5,744
11	Bassein	2,877	929	602	13	9	64	36	1,346
12	Henzada	3,382	1,146	690	27	9	51	29	1,546
13	Myaungmya ...	2,336	766	493	4	1	38	26	1,077
14	Ma-ubin	2,254	688	594	4	6	29	23	972
15	Pyapôn	1,459	476	180	4	1	9	13	803
	Tenasserim Division ...	6,449	999	3,021	4	17	26	79	2,429
16	Toungoo	1,498	309	622	...	4	9	10	567
17	Salween	55	8	18	...	1	2	3	29
18	Thatôn	1,316	163	684	...	10	4	34	469
19	Amherst	2,019	307	956	...	...	1	12	756
20	Tavoy	1,027	126	543	2	2	9	20	358
21	Mergui	534	86	198	2	...	1	...	250
	Magwe Division ...	6,108	1,785	1,430	42	28	177	70	2,893
22	Thayetmyo .	918	181	326	...	4	8	11	411
23	Pakôkku	1,449	404	279	10	...	58	18	766
24	Minbu	1,832	586	396	21	18	73	26	850
25	Magwe	1,909	614	429	11	6	38	15	866
26	Pakôkku Hill Tracts ...	...	...	...	...	...	...	...	...
	Mandalay Division ...	7,944	2,045	3,016	3	13	54	30	2,883
27	Mandalay	6,485	1,721	2,496	1	...	21	20	2,268
	Mandalay City ...	*5,535*	*1,385*	*2,318*	...	...	...	...	*1,832*
28	Bhamo	226	31	128	...	.	...	2	64
29	Myitkyina ...	221	56	62	...	2	5	4	103
30	Katha	1,008	231	330	2	11	28	23	447
31	Putao	4	3	...	...	...	...	...	1
	Sagaing Division ...	6,927	2,320	1,179	67	42	205	97	3,428
32	Shwebo	1,925	597	376	11	29	39	23	952
33	Sagaing	2,575	768	547	26	8	60	50	1,260
34	Lower Chindwin ...	1,620	669	183	13	3	59	15	768
35	Upper Chindwin ...	761	270	72	17	2	47	9	419
36	Chin Hills	46	16	1	..	...	...	...	29
	Meiktila Division ...	7,228	2,170	1,387	27	17	121	72	3,671
37	Kyauksè	745	206	177	4	5	17	3	362
38	Meiktila	2,135	685	376	11	10	51	19	1,074
39	Yamèthin	1,906	538	330	6	2	20	13	1,032
40	Myingyan	2,442	741	498	6	...	33	37	1,203
	Eastern States ...	1,364	311	642	2	9	10	25	411
41	Northern Shan States ..	755	156	336	2	9	9	22	263
42	Southern Shan States ...	546	149	266	...	...	...	3	131
43	Karenni	63	6	40	...	...	1	...	17

PART III.—*Details by districts*—contd.

and the toilet—*continued.*

Group 78.—Shoe, boot and sandal makers.								Group 79.—Makers of umbrellas and of other articles pertaining to dress.								
Total Workers and Dependents.	WORKERS.						DEPENDENTS.	Total Workers and Dependents.	WORKERS.						DEPENDENTS.	Serial No. of District, etc. (column 1).
	Total Workers.		Workers with an agricultural or other subsidiary occupation.						Total Workers.		Workers with an agricultural or other subsidiary occupation.					
			Agricultural.		Other.						Agricultural.		Other.			
	Males.	Females.	Males.	Females.	Males.	Females.			Males.	Females.	Males.	Females.	Males.	Females.		
10	11	12	13	14	15	16	17	18	19	20	21	22	23	24	25	
11,776	5,539	1,162	18	9	76	23	5,075	4,796	2,121	720	4	...	36	10	1,955	
11,496	5,415	1,138	16	8	73	22	4,943	4,781	2,130	707	3	...	36	10	1,954	
78	51	1	...	...	...	...	26	165	60	9	...	...	3	...	96	
53	31	1	...	...	...	...	21	66	31	...	...	...	...	...	35	1
...	...	...	...	...	...	...	..	..	...	...	...	...	...	...	...	2
3	1	...	...	...	...	...	2	23	10	2	...	...	3	...	11	3
22	19	..	..	...	...	...	3	76	19	7	...	...	...	...	50	4
2,870	1,720	66	...	...	4	...	1,084	879	278	177	...	...	6	1	424	
2,157	1,310	51	...	..	2	...	796	706	212	148	...	...	2	1	346	5
28	14	3	...	...	...	..	11	18	7	5	...	...	..	...	6	6
49	29	3	...	..	...	...	17	16	8	...	..	...	1	...	8	7
93	69	5	...	...	1	...	19	54	11	24	...	...	...	...	19	8
81	35	4	...	...	...	...	42	29	10	...	...	...	2	..	19	9
462	263	...	...	...	1	...	199	56	30	...	...	...	1	.	26	10
524	242	35	1	...	3	..	247	829	385	71	...	...	8	2	373	
73	55	..	1	...	...	...	18	684	318	61	...	[illegible]	8	1	305	11
303	110	28	...	...	3	...	165	84	40	3	...	...	...	1	41	12
71	30	3	...	...	...	...	38	40	13	7	...	...	...	...	20	13
31	11	4	...	...	...	...	16	12	7	...	...	..	...	...	5	14
46	36	...	...	...	...	...	10	9	7	...	..	...	...	...	2	15
1,143	656	49	...	...	11	2	438	241	51	7	...	...	7	1	183	
119	49	14	..	...	...	2	56	28	11	...	...	...	...	...	17	16
...	...	...	...	...	...	...	...	...	...	...	..	...	...	...	...	17
364	198	16	...	...	5	...	150	144	38	2	...	...	6	1	110	18
443	274	18	...	...	4	..	151	18	2	...	...	...	...	...	16	19
138	62	1	...	...	1	...	75	44	4	5	...	...	1	...	35	20
79	73	...	...	...	1	...	6	7	2	...	...	...	...	...	5	21
1,073	379	80	3	..	12	1	614	96	37	13	...	...	2	5	46	
640	256	39	...	...	...	...	345	33	5	9	...	...	...	5	19	22
124	30	8	...	...	1	...	86	42	23	..	...	...	2	...	19	23
237	65	20	3	...	11	...	152	13	1	4	...	...	...	...	8	24
72	28	13	...	...	...	1	31	8	8	...	...	...	...	...	...	25
...	...	...	...	...	...	...	...	...	...	...	...	...	...	...	...	26
2,907	1,106	536	...	...	9	...	1,265	1,919	945	369	...	...	1	...	605	
2,801	1,030	533	...	...	9	.	1,238	1,911	942	369	...	...	1	...	600	27
2,670	*978*	*525*	...	...	*8*	...	*1,167*	*1,891*	*936*	*366*	...	...	...	...	*589*	
40	34	..	...	...	...	...	6	3	1	.	...	...	...	...	2	28
19	11	...	...	...	...	...	8	4	1	...	...	...	...	...	3	29
47	31	3	...	...	...	...	13	1	1	...	...	...	...	...	...	30
..	...	...	...	...	...	...	...	...	...	...	...	...	...	...	...	31
2,056	926	30	12	7	26	18	825	585	353	56	3	...	8	1	176	
198	148	11	1	...	..	...	39	125	71	23	3	...	1	...	31	32
814	379	130	6	3	9	4	305	13	3	...	...	...	...	...	10	33
1,028	391	164	5	4	17	14	473	446	278	33	...	...	6	1	135	34
6	6	...	...	...	...	...	...	1	1	...	...	...	1	...	...	35
10	2	...	...	...	...	...	8	.	...	...	...	..	...	...	...	36
845	335	66	...	1	8	1	444	67	11	5	...	...	1	...	51	
110	4	5	...	...	...	.	101	...	...	...	...	...	...	...	...	37
417	176	35	...	...	1	...	206	24	3	2	...	...	1	...	19	38
144	73	2	...	...	...	..	69	36	6	3	...	...	...	...	27	39
174	82	24	...	1	7	1	68	7	2	...	..	...	...	...	5	40
280	124	24	2	1	3	1	132	15	1	13	1	...	...	...	1	
264	115	24	2	1	3	1	125	1	...	...	...	...	...	...	1	41
13	7	..	..	...	...	...	6	14	1	13	1	...	..	...	...	42
3	2	...	...	...	...	...	1	...	...	...	...	...	...	...	...	43

Order XIII.—Dress and

Serial No.	DISTRICT OR STATE.	Group 80.—Washing, cleaning and dyeing articles of dress. Total Workers and Dependents.	WORKERS. Total Workers. Males.	Females.	Workers with an agricultural or other subsidiary occupation. Agricultural. Mls.	Females.	Other. Mls.	Females.	DEPENDENTS.	Group 81.—Barbers, hairdressers, and wig-makers. Total Workers and Dependents.	WORKERS. Total Workers. Males.	Females.	Workers with an agricultural or other subsidiary occupation. Agricultural. Mls.	Females.	Other. Males.	Females.	DEPENDENTS.
	1	2	3	4	5	6	7	8	9	10	11	12	13	14	15	16	17
	Provincial Total ...	17,233	8,078	2,311	6	9	47	24	6,844	5,006	3,324	192	1	...	23	...	1,490
	Divisional Burma ...	17,002	7,965	2,264	6	9	47	24	6,773	4,954	2,294	192	1	...	22	...	1,468
	Arakan Division ...	211	163	1	...	...	2	...	47	532	340	11	1	...	6	...	181
1	Akyab ...	149	129	1	...	...	...	...	19	510	318	11	1	...	4	...	181
2	Hill Dist. of Arakan	2	2	...	...	...	...	...	...	2	2	...	...	...	...	...	...
3	Kyaukpyu ...	13	6	...	...	...	1	...	7	8	8	...	...	...	...	...	...
4	Sandoway ...	47	26	...	...	...	1	...	21	12	12	...	...	...	2	...	...
	Pegu Division ...	7,419	3,817	812	...	3	4	3	2,790	1,911	1,421	7	...	...	5	...	483
5	Rangoon Town ...	4,387	2,412	372	...	...	1	...	1,603	1,384	1,066	...	...	...	1	...	318
6	Insein ...	426	183	46	...	...	...	...	197	110	82	3	...	...	...	...	25
7	Hanthawaddy ...	547	268	65	...	2	1	1	214	177	131	...	...	...	2	...	46
8	Tharrawaddy ...	411	210	17	...	...	...	...	184	108	78	...	...	...	1	...	30
9	Pegu ...	967	432	208	...	1	...	...	327	49	4	2	...	...	1	...	43
10	Prome ...	681	312	104	...	...	2	2	265	83	60	2	...	...	...	...	21
	Irrawaddy Division ...	2,253	1,169	270	3	...	8	...	814	495	370	1	...	...	3	...	124
11	Bassein ...	619	371	68	...	...	1	...	180	232	172	...	...	...	2	...	60
12	Henzada ...	513	214	83	...	...	4	...	216	65	40	...	...	...	...	...	25
13	Myaungmya ...	411	262	16	1	...	2	...	133	19	13	...	...	...	...	...	3
14	Ma-ubin ...	349	181	63	2	...	1	...	105	89	70	1	...	...	1	...	18
15	Pyapôn ...	361	141	40	...	...	...	...	180	93	75	...	...	...	...	...	18
	Tenasserim Division ...	1,956	792	285	2	...	12	7	879	735	500	19	...	...	2	...	216
16	Toungoo ...	461	249	47	...	...	1	...	165	156	113	6	...	...	...	...	37
17	Salween ...	6	3	...	...	...	...	...	3	4	3	...	...	...	...	...	1
18	Thatôn ...	530	197	98	2	...	10	7	235	180	121	6	...	...	...	...	53
19	Amherst ...	577	172	105	...	...	...	...	300	306	197	7	...	...	2	...	102
20	Tavoy ...	174	88	10	...	...	...	...	76	58	38	...	...	...	...	...	20
21	Mergui ...	208	83	25	...	...	1	...	100	31	28	...	...	...	...	...	3
	Magwe Division ...	811	454	70	...	...	8	2	287	122	86	1	...	...	3	...	35
22	Thayetmyo ...	169	42	25	...	...	1	1	102	38	25	...	...	...	...	...	13
23	Pakôkku ...	187	104	7	...	...	5	...	76	27	22	...	...	...	...	...	5
24	Minbu ...	205	109	28	...	...	...	1	68	24	4	...	...	...	3	...	10
25	Magwe ...	249	198	10	...	...	2	...	41	42	34	1	...	...	...	...	7
26	Pakôkku Hill Tracts	1	1	...	...	...	...	...	...	1	1	...	...	...	...	...	...
	Mandalay Division ...	2,779	931	626	...	6	2	10	1,222	872	399	151	...	...	3	...	322
27	Mandalay ...	2,472	840	562	...	6	...	9	1,070	749	322	151	...	...	...	...	276
	Mandalay City ...	*1,901*	*632*	*487*	...	...	...	...	*782*	*465*	*243*	*67*	...	...	...	...	*155*
28	Bhamo ...	88	26	22	...	...	2	...	40	19	13	...	...	...	...	...	6
29	Myitkyina ...	104	40	10	...	...	...	1	54	64	35	...	...	...	...	...	29
30	Katha ...	109	19	32	...	...	...	...	58	33	22	...	...	...	1	...	11
31	Putao ...	6	6	...	...	...	...	...	...	7	7	...	...	...	2	...	...
	Sagaing Division ...	651	266	59	1	...	4	...	326	112	74	1	...	...	...	...	37
32	Shwebo ...	195	65	24	...	...	...	...	106	25	18	1	...	...	...	...	6
33	Sagaing ...	278	125	22	1	...	3	...	131	35	20	...	...	...	...	...	15
34	Lower Chindwin ...	102	41	11	...	...	1	...	50	21	14	...	...	...	...	...	7
35	Upper Chindwin ...	55	27	2	...	...	...	...	26	27	18	...	...	...	...	...	9
36	Chin Hills ...	21	8	...	...	...	...	...	13	4	4	...	...	...	...	...	...
	Meiktila Division ...	922	373	141	...	...	7	2	408	175	104	1	...	...	...	...	70
37	Kyauksè ...	138	62	15	...	...	5	...	61	22	16	1	...	...	...	...	5
38	Meiktila ...	265	102	56	...	...	...	...	107	43	17	...	...	...	...	...	26
39	Yamèthin ...	276	119	14	...	...	2	...	143	78	52	...	...	...	...	...	26
40	Myingyan ...	243	90	56	...	...	...	2	97	32	19	...	...	...	...	...	13
	Eastern States ...	231	113	47	...	...	...	...	71	52	30	...	...	...	...	...	22
41	Northern Shan States	85	36	19	...	...	...	...	30	23	11	...	...	...	1	...	12
42	Southern Shan States	142	76	28	...	...	...	...	38	27	17	...	...	...	...	...	10
43	Karenni ...	4	1	...	...	...	...	...	3	2	2	...	...	...	1	...	...

the toilet—*concluded.* Group 82.—Massagers (*ahneikthè*) and tattooers. Total Workers and Dependents.	Workers. Total Workers. Males.	Workers. Total Workers. Females.	Workers with an agricultural or other subsidiary occupation. Agricultural. Males.	Agricultural. Females.	Other. Males.	Other. Females.	Dependents.	Order XIV.—Furniture. Group 83a.—Cabinet-makers, etc. Total Workers and Dependents.	Workers.* Males.	Workers.* Females.	Dependents.	Group 83b.—Polishers, carriage-painters, etc. Total Workers and Dependents.	Workers.† Males.	Workers.† Females.	Dependents.	Group 84.—Upholsterers, tent-makers, etc. Total Workers and Dependents.	Workers (All without subsidiary occupation). Males.	Females.	Dependents.	Serial No. of District, etc. (column 1).
18	19	20	21	22	23	24	25	26	27	28	29	30	31	32	33	34	35	36	37	
10,569	2,497	3,936	37	38	124	151	4,136	471	237	28	206	322	134	27	161	67	3	42	22	
9,946	2,377	3,628	33	25	114	122	3,941	471	237	28	206	322	134	27	161	67	3	42	22	
108	33	17	...	...	4	...	58	...	...	...	...	...	...	...	...	...	...	...	...	
63	19	6	...	...	1	...	38	...	...	...	...	...	...	...	...	...	...	...	...	1
...	...	...	...	...	...	...	...	...	...	...	...	...	...	...	...	...	...	...	...	2
21	12	2	...	...	3	...	7	...	...	...	...	...	...	...	...	...	...	...	...	3
24	2	9	...	...	...	...	13	...	...	...	...	...	...	...	...	...	...	...	...	4
1,160	359	430	1	1	7	2	371	*172	*57	1	114	22	2	...	20	2	...	...	2	
210	91	32	...	...	...	...	87	*172	*57	1	114	2	2	...	...	2	...	...	2	5
74	27	32	...	...	...	...	15	...	...	...	...	...	...	...	...	...	...	...	...	6
214	60	85	...	...	1	...	69	...	...	...	...	...	...	...	...	...	...	...	...	7
215	63	70	...	...	...	...	82	...	...	...	...	12	...	...	12	...	...	...	...	8
160	40	64	1	...	1	...	56	...	...	...	...	8	...	...	8	...	...	...	...	9
287	78	147	...	1	5	2	62	...	...	...	...	...	...	...	...	...	...	...	...	10
953	243	308	4	4	9	13	402	7	4	...	3	†34	†10	...	24	13	1	5	7	
203	60	57	...	...	3	...	86	...	...	...	...	1	...	...	1	...	...	...	...	11
281	83	85	2	2	2	3	113	7	4	...	3	†33	†10	...	23	3	1	...	2	12
114	5	42	...	...	...	...	67	...	...	...	...	...	...	...	...	...	...	...	...	13
175	52	58	...	1	3	8	65	...	...	...	...	...	...	...	...	10	...	5	5	14
180	43	66	2	1	1	2	71	...	...	...	...	...	...	...	...	...	...	...	...	15
682	170	181	...	1	4	3	331	35	6	17	12	7	3	...	4	...	...	...	...	
140	30	42	...	...	...	...	68	...	...	...	...	4	...	...	4	...	...	...	...	16
9	2	5	...	...	...	...	2	...	...	...	...	...	...	...	...	...	...	...	...	17
161	38	51	...	...	4	1	72	...	...	...	...	...	...	...	...	...	...	...	...	18
160	54	20	...	...	...	1	86	13	1	...	12	2	2	...	...	...	...	...	...	19
137	25	43	...	1	...	1	69	22	5	17	...	1	1	...	...	...	...	...	...	20
75	21	20	...	...	...	...	34	...	...	...	...	...	...	...	...	...	...	...	...	21
1,436	249	656	2	1	17	29	531	10	...	1	9	...	...	...	...	42	...	32	10	
219	38	81	...	...	2	2	100	10	...	1	9	...	...	...	...	...	...	...	...	22
742	142	347	2	1	12	18	253	...	...	...	...	...	...	...	...	4	...	2	2	23
314	56	143	...	...	...	9	115	...	...	...	...	...	...	...	...	...	...	...	...	24
161	13	85	...	...	3	...	63	...	...	...	...	...	...	...	...	38	...	30	8	25
...	...	...	...	...	...	...	...	...	...	...	...	...	...	...	...	...	...	...	...	26
1,127	207	455	2	...	9	4	465	242	170	4	68	43	39	...	4	...	...	...	...	
1,002	155	418	2	...	6	3	429	242	170	4	68	43	39	...	4	...	...	...	...	27
832	*45*	*413*	...	...	*2*	*3*	*374*	*133*	*65*	*4*	*64*	*10*	*6*	...	*4*	...	...	...	...	
36	9	13	...	...	...	1	14	...	...	...	...	...	...	...	...	...	...	...	...	28
9	4	2	...	...	...	...	3	...	...	...	...	...	...	...	...	...	...	...	...	29
80	39	22	...	...	3	...	19	...	...	...	...	...	...	...	...	...	...	...	...	30
...	...	...	...	...	...	...	...	...	...	...	...	...	...	...	...	...	...	...	...	31
3,021	799	1,053	19	13	50	56	1,169	...	...	...	...	†202	†78	†22	102	9	1	5	3	
703	147	266	6	3	7	9	290	...	...	...	...	2	...	...	...	5	...	5	...	32
1,115	282	433	7	4	17	29	400	...	...	...	...	†161	†55	†22	84	...	...	...	...	33
1,091	346	320	6	1	26	17	425	...	...	...	...	39	23	...	16	4	1	...	3	34
112	24	34	...	5	...	1	54	...	...	...	...	...	...	...	...	...	...	...	...	35
...	...	...	...	...	...	...	...	...	...	...	...	...	...	...	...	...	...	...	...	36
1,459	317	528	5	5	14	15	614	5	...	5	...	14	2	5	7	1	1	...	...	
267	95	45	2	5	4	6	127	5	...	5	...	...	...	...	...	...	...	...	...	37
362	65	141	3	...	3	...	156	...	...	...	...	7	...	[illegible]	2	...	...	...	...	38
185	31	80	...	...	2	...	74	...	...	...	...	1	1	...	...	...	...	...	...	39
645	126	262	...	...	5	9	257	...	...	...	...	6	1	...	5	1	1	...	...	40
623	120	308	4	13	10	29	195	...	...	...	...	...	...	...	...	...	...	...	...	
168	18	112	...	2	...	16	38	...	...	...	...	...	...	...	...	...	...	...	...	41
425	98	179	4	11	10	13	148	...	...	...	...	...	...	...	...	...	...	...	...	42
30	4	17	...	...	...	...	9	...	...	...	...	...	...	...	...	...	...	...	...	43

* All without subsidiary occupations except 2 males in Rangoon Town district with a non-agricultural subsidiary occupation.

† All without subsidiary occupations except 1 male in Henzada and Sagaing districts with a non-agricultural subsidiary occupation and 1 female in Sagaing district with an agricultural subsidiary occupation.

Order XV.—

Serial No.	District or State.	Group 85.—Lime-burners, cement-workers. Total Workers and Dependents.	Workers. Total Workers. Males.	Females.	Workers with an agricultural or other subsidiary occupation. Agricultural. Males	Females	Other. Males	Females	Dependents.	Group 86.—Excavators and well sinkers. Total Workers and Dependents.	Workers.* Males.	Females	Dependents.	Group 87.—Stone-cutters and dressers. Total Workers and Dependents.	Workers.† Males.	Females.	Dependents.
	1	2	3	4	5	6	7	8	9	10	11	12	13	14	15	16	17
	Provincial Total ...	3,137	889	260	22	5	61	4	1,988	192	118	8	66	188	21	80	87
	Divisional Burma ...	2,969	838	223	5	1	59	...	1,908	192	118	8	66	188	21	80	87
	Arakan Division ..	6	3	...	...	...	...	...	3	1	1	...	...	...	...	..	...
1	Akyab ...	2	2	...	...	...	...	...	...	...	...	...	...	...	..	...	...
2	Hill Dist. of Arakan	...	...	...	...	...	...	...	...	...	...	...	.	...	...	...	...
3	Kyaukpyu ...	4	1	...	...	...	...	...	3	...	..	...	...	...	...	..	...
4	Sandoway ...	...	...	...	...	...	...	...	...	1	1	...	...	...	...	...	...
	Pegu Division ...	28	28	...	...	..	...	...	...	66	51	...	15	8	...	...	8
5	Rangoon Town ...	...	...	...	...	..	...	...	...	9	2	...	7	...	...	..	...
6	Insein ..	...	...	...	.	...	...	...	...	40	39	...	1	...	...	...	...
7	Hanthawaddy ...	...	...	...	...	...	...	...	...	12	10	...	2	...	...	...	...
8	Tharrawaddy ...	...	...	...	...	..	...	...	...	5	..	..	5	...	...	...	...
9	Pegu ...	..	...	...	...	...	...	...	...	...	..	...	...	..	...	...	..
10	Prome ...	28	28	...	...	..	...	...	...	...	...	...	...	8	...	..	8
	Irrawaddy Division ...	160	84	16	2	...	5	...	60	7	7	...	...	.	...	..	...
11	Bassein ...	...	...	...	...	...	...	...	...	...	...	...	...	...	...	...	...
12	Henzada ..	...	..	...	...	...	...	...	...	7	7	...	...	...	...	...	...
13	Myaungmya ...	160	84	16	2	...	5	...	60	...	...	...	...	...	...	...	...
14	Ma-ubin ...	...	...	...	...	...	-	...	...	...	...	...	...	...	...	...	...
15	Pyapôn ...	...	...	...	...	..	...	...	...	...	...	...	...	...	...	...	...
	Tenasserim Division ...	1,300	368	143	...	...	5	..	789	22	...	...	22	...	...	...	...
16	Toungoo ...	29	12	10	...	...	...	...	7	6	...	...	16	...	...	...	...
17	Salween ...	...	...	...	...	...	...	...	...	...	...	...	...	...	...	...	...
18	Thatôn ...	1,247	352	132	...	...	5	...	763	...	...	..	...	..	...	...	...
19	Amherst ...	9	4	...	...	...	...	...	5	...	...	...	...	...	...	...	...
20	Tavoy ...	6	...	1	...	...	...	...	5	6	...	...	6	...	...	...	...
21	Mergui ...	9	..	...	...	...	...	...	9	...	..	...	...	...	...	...	...
	Magwe Division ...	657	122	32	1	1	29	...	503	57	39	8	10	21	20	...	1
22	Thayetmyo ...	434	103	12	...	...	27	...	319	...	...	...	...	...	...	...	...
23	Pakôkku ...	173	11	11	1	...	2	...	151	...	...	...	...	...	...	...	...
24	Minbu ...	50	8	9	...	1	...	...	33	1	1	...	...	18	17	...	1
25	Magwe ..	...	...	...	...	...	...	...	...	56	38	8	10	3	3	...	...
26	Pakôkku Hill Tracts	...	...	...	...	...	...	...	...	...	...	...	...	.	...	...	...
	Mandalay Division ...	459	176	14	...	...	16	...	269	6	4	...	2	4	...	...	4
27	Mandalay ...	458	175	14	...	..	16	...	269	6	4	...	2	..	...	...	...
	Mandalay City ..	2	...	...	...	...	...	...	2	2	1	...	1	...	...	...	...
28	Bhamo ...	1	1	...	...	...	...	...	...	...	...	...	...	...	...	...	...
29	Myitkyina ...	...	...	...	...	...	...	...	...	...	...	...	...	...	...	...	...
30	Katha ...	...	...	...	...	...	...	...	...	...	...	...	...	4	...	...	4
31	Putao ...	...	...	...	...	...	...	...	...	...	...	...	...	...	...	...	...
	Sagaing Division ...	136	44	9	2	...	4	...	83	*29	*16	...	13	153	1	†80	72
32	Shwebo ...	3	3	...	...	...	...	...	...	4	2	...	2	3	..	3	...
33	Sagaing ...	131	39	9	2	...	3	..	83	...	...	...	...	149	...	†77	72
34	Lower Chindwin ...	...	...	...	...	..	...	..	..	*8	*4	...	4	...	...	...	...
35	Upper Chindwin ...	[illegible]	2	...	...	...	1	...	...	17	10	...	7	1	1	...	...
36	Chin Hills ...	...	...	...	...	...	...	...	...	...	...	...	...	...	...	...	...
	Meiktila Division ...	223	13	9	...	...	..	...	201	4	...	...	4	2	...	...	2
37	Kyauksè ...	157	2	7	...	...	...	...	148	...	...	...	..	..	...	...	...
38	Meiktila ...	[illegible]	9	1	.	...	...	...	2	4	...	...	4	...	...	...	..
39	Yamèthin ...	53	2	1	..	...	...	...	50	...	...	...	...	...	...	...	...
40	Myingyan ...	1	...	...	...	...	...	...	1	...	...	...	...	2	...	...	2
	Eastern States ...	168	51	37	17	4	2	4	80	...	...	...	..	...	..	...	...
41	N. Shan States ...	133	34	37	3	4	2	4	62	...	...	...	...	...	..	...	...
42	S. Shan States ...	35	17	...	14	...	...	..	18	...	...	...	...	...	...	...	...
43	Karenni ...	...	...	...	...	...	...	...	...	...	...	...	...	...	...	...	...

* All without subsidiary occupations except 2 males in Lower Chindwin district with an agricultural subsidiary occupation.
† All without subsidiary occupations except 1 female in Sagaing district with a non-agricultural subsidiary occupation.

PART III.—*Details by districts*—*contd.*

Building.

Group 88.—Brick-layers and masons.								Group 89.—Builders (not using wood, bamboo, etc.), house-painters, plumbers, etc.								
Total Workers and Dependents.	WORKERS. Total Workers. Males.	WORKERS. Total Workers. Females.	Workers with an agricultural or other subsidiary occupation. Agricultural. Males.	Agricultural. Females	Other. Males.	Other. Females.	DEPENDENTS.	Total Workers and Dependents.	WORKERS. Total Workers. Males.	WORKERS. Total Workers. Females.	Workers with an agricultural or other subsidiary occupation. Agricultural. Males.	Agricultural. Females.	Other. Males.	Other. Females	DEPENDENTS.	Serial No. of District, etc. (column 1).
18	19	20	21	22	23	24	25	26	27	28	29	30	31	32	33	
14,741	6,511	792	137	5	189	20	7,438	3,764	1,987	96	6	3	26	...	1,681	
14,324	6,290	790	131	5	168	20	7,244	3,737	1,968	96	6	3	26	...	1,673	
375	172	1	9	...	2	...	202	39	19	1	...	...	...	...	19	
201	102	...	...	...	...	...	99	39	19	1	...	...	...	...	19	1
...	...	...	...	...	...	...	...	..	...	...	...	...	...	...	...	2
113	42	1	9	...	...	...	70	...	...	...	...	...	...	...	...	3
61	28	...	...	...	2	...	33	...	...	...	...	...	...	.	..	4
2,956	1,713	81	6	...	20	3	1,162	2,407	1,422	17	...	...	8	...	968	
1,262	936	4	...	..	7	...	322	2,104	1,266	9	...	...	8	...	829	5
257	149	3	1	...	2	...	105	78	16	4	...	...	...	...	58	6
253	137	3	2	...	2	2	113	41	33	..	...	...	...	...	8	7
456	196	52	...	...	4	...	208	17	8	4	...	...	...	...	5	8
428	174	3	3	...	4	...	245	53	29	...	...	...	...	...	24	9
306	121	16	..	...	1	1	169	114	70	...	...	...	...	...	44	10
1,322	703	26	13	1	12	1	593	99	40	9	...	...	...	...	50	
284	185	6	2	...	2	...	93	65	22	1	...	...	...	...	42	11
418	173	2	5	1	3	1	243	11	8	...	...	...	...	...	3	12
304	186	15	6	..	7	...	103	...	...	..	...	...	...	...	...	13
217	94	3	...	...	...	..	120	23	10	8	...	...	...	...	5	14
99	65	...	...	...	...	...	34	...	...	...	...	...	...	...	...	15
1,679	66	29	10	...	7	...	986	272	119	1	3	...	8	...	152	
168	81	3	1	...	3	...	84	90	20	...	...	...	..	...	70	16
19	16	...	...	...	...	...	3	...	...	...	...	...	...	...	...	17
331	113	...	...	...	...	...	218	20	18	...	...	...	...	...	2	18
727	267	19	3	...	1	...	441	112	49	1	...	...	...	...	62	19
251	90	1	6	...	1	..	160	40	26	...	3	...	8	...	14	20
183	97	6	...	...	2	...	80	10	6	...	...	...	...	...	4	21
1,660	653	55	36	...	39	...	952	6	5	1	...	1	...	...	...	
221	48	7	...	...	3	...	166	..	...	...	...	...	...	...	...	22
619	233	17	3	...	20	...	369	...	...	...	...	...	...	...	...	23
399	102	11	16	...	10	...	286	1	...	1	...	1	...	...	...	24
421	270	20	17	...	6	...	131	5	5	...	...	...	...	...	...	25
...	...	...	...	...	...	...	...	...	...	...	...	...	...	...	...	26
2,697	844	457	10	1	34	3	1,396	735	287	9	...	...	...	...	439	
2,246	584	457	2	1	9	3	1,205	725	280	8	...	...	...	...	437	27
1,770	392	392	...	...	...	1	986	286	102	8	...	...	...	...	176	
203	58	...	...	...	20	...	145	9	6	1	...	...	...	...	2	28
90	73	...	1	...	...	...	17	...	...	...	...	...	...	...	...	29
158	129	...	7	...	5	...	29	1	1	...	...	...	...	...	...	30
...	...	...	...	...	...	..	.	...	...	...	...	...	...	...	...	31
1,985	936	84	36	2	34	8	965	167	70	57	3	2	10	...	40	
421	177	57	5	...	9	6	187	49	5	29	..	...	...	...	15	32
824	400	11	15	1	9	1	413	24	8	...	1	...	...	...	16	33
636	293	15	16	1	14	1	328	93	56	28	2	2	10	...	9	34
87	50	1	...	...	2	...	36	1	1	...	...	.	...	...	...	35
17	16	...	...	...	...	...	1	...	...	...	...	..	...	...	...	36
1,650	605	57	11	1	20	5	988	12	6	1	...	...	...	...	5	
307	119	12	6	...	11	...	196	...	...	...	...	...	...	...	...	37
327	124	3	...	...	3	...	200	5	5	...	...	...	...	...	...	38
274	98	5	...	...	...	...	171	5	...	...	...	...	...	...	5	39
722	264	37	5	1	6	5	421	2	1	1	...	...	...	...	...	40
417	221	2	6	...	21	...	194	27	19	...	...	...	...	...	8	
162	102	1	..	...	3	...	59	26	18	...	...	...	...	...	8	41
234	116	...	6	...	18	...	118	1	1	...	...	...	...	...	...	42
21	3	1	...	...	...	...	17	...	...	...	...	...	...	...	...	43

Order XVI.—Construction of

Serial No.	DISTRICT OR STATE.	Group 90.—Making, assembling or repairing cycles and motor land-vehicles. Total Workers and Dependents.	Workers. Total Workers. Males.	Workers. Total Workers. Females.	Workers with an agricultural or other subsidiary occupation. Agricultural. Males.	Agricultural. Females.	Other. Males.	Other. Females.	DEPENDENTS.	Group 91.—Makers and repairers of other land-vehicles, and wheelwrights. Total Workers and Dependents.	Workers. Total Workers. Males.	Workers. Total Workers. Females.	Workers with an agricultural or other subsidiary occupation. Agricultural. Males.	Agricultural. Females.	Other. Males.	Other. Females.	DEPENDENTS.
	1	2	3	4	5	6	7	8	9	10	11	12	13	14	15	16	17
	Provincial Total ...	1,596	800	17	1	...	24	...	779	3,891	1,273	155	25	2	103	14	2,364
	Divisional Burma ...	1,577	789	17	1	...	24	...	771	3,790	1,337	149	24	2	101	14	2,304
	Arakan Division ...	21	13	...	...	...	...	...	8	32	6	1	...	...	1	1	25
1	Akyab ...	16	10	...	...	..	...	...	6	22	5	...	...	...	...	...	17
2	Hill Dist. of Arakan	...	...	..	...	.	...	...	...	...	...	...	...	..	...	...	...
3	Kyaukpyu ...	...	..	...	...	...	...	..	...	...	...	..	...	...	...	...	...
4	Sandoway ...	5	3	...	...	...	...	...	2	10	1	1	...	...	1	1	8
	Pegu Division ...	1,127	581	7	...	...	17	...	539	665	272	12	2	...	29	...	381
5	Rangoon Town ...	1,059	560	3	...	...	17	...	495	129	60	5	...	..	...	...	64
6	Insein ...	22	3	1	...	...	...	...	18	19	6	3	..	...	2	...	10
7	Hanthawaddy ...	11	5	3	...	...	...	...	3	28	8	...	...	...	1	...	20
8	Tharrawaddy ...	3	2	...	...	...	...	...	1	137	82	...	...	...	17	...	55
9	Pegu ...	22	2	...	...	...	.	...	20	186	57	...	2	...	2	...	129
10	Prome ..	10	9	...	...	...	...	...	1	166	59	4	...	...	7	...	103
	Irrawaddy Division ...	74	24	4	..	...	...	...	46	124	43	8	...	1	3	1	73
11	Bassein ...	37	9	4	...	...	...	...	24	18	...	4	...	1	...	...	14
12	Henzada ...	27	10	...	...	...	...	...	17	20	12	...	...	...	1	...	8
13	Myaungmya ...	1	1	...	.	...	...	...	...	1	...	1	...	...	...	1	...
14	Ma-ubin ...	9	4	...	...	...	..	...	5	78	31	3	...	...	2	...	44
15	Pyapôn ...	...	...	...	...	...	...	...	...	7	...	...	...	...	...	...	7
	Tenasserim Division ...	84	34	...	...	...	1	..	50	637	197	23	3	...	4	1	417
16	Toungoo ...	11	2	...	...	...	1	...	9	230	40	9	...	...	...	1	181
17	Salween ...	...	...	...	...	...	...	..	...	11	1	...	...	...	...	...	10
18	Thatôn ..	12	4	...	.	...	...	...	8	219	109	3	2	...	1	...	107
19	Amherst ...	23	5	...	...	...	...	...	18	175	47	11	1	...	3	...	117
20	Tavoy ...	36	21	...	...	..	...	...	15	2	...	...	...	...	...	...	2
21	Mergui ...	2	2	...	...	...	...	...	...	...	...	...	...	...	...	...	...
	Magwe Division ..	19	8	...	...	...	...	...	11	677	200	82	4	...	16	8	395
22	Thayetmyo ...	8	4	...	..	...	...	...	4	20	2	1	...	...	...	...	17
23	Pakôkku ...	9	4	...	..	...	...	...	5	383	86	75	2	...	9	8	282
24	Minbu ...	2	...	...	...	...	...	...	2	146	47	6	2	...	4	...	93
25	Magwe ...	...	...	...	...	...	...	...	...	128	65	...	...	...	3	...	63
26	Pakôkku Hill Tracts	...	...	...	..	...	...	...	...	...	...	...	...	...	...	...	...
	Mandalay Division ...	190	103	5	...	...	2	...	82	263	77	13	1	...	4	...	173
27	Mandalay ...	187	101	5	...	..	2	...	81	185	49	9	...	..	1	...	107
	Mandalay City ...	*169*	*91*	*5*	...	...	...	...	*73*	*143*	*28*	9	.	...	...	...	*106*
28	Bhamo ...	...	...	...	...	...	...	...	...	1	...	1	...	...	...	...	...
29	Myitkyina ...	3	2	...	...	...	...	...	1	..	...	...	...	...	...	...	...
30	Katha ...	...	...	...	...	...	...	...	...	75	28	3	1	...	3	...	44
31	Putao ...	...	...	...	...	..	...	...	...	2	..	...	...	...	...	...	2
	Sagaing Division ...	28	9	1	1	...	..	...	18	542	257	...	12	...	25	..	285
32	Shwebo ...	10	3	...	1	.	...	..	7	219	101	...	2	...	10	...	118
33	Sagaing ...	12	4	...	.	...	...	...	8	110	57	...	7	...	6	...	53
34	Lower Chindwin ..	6	2	1	...	...	...	...	3	204	95	...	2	...	8	...	109
35	Upper Chindwin ...	...	...	...	...	...	...	...	...	9	4	...	1	...	1	...	5
36	Chin Hills ...	...	...	..	...	...	...	...	...	...	...	...	...	...	...	...	..
	Meiktila Division ...	34	17	...	...	...	4	...	17	850	285	10	2	1	19	3	555
37	Kyauksè ...	3	1	...	...	...	...	...	2	35	13	3	1	...	1	3	19
38	Meiktila ...	14	8	...	...	...	1	...	6	229	100	...	...	...	4	...	129
39	Yamèthin ...	4	1	...	...	...	...	...	3	479	137	3	1	1	10	...	339
40	Myingyan ...	23	7	...	..	...	2	...	6	107	35	4	...	...	4	...	68
	Eastern States ...	19	11	...	...	...	...	..	8	101	35	6	1	...	2	...	60
41	N. Shan States ...	18	11	..	...	...	...	...	7	92	32	6	1	...	2	...	54
42	S. Shan States ...	1	..	...	...	...	...	...	1	8	3	...	...	...	...	...	5
43	Karenni	...	...	...	...	..	...	...	...	1	..	...	...	...	...	..	1

means of transport.								Order XVII.—Production and transmission of physical forces.								
Group 92.—Ship or boat builders.								Group 93.—Gas works, electric light and power and water power.								Serial No. of District, etc. (column 1).
Total Workers and Dependents.	WORKERS.						DEPENDENTS.	Total Workers and Dependents.	WORKERS.						DEPENDENTS.	
	Total Workers.		Workers with an agricultural or other subsidiary occupation.						Total Workers.		Workers with an agricultural or other subsidiary occupation.					
			Agricultural.		Other.						Agricultural.		Other.			
	Males.	Females.	Males.	Females.	Males.	Females.			Males.	Females.	Males.	Females.	Males.	Females.		
18	19	20	21	22	23	24	25	26	27	28	29	30	31	32	33	
3,610	2,187	102	7	...	41	2	1,321	577	177	5	2	...	2	...	395	
3,605	2,187	101	7	...	41	1	1,317	565	177	4	2	...	2	...	384	
502	216	78	1	..	16	...	208	...	...	...	...	...	..	.	..	
464	197	76	1	...	15	...	191	...	...	.	...	...	...	...	...	1
...	...	...	...	...	...	...	...	...	...	...	...	...	...	...	...	2
34	18	2	...	...	...	...	14	...	...	...		...	...	...	...	3
4	1	...	...	...	1	...	3	...	...	...	...	...	...	...	...	4
2,057	1,561	13	1	.	7	...	483	429	103	1	2	...	2	...	325	
1,977	1,517	13	...	...	2	...	447	397	71	1	...	...	2	...	255	5
26	..	...	..	...	...	..	26	67	18	...	...	...	...	...	49	6
43	37	...	1	..	5	...	6	20	4	...	...	...	..	...	16	7
5	2	...	...	...	...	...	3	3	...	..	...	...	..	...	3	8
6	5		...	...	...	...	1	3	2	...	..	...	...	...	1	9
...		...	...	...	...	...	...	9	8	...	2	...	...	...	1	10
284	82	9	5	...	6	...	193	22	9	...	...	...	...	...	13	
158	38	4	4	...	4	...	116	3	2	...	.	..	...	...	1	11
17	3	..	1	...	...	...	14	3	...	...	...	..	...	...	3	12
55	32	2	...	...	1	...	21	...	.	...	...	...	...	...	...	13
19	5	1	...		1	...	13	1	1	...	...	..	...	...	...	14
35	4	2	...	...	...	...	29	15	6	...	...	...	...	..	9	15
689	399	...	...	...	9	...	380	40	18	...	...	...	...	...	22	
374	170	...	...	...	7	...	204	15	6	.	...	...	...	...	9	16
3	...	...	...	...	..	...	3	...	...	...	...	...	...	...	...	17
25	1		...	..	...	...	24	15	7	...	...	...	...	...	8	18
169	95	..	...	...	...	...	74	4	1	...	...	...	...	...	3	19
76	6	...	...	...	1	...	70	4	2	...	...	...	...	...	2	20
42	37	...	...	...	1	...	5	2	2	...	...	...	...	...	...	21
11	...	...	...	.	..	...	11	3	2	...	.	..	...	...	1	
..	...	...	...	...	...	...	...	...	...	.	...	...	...	...	...	22
1	...	...	...	...	...	...	1	...	...	...	...	...	...	...	...	23
10	...	...	..	...	...	...	10	...	...	...	...	...	...	...	...	24
...	...	...	...		...	...	...	3	2	...	...	...	...	...	1	25
...	..	..	...	...	..	...	...	...	...	..	...	...	...	...	...	26
43	10	...	...	...	3	...	33	62	40	3	...	..	...	...	29	
22	1	...	...	...	...	...	21	60	38	3	...	...	...	...	19	27
8	...	...	.	...	...	...	*8*	*56*	*37*	*3*	...	...	...	...	*16*	
16	7	...	...	...	3	...	9	...	...	..	...	...	...	...	...	28
1	1	...	...	...	...	...	...	...	...	...	...	...	...	...	...	29
4	1	...	...	...	...	...	3	2	2	...	...	...	...	...	...	30
...	...	..	...	...	...	...	...	...	...	...	...	...	...	...	...	31
18	8	1	...	...	...	1	9	2	2	...	...	...	...	...	...	
...	...	...	...	...	...	...	...	2	2	...	...	...	...	...	...	32
1	...	...	...	...	...	...	1	...	...	...	...	...	...	...	...	33
12	8	...	..	...	...	...	4	...	...	...	...	...	...	.	...	34
5	...	1	...	...		1	4	...	...	...	...	...	...	...	...	35
...	...	...	...	...	...	...	...	...	...	...	...	...	...	...	...	36
1	1	...	...	...	..	...	...	7	3	...	...	...	.	...	4	
...	...	...	...	...	...	...	...	...	...	...	...	...	...	...	...	37
...	...	.	...	...	...	...	...	..	...	...	...	...	...	...	...	38
...	...	...	...	...	...	...	...	3	3	...	...	...	...	...	...	39
1	1	...	...	...	...	...	...	4	...	...	...	...	...	...	4	40
5	...	1	...	...	.	1	4	12	...	1	...	...	...	...	11	
5	...	1	...	...	...	1	4	12	...	1	...	...	...	...	11	41
...	...	...	...	...	...	...	...	...	...	...	...	...	...	...	...	42
...	...	...	...	...	...	...	...	...	...	...	...	...	...	...	...	43

Order XVIII.—Other industries

Serial No.	District or State.	Group 94.—Printers, lithographers, engravers, etc. Total Workers and Dependents.	Workers. Total Workers. Males.	Total Workers. Females.	Workers with an agricultural or other subsidiary occupation. Agricultural. Mls.	Agricultural. Females	Other. Males	Other. Females.	Dependents.	Group 95.—Bookbinders and stitchers, envelope-makers, etc. Total Workers and Dependents.	Workers.* Males.	Workers.* Females.	Dependents.	Group 96.—Makers of musical instruments. Total Workers and Dependents.	Workers.† Males.	Workers.† Females.	Dependents.
	1	2	3	4	5	6	7	8	9	10	11	12	13	14	15	16	17
	Provincial Total ...	4,441	1,787	38	...	...	8	...	2,616	684	353	6	325	197	101	6	90
	Divisional Burma ...	4,441	1,787	38	...	...	8	...	2,616	683	353	6	324	196	100	6	90
	Arakan Division ...	44	11	6	...	...	...	...	27	11	7	...	4	1	1	...	...
1	Akyab ...	32	9	...	...	...	...	...	23	*7	*5	...	2	...	...	...	...
2	Hill Dist. of Arakan	...	...	...	...	...	...	...	...	...	...	...	...	...	...	...	...
3	Kyaukpyu ...	12	2	6	...	...	...	...	4	3	2	..	1	...	...	...	...
4	Sandoway ...	..	...	...	...	...	...	...	...	1	...	...	1	1	1	...	...
	Pegu Division ...	3,508	1,514	23	...	...	6	...	1,971	533	318	5	210	35	16	2	17
5	Rangoon Town ...	3,161	1,379	17	...	...	5	...	1,765	511	310	4	197	29	15	...	14
6	Insein ..	135	68	5	...	...	...	...	62	6	...	...	6	1	1	...	...
7	Hanthawaddy ...	4	4	...	...	...	...	...	...	...	...	...	...	5	...	2	3
8	Tharrawaddy ...	85	9	...	...	...	...	...	76	1	1	...	...	...	...	...	...
9	Pegu ...	72	25	...	...	...	...	..	47	3	3	...	...	...	...	...	...
10	Prome ...	51	29	1	...	...	1	...	21	12	4	1	7	...	...	...	..
	Irrawaddy Division ...	167	54	...	...	...	1	...	113	10	5	...	5	...	...	...	...
11	Bassein ...	55	6	...	...	...	...	...	49	3	1	...	2	...	...	...	...
12	Henzada ...	74	33	...	..	...	...	...	41	3	3	...	...	...	...	...	...
13	Myaungmya ..	3	3	...	...	...	...	...	..	4	1	...	3	...	...	...	...
14	Ma-ubin ...	8	3	...	...	...	1	...	5	...	...	...	...	...	...	...	.
15	Pyapôn ...	27	9	...	...	...	..	...	18	...	...	...	..	...	...	...	...
	Tenasserim Division ...	189	49	1	...	...	...	...	139	27	7	...	20	57	36	...	
16	Toungoo ...	48	11	...	...	...	...	.	37	...	...	...	...	...	...	...	...
17	Salween ...	...	...	...	...	...	...	...	...	...	...	...	...	...	...	..	..
18	Thatôn	...	...	...	...	..	...	..	...	9	1	...	8	3	3	...	8
19	Amherst ...	121	29	1	...	...	...	...	91	16	4	...	12	10	...	...	10
20	Tavoy	20	9	...	...	...	...	...	11	1	1	...	...	†44	†33	...	11
21	Mergui	...	...	...	...	...	...	...	...	1	1	...	...	...	...	...	...
	Magwe Division ...	27	5	...	...	...	...	...	22	7	2	...	5	70	32	4	34
22	Thayetmyo ...	18	3	...	...	...	...	...	15	...	...	...	..	66	31	3	32
23	Pakôkku ...	7	2	...	...	...	.	...	5	3	1	...	2	1	..	...	1
24	Minbu	2	...	...	...	...	...	...	2	*4	*1	...	3	†3	†1	1	1
25	Magwe	...	...	...	...	...	...	...	...	..	...	...	...	...	...	...	...
26	Pakôkku Hill Tracts	...	...	...	...	...	...	...	...	...	...	...	...	...	...	...	...
	Mandalay Division ...	450	136	8	...	...	1	...	306	61	9	1	51	1	1	...	...
27	Mandalay ...	444	134	8	...	...	...	...	302	51	6	1	44	1	1	...	...
	Mandalay City ...	*381*	*115*	*8*	...	...	...	...	*258*	*25*	*1*	*1*	*23*	*1*	*1*	...	...
28	Bhamo	...	...	...	...	...	...	..	..	6	1	...	5	...	...	...	...
29	Myitkyina ...	4	...	...	...	...	...	...	4	4	2	...	2	...	...	...	...
30	Katha	2	2	...	...	...	1	...	...	...	...	...	...	...	...	...	...
31	Putao	..	...	...	...	...	...	...	...	...	...	...	...	...	...	...	...
	Sagaing Division ...	1	...	...	...	...	...	...	1	4	4	...	...	12	11	...	1
32	Shwebo ...	1	...	...	...	...	...	...	1	...	...	..	...	2	2	...	..
33	Sagaing ...	...	...	...	...	...	...	...	...	2	2	...	...	7	7	...	...
34	Lower Chindwin ...	...	...	...	...	...	...	...	...	1	1	...	...	3	2	...	1
35	Upper Chindwin ...	...	...	...	...	...	...	...	...	1	1	..	...	...	...	...	...
36	Chin Hills ...	...	...	...	...	...	...	...	...	...	..	...	...	...	...	...	...
	Meiktila Division ...	55	18	...	...	...	...	...	37	30	1	...	29	20	3	...	17
37	Kyauksè ...	...	...	...	...	.	...	..	...	...	...	...	...	...	...	...	...
38	Meiktila ...	5	2	...	...	...	...	..	3	9	1	...	8	4	3	...	1
39	Yamèthin ...	32	1	...	...	...	...	...	31	21	...	...	21	16	...	...	16
40	Myingyan ...	18	15	...	...	...	...	...	3	...	...	...	...	...	...	...	...
	Eastern States ...	...	...	...	...	...	...	...	...	1	...	...	1	1	1	...	...
41	Northern Shan States	...	..	...	...	...	...	...	...	1	...	...	1	1	1	...	...
42	Southern Shan States	...	...	...	...	...	...	...	...	...	...	...	...	...	...	...	...
43	Karenni ...	...	...	...	...	...	...	...	...	...	...	...	...	...	...	...	...

* All without subsidiary occupations except 2 males in Akyab and Minbu districts with a non-agricultural subsidiary occupation.

† All without subsidiary occupations except 4 males in Tavoy district with an agricultural subsidiary occupation and 1 male in Minbu district with a non-agricultural subsidiary occupation.

—*contd.*

Group 97.—Makers of watches and clocks and optical, photographic, mathematical and surgical instruments.								Group 98a.—Makers of imitation jewellery.			Group 98b.—Gilders.			Group 98c.—Jewellers, workers in gold, silver and other precious metals, enamellers, etc.								
Total Workers and Dependents.	WORKERS.						DEPENDENTS.	Total Workers and Dependents.	WORKERS (All males without subsidiary occupation.)	DEPENDENTS.	Total Workers and Dependents.	WORKERS.*	DEPENDENTS.	Total Workers and Dependents.	WORKERS.						DEPENDENTS.	Serial No. of District, etc. (column 1).
	Total Workers.		Workers with an agricultural or other subsidiary occupations.												Total Workers		Workers with an agricultural or other subsidiary occupation.					
			Agricultural.		Other.												Agricultural.		Other.			
	Males	Females	Males	Females	Males	Females						Males			Males.	Females	Males	Females	Males	Females		
18	19	20	21	22	23	24	25	26	27	28	29	30	31	32	33	34	35	36	37	38	39	
1,388	421	19	1	...	6	...	948	174	112	62	1,091	718	373	53,365	20,862	1,110	402	106	719	35	31,393	
1,365	414	19	...	...	6	...	932	174	112	62	1,091	718	373	50,272	19,919	1,052	262	104	661	35	29,301	
34	7	...	...	...	...	...	27	...	...	...	...	...	...	4,192	1,735	43	21	...	81	2	2,414	
26	5	...	...	...	...	...	21	...	...	...	...	...	...	3,288	1,438	20	15	...	61	...	1,830	1
...	...	...	...	...	...	...	...	...	...	...	...	...	...	23	12	...	...	...	...	...	11	2
...	...	...	...	...	...	...	...	...	...	...	...	...	...	599	188	23	6	...	9	2	388	3
8	2	...	...	...	...	...	6	...	...	...	...	...	...	282	97	...	...	...	11	...	185	4
615	177	6	...	...	1	...	432	74	21	53	39	24	15	12,809	5,240	160	27	...	93	1	7,409	
448	118	2	...	...	1	...	328	38	10	28	15	...	15	4,022	1,826	30	...	...	4	...	2,176	5
22	11	...	...	...	...	...	11	1	1	...	...	...	...	2,139	462	53	1	...	9	...	624	6
22	7	3	...	...	...	...	12	2	1	1	...	...	...	1,882	676	4	7	...	25	...	1,208	7
38	14	...	...	...	...	...	24	...	...	...	...	...	...	1,919	761	54	11	...	32	...	1,104	8
53	21	...	...	...	...	...	32	33	9	24	...	...	...	2,095	760	5	8	...	17	...	1,330	9
32	6	1	...	...	...	...	25	...	...	...	24	24	...	1,752	755	24	...	...	6	1	973	10
174	55	2	...	...	...	...	117	9	7	2	...	...	...	8,120	3,272	192	23	1	115	10	4,656	
76	23	...	...	...	...	...	53	...	...	...	...	...	...	1,580	672	25	3	...	36	1	883	11
41	13	...	...	...	...	...	28	9	7	2	...	...	...	1,928	732	6	2	...	13	6	1,190	12
12	4	1	...	...	...	...	7	...	...	...	...	...	...	1,696	760	83	3	...	33	2	913	13
39	9	1	...	...	...	...	29	...	...	...	...	...	...	1,417	589	73	9	1	23	1	755	14
6	6	...	...	...	...	...	...	...	...	...	...	...	...	1,493	579	5	6	...	10	...	915	15
243	81	7	...	...	3	...	155	5	2	3	*240	*205	35	6,465	2,340	67	21	...	95	...	4,158	
40	7	...	...	...	1	...	33	...	...	...	2	...	2	1,207	501	14	3	...	22	...	692	16
...	...	...	...	...	...	...	...	...	...	...	...	...	...	57	22	2	...	...	2	...	33	17
60	16	5	...	...	1	...	39	...	...	...	...	...	...	2,021	668	34	4	...	31	...	1,319	18
98	34	...	...	...	...	...	64	5	2	3	...	...	...	2,375	797	10	6	...	28	...	1,568	19
32	11	2	...	...	...	...	19	...	...	...	...	...	...	432	235	3	8	...	12	...	194	20
13	13	...	...	...	1	...	...	...	...	...	*238	*205	33	373	17	4	...	...	...	...	352	21
68	21	2	...	...	...	...	45	...	...	...	*726	*486	240	4,715	1,669	117	21	2	76	9	2,929	
13	3	1	...	...	...	...	9	...	...	...	...	...	...	1,059	327	19	6	...	15	2	713	22
30	6	...	...	...	...	...	24	...	...	...	...	...	...	1,672	683	19	10	1	31	2	1,030	23
13	7	...	...	...	...	...	6	...	...	...	6	6	...	1,565	706	32	5	...	30	2	827	24
12	5	1	...	...	...	...	6	...	...	...	*720	*480	240	419	13	47	...	1	...	3	359	25
...	...	...	...	...	...	...	...	...	...	...	...	...	...	...	...	...	...	...	...	...	...	26
151	42	1	...	...	1	...	108	86	82	4	*78	*1	77	5,682	2,552	162	14	...	41	1	2,968	
118	32	...	...	...	...	...	86	86	82	4	77	...	77	4,165	1,928	127	1	...	1	1	2,110	27
107	*27*	...	...	...	...	...	*80*	*86*	*82*	4	...	...	...	*3,665*	*1,688*	*125*	...	...	...	...	*1,852*	
18	4	...	...	...	...	...	14	...	...	...	...	...	...	202	64	4	...	...	2	...	134	28
8	5	...	...	...	1	...	3	...	...	...	*1	*1	...	311	175	13	7	...	16	...	123	29
7	1	1	...	...	...	...	5	...	...	...	...	...	...	1,004	385	18	6	...	22	...	601	30
...	...	...	...	...	...	...	...	...	...	...	...	...	...	...	...	...	...	...	...	...	...	31
17	12	...	...	...	1	...	5	...	...	...	...	...	...	3,864	1,744	217	122	101	97	4	1,903	
5	3	...	...	...	1	...	2	...	...	...	...	...	...	980	411	29	7	...	15	2	480	32
3	1	...	...	...	...	...	2	...	...	...	...	...	...	1,069	556	6	14	...	22	1	507	33
7	6	...	...	...	...	...	1	...	...	...	...	...	...	881	448	18	9	...	29	...	415	34
2	2	...	...	...	...	...	...	...	...	...	...	...	...	986	326	164	92	101	31	7	496	35
...	...	...	...	...	...	...	...	...	...	...	...	...	...	8	3	...	...	...	...	...	5	36
63	19	1	...	...	...	...	43	...	...	...	8	2	6	4,425	1,467	94	13	...	63	8	2,864	
...	...	...	...	...	...	...	...	...	...	...	...	...	...	621	215	12	3	...	13	2	394	37
8	2	...	...	...	...	...	6	...	...	...	...	...	...	1,195	323	...	...	...	16	...	872	38
34	10	1	...	...	...	...	23	...	...	...	...	...	...	1,197	386	12	4	...	10	...	799	39
21	7	...	...	...	...	...	14	...	...	...	8	2	6	1,412	543	70	6	...	24	6	799	40
23	7	...	1	...	...	...	16	...	...	...	...	...	...	3,093	943	58	140	2	58	...	2,092	
23	7	...	1	...	...	...	16	...	...	...	...	...	...	592	215	43	9	2	20	...	334	41
...	...	...	...	...	...	...	...	...	...	...	...	...	...	1,337	659	8	131	...	37	...	1,670	42
...	...	...	...	...	...	...	...	...	...	...	...	...	...	164	69	7	...	...	1	...	88	43

* One male in Mergui district had an agricultural subsidiary occupation: 4 males in Mergui, 19 males in Magwe and 1 male in Myitkyina districts had non-agricultural subsidiary occupations.

Order XVIII.—

Serial No.	DISTRICT OR STATE.	Group 99.—Makers of bangles or beads or necklaces of other material than glass and makers of spangles, lingams, sacred threads or artificial flowers. Total Workers and Dependents.	WORKERS.* Males.	WORKERS.* Females	DEPENDENTS.	Group 100.—Makers of toys and miscellaneous small articles. Total Workers and Dependents.	WORKERS.† Males.	WORKERS.† Females	DEPENDENTS.	Group 101.—Persons other than performers employed in places of entertainment and persons engaged in connection with sports and games. Total Workers and Dependents.	WORKERS. Total Workers. Males.	WORKERS. Total Workers. Females.	Workers with an agricultural or other subsidiary occupation. Agricultural. M's.	Agricultural. Females	Other. M's.	Other. Females	DEPENDENTS.
	1	2	3	4	5	6	7	8	9	10	11	12	13	14	15	16	17
	Provincial Total ...	625	245	235	145	1,028	507	90	431	3,040	1,302	72	48	1	36	1	1,666
	Divisional Burma ...	613	234	235	144	1,028	507	90	431	2,983	1,268	64	45	1	33	1	1,651
	Arakan Division ...	1	...	1	...	3	...	...	3	10	...	...	...	...	...	...	10
1	Akyab ...	...	...	...	...	...	...	...	...	3	...	...	...	...	...	...	3
2	Hill Dist. of Arakan	...	...	...	...	...	...	...	...	...	...	...	...	...	...	...	...
3	Kyaukpyu ...	1	...	1	...	...	...	...	...	2	...	...	...	...	...	...	2
4	Sandoway ...	...	...	...	...	3	...	...	3	5	...	...	...	...	...	...	5
	Pegu Division ...	148	59	29	60	620	†394	16	210	1,221	458	23	5	...	9	...	740
5	Rangoon Town ...	130	59	19	52	603	†387	16	200	667	306	11	...	...	3	...	3[illegible]0
6	Insein ...	...	...	...	...	...	...	...	...	208	48	8	3	...	1	...	152
7	Hanthawaddy ...	...	...	...	...	1	1	...	...	6	4	...	...	...	...	...	2
8	Tharrawaddy ...	...	...	...	...	9	...	...	9	107	32	...	...	...	...	...	75
9	Pegu ...	18	...	10	8	1	...	...	1	120	52	1	2	...	3	...	67
10	Prome ...	...	...	...	...	6	6	...	...	113	16	3	...	...	2	...	94
	Irrawaddy Division ...	5	*5	...	...	7	...	2	5	569	192	24	26	1	7	1	353
11	Bassein ...	...	...	...	...	1	...	1	...	353	131	12	19	1	6	...	210
12	Henzada ...	...	...	...	...	6	...	1	5	26	7	...	...	...	...	...	19
13	Myaungmya ...	5	*5	...	...	...	...	...	...	92	21	4	4	...	...	...	67
14	Ma-ubin ...	...	...	...	...	...	...	...	...	46	25	8	3	...	1	1	13
15	Pyapôn ...	...	...	...	...	...	...	...	...	52	8	...	...	...	...	...	44
	Tenasserim Division ...	2	...	1	1	2	...	...	2	302	77	4	3	...	...	...	221
16	Toungoo ...	...	...	...	...	2	...	...	2	155	24	1	3	...	...	...	130
17	Salween ...	...	...	...	...	...	...	...	...	2	1	...	...	...	...	...	1
18	Thatôn ...	...	...	...	...	...	...	...	...	43	23	2	...	...	...	...	18
19	Amherst ...	...	...	...	...	...	...	...	...	75	10	1	...	...	...	...	64
20	Tavoy ...	1	...	...	1	...	...	...	...	19	13	...	...	...	...	...	6
21	Mergui ...	1	...	1	...	...	...	...	...	8	6	...	...	...	...	...	2
	Magwe Division ...	...	...	...	...	141	17	12	112	96	47	...	2	...	...	...	49
22	Thayetmyo ...	...	...	...	...	110	...	...	110	13	5	...	...	...	...	...	8
23	Pakôkku ...	...	...	...	...	2	...	2	...	60	31	...	2	...	...	...	29
24	Minbu ...	...	...	...	...	26	14	10	2	23	11	...	...	...	...	...	12
25	Magwe ...	...	...	...	...	3	3	...	...	...	...	...	...	...	...	...	...
26	Pakôkku Hill Tracts	...	...	...	...	...	...	...	...	...	...	...	...	...	...	...	...
	Mandalay Division ...	327	164	97	66	119	20	29	70	459	278	12	2	...	3	...	169
27	Mandalay ...	325	164	97	64	104	18	29	57	402	260	10	2	...	1	...	132
	Mandalay City ...	*325*	*164*	*97*	*64*	*104*	*18*	*29*	*57*	*345*	*228*	*8*	...	...	...	...	*109*
28	Bhamo ...	2	...	...	2	6	...	...	6	18	4	...	...	...	...	...	14
29	Myitkyina ...	...	...	...	...	...	...	...	...	28	7	2	...	...	2	...	19
30	Katha ...	...	...	...	...	7	...	...	7	11	7	...	...	...	...	...	4
31	Putao ...	...	...	...	...	2	2	...	...	...	...	...	...	...	...	...	...
	Sagaing Division ...	130	6	107	17	135	†75	†31	29	164	109	1	1	...	11	...	54
32	Shwebo ...	123	...	*106	17	...	...	...	...	80	57	...	...	...	9	...	23
33	Sagaing ...	1	...	1	...	118	†58	†31	29	49	25	...	1	...	...	...	24
34	Lower Chindwin ...	6	6	...	...	12	12	...	...	31	24	...	...	...	2	...	7
35	Upper Chindwin ...	...	...	...	...	5	5	...	...	1	...	1	...	...	...	...	...
36	Chin Hills ...	...	...	...	...	...	...	...	...	3	3	...	...	...	...	...	...
	Meiktila Division ...	...	...	...	...	1	1	...	...	162	107	...	6	...	3	...	55
37	Kyauksè ...	...	...	...	...	...	...	...	...	4	3	...	...	...	...	...	1
38	Meiktila ...	...	...	...	...	...	...	...	...	67	55	...	3	...	1	...	12
39	Yamèthin ...	...	...	...	...	...	...	...	...	30	18	...	3	...	1	...	12
40	Myingyan ...	...	...	...	...	1	1	...	...	61	31	...	...	...	1	...	30
	Eastern States ...	12	*11	...	1	...	...	...	...	57	34	8	3	...	3	...	15
41	Northern Shan States	11	*11	...	...	...	...	...	...	51	31	8	3	...	3	...	12
42	Southern Shan States	1	...	...	1	...	...	...	...	3	2	...	...	...	...	...	1
43	Karenni ...	...	...	...	...	...	...	...	...	3	1	...	...	...	...	...	2

* One male in Northern Shan States had an agricultural subsidiary occupation: 1 male in Myaungmya, 3 females in Shwebo and 4 males in Northern Shan States had non-agricultural subsidiary occupations.

† Two males in Rangoon Town district and 6 males and 2 females in Sagaing district had agricultural subsidiary occupations: 6 males in Rangoon Town district and 1 female in Sagaing district had non-agricultural subsidiary occupations.

PART III.—*Details by districts*—contd.

Other industries—*concld.* Group 102.* Total Workers and Dependents.	Group 103.—Scavengers and sweepers. Total Workers and Dependents.	Group 103. Workers. Total Workers. Males.	Group 103. Workers. Total Workers. Females	Group 103. Workers with an agricultural or other subsidiary occupation. Agricultural. Males.	Agricultural. Females	Other. Males.	Other. Females	Group 103. Dependents.	Order XIX.† Group 104.† Total Workers and Dependents.	Order XX.—Transport by water. Group 105.—Persons (other than persons of Group 108 and labourers) employed in harbours and docks. Total Workers and Dependents.	Group 105. Workers.‡ Males.	Group 105. Workers.‡ Females	Group 105. Dependents.	Group 106.—Labourers in harbours and docks not of Group 109. Total Workers and Dependents.	Group 106. Workers. (All males without subsidiary occupation). Males.	Group 106. Dependents.	Serial No. of District, etc. (column 1).
18	19	20	21	22	23	24	25	26	27	28	29	30	31	32	33	34	
...	10,569	5,844	738	16	...	37	...	3,987	...	1,475	662	13	800	17	2	15	
...	10,451	5,784	731	10	...	25	..	3,936	...	1,475	662	13	800	17	2	15	
...	378	251	35	...		..	...	92	...	14	5	...	9	...	...	...	
...	326	215	35	...	..	...	...	76	...	14	5	...	9	...	...	...	1
...	7	5	...	...	.	...	...	2	...	..	...	...	...	...	...	...	2
...	3	2	...	...	...	...	...	1	...	...	...	...	...	..	...	...	3
...	42	29	...	.	..	...	...	13	...	...	...	...	...	..	...	...	4
...	5,047	2,578	448	4	.	7	...	2,021	..	941	‡461	...	480	...	...	...	
..	3,684	1,831	372	...	...	1	...	1,481		895	‡450	...	445	...	...	...	5
...	334	132	45	3	...	4	...	157	...	...	..	...	...	..	...	...	6
...	133	96	3	...		1	...	34	...	6	3	...	3	...	...	...	7
...	387	213	15	...	...	...	...	159	...	6	6	...	...	...	...	...	8
...	161	118	1	1	...	...	...	42	...	32	...	...	32	...	...	...	9
...	348	188	12	...	...	1	..	148	...	2	2	...	...	...	...	...	10
...	980	756	39	.	...	3	.	185	...	86	‡63	...	23	8	2	6	
...	446	370	18		.	...	..	58	...	55	49	...	6	...	...	...	11
...	196	126	13	..	...	...	...	57	...	11	‡ 6	...	5	8	2	6	12
..	65	48	3	...	...	..	...	14	...	...	...	...	...	...	...	...	13
...	131	102	3	...	...	3	...	26	..	20	8	...	12	...	..	...	14
...	142	110	2	...	...	.	..	30	...	...	...		...	...	...	...	15
...	749	349	67	...	.	1	...	333	.	31	12	...	19	9	...	9	
...	249	169	15	...	...	1	...	65	...	1	.	...	1	...	...	...	16
..	2	2	.	...	...	...	.	...	...	...	...	...	...	...	...	...	17
...	63	9	7	...	...	.	...	47	...	...	..	..	...	...	...	...	18
...	220	70	25	..	...	...	...	125	...	26	8	...	18	9	...	9	19
...	175	80	1		...	...	...	94	...	...	...	...	...	...	...	...	20
..	40	19	19	...	...	...	...	2	...	4	4	...	...	..	...	...	21
...	674	364	10	1	...	7	...	300	..	251	‡57	13	181	...	...	...	
...	86	49	2	...	...	1	...	35	..	77	‡39	...	38	...	...	...	22
...	193	84	1	1	...	5	...	108	...	139	3	13	123	...	.	...	23
...	156	73	1	...	...	1	...	82		5	1	..	4	...	...	.	24
...	235	154	6	.	...	..	...	75	...	30	14	..	16	...	...	...	25
...	4	4	...	...	...	...	...	...	...	...	...	..	...	..	...	...	26
.	1,546	997	108	...	.	1	...	441	...	69	27	...	42	...	...	...	
...	1,220	800	105	...	.	...	...	315	...	44	17	...	27	...	...	...	27
...	*784*	*479*	*97*	...	...	...	...	*208*	...	*28*	*13*	...	*15*	...	...	...	
..	92	64	...	..	...	..	...	28	...	11	3	...	8	...	...	...	28
...	157	81	2	...	...	..	...	74	...	...	...	...	...	.	...	...	29
..	54	32	..		..	1	..	22	...	14	7	..	7	...	...	...	30
...	23	20	1	..	..	...	.	2	...	...	...	...	...	...	..	...	31
...	456	228	8	5	...	4	..	220	..	72	‡29	..	43	...	...	...	
...	118	53	...	...	...	...	...	65	...	5	4	...	1	.	...	...	32
	93	50	8	4	...	1	...	35	.	50	‡19	...	31	...	...	...	33
..	123	52	..		...	...	...	71	...	10	1	...	9	...	...	...	34
...	75	49	...	1	...	3	...	26	..	7	5	...	2	..	...	...	35
...	47	24	...	...	...	..	...	23	...	...	...	...	..	...	...	...	36
...	621	261	16	..	...	2	...	344	.	11	8	...	3	...	...	...	
...	36	25	1	...	...	...	...	10		...	...	..	.	.	...	...	37
...	243	109	4	...	...	2	.	130	...	...	...	..	...	...	...	...	38
...	220	66	6	...	...	...	...	148	...	...	...	...	...	...	...	...	39
...	122	61	5	..	...	..	...	56	...	11	8	..	3	...	...	...	40
...	118	60	7	...	...	12	...	51	..	...	...	...	...	...	...	...	
...	76	30	6	...	...	2	...	40	..	...	...	...	...	...	...	...	41
..	42	30	1	...	...	10	...	11	...	...	...	...	...	...	...	...	42
.	..	...	...	...	...	...	...	...	...	...	...	...	...	...	...	...	43

* Contractors for the disposal of refuse, dust, etc.

† Transport by air (aeroplanes, etc., and aerodromes).

‡ All without subsidiary occupations except 2 males in Rangoon Town, 1 male in Henzada, 1 male in Thayetmyo and 2 males in Sagaing districts have non-agricultural subsidiary occupations.

Order XX.—

Serial No.	DISTRICT OR STATE.	Group 107a.—Ship-owners, ship-brokers and shipping agents and all their employees not in Group 107b. Total Workers and Dependents.	WORKERS. Total Workers. Males.	Total Workers. Females.	Workers with an agricultural or other subsidiary occupation. Agricultural. Males	Agricultural. Females.	Other. Males	Other. Females.	DEPENDENTS.	Group 107b.—Ships' officers and engineers. Total Workers and Dependents.	WORKERS. Total Workers. Males.	Total Workers. Females.	Workers with an agricultural or other subsidiary occupation. Agricultural. Males.	Agricultural. Females.	Other. Males	Other. Females.	DEPENDENTS.
	1	2	3	4	5	6	7	8	9	10	11	12	13	14	15	16	17
	Provincial Total ...	16,881	13,971	121	40	...	70	.	2,789	5,225	4,128	2	18	...	59	...	1,095
	Divisional Burma ...	16,786	13,876	121	40	...	70	..	2,789	5,216	4,120	2	18	...	59	...	1,094
	Arakan Division ...	2,062	1,945	10	..	..	5	..	107	44	24	...	...	...	1	...	20
1	Akyab ...	2,001	1,924	...	..	...	5	...	77	4	2	..	...	...	...	...	2
2	Hill Dist. of Arakan	3	3	...	...	...	.	...	...	3	3	...	...	...	...	...	...
3	Kyaukpyu ...	41	13	10	...	...	...	...	18	26	9	...	...	...	1	...	17
4	Sandoway ...	17	5	...	..	...	...	...	12	11	10	...	...	...	...	...	1
	Pegu Division ...	10,149	8,150	16	32	...	47	...	1,983	3,003	2,319	1	...	...	5	...	683
5	Rangoon Town ...	9,196	7,381	16	25	...	46	...	1,799	2,780	2,173	...	...	...	5	...	607
6	Insein ...	64	62	...	..	..	...	...	2	50	27	1	...	...	...	...	22
7	Hanthawaddy ...	737	568	..	.	...	...	..	169	44	26	...	...	...	...	...	18
8	Tharrawaddy ...	...	...	...	...	...	...	...	...	80	62	...	..	...	...	...	18
9	Pegu ...	23	17	..	..	...	1	...	6	27	15	...	...	...	...	...	12
10	Prome ...	129	122	...	7	...	...	...	7	22	16	...	...	...	...	...	6
	Irrawaddy Division ...	1,386	1,274	4	..	.	.	...	108	538	425	...	1	...	2	...	110
11	Bassein ...	573	531	..	...	...	...	...	42	25	4	...	...	...	...	...	21
12	Henzada ...	56	51	1	...	...	...	...	4	112	69	...	...	...	...	...	43
13	Myaungmya ...	162	134	2	...	...	...	...	26	109	99	...	1	...	2	...	10
14	Ma-ubin ...	395	360	1	..		...	...	34	172	138	...	...	...	...	...	34
15	Pyapôn ...	200	198	...	...	...	...	..	2	117	115	...	...	...	...	...	2
	Tenasserim Division ...	1,516	1,170	1	3	...	5	...	345	362	258	...	...	...	...	...	104
16	Toungoo ...	4	1	...	.	...	...	...	3	13	2	...	...	...	...	...	11
17	Salween ...	4	...	...	...	...	...	...	4	7	5	...	...	...	...	...	2
18	Thatôn ...	40	33	...	...	...	...	...	7	5	5	...	...	..	...	...	...
19	Amherst ...	1,097	849	...	...	.	..	...	248	221	163	...	...	...	...	...	58
20	Tavoy ...	71	38	...	'	.	.	...	33	64	40	...	...	...	...	...	24
21	Mergui ...	300	249	1	2	...	5	...	50	52	43	...	...	...	...	...	9
	Magwe Division ...	565	352	90	3	...	12	...	123	169	125	...	1	...	4	...	44
22	Thayetmyo ...	256	63	90	...	...	6	...	103	32	24	...	...	...	4	...	8
23	Pakôkku ...	91	82	..	3	...	...	...	9	40	19	...	1	...	...	...	21
24	Minbu ...	22	19	..	...	...	...	...	3	15	10	...	..	...	...	...	5
25	Magwe ...	196	188	...	...	...	6	...	8	82	72	...	...	...	...	...	10
26	Pakôkku Hill Tracts	...	...	...	...	...	...	...	...	...	...	...	...	...	...	...	...
	Mandalay Division ...	737	653	...	2	...	...	...	84	921	804	...	16	...	45	...	117
27	Mandalay ...	551	479	...	...	...	...	...	72	821	741	...	15	...	45	...	80
	Mandalay City ...	*493*	*429*	..	...	...	...	...	*64*	*132*	*59*	...	...	...	...	...	*73*
28	Bhamo ..	76	73	...	...	...	...	...	3	53	30	..	...	...	...	...	23
29	Myitkyina ...	68	60	...	2	...	...	...	8	22	14	...	1	...	...	...	8
30	Katha ...	42	41	...	...	...	..	...	1	25	19	...	...	...	..	...	6
31	Putao ...	...	...	...	...	...	...	...	...	...	...	...	...	...	...	...	...
	Sagaing Division ...	283	261	...	...	...	...	..	22	127	114	1	...	...	1	...	12
32	Shwebo ...	16	16	...	...	..	...	...	...	13	13	...	...	...	1	...	...
33	Sagaing ...	124	108	...	...	...	..	...	16	39	27	...	...	...	...	...	12
34	Lower Chindwin ...	39	33	...	..	...	...	...	6	43	42	1	...	..	...	...	..
35	Upper Chindwin ...	104	104	...	...	...	...	...	...	32	32	...	...	...	...	...	...
36	Chin Hills ...	...	...	...	...	...	...	...	...	...	...	...	...	...	...	...	...
	Meiktila Division ...	88	71	...	...	...	1	...	17	55	51	...	...	...	2	...	4
37	Kyauksè ...	...	...	...	...	...	...	...	...	...	...	...	...	...	...	...	...
38	Meiktila ...	1	1	...	...	...	...	...	...	...	...	...	...	...	..	...	..
39	Yamèthin ...	28	28	...	...	...	...	...	...	31	31	...	...	...	1	...	..
40	Myingyan ...	59	42	.	...	...	1	...	17	24	20	...	...	...	...	...	4
	Eastern States ...	95	95	..	...	...	...	...	...	9	8	...	...	...	1	...	1
41	Northern Shan States	44	44	..	..	...	...	...	...	...	...	..	...	...	...	...	...
42	Southern Shan States	51	51	...	...	...	..	...	...	9	8	..	...	...	...	...	1
43	Karenni ...	...	...	...	...	...	...	...	...	...	...	...	...	...	...	...	...

Transport by water—*contd.*

Group 108.—Persons (other than labourers) employed on the construction and maintenance of harbours, docks, streams, rivers and canals.								Group 109.—Labourers associated with the work of persons of Group 108.			Group 110a.—Boat-owners and their employees other than Group 110b.								
Total Workers and Dependents.	WORKERS. Total Workers.		Workers with an agricultural or other subsidiary occupation. Agricultural.		Other.		DEPENDENTS.	Total Workers and Dependents.	WORKERS. (All, males without subsidiary occupation.)	DEPENDENTS.	Total Workers and Dependents.	WORKERS. Total Workers.		Workers with an agricultural or other subsidiary occupation. Agricultural.		Other.		DEPENDENTS.	Serial No. of District, etc. (column 1).
	Males.	Females.	Males.	Females.	Males.	Females.						Males.	Females.	Males.	Females.	Males.	Females.		
18	19	20	21	22	23	24	25	26	27	28	29	30	31	32	33	34	35	36	
2,084	942	98	31	...	98	2	1,044	25	3	22	15,733	7,081	405	153	...	272	19	8,247	
2,059	933	93	30	...	98	2	1,033	10	3	7	15,715	7,073	405	153	...	272	19	8,237	
2	...	...	...	...	...	...	2	...	...	...	565	90	17	5	...	16	1	458	
...	...	...	...	...	...	...	...	...	...	...	297	18	7	2	...	2	1	272	1
...	...	...	...	...	...	...	...	...	...	...	1	1	...	...	...	...	...	...	2
...	...	...	...	...	...	...	...	...	...	...	53	27	2	...	...	12	...	24	3
2	...	...	...	...	...	...	2	...	...	...	214	44	8	3	...	2	...	162	4
70	48	...	...	...	...	...	22	8	2	6	7,799	4,102	71	61	...	71	2	3,626	
...	...	...	...	...	...	...	...	...	...	...	1,725	1,288	1	...	...	1	...	436	5
...	...	...	...	...	...	...	...	...	...	...	1,985	739	64	12	...	12	2	1,182	6
32	19	...	...	...	...	...	...	6	...	6	3,343	1,699	4	46	...	50	...	1,640	7
47	28	...	...	...	...	...	3	...	...	...	127	39	...	...	...	1	...	88	8
1	1	...	...	...	...	...	19	2	2	...	380	218	2	...	...	3	...	166	9
		...	...	...	...	...	...	...	...	...	239	125	...	3	...	4	...	114	10
21	...	...	...	...	...	...	21	...	...	...	2,550	712	200	8	...	38	2	1,638	
4	...	...	...	...	...	...	4	...	...	...	500	231	...	4	...	16	...	269	11
...	...	...	...	...	...	...	...	...	...	...	491	205	1	4	...	15	...	285	12
...	...	...	...	...	...	...	...	...	...	...	457	74	55	...	...	4	...	328	13
17	...	...	...	...	...	...	17	...	...	...	890	134	139	...	...	3	2	617	14
...	...	...	...	...	...	...	...	...	...	...	212	68	5	...	...	...	...	139	15
201	9	65	...	...	...	...	127	...	...	...	2,908	1,413	83	28	...	41	6	1,412	
...	...	...	...	...	...	...	...	...	...	...	765	436	1	...	...	21	...	328	16
...	...	...	...	...	...	...	...	...	...	...	22	12	...	...	...	...	...	10	17
...	...	...	...	...	...	...	...	...	...	...	393	128	...	6	...	4	...	265	18
197	5	65	...	...	...	...	127	...	...	...	1,223	694	70	19	...	...	6	459	19
4	4	...	...	...	...	...	...	...	...	...	216	56	9	3	...	5	...	145	20
...	...	...	...	...	...	...	...	...	...	...	295	87	3	...	...	11	...	205	21
321	29	9	...	...	4	2	283	1	...	1	1,055	370	4	42	...	41	...	681	
...	...	...	...	...	...	...	...	...	...	...	178	90	...	...	...	...	...	88	22
...	...	...	...	...	...	...	...	...	...	...	194	133	...	35	...	22	...	61	23
319	29	9	...	...	4	2	281	1	...	1	93	27	3	7	...	2	...	63	24
2	...	...	...	...	...	...	2	...	...	...	590	120	1	...	...	17	...	469	25
...	...	...	...	...	...	...	...	...	...	...	...	...	...	...	...	...	...	...	26
32	24	3	...	...	...	...	5	...	...	...	310	145	7	3	...	23	...	158	
11	11	...	...	...	...	...	...	...	...	...	79	26	...	...	...	1	...	53	27
1	1	...	...	...	...	...	...	...	...	...	45	...	...	...	...	...	...	45	
...	...	...	...	...	...	...	...	...	...	...	170	81	7	1	...	17	...	82	28
6	6	...	...	...	...	...	...	...	...	...	11	8	...	2	...	...	...	3	29
15	7	3	...	...	...	...	5	...	...	...	50	30	...	...	...	5	...	20	30
...	...	...	...	...	...	...	...	...	...	...	...	...	...	...	...	...	...	...	31
1,326	781	14	29	...	94	...	521	...	...	...	390	181	15	5	...	35	5	194	
835	469	14	9	...	33	...	352	...	...	...	23	19	4	...	...	3	...	...	32
...	...	...	...	...	...	...	...	...	...	...	202	69	...	5	...	13	...	133	33
11	11	...	1	...	...	...	...	...	...	...	54	39	...	...	...	13	...	15	34
470	301	...	19	...	61	...	169	...	...	...	111	54	11	...	...	6	5	46	35
...	...	...	...	...	...	...	...	...	...	...	...	...	...	...	...	...	...	...	36
96	42	2	1	...	...	...	52	1	1	...	138	60	8	1	...	7	3	70	
15	4	...	...	...	...	...	11	...	...	...	...	...	...	...	...	...	...	...	37
40	16	...	1	...	...	...	24	1	1	...	...	...	...	...	...	...	...	...	38
36	21	2	...	...	...	...	13	...	...	...	...	...	...	...	...	...	...	...	39
5	1	...	...	...	...	...	4	...	...	...	138	60	8	1	...	7	3	70	40
25	9	5	1	...	...	...	11	15	...	15	18	8	...	...	...	...	...	10	
12	1	5	...	...	...	...	6	15	...	15	...	...	...	...	...	...	...	...	41
13	8	...	1	...	...	...	5	...	...	...	17	8	...	...	...	...	...	9	42
...	...	...	...	...	...	...	...	...	...	...	1	...	...	...	...	...	...	1	43

Serial No.	District or State.	Order XX.—Transport by water—*concld.* Group 110b.—Boatmen and towmen. Total Workers and Dependents.	Workers. Total Workers. Males.	Total Workers. Females.	Workers with an agricultural or other subsidiary occupation. Agricultural. Males.	Agricultural. Females.	Other. Males.	Other. Females.	Dependents.	Order XXI.— Group 111.—Persons (other than labourers) employed on construction and maintenance of roads and bridges. Total Workers and Dependents.	Workers. Total Workers. Males.	Total Workers. Females.	Workers with an agricultural or other subsidiary occupation. Agricultural. M's.	Agricultural. Females.	Other. M's.	Other. Females.	Dependents
	1	2	3	4	5	6	7	8	9	10	11	12	13	14	15	16	17
	Provincial Total ..	76,643	38,131	1,711	2,065	22	1,446	174	36,801	4,869	1,703	212	6	4	22	12	2,954
	Divisional Burma .	75,973	37,972	1,545	2,046	18	1,430	139	36,456	4,608	1,606	211	3	4	20	12	2,791
	Arakan Division ...	7,667	6,051	86	1,717	2	187	5	1,530	166	70	...	...	...	1	...	96
1	Akyab	6,852	5,798	64	1,708	..	134	3	990	99	47	...	..	..	.	...	52
2	Hill Dist. of Arakan	8	8	...	...	.	...	..	...	4	1	...	...	...	...	...	3
3	Kyaukpyu ..	190	39	19	5	2	11	2	132	21	8	...	..	..	...	...	13
4	Sandoway ...	617	206	3	4	..	42	..	408	42	14	...	...	...	1	...	28
	Pegu Division ...	22,069	10,912	175	59	6	203	8	10,982	1,355	410	16	2	1	5	...	929
5	Rangoon Town .	7,140	5,719	6	5	...	16	...	1,415	709	228	5	..	...	2	...	476
6	Insein	921	221	56	...	...	7	...	644	163	52	3	..	..	1	...	108
7	Hanthawddy ...	7,774	3,052	64	13	2	26	7	[illegible],658	34	17	...	1	.	...	...	17
8	Tharrawaddy ...	693	289	...	1	...	8	..	404	140	46	...	1	...	1	...	94
9	Pegu	4,357	1,019	5	12	1	77	...	3,333	248	55	8	..	1	...	...	185
10	Prome	1,184	612	44	28	3	69	1	528	61	12	...	...	..	1	...	49
	Irrawaddy Division .	15,865	8,864	493	79	1	275	52	7,308	375	112	4	...	...	1	...	259
11	Bassein ...	2,907	1,576	67	8	...	54	8	1,264	104	54	...	...	...	...	...	50
12	Henzada .	2,327	938	136	18	.	106	35	1,253	106	24	...	...	...	..	...	82
13	Myaungmya ...	1,289	961	26	9	...	35	...	302	71	18	...		...	1	...	53
14	Ma-ubin ...	2,663	1,161	80	6	...	33	1	1,422	75	13	4	...	...	...	...	58
15	Pyapôn ...	6,679	3,428	184	38	1	47	8	3,067	19	3	..	...	...	...	...	16
	Tenasserim Division ...	11,419	5,425	174	80	5	64	12	5,820	861	367	51	...	...	4	...	443
16	Toungoo ..	547	26	49	...	...	..	3	472	255	196	1	..	...	1	...	58
17	Salween ...	68	16	...	..	.	2	...	52	18	8	...	...	...	...	...	10
18	Thatôn ...	2,431	902	65	39	5	35	6	1,464	57	14	...	...	..	...	...	43
19	Amherst ...	5,972	3,176	46	24	...	7	2	2,750	306	62	50	.	.	...	...	164
20	Tavoy	951	423	9	17	...	19	1	519	185	76	.	...	..	3		109
21	Mergui ..	1,450	882	5	...	...	1	...	563	40	11	...	..	.	...	..	29
	Magwe Division ..	8,089	3,106	362	5	4	265	40	4,621	500	81	130	.	3	2	12	289
22	Thayetmyo ..	2,315	801	29	3	...	82	20	1,485	39	11	..		..	1	..	21
23	Pakôkku ..	3,489	1,273	156	...	4	122	13	2,060	32	17	...	...	..	1	...	15
24	Minbu	956	389	59	..	..	35	...	508	338	29	130	...	3	...	12	179
25	Magwe ...	1,329	643	118	2	...	25	7	568	93	23	...	...	...	...	...	70
26	Pakôkku Hill Tracts	...	...	...	..	...	..	...	...	5	1	...	...	...	...	...	4
	Mandalay Division ..	2,338	682	99	5	...	32	...	1,557	498	218	3	1	...	4	...	277
27	Mandalay ...	1,830	479	96	5	...	15	...	1,255	290	147	...	..	...	1	...	143
	Mandalay City ..	*354*	*265*	...	...	..	..	...	*89*	*140*	*86*		...	.	...	...	*54*
28	Bhamo ...	249	107	1	...	...	9	...	141	116	19	2	...	...	...	...	95
29	Myitkyina ..	171	92	2	...	...	8	...	77	58	38	...	...	...	3	...	20
30	Katha	88	4	...	...	...	...	..	84	30	10	1	..	...	...	...	19
31	Putao	...	...		...	...	...	...	...	4	4	...	1	...	..	...	...
	Sagaing Division .	7,817	3,523	128	100	...	373	17	4,166	596	282	6	..	...	3	...	308
32	Shwebo ..	245	72	8	1	...	8	3	165	214	84	5	...	.	...	...	125
33	Sagaing ...	3,259	1,368	88	55	...	87	10	1,795	59	21	1	...	...	..	..	37
34	Lower Chindwin ...	2,192	850	17	13	..	110	3	1,325	125	51	...	...	..	...	...	74
35	Upper Chindwin ...	2,129	1,233	15	31	...	168	1	881	167	110	...	.	...	2	.	57
36	Chin Hills ...	...	...	...	...	...	...	...	...	31	16	...	...	...	1	...	15
	Meiktila Division ...	709	209	28	1	..	31	5	472	257	66	1	...	...	...	...	190
37	Kyauksè ...	276	63	7	1	...	7	..	206	38	6	...	..	...	...	...	32
38	Meiktila ...	3	...	.	...	...	...	...	3	103	25	...	...	..	...	...	78
39	Yamèthin ...	75	9	.	...	...	...	..	66	71	23	1	..	...	...	.	47
40	Myingyan ...	355	137	21	...	...	24	5	197	45	12	...	...	...	...	...	33
	Eastern States ...	670	159	166	19	4	16	35	345	261	97	1	3	...	2	...	163
41	Northern Shan States	303	58	166	6	4	10	35	79	158	62	1	...	...	...	...	95
42	Southern Shan States	366	101	...	13	...	6	...	265	103	35	...	3	..	2	...	68
43	Karenni ...	1	...	...	...	...	...	...	1	...	...	...	...	...	...	...	...

Part III.—*Details by districts*—contd.

Transport on land otherwise than by rail.

Group 112.—Labourers associated with persons of Group 111.								Group 113a.—Drivers and engine-cleaners (excluding private servants) connected with mechanically driven land vehicles (including trams and taxis).								Serial No. of District, etc. (column 1).
Total Workers and Dependents.	WORKERS.						DEPENDENTS.	Total Workers and Dependents.	WORKERS.						DEPENDENTS.	
	Total Workers.		Workers with an agricultural or other subsidiary occupation.						Total Workers.		Workers with an agricultural or other subsidiary occupation.					
			Agricultural.		Other.						Agricultural.		Other.			
	Males.	Females.	Males.	Females	Males.	Females.			Males.	Females.	Males.	Females	Males.	Females		
18	19	20	21	22	23	24	25	26	27	28	29	30	31	32	33	
50,210	26,247	6,137	521	139	850	475	17,826	3,421	1,655	8	3	...	114	...	1,758	
48,912	25,372	6,023	515	139	843	472	17,517	3,244	1,530	8	3	...	9	...	1,706	
3,283	2,803	65	21	1	13	3	415	37	23	...	...	...	...	...	14	
3,009	2,708	13	18	...	10	...	288	35	21	...	...	...	...	...	14	1
5	4	...	...	...	...	...	1	...	...	...	...	...	...	...	...	2
9	8	...	1	...	...	...	1	2	2	...	...	...	...	...	...	3
260	83	52	2	1	3	3	125	...	...	...	...	...	...	...	...	4
7,993	5,452	484	82	5	67	5	2,057	1,912	913	5	...	...	7	...	994	
1,642	1,352	58	...	...	1	...	232	1,669	779	2	...	...	4	...	888	5
1,495	1,204	53	...	...	3	...	238	63	37	3	...	...	1	...	23	6
329	227	15	...	...	...	1	87	36	22	...	...	...	2	...	14	7
1,102	784	29	35	1	19	...	289	28	26	...	...	...	...	...	2	8
1,513	1,155	78	38	4	29	1	280	112	47	...	...	...	...	...	65	9
1,912	730	251	9	...	15	3	931	4	2	...	...	...	...	...	2	10
6,591	4,741	475	51	4	62	1	1,375	100	67	...	...	...	...	...	33	
1,546	1,160	90	46	4	18	...	296	80	66	...	...	...	...	...	14	11
2,503	1,637	193	3	...	7	...	673	12	1	...	...	...	...	...	11	12
903	578	120	2	...	25	1	205	...	...	...	...	...	...	...	...	13
971	795	48	...	...	12	...	128	4	...	...	...	...	.	...	4	14
668	571	24	...	...	...	...	73	4	...	...	...	...	...	...	4	15
5,333	3,777	189	38	1	16	8	1,367	809	369	2	3	...	2	...	438	
644	461	5	8	1	6	...	178	55	7	...	...	...	...	...	48	16
121	111	1	...	...	...	...	9	...	...	...	...	...	...	...	...	17
473	325	21	2	...	2	...	127	47	27	...	...	...	...	...	20	18
2,223	1,428	96	25	...	4	4	699	502	246	2	3	...	...	...	254	19
1,045	840	34	3	...	2	1	171	166	79	...	...	...	2	...	87	20
887	612	32	...	...	2	3	183	39	10	...	...	...	...	...	29	21
8,051	2,981	1,205	112	43	222	83	3,865	36	30	...	...	...	...	...	6	
920	301	67	...	2	2	3	552	7	1	...	...	...	...	...	6	22
3,484	1,341	432	29	6	139	37	1,711	1	1	...	...	...	...	...	...	23
1,004	648	62	27	...	56	2	294	...	...	...	...	...	...	...	...	24
2,641	689	644	56	35	25	41	1,308	28	28	...	...	...	...	...	...	25
2	2	...	...	...	...	...	...	...	...	...	...	...	...	...	...	26
2,144	1,197	120	51	...	68	9	827	124	64	1	...	...	...	...	59	
1,456	750	63	...	...	61	6	643	34	14	1	...	...	...	...	19	27
739	*409*	*11*	...	...	*1*	...	*319*	*19*	*11*	*1*	...	...	...	...	7	
307	148	44	1	...	3	1	135	5	3	...	...	...	...	...	2	28
273	251	4	44	...	...	...	18	10	10	...	...	...	...	...	...	29
88	48	9	6	...	4	2	31	75	37	...	...	...	...	...	38	30
...	...	...	...	...	...	...	...	...	...	...	...	...	...	...	...	31
9,823	2,618	2,279	83	66	263	302	4,926	37	20	...	...	...	...	...	17	
966	122	409	2	9	11	19	435	26	14	...	...	...	...	...	12	32
5,412	1,097	1,320	37	32	134	216	2,995	7	2	...	...	...	...	...	5	33
3,018	1,141	526	44	25	103	62	1,351	...	...	...	...	...	...	...	...	34
426	258	24	...	...	115	5	144	4	4	...	...	...	...	...	...	35
1	...	...	...	...	...	...	1	...	...	...	...	...	...	...	...	36
5,694	1,803	1,206	77	19	132	61	2,685	189	44	...	...	...	...	...	145	
481	199	70	...	3	2	...	212	1	1	...	...	...	...	...	...	37
2,463	642	480	9	6	20	9	1,341	108	16	...	...	...	...	...	92	38
2,399	904	507	68	9	96	17	988	53	12	...	...	...	...	...	41	39
351	58	149	...	1	14	35	144	27	15	...	...	...	...	...	12	40
1,298	875	114	6	...	7	3	309	177	125	...	...	...	105	...	52	
1,145	865	70	6	...	7	3	210	29	7	...	...	...	...	...	22	41
153	10	44	...	...	...	...	99	148	118	...	...	...	105	.	30	42
...	...	...	...	...	...	...	...	...	...	...	...	...	...	...	...	43

Order XXI.—Transport on

Serial No.	DISTRICT OR STATE.	Group 113*b*.—All others (excluding private servants) connected with such vehicles. (See title of Group 113*a*.) — Total Workers and Dependents.	Workers — Total Workers — Males.	Workers — Total Workers — Females.	Workers with an agricultural or other subsidiary occupation — Agricultural — Males	Agricultural — Females	Other — Males	Other — Females	DEPENDENTS.	Group 114.—All (except private servants) connected with transport by vehicles drawn by animals. — Total Workers and Dependents	Workers — Total Workers — Males.	Total Workers — Females	Workers with an agricultural or other subsidiary occupation — Agricultural — Males.	Agricultural — Females	Other — Males.	Other — Females	DEPENDENTS.
	1	2	3	4	5	6	7	8	9	10	11	12	13	14	15	16	17
	Provincial Total ...	3,272	2,859	2	...	...	2	...	411	114413	45,905	5,164	1,128	147	1,860	256	63,344
	Divisional Burma ...	3,267	2,857	2	...	...	2	...	408	105139	41,873	4,541	879	89	1,425	206	58,725
	Arakan Division ...	...	...	...	...	...	...	...	...	802	436	11	2	...	5	1	355
1	Akyab ...	...	...	...	...	...	...	...	...	463	333	3	1	...	2	...	127
2	Hill Dist. of Arakan	...	...	...	...	...	...	...	...	...	...	...	...	...	...	...	...
3	Kyaukpyu ...	...	...	...	...	...	...	...	...	87	33	...	...	...	1	...	54
4	Sandoway ...	...	...	...	...	...	...	...	...	252	70	8	1	...	2	1	174
	Pegu Division ...	2,980	2,707	2	...	...	2	...	271	27,134	12,083	734	199	2	296	14	14,317
5	Rangoon Town ...	2,977	2,707	2	...	...	2	...	268	5,796	3,971	18	3	...	9	...	1,807
6	Insein ...	3	...	...	...	...	...	...	3	4,125	1,732	178	16	1	91	...	2,215
7	Hanthawaddy ...	...	...	...	...	...	...	...	...	2,137	860	54	46	1	35	1	1,523
8	Tharrawaddy ...	...	...	...	...	...	...	...	...	4,721	1,749	145	63	...	45	...	2,897
9	Pegu ...	...	...	...	...	...	...	...	...	5,467	1,957	149	53	...	77	3	3,361
10	Prome ...	...	...	...	...	...	...	...	...	4,588	1,814	190	18	...	39	10	2,584
	Irrawaddy Division ...	9	5	...	...	...	...	...	4	6,481	2,451	287	50	...	113	38	3,743
11	Bassein ...	5	5	...	...	...	...	...	...	1,274	392	61	16	...	23	3	821
12	Henzada ...	...	...	...	...	...	...	...	...	3,850	1,441	172	29	...	59	34	2,237
13	Myaungmya ...	...	...	...	...	...	...	...	...	130	65	5	...	...	4	...	60
14	Ma-ubin ...	...	...	...	...	...	...	...	...	1,182	542	49	5	...	27	1	591
15	Pyapôn ...	4	...	...	...	...	...	...	4	45	11	...	...	...	...	...	34
	Tenasserim Division ...	3	...	...	...	...	...	...	3	20,132	7,947	549	157	5	197	17	11,636
16	Toungoo ...	...	...	...	...	...	...	...	...	4,919	2,089	227	49	2	67	4	2,603
17	Salween ...	...	...	...	...	...	...	...	...	163	84	...	1	...	...	...	79
18	Thatôn ...	...	...	...	...	...	...	...	...	5,214	1,873	130	29	3	57	8	3,211
19	Amherst ...	3	...	...	...	...	...	...	3	6,914	2,583	172	31	...	39	5	4,159
20	Tavoy ...	...	...	...	...	...	...	...	...	2,435	1,120	16	45	...	30	...	1,293
21	Mergui ...	...	...	...	...	...	...	...	...	487	192	4	2	...	4	...	291
	Magwe Division ...	7	7	...	...	...	...	...	...	11,891	4,182	936	216	56	175	34	6,773
22	Thayetmyo ...	...	...	...	...	...	...	...	...	1,551	507	75	2	...	18	5	969
23	Pakôkku ...	2	2	...	...	...	...	...	...	2,590	695	208	55	5	54	10	1,687
24	Minbu ...	5	5	...	...	...	...	...	...	3,576	1,432	256	111	51	76	11	1,888
25	Magwe ...	...	...	...	...	...	...	...	...	4,174	1,548	397	48	...	27	8	2,229
26	Pakôkku Hill Tracts	...	...	...	...	...	...	...	...	...	...	...	...	...	...	...	...
	Mandalay Division ...	263	136	...	...	...	...	...	127	14,875	6,714	501	42	2	223	14	7,660
27	Mandalay ...	263	136	...	...	...	...	...	127	12,000	5,303	422	19	2	111	9	6,275
	Mandalay City .	*256*	*130*	...	...	...	...	...	*126*	*8,090*	*3,421*	*183*	*3*	...	*10*	*2*	*4,486*
28	Bhamo ...	...	...	...	...	...	...	...	...	1,430	759	18	4	...	76	...	653
29	Myitkyina ...	...	...	...	...	...	...	...	...	467	260	16	3	...	6	5	191
30	Katha ...	...	...	...	...	...	...	...	...	967	385	45	16	...	29	...	537
31	Putao ...	...	...	...	...	...	...	...	...	11	7	...	...	...	1	...	4
	Sagaing Division ...	4	1	...	...	...	...	...	3	8,991	3,229	429	118	8	217	44	5,333
32	Shwebo ...	...	...	...	...	...	...	...	...	2,627	922	165	2	...	60	9	1,540
33	Sagaing ...	...	...	...	...	...	...	...	...	3,204	1,121	68	65	1	55	16	2,015
34	Lower Chindwin ...	4	1	...	...	...	...	...	3	2,444	806	168	43	...	70	15	1,470
35	Upper Chindwin ...	...	...	...	...	...	...	...	...	716	380	28	8	7	[illegible]	4	308
36	Chin Hills ...	...	...	...	...	...	...	...	...	...	...	...	...	...	...	...	...
	Meiktila Division ...	1	1	...	...	...	...	...	...	14,833	4,831	1,094	95	16	199	44	8,908
37	Kyauksè ...	...	...	...	...	...	...	...	...	2,474	1,097	52	42	5	57	6	1,325
38	Meiktila ...	1	1	...	...	...	...	...	...	2,091	721	103	14	1	22	2	1,267
39	Yamèthin ...	...	...	...	...	...	...	...	...	6,900	1,036	737	20	3	50	18	4,227
40	Myingyan ...	...	...	...	...	...	...	...	...	3,368	1,077	202	19	7	70	18	2,089
	Eastern States ...	5	2	...	...	...	...	...	3	9,274	4,032	623	249	58	435	50	4,619
41	Northern Shan States	1	...	...	...	...	...	...	1	3,340	1,432	263	38	5	93	18	1,645
42	Southern Shan States	4	2	...	...	...	...	...	2	5,788	2,556	338	211	53	342	31	2,894
43	Karenni ...	...	...	...	...	...	...	...	...	146	44	22	...	...	...	1	80

PART III.—*Details by districts*—contd.

land otherwise than by rail—*concluded.*

Group 115.—Owners and pullers of rickshaws, etc. (excluding private servants). Total Workers and Dependents.	WORKERS.* Males.	WORKERS.* Females.	DEPENDENTS.	Group 116.—Owners and drivers of pack-elephants, mules, bullocks, etc. Total Workers and Dependents.	WORKERS. Total Workers. Males.	Total Workers. Females	Workers with an agricultural or other subsidiary occupation. Agricultural. Males	Agricultural. Females	Other. Males	Other. Females	DEPENDENTS.	Group 117.—Porters and messengers. Total Workers and Dependents.	WORKERS. Total Workers. Males.	Total Workers. Females	Workers with an agricultural or other subsidiary occupation. Agricultural. Males.	Agricultural. Females	Other. Males.	Other. Females	DEPENDENTS.	Serial No. of District, etc. (column 1).
18	19	20	21	22	23	24	25	26	27	28	29	30	31	32	33	34	35	36	37	
2,236	1,751	15	470	1,412	769	141	25	...	46	1	502	19,256	11,216	936	89	3	109	22	7,104	
2,236	1,751	15	470	472	311	20	2	...	6	...	141	18,929	10,999	935	79	3	104	22	6,995	
...	...	...	...	...	...	...	...	...	...	...	...	1,111	645	4	3	...	4	...	462	
...	...	...	...	...	...	...	...	...	...	...	...	273	181	1	1	...	...	...	91	1
...	...	...	...	...	...	...	...	...	...	...	...	25	9	...	...	...	...	...	16	2
...	...	...	...	...	...	...	...	...	...	...	...	668	429	3	2	...	4	...	236	3
...	...	...	...	...	...	...	...	...	...	...		145	26	...	...	...	...	...	119	4
1,804	1,480	6	318	20	17		...	...	...	...	3	6,474	4,963	115	2	...	3	3	1,396	
1,784	1,471	6	307	16	16	...	...	...	...	...	...	4,687	4,219	53	2	...	2	...	415	5
...	...	...	...	...	...	...	...	...	...	...	...	249	103	16	...	...	...	...	130	6
...	...	...	...	...	...	...	...	...	...	...	...	211	105	...	...	...	1	...	106	7
2	2	...	...	1	...	...	...	...	...	...	1	537	252	16	...	...	...	...	269	8
12	1	...	11	3	1	...	...	...	...	...	2	295	94	2	...	...	...	...	199	9
6	6	...	...	...	...	...	...	...	...	...	...	495	190	28	...	...	...	3	277	10
180	112	4	64	...	...	...	...	...	...	...	...	2,452	1,654	45	1	...	12	...	753	
72	39	3	30	...	...	...	...	...	...	...	...	1,045	986	1	...	...	5	...	58	11
...	...	...	...	...	...	...	...	...	...	...	...	624	294	24	1	...	1	...	306	12
3	1	...	2	...	...	...	...	...	...	...	...	258	123	1	...	...	4	...	134	13
6	5	...	1	...	...	...	...	...	...	...	...	209	76	19	...	...	...	...	114	14
99	67	1	31	...	...	...	...	...	...	...	...	316	175	...	...	...	2	...	141	15
246	*159	5	82	95	64	4	2	...	5	...	27	1,149	567	13	...	...	5	...	569	
215	*151	4	60	49	20	4	...	...	1		25	201	35	1	...	...	1	...	165	16
...	...	...	...	9	7	...	1	...	...	...	2	24	15	...	...	...	...	...	9	17
...	...	...	...	...	...	...	...	...	...	...	...	328	179	...	...	...	2	...	149	18
23	...	1	22	5	5		...	...	...	...	...	367	210	12	...	...	2	...	145	19
...	...	...	...	1	1	...	...	...	...	...	—	162	86	...	...	...	...	...	76	20
*8	*8	...	...	31	31	...	1	...	4		...	67	42	...	...	...	...	...	25	21
...	...	...	...	9	9	...	...		...	...	...	3,893	1,583	481	4	...	36	1	1,829	
...	...	...		...	...	...	...	...	...	...	...	381	236	...	...	...	...	...	145	22
...	...	...	...	1	1	...	...	...	...	...	...	1,590	529	125	3	...	10	...	866	23
...	...	...	...	8	8	...	...	...	...	...	...	406	126	38	...	...	8	...	242	24
...	...	...	...	...	...	...	...	...	...	...	...	1,586	692	318	1	...	18	1	576	25
...	...	...	...	...	...	...	...	...	...	...	...	...	...	...	...	...	...	...	...	26
...	...	...	...	171	107	6	...	...	...	...	58	1,541	759	49	61	1	14	...	733	
...	...	...	...	...	...	...	...		...	...	...	1,183	534	45	3	...	7	...	604	27
...		...	...	...	...	...	...	...	...	...	...	*897*	*358*	*45*	...	...	*2*	...	*494*	
...	...	...	...	41	40	...	...	...	...	...	1	47	36	...	...	...	...	...	11	28
...	...	...	...	102	57	4	...	...	...	...	41	175	115	...	58	...	7	...	60	29
...	...	...	...	28	10	2	...	...	...	...	16	120	64	4	...	1	...	...	52	30
...	...	...	...	...	...	...	...	...	...	...	...	16	10	...	...	...	...	...	6	31
...	...	...	...	122	59	10	...	...	1	...	53	1,461	583	228	6	2	24	18	650	
...	...	...	...	...	...	...	...	...	...	...	...	197	98	22	2	...	3	...	77	32
...	...	...	...	...	...		...	...	...	...	...	560	237	78	4	2	14	5	245	33
...	...	...	...	...		...	...	...	...	...	...	461	158	86	...	...	4	6	217	34
...	...	...	...	115	58	10	...	...	1	...	47	216	81	42	...	...	3	7	93	35
...	...	...	...	7	1		...	...	...	...	6	27	9	...	...	...	...	...	18	36
6	...	...	6	55	55	...	...	...	...	...	...	848	245	...	2	...	6	...	603	
...	...	...	...	1	1	...	...	...	...	...	...	256	95	...	...	...	1	...	161	37
...	...	...	...	54	54	...	...	...	...	...	...	379	77	...	2	...	5	...	302	38
6	...	...	6	...	...	...	...	...	...	...	...	46	30	...	...	...	...	...	16	39
...	...	...	...	...	...	...	...	...	...	...	...	167	43	...	...	...	...	...	124	40
...	...	...	...	940	458	121	23	...	40	1	361	327	217	1	10	...	5	...	109	
...	...	...	...	915	444	121	21	...	39	1	350	36	28	1	3	...	...	...	7	41
...	...	...	...	24	13	...	2	...	1	...	11	216	145	...	2	...	5	...	71	42
...	...	...	...	1	1	...	...	...	...	...	...	75	44	...	5	...	...	...	31	43

* All without subsidiary occupations except 4 males in Toungoo and 1 male in Mergui district with non-agricultural subsidiary occupations.

Serial No.	DISTRICT OR STATE.	Order XXII.—Transport by rail.															
		Group 118.—Railway employees of all kinds other than labourers, doctors, police, sweepers and postal service.								Group 119.—Labourers of all kinds associated with railways (excluding sweepers).							
		Total Workers and Dependents.	WORKERS.						DEPENDENTS.	Total Workers and Dependents.	WORKERS.						DEPENDENTS.
			Total Workers.		Workers with an agricultural or other subsidiary occupation.						Total Workers.		Workers with an agricultural or other subsidiary occupation.				
					Agricultural.		Other.						Agricultural.		Other.		
			Males.	Females	Males	Females	Males	Females			Males.	Females	Males	Females	Males.	Females.	
	1	2	3	4	5	6	7	8	9	10	11	12	13	14	15	16	17
	Provincial Total ...	18,000	9,716	322	10	...	36	...	7,962	9,774	6,160	506	4	...	22	2	3,108
	Divisional Burma ...	17,622	9,515	322	10	...	36		7,785	9,355	5,846	461	4	...	22	2	3,048
	Arakan Division	122	86	...	...	...	...	...	36	42	12	8	...	...	...	...	22
1	Akyab ...	122	86	...	...	...	.	..	36	42	12	8	...	...	..	..	22
2	Hill Dist. of Arakan	...	...	...	...	...		..	...	...	...	...	...	...	.	...	..
3	Kyaukpyu ..		...	..		..	...	...	...	...	...	...	...	...	.	...	...
4	Sandoway ...	..	..	..	...	...	...	..	...	...	...	...	...	...	...	...	...
	Pegu Division ...	10,372	5,737	303	4	..	17	...	4,332	4,007	2,804	67	...	..	1	...	1,136
5	Rangoon Town ..	5,405	2,834	243	...	...	2	.	2,328	2,333	1,881	1	..	..	..	...	451
6	Insein ..	2,753	1,605	48	...	...	7	...	1,1[illegible]0	442	327	11	...	...	...	...	104
7	Hanthawaddy ...	150	147	..	...	...	...	...	3	...	...		...	...	..	...	...
8	Tharrawaddy ...	857	525	1	1	.	4	...	331	135	12	5	...	...	...	...	118
9	Pegu ...	919	402	11	3	..	3		506	1,010	534	50	.	..	1	...	426
10	Prome ...	288	224	...	...	..	1	...	64	87	50	...	...	...	..	...	37
	Irrawaddy Division ...	545	224	1	...	...	1	...	320	523	375	12	...	...	5	...	136
11	Bassein ...	223	115	1	...	...	...	...	107	206	173	9	...	..	..	...	24
12	Henzada ...	318	106	...	...	...	1	...	212	317	202	3	...	...	5	.	112
13	Myaungmya ..	4	3	...		...	...	...	1	...	...	...	...	...	...	..	...
14	Ma-ubin ...	..	..	...	...	..	...	...	..	...	...	...	...	...	...	...	..
15	Pyapôn ...	.	...	..	..	.	...	..	...	...	...	...	...	...	...	...	...
	Tenasserim Division ...	2,016	1,025	8	6	...	16	...	983	1,113	849	59	..	...	...	..	205
16	Toungoo ...	1,304	650	5	...	...	10	...	649	170	20	25	...	...	...	...	125
17	Salween ...	...	...	...	...	...	...	...	...	...	...	...	...	..	...	...	...
18	Thatôn ...	471	236	3	6	..	6	...	232	160	108	10	...	...	...	...	42
19	Amherst .	240	138	...	...	.	...	...	102	783	721	24	...	...	.	...	38
20	Tavoy ...	...	...	...	...	...	...	...	..	...	...	.	...	..	...	...	...
21	Mergui ...	1	1	...		...	...	...	..	..	...	...	...	...	...	...	...
	Magwe Division ...	40	40	.	.	...	...		...	11	..	9	...	...	...	...	2
22	Thayetmyo ...	1	1	.	...	...	...	...	...	..	...	...	...	...	...	...	...
23	Pakôkku ...	...	..	...	..	...	...	...	..		...	...	...	...	...	...	...
24	Minbu ...	2	2	...	...	..	...	...	...	...	...	...	...	...	...	...	..
25	Magwe ...	37	37	...	.	...	...	...	..	11	...	9	...	...	...	...	2
26	Pakôkku Hill Tracts	...	..	...	...		...	...	...	...	.	...	...	...	...	...	...
	Mandalay Division ...	2,314	1,490	6	...	..		..	818	1,520	822	137	4	...	6	..	561
27	Mandalay ...	1,945	1,301	5	...	...	...	..	639	1,187	563	126	..	.	...	...	498
	Mandalay City ...	*423*	*211*	...	..	..	..	...	*212*	*536*	*233*	*28*	...		...	...	*275*
28	Bhamo ..	17	3	...	..	..	.	...	14	.	...	...	...	...	...	...	...
29	Myitkyina ...	158	89	...	...	..	...	...	69	199	173	2	1	...	1	...	24
30	Katha ...	191	95	1		..	...	...	95	134	86	9	3	...	5	...	39
31	Putao ...	3	2	...	...	..	...	...	1	...	...	...	...	...	...	...	...
	Sagaing Division ...	761	326	...	...	..	2	..	435	784	398	27	...	...	3	...	359
32	Shwebo .	308	145	...	..	...	2	...	163	258	109	13	..	...	2	..	136
33	Sagaing ...	405	143	...	...	..	...	...	262	430	249	14	...	...	1	...	167
34	Lower Chindwin ...	48	38	..	...	...	...	...	10	96	40	...	...	..	...		56
35	Upper Chindwin ...	...	...	...	...	...	..	...	...	...	...	...	...	...	...	...	...
36	Chin Hills ...	...	...	...	...	...	...	...	...	...	...	...	...	...	...	...	...
	Meiktila Division ...	1,452	587	4	.	...	...	...	861	1,355	586	142	...	...	7	2	627
37	Kyaukse ...	162	53	...	...	...	...	...	109	...	...	...	..	..	...	...	...
38	Meiktila ...	397	147	..	...	...	...	...	250	590	225	53	...	...	3	..	312
39	Yamèthin ...	782	344	4	...	..	...	...	434	656	350	41	...	...	4	2	265
40	Myingyan ...	111	43	...	...	...	...	...	68	109	11	48	...	...	...	...	50
	Eastern States ...	378	201	...	.	.	...	..	177	419	314	45	.	..	...	...	60
41	Northern Shan States	345	183	...	...	...	...	...	162	418	314	45	...	...	...	...	59
42	Southern Shan States	33	18	...	...	...	...	...	15	1	...	...	...	...	...	...	1
43	Karenni ...	.	...	..	...	...	...	...	...	...	...	...	...	...	...	...	...

PART III.—*Details by districts*—contd.

Total Workers and Dependents.	WORKERS. Total Workers. Males.	Females.	Workers with an agricultural or other subsidiary occupation. Agricultural. Males.	Females.	Other. Males.	Females.	DEPENDENTS.	Total Workers and Dependents.	WORKERS. Total Workers. Males.	Females.	Workers with an agricultural or other subsidiary occupation. Agricultural. Males.	Females.	Other. Males.	Females.	DEPENDENTS.	Serial No. of District, etc. (column 1).
* Order XXVI.—Trade in cotton, silk, hair or other textiles or in piece-goods.																
Group 123*a*.—Wholesale dealers and brokers.								Group 123*b*.—Retail dealers and hawkers.								
18	19	20	21	22	23	24	25	26	27	28	29	30	31	32	33	
10,762	4,669	932	83	3	129	35	5,161	44,544	10,212	16,262	114	275	579	874	18,070	
10,447	4,483	913	37	3	118	31	5,051	42,303	9,489	15,745	82	248	497	744	17,069	
60	44	...	1	...	4	...	16	1,841	946	294	8	6	37	8	601	
40	32	...	...	..	3	...	8	1,557	807	259	5	2	30	4	491	1
...	...	...	..	...	...	...	..	18	13	...	...	...	...	...	5	2
1	1	...	...	...	...	...	...	...	...	..	...	...	...	...	...	3
19	11	...	1	..	1	...	8	266	126	35	3	4	7	4	105	4
5,040	2,389	171	...	...	11	1	2,480	8,459	2,160	1,408	4	16	53	41	4,891	
4,118	2,278	53	...	...	9	1	1,787	1,576	363	396	...	...	2	2	817	5
187	36	81	..		...	...	70	287	94	31	...	.	7	...	162	6
32	4	...	...	..	1	...	78	1,880	425	116	4	...	4	23	1,339	7
561	17	28	...	.	...	...	516	818	331	175	3	3	9	3	312	8
1	...	1	.	...	...	...	..	1,247	383	234	1	9	26	5	630	9
141	54	8	...		1	...	79	2,651	564	456	...	4	5	8	1,631	10
1,022	562	50	2	...	27	8	410	3,721	1,071	1,181	3	4	54	40	1,469	
503	264	12	2	...	11	1	227	1,481	542	494	.	1	33	13	445	11
132	79	...	..	...	4	...	53	897	137	236	2	2	7	15	464	12
356	212	37	.	.	12	7	107	169	27	53	...	...	2	3	89	13
30	7	1	...	.	..	...	22	452	34	207		1	5	6	211	14
1	...	...	...	...	...	.	1	782	331	131	1	...	7	3	260	15
1,163	211	444	...	...	3	12	508	4,188	1,522	919	9	2	45	11	1,747	
390	1	191	..	...	.	4	198	814	371	87	2	1	15	2	356	16
21	20	..		...	...	...	1	5	4	1	...	...	...	...	...	17
141	105	1	...	...	1		35	1,123	429	262	2	...	9	1	432	18
126	71	6	...	...	1	..	49	1,876	587	524	5	1	13	8	765	19
240	14	200	...	...	1	8	126	234	77	38	...	...	3	...	119	20
145	...	46	..	...	...	...	99	136	54	7	...	...	5	...	75	21
345	163	12	3	...	12	...	170	10,741	1,100	6,450	26	125	104	478	3,191	
280	133	..	3	...	11	...	147	540	24	344	5	5	4	6	172	22
15	12	...	..	...	...	.	3	8,226	594	5,484	16	109	70	445	2,208	23
33	1	12	...	..	...	...	20	1,273	264	513	3	11	19	24	496	24
17	17	...	...	...	1	..	.	702	218	169	2	...	11	3	315	25
...	...	...	...	...	...	...	...	...	.	...	...	...	...	...	...	26
998	507	80	1	2	10	4	411	3,433	781	1,089	4	8	60	28	1,563	
753	436	6	...	..	6	...	311	2,550	369	964	1	7	20	16	1,217	27
565	*343*	*3*	...	...	*1*	.	*219*	*1,722*	*257*	*584*	...	...	*3*	...	*881*	
66	1	39	..	1	...	2	26	375	186	60	3		6	5	129	28
52	1	32	...	1	1	2	19	336	169	32	...	.	22	..	135	29
127	69	3	1	...	3	...	55	172	57	33	...	1	12	7	82	30
..	...	...	...	...	...	...	...	...	...	.	...	...	...	...	...	31
681	319	45	21	..	38	5	317	5,666	1,196	2,398	24	53	107	76	2,072	
3	1	...	...	...	...	...	2	1,071	295	269	..	8	18	20	507	32
513	237	27	13	..	22	1	249	2,180	193	1,527	4	8	17	8	400	33
42	21	1	2	.	4	...	20	1,819	504	489	19	32	39	42	826	34
123	60	17	6	...	12	4	46	651	204	113	1	5	23	6	334	35
...	...	...	...	...	...	...	..	5	..	..	..	...	...	...	5	36
1,138	288	111	9	1	13	1	739	4,254	713	2,006	4	34	37	62	1,535	
59	32	8	..	...	...	...	19	305	58	116	2	2	7	—	137	37
158	42	30	3	...	6	...	86	2,421	329	1,170	1	27	17	42	929	38
671	212	2	6	...	7	...	457	633	129	332	...	3	1	6	172	39
250	2	71	..	1	.	1	177	895	197	394	1	2	12	14	304	40
315	186	19	46	..	11	4	110	2,241	723	517	32	27	82	130	1,001	
104	62	8	28	..	5	2	34	2,120	716	456	32	13	82	115	948	41
211	124	11	18	...	6	2	76	120	7	61	...	14	...	15	51	42
...	...	...	..	...	...	...	...	1	..	...	...	...	...	...	1	43

* NOTE.—For Groups 120, 121, 122, see Orders XXIII, XXIV, XXV on pages 285, 286, 287 respectively.

Serial No.	DISTRICT OR STATE.	* Order XXVIII.—Trade in wood (not firewood), cork, bark, bamboo, thatch, etc., and articles made from these. Group 125a.—Wholesale dealers and brokers. Total Workers and Dependents.	WORKERS. Total Workers. Males.	Females.	Workers with an agricultural or other subsidiary occupation. Agricultural. Males.	Females.	Other. Males.	Females.	DEPENDENTS.	Group 125b.—Retail dealers and hawkers. Total Workers and Dependents.	WORKERS. Total Workers. Males.	Females.	Workers with an agricultural or other subsidiary occupation. Agricultural. Males.	Females.	Other. Males.	Females.	DEPENDENTS.
	1	2	3	4	5	6	7	8	9	10	11	12	13	14	15	16	17
	Provincial Total ...	9,497	3,191	426	99	4	173	19	5,880	25,022	8,134	3,902	453	74	787	157	12,986
	Divisional Burma ...	9,027	2,929	413	97	3	162	19	5,685	24,394	7,966	3,783	439	69	754	139	12,645
	Arakan Division ...	450	86	38	4	...	7	1	326	1,588	837	51	221	...	170	...	700
1	Akyab ...	312	48	34	1	...	4	1	230	1,509	840	26	221	...	168	...	663
2	Hill Dist. of Arakan	4	1	...	1	...	...	...	3	1	1	...	...	...	...	...	...
3	Kyaukpyu ...	2	...	...	..	...	...	...	2	41	...	21	...	...	...	...	20
4	Sandoway ...	132	37	4	2	...	3	...	91	37	16	4	...	...	2	..	17
	Pegu Division ...	2,685	1,236	82	28	...	52	...	1,367	4,903	1,758	745	13	12	91	20	2,400
5	Rangoon Town ..	775	268	40	...	.	3	...	467	891	442	40	...	...	1	...	409
6	Insein	190	102	8	...	...	...	...	80	697	323	89	5	...	48	...	285
7	Hanthawaddy ...	882	602	4	23	...	30	...	277	605	96	275	...	...	3	4	234
8	Tharrawaddy ...	76	27	10	...	...	6	..	39	503	169	69	5	6	11	1	265
9	Pegu	574	201	9	5	...	11	...	364	1,103	329	133	3	6	24	8	641
10	Prome	187	36	11	..	...	2	...	140	1,104	399	139	...	...	4	7	566
	Irrawaddy Division ...	804	98	104	4	3	7	11	602	3,389	1,192	434	30	3	93	15	1,763
11	Bassein ..	481	18	76	3	3	...	8	387	1,987	799	155	20	...	57	7	1,033
12	Henzada ...	207	35	26	1	..	3	3	146	503	95	108	2	2	15	4	300
13	Myaungmya ...	15	2	1	...	...	...	...	12	246	67	17	7	...	7	..	162
14	Ma-ubin ...	19	8	1	...	...	...	...	10	512	187	137	1	1	7	2	188
15	Pyapôn ...	82	35	...	...	...	4	...	47	141	44	17	...	...	7	2	80
	Tenasserim Division ...	1,586	336	58	6	...	21	1	1,192	2,594	765	383	8	1	24	11	1,446
16	Toungoo ...	531	132	16	..	...	8	...	383	693	219	57	4	1	5	...	417
17	Salween ...	25	7	1	2	...	1	...	17	50	15	12	...	...	...	...	23
18	Thatôn ..	74	63	...	1	...	2	...	11	1,031	373	118	2	...	14	3	540
19	Amherst .	924	132	41	3	...	9	1	751	688	113	175	2	...	4	5	400
20	Tavoy	19	1	...	...	...	1	...	18	105	30	20	...	...	...	3	55
21	Mergui ..	13	1	...	...	...	..	...	12	27	15	1	...	...	1	...	11
	Magwe Division ..	533	135	18	1	...	6	...	380	3,368	1,076	702	32	13	175	37	1,590
22	Thayetmyo ...	87	76	...	1	...	...	...	11	48	1	2	..	...	...	...	45
23	Pakôkku ...	403	45	10	...	...	3	...	348	2,407	746	548	17	...	116	20	1,113
24	Minbu	24	2	8	.	...	...	...	14	765	242	149	12	13	56	17	374
25	Magwe ...	19	12	...	...	...	3	..	7	148	87	3	3	...	3	...	58
26	Pakôkku Hill Tracts	..	...	...	...	...	...	...	...	..	...	...	...	...	...	...	...
	Mandalay Division ...	1,540	557	62	27	...	33	3	921	3,352	735	533	14	11	77	26	2,084
27	Mandalay ...	475	219	14	8	...	10	...	242	1,514	350	311	...	10	2	2	853
	Mandalay City ..	*207*	*51*	*14*	...	...	...	...	*142*	*1,087*	*341*	*166*	...	...	*2*	...	*580*
28	Bhamo ...	527	104	43	2	...	7	3	380	730	214	89	6	...	41	6	427
29	Myitkyina ..	73	13	5	...	...	...	...	55	103	41	3	2	...	8	...	59
30	Katha ...	465	221	...	17	...	16	...	244	1,005	130	130	6	1	26	18	745
31	Putao	..	...	...	...	...	...	...	...	...	...		...	...	...	...	...
	Sagaing Division ..	1,015	336	12	24	...	29	1	667	1,752	618	189	100	3	49	7	945
32	Shwebo ..	274	91	11	2	...	3	1	172	263	86	52	1	..	11	...	125
33	Sagaing ...	58	29	...	...	...	5	...	29	175	44	61	1	1	..	4	69
34	Lower Chindwin ...	323	133	...	4	...	14	...	190	612	205	49	11	...	18	...	358
35	Upper Chindwin ...	357	82	1	18	...	7	..	274	700	282	26	87	2	20	3	392
36	Chin Hills ...	3	1	..	...	...	...	...	2	2	1	...	..	...	...	...	1
	Meiktila Division .	414	145	39	3	..	7	2	230	3,448	985	746	21	26	75	23	1,727
37	Kyauksè ..	45	29	1	1	...	4	1	15	693	147	358	...	22	5	8	188
38	Meiktila ...	132	33	20	2	...	3	1	79	952	217	125	9	2	21	12	680
39	Yamèthin	111	44	17	-	...	..	-	50	1,113	403	191	8	2	19	3	519
40	Myingyan ...	126	39	1	-	...	...	...	86	690	218	72	4	..	30	...	400
	Eastern States ...	470	262	13	2	1	11	...	195	628	168	119	14	5	33	18	341
41	Northern Shan States	421	252	10	2	...	5	...	159	488	120	103	12	5	25	18	265
42	Southern Shan States	47	8	3	...	1	6	...	36	135	48	13	2	..	8	...	74
43	Karenni ...	2	2	...	...	...		-	...	5	...	3	...	..	...	...	2

* NOTE.—For Groups 124 and 126, see Orders XXVII and XXIX on pages 288 and 289 respectively.

PART III.—*Details by districts*—contd.

Order XXX.—Trade in pottery, bricks and tiles.																
Group 127*a*.—Trade in pottery not for domestic use nor for gardening.								Group 127*b*.—Trade in bricks or tiles.								Serial No. of District, etc. (column 1).
Total Workers and Dependents.	WORKERS.						DEPENDENTS.	Total Workers and Dependents.	WORKERS.						DEPENDENTS.	
	Total Workers.		Workers with an agricultural or other subsidiary occupation.						Total Workers.		Workers with an agricultural or other subsidiary occupation.					
			Agricultural.		Other.						Agricultural.		Other.			
	Males.	Females.	Males.	Females	Males.	Females.			Males.	Females.	Males.	Females	Males.	Females		
18	19	20	21	22	23	24	25	26	27	28	29	30	31	32	33	
871	268	201	2	...	7	1	402	732	177	135	33	...	8	18	420	
870	267	201	2	...	7	1	402	732	177	135	33	...	8	18	420	
...	...	...	...	...	...	...	...	...	...	...	...	...	...	...	...	
...	...	...	...	...	...	...	...	...	...	...	...	...	...	...	...	1
...	...	...	...	...	...	...	...	...	...	...	...	...	...	...	...	2
...	...	...	...	...	...	...	...	...	...	...	...	...	...	...	...	3
...	...	...	...	...	...	...	...	...	...	...	...	...	...	...	...	4
156	78	3	1	...	1	...	75	15	...	...	...	...	...	...	15	
25	18	...	...	...	...	...	7	3	...	...	...	...	...	...	3	5
46	29	...	...	...	...	...	17	12	...	...	...	...	...	...	12	6
41	11	2	...	...	...	...	28	...	...	...	...	...	...	...	...	7
21	8	...	1	...	1	...	13	...	...	...	...	...	...	...	...	8
9	1	1	...	...	...	...	7	...	...	...	...	...	...	...	...	9
14	11	...	...	...	...	...	3	...	...	...	...	...	...	...	...	10
148	95	10	1	...	...	...	43	...	...	...	...	...	...	...	...	
127	86	8	...	...	...	...	33	...	...	...	...	...	...	...	...	11
3	1	...	...	...	...	...	2	...	...	...	...	...	...	...	...	12
14	6	1	1	...	...	...	7	...	...	...	...	...	...	...	...	13
4	2	1	...	...	...	...	1	...	...	...	...	...	...	...	...	14
...	...	...	...	...	...	...	...	...	...	...	...	...	...	...	...	15
67	12	11	...	...	...	...	44	692	171	133	33	...	8	18	388	
16	4	...	...	...	...	...	12	...	...	...	...	...	...	...	...	16
...	...	...	...	...	...	...	...	1	...	...	...	...	...	...	1	17
17	3	9	...	...	...	...	5	1	1	...	...	...	...	...	...	18
30	5	2	...	...	...	...	23	690	170	133	33	...	8	18	387	19
...	...	...	...	...	...	...	...	...	...	...	...	...	...	...	...	20
4	...	...	...	...	...	...	4	...	...	...	...	...	...	...	...	21
206	15	125	...	...	...	1	66	20	5	2	...	...	...	...	13	
3	1	1	...	...	...	...	1	...	...	...	...	...	...	...	...	22
1	1	...	...	...	...	...	...	...	...	...	...	...	...	...	...	23
180	2	124	...		...	1	54	20	5	2	...	...	...	...	13	24
22	11	...	...	...	...	...	11	...	...	...	...	...	...	...	...	25
...	...	...	...	...	...	...	...	...	...	...	...	...	...	...	...	26
46	24	...	...	...	...	...	22	...	...	...	...	...	...	...	...	
46	24	...	...	...	...	...	22	...	...	...	...	...	...	...	...	27
42	20	...	...	...	...	...	22	...	...	...	...	...	...	...	...	
...	...	...	...	...	...	...	...	...	...	...	...	...	...	...	...	28
...	...	...	...	...	...	...	...	...	...	...	...	...	...	...	...	29
...	...	...	...	...	...	...	...	...	...	...	...	...	...	...	...	30
...	...	...	...	...	...	...	...	...	...	...	...	...	...	...	...	31
35	14	3	...	...	5	...	18	...	...	...	...	...	...	...	...	
8	3	2	...	...	...	...	3	...	...	...	...	...	...	...	...	32
5	3	1	...	...	...	...	1	...	...	...	...	...	...	...	...	33
17	5	...	...	...	5	...	12	...	...	...	...	...	...	...	...	34
5	3	...	...	...	...	...	2	...	...	...	...	...	...	...	...	35
...	...	...	...	...	...	...	...	...	...	...	...	...	...	...	...	36
212	29	49	...	...	1	...	134	5	1	...	...	...	...	...	4	
...	...	...	...	...	...	...	...	4	...	...	...	...	...	...	4	37
2	...	1	...	...	...	...	1	1	1	...	...	...	...	...	...	38
129	28	15	...	...	1	...	86	...	...	...	...	...	...	...	...	39
81	1	33	...	...	...	...	47	...	...	...	...	...	...	...	...	40
1	1	...	...	...	...	...	...	...	...	...	...	...	...	...	...	
1	1	...	...	...	...	...	...	...	...	...	...	...	...	...	...	41
...	...	...	...	...	...	...	...	...	...	...	...	...	...	...	...	42
...	...	...	...	...	...	...	...	...	...	...	...	...	...	...	...	43

* Order XXXII.—Hotels, cafés, restaurants, etc.

Serial No.	District or State.	Group 129.—Dealers in wine, liquors, aerated waters and ice. Total Workers and Dependents.	Workers. Total Workers. Males.	Workers. Total Workers. Females.	Agricultural. Males.	Agricultural. Females.	Other. Males.	Other. Females.	Dependents.	Group 130.—Owners and managers of hotels, cook-shops, dâk-bungalows, etc., and their employees. Total Workers and Dependents.	Workers. Total Workers. Males.	Workers. Total Workers. Females.	Agricultural. Males.	Agricultural. Females.	Other. Males.	Other. Females.	Dependents.
	1	2	3	4	5	6	7	8	9	10	11	12	13	14	15	16	17
	Provincial Total ...	8,685	4,156	672	30	2	134	50	3,857	40,977	13,411	9,150	89	124	537	299	18,416
	Divisional Burma ...	7,893	3,862	499	23	2	97	22	3,532	38,999	12,705	8,574	74	112	449	224	17,720
	Arakan Division ..	346	121	54	4	1	15	3	171	2,660	654	628	6	2	22	20	1,378
1	Akyab .	140	54	11	...	..	...	2	75	2,505	609	597	5	2	16	19	1,299
2	Hill Dist. of Arakan	...	...	...	...	...	...	...	...	1	...	1	...	...	...	.	...
3	Kyaukpyu ...	10	9	...	1	...	..	...	1	17	7	2	..	...	2	...	8
4	Sandoway ...	196	58	43	3	1	15	1	95	137	38	28	1	...	4	1	71
	Pegu Division ...	2,709	1,503	87	11	...	19	..	1,119	9,506	4,345	1,285	6	32	93	23	3,876
5	Rangoon Town .	986	669	9	.	...	...	..	368	3,726	2,411	135	...	...	5	2	1,180
6	Insein ..	207	80	21	...	...	4	...	106	625	268	72	3	...	27	...	285
7	Hanthawaddy ...	437	213	37	1	...	5	...	187	229	103	8	...	...	..	...	118
8	Tharrawaddy ...	314	140	4	...	...	2	..	170	1,473	360	311	2	9	18	4	802
9	Pegu ...	407	238	7	9	...	7	...	182	1,702	602	286	1	10	31	5	814
10	Prome ...	338	163	9	1	...	1	...	166	1,751	601	473	.	13	12	14	677
	Irrawaddy Division .	1,778	744	142	3	...	13	5	892	5,128	1,735	995	9	14	42	18	2,398
11	Bassein ...	505	239	52	...	...	6	1	274	1,518	545	319	3	4	10	4	654
12	Henzada ...	361	121	30	1	...	1	...	210	1,020	286	237	1	5	9	7	497
13	Myaungmya ...	271	91	36	1	...	6	2	144	869	311	181	3	1	9	3	377
14	Ma-ubin ...	383	151	17	1	...	...	2	215	1,095	317	172	2	4	9	2	607
15	Pyapôn ...	198	142	7	...	...	...	...	49	626	276	87	...	...	5	2	263
	Tenasserim Division ...	1,445	702	64	3	...	16	...	679	4,777	1,562	1,109	...	6	51	14	2,106
16	Toungoo ..	232	115	9	...	...	3	...	108	1,482	552	304	..	...	20	1	606
17	Salween ..	16	6	...	...	...	..	...	10	35	18	...	...	...	2	...	17
18	Thatôn ..	282	143	14		...	1	.	125	1,384	325	396	..	...	11	4	663
19	Amherst ..	757	354	37	3	..	10	..	366	1,323	390	345	...	.	11	9	588
20	Tavoy ...	83	52	3	...	...	2	..	28	311	163	45	...	6	2	...	103
21	Mergui ...	75	32	1	...	..	...	...	42	242	114	19	...	...	5	..	109
	Magwe Division ...	494	244	22	..	...	17	1	228	4,462	1,077	1,397	15	16	57	53	1,988
22	Thayetmyo ...	108	41	7	...	...	...	1	60	740	163	239	...	7	...	3	338
23	Pakôkku ...	145	67	7		...	5	...	71	1,294	350	331	4	3	27	24	613
24	Minbu ...	131	60	8	...	...	3	...	63	891	213	259	4	5	13	12	419
25	Magwe ...	110	76	...	...	...	9	...	34	1,535	351	568	7	1	17	14	616
26	Pakôkku Hill Tracts	...	...	...	...	...	...	..	...	2	...	...	...	...	...	...	2
	Mandalay Division ...	508	295	38	2	...	11	4	175	5,098	1,382	1,321	5	5	53	21	2,395
27	Mandalay ...	350	231	31	2	...	2	..	98	4,012	993	1,126	4	...	14	2	1,893
	Mandalay City ...	*292*	*189*	*30*	...	..	*1*	...	*73*	*3,194*	*741*	*937*		...	*2*	*1*	*1,516*
28	Bhamo ...	63	24	4	...	...	1	4	40	404	133	68	1	..	13	13	203
29	Myitkyina ...	36	20	1	...	...	7	...	15	257	112	55	...	3	16	2	90
30	Katha ...	54	30	2	...	...	1	...	22	425	144	72	.	2	10	4	209
31	Putao ..	...	...	...	..	...	...	...	...	...	...	...	...	...	...	...	...
	Sagaing Division ...	254	106	36	...	...	5	3	112	2,821	786	657	17	16	59	35	1,378
32	Shwebo ...	56	29	4	...	...	2	...	23	865	313	61	6	...	15	1	491
33	Sagaing ...	96	43	8	...	...	1	2	45	909	211	258	4	11	14	22	440
34	Lower Chindwin ...	40	22	...	...	...	1	...	18	766	221	179	7	5	29	5	366
35	Upper Chindwin ...	57	11	24	...	...	1	1	22	281	41	159		...	1	7	81
36	Chin Hills ...	5	1	...	...	...	...	..	4	...	..	...	.	...	...	...	...
	Meiktila Division ..	359	147	56	...	1	1	6	156	4,547	1,164	1,182	16	21	72	40	2,201
37	Kyauksè ..	19	9	1	...	...	1	...	9	876	273	162	8	10	24	3	441
38	Meiktila ...	152	38	42	...	1	..	4	70	1,288	313	329	2	4	25	21	646
39	Yamèthin ...	95	44	3	...	...	...	...	48	1,574	419	398	3	...	13	5	757
40	Myingyan ..	95	56	10	...	...	..	2	29	809	159	293	3	7	10	11	357
	Eastern States .	792	294	173	7	...	37	28	325	1,978	706	576	15	12	88	75	696
41	Northern Shan States	589	233	131	3	...	32	28	225	1,807	662	517	15	12	83	71	628
42	Southern Shan States	200	60	41	4	.	5	...	93	133	32	45	...	...	5	4	56
43	Karenni ...	3	1	1	...	...	...	...	1	38	12	14	...	...	...	...	12

* NOTE.—For Group 128, see Order XXXI on page 291.

PART III.—*Details by districts—contd.*

Order XXXIII.—Other trade in foodstuffs.

Group 131.—Fish. Total Workers and Dependents.	Group 131. Workers. Total Workers. Males.	Group 131. Total Workers. Females.	Group 131. Workers with an agricultural or other subsidiary occupation. Agricultural. Males.	Group 131. Agricultural. Females.	Group 131. Other. Males.	Group 131. Other. Females.	Group 131. DEPENDENTS.	Group 132.—Grocery, vegetable oil, salt and other condiments. Total Workers and Dependents.	Group 132. Workers. Total Workers. Males.	Group 132. Total Workers. Females.	Group 132. Workers with an agricultural or other subsidiary occupation. Agricultural. Males.	Group 132. Agricultural. Females.	Group 132. Other. Males.	Group 132. Other. Females.	Group 132. DEPENDENTS.	Serial No. of District, etc. (column 1).
18	19	20	21	22	23	24	25	26	27	28	29	30	31	32	33	
60,565	10,509	22,388	158	286	570	933	27,668	23,591	5,995	6,262	195	67	479	243	11,334	
60,073	10,441	22,163	158	253	562	904	27,469	21,979	5,402	6,029	150	59	396	214	10,548	
4,988	1,173	1,066	21	21	74	124	2,749	853	322	68	2	2	11	3	463	
4,194	1,090	704	15	3	65	74	2,500	786	293	59	2	2	10	2	434	1
...	...	...	...	...	...	...	...	3	2	1	...	...	...	...	...	2
41	2	21	..	...	...	..	18	6	1	...	...	...	...	...	5	3
653	81	341	6	18	9	40	231	58	26	8	...	..	1	1	24	4
13,855	2,550	3,571	55	49	71	66	7,734	3,691	1,138	845	4	4	33	5	1,708	
2,730	858	609	3	...	6	4	1,203	2,201	780	446	...	...	12	..	975	5
491	55	184	1	5	1	6	252	81	34	17	...	..	1	...	30	6
3,355	553	578	6	..	9	13	2,424	208	73	47	2	2	7	1	88	7
2,614	366	786	20	13	15	19	1,532	345	73	87	2	1	7	1	182	8
2,900	675	634	7	19	27	5	1,591	268	80	57	...	1	6	3	131	9
1,765	243	790	18	12	13	89	732	588	95	191	...	...	..	...	302	10
14,190	3,257	3,963	21	56	170	130	6,970	1,857	377	546	5	1	15	16	934	
4,400	1,024	1,460	...	24	70	48	1,916	503	68	179	2	1	2	8	236	11
2,094	296	584	10	17	18	30	1,214	358	78	70	...	...	3	...	210	12
1,740	376	446	4	1	14	7	918	275	48	86	...	...	3	4	141	13
4,648	1,246	1,185	5	13	50	39	2,217	450	88	159	1	...	5	3	209	14
1,308	315	288	2	1	18	6	705	265	75	52	2	..	2	1	138	15
7,524	719	3,961	14	17	14	42	2,844	2,051	451	489	2	3	9	17	1,111	
912	105	432	1	..	3	13	375	370	40	137	...	...	...	3	193	16
8	...	5	...	..	...	...	3	2	1	...	..	...	..	...	1	17
1,107	178	390	..	3	1	3	539	444	83	111	1	1	4	4	250	18
1,303	122	464	3	4	2	5	717	836	254	85	1	...	2	1	497	19
3,258	200	2,469	10	10	2	21	589	375	68	150	...	2	3	9	157	20
936	114	201	...	...	6	...	621	24	5	6	..	...	...	...	13	21
7,322	972	3,597	19	41	100	140	2,753	5,032	1,304	1,365	69	11	173	58	2,363	
1,420	142	778	1	2	4	17	500	770	150	205	...	...	5	7	415	22
2,190	288	1,194	7	7	35	33	708	1,646	275	587	16	5	27	26	844	23
2,094	266	741	8	12	33	41	1,087	1,206	374	372	14	4	99	19	460	24
1,618	276	884	3	20	28	58	458	1,410	505	261	29	2	42	6	644	25
...	...	...	.	.	...	...	...	...	...	...	...	...	...	...	...	26
4,740	722	2,478	1	30	34	66	1,550	2,699	534	758	5	1	33	18	1,407	
3,008	417	1,610	.	28	5	32	981	1,810	385	613	...	...	6	9	809	27
2,388	76	737	.	...	...	22	575	1,470	312	459	...	...	1	...	699	
691	101	480	1	1	9	15	170	254	53	84	..	..	9	2	217	28
226	26	116	...	1	5	4	84	48	21	10	..	1	6	1	17	29
815	168	332	.	..	15	9	315	587	72	51	5	...	12	6	464	30
..	...	.	...	...	...	...	..	...	.	...	...	..	...	...	...	31
4,698	652	2,365	25	35	80	300	1,621	2,974	626	1,117	43	27	75	74	2,232	
532	119	70	5	1	9	2	342	551	78	250	...	4	3	13	283	32
2,132	144	1,487	7	25	12	238	501	809	128	376	9	5	5	31	315	33
1,587	310	591	9	5	48	51	686	1,038	306	402	23	10	40	25	532	34
448	79	217	4	4	11	11	152	376	123	91	11	8	27	5	162	35
...	...	...	...	..	...	...	...	...	..	...	...	...	...	...	...	36
2,816	406	1,162	2	4	19	35	1,248	2,822	651	842	20	10	47	23	1,330	
230	54	97	...	...	5	1	79	457	134	115	7	1	12	..	208	37
875	76	373	...	1	...	9	426	630	173	160	2	...	8	6	297	38
924	156	283	2	2	14	5	485	673	140	144	5	...	14	...	380	39
787	120	409	...	1	..	20	258	1,062	195	422	6	9	13	17	445	40
492	68	225	...	33	8	29	199	1,612	598	233	45	8	83	29	786	
288	50	81	...	9	6	4	157	1,539	589	185	43	8	83	26	765	41
203	18	143	...	24	2	25	42	72	4	47	2	...	...	3	21	42
1	.	1	...	...	...	...	...	2	...	1	...	...	...	...	...	43

Order XXXIII.—Other trade

Serial No.	DISTRICT OR STATE.	Group 133.—Milk, butter, ghee, poultry, eggs, etc. Total Workers and Dependents.	WORKERS. Total Workers. Males.	Total Workers. Females.	Workers with an agricultural or other subsidiary occupation. Agricultural. Males.	Agricultural. Females.	Other. Males.	Other. Females.	DEPENDENTS.	Group 134.—Sugar, jaggery and sweetmeats. Total Workers and Dependents.	WORKERS. Total Workers. Males.	Total Workers. Females.	Workers with an agricultural or other subsidiary occupation. Agricultural. Males.	Agricultural. Females.	Other. Males.	Other. Females.	DEPENDENTS.
	1	2	3	4	5	6	7	8	9	10	11	12	13	14	15	16	17
	Provincial Total ...	5,165	1,870	749	7	18	49	18	2,546	65,060	11,233	27,925	267	482	533	756	25,902
	Divisional Burma ..	5,047	1,859	649	7	8	49	18	2,539	64,433	11,131	27,628	267	470	524	732	25,674
	Arakan Division ...	115	43	8	...	...	...	...	64	3,222	418	1,165	1	1	4	24	1,639
1	Akyab ...	88	37	6	...	...	...	...	45	3,147	404	1,153	1	1	4	24	1,590
2	Hill Dist. of Arakan	...	...	...	.	. .	...	...	...	9	2	4	...	...	..	...	3
3	Kyaukpyu ...	..	...	...	...	. .	...	...	...	1	1	...	...	..	...	...	...
4	Sandoway ...	27	6	2	...	...	...	...	19	65	11	8	...	..	...	...	46
	Pegu Division ...	1,237	602	57	4	...	12	3	578	11,780	2,890	4,508	83	126	47	69	4,382
5	Rangoon Town ...	507	284	20	.	..	...	...	203	2,375	1,024	471	...	..	5	...	880
6	Insein	121	40	4	4	.	3	...	77	1,147	136	478	...	7	3	5	533
7	Hanthawaddy ...	152	53	11	...	..	1	1	88	880	299	168	3	1	12	2	413
8	Tharrawaddy ...	167	90	5	.	...	..	...	72	1,811	486	673	73	20	11	11	652
9	Pegu	87	43	8	...	...	1	...	36	2,909	530	1,594	3	73	14	20	785
10	Prome	203	92	9	...	..	7	2	102	2,658	415	1,124	4	25	2	31	1,119
	Irrawaddy Division .	439	184	43		.	2	...	212	13,989	2,149	5,991	41	124	73	126	5,849
11	Bassein ...	93	56	10	.	.	...	...	27	6,779	954	3,085	19	73	45	79	2,740
12	Henzada ...	75	22	12	...	..	..	...	41	893	206	273	20	35	4	5	414
13	Myaungmya ...	41	15	7	..	...	1	...	19	509	211	24	2	...	11	1	274
14	Ma-ubin ...	198	81	11	..	..	1	...	106	4,220	581	1,934	...	11	7	38	1,705
15	Pyapôn ...	32	10	3	...	..	...	..	19	1,588	197	675	...	5	6	3	716
	Tenasserim Division ...	973	332	134	..	8	16	1	507	7,191	937	3,409	2	9	26	57	2,845
16	Toungoo ..	190	43	12	...	...	2	...	135	1,100	322	361	1	...	14	3	417
17	Salween ..	2	2	...	..	..	...	...	...	19	7	4		.	.	...	8
18	Thatôn .	494	195	99		8	13	1	200	1,872	160	999	...	1	3	4	713
19	Amherst ...	191	68	15	...	...	...	...	108	2,323	322	1,057	...	...	4	27	944
20	Tavoy	77	18	7	...	...	1	...	52	1,154	115	642	1	8	4	23	397
21	Mergui ..	19	6	1	...	...	...	...	12	723	11	346	...	...	1	.	366
	Magwe Division ...	219	77	46	...	..	1	...	96	11,601	1,853	5,422	58	128	176	227	4,326
22	Thayetmyo ..	58	21	4	..	...	1	...	33	2,246	382	857	7	9	25	21	1,007
23	Pakôkku ..	21	10	...	..	...	..	...	11	5,782	692	2,989	24	56	74	130	2,101
24	Minbu ..	58	9	24	.	...	..	...	25	1,942	476	853	18	49	61	70	613
25	Magwe ..	82	37	18	...	...		..	27	1,631	303	723	9	14	16	6	605
26	Pakôkku Hill Tracts	...	...	..	...	...		...	...	..	...	...	...	...	...	...	...
	Mandalay Division .	1,051	288	265	2	...	5	7	498	3,588	761	1,633	3	6	20	26	1,194
27	Mandalay ...	971	248	256	..	..	3	1	467	2,894	575	1,377	...	4	...	9	942
	Mandalay City .	*872*	*209*	*249*	...	..		..	*414*	*2,222*	*520*	*982*	..	.	...	*1*	*720*
28	Bhamo ...	37	18	7	1	...	1	6	12	387	79	168	..	2	9	14	140
29	Mitkyina	16	9	2	...	.	...	..	5	162	59	55	...	..	5	1	48
30	Katha	27	13	...	1	...	1	...	14	145	48	33	3	...	6	2	64
31	Putao	...	...	.	...	...	..	...	...	...	...	..	...	...	...	..	...
	Sagaing Division ...	353	152	37	1	...	7	5	164	5,260	839	2,437	36	20	95	83	1,984
32	Shwebo ..	84	17	21	.	...	2	4	46	1,412	256	325	4	2	24	11	831
33	Sagaing ...	225	119	16	1	...	5	1	90	1,954	270	1,115	27	...	34	1	499
34	Lower Chindwin ..	43	15	...	..	...	..	...	28	1,741	238	919	4	18	24	71	584
35	Upper Chindwin ...	1	1	...	...	.	..	...	.	149	73	8	1	.	13	...	68
36	Chin Hills ...	...	...	...	...	.	..	...	..	4	2	...	...	..	...	..	2
	Meiktila Division ...	660	181	59	...	.	6	2	420	7,802	1,284	3,063	43	56	83	120	3,455
37	Kyauksè ...	83	26	6	.	...	4	1	51	1,028	179	493	..	32	8	13	356
38	Meiktila ..	190	46	15	...	...	...	1	129	2,561	425	996	35	11	45	47	1,140
39	Yamèthin ...	322	90	20	...	...	2	..	212	1,780	353	487	4	3	16	40	940
40	Myingyan ...	65	19	18	...	...	..	...	28	2,433	327	1,087	4	10	14	50	1,019
	Eastern States .	118	11	100	...	10	...	...	7	627	102	297	...	12	9	24	228
41	Northern Shan States	23	9	9	...	...	...	...	5	453	81	186	...	10	7	14	186
42	Southern Shan States	95	2	91	...	10	.	...	2	173	21	110	...	2	2	10	42
43	Karenni ...	...	.	...	..	...	...	...	...	1	...	1	...	...	...	...	...

PART III.—*Details by districts—contd.*

in foodstuffs—*continued.*

Group 135.—Cardamon, betel-leaf, vegetables, fruit and areca-nut.								Group 136a.—Grain, pulse, flour and bran—wholesale dealers and brokers.								
Total Workers and Dependents.	WORKERS.						DEPENDENTS.	Total Workers, and Dependents.	WORKERS.						DEPENDENTS.	Serial No. of District, etc. (column 1).
	Total Workers.		Workers with an agricultural or other subsidiary occupation.						Total Workers.		Workers with an agricultural or other subsidiary occupation.					
			Agricultural.		Other.						Agricultural.		Other.			
	Males.	Females.	Males.	Females.	Males.	Females.			Males.	Females.	Males.	Females.	Males.	Females.		
18	19	20	21	22	23	24	25	26	27	28	29	30	31	32	33	
64,326	11,432	24,631	186	325	548	817	28,263	59,590	15,645	7,648	295	95	972	454	36,297	
62,929	11,095	24,197	161	296	463	794	27,637	59,339	15,600	7,530	295	88	967	428	36,209	
7,138	1,804	1,952	55	16	87	85	3,382	3,361	1,555	75	36	3	58	2	1,731	
6,753	1,749	1,756	45	8	77	69	3,248	3,051	1,467	58	21	...	43	...	1,526	1
...	...	...	...	...	...	...	...	...	...	...	...	...	...	...	...	2
10	10	...	10	...	...	...	...	42	18	6	9	1	...	...	18	3
375	45	196	..	8	10	16	134	268	70	11	6	2	15	2	187	4
15,828	3,533	6,225	19	97	78	56	6,070	25,643	6,234	2,525	100	22	235	87	16,884	
7,018	2,123	2,709	...	...	18	...	2,186	9,859	2,943	234	3	3	21	5	6,682	5
607	119	271	6	2	3	5	217	1,906	511	113	10	...	31	4	1,282	6
1,812	339	667	2	24	7	2	806	3,977	292	1,483	6	...	20	21	2,202	7
1,670	234	673	5	5	24	8	763	3,529	1,057	184	37	3	109	21	2,288	8
2,576	466	900	5	35	17	11	1,210	3,830	875	240	42	4	46	16	2,715	9
2,145	252	1,005	1	31	9	30	888	2,542	556	271	2	12	8	20	1,715	10
6,029	954	2,357	26	28	52	48	2,718	12,558	3,087	1,608	9	17	299	145	7,863	
1,288	187	554	9	17	28	15	547	2,786	204	635	2	4	26	69	1,947	11
1,051	130	328	11	3	5	3	598	4,642	1,276	386	37	9	113	26	2,980	12
1,069	151	515	1	6	6	18	403	2,754	912	281	7	2	100	42	1,561	13
1,998	380	755	4	...	12	11	923	1,102	271	181	11	2	47	8	650	14
623	166	205	1	2	1	1	252	1,274	424	125	2	...	13	...	725	15
12,537	1,648	4,903	21	54	55	131	5,986	6,409	1,796	705	41	14	108	9	3,908	
5,126	936	1,163	6	14	29	32	3,027	2,673	529	506	11	5	19	3	1,638	16
33	6	8	2	...	1	...	19	3	1	...	...	...	...	...	2	17
1,682	200	710	3	9	10	18	772	686	357	20	4	...	35	...	309	18
2,885	384	1,178	7	9	8	26	1,323	2,589	795	132	20	...	43	4	1,662	19
2,643	115	1,771	3	28	7	55	757	225	61	35	6	9	11	2	129	20
168	7	73	...	...	...	...	88	233	53	12	...	...	...	...	168	21
7,153	1,171	2,713	21	69	104	192	3,269	3,355	811	874	14	11	98	72	1,670	
918	139	312	3	...	5	13	467	124	39	4	...	...	4	...	81	22
2,205	364	847	...	14	41	88	994	2,270	386	761	14	10	53	60	1,123	23
1,914	277	993	6	38	37	59	644	244	14	88	...	1	..	12	142	24
2,116	391	561	12	17	21	32	1,164	717	372	21	...	...	41	...	384	25
...	...	...	...	...	...	...	...	...	...	...	...	...	...	...	...	26
4,464	529	2,212	2	3	10	73	1,723	2,707	672	906	5	2	53	47	1,129	
3,353	377	1,781	1	3	7	51	1,195	1,755	467	519	2	...	13	6	799	27
2,250	*257*	*1,177*	*1*	...	*1*	..	*816*	*1,541*	*354*	*506*	.	...	*1*	*5*	*681*	
688	82	281	...	...	2	18	325	667	94	370	...	2	17	40	203	28
170	17	75	1	...	...	4	78	183	64	11	1	...	17	...	108	29
253	53	75	...	..	1	...	125	102	47	6	2	...	6	1	49	30
...	...	...	...	...	...	...	...	...	...	...	...	...	...	...	...	31
3,164	392	1,522	3	6	36	128	1,250	2,241	671	371	27	16	74	52	1,299	
577	60	303	...	...	7	5	214	1,011	284	174	13	5	27	9	553	32
14,55	101	796	...	4	11	54	558	711	225	153	7	11	23	27	333	33
799	112	258	1	...	7	37	429	339	154	...	7	...	24	...	185	34
333	119	165	2	2	11	32	49	180	8	44	...	...	...	16	128	35
...	...	...	..	..	...	...	...	..	...	...	...	...	...	...	...	36
6,616	1,064	2,313	14	23	41	81	3,239	3,065	774	466	13	3	42	14	1,325	
1,147	176	425	3	6	12	9	546	821	249	48	5	...	11	...	524	37
1,547	207	637	6	...	10	31	683	873	188	271	1	3	13	12	414	38
3,051	483	907	4	12	16	30	1,661	737	109	48	...	...	2	...	580	39
871	178	344	1	5	3	11	349	634	228	99	7	..	16	2	307	40
1,397	337	434	25	29	85	23	626	251	45	118	...	7	5	26	88	
1,105	269	335	13	5	77	19	501	85	25	9	..	...	4	1	51	41
265	67	83	12	24	7	4	115	166	20	109	..	7	1	25	37	42
27	1	16	..	...	1	..	10	...	...	...	...	...	...	...	...	43

Order XXXIII.—Other trade

Serial No.	DISTRICT OR STATE.	Group 136b.—Grain, pulse, flour and bran—retail dealers and hawkers. Total Workers and Dependents.	Workers. Total Workers. Males.	Total Workers. Females.	Workers with an agricultural or other subsidiary occupation. Agricultural. Males.	Agricultural. Females.	Other. Males.	Other. Females.	DEPENDENTS.	Group 137.—Tobacco and opium. Total Workers and Dependents.	Workers. Total Workers. Males.	Total Workers. Females.	Workers with an agricultural or other subsidiary occupation. Agricultural. Males	Agricultural. Females	Other. Males.	Other. Females.	DEPENDENTS.
	1	2	3	4	5	6	7	8	9	10	11	12	13	14	15	16	17
	Provincial Total ...	34,391	9,890	9,177	174	157	653	417	15,324	28,271	4,702	10,153	80	94	310	307	13,416
	Divisional Burma ...	33,244	9,607	8,858	161	153	602	331	14,779	27,254	4,294	9,916	66	84	266	292	13,044
	Arakan Division ...	1,658	835	262	21	1	35	10	561	1,935	394	482	7	11	26	18	1,059
1	Akyab ...	1,619	835	236	21	...	35	8	558	1,635	337	349	7	4	23	11	949
2	Hill Dist. of Arakan	...	...	...	...	...	..	...	...	18	3	1	...	..	...	...	14
3	Kyaukpyu ...	...	...		...	...	...	...	...	11	5	...	...	...	...	...	6
4	Sandoway ...	29	...	26	...	1	...	2	3	271	49	132	...	7	3	7	90
	Pegu Division ...	6,378	1,447	2,124	3	7	19	34	2,807	6,222	1,029	1,963	3	9	28	13	3,230
5	Rangoon Town ..	2,076	864	420	...	...	2	5	1,392	2,070	532	489	...	...	3	...	1,049
6	Insein ...	229	72	64	1	1	2	3	93	285	122	91	...	...	9	...	72
7	Hanthawaddy ...	1,901	103	1,335	1	3	1	8	453	911	66	115	1	6	4	...	730
8	Tharrawaddy ..	260	104	12	1	...	6	...	144	1,311	110	501	1	1	3	3	790
9	Pegu ...	568	164	47	...	..	6	2	357	689	91	282	..	2	9	4	316
10	Prome ...	744	140	246	...	3	2	16	358	956	108	485	1	...	...	6	263
	Irrawaddy Division ...	7,725	3,372	1,074	65	23	152	34	3,279	4,529	517	1,829	1	...	27	28	2,183
11	Bassein ...	4,315	2,705	90	58	7	126	3	1,520	1,179	147	446	...	...	5	8	586
12	Henzada ...	1,016	129	519	..	13	4	3	368	1,307	85	511	1	...	6	4	511
13	Myaungmya ...	479	175	79	2	..	...	11	225	278	89	43	...	...	4	3	146
14	Ma-ubin ...	1,325	142	370	5	2	7	16	813	1,233	133	606	...	...	7	11	494
15	Pyapôn ...	590	221	16	...	1	15	1	353	532	63	223	...	..	5	2	446
	Tenasserim Division ..	3,170	418	749	4	6	21	39	2,003	4,270	531	1,783	4	9	29	62	1,956
16	Toungoo ..	424	102	79	2	1	8	..	243	1,410	263	407	...	1	10	28	719
17	Salween ...	7	4	3	...	...	...	...	...	20	9	2	...	...	...	...	9
18	Thatôn ...	1,189	74	290	..	2	3	14	825	1,104	71	621	3	6	4	11	412
19	Amherst ..	1,203	206	188	2	...	6	8	809	1,036	145	445	1	1	5	18	446
20	Tavoy ...	302	16	185	...	3	2	17	101	260	38	35	...	1	9	5	187
21	Mergui ...	45	16	4	...	...	2	...	25	410	5	273	...	...	1	...	132
	Magwe Division ...	3,918	896	1,691	18	56	96	60	1,331	2,582	462	1,024	18	16	68	58	1,096
22	Thayetmyo ...	976	117	425	...	..	7	10	434	659	66	330	...	...	5	2	263
23	Pakôkku ...	465	139	203	5	...	16	...	123	1,210	225	448	4	12	44	46	537
24	Minbu ...	1,267	327	732	10	48	47	39	208	369	41	197	...	1	3	6	131
25	Magwe ...	1,210	313	331	3	8	26	11	566	344	130	49	14	3	16	4	165
26	Pakôkku Hill Tracts	...	...	...	...	...	..	..	...	...	..	...	.	...	...	...	...
	Mandalay Division ...	3,661	926	896	11	9	91	40	1,839	3,051	424	1,086	2	2	13	23	1,541
27	Mandalay ..	2,140	455	594	...	9	3	15	2,091	2,472	348	997	...	..	4	15	1,127
	Mandalay City ...	*1,694*	*451*	*356*	..	...	*3*	.	*887*	*2,136*	*293*	*870*	...	...	..	...	*973*
28	Bhamo ...	639	229	137	4	...	66	2	273	81	19	31	...	...	3	3	31
29	Myitkyina ...	217	72	57	...	...	6	1	88	63	21	20	1	1	...	...	22
30	Katha ...	665	170	108	7	...	16	22	387	435	36	38	1	1	6	5	361
31	Putao ...	...	...	...	...	..	...	...	...	...	..	...	...	...	...	...	...
	Sagaing Division ...	4,006	1,234	1,086	31	25	152	76	1,686	1,560	442	537	24	18	45	59	581
32	Shwebo ...	393	116	142	1	...	4	...	135	413	108	165	3	2	17	6	140
33	Sagaing	1,082	492	54	8	2	33	3	536	635	231	181	18	6	22	23	233
34	Lower Chindwin ...	1,513	277	675	8	...	32	48	561	463	88	185	3	9	6	21	190
35	Upper Chindwin ...	1,018	349	215	14	23	83	25	454	49	15	6	...	1	...	...	18
36	Chin Hills ...	...	...	...	...	...	..	..	...	...	...	...	...	...	...	...	...
	Meiktila Division ...	2,728	479	976	8	26	36	38	1,273	3,105	495	1,212	7	19	30	40	1,898
37	Kyaukse ...	810	128	362	7	16	14	13	320	255	57	104	4	9	5	7	94
38	Meiktila ..	461	27	129	..	...	3	2	305	665	101	250	1	...	10	12	814
39	Yamethin ...	813	236	251	...	5	14	8	326	1,128	192	519	1	3	6	11	417
40	Myingyan ...	644	88	234	1	5	5	15	322	1,057	145	339	1	7	9	10	573
	Eastern States ...	1,147	283	319	13	4	51	86	545	1,017	408	237	14	10	44	15	372
41	Northern Shan States	1,101	255	318	9	4	42	86	528	813	370	156	10	2	37	10	287
42	Southern Shan States	41	25	...	4	..	9	..	16	172	33	74	4	8	7	5	65
43	Karenni ...	5	3	1	...	...	...	...	1	32	5	7	.	...	...	...	20

in foodstuffs—*concluded.*

Group 138.—Meat, sheep, goats and pigs. Total Workers and Dependents.	Workers. Total Workers. Males.	Total Workers. Females.	Workers with an agricultural or other subsidiary occupation. Agricultural. Males.	Agricultural. Females.	Other. Males.	Other. Females.	Dependents.	Group 139.—Hay, grass and fodder. Total Workers and Dependents.	Workers. Total Workers. Males.	Total Workers. Females.	Workers with an agricultural or other subsidiary occupation. Agricultural. Males.	Agricultural. Females.	Other. Males.	Other. Females.	Dependents.	Serial No. of District, etc. (column 1).
18	19	20	21	22	23	24	25	26	27	28	29	30	31	32	33	
14,648	3,950	2,531	81	31	245	74	8,167	1,433	613	279	1	4	14	20	541	
12,382	3,303	2,195	58	16	201	62	7,084	1,207	539	172	1	...	8	3	496	
143	52	39	...	...	2	3	52	1		...	...	...	..	...	2	
122	49	32	...	...	...	1	41	1	...	...	...	..	...	...	2	1
...	...	...	..	...	...	...	...	...	...	..	...	...	...	...	...	2
14	2	4	...	...	1	...	8	...	...	...	...	...	...	...	...	3
7	1	3	...	..	1	2	3	...	...	...	...	...	...	...	...	4
3,439	1,000	491	4	1	18	10	1,948	317	194	15	...	...	1	...	108	
947	414	68	..	...	...	...	465	305	183	15	...	...	1	...	107	5
229	57	26	...	...	4	...	146	2	2	...	...	...	...	...	...	6
249	69	38	1	...	1	...	142	..	...	...	...	...	~	...	...	7
616	136	47	2	...	8	1	433	4	3	...	...	...	...	...	1	8
236	98	17	1	...	4	...	122	6	6	...	...	...	...	...	...	9
1,162	286	295	...	1	1	9	641	...	...	..	...	...	...	...	...	10
1,143	318	163	1	1	7	8	662	73	26	6	...	...	...	—	41	
390	123	56	...	...	...	1	211	73	26	6	...	...	...	...	41	11
309	36	77	...	1	1	6	196	...	...	...	...	...	...	...	...	12
174	60	11	...	...	4	...	103	...	...	...	...	..	...	...	...	13
111	36	17	1	...	2	1	58	...	...	...	...	...	...	...	...	14
159	63	2	...	...	...	...	94	...	...	...	...	...	...	...	...	15
1,036	297	129	4	5	14	7	610	201	117	4	...	..	...	...	80	
340	98	36	...	...	3	...	206	...	...	...	...	...	...	...	...	16
12	2	3	...	...	...	...	7	..	...	...	...	..	...	...	...	17
336	113	36	4	5	9	7	187	8	1	1	...	...	...	...	6	18
180	46	34	...	...	..	...	100	193	116	3	...	...	...	...	74	19
119	27	12	...	...	2	...	80	...	...	...	...	...	...	...	...	20
49	11	8	...	...	...	...	30	...	...	...	...	.	...	...	...	21
1,812	481	385	30	1	91	8	946	285	104	60	1	...	4	...	121	
175	30	46	...	...	3	1	99	...	...	...	...	...	...	...	...	22
651	214	102	26	...	74	1	335	306	58	52	...	...	3	..	96	23
222	22	83	...	1	4	3	117	83	3	7	...	...	...	...	3	24
764	215	154	4	...	10	3	395	66	43	1	1	...	1	...	22	25
...	...	...	...	...	...	...	...	...	...	...	...	...	...	...	...	26
1,136	261	260	3	...	25	4	615	124	32	34	...	...	...	...	58	
706	121	212	...	..	4	1	373	117	28	32	.	...	...	...	57	27
566	90	198	...	...	..	1	278	114	28	32	...	..	...	...	54	
311	99	35	2	...	18	2	177	2	...	2	...	...	...	...	...	28
11	5	3	...	...	...	...	3	2	2	...	...	...	...	...	...	29
108	36	10	1	...	3	1	62	3	2	...	...	...	...	...	1	30
...	...	...	...	...	...	...	...	...	...	...	...	...	...	...	...	31
1,018	278	222	7	...	12	9	518	77	25	19	...	...	1	...	33	
497	198	73	2	...	8	3	286	...	...	...	...	...	...	...	...	32
300	25	105	...	...	1	6	170	40	19	1	...	...	...	...	20	33
165	46	22	5	...	3	...	97	37	6	18	...	...	1	...	13	34
56	9	22	...	...	...	...	25	...	...	...	...	...	...	...	...	35
...	...	...	...	...	...	...	...	...	...	...	...	...	...	...	...	36
2,855	616	506	9	8	32	13	1,733	129	41	34	...	...	2	3	54	
267	46	48	2	2	...	...	173	...	...	...	...	...	...	...	...	37
803	128	121	2	1	7	6	574	4	2	...	...	...	...	...	2	38
1,020	225	174	3	2	12	1	621	57	24	12	...	...	2	...	21	39
745	217	163	2	3	13	6	365	68	15	22	...		...	3	31	40
2,066	647	336	23	15	44	12	1,083	226	74	107	...	4	6	17	45	
1,503	492	232	15	6	33	5	799	203	71	94	...	4	6	13	38	41
537	153	104	8	9	11	7	280	19	...	13	...	...	...	4	6	42
6	2	...	...	...	...	...	4	4	3	...	...	...	...	...	1	43

Serial No.	District or State.	Order XXXV.*—Trade in household goods. Group 141.*—Furniture and woven furnishings. Total Workers and Dependents.	Workers. Total Workers. Males.	Workers. Total Workers. Females.	Workers with an agricultural or other subsidiary occupation. Agricultural. Males.	Agricultural. Females.	Other. Males.	Other. Females.	Dependents.	Group 142.*—Hardware, glass, gardening tools, etc. Total Workers and Dependents.	Workers. Total Workers. Males.	Workers. Total Workers. Females.	Workers with an agricultural or other subsidiary occupation. Agricultural. Males.	Agricultural. Females.	Other. Males.	Other. Females.	Dependents.
	1	2	3	4	5	6	7	8	9	10	11	12	13	14	15	16	17
	Provincial Total ...	8,691	1,521	4,349	30	73	127	246	2,821	9,216	2,633	2,302	52	29	106	106	4,281
	Divisional Burma ...	8,607	1,506	4,314	30	73	127	243	2,787	8,905	2,441	2,295	33	29	86	106	4,169
	Arakan Division ...	283	27	136	...	...	...	...	120	309	209	4	3	...	3	...	96
1	Akyab ...	275	27	128	...	...	...	...	120	309	209	4	3	...	3	...	96
2	Hill Dist. of Arakan	...	...	...	...	...	...	...	...	...	...	...	...	...	...	...	...
3	Kyaukpyu ...	8	...	8	...	...	...	...	...	...	...	...	...	...	...	...	...
4	Sandoway ...	...	...	...	...	...	...	...	...	...	...	...	...	...	...	...	...
	Pegu Division ...	1,500	220	595	1	45	7	9	685	1,939	544	244	8	1	10	1	1,151
5	Rangoon Town ...	210	92	23	...	...	...	...	95	962	283	51	...	...	...	...	628
6	Insein ...	324	29	254	...	6	...	...	41	74	19	25	...	...	...	...	30
7	Hanthawaddy ...	117	20	45	...	...	1	...	52	254	59	68	1	...	...	...	127
8	Tharrawaddy ...	603	20	176	...	29	5	7	407	163	65	2	4	...	2	...	96
9	Pegu ...	170	40	66	...	5	1	...	64	381	68	93	3	1	8	1	220
10	Prome ...	76	19	31	1	5	...	2	26	105	50	5	...	...	...	...	50
	Irrawaddy Division ...	1,808	244	951	3	6	4	35	613	2,197	811	253	9	4	33	3	1,133
11	Bassein ...	121	53	23	...	...	2	1	45	1,251	594	109	8	4	29	2	548
12	Henzada ...	480	16	316	2	4	1	7	148	121	38	8	...	...	4	...	75
13	Myaungmya ...	415	...	346	...	...	...	5	69	117	49	35	...	...	...	...	33
14	Ma-ubin ...	778	166	262	1	2	1	22	350	619	99	78	1	...	...	1	442
15	Pyapôn ...	14	9	4	...	...	...	...	1	89	31	23	...	...	...	...	35
	Tenasserim Division ...	431	58	249	...	3	1	...	124	712	74	299	...	3	4	16	339
16	Toungoo ...	63	15	5	...	...	1	...	43	141	35	37	...	...	3	4	69
17	Salween ...	...	...	...	...	...	...	...	...	...	...	...	...	...	...	...	...
18	Thatôn ...	145	15	103	...	3	...	...	27	269	10	157	...	3	...	11	102
19	Amherst ...	119	26	64	...	...	...	...	29	207	26	32	...	...	...	1	149
20	Tavoy ...	102	2	77	...	...	...	...	23	79	2	69	...	...	1	...	8
21	Mergui ...	2	...	...	...	...	...	...	2	16	1	4	...	...	...	...	11
	Magwe Division ...	1,855	506	736	16	14	106	42	613	561	111	252	...	3	1	19	198
22	Thayetmyo ...	45	2	20	...	1	...	...	23	40	22	1	...	...	...	...	17
23	Pakôkku ...	859	304	331	16	...	87	29	224	323	11	236	...	3	...	19	76
24	Minbu ...	403	58	167	...	11	9	9	178	33	26	4	...	...	...	...	3
25	Magwe ...	548	142	218	...	2	10	4	188	165	52	11	...	...	1	...	102
26	Pakôkku Hill Tracts	...	...	...	...	...	...	...	...	...	...	...	...	...	...	...	...
	Mandalay Division ...	617	101	356	...	...	2	12	160	1,022	285	285	2	4	6	14	452
27	Mandalay ...	427	49	264	...	...	...	9	114	922	258	248	2	3	5	6	416
	Mandalay City ...	*174*	*43*	*35*	...	...	...	...	*96*	*453*	*142*	*83*	...	...	...	...	*228*
28	Bhamo ...	42	19	2	...	...	...	...	21	36	20	2	...	...	...	...	14
29	Myitkyina ...	5	4	...	...	...	...	...	1	24	2	10	...	...	1	...	12
30	Katha ...	143	29	90	...	...	2	3	24	40	5	25	...	1	...	8	10
31	Putao ...	...	...	...	...	...	...	...	...	...	...	...	...	...	...	...	...
	Sagaing Division ...	691	104	325	...	3	4	14	262	1,279	203	649	3	3	13	49	427
32	Shwebo ...	212	42	116	...	1	2	10	54	441	123	139	...	1	6	4	179
33	Sagaing ...	202	28	78	...	...	1	1	96	652	40	453	1	2	4	36	159
34	Lower Chindwin ...	258	28	126	...	2	1	3	104	182	40	57	2	...	3	9	85
35	Upper Chindwin ...	19	6	5	...	...	...	...	8	4	...	...	...	...	...	...	4
36	Chin Hills ...	...	...	...	...	...	...	...	...	...	...	...	...	...	...	...	...
	Meiktila Division ...	1,422	246	966	10	2	3	131	210	886	204	309	8	11	16	4	373
37	Kyauksè ...	20	16	...	1	...	1	...	4	47	28	1	...	...	2	...	18
38	Meiktila ...	63	42	6	...	1	...	...	15	136	18	58	...	...	1	...	60
39	Yamèthin ...	278	146	40	8	...	2	...	92	430	94	153	4	9	4	3	183
40	Myingyan ...	1,061	42	920	1	1	...	131	99	273	64	97	4	2	9	1	112
	Eastern States ...	84	15	35	...	...	...	3	34	311	192	7	19	...	20	...	112
41	Northern Shan States	38	12	11	...	...	...	3	15	65	37	7	...	...	...	...	21
42	Southern Shan States	46	3	24	...	...	...	...	19	246	155	...	19	...	20	...	91
43	Karenni ...	...	...	...	...	...	...	...	...	...	...	...	...	...	...	...	...

* NOTE.—For Group 140 see Order XXXIV on page 293, and for Group 143 see Order XXXVI on page 294.

Order XXXVII.—Trade in means of transport.

Group 144.—Dealers in and hirers of cycles and all kinds of mechanical transport (not hirers of hackney carriages).				Group 145.—Dealers in and hirers of other carriages, carts, boats, etc. (not hirers of hackney carriages).								Group 146.—Dealers and hirers of elephants, horses, cattle, mules, etc.								
Total workers and dependents.	WORKERS.*		DEPENDENTS.	Total Workers and Dependents.	WORKERS.						DEPENDENTS.	Total Workers and Dependents.	WORKERS.						DEPENDENTS.	Serial No. of District, etc. (column 1).
					Total Workers.		Workers with an agricultural or other subsidiary occupation.						Total Workers.		Workers with an agricultural or other subsidiary occupation.					
							Agricultural.		Other.						Agricultural.		Other.			
	Males	Females			Males.	Females	Males	Females	Males	Females			Males.	Females	Males	Females	Males	Females		
18	19	20	21	22	23	24	25	26	27	28	29	30	31	32	33	34	35	36	37	
330	87	8	235	2,456	803	231	8	5	80	25	1,422	20,953	6,448	2,789	232	95	661	352	11,716	
329	86	8	235	2,336	776	182	7	4	78	16	1,378	19,122	5,874	2,473	176	90	561	258	10,775	
1	...	...	1	307	102	8	2	...	19	...	197	3,215	620	604	45	15	68	70	1,991	
1	..	...	1	168	52	6	...	...	10	...	110	2,848	513	519	30	7	53	57	1,816	1
...	...	...	...	...	...	...	...	...	...	...	...	...	...	...	...	...	..	...	...	2
...	...	...	...	100	40	...	1	...	9	...	60	142	39	41	9	...	3	4	62	3
..	...	...	...	39	10	2	1	...	...	...	27	225	68	44	6	8	12	9	113	4
*184	*73		111	377	151	14	...	..	10	1	212	4,447	1,485	544	54	21	150	32	2,418	
170	66	...	104	83	72	1	...	...	...	...	10	145	32	1	...	...	...	...	112	5
4		...	4	11	5	2	..	...	...	...	4	576	215	89	4	5	24	5	272	6
..	..	...	...	35	27	..	...	...	6	...	8	330	184	21	3	...	19	...	125	7
4	2	...	2	101	16	...	.	...	...	...	85	1,537	423	239	33	11	54	18	875	8
*5	*4	..	1	127	25	11	...	...	4	1	91	1,113	413	130	14	...	51	...	570	9
1	1	...	...	20	6	...	...	...	..	...	14	746	218	64	...	5	2	9	464	10
...	...	...	...	383	59	82	...	4	3	..	242	2,977	956	306	24	18	99	29	1,715	
...	...	...	...	67	14	...	...	...	...	...	53	906	298	56	7	3	38	4	552	11
...	...	...	...	195	12	62	...	4	1	...	121	745	234	130	5	13	36	15	381	12
...	...	...	...	18	...	6	...	...	...	...	12	185	79	14	1	1	5	...	32	13
...	...	...	...	70	22	9	...	...	2	...	39	1,053	240	100	11	1	20	10	713	14
...	...	...	...	33	11	5	...	...	...	...	17	148	105	6	...	...	...	...	37	15
17	4	...	13	140	32	6	1	...	4	...	102	3,056	1,166	267	24	5	89	25	1,623	
.	...	...	...	13	7	...	...	...	3	...	6	1,234	421	154	5	4	53	18	659	16
...	...	...	...	...	...	...	...	...	...	...	...	60	25	...	2	...	2	...	35	17
..	.	...	...	36	9	6	1	...	1	...	21	803	289	68	5	...	18	1	446	18
14	3	...	11	74	5	...	...	...	...	...	69	740	355	33	3	...	3	...	358	19
3	1	...	2	8	6	...	...	...	...	...	2	188	62	12	9	1	12	6	114	20
...	...	...	...	9	5	...	..	...	...	...	4	25	14	...	...	...	1	...	11	21
1	...	...	1	688	320	9	1	...	32	...	359	693	165	178	3	5	17	12	350	
1	...	...	1	11	9	..	...	...	...	...	2	307	34	77	...	2	3	2	196	22
...	...	...	...	634	291	7	...	...	32	...	336	135	63	7	3	...	5	...	65	23
...	...	...	...	35	17	...	...	...	...	...	18	130	30	57	...	2	7	10	43	24
...	..	...	...	8	3	2	1	...	...	...	3	121	38	37	...	1	2	...	46	25
...	...	...	...	...	...	...	...	...	...	...	...	...	...	...	...	...	...	...	...	26
48	8	8	32	97	33	14	...	.	8	10	50	1,720	596	172	11	10	66	44	952	
44	6	8	30	43	9	4	...	...	...	...	30	732	250	4	...	...	3	...	478	27
2	2	...	...	32	...	4	...	...	...	...	28	619	210	4	...	...	...	...	405	
...	...	...	...	26	9	10	...	...	5	10	7	135	50	4	2	...	9	...	81	28
...	...	...	...	...	...	...	..	.	...	...	..	201	62	53	3	...	9	12	86	29
4	2	..	2	28	15	...	...	...	3	...	13	647	233	111	6	10	45	32	303	30
...	...	...	...	...	...	...	...	...	...	...	...	5	1	...	...	...	...	...	4	31
76	...	...	76	135	26	31	1	...	...	5	78	1,252	324	245	6	15	17	33	683	
...	...	...	...	119	22	27	1	...	...	2	70	263	79	18	...	...	2	...	156	32
...	...	..	...	8	3	...	--	...	...	...	5	255	105	2	...	...	6	1	148	33
...	...	...	...	2	1	...	...	...	...	...	1	420	132	40	5	...	6	...	248	34
76	...	...	76	6	...	4	..	...	...	3	2	314	8	175	1	15	3	32	131	35
...	...	...	...	...	...	...	...	.	...	...	...	...	...	...	...	...	...	...	...	36
2	1	...	1	209	53	18	2	...	2	...	138	1,762	562	157	9	1	55	13	1,043	
...	...	...	...	43	10	13	...	...	...	...	20	181	54	16	3	...	5	...	111	37
1	...	...	1	85	10	2	...	...	...	...	73	580	158	53	2	1	17	11	369	38
...	.	...	...	44	10	...	1	...	2	...	34	760	252	64	2	...	32	2	444	39
1	1	...	...	37	23	3	1	...	...	...	11	241	98	24	2	...	1	...	119	40
1	1	...	...	120	27	49	1	1	2	9	44	1,831	574	316	56	5	100	94	941	
...	...	...	...	106	13	49	...	1	.	9	44	793	273	130	27	2	35	45	390	41
1	1	...	...	14	14	...	1	..	2	..	...	1,000	282	185	27	3	64	49	533	42
...	...	...	...	...	...	...	...	...	...	...	...	38	19	1	2	...	1	...	18	43

* All without subsidiary occupations except 1 male in Pegu district with a non-agricultural subsidiary occupation.

Order XXXIX.*—Trade in articles of luxury and articles pertaining to letters or

Serial No.	District or State.	Group 148.—Dealers in precious stones, jewellery (real and imitation), clocks, optical instruments, etc. — Total Workers and Dependents.	Workers — Total Workers — Males.	Workers — Total Workers — Females.	Workers with an agricultural or other subsidiary occupation — Agricultural — Males	Agricultural — Females	Other — Males	Other — Females	Dependents.	Group 149.—Dealers in common bangles, bead necklaces, fans, small articles, toys, hunting and fishing tackle, flowers, etc. — Total Workers and Dependents.	Workers — Total Workers — Males.	Workers — Total Workers — Females.	Workers with an agricultural or other subsidiary occupation — Agricultural — Males	Agricultural — Females	Other — Males	Other — Females	Dependents.
	1	2	3	4	5	6	7	8	9	10	11	12	13	14	15	16	17
	Provincial Total ...	10,216	3,064	1,167	11	6	161	34	5,985	2,883	672	924	3	2	10	20	1,287
	Divisional Burma ...	10,006	2,982	1,116	9	5	158	34	5,908	2,820	653	903	3	2	10	19	1,264
	Arakan Division ...	33	24	...	...	...	...	...	9	41	30	4	...	...	1	2	7
1	Akyab ...	18	17	...	...	...	...	...	1	31	25	...	...	...	...	...	6
2	Hill Dist. of Arakan	...	...	...	...	...	...	...	...	...	...	...	...	...	...	...	...
3	Kyaukpyu ...	3	3	...	...	...	...	...	...	...	...	...	...	...	...	...	...
4	Sandoway ...	12	4	...	...	...	...	...	8	10	5	4	...	...	1	2	1
	Pegu Division ...	1,836	522	197	2	...	9	1	1,117	927	179	332		...	...	...	416
5	Rangoon Town ...	1,149	317	141	...	...	4	...	691	659	1 6	207	...	...	...	...	266
6	Insein ...	142	44	5	1	...	1	...	93	63	18	10	...	...	...	...	35
7	Hanthawaddy ...	37	12	...	1	...	...	...	25	32	3	23	...	...	...	...	6
8	Tharrawaddy ...	149	42	7	...	...	4	...	100	...	...	...	...	...	...	...	...
9	Pegu ...	140	48	6	...	...	...	1	86	49	8	1	...	...	...	...	40
10	Prome ...	219	59	38	...	...	...	...	122	124	24	31	...	...	...	...	69
	Irrawaddy Division ...	621	158	76	...	...	11	7	387	332	55	80	...	1	3	2	197
11	Bassein ...	264	81	9	...	...	9	1	174	5	...	2	...	...	...	...	3
12	Henzada ...	161	41	42	...	...	1	5	78	139	13	45	...	1	3	2	81
13	Myaungmya ...	79	23	10	...	...	1	1	46	2	2	...	...	...	...	...	...
14	Ma-ubin ...	63	6	9	...	...	...	...	48	179	38	31	...	...	...	...	110
15	Pyapôn ...	54	7	6	...	...	...	...	41	2	2	2	...	...	...	...	3
	Tenasserim Division ...	980	305	99	1	...	14		576	204	39	43	...	...	1	1	122
16	Toungoo ...	123	45	7	...	...	5	...	71	21	6	2	...	...	...	...	13
17	Salween ...	...	...	...	...	...	...	...	...	...	...	...	...	...	...	...	...
18	Thatôn ...	266	102	31	...	...	1	...	133	14	4	3	...	...	...	...	7
19	Amherst ...	356	115	33	1	...	7	...	208	136	22	31	...	...	1	...	83
20	Tavoy ...	97	13	22	...	...	1	...	62	22	4	7	...	...	...	1	11
21	Mergui ...	138	30	6	...	...	...	...	102	11	3	...	...	...	...	...	8
	Magwe Division ...	643	90	111	1	1	...	4	442	69	9	35	...	...	...	...	25
22	Thayetmyo ...	31	7	8	...	...	...	...	16	35	6	22	...	...	...	...	7
23	Pakôkku ...	507	40	91	...	1	...	3	376	20	2	5	...	...	...	...	13
24	Minbu ...	73	25	10	...	...	...	1	38	14	1	8	...	...	...	...	5
25	Magwe ...	32	18	2	1	...	...	...	12	...	...	...	...	...	...	...	...
26	Pakôkku Hill Tracts	...	...	...	...	...	...	...	...	...	...	...	...	...	...	...	...
	Mandalay Division ...	5,244	1,679	530	2	2	113	12	3,035	709	169	291	1	...	1	...	249
27	Mandalay ...	2,084	598	381	...	...	12	4	1,105	670	156	289	...	...	...	...	225
	Mandalay City ..	*2,018*	*573*	*369*	...	...	*11*	*4*	*1,076*	*662*	*151*	*289*	...	...	...	...	222
28	Bhamo ...	56	28	12	...	2	1	...	22	11	4	2	...	...	...	...	5
29	Myitkyina ...	562	202	31	2	...	65	3	329	6	...	...	...	...	...	...	6
30	Katha ...	2,542	857	106	...	...	35	5	1,579	22	9	...	1	...	1	...	13
31	Putao ...	...	...	...	...	...	...	...	...	...	...	...	...	...	...	...	...
	Sagaing Division ..	319	103	37	1	.	4	6	179	297	67	87	2	1	4	14	143
32	Shwebo ...	116	33	17	...	...	...	1	66	202	49	59	1	...	4	11	94
33	Sagaing ...	48	33	...	...		3	...	15	83	16	28	1	1	...	3	39
34	Lower Chindwin ...	101	22	12	1	...	...	...	67	11	2	...	...	...	...	...	9
35	Upper Chindwin ...	54	15	8	...	...	1	5	31	1	...	...	...	...	...	...	1
36	Chin Hills ...	..	...	...	...	...	...	...	...	...	...	...	...	...	...	...	...
	Meiktila Division ..	330	101	66	2	2	7	4	163	241	105	31	..	...	..	..	105
37	Kyauksè ...	38	22	1	1	...	2	...	15	14	...	7	...	...	...	...	7
38	Meiktila ...	102	31	13	1	...	4	...	58	66	55	5	...	...	...	...	6
39	Yamèthin ...	69	19	6	...	...	1	...	44	118	26	17	...	...	...	...	75
40	Myingyan ...	121	23	46	...	2	...	4	46	43	24	2	...	...	...	...	17
	Eastern States ...	210	82	51	2	1	3	...	77	63	19	21	...	...	...	1	23
41	Northern Shan States	195	73	50	2	1	3	...	72	54	17	20	...	...		1	17
42	Southern Shan States	9	8	...	...	...	...	...	1	9	2	1	...	...		...	6
43	Karenni ...	6	1	1	...	...	...	...	4	...	...	...	...	...	...	...	...

* NOTE.—For Group 147 see Order XXXVIII on page 295.

PART III.—*Details by districts*—contd.

to the arts or sciences.				Order XL.—Trade of other sorts.											
Group 150.—Publishers, booksellers, stationers, dealers in music, pictures, musical instruments and curiosities.				Group 151.—Dealers in rags or refuse.			Group 152.—General store-keepers and shop-keepers otherwise unspecified.								Serial No. of District, etc. (column 1).
Total Workers and Dependents.	WORKERS.*		DEPENDENTS.	Total Workers and Dependents.	WORKERS.†	DEPENDENTS.	Total Workers and Dependents.	WORKERS.						DEPENDENTS.	
								Total Workers.		Workers with an agricultural or other subsidiary occupation.					
										Agricultural.		Other.			
	Males.	Females.						Males.	Females.	Males.	Females.	Males.	Females.		
18	19	20	21	22	23	24	25	26	27	28	29	30	31	32	
1,077	453	79	545	29	25	4	452,916	103,629	139,856	2,545	2,490	5,612	4,294	209,431	
1,018	424	75	519	29	25	4	412,924	91,416	128,368	1,249	1,748	4,582	3,256	193,140	
42	26	...	16	...	...	...	24,960	6,803	6,527	165	148	281	255	11,630	
42	26	...	16	...	...	...	12,964	4,529	2,428	74	17	138	75	6,007	1
...	..	...	...	.	..	...	208	117	23	1	...	...	...	68	2
...	...	...	...	..	..	..	9,803	1,830	3,423	81	124	119	166	4,550	3
..	...	...	...	..	...	...	1,985	327	653	9	7	24	14	1,005	4
413	*191	26	196	...	...	...	98,658	23,014	26,300	176	482	1,116	460	49,344	
292	144	18	130	...	..	...	19,209	8,197	1,860	11	...	38	4	9,152	5
1	1	...	..	...	...	...	13,042	2,816	4,088	10	43	170	78	7,038	6
17	2	2	13	..	...	..	16,662	3,592	4,197	32	46	453	74	8,873	7
9	*6	...	3	...	...	...	14,167	2,280	5,032	53	96	141	58	6,855	8
38	8	3	27	...	...	...	22,248	4,623	6,280	68	215	207	126	11,345	9
56	*30	3	23	...	...	...	12,430	1,506	4,843	2	82	107	120	6,081	10
76	*19	2	55	1	...	1	120,399	28,168	37,533	366	467	1,259	773	54,698	
14	...	...	14	1	...	1	23,515	5,574	7,585	62	86	322	155	10,406	11
37	*10	1	26		..	...	29,339	5,3[illegible]1	11,002	86	234	248	288	12,986	12
21	7	1	13	...	...	...	31,569	7,881	8,797	120	67	390	204	14,891	13
2	2	...	...	...	...	...	16,845	4,167	5,509	51	39	168	83	7,169	14
2	...	...	2	...	...	...	19,131	5,945	4,640	47	41	131	43	9,246	15
91	31	..	60	19	† 18	1	53,951	11,668	16,439	133	96	546	411	25,844	
4	3	...	1	...	...	...	15,792	3,285	4,376	19	28	109	63	8,131	16
...	...	...	...	..	...	...	986	299	126	3	3	9	2	561	17
7	3	...	4	19	† 18	1	20,194	4,313	6,855	56	39	176	171	9,026	18
45	24	...	21	...	...	...	9,353	2,444	2,455	32	22	141	94	4,454	19
34	...	...	34	...	...	...	3,528	851	1,215	18	13	69	67	1,402	20
1	1	...	...	...	...	...	4,098	476	1,412	5	1	42	14	2,210	21
51	9	4	38	..	...	...	27,078	4,894	9,843	124	182	295	372	12,341	
...	...	...	...	..	...	...	7,340	944	2,172	4	13	36	59	4,224	22
16	..	3	13	...	...	...	6,055	1,121	2,072	36	24	109	118	2,862	23
31	8	...	23	...	...	...	7,440	1,478	2,958	43	102	130	145	3,004	24
4	1	1	2	...	...	...	6,242	1,350	2,641	41	43	20	50	2,251	25
...	...	...	...	..	...	...	1	1	...	...	...	...	...	...	26
273	110	41	122	5	† 5	...	29,896	6,648	9,805	100	63	374	258	13,443	
255	102	40	113	5	5	..	16,398	3,230	6,505	6	40	61	66	6,603	27
247	*98*	*40*	*109*	*5*	*5*	...	*9,702*	*2,034*	*3,409*	...	*1*	*1*	*6*	*4,259*	
...	...	...	...	...	...	...	1,458	331	363	5	...	49	17	764	28
4	4	...	...	...	...	...	1,644	551	390	1	...	85	23	703	29
14	4	1	9	...	...	...	10,355	2,513	2,542	88	13	179	152	5,300	30
...	...	...	..	..	...	...	41	23	5	...	...	...	...	13	31
26	*12	1	13	...	...	..	23,083	4,435	8,606	100	92	434	367	10,842	
5	3	...	2	...	...	..	8,159	1,540	2,974	24	2	133	40	3,645	32
10	2	1	7	...	...	...	5,755	688	2,924	38	33	51	170	2,143	33
11	*7	...	4	...	...	...	3,839	922	1,243	5	28	16	53	1,674	34
...	...	...	...	...	...	...	5,237	1,257	1,465	33	29	232	104	2,515	35
..	...	...	...	...	...	...	93	28	...	...	..	2	...	65	36
46	26	1	19	4	2	2	34,899	5,786	13,315	85	218	277	360	15,798	
5	3	...	2	4	2	2	2,759	266	1,215	6	22	24	22	1,278	37
3	2	1	...	..	...	...	7,217	1,004	3,148	17	67	64	118	3,065	38
37	20	...	17	...	...	...	6,481	1,354	1,615	7	13	43	31	3,512	39
1	1	..	...	...	...	...	18,442	3,162	7,337	55	116	146	189	7,943	40
59	*29	*4	26	..	...	..	39,992	12,213	11,488	1,296	742	1,030	1,038	16,291	
49	*22	*4	23	...	...	...	7,420	2,579	1,751	73	98	221	177	3,090	41
10	7	...	3	...	...	...	28,550	8,344	8,905	1,172	654	707	841	11,301	42
...	...	...	...	..	...	...	4,021	1,290	832	58	30	102	20	1,900	43

* One male in Northern Shan States had an agricultural subsidiary occupation. One male each in Tharrawaddy, Prome, Henzada, and Lower Chindwin districts and 4 males and 1 female in Northern Shan States had non-agricultural subsidiary occupations.

† All males excepting the 5 in the Mandalay district and all without subsidiary occupations except 1 male in Thatôn district with a non-agricultural subsidiary occupation.

Serial No.	DISTRICT OR STATE.	Order XL.—Trade of other sorts—*concluded.* Group 153.—Itinerant traders in miscellaneous or unspecified goods. Total Workers and Dependents.	WORKERS. Total Workers. Males.	Total Workers. Females.	Workers with an agricultural or other subsidiary occupation. Agricultural. Males.	Agricultural. Females.	Other. Males.	Other. Females.	DEPENDENTS.	Group 154.—Other kinds of trade not in the foregoing groups. Total Workers and Dependents.	WORKERS. Total Workers. Males.	Total Workers. Females.	Workers with an agricultural or other subsidiary occupation. Agricultural. Males.	Agricultural. Females.	Other. Males.	Other. Females.	DEPENDENTS.
	1	2	3	4	5	6	7	8	9	10	11	12	13	14	15	16	17
	Provincial Total ...	1,216	351	193	3	3	10	8	672	696	137	209	7	16	10	24	350
	Divisional Burma ...	1,144	296	191	3	3	10	8	657	645	126	209	5	16	10	24	310
	Arakan Division ...	11	...	...	...	...	...	...	11	...	...	...	...	...	...	...	...
1	Akyab ...	9	...	...	...	...	...	...	9	...	...	...	...	...	...	...	...
2	Hill Dist. of Arakan	...	...	...	...	...	...	...	...	...	...	...	...	...	...	...	...
3	Kyaukpyu ...	...	...	...	...	...	...	...	...	...	...	...	...	...	...	...	...
4	Sandoway ...	2	...	...	...	...	...	...	2	...	...	...	...	...	...	...	...
	Pegu Division ...	182	65	27	...	...	1	...	90	93	22	6	...	...	...	...	65
5	Rangoon Town ...	116	53	12	...	...	1	...	51	63	10	4		...	...	...	49
6	Insein ...	...	...	...	...	...	...	...	...	2	...	...	...	...	...	...	2
7	Hanthawaddy ...	19	...	11	...	...	...	...	8	8	1	...	...	...	...	...	7
8	Tharrawaddy ...	11	3	4	...	...	...	...	4	5	5	...	...	...	...	...	...
9	Pegu ...	25	6		...	...	...	...	19	12	4	2	...	...	...	...	6
10	Prome ...	11	3	...	...	...	...	...	8	3	2	...	...	...	...	...	1
	Irrawaddy Division ...	99	1	60	...	...	...	3	38	59	25	3	...	...		...	32
11	Bassein ...	...	...	...	...	...	...	...	...	7	...	...	...	...	...	...	7
12	Henzada ...	50	1	17	...	...	...	2	32	16	3	2	...	...	...	...	11
13	Myaungmya ...	...	...	...	...	...	...	...	...	21	15	...	...	...	...	...	6
14	Ma-ubin ...	7	...	1	...	...	...	1	6	10	4	1	...	...	1	...	5
15	Pyapôn ...	42	...	42	...	...	...	...	...	5	3	...	...	...	...	...	2
	Tenasserim Division ...	64	8	27	...	...	...	...	29	38	7	...	...	...	1	...	32
16	Toungoo ...	1	...	1	...	...	...	...	...	38	2	...	...	...	...	...	26
17	Salween ...	...	...	...	...	...	...	...	...	...	...	...	...	...	...	...	...
18	Thatôn ...	...	...	...	...	...	...	...	...	2	2	...		...	1	...	...
19	Amherst ...	60	7	24	...	...	...	...	29	5	1	...	...	...	...	...	4
20	Tavoy ...	3	1	2	...	...	...	...	...	3	2	...	...	...	...	...	1
21	Mergui ...	...	...	...	...	...	...	...	...	...	...	...	...	...	...	...	...
	Magwe Division ...	363	151	24	...	1	5	2	188	80	39	3	5	...	6	...	38
22	Thayetmyo ...	2	2	...	...	...	...	...	...	1	1	...	...	...	...	...	...
23	Pakôkku ...	290	149	...	...	...	5	...	141	4	2	1	...	...	...	...	1
24	Minbu ...	34	...	1	...	...	...	...	33	63	36	...	5	...	6	...	27
25	Magwe ...	37	...	23	...	1	...	2	14	12	...	2	...	...	...	...	10
26	Pakôkku Hill Tracts	...	...	...	...	...	...	...	...	...	...	...	...	...	...	...	...
	Mandalay Division ...	60	10	29	...	2	...	3	21	310	28	192	...	16	...	21	90
27	Mandalay ...	11	8	...	...	...	...	...	3	64	28	...	...	...	...	...	36
	Mandalay City ...	2	2	...	...	...	...	...	...	43	23	...	...	...	...	...	20
28	Bhamo ...	7	1	5	...	2	...	...	1	4	...	...	...	...	...	...	4
29	Myitkyina ...	20	1	2	...	...	...	...	17	...	...	...	...	...	...	...	...
30	Katha ...	22	...	22	...	...	...	3	...	242	...	192	...	16	...	21	50
31	Putao ...	...	...	...	...	...	...	...	...	...	...	...	...	...	...	...	...
	Sagaing Division ...	29	19	1	2	...	2	...	9	10	1	...	...	...	...	...	9
32	Shwebo ...	...	...	...	...	...	...	...	...	9	1	...	...	...	...	...	8
33	Sagaing ...	12	7	1	2	...	...	...	4	...	...	...	...	...	...	...	...
34	Lower Chindwin ...	17	12	...	...	...	2	...	5	1	...	...	...	...	...	...	1
35	Upper Chindwin ...	...	...	...	...	...	...	...	...	...	...	...	...	...	...	...	...
36	Chin Hills ...	...	...	...	...	...	...	...	...	...	...	...	...	...	...	...	...
	Meiktila Division ...	336	42	23	1	...	2	...	271	55	4	5	...	...	1	3	46
37	Kyauksè ...	16	9	...	...	...	1	...	7	...	...	...	...	...	...	...	...
38	Meiktila ...	235	30	1	1	...	1	...	204	30	3	5	...	...	1	3	22
39	Yamèthin ...	84	2	22	...	...	...	...	60	17	1	...	...	...	...	...	16
40	Myingyan ...	1	1	...	...	...	...	...	...	8	...	...	...	...	...	...	8
	Eastern States ...	72	55	2	...	...	...	...	15	51	11	...	2	...	...	...	40
41	Northern Shan States	72	55	2	...	...	...	...	15	20	5	...	...	...	...	...	15
42	Southern Shan States	...	...	...	...	...	...	...	...	31	6	...	2	...	...	...	25
43	Karenni ...	...	...	...	...	...	...	...	...	...	...	...	...	...	...	...	...

PART III.—*Details by districts*—contd.

Order XLIV.*—Police and professional village-watchmen.											Order XLV.—Public administration.								
Group 159.*—Police.								Group 160 — Professional village watchmen.			Group 161.—General service of the Government of India or a provincial government.								
Total Workers and Dependents.	WORKERS. Total Workers. Males.	WORKERS. Total Workers. Females	Workers with an agricultural or other subsidiary occupation. Agricultural. Males.	Agricultural. Females	Other. Males.	Other. Females	DEPENDENTS.	Total Workers and Dependents.	WORKERS. (All males without subsidiary occupations.)	DEPENDENTS.	Total Workers and Dependents.	WORKERS. Total Workers. Males.	Total Workers. Females	Workers with an agricultural or other subsidiary occupation. Agricultural. Males.	Agricultural. Females.	Other. Males	Other. Females	DEPENDENTS.	Serial No. of District, etc. (column 1).
18	19	20	21	22	23	24	25	26	27	28	29	30	31	32	33	34	35	36	
65,327	29,767	448	212	1	151	39	35,112	47	22	25	35,364	12,071	341	204	2	87	6	22,952	
61,054	27,633	303	165	...	135	28	33,118	47	22	25	32,504	11,295	283	95	...	56	6	20,926	
3,860	1,345	62	3	...	6	..	2,453	...	...	..	2,113	490	2	4	-	3	...	1,621	
1,407	591	1	2	...	...	..	815	...	...	...	1,451	397	...	1	..	1	...	1,054	1
519	249	...	1	...	2	...	270	...	.	...	57	9	...	...	...	...	...	48	2
867	121	61	...	...	...	...	685	...	...	...	253	20	2	...	...	...	...	231	3
1,067	384	...	...	...	4	...	683	...	...	...	352	64	...	3	...	2	...	288	4
13,364	6,068	76	99	...	20	...	7,220	1	.	1	12,578	4,243	195	21	...	15	..	8,140	
3,954	2,276	4	4	-	2	...	1,674	...	...	..	8,445	3,002	173	3	...	7	...	5,270	5
1,507	623	47	...	...	..	..	837	1	...	1	1,248	311	16	11	...	3	...	921	6
1,898	843	21	...	...	1	...	1,031	...		...	285	95	2	2	...	1	...	188	7
2,261	837	..	...	...	1	...	1,424	...	...	...	810	166	...	...	...	3	...	641	8
2,110	865	2	95	...	14	.	1,243	...	...	...	887	245	3	4	...	..	...	639	9
1,634	624	2	..	...	2	...	1,008	...	...	...	903	424	1	1	...	1	...	478	10
7,071	2,864	10	1	...	1	...	4,197	...	...	...	3,703	1,283	20	1	...	4	...	2,400	
2,132	895	...	...	..	...	...	1,237	...	...	...	1,401	561	1	...	...	...	...	839	11
1,848	671	...	..	...	1	...	1,177	..	...		784	290	17	1	..	2	...	477	12
1,163	512	6	..	...	...	...	645	...	...	...	595	201	1	...	...	2	...	393	13
1,015	420	4	...	...	...	...	591	...	..	...	690	183	1	..	...	...	...	506	14
913	366	.	1	...	...	...	547	...	...	...	233	48	...	...	...	...	...	185	15
7,148	3,299	43	3	..	11	19	3,806	1	..	1	4,621	1,869	13	5	..	9	3	2,739	
1,821	980	13	...	...	4	...	828	...	...	...	1,395	711	1	2	...	4	...	683	16
362	238	18	2	...	1	18	106	...	...	...	127	29	...	1	...	...	...	98	17
1,795	648	8	1	...	2	1	1,139	...	...	...	477	169	...	...	...	...	...	308	18
1,604	707	3	...	...	3	...	894	1	..	1	1,447	492	7	1	...	2	3	948	19
910	454	1	1	...	...	...	455	...	...	...	602	239	3	...	...	1	...	360	20
656	272	...	...	...	1	...	384	...	...	...	573	219	2	1	...	2	...	342	21
5,845	2,267	5	1	...	...	...	3,573	...	...	...	1,764	576	7	...	...	5	2	1,181	
1,466	428	...	...	...	...	...	1,038	...	...	...	459	100	...	...	...	2	..	299	22
1,618	474	..	1	...	...	...	1,144	..	...	...	342	135	4		...	2	2	203	23
1,443	580	1	...	...	...	...	862	..	...	...	635	124	2	...	...	...	...	509	24
1,171	655	4	...	...	...	...	512	...	...	...	308	153	1	...	...	1	...	154	25
147	130	...	...	...	...	..	17	...	...	...	20	4	...	...	...	...	...	16	26
11,548	6,558	63	5	...	10	8	4,927	4	4	...	2,839	1,104	15	2	..	5	...	1,720	
4,136	2,338	8	...	...	1		1,790	4	4	...	1,789	718	10	...	..	.	...	1,061	27
1,846	904	...	...	...	...	...	942	4	4	...	1,256	514	6	...	...	...	...	736	
1,468	1,047	...	...	...		...	421	...	...	...	239	54	...	...	...	...	...	185	28
3,517	1,976	3	5	...	2	...	1,538	...	...	...	355	104	3	...	...	...	...	248	29
1,607	626	52	...	...	7	8	929	...	..	...	320	159	2	...	...	5	..	159	30
820	571	...	...	...	...	..	249	...	...	...	136	69	...	2	...	...	...	67	31
6,146	2,925	35	53	...	84	1	3,186	18	2	16	2,532	883	27	44	...	8	1	1,622	
1,670	604	32	...	...	1	...	1,034	...	...	.	694	224	24	4	...	3	...	446	32
807	302	1	...	...	...	1	504	...	...	...	628	230	...	...	...	...	...	398	33
1,341	696	1	...	...	...	...	644	18	2	16	553	220	...	34	...	3	...	333	34
1,384	747	1	...	...	82	...	576	...	...	...	597	195	3	6	...	2	1	399	35
1,004	576	...	53	...	1	.	428	...	...	...	60	14	...	...	...	...	...	46	36
6,072	2,307	9	...	...	3	...	3,756	23	16	7	2,354	847	4	18	...	7	...	1,503	
1,125	346	...	...	..	1	...	779	...	...	...	519	255	...	...	...	...	...	264	37
1,274	520	4	...	...	2	...	750	2	...	2	504	160	1	18	...	5	...	337	38
2,106	895	5	...	...	...	...	1,206	16	16	...	926	215	3	...	...	2	...	708	39
1,567	546	...	..	...	...	...	1,021	5	...	5	405	211	...	...	...	...	...	194	40
4,273	2,134	145	47	1	16	11	1,994	...	...	...	2,860	776	58	109	2	31	..	2,026	
2,064	1,425	132	10	1	11	11	507	...	..	...	1,381	507	28	77	..	26	...	846	41
2,086	680	13	37	...	5	...	1,393	...	...	...	1,185	161	22	23	2	4	...	1,002	42
123	29	...	...	...	...	...	94		...	...	294	108	8	9	...	1	...	178	43

* NOTE.—For Groups 155 and 156 see Order XLI on page 297. Groups 157 and 158 and Orders XLII and XLIII are blank.

Order XLV.—Public administration

Serial No.	District or State.	Group 162.—General service of a Shan, Indian or foreign state. Total Workers and Dependents.	Workers. Total Workers. Males.	Workers. Total Workers. Females.	Workers with an agricultural or other subsidiary occupation. Agricultural. Males.	Agricultural. Females.	Other. Males.	Other. Females.	Dependents.	Group 163.—Municipal and other local (not village) service. Total Workers and Dependents.	Workers. Total Workers. Males.	Workers. Total Workers. Females.	Workers with an agricultural or other subsidiary occupation. Agricultural. Males.	Agricultural. Females.	Other. Males.	Other. Females.	Dependents.
	1	2	3	4	5	6	7	8	9	10	11	12	13	14	15	16	17
	Provincial Total	11,913	5,446	78	3,500	2	421	1	6,389	6,479	2,806	132	11	2	67	2	3,541
	Divisional Burma	227	39	9	8	...	2	...	179	6,213	2,687	103	4	1	59	...	3,423
	Arakan Division	...	...	...	...	...	...	...	...	320	79	6	2	...	2	...	235
1	Akyab	...	...	...	...	...	...	...	...	248	65	4	2	...	1	...	179
2	Hill Dist. of Arakan	...	...	...	...	...	...	...	...	1	...	...	...	...	...	...	1
3	Kyaukpyu	...	...	...	...	...	...	...	...	38	9	1	...	...	1	...	28
4	Sandoway	...	...	...	...	...	...	...	...	33	5	1	...	...	...	...	27
	Pegu Division	11	...	5	...	...	...	...	6	2,255	937	36	...	...	9	...	1,282
5	Rangoon Town	5	...	...	...	...	...	...	5	1,516	646	1	...	...	1	...	869
6	Insein	...	...	...	...	...	...	...	...	129	46	7	...	...	...	...	76
7	Hanthawaddy	...	...	...	...	...	...	...	...	82	19	...	...	...	3	...	63
8	Tharrawaddy	...	...	...	...	...	...	...	...	241	113	2	...	...	5	...	126
9	Pegu	6	...	5	...	...	...	...	1	131	56	1	...	...	...	...	74
10	Prome	...	...	...	...	...	...	...	...	156	57	25	...	...	...	...	74
	Irrawaddy Division	...	...	...	...	...	...	...	...	548	191	14	...	...	6	...	343
11	Bassein	...	...	...	...	...	...	...	...	70	13	1	...	...	...	...	56
12	Henzada	...	...	...	...	...	...	...	...	214	77	10	...	...	1	...	127
13	Myaungmya	...	...	...	...	...	...	...	...	77	33	...	...	...	3	...	44
14	Ma-ubin	...	...	...	...	...	...	...	...	136	45	1	...	...	2	...	90
15	Pyapôn	...	...	...	...	...	...	...	...	51	23	2	...	...	...	...	26
	Tenasserim Division	27	4	...	3	...	...	...	23	1,235	696	4	1	...	8	...	535
16	Toungoo	24	3	...	3	...	...	...	21	332	138	1	...	...	4	...	193
17	Salween	...	...	...	...	...	...	...	...	...	...	...	...	...	...	...	...
18	Thatôn	...	...	...	...	...	...	...	...	263	200	...	...	...	1	...	63
19	Amherst	3	1	...	...	...	...	...	2	479	250	2	...	...	...	...	227
20	Tavoy	...	...	...	...	...	...	...	...	97	67	1	1	...	3	...	29
21	Mergui	...	...	...	...	...	...	...	...	64	41	...	...	...	...	...	23
	Magwe Division	...	...	...	...	...	...	...	...	483	189	16	...	...	25	...	278
22	Thayetmyo	...	...	...	...	...	...	...	...	143	68	2	...	...	...	...	73
23	Pakôkku	...	...	...	...	...	...	...	...	35	22	...	...	...	3	...	13
24	Minbu	...	...	...	...	...	...	...	...	244	68	11	...	...	11	...	165
25	Magwe	...	...	...	...	...	...	...	...	61	31	3	...	...	11	...	27
26	Pakôkku Hill Tracts	...	...	...	...	...	...	...	...	...	...	...	...	...	...	...	...
	Mandalay Division	53	18	...	5	...	2	...	35	495	277	2	...	...	4	...	216
27	Mandalay	...	...	...	...	...	...	...	...	402	238	...	...	...	3	...	164
	Mandalay City	...	...	...	...	...	...	...	...	*297*	*184*	...	...	...	*2*	...	*113*
28	Bhamo	9	5	...	...	...	...	...	4	41	7	1	...	...	1	...	33
29	Myitkyina	22	8	...	...	...	2	...	14	27	16	...	...	...	...	...	11
30	Katha	12	...	...	...	...	...	...	12	25	16	1	...	...	...	...	8
31	Putao	10	5	...	5	...	...	...	5	...	...	...	...	...	...	...	...
	Sagaing Division	136	17	4	...	...	...	...	115	263	111	5	1	...	2	...	147
32	Shwebo	...	...	...	...	...	...	...	...	62	36	4	...	...	1	...	22
33	Sagaing	...	...	...	...	...	...	...	...	156	55	1	1	...	1	...	100
34	Lower Chindwin	...	...	...	...	...	...	...	...	42	19	...	...	...	...	...	23
35	Upper Chindwin	133	17	4	...	...	...	...	112	3	1	...	...	...	...	...	2
36	Chin Hills	3	...	...	...	...	...	...	3	...	...	...	...	...	...	...	...
	Meiktila Division	...	...	...	...	...	...	...	...	614	207	20	...	1	3	...	387
37	Kyauksè	...	...	...	...	...	...	...	...	37	15	...	...	...	1	...	22
38	Meiktila	...	...	...	...	...	...	...	...	207	57	16	...	...	...	...	134
39	Yamèthin	...	...	...	...	...	...	...	...	315	115	4	...	1	1	...	196
40	Myingyan	...	...	...	...	...	...	...	...	55	20	...	...	...	1	...	35
	Eastern States	11,686	5,407	69	3,492	2	419	1	6,210	266	119	29	7	1	8	2	118
41	N. Shan States	1,018	120	24	43	2	4	1	874	200	94	28	5	...	3	2	78
42	S. Shan States	10,602	5,285	44	3,449	...	415	...	5,273	54	22	...	2	...	5	...	32
43	Karenni	66	2	1	...	...	...	...	63	12	3	1	...	1	...	...	8

PART III.—*Details by districts—contd.*

—*concluded.* Group 164.—Village officials and village servants other than watchmen. Total Workers and Dependents.	Workers. Total Workers. Males.	Females.	Workers with an agricultural or other subsidiary occupation. Agricultural. Males.	Agricultural. Females.	Other. Males	Other. Females.	Dependents.	Order XLVI.—Religion. Group 165.—Pongyis, upazins, priests, ministers, etc. Total Workers and Dependents.	Workers. Total Workers. Males.	Females.	Workers with an agricultural or other subsidiary occupation. Agricultural. Males.	Agricultural. Females	Other. Males.	Other. Females.	Dependents.	Serial No. of District, etc. (column 1).
18	19	20	21	22	23	24	25	26	27	28	29	30	31	32	33	
49,285	12,919	441	5,387	84	1,188	33	35,925	106,429	69,593	224	56	9	203	1	36,612	
44,654	12,397	400	5,074	83	1,110	32	31,857	95,174	63,581	171	39	4	84	1	31,422	
2,910	690	17	368	2	38	...	2,203	4,608	2,152	17	11	...	26	1	2,439	
1,631	331	...	167	...	19	...	1,300	2,746	1,292	12	9	...	18	...	1,442	1
57	16	...	8	...	...	...	41	15	10	1	...	...	...	...	4	2
733	206	17	101	2	13	...	510	1,255	581	3	...	...	2	...	671	3
489	137	...	92	...	6	...	352	592	269	1	2	...	6	1	322	4
6,494	1,817	11	535	...	235	...	4,666	17,921	11,435	58	5	...	4	.	6,428	
296	94	...	1	...	5	...	202	4,738	2,604	35	...	...	...	...	2,099	5
1,237	283	3	23	...	14	...	951	1,541	1,059	7	2	...	2	...	475	6
792	349	...	145	...	24	...	443	2,942	1,723	7	...	...	...	...	1,212	7
1,711	434	4	42	...	119	...	1,273	2,521	1,592	5	2	..	2	...	924	8
1,536	395	2	160	...	53	...	1,139	3,184	2,880	4	1	..	...	...	600	9
922	262	2	164	...	20	...	658	2,69[illegible]	1,577	...	...	...	...	...	1,118	10
7,788	2,133	78	888	20	218	13	5,577	10,706	7,337	27	1	..	9	..	3,342	
1,895	530	6	231	2	85	...	1,359	3,076	2,276	12	...	...	...	...	788	11
1,869	543	20	238	14	42	6	1,306	2,550	1,721	6	...	...	3	.	823	12
1,761	474	39	230	...	39	...	1,248	1,364	903	2		...	2	...	459	13
928	258	10	72	1	26	7	660	1,765	1,254	3	1	...	1	...	508	14
1,335	328	3	117	3	26	...	1,004	1,951	1,183	4	...	...	3	..	764	15
5,430	1,401	26	414	2	73	3	4,003	10,568	6,508	29	17	2	18	...	4,031	
1,515	459	3	107	...	21	..	1,053	2,398	1,620	19	12	2	10	...	759	16
81	26	...	9	...	2		55	147	59	...	...	...	1	...	88	17
1,495	356	17	149	2	18	1	1,122	2,665	1,848	1	2	...	...	...	816	18
1,080	288	2	38	...	1	...	796	3,283	1,942	5	...		...	...	1,336	19
501	153	4	71	...	12	2	344	1,219	679	3	1	...	4	...	537	20
752	119	...	40	...	19	...	633	856	360	1	2	...	3	...	495	21
6,693	1,738	59	838	13	213	2	4,896	14,852	10,050	...	...	.	1	...	4,802	
1,605	374	12	172	6	29	1	1,219	2,088	966	...	..	.	1	..	1,122	22
2,414	636	...	377	...	48	.	1,784	5,696	4,234	...	...	..	...	...	1,462	23
1,338	325	3	191	1	21	1	1,010	3,370	1,902	...	...	...	...	...	1,468	24
1,336	409	44	98	6	115	...	883	3,698	2,948	...	.	...	...	...	750	25
...	...	...	...	...	.	...	...	...	...	..	...	...	...	...	...	26
4,348	1,313	89	507	23	146	6	2,946	11,700	7,874	23	2	...	10	...	3,803	
1,448	480	19	47	..	50	...	949	7,006	6,023	6	...	...	3	...	977	27
317	*115*	...	*6*	..	*10*	...	*202*	*4,843*	*4,162*	*5*		...	...	...	*676*	
473	125	1	69	...	25	1	347	760	332	7	1	...	1	...	421	28
489	156	2	88	1	17	...	331	448	269	2	...	...	1	...	177	29
1,937	551	67	302	22	54	5	1,319	3,449	1,218	8	1	...	5	..	2,223	30
1	1	...	1	...	...	...	.	37	32	...	..	..	...	...	5	31
5,451	1,867	62	1,019	11	133	2	3,522	14,419	10,182	4	2	...	1	...	4,233	
1,596	478	58	266	10	25	1	1,060	3,738	2,684	2	1	...	1	...	1,052	32
1,206	365	2	152	1	28	1	839	4,229	3,419	...	1	...	...	..	810	33
703	310	...	160	...	30	...	393	3,677	2,542	2	...	...	...	..	1,133	34
1,570	423	2	230	...	43	...	1,145	2,732	1,525	...	...	..	...	...	1,207	35
376	291	...	205	...	7	...	85	43	12	...	...	...	..	...	31	36
5,540	1,438	58	505	12	54	6	4,044	10,400	8,043	13	1	2	15	...	2,344	
1,190	280	...	176	...	6	...	910	1,400	1,013	5	...	1	...	...	382	37
1,202	284	26	18	8	15	3	892	2,507	2,260	1	...	...	1	...	246	38
1,546	413	32	148	4	22	3	1101	2,571	2,011	7	1	1	14	..	553	39
1,602	461	...	163	...	11	...	1,141	3,922	2,759	...	...	...	...	...	1,163	40
4,631	522	41	313	1	78	1	4,068	11,255	6,012	53	17	5	119		5,190	
1,420	442	1	278	...	75	...	977	3,540	1,925	13	1	1	113	...	1,602	41
3,107	39	39	27	...	3	1	3,029	7,408	3,902	39	16	4	6	...	3,466	42
104	41	1	8	1	...	...	62	307	184	1	...	...	..	...	122	43

Serial No.	District or State.	Order XLVI.—Religion—*concluded.* Group 166.—Nuns, religious mendicants, inmates of monasteries, etc. Total Workers and Dependents.	Workers. Total Workers. Males.	Total Workers. Females	Workers with an agricultural or other subsidiary occupation. Agricultural. Males	Agricultural. Females	Other. Males.	Other. Females	Dependents.	Group 167.—Lay preachers, catechists, readers, church and mission service. Total Workers and Dependents.	Workers.* Males.	Workers.* Females	Dependents.	Group 168.—Temple, burial or burning ground service, circumcisers. Total Workers and Dependents.	Workers.† Males.	Workers.† Females	Dependents.
	1	2	3	4	5	6	7	8	9	10	11	12	13	14	15	16	17
	Provincial Total ...	47,342	26,830	7,745	2	1	110	13	12,767	478	190	7	281	1,061	464	48	549
	Divisional Burma ...	30,326	11,201	6,806	2	1	8	1	12,319	460	179	7	274	1,027	437	48	542
	Arakan Division ...	1,171	386	200	1	...	...	...	585	...	...	...	..	3	3	...	...
1	Akyab ...	880	138	183	1	...	...	...	559	...	...	...	...	2	2	...	...
2	Hill Dist. of Arakan	2	...	1	...	...	...	...	1	...	..	...	...	...	...	...	...
3	Kyaukpyu ...	174	171	...	...	...	...	...	3	...	...	...	...	...	...	...	...
4	Sandoway ...	115	77	16	...	...	...	..	22	...	...	...	..	1	1	...	...
	Pegu Division ..	4,609	1,011	1,402	...	1	...	...	2,196	87	* 25	1	61	386	154	21	211
5	Rangoon Town ...	1,068	49	479	...	...	...	...	540	11	1	1	9	171	48	3	120
6	Insein ...	649	129	134	...	1	.	...	386	1	...	...	1	35	23	...	12
7	Hanthawaddy ..	724	212	210	...	...	...	...	302	...	...	...	...	25	15	...	10
8	Tharrawaddy ...	805	566	166	...	...	...	...	113	41	* 15	...	26	11	4	..	7
9	Pegu ...	593	17	304	...	...	...	...	272	20	2	...	18	134	57	18	59
10	Prome ...	770	98	89	...	...	...	...	583	14	7	...	7	10	7	...	3
	Irrawaddy Division ...	3,631	1,538	685	...	...	...	...	1,408	126	* 46	3	77	103	24	6	73
11	Bassein ..	561	353	136	...	...	...	...	72	14	...	...	14	50	11	...	39
12	Henzada ...	1,283	687	188	...	...	...	...	408	52	* 30	...	22	9	9	..	...
13	Myaungmya ...	620	165	106	...	...	...	...	349	...	...	...	...	10	1	...	9
14	Ma-ubin ..	700	51	138	...	...	...	...	511	38	7	...	25	8	1	...	7
15	Pyapôn ..	467	282	117	...	..	...	...	68	28	9	3	16	26	2	6	18
	Tenasserim Division ..	3,687	1,257	985	...	...	...	...	1,445	103	38	1	64	84	27	2	55
16	Toungoo ...	910	411	179	...	...	...	...	320	4	2	...	2	9	2	1	6
17	Salween ...	39	11	3	...	...	...	...	25	10	6	...	4	...	...	..	...
18	Thatôn ...	875	51	247	...	...	...	...	577	18	...	1	17	35	5	...	30
19	Amherst ...	1,130	579	343	...	...	...	...	208	64	23	...	41	8	7	1	...
20	Tavoy ..	652	180	202	...	...	...	...	270	7	7	...	...	28	11	...	17
21	Mergui ..	81	25	11	...	...	...	...	45	...	...	...	...	4	2	...	2
	Magwe Division ...	2,526	684	438	...	...	...	...	1,404	57	38	...	19	50	† 37	2	11
22	Thayetmyo .	496	16	102	...	...	...	...	378	11	7	...	4	37	26	...	11
23	Pakôkku ...	474	27	211	...	...	...	...	236	16	10	...	6	...	...	...	...
24	Minbu ...	705	1	108	...	...	...	...	596	17	8	...	9	13	† 11	2	...
25	Magwe ...	851	640	17	...	...	...	...	194	13	13	..	...	...	...	...	...
26	Pakôkku Hill Tracts	..	...	...	...	...	...	...	...	...	...	...	...	...	...	...	...
	Mandalay Division ...	2,886	931	607	...	...	5	1	1,348	3	...	1	2	323	161	15	147
27	Mandalay ..	1,587	589	241	...	...	...	...	757	...	...	...	...	319	157	15	147
	Mandalay City ...	*1,174*	*333*	*123*	...	...	...	...	*718*	...	..	...	...	*276*	*149*	*15*	*112*
28	Bhamo ..	146	11	85	...	...	...	...	50	3	...	1	2	3	3	...	.
29	Myitkyina ..	116	77	23	...	...	5	...	16	...	...	...	...	1	1	...	...
30	Katha ...	1,026	253	254	..	...	...	1	519	...	...	..	...	...	...	...	...
31	Putao ...	11	1	4	...	...	...	...	6	...	..	...	...	...	...	...	..
	Sagaing Division ..	7,329	3,544	1,588	...	...	2	...	2,197	45	* 12	1	32	41	22	2	17
32	Shwebo ...	2,397	2,043	238	...	...	...	...	116	25	* 8	1	16	7	7	...	...
33	Sagaing ...	3,020	31	1,078	...	...	...	...	1,911	8	1	...	7	19	6	2	11
34	Lower Chindwin ..	1,633	1,372	114	...	...	2	...	147	10	* 3	...	7	15	9	..	6
35	Upper Chindwin ...	279	98	158	...	...	...	...	23	2	...	...	2	...	...	...	..
36	Chin Hills ..	...	.	...	...	...	...	...	...	...	...	...	...	...	...	...	...
	Meiktila Division ...	4,487	1,850	901	1	...	1	...	1,736	39	* 20	...	19	37	9	...	28
37	Kyauksè ...	190	5	176	1	...	...	...	9	9	4	-	5	...	...	...	...
38	Meiktila ..	1,520	1,033	386	...	...	...	..	101	3	3	...	...	4	3	...	1
39	Yamèthin ..	1,248	505	149	...	...	1	...	596	...	.	...	...	21	5	...	16
40	Myingyan ...	1,529	309	190	...	...	...	...	1,030	27	* 13	..	14	12	1	...	11
	Eastern States ...	17,016	15,629	939	..	...	102	12	448	18	11	...	7	34	27	...	7
41	N. Shan States ..	4,172	3,395	674	...	...	101	12	103	8	6	...	2	5	...	...	5
42	S. Shan States ..	12,793	12,195	257	...	...	1	...	340	10	5	...	5	29	27	...	2
43	Karenni ..	51	38	8	...	...	...	...	5	...	...	...	...	...	...	...	...

* Two males and 11 males respectively in Tharrawaddy and Henzada districts had agricultural subsidiary occupations; 1 male in each of the Shwebo, Lower Chindwin and Myingyan districts had a non-agricultural subsidiary occupation.

† All without subsidiary occupations except 2 males in the Minbu district with non-agricultural subsidiary occupations.

PART III.—*Details by districts*—contd.

Order XLVII.—Law.

Group 169.—Lawyers of all kinds.								Group 170.—Lawyers' clerks, petition writers, etc.								
Total Workers and Dependents.	WORKERS.						DEPENDENTS.	Total Workers and Dependents.	WORKERS.						DEPENDENTS.	Serial No. of District, etc., column 1).
	Total Workers.		Workers with an agricultural or other subsidiary occupation.						Total Workers.		Workers with an agricultutal or other subsidiary occupatoin.					
			Agricultural.		Other.						Agricultural.		Other.			
	Males.	Females.	Males.	Females	Males.	Females.			Males.	Females.	Males.	Females	Males.	Females		
18	19	20	21	22	23	24	25	26	27	23	29	30	31	32	33	
6,4[illegible]3	1,472	41	45	...	63	...	4,900	4,523	1,307	52	19	...	32	2	3,164	
6,359	1,461	32	45	...	63	...	4,866	4,488	1,2[illegible]4	52	19	...	32	[illegible]	3,142	
325	64	...	3	...	2	...	261	285	60	...	1	...	2	...	225	
237	52	..	1	...	1	...	185	239	56	...	1	...	2	...	183	1
...	...	...	...	...	...	...	..	...	...	...	...	...	...	...	..	2
54	7	...	1	...	...	...	47	31	...	...	...	...	...	...	34	3
34	5	...	1	...	1	...	29	12	4	...	...	...	...	...	8	4
1,861	453	7	6	...	10	...	1,401	1,437	353	33	3	...	4	1	1,051	
729	211	..	3	...	10	...	518	589	160	...	...	...	.	...	429	5
209	38	5	...	...	...	...	166	135	48	2	...	...	1	...	85	6
140	26	..	2	...	...	...	114	93	18	...	...	...	...	..	75	7
274	35	...	...	...	...	...	239	137	49	..	...	...	...	...	88	8
330	100	2	1	...	...	...	228	401	54	30	3	...	1	1	317	9
179	43	...	...	...	..	...	136	82	24	1	...	..	2	...	57	10
973	209	...	5	...	7	...	764	801	220	...	...	...	3	..	581	
268	68	...	...	...	...	...	200	168	68	...	...	...	...	...	100	11
134	40	...	1	...	1	...	94	229	41	...	...	...	2	..	188	12
258	43	...	3	...	3	...	215	170	55	...		...	...	.	115	13
151	34	...	1	...	3	...	117	199	50	...	...	...	...	...	149	14
162	24	...	...	...	...	...	138	35	6	...	...	...	1	...	29	15
584	95	1	2	...	3	...	488	644	163	...	5	...	4	...	481	
126	31	..	...	...	1	...	95	99	7	...	...	...	..	...	92	16
14	2	..	...	...	..	..	12	9	3	...	...	...	1	...	6	17
199	30	...	2	...	...	...	169	146	44	..	...	...	...	...	102	18
152	13	1	...	.	...	...	138	241	73	...	5	...	...	...	168	19
56	16	...	...	...	2	...	40	75	14	...	...	...	...	...	61	20
37	3	...	...	...	...	...	34	74	22	...	...	...	3	...	52	21
641	165	...	7	..	17	..	476	323	127	15	2	...	3	1	181	
134	31	...	...	...	...	...	103	148	30	15	...	...	...	1	103	22
92	35	...	1	...	4	...	57	66	46	...	2	...	3	..	20	23
205	35	...	6	...	3	...	170	46	23	..	...	...	...	...	23	24
210	04	...	...	...	10	...	146	62	27	...	...	...	...	...	35	25
...	...	...	...	...	...	...	...	1	1	...	...	..	...	...	...	26
472	124	3	4	...	2	..	345	408	180	1	2	...	9	...	227	
379	103	3	4	...	2	...	273	267	137	...	...	...	7	...	130	27
292	87	3	...	...	...	...	202	172	84	...	...	...	...	...	88	
13	5	...	...	...	...	...	8	25	3	...	...	...	...	...	22	28
15	3	...	...	...	...	...	12	80	25	1	...	...	1	...	54	29
65	13	..	...	...	...	...	52	17	6	..	...	...	1	...	11	30
...	...	..	...	...	...	...	...	19	9	...	2	...	..	...	10	31
552	156	20	13	...	5	...	376	361	116	1	5	...	4	...	244	
159	22	20	...	...	...	...	117	95	95	1	...	...	...	...	69	32
227	78	...	10	...	...	...	149	76	36	...	...	...	...	...	40	33
132	50	...	3	...	4	...	82	64	24	...	3	...	4	...	40	34
34	6	...	...	...	1	...	28	56	13	...	1	...	...	...	43	35
...	...	...	...	...	...	...	...	70	18	...	1	...	...	...	52	36
951	195	1	5	...	17	...	755	229	75	2	1	...	3	...	152	
130	31	...	...	...	9	...	99	18	2	...	...	...	2	..	16	37
271	48	...	3	...	4	...	223	69	26	...	1	...	1	...	43	38
306	56	1	2	...	4	...	249	98	32	2	...	..	...	..	64	39
244	60	...	...	...	...	...	184	44	15	...	...	...	...	...	29	40
54	11	9	...	...	...	...	34	35	13	...	...	...	...	...	22	
28	6	...	...	...	...	...	22	9	2	...	...	...	...	...	7	41
11	2	9	...	...	...	...	...	21	11	...	...	...	...	...	10	42
15	3	...	...	...	...	...	12	5	...	...	...	...	...	...	5	43

Serial No.	DISTRICT OR STATE.	Order XLVIII.—Medicine. Group 171.—Medical practitioners of all kinds. Total Workers and Dependents.	WORKERS. Total Workers. Males.	Fmls.	Workers with an agricultural or other subsidiary occupation. Agricultural. Males.	Fmls.	Other. Males.	Fmls.	DEPENDENTS.	Group 172.—Nurses, midwives, vaccinators, compounders. Total Workers and Dependents.	WORKERS. Total Workers. Males.	Fmls.	Workers with an agricultural or other subsidiary occupation. Agricultural. Males	Fmls.	Other. Males	Fmls.	DEPENDENTS.
	1	2	3	4	5	6	7	8	9	10	11	12	13	14	15	16	17
	Provincial Total ...	49,491	18,883	1,767	710	22	1,168	57	28,841	6,767	1,681	1,565	9	4	37	21	3,521
	Divisional Burma .	45,172	17,064	1,685	491	18	976	55	26,423	6,622	1,633	1,556	9	4	36	21	3,433
	Arakan Division ...	3,185	1,150	75	36	...	38	1	1,960	790	412	28	7	...	10	...	350
1	Akyab	2,120	775	38	9	...	7	1	1,307	724	395	23	7	...	10	...	306
2	Hill Dist. of Arakan	10	7	...	..	...	...	...	3	14	3	...	...	..	..	...	11
3	Kyaukpyu ...	685	234	29	18	.	20	.	422	20	4	3	...	..	...	...	13
4	Sandoway ...	370	134	8	9	...	11	...	228	32	10	2		...	.	...	20
	Pegu Division .	10,289	4,065	223	51	1	196	..	6,001	1,968	434	436	...	..	19	3	1,098
5	Rangoon Town ..	2,603	818	67	1	...	18	...	1,778	902	267	223	...	...	1	...	412
6	Insein	942	487	7	11	...	18	.	448	581	39	71	...	...	...	3	471
7	Hanthawaddy ...	1,601	587	28	13	..	20	...	986	145	52	39	...	...	11	...	54
8	Tharrawaddy .	2,189	750	25	3	...	77	...	1,414	91	23	18	...	..	5	...	50
9	Pegu	1,674	985	10	16	1	34	...	679	114	15	53	...	...	...	...	46
10	Prome	1,220	438	80	7	...	29	...	696	135	38	32	...	.	2	...	65
	Irrawaddy Division ...	9,155	3,431	460	117	10	198	14	5,264	575	101	122	...	...	1	2	352
11	Bassein ...	2,063	806	55	16	2	65	...	1,202	176	22	56	...	..	1	2	98
12	Henzada ...	2,591	931	151	57	6	48	10	1,509	219	30	25	...	..	..	..	164
13	Myaungmya ...	1,466	588	61	14	1	40	1	817	67	25	20	.	..	...	...	22
14	Ma-ubin ...	1,620	575	152	17	1	28	...	893	56	14	18	...	...	...	...	24
15	Pyapôn ...	1,415	531	41	13	...	17	3	843	57	10	3	...	...	...	..	44
	Tenasserim Division ...	6,674	2,402	255	43	1	117	6	4,017	1,122	134	338	1	1	1	7	650
16	Toungoo .	2,171	727	40	8	1	48	1	1,398	127	29	31	.	1	.	..	67
17	Salween ...	58	27	..	1	..	2	...	31	17	5	5	1	...	...	...	7
18	Thatôn ..	1,688	692	41	18	...	45	1	955	359	20	67	...	...	...	2	272
19	Amherst ...	1,521	547	37	2	..	..	4	937	407	32	168	...	..	...	...	207
20	Tavoy	627	237	7	14	...	12	..	383	146	23	51	..	...	..	5	72
21	Mergui .	609	172	124	..	..	10	...	313	66	25	16	...	...	1	...	25
	Magwe Division ...	3,889	1,516	191	59	3	128	8	2,182	313	96	53	...	1	1	2	164
22	Thayetmyo ..	684	255	36	2	...	10	4	393	62	21	2	...	...	...	...	39
23	Pakôkku	1,358	466	52	23	...	57	2	840	67	24	11	...	...	1	...	32
24	Minbu	1,203	473	64	30	3	32	2	666	108	16	40	...	1	...	2	52
25	Magwe .	636	316	39	4	...	29	...	281	73	32	...	...	...	..	...	41
26	Pakôkku Hill Tracts	8	6	...	...	.	...	..	2	3	3	...	...	...	...	...	...
	Mandalay Division ...	3,654	1,364	142	50	.	87	...	2,148	962	274	344	1	1	2	5	344
27	Mandalay .	2,308	797	96	14	...	28	..	1,415	580	101	304	...	..	...	4	175
	Mandalay City ...	*1,390*	*453*	*49*	..	...	*6*	...	*888*	*426*	*67*	*283*	...	..	...	*4*	*126*
28	Bhamo ...	336	131	10	4	...	20	..	195	87	31	9	...	..	..	...	47
29	Myitkyina ...	183	88	3	.	...	11	...	92	156	66	15	...	...	..	..	75
30	Katha	821	346	33	32	...	28	...	442	125	66	16	1	1	2	1	43
31	Putao	6	2	...	...	...	...	...	4	14	10	...	...	...	..	...	4
	Sagaing Division ...	3,552	1,404	113	71	3	122	10	2,035	414	123	77	...	...	2		214
32	Shwebo ...	1,080	390	67	16	3	36	8	629	72	31	13	...	...	1	...	38
33	Sagaing ...	1,059	440	37	21	...	29	...	582	156	29	50	...	...	...	...	77
34	Lower Chindwin ...	619	296	...	10	..	17	..	323	77	39	2	...	...	..	...	36
35	Upper Chindwin ...	763	271	9	24	...	40	2	488	65	14	10	...	...	1	...	41
36	Chin Hills ..	20	7	...	...	...	...	..	13	44	20	2	...	...	...	...	22
	Meiktila Division ...	4,774	1,732	226	64	...	90	16	2,816	478	59	158	..	1	...	2	261
37	Kyauksè ...	838	338	25	10	...	21	...	475	89	9	39	...	1	...		41
38	Meiktila ...	1,201	400	60	30	.	31	4	741	125	29	38	...	.	...	...	58
39	Yamèthin ...	1,429	497	41	15	...	17	3	891	160	7	41	...	...	.	2	112
40	Myingyan ..	1,306	497	100	9	...	21	9	709	104	14	40	...	...	..	..	50
	Eastern States ...	4,319	1,819	82	219	4	192	2	2,418	145	48	9	...	...	1	.	88
41	Northern Shan States	722	373	3	18	...	28	...	346	68	39	3	...	..	1	...	26
42	Southern Shan States	3,256	1,273	73	191	3	152	1	1,910	73	9	3	...	...	...	...	61
43	Karenni ...	341	173	6	10	1	12	1	162	4	...	3	...	...	...	...	1

PART III.—*Details by districts—contd.*

Order XLIX.—Instruction.

Group 173.—Professors and teachers of all kinds.								Group 174.—Clerks and servants connected with education.								
Total Workers and Dependents.	WORKERS. Total Workers. Males.	WORKERS. Total Workers. Females.	Workers with an agricultural or other subsidiary occupation. Agricultural. Males.	Agricultural. Females.	Other. Males.	Other. Females.	DEPENDENTS.	Total Workers and Dependents.	WORKERS. Total Workers. Males.	WORKERS. Total Workers. Females.	Workers with an agricultural or other subsidiary occupation. Agricultural. Males.	Agricultural. Females	Other. Males.	Other. Females	DEPENDENTS.	Serial No. of District, etc. (column 1).
18	19	20	21	22	23	24	25	26	27	28	29	30	31	32	33	
32,801	11,442	2,950	257	22	361	77	18,409	993	498	5	10	...	30	...	490	
31,271	10,847	2,864	196	21	330	76	17,560	966	489	5	10	..	28	.	472	
1,716	721	73	9	...	34	...	922	5		..	...	...	...	..		
1,094	492	36	7	...	20	...	566	4	4	...	...	...	...	...	..	1
5	...	...	...	...	...	...	5	...	...	...	...	...	...	...	...	2
279	118	17	...	...	6	...	144	1	1	...	...	...	...	..	...	3
338	111	20	2	..	8	...	207	...	...	...	...	...	...	..	..	4
10,956	3,574	854	46	1	95	13	6,528	115	67	..	...	...	...	...	48	
4,148	1,517	431	...	...	10	5	2,200	79	64	...	...	..	...	..	15	5
1,230	425	130	3	...	22	4	675	28	...	...	...	...	..	...	28	6
1,123	423	68	8	...	11	...	632	...	...	...	...	...	...	...	...	7
1,652	540	108	15	1	29	2	1,004	1	...	...	...	...	...	...	1	8
1,894	360	50	13	...	10	..	1,484	5	1	..	...	...	...	...	4	9
909	309	67	7	..	13	2	533	2	2	...	...	...	...	...	...	10
6,150	2,153	694	53	13	68	18	3,303	4	3	...	..	...	...	..	1	
1,778	603	187	17	4	31	4	988	...	...	...	...	..	...	...	...	11
1,388	497	178	13	7	12	7	713	3	3	...	..	..	...	...	...	12
1,020	349	121	11	1	5	...	550	...	...	...	...	...	..	...	...	13
1,120	386	135	9		14	5	599	1	..	.	...	...	..	...	1	14
844	318	73	3	1	6	2	453	.	...	...	...	..	...	...	...	15
4,517	1,490	480	34	2	41	11	2,547	44	19	...	..	..	2	...	25	
1,156	510	93	20	2	12	...	553	17	1	...	...	...	...	...	16	16
67	28	2	1	...	...	...	37	...	...	..	...	...	...	...	...	17
1,222	451	92	12	...	11	6	679	12	5	...	...	..	1	..	7	18
1,315	266	228	...	...	3	2	821	3	3	...	...	..	1	...	...	19
410	122	53	...	...	6	3	235	5	4	...	...	...	..	...	1	20
347	113	12	1	...	9	...	222	7	6	..	...	...	...	...	1	21
1,578	697	127	5	1	28	24	754	344	174	...	4	...	20	..	170	
411	129	11	...	..	2	...	271	5	3	...	...	...	...	...	2	22
531	278	77	3	1	13	20	176	280	141	...	4	...	20	...	139	23
372	115	35	2	..	5	4	222	46	17	...	...	.	...	...	29	24
257	175	4	...	...	8	...	78	13	13	...	...	..	...	...	...	25
7	...	...	...	...	...	...	7	..	...	...	...	...	...	...	...	26
2,218	724	241	9	1	8	3	1,253	92	43	3	...	..	1	...	46	
1,557	494	190	3	...	3	...	867	87	42	3	...	..	...	...	42	27
959	*271*	*115*	...	...	...	...	*573*	*56*	*36*	.	...	...	...	...	*20*	
179	56	16	5	1	...	1	107	1	1		...	...	1	...	...	28
161	50	8	1	...	1	..	103	4	...	...	...	...	..	..	4	29
319	122	21	...	...	4	2	176	.	...	.	.	...	...	..	..	30
2	2	...	...	...	...	..	..	...	...	...	...	...	...	...	...	31
2,136	700	171	31	1	39	3	1,265	236	117	2	6	...	5	...	117	
657	247	76	10	1	13	1	334	29	20	1	...	...	1	...	8	32
830	225	52	10	...	15	...	553	161	58	1	3	...	2	...	102	33
368	140	38	6	...	7	2	190	24	24	...	1	...	...	...	..	34
240	77	5	5	...	4	..	158	15	9	...	2	...	2	...	6	35
41	11	...	...	...	...	...	30	7	6	...	...	...	...	...	1	36
2,000	788	224	9	2	17	4	988	126	61	...	..	...	...	..	65	
413	146	35	...	.	7	1	232	.	...	...	..	...	...	...	...	37
469	176	31	4	...	4	1	262	73	28	...	...	...	...	...	45	38
464	221	37	5	1	6	...	206	5	2	.	...	...	...	...	3	39
654	245	121	...	1	...	2	288	48	31	...	...	...	...	..	17	40
1,530	595	86	61	1	31	1	849	27	9	...	...	..	2	..	18	
361	133	20	...	...	1	...	208	15	5	...	...	...	1	..	10	41
970	452	33	61	..	30	...	485	12	4	...	..	...	1	...	8	42
199	10	33	...	1	...	1	156	...	...	...	...	...	...	...	...	43

Order L.—Letters and

Serial No.	District or State.	Group 175.—Public scribes, stenographers, etc.			Group 176.—Architects, surveyors, civil engineers who are not of the Public Works Department, and their employees.				Group 177a.—Photographers.			
		Total Workers and Dependents.	Workers. (All males without subsidiary occupation.) Males.	Dependents.	Total Workers and Dependents.	Workers. (All without subsidiary occupation.) Males.	Workers. (All without subsidiary occupation.) Females.	Dependents.	Total Workers and Dependents.	Workers.* Males.	Workers.* Females.	Dependents.
	1	2	3	4	5	6	7	8	9	10	11	12
	Provincial Total ..	631	349	282	190	2	17	171	844	277	9	558
	Divisional Burma ...	631	349	282	6	2	1	3	768	269	8	491
	Arakan Division ...	...	...	...	...	...	...	...	20	*2	...	18
1	Akyab	...	...	...	...	...	...	...	18	...	...	18
2	Hill Dist. of Arakan ...	..	...	...	...	...	...	...	...	..	...	...
3	Kyaukpyu ...	...		...	...	...	...	...	1	*1	...	...
4	Sandoway ...	.	..	...	...	...	...	...	1	1	...	..
	Pegu Division ..	6	...	6	1	...	1	...	303	* 125	...	178
5	Rangoon Town ...	.	...	...	..	..	...	...	263	* 101	...	162
6	Insein	...	..	...	...	..	...	...	...	...	...	...
7	Hanthawaddy ...	...	...	...	1	..	1	...	14	4	...	10
8	Tharrawaddy ...	6	...	6	...	...	...	...	17	15	...	2
9	Pegu	...	...	...	...	..	...	...	8	5	...	3
10	Prome	...	...	...	...	...	...	...	1	...	...	1
	Irrawaddy Division ...	...	...	...	...	...	...	...	114	* 39	2	73
11	Bassein	..	...	...	...	...	...	...	33	15	1	17
12	Henzada	...	...	...	...	...	..	...	14	6	...	8
13	Myaungmya ...	...	...	...	...	...	...	...	37	8	1	28
14	Ma-ubin	...	...	..	...	...	...	...	9	5	...	4
15	Pyapôn	..	...	...	...	..	...	...	21	*5	...	16
	Tenasserim Division ...	625	349	276	1	1	...	..	87	* 34	...	53
16	Toungoo	...	...	...	...	..	.	...	8	*3	...	5
17	Salween	..	..	...	...	...	...	...	...	...	...	...
18	Thatôn	..	...	.	...	...	..	...	35	7	...	28
19	Amherst	625	349	276	1	1	...	...	14	6	-	8
20	Tavoy	...	...	...	...	...	..	...	21	16	..	5
21	Mergui	...	...	...	...	...	..	...	9	2	...	7
	Magwe Division ...	...	...	...	..	...	...	...	65	* 23	...	42
22	Thayetmyo ..	...	...	...	...	...	...	...	3	* 1	...	2
23	Pakôkku	...	...	...	...	...	...	...	25	8	...	17
24	Minbu	...	...	...	...	...	...	...	37	14	...	23
25	Magwe ...	...	...	...	...	...	..	...	...	..	...	...
26	Pakôkku Hill Tracts ...	...	...	...	...	...	...	...	...	...	...	...
	Mandalay Division ..	..	..	...	3	1	...	2	109	16	6	87
27	Mandalay	...	..	...	3	1	...	2	97	12	6	79
	Mandalay City ..	...	...	...	*3*	*1*	...	*2*	*68*	*3*	*6*	*59*
28	Bhamo	...	...	.	...	...	...	...	3	3	...	...
29	Myitkyina	...	...	...	...	..	...	...	3	...	...	3
30	Katha	...	...	..	.	...	...	...	6	1	...	5
31	Putao	...	...	...	...	...	...	...	..	...	...	...
	Sagaing Division ...	...	...	...	1	...	...	1	25	19	...	6
32	Shwebo	..		...	...	...	...	...	5	5	...	...
33	Sagaing	...	...	...		...	...	...	5	2		3
34	Lower Chindwin ...	...	...	...	...	...	...	...	14	11	...	3
35	Upper Chindwin ...	...	...	...	1	...	...	1	1	1	...	...
36	Chin Hills	.	...	...	...	...	...	...	...	..	...	...
	Meiktila Division ...	...	..	...	...	...	...	...	45	* 11		34
37	Kyauksè	...	..	...	...	...	...	...	9	4	...	5
38	Meiktila	...	...	...	...	...	...	...	4	3	...	1
39	Yamèthin	...	...	..	...	.	...	...	15	* 1	...	14
40	Myingyan	..	...	...	...	..	...	...	17	3	...	14
	Eastern States ...	...		...	184	...	16	168	76	8	1	67
41	Northern Shan States ...	...		..	184	...	16	168	74	6	1	67
42	Southern Shan States ...	..	...	...	...	..	...	..	2	2	..	...
43	Karenni	.	..	.	...	...	...	...	...	...	...	...

* One male in Kyaukpyu, 3 males in Rangoon Town, 1 male in Pyapôn, 1 male in Toungoo, 1 male in Thayetmyo and 1 male in Yamèthin District had non-agricultural subsidiary occupations; no others with subsidiary occupations.

the arts and sciences.

Group 177b.—Horoscope-casters, astrologers and almanac makers.								Group 177c.—Sculptors in stone.								Group 177d.*	
Total Workers and Dependents.	WORKERS. Total Workers.		Workers with an agricultural or other subsidiary occupation. Agricultural.		Other.		DEPENDENTS.	Total Workers and Dependents.	WORKERS. Total Workers.		Workers with an agricultural or other subsidiary occupation. Agricultural.		Other.		DEPENDENTS.	Total Workers and Dependents.	Serial No. of District, etc. (column 1).
	Males.	Females.	Males.	Females.	Males.	Females.			Males.	Females.	Males.	Females.	Males.	Females.			
22	14	15	16	17	18	19	20	21	22	23	24	25	26	27	28	29	
676	258	8	9	...	54	...	420	1,762	780	22	24	8	49	1	959	...	
668	255	8	9	...	53	...	405	1,727	779	19	24	8	49	...	929	...	
11	7	...	...	...	1	...	4	78	47	...	1	...	4	...	31	...	
...	...	...	...	...	...	...	...	...	...	...	...	...	...	...	...	...	1
...	...	...	...	...	...	...	...	...	...	...	...	...	...	...	...	...	2
1	...	...	...	...	...	...	1	71	47	...	1	...	4	...	24	...	3
10	7	...	...	...	1	...	3	7	...	...	...	...	...	...	7	...	4
...	...	...	...	...	...	...	...	254	34	2	...	...	...	...	118	...	
...	...	...	...	...	...	...	...	43	2	2	...	...	...	...	39	...	5
...	...	...	...	...	...	...	...	10	...	...	...	...	...	...	10	...	6
...	...	...	...	...	...	...	...	...	...	...	...	...	...	...	...	...	7
...	...	...	...	...	...	...	...	24	...	...	...	...	...	...	24	...	8
...	...	...	...	...	...	...	...	61	9	...	...	...	...	...	52	...	9
...	...	...	...	...	...	...	...	96	23	...	...	...	...	...	3	...	10
3	2	...	...	...	...	...	1	193	126	...	...	...	...	...	67	...	
...	...	...	...	...	...	...	...	134	84	...	...	...	...	...	50	...	11
3	2	...	...	...	...	...	1	...	...	...	...	...	...	...	...	...	12
...	...	...	...	...	...	...	...	...	...	...	...	...	...	...	...	...	13
...	...	...	...	...	...	...	...	9	...	...	...	...	...	...	9	...	14
...	...	...	...	...	...	...	...	50	42	...	...	...	...	...	8	...	15
4	3	...	...	...	...	...	1	172	44	2	...	...	3	...	126	...	
4	3	...	...	...	...	...	1	14	5	...	...	...	...	...	9	...	16
...	...	...	...	...	...	...	...	...	...	...	...	...	...	...	...	...	17
...	...	...	...	...	...	...	...	120	38	1	...	...	3	...	81	...	18
...	...	...	...	...	...	...	...	30	1	1	...	...	...	...	28	...	19
...	...	...	...	...	...	...	...	...	...	...	...	...	...	...	...	...	20
...	...	...	...	...	...	...	...	8	...	...	...	...	...	...	8	...	21
17	...	...	...	...	...	...	17	381	204	...	9	...	24	...	177	...	
...	...	...	...	...	...	...	...	52	...	...	...	...	...	...	52	...	22
6	...	...	...	...	...	...	6	...	...	...	...	...	...	...	...	...	23
11	...	...	...	...	...	...	11	239	149	...	9	...	24	...	90	...	24
...	...	...	...	...	...	...	...	90	55	...	...	...	...	...	35	...	25
...	...	...	...	...	...	...	...	...	...	...	...	...	...	...	...	...	26
480	184	4	...	...	47	...	292	178	72	...	1	...	6	...	106	...	
467	183	4	...	...	47	...	280	130	34	...	1	...	...	...	96	...	
463	180	3	...	...	46	...	280	102	25	...	...	...	...	...	77	...	27
1	1	...	...	...	...	...	...	3	2	...	...	...	...	...	1	...	28
...	...	...	...	...	...	...	...	...	...	...	...	...	...	...	...	...	29
12	...	...	...	...	...	...	12	46	36	...	...	...	6	...	11	...	30
...	...	...	...	...	...	...	...	...	...	...	...	...	...	...	...	...	31
49	18	...	...	...	2	...	31	430	200	11	13	8	12	...	219	...	
9	5	...	...	...	1	...	4	87	13	...	...	...	...	...	74	...	32
22	4	...	...	...	...	...	18	80	50	...	...	...	3	...	30	...	33
18	9	...	...	...	1	...	9	212	117	3	13	...	6	...	92	...	34
...	...	...	...	...	...	...	...	51	20	8	...	8	3	...	23	...	35
...	...	...	...	...	...	...	...	...	...	...	...	...	...	...	...	...	36
104	41	4	9	...	3	...	59	141	52	4	...	...	...	...	85	...	
...	...	...	...	...	...	...	...	31	1	4	...	...	...	...	26	...	37
50	26	...	9	...	3	...	24	21	13	...	...	...	...	...	8	...	38
...	...	...	...	...	...	...	...	26	...	...	...	...	...	...	26	...	39
54	15	4	...	...	...	...	35	63	38	...	...	...	...	...	25	...	40
8	3	...	...	...	1	...	5	34	1	3	...	...	...	1	30	...	
3	...	...	...	...	...	...	3	33	...	3	...	...	...	...	30	...	41
5	3	...	...	...	1	...	2	1	1	...	...	...	...	1	...	...	42
...	...	...	...	...	...	...	...	...	...	...	...	...	...	...	...	...	43

* Sculptors and image-makers in wood, brass and other materials than stone.

Order L.—Letters and the arts

Serial No.	DISTRICT OR STATE.	Group 177c.—Authors, editors, journalists, poets, artists and all scientists not in Group 177b.								Group 178.—Music composers, band masters players on all kinds of musical instruments (not military), singers, actors and dancers.							
		Total Workers and Dependents.	WORKERS.						DEPENDENTS.	Total Workers and Dependents.	WORKERS.						DEPENDENTS.
			Total Workers.		Workers with an agricultural or other subsidiary occupation.						Total Workers.		Workers with an agricultural or other subsidiary occupation.				
					Agricultural.		Other.						Agricultural.		Other.		
			Males.	Females	Males	Females	Males	Females			Males.	Females	Males	Females	Males.	Females	
	1	2	3	4	5	6	7	8	9	10	11	12	13	14	15	16	17
	Provincial Total ...	2,779	1,618	49	3	...	26	...	1,112	15,851	7,132	1,302	94	12	218	29	7,417
	Divisional Burma ...	2,757	1,601	47	3	...	24	..	1,109	15,330	6,843	1,249	86	9	204	24	7,238
	Arakan Division ..	87	43	..	...	...	..	...	44	530	273	51	3	1	9	...	266
1	Akyab	87	43	...	...	...	...	...	44	336	189	33	1	...	3	...	114
2	Hill Dist. of Arakan	...	...	...	...	...	...	...	...	...	...	...	...	...	...	...	...
3	Kyaukpyu ...	...	...	...	..	...	...	...	...	91	42	18	...	1	2	...	31
4	Sandoway ..	..	...	...	...	...	...	...	...	103	42	...	2	...	4	...	61
	Pegu Division ...	595	239	10	...	...	7	...	346	4,287	1,978	345	14	2	22	3	1,064
5	Rangoon Town ..	262	66	3	..	...	...	...	193	1,716	770	159	...	...	6	...	787
6	Insein	43	26	...	...	...	2	..	17	185	80	20	...	...	..	...	85
7	Hanthawaddy ...	69	30	...	...	...	...	..	39	217	125	4	3	..	2	...	88
8	Tharrawaddy ...	81	64	...	...	...	..	...	17	596	300	30	2	1	...	2	266
9	Pegu	19	11	...	...	...	1	...	8	397	170	64	...	1	...	1	163
10	Prome	121	42	7	.	...	4	...	72	1,176	533	68	9	...	14	...	575
	Irrawaddy Division ...	315	138	5	2	..	3	...	172	2,413	1,151	226	11	...	22	...	1,036
11	Bassein ...	...	...	...	.	...	...	...	...	492	225	45	...	...	...	...	222
12	Henzada ...	213	93	.	2	...	2	...	120	593	186	43	5	...	14	...	364
13	Myaungmya ...	50	12	5	...	...	...	...	33	511	318	68	5	..	2	...	125
14	Ma-ubin ...	39	33	...	..	...	1	...	6	398	210	24	1	...	6	...	164
15	Pyapôn ...	13	...	...	...	...	...	...	13	419	212	46	...	...	...	...	161
	Tenasserim Division ...	58	28	1	...	...	...	...	29	1,578	756	148	11	...	22	...	674
16	Toungoo ...	8	..	..	.	...	...	...	8	415	187	39	...	...	3	..	189
17	Salween	...	...	...	...	...	...	...		18	12	3	2	...	...	...	3
18	Thatôn	...	...	...	...	...	...	...	...	353	186	52	...	...	7	...	115
19	Amherst ...	38	28	1	...	...	...		9	602	262	54	9	...	...	...	286
20	Tavoy	7	...	...	...	...	...	...	7	154	93	...	...	...	12	...	61
21	Mergui ..	5	...	...	...	...	...	..	5	36	16	...	...	...	..	...	20
	Magwe Division ...	449	242	11	...	...	4	...	196	1,849	837	121	2	...	44	6	891
22	Thayetmyo ..	61	18	...	...	...	2	...	43	450	197	...	...	...	...	...	253
23	Pakôkku ...	278	224	3	...	...	2	...	51	778	340	59	...	...	38	3	379
24	Minbu	81	...	4	...	...	...		77	324	135	47	...	...	...	2	142
25	Magwe	29	..	4	...	...	...	...	25	297	165	15	2	...	6	1	117
26	Pakôkku Hill Tracts	...	...	...	...	...	...	...	...	...	...	...	...	...	...	...	...
	Mandalay Division ...	990	834	10	1	..	5	...	146	1,293	514	102	5	...	9	...	677
27	Mandalay ..	971	834	8	1	...	5	...	129	1,012	331	78	5	...	3	...	603
	Mandalay City ...	*883*	*796*	...	.	...	...	...	87	727	263	77	1	..	...	...	387
28	Bhamo ...	14	...	...	...	...	...	..	14	38	28	6	...	...	...	...	4
29	Myitkyina ...	...	...	...	.	...	...	...	...	24	16	...	...	...	...	...	8
30	Katha	5	...	2	...	..	...	...	3	219	139	18	..	...	6	...	62
31	Putao	...	...	...	..	...	...	...	...	...	...	...	...	...	...	...	...
	Sagaing Division ..	122	71	...	..	..	5	...	51	1,982	819	119	33	6	67	14	1,044
32	Shwebo ...	98	71	...	...	...	5	...	27	611	278	72	16	6	10	3	261
33	Sagaing ..	24	...	...	...	...	...	...	24	606	204	4	7	...	9	2	398
34	Lower Chindwin .	...	...	...	...	...	..	...	...	466	230	8	7	...	33	...	228
35	Upper Chindwin ...	...	..	...	...	...	...	...	...	299	107	35	3	..	15	9	157
36	Chin Hills ...	...	...	...	...	...	...	...	...	..	...	...	...	...	...	...	...
	Meiktila Division ...	141	6	10	...	...	...	...	125	1,398	515	137	7	...	9	1	746
37	Kyauksè ..	27	...	4	...	...	..	...	23	361	170	24	5	...	2	...	167
38	Meiktila ...	59	...	2	...	...	...	...	57	257	90	32	...	...	2	...	135
39	Yamèthin ...	9	6	...	...	...	..	...	3	307	74	30	...	...	2	1	203
40	Myingyan ...	46	...	4	...	...	.	...	42	473	181	51	2	...	3	...	241
	Eastern States	22	17	2	...	...	2	...	3	521	289	53	8	3	14	5	179
41	Northern Shan States	15	12	..	...	...	2	...	3	225	154	17	2	..	1	...	54
42	Southern Shan States	7	5	2	...	...	...	...	...	282	131	33	6	3	13	5	118
43	Karenni ...	...	...	..	...	...	...	...	...	14	4	3	...	...	...	...	7

and sciences—*concluded.*								Order LII.*—Domestic service.								
Group 179.—Conjurors, acrobats, fortune-tellers, reciters, exhibitors of curiosities and wild animals.								Group 181.*—Domestic servants (excluding sweepers and all employed on account of animals or vehicles).								
Total Workers and Dependents.	WORKERS. Total Workers.		Workers with an agricultural or other subsidiary occupation. Agricultural.		Other.		DEPENDENTS.	Total Workers and Dependents.	WORKERS. Total Workers.		Workers with an agricultural or other subsidiary occupation. Agricultural.		Other.		DEPENDENTS.	Serial No. of District, etc. (column 1).
	Males.	Females.	Males.	Females	Males.	Females.			Males.	Females.	Males.	Females	Males.	Females		
18	19	20	21	22	23	24	25	26	27	28	29	30	31	32	33	
3,536	1,337	488	20	2	63	11	1,711	58,739	33,421	7,772	210	81	332	104	17,546	
3,434	1,291	488	14	2	59	11	1,655	54,751	31,438	6,631	42	61	261	83	16,682	
372	108	102	8	1	17	5	162	2,431	1,712	405	5	...	6	3	314	
268	73	68	6	..	1	4	127	2,205	1,578	375	5	...	5	3	252	1
...	...	...	...	...	...	...	...	30	26	3	..	...	...	...	1	2
84	32	24	2	1	16	1	28	70	44	10	...	...	1	...	16	3
20	3	10	...	...	...	...	7	126	64	17	...	...	...	...	45	4
550	208	50	...	1	1	...	292	22,498	13,697	2,559	10	46	31	12	6,242	
321	127	14	...	...	..	...	180	16,620	10,160	1,745	5	...	7	...	4,715	5
16	15	...	...	..	...	...	1	1,159	621	194	3	...	3	4	344	6
26	20	...	...	..	..	...	6	1,270	821	174	1	...	3	7	275	7
97	29	10	...	..	...	...	58	962	632	112	...	...	6	...	218	8
18	3	...	...	...	1	...	15	1,320	750	249	1	45	9	...	321	9
72	14	26	...	1	...	...	32	1,167	713	85	...	1	3	1	369	10
356	154	40	2	...	2	1	162	4,635	2,933	637	4	4	50	5	1,065	
120	46	13	...	...	...	1	61	1,681	1,170	127	...	...	31	1	384	11
133	53	20	2	...	2	...	60	955	505	240	...	1	12	3	210	12
33	11	...	...	...	...	...	22	778	440	90	2	...	4	1	248	13
37	19	4	...	...	...	...	14	613	419	71	...	...	2	...	123	14
33	25	3	...	...	...	..	5	608	399	109	2	3	1	...	100	15
172	74	5	.	...	1	1	93	5,941	3,719	649	4	1	94	7	1,573	
58	16	...	...	...	...	...	36	1,145	707	95	...	...	6	...	343	16
1	1	...	...	...	...	...	...	47	34	3	...	...	...	...	10	17
51	33		...	...	1	..	18	864	391	111	...	...	62	...	362	18
4	3	1	...	...	.	...	...	2,620	1,787	254	3	.	14	...	579	19
20	7	1	...	...	.	1	12	626	336	135	...	1	9	7	155	20
44	14	3	...	...	...	...	27	639	464	51	1	...	3	...	124	21
386	166	67	1	...	9	...	153	4,265	2,111	522	..	6	31	5	1,632	
23	14	3	1	...	...	...	6	675	309	41	...	...	3	3	325	22
177	73	42	...	...	8	...	62	1,257	534	210	...	2	6	2	513	23
129	60	11	...	...	1	...	58	842	374	192	..	2	13	...	270	24
57	19	11	...	...	..	...	27	1,470	883	78	...	2	9	..	509	25
...	...	...	...	...	...	...	.	21	11	1	...	...	...	...	9	26
829	281	111	...	..	16	3	437	8,303	4,231	907	1	1	11	1	3,165	
764	246	104	..	.	11	...	414	6,683	3,121	849	..	...	4	1	2,713	27
644	193	62	...	...	9	...	389	4,026	1,872	632	..	...	...	...	1,522	
19	15	3	...	...	1	...	11	507	329	18	...	...	4	...	160	28
8	7	..	...	...	3	...	1	478	330	14	1	...	..	...	134	29
28	13	4	...	...	1	3	11	555	385	23	...	...	2	...	147	30
...	...	...	...	...	...	...	...	80	66	3	...	1	1	...	11	31
389	126	63	3	...	11	1	200	2,481	1,279	264	18	...	16	...	958	
73	32	24	...	...	1	...	17	928	398	102	1	...	1	...	428	32
147	43	27	3	...	6	...	77	591	330	70	1	...	6	...	191	33
92	31	12	...	...	3	1	49	429	225	54	...	...	3	...	156	34
77	20	...	...	...	1	..	57	363	219	36	3	...	6	...	108	35
...	...	...	...	...	...	...	...	170	107	2	13	...	..	...	61	36
380	174	50	...	...	2	...	156	4,197	1,756	688	..	3	22	50	1,753	
63	15	13	...	...	...	...	35	433	230	36	...	...	4	1	167	37
62	31	4	...	...	..	...	27	1,453	533	237	...	...	...	14	683	38
97	34	2	...	...	...	...	61	1,198	588	113	...	3	3	2	497	39
158	94	31	...	...	2	...	33	1,113	405	302	...	...	15	33	406	40
102	46	...	6	...	4	...	56	3,988	1,983	1,141	168	20	71	21	864	
22	12	...	1	...	1	...	10	1,902	800	852	13	...	32	11	250	41
80	34	...	5	..	3	...	46	2,012	1,149	861	155	10	39	10	608	42
...	...	...	...	...	...	..	...	74	34	28	...	10	...	...	12	43

* NOTE.—For Group 180 see Order LI on page 303.

Serial No.	DISTRICT OR STATE.	Order LII.—Domestic service—*concluded.* Group 182.—Domestic servants employed on account of animals or of vehicles moved by animals or by human labour. Total Workers and Dependents.	WORKERS. Total Workers. Males.	Total Workers. Females.	Workers with an agricultural or other subsidiary occupation. Agricultural. Males.	Agricultural. Females	Other. Males.	Other. Females	DEPENDENTS.	Group 183.—Private motor-drivers and cleaners. Total Workers and Dependents.	WORKERS.* Males.	WORKERS.* Females.	DEPENDENTS.
	1	2	3	4	5	6	7	8	9	10	11	12	13
	Provincial Total ...	13,397	8,751	225	597	6	300	11	4,421	1,533	887	4	642
	Divisional Burma ...	2,461	1,462	219	3	6	7	11	780	1,531	885	4	642
	Arakan Division ...	34	13	...	...	...	...	...	21	...	...	...	...
1	Akyab	16	2	...	...	...	...	...	14	...	...	...	...
2	Hill Dist. of Arakan	...	...	...	...	...	...	...	...	...	...	...	...
3	Kyaukpyu ...	4	2	...	...	...	...	...	2	...	...	...	...
4	Sandoway ...	14	9	...	...	...	...	...	5	...	...	...	...
	Pegu Division ...	469	257	29	...	...	1	...	183	1,138	*751	...	387
5	Rangoon Town ...	189	51	24	...	...	...	...	114	1,121	*748	...	373
6	Insein	6	...	...	...	...	...	...	6	5	2	...	3
7	Hanthawaddy ...	16	12	...	...	...	...	...	4	3	...	...	3
8	Tharrawaddy ...	66	60	...	...	...	...	...	6	...	...	...	...
9	Pegu	37	27	...	...	...	1	...	10	4	1	...	3
10	Prome	155	107	5	...	...	...	...	43	5	...	...	5
	Irrawaddy Division ...	134	118	3	...	...	...	...	13	43	15	1	27
11	Bassein	113	98	3	...	...	...	...	12	29	9	...	20
12	Henzada ...	6	6	...	...	...	...	...	...	...	...	...	...
13	Myaungmya ...	...	...	...	...	...	...	...	...	...	...	...	...
14	Ma-ubin ...	13	13	...	...	...	...	...	...	8	...	1	7
15	Pyapôn	2	1	...	...	...	...	...	1	6	6	...	...
	Tenasserim Division ...	485	311	6	...	...	5	...	168	77	7	1	69
16	Toungoo ...	139	94	...	...	...	2	...	45	...	...	...	...
17	Salween	2	1	...	...	...	...	...	1	...	...	...	...
18	Thatôn	18	18	...	...	...	...	...	...	...	...	...	...
19	Amherst ...	284	159	6	...	...	3	...	119	70	...	1	69
20	Tavoy	20	20	...	...	...	...	...	...	4	4	...	...
21	Mergui	22	19	...	...	...	...	...	3	3	3	...	...
	Magwe Division ...	284	195	8	...	...	1	...	81	1	1	...	...
22	Thayetmyo ...	6	2	...	...	...	...	...	4	...	...	...	...
23	Pakôkku ...	8	5	...	...	...	...	...	3	...	...	...	...
24	Minbu	29	14	...	...	...	...	...	15	...	...	...	...
25	Magwe	234	168	8	...	...	1	...	58	1	1	...	...
26	Pakôkku Hill Tracts	7	6	...	...	...	...	...	1	...	...	...	...
	Mandalay Division ...	488	357	4	3	...	...	...	127	228	94	...	134
27	Mandalay ...	366	273	3	...	...	...	...	90	216	85	...	131
	Mandalay City ...	*228*	*183*	*2*	...	...	...	...	*43*	*132*	*26*	...	*106*
28	Bhamo	45	33	...	...	...	...	...	12	1	1	...	...
29	Myitkyina ...	53	46	1	3	...	...	...	6	9	7	...	2
30	Katha	23	4	...	...	...	...	...	19	2	1	...	1
31	Putao	1	1	...	...	...	...	...	...	...	...	...	...
	Sagaing Division ...	357	61	166	...	6	...	11	130	28	*6	...	22
32	Shwebo	26	23	...	...	...	...	...	3	25	3	...	22
33	Sagaing	35	20	...	...	...	...	...	15	...	...	...	...
34	Lower Chindwin ..	271	9	166	...	6	...	11	96	1	*1	...	...
35	Upper Chindwin ..	14	6	...	...	...	...	...	8	2	2	...	...
36	Chin Hills ...	11	3	...	...	...	...	...	8	...	...	...	...
	Meiktila Division ...	210	150	3	...	...	...	...	57	16	11	2	3
37	Kyaukse ...	1	1	...	...	...	...	...	...	...	...	...	...
38	Meiktila ...	45	29	...	...	...	...	...	16	2	2	...	...
39	Yamethin ...	143	105	1	...	...	...	...	37	...	...	...	...
40	Myingyan ...	21	15	2	...	...	...	...	4	14	9	2	3
	Eastern States ...	10,936	7,289	6	594	...	293	...	3,641	2	2	...	...
41	Northern Shan States	73	36	6	...	...	3	...	31	...	...	...	...
42	Southern Shan States	10,858	7,253	...	594	...	290	...	3,605	2	2	...	...
43	Karenni	5	.	...	...	...	...	...	5	...	...	...	...

*Four males in Rangoon Town and 1 male in Lower Chindwin districts had non-agricultural subsidiary occupations.

PART III.—*Details by districts*—contd.

Order LIII.—Insufficiently described occupations.

Group 184.—Manufacturers, business men and contractors otherwise unspecified.								Group 185.—Cashiers, accountants, book-keepers and other clerical employees in unspecified industries or trades.								
Total Workers and Dependents.	WORKERS.						DEPENDENTS.	Total Workers and Dependents.	WORKERS.						DEPENDENTS.	Serial No. of District, etc. (column 1).
	Total Workers.		Workers with an agricultural or other subsidiary occupation.						Total Workers.		Workers with an agricultural or other subsidiary occupation.					
			Agricultural.		Other.						Agricultural.		Other.			
	Males.	Females.	Males.	Females.	Males.	Females.			Males.	Females.	Males.	Females.	Males.	Females.		
14	15	16	17	18	19	20	21	22	23	24	25	26	27	28	29	
110,554	13,323	68,653	793	6,086	869	3,893	28,578	71,478	35,505	1,015	272	..	417	1	34,958	
26,379	6,806	6,680	211	209	289	236	12,893	68,457	34,168	985	84	...	343	1	33,304	
6,866	1,696	2,554	154	121	71	83	2,616	2,487	1,315	22	5	...	17	...	1,150	
894	287	163	7	...	3	...	444	1,843	1,007	13	3	...	4	...	823	1
6	1	...	...	...	...	...	5	44	28	...	...	...	1	...	16	2
5,900	1,384	2,390	146	121	65	83	2,126	394	175	9	1	...	7	...	210	3
66	24	1	1	...	3	...	41	206	105	...	1	...	5	...	101	4
5,246	1,471	914	7	7	32	11	2,861	35,948	19,474	425	27	...	126	...	16,049	
1,801	520	66	2	...	6	...	1,215	15,392	13,927	258	11	...	24	...	1,207	5
1,130	287	320	4	6	10	2	523	2,705	1,217	76	6	...	5	...	1,412	6
1,377	342	349	...	...	12	8	686	3,248	1,804	39	6	...	27	...	1,405	7
141	21	8	...	...	1	...	112	1,097	446	3	2	...	19	...	648	8
445	231	1	...	..	1	...	213	2,280	1,380	18	...	...	37	...	884	9
352	70	170	1	1	2	1	112	1,224	700	31	2	...	14	...	493	10
5,367	1,245	1,754	13	32	60	37	2,368	6,471	3,212	145	18	...	52	...	3,114	
348	83	50	...	14		3	215	1,747	1,036	11	5	...	14	...	700	11
1,611	879	606	...	11	85	13	726	1,039	356	32	3	...	6	...	651	12
3,200	822	1,049	12	7	40	21	1,329	1,216	609	38	3	...	12	...	569	13
30	18	...	1	..	3	...	12	1,047	478	38	4	...	10	...	531	14
178	43	49	..	...	2	...	86	1,422	733	26	3	...	10	...	663	15
2,090	573	376	1	3	12	24	1,141	7,348	3,344	153	4	...	46	...	3,851	
225	75	...	...	..	...	...	150	1,513	985	40	...	...	10	...	488	16
25	7	3	...	...	..	...	15	57	27	...	1	...	2	...	30	17
908	176	300	1	3	7	24	432	1,627	570	55	..	...	17	...	1,002	18
632	239	67	...	...	2	...	326	3,102	1,164	49	1	...	...	...	1,889	19
153	34	3	...	...	2	....	116	534	298	3	2	...	12	..	233	20
87	42	3	...	...	1	...	42	515	300	6	..	...	5	...	209	21
1,948	423	620	13	35	33	54	905	3,019	1,363	25	4	...	27	...	1,631	
129	19	11	...	...	1	...	99	674	165	...	...	...	1	...	509	22
175	44	7	3	...	4	...	124	810	186	1	4	...	4	...	623	23
1,504	299	593	10	35	28	54	612	629	343	18	...	...	21	...	268	24
141	67	9	..	...	...	...	65	894	664	6	...	...	1	...	224	25
6	1	...	...	...	...	...	5	12	5	..	...	...	...	...	7	26
1,581	532	49	10	...	41	5	1,000	7,119	3,042	100	17	...	33	1	3,977	
850	260	24	2	...	4	...	566	5,171	2,302	60	...	...	9	...	2,809	27
511	*184*	*8*	...	...	...	...	*319*	*3,129*	*1,497*	*14*	...	...	*5*	...	*1,618*	
79	26	1	...	...	...	1	52	309	157	1	2	...	3	...	151	28
81	29	...	...	...	1	...	52	331	112	3	1	...	5	...	216	29
570	216	24	8	...	36	4	330	1,304	468	36	14	..	16	1	800	30
1	1	...	...	...	...	...	...	4	3	...	...	...	...	...	1	31
840	201	16	5	1	23	..	623	1,901	685	44	7	...	31	...	1,172	
500	113	15	3	...	11	...	372	1,017	290	26	5	...	12	...	701	32
73	13	...	...	..	1	..	60	168	77	6	...	...	7	...	85	33
61	18	...	...	...	...	...	43	341	161	1	...	...	5	...	179	34
184	54	1	2	1	11	...	129	233	125	11	2	...	7	...	97	35
22	3	...	...	...	...	...	19	142	32	...	...	...	...	...	110	36
2,441	665	397	8	10	17	22	1,379	4,164	1,733	71	2	...	11	...	2,360	
183	63	1	...	...	3	..	119	895	247	40	...	...	...	...	608	37
331	74	46	...	2	2	6	211	740	236	11	...	...	...	...	493	38
633	236	...	7	...	6	...	397	1,110	639	15	...	...	6	...	456	39
1,294	292	350	1	8	6	16	652	1,419	611	5	2	..	5	...	803	40
84,175	6,517	61,973	582	5,877	580	3,657	15,685	3,021	1,337	30	188	...	74	...	1,654	
515	243	30	4	...	5	11	242	1,173	627	18	23	...	27	...	528	41
82,217	5,880	61,514	564	5,877	550	3,642	14,823	1,696	654	11	162	...	46	...	1,031	42
1,443	394	429	14	...	25	4	620	152	56	1	3	...	1	...	95	43

Serial No.	DISTRICT OR STATE.	Order LIII.—Insufficiently described occupations—*concluded.* Group 186.—Mechanics otherwise unspecified. Total Workers and Dependents.	Workers. Total Workers. Males.	Total Workers. F's.	Workers with an agricultural or other subsidiary occupation. Agricultural. Males	Agricultural. F's.	Other. Males	Other. F's.	DEPENDENTS.	Group 187.—Labourers and workmen otherwise unspecified. Total Workers and Dependents.	Workers. Total Workers. Males.	Total Workers. Females	Workers with an agricultural or other subsidiary occupation. Agricultural. Males	Agricultural. Females	Other. Males.	Other. Females	DEPENDENTS.
	1	2	3	4	5	6	7	8	9	10	11	12	13	14	15	16	17
	Provincial Total ...	13,374	7,118	700	19	9	45	29	5,556	378,235	146,683	78,926	1,449	1,760	3,786	3,249	152,626
	Divisional Burma ...	13,074	6,947	700	19	9	45	29	5,427	323,698	125,746	61,350	961	1,109	2,799	2,045	136,602
	Arakan Division	271	150	...	.	...	...	...	121	23,168	8,720	4,089	148	121	281	151	10,359
1	Akyab	248	134	...	...	...	...	...	114	8,501	4,465	632	20	1	58	7	3,404
2	Hill Dist. of Arakan	1	1	...	.	...	...	...	...	79	66	3	...	...	1	...	10
3	Kyaukpyu ...	20	14	...	...	...	...	...	6	10,866	3,151	2,565	110	97	154	88	5,150
4	Sandoway ...	2	1	...	..	...	...	...	1	3,722	1,038	889	18	23	68	56	1,795
	Pegu Division ...	7,139	4,118	36	2	...	25	...	2,985	73,103	39,283	9,056	125	67	436	279	24,764
5	Rangoon Town ...	4,434	2,493	14	...	...	4	..	1,927	12,768	11,061	952	...	...	5	...	1,455
6	Insein	686	405	7	...	...	14	...	274	8,048	3,4[illegible]	1,068	9	3	34	12	3,518
7	Hanthawaddy ...	1,392	925	9	1	...	5	...	458	28,315	16,022	3,372	39	17	217	65	8,921
8	Tharrawaddy ...	69	33	...	...	...	...	...	36	10,946	3,830	2,088	55	29	98	114	5,028
9	Pegu	369	141	5	1	...	2	...	223	6,147	2,750	748	3	5	20	15	2,649
10	Prome	189	121	1	...	...	...	...	67	6,879	2,158	1,528	19	13	62	73	3,193
	Irrawaddy Division ...	1,601	590	639	3	9	3	29	372	40,939	17,225	7,263	198	30	363	167	16,451
11	Bassein	383	156	1	...	...	1	...	226	4,376	2,373	456	7	5	41	4	1,547
12	Henzada ...	783	104	638	...	9	...	29	41	16,807	5,305	4,145	57	22	126	148	7,357
13	Myaungmya ...	211	166	...	3	...	1	...	45	10,425	4,598	1,504	43	...	92	2	4,323
14	Ma-ubin	109	86	...	...	...	1	...	23	4,022	2,262	536	88	1	99	8	1,224
15	Pyapôn	115	78	...	...	...	...	...	37	5,309	2,687	622	3	2	5	5	2,000
	Tenasserim Division ...	1,432	757	7	1	...	4	...	668	41,783	17,832	4,761	73	10	267	125	19,190
16	Toungoo ...	276	149	2	...	...	2	...	125	13,013	4,582	2,172	10	3	61	59	6,259
17	Salween ...	3	...	..	...	...	...	...	3	817	544	48	...	...	2	...	225
18	Thatôn	190	43	1	...	...	...	...	146	17,726	7,760	1,875	54	5	167	61	8,091
19	Amherst ...	634	380	3	...	...	1	...	251	5,473	3,168	281	8	2	19	4	1,924
20	Tavoy	178	84	1	...	...	...	...	93	1,281	506	76	...	...	...	1	699
21	Mergui	151	101	...	1	...	1	...	50	3,473	1,872	209	1	...	18	...	1,998
	Magwe Division ...	366	253	2	..	...	3	...	111	16,267	4,975	4,944	28	32	160	169	6,348
22	Thayetmyo ...	111	65	1	...	...	2	...	45	4,925	1,302	1,425	...	5	19	25	2,198
23	Pakôkku ...	44	21	...	...	...	1	...	23	3,087	848	779	..	5	78	44	1,460
24	Minbu	50	38	...	...	...	...	..	12	5,971	1,679	2,357	27	18	47	86	1,935
25	Magwe	161	129	1	...	...	...	...	31	2,284	1,146	383	1	4	16	14	755
26	Pakôkku Hill Tracts	...	...	...	...	...	...	...	...	...	...	...	...	...	...	...	...
	Mandalay Division ...	1,084	507	2	...	...	2	...	575	35,898	14,072	5,930	148	25	396	160	15,896
27	Mandalay ...	860	357	2	...	-	...	...	501	11,332	3,790	3,127	3	13	20	16	4,415
	Mandalay City ...	412	181	..	..	...	...	-	231	7,256	2,873	2,035	...	..	2	2	2,848
28	Bhamo	24	12	...	..	...	...	...	12	358	275	16	...	...	3	...	67
29	Myitkyina ..	75	52	...	...	...	...	...	23	844	502	126	5	...	10	3	216
30	Katha	123	85	...	...	...	2	...	38	23,297	9,442	2,660	140	12	363	141	11,195
31	Putao	2	1	...	...	...	...	...	1	67	63	1	...	...	...	...	3
	Sagaing Division ...	366	214	7	12	...	5	...	145	22,587	5,898	6,981	97	113	355	302	9,708
32	Shwebo	165	88	5	...	...	...	...	72	16,500	4,616	5,435	89	65	258	167	6,449
33	Sagaing	38	22	...	...	...	...	...	16	2,068	473	555	...	1	20	37	1,040
34	Lower Chindwin ...	82	42	2	...	...	5	...	38	1,071	363	163	5	4	21	8	545
35	Upper Chindwin ...	47	45	...	...	...	...	...	2	2,920	439	823	3	43	56	90	1,656
36	Chin Hills ...	34	17	...	12	...	...	...	17	28	7	3	...	...	...	...	18
	Meiktila Division ...	815	358	7	1	...	3	...	450	69,953	17,741	18,326	144	711	541	692	33,886
37	Kyauksè ...	56	21	1	...	...	...	...	34	13,814	3,341	4,223	68	589	146	200	6,250
38	Meiktila	176	56	...	...	...	...	...	180	5,728	1,577	1,464	25	7	53	35	2,687
39	Yamèthin .	393	189	2	...	...	2	...	202	12,764	3,633	2,28[illegible]	..	...	86	63	6,849
40	Myingyan ...	190	92	4	1	...	1	...	94	37,647	9,190	10,357	51	115	256	394	18,100
	Eastern States ...	300	171	...	...	...	...	...	129	54,537	20,937	17,576	488	651	987	1,204	16,024
41	Northern Shan States	284	166	..	..	...	...	...	118	5,982	2,810	1,065	6	2	42	83	2,107
42	Southern Shan States	16	5	..	...	...	...	...	11	45,225	16,238	15,940	472	642	915	1,119	13,047
43	Karenni	...	...	...	...	...	...	...	...	3,330	1,889	571	10	7	30	11	870

PART III.—*Details by districts*—concld.

Order LV.†—Beggars, vagrants, prostitutes, etc.												
Group 189.†—Beggars, vagrants, wizards, witches, etc.								Group 190.†—Procurers and prostitutes.				Serial No. of District, etc. (column 1).
Total Workers and Dependents.	WORKERS.						DEPENDENTS.	Total Workers and Dependents.	WORKERS. *		DEPENDENTS.	
	Total Workers.		Workers with an agricultural or other subsidiary occupation.									
			Agricultural.		Other.							
	Males.	Females.	Males.	Females.	Males.	Females.			Males.	ales.		
18	19	20	21	22	23	24	25	26	27	8	29	
27,190	10,239	9,323	17	30	108	98	7,628	1,597	277	1,037	83	
23,253	8,897	7,375	8	3	87	62	6,981	1,596	277	1,036	283	
3,577	941	1,224	6	3	9	18	1,412	113	...	109	4	
3,296	873	1,117	6	3	9	18	1,306	110	...	108	2	1
8	4	4	...	..	...	...	...	...	...	...	...	2
221	42	87	...	...	...	...	92	3	...	1	2	3
52	22	16	...	...	...	...	14	...	...	...	...	4
2,882	1,332	827	...	...	12	...	723	808	.79	569	160	
1,033	633	217	...	...	...	...	183	624	33	472	119	5
219	80	33	...	...	...	...	106	...	...	...	...	6
352	168	69	...	...	...	...	115	5	...	5	...	7
247	136	75	...	...	...	...	36	...	...	...	...	8
432	241	135	...	...	12	...	56	136	31	78	27	9
599	74	298	...	...	...	.	227	43	15	14	14	10
1,542	735	368	...	...	6	4	439	250	71	136	43	
208	117	57	...	...	...	...	34	94	26	64	4	11
566	298	96	...	...	...	...	172	1	1	...	...	12
347	143	94	...	...	...	..	110	36	13	19	4	13
311	140	84	...	...	6	4	87	17	5	6	6	14
110	37	37	...	...	...	...	36	102	26	47	29	15
1,447	660	348	...	...	...	9	439	7	...	5	2	
401	233	63	...	...	...	...	105	5	...	3	2	16
5	3	2	...	...	...	...	...	...	...	...	...	17
429	152	118	...	...	...	9	159	...	...	...	...	18
558	250	258	...	...	...	...	150	2	...	2	...	19
17	13	4	...	...	...	...	...	...	...	...	...	20
37	9	3	...	...	...	...	25	...	...	...	...	21
3,297	1,233	1,063	..	...	20	9	1,001	69	*27	23	19	
442	205	34	...	...	...	...	203	...	...	...	...	22
1,438	556	373	...	...	20	1	509	22	*5	8	9	23
1,230	449	527	...	...	...	8	254	43	*18	15	10	24
187	23	189	...	...	...	...	35	4	4	...	...	25
...	...	...	...	...	...	...	...	...	...	...	...	26
3,345	1,150	983	...	...	5	1	1,212	222	*61	127	34	
2,329	848	786	.	...	4	..	695	129	29	85	15	27
618	289	242	...	...	...	...	87	115	23	78	14	
152	39	67	...	...	...	...	46	35	10	20	5	28
35	7	24	...	...	...	...	4	16	5	7	4	29
802	252	103	...	...	1	1	467	42	*17	15	10	30
7	4	3	...	...	...	...	...	...	...	...	...	31
3,333	1,236	1,427	1	...	2	3	670	42	*13	21	8	
1,377	551	446	1	...	1	...	380	1	*1	...	...	32
1,007	258	669	...	...	1	...	80	14	6	2	6	33
778	334	248	...	...	...	2	196	27	6	19	2	34
161	90	60	...	..	...	1	11	...	...	...	...	35
10	3	4	...	...	...	...	3	...	...	...	...	36
3,830	1,610	1,135	1	...	35	18	1,085	85	26	46	13	
907	503	171	...	...	...	1	233	...	...	...	...	37
554	143	295	...	...	...	...	116	8	...	7	1	38
625	294	186	...	...	17	...	145	67	21	39	7	39
1,744	670	483	1	...	18	17	591	10	5	...	5	40
3,937	1,342	1,948	9	27	19	36	647	1	...	1	...	
1,698	519	846	4	2	15	19	333	...	...	...	...	41
2,108	782	1,032	5	25	4	17	294	...	...	...	...	42
131	41	70	...	...	...	...	20	1	...	1	...	43

* One male in Pakôkku, 6 males in Minbu, 1 male in Katha and 1 male in Shwebo districts had non-agricultural subsidiary occupations.
† For Groups 188 and 191 see Orders LIV and LVI which are given on pages 304 and 305 respectively.

IMPERIAL TABLE XVIII.

Subsidiary Occupations.

NOTE 1.—This table furnishes further information relating to those workers who have been shown in Imperial Table XVII as having a subsidiary occupation in addition to the principal occupation according to which they are classified in that table.

NOTE 2.—For this purpose principal occupations have been divided into ten sorts and subsidiary occupations into 35 sorts; and workers of each sex have been classified according to the sort of both their principal and their subsidiary occupation.

NOTE 3.—The table for females for each sort of principal occupation is on the page succeeding the table for males, and the tables for the ten sorts are arranged in the order shown in Note 4 below. In each table the 35 sorts of subsidiary occupations are arranged in the order of their group-numbers; but in each case the sort of principal occupation is naturally omitted, and the tables for the subsidiary occupations of money-lenders or pawn-brokers, and of grain-dealers are compressed by the combination of unimportant figures into one column headed * for which details are given on page 426.

NOTE 4.—The ten sorts of principal occupations for which separate tabulation is given are defined as below in terms of the occupational groups used in Imperial Table XVII. A short title is given for each sort, but this must not be regarded as a rigorous or even adequate definition of the sort, which is defined only by the group-numbers given. The section of the table which comprises the tabulation for each sort is indicated by the letters A to K respectively.

Section of Table.	Name of Sort.	Groups.	Section of Table.	Name of Sort.	Groups.
	Agricultural.			*Non-Agricultural.*	
A	Landlord	1 and 2a	F	Gardener	5, 6a to 6j inclusive, and 7.
B	Cultivating owner ...	3a	G	Money-lender or pawn-broker.	121
C	Cultivating tenant ...	3b	H	Wholesale grain-dealer	136a
D	Agricultural labourer	3c	J	Retail grain-dealer ...	136b
E	Taungya cultivator ...	4	K	Others	All groups not in other sorts.

NOTE 5.—Of the 35 sorts of subsidiary occupations nine are the same as the first nine sorts of principal occupations and the remaining 26 are subdivisions of the tenth sort (*Others*). In the headings of the columns of the table short names are given for the sorts; but as for the sorts of principal occupations these are not to be regarded as defining the content of the sort, which is defined by the group-number or numbers associated with it in the heading, except in the cases of the last four sorts, numbered 1001 to 1004, and the sort *Toddy-drawer or jaggery maker*. This last sort is restricted to persons shown in the enumeration-record as palm-climbers, toddy-drawers or preparers of jaggery and so includes all Group 74 and part of Group 71, but omits those of the latter group who are concerned with kyantaga or dhani-th'gya and not with toddy palms or jaggery. No. 1001 *Durwan or peon* includes all for whom one of these descriptions alone was given without any indication of the group to which they properly belonged, and Nos. 1002, 1003 and 1004 are remainder-sorts.

NOTE 6.—The sorts of subsidiary occupations included in the column headed *Total Agricultural* are those distinguished as agricultural in Note 4 above, and include exactly the occupations defined as agricultural in Imperial Table XVII, Part I, Section A, Article 3.

NOTE 7.—The whole of Part I of Imperial Table XVII applies to this table unless the contrary is indicated by the above Notes.

NOTE 8.—The figures tabulated for the Rangoon Town District represent also Rangoon Town, as for the purposes of the Imperial Census Tables these areas are conterminous.

[*Continued on page 426.*]

IMPERIAL TABLE XVIII, SECTION A.—*Subsidiary Occupations*

Serial No.	District or State.	Total Agricultural.	Total Non-Agricultural.	AGRICULTURAL. 3a. Cultivating owner.	3b. Cultivating tenant.	3c. Agricultural labourer.	4. Taungya cultivator.	5, 6, 7. Gardener, etc.	9a. Charcoal burner.	9b. Wood cutters.	9c. Cutch collectors.	8, 10. All other collectors of forest produce.	11. Herdsman.	37. Fisherman.	97. Cotton-weavers.	94, 18. Silk rearers and spinners.	95. Silk-weavers.
	1	2	3	4	5	6	7	8	9	10	11	12	13	14	15	16	17
	Provincial Total	999	5,831	545	169	178	107	323	1	63	5	14	43	63	17	1	...
	Burma Proper ...	797	5,337	385	168	171	73	308	1	63	5	14	29	58	17	1	...
	Arakan Division ...	188	514	64	39	57	28	39	...	...	...	...	3	15	...	...	...
1	Akyab ...	86	168	28	24	31	3	3	...	...	...	...	3	2	...	...	...
2	Hill Dt. of Arakan	...	...	...	...	...	...	...	...	...	...	...	...	...	...	...	...
3	Kyaukpyu ...	35	176	23	2	5	5	18	...	...	...	...	...	5	...	...	...
4	Sandoway ...	67	170	13	13	21	20	18	...	...	...	...	...	8	...	...	...
	Pegu Division ...	130	943	50	44	24	12	81	1	14	...	5	5	10	5	...	...
5	Rangoon ...	...	2	...	...	...	...	...	...	...	...	...	...	...	...	...	...
6	Insein ...	5	97	3	2	...	...	5	...	1	...	2	...	1	...	...	...
7	Hanthawaddy ..	12	95	3	7	2	...	...	...	...	...	...	...	...	...	...	...
8	Tharrawaddy ...	38	336	24	10	4	...	26	...	2	...	3	...	5	...	...	...
9	Pegu ...	48	177	16	25	6	1	2	...	5	...	...	5	2	1	...	...
10	Prome ...	27	236	4	...	12	11	48	1	6	...	...	...	2	4	...	...
	Irrawaddy Division	139	1,113	78	42	10	9	72	...	4	...	6	...	9	...	...	...
11	Bassein ...	39	269	26	5	1	7	18	...	...	...	4	...	3	...	...	...
12	Henzada ...	26	259	16	5	3	2	34	...	3	...	...	...	1	...	...	...
13	Myaungmya ...	38	349	13	22	3	...	5	...	1	...	2	...	5	...	...	...
14	Ma-ubin ...	31	135	21	8	2	...	14	...	...	...	...	...	...	...	...	...
15	Pyapôn ...	5	101	2	2	1	...	1	...	...	...	...	...	...	...	...	...
	Tenasserim Division	61	422	23	16	6	16	63	...	1	...	2	...	5	...	...	...
16	Toungoo ...	24	136	14	2	5	3	13	...	...	...	...	...	1	...	...	...
17	Salween ...	6	4	...	1	...	5	...	...	...	...	...	...	...	...	...	...
18	Thatôn ...	13	88	2	9	...	2	6	...	...	...	...	...	...	...	...	...
19	Amherst ...	7	81	4	2	1	...	8	...	1	...	2	...	...	...	...	...
20	Tavoy ...	9	108	1	2	...	6	36	...	...	...	...	...	4	...	...	...
21	Mergui ...	2	5	2	...	...	...	...	...	...	...	...	...	...	...	...	...
	Magwe Division ...	146	991	87	10	45	4	32	...	17	5	1	12	6	5	1	...
22	Thayetmyo ...	45	128	20	...	21	4	...	...	11	...	...	8	3	...	...	...
23	Pakôkku ...	25	351	13	1	11	...	3	...	3	3	...	2	...	4	1	...
24	Minbu ...	65	293	48	9	8	...	13	...	3	2	...	1	3	...	...	...
25	Magwe ...	11	219	6	...	5	...	16	...	...	...	1	1	...	1	...	...
26	Pakôkku Hill Tts.	...	...	...	...	...	...	...	...	...	...	...	...	...	...	...	...
	Mandalay Division	14	95	7	1	3	3		...	5	...	...	1	7	...	...	...
27	Mandalay ...	7	34	4	...	3	...	...	...	1	...	...	1	3	...	...	...
	Mandalay City ...	...	...	...	...	...	...	...	...	...	...	...	...	...	...	...	...
28	Bhamo ...	2	3	...	...	...	2	...	...	...	...	...	...	...	...	...	...
29	Myitkyina ...	...	5	...	...	...	...	...	...	...	...	...	...	...	...	...	...
30	Katha ...	5	53	3	1	...	1	2	...	4	...	...	...	4	...	...	...
31	Putao ...	...	...	...	...	...	...	...	...	...		...	...	...	...	...	...
	Sagaing Division	79	808	60	3	16	...	10	...	18	...	...	2	6	4	...	...
32	Shwebo ...	1	35	1	...	...	...	...	...	1	...	-	...	...	...	...	...
33	Sagaing ...	29	336	25	1	3	...	1	...	1	...	...	2	1	...	...	...
34	Lower Chindwin	30	309	22	2	6	...	9	...	3	...	...	...	3	3	...	...
35	Upper Chindwin	19	128	12	...	7	...	...	...	13	...	...	...	2	1	...	...
36	Chin Hills ...	...	...	...	...	...	...	...	...	...	...	...	...	...	...	...	...
	Meiktila Division	40	451	16	13	10	1	9	...	4	...	...	6	...	3	...	...
37	Kyauksê ...	4	78	1	...	3	...	2	...	...	...	...	3	...	...	...	...
38	Meiktila ...	8	169	3	...	5	...	3	...	...	...	...	3	...	2	...	...
39	Yamèthin ...	...	43	...	...	...	...	...	...	3	...	...	...	...	...	...	...
40	Myingyan ...	28	161	12	13	2	1	4	...	1	...	...	...	...	1	...	...
	Eastern States ...	202	494	160	1	7	34	15	...	...	...	...	14	5	...	...	...
41	N. Shan States ...	22	85	2	...	3	17	9	...	...	...	...	3	1	...	...	...
42	S. Shan States ...	180	409	158	1	4	17	6	...	...	...	...	11	4	...	...	...
43	Karenni ...	...	...	...	...	...	...	...	...	...	...	...	...	...	...	...	...

of **Male** *Workers of Sort A—Landlord* (*Groups 1 and 2a*).

48a. Basket-makers.	49. Mat-weavers.	61. Oil-pressers.	65. Rice-pounders.	71, 74. Sweetmeat makers and toddy drawers.	110a. Boat owner.	110b. Boatman or towman.	114. Cart-owner or driver.	121. Money-lender or pawn-broker.	123a. Wholesale cloth seller.	123b. Retail cloth seller.	131. Fish seller.	134. Sweetmeat seller.	135. Vegetable seller.	136a. Wholesale grain-dealer	136b. Retail grain-dealer.	160. Lawyer.	1001. Durwan or peon.	1002. Other labourers.	1003. Other traders.	1004. All others.	Serial No. of District, etc. (column 1).
18	19	20	21	22	23	24	25	26	27	28	29	30	31	32	33	34	35	36	37	38	
60	55	23	11	112	18	23	267	1,374	1	61	30	27	37	338	74	1	10	181	934	1,664	
60	55	23	11	110	18	23	227	1,367	1	60	29	26	25	338	73	1	10	132	852	1,400	
1	...	...	4	10	4	2	3	100	..	2	8	...	11	27	3	...	...	17	67	198	
...	...	...	2	1	2	2	2	12	...	2	4	..	7	18	1	...	...	4	5	104	1
...	...	...	...	...	...	...	...	..	...	...	...	..	..	...	...	...	...	...	..	...	2
...	...	..	1	...	...	...	...	50	...	...	...	...	...	8	1	...	...	13	35	45	3
1	...	..	1	9	2	...	1	38	...	...	4	...	4	7	1	...	...	...	27	49	4
6	7	...	3	8	...	3	39	216	...	12	7	2	3	112	11	...	...	24	158	191	
...	...	...	...	...	..	...	.	...	...	...	...	..	...	1	...	...	...	...	...	1	5
...	...	...	...	...	...	1	2	39	...	...	...	...	...	10	...	...	...	...	22	14	6
...	...	...	...	...	...	1	...	18	...	..	...	...	...	11	4	...	..	17	29	15	7
...	4	...	...	...	...	...	19	88	..	5	4	...	...	61	...	...	...	...	53	66	8
...	1	...	1	...	..	...	9	49	...	3	...	..	...	18	4	...	...	4	33	40	9
6	2	...	2	8	.	1	29	22	...	4	3	2	3	11	3	...	...	3	21	55	10
9	3	...	..	3	2	6	36	407	1	2	5	5	2	109	4	...	...	12	151	265	
...	3	...		...	1	...	2	106	...	.	4	4	1	30	2	...	...	1	29	61	11
2	...	...	...	3	1	1	29	71	1	...	1	...	...	12	1	...	...	6	30	57	12
...	...	...	..	...	...	...	...	148	..	1	...	...	1	16	...	...	...	5	62	103	13
1	..	...	..	...	...	1	5	48	..	...	...	...	...	21	...	...	...	...	18	27	14
...	..	...	...	...	...	4	...	34	...	1	...	1	...	30	1	...	...	...	12	17	15
8	...	...	...	1	2	4	26	94	...	4	...	...	6	17	3	...	...	2	87	97	
...	...	...	..	...	...	...	9	41	...	2	...	...	1	8	...	...	..	...	31	30	16
...	...	...	...	...	...	1	...	...	...	...	...	...	3	...	...	...	...	...	...	...	17
2	...	...	...	...	...	1	5	14	...	...	...	...	...	2	1	...	...	2	37	18	18
1	...	...	...	...	2	2	9	24	...	...	..	...	1	4	1	...	...	...	12	14	19
4	...	...	...	1	...	...	3	14	...	2	...	.	1	3	1	...	...	...	7	32	20
1	...	...	...	...	...	...	..	1	...	...		..	...	...	...	...	...	...	...	3	21
21	35	19	1	56	9	6	55	181	...	24	7	...	...	30	26	1	...	57	145	239	
9	25	14	...	13	...	...	..	1	...	...	–	..	...	13	11	...	...	16	...	4	22
9	5	2	1	30	8	3	18	77	...	16	2	...	..	...	5	...	..	1	69	89	23
3	4	2	...	8	...	2	12	69	...	2	5	...	...	15	9	1	...	3	51	85	24
...	1	1	...	5	1	1	25	34	...	6	...	...	...	2	1	...	...	37	25	61	25
...	...	...	...	.	...	...	...	...	...	...	...	...	..	...	...	...	...	...	...	...	26
1	1	1	1	...	...	...	8	8	...	1	...	1	...	3	...	...	10	1	8	36	
...	...	1	1	...	..	...	5	7	.	1	...	1	...	2	...	...	...	1	3	7	27
...	...	...	...	...	..	...	...	...	...	...	...	...	...	...	...	...	...	...	...	...	
...	...	...	...	...	...	...	...	...	...	...	...	...	...	...	...	...	...	...	..	3	28
...	...	..	...	...	...	...	1	...	...	...	...	...	...	...	...	...	...	...	...	4	29
1	1	...	...	...	...	...	2	1	...	...	..	...	...	1	...	...	10	...	5	22	30
...	...	...	...	...	...	...	...	...	.	...	...	...	...	...	...	...	...	...	...	...	31
13	6	3	...	23	1	2	22	235	...	11	2	10	3	32	19	...	...	4	139	243	
...	...	...	...	1	...	...	2	2	...	8	...	1	...	3	...	...	...	2	6	9	32
2	2	...	..	9	...	...	4	131	..		2	8	...	7	12	...	...	2	69	83	33
7	3	3	...	13	...	...	9	94	...	3	...	1	2	9	4	...	...	...	51	92	34
4	1	...	...	...	1	2	7	8	...	...	...	...	1	13	3	...	...	...	13	59	35
...	...	...	..	...	...	...	...	...	...	...	...	...	...	...	...	...	...	...	...	...	36
1	3	...	2	9	...	...	18	126	...	4	...	8	...	8	7	...	...	15	97	131	
..	2	...	2	3	...	...	5	22	...	...	...	3	...	6	2	...	...	1	11	16	37
...	...	...	...	...	...	...	2	46	..	4	...	...	...	...	...	...	...	6	50	53	38
1	1	...	...	...	...	..	1	9	.	...	...	1	...	...	5	...	...	...	8	14	39
...	...	...	...	6	..	...	10	49	...	...	...	4	...	2	...	...	...	8	28	48	40
...	...	...	...	2	...	...	40	7	...	1	1	1	12	...	1	...	...	49	82	264	
...	...	...	...	...	...	...	3	1	...	...	1	...	1	...	1	...	...	1	14	50	41
...	...	...	...	2	...	...	37	6	...	1	...	1	11	...	...	...	...	48	68	214	42
...	...	...	...	...	...	...	...	...	...	...	...	...	...	...	...	...	...	...	...	...	43

Serial No.	District or State.	Total Agricultural.	Total Non-Agricultural.	AGRICULTURAL. 8a, Cultivating owner.	8b, Cultivating tenant.	8c, Agricultural labourer.	4, Taungya cultivator.	5, 6, 7, Gardener, etc.	9a, Charcoal burner.	9b, Wood cutters.	9c, Cutch collectors.	9d, 10, All other collectors of forest produce.	11, Herdsman.	17, Fisherman.	97, Cotton-weavers.	94, 95, Silk rearers and spinners.	98, Silk-weavers.
	1	2	3	4	5	6	7	8	9	10	11	12	13	14	15	16	17
	Provincial Total ...	1,089	4,570	533	173	274	109	233	...	13	...	15	4	14	1,087	...	20
	Burma Proper ...	896	4,340	445	173	241	37	203	...	13	...	15	3	9	954	...	20
	Arakan Division ...	105	337	62	18	13	12	23	...	2	...	...	...	4	36	...	...
1	Akyab ...	14	109	7	5	...	2	1	...	...	...	...	...	4	23	...	...
2	Hill Dt. of Arakan	...	...	...	...	...	...	...	...	...	...	...	...	...	...	...	...
3	Kyaukpyu ...	37	91	21	7	6	3	10	...	...	...	...	...	...	3	...	...
4	Sandoway ...	54	137	34	6	7	7	12	...	2	...	...	...	...	10	...	...
	Pegu Division ...	89	532	35	17	35	2	35	...	...	...	6	...	1	120	...	...
5	Rangoon ...	...	6	...	...	...	...	...	...	...	...	...	...	...	...	...	...
6	Insein ...	7	37	1	3	3	...	2	...	...	...	2	...	...	1	...	...
7	Hanthawaddy ...	1	15	1	...	...	...	...	...	...	...	...	...	...	...	...	...
8	Tharrawaddy ...	46	122	21	6	19	...	6	...	...	...	4	...	1	9	...	...
9	Pegu ...	23	68	9	8	6	...	2	...	...	...	...	...	...	5	...	...
10	Prome ...	12	284	3	...	7	2	25	...	...	...	...	...	...	105	...	...
	Irrawaddy Division	136	706	68	27	40	1	79	...	1	...	4	2	2	36	...	...
11	Bassein ...	17	190	9	5	3	...	26	...	...	...	2	...	1	9	...	...
12	Henzada ...	81	203	40	12	29	...	12	...	...	...	1	...	...	22	...	...
13	Myaungmya ...	10	182	7	1	1	1	23	...	1	...	...	...	1	...	...	...
14	Ma-ubin ...	26	85	12	7	7	...	16	...	...	...	1	2	...	4	...	...
15	Pyapôn ...	2	46	...	2	...	...	2	...	...	...	...	...	...	1	...	...
	Tenasserim Division	24	268	9	8	4	3	33	...	...	...	1	...	1	31	...	1
16	Toungoo ...	10	56	6	3	...	1	3	...	...	...	1	...	...	9	...	...
17	Salween ...	...	3	...	...	...	...	2	...	...	...	...	...	...	...	...	...
18	Thatôn ...	6	70	2	4	...	...	1	...	...	...	...	...	...	6	...	...
19	Amherst ...	2	57	...	1	1	...	4	...	...	...	...	...	...	13	...	...
20	Tavoy ...	3	76	...	...	1	2	21	...	...	...	...	...	1	3	...	1
21	Mergui ...	3	6	1	...	2	...	2	...	...	...	...	...	...	...	...	...
	Magwe Division ...	162	829	76	6	62	18	20	...	1	...	...	...	...	[illegible]	...	14
22	Thayetmyo ...	51	125	25	4	4	18	7	...	1	...	...	...	...	28	...	...
23	Pakôkku ...	31	359	13	...	18	...	2	...	...	...	...	...	...	198	...	14
24	Minbu ...	63	167	38	2	23	...	5	...	...	...	...	...	...	41	...	...
25	Magwe ...	17	178	...	...	17	...	6	...	...	...	...	...	...	36	...	...
26	Pakôkku Hill Tts.	...	...	...		...	...	...	...	...	...	...	...	...	...	...	...
	Mandalay Division	13	68	2	...	11	...	1	...	...	...	...	...	...	16	...	...
27	Mandalay ...	4	40	...	...	4	...	1	...	...	...	...	...	...	8	...	...
	Mandalay City ...	...	1	...	...	...	...	...	...	...	...	...	...	...	...	...	...
28	Bhamo ...	...	5	...	...	...	...	...	...	...	...	...	...	...	...	...	...
29	Myitkyina ...	...	...	...	...	...	...	...	...	...	...	...	...	...	1	...	...
30	Katha ...	9	23	2	...	7	...	...	...	...	...	...	...	...	...	...	...
31	Putao ...	...	...	...	...	...	...	...	...	...	...	...	...	...	7	...	
	Sagaing Division	272	1,670	158	75	47	...	7	...	6	...	4	1	1	327	...	5
32	Shwebo ...	16	282	...	...	16	...	...	...	1	...	...	...	...	88	...	5
33	Sagaing ...	17	396	3	...	14	...	...	...	...	...	...	1	...	135	...	...
34	Lower Chindwin	216	997	138	67	11		5	...	2	...	...	...	1	104	...	...
35	Upper Chindwin	23	95	9	8	6	...	2	...	3	...	4	...	...	...	...	...
36	Chin Hills ...	...	...	...	...	...	...	...	...	...	...	...	...		...	...	...
	Meiktila Division ..	95	530	43	22	29	1	5	...	3	...	...	...	...	155	...	...
37	Kyaukse ...	12	50	...	...	12	...	...	...	...	...	...	...	...	9	...	...
38	Meiktila ...	5	173	1	1	3	...	2	...	...	...	...	...	...	58	...	...
39	Yamethin ...	16	77	8	1	6	1	1	...	...	...	...	...	...	22	...	...
40	Myingyan ...	62	230	34	20	8	...	2	...	3	...	...	...	...	66	...	...
	Eastern States ...	193	230	88	...	33	72	30	...	...	...	...	1	5	53	...	...
41	N. Shan States ...	7	110	...	...	5	2	24		...	...	...	...	...	...	...	...
42	S. Shan States ..	186	120	88	...	28	70	6	...	...	...	...	...	...	51	...	...
43	Karenni ...	...	...	...	...	...	...	...	...	...	...	...	1	5	2	...	...

of **Female** *Workers of Sort A—Landlord (Groups 1 and 2a).*

45a, Basket-makers.	45b, Mat-weavers.	63, Oil-presser.	65, Rice-pounder.	71, 74, Sweetmeat makers and toddy drawers.	110a, Boat-owner.	110b, Boatman or towman.	114, Cart-owner or driver.	121, Money-lender or pawnbroker.	128a, Wholesale cloth seller.	128b, Retail cloth seller.	131, Fish seller.	134, Sweetmeat seller.	135, Vegetable seller.	138a, Wholesale grain-dealer.	138b, Retail grain-dealer.	160, Lawyer.	1001, Durwan or peon.	1008, Other labourers.	1018, Other traders.	1004, All others.	Serial No. of District, etc. (column 1).
18	19	20	21	22	23	24	25	26	27	28	29	30	31	32	33	34	35	36	37	38	
4	49	11	19	55	4	2	28	667	11	123	36	113	65	50	61	...	...	163	1,085	718	
4	47	11	19	55	4	2	26	665	11	122	36	111	65	50	61	...	...	145	1,057	632	
...	...	...	4	...	3	...	2	49	...	2	4	21	9	2	...	..	...	8	99	69	
...	...	...	3	...	...	...	...	8	...	1	1	...	6	1	...	...	...	...	32	29	1
...	...	...	...	...	...	...	...	...	...	..	...	...	...	...	...	...	...	..	...	...	2
...	...	...	...	...	3	...	...	23	...	...	...	...	...	...	...	...	..	8	28	16	3
...	...	...	1	...	..	..	2	18	...	1	3	21	3	1	...	...	...	...	39	24	4
...	3	1	1	7	..	...	13	80	1	7	6	10	13	18	13	...	...	3	133	61	
...	...	...	...	...	...	...	...	1	...	...	...	...	...	2	...	...	...	...	2	1	5
...	1	...	...	...	...	...	...	17	...	...	...	...	...	...	...	...	...	2	6	6	6
...	...	...	...	...	...	...	1	4	...	1	...	...	...	2	...	...	...	1	5	1	7
...	2	...	1	...	..	..	...	33	1	...	...	1	2	10	1	...	...	...	38	13	8
...	...	1	...	...	...	...	3	18	..	3	2	3	2	3	...	...	...	...	20	6	9
...	...	...	...	7	...	...	9	7	...	3	4	6	9	1	12	...	.	...	62	34	10
1	4	...	...	2	1	1	1	280	2	4	9	15	...	23	10	...	..	24	161	104	
...	...	...	...	...	1	...	...	73	...	1	3	8	...	10	...	...	...	...	30	26	11
1	2	...	..	2	...	..	1	31	2	2	2	4	...	8	6	...	...	13	49	45	12
...	1	...	...	..	...	1	...	77	...	1	2	...	...	...	...	...	...	10	47	18	13
...	1	...	..	...	...	...	...	20	...	...	2	3	...	...	3	...	...	...	22	11	14
..	...	...	...	...	...	...	...	19	...	...	...	...	...	5	1	...	...	1	13	4	15
...	3	...	...	..	...	...	...	24	1	8	..	..	8	2	...	.	..	3	88	64	
...	...	...	...	...	...	...	...	2	...	1	...	...	3	..	...	...	...	3	25	9	16
...	...	...	...	...	...	...	...	...	...	...	...	...	1	...	...	...	..	...	...	...	17
...	...	...	...	...	...	...	...	3	...	1	...	...	1	1	...	...	...	.	40	17	18
...	...	...	...	..	...	..	..	7	...	3	...	...	1	1	...	...	...	...	8	20	19
...	1	...	..	..	...	...	...	12	1	3	...	...	2	...	.	...	...	...	14	17	20
...	2	-	..	...	...	...	...	...	...	...	-	..	...	...	...	...	...	...	1	1	21
...	22	1	4	29	.	1	3	85	5	57	13	23	22	1	17	.	...	15	179	94	
...	20	1	...	...	...	1	1	6	..	5	3	1	2	...	2	...	...	7	27	13	22
...	...	...	3	25	...	...	1	37		36	7	12	5	...	10	...	...	...	40	39	23
...	2	...	1	1	...	...	...	20	5	3	3	9	2	1	3	...	...	8	45	18	24
...	...	..	...	3	...	.	1	22	...	13	..	1	3	...	2	..	...	..	67	24	25
...	...	...	...	...	..	-	...	...	..	.	...	...	...	...	.	...	...	...	...	...	26
...	...	...	...	...	...	...	2	9	...	...	...	2	2	1	.	...	..	3	17	15	
...	...	..	...	...	...	...	2	9	...	...	...	1	1	...	...	...	...	1	13	4	27
..	...	...	..	...	...	...	...	...	...	...	...	...	...	..	...	...	...	1	...	.	
...	...	...	...	...	...	...	...	..	...	...	...	...	...	...	...	...	..	...	...	4	28
...	..	..	...	..	...	...	...	..	...	...	...	...	...	...	...	...	...	...	...	...	29
..	..	...	...	...	...	...	...	...	..	...	...	1	1	1	...	...	...	2	4	7	30
...	..	...	...	...	...	...	...	...	...	...	...	...	...	...	...	...	...	...	...	...	31
3	22	7	7	13	...	...	2	122	2	24	...	28	17	2	8	...	...	75	243	154	
3	1	...	5	..	..	...	1	22	...	18	...	7	3	2	5	..	...	17	60	36	32
...	1	2	...	6	.	...	1	66	...	4	...	8	10	...	3	...	...		88	71	33
...	9	5	2	7	...	...	...	34	2	2	...	13	4	-	.	...	...	..	64	43	34
...	1	...	..	..	...	...	...	...	...	...	...	...	...	...	...	...	...	58	23	4	35
..	...	...	...	...	...	...	...	...	...	...	...	...	.	...	...	...	...	...	...	...	36
...	3	2	3	4	...	.	3	76		20	4	12	4	1	13	...	...	14	137	71	
...	2	...	3	1	...		...	11	...	..	...	4	...	...	...	.	...	...	26	4	37
...	...	...		..	...	...	...	20	..	19	2	2	2	...	3	..	...	...	48	17	38
...	1	...	...	...	..	...	1	8	.	1	...	...	2	1	6	...	...	1	23	10	39
...	...	2	...	3	...	...	2	37	...	...	2	6	...	-	4	..	..	13	50	40	40
...	2	..	...	...	...	...	2	2	...	1	...	2	...	.	...	...	..	18	28	26	
...	2	...	...	...	...	...	1	2	...	1	...	2	...	...	...	...	...	...	17	10	41
...	...		...	..	...	...	1	...	...	...	...	...	...	...	...	...	...	18	11	76	42
...	...	...	...	...	...	...	...	...	...	...	..	...	...	...	...	...	...	...	...	...	43

Serial No.	District or State.	Total Agricultural.	Total Non-Agricultural.	AGRICULTURAL. 1, 2a. Landlord.	2b. Cultivating tenant.	2c. Agricultural labourer.	4. Taungya cultivator.	5, 6, 7, Gardener, etc.	9a. Charcoal burner.	9b. Wood cutters.	9c. Cutch collectors.	9d, 10. All other collectors of forest produce.	11. Herdsman.	17. Fisherman.	97. Cotton-weavers.	94, 16. Silk rearers and spinners.	95. Silk-weavers.
	1	2	3	4	5	6	7	8	9	10	11	12	13	14	15	16	17
	Provincial Total	32,366	183,783	1,898	9,755	7,409	13,304	17,314	212	10,805	1,277	3,005	1,004	4,373	475	6	87
	Burma Proper ...	23,669	145,845	1,718	8,943	6,859	6,149	8,766	211	10,610	1,264	3,001	619	3,351	451	6	87
	Arakan Division ...	2,904	8,679	270	647	586	1,401	1,512	2	39	23	116	43	909	9	...	...
1	Akyab ...	776	2,937	155	276	251	94	152	2	4	...	1	38	61	6	...	...
2	Hill Dt. of Arakan	...	5	..	...	...	...	...	...	...	...	...	...	..	...	...	...
3	Kyaukpyu ...	1,031	3,419	85	281	303	362	637	...	19	22	...	1	319	3	...	...
4	Sandoway ...	1,097	2,318	30	90	32	945	723	...	16	1	115	4	529	...	...	...
	Pegu Division ..	3,073	11,625	253	889	929	1,002	986	27	344	15	691	41	548	32	...	...
5	Rangoon Town ...	...	11	...	...	..	...	...	...	...	...	...	...	...	...	..	...
6	Insein ..	96	445	30	39	26	1	54	10	16	...	24	...	21	...	...	...
7	Hanthawaddy ...	210	544	20	161	28	1	114	..	1	...	2	15	16	...	...	...
8	Tharrawaddy ..	1,326	3,989	99	505	611	111	160	7	48	...	565	11	391	4	...	...
9	Pegu ...	230	1,135	73	66	88	3	4	3	129	...	94	10	60	...	...	...
10	Prome ..	1,211	5,501	31	118	176	886	654	7	150	15	6	5	60	28	...	...
	Irrawaddy Division	2,827	7,661	349	1,274	962	242	2,152	6	192	..	204	15	279	38	...	..1
11	Bassein ...	346	1,432	49	80	99	118	275		45	...	7	3	62	27	...	...
12	Henzada ...	969	3,707	164	316	415	74	1,020	6	95	...	...	1	76	9	...	...
13	Myaungmya	757	903	83	480	144	50	68	.	51	..	193	7	29	1	...	
14	Ma-ubin ...	701	1,382	45	359	297	..	758	...	1	...	1	3	106	...	...	...
15	Pyapôn ...	54	237	8	39	7	...	31	..	...	..	3	1	6	1	...	...
	Tenasserim Division	1,468	8,597	176	465	307	520	1,744	50	242	22	184	142	375	13	...	...
16	Toungoo ...	193	1,406	26	49	72	46	174	5	69	...	146	48	40	1	...	...
17	Salween .	33	424	...	3	4	26	313	...	22	.	...	1	...	...	...	..
18	Thatôn ...	601	2,054	93	298	138	72	253	1	42	...	...	39	61	7	...	...
19	Amherst .	360	2,349	40	64	69	187	486	43	42	...	34	48	47	4	...	..
20	Tavoy ...	174	1,260	15	42	20	97	306		34	21	...	5	96	...	...	...
21	Mergui ..	107	1,104	2	9	4	92	212	1	33	1	4	1	131	1	...	.
	Magwe Division ...	4,046	30,378	223	1,413	1,861	549	679	30	2,004	1,011	15	124	260	73	...	5
22	Thayetmyo ...	1,466	4,450	38	352	552	524	32	...	555	257	3	7	19	29	...	...
23	Pakôkku ..	848	11,529	104	406	313	25	130	27	240	488	8	29	77	31	...	5
24	Minbu ...	956	7,319	55	590	311	...	91	3	994	196	...	18	119	5	...	...
25	Magwe ...	776	7,080	26	65	685	...	426	...	215	70	4	70	45	8	..	...
26	Pakôkku Hill Tts.	...		...	..	..	...	...	..	...	...	...	...	...	...	...	...
	Mandalay Division	2,609	16,707	33	104	269	2,203	317	26	2,189	1	292	35	558	75	6	...
27	Mandalay ...	139	1,945	3	39	97	...	45	24	542	1	6	3	63	38	...	...
	Mandalay City ...	...	...	...		...	...	...	...	...	...	...	...	..	...	..	...
28	Bhamo ...	1,146	2,994	3	7	27	1,109	35	...	814	..	123	5	238	...	...	.
29	Myitkyina ...	478	1,922	...	1	1	476	100	2	64	..	86	14	18	...	...	...
30	Katha ...	738	9,583	25	57	143	513	131	...	769	...	77	13	239	37	6	...
31	Putao ...	108	263	2	...	1	105	6	...	...	...	...	...	...	...	...	..
	Sagaing Division	4,208	42,790	297	2,729	1,054	128	537	6	4,523	86	1,493	131	343	128	...	81
32	Shwebo ...	310	20,250	22	200	178	10	231	1	1,304	...	61	35	35	81	...	12
33	Sagaing ...	1,507	8,238	114	982	411	...	7	.	550	2	12	84	53	13	...	3
34	Lower Chindwin	1,055	6,278	48	920	87	...	164	4	323	44	2	8	28	28	..	66
35	Upper Chindwin	1,336	8,024	113	727	378	118	135	1	2,346	40	1,418	4	233	6	...	...
36	Chin Hills ...	...	...	...	...	...	...	...	...	...	...	...	..	...	...	...	...
	Meiktila Division ..	2,534	19,408	117	1,422	891	104	839	64	1,077	106	6	88	79	83	...	1
37	Kyauksè ...	118	1,567	8	70	40	...	36	...	237	.	6	10	6	3	...	...
38	Meiktila ...	605	6,698	10	185	410	...	244		633	46	...	45	64	27	...	...
39	Yamèthin ...	670	4,282	22	197	347	104	477	51	180	39	...	25	9	7	...	1
40	Myingyan ...	1,141	6,861	77	970	94	...	82	13	27	21	...	8	...	46	...	...
	Eastern States ..	8,697	37,938	180	812	550	7,155	8,548	1	195	13	4	385	1,022	24	...	...
41	N. Shan States ...	4,459	11,417	49	419	132	3,859	4,563	..	189	13	4	379	23	24	...	...
42	S. Shan States ...	4,083	25,947	128	383	316	3,196	3,950	1	6	..	...	6	930	...	...	...
43	Karenni ...	215	574	3	10	102	100	35	...	...	...	...	...	69	...	...	...

of **Male** *Workers of Sort B—Cultivating Owner* (*Group 3a*).

45a, Basket-makers.	45b, Mat-weavers.	61, Oilpresser.	65, Rice-pounder.	71, 74, Sweetmeat makers and toddy drawers.	110a, Boat-owner.	110b, Boatman or towman.	114, Cart-owner or driver.	121, Money-lender or pawn-broker.	128a, Wholesale cloth seller.	128b, Retail cloth seller.	181, Fish seller.	184, Sweetmeat seller.	185, Vegetable seller.	186a, Wholesale grain-dealer.	186b, Retail grain-dealer.	169, Lawyer.	1001, Durwan or peon.	1002, Other labourers.	1003, Other traders.	1004, All others.	Serial No. of District, etc. (column 1).
18	19	20	21	22	23	24	25	26	27	28	29	30	31	32	33	34	35	36	37	38	
1,580	4,450	2,565	208	11,435	96	1,415	27,661	2,365	83	497	584	1,399	1,334	1,751	1041	11	77	16,012	20,831	49,830	
1,498	4,293	2,531	182	11,423	95	1,415	26,204	2,351	65	439	501	1,306	1,149	1,736	914	11	48	11,256	17,037	33,025	
14	20	26	1	9	32	539	88	200	10	8	69	22	106	169	42	...	1	1,100	1,133	2,437	
9	9	2	1	..	20	498	4	74	7	8	34	13	87	85	32	...	...	527	190	1,073	1
...	...	..	...	...	...	...	...	...	...	...	...	...	...	...	...	...	..	...	5	...	2
...	...	7	...	...	3	23	...	91	...	...	...	1	1	76	10	...	1	568	621	1,016	3
5	11	17	...	9	9	18	84	35	3	...	35	8	18	8	...	..	...	5	317	348	4
54	44	32	30	568	11	32	3,601	276	8	47	96	86	40	579	95	1	2	375	1,108	1,856	
..	...	...	...	...	...	...	...	...	...	...	1	...	...	3	1	1	...	...	2	3	5
...	...	1	...	...	...	6	...	39	...	1	...	4	...	53	4	...	...	15	100	97	6
1	1	...	.	..	1	6	34	59	...	.	...	2	2	37	15	...	...	16	102	120	7
15	6	8	6	17	2	6	1,092	83	1	15	74	9	11	262	6	...	2	245	385	618	8
4	1	6	..	...	2	...	303	55	7	11	5	9	1	73	7	..	...	2	139	204	9
34	36	17	24	551	..	14	2,172	40	...	20	16	62	26	151	62	...	...	97	440	814	10
87	81	11	4	39	9	44	966	421	7	16	55	41	58	231	34	...	...	225	926	1,520	
5	2	3	...	...	8	4	101	181	...	6	20	16	17	58	5	...	..	21	148	418	11
77	74	6	4	38	...	8	804	97	6	1	18	13	11	111	13	...	...	135	386	698	12
2	...	...	...	1	1	...	5	82	1	...	...	2	...	...	...	...	...	65	183	212	13
2	2	2	...	...	...	24	54	33	...	6	15	10	28	36	11	...	...	1	144	145	14
1	3	...	...	..	...	8	2	28	...	3	2	...	2	26	5	...	...	3	65	47	15
45	48	29	12	101	30	110	1,437	234	3	12	10	26	74	167	34	...	...	199	940	2,314	
6	34	6	4	5	...	11	335	40	1	1	3	8	23	54	21	...	...	28	130	213	16
..	1	.	...	..	...	...	7	1	...	...	...	..	33	1	..	...	...	...	11	34	17
4	8	6	5	62	10	66	342	26	2	3	1	1	3	28	1	...	...	111	546	426	18
29	...	11	3	7	16	20	496	108	...	2	5	5	6	44	9	...	...	10	186	688	19
2	2	5	...	27	...	...	243	36	...	5	...	12	9	33	...	...	...	41	40	343	20
4	3	1	...	...	4	13	14	23	..	1	1	.	...	7	3	...	...	9	27	610	21
295	2,160	352	19	2,487	10	207	8,217	470	18	126	109	453	279	128	162	...	6	984	3,844	5,851	
17	1,475	27	3	98	3	34	319	38	7	2	8	39	5	11	6	..	..	122	437	897	22
152	412	95	13	1,796	2	86	3,226	262	8	113	30	388	35	39	77	...	3	30	1,090	2,637	23
23	74	119	2	163	...	61	2,451	60	...	9	71	21	29	72	19	...	3	775	885	1,056	24
103	199	111	1	430	5	26	2,221	110	3	2	...	5	210	6	60	...	.	57	1,432	1,261	25
...	...	...	...	...	...	...	...	...	...	...	...	..	...	...	...	...	...	...	...	...	26
88	217	28	21	17	2	94	1,212	64	5	30	84	6	266	116	227	...	16	4,661	1,099	4,955	
...	12	22	2	3	..	35	619	28	...	6	20	1	18	19	21	..	...	17	109	291	27
...	...	...	...	..	...	...	...	...	...	...	.	...	...	..	...	...	...	...	...	...	
4	11	2	8	4	2	31	32	...	...	8	20	...	..	6	95	...	2	21	118	1,415	28
...	12	...	9	..	...	11	106	5	..	12	11	...		17	107	...	11	106	59	1,172	29
84	182	4	2	10	...	17	455	31	5	4	33	5	3	74	4	.	3	4,517	812	2,066	30
...	...	..	...	...	...	...	...	...	...	...	..	...	245	...	...	...	...	...	1	11	31
790	1,215	844	78	6,302	1	384	7,889	341	8	125	37	355	263	279	228	3	23	2,284	4,065	9,948	
338	661	222	17	2,335	...	3	3,917	144	6	46	11	142	202	136	121	1	2	2,238	2,339	5,509	32
188	13	408	...	2,505	...	42	21,16	102	...	7	10	94	30	72	69	2	19	14	922	901	33
84	229	101	4	1,462	1	24	1,405	90	...	43	...	15	16	42	7	...	1	4	607	1,383	34
180	312	13	57	...	..	315	451	5	2	30	16	4	15	29	31	...	1	28	197	2,155	35
...	..	...	...	...	...	..	...	...	...	...	...	...	..	...	...	...	...	...	...	...	36
125	508	1,209	17	1,900	...	5	2,794	345	6	75	41	317	63	67	92	7	.	1,428	3,922	4,144	
13	15	2	10	39		2	519	51	.	6	...	16	23	14	11	...	...	10	208	330	37
61	371	70	3	825	...	...	797	121	5	51	17	247	3	12	48	5	...	263	1,593	1,147	38
28	79	2	4	70	...	...	831	60	1	14	14	31	30	32	20	2	...	164	985	1,126	39
23	43	1,135	..	966	...	3	647	113	...	4	10	23	7	9	13	...	.	991	1,136	1,541	40
82	157	34	26	12	1	...	1,457	14	18	58	83	93	185	15	127	...	29	4,756	3,794	16,805	
77	150	15	24	12	1	...	617	11	6	46	81	83	165	15	120	...	29	109	1,071	3,590	41
5	7	19	2	...	...	...	825	3	12	12	2	10	20	...	...	...	...	4,536	2,456	13,145	42
...	...	...	...	...	...	...	15	...	...	...	...	...	...	..	7	...	...	111	267	70	43

IMPERIAL TABLE XVIII, SECTION B.—*Subsidiary Occupations*

Serial No.	District or State.	Total Agricultural.	Total Non-Agricultural.	Agricultural. 1, 2a. Landlord.	Agricultural. 2b. Cultivating tenant.	Agricultural. 2c. Agricultural labourer.	Agricultural. 4. Taungya cultivator.	5, 6, 7. Gardener, etc.	9a. Charcoal burner.	9b. Wood cutters.	9c. Cutch collectors.	9d, 10. All other collectors of forest produce.	11. Herdsman.	17. Fisherman.	87. Cotton-weavers.	84, 18. Silk rearers and spinners.	86. Silk-weavers.
	1	2	3	4	5	6	7	8	9	10	11	12	13	14	15	16	17
	Provincial Total	18,371	93,923	801	5,385	5,356	6,829	9,179	12	1,294	58	1,986	102	684	25,120	...	94
	Burma Proper ...	13,407	69,904	608	4,667	4,685	3,447	4,058	12	1,194	58	1,985	89	574	20,863	...	94
	Arakan Division ...	1,356	3,799	79	560	305	412	1,004	...	13	...	130	2	253	246	...	2
1	Akyab ...	84	423	13	38	...	33	54	...	...	...	48	2	19	49	...	...
2	Hill Dt. of Arakan	...	...	...	...	...	...	...	...	..	...	...	..	...	...	...	..
3	Kyaukpyu ...	561	2,085	53	148	169	191	643	..	...	...	...	...	69	49	...	...
4	Sandoway ...	711	1,291	13	374	136	188	307	...	13	...	82	...	165	148		2
	Pegu Division ...	983	5,383	107	243	507	126	514	...	20	1	332	...	115	1,290	...	...
5	Rangoon ...	-	3	...	...	...	..	...	...	...	...	...	...	...	...	...	...
6	Insein ...	51	130	14	9	24	4	18	..	1	...	1	...	9	7	...	...
7	Hanthawaddy ...	124	174	9	84	30	1	30	.	...	..	...	...	4	...	...	...
8	Tharrawaddy ...	447	1,833	53	83	308	3	77		3	...	319	...	95	104	...	...
9	Pegu ...	107	284	23	19	59	6	1	...	13	...	12	...	3	13	...	...
10	Prome ...	254	2,959	8	48	86	112	388	.	3	1	...	...	4	1,166	...	...
	Irrawaddy Division	1,410	4,614	96	627	535	152	1,158	...	40	.	147	...	98	519	...	...
11	Bassein ...	182	759	15	49	88	30	140	...	1	...	16	...	89	119	...	...
12	Henzada ...	982	2,156	41	480	342	119	170	.	2	...	21	...	33	386	...	...
13	Myaungmya .	36	547	11	15	10	...	124	...	37	...	96	...	18	...	...	...
14	Ma-ubin ...	192	1,031	24	74	94	...	703	..	...	...	12	...	26	21	...	...
15	Pyapôn ..	18	121	5	9	1	3	21	...	...	...	2	...	2	3	...	...
	Tenasserim Division	609	3,818	20	279	99	211	364	10	5	...	15	8	44	1,129	...	4
16	Toungoo ...	115	253	5	18	21	71	25	4	1	...	5	...	8	12	...	...
17	Salween ..	18	90	...	2	1	15	71	...	...	...	...	...	..	...	...	...
18	Thatôn ...	182	1,580	5	117	37	23	54	1	...	...	..	2	3	394	..	...
19	Amherst ...	116	1,413	7	18	40	51	146	2	1	..	8	6	2	686	...	...
20	Tavoy ...	54	433	2	1	...	51	54	3	3	...	...	...	31	24	...	4
21	Mergui ...	124	49	1	123	...	.	14	..	...	...	2	...	...	3	...	...
	Magwe Division ..	2,843	12,929	88	717	1,601	437	163	...	198	27	3	10	8	4,628	..	44
22	Thayetmyo ...	781	2,352	27	218	102	434	17	...	100	6	...	3	1	989	...	...
23	Pakôkku ...	487	5,462	27	145	313	2	80	...	23	18	3	3	1	2,565	...	44
24	Minbu ..	726	2,630	30	315	380	1	42	..	75	1	...	3	4	553	...	...
25	Magwe ...	849	2,485	4	39	806	..	24	...	.	2	...	1	2	521	...	...
26	Pakôkku Hill Tts.	...	..	...	..	...	..	..	..	...	...	...	...	...	...	...	...
	Mandalay Division	2,795	5,274	9	198	498	2,090	128	...	243	.	146	9	19	2,159	...	...
27	Mandalay ...	341	941	5	28	308	...	13	...	35	...	4	1	3	187	...	...
	Mandalay City ...	...	52	...	..	..	...	...	...	...	..	...	...	..	...	...	...
28	Bhamo ...	1,255	717	...	6	12	1,237	6	..	28	...	84	1	3	39	...	...
29	Myitkyina .	586	238	...	121	10	455	22	...	78	...	3	1	5	3	...	...
30	Katha ..	506	3,291	2	18	168	318		...	102	...	55	6	8	1,930	...	...
31	Putao ...	107	87	2	25	..	80	87	...	..	...	...	..	..	...	...	...
	Sagaing Division	2,277	23,123	160	1,272	839	6	467	1	542	18	1,208	37	28	7,543	...	42
32	Shwebo ...	129	11,372	9	34	86	...	90	...	173		47	17	4	4,400	...	25
33	Sagaing ..	957	6,326	8	567	382	...	3		64	15	.	16	3	2,354	...	...
34	Lower Chindwin	610	2,396	21	557	32	...	96	1	5	3	...	4	2	547	...	1
35	Upper Chindwin	581	3,029	122	114	339	6	278	...	300	...	1,161	...	19	242	...	16
36	Chin Hills .	...	...	...	...	...	...	..	...	...	...		...	..	...	...	...
	Meiktila Division ..	1,134	10,964	49	771	302	13	260	1	133	12	4	23	9	3,359	...	2
37	Kyauksè ...	107	460	6	21	80	...	1		9	..	..	...	1	131	.	...
38	Meiktila ...	119	4,151	13	53	53	...	140	.	93	8	...	5	2	1,234	...	2
39	Yamèthin ...	117	1,282	2	37	73	5	76	1	23	3	4	6	1	313	..	...
40	Myingyan ...	791	5,071	28	660	95	8	43	...	8	1	...	12	5	1,681	..	...
	Eastern States ..	4,964	24,019	193	718	671	3,382	5,121	...	100	...	1	13	110	4,257	...	...
41	N. Shan States .	1,524	9,366	3	27	30	1,464	3,305	...	89	...	1	6	3	4,237	...	..
42	S. Shan States ...	3,071	14,401	186	587	641	1,657	1,783	...	11	..	...	5	107	20	...	...
43	Karenni ...	369	252	4	104	...	261	33	...	...	...	..	2	...	...	...	...

of **Female** *Workers of Sort B—Cultivating Owner (Group 3a).*

45a, Basketmakers.	45b, Mat-weavers.	81, Oil-presser.	85, Rice-pounder.	71, 74, Sweetmeat makers and toddy drawers.	110a, Boat-owner.	110b, Boatman or towman.	114, Cart-owner or driver.	121, Money-lender or pawn-broker.	129a, Wholesale cloth seller.	129b, Retail cloth seller.	131, Fish seller.	134, Sweetmeat seller.	135, Vegetable seller.	136a, Wholesale grain-dealer.	136b, Retail grain-dealer.	139, Lawyer.	1001, Durwan or peon.	1002, Other labourers.	1003, Other traders.	1004, All others.	Serial No. of District, etc. (column 1).
18	19	20	21	22	23	24	25	26	27	28	29	30	31	32	33	34	35	36	37	38	
448	1,367	900	493	5,157	26	20	1,212	630	106	1,353	522	1,641	1,196	230	642		4	3,583	15,220	20,644	
447	1,334	895	466	5,157	26	20	1,146	627	102	1,336	498	1,518	1,129	210	593		4	2,401	13,002	10,066	
...	8	13	12	.	2	1	4	62	.	7	48	37	24	1	1	...	...	121	800	1,008	
...	3	1	6	...	...	...	...	16	..	5	7	...	14	...	..	...	...	17	138	44	1
...	.	..	...	...	...	...	...	...		.	...	...	.	...	...	...	...	...	...	...	2
...	...	6		.	2	1	2	36		...	...		...	...	...	...	..	100	554	623	3
...	5	6	6	...	..	..	2	10	..	2	41	37	10	1	1	..	...	4	108	341	4
4	46	4	3	338	...	...	216	63	17	38	114	148	64	53	96	...	1	84	1,055	767	
...	...	...	..	...	...	...	...	...	...	...	...	...	...	...	1	.	...	...	1	1	5
...	3	...	1	...	...	...	6	11	...	...	...	4	...	...	1	...	...	7	32	29	6
...	1	...	...	...	...	...	3	7	2	2	7	7	4	6	...	...	1	7	53	40	7
.	36	1	2	8	...	...	45	24	14	10	89	31	15	44	6		...	45	570	295	8
...	4	1	...	...	...	...	9	8	.	7	3	17	8	2	...		...	...	74	109	9
4	2	2	...	330	...	...	153	13	1	19	15	89	37	1	88	..	...	25	325	293	10
10	138	6	28	53	22	12	37	171	21	11	63	88	30	79	34	...	...	197	1,006	646	
...	9	...	...	...	1	...	3	85	...	2	16	44	6	18	3	...	...	6	129	142	11
7	61	5	28	53	1	...	31	45	10	3	27	20	11	24	22	...	...	148	654	394	12
3	16	...	...	...	20	...	...	14	11	...	6	1	...	32	...	..	...	42	95	32	13
...	49	1	...	...	...	12	3	7	...	..	14	23	12	1	8	...	...	1	88	60	14
...	3	...	...	...	..	...	...	20	...	6	...	...	1	4	1	.	..	...	40	18	15
3	75	6	9	23	...	1	41	46	3	22	16	33	81	7	16	...	..	30	986	851	
2	9	4	...	15	...	...	17	13	...	3	2	8	13	3	5	...	...	18	61	25	16
..	...	..	..	..	...	...	..	..	.	...	...	...	...	...	...	...	...	..	4	15	17
...	4	...	...	6	..	1	11	7	...	2	2	4	...	2	2	...	...	8	772	305	18
1	9	1	1	1	..	..	11	15	2	14	4	9	27	2	4	..	...	3	80	378	19
...	45	1	8	1	...	...	2	9	1	2	6	11	41	...	5	...	..	1	56	125	20
..	8	...	...	...	...	...	...	2	...	1	2	1	...	...	...	...	.	...	13	3	21
51	421	61	85	749	...	4	312	77	27	716	116	198	345	15	118	...	2	285	2,268	1,998	
4	262	15	17	49	...	...	37	6	.	193	30	24	8		13	...	...	63	323	192	22
16	9	11	42	563	...	2	89	38	3	397	21	88	49	3	39	...	1	9	453	892	23
4	32	25	26	24	...	2	116	17	12	17	62	69	78	8	52	...	1	204	668.	535	24
27	118	10	...	113	...	...	70	16	12	109	3	17	210	4	14	...	...	9	824	379	25
...	...	...	...	...	...	...	...	.	...	...	..	...	...	..	...	...	...	...	.	...	26
4	11	8	43	1	1	1	75	18	...	40	26	36	59	12	79	...	...	354	1,097	705	
...	...	8	2	...	1	..	33	17	...	2	9	14	54	6	9	...	...	7	351	185	27
...	...	...	1	...	...	...	2	1	...	...	.	...	34	...	2	...	...	2	1	9	
...	2	...	37	1	...	1	...	...	..	38	6	4	2	4	64	..	...	2	163	233	28
2	...	...	...	...	...	...	1	1	...	...	...	5	2	2	6	...	...	19	25	63	29
2	9	..	4	...	...	...	41	...	...	...	11	13	1	...	..	...	...	327	558	224	30
..	...	...	...	...	...	...	..	.	..	...	...	...	...	...	...	...	...	...	...	...	31
315	394	146	225	3,514	1	1	325	108	29	241	86	711	297	32	182	...	1	854	3,100	2,675	
209	178	51	51	1,420	1	1	192	38	...	188	11	475	218	17	103	...	1	741	1,289	1,432	32
98	34	79	...	1,316	...	...	26	52	...	33	62	206	61	3	47	...	...	6	1,089	759	33
8	33	16	17	778	...	...	90	18	29	17	2	25	13	2	5	...	...	...	417	267	34
...	149	...	157	...		...	17	...	...	3	11	5	5	10	27	...	...	107	305	217	35
...	...	..	...	...	...	...	..	...	...	..	...	...	...	...	...	..	...	...	...	...	36
60	241	651	61	479	..	...	136	82	5	261	29	267	229	11	67	...	...	476	2,690	1,416	
2	25	2	33	2	...	...	6	12	...	4	1	14	8	1	8	...	...	1	111	88	37
45	178	39	10	204	..	.	32	33	1	149	8	202	114	2	35	..	...	4	1,195	416	38
6	27	..	9	4	...	...	45	12	..	61	4	9	57	4	10	..	..	27	362	218	39
7	11	610	9	269	...	...	53	25	4	47	16	42	50	4	14	...	...	444	1,022	694	40
1	33	5	27	...	...	...	66	3	4	17	24	123	67	20	49	...	...	1,182	2,218	10,578	
...	32	5	27	...	...	...	10	1	1	15	6	54	52	16	47	...	...	42	756	661	41
1	1	...	...	...	...	...	50	...	3	2	18	63	15	4	...	.	...	1,110	1,365	9,843	42
...	...	..	...	...	...	..	6	2	...	...	...	6	..	...	2	...	...	30	97	74	43

Serial No.	District or State.	Total Agricultural.	Total Non-Agricultural.	Agricultural. 1, 2a. Landlord.	3a. Cultivating owner.	8c. Agricultural labourer.	4. Taungya cultivator.	5, 6, 7. Gardener, etc.	9a. Charcoal burner.	9b. Wood cutters.	9c. Cutch collectors.	9d, 10. All other collectors of forest produce.	11. Herdsman.	27. Fisherman.	97. Cotton-weavers.	84, 16. Silk rearers and spinners.	85. Silk-weavers.
	1	2	3	4	5	6	7	8	9	10	11	12	13	14	15	16	17
	Provincial Total	14,641	74,184	279	8,936	3,402	2,024	3,609	147	4,251	947	577	521	1,712	147	...	29
	Burma Proper ..	12,377	67,750	270	7,064	3,310	1,733	2,866	147	4,147	947	577	480	1,449	146	..	29
	Arakan Division ...	1,898	4,545	72	722	478	626	489	..	126	1	21	72	529	3	.	...
1	Akyab ...	801	1,782	42	356	246	157	230	..	73	...	...	63	27	2	...	...
2	Hill Dt. of Arakan		2	...	...	...	...	...	..	...	...	...	...	...	...	...	..
3	Kyaukpyu ...	793	1,593	21	354	214	204	154	...	30	1	...	4	222	...	...	...
4	Sandoway ...	304	1,168	9	12	18	265	105	..	23	...	21	5	280	1	...	...
	Pegu Division ...	1,289	10,528	49	498	360	382	383	63	342	13	153	61	163	17	...	...
5	Rangoon ...	...	8	...	...	...	...	...	.	...	...	...	...	...	...	..	...
6	Insein .	21	1,000	2	13	6	...	69	47	74	...	10	12	29	2	...	...
7	Hanthawaddy	57	1,125	12	35	8	2	64	..	...	...	...	14	8	...	...	...
8	Tharrawaddy ...	517	3,656	15	239	194	69	87	5	51	...	57	5	73	7	...	...
9	Pegu ...	129	1,786	15	79	13	22	18	9	89	...	85	27	25	...	...	...
10	Prome ...	565	2,953	5	132	139	289	145	2	128	13	1	3	28	8	...	...
	Irrawaddy Division	1,478	5,744	51	724	590	113	702	3	253	...	131	62	245	36	..	...
11	Bassein ...	291	918	5	96	150	40	138	1	57	...	17	6	90	16	...	.
12	Henzada .	653	2,852	12	362	233	46	370	2	94	.	...	1	34	20	...	...
13	Myaungmya ...	273	982	22	106	119	26	31	...	97	...	97	45	53	...	...	...
14	Ma-ubin ..	229	646	7	156	66	..	127	...	3	..	...	4	34	...	...	...
15	Pyapôn ...	32	346	5	4	22	1	36	.	2	...	17	6	34	...	...	...
	Tenasserim Division	578	5,545	17	275	97	189	585	32	131	8	49	81	146	22	...	...
16	Toungoo ...	180	1,487	7	97	33	43	93	9	69	...	3	9	17	...	...	...
17	Salween ...	25	28	..	16	...	9	2	...	2	..	...	1	..	...	...	...
18	Thatôn .	79	973	1	32	29	17	47	4	17	...	4	19	11	14	...	...
19	Amherst .	130	1,404	4	72	16	38	158	17	21		42	33	23	8	...	...
20	Tavoy ...	118	1,507	5	16	17	80	272	2	15	8	..	18	90	...	...	...
21	Mergui ...	46	146	...	42	2	2	13	...	7	..	..	1	5	...	...	...
	Magwe Division .	4,124	18,129	54	3,028	664	378	461	6	1,123	904	12	45	88	24	...	21
22	Thayetmyo ..	980	1,327	5	479	140	356	9	5	303	49	...	...	12	8	...	...
23	Pakôkku ...	585	8,116	20	439	104	22	52	..	217	561	...	22	18	7	...	21
24	Minbu ...	1,316	5,968	24	2,093	199		54	1	587	290	..	13	40	6	...	..
25	Magwe ...	243	2,718	5	17	221	...	346	...	16	4	12	10	18	3	...	...
26	Pakôkku Hill Tts.	...	...	..	...	...	...	...	...	...	...	...	..	...	...	...	...
	Mandalay Division	259	2,659	3	88	134	34	17	8	622	...	15	7	80	15	...	1
27	Mandalay ...	138	1,334	3	13	122	...	5	8	445	...	...	2	53	11	...	1
	Mandalay City ...	...	...	...	...	-	...	...	...	...	.	...	...	...	...	...	...
28	Bhamo ...	8	113	...	2	1	5	9	...	20	...	1	...	2	...	...	..
29	Myitkyina ...	2	70	...	...	1	1	.	...	4	...	3	...	2	...	...	.
30	Katha ...	111	1,142	..	73	10	28	3	...	153	...	11	5	23	4	...	...
31	Putao ...	...	...	...	...	...	...	...	...	...	..	...	...	...	...	...	...
	Sagaing Division .	2,113	15,664	14	1,335	753	11	72	6	1,354	17	196	128	173	24	.	6
32	Shwebo .	64	3,928	...	39	25	...	8	...	305	...	...	2	16	8	...	5
33	Sagaing .	1,066	5,510	5	488	564	9	5	1	442	...	43	83	93	6	...	...
34	Lower Chindwin	594	4,924	2	434	157	1	50	3	274	14	11	42	29	9	...	1
35	Upper Chindwin	389	1,302	7	374	7	1	9	2	333	3	142	1	35	1	...	...
36	Chin Hills ...	...	...	...	...	...	...		...	...	...	...	...	...	...	...	...
	Meiktila Division ..	638	4,936	10	394	234	..	157	29	196	4	...	24	25	5	..	1
37	Kyauksè ...	97	940	3	22	72	...	19	..	92	..	...	8	5	...	...	..
38	Meiktila ...	63	1,018	...	34	29	...	29	..	31	3	...	2	10	...	...	..
39	Yamèthin ...	91	1,647	...	35	56	...	87	28	65	...	...	8	8	2	...	1
40	Myingyan ..	387	1,331	7	303	77	...	22	1	8	1	...	6	2	3	...	...
	Eastern States ...	2,264	6,434	9	1,872	92	291	743	...	104	..	...	41	263	1	...	..
41	N. Shan States ...	94	824	..	...	38	56	125	...	104	...	..	5	7	1	...	...
42	S. Shan States ...	2,154	5,513	9	1,857	54	234	616	.		...	..	36	256	...	...	...
43	Karenni ...	16	97	...	15	...	1	2	...	...	...	...	...	...	..	...	...

of **Male** *Workers of Sort C—Cultivating Tenant (Group 3b).*

45a, Basket makers.	45b, Mat-weavers.	61, Oil-presser.	65, Rice-pounder.	71, 74, Sweetmeat makers and toddy drawers.	110a, Boat-owner.	110b, Boatman or towman.	114, Cart-owner or driver.	121, Money-lender or pawn-broker.	128a, Wholesale cloth seller.	128b, Retail cloth seller.	181, Fish seller.	184, Sweetmeat seller.	185, Vegetable seller.	186a, Wholesale grain-dealer.	186b, Retail grain-dealer.	169, Lawyer.	1001, Durwan or peon.	1002, Other labourers.	1003, Other traders.	1004, All others.	Serial No. of District, etc. (column 1).
18	19	20	21	22	23	24	25	26	27	28	29	30	31	32	33	34	35	36	37	38	
555	1,028	871	102	4,567	26	570	21,707	389	27	158	345	369	653	935	329	...	27	5,494	7,599	16,493	
548	1,026	860	101	4,566	26	569	21,473	385	27	157	342	369	641	930	323	...	26	4,353	6,888	13,352	
11	7	12	9	17	7	113	118	24	1	3	94	21	55	70	34	...	3	754	523	1,428	
8	5	2	8	10	3	51	14	10	1	1	56	11	52	53	31	...	...	290	176	605	1
..	...	...	...	...	...	...	..	...	...	...	...	...	...	...	...	...	...	...	2	...	2
...	...	5	...	2	2	33	...	8	...	...	1	..		14	2	...	1	456	256	402	3
3	2	5	1	5	2	29	104	6	...	2	37	10	3	3	1	...	2	8	89	421	4
60	51	11	30	370	4	64	5,000	119	2	33	46	52	35	447	112	...	2	673	781	1,441	
...	...	...	...	...	...	...	4	1	...	...	...	...	...	...	...	...	...	...	1	2	5
7	1	..	...	1	...	17	418	16	1	1	3	6	...	34	...	...	.	33	109	110	6
3	6	...	...	...	4	34	430	50	...	2	3	2	5	52	2	...	.	100	151	195	7
22	13	5	13	10	...	1	1,833	19	...	16	17	11	8	233	8	..	..	476	187	499	8
5	2	2	...	...	...	10	1,019	24	..	5	15	12	9	60	15	...	2	10	132	211	9
23	29	4	17	359	...	2	1,296	9	1	9	8	21	13	68	87	...	..	54	201	424	10
90	71	3	12	19	7	51	1,458	68	4	6	39	47	112	168	12	...	2	328	739	1,076	
4	1	...	...	...	1	3	154	...	...	2	14	18	15	25	4	...	2	34	90	226	11
69	56	3	5	19	2	4	1,024	20	2	1	12	15	81	71	6	...	...	153	329	459	12
10	2	...	4	...	...	...	22	27	2		7	7	3	25	2	...	.	110	198	240	13
4	12	...	1	...	4	12	253	6	...	2	4	5	9	27	...	...	...	8	56	75	14
3	...	...	2	...	..	32	5	15	...	1	2	2	4	20	...	...	...	23	66	76	15
14	13	7	15	110	7	91	1,920	36	13	8	25	14	31	118	25	...	...	164	421	1,459	
2	9	4	12	2	...	24	685	8	11	2	9	3	15	44	12	...	...	47	82	316	16
...	...	...	...	...	..	...	2	...	...	...	..	...	1	...	2	...	...	.	5	13	17
3	4	...	3	14	3	19	341	6	2	...	1	6	3	14	...	..	...	63	190	185	18
5	...	2	..	9	4	46	521	10	...	5	4	..	9	36	10	...	...	29	94	318	19
3	...	1	...	85	...	...	368	11		1	10	4	3	23	1	..	..	23	46	523	20
1	...	...	..	...	...	2	3	1	..	...	1	1	...	1	..	...	...	2	4	104	21
189	607	141	12	2,116	...	128	5,905	48	3	24	102	84	288	35	40	..	3	512	1,892	3,316	
4	284	6	1	15	...	25	103	6	1	...	...	10	2	1	..	...	...	25	156	302	22
143	230	102	7	1,710	...	37	2,404	29	2	17	25	49	130	8	19	...	...	19	659	1,628	23
14	70	13	2	267	..	45	2,441	10	...	5	75	11	17	21	17	...	3	446	655	865	24
28	23	20	2	124	...	21	957	3	...	2	2	14	139	5	4	...	...	22	422	521	25
...	...	...	..	...	...	...	...	...	...	...	...	...	...	...	...	...	...	...	...	..	26
6	12	6	1	1	...	20	567	16	2	5	13	11	3	10	11	..	1	575	177	457	
2	4	6	..	1		19	509	9	...	5	5	8	3	6	2	...	...	...	72	158	27
...	-	...	...	...	...	...	.	...	...	...	...	...	...	...	...	...	...	...	...	...	
1	1	...	..	...	...	1	3	...	...	...	...	...	...	...	9	...	..	...	1	65	28
...	...	...	1	..	...	...	9	2	2	..	...	...	...	...	...	...	...	1	6	40	29
3	7	...	...	...	.	...	46	5	..	...	8	3	...	4	..	..	1	574	98	194	30
...	...	...	...	...	...	...	...	...	..	...	...	...	...	...	...	..	...	...	...	...	31
161	188	541	19	1,638	...	100	4,924	46	2	62	14	104	93	60	68	...	14	662	1,662	3,330	
22	80	34	6	240	...	3	1,095	18	2	25	1	38	45	18	30	...	11	627	502	787	32
82	35	247	1	786	...	17	2,084	12	...		6	29	22	25	23	...	...	18	435	1,015	33
41	40	259	4	612	...	38	1,673	14	...	34	3	32	25	15	14	...	3	8	504	1,172	34
16	33	1	8	...	...	42	72	2	...	3	4	5	1	2	1	...	...	9	221	356	35
..	...	...	...	...	.	...	...	...	...	...	...	...	...	..	...	...	...	...	...	...	36
17	77	139	3	295	1	2	1,586	28	...	16	9	36	24	22	21	...	1	685	693	845	
1	6	1	2	15	...	...	583	3	...	...	..	9	7	9	8	...	...	8	73	91	37
6	6	10	..	149	.	.	223	10		8	2	15	2	...	10	..	...	108	167	227	38
5	62	...	1	15	...	...	466	4	...	4	3	2	15	9	2	...	.	163	293	404	39
5	3	128	...	116	1	2	309	11	...	4	4	10	...	4	1	...	1	406	160	123	40
7	2	11	1	1	...	1	234	4	..	1	3	...	12	5	6	...	1	1,141	711	3,141	
7	2	2	1	1	...	1	45	4	...	1	3	...	12	1	5	...	1	5	130	361	41
...	...	9	...	...	...	...	189	...	...	...	...	...	...	4	...	...	.	1,116	526	2,761	42
...	...	...	...	...	...	...	...	...	...	...	...	...	...	...	1	...	...	20	55	17	43

Serial No.	District or State.	Total Agricultural.	Total Non-Agricultural.	Agricultural. 1, 2a. Landlord.	3b. Cultivating owner.	3c. Agricultural labourer.	4. Taungya cultivator.	5, 6, 7. Gardener, etc.	9a. Charcoal burner.	9b. Wood cutters.	9c. Cutch collectors.	9d, 10. All other collectors of forest produce.	11. Herdsman.	17. Fisherman.	87. Cotton-weavers.	84, 18. Silk rearers and spinners.	85. Silk-weavers.
	1	2	3	4	5	6	7	8	9	10	11	12	13	14	15	16	17
	Provincial Total ...	9,055	27,513	328	4,669	3,112	946	1,406	26	266	62	226	56	273	6,194	...	49
	Burma Proper ..	7,947	25,744	316	3,833	3,044	754	1,136	26	258	62	226	56	252	6,047	...	49
	Arakan Division ...	700	1,456	7	317	178	198	188	...	5	...	50	3	76	110	...	...
1	Akyab ...	121	371	...	64	7	50	42	..	...	...	41	1	4	64	...	...
2	Hill Dt. of Arakan	..	...	...	...	...	...	...	...	...	...	..	.	...	...	.	...
3	Kyaukpyu ...	351	646	3	160	103	85	60	...	4	...	...	2	32	9	..	...
4	Sandoway ..	228	439	4	93	68	63	86	...	1		9	..	40	37	...	...
	Pegu Division ...	522	2,607	14	111	378	19	122	19	22	...	96	1	23	634	...	...
5	Rangoon ...	...	...	.	...	...	...	...	..	...	...	..	...	...	...		...
6	Insein .	42	211	3	5	32	2	31	14	12	...	6	1	6	9	...	..
7	Hanthawaddy .	17	192	1	8	8	...	3	...	...	...	1	...	1	3	...	...
8	Tharrawaddy ..	210	573	3	33	169	5	30	...	4	...	42	...	12	103	...	...
9	Pegu ...	77	391	6	33	37	1	3	5	4	...	47	...	4	37	...	...
10	Prome ...	176	1,240	1	32	132	11	55	...	2	...	...	...	...	482	...	...
	Irrawaddy Division	770	2,364	18	460	257	35	431	...	9	..	36	6	73	288	.	1
11	Bassein ...	122	437	8	32	60	22	67	...	1	...	10		29	56	...	...
12	Henzada ...	447	1,378	6	286	142	13	245	...	3	..	18	1	16	202	...	...
13	Myaungmya ...	20	87	2	13	5		5		5	...	6	5	...	5	...	..
14	Ma-ubin ...	176	319	1	127	48	...	99	...	...	...	1	...	14	21	...	...
15	Pyapôn ...	5	143	1	2	2	..	15	...	...	...	1	...	14	4	...	1
	Tenasserim Division	191	2,096	11	78	27	75	111	6	3	...	11	5	19	512	...	2
16	Toungoo ...	46	340	3	9	3	31	20	1	...	...	...	...	4	29	...	...
17	Salween ...	...	22	..	...	...	...	8	...	...	...	.	...	...	...	...	...
18	Thatôn ...	69	468	7	43	11	8	12		1	...	...	3	1	92	...	...
19	Amherst ...	45	668	...	19	6	20	42	2	1	...	5	2	5	379	.	...
20	Tavoy ...	23	585	1	1	5	16	25	3	1	...	1	...	9	12	...	2
21	Mergui ...	8	13	.	6	2	...	4	...	...	...	5	...	...	...	...	...
	Magwe Division ...	2,902	6,319	6	1,824	791	281	161	...	119	14	6	6	12	1,782	...	37
22	Thayetmyo ...	626	499	.	307	45	274	2		94	2	3	...	...	123	...	...
23	Pakôkku ...	424	2,796	3	206	215	...	8	...	6	9	2	3	2	1,036	..	37
24	Minbu ...	1,572	2,003	3	1,272	291	6	16	...	19	3	1	3	10	392	...	...
25	Magwe ..	280	1,021	...	39	240	1	135	...	...	...	..	...	...	231	...	...
26	Pakôkku Hill Tts.	...	..		..	...	...	...	.	...	...	...	..	...	...	...	...
	Mandalay Division	290	965	8	45	210	27	6	...	26	...	6	...	29	292	...	...
27	Mandalay ..	219	491	8	29	164	18	1	...	15	...	3	...	25	78	...	...
	Mandalay City ...	...	16	...		...	...	.		...	...	..	...	...	...	...	.
28	Bhamo ...	2	64	...	...	1	1	5	...	1	...	...	.	3	1	...	..
29	Myitkyina ...	...	1	...	...	...	...	...	..	..	...	..	...	...	...	...	...
30	Katha ...	69	409	...	16	45	8	...	...	10	...	3	...	1	213	..	
31	Putao ...	..	.	...	...	...	..	...	..	...	...	...	...	...	...	...	.
	Sagaing Division	2,155	7,812	240	825	971	119	57	1	58	48	16	32	19	2,021	..	9
32	Shwebo ...	47	1,782	...	14	33	...	15	..	31	...	9	2	5	312	...	9
33	Sagaing ...	680	3,367	..	240	440	...	.	..	21	45	...	15	13	911	...	..
34	Lower Chindwin	635	2,457	41	321	273	...	34	1	6	3	7	4	1	786	...	...
35	Upper Chindwin	793	206	199	250	225	119	8	..	...	...	..	11	...	12	...	...
36	Chin Hills ...	...	...	...		.	..	...	...	...	...	...	...	...	..	...	...
	Meiktila Division ..	417	2,125	12	173	232	...	60	..	16	...	5	3	1	408	...	...
37	Kyauksè ...	95	191	1	4	90	...	2	...	2	...	...	...	...	32	...	...
38	Meiktila ...	45	398	2	32	11	..	5		4	..	...	...	1	74	...	...
39	Yamèthin ..	21	277	...	2	19	.	26	...	8	...	.	...	...	31	...	...
40	Myingyan ...	256	1,259	9	135	112	...	27	...	2	...	5	3	...	271	...	...
	Eastern States ...	1,108	1,769	12	836	68	192	270	...	8	...	...	...	21	147	...	...
41	N. Shan States	27	385	...	...	10	17	98	...	6	...	...	...	...	144	...	...
42	S. Shan States ...	1,066	1,371	12	834	57	163	172	...	2	...	...	...	21	3	...	...
43	Karenni ...	15	13	...	2	1	12	...	...	...	...	...	...	...	...	...	...

of **Female** *Workers of Sort C—Cultivating Tenant (Group 3b).*

156a, Basket-makers.	158, Mat-weavers.	61, Oil-presser.	65, Rice-pounder.	71, 74, Sweetmeat makers and toddy drawers.	110a, Boat-owner.	110b, Boatman or towman.	114, Cart-owner or driver.	121, Money-lender or pawnbroker.	128a, Wholesale cloth seller.	128b, Retail cloth seller.	131, Fish seller.	134, Sweetmeat seller.	136, Vegetable seller.	136a, Wholesale grain-dealer.	136b, Retail grain-dealer.	159, Lawyer.	1001, Durwan or peon.	1002, Other labourers.	1003, Other traders.	1004, All others.	Serial No. of District, etc. (column 1).
18	19	20	21	22	23	24	25	26	27	28	29	30	31	32	33	34	35	36	37	38	
99	456	208	235	1,643	1	14	694	148	49	392	347	633	627	194	293	...	3	1,383	5,532	6,004	
99	454	207	233	1,643	1	14	693	148	49	392	331	631	624	113	292	...	3	1,231	5,268	5,206	
...	5	5	18	...	.	3	9	9	...	11	48	28	24	2	5	..	2	151	318	386	
..	...	...	7	...	...	...	...	..	..	9	5	3	17	...	5	..	...	65	43	65	1
...	...	...	...	...	..	...	...	..	...	...	...	...	..	...	..	...	...	...	...	...	2
...	...	3	...	...	...	2	...	4	...	...	1	..	...	...	...	...	...	84	236	209	3
...	5	2	11	...		1	9	5	..	2	42	25	7	2	...	...	2	2	39	112	4
5	24	2	9	198	..		156	37	8	20	50	99	53	39	85	...	.	90	462	353	
...	...	.	...	...	.	...	...	...	..		..	...	...	...	...	...	...	...	...	...	5
...	2	...	...	...	..	...	23	9	...	..	8	5	2	...	...	.	...	5	34	44	6
1	1	...	...	1	...	..	19	15	1	2	2	6	4	4	1	...	...	21	50	46	7
1	12	1	9	2	...	...	27	7	7	2	9	10	11	32	3	...	.	50	113	86	8
2	3	1	...	...	..	..	28	4	...	3	18	51	18	...	4	...	..	3	89	67	9
1	6	...	...	195	...	...	49	2	...	13	13	27	18	3	77	...	...	11	176	110	10
3	68	1	27	34	1	6	39	31	10	11	32	91	31	19	28	...	...	109	604	375	
...	6	...	...	...	1	..	3	11	...	4	18	38	10	3	3	...	..	6	84	87	11
2	26	1	26	34	...	..	28	9	10	6	5	25	8	9	20	.	..	97	387	200	12
...	3	...	...	...	...	2	...	3	...	...	6	3	1	1	...	...	...	5	6	31	13
..	33	...	1	..	...	...	7	4	...	1	1	21	9	3	5	...	...	1	76	22	14
1	...	...	...	...	..	4	1	4		...	2	4	3	3	...	.	...	..	51	35	15
2	90	3	9	6	..	3	44	16	2	13	42	69	73	7	28	...	...	40	399	581	
...	7	1	4	4		...	30	2	...	...	1	9	8	3	12	...	...	23	82	100	16
...	...	...	..	...	.	..	...	...	...	...	...	2	...	1	...	...	..	...	4	7	17
2	6	...	...	...	...	...	7	4	...	...	1	13	4	2	1	...	..	15	230	74	18
...	3	1	1	1	..	3	5	9	2	11	2	16	10	1	2	...	..	1	50	114	19
...	70	1	4	1		...	2	1	.	2	38	29	51		13	...	...	1	33	286	20
...	4	...	.	...	...	...	...	...	...	...	...	..	..	...	...	...	...	...	...	...	21
56	105	26	84	380	.	...	200	19	22	168	58	158	140	35	33		1	132	1,355	1,210	
1	56	4	5	7	...	.	1	2	..	3	5	15	4	...	5	.	...	15	71	81	22
36	6	8	38	322	...	...	79	10	..	90	32	30	58	...	19	...	.	45	225	695	23
5	32	7	41	40	...	..	86	7	11	27	21	96	59	35	8	...	1	71	631	381	24
14	11	7	...	11	...	...	34	...	11	48	...	17	19	...	1	...		1	428	53	25
..	...	...	...	..	...	...	...	...	...	...	...	...	...	..	..	...	...	.	...	...	26
...	...	3	1	...		1	8	9	1	.	13	13	21	1	8	..	..	102	127	298	
...	...	3	...	...	...	1	7	6	1	...	11	9	20	1	1	...	...	38	71	200	27
...	..	...	...	...	...	...	...	...	...	...	*1*	...	*8*	...	...	...	.	*6*	*1*	...	
...	...	...	1	...	...	...	...	1	..	...	...	1	...	...	7	...	...	1	7	36	28
...	...	...	...	...	...		...	...	...	...	...	...	1	...	...	.	..	...	...	...	29
...	...	...	...	...	...	...	1	2	...	...	2	3	..	...	...	...	...	63	49	62	30
...	...	..	...	...	.	...	...	..	...	...	...	..	...	...	...	...	...	...	...	...	31
28	139	66	54	876	...	1	168	17	6	110	73	126	253	4	89	...	..	380	1,466	1,695	
21	22	12	24	171	...	..	53	14		93	3	55	53	1	56	..	...	284	292	245	32
7	57	34		491	...	.	32	..	.	4	66	9	70	...	23	..		2	714	853	33
...	60	20	30	214	...	1	69	3	6	13	4	52	130	3	10	...	...	...	403	597	34
...	...	...	...	...	...	...	14	...	...	...	...	10	...	..	...	...	...	94	57	...	35
...	...	...	...	..	...	...	..	...	...	..	...	...	...	...	...	...	...	...	...	...	36
5	23	101	31	149	...	..	69	10	...	59	15	47	29	6	16	..	...	227	537	308	
2	5	...	26		..	..	3	...	...	...	1	14	2	...	1	...	...	1	68	32	37
1	5	3	...	25	...	..	8	1	...	26	4	19	4	...	12	...	...	7	131	68	38
...	10	...	4	..	..	...	19	1		...	3	2	15	1	.	...	.	23	84	50	39
2	3	98	1	124	...	...	39	8	..	33	7	12	8	5	3	...	...	196	254	158	40
...	2	1	2	..	...	...	1	..	.	...	16	2	3	81	1	...	..	152	264	798	
...	2	1	2	...	...	...	...	..	...	.	...	1	3	81	...	...	...	.	4	43	41
...	...	...	...	...	...	...	1	...	...	...	16	1	...	..	...	...	...	151	253	751	42
...	...	...	...	...	...	...	...	..	...	...	...	...	...	...	1	...	...	1	7	4	43

Serial No.	District or State.	Total Agricultural.	Total Non-Agricultural.	AGRICULTURAL. 1, 2a. Landlord.	3a. Cultivating owner.	3b. Cultivating tenant.	4. Taungya cultivator.	5, 6, 7. Gardener, etc.	9a. Charcoal burner.	9b. Wood cutters.	9c. Cutch collectors.	9d, 10. All other collectors of forest produce.	11. Herdsman.	17. Fisherman.	27. Cotton-weavers.	34, 16. Silk rearers and spinners.	35. Silk-weavers.
	1	2	3	4	5	6	7	8	9	10	11	12	13	14	15	16	17
	Provincial Total ...	3,882	50,877	100	1,716	1,176	890	2,056	223	2,653	100	1,183	1,054	2,199	126	3	41
	Burma Proper ...	3,615	49,565	99	1,522	1,170	824	1,854	223	2,637	100	1,182	1,033	2,134	122	3	41
	Arakan Division ...	409	4,332	31	132	81	165	65	15	35	...	11	189	319	2	...	...
1	Akyab ...	324	3,553	29	114	77	104	45	15	21	...	7	179	98	2	...	...
2	Hill Dt. of Arakan	...	..	...	...		...	.	...		..	...	...	..	...	...	...
3	Kyaukpyu ..	81	567	2	18	4	57	17	...	9	...	...	..	142	..	...	...
4	Sandoway ...	4	212	...	...	...	4	3	.	5	..	4	10	79	...	..	...
	Pegu Division ...	1,086	17,940	22	445	512	107	465	155	954	14	702	443	589	38	...	...
5	Rangoon ...	...	2	...	...	...	...	...	..	...	...	...	...	...	...	...	...
6	Insein ..	73	2,589	5	40	25	3	178	102	224	.	150	196	112	2	...	...
7	Hanthawaddy ...	106	2,308	5	70	20	11	64	..	10	..	11	62	54	15	...	...
8	Tharrawaddy ...	606	6,307	6	189	386	25	85	21	328	...	209	31	243	7		...
9	Pegu ..	179	4,052	5	114	59	1	35	8	276	...	331	145	96	...	...	...
10	Prome ...	122	2,682	1	32	22	67	103	24	116	14	1	9	84	14	.	...
	Irrawaddy Division	1,005	8,454	19	449	265	272	737	11	482	1	170	130	573	22	...	39
11	Bassein ..	124	2,112	3	71	8	42	181	3	100	...	...	32	170	10	.	...
12	Henzada ..	632	3,418	6	261	147	218	387	8	306	1	...	10	124	10	...	39
13	Myaungmya ...	126	1,244	...	45	69	12	45	.	59	...	143	49	133	...	...	...
14	Ma-ubin ...	93	1,026	6	56	31	...	95	...	1	...	3	14	107	2	...	...
15	Pyapôn ..	30	654	4	16	10	...	29	..	16	...	24	25	39	...	...	...
	Tenasserim Division	564	8,236	12	274	80	198	332	32	287	19	147	183	366	33	...	...
16	Toungoo ...	85	2,022	1	71	4	9	45	11	144	...	22	20	63	4	...	..
17	Salween ...	2	37	...	1	1	...	3		1	...	..	2	...	...	..	..
18	Thatôn ...	159	2,507	5	55	49	50	115	4	43	...	33	81	40	22	...	...
19	Amherst ...	70	2,138	...	40	10	20	92	17	63	..	92	57	108	7	...	...
20	Tavoy ...	168	1,415	6	37	13	112	69	...	28	19	...	17	142	...	...	...
21	Mergui ...	80	117	.	70	3	7	8	...	8	...	...	6	13	...	..	...
	Magwe Division ...	123	2,126	1	87	30	5	10	2	45	31	2	25	46	2	3	...
22	Thayetmyo ..	56	194	...	50	1	5	...	1	24	1	2	2	...	...	...	...
23	Pakôkku ...	29	770	1	16	12	.	1	..	5	19	...	15	12	...	3	
24	Minbu ...	34	850	...	19	15	...	7	1	11	11	..	2	34	2		...
25	Magwe ..	4	312	...	2	2	...	2	..	5	...		6	...	...		..
26	Pakôkku Hill Tts.	...	...	...	..	...		...	...	...	...		...	...	...	...	...
	Mandalay Division	74	2,116	5	30	20	19	33	3	273	1	27	7	77	5	...	.
27	Mandalay ...	16	833	5	...	11	...	14	2	143	1	...	7	57	3	..	...
	Mandalay City	...	9	...	...			...	...	..	...	...	..	...	...	...	...
28	Bhamo ...	...	128	...	..	.	...	11	...	17	...	7	...	1	...	..	...
29	Myitkyina	3	105	...	..	..	3	4	...	2	..	5	.	4	...	..	...
30	Katha ...	54	1,044	...	30	9	15	4	1	111	..	15	.	15	2	...	...
31	Putao ...	1	6	...	...	..	1		...	...	..	...	...	...	...	...	...
	Sagaing Division ...	174	4,007	3	54	97	20	19	...	403	30	123	35	141	14	...	2
32	Shwebo ...	..	1,123	...	...	...	...	3	..	33	...	3	9	8	8	...	2
33	Sagaing ...	112	1,053	...	18	90	4	...	...	63	1	.	13	79	1	...	...
34	Lower Chindwin	16	642	3	6	7		3	...	13	1	3	6	17	5	...	...
35	Upper Chindwin	46	1,189	...	30	...	16	13	...	294	28	117	7	37	...	...	...
36	Chin Hills ...	...	...	...	...	...	...	....	..	...	...	..	..	..	...	...	..
	Meiktila Division .	180	2,354	6	51	85	38	193	5	158	4	...	21	23	6	...	...
37	Kyauksè ...	31	536	...	3	28	..	57	...	56	...	...	...	6	...	...	...
38	Meiktila	26	460	3	13	10	..	4	...	11	3	..	5	3	..	...	...
39	Yamèthin ..	101	1,104	3	23	37	38	130	5	91	...	..	10	13	1	...	...
40	Myingyan ..	22	254	...	12	10	...	2	.	...	1	...	6	1	5	...	...
	Eastern States ...	267	1,312	1	194	6	66	202	.	16	...	1	21	65	4	...	...
41	N. Shan States ...	67	500	...	22	...	45	105	.	15	...	1	20	14	4	...	...
42	S. Shan States ...	200	798	1	172	6	21	96	...	1	...	...	1	51	...	...	...
43	Karenni ...	...	14	...	...	...	...	1	...	..	...	...	...	...	...	...	

of **Male** *Workers of Sort D—Agricultural Labourer* (*Group 3c*).

40a. Basket-makers.	45b. Mat-weavers.	61. Oil-presser.	68. Rice-pounder.	71, 74. Sweetmeat makers and toddy drawers.	110a. Boat-owner.	110b. Boatman or towman.	114. Cart-owner or driver.	121. Mony-lender or pawn-broker.	128a. Wholesale cloth seller.	128b. Retail cloth seller.	131. Fish seller.	131. Sweetmeat seller.	135. Vegetable seller.	138a. Wholesale grain-dealer.	138b. Retail grain-dealer.	149. Lawyer.	1001. Durwan or peon.	1002. Other labourers.	1003. Other traders.	1004. All others.	Serial No. of District, etc. (column 1).
18	19	20	21	22	23	24	25	26	27	28	29	30	31	32	33	34	35	36	37	38	
685	569	47	377	578	46	1,853	8,449	884	13	55	540	411	559	409	158	...	45	4,616	5,037	15,958	
629	558	46	375	578	46	1,853	8,382	884	13	54	536	407	549	409	153	...	45	4,354	4,900	15,465	
14	18	...	29	1	...	379	10	11	...	2	121	21	119	73	19	...	2	540	316	2,021	
12	17	...	27	...	...	375	4	11	..	2	101	20	119	73	19		...	287	231	1,888	1
...	...	...	...	..	...	...	...	...	...	...	...	..	...	...	..	...	...		.	...	2
...	...	...	...	...	..	...	...	..	...	...	...	...	...	...	...	...	1	249	69	80	3
2	1	...	2	1	.	4	6	...		.	20	1	...	...	...	..	1	4	16	53	4
237	118	6	152	85	31	721	4,703	585	4	21	167	132	188	186	72	...	39	1,611	1,569	3,953	
...	...	.	...	...	...	...	.	...	..		...	...	...	...	..	...	...		1	1	5
33	10	..	3	7	2	147	442	12	2	1	17	19	15	33	...	...	...	137	237	508	6
27	9	...	...	...	2	185	689	6	...	...	20	8	19	19	1	...	27	523	229	328	7
88	64	3	132	41	...	9	1,903	5	...	14	80	50	82	86	37	...		746	405	1,638	8
19	9	3	14	1	...	136	1,669	8	...	6	38	41	42	28	11	..	7	16	368	745	9
70	26	...	3	36	27	244	...	554	2	...	12	14	30	20	23	..	5	189	329	733	10
130	71	...	13	37	...	121	936	222	5	4	146	131	62	53	24	...	1	517	1,396	2,420	
33	4	..	...	...	...	81	154		...	4	96	48	14	...	..	..	...	46	343	793	11
49	51	...	11	32	...	16	524	5	1	..	37	57	10	25	11	.	...	231	605	868	12
14	3	..	2	...	..	24	26	7	...	...	11	9	7	13	...	...	...	160	205	334	13
21	13	...	...	1	...	...	128	196	2	...	2	14	26	9	...	...	...	19	158	215	14
13	...	...	...	4	...	...	104	14	2	...	...	3	5	6	13	...	1	61	85	210	15
56	41	7	31	62	15	443	1,828	32	4	3	51	45	113	74	1	..	1	403	485	3,142	
17	25	1	27	10	...	12	656	.	1	2	5	25	80	47	.	...	...	29	188	588	16
..	...	...	1	1	.	2	1	...	..	...	...	...	2	...	.	....	..	3	2	19	17
10	12	3	1	7	5	173	689	13	..	1	15	13	19	11	...	...	...	276	211	710	18
23	3	..	2	24	10	244	358	15	3	..	20		6	16	1		1	69	51	856	19
5	1	2	..	20	..	...	119	4	..	.	10	7	6		..	...	...	26	31	909	20
1	...	1	...	...	...	12	5	...	..	..	1	...	...	...	...	...	...	..	2	60	21
47	150	4	42	74	..	47	153	6	...	2	15	18	35	7	19	...	.	97	291	953	
4	69	3	2	2	..	6	6	..	...	...	...	...	3	.	...	...	...	5	17	47	22
28	52	1	10	27	...	17	45	3	...	1	9	7	14	3	1	...	...	4	128	365	23
14	26	...	30	35	...	23	97	2	...	1	5	7	11	4	17	...	...	88	97	325	24
1	3	..	...	10		1	5	1	.	...	1	4	7	...	1	...	...	...	49	216	25
...	...		...	...	...	.	...	...	...	...	...	..	...	..	..	...	...	...	...	...	26
22	22	4	11	20	...	29	216	2	..	1	13	8	8	5	6	..	2	554	138	629	
13	5	2	7	16	...	26	178	2	...	1	2	3	3	2	2	...	...	9	57	278	27
...	..	.	...	...	...	..	2	...		...	...	...	1	..	..	...	...	..	...	6	
...	...	2	2	...	..	1	3	...	..	...	1	...	...	1	3	..	...	3	6	70	28
1	1	..	1	...	...	2	3	.	...	...	1	...	...	...	1	...	...	15	6	59	29
8	16	...	1	4	...	...	32	..	...	...	9	5	...	2	...		2	527	69	221	30
	...	...	...	...	...	..	...	...	...	.	...	...	5	..	...	..	...	..	...	1	31
110	86	13	66	227		113	294	9	.	15	12	30	10	7	7	...	..	328	353	1,560	
16	22	1	7	80	...	...	121	5	...	3	1	7	7	5	.	...	...	304	78	400	32
30	9	5	7	96	..	30	78	...	..	1	7	9	...	...	2	...	...	4	153	465	33
29	11	4	2	51	..	1	24	2	...	6	1	8	1	...	1	...	...	4	110	339	34
35	44	3	50	...	...	82	71	2	...	5	3	6	2	2	4	...	...	16	12	356	35
...	...	...	...	...	...	...	..	...	.	...	..	..	...	...	...	...	...	...	...	...	36
13	52	12	31	72	...	...	242	17	...	6	11	22	14	4	5	...	...	304	352	787	
...	8	..	30	24	...	...	50	1	...		2	7	...	...	..	...	.	18	88	189	37
5	4		..	25	.	...	45	7	...	6	2	5		...	4	...	...	67	107	157	38
5	40	6	1	6	...	.	122	6	...	.	7	5	14	4	..	...	...	156	117	365	39
3	...	6	..	17	...	...	25	3	...	...	...	5	..	...	1	...	...	63	40	76	40
6	11	1	2	...	.	...	67	...	...	1	4	4	10	..	5	..	..	262	137	493	
6	10	1	2	...	...		56	...	...	1	4	4	10	.	5	...	...	23	77	142	41
...	1	...	...	..	...	...	11	...	..	...	...	..	...	...	.	...	.	235	51	351	42
...	...	...	...	...	...	...	...	...	.	...	...	...	...	..	..	...	...	4	9	..	43

Serial No.	District or State.	Total Agricultural.	Total Non-Agricultural.	AGRICULTURAL. 1, 8a. Landlord.	8a. Cultivating owner.	8b. Cultivating tenant.	4. Taungya cultivator.	5, 6, 7. Gardeners, etc.	9a. Charcoal burner.	9b. Wood cutters.	9c. Cutch collectors.	9d, 10. All other collectors of forest produce.	11. Herdsman.	17. Fisherman.	27. Cotton-weavers.	34, 16, Silk rearers and spinners.	35, Silk-weavers.
	1	2	3	4	5	6	7	8	9	10	11	12	13	14	15	16	17
	Provincial Total	2,843	28,486	110	1,062	1,186	485	1,099	25	213	3	686	63	279	4,929	...	22
	Burma Proper ...	2,393	27,787	109	9	1,059	236	980	25	213	3	686	62	276	4,735	..	22
	Arakan Division	74	821	1	22	8	43	23	...		..	...	...	25	81	...	...
1	Akyab ...	13	196	...	8	...	5	9	.	...	...	...	...	1	26	...	...
2	Hill Dt. of Arakan	.		.	...	...	...		...	...	...	..	..	.	...	...	.
3	Kyaukpyu ..	51	466	1	13	3	34	14	...	..	..	...	..	18	7	.	...
4	Sandoway ...	10	159	...	1	5	4		..	...	...	...	...	6	48	...	...
	Pegu Division ..	579	9,060	24	200	309	46	335	14	29	1	534	17	50	1,415	...	...
5	Rangoon ...	...	1	..	..	...	...	...	...	..	.	...	.	...	...	...	...
6	Insein ..	13	1,255	1	2	10	...	86	12	16	...	88	2	22	24	...	...
7	Hanthawaddy ...	28	274	13	9	6	..	6	...	..	...	3	...	4	4	...	...
8	Tharrawaddy ...	343	3,470	5	127	179	32	156	.	4	..	245	4	3	385	...	...
9	Pegu ...	148	1,572	3	40	105	...	13	2	6	...	198	10	14	61	...	...
10	Prome ...	47	2,488	2	22	9	14	74		3	1	...	1	7	941	...	..
	Irrawaddy Division	587	5,378	11	360	186	30	471	.	15	..	95	14	103	418	...	...
11	Bassein ...	64	1,847	.	29	24	11	97	..	7		48	3	33	141	...	.
12	Henzada ...	477	2,037	9	297	154	17	258	..	3	...	21	..	17	233	...	
13	Myaungmya ...	...	515	..		...		33	...	5		15	5	23	4	. .	..
14	Ma-ubin ..	42	634	2	33	7	...	63	...	.	...	7	...	21	37	...	...
15	Pyapôn ..	4	345	..	1	1	2	20		...	...	4	6	9	3	..	...
	Tenasserim Division	90	2,785	2	35	11	42	51	7	20	..	15	9	47	655	...	.
16	Toungoo ...	22	1,232	...	4	1	17	13	7	7		12	3	11	39	...	...
17	Salween ...	...	8	...	...	...	...	3	...	...	...	...	.	...	..	...	...
18	Thatôn ...	39	588	1	15	4	19	12	..	13	..	...	3	1	214	...	...
19	Amherst .	18	818	1	12	4	1	19	...		...	2	3	25	395	...	...
20	Tavoy ...	9	118	...	2	2	5	2	.	...	.	.	...	5	4	...	...
21	Mergui ..	2	21	..	2	...	..	2	...	...	...	1	...	5	3	...	...
	Magwe Division ..	85	2,092	6	55	18	6	6	...	5	1	1	5	3	421	...	2
22	Thayetmyo ...	16	64	...	15	1	...	...	..	5	...	1	..	..	16	...	...
23	Pakôkku .	26	726	4	14	8	...	1	...	...	1	...	5	1	216	...	2
24	Minbu ...	36	953	...	24	6	6	3	..	...	...	..	...	2	129	...	...
25	Magwe ...	7	349	2	2	3	...	2	..	...	...	...	...	.	60	...	...
26	Pakôkku Hill Tts.	..	...	...	...	...	..	...	.	...	.	..	...	.	...		...
	Mandalay Division	246	1,253	31	120	45	50	6	.	88	...	22	...	17	181	..	...
27	Mandalay ...	165	652	31	99	34	1	...	...	25	..	2	..	16	57	...	...
	Mandalay City ...	..	*3*	...	...	...	...		...	...	...	..	...	...	...	...	...
28	Bhamo ...	1	62	...		...	1	...	...	5	...	2	...	..	2	.	
29	Myitkyina ..	...	11	...	...	...	..	..	.	...	...	8	...	..	.	...	...
30	Katha .	80	528	...	21	11	48	...	...	58	..	10	...	1	128	...	...
31	Putao . .	...	6	...	...	...	...	6	...	.	...	...	...	...	...	...	...
	Sagaing Division	715	4,041	34	187	476	18	26	...	48	..	19	9	25	1,111	...	18
32	Shwebo ...	53	1,170	10	...	43	..	3	..	3	..	18	4	...	343	...	3
33	Sagaing .	55	2,052	..	31	24	...	.	...	37	.	...	5	25	536	--	...
34	Lower Chindwin	506	569	3	141	362		2	...	...	.	..		...	186	...	...
35	Upper Chindwin	101	250	21	15	47	18	21	.	8	..	1	...	...	46	...	15
36	Chin Hills ...	...	..	...	. .	...	...	...	..	...	.	...	..	...	...	...	...
	Meiktila Division ...	17	2,357	..	10	6	1	62	4	8	1	.	8	6	453	...	2
37	Kyauksè ...	1	781	...	..	.	1	8	...	2	...	...	...	1	69	...	...
38	Meiktila ...	6	438		5	1	..	4	...	2	...	...	2	3	140	...	2
39	Yamèthin .	10	745	...	5	5	.	50	4	4	...	..	1	2	99	...	...
40	Myingyan .	...	393	...	...	...	...	...	...	...	1	...	5	...	145	...	.
	Eastern States ..	450	699	1	73	127	249	119		..	..	..	1	3	194	..	...
41	N. Shan States	26	444	..	...	12	14	89		.	..	...	1	...	192	...	..
42	S. Shan States ...	419	246	1	73	115	230	30	...	...	...	.	.	3	2	..	
43	Karenni .	5	9	...	...	.	5	...	...	..	...	...	...	...	...	...	...

of **Female** *Workers of Sort D—Agricultural Labourer (Group 3c).*

45a, Basket-makers.	46b, Mat-weavers.	61. Oil-presser.	65. Rice-pounder.	71, 74. Sweetmeat makers and toddy drawers.	110a, Boat-owner.	110b. Boatman or towman.	114. Cart-owner or driver.	121. Money-lender or pawn-broker.	123a. Wholesale cloth seller.	123b. Retail cloth seller.	131. Fish seller.	131. Sweetmeat seller.	135. Vegetable seller.	135a. Wholesale grain-dealer.	135b. Retail grain dealer.	180. Lawyer.	1001. Durwan or peon.	1002. Other labourers.	1003 Other traders.	1004. All others.	Serial No. of District, etc. (column 1).
18	19	20	21	22	23	24	25	26	27	28	29	30	31	32	33	34	35	36	37	38	
75	455	43	1,141	259	1	21	370	59	30	158	806	1,570	848	50	541	...	...	1,351	7,443	5,946	
75	455	43	1,127	259	1	21	369	58	30	158	806	1,561	837	49	537	...	...	1,243	7,354	5,802	
...	2	...	42	...	...	...	...	2	...	...	19	30	12	2	2	...	..	131	259	191	
...	2	...	13	...	...	...	...	1	...	...	5	4	10	1	2	...	...	15	25	82	1
...	...	...	...	...	...	...	...	.	...	...	...	...	...	..	...	...	.	...		..	2
...	...	...	...	...	...	...	...	.	...	...	...	.	..	...	...	...	...	116	216	95	3
...	...	...	29	...	...	...	.	1	...	...	14	26	2.	1	...	...	.	...	18	14	4
12	139	...	103	121	...	6	226	9	12	46	335	604	332	31	314	...	...	347	2,426	1,602	
...	...	...	..	...	...	...	...	...	..	...	...	...	...	...	.	..	..	...	1	...	5
...	61	..	8	...	...	4	17	3	...	2	15	54	49	...	5	.	...	66	461	260	6
2	1	...	...	...	..	2	8	.	...	1	1	25	11	1	1	...	..	52	95	56	7
3	56	...	70	24	...	...	133	3	12	6	213	201	70	30	41	...	...	171	904	736	8
1	18	...	25	...	..	...	29	3	...	4	55	216	140	..	28	..	...	5	509	215	9
6	3	...	...	97	...	...	39	..	...	33	51	88	62	...	239	...	.	53	455	335	10
19	144	...	67	19	...	8	34	26	5	8	269	494	97	12	62	...	...	240	1,933	825	
10	6	...	7	...		2	...	8	...	8	195	271	54	1	38	...	...	20	504	393	11
5	52	..	49	19		1	31	...	5	...	41	65	18	8	20		..	179	764	247	12
1	17	...	...	...	..	1	...	18	...	...	7	31	5	...	...		...	26	255	69	13
2	63	...	11	...	...	...	2	...	...	...	15	98	14	..	4		..	2	251	44	14
1	6	...	..	...	...	4	1	...	...	...	10	28	6	3	..		..	13	159	72	15
2	23	37	88	11	1	5	75	5	1	9	29	114	106	2	83	..	...	38	528	824	
1	...	37	63	1	...	...	43	2	...	2	2	83	5[illegible]	1	83	...	...	11	212	517	16
...	...	...	2	...	...	...	...	...	...	...	...	...	...	...	...	...	...	...	2	1	17
...	5	...	1	...	1	2	19	1	1	...	3	7	2	1	...	...	...	22	186	94	18
1	9	...	7	10	...	3	12	2	...	6	17	18	31	...	...	...	...	3	85	169	19
...	6	...	15	...	...	...	1	...	...	1	7	6	21	...	...	...	...	2	10	38	20
...	3	...	...	...	..	...	...	...	..	...	...	...	...	...	...	...	...	...	2	5	21
26	22	1	244	16	..	2	11	3	7	34	20	116	95	..	41	...	...	75	464	471	
...	13	1	7	2	...	...	2	...	...	...	..	1		...	2	...	...	2	6	6	22
25	5	...	101	3	...	2	4	1	2	14	6	31	35	..	2	...	...	8	105	146	23
1	4	...	136	4	...	...	4	2	4	11	10	71	39	...	37	...	...	55	217	224	24
...	...	...	...	7	...	...	1	...	1	9	4	13	21	...	...		...	...	136	95	25
...	..	...	...	...	...	...	...	...	...	...	...	...	...	...	...	...	...	...	...	...	26
...	8	2	12	1	...	...	8	1	2	..	38	14	24	1	7	...	...	154	302	366	
...	1	...	1	...	...	...	5	1	2	...	25	4	24	1	2	..	...	43	146	297	27
...	...	...	...	...	...	...	...	...	...	..	..	...	...	...	..	.	...	...	...	3	
...	...	1	6	...	...	...	...	...	...	..	3	...	...	...	5	...	..	...	16	22	28
...	...	...	...	...	...	...	1	...	...	...	...	...	...	...	...	...	..	1	...	1	29
...	...	...	..	...	...	...	2	...	...	...	10	10	...	...	...	...	..	110	140	46	30
...	7	...	5	1	...	...	...	...	...	...	.	..	...	...	...	...	...	..	...	...	31
15	49	...	199	83	...	...	8	5	3	30	82	136	115	1	14	..	..	135	879	1,031	
7	6	...	100	26	...	...	5	5	...	19	1	53	19	1	4	...	...	130	244	176	32
7	18	...	...	44	...	...	3	...	...	8	75	65	70	...	8	...	..	2	473	676	33
...	3	...	38	13	...	...	..	...	3	3	4	8	20	...	...	...	...	3	130	156	34
1	22	...	61	...	...	...	...	...	...	..	2	10	6	..	2	...	...	...	32	23	35
...	...	...	...	...	...	...	...	...	...	...	...	...	..	...	...	...	...	...	...	...	36
1	68	4	372	8	...	..	7	7	...	31	14	53	56	..	14	...	...	123	563	492	
...	29	...	310	...	...	...	1	1	...		5	31	15	.	1	...	...	3	189	116	37
...	...	1	6	...	..	...	...	3	...	19	2	14	5	..	5	...	...	17	106	107	38
...	38	...	55	..	...	...	6	2	...	3	4	4	32	...	8	...	...	55	193	185	39
1	1	3	1	8	...	...	...	1	...	9	3	4	4	...	...	...	...	48	75	84	40
...	..	..	14	...	...	...	1	1	..	...	...	9	11	1	4			108	89	144	
...	..	...	14	...	...	...	1	...	...	...	..	7	10	1	4	...	...	9	66	50	41
...	...	...	...	...	...	...	..	...	...	...	...	2	1	...	...	...	...	9[illegible]	20	9[illegible]	42
...	...	...	...	...	...	...	...	1	.	...	...	...	...	...	...	...	...	4	3	1	43

Serial No.	District or State.	Total Agricultural.	Total Non-Agricultural.	AGRICULTURAL.				5, 6, 7, Gardeners, etc.	9a, Charcoal burner.	9b, Wood cutters.	9c, Cutch collectors.	9d, 10, All other collectors of forest produce.	11, Herdsman.	17, Fisherman.	87, Cotton-weavers.	84, 88, Silk rearers and spinners.	85, Silk-weavers.
				1, 2a, Landlord.	3a, Cultivating owner.	3b, Cultivating tenant.	3c, Agricultural labourer.										
	1	2	3	4	5	6	7	8	9	10	11	12	13	14	15	16	17
	Provincial Total ...	10,264	36,366	114	8,560	533	1,057	12,372	46	1,678	99	396	479	723	21	...	1
	Burma Proper ...	2,300	11,976	27	1,105	352	816	1,130	44	1,357	90	381	175	596	10	...	...
	Arakan Division ...	643	2,368	2	249	98	294	75	...	335	...	2	33	203	2	...	...
1	Akyab ...	238	1,003	..	54	48	136	8	...	241	...	...	14	13	2	...	...
2	Hill Dt. of Arakan	29	38	...	28	1	..	...	...	...	...	...	...	...	...	...	...
3	Kyaukpyu ...	285	787	1	100	38	146	49	...	5	...	...	...	47	...	...	...
4	Sandoway ...	91	546	1	67	11	12	18	...	89	...	2	19	143	...	...	...
	Pegu Division ...	131	856	4	17	23	87	20	8	116	61	13	20	10	3	...	...
5	Rangoon ...	...	.	...	..	...	...	...	...	...	...	...	...	...	...	...	...
6	Insein ...	13	46	2	...	...	11	6	7	2	...	1	1	...	...	...	...
7	Hanthawaddy ...	4	58	...	...	...	4	1	..	...	...	...	15	1	...	...	...
8	Tharrawaddy ...	4	216	..	2	...	2	7	1	5	...	3	3	6	...	...	...
9	Pegu ...	9	96	...	2	1	6	..	...	24	...	9	1	...	...	...	...
10	Prome ...	101	440	2	13	22	64	6	...	85	61	...	..	3	3	...	...
	Irrawaddy Division	63	194	8	14	8	33	10	1	18	...	2	31	2	...	...	...
11	Bassein ...	22	107	8	9	3	2	4	1	11	...	2	3	2	...	...	...
12	Henzada ...	35	61	...	1	5	29	6	...	2	...	...	26	...	...	...	...
13	Myaungmya ...	6	21	...	4	...	2	..	...	5	...	...	2	...	...	...	...
14	Ma-ubin ...	...	2	...	...	..	.	...	...	...	...	...	...	...	...	...	...
15	Pyapôn ...	...	3	...	...	...	...	...	...	...	...	...	...	...	...	...	...
	Tenasserim Division	672	3,600	11	268	122	271	926	27	254	...	32	62	265	1	...	...
16	Toungoo ...	48	775	5	28	7	8	492	...	18	...	3	1	...	...	...	...
17	Salween ...	123	149	...	42	51	30	55	...	49	...	3	...	...	...	...	...
18	Thatôn ...	232	406	...	107	56	69	157	...	7	...	...	10	...	...	...	...
19	Amherst ...	112	478	5	77	1	29	82	...	50	...	14	33	47	1	...	...
20	Tavoy ...	155	1,548	1	12	7	135	127	27	122	...	...	17	175	...	...	...
21	Mergui ...	2	244	...	2	...	...	13	...	8	...	12	1	43	...	...	...
	Magwe Division ...	184	1,612	1	109	65	9	...	...	90	29	1	8	7	2	...	...
22	Thayetmyo ...	169	1,460	1	103	57	8	...	...	88	4	...	7	2	2	...	...
23	Pakôkku ...	14	105	...	5	8	1	...	...	...	8	...	1	3	...	...	...
24	Minbu ...	1	29	...	1	...	...	..	...	2	17	...	...	2	...	...	...
25	Magwe ...	.	..	...	...	...	...	...	...	...	...	...	...	...	...	...	...
26	Pakôkku Hill Tts.	...	18	...	...	...	...	...	...	...	...	1	...	...	...	...	...
	Mandalay Division	452	2,608	...	396	10	46	53	8	429	...	231	8	92	2	...	...
27	Mandalay ...	...	201	.	...	...	...	1	8	90	...	...	3	...	...	...	...
	Mandalay City ...	...	*28*	..	...	...	...	...	...	...	...	...	...	...	...	...	...
28	Bhamo ...	273	584	...	273	...	...	44	..	248	...	20	...	54	1	...	...
29	Myitkyina ...	105	702	...	80	...	25	4	...	54	...	170	...	12	...	...	...
30	Katha ...	70	1,029	...	39	10	21	4	...	37	...	41	5	26	1	...	...
31	Putao ...	4	92	...	4	...	..	...	..	...	...	...	...	...	...	...	...
	Sagaing Division ...	74	393	...	2	1	71	1	...	93	...	100	11	16	...	...	...
32	Shwebo ...	1	7	..	1	...	...	...	..	2	...	...	...	...	...	...	...
33	Sagaing ...	...	6	...	...	...	...	...	...	..	...	...	...	...	...	...	...
34	Lower Chindwin	...	...	...	..	...	...	..	...	...	...	...	...	...	...	...	...
35	Upper Chindwin	73	351	...	1	1	71	1	...	91	...	100	11	16	...	...	...
36	Chin Hills ...	...	29	...	...	...	...	...	...	...	...	...	...	...	...	...	...
	Meiktila Division ...	81	345	1	50	25	5	45	...	22	...	...	2	1	...	...	...
37	Kyauksè ...	64	41	1	36	22	5	2	...	8	...	...	2	1	...	...	...
38	Meiktila ...	...	177	...	...	..	...	...	..	12	...	..	...	...	...	...	...
39	Yamèthin ...	...	77	...	...	...	...	43	...	2	...	...	...	...	...	...	...
40	Myingyan ...	17	50	...	14	3	..	...	...	...	...	...	...	...	...	...	...
	Eastern States ...	7,964	24,390	87	7,455	181	241	11,242	2	321	9	15	304	127	11	...	1
41	N. Shan States ...	5,725	17,880	14	5,566	25	120	10,535	2	321	9	15	290	42	11	...	1
42	S. Shan States ...	2,156	6,325	73	1,819	145	119	698	...	...	...	...	14	83	...	...	...
43	Karenni ...	83	185	-	70	11	2	9	...	...	...	...	...	2	...	...	...

of Male Workers of Sort E—Taungya Cultivator (Group 4).

45a, Basket-makers.	45b, Mat-weavers.	61. Oil-presser.	65. Rice-pounder.	71, 74. Sweetmeat makers and toddy drawers.	110a. Boat-owner.	110b. Boatman or towman.	114. Cart-owner or driver.	161. Money-lender or pawn-broker.	168a. Wholesale cloth seller.	168b. Retail cloth seller.	181. Fish seller.	184. Sweetmeat seller.	185. Vegetable seller.	186a. Wholesale grain-dealer.	186b. Retail grain-dealer.	189. Lawyer.	1001. Durwan or peon.	1002. Other labourers.	1003. Other traders.	1004. All others.	Serial No. of District, etc. (column 1).
18	19	20	21	22	23	24	25	26	27	28	29	30	31	32	33	34	35	36	37	38	
220	1,668	18	70	63	3	107	1,073	11	5	21	225	48	167	74	115	2	20	4,056	2,823	9,762	
76	1,309	11	35	63	2	55	348	11	2	5	35	33	59	3	13	...	8	1,935	735	3,455	
8	234	...	4	...	..	6	11	4	...	...	15	5	8	2	1	...	...	639	225	556	
2	180	...	...	...	...	2	..	2	...	...	6	1	7	...	1	...	...	99	139	286	1
...	...	...	...	...	...	...	...	...	...	...	...	1	...	...	...	...	...	...	7	24	2
...	...	...	...	...	...	...	...	..	...	...	...	2	...	2	...	...	...	534	67	81	3
6	54	...	4	...	...	4	11	2	...	...	9	1	1	...	...	...	...	6	12	165	4
11	49	3	2	2	...	1	48	...	...	...	15	7	5	.	3	...	2	106	128	223	
...	...	...	...	...	...	...	...	...	...	...	..	...	...	...	...	...	...	...	...	...	5
1	...	...	...	...	...	1	3	...	...	...	...	...	1	...	...	...	1	1	11	10	6
...	1	...	...	...	...	...	5	...	...	...	...	...	1	...	...	...	...	16	5	13	7
4	8	3	...	...	...	...	12	...	...	...	5	1	...	...	...	...	1	60	5	92	8
1	...	...	..	...	...	...	...	...	...	...	...	1	1	...	3	...	...	3	42	11	9
5	40	...	2	2	...	...	28	...	...	...	10	5	2	...	..	...	...	26	65	97	10
12	...	...	12	...	..	1	1	1	...	...	...	10	4	...	...	...	...	11	25	53	
1	..	...	...	...	...	1	1	...	..	...	...	10	2	...	...	...	..	11	14	44	11
10	...	...	12	...	...	...	...	1	...	...	...	...	...	...	...	...	...	...	2	2	12
1	...	...	...	...	...	...	...	...	...	...	...	...	...	...	...	...	...	...	6	7	13
...	...	...	...	...	...	...	...	...	..	...	...	...	2	...	...	...	...	..	..	...	14
..	...	...	...	..	..	...	...	...	...	...	...	...	...	...	...	...	...	...	3	...	15
13	41	1	...	16	1	11	123	2	...	5	4	6	39	1	...	...	...	277	98	1,395	
...	12	...	...	...	...	...	12	...	..	1	...	1	12	...	...	...	...	54	14	155	16
...	1	...	...	...	...	...	2	...	...	...	...	2	6	...	...	...	...	...	6	25	17
3	18	..	...	...	1	4	16	...	...	...	...	1	11	...	...	...	...	87	25	66	18
1	2	...	...	1	...	6	29	...	...	...	...	...	3	2	...	...	...	14	24	170	19
5	...	...	...	15	...	...	64	2	...	4	4	2	7	...	...	...	...	121	26	830	20
4	8	1	...	...	...	1	...	...	...	...	...	...	...	...	...	...	..	1	3	149	21
2	940	3	2	19	...	21	61	3	2	..	..	2	...	...	..	...	...	28	59	333	
2	938	1	2	4	...	19	41	..	1	...	...	2	...	...	...	...	...	24	48	275	22
...	2	2	...	15	...	2	20	3	1	...	...	..	...	...	..	...	...	2	8	38	23
...	...	...	...	...	...	...	...	...	...	...	...	...	...	...	...	...	...	1	3	4	24
...	...	...	...	...	...	...	...	...	...	...	...	...	...	...	...	...	...	...	...	...	25
...	...	...	...	...	...	...	...	...	...	...	...	...	...	...	...	...	...	1	...	16	26
8	27	2	5	...	1	4	57	...	...	...	1	1	3	...	9	...	4	847	98	718	
...	6	1	...	...	1	...	41	...	...	...	...	1	...	...	1	...	...	15	10	23	27
...	2	...	...	...	...	...	22	...	...	...	...	1	...	...	...	...	...	...	...	8	
...	8	...	2	...	...	2	...	...	...	...	...	...	3	...	8	...	3	2	12	177	28
6	3	...	2	...	...	2	1	...	...	...	...	...	...	...	...	...	...	147	6	295	29
2	10	1	1	...	...	...	15	...	...	...	1	...	...	...	...	...	...	681	70	134	30
...	...	...	...	...	...	...	...	...	..	...	...	...	...	...	...	...	1	2	...	89	31
15	3	...	8	...	...	11	12	...	...	...	...	...	...	...	...	...	2	4	38	79	
...	...	...	...	...	...	...	1	...	...	...	...	...	...	..	...	...	...	3	1	...	32
...	...	...	..	...	...	...	...	...	...	...	...	...	...	...	...	...	...	1	...	5	33
...	..	.	..	...	...	..	...	...	...	..	...	...	...	...	..	...	...	...	...	...	34
15	3	...	8	...	...	11	11	...	...	...	...	..	...	...	...	...	2	...	37	45	35
...	...	...	...	...	...	...	...	...	...	...	...	..	...	...	...	...	...	...	...	29	36
7	15	2	2	26	...	...	35	1	...	...	..	2	...	...	...	...	...	23	64	98	
...	...	...	2	1	...	...	6	1	...	...	...	...	...	...	...	...	...	2	8	8	37
7	13	...	...	19	...	...	24	..	...	..	...	..	...	...	...	...	...	15	44	43	38
...	2	1	...	...	..	...	2	...	...	...	...	...	...	...	...	...	...	1	4	22	39
...	...	1	...	6	..	...	3	..	..	...	...	2	...	...	...	...	...	5	8	25	40
144	359	7	35	...	1	52	725	..	3	16	190	15	108	71	102	2	12	2,121	2,088	6,307	
144	353	7	35	...	1	50	654	...	3	16	190	15	101	71	102	...	12	94	1,674	3,132	41
...	6	...	...	...	...	1	71	...	...	...	...	...	7	...	...	2	...	2,018	370	3,055	42
...	..	...	...	...	...	1	...	...	...	...	...	...	...	...	...	...	.	9	44	120	43

Serial No.	District or State.	Total Agricultural.	Total Non-Agricultural.	Agricultural. 1, 2a, Landlord.	3a, Cultivating owner	3b, Cultivating tenant.	3c, Agricultural labourer.	5, 6, 7, Gardeners, etc.	9a, Charcoal burner.	9b, Wood cutters.	9c, Cutch collectors.	9d, 10, All other collectors of forest produce.	11, Herdsman.	17, Fisherman.	87, Cotton-weavers.	84, 86, Silk rearers and spinners.	85, Silk-weavers.
	1	2	3	4	5	6	7	8	9	10	11	12	13	14	15	16	17
	Provincial Total ...	8,884	20,185	175	7,597	351	761	6,401	12	290	9	341	36	200	3,279	...	10
	Burma Proper .	1,392	3,321	46	690	185	471	411	12	79	9	112	8	176	429	...	10
	Arakan Division ...	387	565	5	142	51	189	34	...	7	...	...	2	32	61	...	...
1	Akyab ...	27	198	2	16	6	3	2	...	6	...	...	1	3	45	...	...
2	Hill Dt. of Arakan	47	3	...	45	2	...	...	...	...	...	...	...	...	...	...	...
3	Kyaukpyu ...	241	203	...	61	14	166	18	...	...	..	...	...	8	3	...	...
4	Sandoway ...	72	161	3	20	29	20	14	...	1	...	...	1	21	13	...	...
	Pegu Division ...	77	238	3	16	11	47	4	...	6	9	3	1	2	58	...	...
5	Rangoon ...	...	...	...	...	...	...	...	...	...	...	...	...	...	...	...	...
6	Insein ...	5	21	...	1	1	3	...	...	...	...	2	...	...	...	...	...
7	Hanthawaddy ...	4	13	...	...	...	4	...	...	...	...	...	...	1	...	...	...
8	Tharrawaddy ...	18	20	...	2	1	15	...	...	...	...	1	...	...	...	...	...
9	Pegu ...	7	7	...	...	...	7	1	...	...	...	...	1	...	...	...	...
10	Prome ...	43	177	3	13	9	18	3	...	6	9	...	...	1	58	...	...
	Irrawaddy Division	46	114	3	5	1	37	1	...	8	...	3	2	1	12	...	...
11	Bassein ...	9	47	3	...	...	6	1	...	...	...	2	...	...	...	...	...
12	Henzada ...	36	52	...	5	1	30	...	...	3	...	...	...	1	12	...	
13	Myaungmya ...	1	15	...	...	...	1	...	...	5	...	1	2	...	...	...	...
14	Maubin ...	...	...	...	...	...	...	...	...	...	...	...	...	...	...	...	...
15	Pyapôn ...	...	...	...	...	...	...	...	...	...	...	...	...	...	..	...	...
	Tenasserim Division	243	1,137	32	56	95	60	344	12	6	...	...	3	133	80	...	10
16	Toungoo ...	53	306	24	8	8	13	168	...	...	...	...	...	...	1	...	...
17	Salween ...	21	139	2	2	7	10	104	...	2	...	...	...	...	...	...	...
18	Thatôn ...	100	145	1	15	71	13	38	...	1	...	...	1	...	3	...	...
19	Amherst ...	16	135	...	13	2	1	32	...	..	...	...	1	...	73	...	...
20	Tavoy ...	50	383	5	17	6	22	2	12	2	...	...	1	128	3	...	10
21	Mergui ...	3	29	...	1	1	1	...	..	1	...	..	...	5	...	...	...
	Magwe Division ...	71	297	...	38	21	12	...	...	6	...	...	...	1	78	...	...
22	Thayetmyo ...	55	285	..	32	16	7	...	...	6	...	...	...	1	72	...	...
23	Pakôkku ...	9	11	...	2	3	4	...	..	...	...	...	...	...	6	...	...
24	Minbu ...	7	1	...	4	2	1	...	...	...	...	...	...	...	...	...	...
25	Magwe ...	...	...	...	...	...	...	...	...	...	...	...	...	...	...	...	...
26	Pakôkku Hill Tts.	...	...	...	...	...	...	...	...	...	...	...	...	...	...	...	...
	Mandalay Division	488	654	...	430	4	54	21	...	35	...	35	...	4	37	...	...
27	Mandalay ...	21	62	...	...	...	21	...	...	1	...	...	...	...	3	...	..
	Mandalay City ...	...	...	...	...	...	...	...	...	...	...	...	...	...	...	...	...
28	Bhamo ...	410	73	...	404	...	6	...	..	2	...	5	...	...	9	...	...
29	Myitkyina ...	9	267	...	4	...	5	21	...	31	...	14	...	...	2	...	...
30	Katha ...	48	252	..	22	4	22	...	...	1	..	16	. .	4	23	...	...
31	Putao ...	...	...	...	...	...	..	...	...	.	...	...	...	...	..	...	...
	Sagaing Division ...	67	261	...	...	...	67	5	...	10	...	70	...	3	95	...	...
32	Shwebo ...	2	21	...	...	...	2	3	...	..	...	...	...	...	...	...	...
33	Sagaing ...	...	...	...	...	...	...	...	...	...	...	...	...	...	...	...	...
34	Lower Chindwin	...	2	...	...	...	...	...	...	1	..	...	...	...	...	...	...
35	Upper Chindwin	65	157	...	...	...	65	2	...	9	...	70	...	3	14	...	...
36	Chin Hills ...	...	81	...	...	...	...	...	...	...	...	...	...	...	81	...	...
	Meiktila Division ...	13	55	3	3	2	5	2	...	1	...	1	...	...	8	...	...
37	Kyauksè ...	7	...	3	3	1	...	...	...	...	...	...	...	...	...	...	...
38	Meiktila ...	3	25	...	...	...	3	...	...	...	..	...	...	...	...	...	...
39	Yamèthin ...	...	17	...	...	...	...	2	...	1	...	...	...	...	2	...	...
40	Myingyan ...	3	13	...	...	1	2	...	...	...	...	1	...	...	1	...	...
											...	...	...	...	5	...	...
	Eastern States ...	7,492	16,864	129	6,907	166	290	5,990	...	211	...	229	28	24	2,850	...	...
41	N. Shan States .	3,791	13,152	3	3,667	47	74	5,618	...	211	...	229	25	15	2,849	...	...
42	S. Shan States ...	3,645	3,624	126	3,190	113	216	363	...	...	...	...	...	...	...	...	...
43	Karenni ...	56	88	...	50	6	...	9	...	...	...	...	3	9	1	...	...

of Female Workers of Sort E—Taungya Cultivator (Group 4).

46a, Basket-makers.	46b, Mat-weavers.	61, Oil-presser.	86, Rice-pounder.	71, 74, Sweetmeat makers and toddy drawers.	110a, Boat-owner.	110b, Boatman or towman.	114, Cart-owner or driver.	121, Money-lender or pawn-broker.	168a, Wholesale cloth seller.	168b, Retail cloth seller.	181, Fish seller.	184, Sweetmeat seller.	185, Vegetable seller.	188a, Wholesale grain dealer.	188b, Retail grain-dealer.	160, Lawyer.	100I, Durwan or peon.	100B, Other labourers.	100C, Other traders.	100A, All others.	Serial No. of District, etc. (column 1).
18	19	20	21	22	23	24	25	26	27	28	29	30	31	32	33	34	35	36	37	38	
29	258	4	96	12	...	3	38	45	1	44	78	91	331	3	152	...	...	430	2,229	5,763	
6	229	2	57	10	...	2	17	2	...	10	74	66	129	2	8	...	...	227	538	696	
4	51	2	20	...	...	1	4	2	...	2	34	13	19	1	1	...	...	55	147	73	
2	43	2	3	...	...	1	2	...	...	2	2	...	5	1	...	...	...	5	46	27	1
...	...	...	...	...	...	...	...	...	...	...	...	...	...	...	...	...	...	...	3	...	2
...	...	...	2	...	...	...	...	...	...	...	...	...	12	...	...	...	...	49	85	26	3
2	8	...	15	...	...	...	2	2	...	...	32	13	2	...	1	...	...	1	13	20	4
...	11	...	...	...	...	...	3	...	...	2	17	6	5	...	...	...	...	11	64	36	
...	...	...	...	...	...	...	...	...	...	...	...	...	...	...	...	...	...	...	...	...	5
...	...	...	...	...	...	...	1	...	...	...	...	...	...	...	...	...	...	4	14	...	6
...	...	...	...	...	...	...	1	...	...	...	...	...	2	...	...	...	...	5	4	...	7
...	3	...	...	...	...	...	...	...	...	...	...	1	...	...	...	...	...	...	2	13	8
...	...	...	...	...	...	...	...	...	...	...	...	2	1	...	...	...	...	...	2	...	9
...	8	...	...	...	...	...	1	...	...	2	17	3	2	...	...	...	...	2	42	23	10
...	1	...	...	...	...	1	...	...	...	...	3	14	3	...	...	...	...	6	42	17	
...	...	...	...	...	...	1	...	...	...	...	1	13	3	...	...	...	...	1	13	12	11
...	1	...	...	...	...	...	...	...	...	...	2	...	...	...	...	...	...	5	25	3	12
...	...	...	...	...	...	...	...	...	...	...	...	1	...	...	...	...	...	...	4	2	13
...	...	...	...	...	...	...	...	...	...	...	...	...	...	...	...	...	...	...	...	...	14
...	...	...	...	...	...	...	...	...	...	...	...	...	...	...	...	...	...	...	...	...	15
...	47	...	7	...	...	...	6	...	...	1	13	16	81	1	3	...	...	33	89	252	
...	4	...	1	...	...	...	2	...	...	...	...	1	18	1	...	...	...	8	9	93	16
...	...	...	...	...	...	...	...	...	...	...	...	...	...	...	...	...	...	...	22	11	17
...	9	...	...	...	...	...	1	...	...	...	...	4	1	...	...	...	...	5	19	63	18
...	1	...	1	...	...	...	...	...	...	...	...	...	18	...	...	...	...	...	6	3	19
...	25	...	5	...	...	...	3	...	...	1	13	11	44	...	3	...	...	18	23	79	20
...	8	...	...	...	...	...	...	...	...	...	...	...	...	...	...	...	...	2	10	3	21
1	118	...	6	2	...	...	...	...	...	4	...	11	...	...	...	...	...	3	27	40	
1	118	...	5	2	...	...	...	...	...	4	...	11	...	...	...	...	...	3	23	39	22
...	...	...	1	...	...	...	...	...	...	...	...	...	...	...	...	...	...	...	4	...	23
...	...	...	...	...	...	...	...	...	...	...	...	...	...	...	...	...	...	...	...	1	24
...	...	...	...	...	...	...	...	...	...	...	...	...	...	...	...	...	...	...	...	...	25
...	...	...	...	...	...	...	...	...	...	...	...	...	...	...	...	...	...	...	...	...	26
...	...	...	9	...	...	...	...	...	...	1	...	6	15	...	4	...	...	98	117	272	
...	...	...	...	...	...	...	...	...	...	...	...	...	...	...	...	...	...	...	5	53	27
...	...	...	1	...	...	...	...	...	...	1	...	...	...	...	4	...	...	...	42	9	28
...	...	...	8	...	...	...	...	...	...	...	...	6	15	...	...	...	...	13	11	146	29
...	...	...	...	...	...	...	...	...	...	...	...	...	...	...	...	...	...	85	59	64	30
...	...	...	...	...	...	...	...	...	...	...	...	...	...	...	...	...	...	...	...	...	31
...	1	...	15	6	...	...	...	...	...	...	6	...	6	...	...	...	...	18	23	3	
...	...	...	2	4	...	...	...	...	...	...	...	...	...	...	...	...	...	6	4	2	32
...	...	...	...	...	...	...	...	...	...	...	...	...	...	...	...	...	...	...	...	...	33
...	...	...	1	...	...	...	...	...	...	...	...	...	...	...	...	...	...	...	...	...	34
...	1	...	12	2	...	...	...	...	...	...	6	...	6	...	...	...	...	12	19	1	35
...	...	...	...	...	...	...	...	...	...	...	...	...	...	...	...	...	...	...	...	...	36
1	...	...	...	2	...	...	4	...	...	...	1	...	...	...	...	...	...	3	29	3	
...	...	...	...	...	...	...	...	...	...	...	...	...	...	...	...	...	...	...	...	...	37
1	...	...	...	...	...	...	2	...	...	...	1	...	...	...	...	...	...	2	15	2	38
...	...	...	...	...	...	...	...	...	...	...	...	...	...	...	...	...	...	...	12	...	39
...	...	...	...	2	...	...	2	...	...	...	...	...	...	...	...	...	...	1	2	1	40
23	29	2	39	2	...	1	21	43	1	34	4	25	202	1	144	...	...	203	1,691	5,067	
23	29	2	39	2	...	1	18	41	1	21	4	12	201	1	144	...	...	60	1,391	2,215	41
...	...	...	...	...	...	...	1	...	...	13	...	13	1	...	...	...	...	134	269	2,817	42
...	...	...	...	...	...	...	2	2	...	...	...	...	...	...	...	...	...	9	31	35	43

IMPERIAL TABLE XVIII, SECTION F.—*Subsidiary Occupations*

Serial No.	District or State.	Total Agricultural.	Total Non-Agricultural.	AGRICULTURAL. 1, 2a, Landlord.	3a, Cultivating owner.	3b, Cultivating tenant.	3c, Agricultural labourer.	4, Taungya cultivator.	5, 6, 7, Gardeners, etc.*	9a, Charcoal burner.	9b, Wood cutters.	9c, Cutch collectors.	9d, 10, All other collectors of forest produce.	11, Herdsman.	17, Fisherman.	27, Cotton-weavers.	34, 36, Silk rearers and spinners.	35, Silk-weavers.
	1	2	3	4	5	6	7	8	9	10	11	12	13	14	15	16	17	18
	Provincial Total	5,859	5,613	174	1,865	792	1,344	1,684	19	12	124	...	156	190	163	36	...	...
	Burma Proper ...	2,727	3,916	133	616	489	1,006	483	19	11	119	...	106	72	160	29	...	...
	Arakan Division ...	61	87	..	10	17	12	22	...	...	4	...	5	1	3	...	...	...
1	Akyab ...	20	49	...	1	1	7	11	...	..	...	...	1	1	1	...	...	...
2	Hill Dt. of Arakan	...	...	...	...	...	...	...	...	...	...	...	...	...	...	...	...	...
3	Kyaukpyu ..	33	30	..	4	13	5	11	...	...	4	...	...	...	2	...	...	...
4	Sandoway ...	8	8	..	5	3	...	...	...	.	...	...	4	...	...	...	...	...
	Pegu Division ...	394	829	18	43	101	217	15	..	11	42	...	18	27	59	2	...	..
5	Rangoon ...	10	5	10	...	...	...	...	...	...	...	...	...	...	...	...	...	...
6	Insein ...	58	116	2	2	3	42	9	...	9	7	...	3	3	...	...	...	...
7	Hanthawaddy ...	81	158	2	4	16	54	6	...	...	3	...	...	11	1	1	...	...
8	Tharrawaddy ...	84	151	1	12	17	54	...	...	...	16	...	2	1	11	...	...	...
9	Pegu ...	18	61	...	4	5	9	...	.	...	5	...	11	7	..	...	...	...
10	Prome ...	142	338	3	21	60	58	...	...	2	11	...	2	5	47	1	...	...
	Irrawaddy Division	856	873	34	303	95	403	21	12	...	10	...	30	13	27	3	...	...
11	Bassein ...	275	354	21	27	36	186	5	12	...	2	...	28	8	10	2	...	...
12	Henzada ...	281	323	8	60	26	175	12	...	...	2	..	...	...	5	1	...	...
13	Myaungmya ...	172	150	3	115	30	20	4	...	..	6	...	...	5	10	...	...	...
14	Ma-ubin ..	126	46	2	101	2	21	...	...	...	...	...	2	...	2	...	...	..
15	Pyapôn ...	2	...	...	...	1	1	...	...	...	...	...	...	...	...	...	...	...
	Tenasserim Division	884	969	46	117	109	248	364	...	...	23	...	1	24	70	8	...	...
16	Toungoo ...	189	132	20	16	15	107	31	...	...	4	...	1	...	1	...	...	...
17	Salween ...	31	10	1	4	10	10	6	...	.	.	...	...	...	...	...	...	...
18	Thatôn ...	299	278	1	52	17	65	164	...	...	...	...	...	3	3	8	...	...
19	Amherst ...	142	262	7	33	16	40	46	...	...	8	...	...	10	20	...	...	...
20	Tavoy ...	139	118	6	12	41	22	58	...	...	4	...	...	11	5	...	...	...
21	Mergui ...	84	169	11	...	10	4	59	...	...	7	...	...	...	41	...	...	...
	Magwe Division ...	93	292	1	45	17	30	...	...	...	2	..	...	..	...	14	...	...
22	Thayetmyo ...	2	22	.	1	...	1	...	...	...	1	...	...	...	...	...	...	...
23	Pakôkku ...	14	98	...	7	4	3	...	...	...	...	...	...	...	...	14	...	...
24	Minbu ...	75	161	...	36	13	26	...	...	...	1	...	...	...	...	...	...	...
25	Magwe ...	2	11	1	1	...	...	...	...	..	...	...	...	...	...	...	...	...
26	Pakôkku Hill Tts.	...	...	...	...	...	...	...	...	...	...	...	...	...	...	...	...	...
	Mandalay Division	60	264	4	16	16	19	5	4	...	2	...	17	1	1	...	...	...
27	Mandalay ..	37	148	...	11	10	16	...	...	...	...	...	...	...	...	...	...	...
	Mandalay City ...	...	1	...	...	...	...	..	...	...	...	...	...	1	...	...	...	...
28	Bhamo ...	1	8	..	...	...	...	1	...	...	...	..	...	...	...	...	...	...
29	Myitkyina ...	...	18	..	...	...	...	...	...	...	2	...	...	...	...	...	...	...
30	Katha ...	22	90	4	5	6	3	4	4	...	...	...	...	...	...	...	...	...
31	Putao ...	...	...	...	...	...	...	...	...	..	..	...	17	...	1	...	...	...
	Sagaing Division	161	159	12	39	105	5	...	1	...	17	...	1	...	...	1	...	...
32	Shwebo ...	2	8	...	2	...	...	...	...	...	...	...	...	...	...	...	...	...
33	Sagaing ...	8	44	1	2	3	2	...	...	...	...	...	...	...	...	...	...	...
34	Lower Chindwin	150	86	11	34	102	3	...	...	...	11	...	...	...	...	...	...	...
35	Upper Chindwin	1	21	.	1	...	..	...	1	...	6	...	...	...	...	1	...	...
36	Chin Hills ...	...	...	...	...	...	...	...	...	...	...	...	1	...	...	...	...	...
	Meiktila Division ...	218	443	18	43	29	72	56	2	...	19	...	34	6	...	1	...	...
37	Kyauksè ...	25	39	5	2	11	7	...	...	...	4	...	...	...	...	...	...	...
38	Meiktila ...	44	69	13	20	11	...	...	...	..	...	...	...	...	...	...	...	...
39	Yamèthin ...	107	92	...	3	7	41	56	...	..	15	...	34	5	...	...	...	...
40	Myingyan ...	42	243	...	18	...	24	...	2	...	...	...	...	1	...	1	...	...
	Eastern States ...	3,132	1,697	41	1,249	303	338	1,201	...	1	5	...	50	118	3	7	...	...
41	N. Shan States ...	2,032	1,263	21	347	181	312	1,171										
42	S. Shan States ...	1,093	429	10	897	122	25	29	...	1	5	...	50	117	3	7	...	...
43	Karenni ...	7	5	...	5	...	1	1	...	...	...	...	...	1	...	...	...	...

* Persons shown in this column have a principal occupation of one of the three groups 5, 6, 7 and a subsidiary occupation of one of he other two.

of Male Workers of Sort F—Gardener (Groups 5, 6 and 7).

45a. Basket-makers.	45b. Mat-weavers.	61. Oil presser.	65. Rice pounder.	71, 74. Sweetmeat makers and toddy drawers.	110a. Boat-owner.	110b. Boatman or towman.	114. Cart-owner or driver.	121. Money-lender or pawn-broker.	123a. Wholesale cloth seller.	123b. Retail cloth seller.	131. Fish seller.	134. Sweetmeat seller.	128. Vegetable seller.	136a. Wholesale grain-dealer.	136b. Retail grain-dealer.	160. Lawyer.	1001. Durwan or peon.	1002. Other labourers.	1003. Other traders.	1004. All others.	Serial No. of District, etc. (column 1).
19	20	21	22	23	24	25	26	27	28	29	30	31	32	33	34	35	36	37	38	39	
204	28	50	9	80	7	58	559	71	3	23	46	76	192	45	71	...	2	672	1,316	1,401	
94	22	40	9	79	7	57	468	71	3	12	46	54	164	45	19	...	2	332	765	1,111	
4	1	..	...	...	...	...	...	1	1	1	4	1	2	2	...	...	...	9	16	32	
...	1	...	...	...	...	...	...	...	...	...	4	1	2	1	...	...	.	1	8	28	1
...	...	...	...	...	...	...	...	...	...	...	...	...	...	...	...	...	...	...	...	...	2
3	...	...	...	...	...	...	...	...	1	1	...	...	...	1	...	...	...	8	7	3	3
1	...	.	...	...	..	...	...	1	...	...	...	...	...	...	...	...	...	...	1	1	4
12	...	...	5	11	...	10	80	10	...	8	7	13	54	15	2	...	...	68	172	203	
...	..	...	...	...	...	...	2	...	...	...	...	...	1	...	...	...	..	...	2	...	5
2	...	...	...	1	...	1	10	4	...	...	...	...	7	..	...	...	...	1	44	24	6
4	...	...	...	..	..	3	20	1	...	...	...	2	2	...	...	...	...	28	30	52	7
3	...	.	...	...	...	1	25	..	...	3	4	4	7	5	...	...	...	12	19	38	8
...	...	...	...	...	...	1	4	1	...	1	...	2	3	2	...	...	...	...	20	4	9
3	...	...	5	10	...	4	19	4	...	4	3	5	34	8	2	...	...	27	57	85	10
37	6	2	1	...	..	6	69	7	...	...	11	21	42	18	1	...	1	50	219	287	
9	1	1	...	...	..	3	10	1	...		10	7	32	4	1	...	1	32	64	116	11
24	5	1	1	.	...	...	48	4	...	...	...	8	5	8	...	...	...	11	92	108	12
4	...	...	...	...	...	...	5	2	...	...	...	5	5	2	...	...	...	7	52	47	13
...	...	...	...	...	...	3	6	...	...	...	1	1	...	4	...	...	...	...	11	16	14
...	..	...	...	...	...	...	...	...	...	...	...	...	...	...	..	...	...	...	...	..	15
16	8	1	...	5	5	7	187	46	2	1	10	7	20	8	1	...	1	34	121	363	
...	1	...	...	1	...	...	14	6	...	...	...	...	7	...	...	...	...	...	25	72	16
...	...	...	..	...	...	...	1	...	...	1	...	...	...	...	...	...	...	...	4	4	17
6	7	...	...	...	...	5	95	8	..	..	2	3	8	4	...	...	...	27	19	69	18
7	...	1	...	...	5	1	67	7	1	...	4	1	1	4	1	...	1	1	37	85	19
3	...	...	...	3	...	...	9	3	...	...	4	2	3	...	...	...	...	2	22	57	20
...	...	...	.	1	...	1	...	22	1	...	...	1	1	...	...	...	...	4	14	76	21
12	3	6	1	29	2	14	14	1	...	...	2	...	35	..	11	...	...	18	104	24	
1	3	5	...	..	1	1	1	...	...	...	1	...	...	...	...	...	...	7	...	1	22
11	...	...	...	17	..	...	...	...	...	...	...	...	21	...	...	...	...	...	32	3	23
...	...	...	1	11	...	11	12	1	...	...	.	...	12	...	11	...	...	11	70	20	24
...	...	1	.	1	1	2	1	...	...	...	1	...	2	..	...	...	...	...	2	...	25
...	...	...	.	...	...	...	...	...	...	...	..	...	...	...	...	...	...	...	...	...	26
...	2	...	1	...	...	16	65	2	..	...	11	...	4	...	2	...	...	41	37	58	
...	...	...	...	..	..	16	53	2	...	...	...	...	3	...	2	...	...	27	18	26	27
...	...	...	...	...	...	...	...	...	...	...	..	...	...	...	...	...	...	...	...	1	
...	1	...	...	...	...	...	...	..	...	...	...	...	1	...	...	...	...	...	2	1	28
..	...	...	1	...	...	...	...	...	...	...	...	...	...	...	...	...	...	...	...	13	29
...	1	...	...	...	...	...	12	...	...	..	11	...	...	...	...	...	...	14	17	17	30
...	...	...	...	...	...	...	...	...	...	...	...	...	...	...	..	...	..	...	...	...	31
8	2	...	...	14	...	4	15	1	...	1	1	2	7	...	1	...	...	...	16	67	
...	...	...	..	...	...	...	1	...	...	...	...	...	...	...	...	...	...	...	2	5	32
...	2	...	...	6	...	...	7	...	...	...	...	1	4	...	...	...	...	...	3	10	33
2	...	...	...	8	...	...	7	1	...	1	1	1	2	...	1	...	...	...	11	43	34
6	...	...	...	...	...	4	...	...	...	...	...	...	1	...	...	...	...	...	...	9	35
...	...	...	...	...	...	...	...	...	...	..	...	...	...	...	...	...	...	...	...	...	36
5	...	31	1	20	...	...	38	3	...	1	...	10	..	2	1	...	...	112	80	77	
...	...	...	1	...	...	...	7	3	...	...	...	..	..	2	...	...	...	3	7	12	37
1	...	...	...	...	...	...	7	..	...	...	...	2	...	...	...	...	...	10	22	27	38
3	...	...	.	...	...	...	...	...	...	...	...	7	...	...	...	...	.	...	27	1	39
1	...	31	...	20	...	...	24	...	...	1	...	1	...	...	1	...	...	99	24	37	40
110	6	10	...	1	..	1	91	...	..	11	..	22	28	...	52	...	...	340	551	290	
110	6	...	..	1	...	1	18	...	...	11	...	22	15	...	52	...	...	241	468	135	41
...	...	10	...	...	...	...	73	...	..	...	...	...	13	...	...	...	...	99	80	154	42
...	...	...	...	...	...	...	...	...	...	...	...	...	...	...	...	...	...	..	3	1	43

Serial No.	District or State.	Total Agricultural.	Total Non-Agricultural.	Agricultural. 1, 2a, Landlord.	2a. Cultivating owner.	2b. Cultivating tenant.	2c. Agricultural labourer.	4. Taungya cultivator.	5, 6, 7, Gardeners, etc.*	9a. Charcoal burner.	9b. Wood cutters.	9c. Cutch collectors.	9d, 10. All other collectors of forest produce.	11. Herdsman.	17. Fishermen.	87. Cotton-weavers.	84, 88. Silk rearers and spinners.	86. Silk-weavers.
	1	2	3	4	5	6	7	8	9	10	11	12	13	14	15	16	17	18
	Provincial Total ..	3,421	2,819	65	1,067	182	539	1,568	...	1	338	...	69	5	18	244	...	4
	Burma Proper ...	1,038	1,565	29	299	127	449	134	...	1	26	...	40	4	16	138	...	4
	Arakan Division ...	23	33	..	6	9	5	3	...	...	...	...	...	...	1	4	...	...
1	Akyab ...	...	11	...	...	...	...	...	...	...	...	...	...	...	...	3	...	...
2	Hill Dt. of Arakan	...	...	...	...	...	...	...	...	...	...	...	...	...	...	...	...	...
3	Kyaukpyu ...	13	10	...	3	5	5	...	...	...	...	...	...	...	1	...	...	...
4	Sandoway ...	10	12	...	3	4	...	3	...	...	...	...	...	...	...	1	...	..
	Pegu Division ...	156	369	3	16	24	82	31	...	1	7	..	8	4	3	34	...	...
5	Rangoon .	...	...	...	...	...	...	...	..	...	...	...	...	...	...	...	...	...
6	Insein ...	30	61	...	2	...	28	...		1	1	...	2	...	...	...	...	...
7	Hanthawaddy ..	15	45	...	...	7	4	4			...	...	...	...	...	5	...	...
8	Tharrawaddy ...	56	99	..	7	9	40	...		...	...	...	4	4	...	8	...	...
9	Pegu ...	13	23	...	2	3	8	...	...	...	2	...	2	...	...	...	...	...
10	Prome ...	42	141	3	5	5	2	27	..	...	4	...		...	3	21	...	...
	Irrawaddy Division	539	531	10	190	52	282	5	...	...	2	...	26	...	...	35	...	...
11	Bassein ...	128	170	5	7	16	100	...		...	...	...	22	...	...	6	...	...
12	Henzada ...	204	288	2	35	19	145	3	..	...	...	...	3	...	...	27	...	...
13	Myaungmya ...	99	30	2	68	16	11	2	...	.	...	...	1	...	...	...	...	...
14	Ma-ubin ...	105	39	1	80	...	24	...	...	...	2	...	...	...	...	2	...	...
15	Pyapôn ...	3	4	...	...	1	2	...	-	...	...	...	...	...	...	...	...	...
	Tenasserim Division	217	309	6	50	24	43	94	...	.	10	...	1	..	1	43	..	4
16	Toungoo .	67	46	..	14	3	29	21	...	...	...	...	...	...	...	3	...	...
17	Salween ...	10	5	...	...	4	...	6	...	...	..	...	...	...	...	...	...	...
18	Thaton ...	74	66	1	23	6	11	33	...	...	...	...	...	...	...	26	...	...
19	Amherst ...	24	86	2	2	3	...	17		...	8	...	1	...	1	12	...	...
20	Tavoy ...	29	100	3	5	3	2	16	...	...	2	...	...	..	...	2	...	4
21	Mergui ...	13	6		6	5	1	1	...	.	...	...	...	...	...	...	...	...
	Magwe Division ...	31	93	9	16	2	4	...	...	...	...	...	...	...	...	24	...	..
22	Thayetmyo ...	...		.	..	...	..	...	..	..	...	...	..	...	...	...	...	...
23	Pakôkku ...	9	31	6	1	1	1	..		..	.	...	...	...	...	7	...	...
24	Minbu ...	22	60	3	15	1	3	...	...	...	...	..	...	...	..	6	...	...
25	Magwe ...	...	2	..	...	...	...	...	...	...	...	..	...	...	..	1	.	...
26	Pakôkku Hill Tts.	...	...	..	...	...	...	...	.		...	...	..	...	...	...	..	...
	Mandalay Division	31	182	1	4	10	15	1	...	...	2	...	1	...	11	1	...	..
27	Mandalay ..	26	134	1	4	8	13	...	...	...	...	...	...	...	11	...	...	...
	Mandalay City	...	...	...	...	...	...	...	..	...	...	...	...	...	...	...	...	...
28	Bhamo ...	...	34	...	...	...	...	...	...	...	...	...	...	...	...	...	...	...
29	Myitkyina ...	...	3	...	...	...	...	...	...	...	...	...	...	...	...	..	...	...
30	Katha ..	4	11	...	...	2	1	1	...	..	2	...	1	...	...	1	..	...
31	Putao ...	1	...	...	...	...	1	...	...	...	...	...	...	...	...	...	..	...
	Sagaing Division ...	13	33	...	10	2	1	..	...	...	...	...	4	...	...	5	...	...
32	Shwebo ...	...	2	..	...	...	...	.	..	...	..	...	...	...	...	1	...	...
33	Sagaing ...	3	8	..	1	2	...	.	...	.	...	...	...	...	...	4	...	...
34	Lower Chindwin	1	12	...	...	...	1	..	...	...	...	...	..	...	..	...	..	...
35	Upper Chindwin	9	11	...	9	...	...	...	...	...	...	...	4	...	...	...	...	...
36	Chin Hills ...	.	...	...	...	...	...	...	...	...	...	...	...	...	...	...	..	...
	Meiktila Division ...	28	15	...	7	4	17	...	...	..	5	...	...	...	.	2	...	...
37	Kyauksè ...	...	...	...	...	..	..	...	...	...	...	...	...	...	...	...	...	...
38	Meiktila ...	...	1	.	...	...	...	...	...	..	...	...	...	...	...	1	...	...
39	Yamèthin ...	26	9	...	6	3	17	...	..	..	5	...	...	...	...	...	...	...
40	Myingyan ...	2	5		1	1	...	...	...	...	...	...	...	...	...	1	...	-
	Eastern States ...	2,383	1,254	36	768	55	90	1,434	...	...	312		29	1	2	106	...	...
41	N. Shan States ...	1,787	842	9	324	12	60	1,382	.	...	312	...	29	1	2	106	...	...
42	S. Shan States ...	596	412	27	444	43	30	52		..	...	...	..	...	...	...	...	..
43	Karenni ...	..	...	...	...	...	...	...	...	..	..	...	...	...	..	...	..	...

* See footnote on page 414.

of **Female** *Workers of Sort F—Gardener (Groups 5, 6 and 7).*

65a. Basket-makers.	65, Mat-weavers.	81, Oil pressers.	86, Rice-pounder.	71, 74, Sweetmeat makers and toddy drawers.	110a. Boat-owner.	110b, Boatman or towman.	114, Cart-owner or driver.	121, Money-lender or pawn-broker.	128a, Wholesale cloth seller.	128b, Retail cloth seller.	131, Fish seller.	134, Sweetmeat seller.	138, Vegetable seller.	138a, Wholesale grain-dealer.	138b, Retail grain-dealer.	169, Lawyer.	1001, Durwan or peon.	1002, Other labourers.	1003, Other traders.	1004, All others.	Serial No. of District, etc. (column 1).
19	20	21	22	23	24	25	26	27	28	29	30	31	32	33	34	35	36	37	38	39	
5	41	4	15	12	...	1	28	16	1	27	55	120	340	4	60	1	1	214	677	518	
5	39	3	9	12	...	1	25	15	1	23	55	79	128	4	9	1	1	140	510	276	
...	1	...	3	...	...	...	...	1	...	...	1	4	2	...	...	...	...	1	11	4	
...	1	...	1	...	...	...	...	...	...	...	...	...	2	...	...	...	...	1	1	2	1
...	...	...	...	...	...	...	...	...	...	...	...	...	...	...	...	...	...	...	...	...	2
...	...	...	...	...	...	...	...	1	...	...	...	...	...	...	...	...	...	...	8	...	3
...	...	...	2	...	...	...	...	...	...	...	1	4	...	...	...	...	...	...	2	2	4
...	...	...	...	1	...	...	6	2	1	4	19	34	43	1	4	...	...	17	111	69	
...	...	...	...	...	...	...	...	...	...	...	...	...	...	...	...	...	...	...	...	...	5
...	...	...	...	...	...	...	2	...	...	...	...	2	12	...	...	...	...	4	23	14	6
...	...	...	...	...	...	...	...	...	1	...	...	6	2	...	...	...	...	4	10	17	7
...	...	...	...	...	...	...	...	...	...	2	5	9	14	1	...	...	...	5	36	11	8
...	...	...	...	...	...	...	1	1	...	1	...	1	5	...	1	...	...	...	6	3	9
...	...	...	...	1	...	...	3	1	...	1	14	16	10	...	3	...	...	4	36	24	10
3	20	...	...	1	...	...	3	9	...	...	18	21	16	2	3	...	...	84	192	96	
...	11	...	...	...	...	...	...	1	...	...	7	5	15	...	...	...	...	21	55	27	11
3	2	...	...	1	...	...	3	2	...	...	3	3	...	2	3	...	...	61	116	59	12
...	...	...	...	...	...	...	...	4	...	...	6	3	1	...	...	...	...	2	10	3	13
...	7	...	...	...	...	...	...	...	...	...	2	10	...	...	...	...	...	...	11	5	14
...	...	...	...	...	...	...	...	2	...	...	...	...	...	...	...	...	...	...	...	2	15
2	18	...	6	...	...	1	5	3	...	3	14	11	51	1	1	1	...	4	56	73	
...	...	...	...	...	...	...	...	3	...	...	...	...	7	...	...	...	...	1	9	23	16
...	...	...	4	...	...	...	...	...	...	...	...	...	...	...	...	...	...	...	1	...	17
2	4	...	...	...	...	...	...	...	...	...	1	5	2	1	...	1	...	...	15	9	18
...	4	...	1	...	...	1	4	...	...	2	2	2	11	...	1	...	...	...	22	14	19
...	5	2.	1	...	...	...	1	...	...	1	11	4	31	...	...	...	...	3	8	27	20
...	5	...	...	...	...	...	...	...	...	...	...	...	...	...	...	...	...	...	1	...	21
...	...	2	...	4	...	...	5	...	...	...	3	6	9	...	1	...	...	3	32	14	
...	...	...	...	...	...	...	...	...	...	...	...	...	...	...	...	...	...	...	...	...	22
...	...	...	...	4	...	...	...	...	...	...	...	...	...	...	...	...	...	...	9	11	23
...	...	2	...	...	...	...	4	...	...	...	3	6	9	...	1	...	...	3	23	3	24
...	...	...	...	...	...	...	1	...	...	...	...	...	...	...	...	...	...	...	...	...	25
...	...	...	...	...	...	...	...	...	...	...	...	...	...	...	...	...	...	...	...	...	26
...	...	...	...	...	...	...	3	...	...	16	...	3	5	...	...	...	1	31	95	13	
...	...	...	...	...	...	...	3	...	...	...	...	2	4	...	...	...	...	31	70	13	27
...	...	...	...	...	...	...	...	...	...	...	...	...	...	...	...	...	...	...	...	...	
...	...	...	...	...	...	...	...	...	...	16	...	...	...	...	...	...	...	...	18	...	28
...	...	...	...	...	...	...	...	...	...	...	...	...	1	...	...	...	...	...	2	...	29
...	...	...	...	...	...	...	...	...	...	...	...	1	...	...	...	...	1	...	5	...	30
...	...	...	...	...	...	...	...	...	...	...	...	...	...	...	...	...	...	...	...	...	31
...	...	1	...	6	...	...	1	...	...	...	...	...	1	...	...	...	...	...	11	4	
...	...	...	...	...	...	...	...	...	...	...	...	...	...	...	...	...	...	...	1	...	32
...	...	1	...	6	...	...	1	...	...	...	...	...	1	...	...	...	...	...	3	1	33
...	...	...	...	...	...	...	...	...	...	...	...	...	...	...	...	...	...	...	3	...	34
...	...	...	...	...	...	...	...	...	...	...	...	...	...	...	...	...	...	...	4	3	35
...	...	...	...	...	...	...	...	...	...	...	...	...	...	...	...	...	...	...	...	...	36
...	...	...	...	...	...	...	2	...	...	...	...	...	1	...	...	...	...		2	3	
...	...	...	...	...	...	...	...	...	...	...	...	...	...	...	...	...	...	...	...	...	37
...	...	...	...	...	...	...	...	...	...	...	...	...	...	...	...	...	...	...	...	...	38
...	...	...	...	...	...	...	...	...	...	...	...	...	1	...	...	...	...	...	1	2	39
...	...	...	...	...	...	...	2	...	...	...	...	...	...	...	...	...	...	...	1	1	40
...	2	1	6	...	...	...	3	1	...	4	...	41	212	...	51	...	...	74	167	242	
...	2	1	6	...	...	...	3	1	...	4	...	...	140	...	51	...	...	24	107	53	41
...	...	...	...	...	...	...	...	...	...	...	...	41	72	...	...	...	...	50	60	189	42
...	...	...	...	...	...	...	...	...	...	...	...	...	...	...	...	...	...	...	...	...	43

Imperial Table XVIII, Sections G, H and J.—*Subsidiary Occupations of* Male *Workers of Group*

Serial No.	District or State.	Group 181, Money-lender or Pawn-broker.													Group 188a,			
				Agricultural.					Non-Agricultural.								Agri	
		Total Agricultural.	Total Non-Agricultural.	1, 2a, Landlord.	2a, Cultivating owner.	2b, Cultivating tenant.	2c, Agricultural labourer.	4, Taungya cultivator.	98, Cotton-weaver.	182, Whole-sale grain-dealer.	180, Retail grain-dealer.	* See footnote.	183, Other traders.	184, All others.	Total Agricultural.	Total Non-Agricultural.	1, 2a, Landlord.	2a, Cultivating owner.
	1	2	3	4	5	6	7	8	9	10	11	12	13	14	15	16	17	18
	Provincial Total ...	362	518	212	92	39	9	10	...	90	56	109	193	70	295	972	107	103
	Divisional Burma	346	502	207	87	39	9	4		87	56	105	184	70	295	967	107	103
	Arakan Division ...	35	64	17	12	3	1	2	..	9	9	16	23	7	36	58	18	10
1	Akyab ...	10	22	5	3	...	...	2	...	5	6	4	7	...	21	43	9	7
2	Hill Dt. of Arakan	...	...	...	...	...	...	...	...	..	...	..	...	...	...	...	...	...
3	Kyaukpyu ...	15	21	11	3	...	1	...	...	2	3	4	8	4	9	...	3	3
4	Sandoway	10	21	1	6	3	...	..	..	2	...	8	8	3	6	15	6	...
	Pegu Division ...	42	27	21	5	15	1	...	...	3	...	7	8	9	100	235	31	40
5	Rangoon Town ...	...	7	...	..	...	...	...	...	...	...	3	1	3	3	21	2	...
6	Insein ...	...	...	...	...	..	...	...	...	..	...	...	...	...	10	31	3	1
7	Hanthawaddy ...	17	11	4	3	9	1	...	..	..	...	4	4	3	6	20	4	2
8	Tharrawaddy ...	2	2	2	...	...	...	...	...	1	...	...	...	1	37	109	16	8
9	Pegu ...	21	...	13	2	6	...	...	...	...	..	..	...	...	42	46	6	29
10	Prome ...	2	7	2	..		...	.	...	2	...	...	3	2	2	8	...	...
	Irrawaddy Division	77	136	50	18	7	2	...	...	38	19	18	55	6	59	299	25	19
11	Bassein ...	19	39	9	9	..	1	..	...	5	11	2	21	...	2	16	1	1
12	Henzada ...	17	21	10	7	...	...	...	..	5	3	8	4	1	37	113	17	9
13	Myaungmya ...	26	48	23	1	2	...	..	...	9	5	7	26	1	7	100	3	2
14	Ma-ubin ...	3	28	3	...	..	...	...	...	19	..	1	4	4	11	47	4	7
15	Pyapôn ...	12	...	5	1	5	1	...	..	...	...	...	...	...	2	13	...	...
	Tenasserim Division	30	40	14	11	2	3	...	...	7	8	5	15	5	41	108	12	7
16	Toungoo ...	7	18	4	3	...	...	..	...	4	4	3	4	3	11	19	2	1
17	Salween ...	...	...	...	...	...	...	..	..	...	...	...	..	...	...	...	...	...
18	Thatôn ..	10	6	2	5	1	2	..	...	..	3	...	3	...	4	35	...	2
19	Amherst ...	3	2	...	9	...	...	...	...	..	...	...	2		20	43	8	1
20	Tavoy ...	10	10	8	...	1	1	...	...	3	1	8	4	..	6	11	2	3
21	Mergui ...	...	4	...	...	...	...	...	...	...	...	...	2	2	...	...	...	...
	Magwe Division ...	46	87	24	19	3	...	...	..	7	14	30	19	17	14	98	8	3
22	Thayetmyo ...	7	9	3	4	..	.	...	..	1	...	4	2	2	...	4	...	...
23	Pakôkku ...	29	38	16	11	2	...	..	...	1	4	20	8	5	14	53	8	3
24	Minbu ...	10	12	5	4	1	...	..	...	..	2	2	5	3	...	...	...	...
25	Magwe ...	...	28	...	...	...	...	...		5	8	4	4	7	..	41	...	...
26	Pakôkku Hill Tts.	...	...	...	...	...	...	...		...	...	...	...	..	..	...	...	...
	Mandalay Division	3	35	2	...	1	...	..	...	...	2	9	19	5	5	53	...	5
27	Mandalay ...	2	12	1	...	1	...	...	...	...	2	2	6	2	2	13	...	2
	Mandalay City	...	*1*	..	...	...	..	...	...	...	...	...	...	*1*	...	*1*	...	...
28	Bhamo ...	..	2	...	...	...	...	...	...	...	...	1	..	1	...	17	...	...
29	Myitkyina ...	.	2	...	...	...	...	...	...	...	...	...	2	...	1	17	...	1
30	Katha ...	1	19	1	...	...	...	...	...	...	...	6	11	2	2	6	...	2
31	Putao ...	..	...	...	...	...	...	...	...	...	...	...	...	...	...	...	...	...
	Sagaing Division ...	65	66	41	15	6	1	2	...	17	4	9	25	11	27	74	8	15
32	Shwebo ...	12	13	9	2	1	...	..	...	5	...	1	2	5	13	27	2	8
33	Sagaing ...	19	22	9	6	4	...	...	..	5	3	3	11	...	7	23	2	4
34	Lower Chindwin	29	20	22	5	1	1	...	..	7	1	...	7	5	7	24	4	3
35	Upper Chindwin	5	11	1	2	...	...	2	..	...	...	5	5	1	...	...	...	...
36	Chin Hills ...	..	...	...	...	...	...	...	..	...	...	..	...	...	...	...	...	...
	Meiktila Division ...	48	47	38	7	2	1	.	...	6	..	11	20	10	13	42	5	4
37	Kyaukse ...	...	...	...	...	...	...	...	..	...	...	...	...	...	5	11	2	1
38	Meiktila ...	13	24	9	2	2	...	...	..	...	...	8	12	4	1	13	8	...
39	Yamèthin ...	5	11	4	1	...	...	...	...	6	...	2	1	2	...	2	...	...
40	Myingyan ...	30	12	25	4	...	1	...	...	...	...	1	7	4	7	16	2	3
	Eastern States ...	16	16	5	5	...	..	6		3	...	4	9	...	...	5	...	...
41	N. Shan States ...	4	14	1	3	...	...	...	...	3	...	2	9	...	..	4	...	...
42	S. Shan States ...	12	2	4	2	...	...	6	...	...	...	2	...	...	...	1	...	...
43	Karenni ...	...	...	...	..	...	...	...		...	...	...	...	...	...	...	...	...

* This column accommodates all sorts of subsidiary occupations separately tabulated

121, *Money-lender or Pawn-broker*; 136*a*, *Wholesale Grain-dealer*; and 136*b*, *Retail Grain-dealer*.

WHOLESALE GRAIN-DEALER.								GROUP 136b. RETAIL GRAIN-DEALERS.												Serial No. of District, etc. (column 1).
CULTURAL.			NON-AGRICULTURAL.							AGRICULTURAL.					NON-AGRICULTURAL.					
2b, Cultivating tenant.	2c, Agricultural labourer.	4, Taungya cultivator.	98, Cotton-weaver.	121, Money-lender or pawn-broker.	* See footnote.	136c. Other traders.	100d. All others.	Total Agricultural.	Total Non-Agricultural.	1, 2a, Landlord.	2a, Cultivating owner.	2b, Cultivating tenant.	2c, Agricultural labourer.	4, Taungya cultivator.	98, Cotton-weaver.	121, Money-lender or pawn-broker.	* See footnote.	136c. Other traders.	100d. All others.	
19	20	21	22	23	24	25	26	27	28	29	30	31	32	33	34	35	36	37	38	
38	41	6	9	222	266	296	179	174	653	31	58	41	35	9	6	48	299	193	107	
38	41	6	9	221	264	294	179	161	602	26	55	36	35	9	4	48	275	173	102	
4	...	4	...	18	9	27	4	21	35	2	1	6	12	...	...	11	10	10	4	
4	...	1	...	15	8	16	4	21	35	2	1	6	12	...	..	11	10	10	4	1
...	...	...	...	...	...	...	...	...	...	...	...	...	...	...	...	...	...	...	..	2
...	...	3	...	...	...	...	...	...	...	...	...	...	..	...	...	...	...	...	...	3
...	...	...	...	3	1	11	...	...	...	...	...	...	...	...	...	...	...	...	...	4
12	17	...	...	54	61	64	56	3	19	...	2	...	...	1	...	4	6	4	5	
1	...	...	...	7	1	...	13	...	2	...	...	...	...	...	...	1	...	1	...	5
2	4	...	...	4	6	14	7	1	2	...	...	...	...	1	...	2	...	...	..	6
...	...	...	...	5	...	...	15	1	1	...	1	...	...	...	.	...	...	...	1	7
6	7	...	...	28	29	32	20	1	6	...	1	...	...	...	...	...	5	1	...	8
3	4	...	...	8	22	16	...	...	6	...	...	...	...	...	...	...	1	1	4	9
...	2	..	...	2	3	2	1		2	...	...	...	...	...	...	1	...	1	...	10
6	7	2	4	80	100	63	52	65	152	11	27	22	2	3	...	15	89	34	14	
...	...	...	2	...	4	...	20	58	126	11	21	21	2	3	...	11	85	22	8	11
4	5	2	2	45	22	27	17	...	4	...	.	...	...	...	...	3	...	...	1	12
...	2	...	...	16	47	25	12	2	...	...	1	1	...	...	...	...	...	...	...	13
...	...	...	...	10	27	10	...	5	7	...	5	...	...	...	...	1	3	...	3	14
2	...	...	...	9	..	1	3	...	15	...	...	...	...	...	...	...	1	12	2	15
8	14	...	1	34	26	44	3	4	21	1	3	...	...	...	...	1	2	13	5	
2	6	...	...	7	3	9	...	2	8	1	1	...	...	...	...	1	2	5	...	16
...	...	...	..	...	...	...	...	...	...	...	...	...	...	...	...	...	..	...	...	17
2	...	...	...	18	2	15	...	...	3	...	...	...	...	...	...	...	...	3	...	18
3	8	...	1	5	21	13	3	2	6	...	2	...	...	...	...	...	...	1	5	19
1	...	...	...	4	...	7	...	...	2	...	...	...	...	...	...	...	...	2	...	20
...	...	...	...	...	...	...	...	...	2	...	...	...	...	...	...	...	...	2	...	21
3	...	..	3	10	31	48	6	18	96	4	5	1	8	...	4	4	32	36	20	
...	...	...	...	...	1	3	...	.	7	...	...	...	...	..	...	...	...	4	3	22
3	...	...	3	...	29	18	3	5	16	3	1	1	...	...	4	2	4	6	...	23
...	...	...	...	...	...	...	...	10	47	...	2	...	8	...	...	1	26	8	12	24
...	...	...	.	10	1	27	3	3	26	1	2	...	...	...	...	1	2	18	5	25
...	...	...	...	...	...	...	...	...	...	...	...	...	...	...	...	...	...	...	...	26
...	...	...	1	6	8	11	27	11	91	1	5	2	...	3	...	6	40	9	36	
...	...	...	1	3	1	4	4	...	3	...	...	...	...	...	...	1	...	1	1	27
...	...	...	...	1	...	...	...	...	3	...	...	...	..	...	..	1	...	1	1	
...	...	...	...	...	7	1	9	4	66	...	2	...	...	2	...	...	32	...	34	28
...	...	...	...	1	...	2	14	...	6	...	...	...	...	...	...	3	...	2	1	29
...	...	...	...	2	...	4	...	7	16	1	3	2	...	1	...	2	8	6	...	30
...	...	...	...	...	...	...	...	...	...	...	...	...	...	...	...	...	...	...	...	31
1	3	...	...	17	14	24	19	31	152	6	10	3	10	2	...	4	86	53	9	
1	2	...	...	6	2	11	8	1	4	...	1	...	...	...	...	...	2	2	...	32
...	1	...	...	5	6	6	6	8	33	1	2	1	4	...	...	...	24	2	7	33
...	...	...	..	6	6	7	5	8	32	7	..	...	6	...	...	2	20	10	...	34
...	...	...	...	...	...	...	...	14	83	3	7	2	...	2	...	2	40	39	2	35
...	...		...	...	...	...	...	...	...	...	...	...	..	...	...	...	...	...	...	36
4	...	...	..	2	15	13	12	8	36	1	2	2	3	..	...	3	10	14	9	
2	...	...	...	1	5	3	2	7	14	1	1	2	3	...	...	2	5	2	5	37
...	...	...	...	...	6	4	3	...	3	...	...	...	...	...	...	...	...	1	2	38
...	...	...	...	1	.	...	1	...	14	...	...	...	...	...	...	1	2	11	...	39
2	...	...	...	...	4	6	6	1	5	...	1	...	...	...	...	...	3	...	2	40
..	...	...	...	1	2	2	...	13	51	5	3	5	...	...	2	...	24	20	5	
...	...	...	..	1	1	2	..	9	42	3	2	4	...	...	2	...	21	14	5	41
...	...	...	...	...	1	...	...	4	9	2	1	1	...	...	...	--	3	6	...	42
...	...	...	...	...	...	...	...	...	...	...	...	...	..	...	...	...	...	...	...	43

for other principal occupations but omitted here to save space; for details see the appendix to this table on page 426.

IMPERIAL TABLE XVIII, SECTIONS G, H AND J.—*Subsidiary Occupations of* **Female** *Workers of*

Serial No.	District or State.	GROUP 121, MONEY-LENDER OR PAWN-BROKER.													GROUP 12[illegible].			
				AGRICULTURAL.					NON-AGRICULTURAL.								AGRI[CULTURAL].	
		Total Agricultural.	Total Non-Agricultural.	1, 2a, Landlord.	3a, Cultivating owner.	3b, Cultivating tenant.	3c, Agricultural labourer.	4, Taungya cultivator.	28, Cotton-weaver.	128a, Wholesale grain-dealer.	128b, Retail grain-dealer.	* See footnote.	100B, Other traders.	100A, All others.	Total Agricultural.	Total Non-Agricultural.	1, 2a, Landlord.	3a, Cultivating owner.
	1	2	3	4	5	6	7	8	9	10	11	12	13	14	15	16	17	18
	Provincial Total ...	140	246	57	47	21	15	...	30	18	11	52	95	40	95	454	33	35
	Divisional Burma	136	242	55	45	21	15	...	30	18	11	50	95	38	88	428	32	31
	Arakan Division ...	11	20	6	3	2	..	...	2	2	1	7	5	3	3	2	3	...
1	Akyab ...	...	10	...	...	..	..	...	2	...	1	5	1	1	...	...	...	...
2	Hill Dt. of Arakan	...	...	...	..	...	...	...	...	...	...	...	...	...	..	...	...	...
3	Kyaukpyu ...	6	4	5	1	...	...	...	...	..	...	2	2	...	1	...	1	...
4	Sandoway ...	5	6	1	2	2	...	...	...	2	...	..	2	2	2	2	2	...
	Pegu Division ..	26	25	11	7	...	8	...	6	1	...	4	10	4	22	87	7	11
5	Rangoon Town ...	2	4	2	...	...	...	...	...	...	...	...	1	3	3	5	3	...
6	Insein ...	1	6	...	1	...	...	...	...	...	...	...	3	1	...	4	...	...
7	Hanthawaddy ...	...	..	...	...	...	...	...	...	...	...	2	...	...	...	21	...	...
8	Tharrawaddy ...	6	7	3	...	..	3	...	...	1	...	...	6	...	3	21	...	2
9	Pegu ...	...	...	...	...	...	...	...	...	...	...	..	...	...	4	16	1	...
10	Prome ...	17	8	6	6	...	5	...	6	...	...	2	...	...	12	20	3	9
	Irrawaddy Division	27	64	6	16	4	1	...	...	10	5	10	24	15	17	145	4	4
11	Bassein ...	16	25	3	12	1	...	...	...	4	5	5	11	...	4	69	1	...
12	Henzada ..	5	4	1	3	...	1	...	.	1	...	1	2	...	9	26	...	3
13	Myaungmya ...	...	22	...	...	...	...	...	...	5	...	1	9	7	2	42	2	...
14	Ma-ubin ...	1	12	1	...	...	...	..	...	...	...	3	1	8	2	8	1	1
15	Pyapôn ...	5	1	1	1	3	...	...	...	...	...	...	1	...	...	...	...	...
	Tenasserim Division	4	17	3	1	..	...	...	...	2	1	3	8	3	14	9	5	7
16	Toungoo ...	1	9	1	...	...	...	...	...	2	1	2	4	...	5	3	2	3
17	Salween ...	...	...	...	...	...	...	...	...	...	...	...	...	...	...	...	...	...
18	Thatôn ...	...	4	...	...	...	...	...	...	...	...	1	3	..	...	...	...	...
19	Amherst ...	...	...	...	..	...	...	...	..	...	...	...	...	...	...	4	...	...
20	Tavoy ...	3	4	2	1	...	...	...	.	...	...	...	1	3	9	2	3	4
21	Mergui ...	...	...	..	...	...	...	...	...	...	.	...	...	...	...	...	..	...
	Magwe Division ...	29	48	15	5	3	6	...	7	...	3	13	19	6	11	72	6	4
22	Thayetmyo ...	4	7	3	...	..	1	..	2	.	...	1	4	...	...	...	...	...
23	Pakôkku ...	12	29	6	3	1	2	...	3	...	3	10	11	2	10	60	6	3
24	Minbu ...	6	9	3	1	1	1	...	2	...	...	1	2	4	1	12	...	1
25	Magwe ...	7	3	3	1	1	2	...	...	...	...	1	2	...	...	..	...	...
26	Pakôkku Hill Tts.	...	...	...	...	...	...	...	..	...	...	...	...	...	...	...	...	...
	Mandalay Division	3	11	...	1	2	...	...	1	..	...	1	6	3	2	47	..	...
27	Mandalay ...	3	5	...	1	2	...	...	...	...	...	1	3	1	...	6	...	...
	Mandalay City	..	...	...	...	...	...	...	...	...	...	...	...	...	...	5	...	...
28	Bhamo ...	...	2	..	...	...	...	...	...	..	...	...	...	2	2	40	...	...
29	Myitkyina ..	...	...	...	...	...	...	...	...	...	...	...	...	...	...	...	...	...
30	Katha ...	...	4	...	...	...	...	...	1	...	...	...	3	...	...	1	...	...
31	Putao ...	...	...	...	...	..	...	..	...	...	...	...	...	...	...	...	..	...
	Sagaing Division	20	35	6	6	8	...	..	7	3	1	3	19	2	16	52	6	3
32	Shwebo ...	12	7	4	..	8	...	...	2	3	...	...	2	...	5	9	...	1
33	Sagaing ...	6	16	2	4	...	...	...	4	...	1	3	7	1	11	27	6	2
34	Lower Chindwin	...	4	...	...	...	...	...	1	...	..	...	3	...	...	...	...	...
35	Upper Chindwin	2	8	...	2	...	...	...	...	..	...	...	7	1	...	16	...	...
36	Chin Hills ...	...	...	...	...	.	...	...	...	..	...	..	...	...	...	...	...	...
	Meiktila Division ...	16	22	8	6	2	...	...	7	...	...	9	4	2	3	14	1	2
37	Kyauksè ...	...	.	..	...	...	..	...	...	...	...	...	...	...	...	...	...	...
38	Meiktila ...	7	5	2	4	1	...	...	2	...	..	3	...	...	3	12	1	2
39	Yamèthin ...	...	4	...	...	...	...	...	...	...	...	4	...	...	...	...	...	...
40	Myingyan ...	9	13	6	2	1	...	...	5	...	...	2	4	2	...	2	...	...
	Eastern States ...	4	4	2	2	...	...	...	...	...	..	2	...	2	7	26	1	4
41	N. Shan States	3	2	1	2	.	...	...	...	...	...	1	...	1	..	1	...	...
42	S. Shan States ...	1	1	1	...	...	...	...	...	...	...	1	...	...	7	25	1	4
43	Karenni ...	...	1	...	...	...	...	...	...	...	...	...	...	1	...	...	..	...

* This column accommodates all sorts of subsidiary occupations separately tabulated for other

Group 121, Money-lender or Pawn-broker; 136a, Wholesale Grain-dealer; and 136b, Retail Grain-dealer.

WHOLESALE GRAIN-DEALER.								GROUP 136b, RETAIL GRAIN-DEALER.												
…CULTURAL.			NON-AGRICULTURAL.							AGRICULTURAL.					NON-AGRICULTURAL.					
8b. Cultivating tenant.	8c. Agricultural labourer.	4. Taungya cultivator.	98. Cotton-weaver.	121. Money-lender or pawn-brokers.	* See footnote.	1003. Other traders.	1004. All others.	Total Agricultural.	Total Non-Agricultural.	1, 8a. Landlord.	8a. Cultivating owner.	8b. Cultivating tenant.	8c. Agricultural labourer.	4. Taungya cultivator.	98. Cotton-weaver.	121. Money-lender or pawn-broker.	* See footnote.	1003. Other traders.	1004. All others.	Serial No. of District, etc. (column 1).
19	20	21	22	23	24	25	26	27	28	29	30	31	32	33	34	35	36	37	38	
18	9	.	58	78	90	138	90	157	417	23	27	14	76	17	121	20	91	120	65	
18	7	...	58	78	68	134	90	153	331	23	26	14	74	16	49	20	88	109	65	
..	...	...	...	...	...	2	...	1	10	...	...	...	1	...	5	...	2	2	1	
...	...	...	...	...	...	...	...	...	8	...	...	...	..	...	5	...	2	...	1	1
...	...	...	...	...	...	...	...	...	...	...	...	...	...	...	...	...	...	...	...	2
...	...	...	...	...	...	...	...	...	...	...	...	...	...	...	...	...	...	2	...	3
...	..	...	...	...	...	2	...	1	2	...	.	...	1	...	...	...	...	...	...	4
3	1	...	6	34	9	26	12	7	34	1	4	...	2	...	...	3	9	11	11	
..	...	...	...	1	...	2	2	...	5	...	...	...	...	...	...	...	...	...	5	5
...	...	...	...	1	...	3	...	1	3	...	1	...	...	...	...	...	..	2	1	6
...	...	..	...	19	2	...	...	3	8	...	1	...	2	...	...	3	5	...	...	7
...	1	...	...	5	2	7	7	...	...	...	..	...	...	...	...	...	...	...	...	8
3	...	...	...	4	2	10	...	..	2	...	..	...	...	...	...	...	1	1	...	9
...	...	...	6	4	3	4	3	3	16	1	2	...	...	...	...	...	3	8	5	10
8	1	..	9	35	18	62	21	23	34	10	6	3	4	...	1	5	14	9	5	
2	1	..	2	22	9	19	17	7	3	1	3	3	..	...	1	...	...	2	...	11
6	...	...	5	2	4	14	1	13	3	9	...	..	4	..	...	...	1	2	...	12
..	...	...	2	9	4	24	3	...	11	...	...	...	...	...	...	1	6	2	2	13
...	...	...	...	2	1	5	...	2	16	...	2	...	...	...	...	4	6	3	3	14
...	...	..	...	...	...	...	...	1	1	...	1	...	...	...	...	...	1	...	...	15
2	...	...	1	1	4	2	1	6	39	2	1	...	2	1	4	5	6	7	17	
...	...	...	...	1	...	2	...	1	...	1	...	...	...	...	...	...	...	...	...	16
...	...	...	...	...	...	...	...	...	...	...	...	...	...	...	...	...	...	...	...	17
...	..	..	...	...	...	...	...	2	14	1	1	...	...	...	2	3	3	6	...	18
...	...	...	1	...	2	...	1	...	8	...	...	...	...	...	2	2	2	...	2	19
2	...	...	.	...	2	...	...	3	17	...	...	...	2	1	...	...	1	1	15	20
...	...	...	...	...	...	...	..	..	...	...	...	...	...	...	...	...	...	...	..	21
1	...	...	21	...	15	15	21	56	60	8	6	1	41	...	13	2	16	21	8	
...	...	...	...	...	...	...	...	...	10	..	...	...	...	..	4	...	...	6	...	22
1	...	...	17	...	12	12	19	...	...	...	..	...	...	...	...	...	...	...	...	23
...	...	..	4	...	3	3	2	48	39	5	2	1	40	...	7	...	16	11	5	24
...	...	...	...	...	...	...	...	8	11	3	4	..	1	...	2	2	...	4	3	25
...	...	...	...	...	...	...	...	...	...	...	...	...	...	...	...	...	...	...	...	26
...	2	..	...	3	8	6	30	9	40		2	7	...	...	3	4	15	12	6	
..	...	...	...	3	...	...	3	9	15	...	2	7	...	...	3	2	1	4	5	27
...	...	..		2	...	..	3	...	...		...	...	...	...	..	...	...	...	...	
...	2	...	...	...	8	5	27	...	2	..	...	..	...	...	...	...	2	...	...	28
...	...	...	..	...	...	...	...	...	1	...	...	..	...	...	..	...	...	1	...	29
...	...	...	...	...	...	1	...	...	22	...	...	...	..	...	...	2	12	7	1	30
...	...	...	...	...	...	...	...	...	...	...	...	...	...	...	..	...	...	...	...	31
4	3	...	16	4	13	15	4	25	76	1	4	2	3	15	18	1	13	35	9	
1	3	...	2	2	4	1	..	..	...	...	...	...	...	..	...	...	...	...	..	32
3	...	...	14	2	7	3	1	2	3	...	2	...	..	...	2	...	1	...	...	33
...	...	...	..	...	...	...	...	...	48	...	...	...	...	...	15	1	7	17	8	34
...	..	...	..	..	2	11	3	23	25	1	2	2	3	15	1	...	5	18	1	35
...	...	...	...	...	...	...	...	...	..	...	...	...	...	...	...	...	...	...	...	36
...	...	...	5	1	1	6	1	26	38	1	3	1	21	...	5	..	13	12	8	
...	...		...	...	...	...	...	16	13	...	...	...	16	...	...	...	6	3	4	37
...	...	...	4	1	1	5	1	...	2	...	...	...	...	...	...	...	1	1	...	38
...	...	...	...	...	...	...	...	5	8	...	...	1	4	...	2	...	1	4	1	39
..	...	...	1	...	...	1	...	5	15	1	3	...	1	...	3	...	5	4	3	40
...	2	...	...	.	22	4	...	4	86	...	1	...	2	1	72	...	3	11	...	
...	...	...	...	...	...	1	...	4	86	...	1	...	2	1	72	...	3	11	...	41
...	2	...	...	...	22	3	...	...	...	...	..	...	...	...	..	...	...	...	...	42
...	...	..	...	...	...	...	...	...	...	...	...	...	...	...	...	...	...	...	...	43

* ...principal occupations but omitted here to save space; for details see the appendix to this table on page 426.

IMPERIAL TABLE XVIII, SECTION K.—*Subsidiary Occupations*

Serial No.	District or State.	Total Agricultural.	Total Non-Agricultural.	Agricultural. 1, 2a, Landlord.	3a, Cultivating owner.	3b, Cultivating tenant.	3c, Agricultural labourer.	4, Taungya cultivator.	5, 6, 7, Gardeners, etc.	9a, Charcoal burner.	9b, Wood cutters.	9c, Cutch collectors.	9d, 10, All other collectors of forest produce.	11, Herdsman.	17, Fisherman.	97, Cotton-weavers.	98, 16, Silk rearers and spinners.	96, Silk-weavers.
	1	2	3	4	5	6	7	8	9	10	11	12	13	14	15	16	17	18
	Provincial Total ...	35,724	46,523	3,138	14,128	6,833	9,772	1,853	2,339	59	1,160	100	538	270	1,675	89	1	6
	Burma Proper ...	26,425	39,702	2,721	8,274	5,716	8,452	1,262	1,121	52	1,086	100	536	249	1,431	84	1	6
	Arakan Division ...	3,556	2,414	361	1,048	450	1,410	287	65	...	23	..	12	14	179	2	...	...
1	Akyab ...	2,598	1,194	254	745	262	1,182	155	19	...	7	...	4	2	27	2	...	...
2	Hill Dt. of Arakan	11	4		...	...	...	11	1	...	...	...	...	...	...	...	..	...
3	Kyaukpyu ...	658	720	52	199	116	196	95	31	...	3	...	1	...	48	...	...	...
4	Sandoway ...	289	496	55	104	72	32	26	14	..	13	...	7	12	104	..	...	...
	Pegu Division ...	2,677	6,042	261	730	468	1,183	35	154	8	73	2	143	51	201	7	...	...
5	Rangoon ...	98	477	26	25	23	24	...	5	...	3	...	...	...	...	...	...	...
6	Insein ...	200	884	13	29	35	123	...	28	4	18	...	46	5	17	...	...	...
7	Hanthawaddy ...	495	1,243	27	94	145	229	1	34	...	...	...	...	16	21	...	...	...
8	Tharrawaddy ...	676	1,396	55	260	88	270	3	34	3	11	...	55	14	31	1	..	...
9	Pegu ...	681	1,209	96	217	130	237	1	11	1	36	...	40	13	60	...	...	...
10	Prome ...	526	833	44	105	47	300	30	42	...	5	2	2	3	72	6	...	...
	Irrawaddy Division	3,016	5,393	446	709	422	1,391	48	154	2	111	...	74	38	196	15	...	...
11	Bassein ...	799	1,602	124	108	91	450	26	39	.	43	...	20	4	31	12	...	...
12	Henzada ...	894	1,375	108	262	88	418	18	55	2	32	...	16	17	97	2	...	...
13	Myaungmya ...	638	1,162	118	157	101	258	4	39	.	21	...	24	9	19	..	...	...
14	Ma-ubin ...	380	851	57	108	55	150	...	14	...	6	...	11	6	40	1	...	...
15	Pyapôn ...	305	403	39	74	77	115	...	7	...	9	...	3	2	9	...	...	...
	Tenasserim Division	2,116	3,686	197	624	222	799	274	208	29	85	3	34	23	157	13	...	...
16	Toungoo ...	342	1,020	58	102	43	114	25	45	5	35	...	17	9	34	...	...	...
17	Salween ...	36	50	4	15	3	4	10	2	..	...	...	...	1	1	1	...	...
18	Thatôn ...	492	1,035	39	226	45	126	56	50	6	9	...	4	7	13	11	...	...
19	Amherst ...	513	502	58	157	60	216	22	40	11	4	...	13	3	7	..	...	.
20	Tavoy ...	579	704	28	62	54	321	114	41	4	16	3	...	3	46	...	...	...
21	Mergui ...	154	375	10	62	17	18	47	30	3	21	...	...	...	56	1	...	...
	Magwe Division ...	5,106	7,027	372	1,494	2,088	1,080	72	123	..	137	79	29	40	130	10	...	1
22	Thayetmyo ...	254	640	29	146	30	20	29	9	...	64	..	...	7	33	1	...	...
23	Pakôkku ...	3,330	4,117	151	959	1,800	392	28	71	...	55	55	26	27	46	4	...	1
24	Minbu ...	1,012	1,488	129	242	205	423	13	24	...	18	19	..	4	39	4	...	...
25	Magwe ...	510	782	63	147	53	245	2	19	...	...	5	3	2	12	1	...	...
26	Pakôkku Hill Tts.	...	...	...	..	...	...	..	...	...	...	...	...	..	..	...	...	.
	Mandalay Division	2,031	4,275	546	768	192	365	160	191	9	211	1	78	11	222	9	...	1
27	Mandalay	783	1,413	461	34	62	224	2	34	9	61	...	12	..	14	7	...	1
	Mandalay City ..	*463*	*185*	*451*	*1*	*3*	*6*	*2*	...	...	...	...	...	...	...	*2*	...	*1*
28	Bhamo ...	197	745	12	112	7	24	42	13	...	73	1	30	..	126	...	...	...
29	Myitkyina ...	288	796	45	160	16	13	54	121	...	13	...	8	7	8	...	...	...
30	Katha ...	752	1,316	27	452	107	104	62	23	...	64	...	28	4	74	2	...	...
31	Putao ...	11	5	1	10	...	...	...	...	...	...	...	...	...	...	...	...	...
	Sagaing Division ...	5,795	7,050	376	2,150	1,330	1,658	281	79	1	377	11	165	37	279	24	1	4
32	Shwebo ...	839	1,413	71	459	119	182	2	9	...	52	...	35	2	25	3	...	3
33	Sagaing ...	2,181	1,747	112	709	571	761	28	10	1	53	...	17	22	56	3	...	...
34	Lower Chindwin	1,541	1,855	132	400	564	443	2	27	...	93	5	2	11	83	14	1	1
35	Upper Chindwin	899	2,018	52	461	76	266	44	33	...	179	6	111	2	115	4	...	...
36	Chin Hills ...	335	17	9	121	...	...	205	...	...	...	...	...	..	...	...	...	...
	Meiktila Division ...	2,128	3,815	162	751	544	566	105	147	3	69	4	1	35	67	4	...	...
37	Kyauksè ...	457	674	39	150	52	216	...	13	...	31	...	...	4	18	...	...	...
38	Meiktila ...	515	881	57	197	157	97	7	4	..	21	4	...	13	18	2	...	...
39	Yamèthin ...	551	1,112	17	137	138	167	92	119	1	14	...	1	15	27	...	...	...
40	Myingyan ...	605	1,148	49	267	197	86	6	11	2	3	...	...	3	16	2	...	..
	Eastern States ...	9,299	6,821	417	5,854	1,117	1,320	591	1,218	7	74	...	2	21	244	5	...	...
41	N. Shan States ...	1,165	2,043	60	336	230	184	355	831	...	20	...	2	12	15	5	...	...
42	S. Shan States ...	8,021	4,599	356	5,459	876	1,126	204	384	7	54	...	...	9	208	...	...	...
43	Karenni ...	113	179	1	59	11	10	32	3	...	...	...	...	..	21	...	...	...

of **Male** *Workers of All Other Principal Occupations.*

45a, Basket-makers.	45b, Mat-weavers.	67, Oil presser.	68, Rice pounder.	71, 74, Sweetmeat makers and toddy drawers.	110a, Boat-owner.	110b, Boatman or towman.	114, Cart-owner or driver.	121, Money-lender or pawn-broker.	128a, Wholesale cloth seller.	125 Retail cloth seller.	131, Fish seller.	134, Sweetmeat seller.	135, Vegetable seller.	138a, Wholesale grain-dealer	138b, Retail grain-dealer.	163, Lawyer.	1001, Durwan or peon.	1002, Other labourers.	1003, Other traders.	1004, All others.	Serial No. of District, etc. (column 1).
19	20	21	22	23	24	25	26	27	28	29	30	31	32	33	34	35	36	37	38	39	
548	670	319	240	656	123	856	3,250	1,527	27	262	775	619	454	1,064	361	5	144	3,809	9,538	15,039	
541	659	315	218	656	123	855	2,790	1,505	24	239	764	580	388	1,055	346	5	1 2	2,542	8,387	12,902	
11	160	4	12	3	11	44	16	141	3	6	95	18	55	45	20	...	5	361	366	743	
6	154	4	8	1	7	14	2	78	1	3	84	14	52	36	18	...	3	139	126	383	1
...	...	...	...	...	...	...	..	1	...	...	...	...	...	...	...	..	...	...	1	1	2
...	...	...	..	...	3	5	...	48	..	1	...	1	...	6	...	...	...	203	165	205	3
5	6	...	4	2	1	25	14	14	2	2	11	3	3	3	2	...	2	19	74	154	4
46	50	16	6	37	16	73	648	259	5	34	132	67	56	267	52	1	39	358	1,583	1,658	
...	...	...	...	..	13	2	12	34	1	3	32	1	5	15	7	1	3	1	62	277	5
5	5	1	...	...	...	5	63	47	2	...	10	11	7	49	3	...	..	29	348	181	6
2	15	...	...	...	1	26	70	53	...	5	13	14	13	30	18	...	9	197	405	301	7
9	15	5	4	2	...	5	231	35	...	9	45	[illegible]	14	78	2	...	13	72	369	345	8
12	4	5	2	..	...	26	213	66	...	8	24	26	10	71	16	...	12	24	245	284	9
18	1	5	..	35	2	9	69	21	2	9	8	11	7	24	6	...	2	35	154	270	10
58	42	16	28	8	14	143	132	434	5	21	299	132	31	409	35	...	6	171	1,376	1,433	
18	3	...	3		4	45	45	161	..	7	192	53	5	113	18	...	2	27	303	454	11
19	14	15	19	4	5	39	22	51	3	2	18	20	4	54	3	...	...	49	414	399	12
13	4	.	...	4	1	3	11	131	2	...	32	13	6	130	...	...	...	53	388	315	13
7	19	1	1	..	...	33	53	59	.	11	40	45	3	57	10	...	3	35	241	155	14
1	2	...	5	...	4	23	1	32	...	1	17	1	13	55	4	...	1	7	96	110	15
20	10	26	10	19	22	48	285	171	9	14	44	24	56	94	19	1	5	193	712	1,352	
11	8	14	3	1		10	97	34	5	3	5	9	29	31	1	...	...	33	183	398	16
...	...	1	...	...	...	...	3	1		1	...	...	...	...	...	...	...	...	29	10	17
3	2	7	2	12	11	25	76	40	1	2	9	7	7	22	2	...	4	124	327	250	18
3	...	1	5	1	5	8	65	50	3	1	3	1	7	26	2	1	...	22	49	171	19
2	...	3	...	4	...	...	42	24	...	7	26	4	11	13	3	...	...	8	69	375	20
1	...	...	...	1	6	5	2	21		...	1	3	2	2	11	...	1	6	55	146	21
154	198	193	61	346	54	191	629	179	1	73	62	131	102	61	81	1	9	342	939	2,671	
7	32	2	1	3	1	34	21	28	...	...	5	4	2	5	2	...	...	79	97	203	22
125	145	162	40	302	52	121	463	71	1	61	40	101	45	15	59	1	3	140	344	1,541	23
18	12	4	20	16	1	36	129	40	...	10	15	21	27	29	9	...	6	117	273	597	24
4	9	25	...	25	...	..	16	40	...	2	2	5	28	12	11	...	...	6	225	330	25
...	...	...	...	...	...	...	...	...	...	..	...	...	..	...	..	...	...	...	...	...	26
36	44	5	12	33	...	63	289	77	1	27	50	32	21	52	40	...	64	370	1,070	1,266	
16	17	...	3	31	...	26	229	25	1	14	12	28	11	5	3	...	60	31	383	380	27
...	*8*	...	*1*	...	...	...	*12*	*8*	*1*	...	...	*1*	...	...	*1*	...	*60*	*8*	*18*	*69*	
3	9	4	4	...	...	25	25	2	...	4	14	1	1	5	25	...	...	6	144	230	28
...	1	1	1	...	...	9	16	13	...	5	7	2	2	7	7	...	3	45	227	293	29
17	17	...	4	2	...	3	19	37	...	4	17	...	7	35	5	...	.	288	316	360	30
...	...	...	...	...	...	...	...	...	...	...	...	1	...	...	...	...	1	...	...	3	31
143	122	29	49	138	6	278	375	176	...	34	55	83	39	84	73	...	14	295	1,475	2,604	
11	35	2	6	52	...	7	67	22	...	12	3	32	7	27	5	...	3	210	319	464	32
69	24	16	12	46	5	87	154	52	...	2	9	10	6	25	9	...	..	24	341	694	33
27	27	9	7	40	1	47	94	48	..	14	28	22	10	17	26	...	5	26	338	832	34
36	36	2	24	...	...	137	60	53	...	6	15	18	16	15	33	...	5	35	472	605	35
...	...	...	...	...	...	...	...	1	...	...	...	1	...	...	...	...	1		5	9	36
73	33	26	40	72	.	15	416	68	.	30	27	93	28	43	26	2	...	452	866	1,175	
15	6	...	16	7	...	1	72	10	...	2	...	10	3	28	8	...	..	32	173	231	37
19	11	2	3	...	...	...	55	21	...	13	3	13	2	1	8	...	...	113	220	341	38
29	15	...	21	35	...	...	228	6	...	15	15	48	22	6	6	...	...	42	266	183	39
10	1	24	...	30	...	14	63	31	...	...	9	28	1	8	4	2	...	265	207	420	40
7	11	4	22	...	...	1	460	22	3	23	11	39	66	9	15	..	2	1,267	1,151	2,137	
7	8	3	21	..	...	1	133	4	3	18	9	37	59	9	15	.	2	31	372	426	41
...	3	1	1	...	...	...	324	17	...	5	2	...	7	...	...	...	...	1,207	709	1,661	42
...	...	...	...	...	...	...	3	1	...	...	...	2	...	...	..	...	...	29	70	52	43

Serial No.	District or State.	Total Agricultural.	Total Non-Agricultural.	AGRICULTURAL. 1, 2a, Landlord.	2a. Cultivating owner.	2b. Cultivating tenant.	2c. Agricultural labourer.	4. Taungya cultivator.	5, 6, 7. Gardener, etc.	9a. Charcoal burner.	9b. Wood cutters.	9c. Cutch collectors.	8d, 10. All other collectors of forest produce.	11. Herdsman.	17. Fisherman.	87. Cotton-weavers.	84, 88. Silk rearers and spinners.	86. Silk weavers.
	1	2	3	4	5	6	7	8	9	10	11	12	13	14	15	16	17	18
	Provincial Total	20,645	31,682	710	7,394	1,878	8,741	1,922	970	6	120	4	224	79	499	3,866	...	24
	Burma Proper ...	12,231	24,254	407	2,195	1,628	7,744	257	322	5	108	4	221	63	341	3,591	...	24
	Arakan Division ...	649	1,308	18	71	72	432	56	32	...	...	...	...	1	35	152	...	...
1	Akyab ...	84	613	6	19	14	35	10	13	...	..	...	...	1	3	81	...	...
2	Hill Dt. of Arakan	...	...	...	..	...	...	...	...	...	...	...	...	...	...	...	...	...
3	Kyaukpyu ...	398	404	8	46	46	265	33	12	..	...	...	...	...	22	28	...	...
4	Sandoway ...	167	291	4	6	12	132	13	7	...	...	...	...	...	10	43	...	...
	Pegu Division ...	1,775	2,128	45	301	106	1,305	18	41	...	6	...	53	10	18	181	...	...
5	Rangoon ...	...	38	...	...	...	...	...	...	...	...	.	...	...	...	...	.	...
6	Insein ...	147	267	3	2	8	134	...	8	...	1	...	26	1	..	7	...	...
7	Hanthawaddy ...	158	281	2	74	19	63	...	2	..	..	...	1	...	2	1	...	...
8	Tharrawaddy ...	423	447	7	50	12	354	...	3	...	2	...	13	6	11	28	...	...
9	Pegu ...	520	337	27	155	51	274	13	5	...	2	..	13	2	5	9	...	...
10	Prome ...	527	758	6	20	16	480	5	23	...	1	...	...	1	...	136	...	...
	Irrawaddy Division	1,258	2,579	86	124	87	945	16	50	...	1	..	43	2	54	111	...	...
11	Bassein ...	313	629	17	15	19	248	14	6	...	1	...	12	1	10	26	...	...
12	Henzada ...	552	997	27	75	34	415	1	28	..	...	...	6	1	19	81	..	...
13	Myaungmya ...	107	391	23	15	10	58	1	7	..	..	...	11	...	5	2	...	...
14	Ma-ubin ...	212	456	10	14	14	174	...	5	...	...	...	14	...	19	2	...	..
15	Pyapôn ...	74	106	9	5	10	50	...	4	...	...	...	.	...	1	...	...	...
	Tenasserim Division	611	2,358	42	107	63	306	93	55	3	6	..	19	2	35	262	...	5
16	Toungoo ...	135	341	3	17	11	51	53	6	1	1	...	12	...	3	18	..	...
17	Salween ...	13	31	...	6	...	4	3	13	...	...	...	5	...	...	...	...	...
18	Thatôn ...	162	865	24	40	21	69	8	7	...	1	...	...	1	7	159	..	...
19	Amherst ...	157	575	4	20	17	111	5	20	...	2	...	2	...	2	64	...	...
20	Tavoy ...	139	501	11	21	14	70	23	9	2	2	...	...	1	1	20	...	5
21	Mergui ...	5	45	...	3	...	1	1	...	...	...	...	...	...	22	1	...	...
	Magwe Division ...	2,600	5,276	80	418	635	1,452	15	42	...	25	3	11	19	14	1,256	...	26
22	Thayetmyo ...	135	398	9	19	18	87	2	1	...	15	...	...	1	...	54	...	...
23	Pakôkku ...	1,336	3,248	33	255	551	490	7	23	...	8	...	11	14	6	947	...	26
24	Minbu ...	893	1,249	31	125	56	680	1	6	...	2	1	..	3	8	236	...	...
25	Magwe ...	236	381	7	19	10	195	5	12	.	...	2	.	1	...	19	..	...
26	Pakôkku Hill Tts.	...	...		..	...	...	...	...	...	...	..	...	...	...	...	...	.
	Mandalay Division	539	1,892	16	83	34	389	17	27	...	28	...	26	3	51	182	...	1
27	Mandalay ...	376	962	14	22	21	312	7	17	...	6	...	...	2	38	31	...	1
	Mandalay City ...	9	62	..	3	2	4	..	...	...	...	...	..	...	..	...	...	1
28	Bhamo ...	9	207	...	6	...	1	2	3	...	9	...	1	1	6	3	...	...
29	Myitkyina ...	12	116	...	4	4	4	...	7	...	10	...	5	..	2	...	...	...
30	Katha ...	141	607	2	50	9	72	8	...	...	3	...	20	...	5	148	...	...
31	Putao ...	1	...	...	1	...	...	...	...	...	...	...	...	...	...	...	...	...
	Sagaing Division	2,662	5,332	64	597	404	1,561	36	25	...	35	1	57	15	96	845	...	2
32	Shwebo ...	560	871	18	241	84	217	...	1	...	7	...	4	4	...	132		1
33	Sagaing ...	1,144	2,637	25	199	228	692	...	2	...	7	1	...	5	93	509	..	1
34	Lower Chindwin	596	1,166	17	31	62	486	...	14	...	10	...	...	6	...	138	...	...
35	Upper Chindwin	362	656	4	126	30	166	36	8	...	11	...	53	..	3	66	...	...
36	Chin Hills ...	...	2	...	...	...	...	...	...	...	...	...	...	...	...	...	...	...
	Meiktila Division ...	2,137	3,381	56	494	227	1,354	6	50	2	7	...	12	11	38	602	...	...
37	Kyauksè ...	966	425	4	16	23	923	...	12	...	4	...	...	1	2	30	.	..
38	Meiktila ...	536	907	16	250	74	196	...	19	...	...	...	...	2	5	163	...	...
39	Yamèthin ...	138	401	16	18	19	91	...	10	2	3	...	12	2	1	57	...	...
40	Myingyan ...	497	1,648	25	210	111	144	6	9	..	...	...	...	6	30	352	...	...
	Eastern States ...	8,414	7,428	303	5,199	250	997	1,665	648	1	12	...	3	16	158	275	...	...
41	N. Shan States ...	708	1,248	3	320	38	138	212	213	...	4	...	3	8	4	270	...	...
42	S. Shan States ...	7,655	6,148	299	4,860	209	849	1,438	435	1	8	...	...	8	154	5	..	...
43	Karenni ...	51	38	1	19	3	13	15	...	...	..	...	...	...	...	...	..	...

of Female *Workers of All Other Principal Occupations.*

48a, Basket-makers.	48b, Mat-weavers.	61, Oil presser.	65, Rice pounder.	71, 74, Sweetmeat makers and toddy drawers.	110a, Boat-owner.	110b, Boatman or towman.	114, Cart-owner or driver.	121, Money-lender or pawn-broker.	128a, Wholesale cloth seller.	128b, Retail cloth seller	131, Fish seller.	134, Sweetmeat seller.	135, Vegetable seller.	136a, Wholesale grain-dealer.	136b, Retail grain dealer.	160, Lawyer.	1001, Durwan or peon.	1002, Other labourers.	1003, Other traders.	1004, All others.	Serial No. of District, etc. (column 1).
19	20	21	22	23	24	25	26	27	28	29	30	31	32	33	34	35	36	37	38	39	
82	337	91	819	589	22	51	357	394	102	268	731	1,042	656	138	234	...	5	4,038	6,836	9,098	
82	332	89	804	589	22	51	212	390	97	241	690	871	629	138	203	...	5	1,747	5,434	6,949	
...	36	...	109	1		1	1	10		10	81	44	87	4	10	...	...	121	311	262	
...	33	...	66	1	...	1	...	1	...	9	50	20	72	1	7	...	...	26	80	148	1
..	...	..	...	...	...	...	...	...	..	...	...	...	...	...	...	.	...	...	...	...	2
...	...	...	...	...	...	...	...	5	...	...	..	10	...	...	...	...	...	93	169	65	3
...	3	...	43	...	...	.	1	4	...	1	31	14	15	3	3	...	...	2	62	49	4
2	18	8	12	35	11	24	45	54	7	29	128	95	55	8	25	...	2	212	511	538	
...	...	...	...	...	...	...	..	14	...	...	..	5	...	1	...	...	...	6	3	9	5
1	6	...	1	...	...	...	4	8	...	3	5	11	...	2	...	...	...	19	76	88	6
...	..	...	...	..	...	10	1	8	...	...	8	12	5	2	1	...	2	59	70	97	7
...	8	7	9	...	...	...	8	10	7	5	57	17	2	1	3	...	.	95	87	68	8
...	3	...	2	...	11	...	28	7	...	8	19	25	18	2	2	...	...	3	121	52	9
1	1	1	...	35	...	14	4	7	...	13	39	25	30	...	19	...	...	30	154	224	10
7	113	11	35	...	...	10	23	117	14	7	204	125	79	74	13	...	...	173	765	548	
2	10	...	1	-	...	4	3	43	...	1	119	51	31	15	4	...	...	12	185	142	11
3	35	11	32	...	..	-	13	13	13	..	37	22	25	38	...	...	...	111	369	140	12
1	2	...	...	...	...	1	6	26	...	...	8	12	3	14	4	..	...	32	111	146	13
1	66	...	1	...	...	3	1	27	1	4	38	37	15	5	5	...	...	17	112	83	14
...	...	...	1	...	...	2	...	8	..	2	2	3	5	2	...	...	...	1	38	37	15
16	39	1	31	...	3	3	31	59	5	25	81	125	83	19	15	...	...	127	481	827	
10	3	...	4	..	...	...	16	7	...	5	6	21	12	12	...	...	...	10	61	133	16
3	...	..	...	...	...	...	...	1		...	...	1	1	...	...	...	...	...	5	2	17
2	15	...	4	...	...	2	7	12	5	1	5	55	13	2	3	...	...	104	250	210	18
...	...	1	5	...	...	1	6	19	...	17	12	25	35	3	8	...	...	4	91	258	19
1	20	...	18	...	...	...	2	14	...	2	58	22	22	2	4	...	...	8	68	220	20
..	1	...	...	...	3	...	...	6	...	...	...	1	...	...	...	...	...	1	6	4	21
29	31	27	302	138	..	9	39	51	59	72	88	157	132	10	37	..	2	231	719	1,757	
...	6	...	15	3	...	...	1	6	...	2	9	15	3	...	3	...	...	111	83	70	22
21	13	12	185	83	...	3	14	29	47	58	47	66	69	9	16	...	...	46	248	1,257	23
8	8	..	102	38	..	3	13	11	12	4	27	56	38	1	18	...	2	69	316	264	24
...	4	15	...	14	...	3	11	5	...	8	5	20	22	...	..	...	..	5	72	166	25
...	...	...	...	...	...	...	...	...	...	...	...	...	...	...	...	...	...	...	...	...	26
6	3	1	21	14	1	3	25	35	6	6	59	36	39	10	21	...	...	146	399	743	
..	2	1	10	...	1	1	14	13	6	5	41	25	32	4	4	..	...	32	157	519	27
..	..	...	...	..	..		...	5	...	3	3	1	1	...	1	...	...	...	16	31	
..	...	..	5	...	...	...	...	...	.	1	3	3	6	3	10	...	...	..	60	93	28
...	...	...	2	...	...	2	2	3	...	...	7	1	1	1	6	...	...	2	38	27	29
6	1	...	4	14	...	...	9	19	...	...	8	7	...	2	1	...	...	112	144	104	30
...	...	...	...	...	...	..	...	...	...	...	...	...	...	...	...	..	...	...	...	...	31
16	72	7	169	240	7	...	29	41	6	37	28	192	86	11	53	...	...	310	1,570	1,382	
3	12	1	37	73	...	...	9	5	...	7	2	38	6	4	2	..	...	138	256	129	32
7	38	...	10	144	7	...	3	18	...	14	..	73	45	3	22	...	...	26	837	772	33
6	16	6	87	23	...	...	4	15	6	15	15	70	25	2	14	...	...	..	270	424	34
...	6	...	35	...	...	...	13	3	...	1	11	11	10	2	15	...	...	146	206	56	35
...	...	...	...	...	...	...	..	...	...	...	...	...	...	...	...	...	...	...	1	1	36
6	20	34	125	161	...	1	19	23	...	55	21	97	68	2	29	...	1	427	678	892	
...	11	...	79	3	...	..	1	2	...	1	3	29	10	1	12	.	...	21	93	110	37
3	6	5	17	11	...	...	7	8	...	27	7	54	25	...	6	...	...	97	227	218	38
...	1	...	14	...	...	...	5	4	..	6	...	2	18	...	5	...	...	13	93	153	39
3	2	29	15	147	...	1	6	9	...	21	11	12	15	1	6	...	1	296	265	411	40
...	5	2	15	..	...	...	145	4	5	27	41	171	27	...	31	...	...	2,291	1,402	2,149	
...	5	2	15	..	...	...	20	3	4	26	36	46	25	...	31	...	...	31	282	214	41
...	...	...	...	...	...	...	122	...	1	1	5	125	2	...	...	...	..	2,250	1,111	1,920	42
...	...	...	...	...	...	...	3	1	.	...	...	...	...	...	...	...	...	10	9	15	43

Note 9.—The separate figures which are given for Mandalay City are included in those for the Mandalay District which are shown immediately above them.

Note 10.—A supplement to this table is given as Imperial Table XIX in which a converse tabulation is given of the principal occupations with which five selected sorts of occupations are associated as subsidiary occupations.

Note 11.—In the corresponding table of the census of 1911 in Burma and of the census of 1921 in other provinces the term *Rent-receiver* is used to mean a person with an occupation of Group 1 as that group is defined in Imperial Table XVII. Similarly the term *Rent-payer* is used to correspond to the sum of Groups 3*a*, 3*b* and 4: and *Farm-servants and Field-labourers* (or in some provinces *Agricultural labourers*) to correspond to the sum of Groups 2*a* and 3*c*. As no persons of Group 2*a* in Burma reported a subsidiary occupation either in 1911 or 1921, Section A of this table gives the subsidiary occupations of *Rent-receivers,* and Sections B, C and E together give those of *Rent-payers,* while Section D gives those of *Farm-servants and Field-labourers.*

Appendix to Imperial Table XVIII.—*Provincial totals for the separate sorts of subsidiary occupations included in the columns headed* * *in Sections G, H and J of the Table.*

Sort of Subsidiary Occupations.		Principal Occupation.					
		Money-lender or Pawn-broker (*Section G*).		Wholesale Grain-dealer (*Section H*).		Retail Grain-dealer (*Section J*).	
		Males.	Females.	Males.	Females.	Males.	Females.
1		2	3	4	5	6	7
5, 6, 7	Gardener, etc.	15	13	37	14	63	14
9*a*	Charcoal burner	...	...	1	...	...	...
9*b*	Wood-cutters	1	...	4	...	5	...
9*c*	Cutch-collectors	...	...	...	..	...	...
9*d*, 10	All other collectors of forest produce	...	..	17	4	22	2
11	Herdsman	4	2	1	...	2	...
17	Fisherman	4	...	9	5	5	1
34, 16	Silk-rearers and spinners ...	...	...	...	...	...	...
35	Silk-weavers	...	1	...	8	...	...
45*a*	Basket-makers	4	...	3	...	11	1
45*b*	Mat-weavers	1	3	1	...	21	3
61	Oil presser	1	..	11	..	2	...
65	Rice pounder	...	...	5	1	2	6
71, 74	Sweetmeat-makers and toddy-drawers	12	1	3	8	10	16
110*a*	Boat-owner	11	3	22	10	54	9
110*b*	Boatman or towman	3	2	15	...	25	1
114	Cart-owner or driver	10	1	35	...	34	5
123*a*	Wholesale cloth seller	3	2	2	...	12	...
123*b*	Retail cloth seller	15	6	21	6	4	16
131	Fish seller	4	5	42	11	13	6
134	Sweetmeat seller	10	9	8	3	4	9
135	Vegetable seller	1	...	8	1	5	6
169	Lawyer	3	...	...	...	...	...
1001	Durwan or peon	5	...	1	..	...	...
1002	Other labourers	2	4	20	19	5	11
Total for above sorts of Subsidiary Occupation tabulated under * .		109	52	266	90	299	91

IMPERIAL TABLE XIX.

Supplement to Imperial Table XVIII—Subsidiary Occupations.

NOTE 1.—This table is prepared in five sections A to E, each of which shows the principal occupations of persons who have for their subsidiary occupation one of the occupations which is shown for that section in the following list:—

SECTION A—Landlord or land-agent (Groups 1 and 2*a*).
SECTION B—Money-lenders or pawn-brokers (Group 121).
SECTION C—Grain-dealers (Wholesale or retail—Groups 136*a* and 136*b*).
SECTION D—Silk-weavers (Group 35).
SECTION E—Cotton-weavers (Group 27).

The occupations represented by each of these titles are all the occupations of the occupational-group or groups noted against it; for the full content of any group Imperial Table XVII should be consulted.

NOTE 2.—The principal occupations tabulated are similarly described by short titles, each of which must be understood to include all the occupations of the occupational-groups indicated by the number prefixed to it. The meanings of the headings which have no group-number noted against them are as follows:—

Forestry or Wood.—All occupations of Orders IIB, VIII, XXVIII and XXXVIII as defined in Imperial Table XVII.

Toddy or jaggery.—All toddy climbers and makers of jaggery, but not makers of kyantaga or other sweetmeats (Group 74 and part of Group 71. See Note 5 of Imperial Table XVIII).

Various remainder classes, e.g., *Others, Other Traders.*—For each section of the table these must be interpreted in accordance with the other principal occupations tabulated for that particular section.

NOTE 3.—The section of the table corresponding to each subsidiary occupation thus reproduces the figures corresponding to that subsidiary occupation in each part of Imperial Table XVIII, in each case expanding those of the last part of that table (*Other principal occupations*) to show separate figures for those principal occupations which make any considerable contribution to them.

NOTE 4.—The principal occupations included under the term *Agricultural* are those defined as agricultural in Imperial Table XVII, Part I, Section A, Article 3.

NOTE 5.—The whole of Part I of Imperial Table XVII applies to this table unless the contrary is indicated by the above Notes.

NOTE 6.—The figures tabulated for the Rangoon Town District represent also Rangoon Town, as for the purposes of the Imperial Census Tables these areas are conterminous.

NOTE 7.—The separate figures which are given for Mandalay City are included in those for the Mandalay District which are shown immediately above them.

IMPERIAL TABLE XIX, SECTION A.—*Principal Occupations of Persons who by*

Serial No.	District or State.	MALES. Total. All.	Total. Agricultural.	Total. Non-Agricultural.	Agricultural. 3a. Cultivating owner.	Agricultural. 3b. Cultivating tenant.	Agricultural. 3c. Agricultural labourer.	Agricultural. 4. Taungya cultivator.	Non-Agri… 5, 6, 7. Gardener.	121. Money-lender or pawn-broker.	136a. Wholesale grain-dealer.	136b. Retail grain-dealer.	Forestry or wood.	17. Fisher.	110a & 110b. Boat-owner or boat-man.	114. Cart-owner or driver.
	1	2	3	4	5	6	7	8	9	10	11	12	13	14	15	16
	Provincial Total ...	6,053	2,391	3,662	1,898	279	100	114	174	212	107	31	21	38	179	30
	Divisional Burma ..	5,308	2,114	3,194	1,718	270	99	27	133	207	107	26	21	37	179	14
	Arakan Division ...	773	375	398	270	72	31	2	...	17	18	2	2	6	155	1
1	Akyab ...	496	226	270	155	42	29	...	...	5	9	2	...	3	155	1
2	Hill Dt. of Arakan	...	...	...	...	...	...	...	...	...	...	...	...	...	...	...
3	Kyaukpyu ...	175	109	66	85	21	2	1	...	11	3	...	..	2	...	...
4	Sandoway ...	102	40	62	30	9	...	1	...	1	6	...	2	1	...	...
	Pegu Division ...	659	328	331	253	49	22	4	18	21	31	...	8	...	...	3
5	Rangoon Town ...	38	...	38	...	.	...	...	10	...	2	...	...	...	...	...
6	Insein ...	57	39	18	30	2	5	2	2	...	3	...	...	...	...	...
7	Hanthawaddy ..	74	37	37	20	12	5	...	2	4	4	...	...	...	...	...
8	Tharrawaddy ...	194	120	74	99	15	6	..	1	2	16	...	4	...	...	...
9	Pegu ...	208	93	115	73	15	5	...	.	13	6	...	4	...	...	2
10	Prome ...	88	39	49	31	5	1	2	3	2	...	...	...	...	...	1
	Irrawaddy Division ...	993	427	566	349	51	19	8	34	50	25	11	2	17	4	2
11	Bassein ...	231	65	166	49	3	3	8	21	9	1	11	2	3	1	1
12	Henzada ...	325	182	143	164	12	6	...	8	10	17	...	...	1	1	1
13	Myaungmya .	252	105	147	83	22	..	...	3	23	3	...	..	4	1	..
14	Ma-ubin ...	124	58	66	45	7	6	...	2	3	4	...	...	8	...	...
15	Pyapôn ...	61	17	44	8	5	4	..	...	5	...	...	...	1	1	...
	Tenasserim Division	486	216	270	176	17	12	11	46	14	12	1	...	...	12	2
16	Toungoo ...	124	39	85	16	7	1	5	20	4	2	1	...	...	4	1
17	Salween ...	5	...	5	...	...	..	...	1	...	...	..	...	...	...	...
18	Thatôn ...	141	99	42	93	1	5	...	1	2	...	...	...	..	...	...
19	Amherst ...	122	49	73	40	4	...	5	7	...	8	...	...	...	8	1
20	Tavoy ...	71	27	44	15	5	6	1	6	8	2	...	...	...	...	...
21	Mergui ...	23	2	21	2	...	...	...	11	...	...	...	...	...	...	...
	Magwe Division ...	688	279	409	223	54	1	1	1	24	8	4	2	3	5	3
22	Thayetmyo ...	76	44	32	38	5	...	1	...	3	...	...	1	...	...	...
23	Pakôkku ...	303	125	178	104	20	1	...	..	16	8	3	1	1	3	2
24	Minbu ...	213	79	134	55	24	..	...	...	5	...	...	...	2	1	1
25	Magwe ...	96	31	65	26	5	...	...	1	...	...	1	...	...	1	...
26	Pakôkku Hill Tracts	..	...	...	...	...	...	...	...	...	...	...	...	...	...	...
	Mandalay Division ...	594	41	553	33	3	5	...	4	2	...	1	1	4	...	1
27	Mandalay ...	473	11	462	3	3	5	.	...	1	..	...	...	3	...	...
	Mandalay City ..	*451*	...	*451*	...	...	...	...	...	...	...	...	...	...	...	...
28	Bhamo ...	15	3	12	3	...	...	...	...	...	...	...	...	1	...	...
29	Myitkyina ...	45	...	45	...	...	..	..	...	...	...	...	...	...	...	1
30	Katha ...	58	25	33	25	...	...	...	4	1	...	1	1	...	...	...
31	Putao ...	3	2	1	2	...	...	...	...	...	...	...	...	...	...	...
	Sagaing Division ...	757	314	443	297	14	3	..	12	41	8	6	5	6	2	...
32	Shwebo ...	104	22	82	22	...	...	..	...	9	2	...	...	1	...	...
33	Sagaing ...	244	119	125	114	5	...	...	1	9	2	1	...	3	...	...
34	Lower Chindwin ...	224	53	171	48	2	3	...	11	22	4	2	5	1	...	...
35	Upper Chindwin ...	176	120	56	113	7	...	..	...	1	...	3	...	1	2	...
36	Chin Hills ...	9	...	9	...	...	...	...	...	...	...	...	...	...	...	...
	Meiktila Division	358	134	224	117	10	6	1	18	38	5	1	1	1	1	2
37	Kyauksè ...	59	12	47	8	3	...	1	5		2	1	...	...	...	...
38	Meiktila ..	93	13	80	10	...	3	...	13	9	1	...	...	1	...	2
39	Yamèthin ...	46	25	21	22	...	3	...	...	4	...	...	1	...	...	...
40	Myingyan ...	160	84	76	77	7	...	...	...	25	2	...	...	...	1	...
	Eastern States ...	745	277	468	180	9	1	87	41	5	...	5	...	1	...	16
41	Northern Shan States	148	63	85	49	...	...	14	21	1	...	3	...	...	...	1
42	Southern Shan States	593	211	382	128	9	1	73	20	4	...	2	...	1	...	15
43	Karenni ...	4	3	1	3	...	...	...	...	...	...	...	...	...	...	-

subsidiary occupations are **Landlords or Land Agents** (*Groups 1 and 2a*).

...CULTURAL.					FEMALES.													
					TOTAL.			AGRICULTURAL.				NON-AGRICULTURAL.						
All other dealers in food-stuffs.	Dealers in cloth or clothing.	All other traders.	Lawyers.	Others.	All.	Agricultural.	Non-Agricultural.	2a. Cultivating owner.	2b. Cultivating tenant.	2c. Agricultural labourer.	4. Taungya cultivator.	5, 6, 7. Gardener.	121. Money-lender or pawn-broker.	188a. Wholesale grain-dealer.	188b. Retail grain-dealer.	All other traders.	Others.	Serial No. of District, etc. (column 1).
17	18	19	20	21	22	23	24	25	26	27	28	29	30	31	32	33	34	
28	37	451	29	2,325	2,302	1,414	888	801	328	110	175	65	57	33	23	300	410	
28	35	376	29	2,002	1,625	1,079	546	608	316	109	46	29	55	32	23	234	173	
...	3	39	2	153	119	92	27	79	7	1	5	...	6	3	...	15	3	
...	1	18	1	75	21	15	6	13	...	...	2	...	...	...	...	5	1	1
..	...	...	...	...	...	...	...	...	...	...	...	...	...	...	...	...	...	2
...	...	18	...	32	71	57	14	53	3	1	...	..	5	1	...	6	2	3
...	2	3	1	46	27	20	7	13	4	...	3	...	1	2	...	4	...	4
1	6	58	4	181	215	148	67	107	14	24	3	3	11	7	1	23	22	
...	3	3	2	18	5	...	5	...	..	...	...	...	2	3	...	...	...	5
..	...	2	...	11	21	18	3	14	3	1	...	...	...	...	...	...	3	6
...	...	8	...	19	25	23	2	9	1	13	...	...	...	...	...	..	2	7
...	3	9	...	39	71	61	10	53	3	5	...	...	3	...	...	6	1	8
1	...	31	2	56	60	32	28	23	6	3	...	...	...	1	-	15	12	9
..	..	5	...	38	33	14	19	8	1	2	3	3	6	3	1	2	4	10
6	3	94	6	312	244	128	116	96	18	11	3	10	6	4	10	62	24	
...	1	12	...	104	53	26	27	15	8	...	3	5	3	1	1	13	4	11
3	1	17	1	83	95	56	39	41	6	9	...	2	1	...	9	16	11	12
1	...	37	4	71	40	13	27	11	2	...	..	2	...	2	...	19	4	13
2	...	15	1	31	40	27	13	24	1	2	...	1	1	1	...	7	3	14
...	1	13	...	23	16	6	10	5	1	...	..	...	1	...	..	7	2	15
...	3	38	...	142	123	65	58	20	11	2	32	6	3	5	2	21	21	
...	3	6	...	44	39	32	7	5	3	...	24	...	1	2	1	2	1	16
...	..	1	...	3	2	2	...	...	.	...	2	...	...	...	...	...	...	17
...	...	20	...	19	40	14	26	5	7	1	1	1	...	...	1	11	13	18
...	...	5	...	44	14	8	6	7	..	1	...	2	...	...	...	2	2	19
...	...	3	...	25	27	8	19	2	1	...	5	3	2	3	...	6	5	20
...	...	3	...	7	1	1	...	1	...	...	...	...	...	...	...	...	...	21
3	8	51	11	286	218	100	118	88	6	6	...	9	15	6	8	39	41	
...	...	8	...	20	39	27	12	27	..	...	...	...	3	...	...	0	3	22
3	6	16	1	118	85	34	51	27	3	4	...	6	6	6	...	10	23	23
...	2	21	6	96	75	33	42	30	3	...	...	3	3	...	5	18	13	24
...	...	6	4	52	19	6	13	4	...	2	...	...	3	...	3	5	2	25
..	...	...	..	...	...	...	...	...	...	...	...	...	...	...	..	...	...	26
...	...	5	...	535	65	48	17	9	8	31	...	1	...	...	...	4	12	
...	...	...	...	458	59	44	15	5	8	31	...	1	...	...	...	2	12	27
...	...	..	...	451	...	...	...	...	...	..	...		...	...	...	...	...	
...	...	3	...	8	...	...	...	...	...	...	...	...	...	...	...	...	...	28
...	...	...	...	44	.	...	...	...	...	...	...	...	...	...	...	..	...	29
...	...	1	...	25	4	2	2	2	...	...	.	...	...	...	...	2	...	30
...	...	1	...	...	2	2	...	2	...	...	...	...	...	...	...	...	...	31
18	11	50	2	282	511	434	77	160	240	34	...	...	6	6	1	35	29	
3	...	9	..	58	41	19	22	9		10	...	...	4	...	...	3	15	32
6	...	16	...	87	41	8	33	8	...	...	..	...	2	6	...	17	8	33
6	10	20	2	88	82	65	17	21	41	3	...	...	...	...	...	13	4	34
3	1	...	...	45	347	342	5	132	199	21	...	...	..	...	1	2	2	35
...	...	5	...	4	...	...	..	...	...	...	...	...	...	...	...	...	...	36
...	1	41	4	111	130	64	66	49	12	...	3	...	8	1	1	35	21	
...	...	10	...	29	14	10	4	6	1	...	3	...	...	...	...	3	1	37
...	...	8	3	43	34	15	19	13	2	...	...	...	2	1	...	12	4	38
..	1	9	1	5	12	2	10	2	...	...	...	-	...	...	...	3	7	39
...	...	14	...	34	70	37	33	28	9	...	...	...	6	..	1	17	9	40
...	2	75	...	323	677	335	342	193	12	1	129	36	2	1	...	66	237	
...	2	2	...	55	19	6	13	3	...	...	3	9	1	...		1	2	41
...	...	72	...	268	653	325	328	186	12	1	126	27	1	1	...	65	234	42
...	...	1	...	...	5	4	1	4	...	...	...	...	...	...	...	...	1	43

Imperial Table XIX, Section B.—*Principal Occupations of Persons*

Serial No.	District or State.	MALES.												
		Total.			Agricultural.					Non-Agri…				
		All.	Agricultural.	Non-Agricultural.	1, 2a. Landlord.	3a. Cultivating owner.	3b. Cultivating tenant.	3c. Agricultural labourer.	4. Taungya cultivator.	5, 6, 7. Gardener.	186a. Wholesale grain-dealer.	189. Retail grain dealer.	Forestry or wood.	17. Fisher.
	1	2	3	4	5	6	7	8	9	10	11	12	13	14
	Provincial Total ...	6,891	5,023	1,868	1.374	2,365	389	884	11	71	222	48	13	17
	Divisional Burma ...	6,843	4,998	1,845	1,367	2,351	385	884	11	71	221	48	13	17
	Arakan Division ...	510	339	171	100	200	24	11	4	1	18	11	...	3
1	Akyab ...	213	109	104	12	74	10	11	2	...	15	11	.	1
2	Hill Dt. of Arakan ...	1	...	1	...	..	.	...	...	...	...	...	...	...
3	Kyaukpyu ...	197	149	48	50	91	8	...	...	...		...	...	...
4	Sandoway ...	99	81	18	38	35	6	...	2	1	3	...	...	2
	Pegu Division ...	1,523	1,196	327	216	276	119	585	...	10	54	4	4	3
5	Rangoon Town ...	43	1	42	...	...	1	...	...	...	7	1	...	...
6	Insein ...	163	106	57	39	39	16	12	...	4	4	2	1	8
7	Hanthawaddy ...	192	133	59	18	59	50	6	...	1	5	...	...	...
8	Tharrawaddy ...	258	195	63	88	83	19	5	...	..	28	...	1	...
9	Pegu ...	211	136	75	49	55	24	8	..	1	8	...	1	...
10	Prome ...	656	625	31	22	40	9	554	...	4	2	1	1	1
	Irrawaddy Division ...	1,655	1,119	536	407	421	68	222	1	7	80	15	1	9
11	Bassein ...	460	287	173	106	181	...	..	...	1	...	11	1	3
12	Henzada ...	297	194	103	71	97	20	5	1	4	45	3	...	...
13	Myaungmya ...	413	264	149	148	82	27	7	..	2	16	..	..	...
14	Ma-ubin ...	353	283	70	48	33	6	196	...	...	10	1	...	5
15	Pyapôn ...	132	91	41	34	28	15	14	...	...	9	...	...	1
	Tenasserim Division ...	650	398	252	94	234	36	32	2	46	34	1	3	...
16	Toungoo ...	137	89	48	41	40	8	..	...	6	7	1	1	...
17	Salween ...	2	1	1	...	1	...	...	.	...	...	...	...	...
18	Thatôn ...	125	59	66	14	26	6	13	...	8	18	...	...	...
19	Amherst ...	219	157	62	24	108	10	15	...	7	5	...	2	...
20	Tavoy ...	98	67	31	14	36	11	4	2	3	4	...	...	...
21	Mergui ...	69	25	44	1	23	1	...	...	22	...	...	...	...
	Magwe Division ...	902	708	194	181	470	48	6	3	1	10	4	...	2
22	Thayetmyo ...	73	45	28	1	38	6	...	...	...	.	...	...	...
23	Pakôkku ...	447	374	73	77	262	29	3	3	...	...	2	...	...
24	Minbu ...	183	141	42	69	60	10	2	...	1	...	1	...	2
25	Magwe ...	199	148	51	34	110	3	1	...	...	10	1	...	...
26	Pakôkku Hill Tracts	...	...	...	...	...	...	...	...	.	...	...	...	...
	Mandalay Division ...	181	90	91	8	64	16	2	...	2	6	6	1	...
27	Mandalay ...	77	46	31	7	28	9	2	...	2	3	1	...	...
	Mandalay City. ...	*10*	...	*10*	...	...	...	...	...	...	*1*	*1*	...	...
28	Bhamo ...	2	...	2	...	...	...	...	...	...	...	...	...	...
29	Myitkyina ...	24	7	17	...	5	2	...	...	...	1	3	...	...
30	Katha ...	78	37	41	1	31	5	...	...	...	2	2	1	...
31	Putao ...	...	..	...	...	...	...	...	...	...	...	...	...	...
	Sagaing Division ...	829	631	198	235	341	46	9	...	1	17	4	4	...
32	Shwebo ...	197	169	28	2	144	18	5	...	...	6	...	...	...
33	Sagaing ...	302	245	57	131	102	12	...	...	...	5	...	1	...
34	Lower Chindwin ...	257	200	57	94	90	14	2	...	1	6	2	2	...
35	Upper Chindwin ...	72	17	55	8	5	2	2	...	.	...	2	1	...
36	Chin Hills ...	1	...	1	...	...	...	...	...	..	...	...	...	
	Meiktila Division ..	593	517	76	126	345	28	17	1	3	2	3	...	...
37	Kyauksè ...	94	78	16	22	51	3	1	1	3	1	2	...	...
38	Meiktila ...	205	184	21	46	121	10	7	...	...	...	...	...	
39	Yamèthin ..	87	79	8	9	60	4	6	.	...	1	1	...	...
40	Myingyan ...	207	176	31	49	113	11	3	...	..	...	...	...	...
	Eastern States ...	48	25	23	7	14	4	...	...	...	1	..	..	...
41	Northern Shan States	21	16	5	1	11	4	...	...	...	1	...	...	...
42	Southern Shan States	26	9	17	6	3	...	...	...	...	...	...	...	...
43	Karenni ...	1	...	1	...	...	...	...	...	...	...	...	...	...

who by subsidiary occupations are **Money-lenders or Pawn-brokers.**

...ultural.					Females. Total.			Females. Agricultural.					Females. Non-Agricultural.					
110a and 110b, Boat-owner or boatman.	All other dealers in food stuffs.	Dealers in cloth or clothing.	All other traders.	Others.	All.	Agricultural.	Non-Agricultural.	1, 2a, Landlord.	3a, Cultivating owner.	3b, Cultivating tenant.	3c, Agricultural labourer.	4, Taungya cultivator.	5, 6, 7. Gardener.	188a, Wholesale grain-dealer.	188b, Retail grain-dealer.	Traders.	Others.	Serial No. of District, etc. (column 1).
15	16	17	18	19	20	21	22	23	24	25	26	27	28	29	30	31	32	
20	58	76	785	558	2,057	1,549	508	667	630	148	59	45	16	78	20	289	105	
20	58	75	774	548	2,003	1,500	503	665	627	148	58	2	15	78	20	287	103	
12	...	19	66	41	135	124	11	49	62	9	2	2	1	...	...	9	1	
3	...	19	28	27	26	25	1	8	16	...	1	...	...	...	...	1	...	1
...	...	...	1	..	...	...	...	...	...	..	...	..	...	...	...	...	...	2
9	...	.	31	8	69	63	6	23	36	4	...	..	1	...	..	4	1	3
...	...	...	6	6	40	36	4	18	10	5	1	2	...	...	..	4	...	4
...	4	5	145	98	282	189	93	80	63	37	9	..	2	34	3	27	27	
...	...	...	1	33	16	1	15	1	...	...	...	...	...	1	...	...	14	5
...	1	...	33	10	49	40	9	17	11	9	3	...	...	1	...	7	1	6
...	1	2	38	12	56	26	30	4	7	15	...	..	...	19	3	7	1	7
...	...	...	22	12	82	67	15	33	24	7	3	...	...	5	.	3	7	8
..	2	2	41	20	45	33	12	18	8	4	3	...	1	4	..	4	3	9
...	...	1	10	11	34	22	12	7	13	2	...	..	1	4	...	6	1	10
4	...	19	248	153	614	448	166	220	171	31	26	...	9	35	5	105	12	
4	...	10	89	54	243	177	66	73	85	11	8	...	1	22	...	39	4	11
..	...	2	22	27	102	85	17	31	45	9	...	...	2	2	...	12	1	12
...	...	4	76	51	152	112	40	77	14	3	18	...	4	9	1	24	2	13
...	...	3	34	17	64	31	33	20	7	4	...	...	...	2	4	22	5	14
...	...	...	27	4	53	43	10	19	20	4	...	...	2	...	..	8	...	15
2	...	5	101	60	159	91	68	24	46	16	5	...	3	1	5	37	22	
..	...	2	14	17	30	19	11	2	13	2	2	...	3	1	...	5	2	16
...	...	...	1	...	1	..	1	...	...	...	...	...	...	..	...	1	...	17
...	...	1	22	17	30	15	15	3	7	4	1	...	...	...	3	10	2	18
...	...	1	32	15	54	33	21	7	15	9	2	...	...	...	2	13	6	19
1	.	...	16	7	36	22	14	12	9	1	...	...	...	...	...	8	6	20
1	...	1	16	4	8	2	6	...	2	...	...	...	...	...	...	...	6	21
...	10	2	82	83	237	184	53	85	77	19	3	...	...	...	2	39	12	
...	.	...	6	22	20	14	6	6	6	2	...	...	...	...	...	5	1	22
...	6	2	30	33	115	86	29	37	38	10	1	...	...	...	..	21	8	23
...	2	...	26	10	57	46	11	20	17	7	2	...	...	...	...	8	3	24
...	2	...	20	18	45	38	7	22	16	...	...	...	...	...	2	5	...	25
...	...	...	...	...	...	...	...	...	...	...	...	...	..	...	..	...	...	26
...	...	6	49	21	79	37	42	9	18	9	1	...	...	3	4	19	16	
..	...	5	11	9	51	33	18	9	17	6	1	...	...	3	2	5	8	27
...	...	2	4	2	8	2	7	...	2	...	...	...	...	2	...	3	2	
...	...	...	1	1	1	1	...	...	...	1	...	...	...	...	..	..	...	28
...	...	1	10	2	4	1	3	...	1	...	...	...	...	...	...	3	...	29
...	...	...	27	9	23	2	21	...	...	2	...	...	...	...	2	11	8	30
...	..	...	...	...	...	...	...	...	...	...	...	...	..	...	...	...	...	31
2	44	16	41	69	298	252	46	122	108	17	5	...	.	4	1	33	8	
...	...	4	6	12	86	79	7	22	38	14	5	...	...	2	...	4	1	32
2	8	1	13	27	138	118	20	66	52	...	...	...	...	2	...	15	3	33
...	4	5	17	20	71	55	16	34	18	3	..	...	...	...	1	11	4	34
...	32	6	4	10	3	...	3	..	...	...	...	...	...	...	...	3	...	35
...	...	...	1	...	...	...	...	...	...	...	...	...	...	...	...	...	...	36
...	...	3	42	23	199	175	24	76	82	10	7	...	...	1	...	18	5	
...	...	...	5	5	26	24	2	11	12	...	1	...	...	..	...	2	..	37
...	...	3	10	8	66	57	9	20	33	1	3	...	...	1	...	6	2	38
...	...	...	3	3	27	23	4	8	12	1	2	...	...	...	...	3	1	39
...	...	...	24	7	80	71	9	37	25	8	1	.	...	...	..	7	2	40
...	...	1	11	10	54	49	5	2	3	...	1	43	1	...	...	2	2	
...	...	1	1	2	48	44	4	2	1	..	...	41	1	...	...	1	2	41
...	...	...	10	7	...	...	...	...	...	...	...	...	...	...	...	...	...	42
...	...	...	...	1	6	5	1	...	2	...	1	2	...	...	...	1	...	43

Imperial Table XIX, Section C.—*Principal Occupations of Persons*

Serial No.	District or State.	MALES.												
		Total.			Agricultural.					Non-Agri				
		All.	Agricultural.	Non-Agricultural.	1, 2a. Landlord.	3a. Cultivating owner.	3b. Cultivating tenant.	3c. Agricultural labourer.	4. Taungya cultivator.	5, 6, 7. Gardener.	121. Money-lender or pawn-broker.	Forestry or wood.	17. Fisher.	110a, & 110b. Boat-owner or boatman.
	1	2	3	4	5	6	7	8	9	10	11	12	13	14
	Provincial Total ...	6,911	5,224	1,687	412	2,792	1,264	567	189	116	146	11	29	61
	Divisional Burma ...	6,500	4,892	1,608	411	2,650	1,253	562	16	64	143	11	29	61
	Arakan Division ...	525	440	85	30	211	104	92	3	2	18	...	...	1
1	Akyab ...	373	307	66	13	117	84	92	1	1	11	...	...	1
2	Hill Dt. of Arakan ...	...	...	...	...	...	...	...	...	..	..	...	...	...
3	Kyaukpyu ...	125	113	12	9	86	16	...	2	1	5	...	...	...
4	Sandoway ...	27	20	7	8	8	4	...	...	..	2	...	...	...
	Pegu Division ...	1,956	1,617	339	123	674	559	258	3	17	3	3	7	11
5	Rangoon Town	27	5	22	1	4	...	...	...	..	...	...	...	...
6	Insein ...	186	134	52	10	57	34	33	...	...	...	...	3	4
7	Hanthawaddy ..	189	141	48	15	52	54	20	...	...	...		...	1
8	Tharrawaddy ..	779	693	86	61	268	241	123	...	5	1	1	...	3
9	Pegu ..	308	219	89	22	80	75	39	3	2	...	2	4	...
10	Prome ...	467	425	42	14	213	155	43		10	2	...	..	3
	Irrawaddy Division ...	1,155	635	520	113	265	180	77	...	19	57	1	9	6
11	Bassein ...	276	124	152	32	63	29	...	...	5	16	1	1	3
12	Henzada ..	323	250	73	13	124	77	36	...	8	8	...	1	...
13	Myaungmya ...	202	56	146	16	...	27	13	..	2	14	...	1	2
14	Ma-ubin ...	194	104	90	21	47	27	9	...	4	19	...	5	...
15	Pyapôn ...	160	101	59	31	31	20	19	...	...	...	...	1	1
	Tenasserim Division ...	577	440	137	20	201	143	75	1	9	15	...	2	2
16	Toungoo ...	226	186	40	8	75	56	47	...	...	8	...	...	...
17	Salween ...	3	3	...	...	1	2	.	...	...	...	...	...	...
18	Thatôn ...	88	57	31	3	29	14	11	..	4	3	...	2	1
19	Amherst ...	155	122	33	5	53	46	17	1	5	...	...	...	1
20	Tavoy ...	81	61	20	4	33	24	...	..	...	4	...	...	...
21	Mergui ...	24	11	13	...	10	1	..	...	...	...	...	...	...
	Magwe Division ...	621	447	174	56	290	75	26	...	11	21	...	...	19
22	Thayetmyo ...	50	42	8	24	17	1	..	...	...	1	...	...	3
23	Pakôkku ...	231	152	79	5	116	27	4	...	...	5	..	...	15
24	Minbu ...	225	174	51	24	91	38	21	...	11	2		...	1
25	Magwe ...	115	79	36	3	66	9	1	...	...	13	...	...	...
26	Pakôkku Hill Tracts	...	...	..	...	...	...	...	...		...	...	...	...
	Mandalay Division ...	483	387	96	3	343	21	11	9	2	2	...	9	...
27	Mandalay ...	67	55	12	2	40	8	4	1	2	2	...	1	...
	Mandalay City ...	1	...	1	...	...	...	...	...	...	...	...	...	...
28	Bhamo ...	152	122	30	...	101	9	4	8	..	...	...	8	...
29	Myitkyina ...	139	125	14	...	124	...	1	..	...	...	...	...	...
30	Katha ...	125	85	40	1	78	4	2	...	...	...	...	...	...
31	Putao ...	...	...	...	...	...	...	...	...	...	...	...	...	...
	Sagaing Division ...	879	700	179	52	507	128	14	...	1	21	7	2	18
32	Shwebo	350	313	37	3	257	48	5	..	...	5	1	...	..
33	Sagaing ..	252	210	42	19	141	48	2	..	...	8	..	...	4
34	Lower Chindwin ...	144	92	52	13	49	29	1	..	1	8	3	...	11
35	Upper Chindwin ...	133	85	48	16	60	3	6	...		..	3	2	3
36	Chin Hills ...	...	...	...	..	..	...	..	...	...	..	...	...	..
	Meiktila Division ...	304	226	78	15	159	43	9		3	6	...	...	4
37	Kyauksè ...	88	50	38	8	25	17	...	...	2	...	...	...	...
38	Meiktila ...	83	74	9	...	60	10	4	...	...	...	..	...	...
39	Yamèthin ...	90	72	18	5	52	11	4	...	...	6	..	...	...
40	Myingyan ...	43	30	13	2	22	5	1	...	1	...	...	...	4
	Eastern States ...	411	332	79	1	142	11	5	173	52	3	..	...	...
41	Northern Shan States	399	320	79	1	135	6	5	173	52	3	..	..	...
42	Southern Shan States	4	4	...	...	...	4	...	...	..	...	...	...	..
43	Karenni ...	8	8	...	...	7	1	...	...	..	..	...	...	...

who by subsidiary occupations are **Grain-dealers (Wholesale or Retail).**

[Non-Agri]cultural.					Females. Total.			Agricultural.					Non-Agricultural.				
7II. Cart-owner or driver.	All other dealers in food-stuffs.	Dealers in cloth or clothing.	All other traders.	Others.	All.	Agricultural.	Non-Agricultural.	1, 8a. Landlord.	2a. Cultivating owner.	2b. Cultivating tenant.	3a. Agricultural labourer.	4. Taungya cultivator.	5, 6, 7. Gardener.	III. Money-lender or pawn-broker.	Traders.	Others.	Serial No. of District, etc. (column 1).
15	16	17	18	19	20	21	22	23	24	25	26	27	28	29	30	31	
29	54	51	675	515	2,681	2,216	465	111	872	487	591	155	64	29	230	142	
27	54	49	662	508	2,298	1,915	383	111	803	405	586	10	13	29	201	140	
...	...	5	21	38	34	17	17	2	2	7	4	2	...	3	13	1	
...	...	4	14	35	19	10	9	1	...	5	3	1	...	1	8	...	1
...	...	...	...	...	...	...	...	...	...	...	...	...	...	...	...	...	2
...	...	...	4	2	...	..	...	...	...	...	...	...	..	...	...	...	3
...	...	1	3	1	15	7	8	1	2	2	1	1	...	2	5	1	4
4	9	9	159	117	688	649	39	31	149	124	345	...	5	1	27	26	
...	..	2	2	12	4	3	1	2	1	...	...	...	...	...	...	1	5
2	2	1	31	9	8	6	2	...	1	...	5	...	...	...	2	...	6
...	1	...	24	22	18	15	3	2	6	5	2	...	...	...	3	...	7
.	...	4	42	30	173	167	6	11	50	35	71	...	1	1	...	4	8
2	6	2	51	20	42	37	5	3	2	4	28	...	1	...	...	4	9
..	..	...	9	18	443	421	22	13	89	80	239	...	3	...	12	7	10
3	5	6	261	153	374	267	107	33	113	47	74	...	5	15	54	33	
3	4	1	70	48	104	76	28	10	21	6	39	...	...	9	15	4	11
...	1	4	22	29	161	117	44	14	46	29	28	...	5	1	15	23	12
...	...	...	84	43	56	33	23		32	1	...	...	...	5	16	2	13
...	...	...	42	20	34	24	10	3	9	8	4	...	...	...	6	4	14
...	...	1	43	13	19	17	2	6	5	3	3	...	...	...	2	...	15
2	2	6	55	38	188	149	39	2	23	35	85	4	2	3	20	14	
6	...	3	14	9	123	108	15	...	8	15	84	1	...	3	6	6	16
...	...	...	...	...	1	1	...	...	...	1	...	...	...	...	...	...	17
1	...	1	12	7	15	9	6	1	4	3	1	...	1	...	4	1	18
1	...	2	20	4	22	10	12	1	6	3	...	...	1	...	6	5	19
...	2	...	5	9	27	21	6	...	5	13	...	3	...	...	4	2	20
...	...	...	4	9	...	...	...	...	...	...	...	..	...	...	...	...	21
4	2	5	70	42	311	260	51	18	133	68	41	...	1	3	24	23	
...	...	...	3	1	25	22	3	2	13	5	2	...	...	..	1	2	22
1	2	2	28	26	101	73	28	10	42	19	2	...	...	3	12	13	23
3	...	2	22	10	164	144	20	4	60	43	37	...	1	...	11	8	24
...	...	1	17	5	21	21	...	2	18	1	...	...	...	...	...	...	25
...	...	...	...	...	...	...	...	...	...	...	...	...	...	...	...	...	26
3	1	14	23	32	144	113	31	1	91	9	8	4	...	..	11	20	
7	...	...	2	3	28	20	8	...	15	2	3	...	...	...	4	4	27
2	...	...	...	1	3	2	1	...	2	...	...	...	...	...	...	1	
...	...	...	13	9	97	84	13	...	68	7	5	4	...	...	4	9	28
...	1	5	2	6	15	8	7	...	8	...	..	...	...	...	2	5	29
1	...	9	16	14	4	1	3	1	...	...	...	...	...	...	1	2	30
...	...	...	...	...	..	...	...	...	...	.	...	...	...	...	..	...	31
2	25	4	29	61	400	332	68	10	214	93	15	...	...	4	49	15	
...	1	2	12	16	198	189	9	7	120	57	5	...	...	3	6	...	32
1	4	2	8	15	110	84	26	3	50	23	8	...	...	1	20	5	33
...	1	...	8	20	36	20	16	...	7	13	...	...	...	...	12	4	34
...	29	...	1	10	56	39	17	...	37	...	2	...	...	...	11	6	35
...	...	...	...	...	...	...	...	..	...	..	...	...	...	...	...	..	36
2	...	...	34	27	159	128	31	14	78	22	14	...	...	...	13	18	
...	...	...	13	20	24	11	13	...	9	1	1	...	...	...	4	9	37
...	...	...	6	3	63	57	6	3	37	12	5	...	...	...	5	1	38
2	...	...	8	3	35	30	5	7	14	1	8	...	...	...	1	4	39
...	...	...	7	1	37	30	7	4	18	8	...	...	...	...	3	4	40
2	...	2	13	7	383	301	82	...	69	82	5	145	51	...	29	2	
2	...	2	13	7	376	294	82	...	63	81	5	145	51	...	29	2	41
...	...	...	...	...	4	4	...	...	4	...	...	...	...	...	...	...	42
...	...	...	...	...	3	3	...	...	2	1	...	...	...	...	...	...	43

Serial No.	District or State.	Section D.—Silk Weavers.																		
		MALES.								FEMALES.								Total.		
		Total.			Agricultural.					Total.			Agricultural.							
		All.	Agricultural.	Non-Agricultural.	1, 2a, Landlord.	2a, Cultivating owner.	2b, Cultivating tenant.	2c, Agricultural labourer.	4, Taungya cultivator.	All.	Agricultural.	Non-Agricultural.	1, 2a, Landlord.	2a, Cultivating owner.	2b, Cultivating tenant.	2c, Agricultural labourer.	4, Taungya cultivator.	All.	Agricultural.	Non-Agricultural.
	1	2	3	4	5	6	7	8	9	10	11	12	13	14	15	16	17	18	19	20
	Provincial Total ...	164	158	6	.	87	29	41	1	232	195	37	20	94	49	22	10	926	786	140
	Divisional Burma ..	163	157	6	...	87	29	41	...	232	195	37	20	94	49	22	10	872	746	126
	Arakan Division ...	...	...	...	...	...	...	...	...	2	2	...	...	2	...	...	...	18	16	2
1	Akyab ...	...	...	...	...	...	...	...	...	...	...	...	...	...	...	...	...	14	12	2
2	Hill Dt. of Arakan ...	...	...	...	...	...	..	...	...	..	...	...	...	...	...	...	...	...	...	...
3	Kyaukpyu ...	...	...	...	..	...	...	...	..	...	...	...	...	...	...	...	..	3	3	...
4	Sandoway ...	...	...	...	...	...	.	...	..	2	2	...	...	2	...	...	...	1	1	...
	Pegu Division ...	...	...	...	...	...	...	...	..	3	...	3	...	...	...	...	...	104	95	9
5	Rangoon Town ...	...	...	..	...	...	...	...	...	...	...	...	..	...	...	...	...	...	...	...
6	Insein ...	...	...	...	...	...	...	...	...	...	...	...	...	...	...	...	..	4	4	...
7	Hanthawaddy ...	...	...	...	...	..	...	...	...	...	...	...	...	...	...	..	...	16	15	1
8	Tharrawaddy ...	...	...	...	...	...	...	...	...	...	...	...	...	...	...	...	...	19	18	1
9	Pegu ...	...	...	..	...	...	...	...	...	...	...	..	...	...	...	...	...	1	1	...
10	Prome ...	...	...	...	...	...	...	..	...	3	...	3	..	...	..	...	...	64	57	7
	Irrawaddy Division ...	39	39	...	...	...	..	39	...	1	1	...	...	...	1	...	...	118	96	22
11	Bassein ...	...	...	...	...	...	...	...	...	...	...	...	...	...	...	...	...	69	53	16
12	Henzada ...	39	39	...	...	.	...	39	...	...	...	...	...	...	...	...	...	44	39	5
13	Myaungmya ...	...	...	...	...	...	...	...	...	...	...	...	...	...	.	...	...	1	1	...
14	Ma-ubin ...	...	...	...	...	...	...	...	...	...	...	...	...	...	...	..	...	3	2	1
15	Pyapôn ...	...	..	...	...	...	...	...	...	1	1	...	...	...	1	...	...	1	1	...
	Tenasserim Division ...	...	...	...	...	...	...	...	...	26	17	9	1	4	2	...	10	91	69	22
16	Toungoo ...	...	..	...	...	...	...	...	...	...	...	...	...	...	...	..	...	5	5	...
17	Salween ...	...	...	...	...	...	...	...	...	...	...	...	...	..	...	..	...	1	...	1
18	Thatôn ...	...	...	...	...	...	...	...	...	...	...	...	...	...	...	...	...	62	43	19
19	Amherst ...	...	...	...	...	...	...	...	...	...	...	..	...	..	...	...	..	21	20	1
20	Tavoy ...	...	...	...	...	...	...	...	...	26	17	9	1	4	2	...	10	...	...	...
21	Mergui ...	...	...	...	...	...	...	...	...	...	...	...	...	..	...	...	...	2	1	1
	Magwe Division ...	27	26	1	...	5	21	...	...	116	97	19	14	44	37	2	...	137	106	31
22	Thayetmyo ...	...	...	...	...	...	...	...	...	...	...	...	...	...	...	..	...	40	39	1
23	Pakôkku ...	27	26	1	...	5	21	...	...	116	97	19	14	44	37	2	...	67	42	25
24	Minbu ...	...	...	...	..	...	...	..	...	...	...	...	...	...	...	...	...	17	13	4
25	Magwe ...	...	..	...	..	...	..	...	...	...	...	...	..	...	...	..	...	13	12	1
26	Pakôkku Hill Tracts	...	...	...	...	...	...	...	...	...	...	...	...	...	...	...	..	...	...	...
	Mandalay Division ...	2	1	1	...	...	1	...	...	1	...	1	...	...	...	...	...	107	97	10
27	Mandalay ...	2	1	1	...	..	1	...	...	1	...	1	...	...	...	...	..	60	52	8
	Mandalay City ...	*1*	...	*1*	...	...	...	...	...	*1*	...	*1*	...	...	...	...	...	2	...	2
28	Bhamo ...	...	...	...	...	...	...	...	...	...	...	...	...	...	...	...	...	1	1	...
29	Myitkyina ...	...	...	...	...	..	...	...	...	..	...	...	...	...	...	...	...	...	...	...
30	Katha ...	...	...	...	...	...	...	...	...	...	...	...	...	...	...	..	...	46	44	2
31	Putao ...	...	...	...	...	..	...	...	...	...	..	...	...	...	...	...	...	...	...	...
	Sagaing Division ...	93	89	4	...	81	6	2	...	79	74	5	5	42	9	18	...	195	170	25
32	Shwebo ...	22	19	3	...	12	5	2	..	44	42	2	5	25	9	3	...	100	97	3
33	Sagaing ...	3	3	...	..	3	...	..	...	1	...	1	...	...	...	...	.	23	20	3
34	Lower Chindwin ...	68	67	1	...	66	1	...	...	1	1	...	...	1	...	...	...	60	45	15
35	Upper Chindwin ...	..	...	...	...	...	...	...	..	33	31	2	...	16	...	15	...	12	8	4
36	Chin Hills ...	...	...	..	...	...	...	...	...	...	..	...	...	...	...	...	..	...	...	...
	Meiktila Division ...	2	2	...	.	1	1	...	...	4	4	...	...	2	...	2	...	102	97	5
37	Kyaukse ...	..	.	.	...	...	...	...	...	...	...	...	...	...	..	...	...	3	3	...
38	Meiktila ...	...	...	...	...	...	..	.	...	4	4	...	...	2	...	2	...	31	29	2
39	Yamèthin ...	2	2	...	...	1	1	...	...	...	...	...	...	..	...	...	...	10	10	...
40	Myingyan ...	...	...	...	...	...	...	...	..	...	...	...	...	...	...	...	..	58	55	3
	Eastern States ...	1	1	...	...	...	...	...	1	...	...	...	...	...	...	...	...	54	40	14
41	Northern Shan States	1	1	...	...	...	...	...	1	...	...	...	...	...	...	...	...	54	40	14
42	Southern Shan States	..	...	...	...	...	...	...	..	...	...	...	...	...	.	.	...	...	...	...
43	Karenni ..	..	...	...	...	...	...	..	...	...	...	...	..	...	.	...	...	...	...	...

Persons who by subsidiary occupations are Silk or Cotton Weavers.

Section E.—Cotton Weavers.

MALES.							FEMALES.															
Agricultural.					Non-Agricultural.		Total.			Agricultural.					Non-Agricultural.							
1, 8a, Landlord.	8a, Cultivating owner.	8b, Cultivating tenant.	8c, Agricultural labourer.	4, Taungya cultivator.	5, 6, 7, Gardener.	Others.	All.	Agricultural.	Non-Agricultural.	1, 8a, Landlord.	8a, Cultivating owner.	8b, Cultivating tenant.	8c, Agricultural labourer.	4, Taungya cultivator.	5, 6, 7, Gardener.	191, Money-lender or pawn-broker.	186a, Wholesale grain dealer.	186, Retail grain-dealer.	Toddy or jaggery.	Other traders.	Others.	Serial No. of District, etc. (column 1).
21	22	23	24	25	26	27	28	29	30	31	32	33	34	35	36	37	38	39	40	41	42	
17	475	147	126	21	36	104	44,848	40,529	4,319	1,007	25,120	6,194	4,929	3,279	244	30	58	121	568	1,584	1,714	
17	451	146	122	10	29	97	36,894	33,028	3,866	954	20,863	6,047	4,735	429	138	30	58	49	568	1,354	1,669	
...	9	3	2	2	...	2	697	534	163	36	246	110	81	61	4	2	...	5	...	93	59	
...	6	2	2	2	...	2	298	207	91	23	49	64	26	45	3	2	...	5	...	45	36	1
...	...	...	...	...	...	...	...	...	...	...	...	..	...	...	...	...	...	...	...	...	..	2
...	3	...	..	..		...	99	71	28	3	49	9	7	3	...	...	...	...	...	25	3	3
...	...	1	..	...	...	...	300	256	44	10	148	37	48	13	1	...	...	...	...	23	20	4
5	32	17	38	3	2	7	3,744	3,517	227	120	1,290	634	1,415	58	34	6	6	...	...	105	76	
...	...	...	...	...	...	...	...	...	...	...	...	...	...	...	...	...	...	...	...	...	...	5
...	..	2	2	...	...	...	48	41	7	1	7	9	24	...	..	...	...	...	...	5	2	6
...	...	...	15	...	1	...	13	7	6	...	...	3	4	..	5	...	...	...	...	...	1	7
...	4	7	7	...	...	1	637	601	36	9	104	103	385	.	8	.	...	...	...	6	22	8
1	...	...	...	...	...	...	125	116	9	5	13	37	61	...	...	...	...	...	..	4	5	9
4	28	8	14	3	1	6	2,921	2,752	169	105	1,166	482	941	58	21	6	6	...	...	90	46	10
...	38	36	22	...	3	19	1,429	1,273	156	36	519	288	418	12	35	...	9	1	...	67	44	
...	27	16	10	...	2	14	360	325	35	9	119	56	141	...	6	...	2	1	...	20	6	11
...	9	20	10	...	1	4	968	855	113	22	386	202	233	12	27	...	5	..	..	47	34	12
...	1	...	...	...	...	...	13	9	4	...	...	5	4	...	...	...	2	..	...	...	2	13
...	...	...	2	...	..	1	77	73	4	4	11	21	37	...	2	...	...	...	...	...	2	14
...	1	...	...	...	...	...	11	11	...	1	3	4	3	...	...	...	...	...	...	...	...	15
...	13	22	33	1	8	14	2,707	2,397	310	31	1,119	512	655	80	43	...	1	4	...	89	173	
...	1	...	4	...	...	...	111	90	21	9	12	29	39	1	3	...	...	...	.	7	11	16
...	...	...	...	...	...	1	...	...	...	...	...	...	...	...	...	..	...	...	...	...	...	17
...	7	14	22	...	8	11	896	709	187	6	394	92	214	3	26	...	...	2	...	38	121	18
...	4	8	7	1	..	1	1,625	1,546	79	13	686	379	395	73	12	...	1	2	...	27	37	19
...	...	...	...	...	...	..	68	46	22	3	24	12	4	3	2	...	..	...	...	16	4	20
...	1	...	..	...	...	1	7	6	1	...	3	...	3	...	...	...	...	...	...	1	...	21
5	73	24	2	2	14	17	8,453	7,142	1,311	233	4,628	1,782	421	78	14	7	21	13	405	430	421	
...	29	8	...	2	...	1	1,288	1,228	60	28	989	123	16	72	...	2	...	4	...	14	40	22
4	31	7	...	...	14	11	4,925	3,951	974	128	2,565	1,036	216	6	7	3	17	...	380	263	304	23
...	5	6	2	...	...	4	1,370	1,115	255	41	553	392	129	...	6	2	4	7	25	144	67	24
1	8	3	...	...	...	1	870	848	22	36	521	231	60	...	1	..	..	2	...	9	10	25
...	...	...	...	...	...	...	...	...	...	...	...	...	...	..	...	...	..	...	...	...	..	26
...	75	15	5	2	...	10	2,872	2,685	187	16	2,159	292	181	37	1	1	...	3	...	83	99	
..	38	11	3	..	...	8	367	333	34	8	187	78	57	3	...	...	...	3	...	24	7	27
...	..	...	...	...	...	2	...	...	...	...	...	...	...	...	...	...	...	...	..	...	...	
...	...	...	...	1	...	...	55	52	3	1	39	1	2	9	...	...	...	...	...	3	...	28
...	...	...	...	...	...	...	5	5	...	...	3	..	—	2	...	...	...	...	...	...	...	29
...	37	4	2	1	...	2	2,445	2,295	150	7	1,930	213	122	23	1	1	...	...	...	56	92	30
...	...	...	...	...	...	...	...	...	...	...	...	...	...	...	...	...	...	...	...	...	...	31
4	128	24	14	...	1	24	11,988	11,097	891	327	7,543	2,021	1,111	95	5	7	16	18	131	305	409	
..	81	8	8	...	...	3	5,280	5,143	137	88	4,400	312	343	...	1	2	2	...	1	35	96	32
...	13	6	1	...	...	3	4,469	3,936	533	135	2,354	911	536	...	4	4	14	2	130	212	167	33
3	28	9	5	...	1	14	1,777	1,623	154	104	547	786	186	...	...	1	...	15	...	...	138	34
1	6	1	...	...	..	4	381	314	67	...	242	12	46	14	...	..	...	1	...	58	8	35
...	...	...	...	...	..	...	81	81	...	...	...	...	...	81	...	...	...	...	..	—	...	36
3	83	5	6	...	1	4	5,004	4,383	621	155	3,359	408	453	8	2	7	5	5	32	182	388	
...	3	...	...	.	...	..	271	241	30	9	131	32	69	...	...	...	...	...	...	10	20	37
2	27	...	...	...	...	2	1,678	1,508	170	58	1,234	74	140	2	1	2	4	..	19	87	57	38
...	7	2	1	...	...	...	535	466	59	22	313	31	99	1	...	...	...	2	...	16	41	39
1	46	3	5	...	1	2	2,530	2,168	362	66	1,681	271	145	5	1	5	1	3	13	69	270	40
...	24	1	4	11	7	7	7,954	7,501	453	53	4,257	147	194	2,850	106	...	...	72	...	230	45	
...	24	1	4	11	7	7	7,921	7,473	448	51	4,237	144	192	2,849	106	...	...	72	...	229	41	41
...	...	...	...	...	.	...	33	28	5	2	20	3	2	1	...	...	...	...	...	1	4	42
...	...	...	...	...	...	...	...	...	...	...	...	...	...	...	...	...	...	...	...	..	...	43

IMPERIAL TABLE XX.

Occupations by Race.

NOTE 1.—This table takes account only of principal occupations. In Part I the population associated with each class or sub-class of occupations in Imperial Table XVII is classified by *Peoples*, the statistics being given in each case for the whole province and for selected *Natural Divisions* (which are defined in Note 4 below). Part II gives in a similar statement the numbers of each people associated with selected occupational orders and groups. Part III gives for all occupational sub-classes and orders a similar statement which has however been contracted by combining the 13 peoples into 8 racial divisions and shows only the total figures for the whole province in each case. Parts I and III may also be regarded as giving a classification of each people by principal occupation.

NOTE 2.—The titles given to the *peoples* in the column-headings of the table are only rough indications of their racial compositions which are fully shown in the appendices A and B which follow Part III of the table (page 448). Reference may also be made to Parts IV and V and Note 9 of Imperial Table XIII.

NOTE 3.—The titles of the classes, sub-classes, orders and groups of occupations are explained in Part I of Imperial Table XVII, as also are the terms *Worker* and *Dependent*. The columns headed *Total Supported* show the sum of workers and dependents of both sexes.

NOTE 4.—The *natural divisions* by which statistics are given in Parts I and II are named the *Burman, Chin, Salween, Shan*; and the Burman division is divided into four natural subdivisions called *Delta, Coast, Centre* and *North.* Further particulars of the natural divisions are given in Part II of the Introduction to the report volume. The districts and states included in each of the natural divisions and subdivisions are as follows:—

BURMAN.

Delta.	*Coast.*	*Centre.*	*North.*
Rangoon.	Akyab.	Prome.	Bhamo.
Insein.	Kyaukpyu.	Thayetmyo.	Myitkyina.
Hanthawaddy.	Sandoway.	Pakôkku.	Katha.
Tharrawaddy.	Amherst.	Minbu.	Putao.
Pegu.	Tavoy.	Magwe.	Upper Chindwin.
Bassein.	Mergui.	Mandalay.	
Henzada.		Shwebo.	
Myaungmya.		Sagaing.	
Ma-ubin.		Lower Chindwin.	
Pyapôn.		Kyauksè.	
Toungoo.		Meiktila.	
Thatôn.		Yamèthin.	
		Myingyan.	

CHIN.	SALWEEN.	SHAN.
Hill District of Arakan.	Salween.	Northern Shan States.
Chin Hills.	Karenni States.	Southern Shan States.
Pakôkku Hill Tracts.		

NOTE 5.—This table takes the place of the following Imperial Tables prescribed for other provinces of India:—

Table XX.—Distribution by religion of workers and dependents in different occupations.

Table XXI, Part A.—Occupations of selected castes, tribes or races.

Table XXI, Part B.—Distribution of workers in certain groups of occupations by caste, tribe or race.

Class or Sub-Class of Occupation and Natural Division of the Province.	All Races. Total.	All Races. Workers. Males.	All Races. Workers. Females.	People I—Burma and Mon Groups. Total supported.	Workers. Males.	Workers. Females.	People II—Christian Karens. Total supported.	Workers. Males.	Workers. Females.	People III—Non-Christian Karens. Total supported.	Workers. Males.	Workers. Females.	People IV—Other Indigenous Races. Total supported.	Workers. Males.	Workers. Females.	People V—Chinese. Total supported.	Workers. Males.	Workers. Females.
1	2	3	4	5	6	7	8	9	10	11	12	13	14	15	16	17	18	19
All Occupations	13,169,099	4,080,981	2,734,317	8,998,753	2,514,258	1,921,541	178885	50,223	39,578	1,042,131	306207	240595	1746,737	549992	454400	149060	73,571	57,9[illegible]
Burman	11,496,993	3,520,016	2,283,858	8,803,488	2,452,770	1,873,078	162095	45,651	35,250	791,476	233232	175289	612,576	184387	135620	95,856	51,669	4,987
Delta	4,820,745	1,565,440	859,240	3,326,947	934,418	631,040	147635	41,273	33,601	683,158	201356	152620	53,355	16,532	10,243	64,276	33,866	3,266
Coast	1,598,493	484,740	247,281	1,059,556	286,707	188,256	11,362	2,823	1,333	101,093	29,747	21159	92,371	27,660	17,252	16,258	8,301	909
Centre	4,405,770	1,261,273	1,037,804	4,163,484	1,157,255	1,003,992	2,400	1,021	297	7,075	2,013	1,434	83,529	26,112	19,927	8,220	5,090	39[illegible]
North	671,985	209,063	139,427	253,501	74,390	49,799	698	534	19	150	116	3	383,321	114083	88,198	7,102	4,452	400
Chin	151,030	50,163	51,016	2,282	801	502	22	11	1	1	1	...	145,929	47,863	50,464	53	22	...
Salween	114,229	35,205	23,657	4,302	1,599	496	10,324	2,838	2,725	80,138	21,139	17,215	17,661	6,371	3,179	334	267	15
Shan	1,406,841	457,537	375,993	188,681	59,085	47,463	5,784	1,723	1,612	170,526	51,835	48,166	970,571	318371	265227	52,817	21,683	13,046
CLASSES.																		
A. Production of raw materials ...	9,875,097	2,843,137	2,016,578	6,550,748	1,855,236	1,350,991	159777	44,582	37,294	979,223	286321	215394	1872,442	465586	362834	56,630	22,452	11,9[illegible]
Burman	8,335,093	2,415,098	1,674,817	6,471,442	1,818,460	1,323,482	144972	40,533	33,066	752,857	223260	165631	540,824	160623	122937	14,825	8,317	755
Delta	3,430,448	1,021,021	648,168	2,444,984	695,145	452,204	133028	37,386	31,610	649,024	192860	143879	42,322	13,338	7,501	5,185	2,050	329
Coast	1,234,959	355,259	180,782	819,545	228,157	131,266	10,192	2,473	1,220	97,024	28,431	20,402	85,952	25,412	16,019	7,481	4,568	294
Centre	3,141,375	883,268	726,170	3,024,637	843,211	702,876	1,457	399	232	6,703	1,821	1,348	74,914	22,802	18,029	357	283	22
North	528,321	155,550	119,107	182,276	51,047	37,067	295	275	4	106	28	4	337,636	99,071	81,382	1,802	1,376	110
Chin	146,698	47,848	50,955	1,730	595	486	4	4	..	...	...	...	144,667	47,137	50,439	..	...	—
Salween	97,888	26,414	21,139	1,509	519	148	9,525	2,308	2,656	77,242	19,871	16,704	9,393	3,401	1,622	16	16	...
Shan	1,099,908	353,777	270,251	116,067	35,662	26,944	5,276	1,557	1,572	149,124	43,190	43,064	777,559	254425	187387	41789	15,[illegible]	11,271
B. Industry and commerce ...	2,282,919	727,098	530,819	1,713,062	403,488	468,251	4,881	1,362	697	28,192	6,226	8,266	97,874	27,802	26,298	72,429	38,[illegible]	4,343
Burman	2,116,948	691,293	506,960	1,684,931	393,853	462,958	4,793	1,382	689	22,034	4,200	7,131	41,071	11,650	9,852	65,452	34,686	2,589
Delta	974,554	348,425	175,523	641,203	149,051	152,626	4,211	1,095	639	19,375	3,565	6,441	7,843	2,030	2,294	47,817	26,839	2,376
Coast	254,052	84,060	54,414	169,628	35,963	47,536	350	81	41	2,430	590	609	4,547	1,441	1,065	7,692	3,378	874
Centre	911,291	233,650	261,809	833,102	197,074	253,141	181	115	8	208	34	80	5,110	1,579	1,556	6,729	4,033	296
C. Public service and the professions and liberal arts.	462,007	214,983	27,760	309,429	135,849	12,834	10,393	3,283	969	12,461	6,311	480	58,607	30,942	1,680	2,806	1,098	275
Burman	397,859	178,825	16,128	301,526	131,889	12,489	9,410	2,940	924	6,950	2,785	374	14,876	6,315	611	2,251	838	138
Delta	260,072	67,681	6,706	115,673	47,784	4,324	7,849	2,119	827	5,936	2,265	322	1,117	470	91	1,534	477	111
Coast	45,905	17,664	1,980	33,740	12,185	1,015	679	216	60	868	358	49	1,060	425	41	404	180	18
Centre	162,566	79,672	6,525	140,856	67,913	6,093	667	470	36	136	84	3	2,371	1,326	48	215	126	8
D. Miscellaneous	720,076	275,708	169,266	385,564	119,682	89,465	3,174	997	618	22,265	7,339	6,556	117,813	25,662	64,127	37,185	20,405	1,444
Burman	546,583	134,800	86,536	345,589	108,568	74,218	2,920	866	571	9,635	3,057	2,080	15,805	5,799	2,220	13,328	7,008	425
Delta	255,671	128,313	28,852	125,187	42,458	21,886	2,547	673	535	8,823	2,666	1,978	2,073	694	357	10,840	5,580	360
Coast	63,577	27,257	10,105	36,643	10,402	7,829	141	53	12	771	368	99	812	382	197	941	581	57
Centre	198,538	64,683	43,390	164,889	49,057	41,882	95	57	21	28	14	2	1,134	405	294	919	668	32
SUB-CLASSES.																		
I. **Exploitation of animals or vegetation.**	9,632,020	2,816,117	2,013,577	6,560,721	1,844,847	1,348,898	159635	44,532	37,294	979,017	286076	215336	1467,602	463133	361631	50,680	18,006	11,88[illegible]
Burman	8,299,800	2,394,216	1,671,268	6,449,839	1808,136	1,322,532	144862	40,505	33,066	752,662	223215	165620	536,812	158714	122203	11,567	8,316	726
Delta	3,428,032	1,019,916	647,999	2,443,646	694,734	452,067	133024	37,383	31,610	648,096	192850	143878	42,243	13,310	7,495	5,128	2,034	318
Coast	1,224,528	349,803	180,380	813,875	225,996	130,887	10,096	2,448	1,220	96,857	28,396	20,393	85,289	25,259	15,015	4,815	1,930	281
Centre	3,123,629	872,001	724,8[illegible]	3,021,306	836,174	701,557	1,457	399	232	6,703	1,881	1,348	74,897	22,790	18,028	347	218	22
Shan	1,087,835	347,645	270,215	115,743	35,597	26,944	5,245	1,516	1,572	149,113	43,190	43,064	776,752	253882	187368	30,098	12,479	11,159
Ia. **Control of land or water used for the exploitation of animals or vegetation.**	157,135	36,896	40,732	128,094	28,662	34,279	3,763	806	949	7,114	1,987	2,349	8,288	2,827	1,803	449	200	36
Burman	150,983	34,207	39,449	126,974	28,401	33,883	3,757	803	949	6,786	1,910	2,250	3,558	786	1,108	448	199	36
Delta	60,037	13,821	13,035	46,233	10,014	9,534	3,702	786	943	6,399	1,901	2,108	755	192	875	275	137	28
Coast	23,074	5,152	5,348	16,671	3,986	4,283	47	12	6	324	97	123	450	104	122	139	54	8
Centre	64,980	14,578	20,549	62,292	14,004	19,595	8	5	...	62	11	26	1,319	247	555	33	8	...
Shan	6,090	2,367	1,236	1,118	261	396	3	2	...	250	59	80	4,692	2,036	754	1	1	...
Ib. **Cultivated and wild plants** ..	9,239,997	2,689,311	1945,333	6,264,478	1,785,948	1,293,461	154422	42,820	36,186	967,423	281185	211190	1,445,216	454334	356[illegible]	46,872	16,[illegible]	11,64[illegible]
Burman	7,929,699	2,276,492	1606,852	6,151,422	1,721,313	1,266,499	139663	38,900	31,959	742,107	219355	162,758	527,527	155396	120415	8,318	3,643	585
Delta	3,272,126	968,982	621,743	2,321,100	658,909	431,054	128395	36,143	30,518	639,455	189778	141334	41,228	12,964	7,306	3,596	1,849	193
Coast	1,149,219	325,786	171,543	756,536	209,073	123,895	9,874	2,330	1,211	96,046	27,959	20,201	82,907	24,205	15,613	3,642	1,636	233
Centre	3,002,623	836,029	697,242	2,900,981	805,111	675,656	1,365	316	232	6,561	1,791	1,320	73,032	22,247	17,357	235	156	17
Shan	1,066,422	338,833	266,477	109,642	33,595	26,328	5,236	1,511	1,572	148,199	12,813	42,8[illegible]	763,903	248507	184567	38,539	12,147	11,157
Ic. **Domestic and wild animals** ...	235,080	90,220	27,512	176,249	60,237	21,158	1,450	906	159	4,480	2,104	749	14,218	5,972	2,758	2,360	1,898	207
Burman	219,188	83,517	24,968	171,443	58,428	20,938	1,442	902	158	3,769	1,750	612	5,727	2,532	687	2,801	1,674	166
Delta	95,869	37,183	13,212	76,313	25,811	11,479	927	454	155	3,142	1,271	543	260	154	14	1,259	648	97
Coast	52,235	18,865	3,445	40,668	12,937	2,781	175	106	3	487	340	68	1,932	950	280	1,035	646	40
Centre	57,036	21,394	7,249	48,033	17,959	6,308	84	78	...	80	79	1	546	296	116	79	54	5
Shan	15,321	6,445	2,502	4,783	1,811	220	6	3	...	664	318	136	8,157	3,337	2,047	558	324	42
II. **Exploitation of minerals** ...	40,886	27,020	2,995	31,907	10,389	2,093	142	50	...	196	45	11	4,848	2,453	784	5,948	2,440	48
Burman	35,808	20,882	2,958	21,603	10,324	2,095	110	28	...	195	45	11	4,012	1,909	734	3,238	2,802	29
Delta	2,430	1,805	178	1,338	481	137	14	3	...	28	10	1	79	28	6	57	26	1
Coast	10,431	5,456	453	5,670	2,161	379	96	25	...	167	35	10	663	155	4	2,686	2,232	15
Centre	17,748	12,367	1,330	13,331	7,837	1,589	...	...	...	...	...	...	17	12	1	10	5	—

Classes and Sub-Classes of Occupations by Peoples.

People VI—Burma Moslems.			Peoples VII and VIII—Other Muhomedans (i.e., all not in People V or VI). VII.—Born in Burma.			VIII.—Born outside Burma.			Peoples IX and X—Hindus, Indian Animists, Sikhs, Aryas, and Bramos. IX.—Born in Burma.			X.—Born outside Burma.			People XI—European and allied races.			People XII—Anglo-Indians.			People XIII—Others.		
Total supported.	Workers. Males.	Workers. Females.	Total supported.	Workers. Males.	Workers. Females.	Total supported.	Workers. Males.	Workers. Females.	Total supported.	Workers. Males.	Workers. Females.	Total supported.	Workers. Males.	Workers. Females.	Total supported.	Workers. Males.	Workers. Females.	Total supported.	Workers. Males.	Workers. Females.	Total supported.	Workers. Males.	Workers. Females.
20	21	22	23	24	25	26	27	28	29	30	31	32	33	34	35	36	37	38	39	40	41	42	43
117,957	27,512	23,328	218,046	51,803	15,564	163,770	133,703	3,752	99,763	19,126	6,033	395,655	309,197	18,169	8,317	5,580	375	26,688	4,374	1,159	32,695	15,429	1,756
116,818	27,311	12,277	216,895	51,610	15,414	161,819	131,493	3,693	96,691	18,846	6,162	383,628	279,442	17,972	7,924	3,315	351	16,327	4,238	1,153	32,920	15,002	1,728
19,308	6,211	3,158	31,976	6,516	2,938	96,024	80,200	1,757	67,471	12,473	3,649	280,950	216,041	14,783	4,570	3,051	248	10,955	2,891	853	24,180	10,618	1,172
47,345	12,156	3,909	161,643	41,119	10,397	41,860	33,488	1,541	10,415	2,080	795	41,818	35,666	1,340	540	362	40	1,834	430	138	3,929	2,263	284
38,818	8,057	6,068	13,993	3,212	1,980	18,412	14,074	359	13,989	2,834	1,655	46,371	36,008	1,870	2,643	1,786	70	3,196	771	162	4,380	1,880	302
1,427	887	160	1,283	825	110	3,683	3,121	36	4,816	619	83	15,009	10,727	619	102	116	3	342	146	6	691	847	18
2	2	...	35	7	...	65	58	...	913	96	12	2,500	1,263	29	33	14	4	12	8	...	188	124	2
94	5	3	153	20	23	479	395	3	78	10	1	370	504	3	22	19	1	5	2	.	69	36	5
863	194	38	903	100	122	2,401	1,567	55	2,061	180	58	10,957	9,088	165	336	172	9	344	126	6	838	277	26
54,166	12,877	8,374	166,194	40,648	9,993	25,040	24,821	1,567	45,777	9,426	2,803	103,602	74,895	8,385	877	422	4	805	226	24	9,904	4,665	607
54,048	12,855	5,163	166,083	40,620	9,976	24,868	24,586	1,500	45,279	8,361	2,799	90,517	71,376	8,309	506	375	4	707	192	23	9,755	4,600	595
7,812	1,560	1,078	9,916	2,007	1,280	15,056	12,562	534	37,786	6,718	2,238	76,472	52,967	7,058	140	80	...	305	64	17	7,818	3,642	444
32,517	8,751	2,188	140,815	37,033	7,447	17,605	10,571	455	3,010	981	342	9,800	8,455	576	107	66	1	202	70	6	1,473	691	126
13,018	2,542	1,940	6,870	1,607	1,217	1,559	1,241	84	2,688	452	169	9,053	7,663	363	233	201	2	170	49	...	383	207	13
125	36	17	212	53	26	240	203	12	1,755	210	50	4,102	2,891	412	36	19	1	24	9	...	241	70	8
...	...	...	5	2	...	3	5	...	147	21	9	125	79	19	...	...	...	...	...	...	17	7	2
81	1	2	32	4	3	63	49	1	10	5	1	40	29	...	3	3	...	...	...	...	25	8	8
77	22	10	134	22	14	306	241	6	378	89	14	3,941	3,411	57	68	33	...	58	34	1	107	50	11
47,956	9,609	7,308	36,325	7,339	3,984	96,600	82,566	2,438	31,040	6,037	2,760	173,852	136,642	6,984	2,628	1,749	37	6,892	1,850	220	10,038	4,992	389
47,482	9,514	7,286	35,605	7,471	3,857	94,868	80,354	1,404	30,384	5,970	2,723	170,877	132,962	6,907	2,587	1,727	37	6,804	1,812	220	10,001	4,832	387
16,371	3,240	1,909	17,106	3,263	1,409	63,034	52,918	839	17,275	3,145	953	120,684	99,028	5,580	1,823	1,245	29	4,937	1,112	186	7,198	3,260	232
10,328	2,125	1,532	12,837	2,917	1,762	19,474	17,081	312	5,030	1,544	371	20,352	17,308	556	272	141	...	504	181	10	1,402	976	48
19,742	3,983	3,727	5,350	1,188	685	10,516	8,267	233	7,189	1,275	1,572	20,203	14,997	652	546	306	8	1,328	316	22	1,859	515	99
8,922	1,380	82	9,606	1,012	72	8,625	7,057	90	8,308	2,480	70	28,060	21,659	195	2,760	2,496	276	5,258	1,169	603	3,732	1,286	130
5,855	1,351	81	4,810	1,004	71	8,556	6,702	98	7,081	1,368	67	24,480	18,622	193	3,601	2,419	263	5,144	1,132	599	3,648	1,245	127
1,601	389	20	1,402	288	33	3,374	2,400	68	2,917	558	24	10,354	7,817	119	1,765	1,174	180	3,338	746	404	2,612	854	93
2,135	585	18	2,163	505	20	1,121	963	8	490	108	6	2,143	1,832	10	157	69	34	624	104	85	341	134	15
2,001	416	42	862	196	16	2,782	2,295	16	2,875	536	35	6,137	4,733	54	2,598	2,122	48	1,052	227	107	614	228	19
8,826	2,663	783	20,931	2,805	2,344	23,097	20,459	654	24,626	3,013	598	92,201	76,295	2,605	2,360	854	58	3,724	1,127	321	9,800	4,497	630
8,894	4,590	747	10,647	2,575	1,513	22,587	19,531	637	13,087	3,153	373	88,834	74,482	2,506	1,229	794	57	3,672	2,102	311	9,516	4,325	618
2,524	1,096	151	3,392	894	204	13,740	11,936	316	9,693	2,012	414	66,910	56,832	1,957	842	543	39	2,378	769	246	6,495	2,856	409
2,565	605	831	5,528	1,262	1,103	4,850	4,278	200	2,285	487	70	8,913	8,071	198	106	86	5	809	135	50	714	462	37
2,804	766	239	1,811	361	122	3,415	2,911	51	3,507	571	79	10,278	8,615	321	860	157	12	746	179	33	2,184	942	171
52,096	13,825	8,182	166,089	40,806	9,979	56,094	22,945	1,563	43,548	8,387	2,826	96,042	67,693	8,337	243	154	6	571	146	24	9,779	4,881	607
53,817	13,798	5,841	165,923	40,583	9,963	34,124	23,824	1,556	45,031	8,332	2,728	94,735	66,769	8,264	232	140	4	565	143	23	9,655	4,532	592
7,720	1,535	1,075	9,970	2,034	2,253	15,550	11,451	530	37,751	6,783	2,238	75,442	52,500	7,035	100	60	...	262	53	17	7,810	3,699	444
32,394	8,726	2,819	149,578	37,015	7,412	17,283	10,480	955	3,481	917	335	9,193	7,847	557	55	37	1	154	48	6	1,448	678	126
13,578	3,814	2,937	6,255	2,460	1,212	1,043	718	59	2,949	445	169	5,545	4,284	261	57	38	2	135	35	...	257	148	13
57	16	9	196	13	13	104	69	6	551	29	14	1,362	847	54	11	5	...	8	3	1	84	34	11
2,093	230	434	4,908	604	646	727	298	82	387	67	33	805	604	44	30	22	1	236	45	12	209	35	6
1,293	258	433	4,935	604	686	709	192	82	383	67	30	833	604	43	30	22	1	135	25	22	200	35	4
472	37	74	691	63	71	434	255	41	317	45	25	601	439	31	11	10	...	66	11	9	81	29	3
981	135	285	4,058	513	517	215	107	40	33	5	4	152	120	7	4	2	...	14	3	2	6	4	1
258	184	831	173	25	38	54	27	1	33	17	4	58	88	4	14	10	...	84	10	...	12	2	...
2	1	2	...	...	...	8	5	...	24	...	3	...	...	2	...	...	...	1	...	2	...	...	...
47,272	12,000	4,002	155,628	38,160	9,015	31,020	28,123	2,310	40,398	7,430	2,480	77,789	54,360	7,297	209	109	3	290	107	11	8,978	4,070	578
47,838	12,190	4,305	155,324	38,146	9,089	30,922	21,651	2,310	40,199	7,430	2,430	77,328	54,087	7,165	103	124	3	383	104	11	8,926	4,038	565
6,804	2,397	940	8,447	1,826	1,148	13,925	11,449	480	35,349	6,109	2,059	66,066	44,935	6,452	87	48	...	182	37	7	7,425	3,398	429
20,586	7,038	2,000	141,504	34,983	6,761	16,505	9,879	888	3,853	900	307	7,898	6,679	507	50	35	1	115	41	4	1,284	534	123
18,745	2,841	1,442	5,831	2,300	1,279	304	217	17	732	809	49	1,989	1,700	61	48	27	2	78	22	...	251	86	9
33	10	5	65	9	11	55	43	1	187	83	3	378	237	23	11	5	...	7	3	...	35	10	4
4,309	1,088	396	5,521	1,840	338	2,367	1,820	169	4,820	870	347	17,482	12,725	1,096	4	2	...	48	14	1	706	474	30
4,306	1,350	393	2,474	1,833	334	2,493	1,790	164	4,429	835	326	16,370	12,078	1,058	4	3	...	43	14	1	685	444	28
444	209	52	738	163	64	1,128	749	59	2,080	479	154	9,275	7,136	552	2	2	...	14	5	1	304	222	18
1,847	649	83	3,939	1,517	106	308	474	87	895	82	26	1,188	1,040	43	2	...	...	25	4	...	158	140	2
1,975	481	264	701	189	95	685	467	41	2,257	229	119	3,408	2,450	196	2	1	...	3	3	...	94	60	4
20	5	3	89	6	4	41	22	5	310	16	8	783	580	37	...	...	...	...	...	...	59	24	7
272	60	83	230	44	26	948	876	4	209	29	7	7,680	7,000	48	334	257	...	234	80	...	205	84	...
251	27	82	180	27	13	744	702	4	208	29	7	4,808	4,607	45	274	226	...	144	49	...	182	68	...
92	18	3	46	15	8	100	96	4	35	5	...	830	467	23	40	29	...	43	21	...	8	3	...
123	35	16	37	18	5	187	221	...	129	14	7	692	608	19	52	39	...	54	28	...	25	13	...
33	8	2	25	3	5	586	490	...	39	7	...	3,508	2,479	2	176	163	...	25	14	...	66	49	...

IMPERIAL TABLE XX.—*Occupations by Race.* PART I.—

Class or Sub-Class of Occupation and Natural Division of the Province.	All Races.			People I—Burma and Mon Groups.			People II—Christian Karens.			People III—Non-Christian Karens.			People IV—Other Indigenous races.			People V—Chinese.		
	Total.	Workers. Males.	Workers. Females.	Total supported.	Workers. Males.	Workers. Females.	Total supported.	Workers. Males.	Workers. Females.	Total supported.	Workers. Males.	Workers. Females.	Total supported.	Workers. Males.	Workers. Females.	Total supported.	Workers. Males.	Workers. Females.
1	2	3	4	5	6	7	8	9	10	11	12	13	14	15	16	17	18	19
III. Industry	870,807	280,631	203,217	681,609	175,826	181,950	1,800	516	200	9,554	2,030	2,997	28,285	7,189	8,744	16,800	10,074	967
Burman	843,409	272,456	197,259	671,786	171,597	180,694	1,762	492	201	8,723	1,780	2,918	14,381	3,082	4,203	15,200	9,265	825
Delta	299,108	124,525	43,429	187,799	53,540	35,038	1,530	418	175	7,423	1,471	2,491	3,041	754	1,038	11,350	7,035	476
Coast	90,404	26,976	21,974	64,986	13,979	18,839	184	49	24	1,216	298	370	1,521	317	582	2,313	1,215	287
Centre	432,903	112,827	127,683	407,143	100,364	124,239	43	20	2	78	7	56	3,045	886	1,081	1,124	718	55
IV. Transport	254,274	177,404	15,938	211,782	75,300	13,384	756	228	78	2,057	789	85	9,867	4,235	886	2,600	2,007	28
Burman	339,284	170,266	14,862	206,683	73,298	13,092	747	218	78	1,463	496	59	3,686	1,820	174	1,804	1,278	17
Delta	159,549	88,867	3,628	75,209	26,185	2,446	665	188	77	1,156	386	55	590	213	17	833	534	8
Coast	46,199	27,967	862	20,174	7,888	597	28	6	1	290	100	6	281	92	23	452	283	4
Centre	122,247	47,204	10,065	105,562	36,600	9,856	26	14	...	21	4	...	639	277	43	208	232	...
V. Trade, finance and insurance ...	1,096,828	269,058	321,864	829,621	152,340	270,927	2,305	604	417	16,581	2,445	5,078	59,700	16,878	16,666	[illegible]	26,874	2,348
Burman	1,034,255	249,572	294,840	806,462	148,958	269,272	2,284	607	410	11,848	1,924	4,154	23,074	5,858	5,475	48,428	24,063	2,677
Delta	515,897	135,035	128,466	378,095	69,386	115,142	2,016	489	387	10,796	1,708	3,897	4,212	1,063	1,239	35,334	17,690	1,872
Coast	117,449	29,117	31,578	84,468	14,096	28,100	138	26	16	924	192	233	2,745	1,032	400	4,727	1,874	332
Centre	356,241	73,629	124,061	380,397	60,110	119,046	112	81	6	119	23	24	1,426	416	432	5,344	3,003	241
VI. Public force	76,400	37,628	469	28,303	12,806	268	1,289	900	6	379	294	18	4,708	2,478	85	207	32	26
Burman	68,527	33,479	304	37,416	11,549	189	1,199	854	6	402	185	...	2,627	1,699	52	67	28	4
Delta	24,248	11,148	106	15,118	4,634	74	409	245	5	245	78	...	45	15	3	39	7	4
Coast	6,885	2,834	66	4,511	1,209	60	138	90	1	72	45	...	165	70	...	25	8	...
Centre	27,264	13,255	75	16,236	5,197	48	480	427	...	77	55	...	1,078	949	3	8	8	...
VII. Public administration ...	103,041	23,240	992	61,661	18,071	462	1,904	609	15	2,162	1,040	46	20,418	6,928	224	988	272	264
Burman	82,826	26,029	795	59,686	17,404	438	1,714	523	13	2,101	675	29	4,179	1,296	77	703	180	189
Delta	36,897	11,897	388	24,178	7,053	116	1,501	456	10	1,867	609	27	250	75	8	324	83	157
Coast	10,832	3,113	46	7,112	1,738	17	148	42	2	208	55	2	409	107	10	306	45	1
Centre	28,688	9,107	320	25,523	7,742	277	41	14	...	26	11	...	483	145	6	27	14	1
VIII. The professions and liberal arts	280,966	144,113	26,299	209,455	103,972	12,104	7,180	1,784	948	8,721	4,978	426	[illegible]	22,820	1,272	[illegible]	880	70
Burman	246,616	119,387	15,029	204,484	102,936	11,862	6,407	1,363	905	4,447	1,855	345	8,070	3,480	483	1,481	700	75
Delta	99,027	44,636	6,247	76,377	36,097	4,134	5,879	1,418	802	3,824	1,578	295	828	380	83	981	447	80
Coast	28,188	11,727	2,868	22,127	9,238	1,538	393	84	57	588	258	47	486	248	32	286	187	17
Centre	105,614	57,310	6,140	99,097	54,974	5,768	146	39	36	23	18	3	843	232	30	280	204	7
IX. Persons (not in Sub-class Ia) without an occupation but receiving an income.	13,800	3,030	1,875	7,703	1,704	700	203	40	8	53	17	8	298	60	60	287	80	28
Burman	13,055	3,076	1,104	7,639	1,713	688	183	40	3	81	16	8	290	45	10	281	56	16
Delta	6,039	1,166	569	3,065	430	329	146	30	2	40	12	6	29	2	2	227	44	21
Coast	2,810	428	247	1,212	291	167	8	2	...	7	...	2	76	5	...	25	3	5
Centre	4,485	1,269	264	2,255	948	182	26	4	...	...	...	...	29	8	...	19	9	2
X. Domestic service ...	72,669	43,039	8,001	20,670	8,070	4,898	445	52	284	613	256	190	12,640	6,906	289	2,279	2,280	900
Burman	58,455	33,597	6,845	20,035	7,896	4,491	436	49	281	465	79	155	625	399	39	1,620	1,049	188
Delta	29,756	18,162	3,345	5,798	2,328	1,675	387	37	254	421	68	153	57	33	7	1,058	687	183
Coast	6,723	4,491	849	1,569	598	642	14	3	6	39	9	2	45	15	24	180	109	5
Centre	19,843	9,515	2,556	11,904	4,588	2,114	28	6	20	5	2	1	141	85	3	157	240	5
XI. Insufficiently described occupations.	572,641	202,609	149,094	283,626	88,869	77,379	2,603	847	300	20,634	6,696	6,065	98,079	14,988	[illegible]	[illegible]	6,877	260
Burman	430,332	172,928	69,658	284,710	78,320	62,354	2,198	722	263	8,585	2,577	2,849	13,516	4,727	2,898	72,026	6,400	140
Delta	200,708	97,909	22,947	204,876	30,805	18,022	1,928	567	256	7,997	2,336	1,754	1,894	595	308	[illegible]	4,436	98
Coast	48,875	19,373	7,483	81,317	7,780	6,595	105	35	5	585	239	94	998	247	90	[illegible]	400	6
Centre	147,895	43,839	35,543	131,596	33,579	34,718	48	24	2	14	4	1	780	877	253	668	445	24
XII Unproductive and unclassified	48,966	26,790	10,896	22,345	20,805	6,792	103	55	24	965	320	284	6,486	1,749	1,788	858	587	280
Burman	44,743	25,199	8,929	32,205	20,639	6,685	103	58	24	534	385	68	1,484	628	276	480	360	39
Delta	27,170	11,077	1,991	11,455	8,875	1,278	66	39	23	365	250	65	93	64	20	273	160	28
Coast	6,169	2,975	1,846	2,545	1,733	437	14	13	1	160	127	2	153	128	23	78	60	1
Centre	29,324	10,360	5,037	18,294	9,648	4,859	3	3	...	9	8	1	114	238	28	75	70	1

Classes and Sub-Classes of Occupations by Peoples.

People VI—Burma Moslems.			Peoples VII and VIII—Other Mahomedans (i.e. all not in People V or VI).						Peoples IX and X—Hindus, Indian Animists, Sikhs, Aryas, and Bramos.						People XI—European and allied races.			People XII—Anglo-Indians.			People XIII—Others.		
			VII.—Born in Burma.			VIII.—Born outside Burma.			IX.—Born in Burma.			X.—Born outside Burma.											
Total supported.	Workers.		Total supported.	Workers.		Total supported.	Workers.		Total supported.	Workers.		Total supported.	Workers.		Total supported.	Workers.		Total supported.	Workers.		Total supported.	Workers.	
	Males.	Females.		Males.	Females.		Males.	Females.		Males.	Females.		Males.	Females.		Males.	Females.		Males.	Females.		Males.	Females.
20	21	22	23	24	25	26	27	28	29	30	31	32	33	34	35	36	37	38	39	40	41	42	43
11,307	2,700	1,800	9,052	1,780	1,003	22,104	19,325	236	13,944	2,732	1,512	70,978	56,063	3,623	916	530	11	1,426	440	35	2,002	1,432	196
11,247	2,674	1,529	8,952	1,774	1,218	21,866	19,127	329	13,778	2,717	1,507	70,472	55,663	3,613	907	525	11	1,397	432	35	2,992	1,428	196
3,727	954	273	3,165	645	228	15,538	13,818	136	7,477	1,362	357	54,090	42,729	3,016	592	346	11	1,087	340	30	2,289	1,113	140
2,779	537	393	4,155	743	845	3,353	2,938	116	2,373	683	195	7,178	6,076	241	25	18	...	99	14	...	224	115	22
4,532	1,158	758	1,509	373	143	2,652	2,102	75	3,590	618	945	8,278	6,181	311	267	141	...	189	69	5	453	185	33
7,029	1,880	226	6,403	1,903	140	33,675	31,098	107	8,496	1,978	173	62,475	54,129	826	1,014	770	9	4,058	1,090	83	3,030	1,670	22
6,859	1,853	114	6,223	1,912	115	33,409	31,065	105	8,336	1,958	172	62,114	52,948	822	1,001	760	9	3,096	1,060	83	2,963	1,615	22
8,759	685	44	2,730	795	53	19,330	17,782	67	5,188	1,102	123	45,572	38,722	643	686	551	3	2,754	719	76	2,077	1,073	18
2,102	631	21	2,587	997	47	10,086	9,791	21	1,389	428	29	7,990	7,264	120	126	101	...	305	80	3	389	308	...
1,803	503	47	759	185	12	3,182	2,772	11	1,460	357	20	7,073	5,738	64	177	97	6	842	219	3	453	208	3
29,608	8,029	5,672	20,860	3,826	2,587	40,803	30,952	995	8,602	1,326	1,055	39,398	26,096	2,536	688	449	17	1,417	322	102	4,184	1,886	172
29,375	4,987	5,653	20,490	3,785	2,524	39,593	30,192	970	8,276	1,295	1,044	38,291	25,351	2,472	679	442	17	1,411	320	102	4,046	1,789	170
9,885	1,601	1,592	11,371	1,913	1,128	28,186	21,315	636	4,510	721	473	27,022	17,574	1,930	545	348	15	1,096	253	80	2,829	1,072	75
5,449	957	1,088	5,595	1,177	870	6,035	4,958	175	1,268	233	147	5,184	3,968	205	18	22	...	100	27	7	788	555	24
13,407	2,297	2,942	3,082	630	460	4,683	3,393	147	2,067	300	407	4,852	3,078	277	102	68	2	197	28	14	353	122	63
843	271	8	800	146	11	5,308	4,468	12	2,589	438	10	27,981	25,064	18	1,940	1,437	...	666	290	...	358	164	...
829	269	5	809	144	11	5,273	4,435	12	2,460	346	10	14,594	12,288	26	1,908	1,442	...	655	186	...	294	156	...
226	43	2	276	65	6	1,632	1,362	2	408	133	1	4,559	3,949	9	630	444	...	368	99	...	153	74	...
286	82	1	104	17	1	403	357	1	85	14	1	985	890	1	28	120	...	75	27	...	18	26	...
299	45	2	355	54	2	2,244	1,263	9	685	78	6	4,314	3,533	5	1,226	954	...	167	40	...	108	60	...
2,008	450	18	1,431	270	10	987	784	2	1,644	285	3	4,838	3,263	24	490	293	8	2,202	681	13	2,086	408	4
1,989	449	18	1,410	267	8	975	772	1	1,602	282	3	4,686	3,150	24	430	253	8	2,134	608	13	1,267	409	4
594	129	3	470	89	5	634	483	1	1,128	208	...	3,016	1,887	10	197	126	3	1,512	447	12	1,038	318	4
785	208	5	771	137	...	126	112	...	872	30	2	628	539	3	53	31	3	251	40	1	63	29	...
378	107	9	151	40	3	168	130	...	233	38	1	890	637	11	164	85	2	297	93	...	137	45	...
3,070	742	98	2,363	596	52	2,338	1,805	79	3,095	737	89	5,312	3,330	153	1,332	746	268	2,389	346	590	2,340	718	146
3,027	734	58	2,341	593	52	2,308	1,785	79	3,019	734	54	5,120	3,186	152	1,270	724	255	2,358	338	586	2,087	689	123
781	157	28	656	134	22	1,308	955	65	1,281	223	23	3,279	1,981	100	958	604	177	1,438	200	382	1,423	462	89
2,084	296	12	1,288	351	19	582	494	7	233	64	3	540	403	6	76	28	31	288	37	85	269	89	15
1,124	264	31	356	102	11	370	293	7	1,357	423	28	933	561	38	218	88	46	586	94	107	369	128	19
902	200	98	742	102	96	630	332	47	771	39	30	954	424	54	123	83	10	784	172	60	301	86	14
886	120	98	725	102	96	616	324	47	599	38	29	773	334	54	115	47	9	785	167	60	288	74	14
290	48	30	478	69	26	489	246	39	220	15	21	361	103	32	72	24	7	422	98	44	195	47	10
227	44	18	117	21	20	5	1	3	47	14	6	31	4	11	4	3	1	111	25	14	10	5	...
358	27	50	118	22	9	97	59	5	168	6	1	296	125	20	31	17	...	184	41	2	74	19	4
2,277	544	269	1,289	393	128	6,109	5,271	161	3,548	503	189	27,903	24,463	638	86	53	17	120	48	27	8,920	2,702	420
1,349	534	267	1,263	387	115	6,015	5,304	153	3,502	890	189	17,635	14,229	630	83	52	27	128	47	26	3,414	2,682	404
478	198	46	617	142	56	3,886	3,429	119	2,145	582	125	11,480	9,051	484	64	46	15	71	20	16	3,303	1,633	240
443	194	58	313	144	38	828	746	13	363	104	22	2,483	1,249	28	7	6	1	13	6	...	456	398	21
400	132	61	278	83	20	1,118	952	20	930	254	40	3,238	2,559	109	12	...	11	20	11	9	1,800	103	148
6,243	1,698	287	6,608	1,549	696	15,169	13,609	124	8,272	2,069	324	70,134	60,514	1,800	1,121	744	20	2,690	922	187	3,720	2,620	96
5,686	1,630	251	6,367	1,525	630	14,521	13,010	116	7,868	2,023	300	68,307	58,982	1,489	1,101	681	20	2,649	837	187	3,598	1,304	64
2,380	738	70	2,126	562	104	8,649	7,694	62	5,479	1,384	253	53,434	46,399	1,183	677	460	16	1,744	598	162	2,842	1,135	30
1,299	373	83	3,052	710	419	3,482	3,257	34	793	333	21	6,817	5,703	98	95	77	2	347	47	6	205	129	1
1,886	501	194	1,030	217	88	2,082	1,797	17	1,324	248	25	7,315	5,765	190	283	140	1	525	186	18	493	186	15
696	306	131	2,298	562	714	1,389	946	322	2,025	202	55	2,130	994	393	30	14	2	181	82	38	227	66	126
693	306	231	2,292	561	714	1,388	943	321	2,018	202	55	2,121	987	391	30	14	1	180	81	38	216	65	126
175	215	5	172	125	28	716	567	96	1,849	103	15	1,665	679	258	29	13	2	138	43	24	155	42	109
256	85	72	2,026	387	681	545	269	216	82	36	27	182	115	61	...	...	...	37	7	10	43	20	15
220	106	54	85	49	15	119	103	9	87	63	13	186	166	12	...	...	...	4	1	4	27	4	42

Order No.	Group No.	Names and Areas.	All Races. Total.	All Races. Workers. Males.	All Races. Workers. Females.	People I—Burma and Mon Groups. Total supported.	Workers. Males.	Workers. Females.	People II—Christian Karens. Total supported.	Workers. Males.	Workers. Females.	People III—Non-Christian Karens. Total supported.	Workers. Males.	Workers. Females.	People IV—Other Indigenous races. Total supported.	Workers. Males.	Workers. Females.	People V—Chinese. Total supported.	Workers. Males.	Workers. Females.
		1	2	3	4	5	6	7	8	9	10	11	12	13	14	15	16	17	18	19
I	1	Ownership and rights over land or water used for occupations of sub-class *Ib* or *Ic*	147,-64	33,419	40,732	119,757	26,061	34,288	3,669	768	948	7,081	1,971	2,348	8,191	2,803	1,882	410	192	96
		Delta	56,391	12,681	13,035	43,116	9,216	9,541	3,624	757	942	6,378	1,794	2,100	750	191	175	272	137	58
		Coast	21,644	4,570	5,341	15,450	3,542	4,284	39	8	6	384	97	123	439	104	182	190	52	8
		Centre	60,928	13,221	20,349	58,434	12,696	19,593	2	2	...	60	11	26	1,318	247	555	6	3	—
IIa	All	Cultivation	9,158,932	2657,681	1937,779	6197,266	1730,637	1286,755	153699	42,506	36,170	965,719	281504	222160	1436,751	450762	356408	46,616	15,653	11,628
		Delta	3,245,908	959,112	619,883	2298,607	650,645	429,397	127950	35,934	30,502	638,525	189466	141131	40,702	12,777	7,245	5,571	1,837	292
		Coast	1,140,031	383,350	170,192	750,066	207,453	122,674	9,690	,274	1,207	95,497	37,745	20,177	81,702	24,061	15,554	3,602	1,215	331
		Centre	2,972,098	823,986	694,216	2872,190	793,416	672,652	1,331	302	231	6,551	1,784	1,321	72,722	22,086	17,347	228	149	17
		Agriculture proper—																		
	8a	Cultivating owners	4,054,042	1265,537	903,255	2758,444	767,348	620,578	62,230	18,562	12,797	426,001	123287	105780	697,902	220824	152976	4,905	2,027	774
		Delta	886,424	255,619	184,601	540,221	151,132	109,762	51,429	15,857	10,372	25?,085	74,456	59,144	11,707	3,517	2,282	593	485	46
		Coast	447,530	122,174	79,122	257,230	79,903	56,743	3,572	802	458	44,058	13,818	11,281	27,863	7,890	5,022	730	260	58
		Centre	1,828,866	509,234	452,721	1760,924	491,822	419,990	325	80	47	4,308	1,169	850	42,418	12,964	10,055	71	41	7
	8b	Cultivating tenants	1,814,164	512,362	331,178	1459,371	402,414	274,417	25,723	7,112	5,558	133,624	40,026	28,713	90,259	28,516	16,867	909	318	47
		Delta	750,407	226,218	123,463	560,274	165,301	89,801	25,245	6,987	5,460	117,057	38,995	24,613	7,432	2,357	1,149	489	228	26
		Coast	255,410	66,605	35,919	177,694	45,423	29,589	342	82	56	6,435	1,917	1,835	10,227	2,690	1,650	173	59	17
		Centre	701,973	186,070	150,602	681,628	179,887	146,328	7	7	...	357	96	85	16,331	4,760	3,708	15	11	2
	8c	Agricultural labourers	2,085,806	622,185	405,405	1674,144	476,260	334,760	29,170	8,220	7,238	197,281	59,887	41,431	60,982	19,734	14,256	1,368	778	109
		Delta	1,416,039	419,500	269,385	1126,674	314,284	215,377	28,516	8,083	7,113	185,142	56,140	38,899	11,989	3,?17	2,163	875	513	59
		Coast	254,186	81,203	23,510	182,417	57,028	19,912	544	122	42	8,459	2,607	1,584	5,327	1,628	368	204	84	13
		Centre	349,258	101,209	94,322	343,217	98,862	93,044	9	2	4	348	96	97	3,333	1,180	785	86	66	5
	6b	Rubber cultivation	9,189	5,620	807	3,163	980	409	125	28	4	88	24	15	193	65	30	71	35	4
IID	18	Silk-worms	912	571	205	559	437	39	...	..	...	14	4	7	140	130	...	—	...	—
VI	27	Cotton sizing and weaving	65,913	1,846	46,863	50,083	1,635	41,504	26	1	19	2,107	33	2,648	4,297	78	3,509	41	7	20
		Centre	45,948	1,489	32,099	45,428	1,468	31,753	—	—	—	3	2	1	387	14	251	—	—	—
	28	Silk-weaving	29,436	2,936	18,041	26,752	2,233	16,794	4	4	...	47	...	43	1,439	504	577	87	7	5
		Coast	955	6	718	887	5	685	...	...	...	...	...	—	...	...	...	10	—	8
		Centre	28,371	2,927	17,231	25,887	2,228	16,081	4	4	...	46	—	43	1,370	504	513	5	5	—
VIII		Wood	214,170	79,498	24,870	177,143	58,087	22,706	335	118	37	2,857	850	446	8,405	2,845	1,205	9,336	6,367	148
		Delta	84,845	33,510	9,010	65,077	20,500	8,062	270	98	25	2,295	639	404	1,080	316	317	7,278	5,487	127
		Coast	28,938	11,246	2,246	21,713	6,941	1,783	46	14	9	357	140	33	781	215	275	896	392	5
		Centre	84,248	27,821	12,752	81,692	26,540	12,585	5	...	2	12	2	3	398	168	42	484	307	8
VIII, XIV	44, 88a, 88b	Carpenters, turners, joiners, cabinet-makers, polishers, carriage-painters, etc.	91,762	36,770	2,338	73,480	26,080	1,926	112	4	4	956	359	16	3,444	1,147	231	8,926	6,010	137
IX	All	Metals	41,776	16,690	1,037	32,045	11,509	889	25	12	1	910	317	17	2,702	1,008	73	665	405	11
		Delta	17,600	7,228	277	12,803	4,413	327	25	10	1	572	170	9	282	99	4	324	274	6
		Coast	4,470	1,923	61	2,965	1,096	34	—	...	..	233	112	7	227	82	3	86	56	5
		Centre	15,612	5,807	501	14,824	5,374	585	—	—	—	...	...	..	64	37	2	48	31	...
X	55	Potters and earthen pipe and bowl makers	17,055	3,129	7,628	16,127	2,706	7,442	10	3	6	77	1	18	228	52	105	37	37	—
XIII	77	Tailors, milliners, dress-makers, darners and embroiderers on linen	64,971	19,466	17,635	51,388	13,252	15,120	143	11	81	751	93	379	1,915	281	984	1,520	580	429
	78	Shoe, boot and sandal makers	21,776	5,539	1,162	8,304	3,438	1,052	18	17	—	26	9	—	227	81	27	1,340	903	37
VIII, XIV	88a, 88b, 44	Cabinet-makers, polishers, carriage-painters, carpenters, turners, joiners, etc.	91,762	36,770	2,338	73,480	26,080	1,926	112	40	4	956	359	16	3,444	1,147	231	8,926	6,010	137
XVI	90	Making, assembling, or repairing cycles or motor land-vehicles	1,590	800	17	960	444	3	7	2	—	10	4	3	6	4	—	17	9	—
XXII	118	Railway employees of all kinds other than labourers, doctors, police, sweepers and postal service	18,000	9,716	322	2,465	859	11	79	25	—	14	11	—	49	15	...	66	19	—
	119	Labourers of all kinds associated with railways (excluding sweepers)	9,774	6,160	506	7,323	700	310	2	1	—	2	—	1	185	44	55	126	126	..
XXIII	120	Postal, telegraph and telephone services	9,328	4,503	145	3,419	1,414	68	63	32	—	20	8	—	335	188	1	24	13	...
XXIV	121	Credit, finance and insurance	22,210	8,706	2,909	14,059	5,704	2,595	78	28	13	238	37	64	301	101	55	935	364	40
XXVI	126	Trade in cotton, silk, hair or other textiles or in piece-goods	58,306	14,881	17,104	37,266	6,205	15,458	26	3	10	377	69	87	2,478	635	787	2,112	1,080	186
		Delta	17,918	6,470	2,887	8,783	1,570	2,399	28	3	8	268	33	75	260	80	118	1,071	486	50
		Coast	4,740	1,780	1,115	2,354	368	969	8	—	2	84	23	9	115	35	26	285	96	20
		Centre	28,141	4,038	12,326	24,891	3,781	11,894	—	—	—	1	1	..	154	37	63	338	199	17
XXXIII	136a	Wholesale grain and pulse dealers and brokers	59,590	15,645	7,648	49,395	11,298	6,815	212	54	10	543	150	97	958	171	468	2,339	996	70
		Delta	39,018	9,651	4,388	32,700	7,177	4,126	222	49	9	395	73	80	198	49	26	1,080	789	41
		Coast	6,408	2,464	254	4,256	1,116	194	9	4	1	132	76	7	34	8	6	167	54	22
		Centre	12,778	3,371	9,457	11,944	2,933	7,404	...	...	...	6	1	1	33	12	4	158	111	4
XLIV	159	Police	65,327	29,767	448	37,071	11,386	859	975	662	6	553	266	18	4,098	3,124	85	106	30	95
		Delta	22,417	9,936	105	14,024	4,545	73	4'3	230	5	248	72	...	45	15	3	39	7	4
		Coast	6,511	2,529	66	4,459	1,208	60	128	80	1	71	48	—	165	70	—	13	8	—
		Centre	21,558	9,608	58	15,229	4,868	40	836	188	—	55	35	—	839	727	3	9	5	—
LII	188	Private motor-drivers and cleaners	1,533	887	4	741	458	2	4	3	1	4	4	—	3	—	...	—	..	—

Selected Orders and Groups of Occupations by Peoples.

People VI—Burma Moslems.			Peoples VII and VIII—Other Mahomedans, (i.e. all not in People V or VI). VII.—Born in Burma.			VIII.—Born outside Burma.			Peoples IX and X—Hindus, Indian Animists, Sikhs, Aryas and Bramos. IX.—Born in Burma.			X.—Born outside Burma.			People XI—European and allied races.			People XII—Anglo-Indians.			People XIII—Others.		
Total supported.	Workers. Males.	Workers. Females.	Total supported.	Workers. Males.	Workers. Females.	Total supported.	Workers. Males.	Workers. Females.	Total supported.	Workers. Males.	Workers. Females.	Total supported.	Workers. Males.	Workers. Females.	Total supported.	Workers. Males.	Workers. Females.	Total supported.	Workers. Males.	Workers. Females.	Total supported.	Workers. Males.	Workers. Females.
20	21	22	23	24	25	26	27	28	29	30	31	32	33	34	35	36	37	38	39	40	41	42	43
2,191	351	432	4,876	593	626	633	333	81	374	61	35	468	275	42	3	2	1	41	3	21	70	26	3
441	31	72	672	61	71	382	215	40	298	39	25	360	215	30	1	1	—	34	2	9	63	24	2
212	124	225	4,047	514	517	202	94	40	33	5	4	48	28	6	...	—	—	6	1	2	4	8	1
824	175	131	156	18	38	46	23	1	29	17	1	52	28	4	1	1	...	..	—	—	...	—	—
46,960	12,105	4,197	155,300	38,063	8,908	30,626	21,416	1,304	40,083	7,381	2,436	76,734	53,528	7,146	86	52	3	204	52	11	8,886	4,028	572
6,695	1,348	946	8,338	1,801	1,139	15,790	11,262	399	35,200	6,178	2,056	65,515	44,437	6,443	45	21	...	98	15	7	7,412	3,387	429
28,453	7,901	1,794	142,424	34,928	6,755	16,176	9,801	882	3,201	888	304	7,646	6,524	487	54	28	1	92	29	4	1,249	510	182
10,691	2,820	1,439	5,351	1,297	1,075	277	158	16	704	203	49	1,918	1,646	58	6	3	2	14	8	...	118	74	9
21,420	5,111	2,279	63,721	15,157	5,292	6,164	4,171	427	10,236	1,375	605	11,572	7,140	1,685	9	6	...	28	7	6	2,350	522	96
2,187	396	405	2,923	535	408	2,590	1,908	128	8,495	1,038	438	9,013	5,907	1,536	9	6	..	15	..	4	2,079	382	76
12,584	3,039	1,029	56,252	13,517	4,029	3,151	2,106	286	1,032	229	127	717	516	75	...	...	...	7	2	2	174	92	12
6,618	1,665	834	4,458	2,079	846	127	79	10	267	71	27	299	236	12	—	...	—	6	5	—	45	25	8
13,761	5,511	991	46,385	10,928	2,265	10,620	6,252	577	12,577	1,525	470	17,178	10,539	1,055	1	1	...	14	3	2	3,642	1,222	216
2,254	411	274	2,495	466	361	4,020	3,204	120	11,732	1,286	412	16,427	9,995	1,003	2	1	...	9	3	...	2,972	984	154
8,898	2,351	425	43,247	10,315	1,739	6,534	2,907	452	778	199	45	502	353	40	...	—	—	3	...	2	637	219	61
2,649	747	291	602	137	163	51	58	4	140	35	13	170	139	7	...		—	2		...	21	13	..
10,561	3,194	776	43,817	11,693	1,303	12,905	10,337	250	15,544	4,080	1,238	36,426	25,918	3,798	6	2	2	29	23	3	3,578	2,069	241
2,098	497	253	2,440	726	318	6,797	5,850	129	14,259	3,648	1,140	34,031	23,931	3,682	2	1	...	24	10	3	3,201	1,980	189
7,168	2,311	218	41,111	10,895	919	6,048	4,435	121	998	353	90	1,587	1,408	62	—	—	..	—	—	...	385	132	46
1,264	385	298	252	69	64	44	36	..	110	41	4	549	464	13	4	1	2	5	3	...	57	26	6
198	47	11	99	27	2	91	78	7	263	52	15	4,730	4,180	310	44	35	—	112	28	—	54	41	—
124	—	103	39	..	37	...	...	...	36	...	29	...	...	—	—	...	—	—	...	...	...	—	—
91	...	71	135	1	22	7	5	..	95	2	68	13	10	2	...	...	...	...	...	—	18	14	...
60	—	49	15	1	9	6	4	—	47	—	36	—	..	—	...	...	—	...	—	—	—	...	...
301	60	134	29	9	12	19	10	...	795	95	466	12	10	...	—	...	...	—	...	—	22	4	10
80	...	25	—	—	—	1	1	—	...	...	...	—	..	...	...	..	—	—	...	—	7	...	3
221	60	109	29	9	12	17	8	...	795	95	466	12	10	—	...	—	—	...	...	...	15	4	7
1,661	478	105	1,240	287	77	1,982	1,838	5	1,151	191	61	9,324	8,185	76	112	78	...	154	46	1	269	128	2
875	177	19	310	67	9	1,001	913	1	496	100	4	6,165	5,531	40	45	32	...	68	22	1	188	88	1
802	170	29	836	197	62	823	776	4	402	56	21	2,333	2,096	24	14	10	...	59	9	—	65	31	1
438	122	58	74	21	6	236	127	—	227	31	36	707	462	12	37	22	...	23	11	—	17	8	—
653	202	8	480	137	2	926	853	2	474	116	3	2,120	1,746	8	9	5	...	6	2	—	176	73	1
847	137	13	433	65	15	1,133	1,039	3	661	200	8	2,557	1,954	7	13	7	—	39	9	...	56	28	—
199	49	6	276	44	13	910	854	1	336	58	4	1,793	1,321	6	10	5	—	37	7	—	45	24	—
170	44	6	84	12	2	63	54	2	242	128	2	398	377	—	1	1	—	—	...	—	2	1	—
158	40	1	55	5	—	146	119	—	47	10	2	257	186	1	2	1	...	2	2	...	9	2	—
12	1	3	83	13	6	66	38	12	85	10	5	360	272	38	...	—	...	...	—	—	—	...	—
1,651	342	264	1,402	286	141	4,333	3,786	48	274	66	28	1,357	820	125	9	8	...	42	14	8	186	90	28
84	28	7	53	17	1	114	70	1	305	81	1	1,250	877	33	...	—	—	—	...	—	37	18	3
683	202	8	480	137	2	926	853	2	474	116	3	2,120	1,746	8	9	5	—	6	2	—	176	73	1
190	69	5	64	11	6	52	28	...	19	8	—	211	187	...	31	23	—	14	5	...	15	6	—
531	206	2	650	167	4	2,132	1,728	6	1,746	271	35	7,781	5,680	237	198	127	6	2,334	406	12	985	309	9
83	41	4	145	20	16	391	277	5	495	93	16	5,664	4,823	100	1	1	...	301	3	...	58	22	2
356	94	.	398	93	3	563	415	4	554	89	...	2,238	1,708	8	102	72	3	931	265	57	336	147	4
283	32	34	279	29	26	282	210	8	543	107	21	4,663	3,801	20	93	71	—	150	22	32	329	200	2
2,648	884	400	1,665	277	101	5,411	4,314	72	547	73	48	2,390	1,567	51	16	13	...	22	2	1	344	149	83
852	186	59	1,137	129	58	4,012	3,194	47	157	21	11	1,100	684	25	15	12	...	20	2	1	223	70	53
299	73	82	254	77	23	671	574	13	50	10	...	567	471	1	...	—	...	1	—	—	74	50	—
2,375	288	269	226	64	20	436	307	6	248	27	34	448	258	13	1	1	...	1	...	...	28	5	20
1,260	279	61	989	231	40	1,359	1,157	10	407	65	15	1,682	1,127	35	16	14	...	67	23	10	343	82	19
689	152	28	587	99	28	696	550	6	296	42	7	963	584	23	14	12	...	56	20	6	300	55	21
329	64	12	383	113	2	565	546	1	28	11	—	540	444	5	2	2	...	9	3	4	24	25	—
242	59	21	62	16	12	68	59	2	61	11	8	133	74	1	..	—	—	2	...	—	9	5	—
788	162	3	741	136	10	3,297	2,683	9	2,847	318	10	13,611	11,586	12	212	118	—	578	173	—	251	126	—
197	39	2	270	65	6	1,398	1,156	2	308	68	1	4,001	3,526	9	111	49	—	335	96	...	134	63	—
285	81	1	104	17	1	275	238	1	82	13	1	787	722	1	12	5	—	72	26	—	18	18	—
275	40	—	286	45	2	1,167	911	6	554	65	6	2,480	2,034	1	90	38	—	113	26	—	68	28	—
200	86	1	65	4	—	76	84	...	44	9	...	380	280	—	...	—	—	25	20	...	15	9	—

SUB-CLASS OR ORDER. (Sub-Classes distinguished by italics.)	All Races.			Peoples I to IV—Indigenous Races.			People V—Chinese.		
	Total supported.	WORKERS.		Total supported.	WORKERS.		Total supported.	WORKERS.	
		Males.	Females.		Males.	Females.		Males.	Females
1	2	3	4	5	6	7	8	9	10
All Occupations	13,169,099	4,060,921	2,734,517	11,965,846	3,420,677	2,656,204	149,060	73,871	[illegible]
Ia } Control of land or water used for the exploitation of animals or I } vegetation.	157,135	36,596	40,732	147,259	34,282	39,460	449	200	36
Ib—Cultivated and wild plants ...	9,239,997	2,689,311	1,945,333	8,831,639	2,535,287	1,908,927	46,873	15,806	11,642
IIa—Cultivation	9,158,932	2,657,681	1,937,779	8,753,435	2,505,409	1,901,493	46,616	15,653	11,625
IIb—Forestry	81,065	31,630	7,554	78,104	29,878	7,434	257	153	17
Ic—Domestic and wild animals ...	235,080	90,210	27,512	196,297	69,219	24,824	3,360	1,998	207
IIc—Raising of farm-stock ...	72,611	34,985	10,205	45,996	20,362	8,153	2,426	1,380	174
IId—Raising of other animals ..	1,660	768	382	1,139	629	185	227	95	21
IIe—Exploitation of wild animals ...	160,809	54,457	16,925	149,162	48,228	16,486	707	523	[illegible]
II—Exploitation of minerals ...	42,885	27,020	2,995	27,086	12,937	2,858	5,948	5,449	41
III—Coal, petroleum and metals ...	28,136	19,486	856	14,764	7,288	804	4,729	4,384	23
IV—Minerals not of Order III or V ..	10,787	5,989	1,720	8,594	4,205	1,639	1,027	980	15
V—Minerals soluble in water ...	3,962	1,545	419	3,728	1,444	415	192	85	3
III—Industry	870,827	280,631	203,317	721,268	185,563	193,893	16,820	10,074	967
VI—Textiles	115,338	8,859	75,018	1,11,834	7,840	73,902	72	21	27
VII—Hides, feathers, bristles and hard materials from the animal kingdom.	1,067	537	53	700	230	39	97	77	4
VIII—Wood	214,170	79,498	24,870	188,741	61,900	24,394	9,536	6,367	148
IX—Metals	41,776	16,690	1,037	35,682	12,846	980	665	405	11
X—Ceramics	30,602	9,901	9,771	26,439	6,501	9,641	91	87	...
XI—Manufacture or refining of chemical products and analogous substances.	20,324	9,021	1,778	12,565	2,988	1,714	182	77	2
XII—Food	223,528	68,293	60,807	180,644	39,277	56,974	2,153	1,084	267
XIII—Dress and the toilet ..	114,864	41,144	26,057	82,739	23,045	23,233	3,092	1,546	473
XIV—Furniture	860	374	97	587	190	88	21	4	...
XV—Building	22,022	9,526	1,236	15,476	5,608	1,166	270	148	[illegible]
XVI—Construction of means of transport.	9,097	4,359	274	6,426	2,354	238	175	116	8
XVII—Production and transmission of physical forces.	577	177	5	311	85	5	20	10	..
XVIII—Other industries ...	76,602	32,252	2,314	59,134	22,699	1,519	446	192	32
IV—Transport	354,274	177,404	15,938	224,462	80,637	14,433	2,620	2,027	28
XIX—Transport by air (aeroplanes, etc., and aerodromes).	...	...	..	...	...	...	...	...	...
XX—Transport by water	118,083	64,920	2,350	76,496	28,771	2,076	589	404	5
XXI—Transport on land otherwise than by rail.	199,089	92,105	12,615	139,010	48,602	11,717	1,815	1,465	23
XXII—Transport by rail	27,774	15,876	828	5,119	1,655	374	192	145	...
XXIII—Postal, telegraph and telephone services.	9,328	4,503	145	3,837	1,609	66	24	13	...
V—Trade, finance and insurance ...	1,096,818	269,058	311,564	898,239	172,687	295,080	52,999	26,514	2,348
XXIV—Credit, finance and insurance	22,210	8,706	2,909	14,676	3,870	2,727	933	364	40
XXV—Brokerage, commission and auditing.	16,409	6,940	586	10,812	3,854	509	548	264	18
XXVI—Trade in cotton, silk, hair or other textile or in piece-goods.	55,306	14,881	17,194	40,151	6,912	16,349	2,128	1,020	156

and Orders by Eight Groups of Peoples.

People VI—Burma Moslems.			Peoples VII to X—Indians other than Buddhists, Christians, Jains and Parsis.						People XI—European and allied races.			People XII—Anglo-Indians.			People XIII—Others.		
			VII and IX.—Born in Burma.			VIII and X.—Born outside Burma.											
Total supported	WORKERS.		Total supported	WORKERS.		Total supported	WORKERS.		Total supported.	WORKERS.		Total supported.	WORKERS.		Total supported.	WORKERS.	
	Males.	Females		Males.	Females		Males.	Females		Males.	Females		Males.	Females		Males.	Females
11	12	13	14	15	16	17	18	19	20	21	22	23	24	25	26	27	28
117,257	27,511	13,318	387,809	70,929	21,797	560,427	442,900	21,920	8,317	5,520	375	14,688	4,374	1,159	33,695	15,439	1,756
2,295	359	434	5,322	671	659	1,542	1,002	126	30	22	1	136	25	12	102	35	4
47,271	12,201	4,211	195,959	45,610	11,457	108,785	76,099	8,509	209	129	3	390	107	11	8,971	4,072	578
46,962	12,105	4,197	195,383	45,444	11,428	107,360	74,944	8,450	86	52	3	204	52	11	8,886	4,022	572
309	96	14	576	166	29	1,425	1,155	59	123	77	...	186	55	...	85	50	1
4,329	1,255	506	10,331	2,710	679	20,008	14,537	1,265	4	2	..	45	14	1	706	474	30
1,693	523	228	6,487	1,705	461	15,579	10,776	1,159	1	1	...	16	5	1	413	233	29
147	1	116	97	3	57	49	40	3	...	...	...	...	...	...	1	...	...
2,489	731	162	3,747	1,002	161	4,380	3,721	103	3	2	..	29	9	...	292	242	1
271	62	23	859	73	21	8,528	8,078	52	334	257	...	234	80	..	125	84	...
163	46	1	144	35	7	7,669	7,322	21	331	256	...	220	77	...	116	78	...
101	15	22	182	25	13	859	756	31	3	1	...	13	2	...	8	5	...
7	1	...	33	13	1	...	...	...	...	...		1	1	...	1	1	...
11,327	2,700	1,920	22,996	4,513	2,737	92,082	75,278	3,958	926	530	11	1,416	440	35	3,002	1,422	196
808	161	333	1,971	340	737	580	475	9	...	..	..	5	...	...	48	22	10
7	1	..	38	27	...	224	201	10	..	...	..		...	...	1	...	...
1,661	478	106	2,391	478	138	11,306	10,023	81	112	78	...	154	46	1	269	128	2
547	137	13	1,084	265	23	3,690	2,993	10	13	7	...	39	9	...	56	28	...
91	27	8	494	164	23	3,441	3,094	97	...		.	...	...	...	46	28	2
325	78	6	451	129	11	5,626	5,185	31	454	266	..	489	186	4	242	110	18
3,005	559	646	4,847	713	938	32,095	26,840	1,937	181	99	5	249	64	7	354	237	33
2,419	558	359	6,669	1,352	691	19,303	14,393	1,207	18	16	...	61	17	8	563	283	66
59	21	4	45	21	..	148	138	5	...	...	...	...	.	...	...	...	..
1,074	276	19	1,177	247	20	3,873	3,185	30	8	2	...	25	9	...	110	51	...
437	150	7	201	55	8	1,752	1,622	19	47	32	...	40	21	...	19	9	...
40	10	..	38	6	...	69	41	...	8	4	...	69	13	..	22	8	...
834	264	19	3,590	716	148	10,975	7,687	522	75	32	6	285	75	15	1,263	587	53
7,019	1,880	116	14,899	3,901	315	97,150	85,427	933	1,014	770	9	4,058	1,090	83	3,052	1,672	21
...	...	...	...	...	...	...	.	...	...	...	...	...	...	...	...	...	...
1,359	250	8	2,544	804	25	34,874	33,447	29	599	517	...	916	213	5	706	520	2
4,690	1,389	102	8,372	2,364	216	43,537	37,356	543	114	59	...	576	205	9	975	665	5
614	147	6	3,034	551	71	15,938	12,501	349	199	128	6	1,635	409	12	1,043	340	10
356	94	...	949	182	3	2,801	2,185	10	102	72	3	931	263	57	328	227	4
29,608	5,029	5,672	29,462	5,162	3,642	80,221	57,009	3,631	688	449	17	1,417	320	102	4,184	1,886	170
253	32	34	821	136	47	4,945	4,181	28	93	71	...	150	22	31	330	100	2
557	144	13	634	102	11	3,376	2,395	30	69	50	2	95	38	3	218	98	...
2,648	554	400	2,212	350	149	7,801	5,881	123	16	13	...	22	2	1	344	149	23

SUB-CLASS OR ORDER. (Sub-Classes distinguished by italics.)	All Races.			Peoples I to IV—Indigenous Races.			People V—Chinese.		
	Total supported.	WORKERS.		Total supported.	WORKERS.		Total supported.	WORKERS.	
		Males.	Females.		Males.	Females.		Males.	Females.
1	2	3	4	5	6	7	8	9	10
V—Trade, finance and insurance—concld.									
XXVII—Trade in skins, leather, furs, feathers, horn, etc., and articles made from these not included in Order XXXIV or other order.	2,811	962	342	2,033	635	311	193	109	12
XXVIII—Trade in wood (not firewood), cork, bark, bamboo, thatch, etc., and articles made from these.	34,519	11,325	4,328	32,082	10,291	4,216	453	206	18
XXIX—Trade in metals, machinery, knives, tools, etc.	4,795	1,240	954	3,013	584	906	59	28	2
XXX—Trade in pottery, bricks and tiles	1,603	445	336	1,247	271	319	11	4	1
XXXI—Trade in chemical products ..	9,941	2,717	1,982	8,080	1,887	1,827	414	200	15
XXXII—Hotels, cafés, restaurants, etc.	49,662	17,567	9,822	30,888	6,152	8,814	7 565	4,413	369
XXXIII—Other trade in foodstuffs ..	357,040	75,839	111,743	303,482	53,006	105,581	10,293	4,647	712
XXXIV—Trade in ready-made clothing and other articles of dress and the toilet	8,410	2,[illegible]81	1,597	7,071	2,038	1,502	265	111	15
XXXV—Trade in household goods ...	17,907	4,154	6,651	15,612	3,281	6,421	177	104	5
XXXVI—Trade in building materials (other than bricks, tiles, thatch and woody materials).	11,865	2,205	5,827	11,464	2,015	5,785	75	21	34
XXXVII—Trade in means of transport	23,739	7,338	3,028	19,456	5,793	2,755	359	159	73
XXXVIII—Trade in fuel	11,568	3,732	1,832	9,488	2,648	1,656	188	134	8
XXXIX—Trade in articles of luxury and articles pertaining to letters or to the arts or sciences.	14,176	4,189	2,170	11,558	3,025	2,003	384	165	14
XL—Trade of other sorts	454,857	104,137	140,263	377,126	66,425	133,4[illegible]6	28,970	14,571	1,857
VI—Public force	*76 400*	*37,628*	*469*	*44,896*	*15,495*	*377*	*107*	*33*	*36*
XLI—Army	11,026	7,839	21	1,963	1,042	9	5	3	...
XLII—Navy	...	...	..	...	..	...	...	...	...
XLIII—Air force	...	...	...	.	...	...	...	...	..
XLIV—Police and professional village watchmen.	65,374	29,789	448	42,933	14,453	368	108	30	36
VII XLV } *Public administration* ...	*103,041*	*33,242*	*992*	*87,161*	*26,657*	*747*	*993*	*208*	*164*
VIII—The professions and liberal arts	*282,566*	*144,118*	*16,299*	*258,828*	*134,233*	*14,839*	*1,706*	*862*	*75*
XLVI—Religion	155,310	97,077	8,024	150,997	95,189	7,859	238	103	15
XLVII—Law	10,936	2,779	93	8,464	9,004	86	52	13	...
XLVIII—Medicine	56,258	20,564	3,332	49,026	17,726	2,817	611	276	6
XLIX—Instruction	33,794	11,940	2,955	27,456	9,274	2,330	573	303	45
L—Letters and arts and sciences ...	26,268	11,753	1,895	22,880	10,140	1,745	232	167	9
IX LI } *Persons (not in Sub-class Ia) without an occupation but receiving an income.*	*13,800*	*8.230*	*1,175*	*8,377*	*1,845*	*778*	*267*	*59*	*28*
X LII } *Domestic service*	*73,669*	*43,059*	*8,001*	*35,368*	*17,405*	*5,361*	*2,379*	*1,252*	*901*
XI LIII } *Insufficiently described occupations.*	*573,641*	*202,629*	*149,294*	*445,962*	*111,297*	*145,773*	*13.641*	*8,677*	*268*
XII—Unproductive and unclassified ...	*48,966*	*26,790*	*10,896*	*39,109*	*23,133*	*8,854*	*898*	*517*	*252*
LIV—Prisoners in jails, etc., and inmates of asylums and alms-houses.	16,324	15,827	497	14,381	14,043	338	343	342	1
LV—Beggars, vagrants, prostitutes, etc.	28,787	10,516	10,360	23,405	8,667	8.493	553	174	251
LVI—Other unproductive occupations and unclassified.	3,855	447	39	1,323	423	23	2	1	...

and Orders by Eight Groups of Peoples—concluded.

People VI—Burma Moslems.			Peoples VII to X—Indians other than Buddhists, Christians, Jains and Parsis. VII and IX.—Born in Burma.			VIII and X.—Born outside Burma.			People XI—European and allied races.			People XII—Indians.			People XIII—Others.		
Total supported	WORKERS. Males.	WORKERS. Females	Total supported	WORKERS. Males.	WORKERS. Females	Total supported	WORKERS. Males.	WORKERS. Females	Total supported.	WORKERS. Males.	WORKERS. Females	Total supported.	WORKERS. Males.	WORKERS. Females	Total supported.	WORKERS. Males.	WORKERS. Females
11	12	13	14	15	16	17	18	19	20	21	22	23	24	25	26	27	28
208	44	9	128	16	1	234	148	9	7	6	...	5	1	..	3	3	...
461	73	43	469	88	11	881	586	35	25	18	...	25	11	1	123	52	4
267	67	12	379	81	12	1,029	467	20	5	1	...	10	5	2	33	13	...
68	20	4	110	20	11	161	128	1	...	..	...	4	1	..	2	1	...
406	85	97	277	43	24	628	452	10	11	10	...	73	10	8	52	30	1
1,662	293	312	1,700	363	146	7,523	6,187	169	22	12	1	56	34	1	246	113	10
10,535	1,560	2,485	8,720	1,439	1,286	22,591	14,617	1,583	42	34	1	289	55	15	1,088	481	81
232	68	33	174	26	10	648	427	36	..	...	...	...	..	..	20	11	1
293	36	50	696	89	61	1,078	622	111	5	4	...	9	...	1	37	18	2
83	23	3	83	19	3	157	125	2	...	...	..	...	...	...	3	2	...
1,818	378	60	1,004	196	94	972	769	45	5	4	...	63	13	...	62	26	1
221	34	9	324	53	27	1,317	851	131	7	2	...	6	2	...	17	8	1
638	127	103	362	63	32	1,030	720	15	15	9	...	29	8	2	160	72	1
9,258	1,491	2,005	11,369	2,078	1,717	25,850	18,523	1,183	366	215	13	581	125	37	1,337	709	45
843	*171*	*5*	*4,411*	*584*	*21*	*23,219*	*19,532*	*30*	*1,940*	*1,457*	...	*666*	*192*	...	*318*	*164*	...
59	8	2	828	128	1	6,290	5,263	9	1,728	1,342	..	91	19	...	62	34	...
...	...	...	...	...	...	...	...	...	...	...	..	...	...	...	...	...	...
..	...	...	...	...	...	...	...	...	...	...	...	..	...	..	...	...	...
784	163	3	3,583	456	20	16,929	14,269	21	212	115	...	575	173	...	256	130	...
2,008	*450*	*18*	*3,075*	*555*	*13*	*5,825*	*4,047*	*25*	*490*	*293*	*8*	*2,203*	*631*	*13*	*1,286*	*406*	*4*
3,070	*741*	*58*	*5,448*	*1,332*	*111*	*7,649*	*5,137*	*232*	*1,332*	*746*	*268*	*2,389*	*346*	*590*	*2,149*	*716*	*126*
670	159	6	987	238	17	1,473	1,139	17	327	149	74	353	27	28	265	73	8
669	135	1	612	98	4	697	393	...	52	22	1	204	59	...	186	55	1
840	160	25	1,443	237	30	2,813	1,824	110	227	34	96	587	79	194	711	228	54
762	262	22	1,055	263	32	1,558	1,140	18	635	464	92	1,077	135	354	678	199	60
129	25	4	1,351	496	28	1,108	641	87	91	77	5	168	46	14	309	161	3
902	*120*	*98*	*1,512*	*141*	*86*	*1,584*	*757*	*101*	*123*	*53*	*10*	*734*	*173*	*60*	*301*	*82*	*14*
1,377	*544*	*169*	*4,837*	*1,296*	*307*	*24,012*	*19,834*	*799*	*86*	*53*	*27*	*120*	*48*	*27*	*5,490*	*2,727*	*410*
6,243	*1,693*	*357*	*14,880*	*3,618*	*980*	*85,303*	*74,123*	*1,644*	*1,121*	*744*	*20*	*2,699*	*855*	*187*	*3,792*	*1,622*	*70*
694	*306*	*131*	*4,318*	*763*	*769*	*3,519*	*1,940*	*715*	*30*	*14*	*1*	*181*	*51*	*38*	*217*	*66*	*136*
150	145	5	326	302	24	967	901	66	13	13	...	79	45	34	65	36	29
497	159	126	2,300	460	745	1,880	1,027	634	1	1	..	5	...	4	146	28	107
47	2	...	1,698	1	...	672	12	15	16	...	1	97	6	...	6	2	...

APPENDICES TO IMPERIAL TABLE XX.

A.—*The Racial Composition of each People.*

NOTE.—Particulars are not given for Peoples II, III, V, VI and XII as their titles alone are sufficient. The detailed constitution of People XI is given in Imperial Table XVI.

	Race or Group.	Males.	Females.
	People I.		
A	Burma Group * ...	4,247,900	4,426,539
K	Talaing	163,830	159,679
S2	Zerbadi Buddhists ...	484	280
	Zerbadi Animists ..	8	16
S3	Arakan-Kaman Buddhists	10	7
	Total ..	4,412,232	4,586,521
	People IV.		
B	Lolo-Muso ..	39,494	36,351
C	Kuki-Chin * ...	140,638	141,236
D	Naga	197	209
E	Kachin	70,611	76,234
F	Sak	24,497	25,229
G	Mishmi	9	4
H	Mro	7,520	7,251
I	Shan	508,975	509,012
J	Malay *	942	1,025
L	Palaung-Wa ...	78,674	78,029
M	Khasi	2	1
O	Man	338	259
	Total ...	871,897	874,840

Race.	Males.	Females.
People XIII.		
Indian Buddhists ...	5,829	1,333
Indian Christians ...	13,674	8,928
Armenians ...	185	163
Zerbadi Christians ...	27	19
Jains	856	269
Parsis	229	151
Other Indians ..	11	6
Goa-Portuguese ...	47	17
Japanese	269	261
Jews ...	622	570
Mauritian ...	1	2
Negro	18	4
Nicobarese ...	6	4
Philippino ...	53	15
Singhalese ..	108	11
Turk	1	2
Total ..	21,939	11,756

	Race.	Males.	Females	Males.	Females.
		People	*VII.*	*People*	*VIII.*
A1	Burmese	2,683	5,913	...	...
C1	Kathè	1	33	35	15
J1	Malay	2,191	2,169	11	315
S3	Arakan-Kaman ...	1,044	1,119	...	...
X	Indian	103,461	99,429	146,139	17,242
Z	African	...	...	1	...
	Singhalese	...	...	14	...
	Turk	2	1	...	...
	Total	109,382	108,664	146,200	17,572
		People	*IX.*	*People*	*X.*
C1	Kathè	2,055	3,016	1,589	229
X	Indians—				
	Hindus and Animists	51,328	42,397	328,801	62,030
	Sikhs, Aryas and Brahmos	506	455	3,743	857
Z	Singhalese ...	3	3	6	...
	Total ...	53,892	45,871	333,539	63,116

B.—*Relation of Peoples to Indigenous Races.*

People; Race, etc.	Males.	Females.
People I ...	4,412,232	4,586,521
People II ..	88,879	89,346
People III ...	523,237	518,894
People IV ...	871,897	874,840
Burmese Mahomedans	2,683	5,913
Kathè Hindus ...	3,644	3,245
Kathè Mahomedans ...	36	48
Malay Mahomedans ...	2,202	2,484
Total ..	5,904,810	6,081,291
Deduct the following	*included in*	*People I:*
Zerbadi Buddhist ..	484	280
Zerbadi Animists ..	8	16
Arakan-Kaman Buddhists	10	7
Indigenous Races † ...	5,904,308	6,080,988

* Indicates that Hindus and Mahomedans are excluded.
† Agreeing with total of Race-groups A to O inclusive.

C.—*The Numbers of Home Races.*

People or Race.	Males.	Females.
Indigenous Races ... (*Total of Groups A to O or as in Appendix B*)	5,904,308	6,080,988
Indo-Burman Races (*Group S*)	59,442	60,829
Total Home Races	5,963,750	6,141,817
Peoples I to IV and VI	5,954,114	6,128,989
Burmese Mahomedans	2,683	5,913
Kathè Hindus ..	3,644	3,245
Kathè Mahomedans	36	48
Malay Mahomedans	2,202	2,484
Zerbadi Christians ...	27	19
Arakan-Kaman Mahomedans	1,044	1,119
Total Home Races ...	5,963,750	6,141,817

IMPERIAL TABLE XXII-A.

The Special Industrial Census (All Industries).

NOTE 1.—The statistics of this table have been obtained from the schedules of the Special Industrial Census, which was quite distinct from the ordinary census and related to all Industrial Establishments which employed 10 or more persons. For further particulars Chapter XIII of the Report Volume should be consulted.

NOTE 2.—All establishments have been classified in Groups A, B, C......of classes of industries which are distinguished in each group by serial numbers. Column 1 of Part I of the table shows the classes included in each group. Some establishments practise more than one kind of industry, *e.g.*, many rice mills saw timber.

NOTE 3.—The table is presented in four principal parts as follows:—

Part I.—Classification of all Industrial Establishments and of the persons employed in them.

Part II.—Distribution by districts of the statistics in Part I of the table.

Part III.—Power used in Industrial Establishments.

Part IV.—Looms in textile establishments.

NOTE 4.—Part III is further subdivided into three parts as follows:—

Part IIIA.—Power in establishments deriving it directly from Steam, Oil, Gas or Water.

Part IIIB.—Power in establishments using electric power generated on their premises.

Part IIIC.—Power in establishments using electricity supplied from outside.

An establishment which uses more than one source of power coming under Part IIIA of the table is entered in columns 3, 4 and 5 of that table once for each source, and if in addition electric power is generated on the premises it will be entered one or more times in columns 4 to 7 of Part IIIB.

Engines which are used principally to drive the characteristic machinery of an establishment but are also coupled to dynamos when electric current is required are entered only in Part IIIA and are not shown again in columns 4 to 7 inclusive of Part IIIB; the entries in those columns thus relate to engines used for no other purposes than to drive dynamos.

All the power represented in Part IIIC is included already in Part IIIB under Group P for Mandalay or under Group Q. Some of the establishments shown in Part IIIB have electric motors which are shown nowhere in the table.

As many managers of establishments are unable to describe correctly the engines and dynamos which they use, the whole of Part III is particularly liable to error although a very large number of references have been made to managers to get corrections of doubtful records.

NOTE 5.—For the definition of *Skilled* Occupations see the appendix at the end of Part IV of the table.

NOTE 6.—The term *Home Races* includes all Indigenous and Indo-Burman Races, that is races of Groups A to O inclusive and also of Group S of Imperial Table XIII. It differs slightly from the sum of Peoples I to IV and VI by including Mahomedans of indigenous races and those Zerbadis who are neither Mahomedans nor Buddhists (see the appendices to Imperial Table XX). The number amongst those tabulated under *Others* who are not Indians has not been tabulated; for both Skilled and Unskilled Labourers it is either *nil* or negligibly small.

NOTE 7.—Armenians are included under the description *European* for the purposes of this table.

NOTE 8.—The Group *Age under 14* includes all who have not *completed* 14 years of age; the group *Age 18 or over* includes all who have completed 18 years of age or more.

NOTE 9.—All the owners, directors and managers of the establishments shown in the table are British subjects except as shown in the footnotes of Part I of the table.

NOTE 10.—Imperial Table XXIIB gives further statistics for a selection of the most important industries shown in this table.

IMPERIAL TABLE XXIIA.—THE SPECIAL INDUSTRIAL CENSUS. PART I.—

NOTE.—For col. 2 all establishments have been classified, according to the total number of persons they employ in any capacity in six magni

ESTABLISHMENTS.			TOTAL EMPLOYEES.			CLASSIFICATION OF SUPERIOR EMPLOYEES. N.B.—In these columns all are males unless the contrary is indicated.												
						Managers.			Supervising and Technical Staff.			Clerical Staff.			Skilled Labourers.			
DESCRIPTION (with Group-letters and Serial Nos. of Classes in each Group).	MAGNITUDE. (See Note below title of table on this page and the next).	Number of Establishments.	Persons.	Males.	Females.	Europeans and Anglo-Indians.	Home Races.	Others.	Europeans and Anglo-Indians.	Home Races.	Others.	Europeans and Anglo-Indians.	Home Races.	Others.	Europeans and Anglo-Indians.	Home Races.	Chinese and Japanese.	Others.
1	2	3	4	5	6	7	8	9	10	11	12	13	14	15	16	17	18	19
All Industrial Establishments	..	1198	118,443	112,945	5498	M-233 F-3	M-513 F-26	M-425 F-2	M-1,260 F-15	M-651 F-84	M-994 F-1	M-269 F-29	M-3,826 F-11	M-2,255 F-3	M-363 F-58	M-7,443 F-605	M-1,542 F-3	12533
A. Cultivation for special products	...	44	5,881	4,976	905	28	6	10	48	50	47	10	15	19	1	41	8	24
1. Coffee— *With mechanical power*	20-49	1	20	20	...	...	...	1	1	6	1	1	...	..	..	6	...	...
2. Sugar-cane—	Total	2	32	27	5	...	1	1	...	...	...	...	...	...	...	...	...	...
Without mech. power	10-19	1	12	12	..		...	1		...	...	...	...	...	...	...	..	..
	20-49	1	20	15	5	..	1	...	...	...	.	..	...	...	..	..	...	...
3. Cinchona— *Without mech. power*	50-99	1	54	49	5	1	...	...	...	1	.	...	...	..	..	...	...	...
4. Rubber—*	Total	39	5,720	4,842	878	26	5	8	47	43	46	9	14	19	1	33	8	24
(i) *With mechanical power*	...	*12*	*2,953*	*2,341*	*612*	*10*	.	*2*	*28*	*19*	*31*	7	*2*	*11*	*1*	*24*	*6*	*19*
	20-49	1	45	45	.	1	.	...	1	5	16	1	1	...	...	4	...	2
	50-99	2	126	102	24	1	...	1	1	2	1	...	.	...	.	1	...	1
	100-199	3	412	352	60	3	.	..	7	3	2	1	...	5	..	6	...	5
	200-399	4	1,147	913	234	3	..	1	5	6	8	4	1	4	1	11	2	5
	400 & over.	2	1,223	929	294	2	.	...	14	3	4	1	..	2	.	2	4	6
(ii) *Without mech. power*	.	*27*	*2,767*	*2,501*	*266*	*16*	*5*	*6*	*19*	*24*	*15*	*2*	*12*	*8*	.	*9*	*2*	*5*
	10-19	2	33	33	..	1	.	1	...	1	1	...	.	.	...	...	...	..
	20-49	9	284	252	32	5	3	1	3	4	1	...	4	3	.	1	...	...
	50-99	5	367	314	53	3	1	1	4	6	1	...	1	...	...	...	..	...
	100-199	7	1,015	947	68	4	1	2	5	8	9	.	4	4	...	3	2	3
	200-399	4	1,068	955	113	3	.	1	7	5	3	2	3	1	..	5	...	2
5. Camphor— *With mechanical power*	50-99	1	55	38	17	1	.	...	...	...	..	...	1	...	..	2	...	...
B. Mines ...	...	70	10,559	10,208	351	26	M24 F-4	16	M186 F-1	38	31	M35 F-2	158	203	25	369	74	518
1. Petroleum wells—	Total	22	1,134	1,039	95	7	M11 F-3	1	16	8	2	1	24	11	..	115	...	27
(i) *With mechanical power*	...	*10*	*934*	*908*	*26*	†7	*3*	...	*16*	*8*	*2*	*1*	*24*	*11*	..	*112*	...	*26*
	20-49	6	181	181	...	3	3	...	3	2	..	1	6	3	..	34	...	7
	50-99	1	64	64	...	1	.	.	1	..		.	1	.	...	1	...	2
	100-199	2	364	338	26	2	.	.	5	6	2	...	3	2	...	49	..	15
	200-399	1	325	325	...	1	..	...	7	.	..	...	14	6	..	29	...	2
(ii) *Without mech. power*	...	*12*	*200*	*131*	*69*	...	*M 8 F-3*	*1*	...	...	...	...	.	...	...	*2*	...	*1*
	10-19	8	115	76	39	..	M-5 F-2	1	..	..	...	...	...	...	...	2	...	1
	20-49	4	85	55	30	..	M-3 F-1	...	...	..		...	...	...	...	...	...	...
2. Tin and Wolfram mines—	Total	41	4,076	3,838	238	15	12	14	34	17	26	4	45	23	2	74	37	88
(i) *With mechanical power*	...	*6*	*627*	*627*	...	*5*	...	*1*	*21*	.	*7*	*2*	*13*	*11*	*1*	*45*	*25*	*74*
	20-49	4	164	164	...	3	.	1	8	...	4	..	6	6	...	13	7	7
	200-399	2	463	463	...	2	...	...	13	.	3	2	7	5	1	32	18	67
(ii) *Without mech. power*		*35*	*3,449*	*3,211*	*238*	*10*	*12*	*13*	*13*	*17*	*19*	*2*	*32*	*12*	*1*	*29*	*12*	*14*
	10-19	9	152	111	11	..	6	3	1	4	4		4	2	...	...	1	..
	20-49	11	398	387	11	1	5	5	2	2	2	2	7	4	..	7	3	...
	50-99	6	375	334	41	3	..	3	2	2	2	...	11	3	1	...	...	..
	100-199	7	885	725	160	4	1	2	2	1	...	...	10	3	...	2	4	8
	200-399	1	276	261	15	1	...	...	.	2	1	...	...	...	...	1	...	...
	400 and over.	1	1,363	1,363	..	1	...	...	6	6	10	...	...	...	...	19	4	6
3. Silver and Lead mines—	Total	3	4,310	4,298	12	‡1	M-0 F-1	1	M103 F-1	2	2	M29 F-2	77	167	21	108	33	390
(i) *With mechanical power*	400 and over.	1	4,252	4,244	8	1	...	...	M103 F-1	2	1	M29 F-2	77	167	21	108	33	390
(ii) *Without mech power*	20-49	2	58	54	4	...	F-1	1	...	..	1	...	..	...	..	...	...	...

* Includes one estate in Dutch ownership managed by a British subject and two in French ownership managed by French subjects.
† Two are American subjects.
‡ American subject.

Classification of all Industrial Establishments and of the Persons employed in them.

tudes, namely: 10-19, 20-49, 50-99, 100-199, 200-399, 400 and over. For definitions of other column-headings *see* the Notes on the title-page.

CLASSIFICATION OF UNSKILLED LABOURERS.

Total.			Males.										Females.									
			Europeans and Anglo-Indians.	Home Races.			Chinese and Japanese			Others.			Europeans and Anglo-Indians.	Home Races.			Chinese and Japanese.			Others.		
Persons.	Males.	Females.		Age 18 or over.	Age 14 to 18.	Age under 14.	Age 18 or over.	Age 14 to 18.	Age under 14.	Age 18 or over.	Age 14 to 18.	Age under 14.		Age 18 or over.	Age 14 to 18.	Age under 14.	Age 18 or over.	Age 14 to 18.	Age under 14.	Age 18 or over.	Age 14 to 18.	Age under 14.
20	21	22	23	24	25	26	27	28	29	30	31	32	33	34	35	36	37	38	39	40	41	42
85,296	80,638	4,658	164	14,810	1011	236	3,074	61	9	57,930	2564	779	6	2,875	807	246	6	3	5	585	61	64
5,574	4,669	905	1	502	123	46	8	.	...	3 460	354	175	...	405	205	53	1	..	...	202	18	21
4	4	...	...	1	...	..		..	...	3	...	...	...	...	.	...	.	...		...	..	...
30	25	5	...	16	5	.	1	..	...	3	...	...	...	3	2	...	...	...	...	...	...	...
11	11	...	...	6	2	..	1	...	...	2	.	...	...	...	...	...	..		...	...	...	...
19	14	5	..	10	3	...		...	...	1	..	..	..	3	2	...	...	...	..	...	...	...
52	47	5	...	...	...	...	.	...	...	47	..	...	.	..	...	...	...	...	..	5	..	..
5,437	4,559	878	1	456	116	44	7	...	..	3,406	354	175	...	394	197	50	1	...	...	197	18	21
2,793	2,181	612	1	239	82	33	7	.	.	1,510	216	93	...	286	148	38	...	...	...	115	15	10
14	14	...	1	1	...	...	...	..	...	12	.	...	...	..	...	..	...	..	.	...	..	...
118	94	24	...	20	7	5	...		.	43	7	12	...	18	6	...	...	..	.	...	...	...
380	320	60	.	3	2	..	6	.	..	266	40	3	...	4	1	...	...	..	..	46	7	2
1,096	862	234	...	50	23	10	1	.	..	648	88	42	..	104	73	7	...	...	...	38	8	4
1,185	891	294	...	165	50	18	...	..	...	541	81	36	...	160	68	31	...	...	...	31	...	4
2,644	2,378	266	..	217	34	11	.		...	1,896	138	82	...	108	49	12	1	...	...	82	3	11
29	29	...	...	3	...	...		..	...	25	1	...	...	...	...	...	...	...	...	...	...	...
259	227	32	..	52	7	4	..	...	.	149	9	6	...	12	8	...	...	...	...	10	...	2
340	297	53	...	48	11	1	..	..	...	215	17	5	...	20	25	2	...	...	.	6	...	...
970	902	68	..	46	5	3	..	.	.	763	66	19	...	27	8	2	1	...	...	30	...	...
1,036	923	113	..	68	11	3	...	...	...	744	45	52	..	49	8	8	...	...	...	36	3	9
51	34	17	...	29	2	2	...	.	...	1	...	...	..	8	6	3	...	...	...	...	...	...
8,849	8,505	344	16	2,327	96	60	2,625	37	5	3,234	85	20	...	240	34	40	...	...	2	17	5	6
908	816	92	.	571	6	1	...	.	..	235	2	1	...	78	11	3	...	...		...	...	...
723	697	26	..	459	5	1	...	...	...	229	2	1	...	13	10	3	...	...	..	..	...	...
119	119	...	...	64	2	1	...	..	...	51	...	1		...	...	..	..	...	...	...	...	...
58	58	..	...	51	...	..	...	...	...	7	...	...	...	...	..	...	...	...	...	...	...	...
280	254	26	...	175	3	..		...	...	74	2	..	...	13	10	3	...	.	.	.	...	...
266	266	...	...	169	.	..	.	..	..	97	...	...	...	..	...	...	..	..	..	...	...	...
185	119	66	...	112	1	..	...	...	..	6	...	...	...	65	1	...	..	...	...	...	...	..
104	67	37	.	60	1	...	...	.	..	6		...	...	36	1	..	...	...	...	...	..	...
81	52	29	...	52	...			...	...	...	..	...	...	29	...	...	...	...	...	...	..	...
3,685	3,447	238	...	563	31	46	1,991	2	1	800	9	4	...	157	22	35	...	...	2	12	4	6
422	422	..	...	52	7	2	23	...		332	5	1	...	...	...	...	...	...	...	...	...	...
109	109	...	..	20	...	...	19	...	..	64	...	...	...	...	...	...	...	...	...	...	...	...
313	313	...	..	26	7	2	4	..		268	5	1	...	...	...	...	.	...	...	...	...	...
3,263	3,025	238	...	511	24	44	1,968	2	1	468	4	3	...	157	22	35	...		2	12	4	6
127	116	11	.	24	...	...	81	...	.	10	1	..	..	10	...	1	..	..	...	...	...	...
358	347	11	..	111	1	3	142	...	...	90		..	...	8	1	2	...	...	...	...	...	...
348	307	41	..	24	4	6	167	..	...	103	1	2	...	26	5	7	...	...	...	...	2	1
848	688	160	..	144	16	31	407	1	...	87	1	1	...	104	16	25	.	...	...	8	2	5
271	256	15	...	10	2	4	117	1	1	120	1	...	...	9	...	..	...	...	2	4	...	...
1,311	1,311	...	...	198	1	..	1,054	..		58	..	.	...	...	...	..	...	...	...	...	...	...
3,372	3,364	8	16	563	37	13	563	34	4	2,049	70	15	..	5	1	2	..	...	...	..	...	...
3,317	3,312	5	16	521	27	13	563	34	4	2,049	70	15	...	4	1	...	...	...	...	...	...	...
55	52	3	...	42	10	...	...	.	...	...	...	...	...	1	...	2	...	..	...	...	...	...

IMPERIAL TABLE XXIIA.—THE SPECIAL INDUSTRIAL CENSUS. PART I.—

ESTABLISHMENTS. DESCRIPTION (with Group-letters and Serial Nos. of Classes in each Group).	MAGNITUDE. (See Note below title of table on pages 450 and 451.)	Number of Establishments.	TOTAL EMPLOYEES. Persons.	Males.	Females.	CLASSIFICATION OF SUPERIOR EMPLOYEES. N.B.—In these columns all are males unless the contrary is indicated. Managers. Europeans and Anglo-Indians.	Managers. Home Races.	Managers. Others.	Supervising and Technical Staff. Europeans and Anglo-Indians.	Supervising and Technical Staff. Home Races.	Supervising and Technical Staff. Others.	Clerical Staff. Europeans and Anglo-Indians.	Clerical Staff. Home Races.	Clerical Staff. Others.	Skilled Labourers. Europeans and Anglo-Indians.	Skilled Labourers. Home Races.	Skilled Labourers. Chinese and Japanese.	Skilled Labourers. Others.
1	2	3	4	5	6	7	8	9	10	11	12	13	14	15	16	17	18	19
B. Mines—concld.																		
4. Ruby mines— *With mechanical power*	400 and over.	1	940	940	...	1	..	...	28	10	1	1	10	2	2	72	4	13
5. Other mines*— *Without mech. power*	Total	3	99	93	6	2	1		5	1	...	...	2	...	...	...	...	...
	10-19	1	17	17	...	1	.	...	1	1	...	...	1	...	...	..	...	...
	20-49	2	82	76	6	1	1		4	..	...	.	1	...	...	...	..	...
C. Stone Quarries ...	...	15	1,436	1,320	116	1	3	11	1		6	1	3	9	..	1	...	13
(i) *With mechanical power*	...	3	693	662	31	..	...	3	1	..	4	...	..	3	...	1	...	8
	20-49	1	27	27	...	...	..	1		.	2	...	...	2	..	...	...	1
	100-199	1	193	193	..	.	..	1	...	...	1	...	...	1	...	1	...	7
	400 and over.	1	473	442	31	.	...	1	1	...	1	...	...	...	...	...	...	...
(ii) *Without mech. power*	...	12	743	658	85	1	3	8	.	...	2	1	3	6	...	...	...	5
	10-19	2	34	34	...	..	.	2	...	...	...	..	...	...	...	...	...	...
	20-49	9	304	221	83	1	3	5	...	...	1	1	3	3	...	...	...	3
	400 and over.	1	405	403	2	...	...	1	...	...	1	...	...	3	..	...	..	2
D. Textiles—	...	39	2,437	1,575	862	5	M20 F-1	14	5	M16 F-30	16	3	90	67	...	M184 F-162	1	116
1. Cotton-ginning, cleaning and pressing.	Total	24	1,585	1,076	509	3	10	11	2	9	16	2	79	58	...	63	...	92
(i) *With mechanical power*	...	23	1,570	1,075	495	3	9	11	2	9	16	2	79	58	...	63	...	92
	10-19	4	59	32	27	...	2	2	...	1	1	...	1	2	...	5	...	...
	20-49	12	391	240	151	1	6	4	1	7	2	2	14	14	...	21	...	20
	50-99	3	180	107	73	.	1	2	...	1	3	...	15	4	...	7	...	7
	100-199	1	118	118	...	...	.	2	...	...	1	...	13	10	...	3	...	11
	200-399	3	822	578	244	2	...	1	1	...	9	...	36	28	...	27	..	54
(ii) *Without mech. power*	10-19	1	15	1	14		1	..	...	...	...	.	...	...	...	...	...	...
2. Cotton-weaving—	Total	6	202	21	181		M-5 F-1	..	..	M-3 F-30	...	...	2	...	...	M-11 F-91	...	...
Without mech. power	10-19	2	34	8	26		2	...	...	2	..	...	1	...	...	M-3 F-22	--	...
	20-49	3	107	12	95	...	M-2 F-1	..	...	1	...	...	1	...	.	M-8 F-57	...	...
	50-99	1	61	1	60	...	1	..	...	F-30	...	...	...	...	...	F-12	...	...
3. Rope-making—	Total	4	441	340	101	2	.	2	3	1	...	...	2	9	...	8	1	20
(i) *With mechanical power*	100-199	2	301	242	59	1	...	1	1	1	...	...	1	7	...	4	1	15
(ii) *Without mech. power*	...	2	140	98	42	1	..	1	2	...	..	1	1	2	...	4	...	5
	20-49	1	23	16	7	...	...	1	..	...	...	..	..	1	...	...	...	...
	100-199	1	117	82	35	1	...	...	2	...	...	1	1	1	...	4	...	5
4. Silk-weaving—	Total	5	209	138	71	...	5	1	...	3	...	...	7	...	...	M102 F-71	...	4
Without mech. power	20-49	4	137	95	42	...	5	..	...	...	.	...	6	..	..	M-71 F-42	...	...
	50-99	1	72	43	29	.	...	1	...	3	...	...	1	...	...	M-31 F-29	...	4
E. Leather and Bone—	..	15	451	440	11	4	3	8	5	6	6	2	7	33	...	2	14	56
1. Tanneries— *Without mech. power*	Total	9	203	203	...	...	3	6	..	1	3	...	4	5	...	...	13	19
	10-19	5	80	80	...		2	3	..	1	1	...	1	3	...	...	7	10
	20-49	4	123	123	...	...	1	3	...	.	2	...	3	2	..	...	6	9
2. Leather factories—† *Without mech. power*	Total	5	219	208	11	4	...	1	4	5	2	2	3	26	...	2	...	32
	10-19	1	11	11	...	1	...	...	1	...	...	...	2	...	...	..	...	...
	20-49	3	97	86	11	2	...	1	1	...	1	2	...	6	...	2	...	32
	100-199	1	111	111	...	1	...	...	2	5	1	...	1	20	...	...	...	...
3. Bone mills— *With mechanical power*	20-49	1	29	29	...	...	...	1	1	..	1	...	...	2	...	...	1	5

* Copper (prospecting), steatite and coal mines; one establishment each. See also in Part II of the table.

† Includes one owned by a company of which some of the directors are Belgian subjects; the manager is a Greek who is a British subject.

Classification of all Industrial Establishments and of the Persons employed in them—continued.

CLASSIFICATION OF UNSKILLED LABOURERS.																						
TOTAL.			MALES.										FEMALES.									
			Europeans and Anglo-Indians.	Home Races.			Chinese and Japanese			Others.			Europeans and Anglo-Indians.	Home Races.			Chinese and Japanese.			Others.		
Persons.	Males.	Females.		Age 18 or over.	Age 14 to 18.	Age under 14.	Age 18 or over.	Age 14 to 18.	Age under 14.	Age 18 or over.	Age 14 to 18.	Age under 14.		Age 18 or over.	Age 14 to 18.	Age under 14.	Age 18 or over.	Age 14 to 18.	Age under 14.	Age 18 or over.	Age 14 to 18.	Age under 14.
20	21	22	23	24	25	26	27	28	29	30	31	32	33	34	35	36	37	38	39	40	41	42
796	796	...	...	585	18	...	71	1	...	118	3	...	...	...		..	...	...	..	...	..	...
88	82	6	...	45	4	...	...		...	32	1	.	...		...	..	...	...	...	5	1	...
13	13	...	.	13	...	.	...	..	.	...	..	..	...	...	...	...	...	...	...	...	...	...
75	69	6	..	32	4	..	...	...	...	32	1	...	..	...	.	...	...	...	...	5	1	...
1,387	1,271	116	...	119	3	..	1	...	...	1,057	66	25	...	89	17	3	..	...	...	7	.	...
673	642	31	...	9	3	...	...	...	...	545	60	25	...	19	12		...	...	...	...	...	...
21	21	..	...	1	..	..	...	...	...	20	...		...	...	...	...	..	...	...	...	...	...
182	182	...	.	2	.	...	...	...	...	168	10	2	...	...	...	.	..	...	..	...	...	...
470	439	31	...	6	3	...	...	..	...	357	50	23	...	19	12	...		...	..	...	...	...
714	629	85	...	110	...	..	1	...	...	512	6	...	...	70	5	3	...	...	..	7	...	..
32	32	...	...	...	..	...	1	...	...	31	...	...	...	...	...	...	...	...	...	...	...	...
284	201	83	...	83	...	..	...	...	...	112	6	...	..	68	5	3	...	...	...	7	..	...
398	396	2	...	27	.	..	...	..	...	369	...	..	...	2	.	...	...	...	...	...	..	...
1,707	1,038	669	...	251	46	17	...	...	...	658	33	33	...	416	210	43	...	...	.	...	..	...
1,240	731	509	...	189	39	17	..	..	.	471	12	3	...	280	200	29	...	...	...	...	...	..
1,226	731	495	...	189	39	17	...	...	...	471	12	3	...	268	198	29	...	..	...	...	...	...
45	18	27	.	6	2	..	...	..		10	...	..	...	17	10	...	...	...	..	...	...	...
299	148	151	...	68	11	15	...	.	.	54	...	...	...	89	37	25	...	...	..	...	...	...
140	67	73	...	25	3	1	..	...	...	36	2	.	...	45	24	4	...	...	..	..	..	..
78	78	...	...	6	...	...	...	...	...	72	...	...	.	...	..	...	...	...	...	..	...	...
664	420	244	...	84	23	1	...	...	..	299	10	3	.	117	127	...	...	.	..	..	...	...
14	...	14	..	...	...	..	...	...	...	...	...	...	...	12	2	...	...	..	...	...	..	...
59	...	59	...	...	...	...	...	...	...	...	...	..	...	42	4	13	...	..	...	...	..	..
4	...	4	...	...	..	...	..	...	..	...		...	...	...	2	2	...	...	...	..	...	..
37	...	37	...	..	...	...	.	...	...	..	...	..	...	31	2	4	...		...	...	...	...
18	...	18	...	...	...	...	..	...	..	...	.	.	...	11	...	7	...	...	...	...	...	...
392	291	101	...	47	7	...	...	...	...	186	21	30	...	94	6	1	..	...	...	..	...	...
269	210	59	...	37	1	...	...	...	..	124	18	30	...	59	..	...	...	...	...	...	...	...
123	81	42	...	10	6	...	...	...	...	62	3	...	...	35	6	1	...	..	...	..	...	..
21	14	7		3	1	...	...	...	..	10	...	...	...	4	2	1	...	...	...	...	...	...
102	67	35	...	7	5	...	...	...	..	52	3	..	...	31	4	...	...	...	...	...	...	...
16	16	...	...	15	...	.	...	...	...	1	...	...	...	...	...	...	...	...	...	...	...	...
13	13	...	...	13	...	...	...	...	...	...	...	.	...	...	...	...	...	...	...	...	...	...
3	3	...	...	2	...	...	...	...	...	1	...	.	...	...	.	...	...	...	...	...	...	...
305	294	11	...	9	...	...	6	...	...	273	3	3	...	...	...	...	1	.	.	6	2	2
149	149	...	...	6	...	..	3	...	...	140	.	...	...	...	...	...	...	..	...	..	...	...
52	52	...	..	6	...	..	2	...	...	44	...	...	...	...	...	...	...	...	...	..	...	..
97	97	...	...	...	...	...	1	...	...	96	...	..	..	...	...	.	.	..	...	...	...	...
138	127	11	...	3	..	...	3	...	...	115	3	3	...	..	...	...	1	...	...	6	2	2
7	7	...	...	...	...	...	...	...	...	7	...	...	...	...	...	...	...	...	...	...	...	...
50	39	11	..	...	...	...	3	...	...	31	2	3	...	...	...	...	1	...	...	6	2	2
81	81	...	...	3	...	...	...	...	...	77	1	...	...	...	...	...	...	...	...	...	...	...
18	18	...	...	...	...	...	...	...	...	18	...	...	...	...	...	...	...	...	...	...	...	...

ESTABLISHMENTS. DESCRIPTION (with Group-letters and Serial Nos. of Classes in each Group).	MAGNITUDE. (See Note below title of table on pages 46 and 451.)	Number of Establishments.	TOTAL EMPLOYEES. Persons.	Males.	Females.	Managers. Europeans and Anglo-Indians.	Managers. Home Races.	Managers. Others.	Supervising and Technical Staff. Europeans and Anglo-Indians.	Supervising and Technical Staff. Home Races.	Supervising and Technical Staff. Others.	Clerical Staff. Europeans and Anglo-Indians.	Clerical Staff. Home Races.	Clerical Staff. Others.	Skilled Labourers. Europeans and Anglo-Indians.	Skilled Labourers. Home Races.	Skilled Labourers. Chinese and Japanese.	Skilled Labourers. Others.
1	2	3	4	5	6	7	8	9	10	11	12	13	14	15	16	17	18	19
F. Wood—	...	150	13,931	1,3642	289	24	M53 F-1	72	73	M78 F-6	68	M-8 F-1	M731 F-5	266	2	1,195	176	1,347
1. Carpentry— *Without mech. power*	Total	11	219	219	...	..	2	9	1	...	7	..	.	21	...	13	104	3
	10-19	6	76	76	...	...	2	4	...	...	1	...	..	...	...	13	24	3
	20-29	5	143	143	...	..	...	5	1	...	6	...	..	21	...	...	80	...
2. Sawmills and timber yards†—	Total	139	13,712	13,423	289	24	M51 F-1	63	72	M78 F-6	61	M-8 F-1	M731 F-5	245	2	1,182	72	1,344
(i) *With mechanical power* (a) *The whole Province*	...	132	13,601	13,313	288	24	M44 F-1	63	72	M77 F-6	61	M-8 F-1	M727 F-5	245	2	1,117	66	1,343
	10-19	8	114	112	2	...	3	5	...	...	3	...	8	9	...	19	3	17
	20-49	64	2,292	2,183	109	2	M28 F-1	33	6	M36 F-1	31	7	104	83	...	211	17	219
	50-99	26	1,592	1,474	118	2	11	13	3	M17 F-5	18	...	M-81 F-5	29	...	166	7	101
	100-199	19	2,555	2,516	39	6	2	11	6	23	6	...	63	56	1	180	6	218
	200-399	9	2,810	2,791	19	8	...	1	14	1	3	F-1	167	36	1	204	4	208
	400 and over.	6	4,298	4,297	1	6	...	...	43	...	...	1	304	32	...	337	29	580
(b) *Arakan Division* ...	20-49	2	40	40	...	...	2	.	..	1	..	..	1	...	...	6	...	4
(c) *Rangoon* ...	...	26	6,469	6,467	2	10	3	13	41	10	9	.	338	103	1	331	31	787
	10-19	3	45	44	1	...	..	3	...	..	2	...	3	5	...	...	1	8
	20-49	4	123	123	..	...	2	2	...	4	1	..	7	5	...	4	...	13
	50-99	1	55	55	.	...	...	1	...	...	1	...	1	2	.	4	...	10
	100-199	9	1,162	1,162	..	2	1	6	2	6	2	..	18	29	1	25	2	121
	200-399	4	1,279	1,279	...	3	...	1	4	..	3	..	41	30	..	40	...	118
	400 and over.	5	3,805	3,804	1	5	...	...	35	.	...	...	268	32	...	258	28	517
(d) *Pegu Division (less Rangoon)* *	...	17	670	662	8	...	6	11	..	1	20	.	34	25	..	30	3	59
	10-19	1	13	13	...	.	1	..	...	..	1	.	1	1	...	...	.	4
	20-49	13	497	495	2	..	4	9	.	1	14	..	25	24	...	22	3	48
	50-99	3	160	154	6	..	1	2	...	...	5	..	8	...	...	8	...	7
(e) *Irrawaddy Division*	...	7	181	180	1	...	6	1	1	8	...	5	15	2	...	26	...	38
	10-19	2	22	21	1	...	2	...	...	...	...	...	3	...	...	14	..	...
	20-49	5	159	159	...	...	4	1	1	8	...	5	12	2	..	12	...	38
(f) *Toungoo and Thatôn districts.*	...	16	750	721	29	1	M-2 F-1	12	3	7	3	2	31	39	...	33	12	85
	20-49	9	292	285	7	...	M-1 F-1	7	1	4	...	2	10	21	...	12	9	57
	50-99	7	458	436	22	1	1	5	2	3	3	...	21	18	...	21	3	28
(g) *Amherst, Salween, Tavoy and Mergui districts.*	...	19	3,064	3,060	4	6	6	7	19	20	6	M-1 F-1	182	26	1	294	12	274
	20-49	4	160	157	3	...	2	2	..	2	1	...	5	5	...	19	...	16
	50-99	4	290	290	...	...	3	1	...	2	3	...	11	2	...	33	3	33
	100-199	6	813	813	...	1	1	4	1	15	2	..	13	13	...	80	4	77
	200-399	4	1,308	1,307	1	4	...	...	10	1	...	F-1	117	6	1	83	4	85
	400 and over.	1	493	493	...	1	...	...	8	...	..	1	36	...	...	79	1	63
(h) *Upper Burma and the Shan States.*	...	45	2,427	2,183	244	7	19	19	8	M30 F-6	23	...	M126 F-5	50	..	397	8	96
	10-19	2	34	34	...	...	...	2	...	...	...	.	1	3	...	5	2	5
	20-49	27	961	864	97	2	13	12	4	M16 F-1	15	...	44	26	...	136	5	43
	50-99	11	629	539	90	1	6	4	1	M12 F-5	6	..	M-40 F-5	7	...	100	1	23
	100-199	4	580	541	39	3	...	1	3	2	2		32	14	...	75	..	20
	200-399	1	223	205	18	1	...	...	.	...	...	...	9	...	...	81	...	5
(ii) *Without mech. power The whole Province (But for Lower Burma the figures are nil).*	...	7	111	110	1	...	7	...	...	1	...	...	4	...	...	65	6	1
	10-19	5	69	68	1	...	5	..	...	1	...	...	3	..	...	42	5	1
	20-49	2	42	42	...	...	2	...	...	...	...	...	1	..	...	23	1	...

N.B.—In these columns (7–19) all are males unless the contrary is indicated.

* That is, the Insein, Hanthawaddy, Tharrawaddy, Pegu and Prome districts.

† Includes one owned by a company of which some directors are American subjects.

Classification of all Industrial Establishments and of the Persons employed in them—continued.

CLASSIFICATION OF UNSKILLED LABOURERS.																						
TOTAL.			MALES.										FEMALES.									
			Europeans and Anglo-Indians.	Home Races.			Chinese and Japanese.			Others.			Europeans and Anglo-Indians.	Home Races.			Chinese and Japanese.			Others.		
Persons.	Males.	Females.		Age 18 or over.	Age 14 to 18.	Age under 14.	Age 18 or over.	Age 14 to 18.	Age under 14.	Age 18 or over.	Age 14 to 18.	Age under 14.		Age 18 or over.	Age 14 to 18.	Age under 14.	Age 18 or over.	Age 14 to 18.	Age under 14.	Age 18 or over.	Age 14 to 18.	Age under 14.
20	21	22	23	24	25	26	27	28	29	30	31	32	33	34	35	36	37	38	39	40	41	42
9,825	9,549	276	1	1,424	138	8	76	8	...	7,282	528	94	...	209	44	10	...	...	...	12	...	1
59	59		...	8	...	...	16	5	...	...	...	...	...	...	...	...	...	...	...	...	...	...
29	29		...	8	...	...	16	5	...	...	...	...	...	...	...	...	...	...	...	...	...	...
30	30		...	...	...	...	30	...	...		...	...	...	...	...	...	...	...	...	...	...	...
9,766	9,490	276	1	1,416	138	8	30	3	...	7,282	518	94	...	209	44	10	...	...	...	12	...	1
9,739	9,464	275	1	1,400	138	8	20	3	...	7,282	518	94	...	208	44	10	...	...	...	12	...	1
47	45	2	...	16	...	...	...	...	...	26	1	2	...	1	...	1	...	...	...	...	...	...
1,453	1,346	107	...	467	41	2	7	...	...	796	29	4	...	81	17	5	...	...	...	3	...	1
1,134	1,026	108	...	360	26	4	12	2	...	584	27	11	...	85	12	2	...	...	...	9	...	...
1,977	1,938	39	...	287	48	1	...	...	...	1,369	191	42	...	28	9	2	...	...	...	...	...	...
2,162	2,144	18	1	157	21	1	...	1	...	1,801	127	35	...	12	6	...	...	...	...	...	...	...
2,966	2,965	1	...	113	2	...	1	...	...	2,706	143	...	...	1	...	...	...	...	...	...	...	...
26	26	...	...	12	...	...	...	...	...	14	...	...	...	...	...	...	...	...	...	...	...	...
4,792	4,790	2	...	102	8	...	1	...	...	4,206	409	73	...	1	...	1	...	...	...	...	...	...
23	22	1	...	...	...	...	...	...	...	20	1	1	...	...	...	1	...	...	...	...	...	...
85	85	...	...	4	...	...	...	...	...	62	15	4	...	...	...	...	...	...	...	...	...	...
36	36	...	...	...	...	...	...	...	...	28	7	1	...	...	...	...	...	...	...	...	...	...
947	947	...	...	1	2	...	...	...	...	768	141	35	...	...	...	...	...	...	...	...	...	...
1,039	1,039	...	...	11	4	...	...	...	...	899	95	32	...	...	...	...	...	...	...	...	...	...
2,662	2,661	1	...	86	2	...	1	...	...	2,429	143	...	...	1	...	...	...	...	...	...	...	...
481	473	8	...	81	5	3	12	...	...	357	8	7	...	4	3	1	...	...	...	...	...	...
5	5	...	...	...	...	...	...	...	...	4	...	1	...	...	...	...	...	...	...	...	...	...
347	345	2	...	45	4	1	2	...	...	286	7	...	...	2	...	...	...	...	...	...	...	...
129	123	6	...	36	1	2	10	...	...	67	1	6	...	2	3	1	...	...	...	...	...	...
79	78	1	...	22	...	...	...		...	56	...	...	...	1	...	...	...	...	...	...	...	...
3	2	1	...	2	...	...	...	...	...	...	...	...	...	1	...	...	...	...	...	...	...	...
76	76	...	...	20	...	...	...	...	...	56	...	...	...	...	...	...	...	...	...	...	...	...
519	491	28	...	72	3	1	3	2		391	16	4	...	24	4	...	...	...	...	...	...	...
167	161	6	...	13	2	...	1	...	...	142	3	...	...	3	3	...	...	...	...	...	...	...
352	330	22	...	59	1	1	2	2		249	12	4	...	21	1	...	...	...	...	...	...	...
2,209	2,206	3	1	179	19	2	2	1	...	1,903	99	9	...	...	...	...	...	...	...	2	...	1
108	105	3	...	12	...	...	2	...	...	88	3	...	...	...	...	...	...	...	...	...	...	...
199	199	...	...	35	6	...	...	...	...	153	5	...	...	...	...	...	...	...	...	2	...	1
602	602	...	...	45	8	1	...	...	...	493	49	6	...	...	...	...	...	...	...	...	...	...
996	996	...	1	60	5	1		1	...	892	33	3	...	...	...	...	...	...	...	...	...	...
304	304	...	...	27	...	...	...	...	...	277	...	...	...	...	...	...	...	...	...	...	...	...
1,633	1,400	233	...	932	103	2	2	...	...	355	5	1	...	178	37	8	...	...	...	10	...	...
16	16	...	...	14	...	...		...	...	2	...	...	...	...	...	...	...	...	...	...	...	...
644	548	96	...	361	35	1	2	...	...	148	1	...	...	76	14	5	...	...	...	1	...	...
418	338	80	...	230	18	1	...	...	...	87	2	...	...	60	8	1	...	...	...	9	...	...
428	389	39	...	241	38	...	...	...	...	108	1	1	...	28	9	2	...	...	...	...	...	...
127	109	18	...	86	12	...	...	...	...	10	1	...	...	12	6	...	...	...	...	...	...	...
27	26	1	...	16	...	...	10	...	...	...	...	...	...	1	...	...	...	...	...	...	...	...
12	11	1	...	9	...	...	2	...	...	...	...	...	...	1	...	...	...	...	...	...	...	...
15	15	...	...	7	...	...	8	...	...	...	...	...	...	...	...	...	...	...	...	...	...	...

ESTABLISHMENTS. DESCRIPTION (with Group-letters and Serial Nos. of Classes in each Group).	MAGNITUDE. (*See* Note below title of table on pages 45. and 461.)	Number of Establishments.	TOTAL EMPLOYEES. Persons.	Males.	Females.	CLASSIFICATION OF SUPERIOR EMPLOYEES. *N.B.*—In these columns all are males unless the contrary is indicated. Managers. Europeans and Anglo-Indians.	Managers. Home Races.	Managers. Others.	Supervising and Technical Staff. Europeans and Anglo-Indians.	Supervising and Technical Staff. Home Races.	Supervising and Technical Staff. Others.	Clerical Staff. Europeans and Anglo-Indians.	Clerical Staff. Home Races.	Clerical Staff. Others.	Skilled Labourers. Europeans and Anglo-Indians.	Skilled Labourers. Home Races.	Skilled Labourers. Chinese and Japanese.	Skilled Labourers. Others.
1	2	3	4	5	6	7	8	9	10	11	12	13	14	15	16	17	18	19
G. Metals	...	32	2,448	2,448	...	10	9	13	48	4	28	6	31	66	35	417	74	683
1. Iron-foundries—	Total	10	727	727	...	1	5	4	11	1	1	3	16	8	12	220	17	145
(i) *With mechanical power*	...	*6*	*620*	*620*	...	*1*	*2*	*3*	*11*	*1*	*1*	*3*	*16*	*8*	*12*	*188*	*7*	*145*
	20-49	4	103	103	.	...	1	3	1	..	1	...	...	3	...	28	...	36
	50-99	1	72	72	.	..	1	...	...	1	...	...	1	...	...	31	...	9
	400 and over.	1	445	445	..	1	..	...	10	...	...	3	15	5	12	129	7	100
(ii) *Without mech. power*	...	4	*107*	*107*	.	..	*3*	*1*	...	...	...	...	...	...	...	*32*	*10*	...
	10-19	1	18	18	...	...	1	...	...	...	..	...	...	...	...	8	...	...
	20-49	3	89	89	..	...	2	1	...	..	..	.	...	..	...	24	10	...
2. Iron and steel-works*—	Total	9	150	150	...	...	3	6	...	2	14	..	..	3	...	33	29	19
(i) *With mechanical power*	10-19	*1*	*12*	*12*	..	...	*1*	..	...	*1*	...		...	..	..	*2*	...	...
(ii) *Without mech. power*	...	*8*	*138*	*138*	...	...	*2*	*6*	...	*1*	*14*	.	...	*3*	...	*31*	*29*	*19*
	10-19	5	63	63		...	1	4	...	..	1	...	...	2	...	10	10	17
	20-49	3	75	75		...	1	2	.	1	13	..	...	1	...	21	19	2
3. Arsenals— *With mechanical power*	200-399	1	396	396	...	1	.	...	25	...	1	1	4	18	...	12	...	148
4. Machinery and engineering workshops—	Total	11	1,046	1,046	...	7	1	3	9	1	12	2	10	35	21	136	28	291
(i) *With mechanical power*	...	*9*	*833*	*833*	...	*5*	*1*	*3*	*8*	*1*	*12*	*2*	*10*	*31*	*7*	*134*	*28*	*207*
	20-49	3	89	89	...	1	...	2	2	1	2	...	..	3	...	18	4	31
	50-99	2	127	127	...	2	...	...	4	...	5	1	2	8	..	...	18	8
	100-199	3	395	395	..	1	1	1	1	...	5	1	5	16	4	61	6	120
	200-399	1	222	222	...	1	...	...	1	...	..	..	3	4	3	55	...	48
(ii) *Without mech. power*	...	*2*	*213*	*213*	...	*2*	...	...	*1*	...	...	...	...	*4*	*14*	*2*	...	*84*
	20-49	1	33	33	...	1	...	...	1	...	...	...	...	1	...	1	...	7
	100-199	1	180	180	...	1	...	..	...		...	...	...	3	14	1	...	77
5. Sewage pumping-station workshop— *With mechanical power*	100-199	1	129	129	...	1	.	...	3	...	..	...	1	2	2	16	...	80
H. Glass and Earthenware	...	83	4,106	3,709	397	...	47	36	...	6	46	...	14	16	..	M288 F-23	...	543
1. Pottery works—	Total	11	180	159	21	...	10	1	...	...	10	..	..	...	...	M-48 F-7	..	10
Without mech. power	10-19	9	112	101	11	...	9	...	...	...	...	...		..	..	M-44 F-6	...	...
	20-49	2	68	58	10	...	1	1	...	...	10	...	...	...	...	M-4 F-1	...	10
2. Brick, tile and firebrick factories—	Total	72	3,926	3,550	376	..	37	35	...	6	36	...	14	16	.	M240 F-16	...	533
Without mech. power	10-19	11	156	142	14	...	8	3	.	4	3	...	3	...	...	M-60 F-1	...	3
	20-49	37	1,128	883	245	...	26	11	...	2	8	...	11	2	...	M131 F-11	...	26
	50-99	15	1,077	1,010	67	...	2	13	...	..	19	..	...	7	...	M-23 F-2	...	129
	100-199	7	874	825	49	...	1	6	...	...	...	...	..	5	...	M-26 F-2	...	140
	200-399	1	279	278	1	...	..	1	.	...	5	...	...	2	..	...	...	48
	400 and over.	1	412	412	...	.	..	1	...	..	1	...	...	...	...	...	...	187
J. Chemical products ...	...	78	34,963	34,414	549	28	29	21	514	M63 F-11	66	M87 F-9	M 1349 F-4	M594 F-3	50	1,478	260	3,092
1. Salt refineries—	Total	3	57	30	27	...	3	..	...	M 1 F-3	...	...	F-2	..	...	...	...	...
Without mech. power	10-19	1	15	8	7	...	1	..	...	M-1 F-1	..	...	.	...	...	...	...	...
	20-49	2	42	22	20	...	2		...	F-2	...	..	F-2	...	...	...	...	...
2. Aerated water factories— *With mechanical power*	Total	5	337	337	..	2	1	2	4	9	11	.	6	11	...	13	...	46
	10-19	1	13	13	..	...	..	1	...	...	.	..	...	1	...	...	...	..
	20-49	1	28	28	...	.	..	1	2	1	...	...	6	...	...	2	...	...
	50-99	2	186	186	...	1	1	...	2	8	11	..	...	10	...	5	...	19
	100-199	1	110	110	...	1		..	...	...	...	...	...	...	...	6	...	34

* Including blacksmiths and trades working with iron sheets, *e.g.*, making galvanised iron buckets, steel trunks, despatch-boxes.

Classification of all Industrial Establishments and of the Persons employed in them—continued.

CLASSIFICATION OF UNSKILLED LABOURERS.

Total.			Males.										Females.									
			Europeans and Anglo-Indians.	Home Races.			Chinese and Japanese.			Others.			Europeans and Anglo-Indians.	Home Races.			Chinese and Japanese.			Others.		
Persons.	Males.	Females.		Age 18 or over.	Age 14 to 18.	Age under 14.	Age 18 or over.	Age 14 to 18.	Age under 14.	Age 18 or over.	Age 14 to 18.	Age under 14.		Age 18 or over.	Age 14 to 18.	Age under 14.	Age 18 or over.	Age 14 to 18.	Age under 14.	Age 18 or over.	Age 14 to 18.	Age under 14.
20	21	22	23	24	25	26	27	28	29	30	31	32	33	34	35	36	37	38	39	40	41	42
1,084	1,084	...	3	118	37	6	7	...	...	852	23	38	...	...	...	...	...	...	...	...	...	...
283	283	...	...	38	23	4	7	...	...	178	13	20	...	...	...	...	...	...	...	...	...	...
222	222	...	...	11	3	1	...	...	...	175	12	20	...	...	...	...	...	...	...	...	...	...
30	30	...	...	7	3	1	...	...	...	11	6	2	...	...	...	...	...	...	...	...	...	...
29	29	...	...	3	...	...	...	...	...	25	1	...	...	...	...	...	...	...	...	...	...	...
163	163	...	...	1	...	...	...	...	...	139	5	18	...	...	...	...	...	...	...	...	...	...
61	61	...	...	27	20	3	7	...	...	2	1	...	...	...	...	...	...	...	...	...	...	...
9	9	...	...	4	4	1	...	...	...	...	...	...	...	...	...	...	...	...	...	...	...	...
52	52	...	...	23	16	2	7	...	...	3	1	...	...	...	...	...	...	...	...	...	...	...
41	41	...	...	19	7	1	...	...	...	14	...	...	...	...	...	...	...	...	...	...	...	...
8	8	...	...	2	6	...	...	...	...	...	...	...	...	...	...	...	...	...	...	...	...	...
33	33	...	...	17	1	1	...	...	...	14	...	...	...	...	...	...	...	...	...	...	...	...
18	18	...	...	9	...	...	...	...	...	9	...	...	...	...	...	...	...	...	...	...	...	...
15	15	...	...	8	1	1	...	...	...	5	...	...	...	...	...	...	...	...	...	...	...	...
186	186	...	...	1	...	...	...	...	...	165	3	17	...	...	...	...	...	...	...	...	...	...
490	490	...	3	56	7	1	...	...	...	415	7	1	...	...	...	...	...	...	...	...	...	...
384	384	...	3	49	7	1	...	...	...	317	7	...	...	...	...	...	...	...	...	...	...	...
25	25	...	...	1	...	...	...	...	...	24	...	...	...	...	...	...	...	...	...	...	...	...
79	79	...	...	3	...	...	...	...	...	75	1	...	...	...	...	...	...	...	...	...	...	...
173	173	...	1	32	4	1	...	...	...	130	5	...	...	...	...	...	...	...	...	...	...	...
107	107	...	2	13	3	...	...	...	...	88	1	...	...	...	...	...	...	...	...	...	...	...
106	106	...	...	7	...	...	...	...	...	98	...	1	...	...	...	...	...	...	...	...	...	...
22	22	...	...	4	...	...	...	...	...	18	...	...	...	...	...	...	...	...	...	...	...	...
84	84	...	...	3	...	...	...	...	...	80	...	1	...	...	...	...	...	...	...	...	...	...
84	84	...	...	4	...	...	...	...	...	80	...	...	...	...	...	...	...	...	...	...	...	...
3,087	2,713	374	...	544	59	24	...	...	...	2,056	23	7	...	257	54	29	...	...	...	33	1	...
94	80	14	...	27	2	1	...	...	...	50	...	...	...	12	1	...	...	...	...	1	...	...
53	48	5	...	14	1	...	...	...	...	33	...	...	...	4	1	...	...	...	...	...	...	...
41	32	9	...	13	1	1	...	...	...	17	...	...	...	8	...	...	...	...	...	1	...	...
2,893	2,633	360	...	517	57	23	...	...	...	2,006	23	7	...	245	53	29	...	...	...	32	1	...
71	58	13	...	34	3	...	...	...	...	21	...	...	...	11	2	...	...	...	...	...	...	...
900	666	234	...	310	37	17	...	...	...	298	3	1	...	170	36	21	...	...	...	6	1	...
882	817	65	...	92	5	3	...	...	...	703	8	6	...	31	5	6	...	...	...	23	...	...
694	647	47	...	81	10	3	...	...	...	539	12	...	...	33	10	2	...	...	...	2	...	...
223	222	1	...	...	...	...	...	...	...	222	...	...	...	...	...	...	...	...	...	1	...	...
223	223	...	...	...	...	...	...	...	...	223	...	...	...	...	...	...	...	...	...	...	...	...
27,305	26,783	522	72	6,521	236	29	70	1	1	18,698	904	252	1	421	77	26	...	...	...	7	...	...
48	26	22	...	21	1	4	...	...	...	...	...	...	...	12	2	8	...	...	...	...	...	...
12	6	6	...	6	...	...	...	...	...	...	...	...	...	4	1	1	...	...	...	...	...	...
36	20	16	...	15	1	4	...	...	...	...	...	...	...	8	1	7	...	...	...	...	...	...
232	232	...	...	2	1	...	...	...	...	228	1	...	...	...	...	...	...	...	...	...	...	...
11	11	...	...	...	1	...	...	...	...	10	...	...	...	...	...	...	...	...	...	...	...	...
16	16	...	...	1	...	...	...	...	...	15	...	...	...	...	...	...	...	...	...	...	...	...
136	136	...	...	...	...	...	...	...	...	135	1	...	...	...	...	...	...	...	...	...	...	...
69	69	...	...	1	...	...	...	...	...	68	...	...	...	...	...	...	...	...	...	...	...	...

ESTABLISHMENTS.			TOTAL EMPLOYEES.			CLASSIFICATION OF SUPERIOR EMPLOYEES. *N.B.*—In these columns all are males unless the contrary is indicated.												
						Managers.			Supervising and Technical Staff.			Clerical Staff.			Skilled Labourers.			
DESCRIPTION (with Group-letters and Serial Nos. of Classes in each Group).	MAGNITUDE. (*See* Note below title of table on pages 450 and 451.)	Number of Establishments.	Persons.	Males.	Females.	Europeans and Anglo-Indians.	Home Races.	Others.	Europeans and Anglo-Indians.	Home Races.	Others.	Europeans and Anglo-Indians.	Home Races.	Others.	Europeans and Anglo-Indians.	Home Races.	Chinese and Japanese.	Others.
1	2	3	4	5	6	7	8	9	10	11	12	13	14	15	16	17	18	19
J. 3. Dye-works—	Total	4	75	75	..	...	1	3	...	3	...	...	...	4	...	8	...	16
(i) *With mechanical power*	20-49	*1*	*23*	*23*	...	...	...	*1*	...	*3*	...	...	...	*2*	...	*2*	...	..
(ii) *Without mech. power*	..	*3*	*52*	*52*	..	...	*1*	*2*	.	...	...	...	..	*2*	...	*6*	...	*16*
	10-19	2	32	32	..	...	...	2	..	..	...	...	...	2	...	...	...	10
	20-49	1	20	20	...	...	1	...	...	...	...	..	...	...	...	6	...	6
4. Petroleum refineries*—	Total	24	33,080	32,715	365	21	1	2	503	29	25	M85 F-9	1,294	M524 F-3	50	1,407	258	2,957
(i) *With mechanical power*	..	*22*	*32,905*	*32,540*	*365*	*19*	*1*	*2*	*496*	*29*	*25*	*M82* *F-9*	*1,289*	*M523* *F-3*	*50*	*1,365*	*258*	*2,955*
	20-49	3	86	84	2	1	1	1	3	2	2	...	4	3	...	4	...	4
	50-99	4	319	319	...	4	...	...	8	6	...	...	5	5		29	...	44
	100-199	4	485	475	10	4	...	...	9	...	..	1	5	18	...	35	...	32
	200-399	1	206	205	1	1	...	...	2	1	2	...	3	1	...	13	...	7
	400 and over.	10	31,809	31,457	352	9	...	1	474	20	21	M81 F-9	1,272	M502 F-3	50	1,284	258	2,868
(ii) *Without mech. power*	50-99	*2*	*175*	*175*	...	*2*	...	...	*7*	...	...	*3*	*5*	*1*	...	*42*	...	*2*
5. Bulk-oil installations*— *With mechanical power*	50-99	1	95	95	..	1	...	..	...	...	..	...	...	8	...	1	...	6
6. Chemical drug and medicine works—	Total	4	206	206	..	2	..	2	4	2	4	1	2	12	...	19	...	9
(i) *With mechanical power*	50-99	*2*	*173*	*173*	...	*2*	...	...	*4*	*2*	*3*	*1*	*2*	...	...	*19*	...	*9*
(ii) *Without mech. power*	...	*2*	*33*	*33*	...	...	...	*2*	...	...	*1*	...	...	*12*	...	...	...	...
	10-19	1	12	12	...	...	...	1	..	...	1	...	...	2	...	...	...	...
	20-49	1	21	21	...	.	...	1	...	..	...	...	...	10	...	...	...	...
7. Vegetable-oil mills—	Total	37	1,113	956	157	2	23	12	3	M19 F-8	26	1	M-47 F-2	35	..	30	2	58
(i) *With mechanical power*	...	*29*	*925*	*827*	*98*	*1*	*16*	*12*	*2*	*M12* *F-8*	*26*	*1*	*M-40* *F-2*	*35*	...	*30*	*2*	*58*
	10-19	10	139	105	34	...	10	...	...	7	1	...	M-8 F-2	...	...	10	...	4
	20-49	16	481	427	54	...	6	10	1	2	13	1	14	16	...	17	2	36
	50-99	2	108	100	8	...	.	2	..	M-3 F-8	9	...	3	11	...	...	...	8
	100-199	1	197	195	2	1	...	...	1	...	3	...	15	8	...	3	...	10
(ii) *Without mech. power*	...	*8*	*188*	*129*	*59*	*1*	*7*	...	*1*	*7*	...	...	*7*	...	...	...	...	...
	10-19	7	102	80	22	...	7	...	...	7	...	...	7	...	...	...	...	...
	50-99	1	86	49	37	1	...	...	1	...	..	...	...	...	...	...	...	...
K. Food	...	482	24,080	22,251	1,829	M54 F-2	M 274 F-15	M 139 F-1	M 162 F-2	M 280 F-35	481	17	M 1005 F-2	436	18	M 692 F-389	M 227 F-3	994
1. Biscuit factories— *Without mech. power*	10-19	1	12	12	...	...	...	1	...	...	...	...	...	.	...	...	...	...
2. Flour mills— *With mechanical power*	20-49	3	108	106	2	...	...	3	1	...	1	...	...	4	...	...	...	11
3. Rice mills†— *With mechanical power*	Total	388	21,678	20,658	1,020	44	M 218 F10	M 127 F-1	144	M 230 F26	391	14	M998 F-2	397	18	671	226	932
(a) *The whole Province*	10-19	103	1,576	1,478	98	2	M72 F-1	M27 F-1	...	M37 F-2	43	...	M115 F-1	29	1	113	1	114
	20-49	204	5,948	5,546	402	9	M 126 F-6	63	10	M 117 F-9	126	5	M411 F-1	161	...	340	15	380
	50-99	36	2,381	2,238	143	4	M19 F-3	12	8	M47 F-15	30	...	124	45	...	69	9	69
	100-199	19	2,440	2,397	43	8	1	10	20	22	25	2	52	65	6	43	54	77
	200-399	20	5,347	5,298	49	17	...	3	81	5	166	7	245	61	6	80	95	207
	400 and over.	6	3,986	3,701	285	4	...	2	25	2	1	..	51	36	5	26	52	83
(b) *Arakan Division*	...	*10*	*951*	*944*	*7*	*7*	*1*	*2*	*17*	*2*	*1*	..	*38*	*6*	...	*17*	*25*	*28*
	20-49	1	23	23	...	...	...	1	1	...	...	...	1	...	...	...	...	...
	50-99	4	273	271	2	3	1	...	5	2	..	..	18	..	..	1	...	4
	100-199	5	655	650	5	4	...	1	11	...	1	...	19	6	...	3	4	10
																13	21	14

* Pipe-line pumping stations have been included in J4, Petroleum refineries.

† Includes one owned by a company of which some directors are American subjects, and three owned by one company of which some directors are Belgian subjects.

Classification of all Industrial Establishments and of the Persons employed in them—continued.

CLASSIFICATION OF UNSKILLED LABOURERS.																						
TOTAL.			MALES.										FEMALES.									
			European and Anglo-Indians.	Home Races.			Chinese and Japanese.			Others.			European and Anglo-Indians.	Home Races.			Chinese and Japanese.			Others.		
Persons.	Males.	Females.		Age 18 or over.	Age 14 to 18.	Age under 14.	Age 18 or over.	Age 14 to 18.	Age under 14.	Age 18 or over.	Age 14 to 18.	Age under 14.		Age 18 or over.	Age 14 to 18.	Age under 14.	Age 18 or over.	Age 14 to 18.	Age under 14.	Age 18 or over.	Age 14 to 18.	Age under 14.
20	21	22	23	24	25	26	27	28	29	30	31	32	33	34	35	36	37	38	39	40	41	42
40	40	...	...	1	...	...	...	...	...	33	2	4	...	...	...	...	...	...	...	...	...	...
15	*15*	...	...	*1*	...	...	...	...	...	*14*	...	...	...	...	...	...	...	...	...	...	...	...
25	*25*	...	...	...	...	...	...	...	...	*19*	*2*	*4*	...	...	...	...	...	...	...	...	...	...
18	18	...	...	...	...	...	...	...	...	12	2	4	...	...	...	...	...	...	...	...	...	...
7	7	...	...	...	...	...	...	...	...	7	...	...	...	...	...	...	...	...	...	...	...	...
25,912	25,559	353	72	6,170	200	24	24	...	...	17,942	884	243	1	291	51	5	...	...	...	5	...	...
25,799	*25,446*	*353*	72	*6,124*	*198*	*24*	*24*	...	...	*17,877*	884	*243*	*1*	*291*	*51*	*5*	...	...	...	*5*	...	...
61	59	2	...	22	1	...	...	...	...	35	...	1	...	2	...	...	...	...	...	...	...	...
218	218	...	1	43	2	...	...	...	...	165	7	...	...	...	...	...	...	...	...	...	...	...
387	377	10	...	190	7	3	1	...	...	167	3	6	...	6	3	...	...	...	...	1	...	...
176	175	1	...	68	1	...	...	...	...	105	1	...	...	1	...	...	...	...	...	...	...	...
24,957	24,617	340	71	5,801	187	21	23	...	...	17,405	873	236	1	282	48	5	...	...	...	4	...	...
113	*113*	...	...	*46*	*2*	...	...	...	...	*65*	...	...	...	...	...	...	...	...	...	...	...	...
79	79	...	...	1	...	...	...	...	...	76	2	...	...	...	...	...	...	...	...	...	...	...
149	149	...	...	9	...	...	16	1	1	111	10	1	...	...	...	...	...	...	...	...	...	...
131	*131*	...	...	*9*	...	...	...	...	...	*111*	*10*	*1*	...	...	...	...	...	...	...	...	...	...
18	*18*	...	...	...	...	...	*16*	*1*	*1*	...	...	...	...	...	...	...	...	...	...	...	...	...
8	8	...	...	...	...	...	7	...	1	...	...	...	...	...	...	...	...	...	...	...	...	...
10	10	...	...	...	...	...	9	1	...	...	...	...	...	...	...	...	...	...	...	...	...	...
845	698	147	...	317	34	1	30	...	...	308	5	3	...	118	24	3	...	...	...	2	...	...
680	*592*	*88*	...	*226*	*26*	...	*30*	...	...	*302*	*5*	*3*	...	*74*	*12*	...	...	...	...	*2*	...	...
97	65	32	...	49	6	...	...	...	...	8	2	...	...	28	4	...	...	...	...	...	...	...
363	309	54	...	109	6	...	13	...	...	177	1	3	...	44	8	...	...	...	...	2	...	...
64	64	...	...	8	...	...	17	...	...	39	...	...	...	...	...	...	...	...	...	...	...	...
156	154	2	...	60	14	...	...	...	...	78	2	...	...	2	...	...	...	...	...	...	...	...
165	*106*	*59*	...	*91*	*8*	*1*	...	...	...	*6*	...	...	...	*44*	*12*	*2*	...	...	...	...	...	...
81	59	22	...	50	8	1	...	...	...	...	...	...	...	19	2	1	...	...	...	...	...	...
84	47	37	...	41	...	...	...	...	...	6	...	...	...	25	10	2	...	...	...	...	...	...
18,852	17,472	1,380	15	2,213	177	42	190	6	1	14,432	324	72	...	805	155	49	4	3	3	297	25	23
11	11	...	...	6	4	1	...	...	...	...	...	...	...	...	...	...	...	...	...	...	...	...
88	86	2	...	...	...	...	...	...	...	85	1	...	...	...	...	...	...	...	...	2	...	...
17,239	16,258	981	10	1,715	137	23	143	2	...	13,845	311	72	...	512	119	12	...	...	...	277	35	33
1,017	984	93	...	384	19	1	5	...	...	558	17	...	...	75	17	...	...	...	...	1	...	...
4,167	3,781	386	...	816	61	3	22	...	...	2,803	60	14	...	286	72	3	...	...	...	23	2	...
1,907	1,802	125	...	195	25	11	4	...	...	1,513	36	18	...	97	14	9	...	...	...	5	...	...
2,055	2,012	43	...	148	10	4	82	2	...	1,734	28	4	...	27	4	...	...	...	...	13	...	...
4,374	4,325	49	...	132	22	3	10	...	...	4,048	103	7	...	17	5	...	...	...	...	24	4	2
3,699	3,414	285	10	100	...	1	20	...	...	3,189	65	29	...	10	...	...	...	...	...	212	32	31
807	800	7	...	26	4	...	...	...	...	750	18	2	...	7	...	...	...	...	...	...	...	...
15	15	...	...	...	...	...	...	...	...	15	...	...	...	...	...	...	...	...	...	...	...	...
227	225	2	...	7	...	...	...	...	...	208	8	2	...	2	...	...	...	...	...	...	...	...
565	560	5	...	19	4	...	...	...	...	527	10	...	...	5	...	...	...	...	...	...	...	...

Imperial Table XXIIa.—The Special Industrial Census. Part I.—

ESTABLISHMENTS. Description (with Group-letters and Serial Nos. of Classes in each Group).	Magnitude. (See Note below title of table on pages 450 and 451.)	Number of Establishments.	Total Employees. Persons.	Males.	Females.	Managers. Europeans and Anglo-Indians.	Managers. Home Races.	Managers. Others.	Supervising and Technical Staff. Europeans and Anglo-Indians.	Supervising and Technical Staff. Home Races.	Supervising and Technical Staff. Others.	Clerical Staff. Europeans and Anglo-Indians.	Clerical Staff. Home Races.	Clerical Staff. Others.	Skilled Labourers. Europeans and Anglo-Indians.	Skilled Labourers. Home Races.	Skilled Labourers. Chinese and Japanese.	Skilled Labourers. Others.
						Classification of Superior Employees. N.B.—In these columns all are males unless the contrary is indicated.												
1	2	3	4	5	6	7	8	9	10	11	12	13	14	15	16	17	18	19
K. 3. Rice mills—concld.																		
(c) *Rangoon* ...	...	50	8,317	7,993	324	15	14	21	72	40	70	1	250	186	10	129	136	304
	10-19	2	33	33	...	...	...	2	...	...	4	...	2	1	...	1	...	1
	20-49	17	498	498	...	...	10	7	...	12	13	...	54	40	...	23	3	50
	50-99	5	367	366	1	1	3	1	2	2	8	...	30	27	...	11	2	14
	100-199	10	1,309	1,296	13	2	1	7	5	22	23	1	20	51	3	17	23	50
	200-399	11	2,773	2,747	26	9	...	2	40	2	21	...	98	37	5	54	61	116
	400 and over.	5	3,337	3,053	284	3	...	2	25	2	1	.	46	30	2	23	47	73
(d) *Pegu Division (less Rangoon).**	...	119	5,088	4,906	182	7	M68 F-3	42	13	M50 F-1	226	3	249	103	7	187	24	267
	10-19	32	489	488	1	...	17	15	..	8	13	...	34	14	...	31	...	50
	20-49	70	2,033	1,900	133	2	M44 F-2	22	...	29	58	3	154	56	...	121	...	133
	50-99	11	734	701	33	...	M-7 F-1	4	1	M10 F-1	10	...	32	12	...	19	1	18
	100-199	2	256	250	6	2	...	...	3	...	...	...	5	...	3	6	9	6
	200-399	3	927	919	8	2	...	1	9	3	145	...	19	15	1	7	9	50
	400 and over.	1	649	648	1	1	...	...	...	...	...	...	5	6	3	3	5	10
(e) *Irrawaddy Division*	...	96	4,348	4,252	96	9	M63 F-2	23	32	55	58	9	M282 F-1	52	...	106	26	201
	10-19	24	372	372	...	1	18	5	...	10	12	...	32	6	...	19	...	24
	20-49	56	1,710	1,677	33	2	40	14	...	38	43	2	M-91 F-1	33	...	59	1	116
	50-99	10	619	571	48	...	M-5 F-2	4	...	7	3	...	31	4	...	9	...	20
	200-399	6	1,647	1,632	15	6	...	...	32	...	...	7	128	9	...	19	25	41
(f) *Toungoo and Thatôn districts.*	...	32	808	757	51	1	M24 F-3	M-3 F-1	1	M17 F-4	5	...	M-42 F-1	13	...	72	8	84
	10-19	14	196	186	10	.	M11 F-1	M-1 F-1	...	M-6 F-1	3	..	M-15 F-1	2	...	19	...	21
	20-49	15	389	383	6	1	M11 F-2	1	1	M11 F-3	1	...	22	4	...	46	3	27
	50-99	2	109	93	16	...	2	...	...	...	...	...	2	..	...	5	...	2
	100-199	1	114	95	19	...	...	1	...	...	1	...	3	7	...	3	...	4
(g) *Amherst, Salween, Tavoy and Mergui districts.*	...	30	1,056	988	68	4	M11 F-1	14	9	20	11	1	80	29	...	76	11	43
	10-19	4	59	59	...	..	4	...	...	4	1	...	6	1	...	6	1	2
	20-49	22	691	638	53	4	M-6 F-1	11	8	12	10	...	58	25	...	47	7	33
	50-99	3	200	185	15	...	1	2	...	4	...	...	11	2	...	19	2	5
	100-199	1	106	106	...	...	..	1	1	...	...	1	5	1	...	4	1	3
(h) *Upper Burma and the Shan States.*	...	51	1,110	818	292	1	M37 F-1	12	.	M46 F-21	20	.	57	8	1	83	1	25
	10-19	27	427	340	87	1	22	4	...	M-9 F-1	10	...	26	5	1	37	...	16
	20-49	23	604	427	177	...	M15 F-1	7	...	M15 F-6	1	..	31	3	...	43	1	19
	50-99	1	79	51	28	...	...	1	...	M22 F-14	9	...	...	...	..	3	...	...
4. Bakeries and confectioneries—	Total	11	245	241	4	M-4 F-1	...	7	M-5 F-2	...	27	2	2	14	.	...	...	...
(i) *With mechanical power*	20-49	1	21	21	...	...	...	1	...	...	9	...	...	1	...	...	...	...
(ii) *Without mech. power*	...	10	224	220	4	M-4 F-1	..	6	M-5 F-2	...	18	2	2	13	...	...	...	...
	10-19	5	81	81	...	1	...	4	1	...	...	1	...	1	...	...	...	...
	20-49	5	143	139	4	M-3 F-1	...	2	M-4 F-2	...	18	1	2	12	...	...	...	...
5. Dairy farms— *With mechanical power*	20-49	1	48	33	15	F-1	...	..	...	...	...	...	...	...	...	...	...	...
6. Slaughter-houses— *With mechanical power*	20-49	1	23	23	...	1	...	...	1	...	...	...	...	...	...	...	...	1
7. Sugar factories— *Without mech. power*	Total	54	945	640	305	...	52	2	...	40	15	...	...	...	...	...	...	...
	10-19	36	471	330	141	...	36	...	...	1	..	...	..	...	...	...	...	...
	20-49	17	421	257	164	...	15	2	...	13	15	...	...	...	...	...	...	...
	50-99	1	53	53	...	...	1	...	...	26	...	..	...	...	...	...	...	...

* That, is the Insein, Hanthawaddy, Tharrawaddy, Pegu and Prome districts.

Classification of all Industrial Establishments and of the Persons employed in them—continued.

CLASSIFICATION OF UNSKILLED LABOURERS.																						
TOTAL.			MALES.										FEMALES.									
			Europeans and Anglo-Indians.	Home Races.			Chinese and Japanese.			Others.			Europeans and Anglo-Indians.	Home Races.			Chinese and Japanese.			Others.		
Persons.	Males.	Females.		Age 18 or over.	Age 14 to 18.	Age under 14.	Age 18 or over.	Age 14 to 18.	Age under 14.	Age 18 or over.	Age 14 to 18.	Age under 14.		Age 18 or over.	Age 14 to 18.	Age 14 to 18.	Age 18 or over.	Age 14 to 18.	Age under 14.	Age 18 or over.	Age 14 to 18.	Age under 14.
20	21	22	23	24	25	26	27	28	29	30	31	32	33	34	35	36	37	38	39	40	41	42
7,069	6,745	324	10	164	5	4	106	2	...	6,292	130	32	...	11	...	...	...	...	...	247	22	22
22	22	...	...	...	...	...	...	...	...	21	1	...	...	...	...	...	...	...	...	...	...	...
286	286	...	...	11	...	...	...	...	...	266	9	...	...	...	...	...	...	...	...	...	...	...
266	265	1	...	1	1	...	...	...	...	263	...	...	...	...	...	...	...	...	...	1	...	...
1,084	1,071	13	...	98	4	3	78	2	...	869	16	1	...	1	...	...	...	...	...	12	...	...
2,328	2,302	26	...	23	...	...	8	...	...	2,223	46	2	...	...	...	...	...	...	...	23	1	2
3,083	2,799	284	10	31	...	1	20	...	...	2,650	58	29	...	10	...	...	...	...	...	211	32	31
3,838	3,660	178	...	588	45	7	17	...	...	2,926	60	17	...	133	27	6	...	...	...	11	1	...
307	306	1	...	73	3	...	5	...	...	217	8	...	...	1	...	...	...	...	...	...	...	...
1,409	1,278	131	...	303	28	2	9	...	...	919	14	3	...	101	21	1	...	...	...	7	1	...
618	587	31	...	74	13	5	...	...	...	462	19	14	...	22	1	5	...	...	...	3	...	...
222	216	6	...	8	...	...	3	...	...	205	...	...	...	5	1	...	...	...	...	...	...	...
666	658	8	...	61	1	...	...	...	...	584	12	...	...	4	4	...	...	...	...	...	...	...
616	615	1	...	69	...	...	...	...	...	539	7	...	...	...	...	...	...	...	...	1	...	...
3,429	3,336	93	...	251	42	5	7	...	...	2,840	83	8	...	66	8	...	...	...	...	18	1	...
245	245	...	...	68	4	1	...	...	...	170	2	...	...	...	...	...	...	...	...	...	...	...
1,270	1,238	32	...	169	10	...	1	...	...	1,027	29	2	...	12	3	...	...	...	...	16	1	...
534	488	46	...	66	7	1	4	...	...	402	7	1	...	41	4		...	...	...	1	...	...
1,380	1,365	15	...	48	21	3	2	...	...	1,241	45	5	...	13	1	...	...	...	...	1	...	...
563	521	42	...	121	4	1	1	...	...	382	11	1	...	33	8	...	...	...	...	1	...	...
114	108	6	...	39	2	...	...	...	...	63	4	...	...	5	...	...	...	...	...	1	...	...
256	255	1		46	...	...	...	...	...	203	6	...	...	1	...	...	...	...	...	...	...	...
98	82	16	...	16	...	...	...	...	...	64	1	1	...	11	5	...	...	...	...	...	...	...
95	76	19	...	20	2	1	1	...	...	52	...	...	...	16	3	...	...	...	...	...	...	...
746	679	67	...	132	14	1	2	...	...	513	5	12	...	62	5	...	...	...	...	...	...	...
34	34	...	...	8	1	...	...	...	...	25	...	...	...	...	...	...	...	...	...	...	...	...
469	417	52	...	95	9	1	2	...	...	299	2	9	...	50	2	...	...	...	...	...	...	...
154	139	15	...	26	4	...	...	...	...	108	1	...	...	12	3	...	...	...	...	...	...	...
89	89	...		3	...	...	...	...	...	81	2	3	...	...	...	...	...	...	...	...	...	...
787	517	270	...	333	23	5	10	...	...	142	4	...	...	200	64	6	...	...	...	...	...	...
295	209	86	...	136	9	...	...	...	...	62	2	...	...	69	17	...	...	...	...	...	...	...
462	292	170	...	192	14	...	10	...	...	74	2	...	...	122	46	2	...	...	...	...	...	...
30	16	14	...	5	...	5	...	...	...	6	...	...	...	9	1	4	...	...	...	...	...	...
181	180	1	5	2	2	1	5	4	...	161	...	...	...	1	...	...	...	...	...	...	...	...
10	10	...	...	...	...	...	...	...	...	10	...	...	...	...	...	...	...	...	...	...	...	...
171	170	1	5	2	2	1	5	4	...	151	...	...	...	1	...	...	...	...	...	...	...	...
73	73	...	2	...	...	...	...	...	...	71	...	...	...	...	...	...	...	...	...	...	...	...
98	97	1	3	2	2	1	5	4	...	80	...	...	...	1	...	...	...	...	...	...	...	...
47	33	14	...	...	...	...	...	...	...	32	1	...	...	8	...	3	...	...	...	3	...	...
20	20	...	...	...	...	...	...	...	...	19	1	...	...	...	...	...	...	...	...	...	...	...
836	531	305	...	482	33	16	...	...	...	...	...	...	...	242	37	26	...	...	...	...	...	...
434	293	141	...	270	15	8	...	...	...	...	...	...	...	112	17	12	...	...	...	...	...	...
376	212	164	...	186	18	8	...	...	...	...	...	...	...	130	20	14	...	...	...	...	...	...
26	26	...	...	26	...	...	...	...	...	...	...	...	...	...	...	...	...	...	...	...	...	...

ESTABLISHMENTS.			TOTAL EMPLOYEES.			CLASSIFICATION OF SUPERIOR EMPLOYEES. N.B.—In these columns all are males unless the contrary is indicated.												
						Managers.			Supervising and Technical Staff.			Clerical Staff.			Skilled Labourers.			
DESCRIPTION (with Group-letters and Serial Nos. of Classes in each Group).	MAGNITUDE. (See Note below title of table on pages 450 and 451.)	Number of Establishments.	Persons.	Males.	Females.	Europeans and Anglo-Indians.	Home Races.	Others.	Europeans and Anglo-Indians.	Home Races.	Others.	Europeans and Anglo-Indians.	Home Races.	Others.	Europeans and Anglo-Indians.	Home Races.	Chinese and Japanese.	Others.
1	2	3	4	5	6	7	8	9	10	11	12	13	14	15	16	17	18	19
K. 8. Breweries and distilleries—	Total	2	183	183	...	1	...	1	3	5	34	...	1	19	...	9	...	26
(i) *With mechanical power*	100-199	1	154	154	...	1	...	...	3	5	33	...	1	5	...	9	...	26
(ii) *Without mech. power*	20-49	1	29	29	...	...	...	1	...	...	1	...	...	14	...	...	..	...
9. Water-works—	Total	4	256	241	15	3	..	1	8	5	6	...	3	...	...	7	..	23
With mechanical power		3	135	135	...	2	...	1	5	3	6	.	1	..	...	5	...	21
	20-49	2	78	78	...	1	.	1	2	3	6	...	1	...	...	2	...	19
	50-99	1	57	57	...	1	...	..	3	...	..	...	...	...	...	3	...	2
Without mech. power	100-199	1	121	106	15	1	...	...	3	2	..	...	2	..	...	2	...	2
10. Tobacco, cigar or cigarette factories—	Total	17	582	114	468	1	M-4 F-5	7	...	F-9	7	1	1	2	...	M-5 F389	M-1 F-3	1
(i) *With mechanical power*	20-49	1	44	22	22	1	...	...	..	...	2	1	1	...	...	M-1 F-1	1	1
(ii) *Without mech. power*	...	16	538	92	446	...	M-4 F-5	7	...	F-9	5	...	...	2	...	M-4 F-388	F-2	...
	10-19	7	104	32	72	...	M-3 F-2	2	...	...	1	.	...	...	...	M-1 F-65	...	...
	20-49	8	226	49	177	...	M-1 F-3	4	...	F-9	4	...	...	...	...	M-3 F-129	..	...
	200-399	1	208	11	197	...	...	1	...	...	...	..	...	2	...	F-194	F-3	...
L. Clothing ...	...	48	1,033	979	54	M-5 F-1	10	32	M-9 F-2	5	63	..	2	29	M-1 F-2	M191 F-24	165	305
1. Tailoring works—	Total	26	461	461	..	4	1	21	9	4	37	...	1	24	1	19	60	226
Without mech. power	10-19	20	263	263	...	1	1	18	3	...	5	...	..	5	...	16	91	153
	20-49	6	198	198	...	3	...	3	6	4	32	...	1	19	1	3	39	73
2. Dress makers and milliners— *Without mech. power*	20-49	2	47	27	20	M-1 F-1	...	...	F-2	..	...	..	...	...	F-2	...	...	17
3. Boot and shoe factories *—	Total	14	287	280	7	...	4	10	...	...	25	..	...	5	...	M-49 F-6	105	39
Without mech. power	10-19	10	145	138	7	...	3	7	..	...	1	..	...	3	...	M-26 F-6	79	5
	20-49	4	142	142	...	..	1	3	...	...	24	...	...	2	...	23	26	34
4. Umbrella factories—	Total	6	238	211	27	...	5	1	...	1	1	...	1	...	...	M123 F-18	...	23
Without mech. power	10-19	2	28	24	4		2	...	.	1	...	...	...	...	...	M-20 F-4	...	...
	20-49	2	62	61	1	...	2	...	...	...	...	...	1	...	...	M-58 F-1	...	...
	50-99	2	148	126	22	...	1	1	...	...	1	...	...	...	...	M-45 F-13	...	23
M. Furniture ...	...	12	598	597	1	3	M-1 F-1	7	13	34	23	...	14	8	...	119	75	32
Without mech. power	10-19	5	70	69	1	...	F-1	4	...	...	...	...	...	1	...	1	37	1
	20-49	4	111	111	...	1	...	3	1	...	23	.	1	1	...	1	38	...
	50-99	1	59	59	...	...	1	...	..	...	...	...	...	5	...	...	...	...
	100-199	1	123	123	...	1	...	...	2	2	...	...	...	...	...	22	...	30
	200-399	1	235	235	...	1	...	...	10	32	...	...	13	1	...	95	...	...
N. Building ...	...	17	1,270	1,259	11	3	9	5	13	1	15	M-1 F-2	43	15	12	119	34	180
1. Stone, marble and cement works— *Without mech. power*	...	2	85	85	...	...	2	...	...	...	...	..	14	...	...	56	..	...
	20-49	1	34	34	...	...	1	...	...	...	...	...	1	...	...	27	..	...
	50-99	1	51	51	...	...	1	...	...	...	...	...	13	...	...	29	...	...
2. Lime-works and kilns—	Total	11	312	303	9	...	7	4	...	...	4	1	...	1	...	3	...	...
Without mech. power	10-19	6	92	92	...	...	5	1	...	...	1	..	...	...	...	...	...	...
	20-49	4	133	130	3	...	2	2	...	...	3	1	...	...	...	3	...	...
	50-99	1	87	81	6	...	...	1	...	...	...	...	...	1	...	...	...	...

* Including factories using feather, wood or any other material.

Classification of all Industrial Establishments and of the Persons employed in them—continued.

CLASSIFICATION OF UNSKILLED LABOURERS.																						
TOTAL.			MALES.										FEMALES.									
			Europeans and Anglo-Indians.	Home Races.			Chinese and Japanese.			Others.			Europeans and Anglo-Indians.	Home Races.			Chinese and Japanese.			Others.		
Persons.	Males.	Females.		Age 18 or over.	Age 14 to 18.	Age under 14.	Age 18 or over.	Age 14 to 18.	Age under 14.	Age 18 or over.	Age 14 to 18.	Age under 14.		Age 18 or over.	Age 14 to 18.	Age under 14.	Age 18 or over.	Age 14 to 18.	Age under 14.	Age 18 or over.	Age 14 to 18.	Age under 14.
20	21	22	23	24	25	26	27	28	29	30	31	32	33	34	35	36	37	38	39	40	41	42
84	84	...	...	...	...	...	13	...	...	67	4	...	...	...	...	...	...	...	...	...	...	...
71	71	...	...	...	...	...	...	...	...	67	4	...	...	...	...	...	...	...	...	...	...	...
13	13	...	...	...	...	...	13	...	...	...	...	...	...	...	...	...	...	...	...	...	...	...
200	185	15	...	8	1	...	...	...	...	175	1	...	...	...	...	...	...	...	...	15	...	...
91	91	...	...	3	...	...	...	...	...	88	...	...	...	...	...	...	...	...	...	...	...	...
43	43	...	...	1	...	...	...	...	...	42	...	...	...	...	...	...	...	...	...	...	...	...
48	48	...	...	2	...	...	...	...	...	46	...	...	...	...	...	...	...	...	...	...	...	...
109	94	15	...	5	1	...	...	...	...	87	1	...	...	...	...	...	...	...	...	15	...	...
146	84	62	...	...	...	1	29	...	1	48	5	...	...	38	6	8	4	3	3	...	...	...
35	14	21	...	...	...	...	...	...	...	14	...	...	...	17	4	...	...	...	...	...	...	...
111	70	41	...	...	...	1	29	...	1	34	5	...	...	21	2	8	4	3	3	...	...	...
30	25	5	...	...	...	...	...	...	...	22	3	...	...	4	1	...	...	...	...	...	...	...
73	37	36	...	...	...	1	29	...	1	4	2	...	...	17	1	8	4	3	3	...	...	...
8	8	...	...	...	...	...	...	...	...	8	...	...	...	...	...	...	...	...	...	...	...	...
187	162	25	...	26	10	1	2	2	1	103	12	5	5	14	6	...	...	...	...	...	...	...
54	54	...	...	1	...	...	1	2	1	37	9	3	...	...	...	...	...	...	...	...	...	...
40	40	...	...	1	...	...	...	...	1	29	7	2	...	...	...	...	...	...	...	...	...	...
14	14	...	...	...	...	...	1	2	...	8	2	1	...	...	...	...	...	...	...	...	...	...
24	9	15	...	...	...	...	...	...	...	7	2	...	5	8	2	...	...	...	...	...	...	...
44	43	1	...	11	8	1	1	...	...	21	...	1	...	1	...	...	...	...	...	...	...	...
15	14	1	...	4	8	1	1	...	...	...	...	...	...	1	...	...	...	...	...	...	...	...
29	29	...	...	7		...	...	...	...	21	...	1	...	...	...	...	...	...	...	...	...	...
65	56	9	...	14	2	...	...	...	...	38	1	1	...	5	4	...	...	...	...	...	...	...
1	1	...	...	...	1	...	...	...	...	...	...	...	...	...	...	...	...	...	...	...	...	...
...	...	...	...	...	...	...	...	...	...	...	...	...	...	...	...	...	...	...	...	...	...	...
64	55	9	...	14	1	...	...	...	...	38	1	1	...	5	4	...	...	...	...	...	...	...
269	269	...	...	98	...	...	19	...	1	133	11	7	...	...	...	...	...	...	...	...	...	...
25	25	...	...	6	...	...	2	...	...	16	...	1	...	...	...	...	...	...	...	...	...	...
42	42	...	...	1	...	...	17	...	1	8	9	6	...	...	...	...	...	...	...	...	...	...
53	53	...	...	1	...	...	...	...	...	52	...	...	...	...	...	...	...	...	...	...	...	...
66	66	...	...	7	...	...	...	...	...	57	2	...	...	...	...	...	...	...	...	...	...	...
83	83	...	...	83	...	...	...	...	...	...	...	...	...	...	...	...	...	...	...	...	...	...
828	809	9	1	163	14	...	33	1	...	584	10	3	...	6	...	...	...	...	...	2	...	1
13	13	...	...	6	7	...	...	...	...	...	...	...	...	...	...	...	...	...	...	...	...	...
5	5	...	...	2	3	...	...	...	...	...	...	...	...	...	...	...	...	...	...	...	...	...
8	8	...	...	4	4	...	...	...	...	...	...	...	...	...	...	...	...	...	...	...	...	...
292	283	9	...	149	6	...	32	1	...	89	3	3	...	6	...	...	...	...	...	2	...	1
82	82	...	...	66	5	...	...	...	...	11	...	...	...	...	...	...	...	...	...	...	...	...
125	122	3	...	43	1	...	3	...	...	69	3	3	...	...	...	...	...	...	...	2	...	1
85	79	6	...	40	...	...	29	1	...	9	...	...	...	6	...	...	...	...	...	...	...	...

ESTABLISHMENTS.			TOTAL EMPLOYEES.			CLASSIFICATION OF SUPERIOR EMPLOYEES. *N.B.*—In these columns all are males unless the contrary is indicated.												
						Managers.			Supervising and Technical Staff.			Clerical Staff.			Skilled Labourers.			
DESCRIPTION (with Group-letters and Serial Nos. of Classes in each Group).	MAGNITUDE. (*See* Note below title of table on pages 450 and 451.)	Number of Establishments.	Persons.	Males.	Females.	Europeans and Anglo-Indians.	Home Races.	Others.	Europeans and Anglo-Indians.	Home Races.	Others.	Europeans and Anglo-Indians.	Home Races.	Others.	Europeans and Anglo-Indians.	Home Races.	Chinese and Japanese.	Others.
1	2	3	4	5	6	7	8	9	10	11	12	13	14	15	16	17	18	19
N. Building—concld.																		
3. Plumbing and sanitary engineering— *Without mech. power*	50-99	2	153	153	...	1	...	1	4	...	5	...	3	10	...	2	1	50
4. Constructional engineers— *With mechanical power*	..	2	720	718	2	2	..	..	9	1	6	F-2	26	4	12	58	33	130
	100-129	1	147	147	...	1	...	...	1	.	...	...	1	2	12	33	17	34
	400 and over.	1	573	571	2	1	...	...	8	1	6	F-2	25	2	...	25	16	96
P. Construction of means of transport or communication—	Total	41	11,191	11,121	70	23	M-2 F-1	M13 F-1	M134 F-5	16	M12 F-1	M47 F-10	189	261	M 190 F-51	1,845	425	3,452
1. Railway works—	Total	6	3,004	3,004	...	5	...	1	41	...	1	1	15	112	59	169	166	1,396
(i) *With mechanical power*	...	*5*	*2,982*	*2,982*	...	*5*	...	...	*41*	...	*1*	*1*	*15*	*111*	*58*	*168*	*166*	*1,391*
	100-199	2	338	338	...	2	...	...	14	...	1	1	5	44	28	23	1	47
	200-399	1	333	333	...	1	...	...	5	...	...	...	1	4	21	...	...	107
	400 and over.	2	2,311	2,311	..	2	...	...	22	...	...	...	9	63	9	145	165	1,237
(ii) *Without mech. power*	20-49	*1*	*22*	*22*	...	...	...	*1*	...	...	...	...	...	*1*	*1*	*1*	...	*5*
2. Tramway works—	Total	2	667	666	1	2	...	...	6	2	...	1	74	2	18	179	9	67
With mechanical power	200-399	1	257	257	...	1	...	..	3	...	..	...	3	1	10	59	7	47
	400 and over.	1	410	409	1	1	...	...	3	2	...	1	71	1	8	120	2	20
3. Bridge-works— *With mechanical power*	200-399	1	259	259	..	1	...	...	3	...	...	...	...	13	3	1	...	23
4. Coach-building works—	Total	3	55	54	1	...	F-1	2	...	...	...	...	1	1	...	6	29	8
Without mech. power	10-19	2	29	28	1	...	F-1	1		...	...	...	..	1	...	5	14	1
	20-49	1	26	26	...	...	...	1	...	...	...	...	1	..	...	1	15	7
5. Motor-car works—	Total	11	1,125	1,119	6	7	1	3	M-34 F-1	3	2	M26 F-5	36	78	48	384	24	158
(i) *With mechanical power*	...	*10*	*1,112*	*1,106*	*6*	*7*	*1*	*2*	*M-34 F-1*	*3*	*2*	*M26 F-5*	*35*	*78*	*48*	*375*	*24*	*158*
	20-49	3	95	95	...	...	1	2	...	1	...	1	2	10	...	27	4	14
	50-99	4	282	282	...	4	...	...	12	1	.	9	12	14	16	135	7	35
	100-199	2	287	283	4	2	...	...	M-8 F-1	1	2	M11 F-3	14	42	5	45	3	14
	400 and over.	1	448	446	2	1	...	...	14	...	...	M-5 F-2	7	12	27	168	10	95
(ii) *Without mech. power*	10-19	*1*	*13*	*13*	...	...	...	*1*	...	...	...	...	*1*	...	...	*9*	...	...
6. Shipyards, boat-building yards, dock-yards and Port Authorities' workshops—	Total	15	5,756	5,753	3	7	1	M-5 F-1	34	4	M-3 F-1	16	59	38	60	1,100	185	1,776
(i) *With mechanical power*	...	*7*	*5,433*	*5,433*	...	*6*	...	...	*34*	*4*	...	*16*	*54*	*30*	*60*	*1,072*	*147*	*1,726*
	109-199	2	301	301	...	1	...	...	2	...	...	1	..	2	12	152	2	23
	200-399	2	493	493	...	2	...	...	3	...	...	...	13	2	8	67	6	229
	400 and over.	3	4,639	4,639	...	3	...	...	29	4	...	15	41	26	40	853	139	1,474
(ii) *Without mech. power*	...	*8*	*323*	*320*	*3*	*1*	*1*	*M-5 F-1*	...	...	*M-3 F-1*	...	*5*	*8*	...	*28*	*38*	*50*
	10-19	3	41	39	2	...	1	M-1 F-1	...	...	F-1	...	1	...	...	16	8	...
	20-49	3	90	90	...	...	...	3	...	...	3	...	1	4		8	30	11
	50-99	1	81	81	...	1	...	...	...	...	...	...	3	...	...	4	...	5
	100-199	1	111	110	1	...	...	1	...	...	...	...	...	4	...	...	...	34
7. Telephone system— *With mechanical power*	100-199	1	181	122	59	1	...	...	M-10 F-4	6	4	M-3 F-4	4	12	M-2 F-51	6	2	24
8. Stone-breaking yards and workshops connected with road-making—	Total	2	144	144	...	...	...	2	6	1	2	...	..	5	...	...	...	..
(i) *With mechanical power*	50-99	*1*	*67*	*67*	...	...	...	*1*	*6*	*1*	..	...	...	*2*	...	...	...	...
(ii) *Without mech. power*	50-99	*1*	77	77	...	...	...	*1*	...	...	*2*	...	...	*3*	...	...	...	...

Classification of all Industrial Establishments and of the Persons employed in them—continued.

CLASSIFICATION OF UNSKILLED LABOURERS.

Total.			Males.										Females.									
			Europeans and Anglo-Indians.	Home Races.			Chinese and Japanese			Others.			Europeans and Anglo-Indians.	Home Races.			Chinese and Japanese.			Others.		
Persons.	Males.	Females.		Age 18 or over.	Age 14 to 18.	Age under 14.	Age 18 or over.	Age 14 to 18.	Age under 14.	Age 18 or over.	Age 14 to 18.	Age under 14.		Age 18 or over.	Age 14 to 18.	Age under 14.	Age 18 or over.	Age 14 to 18.	Age under 14.	Age 18 or over.	Age 14 to 18.	Age under 14.
20	21	22	23	24	25	26	27	28	29	30	31	32	33	34	35	36	37	38	39	40	41	42
76	76	...	...	1	...	...	...	...	...	73	2	...	...	...		...	...	...	...	...	...	...
437	437	...	1	7	1	...	1	...	...	422	5	...	...	...	...	...	...	...	...	...	...	...
46	46	...	1	2	...	...	...	...	...	43	...	...	...	...	...	...	...	...	...	...	...	...
391	391	...	...	5	1	...	1	...	...	379	5	...	...	...	...	...	...	...	...	...	...	...
4,523	4,522	1	46	299	31	2	33	5	...	3,925	147	34	...	...	...	...	...	...	...	1	...	...
1,038	1,038	...	14	25	1	...	1	...	...	956	41	...	...	...	...	...	...	...	...	...	...	...
1,025	1,025	...	14	21	1	...	1	...	...	947	41	...	...	...	...	...	...	...	...	...	...	...
172	172	...	1	1	...		...	...	...	164	6	...	...	...	...	...	...	...	...	...	...	...
194	194	...	13	...	...	...	...	...	...	181	...	...	...	...	...	...	...	...	...	...	...	...
659	659	...	...	20	1	...	1	...	...	602	35	...	...	...	...	...	...	...	...	...	...	...
13	13	...	...	4	...	...	...	...	...	9	...	...	...	...	...	...	...	...	...	...	...	...
306	306	...	4	108	8	2	2	...	...	183	...	...	...	...	...	...	...	...	...	...	...	...
125	126	...	3	2	2	...	2	...	...	118	...	...	...	...	...	...	...	...	...	...	...	...
180	180	...	1	106	6	2	...	...	...	65	...	...	...	...	...	...	...	...	...	...	...	...
215	215	...	...	...	...	...	...	...	...	215	...	...	...	...	...	...	...	...	...	...	...	...
7	7	...	...	4	2	...	...	...	...	1	...	...	...	...	...	...	...	...	...	...	...	...
6	6	...	...	4	2	...	...	...	...	...	...	...	...	...	...	...	...	...	...	...	...	...
1	1	...	...	...	...	...	...	...	...	1	...	...	...	...	...	...	...	...	...	...	...	...
315	315	...	21	46	6	...	3	...	...	228	10	1	...	...	...	...	...	...	...	...	...	...
313	313	...	21	46	6	...	3	...	...	226	10	1	...	...	...	...	...	...	...	...	...	...
33	33	...	1	6	...	...	...	...	...	26	...	...	...	...	...	...	...	...	...	...	...	...
37	37	...	...	2	...	...	...	...	...	35	...	...	...		...	...	...	...	...	...	...	...
136	136	...	8	15	2	...	3	...	...	105	2	1	...	...	...	...	...	...	...	...	...	...
107	107	...	12	23	4	...	...	...	...	60	8	...	...	...		...	...	...	...	...	...	...
2	2	...	...	...		...	...	...	...	2	...	...	...	...	...	...	...	...	...	...	...	...
2,466	2,465	1	4	105	14	...	25	4	...	2,189	93	31	...	...	...	...	...	...	...	1	...	...
2,284	2,284	...	3	88	12	...	24	...	...	2,041	86	30	...	...	...	...	...	...	...	...	...	...
106	106	...	...	34	...	...	...	...	...	72	...	...	...	...	...	...	...	...	...	...	...	...
163	163	...	...	...	...	...	...	...		163	...	...	...	...	...	...	...	...	...	...	...	...
2,015	2,015	...	3	54	12	...	24	...	...	1,806	86	30	...	...	...	...	...	...	...	...	...	...
182	181	1	1	17	2	...	1	4	...	148	7	1	...	...	...	...	...	...	...	1	...	...
12	12	...	...	10	...	...	1	1	...	...	...	...	...	...	...	...	...	...	...	...	...	...
30	30	...	...	...	...		...	3	...	27	...	...	...	...	...	...	...	...	...	...	...	...
68	68	...	1	7	2	...	...	...	...	58	...	...	...	...	...	...	...	...	...	...	...	...
72	71	1	...	...	...	...	...	...	...	63	7	1	...	...	...	...	...	...	...	1	...	...
48	48	...	...	5	...		...	1	...	39	3	...	...	...	...	...	...	...	...	...	...	...
128	128	...	3	6		...	3	...	...	114	...	2	...	...	...	...	...	...	...	...	...	...
57	57	...	3	6	...	...	3	...	...	43	...	2	...	...	...	...	...	...	...	...	...	...
71	71	...	...	...	...	...	...	...	...	71	...	...	...	...	...	...	...	...	...	...	...	...

IMPERIAL TABLE XXIIA.—THE SPECIAL INDUSTRIAL CENSUS. PART I.—

ESTABLISHMENTS. DESCRIPTION (with Group-letters and Serial Nos. of Classes in each Group.)	MAGNITUDE. (See Note below title of table on pages 460 and 461.)	Number of Establishments.	TOTAL EMPLOYEES. Persons.	Males.	Females.	CLASSIFICATION OF SUPERIOR EMPLOYEES. N.B.—In these columns all are males unless the contrary is indicated. Managers. Europeans and Anglo-Indians.	Managers. Home Races.	Managers. Others.	Supervising and Technical Staff. Europeans and Anglo-Indians.	Supervising and Technical Staff. Home Races.	Supervising and Technical Staff. Others.	Clerical Staff. Europeans and Anglo-Indians.	Clerical Staff. Home Races.	Clerical Staff. Others.	Skilled Labourers. Europeans and Anglo-Indians.	Skilled Labourers. Home Races.	Skilled Labourers. Chinese and Japanese.	Skilled Labourers. Others.
1	2	3	4	5	6	7	8	9	10	11	12	13	14	15	16	17	18	19
Q. Electricity, light and heat	...	10	690	686	4	5	3	2	M-18 F-2	4	2	M-8 F-2	30	14	3	56	1	50
1. Ice factories—	Total	5	165	165	..	1	2	2	3	4	2	1	5	5	...	8	...	17
With mechanical power	10-19	1	13	13	...	...	...	1	1	..	...	1	...	...	...	...	...	3
	20-49	3	90	90	...	1	2	...	...	3	2	-	5	4	...	6	...	5
	50-99	1	62	62	...	...	..	1	2	1	...	...	...	1	...	2	...	9
2. Electric works*—	Total	5	525	521	4	4	1	...	M-15 F-2	...	...	M-7 F-2	25	9	3	48	1	33
With mechanical power	20-49	1	21	21	..	1	...	.	2	...	...	...	1	..	...	1	...	1
	50-99	2	124	124	...	1	1	...	1	...	...	...	12	3	1	24	...	3
	100-199	1	109	105	4	1	...	...	M-6 F-2	...	...	M-4 F-2	12	4	...	11	1	5
	200-399	1	271	271	...	1	...	...	6	...	..	3	.	2	2	12	..	24
R. Other Industries	.	62	3,369	3,320	49	14	M20 F-3	26	M-31 F-3	M50 F-2	84	M44 F-3	145	219	M26 F-5	M 446 F-7	18	1,189
1. Printing†—	Total	48	2,950	2,936	14	11	M15 F-1	21	M-18 F-2	35	80	M38 F-3	131	156	M21 F-5	382	3	1,071
(i) *With mechanical power*	...	*21*	*2,335*	*2,323*	*12*	*10*	*5*	*6*	*M-18 F-2*	*23*	*54*	*M37 F-3*	*71*	*114*	*M21 F-5*	*260*	*3*	*925*
	10-19	4	63	63	..	2	2	...	1	2	3	...	2	4	...	7	...	24
	20-49	8	263	262	1	3	2	3	M-3 F-1	3	13	3	18	20	..	62	2	77
	50-99	3	208	208	...	1	..	2	...	...	3	1	8	23	1	10	...	95
	100-199	2	232	232	...	...	1	1	...	17	35	...	23	17	...	38	...	49
	200-399	2	492	481	11	2	...	..	M-9 F-1	1	...	M-6 F-3	9	21	M-1 F-5	23	..	213
	400 and over.	2	1,077	1,077	...	2	...	...	5	...	..	27	11	29	19	120	1	467
(ii) *Without mech. power*	...	*27*	*615*	*613*	*2*	*1*	*M10 F-1*	*15*	...	*12*	*26*	*1*	*60*	*42*	...	*122*	...	*146*
	10-19	15	207	206	1	..	M-5 F-1	9	...	1	3	1	7	10	..	41	...	71
	20-49	11	342	341	1	1	5	5	...	7	10	...	32	32	...	67	...	71
	50-99	1	66	66	..	...	..	1	...	4	13	...	21	...	...	14	...	4
2. Goldsmiths, silversmiths and jewellers—	Total	6	221	216	5	2	M-1 F-1	2	6	M13 F-2	...	1	7	51	1	M-28 F-2	15	61
(i) *With mechanical power*	50-99	*1*	*83*	*83*	..	*1*	..	..	*5*	...	...	*1*	*7*	*34*	...	...	..	*22*
(ii) *Without mech. power*	...	*5*	*138*	*133*	*5*	*1*	*M-1 F-1*	*2*	*1*	*M13 F-2*	..	...	...	*17*	*1*	*M-28 F-2*	*15*	*39*
	10-19	2	27	27	...	...	1	1	...	...	..	...	...	..	...	10	...	10
	20-49	3	111	106	5	1	F-1	1	1	M13 F-2	..	...	...	17	1	M-18 F-2	15	29
3. Book-binding works—	Total	2	41	41	...	...	..	2	..	...	1	...	..	...	...	...	...	32
Without mech. power	10-19	1	12	12	...	...	...	1	..	...	1	...	..	...	...	...	...	10
	20-49	1	29	29	..	...	...	1	...	...	...	..	...	...	...	..	..	22
4. Photographic studio— *Without mech. power*	20-49	1	44	44	...	...	...	1	...	...	1	2	2	9	...	3	...	14
5. Musical instrument workshop— *Without mech. power*	20-49	1	42	41	1	1	...	..	M-7 F-1	2	2	3	5	3	4	2	...	11
6. Fan making— *Without mech. power*	10-19	2	29	23	6	...	M-2 F-1	...	...	...	..	..	...	...	...	M-21 F-5	...	..
7. Carving of ivory and wood— *Without mech. power*	10-19	1	11	11	...	...	1	...	...	...	...	..	...	...	...	10	...	...
8. Making paper cartons— *Without mech. power*	20-49	1	31	8	23	...	1	...	...	...	...	...	..	...	...	...	...	...

* One in class 200—399 and one in class 50—99 are generating-stations; the others make or repair electrical machinery and apparatus.

† Includes one press managed by an American subject and owned by a company of which all the directors are American subjects.

Classification of all Industrial Establishments and of the Persons employed in them—concluded.

CLASSIFICATION OF UNSKILLED LABOURERS.																						
TOTAL.			MALES.										FEMALES.									
			European and Anglo-Indians.	Home Races.			Chinese and Japanese.			Others.			European and Anglo-Indians.	Home Races.			Chinese and Japanese.			Others.		
Persons.	Males.	Females.		Age 18 or over.	Age 14 to 18.	Age under 14.	Age 18 or over.	Age 14 to 18.	Age under 14.	Age 18 or over.	Age 14 to 18.	Age under 14.		Age 18 or over.	Age 14 to 18.	Age under 14.	Age 18 or over.	Age 14 to 18.	Age under 14.	Age 18 or over.	Age 14 to 18.	Age under 14.
20	21	22	23	24	25	26	27	28	29	30	31	32	33	34	35	36	37	38	39	40	41	42
490	490	...	4	81	7	...	4	1	...	381	12	...	...	...	...	...	...	...	...	...	...	...
115	115	...	...	12	...	...	...	...	...	103	...	...	...	...	...	...	...	...	...	...	...	...
7	7	...	...	...	...	...	...	...	...	7	...		...	...	...	...	...	...	...	...	...	...
62	62	...	...	12	...	...	...	...	...	50	...	...	...	...	...	...	...	...	...	...	...	...
46	46	...	...	...	...	...	...	...	...	46	...	...	...	...	...	...	...	...	...	...	...	...
375	375	...	4	69	7	...	4	1	...	278	12	...	...	...	...	...	...	...	...	...	...	...
15	15	...	...	6	...	...	...	...	...	9	...	...	...	...	...	...	...	...	...	...	...	...
78	78	...	...	26	7	...	...	1	...	44	...	...	...	...	...	...	...	...	...	...	...	...
61	61	...	...	36	...	...	4	...	...	18	3	...	...	...	...	...	...	...	...	...	...	...
221	221		4	1	...	...	...	...	...	207	9	...	...	...	...	...	...	...	...	...	...	...
1,034	1,008	26	5	115	34	1		...		802	39	12	...	17	5	3	...	...	...	1	...	...
957	954	3	5	111	34	1	...	...	...	760	36	7	...	2	...	...	...	...	...	1	...	...
778	776	2	5	66	20	1	...	...	...	646	34	4	...	2	...	...	...	...	...	...	...	...
16	16	...	...	3	1	1	...	...	...	9	2	...	...	...	...	...	...	...	...	...	...	...
53	53	...	...	7	...	...	...	...	...	45	1	...	...	...	...	...	...	...	...	...	...	...
64	64	...	1	3	1	...	...	...	...	59	...	...	...	...	...	...	...	...	...	...	...	...
51	51	...	...	7	...	...	...	...	...	44	...	...	...	...	...	...	...	...	...	...	...	...
198	196	2	...	15	12	...	...	...	...	167	...	2	...	2	...		...	...	...	...	...	...
396	396	...	4	31	6	...	...	...	...	322	31	2	...	...	...	...	...	...	...	...	...	...
179	178	1	...	45	14	...	...	...	...	114	2	3	...	...	...	...	...	...	...	1	...	...
58	58	...	...	8	10	...	...	...	...	38	1	1	...	...	...	...	...	...	...	...	...	...
112	111	1	...	37	4	...	...	...	...	67	1	2	...	...	...	...	...	...	...	1	...	...
9	9	...	...	...	...	...	...	...	...	9	...	...	...	...	...	...	...	...	...	...	...	...
28	28	...	...	2	...	...	...	...	...	23	2	1	...	...	...	...	...	...	...	...	...	...
13	13	...	...	...	...	...	...	...	...	10	2	1	...	...	...	...	...	...	...	...	...	...
15	15	...	...	2	...	...	...	...	...	13	...	...	...	...	...	...	...	...	...	...	...	...
5	5	...	...	...	...	...	...	...	...	5	...	...	...	...	...	...	...	...	...	...	...	...
10	10	...	...	2	...	...	...	...	...	8		...	...	...	...	...	...	...	...	...	...	...
6	6	...	...	...	...	...	...	...	...	2	...	4	...	...	...	...	...	...	...	...	...	...
...	...	...	...	...	...	...	...	...	...	...	...	...	...	...	...	...	...	...	...	...	...	...
6	6	...	...	...	...	...	...	...	...	2	...	4	...	...	...	...	...	...	...	...	...	...
12	12	...	...	1	...	...	...	...	...	10	1	...	...	...	...	...	...	...	...	...	...	...
1	1	...	...	...	...	...	...	...	...	1	...	...	...	...	...	...	...	...	...	...	...	...
...	...	...	...	...	...	...	...	...	...		...	...	...	...	...	...	...	...		...	...	...
...	...	...	...	...	...	...	...	...	...	...	...	...	...	...	...	...	...	...	...	...	...	...
30	7	23	...	1	...	...	...	...	...	6	...	...	...	15	5	3	...	...	...	...	...	...

Imperial Table XXIIa.—The Special Industrial Census. Part II.—

DESCRIPTION OF ESTABLISHMENT (with Group-letters and Serial Nos. of Classes in each Group).	DISTRICT.	Number of Establishments.	TOTAL EMPLOYEES.			CLASSIFICATION OF SUPERIOR EMPLOYEES. N.B.—In these columns all are males unless the contrary is indicated.												
						Managers.			Supervising and Technical Staff.			Clerical Staff.			Skilled Labourers.			
			Persons.	Males.	Females.	Europeans and Anglo-Indians.	Home Races.	Others.	Europeans and Anglo-Indians.	Home Races.	Others.	Europeans and Anglo-Indians.	Home Races.	Others.	Europeans and Anglo-Indians.	Home Races.	Chinese and Japanese.	Others.
1	2	3	4	5	6	7	8	9	10	11	12	13	14	15	16	17	18	19
A. Cultivation for special products.	...	44	5,881	4,976	905	28	6	10	48	50	47	10	15	19	1	41	8	24
1. Coffee— *With mechanical power*	Toungoo ...	1	20	20	...	...	...	1	1	6	1	1	...	...	...	6	...	...
2. Sugar-cane— *Without mech power*	Total ...	2	32	27	5	...	1	1	..	.	...	...	...	...	...	..	...	...
	Prome ...	1	20	15	5	...	1	...	...	...	...	...	...	...	...	...	...	...
	S. Shan States	1	12	12	...	...	..	1	...	...	...	..	...	...	...	...	...	...
3. Cinchona— *Without mech. power*	Tavoy ...	1	54	49	5	1	...	...	...	1	...	...	...	...	...	...	...	...
4. Rubber—	Total .	39	5,720	4,842	878	26	5	8	47	43	46	9	14	19	1	33	8	24
(i) *With mechanical power*	...	*12*	*2,953*	*2,341*	*612*	*10*	...	*2*	*28*	*19*	*31*	*7*	*2*	*11*	*1*	*24*	*6*	*19*
	Insein ...	1	75	51	24	...	...	1	...	...	1	...	...	..	...	1	...	.
	Hanthawaddy	1	769	504	265	1	..	...	7	...	4	1	...	..	...	2	3	...
	Toungoo ...	1	51	51	...	1	...	..	1	2	...	...	...	...	...	...	...	1
	Thatôn ...	2	441	334	107	1	...	1	2	5	6	...	..	3	.	4	1	2
	Amherst ..	2	604	505	99	2	...	...	5	1	1	4	1	2	1	8	...	2
	Mergui ...	5	1,013	896	117	5	..	...	13	11	19	2	1	6	...	9	2	14
(ii) *Without mech. power*	...	*27*	*2,767*	*2,501*	*266*	*16*	*5*	*6*	*19*	*24*	*15*	*2*	*12*	*8*	...	*9*	*2*	*5*
	Insein ...	4	327	305	22	2	1	1	2	...	3	...	1	..	...	...	...	...
	Hanthawaddy	4	578	511	67	2	...	2	4	1	3	1	3	...	.	...	1	.
	Henzada ...	2	47	47	...	1	1	...	1	2	...	...	1	1	...	1	...	...
	Toungoo ..	2	199	171	28	2	..	...	1	2	...	..	2	...	...	...	...	...
	Thatôn ..	6	554	493	61	2	2	2	2	8	8	...	4	3	...	1	1	.
	Amherst ..	2	54	48	6	1	...	1	..	1	..	...	...	1	...	...	...	...
	Tavoy ...	2	113	96	17	1	1	...	...	4	...	.	...	1	...	...	...	...
	Mergui ...	5	895	830	65	5	...	..	9	6	1	1	1	2	...	7	...	5
5. Camphor— (i) *With mechanical power*	S. Shan States	1	55	38	17	1	...	...	...	...	..	...	1	...	...	2	...	...
B. Mines	...	70	10,559	10,208	351	26	M24 F-4	16	M186 F-1	38	31	M35 F-2	158	203	25	369	74	518
1. Petroleum wells—	Total ...	22	1,134	1,039	95	7	M11 F-3	1	16	8	2	1	24	11	...	115	..	27
(i) *With mechanical power*	...	*10*	*934*	*908*	*26*	*7*	*3*	..	*16*	*8*	*2*	*1*	*24*	*11*	...	*113*	...	*26*
	Thayetmyo	2	497	472	25	2	..	..	10	2	...	..	15	6	...	68	...	6
	Minbu ...	8	437	436	1	5	3	...	6	6	2	1	9	5	...	45	...	20
(ii) *Without mech. power*	...	*12*	*200*	*131*	*69*	...	*M-8 F-3*	*1*	...	...	...	...	..	...	..	*2*	...	*1*
	Thayetmyo	1	15	15	...	.	...	1	..	..	...	..	...	...	...	2	...	1
	Mergui ...	11	185	116	69	..	M-8 F-3	..	..	...	...	...	...	...	...	...	...	..
2. Tin and Wolfram mines—	Total ..	41	4,076	3,838	238	15	12	14	34	17	26	4	45	23	2	74	37	88
(i) *With mechanical power*	...	*6*	*627*	*627*	..	*5*	..	*1*	*21*	...	*7*	*2*	*13*	*11*	*1*	*45*	*25*	*74*
	Tavoy ...	5	581	581	...	4	...	1	18	...	5	2	10	11	1	38	23	71
	Mergui ...	1	46	46	...	1	...	.	3	...	2	...	3	...	..	7	2	3
(ii) *Without mech. power*	...	*35*	*3,449*	*3,211*	*238*	*10*	*12*	*13*	*13*	*17*	*19*	*2*	*32*	*12*	*1*	*29*	*12*	*14*
	Amherst ...	1	113	72	41	1	...	...	1	...	...	...	4	1	.	1	2	..
	Tavoy	17	2,501	2,333	168	6	7	4	7	12	15	1	10	7	...	21	6	14
	Mergui ...	17	835	806	29	3	5	9	5	5	4	1	18	4	1	7	4	.
3. Silver and Lead mines—	Total ...	3	4,310	4,298	12	1	M-0 F-1	1	M103 F-1	2	2	M29 F 2	77	167	21	108	33	390
(i) *With mechanical power*	N. Shan States	*1*	*4,252*	*4,244*	*8*	*1*	...	..	*M103 F-1*	*2*	*1*	*M29 F-2*	*77*	*167*	*21*	*108*	*33*	*390*
(ii) *Without mech. power*	S. Shan States	*2*	*58*	*54*	*4*	.	*M-0 F-1*	*1*	...	...	*1*	...	...	..	...	...	...	...
4. Ruby mines— (i) *With mechanical power*	Katha ...	1	940	940	...	1	...	...	28	10	1	1	10	2	2	72	4	13
5. Other mines—	Total ..	3	99	93	6	2	1	...	5	1	...	...	2	...	...	...	...	...
(a) Copper (prospecting). *Without mech. power.*	Henzada ...	1	17	17	...	1	...	..	1	1	...	..	1	...	...	...	...	...
(b) Steatite ... *Without mech. power.*	Minbu	1	36	36	...	...	1	...	...	...	...	...	1	...	...	...	...	...
(c) Coal ... *Without mech. power.*	S. S. States	1	46	40	6	1	...	...	4	...	...	...	...	...	...	...	...	...

Distribution by Districts of the Statistics in Part I of this Table.

CLASSIFICATION OF UNSKILLED LABOURERS.																						
TOTAL.			MALES.										FEMALES.									
			Europeans and Anglo-Indians.	Home Races.			Chinese and Japanese.			Others.			Europeans and Anglo-Indians.	Home Races.			Chinese and Japanese.			Others.		
Persons.	Males.	Females.		Age 18 or over.	Age 14 to 18.	Age under 14.	Age 18 or over.	Age 14 to 18.	Age under 14.	Age 18 or over.	Age 14 to 18.	Age under 14.		Age 18 or over.	Age 14 to 18.	Age under 14.	Age 18 or over.	Age 14 to 18.	Age under 14.	Age 18 or over.	Age 14 to 18.	Age under 14.
20	21	22	23	24	25	26	27	28	29	30	31	32	33	34	35	36	37	38	39	40	41	42
5,574	4,669	905	1	502	123	46	8	...	...	3,460	354	175	...	405	205	53	1	...	...	202	18	21
4	4	...	...	1	...	...	...	...	...	3	...	...	...	...	...	...	...	...	...	...	...	...
30	25	5	...	16	5	...	...	...	...	3	...	...	...	3	2	...	...	...	...	...	...	...
19	14	5	...	10	3	...	...	...	...	1	...	...	...	3	2	...	...		...	...	...	...
11	11	...	.	6	2	...	1	...	...	2	...	...	...	...	...	...	...	.	...	...	...	...
52	47	5	...	...	...	...	...	...	...	47	...	...	...	...	...	...	...	...	...	5	...	...
5,437	4,559	878	1	456	116	44	7	...	...	3,406	354	175	.	394	197	50	1	...	...	197	18	21
2,793	2,181	612	1	239	82	33	7	...	...	1,510	216	93	...	286	148	38	...	...	...	115	15	10
72	48	24	...	18	7	3	.	...	...	17	2	1	...	18	6	...	...	...	...	...	...	.
751	486	265	...	161	50	18	...		...	230	14	13	...	160	68	31	...	...	...	4	...	2
46	46	...	...	2	...	2	...	...	...	26	5	11	...	...	...	...	...	...	...	...	...	...
416	309	107	...	28	8	7	1	.	...	216	27	22	...	61	27	1	...	...	...	13	5	...
577	478	99	...	25	16	3	...	...	...	364	56	14	...	45	46	6	...	...	...	2	...	...
931	814	117	1	5	1	...	6	...	...	657	112	32	...	2	1	...	...		...	96	10	8
2,644	2,378	266	...	217	34	11	.	...	...	1,896	138	82	...	108	49	12	1	...	...	82	3	11
317	295	22	...	31	5	2	...	...	...	234	17	6	...	17	5	...	...	...	...	...	...	...
561	494	67	...	51	10	3	...	...	...	410	18	2	...	45	11	8	1	...	...	2	...	...
39	39	...	...	23	1	1	...	...	...	12	1	1	...	...	...	...	...	...	...	...	...	...
192	164	28	...	20	1	...	...	...	...	127	5	11	...	10	4	2	...	...	...	11	...	1
521	460	61	...	69	9	4	...	...	...	343	32	3	...	31	26	2	...	...	...	2	...	...
50	44	6	...	6	2	1	...	...	...	29	3	3	...	3	...	...	...	...	...	2	...	1
106	89	17	...	10	5	...	...	...	...	66	5	3	...	2	3	...	...	...	...	12	...	...
858	793	65	...	7	1	...	...	.	...	675	57	53	...	...	...	...	...	...	...	53	3	9
51	34	17	...	29	2	2	...	...	...	1	...	...	...	8	6	3	...	...	...	...	...	...
8,849	8,505	344	16	2,327	96	60	2,625	37	5	3,234	85	20	...	240	34	40	...	...	2	17	5	6
908	816	92	...	571	6	1	...	...	...	235	2	1	...	78	11	3	...	...	...	...	...	...
723	697	26	...	459	5	1	...	.	...	229	2	1	...	13	10	3	...	...	...	...	...	...
388	363	25	...	260	1	...	...	...	...	102	...	...	...	12	10	3	...	...	...	...	...	...
335	334	1	...	199	4	1	...	...	...	137	2	1	...	1	...	...	...	...	...	...	...	...
185	119	66	...	112	1	...	...	...	...	6	...	...	...	65	1	...	...	...	...	...	...	...
11	11	...	...	5	...	...	...	...	...	6	...	...	.	...	...	...	...	...	...	...	...	...
174	108	66	.	107	1	...	...	.	...	...	...	...	...	65	1	...	...	...	...	...	...	...
3,685	3,447	238	...	563	31	46	1,991	2	1	800	9	4	...	157	22	35	...	...	2	12	4	6
422	422	...	...	52	7	2	23	...	...	332	5	1	...	...	...	...	...	...	...	...	...	...
397	397	...	...	45	7	2	23	...	...	314	5	1	...	...	...	.	...	...	...	...	...	...
25	25	...	...	7	...	...	...	...	.	18	.	...	...	...	...	.	...	...	...	...	...	...
3,263	3,025	238	...	511	24	44	1,968	2	1	468	4	3	...	157	22	35	...	...	2	12	4	6
103	62	41	...	37	4	6	6	...	...	9	...	...	...	31	4	3	...	...	...	2	...	1
2,391	2,223	168	...	350	19	37	1,518	2	1	291	2	3	...	99	18	30	...	...	2	10	4	5
769	740	29	...	124	1	1	444	...	...	168	2	...	...	27	...	2	...	...	...	...	...	...
3,372	3,364	8	16	563	37	13	563	34	4	2,049	70	15	...	5	1	2	...	...	...	...	...	...
3,317	3,312	5	16	521	27	13	563	34	4	2,049	70	15	...	4	1	...	...	...	...	...	...	...
55	52	3	...	42	10	...	...	...	...	...	...	...	...	1	...	2	...	...	...	...	...	...
796	796	...	...	585	18	...	71	1	...	118	3	...	...	...	...	...	...	...	...	...	...	...
88	82	6	...	45	4	...	...	...	...	32	1	.	...	...	...	...	...	...	...	5	1	...
13	13	...	...	13	...	.	...	.	...	...	...	...	...	...	...	...	...	...	...	...	...	...
34	34	...	...	30	4	...	...	...	...	...	...	...	...	...	...	...	...	...	...	...	...	...
41	35	6	...	2	...	.	...	...	...	32	1	...	...	...	...	...	...	...	...	5	1	...

DESCRIPTION OF ESTABLISHMENT (with Group-letters and Serial Nos. of Classes in each group).	DISTRICT.	Number of Establishments.	TOTAL EMPLOYEES.			CLASSIFICATION OF SUPERIOR EMPLOYEES. N.B.—In these columns all are males unless the contrary is indicated. Managers.			Supervising and Technical Staff.			Clerical Staff.			Skilled Labourers.			
			Persons.	Males.	Females.	Europeans and Anglo-Indians.	Home Races.	Others.	Europeans and Anglo-Indians.	Home Races.	Others.	Europeans and Anglo-Indians.	Home Races.	Others.	Europeans and Anglo-Indians.	Home Races.	Chinese and Japanese.	Others.
1	2	3	4	5	6	7	8	9	10	11	12	13	14	15	16	17	18	19
C. Stone quarries—	...	15	1,436	1,320	116	1	3	11	1	...	6	1	3	9	...	1	...	13
(i) *With mechanical power*	...	*3*	*693*	*662*	*31*	...	...	*3*	*1*	...	*4*	...	...	*3*	...	*1*	...	*8*
	Thatôn ...	2	666	635	31	...	...	2	1	...	2	...	...	1	..	1	...	7
	Tavoy ...	1	27	27	...	...	...	1	...	...	2	...	...	2	...	...	...	1
(ii) *Without mech. power*	...	*12*	*743*	*658*	*85*	*1*	*3*	*8*	...	...	*2*	*1*	*3*	*6*		...	...	*5*
	Bassein ...	1	49	49	...	1	...	...	...	.	...	...	1	..	...	...	...	1
	Henzada ...	1	24	24	...	...	...	1	...	...	...	1	2	3	...	...	...	...
	Thatôn ..	3	470	461	9	.	...	3	...	...	2	..	...	3	...	...	...	4
	Tavoy ...	5	123	79	44	...	2	3	..	.	..	...	...	...	...	...	...	...
	Kyauksè ...	1	41	24	17	...	1	...	...	...	...	...	...	...	...	...	...	...
	Yamèthin ...	1	36	21	15	...	...	1	...	...	...	..	...	...	...	...	...	...
D. Textiles—	...	39	2,437	1,575	862	5	M 20 F-1	14	5	M 16 F-30	16	3	90	67	...	M 184 F-162	1	116
1. Cotton ginning, cleaning and pressing—	Total ...	24	1,585	1,076	509	3	10	11	2	9	16	2	79	58	...	63	.	92
(i) *With mechanical power*	...	*23*	*1,570*	*1,075*	*495*	*3*	*9*	*11*	*2*	*9*	*16*	*2*	*79*	*58*	...	*63*	.	*92*
	Thayetmyo	4	335	296	39	...	...	4	...	1	6	...	2	11	..	20	...	21
	Bhamo ...	1	66	34	32	.	1	...	..	1	1	..	10	...	..	2	...	3
	Sagaing ...	4	126	97	29	1	2	1	1	1	1	2	6	3	..	12	...	3
	L. Chindwin	1	12	12	...	...	...	1	...	..	...	...	..	1	...	1	...	...
	Meiktila .	5	143	87	56	..	5	.	...	6	...	...	10	3	...	6	...	6
	Myingyan ...	8	888	549	339	2	1	5	1	..	8	...	51	40	...	22	...	59
(ii) *Without mech. power*	Sagaing ...	*1*	*15*	*1*	*14*	...	*1*	...	...	...	...	...	...	...	...	...	...	...
2. Cotton-weaving—	Total	6	202	21	181	...	M 5 F-1	...	...	M 3 F-30	...	...	2	...	...	M-11 F-91	...	...
(i) *Without mech. power*	Meiktila ...	4	159	14	145	...	4	...	...,	M 1 F 30	...	...	1	...	...	M-8 F-81	...	...
	Sagaing ...	1	26	...	26	..	F-1	...	...	...	...	..	...	...	...	...	...	...
	L. Chindwin	1	17	7	10	...	1	...	...	2	...	...	1	...	...	M-3 F-10	..	..
3. Rope-making—	Total	4	441	340	101	2	...	2	3	1	...	...	2	9	..	8	1	20
(i) *With mechanical power*	...	*2*	*301*	*242*	*59*	*1*	...	*1*	*1*	*1*	...	...	*1*	*7*	..	*4*	*1*	*15*
	Rangoon ..	1	138	138	...	1	...	..	1	1	...	..	1	5	...	4	1	13
	Insein ...	1	163	104	59	...	...	1	...	...	...	...	...	2	...	...	...	2
(ii) *Without mech. power*	...	*2*	*140*	*98*	*42*	*1*	...	*1*	*2*	...	...	*1*	*1*	*2*	...	*4*	...	*5*
	Rangoon ...	1	117	82	35	1	...	...	2	.	...	1	1	1	...	4	...	5
	Insein ...	1	23	16	7	...	...	1	...	.	...	...	...	1	...	...	.	...
4. Silk-weaving— *Without mech. power*	Mandalay ...	5	209	138	71	..	5	1	...	3	...	...	7	...	...	M 102 F-71	...	4
E. Leather and Bone—	...	15	451	440	11	4	3	8	5	6	6	2	7	33	...	2	14	56
1. Tanneries— *Without mech. power*	Total ...	9	203	203	...	...	3	6	...	1	3	...	4	5	...	...	13	19
	Rangoon ...	1	38	38	...	...	1	...	...	...	...	...	3	...	...	...	...	...
	Insein ...	5	116	116	...	...	...	5	.	...	3	...	...	2	...	...	9	9
	Mandalay ...	3	49	49	..	...	2	1	...	1	...	...	1	3	...	...	4	10
2. Leather factories— *Without mech. power*	Total ...	5	219	208	11	4	...	1	4	5	2	2	3	26	...	2	...	32
	Rangoon	3	171	171	..	3	...	...	3	5	1	2	1	25	...	2	...	32
	Prome ..	2	48	37	11	1	...	1	1	...	1	...	2	1	..	...	..	[illegible]
3. Bone mills— *With mechanical power*	Rangoon ...	1	29	29	...	...	...	1	1	...	1	..	...	2	..	...	1	5
F. Wood—	...	150	13,931	13,642	289	24	M 53 F-1	72	73	M 78 F-6	68	M-8 F-1	M 731 F-5	266	2	1,195	176	1,347
1. Carpentry— *Without mech. power*	Total ...	11	219	219	..	...	2	9	1	...	7	...	...	21	...	13	104	3
	Rangoon ...	9	193	193	...	...	...	9	1	...	7	...	...	21	...	...	104	...
	Mandalay ...	2	26	26	...	..	2	...	...	...	...	...	...	.	...	13	...	3
2. Sawmills and timber yards.	Total ...	139	13,712	13,423	289	24	M 51 F-1	63	72	M 78 F-6	61	M 8 F-1	M 731 F-5	245	2	1,182	72	1,344
(i) *With mechanical power*	*Province* ...	*132*	*13,601*	*13,313*	*288*	*24*	*M 44* *F-1*	*63*	*72*	*M 77* *F-6*	*61*	*M-8* *F-1*	*M 727* *F-5*	*245*	*2*	*1,117*	*66*	*1,343*
	Arakan Division.	*2*	*40*	*40*	..	...	*2*	...	...	*1*	...	...	*1*	...		*6*	...	*4*
	Rangoon ..	*26*	*6,469*	*6,467*	*2*	*10*	*3*	*13*	*41*	*10*	*9*	...	*338*	*103*	*1*	*331*	*31*	*787*
	*Pegu Division (less Rangoon).**	*17*	*670*	*662*	*8*	...	*6*	*11*	...	*1*	*20*	..	*34*	*25*	...	*30*	*3*	*59*

* That is, the Insein, Hanthawaddy, Tharrawaddy, Pegu and Prome districts.

Distribution by Districts of the Statistics in Part I of this Table—continued.

CLASSIFICATION OF UNSKILLED LABOURERS.

Total: Persons.	Total: Males.	Total: Females.	Males: Europeans and Anglo-Indians.	Males: Home Races: Age 18 or over.	Males: Home Races: Age 14 to 18.	Males: Home Races: Age under 14.	Males: Chinese and Japanese: Age 18 or over.	Males: Chinese and Japanese: Age 14 to 18.	Males: Chinese and Japanese: Age under 14.	Males: Others: Age 18 or over.	Males: Others: Age 14 to 18.	Males: Others: Age under 14.	Females: Europeans and Anglo-Indians.	Females: Home Races: Age 18 or over.	Females: Home Races: Age 14 to 18.	Females: Home Races: Age under 14.	Females: Chinese and Japanese: Age 18 or over.	Females: Chinese and Japanese: Age 14 to 18.	Females: Chinese and Japanese: Age under 14.	Females: Others: Age 18 or over.	Females: Others: Age 14 to 18.	Females: Others: Age under 14.
20	21	22	23	24	25	26	27	28	29	30	31	32	33	34	35	36	37	38	39	40	41	42
1,387	1,271	116	...	119	3	...	1	...	...	1,057	66	25	...	89	17	3	...	...	...	7	...	...
673	642	31	...	9	3	...	...	...	...	545	60	25	...	19	12	...	...	...	...	...	...	...
652	621	31	...	8	3	...	...	...	...	525	60	25	...	19	12	...	...	...	...	...	...	...
21	21	...	...	1	...	...	...	...	...	20	...	...	...	...	...	...	...	...	...	...	...	...
714	629	85	...	110	...	...	1	...	...	512	6	...	...	70	5	3	...	...	...	7	...	...
46	46	...	...	...	...	...	...	...	...	43	3	...	...	...	...	...	...	...	...	...	...	...
17	17	...	...	11	...	...	...	...	...	4	2	...	...	...	...	...	...	...	...	...	...	...
458	449	9	...	34	...	...	...	...	...	414	1	...	...	2	...	...	...	...	...	7	...	...
118	74	44	...	22	...	...	1	...	...	51	...	...	...	40	2	2	...	...	...	...	...	...
40	23	17	...	23	...	...	...	...	...	...	...	...	...	17	...	...	...	...	...	...	...	...
35	20	15	...	20	...	...	...	...	...	...	...	...	...	11	3	1	...	...	...	...	...	...
1,707	1,038	669	...	251	46	17	...	...	...	658	33	33	...	416	210	43	...	...	...	...	...	...
1,240	731	509	...	189	39	17	...	...	...	471	12	3	...	280	200	29	...	...	...	...	...	...
1,226	731	495	...	189	39	17	...	...	...	471	12	3	...	268	198	29	...	...	...	...	...	...
270	231	39	...	54	15	5	...	...	...	151	4	2	...	15	19	5	...	...	...	...	...	...
48	16	32	...	11	2	...	...	...	...	1	2	...	...	24	8	...	...	...	...	...	...	...
93	64	29	...	17	...	5	...	...	...	42	...	...	...	17	6	6	...	...	...	...	...	...
9	9	...	...	2	...	...	...	...	...	7	...	...	...	...	...	...	...	...	...	...	...	...
107	51	56	...	38	5	6	...	...	...	2	...	...	...	35	8	13	...	...	...	...	...	...
699	360	339	...	67	17	1	...	...	...	268	6	1	...	177	157	5	...	...	...	...	...	...
14	...	14	...	...	...	...	...	...	...	...	...	...	...	12	2	...	...	...	...	...	...	...
59	...	59	...	...	...	...	...	...	...	...		...	...	42	4	13	...	...	...	...	...	...
34	...	34	...	...	...	...	...	...	...	...	...	...	...	17	4	13	...	...	...	...	...	...
25	...	25	...	...	...	...	...	...	...	...	...	...	...	25	...	...	...	...	...	...	...	...
...	...	...	...	...	...	...	...	...	...	...	...	...	...	...	...	...	...	...	...	...	...	...
398	291	101	...	47	7	...	...	...	...	186	21	30	...	94	6	1	...	...	...	...	...	...
269	210	59	...	37	1	...	...	...	...	124	18	30	...	59	...	...	...	...	...	...	...	...
111	111	...	...	...	1	...	...	...	...	72	14	24	...	...	...	...	...	...	...	...	...	...
158	99	59	...	37	...	...	...	...	...	52	4	6	...	59	...	...	...	...	...	...	...	...
123	81	42	...	10	6	...	...	...	...	62	3	...	...	35	6	1	...	...	...	...	...	...
102	67	35	...	7	5	...	...	...	...	52	3	...	...	31	4	...	...	...	...	...	...	...
21	14	7	...	3	1	...	...	...	...	10	...	...	...	4	2	1	...	...	...	...	...	...
16	16	...	...	15	...	...	...	...	...	1	...	...	...	...	...	...	...	...	...	...	...	...
305	294	11	...	9	...	...	6	...	...	273	3	3	...	...	...	...	1	...	...	6	2	2
149	149	...	...	6		...	3	...	...	140	...	...	...	...	...	...	...	...	...	...	...	...
34	34	...	...	...	...	...	...	...	...	34	...	...	...	...	...	...	...	...	...	...	...	...
88	88	...	...	...	...	...	3	...	...	85	...	...	...	...	...	...	...	...	...	...	...	...
27	27	...	...	6	...	...	...	...	...	21	...	...	...	...	...	...	...	...	...	...		...
138	127	11	...	3	...	...	3	...	...	115	3	3	...	...	...	...	1		...	6	2	2
97	97	...	...	3	...	...	...	...	...	91	2	1	...	...	...	...	...	...	...	...	...	...
41	30	11	...	...	...	...	3	...	...	24	1	2	...	...	...	...	1	...	...	6	2	2
18	18	...	...	...	...	...	...	...	...	18	...	...	...	...	...	...	...	...	...	...	...	...
9,825	9,549	276	1	1,424	138	8	76	8	...	7,282	518	94	...	209	44	10	...	...	...	12	...	1
59	59	...	...	8	...	...	46	5	...	...	...	...	...	...	...	...	...	...	...	...	...	...
51	51	...	...	...	...	...	46	5	...	...	...	...	...	...	...	...	...	...	...	...	...	...
8	8	...	...	8	...	...	...	...	...	...	...	...	...	...	...	...	...	...	...	...	...	...
9,766	9,490	276	1	1,416	138	8	30	3	...	7,282	518	94	...	209	44	10	...	...	...	12	...	1
9,739	9,464	275	1	1,460	138	8	20	3	...	7,282	518	94	...	208	44	10	...	...	...	12	...	1
26	26	...	...	12	...	...	...	...	...	14	...	...	...	...	...	...	...	...	...	...	...	...
4,792	4,790	2	...	102	8	...	1	...	...	4,206	400	73	...	1	...	1	...	...	...	...	...	
481	473	8	...	81	5	3	12	...	...	357	8	7	...	4	3	1	...	...	...	...	...	

CLASSIFICATION OF SUPERIOR EMPLOYEES. *N.B.*—In these columns all are males unless the contrary is indicated.

DESCRIPTION OF ESTABLISHMENT (with Group-letters and Serial Nos. of Classes in each group).	DISTRICT.	Number of Establishments.	Total Employees: Persons.	Total Employees: Males.	Total Employees: Females.	Managers: Europeans and Anglo-Indians.	Managers: Home Races.	Managers: Others.	Supervising and Technical Staff: Europeans and Anglo-Indians.	Supervising and Technical Staff: Home Races.	Supervising and Technical Staff: Others.	Clerical Staff: Europeans and Anglo-Indians.	Clerical Staff: Home Races.	Clerical Staff: Others.	Skilled Labourers: Europeans and Anglo-Indians.	Skilled Labourers: Home Races.	Skilled Labourers: Chinese and Japanese.	Skilled Labourers: Others.
1	2	3	4	5	6	7	8	9	10	11	12	13	14	15	16	17	18	19
F. 2. Sawmills and timber yards—concld.																		
(i) *With mechanical power*	*Irrawaddy Division.*	7	181	180	1	..	6	1	1	8	...	5	15	2	..	26	...	38
	Tenasserim Division.	35	3,814	3,781	33	7	M-8 F-1	19	22	27	9	M-3 F-1	213	65	1	327	24	359
	Upper Burma and Shan States.	45	2,427	2,183	244	7	19	19	8	M30 F-6	23	...	M126 F-5	50	...	397	8	96
	Akyab .	2	40	40	...	...	2	...	...	1	...	...	1	..	...	6	...	4
	Rangoon ...	26	6,469	6,467	2	10	3	13	41	10	9	...	338	103	1	331	31	787
	Insein ...	2	50	50	...	...	1	1	..	...	2	...	2	2	...	2	...	10
	Tharrawaddy	6	245	241	4	...	2	4	...	...	3	...	11	7	...	14	...	18
	Pegu ...	5	197	197	...	...	2	3	...	1	5	...	12	6	...	12	3	28
	Prome ..	4	178	174	4	...	1	3	...	...	10	...	9	10	...	2	...	9
	Bassein ..	4	139	139	...	...	4	...	.	8	...	...	10	..	..	12	...	29
	Henzada ..	3	42	41	1	...	2	1	1	...	...	5	5	2	...	14	...	9
	Toungoo ...	13	638	609	29	1	M-1 F-1	10	3	5	2	...	27	39	...	24	12	68
	Thatôn ...	3	112	112	...	...	1	2	...	2	1	2	4	..	...	9	...	17
	Amherst ..	17	2,987	2,986	1	6	5	6	19	18	6	M-1 F-1	178	25	1	290	19	269
	Mergui	2	77	74	3	...	1	1	...	2	...	...	4	1	..	4	..	5
	Pakôkku ..	2	83	77	6	...	2	...	..	2	..	...	3	1	...	7	...	1
	Minbu ...	1	113	113	...	1	...	...	2	1	...	...	4	...	...	7	...	...
	Mandalay ...	17	1,182	1,076	106	3	9	5	1	8	7	...	70	5	...	291	1	19
	Katha ...	1	31	31	..	1	...	...	1	3	5	...	2	...	..	3	1	3
	Shwebo ..	2	79	67	12	..	2	...	...	3	...	...	6	...	...	10	...	2
	Sagaing ..	1	25	15	10	...	...	1	...	M-4 F-1	...	...	...	...	...	4	...	...
	L. Chindwin	2	40	40	...	...	...	2	...	...	...	..	...	2	...	6	2	5
	Meiktila ..	1	62	53	9	1	...	...	1	1	1	...	6	...		1	...	3
	Yamèthin ...	17	774	678	96	1	5	11	3	M-7 F-5	9	...	M-33 F-5	42	...	60	4	62
	Myingyan .	1	38	33	5	..	1	...	..	1	1	...	2	...	...	8	..	1
(ii) *Without mech. power*		7	111	110	1	..	7	...	...	1	...	.	4	..	...	65	6	1
	Pakôkku .	4	65	65	..	..	4	...	...	1	...	...	4	...	..	53	...	...
	S. Shan States	3	46	45	1	...	3	...	.	...	...	...	...	...	...	12	6	1
G. Metals	...	32	2,448	2,448	..	10	9	13	48	4	28	6	31	66	35	417	74	623
1. Iron-foundries—	Total .	10	727	727	...	1	5	4	11	1	1	3	16	8	12	220	17	145
(i) *With mechanical power*	...	6	620	620	..	1	2	3	11	1	1	3	16	8	12	188	7	145
	Rangoon ...	5	600	600	...	1	1	3	11	1	1	3	16	8	12	181	7	143
	Mandalay ...	1	20	20	...	..	1	..	...	...	...	...	...	...	...	7	...	2
(ii) *Without mech. power*	...	4	107	107	...	...	3	1	...	...	...		...	...		32	10	...
	Rangoon ...	1	20	20	...	...	...	1	...	...	...		...	...		...	10	...
	Mandalay ...	3	87	87	...		3	...	...	..	...	...	..	...	.	30	...	...
2. Iron and steel-works*—	Total ...	9	150	150	...	..	3	6	...	2	14	...	...	3	...	33	29	19
(i) *With mechanical power*	Rangoon ..	1	12	12	...	..	1	...	..	1	...	...	...	...	...	2	...	...
(ii) *Without mech. power*	Rangoon ..	8	138	138	...	...	2	6	...	1	14		...	3	...	31	29	19
3. Arsenals— *With mechanical power*	Rangoon ..	1	396	396	...	1	...	...	25	...	1	1	4	18	...	12	...	148
4. Machinery and Engineering Workshops—	Total ..	11	1,046	1,046	...	7	1	3	9	1	12	2	10	35	21	136	28	291
(i) *With mechanical power*	...	9	833	833	...	5	1	3	8	1	12	2	10	31	7	134	28	207
	Rangoon ..	8	768	768	...	4	1	3	7	1	12	2	10	30	7	134	28	202
	Pegu ...	1	65	65	...	1	...	...	1	...	...	...	..	1	...	..	...	5
(ii) *Without mech. power*	...	2	213	213	...	2	...	...	1	...	--	...	...	4	14	2	..	84
	Pegu ...	1	180	180	...	1	...	...	.	...	...	...	...	3	14	1	...	77
	Shwebo ..	1	33	33	...	1	..	...	1	...	...	...	...	1	...	1	...	7
5. Sewage pumping-station workshop— *With mechanical power*	Rangoon ...	1	129	129	...	1	..	...	3	.	...	...	1	2	2	16	...	20

* Including blacksmiths and trades working with iron sheets, *e.g.*, making galvanised iron buckets, steel trunks, despatch boxes.

Distribution by Districts of the Statistics in Part I of this table—continued.

CLASSIFICATION OF UNSKILLED LABOURERS.

Total.			Males.										Females.									
			Europeans and Anglo-Indians.	Home Races.			Chinese and Japanese			Others.			Europeans and Anglo-Indians.	Home Races.			Chinese and Japanese.			Others.		
Persons.	Males.	Females.		Age 18 or over.	Age 14 to 18.	Age under 14.	Age 18 or over.	Age 14 to 18.	Age under 14.	Age 18 or over.	Age 14 to 18.	Age under 14.		Age 18 or over.	Age 14 to 18.	Age under 14.	Age 18 or over.	Age 14 to 18.	Age under 14.	Age 18 or over.	Age 14 to 18.	Age under 14.
20	21	22	23	24	25	26	27	28	29	30	31	32	33	34	35	36	37	38	39	40	41	42
79	78	1	...	22	...		...	...	...	56	...	...	...	1	...	...	...	...	...	...	...	...
2,728	2,697	31	1	251	22	3	5	3	...	2,294	105	13	...	24	4	...	...	...	...	2	...	1
1,633	1,400	233	...	932	103	2	2	...	...	355	5	1	...	178	37	8	...	...	...	10	...	...
26	26	...	...	12	...	...	...	...	...	14	...	...	...	...	...	...	...	...	...	...	...	...
4,792	4,790	2	...	102	8	...	1	...	...	4,206	400	73	...	1	...	1	...	...	...	...	...	...
30	30	...	...	2	...	...	...	...	...	26	1	1	...	...	...	...	...	...		...	...	...
192	188	4	...	32	1	1	...	...	...	151	1	2	...	1	2	1	...	...	...	...	...	...
125	125	...	...	13	2	...	2	...	...	104	4	...	...	...	...	...	...	...	...	...	...	...
134	130	4	...	34	2	2	10	...	...	76	2	4	...	3	1	...	...	...	...	...	...	...
76	76	...	...	20	...	...	...	...	...	56	...	...	...	...	...	...	...	...	...	...	...	...
3	2	1	...	2		...	...	...	...	...	...	...	...	1	...	...	...	...	...	...	...	...
445	417	28	...	71	3	1	3	2	...	321	12	4	...	24	4	...	...	...	...	...	...	...
74	74	...	...	1	...	...	...	...	...	70	3	...	...	...	...	...	...	...	...	...	...	...
2,150	2,150	...	1	174	19	2	...	1	...	1,857	87	9	...	...	...	...	...	...	...	...	...	...
59	56	3	...	5	...	...	2	...		46	3	...	...		...	...	...	...	...	2	...	1
67	61	6	...	35	14	...	...	...	...	12	...	...	...	6	...	...	...	...	...	...	...	...
98	98	...	...	95	2	...	...	...	...	1	...	...	...	...	...	...	...	...	...	...	...	...
763	657	106	...	522	73	...	...	...	...	61	1	...	...	75	21	2	...	...	...	8	...	...
12	12		...	11	...	...	1	...	...	...	...	...	...	...	...	...	...	...	...	...	...	...
56	44	12	...	38	2	...	...	...	...	4	...	...	...	8	2	1	...	...	...	1	...	...
15	6	9	...	6	...	...	...	...	...	...	...	...	...	9	...	...	...	...	...	...	...	...
23	23	...	...	16	...	...	...	...	...	7	...	...	...	...	...	...	...	...	...	...	...	...
48	39	9	...	8	...	...	...	...	...	31	...	...	...	9	...	...	...	...	...	...	...	...
527	441	86	...	184	21	2	1	...	...	238	4	1	...	66	14	5	...	...	...	1	...	...
24	19	5	...	17	1	...		...	...	1	...	...	...	5	...	...	...	...	...	...	...	...
27	26	1	...	16	...	...	10	...	...	...	...	...	...	1	...	...	...	...	...	...	...	
3	3	...	...	3	...	...	...	...	...	...	...	...	...	...	...	...	...	...	...	...	...	...
24	23	1	...	13	...	...	10	...	...	...	...	...	...	1	...	...	...	...	...	...	...	...
1,084	1,084	...	3	118	37	6	7	...	...	852	23	38	...	...	...	...	...	...	...	...	...	...
283	283	...	...	38	23	4	7	...	...	178	13	20	...	...	...	...	...	...	...	...	...	...
222	222	...	...	11	3	1	...	...	...	175	12	20	...	...	...	...	...	...	...	...	...	...
212	212	...	...	5	...	1	...	...	...	175	12	19	...	...	...	...	...	...	...	...	...	...
10	10	...	...	6	3	...	...	...	...	...	...	1	...	...	...	...	...	...	...	...	...	...
61	61	...	...	27	20	3	7	...	...	3	1	...	...	...	...	...	...	...	...	...	...	...
9	9	...		...	...	...	7	...	...	2	...	...	...	...	...	...	...	...	...	...	...	...
52	52	...	...	27	20	3	...	...	...	1	1	...	...	...	...	...	...	...	...	...	...	...
41	41	...	...	19	7	1	...	...	...	14	...	...	...	...	...	...	...	...	...	...	...	...
8	8	...	...	2	6	...	...	...	...	...	...	...	...	...	...	...	...	...	...	...	...	...
33	33	...	...	17	1	1	...	...	...	14	...	...	...	...	...	...	...	...	...	...	...	...
186	186	...	...	1	...	...	...	...	...	165	3	17	...	...	...	...	...	...	...	...	...	...
490	490	...	3	56	7	1	...	...	...	415	7	1	...	...	...	...	...	...	...	...	...	...
384	384	...	3	49	7	1	...	...	...	317	7	...	...	...	...	...	...	...	...	...	...	...
327	327	...	3	46	7	1	...	...	...	264	6	...	...	...	...	...	...	...	...	...	...	...
57	57	...	...	3	...	...	...	...	...	53	1	...	...	...	...	...	...	...	...	...	...	...
106	106	...	...	7	...	...	...	...	...	98	...	1	...	...	...	...	...	...	...	...	...	...
84	84	...	...	3	...	...	...	...	...	80	...	1	...	...	...	...	...	...	...	...	...	...
22	22	...	...	4	...	...	...	...	...	18	...	...	...	...	...	...	...	...	...	...	...	...
84	84	...	...	4	...	...	...	...	...	80	...	...	...	...	...	...	...	...	...	...	...	...

Imperial Table XXIIA.—The Special Industrial Census. Part II.—

Description of Establishment (with Group-letters and Serial Nos. of Classes in each group).	District.	Number of Establishments.	Total Employees.			Classification of Superior Employees. N.B.—In these columns all are males unless the contrary is indicated.												
						Managers.			Supervising and Technical Staff.			Clerical Staff.			Skilled Labourers.			
			Persons.	Males.	Females.	Europeans and Anglo-Indians.	Home Races.	Others.	Europeans and Anglo-Indians.	Home Races.	Others.	Europeans and Anglo-Indians.	Home Races.	Others.	Europeans and Anglo-Indians.	Home Races.	Chinese and Japanese.	Others.
1	2	3	4	5	6	7	8	9	10	11	12	13	14	15	16	17	18	19
H. Glass and Earthenware	...	83	4,106	3,709	397	...	47	36	...	6	46	..	14	16	..	M288 F-23	...	543
1. Pottery work—	Total ...	11	180	159	21	...	10	1	..	...	10		...	...	...	M.48 F-7	...	10
Without mech. power	Rangoon	1	34	34	...	...	...	1	...	.	10	..	...	...	...	...	...	10
	Hanthawaddy	10	146	125	21	...	10	..	...	...	...	...	...	...	...	M-48 F-7	...	...
2. Brick, tile and firebrick factories—	Total ..	72	3,926	3 550	376	...	37	35	...	6	36	...	14	16	...	M240 F-16	...	533
Without mech. power	Rangoon	2	488	488	...	...	...	2	...	...	2	...	..	...	...	...	...	198
	Hanthawaddy	25	798	676	122	...	19	6	...	...	2	:	5	3	...	M106 F-4	..	35
	Insein ...	24	1,905	1,834	71	...	2	22	...	1	31	...	...	11	...	M-58 F-6	...	290
	Tharrawaddy	4	116	94	22	...	1	3	...	...	...	...	1	1	..	...	...	8
	Pegu ...	3	190	151	39	...	2	1	...	..	...		...	...	...	19	...	1
	Prome ..	2	75	69	6	...	1	1	...	1	1	...	1	1	...	...	...	1
	Pakôkku ...	1	12	12	...	...	1	...	...	...	...	...	...	...	...	6	...	...
	Minbu ...	2	108	53	55	...	2	...	...	...	...	...	...	...	...	...	...	...
	Mandalay ...	9	234	173	61	...	9	...	...	4	...	...	7	...	...	M-51 F-6	...	...
J. Chemical Products ...	...	78	34,963	34,414	549	28	29	21	514	M63 F-11	66	M87 F-9	M1349 F-4	M594 F-3	50	1478	260	3092
1. Salt refineries— *Without mech. power*	Hanthawaddy	3	57	30	27	...	3	...	...	M-1 F-3	...	...	F-2	...	...	...	...	..
2. Aerated waters factories—	Total ...	5	337	337	..	2	1	2	4	9	11	...	6	11	..	13	...	46
With mechanical power	Akyab ...	1	13	13	...	...	...	1	...	..	...	...	...	1	...	...	...	..
	Rangoon ...	4	324	324	...	2	1	1	4	9	11	...	6	10	...	13	...	46
3. Dye works—	Total ...	4	75	75	...	...	1	3	...	3	..	...	...	4	...	8	...	16
With mechanical power	Insein ..	1	23	23	..	...	...	1	...	3	...	...	..	2	...	2	...	...
Without mech. power	Rangoon ...	3	52	52	...	...	1	2	...	..	...	...	...	2	...	6	...	16
4. Petroleum refineries*—	Total .	24	33,080	32,715	365	21	1	2	503	29	25	M85 F-9	1,294	M524 F-3	50	1,407	258	2957
(i) *With mechanical power*	...	22	32,905	32,540	365	19	1	2	496	29	25	M82 F-9	1,289	M523 F-3	50	1,365	258	2955
	Rangoon ...	1	2,698	2,684	8	1	...	...	16	...	...	M35 F-7	78	46	5	61	42	380
	Hanthawaddy	5	10,365	10,285	80	5	...	...	139	19	11	11	147	M111 F-3	25	277	184	1490
	Insein ..	1	63	63	...	1	...	..	1	...	...	...	...	4	...	1	...	3
	Tharrawaddy	1	95	95	...	1	...	...	2	3	...	...	1	1	...	4	...	14
	Prome ...	1	65	65	..	1	...	...	3	3	...	...	2	...	...	5	...	6
	Thayetmyo	1	206	205	1	1	—	...	2	1	2	...	3	1	..	13	...	7
	Pakôkku ...	3	773	767	6	3	...	...	4	...	...	1	12	2	...	100	...	61
	Magwe ...	7	18,404	18,141	263	4	1	2	326	3	12	M35 F-2	1,044	346	20	893	32	986
	U. Chindwin	2	242	235	7	2	...	...	3	...	...	...	2	12	...	11	..	6
(ii) *Without mech. power*	...	2	175	175	...	2	...	...	7	...	...	3	5	1	...	42	...	2
	Thayetmyo	1	80	80	...	1	...	...	1	...	...	1	..	...	...	1	...	1
	Magwe ...	1	95	95	...	1	...	...	6	...	...	2	5	1	...	41	...	1
5. Bulk-oil installations*— *With mechanical power*	Rangoon ..	1	95	95	...	1	...	..	...	...	..	...	...	8	..	1	...	6
6. Chemical drug and medicine works—	Total ...	4	206	206	-	2	...	2	4	2	4	1	2	12	...	19	...	9
With mechanical power	...	2	173	173	...	2	...	...	4	2	3	1	2	...	...	19	...	9
	Rangoon ...	1	76	76	...	1	...	...	4	1	...	...	2	...	...	16	...	4
	Insein ...	1	97	97	...	1	...	...	...	1	3	1	...	...	...	3	...	5
Without mech. power	Rangoon ...	2	33	33	...	...	...	2	...	...	1	...	...	12	...	...	...	...
7. Vegetable-oil mills—	Total ...	37	1,113	956	157	2	23	12	3	M19 F-8	26	1	M-47 F-2	35	.	30	2	58
(i) *With mechanical power*	...	29	925	827	98	1	16	12	2	M12 F-8	26	1	M-40 F-2	35	...	30	2	58
	Rangoon ...	6	196	185	11	...	2	4	..	M-3 F-8	11	...	5	16	...	1	...	14
	Insein ...	4	114	114	...	..	...	4	...	1	5	...	...	7	...	...	2	13
	Henzada ...	1	26	26	...	...	1	.	...	...	...	...	2	...	...	2	...	...

* Pipe-line pumping-stations have been included in J4, Petroleum refineries.

Distribution by Districts of the Statistics in Part I of this table—continued.

CLASSIFICATION OF UNSKILLED LABOURERS.																						
TOTAL.			MALES.										FEMALES.									
			Europeans and Anglo-Indians.	Home Races.			Chinese and Japanese.			Others.			Europeans and Anglo-Indians.	Home Races.			Chinese and Japanese.			Others.		
Persons.	Males.	Females.		Age 18 or over.	Age 14 to 18.	Age under 14.	Age 18 or over.	Age 14 to 18.	Age under 14.	Age 18 or over.	Age 14 to 18.	Age under 14.		Age 18 or over.	Age 14 to 18.	Age under 14.	Age 18 or over.	Age 14 to 18.	Age under 14.	Age 18 or over.	Age 14 to 18.	Age under 14.
20	21	22	23	24	25	26	27	28	29	30	31	32	33	34	35	36	37	38	39	40	41	42
3,087	2,713	374	...	544	59	24	...	...	...	2,056	23	7	...	257	54	29	...	...	...	33	1	1
94	80	14	...	27	2	1	...	...	...	50	...	...	...	12	1	...	...	...	...	1	...	...
13	13	...	...	...	...	...	...	...	...	13	...	...	...	...	...	...	...	...	...	...	...	...
81	67	14	...	27	2	1	...	...	...	37	...	...	...	12	1	...	...	...	...	1	...	...
2,993	2,633	360	...	517	57	23	...	...	...	2,006	23	7	...	245	53	29	...	...	...	32	1	...
286	286	...	...	...	...	...	...	...	...	280	3	3	...	...	...	...	...	...	...	...	...	...
618	500	118	...	172	19	9	...	...	...	292	5	3	...	92	21	5	...	...	...	...	...	...
1,484	1,419	65	...	151	7	5	...	...	...	1,242	13	1	...	31	11	5	...	...	...	18	...	...
102	80	22	...	10	9	2	...	...	...	57	2	...	...	9	5	5	...	...	...	2	1	...
167	128	39	...	43	6	...	...	...	...	79	...	...	...	25	4	...	...	...	...	10	...	...
68	62	6	...	3	1	2	...	...	...	56	...	...	...	3	...	1	...	...	...	2	...	...
5	5	...	...	5	...	...	...	...	...	...	...	...	...	...	...	...	...	...	...	...	...	...
106	51	55	...	43	6	2	...	...	...	...	...	...	...	40	6	9	...	...	...	...	...	...
157	102	55	...	90	9	3	...	...	...	...	...	...	...	45	6	4	...	...	...	...	...	...
27,305	26,783	522	72	6,521	236	29	70	1	1	18,698	904	251	1	421	77	16	...	...	...	7	...	...
48	26	22	...	21	1	4	...	...	...	...	...	...	...	12	2	8	...	...	...	...	...	...
232	232	...	...	2	1	...	...	...	...	228	1	...	...	...	...	...	...	...	...	...	...	...
11	11	...	...	...	1	...	...	...	...	10	...	...	...	...	...	...	...	...	...	...	...	...
221	221	...	...	2	...	...	...	...	...	218	1	...	...	...	...	...	...	...	...	...	...	...
40	40	...	...	1	...	...	...	...	...	33	2	4	...	...	...	...	...	...	...	...	...	...
15	15	...	...	1	...	...	...	...	...	14	...	...	...	...	...	...	...	...	...	...	...	...
25	25	...	...	...	...	...	...	...	...	19	2	4	...	...	...	...	...	...	...	...	...	...
25,912	25,559	353	72	6,170	200	24	24	...	...	17,942	884	243	1	291	51	5	...	...	...	5	...	...
25,799	*25,446*	*353*	72	*6,124*	*198*	*24*	24	...	...	*17,877*	884	*243*	*1*	*291*	*51*	*5*	...	...	...	*5*	...	...
2,019	2,018	1	18	8	...	...	...	...	...	1,728	225	39	1	...	...	...	...	...	...	...	...	...
7,943	7,866	77	46	216	22	2	20	...	...	7,113	408	39	...	63	14	...	...	...	...	...	...	...
53	53	...	...	2	...	...	...	...	...	51	...	...	...	...	...	...	...	...	...	...	...	...
69	69	...	...	10	...	...	...	...	...	59	...	...	...	...	...	...	...	...	...	...	...	...
45	45	...	1	19	1	...	...	...	...	24	...	...	...	...	...	...	...	...	...	...	...	...
176	175	1	...	68	1	...	...	...	...	105	1	...	...	1	...	...	...	...	...	...	...	...
590	584	6	...	351	1	...	1	...	...	212	7	12	...	3	3	...	...	...	...	...	...	...
14,698	14,437	261	7	5,341	170	19	2	...	...	8,506	241	151	...	218	34	5	...	...	...	4	...	...
206	199	7	...	109	3	3	1	...	...	79	2	2	...	6	...	...	...	...	...	1	...	...
113	*113*	...	...	*46*	*2*	...	...	...	...	*65*	...	...	...	...	...	...	...	...	...	...	...	...
75	75	...	...	18	2	...	...	...	...	55	...	...	...	...	...	...	...	...	...	...	...	...
38	38	...	...	28	...	...	...	...	...	10	...	...	...	...	...	...	...	...	...	...	...	...
79	*79*	...	...	*1*	...	...	...	...	...	*76*	*2*	...	...	...	...	...	...	...	...	...	...	...
149	149	...	...	9	...	...	16	1	1	111	10	1	...	...	...	...	...	...	...	...	...	...
131	*131*	...	...	9	...	...	...	...	...	*111*	*10*	*1*	...	...	...	...	...	...	...	...	...	...
48	48	...	...	5	...	...	...	...	...	39	4	...	...	...	...	...	...	...	...	...	...	...
83	83	...	...	4	...	...	...	...	...	72	6	1	...	...	...	...	...	...	...	...	...	...
18	*18*	...	...	...	...	...	*16*	*1*	*1*	...	...	...	...	...	...	...	...	...	...	...	...	...
845	698	147	...	317	34	1	30	...	...	308	5	3	...	118	24	3	...	...	...	2	...	...
680	*592*	*88*	...	*226*	*26*	...	*30*	...	...	*302*	*5*	*3*	...	*74*	*12*	...	...	...	...	2	...	...
132	129	3	...	8	...	...	17	...	...	102	2	...	...	1	...	...	...	...	...	2	...	...
82	82	...	...	20	...	...	13	...	...	49	...	...	...	...	...	...	...	...	...	...	...	...
21	21	...	...	6	...	...	...	...	...	14	1	...	...	...	...	...	...	...	...	...	...	...

CLASSIFICATION OF SUPERIOR EMPLOYEES. N.B.—In these columns all are males unless the contrary is indicated.

DESCRIPTION OF ESTABLISHMENT (with Group-letters and Serial Nos. of Classes in each group).	DISTRICT.	Number of Establishments.	TOTAL EMPLOYEES. Persons.	TOTAL EMPLOYEES. Males.	TOTAL EMPLOYEES. Females.	Managers. Europeans and Anglo-Indians.	Managers. Home Races.	Managers. Others.	Supervising and Technical Staff. Europeans and Anglo-Indians.	Supervising and Technical Staff. Home Races.	Supervising and Technical Staff. Others.	Clerical Staff. Europeans and Anglo-Indians.	Clerical Staff. Home Races.	Clerical Staff. Others.	Skilled Labourers. Europeans and Anglo-Indians.	Skilled Labourers. Home Races.	Skilled Labourers. Chinese and Japanese.	Skilled Labourers. Others.
1	2	3	4	5	6	7	8	9	10	11	12	13	14	15	16	17	18	19
J.7. Vegetable-oil mills—concld. (i) *With mechanical power*—concld.	Thayetmyo	1	13	13	...	...	1	...	...	...	...	...	1	...	...	...	...	...
	Pakôkku ...	7	129	86	43	..	5	2	...	6	1	...	4	3	...	8	...	3
	Magwe .	1	40	34	6	...	...	1	...	...	...	1	2	.	...	1	...	4
	Mandalay ...	2	47	37	10	...	2	...	...	...	...	...	M-5 F-2	...	...	7	...	6
	Myingyan ...	3	247	227	20	1	2	...	1	1	5	...	19	8	.	7	...	12
	Amherst ...	1	37	37	...	...	...	1	1	...	...	...	...	1	...	1	...	1
	L. Chindwin	1	11	11	...	...	1	...	...	...	...	...	...	...	...	2	...	1
	Prome ...	2	65	57	8		2	.	..	1	4	...	2	..	...	1	...	4
(ii) *Without mech. power*	...	8	188	120	59	1	7	...	1	7	...	.	7	...	...	...	...	...
	Pakôkku ...	7	102	0	22	...	7	...	...	7	...	...	7	...	.	...	...	...
	Amherst ...	1	86	49	37	1	...	.	1	...	...	...	...	..	...	...		...
K. Food—	...	482	24,080	22,251	1829	M54 F-2	M274 F-15	M139 F-1	M162 F-2	M280 F-35	481	17	M1005 F-2	436	18	M692 F389	M227 F-3	994
1. Biscuit factories—*Without mech. power*	Rangoon ...	1	12	12	...	...	...	1	..	...	...	...	...	..	..	...	...	...
2. Flour mills—*With mechanical power*	Rangoon ...	3	108	106	2	...	..	3	1	...	1	..	...	4	...	...	...	11
3. Rice mills—	Province ...	388	21678	20658	1020	44	M218 F-10	M-117 F-1	144	M230 F-26	391	14	M-998 F-2	397	18	671	226	932
All with mech. power	*Arakan Division.*	*10*	*951*	*944*	*7*	*7*	*1*	*2*	*17*	*2*	*1*	...	*38*	*6*	...	*17*	*25*	*28*
	Rangoon ...	*50*	*8,317*	*7,993*	*324*	*15*	*14*	*21*	*72*	*40*	*70*	*1*	*250*	*186*	*10*	*129*	*136*	*304*
	*Pegu Division (less Rangoon).**	*119*	*5,088*	*4,906*	*182*	*7*	*M-68 F-3*	*42*	*13*	*M-50 F-1*	*226*	*3*	*249*	*103*	*7*	*187*	*24*	*267*
	Irrawaddy Division.	*96*	*4,348*	*4,252*	*96*	*9*	*M-63 F-2*	*23*	*32*	*55*	*58*	*9*	*M-282 F-1*	*52*	...	*106*	*26*	*201*
	Tenasserim Division.	*62*	*1,864*	*1,745*	*119*	*5*	*M-35 F-4*	*M-17 F-1*	*10*	*M-37 F-4*	*16*	*1*	*M-122 F-1*	*42*	...	*149*	*14*	*97*
	Upper Burma and Shan States.	*51*	*1,110*	*818*	*292*	*1*	*M-37 F-1*	*12*	...	*M-46 F-21*	*20*	...	*57*	*8*	*1*	*83*	*1*	*35*
	Akyab ...	10	951	944	7	7	1	2	17	2	1	...	38	6	...	17	25	28
	Rangoon ...	50	8,317	7,993	324	15	14	21	72	40	70	1	250	186	10	129	136	304
	Hanthawaddy	32	2,500	2,460	40	6	14	12	12	7	150	...	61	38	7	48	24	121
	Insein ...	8	306	283	23	...	M-4 F-1	3	..	5	13	...	21	4	...	14	...	6
	Tharrawaddy	40	1,196	1,113	83	1	M-28 F-1	10	...	16	4	3	103	23	...	68	...	71
	Pegu ...	21	591	579	12	...	M-11 F-1	10	1	M-10 F-1	42	...	26	27		18	...	41
	Prome ...	18	495	471	24	...	11	7	..	12	17	..	38	11	...	39	...	28
	Bassein ...	25	2,067	2,052	15	7	11	7	32	9	12	7	161	22	...	37	25	61
	Henzada ...	12	321	299	22	1	10	1	...	18	24	2	31	14	...	22	...	20
	Myaungmya	25	695	694	1	...	21	4	...	11	14	...	M-30 F-1	7	.	13	...	50
	Ma-ubin ..	11	245	244	1	..	9	2	...	6	4	...	18	2	.	13	...	16
	Pyapôn ...	23	1,020	963	57	1	M-12 F 2	9	...	11	4	...	40	7	...	21	1	54
	Toungoo ...	8	281	246	35	1	6	1	...	3	2	...	21	7	...	12	...	10
	Thatôn ...	24	527	511	16	...	M-18 F-3	M-2 F-1	1	M-14 F-4	3	...	M-21 F-1	6	...	61	3	44
	Amherst ...	20	732	731	1	4	M-6 F-1	9	8	13	7	1	68	18	...	36	11	33
	Tavoy ...	7	244	186	58	...	3	4	1	4	3	...	8	7	...	32	...	5
	Mergui ...	3	80	71	9	...	2	1	...	3	1	...	4	4	...	8	...	5
	Minbu ...	5	126	84	42	...	4	1	...	2	1	...	4	...	...	1	...	6
	Mandalay ...	21	440	344	96	1	M-18 F-1	1	...	4	1	...	28	...	...	38	...	15
	Katha ...	3	136	85	51	..	...	3	...	M-29 F-20	9	...	1	...	...	9	...	...
	Putao ...	1	21	21	...	...	...	1	...	...	...	...	...	...	..	...	1	...
	Shwebo ...	15	286	191	95	...	12	3	...	M-8 F-1	4	...	19	1	...	29	...	10
	Sagaing ...	2	30	27	3	...	1	1	...	2	3	...	1	1	...	2	...	...
	Kyauksè ...	2	28	23	5	...	2	...	...	1	1	...	2	...	1	4	...	2
	Yamèthin ...	2	43	43	...	...	...	2	...	...	1	...	2	6	...	...	...	2

* That is, the Insein, Hanthawaddy, Tharrawaddy, Pegu and Prome districts.

Distribution by Districts of the Statistics in Part I of this table—continued.

CLASSIFICATION OF UNSKILLED LABOURERS.

Total.			Males.										Females.									
			Europeans and Anglo-Indians.	Home Races.			Chinese and Japanese.			Others.			Europeans and Anglo-Indians.	Home Races.			Chinese and Japanese.			Others.		
Persons.	Males.	Females.		Age 18 or over.	Age 14 to 18.	Age under 14.	Age 18 or over.	Age 14 to 18.	Age under 14.	Age 18 or over.	Age 14 to 18.	Age under 14.		Age 18 or over.	Age 14 to 18.	Age under 14.	Age 18 or over.	Age 14 to 18.	Age under 14.	Age 18 or over.	Age 14 to 18.	Age under 14.
20	21	22	23	24	25	26	27	28	29	30	31	32	33	34	35	36	37	38	39	40	41	42
11	11	...	...	10	1	...	..	...	...	..	...	...	...	...	...	...	...	...	...	...	...	...
97	54	43	...	51	3	...	...	...	...	...	...	...	...	38	5	...	..	...	...	...	...	...
31	25	6	...	15	5	...	...	...	...	5	...	...	...	4	2	...	...	...	...	...	...	...
25	17	8	..	15	..	...	...	...	...	2	...	...	...	8	...	...	...	...	...	...	...	...
191	171	20	...	73	17	...	...	...	...	79	2	...	...	15	5	...		...	...	...	...	...
32	32	..	...	.	...	...	...	...	...	29	...	3	...	...	...	...	...	...	...	...	...	...
7	7	..	...	7	..	...	...	...	...	...	...	...	...	...	..	...	...	...	...	...	...	...
51	43	8	...	21	...	...	.	...	...	22	...	...	...	8	...	...	...	...	...	...	...	...
165	106	59	..	91	8	1	...	...	...	6	...	...	...	44	12	3	...	...	...	...	...	...
81	59	22	...	50	8	1	...	...	..	...	...	...	..	19	2	1	...	...	...	...	...	...
84	47	37	...	41	...	..	...	...	...	6	...	...	...	25	10	2	...	..	...	...	...	...
18,852	17,472	1,380	15	2,213	177	42	190	6	1	14,432	324	72	...	801	155	49	4	3	3	297	35	33
11	11	...	...	6	4	1	...	...	...	..	...	..	...	...	...	..	...	...	...	...	...	...
88	86	2	..	...	...	...	...	...	...	85	1	...	...	...	...	...	...	...	..	2	...	...
17,239	16,258	981	10	1,715	137	23	143	2	...	13,845	311	72	...	512	112	12	...	...	...	277	35	33
807	800	7	...	26	4	..	...	...	..	750	18	2	...	7	...	...	...	...	...	...	...	...
7,069	6,745	324	10	164	5	4	106	2	...	6,292	130	32	...	11	...	...	...	...	...	247	33	33
3,838	3,660	178	...	588	45	7	17	...	..	2,926	60	17	...	133	27	6	...	...	...	11	1	...
3,429	3,336	93	...	351	42	5	7	.	...	2,840	83	8	...	66	8	...	...	...	..	18	1	...
1,309	1,200	109	..	253	18	2	3	...		895	16	13	..	95	13	..	...	...	...	1	...	...
787	517	270	...	333	23	5	10	...	...	142	4	...	...	200	64	6	...	...	...	...	...	...
807	800	7	..	26	4	...	...	...	...	750	18	2	...	7	...	...	...	...	...	...	...	...
7,069	6,745	324	10	164	5	4	106	2	...	6,291	130	32	...	11	...	...	...	...	...	247	33	33
2,000	1,960	40	...	186	6	..	4	...	...	1,731	30	3	...	27	6	...	...	...	...	6	1	...
235	213	22	...	44	5	2	2	...	...	155	5	...	...	18	1	2	...	...	...	1	...	...
868	786	82	...	210	16	1	4	...	...	552	3	...	...	67	12	1	...	...	...	2	...	...
403	393	10	...	49	6	4	7	...	...	308	9	10	...	5	...	3	...	...	...	2	...	...
332	308	24	...	99	12	...	...	...	...	180	13	4	...	16	8	...	...	...	...	...	...	...
1,676	1,661	15	...	100	25	3	3	...	...	1,479	46	5	...	13	1	...	...	...	...	1	...	...
178	156	22	...	82	3	1	...	...	...	69	1	...	...	20	2	...	...	...	...	...	...	...
542	542	...	...	47	1	...	...	...	...	471	21	2	...	...	...	...	...	...	...	...	...	...
175	174	1	...	36	4	...	...	...	...	133	1	...	...	1	...	...	...	...	...	...	...	...
858	803	55	..	86	9	1	4	...	...	688	14	1	...	32	5	...	...	...	...	17	1	...
218	183	35		58	3	1	1	...	...	115	5	..	...	27	8	...	...	...	...	...	...	...
345	338	7	...	63	1	...	...	...	...	267	6	1	...	6	...	...	...	...	...	1	...	...
517	517	...	...	39	4	1	...	...	...	458	3	12	...	...	...	...	...	...	...	...	...	...
177	119	58	...	79	10	...	...	...	...	29	1	...	...	53	5	...	...	...	...	...	...	...
52	43	9	...	14	...	...	2	...	...	26	1	...	...	9	...	...	...	...	...	...	...	...
107	65	42	...	41	4	...	...	...	...	19	1	...	...	24	16	2	...	...	...	...	...	...
333	238	95	...	172	11	...	..	...	...	54	1	...	...	81	14	...	...	...	...	...	...	...
65	34	31	...	17	1	5	...	...	...	11	...	...	...	16	11	4	...	...	...	...	...	...
19	19	...	...	9	...	...	10	...	...	..	...	...	...	...	...	...	...	...	...	...	...	...
199	105	94	...	79	4	...	...	...	...	22	...	...	...	72	22	..	...	...	...	...	...	...
19	16	3	...	7	1	...	...	...	...	8	...	...	...	3	...	...	...	...	...	...	...	...
15	10	5	...	5	2	...	...	...	...	3	...	...	...	4	1	...	...	...	...	...	...	...
30	30	...	...	3	...	...	...	...	...	25	2	...	...	...	...	...	...	...	...	...	...	...

DESCRIPTION OF ESTABLISHMENT (with Group-letters and Serial Nos. of Classes in each group).	DISTRICT.	Number of Establishments.	TOTAL EMPLOYEES.			CLASSIFICATION OF SUPERIOR EMPLOYEES. N.B.—In these columns all are males unless the contrary is indicated.												
						Managers.			Supervising and Technical Staff.			Clerical Staff.			Skilled Labourers.			
			Persons.	Males.	Females.	Europeans and Anglo-Indians.	Home Races.	Others.	Europeans and Anglo-Indians.	Home Races.	Others.	Europeans and Anglo-Indians.	Home Races.	Others.	Europeans and Anglo-Indians.	Home Races.	Chinese and Japanese.	Others.
1	2	3	4	5	6	7	8	9	10	11	12	13	14	15	16	17	18	19
K. Food—concld.																		
4. Bakeries and confectioneries—	Total ...	11	245	241	4	M-4 F-1	...	7	M-5 F-2	...	27	2	2	14	...	...	...	...
(i) *With mechanical power*	Rangoon ...	1	21	21	...	...	.	1	...	...	9	...	...	1	...	...	...	...
(ii) *Without mech. power*	Rangoon ...	10	224	220	4	M-4 F-1	...	6	M-5 F-2	...	18	2	2	13	...	...	...	...
5. Dairy Farms— *With mechanical power*	S. Shan States	1	48	33	15	F-1	...	...	...	...	...	...	...	...	...	...	...	...
6. Slaughter-houses— *With mechanical power*	Rangoon ...	1	23	23	..	1	...	...	1	..	...	...	...	...	.	...	...	1
7. Sugar-factories—	Total ...	54	945	640	305	...	52	2	...	40	15	..	...	...	...	...	..	...
Without mech. power	Kyauksè ...	3	111	111	...	...	1	2	...	39	15	...	...	...	.	...	...	...
	Yamèthin ...	51	834	529	305	...	51	...	...	1	...	...	...	...	..	...	...	..
8. Breweries and distilleries—	Total ...	2	183	183	...	1	...	1	3	5	34	..	1	19	...	9	...	26
(i) *With mechanical power*	Mandalay ...	1	154	154	..	1	...	...	3	5	33	...	1	5	..	9	...	26
(ii) *Without mech. power*	Rangoon ...	1	29	29	...	...	...	1	...	..	1	...	...	14	...	...	...	...
9. Water-works—	Total ...	4	256	241	15	3	...	1	8	5	6	...	3	...	...	7	...	23
(i) *With mechanical power*	...	*3*	*135*	*135*	..	*2*	...	*1*	*5*	*3*	*6*	...	*1*	.	...	*5*	...	*21*
	Rangoon .	1	45	45	...	...	...	1	1	...	...	...	...	...	...	...	...	9
	Insein ...	1	57	57	...	1	...	...	3	...	...	...	...	...	.	3	...	2
	Prome ...	1	33	33	..	1	...	...	1	3	6	..	1	...	...	2	...	10
(ii) *Without mech. power*	Insein ...	*1*	*121*	*106*	*15*	*1*	...	...	*3*	*2*	...	...	*2*	..	...	*2*	...	*2*
10. Tobacco, cigar or cigarette factories—	Total ...	17	582	114	468	1	M-4 F-5	7	...	F-9	7	1	1	2	...	M-5 F-389	M-1 F-3	1
(i) *With mechanical power*	Rangoon ...	*1*	*44*	*22*	*22*	*1*	...	..	...	...	*2*	*1*	*1*	...	..	*M-1 F-1*	*1*	*1*
(ii) *Without mech. power*	...	*16*	*538*	*92*	*446*	...	*M-4 F-5*	*7*	...	*F-9*	*5*	...	...	*2*	...	*M-4 F-388*	*F-3*	...
	Rangoon ...	11	447	88	359	...	M-1 F-3	7	...	F-9	5	.	..	2	..	M-3 F-308	F-3	...
	Prome ...	3	59	4	55	...	3	...	...	...	...	...	...	...	...	M-1 F-55	...	..
	Henzada ...	1	20	...	20	...	F-1	...	...	..	...	...	...	...	...	F-19	...	...
	Mandalay ...	1	12	...	12	...	F-1	..	...	...	...	...	...	...	...	F-6	...	...
L. Clothing ...	...	48	1,033	979	54	M-5 F-1	10	32	M-9 F-2	5	63		2	29	M-1 F-2	M-191 F-24	165	305
1. Tailoring works—	Total ...	26	461	461	...	4	1	21	9	4	37	...	1	24	1	19	60	226
Without mech. power	Rangoon ...	25	444	444	...	4	...	21	9	4	37	...	1	24	1	3	60	226
	Henzada ..	1	17	17	...	...	1	...	...	...	..	...	...	...	...	16	...	...
2. Dress makers and milliners— *Without mech. power*	Rangoon ...	2	47	27	20	M-1 F-1	...	...	F-2	...	...	...	...	...	F-2	...	...	17
3. Boot and shoe factories*—	Total ...	14	287	280	7	...	4	10	...	...	25	...	...	5	...	M-49 F-6	105	39
Without mech. power	Rangoon ...	11	215	213	2	...	1	10	...	...	25	...	...	5	...	M-13 F-2	105	29
	Thayetmyo	1	41	41	...	...	1	...	...	...	...	...	...	...	...	23	...	10
	Mandalay ...	1	12	12	...	...	1	...	...	...	...	...	...	...	...	4	...	...
	Sagaing ...	1	19	14	5	..	1	...	...	...	...	...	...	...	...	M-9 F-4	...	...
4. Umbrella factories—	Total ...	6	238	211	27	...	5	1	...	1	1	...	1	...	...	M-123 F-18	...	23
Without mech. power	Bassein ...	5	160	146	14	...	5	...	...	1	..	..	1	...	...	M-123 F-5	...	...
	Insein ...	1	78	65	13	...	...	1	...	...	1	...	...	...	..	F-13	...	23
M. Furniture ...	...	12	598	597	1	3	M-1 F-1	7	13	34	23	...	14	8	...	119	75	31
Without mech. power	Rangoon ...	11	363	362	1	2	M-1 F-1	7	3	2	23	...	1	7	..	24	75	31
	Mandalay ...	1	235	235	...	1	...	...	10	32	...	...	13	1	...	95	..	...

* Includes factories using leather, wood or any other material.

Distribution by Districts of the Statistics in Part I of this table—continued.

CLASSIFICATION OF UNSKILLED LABOURERS.																						
Total.			Males.										Females.									
			Europeans and Anglo-Indians.	Home Races.			Chinese and Japanese.			Others.			Europeans and Anglo-Indians.	Home Races.			Chinese and Japanese.			Others.		
Persons.	Males.	Females.		Age 18 or over.	Age 14 to 18.	Age under 14.	Age 18 or over.	Age 14 to 18.	Age under 14.	Age 18 or over.	Age 14 to 18.	Age under 14.		Age 18 or over.	Age 14 to 18.	Age under 14.	Age 18 or over.	Age 14 to 18.	Age under 14.	Age 18 or over.	Age 14 to 18.	Age under 14.
20	21	22	23	24	25	26	27	28	29	30	31	32	33	34	35	36	37	38	39	40	41	42
181	180	1	5	2	2	1	5	4	...	161	...	...	...	1	...	...	...	...	...	...	...	...
10	10	...	...	...		...	...	...	...	10	...	...	...	...	...	...	...	...	...	...	...	...
171	170	1	5	2	2	1	5	4	...	151	...	...	...	1	...	...	...	...	...	...	...	...
47	33	14	...	...	...	...	...	...	...	32	1	...	...	8	...	3	...	...	...	3	...	...
20	20	...	...	...	...	...	...	...	...	19	1	...	...	...	...	...	...	...	...	...	...	...
836	531	305	...	482	33	16	...	...	...	...		...	...	242	37	26	...	...	...	...	...	...
54	54	...	...	54	...	...	...	...	...	...	...	...	...	...	...	...	...	...	...	...	...	...
782	477	305	...	428	33	16	...	...	...	...	...	...	...	242	37	26	...	...	...	...	...	...
84	84	...	...	...	...	...	13	...	...	67	4	...	...	...	...	...	...	...	...	...	...	...
71	71	...	...	...	...	...	...	...	...	67	4	...	...	...	...	...	...	...	...	...	...	...
13	13	...	...	...	...	...	13	...	...	...	...	...	...	...	...	...	...	...	...	...	...	...
200	185	15	...	8	1	...	...	...	...	175	1		...	...	...	...	...	...	...	15	...	...
91	*91*	...	...	*3*	...	...	...	...	...	*88*	...	...	...	...	...	...	...	...	...	...	...	...
34	34	...	...	...	...	...	...	...	...	34	...	...	...	...	...	...	...	...	...	...	...	...
48	48	...	...	2	...	...	...	...	...	46	...	...	...	...	...	...	...	...	...	...	...	...
9	9	...	...	1	...	...	...	...	...	8	...	...	...	...	...	...	...	...	...	...	...	...
109	*94*	*15*	...	*5*	*1*	...	...	...	...	*87*	*1*	...	...	...	...	...	...	...	...	*15*	...	...
146	84	62	...	...	...	1	29	...	1	48	5	...	...	38	6	8	4	3	3	...	...	...
35	*14*	*21*	...	...	...	...	...	...	...	*14*		...	...	*17*	4	...	...	...	...	...	...	...
111	*70*	*41*	...	...	...	*1*	*29*	...	*1*	*34*	*5*	...	...	*21*	*2*	*8*	*4*	*3*	*3*	...	...	...
106	70	36	...	...	...	1	29	...	1	34	5	...	...	17	1	8	4	3	3	...	...	...
...	...	...		...	...	...	...	...	...	...	...	...	...	...	...	...	...	...	...	...	...	...
...	...	...	...	...	...	...	...	...	...	...	...	...	...	...	...	...	...	...	...	...	...	...
5	...	5	...	...	...	...	...	...	...	...	...	...	...	4	1	...	...	...	...	...	...	...
187	162	25	...	26	10	1	2	2	1	103	12	5	5	14	6	...	...	...	...	...	...	...
54	54	...	...	1	...	...	1	2	1	37	9	3		...	...	...	...	...	...	...	...	...
54	54	...	...	1	...	...	1	2	1	37	9	3	...	...	...	...	...	...	...	...	...	...
...	...	...	...	...	...	...	...	...	...	...	...	...	...	...	...	...	...	...	...	...	...	...
24	9	15	...	...	...	...	...	...	...	7	2		5	8	2	...	...	...	...	...	...	...
44	43	1	...	11	8	1	1	...	...	21	...	1	...	1	...	...	...	...	...	...	...	...
25	25	...	...	...	1	1	1	...	...	21	...	1	...	...	...	...	...	...	...	...	...	...
7	7	...	...	7	...	...	...	...	...	...	...	...	...	...	...	...	...	...	...	...	...	...
7	7	...	...	...	7	...	...	...	...	...	...	...	...	...	...	...	...	...	...	...	...	...
5	4	1	...	4	...	...	...	...	...	...	...	...	...	1	...	...	...	...	...	...	...	...
65	56	9	...	14	2	...	...	...	...	38	1	1	...	5	4	...	...	...	...	...	...	...
25	16	9	...	14	2	...	...	...	...	...		...	...	5	4	...	...	...	...	...	...	...
40	40	...	...	...	...	...	...	...	...	38	1	1	...	...	...	...	...	...	...	...	...	...
269	269	...	...	98	...	...	19	...	1	133	11	7	...	...	...	...	...	...	...	...	...	...
186	186	...	...	15	...	...	19	...	1	133	11	7	...	...	...	...	...	...	...	...	...	...
83	83	...	...	83	...	...	...	...	...	...	...	...	...	...	...	...	...	...	...	...	...	...

IMPERIAL TABLE XXIIA.—THE SPECIAL INDUSTRIAL CENSUS. PART II.—

DESCRIPTION OF ESTABLISHMENT (with Group-letters and Serial Nos. of Classes in each group).	DISTRICT.	Number of Establishments.	TOTAL EMPLOYEES. Persons.	TOTAL EMPLOYEES. Males.	TOTAL EMPLOYEES. Females.	CLASSIFICATION OF SUPERIOR EMPLOYEES. (N.B.—In these columns all are males unless the contrary is indicated.) Managers. Europeans and Anglo-Indians.	Managers. Home Races.	Managers. Others.	Supervising and Technical Staff. Europeans and Anglo-Indians.	Supervising and Technical Staff. Home Races.	Supervising and Technical Staff. Others.	Clerical Staff. Europeans and Anglo-Indians.	Clerical Staff. Home Races.	Clerical Staff. Others.	Skilled Labourers. Europeans and Anglo-Indians.	Skilled Labourers. Home Races.	Skilled Labourers. Chinese and Japanese.	Skilled Labourers. Others.
1	2	3	4	5	6	7	8	9	10	11	12	13	14	15	16	17	18	19
N. Building	...	17	1,270	1,259	11	3	9	5	13	1	15	M-1 F-2	43	15	12	119	34	180
1. Stone, marble and cement works—*Without mech. power*	Mandalay ..	2	85	85	...	...	2	...	..	...	..	...	14	...	...	56	...	...
2. Lime works and kilns—	Total ...	11	312	303	9	...	7	4	...	...	4	1		1	...	3	...	...
Without mech. power	Rangoon ...	2	57	56	1	...	...	2	...	...	4	1	...	...	..	...	...	...
	Mandalay ...	2	45	45	...	..	2	...	...	..	...	...	...	...	...	3	...	...
	S. Shan State	7	210	202	8	...	5	2	...	...	..	...	...	1	...	...	...	...
3. Plumbing and sanitary engineering—*Without mech. power*	Rangoon ...	2	153	153	...	1	.	1	4	..	5	..	3	10	...	2	1	50
4. Constructional engineers—*With mechanical power*	Rangoon ...	2	720	718	2	2	...	...	9	1	6	F-2	26	4	12 M	58	33	130
P. Construction of means of transport or communication.	..	41	11,191	11,121	70	23	M-2 F-1	M13 F-1	M134 F-5	16	M12 F-1	M47 F-10	189	261	190 F-51	1,845	415	3,452
1. Railway works—	Total ...	6	3,004	3,004	...	5	...	1	41	...	1	1	15	112	59	169	166	1,396
(i) *With mechanical power*	...	5	2,982	2,982	...	5	...	...	41	...	1	1	15	111	58	168	166	1,391
	Rangoon ...	3	905	905	...	3	...	...	17	...	...	1	4	17	34	11	21	267
	Insein ...	1	187	187	...	1	...	...	11	...	1	..	4	38	15	21	1	10
	Mandalay ...	1	1,890	1,890	...	1	...	...	13	...	..	...	7	56	9	136	144	1,114
(ii) *Without mech. power*	Akyab ...	1	22	22	...	...	..	1	...	...	...	..	..	1	1	1	...	5
2. Tramway works—	Total ...	2	667	666	1	2	...	...	6	2	.	M-1 F-1	74	2	18	179	. 9	67
With mechanical power	Rangoon ...	1	257	257	..	1	..	...	3	...	...	.	3	1	10	59	7	47
	Mandalay ...	1	410	409	1	1	...	...	3	2	...	M-1 F-1	71	1	8	120	2	20
3. Bridge works—*With mechanical power*	Insein ...	1	259	259	...	1	...	...	3	...	...	...	...	13	3	1	...	23
4. Coach-building Works—	Total ...	3	55	54	1	...	F-1	2	...	...	...	...	1	1	...	6	29	8
Without mech. power	Rangoon ...	2	43	43	...	..	...	2	...	...	...	...	1	1	...	1	29	8
	Mandalay ...	1	12	11	1	...	F-1	...	...	...	...	...	...	...	...	5	...	...
5. Motor-car works—	Total ...	11	1,125	1,119	6	7	1	3	M-34 F-1	3	2	M26 F-5	36	78	48	384	24	158
(i) *With mechanical power*	...	10	1,112	1,106	6	7	1	2	M-34 F-1	3	2	M26 F-5	35	78	48	375	24	158
	Rangoon .	9	1,040	1,034	6	6	1	2	M-32 F-1	3	2	M21 F-5	33	71	44	339	24	151
	Mandalay ...	1	72	72	...	1	...	...	2	...	..	5	2	7	4	36	...	7
(ii) *Without mech. power*	Rangoon ...	1	13	13	...	...	...	1	...	...	..	...	1	..	...	9	...	...
6. Shipyards, boat-building yards, dockyards and Port Authorities' workshops—	Total ...	15	5,756	5,753	3	7	1	M-5 F-1	34	4	M-3 F-1	16	59	38	60	1,100	185	1,776
(i) *With mech. power*	...	7	5,433	5,433	...	6	...	...	34	4	...	16	54	30	60	1,072	147	1,726
	Akyab ...	1	222	222	...	1	...	...	2	...	...	...	13	...	...	25	5	104
	Rangoon ...	4	4,910	4,910	...	4	..	..	30	4	...	15	41	28	48	895	140	1,599
	Amherst ...	1	132	132	...	1	...	..	...	...	...	1	...	1	4	56	2	14
	Mandalay ...	1	169	169	...	...	...	...	2	...	..	...	...	1	8	96	...	9
(ii) *Without mech. power*	...	8	323	320	3	1	1	M-5 F-1	...	...	M-3 F-1	...	5	8	...	28	38	50
	Rangoon ...	7	242	239	3	...	1	M-5 F-1	...	...	M-3 F-1	...	2	8	...	24	38	45
	Bassein ...	1	81	81	...	1	...	...	...	...	...	...	3	..	...	4	...	5
7. Telephone system—*With mechanical power*	Rangoon ...	1	181	122	59	1	...	...	M-10 F-4	6	4	M-3 F-4	4	12	M-2 F-51	6	2	24

Distribution by Districts of the Statistics in Part I of this table—continued.

CLASSIFICATION OF UNSKILLED LABOURERS.

Total. Persons.	Total. Males.	Total. Females.	Males. Europeans and Anglo-Indians.	Males. Home Races. Age 18 or over.	Males. Home Races. Age 14 to 18.	Males. Home Races. Age under 14.	Males. Chinese and Japanese. Age 18 or over.	Males. Chinese and Japanese. Age 14 to 18.	Males. Chinese and Japanese. Age under 14.	Males. Others. Age 18 or over.	Males. Others. Age 14 to 18.	Males. Others. Age under 14.	Females. Europeans and Anglo-Indians.	Females. Home Races. Age 18 or over.	Females. Home Races. Age 14 to 18.	Females. Home Races. Age under 14.	Females. Chinese and Japanese. Age 18 or over.	Females. Chinese and Japanese. Age 14 to 18.	Females. Chinese and Japanese. Age under 14.	Females. Others. Age 18 or over.	Females. Others. Age 14 to 18.	Females. Others. Age under 14.
20	21	22	23	24	25	26	27	28	29	30	31	32	33	34	35	36	37	38	39	40	41	42
818	809	9	1	163	14	...	33	1	...	584	10	3	...	6	...	...	...	...	...	2	...	1
13	13	...	...	6	7	...	...	...	...	...	...	...	...	...	...	...	...	...	...	...	...	...
292	283	9	...	149	6	...	32	1	...	89	3	3	...	6	...	...	...	...	...	2	...	1
50	49	1	...	2	...	...	...	...	...	45	1	1	...	...	...	...	...	...	...	1	...	...
40	40	...	...	37	...	...	3	...	...	...	...	...	...	...	...	...	...	...	...	...	...	...
202	194	8	...	110	6	...	29	1	...	44	2	2	...	6	...	...	...	...	...	1	...	1
76	76	...	...	1	...	...	...	...	...	73	2	...	...	...	...	...	...	...	...	...	...	...
437	437	...	1	7	1	...	1	...	...	422	5	...	...	...	...	...	...	...	...	...	...	...
4,523	4,522	1	46	299	31	2	33	5	...	3,925	147	34	...	...	...	...	...	...	...	1	...	...
1,038	1,038	...	14	25	1	...	1	...	...	956	41	...	...	...	...	...	...	...	...	...	...	...
1,025	*1,025*	...	*14*	*21*	*1*	...	*1*	...	...	*947*	*41*	...	...	...	...	...	...	...	...	...	...	...
530	530	...	14	13	...	...	1	...	...	497	5	...	...	...	...	...	...	...	...	...	...	...
85	85	...	...	...	...	...	...	...	...	84	1	...	...	...	...	...	...	...	...	...	...	...
410	410	...	...	8	1	...	...	...	...	366	35	...	...	...	...	...	...	...	...	...	...	...
13	*13*	...	...	*4*	...	...	...	...	...	*9*	...	...	...	...	...	...	...	...	...	...	...	...
306	306	...	4	108	8	2	1	...	...	183	...	...	...	...	...	...	...	...	...	...	...	...
126	126	...	3	2	2	...	1	...	...	118	...	...	...	...	...	...	...	...	...	...	...	...
180	180	...	1	106	6	2	...	...	...	65	...	...	...	...	...	...	...	...	...	...	...	...
215	215	...	...	...	...	...	...	...	...	215	...	...	...	...	...	...	...	...	...	...	...	...
7	7	...	...	4	2	...	...	...	...	1	...	...	...	...	...	...	...	...	...	...	...	...
1	1	...	...	...	...	...	...	...	...	1	...	...	...	...	...	...	...	...	...	...	...	...
6	6	...	...	4	2	...	...	...	...	...	...	...	...	...	...	...	...	...	...	...	...	...
315	315	...	21	46	6	...	3	...	...	228	10	1	...	...	...	...	...	...	...	...	...	...
313	*313*	...	*21*	*46*	*6*	...	*3*	...	...	*226*	*10*	*1*	...	...	...	...	...	...	...	...	...	...
305	305	...	21	44	6	...	3	...	...	220	10	1	...	...	...	...	...	...	...	...	...	...
8	8	...	...	2	...	...	...	...	...	6	...	...	...	...	...	...	...	...	...	...	...	...
2	2	...	...	...	...	...	...	...	...	2	...	...	...	...	...	...	...	...	...	...	...	...
2,466	2,465	1	4	105	14	...	25	4	...	2,189	93	31	...	...	...	...	...	...	...	1	...	...
2,284	*2,284*	...	*3*	*88*	*12*	...	*24*	...	...	*2,041*	*86*	*30*	...	...	...	...	...	...	...	...	...	...
72	72	...	...	...	...	...	...	...	...	72	...	...	...	...	...	...	...	...	...	...	...	...
2,106	2,106	...	3	54	12	...	24	...	...	1,897	86	30	...	...	...	...	...	...	...	...	...	...
53	53	...	...	1	...	...	...	...	...	52	...	...	...	...	...	...	...	...	...	...	...	...
53	53	...	...	33	...	...	...	...	...	20	...	...	...	...	...	...	...	...	...	...	...	...
182	*181*	*1*	*1*	*17*	*2*	...	*1*	*4*	...	*148*	*7*	*1*	...	...	...	...	...	...	...	*1*	...	...
114	113	1	...	10	...	...	1	4	...	90	7	1	...	...	...	...	...	...	...	1	...	...
68	68	...	1	7	2	...	...	...	...	58	...	...	...	...	...	...	...	...	...	...	...	...
48	48	...	...	5	...	...	...	1	...	39	3	...	...	...	...	...	...	...	...	...	...	...

IMPERIAL TABLE XXIIA.—THE SPECIAL INDUSTRIAL CENSUS. PART II.—

DESCRIPTION OF ESTABLISHMENT (with Group-letters and Serial Nos. of Classes in each group).	DISTRICT.	Number of Establishments.	TOTAL EMPLOYEES.			CLASSIFICATION OF SUPERIOR EMPLOYEES. N.B.—In these columns all are males unless the contrary is indicated.												
						Managers.			Supervising and Technical Staff.			Clerical Staff.			Skilled Labourers.			
			Persons.	Males.	Females.	Europeans and Anglo-Indians.	Home Races.	Others.	Europeans and Anglo-Indians.	Home Races.	Others.	Europeans and Anglo-Indians.	Home Races.	Others.	Europeans and Anglo-Indians.	Home Races.	Chinese and Japanese.	Others.
1	2	3	4	5	6	7	8	9	10	11	12	13	14	15	16	17	18	19
P. 8. Stone-breaking yards and workshops connected with road-making—	Total ...	2	144	144	...	...	...	2	6	1	2	..	...	5	...	...	...	...
(i) *With mechanical power*	Rangoon ...	1	67	67	...	...	...	1	6	1	...	...	...	2	...	...	...	...
(ii) *Without mech. power*	Rangoon ..	1	77	77	...	...	...	1	...		2	...	...	3	...	...	...	...
Q. Electricity, light and heat.	...	10	690	686	4	5	3	2	M18 F-2	4	2	M-8 F-2	30	14	3	56	1	50
1. Ice factories— *With mechanical power*	Total ..	5	165	165	...	1	2	2	3	4	2	1	5	5	...	8	...	17
	Rangoon ...	1	62	62	...	...	...	1	2	1	...	...	...	1	...	2	...	9
	Insein ...	1	35	35	...	...	1	...	...	1	...	...	1	...	...	1	...	1
	Pegu ...	1	26	26	...	...	1	...	...	2	2	...	2	2	...	2	...	1
	Bassein ...	1	29	29	...	1	...	...	...	...	...	...	2	2	...	3	...	3
	Mandalay ...	1	13	13	...	...	...	1	1	...	...	1	...	...	...	...	...	3
2. Electric works*— *With mechanical power*	Rangoon ...	5	525	521	4	4	1	...	M15 F-2	...	...	M-7 F-2	25	9	3	48	1	33
R. Other Industries ...	...	62	3,369	3,320	49	14	M20 F-3	26	M31 F-3	M50 F-2	84	M44 F-3	145	219	M26 F-5	M-446 F-7	18	1,189
1. Printing	Total ...	48	2,950	2,936	14	11	M15 F-1	21	M18 F-2	35	80	M38 F-3	131	156	M21 F-5	382	3	1,071
(i) *With mechanical power*	...	21	2,335	2,323	12	10	5	6	M18 F-2	23	54	M37 F-3	71	114	M21 F-5	260	3	925
	Rangoon ...	20	2,295	2,283	12	9	5	6	M18 F-2	23	54	M37 F-3	71	111	M21 F-5	254	3	907
	Mandalay ...	1	40	40	...	1	...	...	...	...	...	...	...	3	...	6	...	18
(ii) *Without mech. power*	...	27	615	613	2	1	M10 F-1	15	...	12	26	1	60	42	...	122	...	146
	Akyab ...	1	10	10	...	...	1	...	...	...	...	...	...	...	...	7	...	...
	Rangoon ...	23	544	542	2	...	M-7 F-1	15	...	11	26	1	54	42	...	99	...	145
	Mandalay ...	3	61	61	..	1	2	...	...	1	...	...	6	...	...	16	...	1
2. Goldsmiths, silversmiths and jewellers—	...	6	221	216	5	2	M-1 F-1	2	6	M13 F-2	...	1	7	51	1	M-28 F-2	15	61
(i) *With mechanical power*	Rangoon ..	1	83	83	...	1	...	...	5	...	..	1	7	34	...	...	...	22
(ii) *Without mech. power*	...	5	138	133	5	1	M-1 F-1	2	1	M13 F-2	...	...	...	17	1	M-28 F-2	15	39
	Rangoon ...	4	127	122	5	1	F-1	2	1	M13 F-2	...	...	...	17	1	M-18 F-2	15	39
	Henzada ..	1	11	11	...	...	1	...	...	...	...	...	...	...	...	10	...	...
3. Book binding— *Without mech. power*	Rangoon ...	2	41	41	...	...	...	2	...	...	1	...	...	...	...	...	...	32
4. Photographic studio— *Without mech. power*	Rangoon ...	1	44	44	...	...	...	1	...	...	1	2	2	9	...	3	...	44
5. Musical instruments workshop— *Without mech. power*	Rangoon ...	1	42	41	1	1	...	...	M-7 F-1	2	2	3	5	3	4	2	...	41
6. Fan making— *Without mech. power*	Total ...	2	29	23	6	...	M-2 F-1	...	...	...	...	...	...	...	...	M-21 F-5	...	...
	Henzada ...	1	17	16	1	...	M-1 F-1	...	...	...	..	...	...	...	...	15	...	...
	Mandalay ...	1	12	7	5	...	1	...	...	...	...	...	...	...	...	M-6 F-5	...	...
7. Carving of ivory and wood— *Without mech. power*	Rangoon ...	1	11	11	...	..	1	...	...	...	...	...	..	...	.	10	...	..
8. Making paper cartons— *Without mech. power*	Hanthawaddy	1	31	8	23	...	1	...	...	...	...	...	...	...	...	...	...	...

* Of these, two with 341 employees are generating stations; the other three make or repair electrical machinery and apparatus.

Distribution by Districts of the Statistics in Part I of this table—concluded.

CLASSIFICATION OF UNSKILLED LABOURERS.																						
Total.			Males.										Females.									
				Home Races.			Chinese and Japanese.			Others.				Home Races.			Chinese and Japanese.			Others.		
Persons.	Males.	Females.	Europeans and Anglo-Indians.	Age 18 or over.	Age 14 to 18.	Age under 14.	Age 18 or over.	Age 14 to 18.	Age under 14.	Age 18 or over.	Age 14 to 18.	Age under 14.	Europeans and Anglo-Indians.	Age 18 or over.	Age 14 to 18.	Age under 14.	Age 18 or over.	Age 14 to 18.	Age under 14.	Age 18 or over.	Age 14 to 18.	Age under 14.
20	21	22	23	24	25	26	27	28	29	30	31	32	33	34	35	36	37	38	39	40	41	42
128	128	...	3	6	...	...	3	...	...	114	-	2	...	...	...	...	...	...	...	...	...	...
57	57	...	3	6	...	...	3	...	...	43	...	2	...	...	...	...	...	...	...	...	...	...
71	71	...	...	...	...	...	...	...	...	71	...	...	...	...	...	...	...	...	...	...	...	...
490	490	...	4	81	7	...	4	1	...	381	12	...	...	...	...	...	...	...	...	...	...	...
115	115	...	...	12	...	...	...	...	...	103	...	...	...	...	...	...	...	...	...	...	...	...
46	46	...	...	...	...	...	...	...	...	46	...	...	...	...	...	...	...	...	...	...	...	...
30	30	...	...	10	...	...	...	...	...	20	...	...	...	...	...	...	...	...	...	...	...	...
14	14	...	...	...	...	...	...	...	...	14	...	...	...	...	...	...	...	...	...	...	...	...
18	18	...	...	2	...	...	...	...	...	16	...	...	...	...	...	...	...	...	...	...	...	...
7	7	...	...	...	...	...	...	...	...	7	...	...	...	...	...	...	...	...	...	...	...	...
375	375	...	4	69	7	...	4	1	...	278	12	...	...	...	...	...	...	...	...	...	...	...
1,034	1,008	26	5	115	34	1	...	...	...	802	39	12	...	17	5	3	...	...	...	1	...	...
957	954	3	5	121	34	1	...	...	...	760	36	7	...	2	...	...	...	...	...	1	...	...
778	776	2	5	66	20	1	...		...	646	34	4	...	2	...	...	...	...	...	...	...	...
766	764	2	5	64	20	1	...	...	...	637	33	4	...	2	...	...	...	...	...	...	...	...
12	12	...	...	2	...	...	...	...	...	9	1	...	...	...	...	...	...	...	...	...	...	...
179	178	1	...	45	14	...	...	...	...	114	2	3	...	...	...	...	...	...	...	1	...	...
2	2	...	...	2	...	...	...	...	...	...	...	...	...	...	...	...	...	...	...	...	...	...
143	142	1	...	21	5	...	...	...	...	111	2	3	...	...	...	...	...	...	...	1	...	...
34	34	...	...	22	9	...	...	...	...	3	...	...	...	...	...	...	...	...	...	...	...	...
28	28	...	...	2	...	...	...	...	...	23	2	1	...	...	...	...	...	...	...	...	...	...
13	13	...	...	...	...	...	...	...	...	10	2	1	...	...	...	...	...	...	...	...	...	...
15	15	...	...	2	...	...	...	...	...	13	...	...	...	...	...	...	...	...	...	...	...	...
15	15	...	...	2	...	...	...	...	...	13	...	...	...	...	...	...	...	...	...	...	...	...
...	...	...	...	...	...	...	...	...	...	...	...	...	...	...	...	...	...	...	...	...	...	...
6	6	...	...	...	...	...	...	...	...	2	...	4	...	...	...	...	...	...	...	...	...	...
12	12	...	...	1	...	...	...	...	...	10	1	...	...	...	...	...	...	...	...	...	...	...
1	1	...	...	...	...	...	...	...	...	1	...	...	...	...	...	...	...	...	...	...	...	...
...	...	...	...	...	...	...	...	...	...	...	...	...	...	...	...	...	...	...	...	...	...	...
...	...	...	...	...	...	...	...	...	...	...	...	...	...	...	...	...	...	...	...	...	...	...
...	...	...	...	...	...	...	...	...	...	...	...	...	...	...	...	...	...	...	...	...	...	...
...	...	...	...	...	...	...	...	...	...	...	...	...	...	...	...	...	...	...	...	...	...	...
30	7	23	...	1	...	...	...	...	...	6	...	...	...	15	5	3	...	...	...	...	...	...

IMPERIAL TABLE XXIIA.—THE SPECIAL INDUSTRIAL CENSUS. PART IIIA.—
Power in establishments deriving it directly from Steam, Oil, Gas or Water.

NOTE.—In the columns headed *Gas or Water* all entries relate to *Gas* unless marked *W*.

Description of Establishment.	District.	Number of Establishments employing			Number of Engines.			Total Horse-power.		
		Steam.	Oil.	Gas or Water.	Steam.	Oil.	Gas or Water.	Steam.	Oil.	Gas or Water.
1	2	3	4	5	6	7	8	9	10	11
A. Cultivation for special products.	...	8	5	G-5 W-1	12	8	G-6 W-1	439	117	G-307 W250
1. Coffee ...	Toungoo ...	...	1	...	...	1	...	...	5	...
4. Rubber ...	Total ...	7	4	G-5 W-1	12	5	G-6 W-1	439	89	G-307 W250
	Insein ...	...	1	...	...	1	...	...	7	...
	Hanthawaddy ...	...	...	1	...	...	1	...	...	65
	Toungoo ...	1	...	1	1	...	2	4	.	100
	Thatôn ..	1	...	1	2	...	1	12	..	48
	Amherst ...	2	1	1	5	1	1	43	16	47
	Mergui ...	3	2	G-1 W-1	4	3	G-1 W-1	380	66	G-47 W250
5. Camphor ...	S. Shan States ...	1	...	...	...	2	...	...	23	...
B. Mines ...	...	14	4	1	76	5	22	1,869	49	24
1. Petroleum wells	Tota ...	10	2	1	62	3	22	666	7	24
	Thayetmyo ...	2	1	...	5	2	...	78	5	...
	Minbu ...	8	1	1	57	1	22	588	2	24
2. Tin and Wolfram mines.	Total ...	3	2	...	12	2	...	203	42	...
	Tavoy ...	2	1	...	8	1	...	152	30	...
	Mergui ...	1	1	...	4	1	...	51	12	...
3. Silver and Lead mines.	N. Shan States ...	1	...	...	2	...	...	1,000	...	...
C. Stone quarries ...	...	2	1	...	3	3	...	32	44	...
	Thatôn ...	1	1	...	2	3	...	16	44	...
	Tavoy ...	1	...	...	1	...	...	16	...	...
D. Textiles ...	...	14	16	...	28	21	...	1,235	1,144	...
1. Cotton ginning, cleaning and pressing.	Total ...	12	16	...	24	21	...	1,154	1,144	...
	Thayetmyo ...	3	2	...	10	2	...	213	88	...
	Bhamo ...	...	1	...	...	1	...	..	75	...
	Sagaing ...	2	3	...	2	5	...	23	255	...
	Lower Chindwin ...	...	1	...	...	1	...	...	55	...
	Meiktila ...	3	3	...	3	3	...	101	65	...
	Myingyan ...	4	6	...	9	9	...	817	606	...
3. Rope-making ...	Total ...	2	...	...	4	...	...	81	...	...
	Rangoon ...	1	...	...	2	...	...	32	...	...
	Insein ...	1	..	...	2	...	...	49	...	...
E. Leather and Bone	...	1	...	...	5	...	...	77	...	...
3. Bone-mills ...	Rangoon ..	1	...	...	5	...	...	77	...	..
F. Wood— a Sawmills and timber-yards.	Total ...	129	4	.	226	4	...	8,780	123	...
	Arakan Division	...	2	...	...	2	...	...	100	...
	Rangoon ...	25	2	...	67	2	...	4,164	23	...
	Pegu Division (less Rangoon) *	17	...	...	21	...	..	464	...	...
	Toungoo and Thatôn	16	...	...	16	...	...	458	...	...
	Irrawaddy Division	7	...	...	10	...	...	226	...	...
	Amherst, Salween, Tavoy and Mergui.	20	...	...	53	...	...	1,839	...	...
	Upper Burma and the Shan States.	45	...	...	62	...	...	1,712	...	...
	Akyab ...	...	2	...	...	2	...	...	100	...
	Rangoon ...	25	2	...	67	2	...	4,164	23	...
	Insein ...	2	...	...	2	...	...	30	...	...
	Tharrawaddy ...	6	...	...	7	...	...	164	...	...

* That is, the Insein, Hanthawaddy, Tharrawaddy, Pegu and Prome districts.

IMPERIAL TABLE XXIIA.—THE SPECIAL INDUSTRIAL CENSUS. PART IIIA.—*Power in establishments deriving it directly from Steam, Oil, Gas or Water*—contd.

Description of Establishment.	District.	Number of Establishments employing			Number of Engines.			Total Horse-power.		
		Steam.	Oil.	Gas or Water.	Steam.	Oil.	Gas or Water.	Steam.	Oil.	Gas or Water.
1	2	3	4	5	6	7	8	9	10	11
F. Wood—concld.										
2. Sawmills and timber-yards.	Pegu	5	...		7	...	...	172	..	...
	Prome ...	4	...	...	5	...	...	98	...	...
	Bassein ...	4	...	...	6	...	...	150	...	...
	Henzada ...	3	...	...	4	...	...	76	...	...
	Toungoo ...	13	...	...	13	...	...	367	...	...
	Thatôn ...	3	...	...	3	...	...	91	...	...
	Amherst ...	17	...	...	46	...	...	1,712	...	...
	Mergui ...	2	...	...	4	...	...	44	...	...
	Pakôkku ...	2	..	...	2	...	...	30	...	...
	Minbu ...	1	...	...	1	...	...	40	..	...
	Mandalay ...	17	...	...	27	...	...	704	...	...
	Katha ...	1	...	...	1	...	...	14	...	...
	Shwebo ...	2	...	...	2	...	...	232	...	...
	Sagaing ...	1	...	...	1	...	...	43	...	...
	Lower Chindwin ...	2	...	...	2	...	...	60	...	...
	Meiktila ...	1	...	...	1	...	...	25	...	...
	Yamèthin ...	17	...	...	24	...	...	549	...	...
	Myingyan ...	1	...	...	1	...	...	15	...	...
G. Metals ...	......	11	1	1	23	1	1	1,314	9	53
	Rangoon ...	9	1	1	18	1	1	1,228	9	53
	Pegu ...	1	...	...	3	...	...	40	...	...
	Mandalay ...	1	...	...	2	...	...	46	...	...
J. Chemical products	......	44	22	2	1,893	218	49	30,769	4,869	67
2. Aerated water factories.	Total ...	2	4	...	4	9	...	114	337	...
	Akyab ...	...	1	...	...	1	...	...	3	...
	Rangoon ...	2	3	...	4	8	...	114	334	...
3. Dye-works ...	Insein ...	1	...	-	1	...	...	12	...	...
4. Petroleum refineries.*	Total ..	19	10	2	1,843	198	49	30,063	4,236	67
	Rangoon ...	1	1	..	4	5	..	66	75	...
	Hanthawaddy ..	5	2	...	517	13	...	6,669	660	...
	Insein ...	...	1	...	..	2	...	...	160	...
	Tharrawaddy ...	1	...	...	2	...	...	75	...	...
	Prome ...	1	...	...	11	...	...	353	...	...
	Thayetmyo ...	1	...	...	2	...	...	150	...	..
	Pakôkku ...	1	3	1	30	5	46	50	53	47
	Magwe ...	7	2	...	1,268	175	...	22,626	3,280	...
	Upper Chindwin ...	2	1	1	9	1	3	74	8	20
5. Bulk-oil installations.	Rangoon ...	...	1	..	...	2	...	...	160	...
6. Chemical, drug and medicine works.	Total ...	2	1	...	17	1	...	123	5	...
	Rangoon ...	1	1	...	12	1	...	96	5	...
	Insein ...	1	...	...	5	...	...	27	...	...
7. Vegetable-oil mills.	Total ...	20	7	...	28	8	...	457	131	...
	Rangoon ...	5	...	...	6	...	...	68	...	...
	Insein ...	4	...	...	7	...	...	185	...	...
	Prome ...	2	...	...	3	..	...	22	...	..
	Henzada ...	1	...	...	2	...	...	20	...	...
	Amherst ...	...	1	...	...	2	..	...	9	...
	Thayetmyo ...	1	...	...	1	...	...	20	...	...
	Pakôkku ...	1	6	...	1	6	...	14	122	...
	Mandalay ...	2	...	...	2	...	...	30	...	...
	Lower Chindwin ...	1	...	...	1	...	...	12	...	...
	Myingyan ...	3	...	...	5	...	...	86	...	...
K. Food ...	......	397	14	W-1	703	15	W-1	23,287	112	W-15
2. Flour mills ...	Rangoon ...	3	...	...	3	..	...	94	...	...

* Pipe-line pumping-stations have been included in J4. Petroleum refineries.

Imperial Table XXIIa.—The Special Industrial Census. Part IIIa.—*Power in establishments deriving it directly from Steam, Oil, Gas or Water*—concld.

Description of Establishment.	District.	Number of Establishments employing			Number of Engines.			Total Horse-power.		
		Steam.	Oil.	Gas or Water.	Steam.	Oil.	Gas or Water.	Steam.	Oil.	Gas or Water.
1	2	3	4	5	6	7	8	9	10	11
K. 3. Rice mills ...	Total ...	387	13	W-1	662	14	W-1	22,434	100	W-15
	Arakan Division ...	10	4	...	26	4	...	1,518	24	...
	Rangoon ...	50	3	...	169	3	...	9,361	16	...
	*Pegu Division (less Rangoon).**	119	3	...	201	4	...	3,777	29	...
	Toungoo and Thatôn	32	...	...	37	...	...	539	...	..
	Irrawaddy Division	96	2	...	122	2	...	4,575	24	...
	Amherst, Salween, Tavoy and Mergui.	30	1	...	50	1	...	1,693	7	...
	Upper Burma and the Shan States.	50	...	W-1	57	...	W-1	971	...	W-15
	Akyab .	10	4	...	26	4	...	1,518	24	...
	Rangoon ...	50	3	...	169	3	...	9,361	16	...
	Hanthawaddy ...	32	1	...	67	1	...	1,844	4	...
	Insein ...	8	...	...	13	...	...	326	...	...
	Tharrawaddy ...	40	...	...	57	...	...	717	...	...
	Pegu	21	...	...	35	...	...	507	...	...
	Prome ...	18	2	...	29	3	...	383	25	...
	Bassein ...	25	2	...	41	2	...	3,373	24	...
	Henzada ...	12	..	...	14	...	...	209	...	...
	Myaungmya ...	25	...	...	26	...	...	446	...	...
	Ma-ubin ...	11	...	...	12	...	...	177	...	...
	Pyapôn ...	23	...	...	29	...	..	370	...	...
	Toungoo ...	8	...	...	10	...	...	135	...	...
	Thatôn ...	24	...	...	27	...	...	404	...	...
	Amherst ...	20	1	...	36	1	...	1,382	7	...
	Tavoy ...	7	...	...	8	...	...	231	...	...
	Mergui ...	3	...	...	6	...	...	80	...	...
	Minbu ...	5	...	...	6	...	...	86	...	...
	Mandalay ...	21	...	...	28	...	...	371	...	...
	Katha ...	3	...	...	3	...	...	44	...	...
	Shwebo ...	15	...	...	15	...	...	224	...	...
	Putao ...	...	...	W-1	...	...	W-1	...	...	W-15
	Sagaing ...	2	...	...	4	...	...	71	...	...
	Kyauksè ...	2	...	...	2	...	...	23	...	...
	Yamèthin ...	2	...	...	5	...	...	152	...	...
5. Dairy farms ...	S. Shan States ...	...	1	...	..	1	...	...	12	...
6. Slaughter-houses	Rangoon ...	1	...	...	2	...	...	38	...	...
8. Breweries and distilleries.	Mandalay ...	1	...	..	6	...	...	89	...	...
9. Water-works ...	Total ...	5	..	...	30	...	...	632	..	...
	Rangoon ...	3	...	...	16	...	...	323	...	...
	Insein ..	1	...	...	6	...	...	122	...	...
	Prome ...	1	...	...	8	...	...	187	...	...
N. Building ...	......	2	...	...	7	..	...	118	...	...
4. Constructional engineers.	Rangoon ...	2	...	...	7	...	...	118	...	...
P. Construction of means of transport or communication.	......	9	4	...	28	21	...	589	360	...
	Akyab ...	...	1	...	...	1	...	...	25	...
	Rangoon ...	5	3	...	14	20	...	246	335	...
	Insein ...	2	...	...	9	...	...	250	...	...
	Amherst ...	1	...	...	1	...	...	20	...	...
	Mandalay ...	1	...	...	4	...	...	73	...	...
Q. Electricity, light and heat.	......	6	3	...	26	11	...	535	240	...
Ice factories ...	Total ...	5	2	...	9	2	...	182	64	...
	Rangoon ...	1	1	...	2	1	...	55	60	...
	Insein ...	1	...	...	1	...	...	14	...	...
	Pegu ...	1	...	...	1	...	...	9	...	...
	Bassein ...	1	1	...	2	1	...	22	4	...
	Mandalay ...	1	...	...	3	...	..	22	...	...
2. Electric works ...	Rangoon ...	1	1	...	17	9	...	413	196	...
R. Other Industries ...	......	1	3	.	1	6	...	20	56	...
1. Printing ...	Rangoon ...	1	3	...	1	6	...	20	56	...

* That is, the Insein, Hanthawaddy, Tharrawaddy, Pegu and Prome districts.

Imperial Table XXIIA.—The Special Industrial Census. Part IIIb.

—*Power in establishments using electricity generated on their premises.*

Description of Establishment.	Number of Establishments.		Prime Movers.				Electric Power.	
	Total.	Using special engine to drive dynamos	Steam or Water.*		Oil.		Number of dynamos	Power in Kilo-watts.
			No. of Engines.	Horse-power.	No. of engines.	Horse-power.		
1	2	3	4	5	6	7	8	9
A.—Cultivation for special products—								
4. Rubber	*3*	...	...	...	...	...	*3*	*10*
Toungoo	1	...	...	...	...	...	1	6
Thatôn	1	...	...	...	...	...	1	3
Mergui	1	...	...	...	...	...	1	1
B.—Mines—								
2. Tin and Wolfram mines ...	*3*	*2*	S-*1* W-3	S-*13* W-376	*4*	*135*	*5*	*460*
Pegu	1	...	...	...	...	...	1	10
Tavoy	2	2	S-1 W-3	S-13 W-376	4	135	4	450
3. Silver and Lead mines (N. Shan States)	1	1	W-3	W-9,000	2	2,000	5	8,000
4. Ruby mines (Katha)	1	1	W-2	W-600	..	...	3	300
D.—Textiles—								
1. Cotton ginning, cleaning and pressing	*9*	...	...	...	...	...	*11*	*259*
Thayetmyo	2	...	...	...	...	...	2	13
Sagaing	1	...	...	...	...	...	1	6
Lower Chindwin	1	...	...	...	...	...	1	4
Meiktila	1	...	...	...	...	...	1	100
Myingyan	4	...	...	...	...	...	6	136
E.—Leather and Bone—								
3. Bone mills (Rangoon)	1	...	...	...	...	...	1	2
F.—Wood—								
2. Sawmills and timber-yards ...	*7*	*5*	*6*	*45*	...	...	*15*	*1,501*
Rangoon	3	2	2	9	...	...	9	1,051
Henzada	1	...	...	...	...	...	1	5
Amherst	3	3	4	36	...	...	5	445
J.—Chemical products—								
4. Petroleum refineries †	*15*	*12*	*45*	*496*	*4*	*174*	*61*	*826*
Rangoon	1	1	5	38	1	100	5	52
Hanthawaddy	4	3	20	176	2	58	30	538
Insein	1	...	..	...	...	...	1	8
Tharrawaddy	1	1	2	5	...	...	2	22
Prome	1	1	2	5	...	...	2	26
Thayetmyo	1	1	2	40	...	...	2	22
Pakôkku	3	3	2	17	1	16	3	17
Magwe	2	2	12	215	...	...	15	140
Upper Chindwin	1	...	...	...	...	...	1	1
5. Bulk-oil installations † (Rangoon) ...	1	...	...	...	...	...	1	3
6. Chemical, drug and medicine works (Rangoon).	1	1	...	...	1	5	1	3
7. Vegetable-oil mills (Amherst) ...	1	...	...	...	-	...	1	4
K.—Food—								
3. Rice mills	*127*	*49*	*51*	*556*	*5*	*21*	*146*	*1,993*
Akyab	8	...	...	...	...	...	8	105
Rangoon	35	18	22	277	2	11	49	730
Hanthawaddy	12	3	1	6	2	4	14	381
Insein	4	...	...	...	...	...	4	78
Tharrawaddy	18	9	9	47	...	...	18	102
Pegu	1	...	...	...	...	...	1	4
Prome	5	1	1	4	...	...	5	95
Bassein	8	4	5	121	...	...	12	290
Henzada	3	1	1	6	...	...	3	13
Myaungmya	5	...	...	...	...	...	5	63
Ma-ubin	2	1	1	5	...	...	1	2
Pyapôn	8	3	3	[illegible]	...	...	8	39
Toungoo	2	1	1	4	...	...	2	10
Thatôn	3	...	...	...	...	...	3	6
Amherst	11	8	7	64	1	6	11	76
Tavoy	1	...	...	...	...	...	1	41
Shwebo	1	...	...	...	...	...	1	2
6. Slaughter-houses (Rangoon) ...	1	...	...	...	...	...	1	10
P.—Construction of means of transport or communication—	*11*	*6*	*11*	*1,467*	*4*	*899*	*25*	*2,018*
Rangoon	7	3	5	87	1	9	15	459
Insein	2	1	2	80	...	..	3	64
Mandalay	2	2	4	1,300	3	890	7	1,525
Q.—Electricity, light and heat—								
2. Electric works (Rangoon) ...	1	1	6	14,750	...	...	14	15,954
R.—Other industries—								
2. Goldsmiths, silversmiths and jewellers (Rangoon).	1	...	...	...	...	...	1	10

* All engines shown in these columns are worked by steam unless marked W.

† Pipe-line pumping stations have been included in J4. Petroleum refineries.

IMPERIAL TABLE XXIIA.—THE SPECIAL INDUSTRIAL CENSUS. PART IIIc. —*Power in establishments using electricity supplied from outside.*

Description of Establishment and district.	Number of Establishments.	Number of motors installed.	Total Horse-power.
1	2	3	4
F. Wood—			
2. Sawmills and timber-yards (Rangoon) ...	1	6	32
G. Metals—			
Rangoon	7	11	74
J. Chemical products—			
7. Vegetable-oil mills	2	2	70
Rangoon	1	1	10
Magwe	1	1	60
K. Food—			
4. Bakeries and confectioneries (Rangoon) ...	1	1	20
9. Water-works (Rangoon)	1	2	50
10. Tobacco, cigar or cigarette factories (Rangoon) ...	1	2	20
P. Construction of means of transport or communication—	*14*	*52*	*448*
Rangoon	13	51	443
Mandalay	1	1	5
Q. Electricity, light and heat—			
2. Electric works (Rangoon)	4	8	61
R. Other industries—			
1. Printing	20	78	278
Rangoon	19	77	275
Mandalay	1	1	3
2. Goldsmiths, silversmiths and jewellers (Rangoon)	1	3	15

PART IV.—*Looms in Textile Establishments employing* 10 *or more persons.*

District.	Cotton-weaving Establishments.				Silk-weaving Establishments.			
	Number of Establishments.	Number of looms at work.			Number of Establishments.	Number of looms at work.		
		Worked by power.	Worked by hand.			Worked by power.	Worked by hand.	
			With fly-shuttle.	Without flyshuttle.			With fly-shuttle.	Without flyshuttle.
1	2	3	4	5	6	7	8	9
Total ..	6	...	54	53	5	...	104	62
Mandalay	...	...	...	...	5	...	104	62
Sagaing	1	...	...	20	...	...	...	...
Lower Chindwin ...	1	..	16	1	...	...	...	...
Meiktila	4	...	38	32	...	...	...	...

APPENDIX TO IMPERIAL TABLE XXIIA.

Skilled and Unskilled Occupations.

The following list of occupations treated as skilled is possibly not complete, but probably no occupations treated as skilled and practised by more than a few persons are omitted. A list is first given of occupations which are found in many groups and classes, a few other occupations being inserted which are peculiar to one group or class and could be shown more shortly in this list. Then some additional occupations are shown for the industries indicated. For further information the relevant article in Part A of Chapter XIII of the Report Volume should be consulted :—

All Industries.

Blacksmith.
Bricklayer
Boilermaker.
Bookbinder.
Bucket-maker (metal).

Carpenter.
Carver.
Cooper.
Coppersmith.

Driller.
Dyer.

Electrician.
Electric lineman.
Engineer.
Engine driver.

Fireman.
Fitter.
Foreman.
Furniture-maker.

Latheman.
Leather worker.

Mason.
Mechanic.
Moulder.

Overseer.

Painter.
Pattern-maker.
Planer.
Plater.
Plumber.
Potter.

Rivetter.

Saddler.
Sailmaker.
Saw sharpener.
Sawyer.
Serang.
Secunni.

Tailor.
Tinsmith.
Turner.

Viceman (= Fitter).

B1. Petroleum wells.

Boiler maistry.
Motor-driver.
Rod puller.

B1. Silver and Lead mines.

Carriage foreman.
Carriage repairer.
Pipe foreman.
Workshop foreman.

C. Stone Quarries.

Blaster.

D1. Cotton-ginning, cleaning and pressing.

Belting man.
Gin fitter.

D2. Cotton-weaving.

Heddle threader.
Heddle maker.
Spinner.
Thread extender.

D3. Rope-making.

Rope maistry.
Spinner.

D4. Silk-weaving.

Printer.
Weaver.

E1. Tanneries.

Currier.
Tanner.

E2. Leather factories.

Boot maker.
Flesher.
Harness maker.
Hood maker.
Setter.

F2. Saw mills and timber yards.

Gunner.
Launch driver.

G1. Iron foundries.

Iron worker.
Machine man.

G3. Arsenals.

Armourer.
Fileman.
Melter.
Ropemaker.

G4. Machinery and engineering workshops.

Carriage examiner.
Carriage lifter.
Craneman.
Motor mechanic.
Stone dresser.

H2. Brick, tile and fire-brick factories.

Brick maker.
Brick manufacturer.
Brick moulder.
Brick-mould maker.
Clay moulder.
Pipe maker.
Pot maker.
Tile maker.

J4. Petroleum refineries.

Motor-boat driver.
Oilstillsman.
Stamp cutter.

3K. Rice mills.

Gunner.
Launch driver.
Mill foreman.
Motor-boat driver.
Moter driver.

K10. Cigar factories.

Cigar roller.

L1. Tailoring works.

Cutter.
Ironer.
Stitcher.

L3. Boot and shoe factories.

Shoemaker.
Solefitter.
Sole maker.
Upper sewer.
Wooden-shoe maker.

L4. Umbrella factories.

Covesor.
Cutter.
Handle-maker.
Painter.

N1. Stone, marble and cement works.

Engraver.

P1. Railway works.

Beltmaker.
Carriage examiner.
Chargeman.
Erector.
Leadburner.
Steam-hammer driver.

P2. Tramway works.

Armature winder.
Driver.
Improver.
Roller driver.
Wireman.

P5. Motor-car works.

Cushionman.
Hoodman.
Nickelplater.
Vulcanizer.
Welder (with electricity or acetylene).

P6. Shipyards, etc.

Driver.

P7. Telephone system.

Switchboard fitter.
Telephone fitter.

Q2. Electric works.

Lighting Inspector.

R1. Printing.

Compositor.
Copper-plate printer.
Draftsman.
Engraver.
Gilder.
Linotype operator.
Lithographer.
Machineman.

R1. Printing—concld.

Printer.
Proof-reader.
Punch cutter.
Reviser.
Stereo maker.
Stereo typer.
Type caster.
Type founder.
Type setter.

R3. Goldsmiths, etc.

Draftsman.
Engraver.
Jeweller.
Lapidary.

R4. Photographic studio.

Developer.
Finisher.
Photographer.
Printer.

R6. Fan-making.

Bamboo-work maker.
Fan-maker.
Painter.

IMPERIAL TABLE XXII-B.

The Special Industrial Census (Selected Industries).

NOTE 1.—This table supplements Imperial Table XXIIA by giving further statistics for the specially important groups or classes of industrial establishments which are listed in column 1 of Part I of the table.

NOTE 2.—The table is in three parts as follows:—

Part I.—Ownership and management of establishments.

Part II.—Classification and birthplaces of labourers.

Part III.—Duration of residence in Burma of labourers born outside Burma.

Part II is in eleven sections dealing with skilled and unskilled labourers in the classes indicated by the titles of the sections. Part III is also subdivided into two parts IIIA and IIIB for males and females respectively.

NOTE 3.—All the owners, directors and managers of the establishments shown in Part I of the table are British subjects except as indicated in the footnotes of Part I of Imperial Table XXIIA.

NOTE 4.—The term *Home Races* includes all Indigenous and Indo-Burman Races, that is races of Groups A to O inclusive and also of Group S of Imperial Table XIII. It differs slightly from the sum of Peoples I to IV and VI by including Mahomedans of indigenous races and those Zerbadis who are neither Mahomedans nor Buddhists (see the appendices to Imperial Table XX).

NOTE 5.—In column 16 of Part I of the table under the heading *Chinese and Others* all the figures relate to Chinese except the one establishment shown for Class F2. Similarly in column 23 for all except 3 of Class K3 with power and 1 of Group P with power. Column 9 includes only Chinese.

NOTE 6.—Armenians have been regarded for this table as Europeans.

NOTE 7.—The complete list of races used in the tabulation in Part II of the table is shown in Section 2 of that part. The terms *Other Hindustanis, All other Mahomedans, All Others* and all other terms used in Section 2 of Part I have the same meaning throughout the table. In particular the term *Burmese* includes Tavoyans, Merguese, Yanbye, Chaungtha and non-Mahomedan Arakanese but not Arakan-Mahomedans nor Zerbadis.

NOTE 8.—For the definition of *Skilled Occupations* see the appendix to Imperial Table XXIIA on the last two pages before this.

NOTE 9.—The group *Age under 14* includes all who have not completed 14 years of age; the group *Age 18 or over* includes all who have completed 18 years of age or more.

NOTE 10.—Persons under 18 years of age have been excluded from column 9 in Part II of the table; they are few and their number is shown in Subsidiary Table IV of Chapter XIII of the Report volume.

NOTE 11.—Labourers are classified in Part III as *Permanent Residents* if they stated at the time of enumeration that they intended to make their home in Burma for the rest of their lives. The number of years of residence shown is the number of completed years.

IMPERIAL TABLE XXIIB.—THE SPECIAL INDUSTRIAL CENSUS (SELECTED INDUSTRIES).

PART I.—*Ownership and Management of Establishments.*

NOTE.—Except as shown by the foot-notes *all* the owners or directors of each establishment are of the race-class under which the establishment is tabulated. Establishments owned by Government or by a local authority are included in columns 17 to 23 and distinguished by an asterisk* in column 17.

DESCRIPTION OF ESTABLISHMENT. (All with mechanical power unless *without* is shown.)	Total Number of Establishments.	Establishments whose owners or directors are of Home Races.							Establishments whose owners or directors are of Indian Races.							Establishments whose owners or directors are of other Races.*						
		Total number.	Classified by ownership.		Classified by Race of Manager.				Total number.	Classified by ownership.		Classified by Race of Manager.				Total number.	Classified by ownership.		Classified by Race of Manager.			
			Private.	Company.	Home Races.	Indian.	European and Anglo-Indian.	Chinese.		Private.	Company.	Home Races.	Indian.	European and Anglo-Indian.	Chinese and others.		Private.	Company.	Home Races.	Indian.	European and Anglo-Indian.	Chinese and others.
1	2	3	4	5	6	7	8	9	10	11	12	13	14	15	16	17	18	19	20	21	22	23
A4. Rubber cultivation																						
With	12	...	...	..	...	..	...	...	...	..	...	...	...	...	...	12	4	8	...	...	10	2
Without	27	4	3	1	4	...	...	...	4	4	...	.	3	1	...	19	6	13	1	1	15	2
B1. Petroleum wells—																						
With	10	1		1	1	...	...	.	...	...	..	.	...	..	...	9	...	9	2	...	7	...
Without	12	11	9	2	11	..	..	.	...	...	...	..	...	...	...	1	...	1	..	1	...	...
B2. Tin and Wolfram mines—																						
With	6	.	...	..				...	.	...	...	...	...		...	6	1	5	...	...	5	1
Without	35	8	8	.	8	..	...	...	3	2	1	2	...	...	1	24	12	12	2	1	10	11
B3. Silver and Lead mines																						
With	1	..	.	..	..	...		...	...		...	...	...	...	...	1	..	1	...	..	1	..
Without	2	1	1	...	1	...	...	...	...	...	...	...	...	...	..	1	1	...	...	...	.	1
B4. Ruby mines ...	1	..	..	...	...	.	...	...	...	...	...	.	...	...	...	1	...	1	...	...	1	...
B5. Other mines—																						
Without	3	1	1		1	...	...	.	.	...	...	...	...	...	..	2	1	1	..	...	2	...
F2. Sawmills and timber-yards. With	132	42	39	3	40	1	..	1	43	35	8	1	39	2	1	47	15	32	4	1	22	20
Without	7	7	7	..	7	...	..		...	...	...	..	..	.	..	..	...	..	...	...	...	...
Arakan Division ...	2	2	2	...	2	.	...	..	..	..	...	..	..	...	...	...	..	...	...	...	...	...
Rangoon ...	25	2	1	1	2	..	...		7	4	3	.	7	...	...	16	2	14	1	1	10	4
Pegu Division (less Rangoon).†	17	6	6	...	6	...	..	..	7	7	...	...	7	...	..	4	2	2	...	...	..	4
Irrawaddy Division	7	6	(b)5	1	6	.	..	...	1	...	1	...	1	...	..	...	...	...	...	...	...	...
Toungoo and Thatôn	16	4	4	...	3	..	..	1	7	5	2	...	7	...	...	5	3	2	...	..	1	4
Amherst, Salween, Tavoy and Mergui.	20	6	(a)6	.	5	1	...	.	6	5	1	...	5	1	...	8	(c)2	6	1	...	5	2
Upper Burma and the Shan States—																						
With	45	16	15	1	16	...	.	...	15	14	1	1	12	1	1	14	6	8	2	...	6	6
Without	7	7	7	...	7	...	...	...	.	...	...	...	...	...	...	...	...	..	...	...	...	...
G. Metal industries—																						
With	18	3	3	...	3	..	..	..	6	4	2	...	6	...	...	7 2*	2 2	5 ...	1 ..	... ...	6 2	... ...
Without	14	4	4	...	4	...		...	5	5	...	1	4	...	...	5	3	2	...	.	2	3
J4. Petroleum refineries and pipe line pumping stations— With	22	1	...	1	1	..	...	...	2	1	1	...	2	..	...	19	...	19	...	...	19	..
Without	2	..	..	...	...	...	..	...	...	...	.	...	..	...	...	2	..	2	...	...	2	...
K3. Rice mills ...	388	224	210	14	220	1	...	3	61	52	9	4	57	..	...	103	49	54	2	3	45	53
Arakan Division ...	10	1	1	..	1	...		...	1	1	...	...	1	...	...	8	1	7	...	...	7	1
Rangoon ..	50	(e)13	13	..	13	.	...	..	8	5	3	1	7	...	...	29	5	24	...	3	15	11
Pegu Division (less Rangoon).	119	66	(f)64	2	66	.	...	.	30	(d)24	6	2	28	...	..	23	17	6	2	...	8	13
Irrawaddy Division	96	65	60	5	64	...	...	1	11	11	...	...	11	...	...	20	(c)11	9	...	...	9	11
Toungoo and Thatôn	32	27	25	2	26	1	.	...	4	4	..	1	3	...	...	1	1	...	...	.	1	...
Amherst, Salween, Tavoy and Mergui.	30	14	11	3	12	.	..	2	3	3	..	...	3	...	..	13	7	6	...	...	4	9
Upper Burma and the Shan States.	51	38	36	2	38	...	..	...	4	4	...	...	4	...	...	9	7	(g)2	...	...	1	8
P. Construction of means of transport or communication— With	27	..	...	...	...	...	...	...	2	1	1	..	2	...	..	21 4*	(h)2 4	(k)19 ...	1 ...	... 1	19 3	1 ...
Without	14	2	2	.	2	..	...	...	3	2	1	2	1	..	...	9	8	(l)1	...	1	1	7

* See the note above the table.

† That is, the Insein, Hanthawaddy, Tharrawaddy, Pegu and Prome districts.

(a) Includes 1 establishment of which more than half the owners are of Home races, the remainder being chiefly Indians.
(b) " 1 " " more " " " *Others.*
(c) " 1 " " less " " " *Others.*
(d) " 2 " " less " " " Indians.
(e) " 1 " " more than half the directors are of Home races, the remainder being chiefly Indians.
(f) " 1 " " more " " " Indians.
(g) " 2 " " less " " " *Others.*
(h) " 1 " " half the directors are Indians and half are Europeans. " *Others.*
(k) " 1 " " more than half the directors are Europeans and the remainder are Chinese and Indians.
(l) " 1 " " more " " " Indians.

IMPERIAL TABLE XXIIB.—THE SPECIAL INDUSTRIAL CENSUS (SELECTED INDUSTRIES).

PART II.—*Classification and Birthplaces of Labourers.*

Industry, Skill, Occupation and Race.	Total Number.	Born in Burma.			Born outside Burma.			See foot-note.
		Age 18 and over.	Age 14 to 18.	Age under 14.	Age 18 and over.	Age 14 to 18.	Age under 14.	
1	2	3	4	5	6	7	8	9
Section 1.—Total Unskilled and Skilled by Sex.								
Total workers ...	90,083	20,633	1,435	347	64,547	2,436	685	7,813
Males ...	87,199	18,935	974	218	64,056	2,383	633	7,485
Unskilled ...	*69,977*	*12,601*	*830*	*217*	*53,401*	*2,297*	*631*	*5,244*
Skilled ...	*17,222*	*6,334*	*144*	*1*	*10,655*	*86*	*2*	*2,241*
Females ...	2,884	1,698	461	129	491	53	52	328
Unskilled ...	*2,833*	*1,668*	*448*	*129*	*484*	*52*	*52*	*316*
Skilled ...	*51*	*30*	*13*	...	*7*	*1*	...	*12*
Section 2.—Total Unskilled Males by Race.								
UNSKILLED MALES ...	69,977	12,601	830	217	53,401	2,297	631	5,244
Home races ...	13,423	12,053	750	167	448	5	...	5,031
Burmese ...	11,821	11,042	645	134	...	...	...	4,543
Arakanese ...	*48*	*44*	*4*	...	...	...	...	*7*
Zerbadi ...	216	183	26	7	...	...	...	41
Arakan-Mahomedan ...	3	3	...	...	...	...	...	3
Other Home races ...	1,383	825	79	25	448	5	...	444
Danu ...	*52*	*42*	*10*	...	...	...	...	...
Lashi ...	*1*	*1*	...	...	...	...	...	*1*
Maingtha ...	*162*	*23*	*1*	...	*135*	*3*	...	*11*
Chin ...	*16*	*14*	*2*	...	...	...	...	*7*
Kachin ...	*11*	*11*	...	...	...	...	...	*10*
Kadu ...	*2*	*2*	...	...	...	...	...	*1*
Shan ...	*839*	*481*	*36*	*12*	*308*	*2*	...	*333*
Talaing ...	*88*	*68*	*13*	*7*	...	...	...	*11*
Palaung ...	*12*	*12*	...	...	...	...	...	*12*
Khamuk ...	*5*	...	...	...	*5*	...	...	...
Karen ...	*195*	*171*	*17*	*7*	...	...	...	*58*
Chinese and Japanese	2,981	74	4	1	2,795	43	4	46
Yünnanese ...	875	22	...	...	517	33	3	21
Other Chinese ...	2,346	52	4	1	2,278	10	1	25
Japanese ...	...	...	...	...	...	...	...	...
European ...	22	...	...	...	22	...	...	...
Anglo-Indian ...	127	66	2	...	58	1	...	41
Indian ...	53,484	408	74	49	50,078	2,248	627	126
Sikh ...	106	4	...	...	100	2	...	...
Punjabi Mahomedans and Pathans.	205	2	3	1	195	3	1	1
Other Punjabis ...	276	2	...	...	265	8	1	2
Hindustani Mahomedans.	869	9	4	2	839	12	3	4
Other Hindustanis ...	7,231	24	3	2	6,971	196	35	7
Bengali and Chittagonian Mahomedans.	9,013	94	7	...	8,702	197	13	95
Other Bengalis and Chittagonians.	723	5	...	...	689	28	1	3
Oriya ...	10,719	8	8	2	10,086	478	137	3
Tamil ...	759	92	24	13	603	16	11	39
Telugu ...	22,132	126	21	26	20,266	1,274	419	32
All other Mahomedans	110	18	...	...	89	3	...	4
All others ...	1,341	24	4	3	1,273	31	6	6
Section 3.—Total Skilled Males by Race.								
SKILLED MALES ...	17,222	6,334	144	1	10,655	86	2	2,241
Home races ...	5,924	5,819	103	1	1	...	...	2,049
Burmese ...	5,512	5,420	92	...	...	...	...	1,887
Arakanese ...	*49*	*49*	...	...	...	...	...	*4*
Zerbadi ...	304	294	9	...	...	...	...	101
Arakan-Mahomedan ...	2	1	1	...	...	...	...	1
Other Home races ...	106	103	1	1	1	...	...	60
Danu ...	*1*	*1*	...	...	...	...	...	...
Maingtha ...	*1*	...	...	...	*1*	...	...	...
Kachin ...	*2*	*2*	...	...	...	...	...	*1*
Kadu ...	*1*	*1*	...	...	...	...	...	*1*
Shan ...	*35*	*35*	...	...	...	...	...	*23*
Talaing ...	*10*	*10*	...	...	...	...	...	*3*
Palaung ...	*1*	*1*	...	...	...	...	...	*1*
Karen ...	*55*	*53*	*1*	*1*	...	...	...	*31*
Chinese and Japanese	1,128	71	...	...	1,056	1	...	24
Yünnanese ...	4	...	...	...	4	...	...	...
Other Chinese ...	1,122	71	...	...	1,050	1	...	24
Japanese ...	2	...	...	...	2	...	...	...
European ...	39	...	...	...	38	1	...	...
Anglo-Indian ...	282	167	14	...	92	9	...	81
Indian ...	9,849	277	27	...	9,468	75	2	87
Sikh ...	90	5	...	...	84	1	...	2
Punjabi-Mahomedans and Pathans.	150	3	3	...	144	...	...	2
Other Punjabis ...	464	6	2	...	450	6	...	3
Hindustani Mahomedans.	243	7	1	...	235	...	...	3
Other Hindustanis ...	1,521	26	2	...	1,483	9	1	14
Section 3.—Total Skilled Males by Race—concld.								
Bengali and Chittagonian Mahomedans.	3,380	43	2	...	3,305	30	...	7
Other Bengalis and Chittagonians.	413	21	1	...	391	...	...	3
Oriya ...	905	6	...	...	892	7	...	...
Tamil ...	539	69	8	...	452	10	...	35
Telugu ...	1,956	74	8	...	1,862	11	1	13
All other Mahomedans	46	8	...	...	37	1	...	5
All others ...	142	9	...	...	133	...	...	2
Section 4.—Total Unskilled Females by Race.								
UNSKILLED FEMALES ...	2,833	1,668	448	129	484	52	52	316
Home races ...	2,201	1,646	438	117	...	...	...	310
Burmese ...	1,892	1,440	362	90	...	...	...	287
Arakanese ...	*8*	*8*	...	...	...	...	...	...
Zerbadi ...	21	10	10	1	...	...	...	1
Arakan-Mahomedan ...	...	...	...	...	...	...	...	...
Other Home races ...	288	196	66	26	...	...	...	21
Danu ...	*3*	*1*	...	*2*	...	...	...	...
Shan ...	*65*	*47*	*10*	*8*	...	...	...	*7*
Talaing ...	*92*	*70*	*15*	*4*	...	...	...	*7*
Karen ...	*128*	*78*	*38*	*12*	...	...	...	*8*
Chinese and Japanese	3	...	...	2	1	...	...	...
Yünnanese ...	...	...	...	...	...	...	...	...
Other Chinese ...	3	...	...	2	1	...	...	...
Japanese ...	...	...	...	...	...	...	...	...
European ...	1	...	...	...	1	...	...	...
Anglo-Indian ...	...	...	...	...	...	...	...	...
Indian ...	628	22	10	10	482	52	52	6
Sikh ...	...	...	...	...	...	...	...	...
Punjabi-Mahomedans and Pathans.	1	...	...	...	1	...	...	...
Other Punjabis ...	...	...	...	...	...	...	...	...
Hindustani Mahomedans.	1	...	...	...	1	...	...	...
Other Hindustanis ...	3	...	...	...	3	...	...	...
Bengali and Chittagonian Mahomedans.	2	2	...	...	...	...	...	...
Other Bengalis and Chittagonians.	...	...	...	...	...	...	...	...
Oriya ...	26	...	2	...	20	...	4	...
Tamil ...	36	3	2	1	29	1	...	...
Telugu ...	529	16	5	6	415	43	44	6
All other Mahomedans	1	1	...	...	...	...	...	...
All others ...	29	...	1	3	13	8	4	...
Section 5.—Total Skilled Females by Race.								
SKILLED FEMALES ...	51	30	13	...	7	1	...	12
Anglo-Indian ...	51	30	13	...	7	1	...	12
Section 6.—Total Unskilled Males in each Industry.								
A4. Rubber cultivation ...	4,559	489	126	49	3,381	344	170	105
B1. Petroleum wells ...	816	579	6	1	227	2	1	72
B2. Tin and Wolfram mines.	3,447	589	33	48	2,765	9	3	122
B3. Silver and Lead mines	3,364	482	36	13	2,702	105	19	328
B4. Ruby mines ...	796	267	17	...	507	5	...	263
B5. Other mines ...	82	45	4	...	32	1	...	2
F2. Sawmills and timber-yards.	9,490	1,493	150	10	7,236	503	92	368
G. Metals ...	1,084	143	39	15	837	21	29	28
J4. Petroleum refineries	25,559	6,265	219	34	17,940	868	233	3,447
K3. Rice mills ...	16,258	1,861	152	43	13,852	298	52	432
P. Construction of means of transport or communication.	4,522	388	42	4	3,915	141	32	77
Total ...	69,977	12,601	830	217	53,401	2,297	631	5,244
Section 7.—Total Skilled Males in each Industry.								
A4. Rubber cultivation ...	66	37	...	...	29	...	...	11
B1. Petroleum wells ...	142	115	...	...	27	...	...	41
B2. Tin and Wolfram mines.	201	75	...	...	126	...	...	49
B3. Silver and Lead mines	552	120	2	...	430	...	...	116
B4. Ruby mines ...	91	78	...	...	13	...	...	77
B5. Other mines ...	...	...	...	...	...	...	...	...
F2. Sawmills and timber yards.	2,600	1,255	5	...	1,335	5	...	288
G. Metals ...	1,149	463	22	1	653	9	1	125
J4. Petroleum refineries	4,672	1,458	17	...	3,172	24	1	849
K3. Rice mills ...	1,847	701	10	...	1,130	6	...	219
P. Construction of means of transport or communication.	5,902	2,032	88	...	3,740	42	...	466
Total ...	17,222	6,334	144	1	10,655	86	2	2,241

Column 9 shows the number of age 18 or over who were born in Burma outside the district in which they were employed at the time of the Census

IMPERIAL TABLE XXIIB.—THE SPECIAL INDUSTRIAL CENSUS (SELECTED INDUSTRIES).

PART II.—*Classification and Birthplaces of Labourers*—continued.

Industry, Skill, Occupation and Race.	Total Number	Born in Burma. Age 18 and over.	Born in Burma. Age 14 to 18.	Born in Burma. Age under 14.	Born outside Burma. Age 18 and over.	Born outside Burma. Age 14 to 18.	Born outside Burma. Age under 14.	See foot-note.
1	2	3	4	5	6	7	8	9
Section 8.—Total Unskilled Females in each Industry.								
A4. Rubber cultivation ...	878	399	197	51	193	18	20	56
B1. Petroleum wells ...	92	78	11	3	...	...	...	4
B2. Tin and Wolfram mines.	238	157	23	40	12	3	3	16
B3. Silver and Lead mines	8	5	1	2	...	...	...	4
B5. Other mines ...	6	...	...	...	...	5	1	...
F9. Sawmills and timber-yards.	276	216	44	10	5	...	1	66
J4. Petroleum refineries	353	291	51	5	6	...	...	104
K3. Rice mills ...	981	522	121	18	267	26	27	66
P. Construction of means of transport or communication.	1	...	...	...	1	...	...	...
Total ...	2,833	1,668	448	129	484	52	52	316
Section 9.—Total Skilled Females in each Industry.								
P. Construction of means of transport or communication (P-4 Telephone system).	51	30	13	...	7	1	...	12
Section 10.—Male Labourers of each selected Industry by Race and Occupation.								
A4. Rubber Cultivation	4,625	526	126	49	3,420	344	170	116
All Unskilled Occupations	4,559	489	126	49	3,381	344	170	105
Burmese ...	469	341	92	36	...	...	...	69
Zerbadi ...	9	7	2	...	...	...	...	2
Other Home races ..	138	108	22	8	...	...	...	24
Chinese ...	7	1	...	...	6	...	...	...
Anglo-Indian ...	1	1	...	...	...	...	...	...
Sikh ...	1	...	...	...	1	...	...	...
Punjabi Mahomedans and Pathans.	1	...	...	...	1	...	...	...
Other Punjabis ...	4	...	...	...	4	...	...	.
Hindustani Mahomedans.	15	...	...	...	15	...	...	.
Other Hindustanis ...	40	...	...	...	40	...	...	...
Bengali and Chittagonian Mahomedans.	20	3	1	...	15	1	...	
Other Bengalis and Chittagonians.	1	...	...	.	1	...	...	...
Oriya ...	1,737	5	2	1	1,536	138	57	1
Tamil ...	37	8	3	4	22	...	...	3
Telugu ...	2,065	11	3	..	1,734	204	113	6
All other Mahomedans	3	2	...	...	1	...	...	...
All others ...	11	4	1	...	5	1	...	...
All Skilled Occupations .	66	37	...	...	29	...	...	11
Burmese ...	28	28	...	...	...	...	...	7
Zerbadis ...	3	3	...	...	...	...	...	3
Other Home races ...	2	2	...	...	...	...	...	...
Chinese ...	8	2	...	...	6	...	...	1
Anglo-Indian ...	1	1	...	...	...	...	...	...
Bengali and Chittagonian Mahomedans.	17	1	...	...	16	...	...	...
Tamil ...	1	...	...	...	1	...	...	...
Telugu ...	5	.	...	...	5	...	...	...
All other Mahomedans	1	...	...	...	1	...	...	...
Carpenter ...	28	19	...	...	9	...	...	6
Burmese ...	18	18	...	...	...	...	...	5
Chinese ...	7	1	...	...	6	...	...	1
Indians ...	3	...	...	...	3	...	...	...
Engineer—Bengali and Chittagonian Mahomedans.	1	...	...	...	1	...	...	...
Engine-driver ...	16	9	...	...	7	...	...	3
Home races ..	8	8	...	...	...	...	...	3
Chinese	1	1	...	...	...	...	...	...
Bengali and Chittagonian Mahomedans.	7	...	...	...	7	...	...	...
Fireman ...	5	1	...	...	4	...	...	...
Burmese ...	1	1	...	...	...	...	...	...
Indians ...	4	...	...	...	4	...	...	...
Fitter ...	10	7	.	...	3	...	...	2
Home races ...	5	5	...	...	...	...	...	2
Anglo-Indian ...	1	1	...	...	...	...	...	...
Indians ...	4	1	...	...	3	...	...	...
Serang—Bengali and Chittagonian Mahomedans.	3	...	...	...	3	...	...	...
Secunni—Bengali and Chittagonian Mahomedans.	2	...	...	...	2	...	...	...
Tinsmith—Burmese ...	1	1	...	...	...	...	...	...
B1. Petroleum Wells ...	958	694	6	1	254	2	1	123
All Unskilled Occupations	816	579	6	1	227	2	1	72
Burmese ...	566	559	6	1	...	...	...	70
Zerbadis ...	9	9	...	...	...	...	...	..
Other Home races ...	3	3	...	...	.	...	...	2
Sikh ...	1	...	...	...	1	...	...	...
Punjabi Mahomedans and Pathans.	3	...	...	...	3	...	...	...
Other Punjabis ...	4	...	...	...	4	...	...	...
Hindustani Mahomedans.	24	...	...	...	24	...		...
Other Hindustanis ...	59	...	...	...	57	2	...	...
Bengali and Chittagonian Mahomedans.	7	...	...	...	7	...	...	...
Other Bengalis and Chittagonians.	11	...	...	...	11	...	...	...
Oriya ...	69	...	...	...	69	...	...	..
Tamil ...	19	7	...	...	12	...	...	...
Telugu ...	29	1	...	...	27	...	1	...
All other Mahomedans	1	...	...	...	1	...	...	...
All others ...	11	...	...	...	11	...	...	...
All Skilled Occupations ...	142	115	...	...	27	...	...	41
Burmese ...	115	115	...	...	...	...	...	41
Punjabi Mahomedans and Pathans.	2	.	...	...	2	...	..	...
Hindustani Mahomedans.	7	...	...	...	7	...	...	...
Other Hindustanis ...	1	...	...	...	1	...	..	...
Bengali and Chittagonian Mahomedans.	3	...	..	...	3	...	...	...
Oriya ...	5	...	...	...	5	...	...	...
Telugu ...	9	...	...	...	9	...	...	...
Black-smith—Burmese ...	1	1	...	...	..	...	...	...
Boiler-maistry—Telugu	1	...	...	...	1	...	...	...
Carpenter—Burmese ...	67	67	...	...	...	...	...	27
Driller—Burmese ...	10	10	...		...	...	...	2
Engine-driver ...	11	7	...	...	4	...	...	3
Burmese ...	7	7	...	...	..	...	...	3
Indians ...	4	...	..	...	4	...	...	...
Fireman ...	27	6	..	...	21	...	...	3
Burmese ...	6	6	...	...	...	...	...	3
Indians ...	21	...	...	...	21	...	...	...
Fitter ...	10	9	...	...	1	...	...	4
Burmese ...	9	9	...	...	...	..	...	4
Oriya ...	1	...	...	...	1	..	...	...
Motor-driver—Burmese	1	1	...	...	...	...	...	1
Rod-puller—Burmese ..	14	14	...	...	...	...	...	1
B2. Tin and Wolfram Mines.	2,648	664	33	48	2,892	9	3	271
All Unskilled Occupations	3,447	589	33	48	2,765	9	3	122
Burmese ...	544	481	25	38	...	...	...	102
Zerbadi ...	4	4	...	...	...	...	...	2
Other Home races ...	92	78	6	8	...	...	...	11
Chinese ...	1,994	6	1	1	1,985	1	...	1
Punjabi Mahomedans and Pathans.	30	...	...	...	30	...	...	...
Other Punjabis ...	21	...	...	...	21	...	...	...
Hindustani Mahomedans	17	...	...	...	17	...	...	...
Other Hindustanis .	46	...	...	..	46	...	...	...
Bengali and Chittagonian Mahomedans.	32	...	..	...	32	...	...	...
Other Bengalis and Chittagonians.	20	...	..	.	20	...	...	...
Oriya ...	301	...	..	...	297	4	...	...
Tamil ...	11	1	...	...	10	...	...	1
Telugu ...	80	3	...	...	74	2	1	3
All others ...	255	16	1	1	233	2	2	8
All Skilled Occupations...	201	75	...	..	126	...	...	49
Burmese ...	71	71	...	...	...	...	...	46
Zerbadi ...	2	2	...	...	...	...	...	2
Other Home races . ..	1	1	...	...	...	...	...	1
Chinese ...	37	1	...	...	36	...	..	...
European ...	1	...	..	...	1	...	..	...
Anglo-Indian ...	1	...	...	...	1	...	...	...
Punjabi Mahomedans and Pathans.	3	...	...	...	3	...	...	...
Other Punjabis ...	12	...	...	...	12	...	...	...
Hindustani Mahomedans.	1	...	...	...	1	...	...	...
Other Hindustanis ...	15	...	...	...	15	...	...	...
Bengali and Chittagonian Mahomedans.	39	...	...	...	39	...	...	..
Other Bengalis and Chittagonians.	1	...	..	...	1	...	...	...
Oriya ...	10	...	...	...	10	...	...	...
Tamil ...	1	...	..	...	1	...	...	...
Telugu ...	5	...	..	...	5	...	...	...
All other Mahomedans	1	...	...	...	1	...	...	...

Column 9 shows the number of age 18 or over who were born in Burma outside the district in which they were employed at the time of the Census.

IMPERIAL TABLE XXIIB.—THE SPECIAL INDUSTRIAL CENSUS (SELECTED INDUSTRIES).

PART II.—*Classification and Birthplaces of Labourers*—continued.

Industry, Skill, Occupation and Race.	Total Number.	Born in Burma. Age 18 and over.	Born in Burma. Age 14 to 18.	Born in Burma. Age under 14.	Born outside Burma. Age 18 and over.	Born outside Burma. Age 14 to 18.	Born outside Burma. Age under 14.	See foot-note.
1	2	3	4	5	6	7	8	9
B2. Tin and Wolfram Mines—*concld.*								
Blacksmith	19	5	...	...	14	...	...	5
Burmese	5	5	...	...	...	...	...	5
Chinese	2	...	...	...	2	...	...	...
Indians	12	...	...	...	12	...	...	...
Carpenter	47	24	...	...	23	...	...	18
Home races	24	24	...	...	...	...	...	18
Chinese	20	...	...	...	20	...	...	...
Other Hindustanis	3	...	...	...	3	...	...	...
Driller—Bengali and Chittagonian Mahomedans.	2	...	...	...	2	...	...	...
Engineer—European	1	...	...	...	1	...	...	...
Engine-driver	25	5	...	...	20	...	...	4
Burmese	5	5	...	...	...	...	...	4
Indians	20	...	...	...	20	...	...	...
Fireman	8	1	...	...	7	...	...	...
Burmese	1	1	...	...	...	...	...	...
Indians	7	...	...	...	7	...	...	...
Fitter	53	26	...	...	27	...	...	17
Home races	26	26	...	...	...	...	...	17
Chinese	2	...	...	...	2	...	...	...
Indians	25	...	...	...	25	...	...	...
Mason—Other Hindustanis.	3	...	...	...	3	...	...	...
Mechanic	3	...	...	...	3	...	...	...
Chinese	2	...	...	...	2	...	...	...
Other Punjabis	1	...	...	...	1	...	...	...
Overseer	7	2	...	...	5	...	...	1
Burmese	1	1	...	...	...	...	...	1
Chinese	2	1	...	...	1	...	...	...
Anglo-Indian	1	...	...	...	1	...	...	...
Indians	3	...	...	...	3	...	...	...
Rivetter	21	...	...	...	21	...	...	...
Chinese	9	...	...	...	9	...	...	...
Indians	12	...	...	...	12	...	...	...
Sawyer—Burmese	10	10	...	...	...	...	...	2
Turner—Burmese	2	2	...	...	...	...	...	2
B3. Silver and Lead Mines.	3,916	660	32	13	3,139	105	19	444
All Unskilled Occupations	3,364	480	30	13	2,709	105	19	328
Burmese	105	100	4	1	...	...	...	98
Zerbadi	7	3	...	4	...	...	...	3
Other Home races	501	338	30	8	122	3	...	187
Chinese	601	27	...	...	536	34	4	26
European	1	...	...	...	1	...	...	...
Anglo-Indian	15	7	...	...	8	...	...	7
Punjabi Mahomedans and Pathans.	13	...	...	...	13	...	...	...
Other Punjabis	156	...	...	...	149	6	1	...
Hindustani Mahomedans.	70	2	1	...	66	1	...	2
Other Hindustanis	89	...	...	...	88	1	...	...
Bengali and Chittagonian Mahomedans.	181	...	...	...	176	5	...	...
Other Bengalis and Chittagonians.	42	...	...	...	38	4	...	...
Oriya	1,081	...	...	...	1,033	36	12	...
Tamil	33	3	1	...	29	...	...	3
Telugu	4	1	...	...	3	...	...	1
All other Mahomedans	4	1	...	...	3	...	...	1
All others	461	...	...	...	444	15	2	...
All Skilled Occupations	552	180	2	...	430	...	...	116
Burmese	91	90	1	...	...	...	...	87
Zerbadi	4	4	...	...	...	...	...	4
Other Home races	13	12	...	...	1	...	...	11
Chinese	33	6	...	...	27	...	...	6
European	1	...	...	...	1	...	...	...
Anglo-Indian	20	5	1	...	14	...	...	5
Punjabi Mahomedans and Pathans.	15	...	...	...	15	...	...	...
Other Punjabis	121	...	...	...	121	...	...	...
Hindustani Mahomedans.	14	...	...	...	14	...	...	...
Other Hindustanis	37	...	...	...	37	...	...	...
Bengali and Chittagonian Mahomedans.	90	1	...	...	89	...	...	1
Other Bengalis and Chittagonians.	38	1	...	...	37	...	...	1
Oriya	28	...	...	...	28	...	...	...
Tamil	13	1	...	...	12	...	...	1
Telugu	1	...	...	...	1	...	...	...
All other Mahomedans	2	...	...	...	2	...	...	...
All others	31	...	...	...	31	...	...	...
Blacksmith	45	9	...	...	36	...	...	9
Burmese	9	9	...	...	...	...	...	9
Indians	36	...	...	...	36	...	...	...

Industry, Skill, Occupation and Race.	Total Number.	Born in Burma. Age 18 and over.	Born in Burma. Age 14 to 18.	Born in Burma. Age under 14.	Born outside Burma. Age 18 and over.	Born outside Burma. Age 14 to 18.	Born outside Burma. Age under 14.	See foot-note.
1	2	3	4	5	6	7	8	9
B3. Silver and Lead Mines—*concld.*								
Boiler-maker—Indians	3	...	...	...	3	...	...	...
Carpenter	115	42	...	...	73	...	...	39
Burmese	36	36	...	...	...	...	...	33
Chinese	29	6	...	...	23	...	...	6
Anglo-Indian	1	...	...	...	1	...	...	...
Indians	49	...	...	...	49	...	...	...
Carriage-repairer—Other Punjabis.	1	...	...	...	1	...	...	...
Driller—Indians	4	...	...	...	4	...	...	...
Electrician—Anglo-Indian	3	2	...	...	1	...	...	2
Engine-driver	52	5	...	...	47	...	...	5
Other Home races	5	5	...	...	...	...	...	5
Chinese	1	...	...	...	1	...	...	...
European	1	...	...	...	1	...	...	...
Anglo-Indian	9	...	...	...	9	...	...	...
Indians	36	...	...	...	36	...	...	...
Fireman—Other Punjabis	2	...	...	...	2	...	...	...
Fitter	250	48	2	...	200	...	...	47
Zerbadi	4	4	...	...	...	...	...	4
Home races	42	40	1	...	1	...	...	39
Chinese	3	...	...	...	3	...	...	...
Anglo-Indian	6	2	1	...	3	...	...	2
Indians	195	2	...	...	193	...	...	2
Foreman—Other Punjabis	1	...	...	...	1	...	...	...
Mason	28	8	...	...	20	...	...	8
Other Home races	8	8	...	...	...	...	...	8
Indians	20	...	...	...	20	...	...	...
Painter—Indians	2	...	...	...	2	...	...	...
Rivetter—Indians	28	1	...	...	27	...	...	1
Tinsmith—All others	1	...	...	...	1	...	...	...
Turner	17	5	...	...	12	...	...	5
Burmese	4	4	...	...	...	...	...	4
Anglo-Indian	1	1	...	...	...	...	...	1
Indians	12	...	...	...	12	...	...	...
B4. Ruby Mines	887	345	17	...	520	5	...	340
All Unskilled Occupations	796	267	17	...	507	5	...	263
Burmese	87	81	6	...	...	...	...	81
Other Home races	516	183	10	...	321	2	...	180
Chinese	72	1	...	...	70	1	...	1
Punjabi Mahomedans and Pathans.	3	...	1	...	2	...	...	...
Other Punjabis	4	...	...	...	4	...	...	...
Hindustani Mahomedans.	6	...	...	...	6	...	...	...
Other Hindustanis	14	1	...	...	12	1	...	...
Other Bengalis and Chittagonians.	2	...	...	...	2	...	...	...
All others	92	1	...	...	90	1	...	1
All Skilled Occupations	91	78	...	...	13	...	...	77
Burmese	51	51	...	...	...	...	...	50
Zerbadi	6	6	...	...	...	...	...	6
Other Home races	15	15	...	...	...	...	...	15
Chinese	4	1	...	...	3	...	...	1
European	1	...	...	...	1	...	...	...
Anglo-Indian	1	1	...	...	...	...	...	1
Punjabi Mahomedans and Pathans.	3	1	...	...	2	...	...	1
Other Punjabis	2	1	...	...	1	...	...	1
Hindustani Mahomedans.	3	1	...	...	2	...	...	1
Other Hindustanis	1	...	...	...	1	...	...	...
All others	4	1	...	...	3	...	...	1
Blacksmith	6	3	...	...	3	...	...	2
Burmese	2	2	...	...	...	...	...	2
Indians	4	1	...	...	3	...	...	1
Carpenter	14	11	...	...	3	...	...	11
Burmese	11	11	...	...	...	...	...	11
Chinese	3	...	...	...	3	...	...	...
Electrician—Shan	1	1	...	...	...	...	...	1
Engine-driver	6	5	...	...	1	...	...	4
Home races	5	5	...	...	...	...	...	4
Indians	1	...	...	...	1	...	...	...
Fitter	44	39	...	...	5	...	...	39
Home races	36	36	...	...	...	...	...	36
Anglo-Indian	1	1	...	...	...	...	...	1
Indians	7	2	...	...	5	...	...	2
Foreman—European	1	...	...	...	1	...	...	...
Moulder—Home races	10	10	...	...	...	...	...	10

Column 9 shows the number of age 18 or over who were born in Burma outside the district in which they were employed at the time of the Census.

IMPERIAL TABLE XXIIB.—THE SPECIAL INDUSTRIAL CENSUS (SELECTED INDUSTRIES).

PART II.—*Classification and Birthplaces of Labourers*—continued.

Industry, Skill, Occupation and Race.	Total Number.	Born in Burma. Age 18 and over.	Born in Burma. Age 14 to 18.	Born in Burma. Age under 14.	Born outside Burma. Age 18 and over.	Born outside Burma. Age 14 to 18.	Born outside Burma. Age under 14.	See foot-note.
1	2	3	4	5	6	7	8	9
B4. Ruby Mines—*concld.*								
Tinsmith—Burmese ...	1	1	...	...	...	...	...	1
Turner	8	8	...	...	...	...	...	8
Burmese ...	6	6	...	...	...	...	...	6
Chinese	1	1	...	...	...	...	...	1
All others	1	1	...	...	...	...	...	1
B5. Copper, Steatite and Coal Mines.								
All Unskilled Occupations	82	45	4	...	32	1	...	2
Burmese ...	47	43	4	...	...	...	...	...
Other Home races ...	2	2	...	...	...	...	...	2
Hindustani Mahomedans.	1	...	...	...	1	...	...	...
All others	32	...	...	...	31	1	...	...
F2. Sawmills and Timber-yards.	12,050	2,748	161	10	8,571	508	92	656
All Unskilled Occupations	9,490	1,493	156	10	7,236	503	92	368
Arakan Division ...	26	13	..	...	13	...	...	...
Rangoon	4,790	106	10	1	4,203	398	72	50
*Pegu Division * (less Rangoon).*	473	87	5	4	363	8	6	31
Irrawaddy Division ...	78	22	...	...	56	...	..	..
Amherst, Salween, Tavoy and Mergui.	2,697	305	35	3	2,246	95	13	40
Upper Burma and the Shan States.	1,426	960	106	2	355	2	1	247
Burmese	1,467	1,329	131	7	...	...	...	343
Zerbadi	42	36	5	1	...	...	..	1
Other Home races ...	53	46	2	...	5	...	...	18
Chinese	33	3	1	...	27	2	...	...
Anglo-Indian ...	1	1	..	...	..	...	...	...
Sikh	4	...	..	...	4	...	...	...
Punjabi Mahomedans and Pathans.	14	...	...	...	14	...	...	...
Other Punjabis ...	1	.	...	...	1	...	...	...
Hindustani Mahomedans.	58	...	...	...	58	...	...	...
Other Hindustanis ...	644	2	1	...	586	41	14	...
Bengali and Chittagonian Mahomedans.	651	27	4	...	613	6	1	1
Other Bengalis and Chittagonians.	29	...	..	...	29	...		...
Oriya	949	1	4	...	895	38	11	1
Tamil	79	7	1	..	71	..	...	...
Telugu	5,451	38	7	2	4,922	416	66	3
All other Mahomedans	4	3	...	...	1	...	..	1
All others	10	...	...	...	10	...	...	...
All Skilled Occupations ..	2,600	1,255	5	...	1,335	5	..	288
Arakan Division ...	10	6	...	...	4	...	...	...
Rangoon	1,150	338	3	...	804	5	...	158
Pegu Division (less Rangoon).*	92	36	.	...	56	...	...	15
Irrawaddy Division	64	31	..	..	33	..	...	5
Amherst, Salween, Tavoy and Mergui.	711	381	...	...	330	..	...	48
Upper Burma and the Shan States.	573	463	2	...	108	...	...	82
Burmese	1,094	1,089	5	...	...	..	..	259
Zerbadi	70	70	...	...	...	...	...	15
Other Home races ...	18	18	...	...	..	...	...	5
Chinese	72	14	..	...	58	...	...	5
Anglo-Indian .	2	2	...	...	...	...	..	1
Other Punjabis ...	1	...	...	...	1	...	...	...
Hindustani Mahomedans.	5	1	...	..	4	..	...	1
Other Hindustanis ...	57	...	...	...	56	1	...	...
Bengali and Chittagonian Mahomedans.	294	11	..	..	283	...	...	2
Other Bengalis and Chittagonians.	18	3	...	...	15	...	...	...
Oriya	40	...	...	...	39	1	...	...
Tamil	16	9	...	...	7	...	..	...
Telugu	912	38	...	...	871	3	...	...
All others	1	...	...	...	1	...	...	...
Blacksmith	84	51	1	...	32	..	..	15
Home races ...	52	51	1	...	...	...	.	15
Chinese	1	...	...	...	1	...	...	...
Indians	31	...	...	...	31	...	...	...
Bricklayer—Telugu ...	2	...	...	...	2	...	...	...
Carpenter	209	161	1	...	47	...	...	54
Home races ...	157	156	1	...	...	...	...	52
Chinese	44	5	...	...	39	...	...	2
Indians	8	...	...	...	8	...	...	...
Driller—Burmese ...	3	3	...	...	...	...	...	...
Engineer	22	15	...	...	7	...	...	9
Home races ...	13	13	...	...	...	...	...	7
Chinese	1	1	...	...	...	...	...	1
Anglo-Indian ...	1	1	...	...	...	...	...	1
Indians	7	...	...	...	7	...	...	...

Industry, Skill, Occupation and Race.	Total Number.	Born in Burma. Age 18 and over.	Born in Burma. Age 14 to 18.	Born in Burma. Age under 14.	Born outside Burma. Age 18 and over.	Born outside Burma. Age 14 to 18.	Born outside Burma. Age under 14.	See foot-note.
1	2	3	4	5	6	7	8	9
F2. Sawmills and Timber-yards—*concld.*								
Engine-driver ...	221	37	...	...	184	...	...	9
Home races ...	34	34	..	..	...	...	...	8
Chinese	2	...	...	..	2	...	...	...
Indians	185	3	...	...	182	...	...	1
Fireman	128	17	...	...	111	...	...	4
Home races ..	10	10	...	...	...	...	...	3
Indians	118	7	...	...	111	...	...	1
Fitter	208	168	...	...	40	...	...	39
Home races ...	163	163	...	...	...	...	...	39
Anglo-Indian ...	1	1	..	...	...	...	...	...
Indians	44	4	...	...	40	...	...	..
Foreman—Indians ...	2	...	...	...	2	...	...	...
Gunner	223	157	...	...	65	1	...	56
Home races ...	152	152	...	...	...	...	...	54
Chinese	5	4	...	...	1	...	...	2
Indians	66	1	...	...	64	1	...	...
Launch-driver—Bengali and Chittagonian Mahomedans.	1	...	...	.	1	...	...	...
Moulder ... —	13	12	...	...	1	...	...	1
Burmese	12	12	...	...	..	...	...	1
Telugu	1	...	...	...	1	...	...	...
Planer	40	31	1	...	8	...	...	9
Home races ..	30	29	1	...	..	...	...	8
Chinese	4	1	...	..	3	...	...	...
Indians	6	1	...	..	5	...	...	1
Rivetter—Indians ...	2	...	...	...	2	...	...	...
Sail-maker—Bengali and Chittagonian Mahomedans.	1	...	...	...	1	...	...	...
Saw-sharpener ..	123	64	2	...	57	...	...	22
Home races ...	64	62	2	...	...	...	...	22
Indians	59	2	...	...	57	...	...	...
Sawyer	1,261	512	...	...	745	4	...	78
Home races ...	471	471	...	...	...	...	...	78
Chinese	15	3	...	...	12	...	...	...
Indians	775	38	...	...	733	4	...	...
Serang	20	1	...	..	19	...	...	...
Karen	1	1	...	...	...	...	...	...
Indians	19	...	...	...	19	..	...	...
Secunni—Bengali and Chittagonian Mahomedans.	2	...	...	...	2	...	...	...
Turner	35	26	...	...	9	...	...	2
Burmese	20	20	...	...	...	...	..	2
Indians	15	6	...	...	9	..	...	...
G. Metal Industries ...	2,233	606	61	16	1,490	30	30	153
All Unskilled Occupations	1,084	143	39	15	837	21	29	28
Burmese	143	103	34	6	...	..	...	13
Zerbadi	17	14	3	...	...	...	...	2
Other Home races ...	1	1	...	...	...	...	...	1
Chinese	7	...	..	...	7	...	..	...
Anglo-Indian ...	3	1	..	...	2	...	...	1
Sikh	7	2	...	...	5	..	...	...
Punjabi Mahomedans and Pathans.	4	...	.	...	4	...	...	...
Other Punjabis ..	1	...	...	..	1	...	...	...
Hindustani Mahomedans.	79	...	...	..	79	...	...	...
Other Hindustanis ...	152	1	...	...	145	2	4	1
Bengali and Chittagonian Mahomedans.	90	2	1	...	78	7	2	1
Other Bengalis and Chittagonians.	22	...	...	..	19	3	...	...
Oriya	54	...	...	...	51	...	3	...
Tamil	131	16	...	8	97	3	7	9
Telugu ...	370	3	1	1	347	5	13	...
All other Mahomedans	2	...	...	...	1	1	...	...
All others	1	...	...	...	1	...	...	...
All Skilled Occupations..	1,149	463	22	1	653	9	1	125
Burmese	374	362	12	...	...	...	...	85
Zerbadi	34	34	...	..	...	...	...	10
Other Home races ...	9	7	1	1	...	..	...	5
Chinese	74	4	...	...	70	...	...	1
European	1	...	...	...	1	...	...	..
Anglo-Indian ...	34	18	...	...	16	...	...	9
Sikh	8	1	...	...	7	...	...	...
Punjabi Mahomedans and Pathans.	19	...	2	.	17	...	...	...
Other Punjabis ...	20	...	..	...	20	...	...	...
Hindustani Mahomedans.	55	2	...	...	53	...	...	..
Other Hindustanis ...	92	5	..	...	87	...	...	4
Bengali and Chittagonian Mahomedans.	88	1	...	...	84	3	...	...

Column 9 shows the number of age 18 or over who were born in Burma outside the district in which they were employed at the time of the Census.

* That is the Insein, Hanthawaddy, Tharrawaddy, Pegu and Prome districts.

Imperial Table XXIIb.—The Special Industrial Census (Selected Industries).

Part II.—*Classification and Birthplaces of Labourers*—continued.

Industry, Skill, Occupation and Race.	Total Number.	Born in Burma.			Born outside Burma.			See foot-note.
		Age 18 and over.	Age 14 to 18.	Age under 14.	Age 18 and over.	Age 14 to 18.	Age under 14.	
1	2	3	4	5	6	7	8	9
G. Metal Industries—*contd.*								
Other Bengalis and Chittagonians.	49	6	...	...	43	...	...	1
Tamil	137	16	4	...	113	4	...	8
Oriya	47	3	...	...	43	1	...	...
Telugu	89	2	3	...	82	1	1	...
All other Mahomedans	6	2	...	...	4	...	...	2
All others ...	13	...	...	...	13	...	...	...
Armourer	42	3	7	...	28	4	...	1
Other Home races ...	2	2	...	...	...	...	...	1
Indians	40	1	7	...	28	4	...	...
Blacksmith	96	8	...	...	88	...	...	2
Burmese	4	4	...	...	...	...	...	2
Chinese	32	...	...	...	32	...	...	...
Indians	60	4	...	...	56	...	...	...
Boilermaker ...	40	5	1	...	34	...	...	...
Home races ...	6	5	1	...	...	...	...	...
Chinese	9	...	...	...	9	...	...	...
Indians	25	...	...	...	25	...	...	...
Bookbinder—Indian ...	1	...	...	...	1	...	...	...
Bucket-maker ...	15	12	2	...	1	...	...	...
Burmese	14	12	2	...	...	...	...	...
Indian	1	...	...	...	1	...	...	...
Carpenter	107	74	1	...	32	...	...	34
Other Home races ...	72	71	1	...	...	...	...	33
Chinese	15	1	...	...	14	...	...	...
Indians	20	2	...	...	18	...	...	1
Carriage-examiner—Indians ...	4	...	...	...	4	...	...	...
Carriage-lifter—Indians	7	...	...	...	7	...	...	...
Coppersmith—Indians ...	6	...	...	...	6	...	...	...
Craneman—Indians	5	...	...	...	5	...	...	...
Driller—Indians ...	4	...	...	...	4	...	...	...
Engine-driver ...	50	1	...	...	49	...	...	...
European	1	...	...	...	1	...	...	...
Anglo-Indian ...	9	1	...	...	8	...	...	...
Indians	40	...	...	...	40	...	...	...
Fileman—Indians ...	10	2	...	...	7	1	...	2
Fireman	32	5	...	...	27	...	...	4
Zerbadi	1	1	...	...	...	...	...	1
Anglo-Indian ...	4	4	...	...	...	...	...	3
Indians	27	...	...	...	27	...	...	...
Fitter	281	125	3	...	152	1	...	39
Home races ...	105	103	2	...	...	...	...	30
Chinese	5	3	...	...	2	...	...	1
Anglo-Indian ...	18	12	...	...	6	...	...	6
Indians	153	7	1	...	144	1	...	2
Foreman	6	1	...	...	5	...	...	...
Burmese	1	1	...	...	...	...	...	...
Anglo-Indian ...	1	...	...	...	1	...	...	...
Indians	4	...	...	...	4	...	...	...
Iron-worker ...	4	3	...	...	1	...	...	...
Burmese	3	3	...	...	...	...	...	...
Anglo-Indian ...	1	...	...	...	1	...	...	...
Latheman—Indian ...	1	...	...	...	1	...	...	...
Leather-sewer—Indians	14	3	...	...	11	...	...	3
Machineman—Home races ...	19	17	2	...	...	...	...	...
Mason—Indian	1	...	...	...	1	...	...	...
Melter—Indians ...	7	...	...	...	7	...	...	...
Motor-mechanic—Indian	1	1	...	...	...	...	...	1
Moulder	159	120	3	...	36	...	...	16
Home races ...	118	115	3	...	...	...	...	16
Chinese	7	...	...	...	7	...	...	...
Anglo-Indian ...	1	1	...	...	...	...	...	...
Indians	33	4	...	...	29	...	...	...
Painter—Indians ...	10	2	...	...	8	...	...	2
Pattern-maker—Burmese	1	1	...	...	...	...	...	1
Plater	30	8	...	...	22	...	...	2
Burmese	7	7	...	...	...	...	...	2
Chinese	4	...	...	...	4	...	...	...
Indians	19	1	...	...	18	...	...	...
Rivetter	32	1	...	...	30	...	1	...
Zerbadi	1	1	...	...	...	...	...	...
Chinese	1	...	...	...	1	...	...	...
Indians	30	...	...	...	29	...	1	...
G. Metal Industries—*concld.*								
Rope-maker—Indians ...	5	...	...	...	5	...	...	...
Saddler—Indians ...	6	1	...	...	5	...	...	1
Sawyer—Indians ...	2	...	...	...	2	...	...	...
Serang—Indian ...	1	...	...	...	1	...	...	...
Stone-dresser—Indians ...	2	...	...	...	2	...	...	...
Tailor—Indians ...	18	1	...	...	17	...	...	1
Tinsmith	27	19	2	...	6	...	...	3
Burmese	18	17	1	...	...	...	...	3
Zerbadi	2	2	...	...	...	...	...	...
Indians	7	...	1	...	6	...	...	...
Turner	103	50	1	1	48	3	...	10
Home races ...	43	41	1	1	...	...	...	8
Chinese	1	...	...	...	1	...	...	...
Indians	59	9	...	...	47	3	...	2
J4. Petroleum Refineries.*	30,231	7,723	236	34	21,112	892	234	4,095
All Unskilled Occupations	25,559	6,165	219	34	17,940	868	233	3,247
Burmese	6,343	6,129	191	23	...	...	...	[illegible]
Zerbadi	40	36	4	...	...	...	...	23
Other Home races ...	11	5	5	1	...	...	...	3
Chinese	24	9	...	...	15	...	...	2
European	21	...	...	...	21	...	...	...
Anglo-Indian ...	51	28	2	...	20	1	...	22
Sikh	17	...	...	...	16	1	...	...
Punjabi Mahomedans and Pathans.	72	2	2	1	66	1	...	1
Other Punjabis ...	62	1	...	...	60	1	...	1
Hindustani Mahomedans.	412	1	...	1	400	8	2	1
Other Hindustanis ...	3,449	8	...	1	3,305	119	16	4
Bengali and Chittagonian Mahomedans.	1,666	7	1	...	1,625	31	2	7
Other Bengalis and Chittagonians.	144	3	...	...	140	1	...	3
Oriya	5,348	4	1	1	5,090	215	37	1
Tamil	146	22	12	...	107	2	3	17
Telugu	7,443	5	1	3	6,785	477	172	2
All other Mahomedans	23	3	...	...	20	...	...	1
All others	287	2	...	2	270	11	2	2
All Skilled Occupations ..	4,672	1,458	17	...	3,172	24	1	849
Burmese	1,374	1,361	13	...	...	...	...	793
Zerbadi	28	27	1	...	...	...	...	9
Other Home races ...	5	5	...	...	...	...	...	5
Chinese	258	6	...	...	251	1	...	1
European	9	...	...	...	9	...	...	...
Anglo-Indian ...	41	28	...	...	13	...	...	23
Sikh	14	...	...	...	14	...	...	...
Punjabi Mahomedans and Pathans.	43	...	...	...	43	...	...	...
Other Punjabis ...	154	...	...	...	151	3	...	...
Hindustani Mahomedans.	39	1	...	...	38	...	...	1
Other Hindustanis ...	450	2	...	...	443	4	1	1
Bengali and Chittagonian Mahomedans.	1,396	8	1	...	1,377	10	...	3
Other Bengalis and Chittagonians.	128	1	...	...	127	...	...	1
Oriya	120	...	...	...	119	1	...	...
Tamil	50	12	1	...	37	...	...	7
Telugu	517	6	1	...	505	5	...	4
All other Mahomedans	4	1	...	...	3	...	...	1
All others	42	...	...	...	42	...	...	...
Blacksmith	183	118	...	...	65	...	...	51
Burmese	115	115	...	...	...	...	...	49
Indians	68	3	...	...	65	...	...	2
Boilermaker ...	46	20	...	...	26	...	...	11
Burmese	19	19	...	...	...	...	...	10
Indians	27	1	...	...	26	...	...	1
Bricklayer—Indians ...	167	...	...	...	167	...	...	...
Carpenter	850	588	2	...	259	1	...	411
Burmese	588	586	2	...	...	...	...	411
Chinese	239	2	...	...	236	1	...	...
Indians	23	...	...	...	23	...	...	...
Cooper—Indians ...	98	...	...	...	98	2	1	...
Coppersmith—Indians ...	5	...	...	...	4	1	...	...
Driller—Burmese ...	7	7	...	...	...	...	...	5
Electrician	10	6	1	...	3	...	...	3
Burmese	5	5	...	...	...	...	...	2
Zerbadi	1	...	1	...	...	...	...	...
Chinese	2	...	...	...	2	...	...	...
Indians	2	1	...	...	1	...	...	1
Engineer—Burmese ...	4	4	...	...	...	...	...	4

Column 9 shows the number of age 18 or over who were born in Burma outside the district in which they were employed at the time of the Census.

* Pipe-line pumping-stations are also included here.

IMPERIAL TABLE XXIIB.—THE SPECIAL INDUSTRIAL CENSUS (SELECTED INDUSTRIES).

PART II.—*Classification and Birthplaces of Labourers*—continued.

Industry, Skill, Occupation and Race.	Total Number	Born in Burma. Age 18 and over.	Born in Burma. Age 14 to 18.	Born in Burma. Age under 14.	Born outside Burma. Age 18 and over.	Born outside Burma. Age 14 to 18.	Born outside Burma. Age under 14	*See foot-note.*
1	2	3	4	5	6	7	8	9
J4. Petroleum Refineries—*concld.*								
Engine-driver ...	241	28	...	...	213	...	...	22
Burmese ...	10	10	...	...	...	...	...	8
Zerbadi ...	1	1	...	...	...	...	...	...
Anglo-Indian ...	20	16	...	...	4	...	...	13
Indians ...	210	1	...	...	209	...	...	1
Fireman ...	564	8	...	...	556	...	...	3
Burmese ...	7	7	...	...	...	...	...	3
European ...	3	...	...	...	3	...	...	...
Anglo-Indian ...	1	...	...	...	1	...	...	...
Indians ...	553	1	...	...	552	...	...	...
Fitter ...	1,151	368	4	...	773	9	...	202
Burmese ...	323	319	4	...	...	...	...	177
Zerbadi ...	18	18	...	...	...	...	...	6
Other Home races ...	5	5	...	...	...	...	...	5
Chinese ...	1	1	...	...	...	...	...	...
European ...	2	...	...	...	2	...	...	...
Anglo-Indian ...	12	7	...	...	5	...	...	6
Indians ...	790	15	...	...	766	9	...	8
Foreman ...	4	2	...	...	2	...	...	2
Anglo-Indian ...	3	2	...	...	1	...	...	2
Indians ...	1	...	...	...	1	...	...	...
Mason ...	250	29	...	...	221	...	...	29
Burmese ...	27	27	...	...	...	...	...	27
Indians ...	223	2	...	...	221	...	...	2
Motor-boat-driver—Burmese ...	2	2	...	...	...	...	...	2
Moulder ...	96	41	2	...	47	6	...	21
Burmese ...	38	37	1	...	...	...	...	20
European ...	1	...	...	...	1	...	...	...
Anglo-Indian ...	1	1	...	...	...	...	...	...
Indians ...	56	3	1	...	46	6	...	1
Oil-stills-man—Indians ...	397	...	...	...	397	...	...	...
Overseer ...	10	4	...	...	6	...	...	3
Burmese ...	1	1	...	...	...	...	...	...
European ...	3	...	...	...	3	...	...	...
Anglo-Indian ...	4	2	...	...	2	...	...	2
Indians ...	2	1	...	...	1	...	...	1
Painter ...	9	...	...	...	9	...	...	...
Chinese ...	3	...	...	...	3	...	...	...
Indians ...	6	...	...	...	6	...	...	...
Pattern-maker ...	22	1	...	...	21	...	...	1
Burmese ...	1	1	...	...	...	...	...	1
Chinese ...	10	...	...	...	10	...	...	...
Indians ...	11	...	...	...	11	...	...	...
Planer ...	4	1	...	...	3	...	...	1
Burmese ...	1	1	...	...	...	...	...	1
Indians ...	3	...	...	...	3	...	...	...
Rivetter ...	204	86	5	...	112	1	...	12
Burmese ...	85	81	4	...	...	...	...	11
Zerbadi ...	2	2	...	...	...	...	...	1
Chinese ...	2	2	...	...	...	...	...	...
Indians ...	115	1	1	...	112	1	...	...
Saw-sharpener—Burmese	1	1	...	...	...	...	...	1
Sawyer—Burmese ...	17	17	...	...	...	...	...	16
Serang—Indians ...	17	...	...	...	17	...	...	...
Stamp-cutter ...	28	5	...	...	23	...	...	2
Burmese ...	4	4	...	...	...	...	...	1
Chinese ...	1	1	...	...	...	...	...	1
Indians ...	23	...	...	...	23	...	...	...
Secunni—Indians ...	8	...	...	...	8	...	...	...
Tinsmith ...	130	88	1	...	41	...	...	26
Burmese ...	87	87	...	...	...	...	...	26
Zerbadi ...	1	1	...	...	...	...	...	...
Indians ...	42	...	1	...	41	...	...	...
Turner ...	147	37	2	...	104	4	...	21
Burmese ...	32	30	2	...	...	...	...	18
Zerbadi ...	5	5	...	...	...	...	...	2
Indians ...	110	2	...	...	104	4	...	1
K3. Rice-mills ...	18,145	2,562	162	43	14,982	304	52	651
All Unskilled Occupations	16,298	1,861	152	43	13,852	298	52	432
Arakan Division ...	800	28	5	...	748	17	2	1
Rangoon ...	6,745	191	13	11	6,381	124	25	80
*Pegu Division * (less Rangoon).*	3,660	626	47	14	2,905	58	10	176
Irrawaddy Division ...	3,336	381	46	5	2,817	79	8	81
Toungoo and Thatôn ...	521	131	4	2	373	11	...	25
Amherst, Salween, Tavoy and Mergui.	679	168	14	6	479	5	7	3
Upper Burma and the Shan States.	517	336	23	5	149	4	...	66
K3. Rice-mills—*contd.*								
Burmese ...	1,744	1,599	125	20	...	...	...	365
Zerbadi ...	66	56	8	2	...	...	...	7
Other Home races ...	65	60	4	1	...	...	...	15
Chinese ...	145	20	...	...	123	2	...	14
Anglo-Indian ...	10	2	...	...	8	...	...	...
Sikh ...	20	...	...	...	20	...	...	...
Punjabi Mahomedans and Pathans.	16	...	...	...	15	...	1	...
Other Punjabis ..	9	...	...	...	8	1	...	...
Hindustani Mahomedans.	78	2	1	...	74	1	...	...
Other Hindustanis ...	1,869	1	...	1	1,850	16	1	1
Bengali and Chittagonian Mahomedans.	6,085	50	...	...	5,890	137	8	16
Other Bengalis and Chittagonians.	435	1	...	...	415	18	1	...
Oriya ...	450	...	1	...	437	9	3	...
Tamil ...	216	8	3	...	199	4	2	2
Telugu ...	4,918	56	8	19	4,690	109	36	11
All other Mahomedans	54	6	...	...	47	1	...	1
All others ...	78	...	2	...	76	...	...	...
All Skilled Occupations ..	1,847	701	10	...	1,130	6	...	219
Arakan Division ...	70	25	...	...	45	...	...	2
Rangoon ...	579	139	4	...	434	2	...	52
*Pegu Division * (less Rangoon).*	485	185	4	...	294	2	...	70
Irrawaddy Division ...	333	107	2	...	222	2	...	91
Toungoo and Thatôn ...	130	76	...	...	54	...	...	29
Amherst, Salween, Tavoy and Mergui.	130	85	...	...	45	...	...	7
Upper Burma and the Shan States.	120	84	...	...	36	...	...	98
Burmese ...	600	592	8	...	...	...	...	189
Zerbadi ...	45	44	1	...	...	...	...	20
Other Home races ...	26	26	...	...	...	...	...	5
Chinese ...	226	8	...	...	218	...	...	...
European ...	12	...	...	...	12	...	...	...
Anglo-Indian ...	6	3	...	...	3	...	...	3
Sikh ...	3	...	...	...	3	...	...	...
Punjabi Mahomedans and Pathans.	3	1	...	...	2	...	...	...
Hindustani Mahomedans.	6	...	...	...	6	...	...	...
Other Hindustanis ...	18	...	...	...	18	...	...	...
Bengali and Chittagonian Mahomedans.	822	13	1	...	802	6	...	...
Other Bengalis and Chittagonians.	14	1	...	...	13	...	...	...
Oriya ...	10	2	...	...	8	...	...	...
Tamil ...	2	1	...	...	1	...	...	...
Telugu ...	52	8	...	...	44	...	...	3
All other Mahomedans	2	2	...	...	...	...	...	2
All others ...	...	...	...	...	...	...	...	...
Blacksmith ...	95	65	1	...	29	...	...	15
Home races ...	63	62	1	...	...	...	...	15
Indians ...	32	3	...	...	...	...	...	...
Boilermaker—Burmese	4	4	...	...	...	...	...	...
Carpenter ...	435	206	...	...	227	...	...	78
Home races ...	204	202	2	...	...	...	...	75
Chinese ...	220	4	...	...	216	...	...	...
Indians ...	11	...	...	...	11	...	...	...
Electrician—Indians ...	5	1	...	...	4	...	...	...
Engineer ...	40	16	...	...	24	...	...	8
Home races ...	12	12	...	...	...	...	...	6
Chinese ...	2	1	...	...	1	...	...	...
European ...	12	...	...	...	12	...	...	...
Anglo-Indian ...	3	2	...	...	1	...	...	...
Indians ...	11	1	...	...	10	...	...	...
Engine-driver ...	493	207	...	...	285	1	...	46
Home races ...	105	105	...	...	...	...	...	44
Indians ...	388	102	...	...	285	1	...	2
Fireman ...	383	62	...	...	318	3	...	12
Home races ...	58	58	...	...	...	...	...	11
Indians ...	325	4	...	...	318	3	...	1
Fitter ...	219	149	5	...	63	2	...	39
Home races ...	147	142	5	...	...	...	...	39
Chinese ...	5	3	...	...	2	...	...	...
Anglo-Indian ...	2	...	...	...	2	...	...	...
Indians ...	65	4	...	...	59	2	...	...
Foreman ...	62	30	...	...	32	...	...	5
Home races ...	28	28	...	...	...	...	...	5
Indians ...	34	2	...	...	32	...	...	...
Gunner—Zerbadi ...	2	1	1	...	...	...	...	...
Launch-driver—Bengali and Chittagonian Mahomedans.	2	...	...	...	2	...	...	...
Mason ...	2	1	...	...	1	...	...	1
Zerbadi ...	1	1	...	...	...	...	...	1
Bengali and Chittagonian Mahomedans.	1	...	...	...	1	...	...	...

Column 9 shows the number of age 18 or over who were born in Burma outside the district in which they were employed at the time of the Census.

* That is, the Insein, Hanthawaddy, Tharrawaddy, Pegu and Prome districts.

IMPERIAL TABLE XXIIB.—THE SPECIAL INDUSTRIAL CENSUS (SELECTED INDUSTRIES).

PART II.—*Classification and Birthplaces of Labourers*—continued.

Industry, Skill, Occupation and Race.	Total Number	Born in Burma. Age 18 and over.	Born in Burma. Age 14 to 18.	Born in Burma. Age under 14.	Born outside Burma. Age 18 and over.	Born outside Burma. Age 14 to 18.	Born outside Burma. Age under 14.	See foot-note.
1	2	3	4	5	6	7	8	9
K3. Rice-mills—*concld.*								
Mechanic	9	2	...	...	7	...	...	...
Burmese	2	2	...	...	...	...	...	...
Indians	7	...	...	...	7	...	...	...
Mill-foreman ...	32	18	...	...	14	...	...	11
Burmese	17	17	...	...	...	...	...	10
Anglo-Indian ...	1	1	...	...	...	...	...	1
Indians	14	...	...	...	14	...	...	...
Motor-driver	5	4	...	...	1	...	...	...
Burmese	3	3	...	...	...	...	...	...
Bengali and Chittagonian Mahomedans.	2	1	...	...	1	...	...	...
Motor-boat-driver ...	2	1	...	...	1	...	...	...
Burmese	1	1	...	...	...	...	...	...
Bengali and Chittagonian Mahomedans.	1	...	...	...	1	...	...	...
Moulder—Burmese ...	1	1	...	...	...	...	...	1
Rivetter—Telugu ...	1	...	...	...	1	...	...	...
Sawyer	7	5	...	...	2	...	...	1
Burmese	4	4	...	...	...	...	...	...
Telugu	3	1	...	...	2	...	...	1
Serang—Indians ...	15	...	...	...	15	...	...	...
Tinsmith—Burmese ...	4	4	...	...	...	...	...	1
Turner	29	17	1	...	11	...	...	4
Home races ..	15	15	...	...	...	...	...	4
Indians	14	2	1	...	11	...	...	...
P. Construction of means of transport or communication.	10,424	2,420	230	4	7,655	183	32	543
All Unskilled Occupations	4,522	388	42	4	3,915	141	32	77
Burmese	306	277	27	2	...	...	...	45
Zerbadi	22	18	4	...	...	...	...	1
Other Home races ...	1	1	...	...	...	...	...	1
Chinese	38	7	2	...	26	3	...	2
Anglo-Indian ...	46	26	...	...	20	...	...	11
Arakan Mahomedans.	3	3	...	...	...	...	...	3
Sikh	56	2	...	...	53	1	...	...
Punjabi Mahomedans and Pathans.	49	...	...	...	47	2	...	...
Other Punjabis ...	14	1	...	...	13	...	...	1
Hindustani Mahomedans.	109	4	2	1	99	2	1	1
Other Hindustanis ...	869	11	2	...	842	14	...	1
Bengali and Chittagonian Mahomedans.	281	5	...	...	266	10	...	...
Other Bengalis and Chittagonians.	17	1	...	...	14	2	...	...
Oriya	730	...	...	...	678	38	14	...
Tamil	87	20	4	...	56	7	...	4
Telugu	1,772	8	1	1	1,684	61	17	6
All other Mahomedans	19	3	...	...	15	1	...	...
All others	103	1	...	...	102	...	...	1
All Skilled Occupations...	5,902	2,032	88	...	3,740	42	...	466
Burmese	1,714	1,661	53	...	...	...	...	330
Zerbadi	112	105	7	...	...	...	...	32
Arakan Mahomedans	2	1	1	...	...	...	...	1
Other Home races ...	17	17	...	...	...	...	...	15
Chinese	413	29	...	...	384	...	...	9
Japanese	3	...	...	...	2	...	...	...
European	14	...	...	...	13	1	...	...
Anglo-Indian ...	176	109	13	...	45	9	...	39
Sikh	65	4	...	...	60	1	...	2
Punjabi Mahomedans and Pathans.	62	1	1	...	60	...	...	1
Other Punjabis ...	154	5	2	...	144	3	...	2
Hindustani Mahomedans.	113	2	1	...	110	...	...	...
Other Hindustanis ...	850	[illegible]	2	...	825	4	...	6
Bengali and Chittagonian Mahomedans.	631	8	...	...	612	11	...	1
Other Bengalis and Chittagonians.	165	9	1	...	155	...	...	...
Oriya	645	1	...	...	640	4	...	...
Tamil	320	30	3	...	281	6	...	17
Telugu	366	20	4	...	340	2	...	6
All other Mahomedans	30	3	...	...	26	1	...	1
All others	51	8	...	...	43	...	...	1
Armateur-winder ...	8	6	2	...	2	...	...	2
Burmese	7	5	2	...	...	...	...	1
Anglo-Indian ...	1	1	...	...	...	...	...	1
Belt-maker—Other Hindustanis ...	1	...	...	...	...	...	...	...
Blacksmith	279	29	...	...	250	...	...	5
Home races ...	25	25	...	...	...	...	...	4
Chinese	12	...	...	...	12	...	...	...
Anglo-Indian ...	1	...	...	...	1	...	...	...
Indians	241	4	...	...	237	...	...	1

Industry, Skill, Occupation and Race.	Total Number	Born in Burma. Age 18 and over.	Born in Burma. Age 14 to 18.	Born in Burma. Age under 14.	Born outside Burma. Age 18 and over.	Born outside Burma. Age 14 to 18.	Born outside Burma. Age under 14.	See foot-note.
1	2	3	4	5	6	7	8	9
P. Construction of means of transport or communication—*contd.*								
Boilermaker ...	263	67	...	...	192	4	...	1
Burmese	63	63	...	...	...	...	...	...
Chinese	31	2	...	...	29	...	...	...
Anglo-Indian ...	1	1	...	...	...	...	...	1
Indians	168	1	...	...	163	4	...	...
Carpenter	1,305	746	11	...	545	3	...	170
Home races ...	730	720	10	...	...	...	...	165
Chinese	329	11	...	...	318	...	...	1
Anglo-Indian ...	1	1	...	...	...	...	...	...
Indians	245	14	1	...	227	3	...	4
Carriage-examiner .	16	1	...	...	15	...	...	...
Burmese	1	1	...	...	...	...	...	...
Indians	15	...	...	...	15	...	...	...
Chargeman	14	5	...	...	9	...	...	5
Burmese	1	1	...	...	...	...	...	1
Chinese	1	1	...	...	...	...	...	1
Anglo-Indian ...	7	2	...	...	5	...	...	2
Indians	5	1	...	...	4	...	...	1
Coppersmith	17	3	...	...	14	...	...	...
Burmese	2	2	...	...	...	...	...	...
Indians	15	1	...	...	14	...	...	...
Cushion-man—Other Hindustanis.	5	...	...	...	5	...	...	...
Draftsman	3	1	...	...	2	...	...	1
Burmese	1	1	...	...	...	...	...	1
Indians	2	...	...	...	2	...	...	...
Driller	51	2	...	...	49	...	...	...
Burmese	2	2	...	...	...	...	...	...
Indians	49	...	...	...	49	...	...	...
Driver	208	83	...	...	125	...	...	7
Home races ...	54	54	...	...	...	...	...	5
Chinese	2	2	...	...	...	...	...	...
European	1	...	...	...	1	...	...	...
Anglo-Indian ...	28	18	...	...	10	...	...	1
Indians	123	9	...	...	114	...	...	1
Electrician	49	30	...	...	19	...	...	5
Home races ...	24	24	...	...	...	...	...	4
Chinese	19	3	...	...	16	...	...	...
Anglo-Indian ...	1	1	...	...	...	...	...	1
Indians	5	2	...	...	3	...	...	...
Electric Linesman—Indians.	20	...	...	...	20	...	...	...
Engineer	110	83	7	...	16	4	...	34
Home races ...	38	36	2	...	...	...	...	16
Chinese	1	1	...	...	...	...	...	1
European	8	...	...	...	8	...	...	...
Anglo-Indian ...	55	45	5	...	4	3	...	17
Indians	8	3	...	...	4	1	...	...
Erector	3	1	...	...	2	...	...	...
European	1	...	...	...	1	...	...	...
Anglo-Indian ..	1	1	...	...	...	...	...	...
Goanese	1	...	...	...	1	...	...	...
Fireman	112	18	...	...	94	...	...	8
Home races ...	8	8	...	...	...	...	...	2
European	1	...	...	...	1	...	...	...
Anglo-Indian ...	5	4	...	...	1	...	...	2
Indians	98	6	...	...	92	...	...	4
Fitter	1,563	464	15	...	1,079	5	...	134
Home races ...	414	406	8	...	...	...	...	104
Chinese	14	7	...	...	7	...	...	4
Japanese	2	...	...	...	2	...	...	...
European	1	...	...	...	1	...	...	...
Anglo-Indian ...	40	23	4	...	12	1	...	10
Indians	1,092	28	3	...	1,057	4	...	16
Foreman	14	6	...	...	7	1	...	4
Burmese	1	1	...	...	...	...	...	1
Chinese	1	1	...	...	...	...	...	1
European	1	...	...	...	...	1	...	...
Anglo-Indian ...	11	4	...	...	7	...	...	2
Gunner—Anglo-Indian ...	1	...	...	...	1	...	...	...
Hoodman—Telugu ...	1	...	...	...	1	...	...	...
Improver	7	3	...	...	4	...	...	...
Burmese	2	2	...	...	...	...	...	...
Indians	5	1	...	...	4	...	...	...
Iron-worker—Indians ...	20	...	...	...	20	...	...	...
Latheman	6	1	...	...	5	...	...	...
Burmese	1	1	...	...	...	...	...	...
Indians	5	...	...	...	5	...	...	...
Lead-burner—Tamil ...	1	...	...	...	1	...	...	...
Leather-sewer ...	9	3	...	...	6	...	...	1
Burmese	2	2	...	...	...	...	...	...
Indians	7	1	...	...	6	...	...	1

Column 9 shows the number of age 18 or over who were born in Burma outside the district in which they were employed at the time of the Census.

IMPERIAL TABLE XXIIB.—THE SPECIAL INDUSTRIAL CENSUS (SELECTED INDUSTRIES).

PART II.—*Classification and Birthplaces of Labourers*—concluded.

Industry, Skill, Occupation and Race.	Total Number	Born in Burma. Age 18 and over.	Born in Burma. Age 14 to 18.	Born in Burma. Age under 14.	Born outside Burma. Age 18 and over.	Born outside Burma. Age 14 to 18.	Born outside Burma. Age under 14.	See foot-note.
1	2	3	4	5	6	7	8	9
P. Construction of means of transport or communication—*concld.*								
Machineman ...	94	28	...	...	65	1	...	5
Burmese ...	28	28	...	...	...	...	...	5
Indians ...	66	...	...	...	65	1	...	...
Mason—Hindustani Mahomedans.	2	...	...	...	2	...	...	...
Mechanic ...	179	117	19	...	39	4	...	24
Home races	120	104	16	...	...	...	...	21
Chinese ...	1	1	...	...	...	...	...	1
European ...	1	...	...	...	1	...	...	...
Anglo-Indian	17	7	3	...	4	3	...	1
Indians ...	40	5	...	...	34	1	...	1
Moulder ...	140	88	5	...	45	2	...	10
Home races	92	87	5	...	...	...	...	10
Indians ...	48	1	...	...	45	2	...	...
Nickel-plater	9	9	...	...	...	...	...	...
Zerbadi ...	7	7	...	...	...	...	...	...
Tamil ...	2	2	...	...	...	...	...	...
Painter ...	382	56	7	...	311	8	...	16
Home races	45	43	2	...	...	...	...	12
Chinese ...	1	...	...	...	1	...	...	...
Indians ...	336	13	5	...	310	8	...	4
Pattern-maker—Burmese	9	7	2	...	...	...	...	2
Plater—Indians ...	119	...	...	...	119	...	...	...
Plumber ...	10	2	...	...	8	...	...	...
Burmese ...	2	2	...	...	...	...	...	...
Indians ...	8	...	...	...	8	...	...	...
Rivetter ...	532	60	3	...	467	2	...	9
Home races	58	57	1	...	...	...	...	7
Indians ...	474	3	2	...	467	2	...	2
Roller-driver—Burmese	1	1	...	...	...	...	...	...
Sail-maker ...	41	1	...	...	40	...	...	...
Zerbadi ...	1	1	...	...	...	...	...	...
Indians ...	40	...	...	...	40	...	...	...
Sawyer ...	38	4	...	...	34	...	...	3
Burmese ...	4	4	...	...	...	...	...	3
Indians ...	34	...	...	...	34	...	...	...
Serang—Indians ...	11	...	...	...	11	...	...	...
Steam-hammer-driver—Tamil ...	2	1	...	...	1	...	...	1
Tailor ...	29	5	...	...	21	3	...	2
Zerbadi ...	1	1	...	...	...	...	...	...
Indians ...	28	4	...	...	21	3	...	2
Telephone-fitter—Other Hindustanis.	3	...	...	...	3	...	...	...
Tinsmith ...	45	17	9	...	18	1	...	5
Burmese ...	1	1	...	...	...	...	...	...
Other Home races ...	22	15	7	...	...	...	...	5
Anglo-Indian ...	2	...	2	...	...	...	...	...
Indians ...	20	1	...	...	18	1	...	...
Turner ...	126	49	3	...	72	2	...	7
Home races	40	40	...	...	...	...	...	5
Indians ...	86	9	3	...	72	2	...	2
Vulcanizer ...	23	22	1	...	...	...	...	4
Home races	19	19	...	...	...	...	...	3
Anglo-Indian	4	3	1	...	...	...	...	1
Watch-repairer—Other Bengalis and Chittagonians.	1	...	...		1	...	...	...
Welder ...	2	1	...	...	1	...	...	1
Burmese ...	1	1	...	...	...	...	...	1
Chinese ...	1	...	...	...	1	...	...	...
Wireman—Burmese ...	18	12	6	...	...	...	...	...

Industry, Skill, Occupation and Race.	Total Number	Born in Burma. Age 18 and over.	Born in Burma. Age 14 to 18.	Born in Burma. Age under 14.	Born outside Burma. Age 18 and over.	Born outside Burma. Age 14 to 18.	Born outside Burma. Age under 14.	See foot-note.
1	2	3	4	5	6	7	8	9
Section II.—Female Labourers of each selected Industry by Race and Occupation.								
A4. Rubber cultivation.								
All Unskilled Occupations	878	399	197	51	193	18	20	56
Burmese ...	460	282	147	31	...	...	...	41
Zerbadi ...	12	5	6	1	...	...	...	1
Other Home races ...	169	107	44	18	...	...	...	12
Chinese ...	1	...	...	...	1	...	...	...
Oriya ...	19	...	...	...	15	...	4	...
Tamil ...	5	2	...	1	2	...	...	...
Telugu ...	210	2	...	...	174	18	16	2
All other Mahomedans	1	1	...	...	...	...	...	...
All others ...	1	...	...	...	1	...	...	...
B1. Petroleum wells.								
All Unskilled Occupations Burmese ...	92	78	11	3	...	...	...	4
B2. Tin and Wolfram mines.								
All Unskilled Occupations	238	157	23	40	12	3	3	16
Burmese ...	160	119	12	29	...	...	...	11
Other Home races ...	54	38	10	6	...	...	...	5
Chinese ...	2	...	...	2	...	...	...	...
Punjabi Mahomedans and Pathans.	1	...	...	...	1	...	...	...
All others ...	21	...	1	3	11	3	3	...
B3. Silver and Lead mines.								
All Unskilled Occupations	8	5	1	2	...	...	...	4
Burmese ...	4	3	1	...	...	...	...	3
Other Home races ...	4	2	...	2	...	...	...	1
B5. Copper, Steatite and Coal mines.								
All Unskilled Occupations All others ...	6	...	...	...	...	5	1	...
J4. Petroleum refineries.								
All Unskilled Occupations	353	291	51	5	6	...	...	104
Burmese ...	189	245	39	5	...	...	...	100
Other Home races ...	58	46	12	...	...	...	...	4
European ...	1	...	...	...	1	...	...	...
Oriya ...	2	...	...	...	2	...	...	...
Telugu ...	3	...	...	...	3	...	...	...
P. Construction of means of transport or communication.								
All Unskilled Occupations Telugu ...	1	...	...	...	1	...	...	...
All Skilled Occupations Telephone Operator—Anglo-Indian ...	51	30	13	...	7	1	...	12
F2. Saw-mills.								
All Unskilled Occupations	276	216	44	10	5	...	1	66
Burmese ...	260	[illegible]	44	10	...	...	...	64
Zerbadi ...	2	2	...	...	...	...	...	...
Other Home races ...	1	1	...	...	...	...	...	...
Tamil ...	1	...	...	...	1	...	...	...
Telugu ...	11	7	...	...	3	...	1	2
All others ...	1	...	...	...	1	...	...	...
K3. Rice-mills.								
All Unskilled Occupations	981	522	121	18	267	26	27	466
Burmese ...	627	507	108	12	...	...	...	64
Zerbadi ...	7	3	4	...	...	...	...	...
Other Home races ...	2	2	...	...	...	...	...	...
Hindustani Mahomedans.	1	...	...	...	1	...	...	...
Other Hindustanis ...	3	...	...	...	3	...	...	...
Bengali and Chittagonian Mahomedans.	2	2	...	...	...	...	...	...
Oriya ...	5	...	2	...	3	...	...	...
Tamil ...	30	1	2	...	26	1	...	...
Telugu ...	304	7	5	6	234	25	27	2

Column 9 shows the number of age 18 or over who were born in Burma outside the district in which they were employed at the time of the Census.

IMPERIAL TABLE XXIIb.—THE SPECIAL INDUSTRIAL CENSUS (SELECTED INDUSTRIES).

PART IIIa.—*Duration of residence in Burma of* Male *labourers born outside Burma.*

NOTE.—This table relates to all labourers employed in the Selected Industries who were born outside Burma. The *Permanent Residents* are those amongst the labourers tabulated in the other columns who stated that they intended to complete their lives in Burma.

Race and Skill.	Age-group.	All labourers born outside Burma. Total Number.	Completed years of residence. 0	1	2	3, 4	5–9	10 or over.	Permanent Residents in Burma. Total Number.	Completed years of residence. 0	1	2	3, 4	5–9	10 or over.
1	2	3	4	5	6	7	8	9	10	11	12	13	14	15	16
All races ..	...	67,072	11,945	10,270	10,271	11,459	11,983	11,144	3,099	191	222	278	334	499	1,575
Skilled ...	...	10,743	1,115	910	1,196	1,645	2,164	3,713	769	22	10	20	33	109	575
	0–14	2	1	...	...	...	...	1	...	...	...	...	...	...	...
	14–18	86	23	12	19	13	9	10	6	3	...	...	...	2	1
	18 & over.	10,655	1,091	898	1,177	1,632	2,155	3,702	763	19	10	20	33	107	574
Unskilled ...	...	56,329	10,830	9,360	9,075	9,814	9,819	7,431	2,330	169	212	258	301	390	1,000
	0–14	631	172	221	123	84	23	8	6	2	...	1	...	1	2
	14–18	2,297	660	563	562	343	114	55	85	12	29	13	8	4	19
	18 & over.	53,401	9,998	8,576	8,390	9,387	9,682	7,368	2,239	155	183	244	293	385	979
Yünnanese ...	...	557	238	43	86	98	71	21	10	...	...	...	...	1	9
Skilled ..	18 & over.	4	1	...	...	1	1	1	1	...	...	...	...	...	1
Unskilled ...	...	553	237	43	86	97	70	20	9	...	...	...	...	1	8
	0–14	3	2	...	...	1	...	...	...	...	...	...	...	...	...
	14–18	33	23	3	3	4	...	...	...	...	...	...	...	...	...
	18 & over.	517	212	40	83	92	70	20	9	...	...	...	...	1	8
Chinese ..	..	3,340	155	222	213	450	1,430	870	320	29	1	7	24	75	184
Skilled ..	...	1,051	46	54	77	150	293	431	130	6	...	2	5	27	90
	14–18	1	...	...	...	1	...	...	...	...	...	...	...	...	...
	18 & over.	1,050	46	54	77	149	293	431	130	6	...	2	5	27	90
Unskilled ...	...	2,289	109	168	136	300	1,137	439	190	23	1	5	19	48	94
	0–14	1	1	...	...	...	...	...	...	...	...	...	...	...	...
	14–18	10	5	...	...	3	1	1	1	1	...	...	...	...	...
	18 & over.	2,278	103	168	136	297	1,136	438	189	22	1	5	19	48	94
Japanese															
Skilled ...	18 & over.	2	1	...	...	1	...	...	...	...	...	...	...	...	...
Maingtha, Shan, and Khamuk.	...	454	149	60	38	51	67	89	78	...	...	...	...	8	70
Skilled ...	18 & over.	1	...	1	...	...	...	...	...	...	...	...	...	...	...
Unskilled ...	...	453	149	59	38	51	67	89	78	...	...	...	...	8	70
	14–18	5	3	1	...	...	1	...	...	...	...	...	...	...	...
	18 & over.	448	146	58	38	51	66	89	78	...	...	...	...	8	70
European ...	...	61	17	3	2	2	11	26	12	2	...	...	...	4	6
Skilled ..	...	39	13	3	1	...	7	15	8	2	...	...	...	1	5
	14–18	1	1	...	...	...	...	...	1	1	...	...	...	...	...
	18 & over.	38	12	3	1	...	7	15	7	1	...	...	...	1	5
Unskilled ...	18 & over.	22	4	...	1	2	4	11	4	...	...	...	...	3	1
Anglo-Indian ...	...	160	16	2	7	12	20	103	81	5	...	2	4	3	67
Skilled ...	...	101	8	1	4	6	10	72	59	2	...	2	4	2	49
	14–18	9	3	...	2	...	1	3	2	1	...	...	...	...	1
	18 & over.	92	5	1	2	6	9	69	57	1	...	2	4	2	48
Unskilled ...	...	59	8	1	3	6	10	31	22	3	...	...	...	1	18
	14–18	1	...	...	...	...	...	1	...	...	...	...	...	...	...
	18 & over.	58	8	1	3	6	10	30	22	3	...	...	...	1	18

IMPERIAL TABLE XXIIB.—THE SPECIAL INDUSTRIAL CENSUS (SELECTED INDUSTRIES).

PART IIIA.—*Duration of residence in Burma of* Male *labourers born outside Burma.*

NOTE.—This table relates to all labourers employed in the Selected Industries who were born outside Burma. The *Permanent Residents* are those amongst the labourers tabulated in the other columns who stated that they intended to complete their lives in Burma.

Race and Skill.	Age-group.	All labourers born outside Burma. Total Number.	Completed years of residence. 0	1	2	3, 4	5–9	10 or over.	Permanent Residents in Burma. Total Number.	Completed years of residence. 0	1	2	3, 4	5–9	10 or over.
1	2	3	4	5	6	7	8	9	10	11	12	13	14	15	16
Sikh ...	...	187	20	15	26	20	32	74	11	1	...	2	...	2	6
Skilled ...	...	85	5	3	7	10	19	41	3	...	...	...	...	1	2
	14–18	1	...	...	1	...	...	...	...	...	...	...	...	...	...
	18 & over.	84	5	3	6	10	19	41	3	...	...	...	...	1	2
Unskilled ...	...	102	15	12	19	10	13	33	8	1	...	2	...	1	4
	14–18	2	2	...	...	...	...	...	...	...	...	...	...	...	...
	18 & over.	100	13	12	19	10	13	33	8	1	...	2	...	1	4
Punjabi Mahomedans and Pathan.	...	343	40	30	36	55	72	110	29	1	...	1	1	3	23
Skilled ...	18 & over.	144	17	12	14	21	32	48	11	...	...	...	...	1	10
Unskilled ...		199	23	18	22	34	40	62	18	1	...	1	1	2	13
	0–14	1	...	...	1	...	...	...	...	...	...	...	...	...	...
	14–18	3	1	2	...	...	...	...	...	...	...	...	...	...	...
	18 & over.	195	22	16	21	34	40	62	18	1	...	1	1	2	13
Other Punjabis (*i.e.* not Sikh nor Mahomedan).	...	730	109	109	92	122	110	188	18	...	...	...	...	...	18
Skilled ...	...	456	75	44	52	71	80	134	7	...	...	...	...	...	7
	14–18	6	...	1	1	2	...	2	...	...	...	...	...	...	...
	18 & over.	450	75	43	51	69	80	132	7	...	...	...	...	...	7
Unskilled ...	...	274	34	65	40	51	30	54	11	...	...	...	...	...	11
	0–14	1	...	1	...	...	...	...	...	...	...	...	...	...	...
	14–18	8	2	3	1	1	...	1	...	...	...	...	...	...	...
	18 & over.	265	32	61	39	50	30	53	11	...	...	...	...	...	11
Hindustani Mahomedans.	...	1,089	234	118	139	173	198	227	52	1	1	3	9	7	31
Skilled ...	18 & over.	235	27	12	17	36	49	94	16	...	...	...	...	3	13
Unskilled ...	...	854	207	106	122	137	149	133	36	1	1	3	9	4	18
	0–14	3	1	...	1	...	1	...	...	...	...	...	...	...	...
	14–18	12	4	2	3	2	1	...	...	...	...	...	...	...	...
	18 & over.	839	202	104	118	135	147	133	36	1	1	3	9	4	18
Other Hindustanis	...	8,695	1,565	1,053	1,327	1,517	1,669	1,564	264	26	23	27	31	39	118
Skilled ...	...	1,493	160	93	179	235	344	482	46	...	1	2	1	8	34
	0–14	1	1	...	...	...	...	...	...	...	...	...	...	...	...
	14–18	9	4	2	3	...	...	...	...	...	...	...	...	...	...
	18 & over.	1,483	155	91	176	235	344	482	46	...	1	2	1	8	34
Unskilled ...	...	7,202	1,405	960	1,148	1,282	1,325	1,082	218	26	22	25	30	31	84
	0–14	35	7	6	17	3	2	...	1	...	...	1	...	...	...
	14–18	196	45	43	72	28	4	4	4	1	2	...	1	...	...
	18 & over.	6,971	1,353	911	1,059	1,251	1,319	1,078	213	25	20	24	29	31	84
Bengali and Chittagonian Mahomedans.	...	12,247	2,357	1,512	1,782	1,983	2,069	2,544	531	21	22	45	62	96	285
Skilled ...	...	3,335	438	354	381	497	626	1,039	148	5	3	7	9	24	100
	14–18	30	10	7	4	6	2	1	...	...	...	...	...	...	...
	18 & over.	3,305	428	347	377	491	624	1,038	148	5	3	7	9	24	100
Unskilled ...	...	8,912	1,919	1,158	1,401	1,486	1,443	1,505	383	16	19	38	53	72	185
	0–14	13	9	3	1	...	...	...	...	...	...	...	...	...	...
	14–18	197	65	60	37	21	8	6	9	1	4	2	2	...	...
	18 & over.	8,702	1,845	1,095	1,363	1,465	1,435	1,499	374	15	15	36	51	72	185

IMPERIAL TABLE XXIIB.—THE SPECIAL INDUSTRIAL CENSUS (SELECTED INDUSTRIES).

PART IIIA.—*Duration of residence in Burma of* **Male** *labourers born outside Burma.*

NOTE.—This table relates to all labourers employed in the Selected Industries who were born outside Burma. The *Permanent Residents* are those amongst the labourers tabulated in the other columns who stated that they intended to complete their lives in Burma.

Race and Skill.	Age-group.	All labourers born outside Burma. Total Number.	Completed years of residence. 0	1	2	3, 4	5–9	10 or over.	Permanent Residents in Burma. Total Number.	Completed years of residence. 0	1	2	3, 4	5–9	10 or over.
1	2	3	4	5	6	7	8	9	10	11	12	13	14	15	16
Other Bengalis and Chittagonians.	...	1,109	244	127	173	188	162	215	37	3	...	1	3	8	22
Skilled ...	18 & over.	391	56	37	61	59	60	118	14	1	...		...	1	12
Unskilled	...	718	188	90	112	129	102	97	23	2	...	1	3	7	10
	0–14	1	1	...	...	...	...	...	...	...	...	...	...	...	...
	14–18	28	12	7	5	4	...	...		...	...	...	...	...	...
	18 & over.	689	175	83	107	125	102	97	23	2	...	1	3	7	10
Oriya ...	...	11,600	2,471	2,552	2,039	2,000	1,695	843	351	21	47	66	67	59	91
Skilled ...	...	899	85	100	124	172	206	212	26	...	...	2	2	2	20
	14–18	7	1	...	4	1	1	...	...	...	...	...	...	...	...
	18 & over.	892	84	100	120	171	205	212	26	...	...	2	2	2	20
Unskilled ...	...	10,701	2,386	2,452	1,915	1,828	1,489	631	325	21	47	64	65	57	71
	0–14	137	50	53	20	10	1	3	...	...	...	...	...	...	...
	14–18	478	145	132	116	69	14	2	1	...	...	...	1	...	...
	18 & over.	10,086	2,191	2,267	1,779	1,749	1,474	626	324	21	47	64	64	57	71
Tamil ...	...	1,092	97	72	103	129	221	470	171	4	2	6	4	16	139
Skilled ...	...	462	31	17	32	38	91	253	89	3	...	3	4	8	71
	14–18	10	2	1	2	...	3	2	3	1	...	...	...	2	...
	18 & over.	452	29	16	30	38	88	251	86	2	...	3	4	6	71
Unskilled ...	...	630	66	55	71	91	130	217	82	1	2	3	...	8	68
	0–14	11	1	2	1	1	4	2	3	...	...	...	...	1	2
	14–18	16	3	1	4	1	2	5	...	...	...	...	...	...	...
	18 & over.	603	62	52	66	89	124	210	79	1	2	3	...	7	66
Telugu ...	...	23,833	3,829	4,181	3,982	4,409	3,882	3,550	1,014	70	124	113	126	147	434
Skilled ...	...	1,874	127	170	233	322	309	713	194	3	5	1	8	29	148
	0–14	1	...	...	...	...	...	1	...	...	...	...	...	...	...
	14–18	11	2	1	2	3	2	1	...	...	...	...	...	...	...
	18 & over.	1,862	125	169	231	319	307	711	194	3	5	1	8	29	148
Unskilled ...	...	21,959	3,702	4,011	3,749	4,087	3,573	2,837	820	67	119	112	118	118	286
	0–14	419	99	155	82	68	13	2	2	2	...	...	...	...	...
	14–18	1,274	331	307	317	207	80	32	65	8	23	11	4	3	16
	18 & over.	20,266	3,272	3,549	3,350	3,812	3,480	2,803	753	57	96	101	114	115	270
Other Mahomedans	...	130	23	7	22	11	19	48	22	1	1	...	2	2	16
Skilled ...	...	38	8	1	3	1	6	19	6	...	1	...	...	...	5
	14–18	1	...	...	...	...	...	1	...	...	...	...	...	...	...
	18 & over.	37	8	1	3	1	6	18	6	...	1	...	...	...	5
Unskilled ...	...	92	15	6	19	10	13	29	16	1	...	...	2	2	11
	14–18	3	2	...	1	...	...	...	...	...	...	...	...	...	...
	18 & over.	89	13	6	18	10	13	29	16	1	...	...	2	2	11
Others—Not Mahomedans	...	1,443	380	164	204	238	255	202	98	6	1	5	1	29	56
Skilled ...	18 & over.	133	17	8	11	25	31	41	11	...	...	1	...	2	8
Unskilled ...	...	1,310	363	156	193	213	224	161	87	6	1	4	1	27	48
	0–14	6	1	1	...	1	2	1	...	...	...	...	...	...	...
	14–18	31	17	2	3	3	3	3	5	1	...	...	...	1	3
	18 & over.	1,273	345	153	190	209	219	157	82	5	1	4	1	26	45

IMPERIAL TABLE XXIIB.—THE SPECIAL INDUSTRIAL CENSUS (SELECTED INDUSTRIES).

PART IIIB.—*Duration of residence in Burma of* **Female** *labourers born outside Burma.*

NOTE.—(1) This table relates to all labourers employed in the Selected Industries who were born outside Burma. The *Permanent Residents* are those amongst the labourers tabulated in the other columns who stated that they intended to complete their lives in Burma.

(2) No Mahomedan females of any race not shown in this table were recorded, neither were any females of any religion of the following races for which entries are given for males in the preceding table, Japanese, Maingtha, Shan, Khamuk, Sikh, Other Punjabis, Bengali Chittagonian.

Race and Skill.	Age-group.	All labourers born outside Burma. Total Number.	Completed years of residence: 0	1	2	3, 4	5–9	10 or over.	Permanent Residents in Burma. Total Number.	Completed years of residence: 0	1	2	3, 4	5–9	10 or over.
1	2	3	4	5	6	7	8	9	10	11	12	13	14	15	16
All Races ...	...	596	110	49	97	141	114	85	17	1	...	..	1	3	12
Skilled ..	...	8	...	...	...	1	2	5	8	...	...	..	1	2	5
	0–14	...	.	...	...	...	..	...	...	...	...	...	...	-	...
	14–18	1	...	...	..	...	1	...	1	..	...	...	...	1	...
	18 & over.	7	..	...	...	1	1	5	7	..	.	...	1	1	5
Unskilled ...	...	588	110	49	97	140	112	80	9	1	...	...	...	1	7
	0–14	52	9	8	14	10	10	1	..	..	...	...	...	...	...
	14–18	52	16	5	5	15	9	2	2	...	...	...	...	1	1
	18 & over.	484	85	36	78	115	93	77	7	1	...	...	...	...	6
Yünnanese ...	All	...	...	...	...	...	...	..	...	...	..	...	..	...	..
Other Chinese															
Unskilled ...	18 & over.	1	.	...	...	..	...	1	1	...	...	...	...	...	1
European															
Unskilled ...	15 & over.	1	1	..	...	...	...	...	...	...	...	...	...	...	...
Anglo-Indian															
Skilled ...	...	8		..	...	1	2	5	8	...	...	...	1	2	5
	14–18	1	.	...	...	...	1	...	1	...	...	...	..	1	...
	18 & over.	7	..	...	...	1	1	5	7	...	...	...	1	1	5
Punjabi Mahomedans and Pathans.															
Unskilled ...	18 & over.	1	...	...	...	1	...	..	...	...	...	...	...	...	...
Hindustani Mahomedans															
Unskilled ...	18 & over.	1	...	1	...	...	...	...	..	...	...	...	...	...	...
Other Hindustanis															
Unskilled ...	18 & over.	3	...	...	2	...	...	1	...	...	...	...	...	...	...
Oriya															
Unskilled ...	...	24	10	1	2	2	5	4	...	...	...	...	...	...	...
	0–14	4	1	1	...	...	1	1	...	...	...	...	..	...	...
	18 & over.	20	9	...	2	2	4	3	...	...	...	...	...	...	...
Tamil															
Unskilled ...	...	30	...	...	3	6	9	12	3	..	...	...	...	1	2
	14–18	1	...	...	...	...	1	..	1	...	.	...	...	1	...
	18 & over.	29	...	...	3	6	8	12	2	..	...	...	...	...	2
Telugu															
Unskilled ...	...	502	98	47	88	127	88	54	4	1	...	...	...	...	3
	0–14	44	7	7	13	10	7	...	...	...	...	...	...	...	...
	14–18	43	16	5	5	11	5	1	1	...	...	...	...	...	1
	18 & over.	415	75	35	70	106	76	53	3	1	...	...	...	...	2
Others															
Unskilled ...	...	25	1	...	2	4	10	8	1	...	...	...		...	1
	0–14	4	1	...	1	...	2	...	...	...	...	...	...	...	...
	14–18	8	...	...	...	4	3	1	...	...	...	...	...	...	...
	18 & over.	13	...	...	1	...	5	7	1	...	...	...	...	...	1

PROVINCIAL TABLE I.

Area and Population of Townships, States and Hill-Tracts.

NOTE 1.—Numbers added in brackets after the names in column 1 of the table are references to the notes below bearing those numbers.

NOTE 2.—The term *town* in column 3 connotes only towns defined as such under the Burma Towns Act and differs therefore from the term *Census town* used in Imperial Tables I, III, IV and V. Note 3 of Imperial Table IV and column 3 of Imperial Tables IV and V indicate the relationship of the two meanings.

NOTE 3.—For the Hill District of Arakan, the Pakôkku Hill-Tracts, the Chin Hills district, the Eastern States and all hill-tracts included in other districts the figures given in column 4 represent *villages*. For other areas there is no record of the total number of villages available; column 4 for these areas (except Putao district) shows *village-tracts* and not villages. A village-tract is defined by law as the local area under the jurisdiction of a headman, including a village or group of villages and adjacent lands. In practice it may include no true village at all but only a number of small clusters of houses scattered through a comparatively extensive area. On the other hand a village may be shared by two or more village-tracts, some of which may include parts or wholes of other villages. On account of numerous recent revisions of village-tract boundaries in some townships the numbers given in column 4 must be regarded only as close approximations for the early part of the year 1922. For Putao district see the foot-note added to the entry.

NOTE 4.—No entry for villages has been made in column 4 for the Somra Tract (item No. 208) or East Manglün (item No. 236) which are two of the areas in which the census was made by estimate only. Totals for all areas including these are affected accordingly. The third area in which the census was by estimate was the part of the Pakôkku Hill-Tracts represented by item No. 141 for which however all columns except column 6 have been filled.

NOTE 5.—No town as defined for this table can include the whole or any part of a village-tract; for this reason the number of village-tracts shown in Imperial Tables I and III differs from that shown in this table which is in each case the correct number of statutory village-tracts as nearly as that could be determined.

NOTE 6.—Columns 5 and 6 do not relate to village-tracts but to villages in the sense of continuous blocks of residences within a single village-tract. For these columns the divisions of a continuous block of residences made by a village-tract boundary crossing it are regarded as separate villages. *Town* has for these columns also the meaning given to it in Note 2 above.

NOTE 7.—The definition of a house on which the numbers in columns 5 to 7 depend was ordinarily as follows:—

> A *house* means the separate residence of a family. A residence is considered to be separate when it has a separate entrance from a common way.
>
> If one building is jointly occupied by two or more families it should be treated as one house if the families share meals, but as two or more if they cook and eat separately.
>
> *Monasteries, Zayats, Schools, Godowns and Field Huts* and all other buildings are to be included in the term "House" if used as dwelling-places, whether used at night or not. They must always be included if a watchman or durwan lives there.

In Rangoon Town and occasionally in other towns *house* was taken to mean a tenement; and this definition was generally substituted for the ordinary one for lodging-houses and coolie-lines and similar cases. Amongst some tribes in which there is a custom of building extensions of a house for all descendants of the original householder, the term house was generally taken to mean the residence of the whole group of relations; this variation from the normal definition would only affect the figures in a few remote areas.

NOTE 8.—Adjustments of population have been made throughout so as to give in column 11 the population in 1911 of the area which was included at the census of 1921 in the township or other administrative unit named in column 1, and in column 12 the rate of variation for that area. For districts a similar adjustment has also been made for the population in 1901, so that the figures of column 13 also relate to the area included in each district in 1921. No such adjustments however have been made for the population of townships in 1901; the figures given for townships in column 13 represent, therefore, the variation of population in the period 1901 to 1911 found in 1911 for the area which at the time of the census of 1911 was included in the township named in column 1. In some cases where that unit has been newly formed since 1911 and differs greatly from any similar unit existing then, column 13 has been left blank. For the purposes of this note the Northern Shan States, the Southern Shan States and Karenni are to be regarded as three districts, while the states included in them are to be regarded as townships.

NOTE 9.—The following items in the table include areas in which no census was made in 1911, and for which therefore the figures of columns 8 and 11 are not strictly comparable :—

District.		Area omitted in 1911 and number of item in the table which includes it.					
				Census of 1921.			
Serial No.	Name.	Item No.	Description.	Kind of Enumeration.	Persons.	Males.	Females.
6	Hanthawaddy ...	28*	Coco Islands ...	Synchronous ...	46	40	6
28	Myitkyina ...	155	Htawgaw Kachin Hill Tracts.	Non-synchronous.	17,305	8,745	8,560
		158*	Sana Kachin Hill Tracts.	Do.	979	484	495
		157*			2,773	1,331	1,442
30	Putao ...	174	Hkamti Lông States	Do.	7,673	4,144	3,529
34	Upper Chindwin ...	208	Somra Tract ...	Estimate ..	7,636	3,719	3,917
40	Northern Shan States	236*	East Manglün ...	Do. ...	26,701	13,527	13,174
* Included in this item of the table but not constituting the whole of it.				Total ...	63,113	31,990	31,123

Totals for all areas which include these areas are effected by this extension of the census if comparison with the census of 1911 is made. In calculating the figures for column 12 of the table the above figures have first been deducted from the 1921 figures.

NOTE 10.—The number of square miles given for Rangoon Municipality excludes the area covered by the rivers and lakes and thus differs from the statement of 27·97 square miles which was adopted for the corresponding table of 1911, although it represents the same area of habitations. The area covered by water has been added to that of the Port in column 2.

NOTE 11.—Some of the entries for area given in column 2 of the table (especially for units which lie along the inland boundary of the province) include estimates or approximations reached by rough surveys, and in some such cases revised figures have been adopted since the census of 1911. In some other cases area-figures, although based on complete survey, have been changed by a revision of the survey or as a consequence of erosion or accretion by rivers. Some district or township boundaries and areas have been changed since 1911 by the transfer of land which in some cases had no population in 1911.

NOTE 12.—An effort has been made to get the account of changes in townships and districts which is given in Notes 13 to 19 below as complete as possible; and it is hoped that any omissions are insignificant.

NOTE 13.—In the following districts there was no change in township names or boundaries between the census of 1911 and that of 1921 :—

(1) Akyab, (2) Hill District of Arakan, (3) Kyaukpyu, (4) Sandoway, (15) Pyapôn, (17) Salween, (20) Tavoy, (27) Mandalay, (32) Shwebo, (33) Sagaing.

NOTE 14.—In the cases shown in the margin the name of a township shown in one district in the table of 1911 has been shown under a different district in 1921. The Karenni States are also shown separately in this table instead of being shown as parts of the Southern Shan States.

Township.		District.	
		1921.	1911.
22	Hlègu ...	Insein ...	Pegu ...
23	Insein ...	Insein ...	Hanthawaddy ...
24	Taikkyi .	Insein ...	Hanthawaddy ...
25	Tantabin ...	Insein ...	Hanthawaddy ...
136	Sale ...	Magwe ...	Myingyan ...

NOTE 15.—In the Upper Chindwin District (No. 35) the name of township No. 204 has been changed from Kindat to Mawlaik without a change of boundaries.

NOTE 16.—The following are new names in the table which represent townships formed since 1911 by re-arranging boundaries of townships existing in 1911:—

	District.	Township.		District.	Township.		District.	Township.
7	Hanthawaddy.	Kungyangôn N. Kungyangôn S. Syriam.	8	Tharrawaddy.	Letpadan East. Letpadan West. Minhla East. Minhla West. Zigôn.	13	Myaungmya	Labutta.
11	Bassein	Bassein East. Bassein West.				19	Amherst ...	Kya-in.
						22	Thayetmyo	Sinbaungwè.

NOTE 17.—No townships of the corresponding table of 1911 have been simply divided into two townships without other change of boundary.

NOTE 18.—The Bassein township, which was included in the table of 1911, does not appear in this table because it has been shared (with other areas) by the Bassein East and Bassein West townships (Nos. 54 and 55). Similarly the Sinbo Kachin Hills are now included in the Myitkyina Kachin Hills (No. 158) and the Namkhai State in the Loilong State (No. 274).

NOTE 19.—The townships, states and tracts shown in the following list have suffered a change in boundary in the interval between the census of 1911 and that of 1921 without a change of name :—

	District.	Township.		District.	Township.
6	Insein ...	Hlègu.	22	Thayetmyo	Minhla, Allanmyo.
7	Hanthawaddy	Kyauktan, Thôngwa, Kayan.	23	Pakôkku	Pakôkku.
8	Tharrawaddy	Tharrawaddy, Nattalin, Mônyo, Gyobingauk.	24	Minbu	Pwinbyu, Salin.
			25	Magwe	Sale, Yenangyaung.
9	Pegu ...	Kawa, Thanatpin, Pegu, Daiku, Nyaunglebin.	28	Bhamo	Shwegu, Kachin Hill Tracts.
10	Prome ...	Prome, Paukkaung, Hmawza, Shwedaung.	29	Myitkyina	Myitkyina, Mogaung, Kamaing ; and Myitkyina, Mogaung, Kamaing and Sima Kachin Hill Tracts.
11	Bassein ...	Thabaung.			
12	Henzada ...	Lemyethna.	34	L. Chindwin	Budalin, Mônywa, Salingyi, Pale, Kani.
13	Myaungmya	Myaungmya, Wakèma, Mawlamyainggyun.	35	U. Chindwin	Thaungdut State.
14	Ma-ubin ...	Ma-ubin, Pantanaw, Yandoon, Danubyu.	37	Kyauksè	Myittha.
			38	Meiktila	Thazi, Wundwin.
16	Toungoo ..	Kyaukgyi, Leiktho, Shwegyin, Toungoo, Yedashe.	39	Yamèthin	Yamèthin, Pyawbwè, Lewè.
			40	Myingyan	Pagan, Kyaukpadaung, Taungtha, Myingyan, Natogyi.
18	Thatôn ...	Kyaikto, Paung, Thatôn, Bilin.			
19	Amherst ..	Kawkareik, Kyaikmaraw.	41	N. Shan States	Möngmit.
			42	S. Shan States	Loilong, Hsa Möng Hkam.

NOTE 20.—There is some difficulty about the figures in column 21 for the Somra Tract and for Thaungdut State which are items Nos. 208 and 210 of the table. It was originally stated that the whole Somra Tract had been omitted from the 1911 census, but later it was reported by the local officers that an area which was transferred to the tract from Thaungdut State in 1920 had been censused in 1911 as part of that state and had a population of 259. Meanwhile Note 8 of Imperial Table II, Note 9 of this table and other statements had been prepared in which the whole population estimated in the Somra Tract was associated with the extension of the census area to include that tract. The number of 259 involved is negligible for all purposes except the calculation of the variation of population in Thaungdut State. Accordingly the whole of the Somra Tract has been uniformly regarded as an extension of the census area throughout the census report, except in this table, where the 259 persons of 1911 have been entered for the Somra Tract so as to maintain the correct total for the Upper Chindwin district while still giving correct figures for Thaungdut State in 1911.

PROVINCIAL TABLE I.—*Area and Population of Townships, etc.*

Serial No.	Township, State, etc.	Area in square miles.	Number of: Towns under the Burma Towns Act.	Number of: Village Tracts.	Number of Villages (Towns excluded): Exceeding 100 houses.	Number of Villages (Towns excluded): Having 40 to 99 houses.	Total number of occupied houses, 1921.	Population 1921: Persons.	Population 1921: Males.	Population 1921: Females.	Population 1911: Persons.	Percentage of variation of total population: 1911 to 1921.	Percentage of variation of total population: 1901 to 1911.	Number of persons per square mile in 1921.
	1	2	3	4	5	6	7	8	9	10	11	12	13	14
	Provincial Total (3, 4)	**233,707**	**54**	**35,090**	**4,711**	**15,067**	**2,727,451**	**13,212,192**	**6,756,969**	**6,455,223**	**12,115,217**	**+ 8·5***	**+ 15·0***	**57**
	Divisional Burma (3, 4) ...	*173,114*	*54*	*16,367*	*4,624*	*14,151*	*2,427,151*	*11,714,800*	*5,999,549*	*5,715,251*	*10,702,849*	*+9·1**	*+ 14·9**	*68*
	Eastern States (3, 4) ...	*60,593*	...	*18,723*	*87*	*916*	*300,300*	*1,497 392*	*757,420*	*739,972*	*1,412,368*	*+4·1**	*+ 15·7**	...
	Arakan Division.	**14,807**	**3**	**1,442**	**275**	**1,336**	**189,892**	**909,246**	**472,227**	**437,019**	**839,896**	**+ 8**	**+ 10**	**61**
	1. Akyab District.	*5,136*	*1*	*870*	*189*	*884*	*117,396*	*576,430*	*309,564*	*266,866*	*529,943*	*+ 9*	*+ 10*	*112*
1	Akyab	72	1	18	8	22	9,516	48,188	33,894	14,294	49,539	— 3	+ 4	669
2	Buthidaung	796	...	95	19	112	14,300	78,497	40,835	37,662	63,679	+ 23	+ 6	99
3	Kyauktaw	562	...	96	22	127	12,597	58,274	31,642	26,632	55,820	+ 4	+ 4	104
4	Maungdaw	440	...	141	32	157	20,981	118,205	59,461	58,744	101,134	+ 17	+ 21	269
5	Minbya	899	...	92	12	93	10,941	51,388	27,729	23,659	47,795	+ 8	+ 14	57
6	Myohaung	567	...	124	16	109	13,664	61,089	33,446	27,643	58,032	+ 5	+ 26	108
7	Pauktaw	656	...	79	17	77	11,008	45,615	23,902	21,713	45,350	+ 1	+ 4	70
8	Pônnagyun	783	...	147	23	108	12,227	53,581	27,327	26,254	51,805	+ 3	+ 4	68
9	Rathedaung	361	.	78	41	79	12,162	61,593	31,328	30,265	56,789	+ 8	+ 7	171
	2. Hill District of Arakan (8).	*1,500*	...	*41*	*25*	*13*	*5,303*	*20,914*	*10,790*	*10,124*	*22,234*	*— 6*	*+ 7*	*14*
10	Paletwa	1,500	..	41	25	13	5,303	20,914	10,790	10,124	22,234	— 6	+ 7	14
	3. Kyaukpyu District.	*4,387*	*1*	*354*	*31*	*314*	*44,659*	*199,873*	*96,569*	*103,304*	*184,916*	*+ 8*	*+ 10*	*46*
11	An	1,877	...	64	2	14	7,957	35,079	17,980	17,099	32,855	+ 7	+ 12	19
12	Cheduba	308	...	51	13	47	7,188	32,521	15,389	17,132	30,197	+ 8	+ 12	106
13	Kyaukpyu	594	1	92	6	77	11,652	51,134	24,809	26,325	46,195	+ 11	+ 8	86
14	Myebôn	1,008	...	70	6	29	6,427	30,698	15,664	15,034	28,880	+ 6	+ 19	30
15	Ramree	600	...	77	4	147	11,435	50,441	22,727	27,714	46,789	+ 8	+ 1	84
	4. Sandoway District.	*3,784*	*1*	*177*	*30*	*125*	*22,534*	*112,029*	*55,304*	*56,725*	*102,803*	*+ 9*	*+ 13*	*30*
16	Gwa	803	...	42	6	23	4,705	23,702	12,026	11,676	21,963	+ 8	+ 19	30
17	Sandoway	1,318	1	81	11	52	9,596	48,116	23,777	24,339	43,215	+ 12	+ 9	37
18	Taungup	1,663	...	54	13	50	8,233	40,211	19,501	20,710	37,625	+ 7	+ 14	24
	Pegu Division.	**13,707**	**11**	**2,279**	**778**	**2,593**	**462,141**	**2,309,293**	**1,258,914**	**1,050,379**	**2,085,487**	**+ 11**	**+ 14**	**168**
	5. Rangoon Town District.	*76*	*2*	...	...	...	*58,047*	*341,962*	*236,689*	*105,273*	*293,316*	*+ 17*	*+ 20*	..
19	Municipality (10)	21·95	1	...	..	...	56,481	321,690	218,719	102,941	274,967	+ 17	+ 31	14,656
20	Cantonment—Civil and Military	1·47	1	...	...	.	919 647	3,897 2,574	2,870 1,670	1,027 904	} 8,381	— 23	— 39	4,403
21	Port (10)	52·52	...	...	..	...	...	13,801	13,400	401	9,968	...	...	...
	6. Insein District.	*1,904*	*1*	*375*	*102*	*378*	*60,110*	*293,083*	*156,794*	*136,289*	*265,245*	*+ 10*	*+ 17*	*154*
22	Hlègu (14, 29)	595	...	84	25	92	11,513	58,076	30,059	28,017	58,705	— 1	+ 17	98
23	Insein (14)	396	1	148	53	103	22,579	110,849	62,721	48,128	101,650	+ 9	+ 15	280
24	Taikkyi (14)	585	..	72	11	101	15,828	69,183	36,158	33,025	58,221	+ 19	+ 18	118
25	Tantabin (14)	328	...	71	13	82	10,190	54,975	27,856	27,119	46,669	+ 18	+ 16	168
	7. Hanthawaddy District (9).	*1,866*	*2*	*468*	*252*	*384*	*70,571*	*364,624*	*201,043*	*163,581*	*332,569*	*+ 10*	*+ 12*	*195*
26	Kayan (19)	272	...	67	30	65	10,641	59,706	31,951	27,755	52,603	+ 14	+ 11	220
27	Kungyangôn North (16) ...	243	...	67	98	55	9,429	47,256	25,089	22,167	44,215	+ 7	...	194
28	Kungyangôn South (9, 16) ...	220	...	57	31	44	8,234	40,888	21,597	19,291	36,934	+ 11	...	186
29	Kyauktan (19)	350	...	60	34	47	9,912	51,510	28,313	23,197	46,720	+ 10	+ 11	147
30	Syriam (16) ...	45	1	15	9	11	5,636	27,551	19,237	8,314	22,167	+ 24	..	612
31	Thôngwa (19)	374	1	80	18	68	10,634	56,171	29,854	26,317	46,228	+ 22	+ 10	150
32	Twante	362	...	122	32	94	16,085	81,542	45,002	36,540	83,702	— 3	+ 11	225
	8. Tharrawaddy District.	*2,863*	*3*	*553*	*110*	*832*	*101,359*	*492,429*	*246,261*	*246,168*	*433,320*	*+ 14*	*+ 10*	*172*
33	Gyobingauk (19)	264	1	69	9	91	11,405	56,628	28,132	28,496	54,423	+ 4	+ 8	214
34	Letpadan East (16)	375	1	36	4	57	8,451	40,805	20,839	19,966	38,808	+ 5	...	109
35	Letpadan West (16)	271	..	62	10	91	11,961	62,800	31,476	31,324	45,173	+ 39	...	232
36	Minhla East (16)	297	..	66	13	88	9,457	42,743	21,546	21,197	41,587	+ 3	...	144
37	Minhla West (16)	243	...	62	10	70	9,405	44,670	22,276	22,394	38,329	+ 17	...	184
38	Mônyo (19)	264	..	48	14	58	10,305	52,920	26,488	26,432	41,826	+ 27	+ 1	200
39	Nattalin (19)	483	..	86	21	150	14,755	68,070	33,796	34,274	62,789	+ 8	+ 4	141
40	Tharrawaddy (19)	401	1	61	19	94	14,463	69,567	34,819	34 748	59,592	+ 17	+ 12	173
41	Zigôn (16)	265	...	64	10	103	11,157	54,226	26,889	27,337	50,793	+ 7	...	205
	9. Pegu District.	*4,083*	*1*	*439*	*183*	*887*	*88,699*	*445,620*	*235,324*	*210,296*	*382,166*	*+ 17*	*+ 28*	*109*
42	Daik-u (19)	1,006	...	81	17	40	18,230	89,597	47,296	42,301	76,557	+ 17	+ 44	89
43	Kawa (19)	372	...	84	35	67	13,143	70,525	36,529	33,996	63,823	+ 1	+ 18	190
44	Nyaunglebin (19)	800	..	77	28	147	20,922	99,006	52,395	46,611	83,367	+ 19	+ 29	124
45	Pegu (19)	1,201	1	82	42	98	21,777	106 945	56,957	49,988	87,331	+ 22	+ 20	89
46	Thanatpin (19)	704	...	115	61	35	14,627	79,547	42,147	37,400	65,088	+ 22	+ 30	113
	10. Prome District.	*2,916*	*2*	*444*	*131*	*612*	*83,355*	*371,575*	*182,803*	*188,772*	*378,871*	*— 2*	*+ 4*	*127*
47	Hmawza (19)	205	...	56	14	105	11,194	47,846	23,014	24,832	51,459	— 7	+ 7	233
48	Padaung	968	...	73	25	94	11,401	50,921	25,507	25,414	53,191	— 4	+ 2	53
49	Paukkaung (19)	629	...	58	6	47	6,908	29,770	14,856	14,914	28,603	+ 4	— 4	47
50	Paungdè	369	1	74	27	89	14,811	68,515	33,604	34,911	66,189	+ 4	+ 9	186
51	Prome (19)	209	1	42	10	64	11,087	50,602	26,293	24,309	50,024	+ 1	†	248
52	Shwedaung (19)	294	..	80	19	100	13,773	61,116	29,221	31,895	62,687	— 3	— 4	208
53	Thègôn	241	...	61	30	113	14,181	62,805	30,308	32,497	66,718	— 6	+ 9	261

* Increase due to extension of census area excluded in calculating the figure.
† In 1911 Prome township consisted only of Prome town; in 1921 it included so much rural area that the entry of any figures for the 1911 area would be misleading.

PROVINCIAL TABLE I.—*Area and Population of Townships, etc.*

Serial No.	Township, State, etc.	Area in square miles.	Number of: Towns under the Burma Towns Act.	Number of: Village Tracts.	Number of Villages (Towns excluded): Exceeding 100 houses.	Number of Villages (Towns excluded): Having 40 to 99 houses.	Total number of occupied houses, 1921.	Population 1921: Persons.	Population 1921: Males.	Population 1921: Females.	Population 1911: Persons.	Percentage of variation of total population: 1911 to 1921.	Percentage of variation of total population: 1901 to 1911.	Number of persons per square mile in 1921.
	1	2	3	4	5	6	7	8	9	10	11	12	13	14
	Irrawaddy Division.	**13,437**	**12**	**2,591**	**393**	**2,376**	**395,938**	**2,030,044**	**1,048,377**	**981,667**	**1,869,485**	**+ 9**	**+ 12**	**151**
	11. Bassein District.	*4,127*	*2*	*693*	*90*	*558*	*95,041*	*489,473*	*252,947*	*236,526*	*440,988*	*+ 11*	*+ 13*	*119*
54	Bassein East (16, 18) ...	350	...	108	15	78	12,816	65,882	32,869	33,013	97,471	− 32	...	188
55	Bassein West (16, 18) ...	352	1	59	2	83	14,512	76,752	45,659	31,093	29,423	+161	...	218
56	Kyaunggon	263	...	79	6	78	11,699	59,146	29,475	29,671	55,799	+ 6	+ 2	225
57	Kyonpyaw	320	...	115	21	142	18,676	92,893	46,359	46,524	90,704	+ 2	+ 10	290
58	Ngaputaw	1,457	...	109	16	87	11,413	60,435	31,502	28,933	46,379	+ 30	+ 25	41
59	Ngathainggyaung	336	1	133	22	80	16,474	83,934	41,818	42,116	77,324	+ 9	+ 19	250
60	Thabaung (19)	1,049	...	90	8	60	9,451	50,431	25,255	25,176	43,888	+ 15	+ 16	48
	12. Henzada District.	*2,872*	*3*	*621*	*111*	*714*	*114,800*	*550,920*	*273,439*	*277,481*	*532,357*	*+ 3*	*+ 10*	*192*
61	Henzada	360	1	152	31	153	29,389	142,357	71,421	70,936	140,205	+ 2	+ 6	395
62	Ingabu	727	...	99	21	140	21,048	102,734	50,626	52,108	93,260	+ 10	+ 11	141
63	Kyangin	388	1	62	10	74	11,745	48,371	24,372	23,999	50,329	− 4	+ 8	125
64	Lemyethna (19)	369	...	92	10	110	13,724	67,000	33,329	33,671	64,242	+ 4	+ 6	182
65	Myanaung	736	1	105	19	137	21,742	106,008	51,930	54,078	106,943	− 1	+ 16	144
66	Zalun	292	...	111	20	100	17,152	84,450	41,761	42,689	77,378	+ 9	+ 11	289
	13. Myaungmya District.	*2,660*	*2*	*590*	*55*	*385*	*71,604*	*370,551*	*196,757*	*173,794*	*334,852*	*+ 11*	*+ 18*	*140*
67	Eiamè	285	...	118	13	42	14,450	73,450	37,318	36,132	71,790	+ 2	+ 21	258
68	Labutta (16)	950	...	43	9	43	7,533	35,507	19,482	16,025	24,972	+ 42	...	37
69	Mawlamyainggyun (19) ...	421	...	131	11	158	15,789	82,899	44,751	38,148	80,570	+ 3	+ 19	197
70	Myaungmya (19)	543	1	145	11	61	15,187	80,676	43,174	37,502	67,383	+ 20	+ 11	149
71	Wakèma (19)	451	1	153	12	81	18,645	98,019	52,032	45,987	90,137	+ 9	+ 23	217
	14. Ma-ubin District	*1,640*	*3*	*312*	*74*	*387*	*62,692*	*330,106*	*168,513*	*161,593*	*305,073*	*+ 8*	*+ 10*	*201*
72	Danubyu (19)	290	1	96	25	95	16,382	87,240	43,333	43,907	89,287	− 2	+ 8	301
73	Ma-ubin (19)	509	1	94	15	113	16,703	89,502	47,116	42,386	80,069	+ 12	+ 9	176
74	Pantanaw (19)	501	...	66	19	71	15,638	81,238	41,126	40,112	71,239	+ 14	+ 15	162
75	Yandoon (19)	340	1	56	15	108	13,969	72,126	36,938	35,188	64,478	+ 12	+ 7	212
	15. Pyapon District.	*2,148*	*2*	*375*	*63*	*332*	*51,801*	*288,994*	*156,721*	*132,273*	*256,215*	*+ 13*	*+ 13*	*135*
76	Bogalè	1,165	...	77	19	114	15,164	84,896	46,882	38,014	58,919	+ 44	+ 35	73
77	Dedayè	365	...	116	20	80	13,692	73,946	39,728	34,218	71,442	+ 4	+ 7	203
78	Kyaiklat	284	1	111	7	99	14,022	78,241	41,441	36,800	75,676	+ 3	+ 5	275
79	Pyapôn	334	1	71	17	39	8,923	51,911	28,670	23,241	50,178	+ 3	+ 14	155
	Tenasserim Division.	**35,788**	**8**	**1,714**	**707**	**1,263**	**311,372**	**1,613,523**	**847,445**	**766,078**	**1,417,544**	**+ 14**	**+ 23**	**45**
	16. Toungoo District.	*6,135*	*3*	*560*	*98*	*687*	*85,827*	*381,883*	*197,505*	*184,378*	*351,076*	*+ 9*	*+ 26*	*62*
80	Kyaukkyi (19)	922	...	57	9	67	8,196	38,647	20,168	18,479	34,855	+ 11	+ 25	42
81	Leiktho (19)	703	...	119	2	34	3,820	16,922	8,327	8,595	16,123	+ 5	+ 10	24
82	Oktwin	924	...	56	18	84	12,423	52,175	26,164	26,011	49,753	+ 5	+ 13	57
83	Pyu ... -	773	1	66	13	149	16,417	76,795	39,694	37,101	70,300	+ 9	+ 21	99
84	Shwegyin (19)	746	1	75	4	68	9,331	39,745	21,983	17,762	33,968	+ 17	+ 50	53
85	Tantabin	889	...	72	21	60	10,096	46,971	23,791	23,180	41,568	+ 13	+ 68	53
86	Toungoo (19)	340	1	58	9	100	13,083	58,687	30,935	27,752	54,650	+ 7	+ 25	173
87	Yedashè (19)	838	...	57	22	125	12,481	51,941	26,443	25,498	49,859	+ 4	+ 17	62
	17. Salween District.	*2,666*	*...*	*89*	*1*	*29*	*11,256*	*50,379*	*26,811*	*23,568*	*46,608*	*+ 8*	*+ 23*	*19*
88	Papun	2,666	...	89	1	29	11,256	50,379	26,811	23,568	46,608	+ 8	+ 23	19
	18. Thaton District.	*4,831*	*2*	*385*	*333*	*37*	*87,569*	*471,100*	*245,909*	*225,191*	*405,225*	*+ 16*	*+ 21*	*98*
89	Bilin (19)	750	...	58	48	7	13,481	68,622	35,955	32,667	60,269	+ 14	+ 9	91
90	Hlaingbwè	1,764	...	76	66	4	12,846	75,145	39,004	36,141	60,752	+ 24	+ 39	43
91	Kyaikto (19)	425	1	40	35	5	9,487	48,649	25,748	22,901	40,772	+ 19	+ 16	114
92	Pa-an	1,007	...	105	98	6	22,013	120,341	61,377	58,964	102,490	+ 17	+ 34	120
93	Paung (19)	399	...	54	45	7	13,002	73,492	39,333	34,159	63,578	+ 16	+ 18	184
94	Thatôn (19)	486	1	52	41	8	16,740	84,851	44,492	40,359	77,364	+ 10	+ 12	175
	19. Amherst District.	*7,059*	*1*	*354*	*174*	*290*	*71,480*	*417,910*	*223,348*	*194,562*	*367,918*	*+ 14*	*+ 23*	*59*
95	Chaungzôn	193	...	48	39	19	9,095	53,898	27,778	26,120	49,271	+ 9	+ 18	279
96	Kawkareik (19)	1,963	...	68	18	71	10,458	61,878	32,238	29,640	54,440	+ 14	+ 50	32
97	Kyaikkami	928	...	22	13	26	5,264	29,821	15,969	13,852	23,105	+ 29	+ 47	32
98	Kyaikmaraw (19)	1,219	...	55	21	56	8,334	51,542	26,323	25,219	45,417	+ 13	+ 12	42
99	Kyain (16)	1,258	..	68	8	32	7,623	42,509	22,149	20,360	34,914	+ 22	..	34
100	Moulmein	30	1	13	9	16	13,585	75,795	45,837	29,958	65,383	+ 16	+ 19	2,526
101	Mudôn	230	...	50	51	13	10,008	60,154	30,776	29,378	59,808	+ 1	+ 15	262
102	Yelamaing	1,258	...	30	15	37	7,163	42,318	22,278	20,035	35,580	+ 19	+ 58	34
	20. Tavoy District.	*5,308*	*1*	*179*	*83*	*123*	*29,949*	*156,786*	*80,994*	*75,792*	*135,293*	*+ 16*	*+ 23*	*30*
103	Launglôn	313	...	52	36	38	8,654	47,153	23,670	23,483	41,081	+ 15	+ 24	151
104	Tavoy	2,412	1	38	14	24	9,300	46,888	24,826	22,062	39,222	+ 20	+ 16	19
105	Thayetchaung	981	...	48	25	39	7,928	41,893	20,845	20,748	37,858	+ 10	+ 24	42
106	Yebyu	1,600	...	41	8	22	4,067	21,152	11,653	9,499	17,132	+ 24	+ 36	13
	21. Mergui District.	*9,789*	*1*	*147*	*18*	*97*	*25,291*	*135,465*	*72,878*	*62,587*	*111,424*	*+ 22*	*+ 26*	*14*
107	Bokpyin	2,605	..	22	...	...	2,129	10,716	5,939	4,777	8,575	+ 25	+ 18	4
108	Mergui	1,377	1	49	8	58	11,631	63,924	34,887	29,037	53,466	+ 20	+ 24	46
109	Palaw	785	...	35	9	31	6,292	33,384	16,953	16,431	28,588	+ 17	+ 27	43
110	Tenasserim	4,033	...	23	1	14	2,985	16,510	8,845	7,665	12,583	+ 31	+ 18	4
111	Maliwun	989	...	18	...	...	1,781	8,441	4,726	3,715	8,212	+ 3	+ 96	9
112	Salons living in boats ...	...	...	...	...	...	511	1,825	875	950	*	...	...	...
113	Settlement and Survey Parties...	...	...	...	...	...	22	665	653	12	...	...	...	...

* The Salons were included in the figures for various townships in 1911, when there were 1,020 males and 964 females. In 1921 there were altogether 929 males and 1,012 females, of whom the numbers shown in the table lived in 512 boats and the remainder on shore in the various townships.

PROVINCIAL TABLE I.—*Area and Population of Townships, etc.*

Serial No.	Township, State, etc.	Area in square miles.	Number of: Towns under the Burma Towns Act.	Number of: Village Tracts.	Number of Villages (Towns excluded): Exceeding 100 houses.	Number of Villages (Towns excluded): Having 40 to 99 houses, 1921.	Total number of occupied houses, 1921.	Population 1921: Persons.	Population 1921: Males.	Population 1921: Females.	Population 1911: Persons.	Percentage of variation of total population: 1911 to 1921.	Percentage of variation of total population: 1901 to 1911.	Number of persons per square mile in 1921.
	1	2	3	4	5	6	7	8	9	10	11	12	13	14
	Magwe Division.	**21,040**	**7**	**2,533**	**729**	**2,167**	**306,218**	**1,447,530**	**709,454**	**738,076**	**1,308,267**	**+ 11**	**+ 16**	**69**
	22. Thayetmyo District.	*4,750*	*2*	*641*	*86*	*455*	*57,172*	*255,406*	*125,283*	*130,123*	*248,275*	*+ 3*	*+ 4*	*54*
114	Allanmyo (19)	1,102	1	157	23	110	14,600	66,319	31,935	34,384	69,541	− 5	+ 3	60
115	Kama	503	...	91	14	69	8,674	37,326	18,184	19,142	34,103	+ 9	Nil	74
116	Mindôn	1,033	...	107	6	78	9,361	36,082	17,839	18,243	36,598	− 1	+ 2	35
117	Minhla (19)	902	...	98	8	52	7,085	33,765	16,935	16,830	30,250	+ 12	+ 5	37
118	Sinbaungwe (16)	755	...	100	16	65	7,301	35,738	17,173	18,565	33,008	+ 8	+ 2	47
119	Thayetmyo	455	1	86	19	81	10,151	46,176	23,217	22,959	44,775	+ 3	+ 9	101
	23. Pakokku District.	*6,210*	*1*	*742*	*285*	*752*	*98,422*	*465,771*	*223,943*	*241,828*	*409,823*	*+ 14*	*+ 15*	*75*
120	Gangaw	1,400	...	100	17	38	7,123	38,306	19,151	19,155	30,739	+ 25	+ 27	27
121	Myaing	780	...	131	57	171	20,361	93,482	43,676	49,806	78,969	+ 18	+ 10	120
122	Pakôkku (19)	403	1	77	64	133	20,729	98,352	37,578	50,774	86,415	+ 14	+ 11	244
123	Pauk	977	...	97	25	109	10,814	54,499	26,909	27,590	50,137	+ 9	+ 22	56
124	Saw	1,011	...	83	5	50	5,131	25,591	12,935	12,656	22,462	+ 14	+ 15	25
125	Seikpyu	774	...	62	18	77	7,168	34,436	16,714	17,722	30,693	+ 12	+ 15	44
126	Tilin	488	...	56	3	19	2,859	15,525	7,840	7,685	14,652	+ 6	+ 20	32
127	Yesagyo	377	...	136	96	155	24,177	105,580	49,140	56,440	95,756	+ 10	+ 8	280
	24. Minbu District.	*3,293*	*2*	*339*	*128*	*402*	*60,888*	*274,302*	*134,495*	*139,807*	*262,380*	*+ 5*	*+ 13*	*83*
128	Ngape	355	...	45	5	21	3,797	16,827	8,488	8,339	16,735	+ 1	+ 4	47
129	Pwinbyu (19)	461	...	53	51	99	16,364	74,106	36,530	37,576	61,233	+ 21	+ 9	161
130	Sagu	787	1	71	31	71	13,813	64,552	31,967	32,585	62,791	+ 3	+ 15	82
131	Salin (19)	763	1	117	38	177	21,756	95,497	45,737	49,760	98,672	− 3	+ 15	125
132	Sidôktaya	927	...	53	3	34	5,158	23,320	11,773	11,547	22,949	+ 2	+ 15	25
	25. Magwe District.	*3,687*	*2*	*466*	*230*	*546*	*83,424*	*423,252*	*211,686*	*211,566*	*361,538*	*+ 17*	*+ 28*	*115*
133	Magwe	637	1	75	42	88	16,848	87,675	43,613	44,062	71,594	+ 22	+ 26	138
134	Myothit	626	...	74	36	86	11,335	57,197	27,584	29,613	53,454	+ 7	+ 31	91
135	Natmauk	880	...	94	62	99	15,681	85,476	41,163	44,313	73,217	+ 17	+ 24	97
136	Sale (14, 19)	364	...	73	24	91	12,512	60,132	30,422	29,710	43,070	+ 40	+ 28	165
137	Satthwa	563	...	59	10	71	6,309	29,478	14,103	15,375	32,811	− 10	+ 31	52
138	Taungdwingyi	223	1	48	21	44	7,222	35,750	17,205	18,545	35,531	+ 1	+ 20	160
139	Yenangyaung (19)	394	...	43	28	67	13,547	67,544	37,596	29,948	51,861	+ 30	+ 40	171
	26. Pakokku Hill-Tracts (3).	*3,100*	...	*345*	...	*12*	*6,312*	*28,799*	*14,047*	*14,752*	*26,251*	*+ 10*	...	*9*
140	Administered Area	2,250	...	302	...	12	4,510	20,043	9,840	10,203	17,128	+ 17	+ 31	9
141	Unadministered Area ...	850	...	43	...	?	1,802	8,756	4,207	4,549	9,123	− 4	...	10
	Mandalay Division.	**28,788**	**5**	**2,355**	**273**	**939**	**184,382**	**849,361**	**435,894**	**413,467**	**779,755**	**+ 5‡**	**+ 7**	**30**
	27. Mandalay District.	*2,117*	*4*	*333*	*207*	*389*	*83,630*	*356,621*	*182,999*	*173,622*	*340,770*	*+ 5*	*− 7*	*168*
142	Mandalay City	25	1	...	...	...	34,638	148,917	77,763	71,154	138,299	+ 8	− 15	5,957
143	Amarapura	85	1	50	61	112	9,661	47,928	23,531	24,397	44,021	+ 9	Nil	564
144	Madaya	321	..	87	55	105	11,303	51,038	25,015	26,023	54,550	− 6	+ 3	159
145	Maymyo	761	1	59	5	28	8,950	34,257	20,349	13,908	28,265	+ 21	+ 32	45
146	Patheingyi	213	...	67	32	65	8,163	32,324	15,604	16,720	34,837	− 7	+ 22	152
147	Singu	711	...	70	54	68	9,915	42,157	20,737	21,420	40,898	+ 3	+ 14	59
	28. Bhamo District (3).	*6,903*	*1*	*556*	*18*	*156*	*24,532*	*112,960*	*56,888*	*56,072*	*107,811*	*+ 5*	*+ 36*	*16*
148	Bhamo	3,643	1	125	9	51	8,465	37,222	19,879	17,343	36,558	+ 2	} + 40§	} 10
149	Shwegu	448	...	91	4	33	4,477	22,001	11,911	10,091	21,149	+ 4	} + 24	} 49
150	Shwegu Kachin H. Tracts (3, 19)	1,212	...	73	...	3	1,127	5,608	2,788	2,820	6,069	− 8	}	} 5
151	Sinlum Kachin Hill Tracts (3)	1,600	...	276	5	69	10,463	48,128	22,320	25,808	44,035	+ 9	...	30
	29. Myitkyina District (3, 9).	*10,651*	...	*772*	*15*	*64*	*24,954*	*118,382*	*63,419*	*54,963*	*85,577*	*+ 14‡*	*+ 25*	*11*
152	Kamaing (19)	1,348	...	35	6	14	2,917	13,638	8,841	4,797	13,312	+ 2	...	10
153	Mogaung (19)	1,257	..	50	5	24	4,277	19,187	10,228	8,959	10,504	+ 83	...	15
154	Myitkyina (19)	1,248	..	80	4	26	5,107	21,536	12,278	9,258	17,779	+ 21	...	17
155	Htawgaw Kachin H. Tracts (3, 9)	1,574	...	75	...	...	3,138	17,305	8,745	8,560	*	...	...	11
156	Kamaing Kachin H. Tracts (3, 19)	1,348	...	14	...	...	1,258	7,057	3,951	3,106	5,671	+ 25	..	5
157	Mogaung Kachin H. Tts (3, 9, 19)	1,257	..	38	...	...	1,944	10,467	5,095	5,372	6,992	+ 10	...	8
158	Myitkyina Kachin Hill Tracts (3, 9, 18, 19).	1,248	...	143	...	...	1,255	6,431	3,229	3,202	6,064	− 18	...	5
159	Sadon Kachin Hill Tracts (3) ...	726	..	185	...	...	2,737	12,355	6,039	6,316	13,066	− 5	...	17
160	Sima Kachin Hill Tracts (3, 19)	645	..	152	...	...	2,321	10,416	5,023	5,393	10,541	− 1	...	16
...	Military Camps	...	...	...	...	...	...	...	...	...	1,648	...	...	...
	30. Katha District (3).	*6,917*	...	*686*	*29*	*327*	*49,762*	*253,725*	*128,444*	*125,281*	*245,597*	*+ 3*	*+ 12*	*28*
161	Banmauk	1,232	...	87	...	28	5,995	28,677	13,613	15,064	29,589	− 3	+ 4	23
162	Indaw	415	...	44	2	14	3,364	16,469	8,367	8,102	15,572	+ 6	+ 9	40
163	Katha	402	...	51	6	54	4,998	22,254	11,659	10,595	20,464	+ 9	...	55
164	Kawlin	536	...	80	3	79	3,305	35,070	17,557	17,513	33,135	+ 6	+ 18	65
165	Mawlu	1,053	...	44	1	53	5,286	26,689	14,001	12,688	19,593	+ 36	...	25
166	Mogôk	610	...	76	11	25	5,991	25,436	14,161	11,275	26,381	− 4	+ 7	42
167	Pinlebu	1,368		97	2	19	6,414	31,466	14,754	16,712	32,685	− 4	+ 11	23
168	Tagaung	618	...	31	1	12	2,467	12,548	6,543	6,005	10,785	+ 16	+ 25	20
169	Thabeitkyin	688	...	30	8	15	2,428	9,837	5,252	4,585	10,238	− 4	+ 5	14
170	Tigyaing	352	...	49	1	31	3,625	17,188	8,602	8,586	17,582	− 2	+ 9	49
171	Wuntho	592	...	74	1	17	4,803	22,390	11,128	11,262	23,664	− 5	+ 3	38
172	Katha Kachin Hill-Tracts (3) ...	750	...	11	...	...	155	908	480	428	4,964	− 83	...	1
173	Mawlu Kachin Hill-Tracts (3) ...	300	..	19	...	...	941	4,793	2,327	2,466	1,015	+378	...	16
	31. Putao District (9).	*200*	...	*9*	*4*	*3*	*1,504*	*7,673*	*4,144*	*3,529*	*	*	*	*38*
	Putao Subdivision—													
174	(i) Hkamti Lông Shan States (9)	200	...	9†	4	3	1,504	7,673	4,144	3,529	*	*	*	38
175	(ii) *Remainder*	4,800	...	143	} Omitted from the census and excluded from district totals accordingly.									
176	*Kenglu Subdivision*	3,200	...	357										
177	*Laxa (or Sumpra Bum Subdivision)*	2,400	...	238										

* Omitted from the census of 1911.
† Really, 8 Shan States and 1 Civil Station.
‡ Allowing for extension of census area in 1921.
§ This figure is for items 148 and 151 combined.

PROVINCIAL TABLE I.—*Area and Population of Townships, etc.*

Serial No.	Township, State, etc.	Area in square miles.	Number of: Towns under the Burma Towns Act.	Number of: Village Tracts.	Number of Villages (Towns excluded): Exceeding 100 houses.	Number of Villages (Towns excluded): Having 40 to 99 houses.	Total number of occupied houses, 1921.	Population, 1921: Persons.	Population, 1921: Males.	Population, 1921: Females.	Population, 1911: Persons.	Percentage of variation of total population: 1911 to 1921.	Percentage of variation of total population: 1901 to 1911.	Number of persons per square mile in 1921.
	1	2	3	4	5	6	7	8	9	10	11	12	13	14
	Sagaing Division.	**35,056**	**4**	**2,221**	**821**	**1,632**	**317,853**	**1,358,832**	**645,009**	**713,023**	**1,274,827**	**+ 17***	**+ 16**	**38**
	32. Shwebo District.	*5,714*	*1*	*633*	*236*	*553*	*90,799*	*391,284*	*184,708*	*206,576*	*356,363*	*+ 10*	*+ 24*	*68*
178	Kanbalu	1,336	...	121	28	96	13,100	54,560	26,856	27,704	51,895	+ 5	+ 16	36
179	Kin-u	309	...	81	36	59	10,232	45,090	21,364	23,726	42,404	+ 6	+ 35	146
180	Kyunhla	988	...	37	...	21	3,048	14,946	7,485	7,461	13,742	+ 9	+ 61	15
181	Shwebo	428	1	79	43	64	14,802	63,104	30,846	32,258	60,292	+ 5	+ 18	147
182	Tabayin	613	...	90	23	90	12,730	54,862	25,267	29,595	45,859	+ 20	+ 17	89
183	Tamadaw	600	...	36	5	58	6,119	25,666	10,988	14,678	23,820	+ 8	+ 21	43
184	Tazè	588	...	45	22	53	8,325	36,838	16,928	19,910	34,204	+ 8	+ 21	63
185	Wetlet	512	...	87	58	64	14,686	63,636	30,345	33,291	54,675	+ 16	+ 38	124
186	Ye-u	140	...	57	21	48	7,757	32,582	14,629	17,953	29,472	+ 11	+ 22	233
	33. Sagaing District.	*1,826*	*1*	*282*	*232*	*259*	*72,488*	*326,908*	*155,054*	*171,854*	*312,111*	*+ 5*	*+ 12*	*179*
187	Chaungu	188	...	22	25	33	7,249	32,485	14,993	17,492	33,512	− 3	+ 1	173
188	Myaung	177	...	40	36	28	8,974	45,994	21,805	24,189	40,498	+ 14	+ 18	260
189	Myinmu	295	...	38	33	35	9,944	40,633	19,092	21,541	41,314	− 2	+ 7	138
190	Ngazun	331	...	41	23	33	12,736	59,970	28,524	31,446	54,619	+ 10	+ 12	181
191	Sagaing	474	1	77	68	72	20,328	88,836	42,441	46,395	87,842	+ 1	+ 15	87
192	Tada-u	360	...	64	47	68	13,257	58,990	28,199	30,791	54,326	+ 9	+ 16	164
	34. Lower Chindwin District.	*3,480*	*1*	*361*	*258*	*482*	*92,176*	*342,880*	*156,693*	*186,187*	*316,175*	*+ 8*	*+ 14*	*99*
193	Budalin (19)	451	...	80	55	92	19,384	76,561	34,171	42,390	74,905	+ 2	+ 16	170
194	Kani (19)	1,788	...	88	48	108	16,513	63,761	29,791	33,970	57,131	+ 12	+ 17	36
195	Monywa (19)	487	1	72	72	104	27,085	100,275	45,522	54,753	88,533	+ 13	+ 10	206
196	Palè (19)	488	...	76	47	75	14,488	51,321	23,786	27,535	48,392	+ 6	+ 15	112
197	Salingyi (19)	296	...	45	36	103	14,766	50,962	23,423	27,539	47,214	+ 8	+ 19	172
	35. Upper Chindwin District (9).	*16,037*	*1*	*466§*	*43*	*186*	*38,107*	*186,881*	*94,432*	*92,449*	*170,622*	*+ 5**	*+ 11*	*12*
198	Homalin	2,524	...	52	3	25	4,239	23,936	12,121	11,815	23,608	+ 1	+ 34	9
199	Kale	812	...	50	11	21	4,029	19,085	9,869	9,216	15,064	+ 27	+ 18	24
200	Kalewa	176	...	9	1	1	850	3,589	1,870	1,719	4,015	− 11	+ 9	20
201	Kyabin	640	...	45	5	19	2,574	11,649	5,792	5,857	11,234	+ 4	+ 13	18
202	Maingkaing	4,665	...	48	1	10	3,289	18,605	9,159	9,446	18,618	...	− 16	4
203	Masein	768	...	42	1	21	3,188	14,262	7,220	7,042	13,909	+ 3	+ 15	19
204	Mawlaik (15)	1,088	1	34	4	11	3,692	16,641	8,904	7,737	15,225	+ 9	+ 9	15
205	Mingin	872	...	51	10	54	5,200	23,890	11,727	12,163	22,336	+ 7	+ 12	27
206	Paungbyin	1,316	...	62	5	28	6,152	31,865	16,016	15,849	30,440	+ 5	+ 15	22
207	Tamu	540	...	19	2	11	1,310	6,393	3,384	3,009	5,918	+ 8	+ 22	12
208	Somra Tract (4, 9, 20)	924	...	5	...	...	1,834	7,636	3,719	3,917	859	...	...	8
209	Kanti State †	963	...	20	...	1	422	2,287	1,193	1,094	2,560	− 11	+ 25	2
210	Thaungdut State ‡ (19, 20)	529	...	36	2	7	1,328	7,043	3,458	3,585	7,438	− 5	+ 5	13
	36. Chin Hills District (3).	*8,000*	...	*479*	*52*	*152*	*23,483*	*110,079*	*54,122*	*55,957*	*119,556*	*− 8*	*+ 37*	*14*
211	Falam (Subdivision)	890	...	173	34	67	10,127	40,883	19,399	21,484	43,213	− 5	+ 17	46
212	Haka	5,100	...	155	19	47	7,514	33,629	17,011	16,618	44,428	− 24	+ 31	7
213	Tiddim	2,010	...	151	9	38	5,842	35,567	17,712	17,855	31,918	+ 11	+ 94	18
	Meiktila Division.	**10,491**	**4**	**1,232**	**648**	**1,845**	**260,155**	**1,197,771**	**582,229**	**615,542**	**1,127,588**	**+ 6**	**+ 17**	**116**
	37. Kyaukse District.	*1,282*	*1*	*277*	*80*	*285*	*36,509*	*142,677*	*70,449*	*72,228*	*141,598*	*+ 1*	*Nil*	*111*
214	Kyauksè	180	1	99	30	110	13,998	53,409	26,319	27,090	52,348	+ 2	Nil	297
215	Myittha (19)	251	...	110	27	99	12,950	50,931	25,422	25,509	49,459	+ 3	− 3	203
216	Singaing	851	...	68	23	76	9,561	38,337	18,708	19,629	39,791	− 4	+ 3	45
	38. Meiktila District.	*2,287*	...	*401*	*143*	*565*	*62,335*	*289,897*	*137,573*	*152,324*	*280,690*	*+ 3*	*+ 11*	*127*
217	Mahlaing	426	...	79	39	159	15,448	74,089	34,565	39,524	67,805	+ 9	+ 8	174
218	Meiktila	470	...	99	33	159	19,204	90,149	43,090	47,059	83,257	+ 8	+ 8	192
219	Thazi (19)	929	...	108	28	104	13,190	61,030	29,847	31,183	60,527	+ 1	+ 19	66
220	Wundwin (19)	462	...	115	43	113	14,496	64,629	30,071	34,558	69,101	− 6	+ 10	140
	39. Yamethin District.	*4,176*	*2*	*357*	*151*	*508*	*69,654*	*323,189*	*160,913*	*162,276*	*306,379*	*+ 5*	*+ 26*	*77*
221	Lewè (19)	816	...	62	30	86	12,450	61,173	31,811	29,362	49,661	+ 23	+ 62	75
222	Pyawbwè (19)	246	...	45	23	66	9,856	43,464	20,523	22,941	46,923	− 7	+ 12	177
223	Pyinmana	1,474	1	97	35	116	20,531	91,396	46,889	44,507	80,380	+ 14	+ 31	62
224	Yamèthin (19)	1,089	1	85	41	140	16,394	75,809	37,186	38,623	80,150	− 5	+ 18	70
225	Yanaung	551	...	68	22	100	10,423	51,347	24,504	26,843	49,265	+ 4	+ 21	93
	40. Myingyan District.	*2,746*	*1*	*197*	*274*	*487*	*91,657*	*442,008*	*213,294*	*228,714*	*398,921*	*+ 11*	*+ 22*	*161*
226	Kyaukpadaung (19)	766	...	47	44	171	20,214	100,561	48,119	52,442	89,169	+ 13	+ 32	131
227	Myingyan (19)	404	1	43	68	65	21,450	102,765	50,597	52,168	92,884	+ 11	+ 14	254
228	Natogyi (19)	481	...	34	63	76	16,281	73,803	34,776	39,027	72,872	+ 1	+ 19	153
229	Pagan (19)	574	...	29	45	76	16,041	79,857	38,854	41,003	70,438	+ 13	+ 24	139
230	Taungtha (19)	521	...	44	54	99	17,671	85,042	40,968	44,074	73,558	+ 16	+ 27	163

* Allowing for extension of census area in 1921. § Also called Singkaling Hkamti. ‡ Also called Hsawnghsup.

PROVINCIAL TABLE I.—*Area and Population of States, etc.*

Serial No.	Subdivision, State, Notified Area, etc.	Area in square miles.	Number of Towns under the Burma Towns Act.	Number of Villages. Total.	Having 100 houses or more.	Having 40 to 99 houses.	Total number of occupied houses, 1921.	Population. 1921. Persons.	Males.	Females.	1911. Persons.	Percentage of variation of total population. 1911 to 1921.	1901 to 1911.	Number of persons per square mile in 1921.
	1	2	3	4	5	6	7	8	9	10	11	12	13	14
	Eastern States.	**60,593**	...	**18,723***	**87***	**916***	**300,300**	**1,497,392**	**757,420**	**739,972**	**1,412,368***	**+ 4·1¶**	**+ 16¶**	**25**
	41. Northern Shan States.	**20,156**	...	...	...	...	**113,979**	**585,924**	**299,227**	**286,697**	...	...	...	**29**
	Northern Shan States (omitting East Manglün).	**17,856**	...	**6,614**	**26**	**326**	**109,124**	**559,223**	**285,700**	**273,523**	**512,166**	**+ 9**	**+ 28¶**	**31**
231	*Lashio Notified Area* ...	*5*	...	*1*	*1*	...	*640*	*3,448*	*2,046*	*1,402*	*4,055*	...	...	*690*
232	*Hsipaw State* ...	*4,400*	...	*1,654*	*4*	*60*	*25,938*	*131,450*	*67,848*	*63,602*	*122,129*	*+ 8*	*+ 9*	*30*
233	*Mõng Mit State (19)* ...	*3,562*	...	*411*	*1*	*106*	*12,269*	*56,498*	*28,349*	*28,149*	*53,214*	*+ 6*	*+ 19*	*16*
	Mõng Mit (State proper)†	2,802	...	106	18	52	6,761	30,022	15,834	14,188	28,757	+ 4	+ 27	11
	Kodaung Hill Tracts ...	760	...	305	...	26	5,508	26,476	12,515	13,961	24,457	+ 8	+ 10	35
234	*Tawngpeng State* ...	*778*	..	*253*	*6*	*25*	*8,323*	*41,898*	*23,957*	*17,941*	*31,976*	*+ 31*	*+ 41*	*54*
235	*South Hsenwi*	*2,281*	...	*1,002*	*1*	*38*	*14,881*	*84,141*	*42,108*	*42,033*	*85,110*	*— 1*	*+ 25*	*37*
236	*North Hsenwi (omitting East Manglün):*	*6,830*	...	*3,293*	*13*	*97*	*47,073*	*241,788*	*121,492*	*120,396*	*215,682*	*+ 12*	*+ 82*	*36*
	Shan Tracts § ..	} 6,330	... {	1,648	12	67	26,765	138,925	70,621	68,304	121,699	+ 14	+ 31	} 35
	Kachin Tracts ...			1,349	1	24	16,592	82,866	40,335	41,931	75,421	+ 9	+ 67	
	East Manglün ...	Census	estima	ted only	, see	separate	entry, next	but one	below.					
	West Manglün ...	500	...	296	...	6	3,716	20,597	10,436	10,161	18,562	+ 11	...	41
	East Manglün (4) ...	*2,300*	...	...	...	...	*4,855*	*26,701*	*13,527*	*13,174*	...	...	...	*12*
	42. Southern Shan States.	**36,157**	...	**11,417**	**48**	**534**	**178,494**	**847,618**	**427,064**	**420,554**	**836,574**	**+ 1**	**+ 10**	**23**
237	*Taunggyi Notified Area* ...	*3·4*	...	*1*	...	*1*	*1,107*	*6,016*	*3,311*	*2,705*	*5,180*	*+ 16*	...	*177*
	Civil Population ...	...	..	..	...	...	*948*	*5,210*	*2,734*	*2,476*	...	..	...	...
	Military Police ...	...	...	...	...	...	*159*	*806*	*577*	*229*	...	...	...	...
238	*Loilem Notified Area* ...	*3.0*	...	*1*	...	*1*	*225*	*998*	*552*	*446*	*751*	*+ 37*	...	*333*
	Civil Population ...	...	-	...	-	...	*191*	*876*	*450*	*426*	...	...	...	...
	Military Police ...	...	...	...	...	...	*34*	*122*	*102*	*20*	...	...	...	...
239	*Kalaw Notified Area* ...	*9·25*	...	*1*	...	*1*	*608*	*2,997*	*1,822*	*1,175*	...	...	...	*324*
	Civil Population ...	...	...	...	...	...	*603*	*2,891*	*1,727*	*1,164*	...	...	...	...
	Military Police ...	.	...	...	...	...	*5*	*106*	*95*	*11*	...	...	...	...
240	*Yawnghwe State* ...	*1,299*	...	*1,018*	*9*	*124*	*22,639*	*105,512*	*52,157*	*53,355*	*106,377*	...	*+ 12*	*81*
241	*Kengtung State* ...	*12,400*	...	*2,797*	*5*	*131*	*42,260*	*208,761*	*107,513*	*101,248*	*200,344*	*+ 4*	*+ 5*	*17*
	North-Eastern Subdivision.	*6,540*	...	*3,073*	*6*	*34*	*33,389*	*173,978*	*86,539*	*87,439*	*175,536*	*— 1*	*+ 9*	*27*
242	Laihka ...	1,557	...	668	1	6	6,041	32,827	16,430	16,397	30,196	+ 9	+ 17	21
243	Mõng Kung	1,593	...	578	2	8	6,735	34,714	17,413	17,301	35,222	— 1	+ 16	22
244	Kehsi Mansam ...	497	...	345	...	4	3,705	18,028	8,869	9,159	18,393	— 2	— 17	36
245	Kenglön	54	...	77	...	2	1,054	4,509	2,169	2,340	5,891	— 15	+ 24	83
246	Mong Hsu	470	...	303	...	3	3,661	18,898	9,421	9,477	20,913	— 10	+ 20	40
247	Mõng Nawng	1,646	...	708	1	7	7,730	42,372	20,923	21,449	42,538	...	+ 9	26
248	Mõng Sit	357	...	136	1	.	1,415	6,727	3,409	3,318	7,338	— 14	— 13	19
249	Mõng Pawn	366	...	258	1	4	3,048	15,903	7,905	7,998	15,145	+ 5	+ 15	43
	Central Subdivision.	*4,526*	...	*1,877*	*12*	*81*	*23,055*	*111,261*	*56,502*	*54,759*	*114,084*	*— 2*	*+ 6*	*25*
250	Samka	314	...	220	1	7	3,428	14,135	7,189	6,946	15,742	— 10	— 11	45
251	Hsahtung	471	...	163	...	3	1,878	10,164	5,248	4,916	11,453	— 11	+ 8	22
252	Namhkok	108	...	71	1	9	1,394	7,160	3,639	3,521	6,920	+ 3	+ 3	66
253	Nawn Wawn	28		59	1	3	815	4,039	2,066	1,973	4,143	— 3	— 14	144
254	Mõng Pai	730	...	154	4	32	4,496	20,994	10,615	10,379	20,287	+ 3	+ 5	29
255	Wanyin	219	...	172	1	4	2,153	11,544	5,782	5,762	11,254	+ 3	*Nil*	53
256	Sakoi	82	...	37	...	1	489	1,996	1,029	967	2,162	— 8	+ 56	24
257	Hopong	212	...	131	1	5	2,313	11,871	5,967	5,904	13,153	— 10	+ 18	56
258	Lawksawk	2,362	...	370	3	17	6,089	29,358	14,967	14,391	28,970	+ 1	+ 17	12
	South-Eastern Subdivision.	*8,288*	...	*1,865*	*6*	*39*	*21,859*	*112,701*	*56,492*	*56,209*	*104,230*	*+ 8*	*+ 9*	*14*
259	Mõng Nai	3,100	..	1,108	2	4	10,523	55,647	27,781	27,866	53,784	+ 3	+ 9	18
	Kenghkam	*196*	...	*118*	...	*1*	*1,138*	*5,833*	*2,888*	*2,945*	*5,936*	*— 2*	*+ 9*	*30*
	Kengtawng	} *2,904*	...	{ *270*	*1*	*2*	*2,269*	*12,681*	*6,329*	*6,352*	*12,225*	*+ 4*	*+ 27*	} *17*
	Remainder		.	*720*	*1*	*1*	*7,116*	*37,133*	*18,564*	*18,569*	*35,623*	*+ 4*	*+ 3*	
260	Mawkmai	2,200	...	489	3	21	7,005	35,326	17,580	17,746	31,892	+ 11	+ 8	16
261	Mõng Pan	2,988		268	1	14	4,331	21,728	11,131	10,597	18,554	+ 17	+ 9	7
	Western Subdivision.	*3,089*	...	*1,284*	*10*	*122*	*25,352*	*125,394*	*62,176*	*63,218*	*130,072¶*	*— 4*	*+ 9*	*40*
262	Hsa Mõng Hkam (19)** ..	287	.	189	2	10	3,295	14,664	7,572	7,092	15,509‖	— 5	+ 23	50
263	Kyon	24	..	24	..	4	610	2,523	1,248	1,275	2,577	— 2	+ 10	105
264	Pwela	102	...	60	2	15	2,032	9,348	4,526	4,822	8,835	+ 6	+ 12	92
265	Mawson	43	...	38	1	6	974	4,061	1,913	2,148	3,792	+ 7	+ 7	94
266	Pangtara	86	...	92	2	19	2,865	15,580	7,542	8,038	16,789	— 7	+ 12	181
267	Kyawkku	76	...	33	...	7	773	4,790	2,349	2,441	4,636	+ 3	— 3	63
268	Ye-ngan	359	...	55	2	12	1,629	9,152	4,606	4,546	10,107	— 9	+ 1	28
269	Maw	741	...	55	1	10	1,474	7,406	3,755	3,651	8,262	— 10	+ 7	10
270	Mawnang	39	...	11	..	7	1,041	4,275	2,058	2,217	4,644	— 8	+ 24	110
271	Pinmi	30	...	37	...	3	624	3,001	1,521	1,480	3,529	— 15	+ 2	100
272	Loimaw	48	...	50	...	2	919	4,665	2,263	2,402	5,045	— 8	+ 10	97
273	Loi Ai	156	...	114	...	2	1,470	7,492	3,680	3,812	5,939	+ 26	+ 9	48
274	Loi Long (18, 19)	1,084	...	450	...	24	7,422	37,607	18,722	18,885	39,498	— 5	+ 8	35
275	Namtok	14	...	16	...	1	224	830	421	409	910	— 9	+ 17	59
	43. Karenni.	**4,280**	...	**692**	**13**	**56**	**15,827**	**63,850**	**31,129**	**32,721**	**63,628**	...	**+ 30**	**15**
276	Kantarawadi	3,000	...	420	8	24	8,834	36,621	18,020	18,601	39,198	— 7	+ 49	12
277	Bawlakè	500	...	90	5	11	2,756	10,754	5,640	5,114	8,649	+ 24	+ 52	22
278	Kyebogyi	700	...	130	...	21	3,610	14,104	6,274	7,830	12,785	+ 10	+ 30	20
279	Naungpale	30	...	20	...	...	263	966	508	458	1,153	— 16	— 9	32
280	Nammekon	50	...	32	...	...	359	1,405	687	718	1,843	— 24	— 30	28

* Omitting East Manglün.

¶ Allowing for extension of Census Area.

‖ The separate 1911 figures for Kalaw are not available; they were chiefly included in those given for Hsa Mõng Hkam State in the Western Subdivision, but some were also included in the Yamèthin District.

** Known to Burmans as Thamakan.

† Includes the Ngadaung tract separately listed in 1911 and also Mõng Leng.

§ Includes Kokang Circle separately listed in 1921.

PROVINCIAL TABLE II.

Population of Townships, States and Hill-Tracts Classified by Religion.

NOTE 1.—All totals given in this table for parts of the province which include either the Pakôkku Hill Tracts, the Upper Chindwin district, or North Hsenwi of the Northern Shan States differ from the corresponding totals in Provincial Table I by the omission of figures for the area in which in the census was only an estimate of the total population and no classification by religion could be effected. These areas are shown with their total populations in Provincial Table I as items Nos. 141, 208 and 236.

NOTE 2.—The figures given for Christians in this table include all who follow the Christian religion and also all those members of Christian races who do not individually follow that religion. The total of the latter for the province is 45 males and 20 females, of whom 15 and 16 respectively are Buddhists; the distribution of these by religion and district is given in Note 3 of Imperial Table VIA.

NOTE 3.—Details of *Others* by whole districts are given in Imperial Table VIA.

NOTE 4.—Notes 9 and 13 to 19 inclusive of Provincial Table I apply also to this table if comparison with the corresponding table of 1911 is instituted.

NOTE 5.—A table in the same form as this, but giving particulars for each village-tract in the district, is included in the B volume of the gazetteer of each district.

PROVINCIAL TABLE II.—*Population of Townships, etc., Classified by Religion.*

Serial No.	Township, State, etc.	Total. Males.	Total. Females.	Buddhists. Males.	Buddhists. Females.	Animists. Males.	Animists. Females.	Hindus. Males.	Hindus. Females.	Mahomedans. Males.	Mahomedans. Females.	Christians. Males.	Christians. Females.	Others. Males.	Others. Females.
	1	2	3	4	5	6	7	8	9	10	11	12	13	14	15
	PROVINCIAL TOTAL.*	6,735,516	6,433,583	5,525,144	5,676,768	369,188	333,399	378,177	106,255	314,527	186,065	132,543	124,628	15,937	6,468
	*Divisional Burma.**	5,991,623	5,706,785	4,932,834	5,085,632	248,426	212,678	367,516	103,911	311,098	184,660	121,020	113,483	15,729	6,421
	*Eastern States.**	743,893	726,798	592,310	591,136	125,762	120,721	10,661	2,344	3,429	1,405	11,523	11,145	208	47
	Arakan Division.	472,227	437,019	295,258	301,436	38,998	36,633	14,748	1,556	122,108	96,629	992	732	153	33
	1. Akyab District.	309,564	266,866	159,722	155,418	19,124	17,682	13,401	1,318	116,736	92,225	428	190	153	33
1	Akyab	33,894	14,294	9,682	9,340	330	118	8,087	440	15,319	4,212	393	162	83	22
2	Buthidaung	40,835	37,662	15,120	14,474	2,424	2,318	972	273	23,299	20,595	11	8	9	...
3	Kyauktaw	31,642	26,632	15,025	14,100	3,816	3,665	626	88	12,147	8,768	6	4	22	7
4	Maungdaw	59,461	58,744	11,171	11,592	1,669	1,502	1,077	471	45,540	45,174	4	5	...	...
5	Minbya	27,729	23,659	18,413	17,214	4,551	4,185	637	7	4,088	2,245	12	8	8	...
6	Myohaung	33,446	27,643	23,796	22,024	2,532	2,352	983	9	6,220	3,205	...	...	...	3
7	Pauktaw	23,902	21,713	20,356	19,644	452	373	196	17	2,891	1,676	1	3	6	...
8	Pônnagyun	27,327	26,252	22,842	22,951	2,848	2,760	462	1	1,150	541	1	...	24	1
9	Rathedaung	31,328	30,265	23,317	24,089	502	415	416	12	7,092	5,749	...	...	1	...
	2. Hill District of Arakan.	10,790	10,124	1,220	1,005	9,109	8,945	407	168	43	3	11	3	...	...
10	Paletwa	10,790	10,124	1,220	1,005	9,109	8,945	407	168	43	3	11	3	...	...
	3. Kyaukpyu District.	96,669	103,304	84,901	93,550	8,414	7,759	609	25	2,580	1,899	65	71	...	...
11	An	17,980	19,099	11,492	11,259	6,336	5,814	78	1	61	...	16	12	...	...
12	Cheduba	15,389	17,132	15,236	17,036	74	72	24	...	83	25	2	...	...	...
13	Kyaukpyu	24,800	26,325	23,781	25,765	130	101	260	21	612	424	10	14	...	...
14	Myebôn	15,664	15,034	12,831	13,054	1,573	1,521	226	2	997	416	37	41	...	...
15	Ramree	22,727	27,714	21,861	26,438	283	242	24	1	887	1,034	...	1	...	...
	4. Sandoway District.	5,304	56,725	49,415	51,463	2,321	2,247	331	45	2,749	2,502	488	468	...	...
16	Gwa	12,026	11,676	11,264	11,145	186	160	73	8	212	87	289	276	...	...
17	Sandoway	23,777	24,339	20,281	21,141	700	662	204	35	2,434	2,357	158	144	...	...
18	Taungup	19,501	20,710	17,870	19,177	1,435	1,428	52	2	103	58	41	48	...	...
	Pegu Division.	1,258,914	1,050,379	922,188	926,780	17,273	7,133	195,953	56,577	77,881	24,214	34,498	28,593	11,121	5,092
	5. Rangoon District.	236,689	105,273	58,077	53,473	2,136	747	102,313	22,689	49,520	12,434	14,236	11,079	10,407	4,851
19	Municipality	218,749	102,941	56,365	52,727	1,998	721	93,307	21,820	44,735	12,308	12,018	10,487	10,338	4,838
20	Cantonment { Civil Area ...	2,870	1,027	81	87	...	...	1,345	559	325	65	1,118	345	1	1
	Cantonment { Military Area ...	1,670	906	894	452	34	12	635	226	208	83	275	163	27	4
21	Port	13,400	401	1,237	257	104	14	7,029	90	4,257	8	825	44	51	8
	6. Insein District.	156,794	136,289	122,368	119,113	2,358	853	18,872	5,786	5,391	2,599	7,688	7,891	117	47
22	Hlegu	30,059	28,017	25,142	24,713	338	132	1,906	803	675	376	1,990	1,986	8	7
23	Insein	62,721	48,128	42,648	39,971	1,099	409	13,644	3,934	2,882	1,267	2,397	2,511	101	36
24	Taikkyi	36,158	33,025	30,694	30,093	513	158	1,920	423	1,368	729	1,655	1,618	8	4
25	Tantabin	27,856	27,119	23,884	24,336	408	154	1,402	626	516	227	2,646	2,776	...	...
	7. Hanthawaddy District.	201,043	163,581	148,754	145,006	3,997	1,205	35,365	11,961	9,551	3,260	3,028	2,058	348	92
26	Kayan	31,981	27,755	24,735	24,097	584	197	5,693	3,074	826	320	806	67	7	...
27	Kungyangôn North	25,089	22,167	20,934	20,401	254	59	2,343	920	857	265	692	526	9	...
28	Kungyangôn South	21,597	19,291	17,949	17,481	311	93	1,683	697	1,515	972	90	46	51	2
29	Kyauktan	28,313	25,197	20,381	19,898	373	101	6,287	2,781	976	245	293	170	3	2
30	Syriam	19,337	8,314	6,093	6,080	233	41	8,880	1,013	3,248	755	519	343	264	82
31	Thôngwa	29,854	26,317	24,229	23,578	644	221	3,908	1,968	442	201	630	349	1	...
32	Twante	45,002	35,540	34,433	33,470	1,598	493	6,571	1,508	1,689	506	698	557	13	6
	8. Tharrawaddy District.	246,261	246,168	229,477	238,081	1,600	529	7,422	1,757	3,736	1,685	3,970	4,104	56	12
33	Gyobingauk	28,132	28,496	26,233	27,775	229	75	914	190	405	140	332	307	19	...
34	Letpadan East	20,839	19,966	18,332	18,781	221	54	1,204	378	618	268	457	483	7	9
35	Letpadan West	31,476	31,324	29,169	30,223	182	21	1,089	246	437	186	898	648	1	...
36	Minhla East	21,546	21,197	20,308	20,743	91	34	711	122	203	57	232	281	1	...
37	Minhla West	22,276	22,094	20,784	21,834	231	89	613	158	500	181	148	132	...	...
38	Mênyo	26,488	26,432	26,094	26,240	30	3	140	16	68	14	156	159	...	...
39	Nattalin	33,796	34,274	32,801	33,990	100	28	527	84	228	106	140	126	...	...
40	Tharrawaddy	34,819	34,748	30,453	31,771	241	77	1,404	423	980	597	1,774	1,870	27	[illegible]
41	Zigôn	26,889	27,337	25,303	26,784	275	148	820	150	387	137	133	128	1	...
	9. Pegu District.	235,324	210,296	191,185	187,152	4,533	2,174	27,554	13,302	6,996	2,749	4,919	4,872	137	47
42	Daiku	47,296	42,201	39,788	38,891	1,331	745	3,312	936	1,466	568	1,394	1,459	8	8
43	Kawa	36,539	33,996	30,871	30,001	472	232	3,247	1,690	631	348	1,844	1,219	34	16
44	Nyaunglebin	52,395	46,611	40,089	39,883	1,253	626	7,446	3,937	2,048	639	1,557	1,817	28	9
45	Pegu	56,987	49,088	45,868	44,624	747	271	7,831	3,738	1,885	812	864	829	62	17
46	Thanatpin	42,147	37,400	34,569	33,553	730	310	5,718	3,004	939	383	180	148	11	...
	10. Prome District.	182,803	188,772	172,327	183,956	2,649	1,625	4,427	1,082	2,687	1,487	657	589	56	33
47	Hmawza	23,014	24,832	22,513	24,663	93	55	255	45	112	33	40	35	1	1
48	Padaung	25,807	25,424	24,477	24,558	601	576	120	8	124	115	185	155	...	2
49	Paukkaung	14,856	14,914	14,252	14,494	437	368	86	11	40	19	25	16	16	6
50	Paungdè	33,604	34,911	31,655	34,318	305	83	1,091	199	466	225	62	68	25	18
51	Prome	26,293	24,309	21,548	22,225	990	423	2,053	680	1,441	745	248	230	13	6
52	Shwedaung	29,221	31,896	28,685	31,618	88	31	179	45	259	186	9	17	1	...
53	Thêgôn	30,308	32,497	29,197	32,080	138	89	643	96	245	164	88	68	...	...

* See Note 1 on the title-page of the table.

PROVINCIAL TABLE II.—*Population of Townships, etc., Classified by Religion.*

Serial No.	Township, State, etc.	Total. Males.	Total. Females.	Buddhists. Males.	Buddhists. Females.	Animists. Males.	Animists. Females.	Hindus. Males.	Hindus. Females.	Mahomedans. Males.	Mahomedans. Females.	Christians. Males.	Christians. Females.	Others. Males.	Others. Females.
	1	2	3	4	5	6	7	8	9	10	11	12	13	14	15
	Irrawaddy Division.	**1,048,377**	**981,067**	**917,736**	**917,290**	**11,762**	**3,095**	**46,165**	**8,282**	**28,588**	**9,790**	**43,464**	**43,144**	**882**	**148**
	11. Bassein District.	*252,947*	*236,526*	*213,811*	*214,735*	*2,696*	*860*	*13,151*	*1,796*	*7,082*	*2,912*	*16,207*	*16,423*	...	...
54	Bassein East	32,869	33,013	29,030	29,835	299	115	611	159	528	255	2,401	2,649	...	...
55	Bassein West	45,659	31,093	26,873	24,003	1,031	233	9,758	1,339	4,209	1,670	3,788	3,788	...	...
56	Kyaunggôn	29,475	29,671	26,410	27,285	271	65	291	41	579	283	1,924	1,597	...	...
57	Kyônpyaw	46,369	46,524	42,517	43,911	314	63	855	78	620	271	2,063	2,171	...	...
58	Ngaputaw	31,502	28,933	28,008	26,701	325	55	562	25	279	104	2,328	2,048	...	...
59	Ngathainggyaung	41,818	42,216	39,020	40,658	291	80	856	80	654	275	997	983	...	...
60	Thabaung	25,255	25,176	21,953	22,872	165	49	818	14	213	54	2,706	2,787	...	...
	12. Henzada District.	*273,439*	*277,481*	*257,027*	*268,204*	*1,632*	*388*	*5,712*	*991*	*3,323*	*1,888*	*5,711*	*6,031*	*34*	*28*
61	Henzada	71,421	70,936	64,118	67,561	774	138	3,301	645	1,396	694	1,812	1,877	20	22
62	Ingabu	50,626	52,108	48,842	50,887	192	76	396	69	342	156	849	920	5	...
63	Kyangin	24,372	23,999	23,664	23,701	75	20	360	40	178	141	92	97	3	...
64	Lemyethna	33,329	33,671	32,143	33,044	197	22	407	71	254	176	325	353	3	2
65	Myanaung	51,930	54,078	49,716	52,699	137	29	595	106	673	403	806	838	3	3
66	Zalun	41,761	42,689	38,544	40,312	257	53	653	60	480	318	1,827	1,946	...	...
	13. Myaungmya District.	*196,757*	*173,794*	*165,260*	*159,055*	*3,292*	*735*	*8,544*	*989*	*8,990*	*2,461*	*10,645*	*10,653*	*26*	*1*
67	Einme	37,318	36,132	31,264	32,121	607	135	558	289	1,858	780	2,626	2,807	5	...
68	Labutta	19,482	16,025	16,787	15,014	414	53	832	22	506	86	943	890	...	...
69	Mawlamyainggyun	44,751	38,148	37,458	35,564	681	230	2,361	255	2,526	381	1,720	1,678	5	...
70	Myaungmya	43,174	37,502	36,760	33,975	782	131	1,618	220	1,162	361	2,962	2,814	10	1
71	Wakema	52,032	45,987	42,991	42,381	865	186	2,775	163	2,938	853	2,454	2,404	6	...
	14. Ma-ubin District.	*168,513*	*161,593*	*150,413*	*152,449*	*1,244*	*492*	*5,954*	*879*	*4,350*	*1,651*	*5,976*	*6,008*	*576*	*114*
72	Danubyu	43,333	43,907	39,219	41,335	207	71	1,196	132	975	476	1,733	1,887	89	6
73	Ma-ubin	47,116	42,386	40,275	40,025	209	63	3,081	369	1,737	462	1,505	1,388	332	72
74	Pantanaw	41,126	40,112	37,264	37,406	365	296	492	97	810	348	1,986	1,961	9	41
75	Yandoon	36,938	35,188	33,655	33,683	263	62	1,273	281	848	365	750	772	149	25
	15. Pyapon District.	*156,721*	*132,273*	*131,226*	*122,847*	*2,898*	*873*	*12,804*	*3,627*	*4,843*	*797*	*4,925*	*4,129*	*26*	...
76	Bogale	46,882	38,014	39,875	35,578	849	167	3,344	793	1,215	127	1,899	1,355	...	...
77	Dedayè	39,728	34,218	33,481	32,192	656	197	3,153	897	1,309	225	1,128	797	1	...
78	Kyaiklat	41,441	36,800	35,511	34,219	679	261	2,387	501	1,268	259	1,580	1,560	16	...
79	Pyapôn	28,670	23,141	22,358	20,864	714	248	3,920	1,436	1,051	186	618	507	9	...
	Tenasserim Division.	**847,445**	**786,078**	**690,077**	**669,487**	**32,981**	**25,069**	**56,680**	**10,700**	**38,234**	**24,062**	**28,250**	**27,633**	**223**	**108**
	16. Toungoo District.	*197,505*	*184,378*	*149,783*	*148,197*	*11,268*	*9,431*	*13,316*	*6,259*	*5,498*	*2,665*	*17,624*	*17,818*	*16*	*8*
80	Kyaukkyi	20,168	18,479	12,695	11,800	5,844	5,459	392	59	246	31	1,030	1,040	...	...
81	Leiktho	8,327	8,595	468	379	3	4	..	..	1	...	7,855	8,212	...	...
82	Oktwin	26,164	26,011	23,867	24,784	614	422	778	210	558	230	347	365	...	...
83	Pyu	39,694	37,101	30,765	30,971	1,032	594	6,262	4,582	1,112	900	523	454	...	...
84	Shwegyin	21,983	17,762	18,042	16,265	593	401	1,632	160	1,125	446	591	490	...	...
85	Tantabin	23,791	23,180	16,828	16,614	1,600	1,502	204	33	162	71	4,997	4,960	...	...
86	Toungoo	30,935	27,752	23,026	23,097	712	391	3,224	1,037	1,987	1,219	1,960	2,000	16	8
87	Yedashe	26,443	25,498	24,131	24,197	870	658	824	178	897	168	321	297	...	...
	17. Salween District.	*26,811*	*23,568*	*14,413*	*11,914*	*11,200*	*11,207*	*307*	*48*	*449*	*83*	*442*	*316*	...	...
88	Papun	26,811	23,568	14,413	11,914	11,200	11,207	307	48	449	83	442	316	...	...
	18. Thaton District.	*245,909*	*225,191*	*218,580*	*211,749*	*1,615*	*688*	*14,794*	*6,318*	*8,912*	*4,493*	*1,920*	*1,891*	*88*	*52*
89	Bilin	35,955	32,667	32,828	31,678	210	75	1,895	505	895	324	45	35	32	50
90	Hlaingbwè	39,004	36,141	36,435	34,443	70	24	240	101	1,455	701	804	872	...	...
91	Kyaikto	25,748	22,901	21,813	21,259	353	122	2,553	1,039	993	455	36	32	...	1
92	Pa-an	61,377	58,964	56,728	56,246	211	83	1,961	1,153	1,010	855	569	627	1	...
93	Paung	37,333	34,159	32,281	30,544	278	169	5,019	2,379	1,623	977	130	89	2	1
94	Thatôn	44,492	40,359	38,498	37,579	493	215	3,126	1,148	2,036	1,181	336	236	3	...
	19. Amherst District.	*223,348*	*194,562*	*181,489*	*173,686*	*2,446*	*996*	*19,468*	*5,947*	*16,261*	*10,417*	*3,596*	*3,478*	*88*	*38*
95	Chaungzôn	27,778	26,120	25,258	24,698	129	41	1,105	448	1,139	882	47	52	...	...
96	Kawkareik	32,238	29,640	29,097	27,478	241	158	764	357	1,877	1,466	259	244	...	...
97	Kyaikkami	15,969	13,852	14,256	13,210	135	38	892	76	536	394	149	134	1	...
98	Kyaikmaraw	26,383	25,219	22,226	22,113	47	12	892	482	3,007	2,465	151	147	...	...
99	Kya-in	22,149	20,360	20,440	19,062	1	1	78	7	475	195	1,155	1,095	...	...
100	Moulmein	48,837	29,958	20,265	19,444	1,200	803	14,623	4,084	8,054	4,365	1,854	1,804	81	38
101	Mudôn	30,776	29,378	28,515	27,934	445	119	898	451	708	573	207	231	6	...
102	Yelamaing	22,278	20,035	21,432	19,747	158	37	229	42	365	137	94	72	...	...
	20. Tavoy District.	*80,994*	*75,792*	*72,612*	*72,534*	*2,194*	*579*	*2,953*	*366*	*1,844*	*1,029*	*1,371*	*1,274*	*20*	*10*
103	Launglon	23,670	23,483	23,331	23,339	46	6	107	15	161	98	24	24	1	1
104	Tavoy	24,826	22,062	18,789	19,816	1,844	558	2,176	321	1,382	773	690	585	15	9
105	Thayetchaung	20,845	20,748	20,347	20,404	50	8	101	2	152	121	195	213	...	...
106	Yebyu	11,653	9,499	10,145	8,975	254	7	869	28	179	37	262	452	4	...
	21. Mergui District.	*72,878*	*62,587*	*53,200*	*51,417*	*4,258*	*2,168*	*5,842*	*771*	*6,270*	*5,375*	*3,297*	*2,856*	*11*	...
107	Bôkpyin	5,139	4,777	4,158	3,488	432	110	2	...	1,076	996	271	175	...	...
108	Mergui	34,887	29,037	25,078	24,579	1,701	878	4,032	532	3,181	2,658	888	690	7	...
109	Palaw	16,953	16,431	14,114	14,216	553	464	591	47	99	21	1,506	1,663	...	...
110	Tenasserim	8,845	7,665	7,345	6,901	172	5	472	88	403	397	483	274	...	...
111	Maliwun	4,726	3,718	2,325	2,225	530	56	374	102	1,425	1,301	78	38	...	...
112	Salons living in boats	875	956	...	...	868	945	...	...	4	2	3	3	...	...
113	Settlement and Survey Parties	683	13	180	8	2	...	371	2	88	...	84	2	4	...

PROVINCIAL TABLE II.—*Population of Townships, etc., Classified by Religion.*

Serial No.	Township, State, etc.	Total. Males.	Total. Females.	Buddhists. Males.	Buddhists. Females.	Animists. Males.	Animists. Females.	Hindus. Males.	Hindus. Females.	Mahomedans. Males.	Mahomedans. Females.	Christians. Males.	Christians. Females.	Others. Males.	Others. Females.
	1	2	3	4	5	6	7	8	9	10	11	12	13	14	15
	Magwe Divisions.*	**706,247**	**733,527**	**667,197**	**714,249**	**20,233**	**19,582**	**10,671**	**1,538**	**5,473**	**2,295**	**1,343**	**768**	**330**	**95**
	22. Thayetmyo District.	*126,283*	*130,123*	*116,712*	*128,014*	*5,725*	*5,544*	*1,405*	*541*	*1,177*	*817*	*261*	*204*	*3*	*3*
114	Allanmyo	31,938	34,384	30,119	32,947	998	1,018	370	121	372	253	79	45	...	...
115	Kama	18,184	19,142	17,047	18,049	1,020	1,015	40	8	39	27	38	43	...	...
116	Mindon	17,839	18,243	15,308	15,762	2,502	2,475	15	1	5	2	9	3	...	...
117	Minhla	16,935	16,830	15,529	15,850	1,057	939	132	16	196	43	21	2	...	...
118	Sinbaungwe	17,173	18,565	17,055	18,547	4	3	68	4	40	9	6	2	...	...
119	Thayetmyo	23,217	22,959	21,654	21,879	147	94	780	391	525	483	108	109	3	3
	23. Pakokku District.	*223,943*	*241,828*	*220,496*	*239,663*	*1,756*	*1,589*	*702*	*140*	*701*	*321*	*211*	*97*	*78*	*18*
120	Gangaw	19,151	19,155	17,327	17,622	1,485	1,507	64	12	22	9	46	5	7	...
121	Myaing	43,676	49,806	43,661	49,802	2	...	8	1	5	3	...	...	...	...
122	Pakôkku	47,578	50,774	46,116	50,239	155	35	546	118	586	289	133	82	42	11
123	Pauk	26,909	27,590	26,833	27,579	1	...	19	...	33	5	16	4	8	2
124	Saw	12,935	12,656	12,884	12,648	26	7	7	...	2	...	3	...	13	1
125	Seikpyu	16,714	17,722	16,656	17,706	2	...	28	3	17	5	4	4	7	4
126	Tilin	7,840	7,685	7,785	7,644	45	37	6	3	3	1	1	...	...	...
127	Yesagyo	49,140	56,440	49,034	56,423	40	3	24	3	33	9	8	2	1	...
	24. Minbu District.	*134,495*	*139,807*	*129,039*	*136,846*	*2,620*	*2,240*	*1,752*	*243*	*842*	*381*	*118*	*56*	*124*	*41*
128	Ngape	8,488	8,339	6,498	6,394	1,977	1,944	12	1	1	...	...	...	...	...
129	Pwinbyu	36,530	37,576	35,351	37,482	69	17	844	70	179	45	8	1	79	21
130	Sagu	31,967	32,585	30,529	32,101	173	51	665	130	479	239	89	48	32	16
131	Salin	45,737	49,760	45,128	49,575	179	35	219	42	178	97	20	7	13	4
132	Sidôktaya	11,773	11,547	11,533	11,354	222	193	12	...	5	...	1	...	...	...
	25. Magwe District.	*211,686*	*211,566*	*200,865*	*209,683*	*533*	*96*	*6,669*	*574*	*2,748*	*773*	*746*	*407*	*125*	*33*
133	Magwe	43,613	44,062	42,240	43,622	178	45	689	165	422	155	74	67	10	8
134	Myothit	27,584	29,613	27,500	29,592	2	...	5	...	55	21	22	...	...	...
135	Natmauk	41,163	44,313	41,107	44,279	1	...	25	16	28	18	1	...	1	...
136	Sale (transferred from Myingyan District).	30,422	29,710	29,035	29,510	84	16	757	36	402	75	136	69	8	4
137	Satthwa	14,103	15,375	14,027	15,338	...	...	34	1	14	...	28	36	...	...
138	Taungdwingyi	17,335	18,545	16,854	18,364	30	6	152	48	122	81	26	33	21	13
139	Yenangyaung	37,596	29,948	30,102	28,978	238	29	5,007	308	1,705	423	459	202	85	8
	*26. Pakokku Hill Tracts.**	*9,840*	*10,203*	*86*	*43*	*9,599*	*10,113*	*143*	*40*	*5*	*3*	*7*	*4*	*...*	*...*
140	Administered Area	9,840	10,203	86	43	9,599	10,113	143	40	5	3	7	4	...	...
141	Unadministered Area *	Not classified by religion.													
	Mandalay Division.	**435,894**	**413,467**	**316,866**	**321,258**	**65,049**	**63,018**	**26,382**	**10,892**	**17,752**	**11,209**	**7,659**	**6,493**	**2,192**	**597**
	27. Mandalay District.	*182,999*	*173,622*	*146,206*	*153,122*	*2,301*	*397*	*15,591*	*6,470*	*13,665*	*9,544*	*4,506*	*3,823*	*731*	*266*
142	Mandalay City	77,763	71,154	56,811	58,343	1,320	292	7,434	3,561	9,638	6,735	2,083	2,077	477	146
143	Amarapura	23,531	24,397	19,327	21,552	42	20	2,086	947	1,823	1,738	113	90	140	56
144	Madaya	25,015	26,023	24,617	25,901	7	1	227	35	118	69	24	11	28	16
145	Maymyo	20,349	13,908	9,863	9,387	911	72	5,390	1,914	1,857	857	2,254	1,639	74	39
146	Patheingyi	15,604	16,720	15,037	16,604	14	12	422	23	140	68	9	4	12	9
147	Singu	20,737	21,420	20,380	21,335	7	...	32	...	95	83	23	2	...	...
	28. Bhamo District.	*56,888*	*56,072*	*28,193*	*27,629*	*22,850*	*25,509*	*1,097*	*300*	*1,541*	*419*	*2,056*	*1,996*	*1,151*	*219*
148	Bhamo	19,879	17,343	14,220	14,719	2,090	1,405	693	228	1,300	371	517	434	1,059	186
149	Shwegu	11,911	10,091	10,965	9,769	491	226	103	38	145	37	185	19	22	4
150	Shwegu Kachin Hill Tracts	2,788	2,580	128	21	2,652	2,790	..	...	...	...	8	9	...	...
151	Sinlum Kachin Hill Tracts	22,310	25,818	2,880	3,120	17,617	21,090	301	34	96	11	1,346	1,534	70	29
	29. Myitkyina District.	*63,419*	*54,963*	*21,587*	*18,373*	*34,135*	*32,792*	*5,980*	*2,849*	*899*	*384*	*536*	*459*	*282*	*106*
152	Kamaing	8,841	4,797	6,693	4,486	1,560	164	518	131	51	9	10	5	9	2
153	Mogaung	10,228	8,059	8,437	8,222	607	250	989	274	154	86	24	17	17	20
154	Myitkyina	12,278	9,358	5,704	5,116	2,122	1,480	3,362	2,080	595	279	361	277	136	56
155	Htawgaw Kachin Hill Tracts	8,745	8,560	5	2	8,385	8,447	318	106	84	1	8	3	15	1
156	Kamaing Kachin Hill Tracts	3,961	3,106	172	21	3,749	3,085	35	...	1	...	2	...	2	...
157	Mogaung Kachin Hill Tracts	5,095	5,372	138	138	4,876	5,190	40	13	...	...	26	31	15	...
158	Myitkyina Kachin Hill Tracts	3,809	3,202	45	10	3,046	3,147	119	10	67	...	28	35	4	...
159	Sadôn Kachin Hill Tracts	6,030	6,316	363	359	5,305	5,735	320	112	12	6	58	67	84	27
160	Sima Kachin Hill Tracts	5,023	5,393	30	19	4,685	5,234	281	283	5	3	22	24	...	...
	30. Katha District.	*128,444*	*126,281*	*117,983*	*118,903*	*5,362*	*4,258*	*2,935*	*1,055*	*1,620*	*858*	*537*	*207*	*7*	*...*
161	Banmauk	13,613	15,064	13,462	15,037	39	17	65	6	21	2	22	2	4	...
162	Indaw	8,367	8,102	7,832	7,985	103	13	265	28	151	82	16	14	...	...
163	Katha	11,659	10,595	10,560	10,153	222	67	339	87	443	233	94	55	1	...
164	Kawlin	17,557	17,513	17,180	17,361	110	50	94	20	168	81	5	1	...	...
165	Mawlu	14,001	12,688	13,263	12,465	232	76	347	62	157	78	42	7	...	...
166	Mogôk	14,161	11,275	10,435	9,957	1,714	1,087	1,492	785	420	266	99	80	1	...
167	Pinlebu	14,754	16,712	14,681	16,700	2	...	36	5	28	...	7	7	...	...
168	Tagaung	6,543	6,005	6,337	5,945	11	3	56	14	44	32	95	11	...	...
169	Thabeitkyin	5,252	4,585	4,982	4,511	40	36	114	20	39	13	77	5	...	...
170	Tigyaing	8,602	8,586	8,457	8,525	38	5	25	4	78	49	4	3	...	...
171	Wuntho	11,128	11,262	10,788	11,168	63	13	141	24	71	42	64	21	1	...
172	Katha Kachin Hill Tracts	480	428	2	...	466	428	1	...	...	...	11	...	...	...
173	Mawlu Kachin Hill Tracts	2,327	2,466	4	2	2,322	2,463	...	...	...	...	1	1	...	...
	31. Putao District.	*4,144*	*3,529*	*2,892*	*3,231*	*401*	*62*	*779*	*218*	*27*	*4*	*24*	*8*	*21*	*6*
	Putao Subdivision—														
174	(i) Hkamti Long Shan States	4,144	3,529	2,892	3,231	401	62	779	218	27	4	24	8	21	6
175	(ii) Remainder	Omitted from the census and excluded from district totals accordingly.													
176	Kaugin Subdivision														
177	Laza (or Sumpra Bum Subdivision)														

* See Note 1 on the title-page of this table.

PROVINCIAL TABLE II.—*Population of Townships, etc., Classified by Religion.*

Serial No.	Township, State, etc.	Total.		Buddhists.		Animists.		Hindus.		Mahomedans.		Christians.		Others.	
		Males.	Females.	Males.	Females.	Males.	Females.	Males.	Females.	Males.	Females.	Males.	Females.	Males.	Females.
	1	2	3	4	5	6	7	8	9	10	11	12	13	14	15
	Sagaing Division.*	**641,290**	**709,106**	**568,431**	**642,570**	**54,873**	**56,825**	**7,895**	**2,763**	**7,068**	**5,449**	**2,503**	**2,309**	**520**	**190**
	32. Shwebo District.	*184,708*	*206,576*	*177,347*	*201,117*	*305*	*83*	*1,925*	*613*	*3,922*	*3,688*	*1,016*	*993*	*193*	*82*
178	Kanbalu	26,856	27,704	23,780	24,888	117	30	412	145	2,436	2,563	73	67	38	11
179	Kin-u	21,364	23,726	20,836	23,309	8	3	91	25	277	221	140	160	18	8
180	Kyunhla	7,485	7,461	7,374	7,372	18	3	19	5	63	81	11	...	...	...
181	Shwebo	30,846	32,258	28,557	30,954	104	30	840	279	797	578	420	357	128	60
182	Tabayin	25,267	29,595	25,152	29,565	...	...	77	20	19	7	16	1	3	2
183	Tamadaw	10,988	14,678	10,976	14,678	...	...	4	...	1	...	7	...	...	...
184	Taze	16,928	19,910	16,880	19,901	2	1	26	2	18	6	2	...	...	...
185	Wetlet	30,345	35,291	29,886	33,049	19	6	217	66	186	139	31	30	6	1
186	Ye-u	14,629	17,953	13,906	17,401	43	10	239	71	125	93	316	378	...	...
	33. Sagaing District.	*155,054*	*171,854*	*151,524*	*169,492*	*84*	*13*	*1,382*	*574*	*1,563*	*1,248*	*446*	*502*	*55*	*25*
187	Chaungu	14,993	17,492	14,736	17,267	4	...	50	8	23	25	164	183	16	9
188	Myaung	21,805	24,189	21,613	23,971	9	...	5	...	42	38	132	180	4	...
189	Myinmu	19,092	21,541	18,607	21,278	37	5	207	66	232	188	9	4	...	...
190	Ngazun	28,524	31,446	28,327	31,272	8	2	16	5	170	164	2	2	1	1
191	Sagaing	42,441	46,395	40,225	45,038	25	6	1,064	489	956	785	137	132	34	15
192	Tada-u	28,199	30,791	28,016	30,666	1	...	40	6	140	118	2	1	...	...
	34. Lower Chindwin District.	*156,693*	*186,187*	*154,557*	*185,508*	*126*	*15*	*1,006*	*293*	*794*	*231*	*194*	*140*	*16*	...
193	Budalin	34,171	42,390	34,112	42,377	1	...	46	10	12	2	...	1	...	...
194	Kani	29,791	33,970	29,689	33,966	...	...	85	2	12	...	5	2	...	...
195	Mônywa	45,522	54,753	45,709	54,112	108	13	784	278	722	215	183	135	16	...
196	Palè	23,786	27,535	23,749	27,538	...	...	32	...	5	...	...	...	...	...
197	Salingyi	23,423	27,539	23,298	27,518	17	2	59	3	43	14	6	2	...	...
	*35. Upper Chindwin District.**	*90,713*	*88,532*	*84,914*	*85,408*	*1,932*	*1,733*	*2,472*	*751*	*758*	*265*	*397*	*298*	*240*	*77*
198	Homalin	12,121	11,815	11,275	11,535	207	162	442	69	98	21	13	4	86	26
199	Kale	9,869	9,216	8,312	8,033	785	722	404	144	93	50	275	267	...	...
200	Kalewa	1,870	1,719	1,709	1,674	12	4	108	21	37	20	4	...	...	...
201	Kyabin	5,792	5,857	5,782	5,857	3	...	5	...	1	...	...	...	1	...
202	Maingkaing	9,159	9,446	9,061	9,404	...	...	64	26	16	7	4	...	14	9
203	Masein	7,220	7,042	7,188	7,035	8	...	12	5	4	...	2	...	6	2
204	Mawlaik	8,904	7,737	7,587	7,406	97	18	758	176	324	91	55	22	83	24
205	Mingin	11,727	12,163	11,517	12,088	1	...	87	37	98	30	2	3	22	5
206	Paungbyin	16,016	15,849	15,756	15,753	5	...	154	58	77	34	9	2	15	2
207	Tamu	3,384	3,009	2,682	2,387	466	511	191	95	8	12	33	...	4	4
208	Somra Tract	Not classified by religion. See Provincial Table I.													
209	Kanti State	1,193	1,094	1,005	959	157	135	31	...	...	...	...	...	...	...
210	Thaungdut State	3,458	3,585	3,040	3,279	191	181	316	120	2	...	...	...	9	5
	36. Chin Hills District.	*54,122*	*55,957*	*89*	*45*	*52,426*	*54,981*	*1,110*	*532*	*31*	*17*	*450*	*376*	*16*	*6*
211	Falam	19,399	21,484	65	33	18,674	21,046	531	298	15	11	100	90	14	6
212	Haka	17,011	16,618	10	3	16,540	16,479	338	78	12	5	109	55	2	...
213	Tiddim	17,712	17,855	14	9	17,212	17,456	241	156	4	3	241	231	...	...
	Meiktila Division.	**582,229**	**615,542**	**555,087**	**598,552**	**2,287**	**1,320**	**9,022**	**2,594**	**12,994**	**11,093**	**2,311**	**1,811**	**528**	**172**
	37. Kyaukse District.	*70,449*	*72,228*	*66,277*	*68,805*	*110*	*47*	*821*	*207*	*2,896*	*2,844*	*292*	*300*	*53*	*25*
214	Kyauksè	26,319	27,090	24,143	25,250	28	6	394	106	1,591	1,567	119	138	44	23
215	Myittha	25,422	25,509	24,624	25,083	82	41	330	70	343	284	37	30	6	2
216	Singaing	18,708	19,629	17,510	18,472	...	...	97	31	962	993	136	132	3	1
	38. Meiktila District.	*137,573*	*152,324*	*132,184*	*149,434*	*305*	*44*	*2,005*	*639*	*2,369*	*1,914*	*532*	*240*	*178*	*53*
217	Mahlaing	34,565	39,524	34,276	39,406	32	16	116	34	130	66	2	...	9	2
218	Meiktila	43,090	47,059	40,689	45,706	61	16	890	339	964	823	342	130	144	45
219	Thazi	29,847	31,283	27,343	29,824	156	8	895	250	1,206	986	182	109	25	6
220	Wundwin	30,071	34,558	29,876	34,498	16	4	104	16	69	39	6	1	...	...
	39. Yamethin District.	*160,913*	*162,276*	*146,086*	*152,479*	*1,577*	*1,142*	*4,797*	*1,423*	*6,896*	*6,012*	*1,285*	*1,131*	*272*	*89*
221	Lewè	31,811	29,362	29,402	28,519	137	64	1,383	119	670	477	169	166	20	17
222	Pyawbwè	20,523	22,941	18,750	21,820	105	29	630	350	826	686	65	15	107	41
223	Pyinmana	46,889	44,507	40,807	40,559	1,178	958	1,896	644	2,088	1,544	902	799	18	3
224	Yamèthin	37,180	38,623	34,265	36,601	155	89	817	280	1,708	1,481	148	147	93	25
225	Yanaung	24,504	26,843	22,822	24,980	2	2	71	30	1,604	1,824	1	4	4	3
	40. Myingyan District.	*213,294*	*228,714*	*210,540*	*227,834*	*295*	*87*	*1,399*	*325*	*833*	*323*	*202*	*140*	*25*	*5*
226	Kyaukpadaung	48,119	52,442	48,081	52,422	...	...	27	17	9	3	2	...	...	...
227	Myingyan	50,597	52,168	48,365	51,451	236	69	1,145	271	656	238	187	134	8	5
228	Natogyi	34,776	39,027	34,773	39,027	...	...	1	...	2	...	...	...	...	...
229	Pagan	38,834	41,005	38,494	40,904	47	8	144	22	124	66	8	5	17	...
230	Taungtha	40,968	44,084	40,827	41,030	12	10	82	15	42	16	5	3	...	...

* See Note 1 on the title-page of this table.

PROVINCIAL TABLE II.—*Population of States, etc., Classified by Religion.*

Serial No.	Subdivision, State, Notified Area, etc.	Total. Males.	Total. Females.	Buddhists. Males.	Buddhists. Females.	Animists. Males.	Animists. Females.	Hindus. Males.	Hindus. Females.	Mahomedans. Males.	Mahomedans. Females.	Christians. Males.	Christians. Females.	Others. Males.	Others. Females.
	1	2	3	4	5	6	7	8	9	10	11	12	13	14	15
	Eastern States. *	**743,393**	**726,798**	**592,310**	**581,136**	**125,762**	**120,721**	**10,661**	**2,344**	**3,429**	**1,405**	**11,523**	**11,145**	**288**	**47**
	41. Northern Shan States. *	**285,700**	**273,523**	**208,446**	**207,447**	**67,495**	**63,562**	**6,686**	**1,118**	**1,815**	**471**	**1,050**	**879**	**288**	**46**
231	*Lashio Notified Area*	*2,046*	*1,402*	*978*	*903*	*139*	*60*	*818*	*360*	*49*	*45*	*49*	*31*	*13*	*3*
232	*Hsipaw State*	*67,848*	*63,602*	*63,746*	*62,294*	*2,029*	*747*	*1,357*	*277*	*651*	*227*	*63*	*55*	*2*	*2*
233	*Mong Mit State*	*28,349*	*28,149*	*21,682*	*20,857*	*6,352*	*7,125*	*138*	*23*	*60*	*12*	*102*	*130*	*15*	*2*
	Möng Mit (State proper) ...	15,834	14,188	14,723	13,444	911	692	108	23	59	12	20	15	13	2
	Kodaung Hill Tracts ...	12,515	13,961	6,959	7,413	5,441	6,433	30	...	1	...	82	115	2	...
234	*Taunpeng State*	*23,957*	*17,941*	*15,220*	*15,592*	*4,063*	*1,711*	*3,315*	*264*	*828*	*137*	*381*	*203*	*150*	*34*
235	*South Hsenwi*	*42,108*	*42 033*	*39,434*	*39,751*	*2,412*	*2,232*	*223*	*24*	*37*	*26*	*2*	...	...	...
236	*North Hsenwi* *	*121,492*	*120,396*	*67,386*	*68,050*	*52,500*	*51,687*	*835*	*170*	*190*	*24*	*453*	*460*	*28*	*5*
	Shan Tracts ...	70,621	68,304	46,839	47,469	22,460	20,362	804	167	186	24	304	277	28	5
	Kachin Tracts ...	40,335	41,931	11,173	11,396	28,978	30,349	31	3	4	...	149	183	...	...
	East Manglün * ...				Not class-	ified by	religion.	See Pr-	ovincial	Table I.					
	West Manglün ...	10,436	10,161	9,374	9,185	1,062	976	...	...	...	...	...	...	...	...
	42. Southern Shan States.	**427,064**	**420,554**	**373,459**	**374,601**	**42,672**	**38,539**	**3,721**	**1,187**	**1,467**	**843**	**5,754**	**5,383**	...	**1**
237	*Taunggyi Notified Area* ...	*3,311*	*2,705*	*1,670*	*1,769*	*109*	*28*	*987*	*460*	*374*	*305*	*171*	*143*	...	...
	Civil Population	*2,734*	*2,476*	*1,666*	*1,760*	*109*	*28*	*420*	*246*	*368*	*299*	*171*	*143*	...	...
	Military Police	*577*	*229*	*4*	*9*	...	...	*567*	*214*	*6*	*6*	...	...	...	...
238	*Loilem Notified Area*	*552*	*446*	*329*	*352*	*12*	*2*	*173*	*66*	*25*	*16*	*13*	*10*	...	...
	Civil Population	*450*	*426*	*329*	*352*	*12*	*2*	*72*	*46*	*24*	*16*	*13*	*10*	...	...
	Military Police	*102*	*20*	...	...	...	...	*101*	*20*	*1*	...	...	...	...	...
239	*Kalaw Notified Area*	*1,822*	*1,175*	*848*	*887*	*103*	*20*	*644*	*107*	*134*	*67*	*93*	*94*	...	...
	Civil Population	*1,727*	*1,164*	*848*	*887*	*103*	*20*	*549*	*96*	*134*	*67*	*93*	*94*	...	...
	Military Police	*95*	*11*	...	...	...	...	*95*	*11*	...	...	...	...	...	...
240	*Yawnghwe State*	*52,157*	*53,355*	*51,122*	*52,857*	*127*	*42*	*450*	*158*	*332*	*194*	*126*	*104*	...	...
241	*Kengtung State*	*107,513*	*101,248*	*72,446*	*69,893*	*31,721*	*28,746*	*690*	*262*	*180*	*55*	*2,476*	*2,303*	...	...
	North-Eastern Subdivision ...	*86,539*	*87,439*	*85,783*	*86,980*	*564*	*377*	*94*	*10*	*74*	*53*	*24*	*19*	...	...
242	Laihka	16,430	16,397	16,293	16,330	53	13	27	5	40	35	17	15	...	...
243	Möng Kung	17,413	17,301	17,352	17,293	45	5	7	...	9	2	...	1	...	...
244	Kehsi Mansam	8,869	9,159	8,832	9,139	27	19	10	1	...	...	...	...	...	...
245	Kenglon	2,169	2,340	2,169	2,340	...	...	...	...	...	...	...	...	...	...
246	Möng Hsee	9,421	9,477	9,402	9,472	14	2	...	...	...	...	5	3	...	...
247	Möng Nawng	20,923	21,449	20,807	21,422	65	20	38	...	11	7	2	...	...	...
248	Möng Sit	3,409	3,318	3,317	3,243	92	75	...	...	...	...	...	...	...	...
249	Möng Pawn	7,903	7,998	7,611	7,741	265	244	13	4	14	9	...	...	...	...
	Central Subdivision ...	*56,502*	*54,759*	*47,141*	*45,905*	*6,395*	*6,182*	*134*	*17*	*81*	*36*	*2,751*	*2,619*	...	...
250	Samka	7,189	6,946	7,153	6,919	27	25	6	...	3	2	...	...	...	...
251	Hsahtung	5,248	4,916	5,098	4,885	127	22	3	...	19	9	1	...	...	...
252	Namhkok	3,639	3,521	3,632	3,521	3	...	2	...	2	...	...	...	...	...
253	Nawn Wawn	2,066	1,973	2,043	1,971	...	...	9	...	14	2	...	...	...	...
254	Mong Pai	10,615	10,379	2,003	1,946	5,861	5,809	...	...	3	5	2,748	2,619	...	...
255	Wanyin	5,782	5,762	5,571	5,564	189	189	6	...	16	9	...	...	...	...
256	Sakoi	1,029	967	887	833	137	132	1	...	3	2	1	...	...	...
257	Hopong	5,967	5,904	5,888	5,896	39	3	33	5	7	...	...	...	...	...
258	Lawksawk	14,967	14,391	14,866	14,370	12	2	74	12	14	7	1	...	...	...
	South-Eastern Subdivision ...	*56,492*	*56,209*	*53,855*	*53,983*	*2,360*	*2,066*	*103*	*27*	*109*	*53*	*75*	*79*	...	*1*
259	Möngnai	27,781	27,866	27,488	27,684	65	52	96	25	65	29	67	75	...	1
	Kengham	*2,888*	*2,945*	*2,876*	*2,945*	*5*	...	*7*	...	...	...	...	...	...	...
	Kengtawng	*6,329*	*6,352*	*6,259*	*6,299*	*54*	*52*	*11*	...	*5*	*1*	...	...	...	...
	Remainder	*18,564*	*18,569*	*18,353*	*18,440*	*6*	...	*78*	*25*	*60*	*28*	*67*	*75*	...	*1*
260	Mawkmai	17,580	17,746	16,717	16,962	815	763	6	2	38	19	4	...	...	...
261	Möng Pan	11,131	10,597	9,650	9,337	1,470	1,251	1	...	6	5	4	4	...	...
	Western Subdivision	*62,176*	*63,218*	*60,256*	*61,975*	*1,291*	*1,077*	*446*	*90*	*158*	*64*	*25*	*12*	...	...
262	Hsa Möng Hkam †	7,572	7,092	6,943	6,928	111	17	363	83	131	52	24	12	...	...
263	Kyon	1,248	1,275	1,248	1,275	...	...	...	...	...	...	...	...	...	...
264	Pwela	4,526	4,822	4,484	4,818	1	...	37	...	4	4	...	...	...	...
265	Mawson	1,913	2,148	1,912	2,148	...	...	...	...	1	...	...	...	...	...
266	Pangtara	7,542	8,038	7,504	8,036	13	...	21	2	4	...	...	...	...	...
267	Kyawkku	2,349	2,441	2,345	2,441	...	...	3	...	1	...	...	...	...	...
268	Yengan	4,606	4,546	4,600	4,543	...	...	5	3	...	...	1	...	...	...
269	Maw	3,755	3,651	3,753	3,651	...	...	...	...	2	...	...	...	...	...
270	Mawnang	2,058	2,217	2,055	2,216	...	...	3	1	...	...	...	...	...	...
271	Pinmi	1,521	1,480	1,521	1,480	...	...	...	...	...	...	...	...	...	...
272	Loimaw	2,263	2,402	2,263	2,402	...	...	...	...	...	...	...	...	...	...
273	Loi Ai	3,680	3,812	3,676	3,811	1	...	1	...	2	1	...	...	...	...
274	Loi Long	18,722	18,885	17,574	17,865	1,123	1,012	13	1	13	7	...	...	...	...
275	Namtok	421	409	378	361	43	48	...	...	...	...	...	...	...	...
	43. Karenni.	**31,129**	**32,721**	**10,614**	**9,088**	**15,595**	**18,620**	**254**	**39**	**147**	**91**	**4,719**	**4,883**	...	...
276	Kantarawadi	18,020	18,601	8,386	7,596	9,234	10,807	125	37	119	80	153	81	...	...
277	Bawlakè	5,640	5,114	1,309	892	1,491	1,442	126	2	28	11	2,686	2,767	...	...
278	Kyebogyi	6,274	7,890	224	180	4,280	5,742	...	...	...	...	1,770	1,929	...	...
279	Naungpale	508	458	189	151	209	201	...	...	...	...	110	106	...	...
280	Nammekon	687	718	306	290	381	428	...	...	...	...	...	...	...	...

* The population of East Manglün (No. 236) is omitted. † Also called Thamakan.